Professor Effie Maclellan
School of Education
University of Strathclyde
GLASGOW G13 1PP
Tel:- 0141 950 3355
e.maclellan@strath.ac.uk

The SAGE
Handbook of
Writing
Development

The SAGE
Handbook of

Writing
Development

Edited by
Roger Beard, Debra Myhill,
Jeni Riley and Martin Nystrand

Los Angeles • London • New Delhi • Singapore • Washington DC

SAGE Publications Ltd
1 Oliver's Yard
55 City Road
London EC1Y 1SP

SAGE Publications Inc.
2455 Teller Road
Thousand Oaks, California 91320

SAGE Publications India Pvt Ltd
B 1/I 1 Mohan Cooperative Industrial Area
Mathura Road
New Delhi 110 044

SAGE Publications Asia-Pacific Pte Ltd
33 Pekin Street #02-01
Far East Square
Singapore 048763

Library of Congress Control Number: 2008936644

British Library Cataloguing in Publication data

A catalogue record for this book is available from the British Library

ISBN 978-1-4129-4846-3

Typeset by CEPHA Imaging Pvt. Ltd., Bangalore, India
Printed in Great Britain by MPG Books Group
Printed on paper from sustainable resources

Contents

Notes on Contributors

EDITORS

Roger Beard taught in primary schools, at University College, Northampton, and at the University of Leeds before becoming Professor of Primary Education and Head of the Department of Early Childhood and Primary Education at the Institute of Education, University of London. He has published widely on both reading and writing and has written literature reviews for the National Literacy Strategy in England and for the Brazilian and European Parliaments. His books include *Children's Writing in the Primary School*, *Developing Reading 3–13*, *Teaching Literacy: Balancing Perspectives*; *Rhyme, Reading and Writing*; *Developing Writing 3–13* (all published by Hodder & Stoughton) and *Reading Development and the Teaching of Reading* (with Jane Oakhill and published by Blackwell).

Debra Myhill is Professor of Education at the University of Exeter, and is Head of the School of Education and Lifelong Learning. Until recently, she was Head of Initial Teacher Education, leading the School's teacher education courses to national recognition for their excellence. Her research interests focus principally on aspects of language and literacy teaching, including underachievement, writing, and talk in the classroom, and she has published widely in this area. She is the author of *Better Writers* (Courseware Publications), and *Talking, Listening, Learning: Effective Talk in the Primary Classroom* (Open University Press).

Jeni Riley is a Reader in Literacy in Primary Education in the Department of Early Childhood and Primary Education, at the Institute of Education, University of London. She is passionately committed to enhancing the teaching and learning in early years settings and primary schools through her teaching, research and writing. Before her appointment to the Institute of Education, Jeni was an early years teacher and educational adviser in Oxfordshire. Since her appointment to the Institute, she has focused her research energies on the teaching and learning of language and literacy in the early years of education. Her most recent funded research project, *StoryTalk,* investigated ways of effectively enhancing the spoken language skills of reception class children in inner city, multicultural schools. Jeni led both a large primary initial teacher education course for 10 years and the Department of Primary Education, before becoming the Head of the School of Early Childhood and Primary Education at the Institute of Education. Currently, she is Consultancy Co-ordinator for the Faculty of Children and Health. She is on the editorial board of the *Journal of Early Childhood Literacy,* and her recent books are: Riley, J.L. and Reedy, D. (2000) *Developing Writing for Different Purposes: Teaching about Genre in the Early Years*; Riley, J.L. (2006) *Language and Literacy 3–7* and Riley, J.L. (ed.) (2007) *Learning in the Early Years 3–7*, all published by Paul Chapman Publishing.

CHAPTER 1

David R. Olson is University Professor Emeritus, OISE/University of Toronto. He is author or editor of 19 books including *The World on Paper: The conceptual and cognitive implications of writing and reading* (Cambridge University Press, 1994), *Psychological theory and Educational Reform: How school remakes mind and society* (Cambridge University Press, 2003) and *Jerome Bruner: The cognitive revolution in educational theory* Continuum, 2006). He is editor with Nancy Torrance of the forthcoming *Cambridge Handbook of Literacy.*

CHAPTER 2

Denis Alamargot is Senior Lecturer in cognitive and developmental psychology at the University of Poitiers (France). He is the director of the French CNRS 'Group of Research on writing' and the European COST Action *Learning to Write Effectively.* He does research on eye movements during writing in children, students and professional writers. He publishes various syntheses and experimental papers on writing processes, and wrote *Through the Models of Writing* (in collaboration with Lucile Chanquoy). He is the co-inventor (with David Chesnet) of the *Eye and Pen* © software.

Michel Fayol is full Professor in cognitive and developmental psychology at the Blaise Pascal University of Clermont-Ferrand (France) and program officer at the Agence Nationale de la Recherche, Paris (France) (National Research Agency). He has been the director of two CNRS teams, from 1984 to 1998, the LEAD CNRS in Dijon, and from 1998 to 2007, the LAPSCO CNRS in Clermont-Ferrand. He has published more than a hundred papers in referenced journals and many chapters and books, more specifically *Processing Interclausal Relationships* (Erlbaum) with Jean Costermans, and *Learning to Spell* (Erlbaum) with C. Perfetti and L. Rieben.

CHAPTER 3

David Galbraith is Senior Lecturer in Psychology and Director of the Centre for Educational Psychology Research at Staffordshire University in the UK. He researches into cognitive processes in writing (particularly the effects of writing on cognition) and into the uses of writing in educational and therapeutic contexts. He is a committee member of the British Psychological Society's Psychology of Education Section and of the European Research Network for Learning to Write Effectively funded by the European Science Foundation. He was coordinator of the European Association for Learning and Instruction's Special Interest Group on Writing and is currently an Associate Editor of the *Journal of Writing Research* and a member of the Editorial Board for the Educational Research Review.

CHAPTER 4

John Hayes is Professor of Psychology at Carnegie Mellon University. He has carried out many empirical studies of factors involved in adult writing and has been active in the development of models of adult writing processes. He is currently interested in trying to model the sequence of events by which beginning and developing writers become adult writers.

CHAPTER 5

Lucile Chanquoy is Professor of Cognitive Development at the University of Nice – Sophia Antipolis in France. She teaches graduate and postgraduate courses in developmental psychology and statistics; she has written two students books on these topics (in French, Hachette Editor). She conducts research in writing, more precisely, in a developmental perspective, she is interested in the revising process, and the possibility of helping children to develop revising strategies, and in spelling to explain grammatical errors that occur both in adults and in children. She is currently the head of her research Laboratory (Laboratory of Cognitive and Social Psychology), and she is a member of a French group of writing researchers (called Groupe de Recherche sur la Production Verbale Ecrite) which is affiliated to the French National Research Centre. In this group, she acts as co-responsible for a specific axis of research about the constraints on writing processes.

CHAPTER 6

Triantafillia Kostouli is an Associate professor at the Department of Education, Aristotle University of Thessaloniki, in Greece. She teaches (undergraduate, graduate and in-service teacher education) courses on literacy education, sociocultural linguistics and critical discourse analysis. She has published on Greek children's school writing practices, classroom interaction and on Greek students' writing in academic contexts. Her research interests include the discursive construction of schools as learning communities, the intertextual construction of ideology in and through classroom practices, the relation between identities and learning, and the design of literacy courses (through university–school collaboration) that work for social change.

CHAPTER 7

Jon Smidt is Professor of Norwegian Language and Literature in Teacher Education at Sør-Trøndelag University College in Trondheim, Norway. He has been involved since 1982 in classroom research in reading and writing processes and the teaching of literature and writing in secondary schools, with special interest in the dialogical relationships between students, teachers, texts and sociocultural contexts. At present, he leads a research project about writing in the disciplines and across the curriculum from kindergarten to upper secondary school, besides teaching and supervising master students in teacher education. He is an honorary doctor at Uppsala University, Sweden, has been involved in the development of the current Norwegian school curriculum of Norwegian as a subject, and has conducted international comparative studies, in the International Mother Tongue Education Network (IMEN), and for the Language Division of the Council of Europe.

CHAPTER 8

Hilary Janks is a Professor in Applied English Language Studies at the University of the Witwatersrand, Johannesburg, South Africa. Her research is in the area of critical literacy, and she is best known for the Critical Language Awareness Series, a collection of classroom materials for teaching students about the relationship between language and power, which she edited. While her earlier work focused on power as negative and oppressive, she is now trying to understand the relationship between literacy and a productive theory of power in the hope that critical literacy can do both deconstructive and reconstructive work.

CHAPTER 9

Brian Street is Professor of Language in Education at King's College, London University, and Visiting Professor of Education in both the Graduate School of Education, University of Pennsylvania and in the School of Education and Professional Development, University of East Anglia. He has written and lectured extensively on literacy practices from both a theoretical and an applied perspective. He has a longstanding commitment to linking ethnographic-style research on the cultural dimension of language and literacy with contemporary practice in education and in development and has recently extended this to research on social dimensions of numeracy practices. He was the 2008 winner of the National Reading Conference's Distinguished Scholar Lifetime Achievement Award. During 2007, he has published four books, he recently published a reader on literacy studies entitled *Literacy: A resource Handbook*, Routledge (jointly with Adam Lefstein) and edited a volume on literacy in the Springer *Encyclopedia of Language & Education* . He is co-author of a volume on ethnography (for the National Council for Research in Language and Literacy) with Shirley Heath and co-editor with Viv Ellis and Carol Fox of *Rethinking English in Schools* published by Continuum Books.

CHAPTER 10

David Rose is the director of *Reading to Learn*, an international literacy program that trains teachers across school and university sectors (www.readingtolearn.com.au). He is also an Associate of both the Faculty of Education and Social Work and the Department of Linguistics at the University of Sydney. His research interests include literacy pedagogy and teacher education, language and cultural contexts and language evolution. He is the author of *The Western Desert Code: an Australian cryptogrammar* (Canberra: Pacific Linguistics, 2001), *Working with Discourse: meaning beyond the clause* (with J.R. Martin) (London: Continuum, 2003/2007) and *Genre Relations: mapping culture* (also with J.R. Martin) (London: Equinox, 2008).

CHAPTER 11

Gunther Kress is Professor of Semiotics and Education at the Institute of Education, University of London. His interests are in understanding principles of representation, meaning-making and communication in contemporary social environments. This involves a continuing interest in the development of a social semiotic theory of multimodal representation and communication. For him, this implies a focus on the processes and forms of communication in all modes including those of speech and writing. Some of his publications in this area are *Learning to Write* (1982/1994); *Linguistic Processes in Sociocultural Practices* (1984/1989); *Social Semiotics* (1988, with R. Hodge); *Before Writing: rethinking the paths to literacy* (1996); *Reading Images: the grammar of graphic design* (1996/2006, with T. van Leeuwen); *Multimodal Discourse: the modes and media of contemporary communication* (2002, with T. van Leeuwen); *Literacy in the New Media Age* (2003); *English in Urban Classrooms* (2005, with C. Jewitt, J. Bourne, A. Franks, J. Hardcastle, K. Jones, E. Reid). Current research projects are 'Museums, exhibitions and the visitor' (funded by the Swedish National Research Foundation) and 'Gains and Losses: changes in teaching materials 1935–2005' (funded by the Economic and Social Science Research Council, UK).

Jeff Bezemer is co-organizer of a 3-year training programme on ethnography, language and communication under the ESRC's Researcher Development Initiative. The programme is run by Jan Blommaert, Jeff Bezemer and Carey Jewitt from the Institute of Education and Ben Rampton, Adam Lefstein and Celia Roberts from King's College London. It is intended to provide researchers from across the social sciences UK-wide with sociolinguistic tools for the analysis of textual data.

CHAPTER 12

Terry Locke is Associate Professor and Chairperson in the Arts and Language Education Department at the School of Education, University of Waikato. His research interests include the efficacy of grammar teaching, teacher professionalism, constructions of English as a subject (in relation to curriculum and assessment reforms), literature teaching pedagogies and the relationship between English/literacy and ICTs. He is widely published in all of these areas. His recent books are *Resisting qualifications reforms in New Zealand: The English Study Design as constructive dissent* (Sense Publishers, 2007) and *Critical Discourse Analysis* (Continuum, 2004). He is coordinating editor of the refereed, online journal *English Teaching: Practice and Critique.* He is currently working directly on a major New Zealand-based project on teaching literature in the multicultural classroom.

CHAPTER 13

Craig Hancock has taught at the college level for over three decades, with the last twenty-one years as teacher of writing for the nationally recognized Educational Opportunity Program at the University at Albany. From the beginning, he has looked for approaches to grammar that work in harmony with higher-end concerns, approaches that empower and not just correct or constrain. His book *Meaning Centered Grammar* (Equinox, 2005) has been called 'an excellent introduction to traditional grammar viewed within a functional perspective'. He has been very active in NCTE sub-groups, including the Assembly for the Teaching of English Grammar and the Conference on College Composition and Communication, writing and presenting frequently on the value of language awareness, on form/meaning connections, and on meaning-centered approaches to grammar. He is a founding member of *New Public Grammar*, an advocacy group for the reintegration of scientifically grounded grammar instruction in US public schools.

CHAPTER 14

Deborah Wells Rowe is Associate Professor of Early Childhood Education in the Department of Teaching & Learning, Vanderbilt University, Nashville, Tennessee, in the United States. She conducts ethnographic research in school settings on preschool and primary grades children's literacy learning. She is co-principal investigator of the Write Start! Project – a 3-year longitudinal study of connections between preschoolers' writing and patterns of personal play interests, and of Enhanced Language and Literacy Success – a grant funded to assist preschoool teachers in implementing research-based reading and writing instruction. At Vanderbilt, she teaches undergraduate and graduate courses related to literacy instruction, literacy learning and qualitative research methods.

CHAPTER 15

Anne Haas Dyson is a former teacher of young children and, currently, a professor of education at the University of Illinois at Urbana-Champaign. Previously, she was on the faculty of the University of Georgia, Michigan State University and the University of California, Berkeley, where she was a recipient of the campus Distinguished Teaching Award. She studies the childhood cultures and literacy learning of young schoolchildren. Among her publications are *Social Worlds of Children Learning to Write in an Urban Primary School*, which was awarded NCTE's David Russell Award for Distinguished Research, *Writing Superheroes*, and *The Brothers and Sisters Learn to Write: Popular Literacies in Childhood and School Cultures*. She recently co-authored two books with Celia Genishi, *On the Case*, on interpretive case study methods, and *Children, Language, and Literacy in Diverse Times*.

CHAPTER 16

Stuart McNaughton, PhD, is Professor of Education at the University of Auckland and Director of the Woolf Fisher Research Centre (established 1998). The Centre has a national and international reputation for excellence in research on teaching, learning and development with culturally and linguistically diverse communities. He has research and teaching interests in developmental and educational psychology with a focus on the development of language and literacy, and processes of education, socialisation and culture. Publications include books on reading and instruction (*Being Skilled: The Socialisation of Learning to Read* – Methuen, 1987) and emergent literacy (*Patterns of Emergent Literacy: Processes of Development and Transition* – Oxford University Press, 1995); and papers and presentations on many aspects of teaching, learning and development in family and school settings. His most recent book (*Meeting of Minds* – Learning Media, 2002) develops theory about and extensive examples of effective literacy instruction for culturally and linguistically diverse children. Current research is focused on properties of effective teaching of literacy and language in the context of research-based interventions with clusters of schools. Research and development interventions which have successfully raised achievement levels with schools have involved over 10,000 children and their teachers in more than 50 schools, including large urban multicultural schools and rural isolated schools. He has been Head of the School of Education at the University of Auckland and Director of the University of Auckland at Manukau programme. He was a member of the New Zealand government appointed Literacy Task Force and was chair of the New Zealand Literacy Experts Group and sits on literacy advisory committees for the New Zealand Ministry of Education. He is an international consultant on instructional changes in educational systems and the design and implementation of research and development collaborations with schools for innovation and change.

Judy Parr is an Associate Professor in the Faculty of Education at the University of Auckland. Her research interests are broadly in developmental and educational psychology but focus on optimising the development of literacy, particularly writing. Current work includes that of a researcher nested within and informing the national Literacy Professional Development Project and as part of a lead team involved in evaluating and, concurrently, building the evaluative capability of, schools within the national Schooling Improvement initiatives. She has published in a range of journals including *Assessment in Education, Professional Development in Education, Journal of Adolescent and Adult Literacy, Journal of Technology and Teacher Education* and *Journal of Educational Change*. She is a co-author of the book *Using Evidence in Teaching Practice*. Funded research projects completed recently include: effective practice in use of ready-made literacy materials in classrooms; assessment tools for teaching and learning in writing (asTTle); a study of effective practitioners of writing, and a Teaching and Learning Research Initiative project with partner schools to produce a tool for peer observation and feedback of practice in literacy classrooms.

Rebecca Jesson is a Project Researcher and PhD student at the Woolf Fisher Research Centre at the University of Auckland. With a teaching background in primary education and Reading Recovery, she currently facilitates teacher professional development in writing, assessment and moderation in schooling improvement contexts in New Zealand. Her research interests include theories of critical thinking, inter-textuality and transfer, and the application of these to literacy education.

CHAPTER 17

Charles Read is Professor of Linguistics, Emeritus, at the University of Wisconsin-Madison in the United States. His research has focused on the linguistic foundations of reading and writing, particularly the relationships between sound systems and writing systems. He discovered unexpected phonetic influences on children's beginning spelling and has studied phonological awareness in readers of Chinese and in adults of low literacy. He also co-authored a text and articles about the acoustic analysis of speech. For 10 years, Read served as Dean of the highly regarded School of Education at Wisconsin, leading a period of growth in teacher education, research–doctoral preparation and private support.

CHAPTER 18

Nigel Hall is Professor of Literacy Education at Manchester Metropolitan University and has interests in young children's developing knowledge of language and literacy, particularly with respect to punctuation, play and literacy, and writing. He is also interested in literacy as a social practice, both currently and historically, and how this notion relates to primary-school literacy education. He is the Director of The Punctuation Project which, supported by three ESRC awards, is seeking to understand how children make sense of punctuation and how teachers might best teach it. A more recent specialist interest is in the field of child language brokering. He headed a recent ESRC seminar series on the topic Children and Adolescents as Language Brokers and has edited a book on child language brokering for the Dutch publisher John Benjamins. He is a co-founder and joint-editor of the international research journal, the *Journal of Early Childhood Literacy*. Nigel's current areas of post-graduate research supervision are: The nature of learning primary science through fieldwork learning experiences; the young child as a cultural broker; adult learners in FE; how young children learn to use the apostrophe; and the development of the concept of the sentence in children between the ages of 7 and 11. Recent publications are: Hall, N., Larson, J. and Marsh, J. (eds) (2004) *Handbook of Early Childhood Literacy* (Sage); Hall, N. and Sham, S. (2007) 'Language brokering as young people's work: evidence from Chinese adolescents in England', *Language and Education*, 21, 1:16–30; Hall, N. (2004) 'The Child in the Middle: agency and diplomacy in language brokering events' in Hansen, G., Malmkjar, K. and Gile, D. (eds) *Claims, Changes and Challenges in Translation Studies* (Amsterdam: John Benjamins); Hall, N. and Robinson, A. (2003) *Exploring Writing and Play in the Early Years*, 2nd edition (David Fulton).

CHAPTER 19

After teaching Educational Psychology for many years at University of Queensland, **Carol Christensen** is currently working as a consultant in literacy. Much of her work focuses on the application of research to school practice. She is particularly interested in the way in which the development of automaticity of component skills can promote student performance in complex, intellectual tasks. She has conducted a number studies looking at the impact of handwriting on student's capacity to write high-quality text and feels that a greater understanding of effective approaches to teaching handwriting will result in substantial benefits in terms of students' written language skills.

CHAPTER 20

Pietro Boscolo is Professor of Educational Psychology in the Faculty of Psychology at the University of Padova (Italy). He also teaches academic writing to undergraduate students. He conducts research in writing at different school levels, from elementary school to university. His recent production focuses in particular on two fields: the improvement of writing competence of struggling writers in primary and middle school, and the affective aspects of writing including the co-editing (with S. Hidi) of *Writing and Motivation* (2007). He is currently (2007–2009) President of the European Association for Research in Learning and Instruction (EARLI).

CHAPTER 21

Jackie Marsh is Professor of Education at the University of Sheffield, UK, where she directs the EdD programme. She is involved in research relating to the nature and role of popular culture, media and new technologies in young children's literacy development. She has conducted national studies of children's out-of-school use of technologies and has been engaged in numerous projects that have explored how these interests can be built upon in the literacy curriculum. She is a past president of the United Kingdom Literacy Association. Jackie's publications include *Desirable Literacies* (co-edited with E. Hallett, 2nd edition, Sage, 2008; Literacy *and Social Inclusion: Closing the Gap* (co-edited with E. Bearne) Trentham, 2008; *Popular Culture, New Media and Digital Literacy in Early Childhood* (Ed.), RoutledgeFalmer, 2005; and *Making Literacy Real* (co-authored with J. Larson), Sage, 2005.

CHAPTER 22

Peter Bryant's research is on perceptual and cognitive development in children from birth to adolescence. In recent years, he has worked with Terezinha Nunes on children's reading and spelling and on their mathematics. He was the Watts Professor of Psychology, University of Oxford from 1980 until he retired in 2004, when he became Senior Research Fellow at the department of Education, University of Oxford and Visiting Professor (2004–9) at Oxford Brookes University. He was the founding editor of the *British Journal of Developmental Psychology* (1983–1988) and the editor of *Cognitive Development* (2000–2006). In 1991, he was elected a Fellow of the Royal Society. He has authored or co-authored the following books: P. Bryant (1974) *Perception and Understanding in Young Children* (Methuen); L. Bradley and P. Bryant (1985) *Rhyme and Reason in Reading and Spelling* (University of Michigan Press); P. Bryant and L. Bradley (1985) *Children's Reading Problems* (Blackwell); U. Goswami and P. Bryant (1990) *Phonological Skills and Learning to Read* (Psychology Press); T. Nunes and P. Bryant (1996) *Children Doing Mathematics* (Blackwell); T. Nunes and P. Bryant (2006) *Improving Literacy through Teaching Morphemes* (Routledge); T. Nunes and P. Bryant (2009, in press) *Children's Reading and Spelling: Beyond the first steps* (Blackwell).

Terezinha Nunes is Professor of Educational Studies in the Department of Education, University of Oxford, and a Fellow of Harris Manchester College. Her research spans the domains of children's literacy and numeracy, including hearing and deaf children's learning. Her focus of analysis covers both cognitive and cultural issues, with a particular interest in educational applications. She was awarded a Research Readership by British Academy and a prize for her monograph on *Alfabetização e Pobreza* (*Literacy and Poverty*) by the Brazilian Society for the Progress of Science. Among her books are *Street Mathematics, School mathematics* (Cambridge University Press); *Children doing Mathematics* (Blackwell); *Teaching Mathematics to Deaf Children* (Wiley), *Improving Literacy by Teaching Morphemes* (Routledge); and *Children's Reading and Spelling: Beyond the First Steps* (Wiley-Blackwell).

CHAPTER 23

Richard Hudson is Emeritus Professor of Linguistics at University College London, where he spent all his working life. His main research activity has always been in the area of grammar, where he has built an original theory of grammatical and cognitive structure called *Word Grammar* and published over a hundred books and articles. For three years he was the president of the Linguistics Association of Great Britain (LAGB), and he is a Fellow of the Linguistics and Philology section of the British Academy. But, alongside this central focus on language structure, he has strong interests in sociolinguistics, psycholinguistics and educational linguistics, the area where he has been most active in recent years. The educational focus started early in his career, during six years as research assistant to Michael Halliday, and he is a founding member of the Committee for Linguistics in Education and also instigated the Education Committee of the LAGB. One of his books is *Teaching Grammar. A Guide to the National Curriculum*, (Blackwell, 1992), and he has written a number of articles about educational linguistics, both for teachers and for general linguists. His website is www.phon.ucl.ac.uk/home/dick/home.htm.

CHAPTER 24

Peter Smagorinsky is Professor of English Education at The University of Georgia. His research investigates teaching and learning from a sociocultural perspective, drawing on the work of L.S. Vygotsky and his followers. His research has included studies of writing, composing across the secondary school curriculum, the use of arts in literary interpretation, teachers' transitions from teacher education programs to their first jobs, and the discourse of character education. He has also written extensively about instructional practice, with a number of books and articles outlining practical ways of applying research findings to classrooms.

CHAPTER 25

Brenton Doecke is an Associate Professor in the Faculty of Education at Monash University, Melbourne, Victoria. He has published extensively in the field of English curriculum and pedagogy, including articles, edited collections, and classroom resources, many in collaboration with secondary English teachers. He was formerly editor of *English in Australia*, the journal of the Australian Association for the Teaching of English (AATE), and a member of the AATE's executive. He played a leading role in the development of the Standards for Teachers of English Language and Literacy in Australia (STELLA) and is currently heavily engaged in research and debate on standards-based reforms in Australia. Brenton is an associate editor of *English Teaching: Practice and Critique* and *L1-Educational Studies in Language and Literature* and has guest-edited issues for both journals.

Douglas McClenaghan is an English and Literature teacher at Viewbank College, a state secondary school in Melbourne, Australia. He has published articles and book chapters in the field of English curriculum and pedagogy, particularly in the field of student writing. His teaching and research interests lie in the exploration of reflective teaching practice and the development of alternative understandings of student literacy practices and their place in the English curriculum.

CHAPTER 26

Anthony Wilson is Programme Director of Primary PGCE at Exeter University, School of Education and Lifelong Learning. A published poet, his research interests focus on poetry writing pedagogy, particularly on the cognitive demands of poetry upon children, and on teachers' beliefs and values regarding the place of poetry in the curriculum. He teaches on undergraduate and graduate programmes in the field of creativity and learning, as well as literacy. He is currently submitting an ESRC research bid on poetry writing and cognition.

CHAPTER 27

Debra Myhill See above

CHAPTER 28

Ellen Lavelle is Professor in the Department of Internal Medicine at University of Arkansas for Medical Sciences in Little Rock, Arkansas. Her duties include providing instructional and educational research support for graduate medical education and consulting on assessment issues across campus. Her research interests include the assessment of writing approaches of nursing students, teaching residents to teach and the development of a multi-rater evaluation for professional skills in resident education.

CHAPTER 29

Brian Huot has been working in writing assessment for two decades. While the majority of his work has focused on assessment outside the classroom, he has continued to develop theory and practice in which assessment is a valuable component for teaching and learning. He has co-edited several collections including *Validating Holistic Scoring: Theoretical and empirical foundations*; *Assessing Writing Across the Curriculum: Diverse Approaches and Practices*; and *Assessing Writing: A critical sourcebook*. His monograph (*Re*)-*Articulating Writing Assessment for Teaching and Learning* appeared in 2002. With Kathleen Yancey he founded two journals devoted to writing assessment: *Assessing Writing* and *The Journal of Writing Assessment* which he continues to edit. Brian is professor of English at Kent State University where he coordinates the Writing Program.

R. Jeff Perry is Assistant Professor of English and director of The Writing Center at North Carolina Wesleyan College. His scholarship focuses on the politics of literacy and institutional writing assessments. As a socially progressive researcher, his work attempts to merge scholarship from educational testing and critical theories of reproduction to better understand the ways in which external writing assessments, and pressures to achieve cost efficiency and reliability, undermine writing programs' and writing instructors' ability to educate students.

CHAPTER 30

Martine Braaksma, **PhD**, is postdoctoral fellow at the Graduate School of Teaching and Learning of the University of Amsterdam. She is member of the Research Group in Language & Literature Education and conducts a research project on 'Hypertext writing' (funded by Netherlands Organization for Scientific Research) and a review study on empirical studies about the subject Dutch in secondary education. Martine teaches a course Communication to Masters students Biology and Science at the University of Amsterdam.

Michel Couzijn, PhD, is researcher and teacher educator at the Graduate School of Teaching and Learning of the University of Amsterdam, and member of the Research Group in Language & Literature Education. His research interests include effective language education and transfer, writing instruction, literary and argumentation skills. Currently, he conducts a research project on inquiry learning and writing in pre-academic streams, funded by the Netherlands Organization for Scientific Research (NWO).

Tanja Janssen is a senior researcher at the Graduate School of Teaching and Learning of the University of Amsterdam and member of the Research Group in Language & Literature Education. She has written on research in the teaching and learning of literature and writing in secondary schools. Currently, she conducts research in arts education, literature education and creative writing, and she coaches teachers-as-researchers in secondary schools.

Marleen Kieft, PhD, was a member of the Research Group in Language & Literature Education at the Graduate School of Teaching and Learning of the University of Amsterdam from 2001–2007. As a PhD candidate and a postdoctoraral fellow, she conducted research in the field of writing education and writing-to-learn in upper secondary education. Currently, she works as a researcher in educational consultancy.

Mariet Raedts holds a PhD in Language and Literature. She currently works as a postdoctoral researcher and lecturer at HUBrussel, Belgium. Her research interests include observational learning, academic writing and the relationship between self-efficacy beliefs and writing per-formance. She teaches different writing courses, including academic and argumentative writing.

Gert Rijlaarsdam, PhD, is a member of the Research Group in Language & Literature Education at the Graduate School of Teaching and Learning at the University of Amsterdam. His research focuses on writing in L1 and L2, and supervises research on language and litera-ture education. He is editor-in-chief of *L1-Educational Studies in Language and Literature* and of *Journal of Writing Research* and founded, with Ken Watson (Australia), the International Association for the Improvement of Mother Tongue Education (IAIMTE).

Anne Toorenaar is a PhD candidate at the Graduate School of Teaching and Learning (GSTL), University of Amsterdam, and member of the Research Group in Language & Literature Education. After a career in educational consultancy, she specialized in L2 education in middle vocational schools and guided research in pre-vocational schools with teachers to create new forms of language education. Her thesis on 'Community of Learners for L1-learning in Dutch pre-vocational secondary education' is funded by Netherlands Organization for Scientific Research.

Huub van den Bergh is a professor at the Department of Dutch at the University of Utrecht and at the Graduate School of Teaching and Learning at the University of Amsterdam, the Netherlands. He has been involved in nation-wide studies on educational effectiveness, as well as in experimental studies on effective pedagogy in language education and smaller-scale stud-ies on writing and reading processes. He is a member of the Research Group in Language & Literature Education.

Elke Van Steendam, PhD, works at the University of Antwerp. Her research deals with effec-tive methods to teach foreign language learners how to improve their revision and writing skills. More specifically, she focuses on collaborative revision, strategy instruction and obser-vational learning. She teaches business communication in English and German.

CHAPTER 31

Paul Kei Matsuda is Associate Professor of English at Arizona State University, where he works with doctoral students in Rhetoric, Composition and Linguistics as well as Applied Linguistics. Founding Chair of the Symposium on Second Language Writing and editor of the Parlor Press Series on Second Language Writing, he has published widely on second language writing, history of composition and applied linguistics, and identity in written discourse. His publications appear in journals such as *College English*, *College Composition and Communication*, *Composition Studies*, *English for Specific Purposes*, *International Journal of Applied Linguistics*, *Journal of Basic Writing*, *Journal of Second Language Writing*, and *Written Communication*.

Aya Matsuda is Assistant Professor of Language and Literacy at Arizona State University, where she teaches graduate courses in applied linguistics. She also teaches courses and gives workshops for K-12 teachers interested in learning how to work with English Language Learners. Her research interests include the use of English as an international language, linguistic and pedagogical implications of the global spread of English, and identity negotiation of bilingual writers. Her work has appeared in various books and journals including *English Today*, *JALT Journal*, *TESOL Quarterly* and *World Englishes*. She currently serves on the editorial advisory board for *TESOL Quarterly*.

Christina Ortmeier-Hooper is an Assistant Professor of Composition Studies at the University of New Hampshire in the United States. She conducts research on the writing development of immigrant second language students in secondary schools and higher education, with a focus on issues of writer identity, educational policy, and teacher education. Currently she is the co-chair of the CCCC Committee on Second Language Writing, and she served as the founding chair of the Second Language Writing Section at TESOL. She has edited two collections on second language writing, and her work has been published in *TESOL Journal* and *College Composition and Communication*. Professor Ortmeier-Hooper teaches undergraduate courses on writing and graduate-level courses on literacy and identity, research methodology, English education, and second language writing.

CHAPTER 32

Suresh Canagarajah is the Kirby Professor in Language Learning and Director of the Migration Studies Project at Pennsylvania State University. He teaches World Englishes, Teaching and Research in Second Language Writing, Postcolonial Studies, and Theories of Rhetoric and Composition in the departments of English and Applied Linguistics. He has taught in the University of Jaffna, Sri Lanka, and the City University of New York (Baruch College and the Graduate Center). He has published on bilingual communication, learning of writing, and English language teaching in professional journals. His book *Resisting Linguistic Imperialism in English Teaching* (OUP, 1999) won Modern Language Association's Mina Shaughnessy Award for the best research publication on the teaching of language and literacy. His subsequent publication *Geopolitics of Academic Writing*, U. Pittsburgh Press, 2002, won the Gary Olson Award for the best book in social and rhetorical theory. His edited collection *Reclaiming the Local in Language Policy and Practice*, Erlbaum, 2005, examines linguistic and literacy constructs in the context of globalization. His study of World Englishes in Composition won the 2007 Braddock Award for the best article in the *College Composition* *and Communication* journal. Suresh edits *TESOL Quarterly*. He is currently analyzing interview transcripts and survey data from South Asian immigrants in Canada, the United States, and the United Kingdom to consider questions of identity, community and heritage languages in diaspora communities.

Maria Jerskey is Assistant Professor of Education and Language Acquisition at LaGuardia Community College and the former Writing Center Director at Baruch College – both of the City University of New York. Her research and practice have focused on developing writing programs and creating teaching materials for multilingual writers from diverse linguistic and literacy backgrounds. Maria is the co-author, with Ann Raimes, of two writing handbooks, The Open Handbook (© 2007) and Universal Keys for Writers (© 2008). She is also a contributing author to *Transformative Spaces: Designing Creative Sites for Teaching and Learning in Higher Education* with Springer Publishing (© 2009). Her research interests include multilingual writers of English, rhetoric and composition, applied linguistics and education reform. She teaches undergraduate and graduate courses in writing and linguistics.

CHAPTER 33

Julie Dockrell (AcSS, FRCSLT) is Professor of Psychology and Special Needs at the Institute of Education, London. She trained as a clinical and educational psychologist and has worked with children who have language and communication difficulties for over 25 years. She continues to do work in schools, collaborate with voluntary agencies and advice the government on ways supporting children with special educational needs. Her major research interests are in patterns of development and the ways in which developmental difficulties impact on children's learning, interaction and attainments. She has a special research interest in vocabulary learning and the ways in which vocabulary knowledge underpins educational attainments. A central theme in this research has been the application of evidence-based research and evaluating interventions to support children with language and communication. She has been Editor of the *British Journal of Educational Psychology* and the *International Journal of Language and Communication Difficulties*.

CHAPTER 34

Doreen Starke-Meyerring is an Assistant Professor of Rhetoric and Writing Studies in the Department of Integrated Studies in Education at McGill University in Montréal, Canada, where she co-directs the Centre for the Study and Teaching of Writing. Focused on discourse studies and writing development in higher education, her research examines changes in writing practices in increasingly digital, globalizing, and knowledge-intensive settings and derives pedagogical models for writing development that address these changes. Currently, she is conducting a three-year collaborative research project on the state of writing development in doctoral education at Canadian research-intensive universities. She teaches undergraduate and graduate courses in academic writing, business communication, and critical internet studies. She is the co-editor of *Designing Globally Networked Learning Environments*, Sense Publishers, 2008; *Research Communication in the Social and Human Sciences*, Cambridge

Scholars Press, 2008; and *Writing (in) the Knowledge Society*, Parlor Press/WAC Clearinghouse, forthcoming.

CHAPTER 35

Christina Haas received her PhD From Carnegie Mellon University. She is currently Associate Professor of English and Faculty Associate for Undergraduate Research at Kent State University, Kent, Ohio, in the United States, where she teaches in the doctoral program in Literacy, Rhetoric, and Social Practice and directs the Writing Internship Program. She has published in the area of writing technologies in numerous venues in the last 20 years, including *Research in the Teaching of English*, *Written Communication*, *Technical Communication*, *Journal of Business and Technical Communication*, *Computers and Composition*, *Works & Days*, *Publications of the ACM*, and *Human–Computer Interaction*. Her book, *Writing Technologies: Studies on the Materiality of Literacy* was published in 1996 by Erlbaum. Her current research projects include a study of the language of IM, TM, and Facebook (with Pamela Takayoshi), an examination the human hand as a site of the interplay of body and technology in writing, and collaborations with undergraduates in the study of new literacies.

Chad Wickman is completing his doctorate in Rhetoric and Composition, with specialization in Literacy, Rhetoric, and Social Practice, at Kent State University in Kent, Ohio, in the United States. His research, focusing on writing and visual representation in scientific practice, examines the distributed and technologically mediated processes whereby scientists transform their laboratory work into rhetorically persuasive texts. Chad has presented his research at national and international writing and physics conferences, and he has been involved in interdisciplinary collaborations that link writing studies with scholarship in the physical sciences.

CHAPTER 36

Marian Sainsbury is Head of Literacy Assessment Research in the Department for Research in Assessment and Measurement at the National Foundation for Educational Research. She is currently directing the Foundation's research into formative uses of e-assessment, together with projects developing single-level tests in reading and assessments of communication skills for Wales. She is international reading co-ordinator for PIRLS. Her assessment research experience with NFER since 1989 has focused mainly on the assessment of literacy in primary schools. Her higher degrees are in philosophy of education, and her recent publications include *Assessing Reading: From theories to classrooms* (NFER, 2006).

CHAPTER 37

Beverly J. Moss is Associate Professor of English in the rhetoric, composition, and literacy program at the Ohio State University iin the United States. She teaches undergraduate writing and literacy courses as well as graduate courses in composition theory, literacy and race, and qualitative research methods. Her scholarly interests include examining literacy in community settings, and the teaching of writing. Currently, Beverly is conducting an ethnographic study of literacy in an African-American woman's service club.

CHAPTER 38

Robert Gundlach is founding Director of the Writing Program and Professor in the Department of Linguistics at Northwestern University in the United States. Combining his interest in writing instruction and his interest in children's language development, he has long been engaged with questions related to how children learn to write and how people continue to develop writing ability through childhood, adolescence and adulthood. He has been a consultant or advisory board member for many organizations, including the National Institute of Education, the National Assessment of Educational Progress, The College Board, the New York State Board of Education, the Illinois State Board of Education, the Center for the Study of Writing and Literacy at the University of California-Berkeley, and the Center for English Learning and Achievement at the University of Wisconsin. He has also served on the editorial boards of *Written Communication and Discourse Processes.*

General Introduction

The origins of this *Handbook* lie in an international seminar series, *Reconceptualising Writing 5–16: cross-phase and cross-disciplinary perspectives*[1] that was held at the Universities of Leeds, Exeter, and London in 2003-4. The seminars were funded by the United Kingdom Economic and Social Research Council and were planned in response to national concerns about children's writing in English schools that had been the focus of national debate in the preceding years (e.g., Beard, 1999, 2000a and b; HMI, 2000; Myhill, 1999, 2001; Riley and Reedy, 2000, 2002; Earl et al., 2003). This was a debate that had been fuelled by central government policies to raise standards of literacy. The policies had appeared to have had at least some short-term impact on the reading attainment of eleven-year-olds but considerably less impact on writing, according to national test data (e.g., DfES, 2002).

Such debates raise important issues, including what is meant by 'attainment', how 'standards' are assessed and, more fundamentally, what 'literacy' is taken to be. However, as will be evident in the following sections, the seminars went substantially beyond discussions on the writing attainment of 11-year-olds. As *Handbooks* are generally compiled to review work in a particular area of enquiry, to summarize key debates and to consider where the work is going, the subtitles of the seminar series—*cross-phase and cross-disciplinary perspectives*—provided some helpful directions in planning the structure of a *Handbook of Writing Development*.

CROSS-DISCIPLINARY ASPECTS

It was evident that, although international research interest in writing and writing processes was widespread, a variety of research perspectives were being used, most notably linguistic, psychological and sociocultural. It also appeared that the insights that these research perspectives on writing can offer had only rarely been *jointly* exploited. There appeared to be a need for an interdisciplinary exploration of writing, to explore a more coherent conceptualization of the field.

Reviews of the literature suggested some additional issues. Some promising outcomes from research findings had apparently not been widely used to develop educational policy and practice, for example specific techniques to develop pupil revision strategies (e.g., Galbraith and Rijlaarsdam, 1999; Chanquoy, 2001) or to enhance syntactical structure (e.g., Beard, 2000a).

Other recent empirical studies had suggested that some key features of writing development warranted further investigation, such as the role of subordination in the development of sustained written discourse (Allison et al., 2002). Although the research base on the use of ICT to improve writing appeared largely inconclusive (Beard, 2000a; see also Torgerson and Zhu, 2003), valuable insights had been suggested from an examination of writing development within a broader notion of 'creative design' (Sharples, 1999; see also Maun and Myhill, 2005).

The seminars also highlighted other possibilities for more research-informed practice. The teaching of writing had not been properly informed by basic models of composition such as knowledge-telling and knowledge-transforming, in some ways analogous to the distinction between casual and critical reading. The knowledge-telling model makes writing a relatively natural task, using existing cognitive structures to overcome difficulties and to minimize the extent to which new challenges are introduced. In contrast, the knowledge-transforming model makes writing a task, which grows in complexity to match the expanding competence of the reflective writer and goes beyond the individual's normal linguistic achievement, reprocessing knowledge through the writer's own cognitive activity (Bereiter and Scardamalia, 1987, 1993; Riley and Reedy, 2002).

Other work suggested that higher pupil achievements might result from increased topic choice and the greater use of peer review and publication procedures (Graves, 1994), although some researchers had reported the dilemmas raised by certain student topic choices (e.g., Gilbert, 1989; Lensmire, 1994). Meta-analyses suggested the value of more guided or 'environmental' approaches that address discourse features and promote pupil approximation of genre features for review and presentation to critical audiences

(Hillocks, 1984, 1986, 1995; Harrison, 2002). At the same time, sociocultural critiques had pointed out the limitations of 'school literacy' and highlighted the need for pupils to be engaged in writing tasks that reflect the authentic communicative practices of the real world (e.g., Barton and Hall, 2000).

The *Handbook* was thus planned to ensure that there was extensive examination of a range of perspectives that can contribute to theoretical and empirical advances in writing development. This range is particularly evident in Section I. The chapters in this section also specifically review key components of the writing process, such as composing, translating and revising, as well as newer semiotics-based investigations into multimodality.

In addition, some chapters in Section I address topics that remain the subject of considerable debate, such as the long-running one on grammar and writing, and more recent ones that discuss multiliteracies and the relationships between writing, language, and power.

Such an examination of theoretical frameworks may also be thrown into sharper relief by the use of a basic historical perspective. This is provided in the very first chapter of the *Handbook*, which reviews the history of writing within a broad view that begins with the use of created visual marks and other artefacts for communication and expression. This beginning helps to clarify how written communication relates more specifically to language, an underlying concern in much of the content of the *Handbook*.

CROSS-PHASE ASPECTS

It was also evident that, historically, research and practice in the teaching of writing had tended to be focused upon specific age ranges, usually characterized by an interest in Early Years education, Primary/Elementary education, or Secondary Education. Age-specific publications in this field often lack attention to cross-phase implications. A relatively narrow disciplinary perspective may limit the research-policy interface and constrain the synergetic potential of cross-disciplinary inquiry and discussion. There appeared to have been little cross-fertilization of academic ideas in a cross-phase context.

Cross-phase perspectives inform Sections II and II of the *Handbook*. Research publications consistently acknowledge that the transformation of spoken language into a written form is hugely challenging for young children and that it is vital to appreciate the multidimensional nature of the task. Sections II and III have been planned to address some of the key dimensions that embrace early written communication, within the contexts of personal experience, identity, and popular culture, in and out of school. These sections also focus on dimensions that schools have long been specifically mandated to promote: handwriting, punctuation, vocabulary, syntax, and the general handling of the alphabetic code. Additional dimensions of development are discussed that have only recently been systematically investigated, including morphology and the 'architecture' of textuality.

As behoves a volume coedited by teacher educators with substantial experience of working with school children and students, these sections reveal a concern for the quality of young people's learning, through the developmental issues of motivation and the content of writing. One chapter specifically addresses a possible casualty of a test-driven curriculum: the writing of poetry. The central concern with the notion of development is maintained through chapters on writing in the secondary/high school years and on writing through college, with a particular focus on self-efficacy.

THE ISSUE OF DEVELOPMENT

A number of issues run across both the cross-phase and cross-disciplinary perspectives. In preparing the *Handbook*, it was noted that a rigorous consideration of the nature of writing development needs to include interrogation of the notion of progression beyond the blinkers of age-related expectations. One of the objectives of the original seminar series was 'to identify aspects of pupil writing that are in need of further investigation'. As one of the participants suggested in the first seminar, more research needs to be done on what constitutes progression in writing and to conceptualize what that progression looks like (Seminar 1 transcripts, para. 49).

The response of the editors was to accept that such issues offer challenges that often stretch far beyond the conceptual reach of a single discipline and that the challenges have complexities that may be most productively tackled by drawing upon the widest research base that is operationally feasible. Section IV of the *Handbook* was designed to allow an examination of some of the most salient challenges that writing development currently presents.

It is evident that issues of writing development have always been shaped by sociocultural contexts, especially demographic and cultural shifts that have shaped development and made it critical to users. This was true in eighteenth-century provincial colleges in America and Britain, where writing was first taught to meet the demands of an expanding upwardly mobile middle class with enough leisure time, interest, and money to take advantage of newly cheap print, and who strove to improve their social class status (Miller, 1997). It was true after the American Civil War as the rise of the modern university made skill in writing an essential credential for professional and economic success. It was true after World War II in America and the UK, as a generation of returning war veterans rapidly expanded state university campuses and enrolments, and in the 1970s US War on Poverty when a new generation of nontraditional, first-generation college students challenged traditional concepts of writing development in these contemporary contexts. In the twenty-first century, writing development is being shaped by new sociocultural transformations in increasingly multiracial, multicultural, and bilingual societies. New information and computer technologies (ICT) are accelerating these transformations, and state and public education authorities, responding to the pace of change and pressures of globalization, are setting standards and mandating high-stakes standardized assessments.

Section IV has been structured to allow reviews of some of these key transformations, with chapters on bilingual writing development from early and advanced learning perspectives. This section also includes chapters that address information and computer technologies: one examines work on hypertext and writing on line; another looks in detail at the 'contested materialities' of writing in new digital environments. The challenge of using research to inform practice is again evident in a chapter that reports investigations into the role of readers in writing development.

Elsewhere in Section IV, the new global and political and social context, in which high-stakes assessment has become prominent, is discussed. One chapter has been planned to set out current views of test validity, which are then related to specific examples of high-stakes writing assessment. This may be counterposed with another chapter. which explores new understandings of classroom writing assessment.

The enduring challenges raised by delays and difficulties in writing development are also reviewed in this final section. As is evident elsewhere, models of the development of writing skills are seen as necessary to understand the nature of the difficulties that children and young people experience.

The ecological validity of educational practices is highlighted by another chapter, which is concerned with writing in the wider community. The conceptual validity of the Handbook as a whole is raised by a final chapter, concerned with the future of writing.

The *Handbook of Writing Development* critically examines research and theoretical issues that impact upon writing development from the early years to adulthood. It is planned to be a pivotal text, whose main purpose is to provide those researching, studying, or teaching literacy with one of the most academically authoritative and comprehensive bodies of work in the field. In bringing together the *Handbook*, the editors have been privileged to work with many of the leading figures in the field from across the world. The editors hope that the cross-phase, cross-disciplinary, and developmental perspectives will encourage synergy in building new theories and in raising new issues for research. If that hope is fulfilled, then the impact of the *Handbook* will offer far-reaching implications for children and young people.

NOTE

1 <http://www.ioe.ac.uk/schools/ecpe/ ReconceptualisingWriting5-16/index.html> (accessed 14 March, 2007).

REFERENCES

Allison, P., Beard, R., and Willcocks, J. (2002) 'Subordination in children's writing', *Language and Education*, 16(2): 97–111.

Barton, D. and Hall, N. (eds) (2000) *Letter Writing as a Social Practice*, Amsterdam: John Benjamins Pub.Co.

Beard, R. (1999) *The National Literacy Strategy: Review of Research and Other Related Evidence*, London: Department for Education and Employment.

Beard, R. (2000a) *Developing Writing 3–13*, London: Hodder and Stoughton.

Beard, R. (2000b) 'Research and the National Literacy Strategy', *Oxford Review of Education*, 26, 3/4: 421–436.

Bereiter, C. and Scardamalia, M. (1987) *The Psychology of Written Composition*, Hillsdale, NJ: Lawrence Erlbaum.

Bereiter, C. and Scardamalia, M. (1993) 'Composing and writing', in R. Beard (ed), *Teaching Literacy: Balancing Perspectives*, London: Hodder and Stoughton.

Chanquoy, L. (2001) 'How to make it easier for children to revise their writing: A study of text revision from 3rd to 5th grades', *British Journal of Educational Psychology*, 71:15–41.

Department for Education and Skills (2002) 'Autumn Package', London: Department for Education and Employment.

Earl, L., Watson, N., Levin, B., Leithwood, K., Fullan, M., and Torrance, N. (2003) 'Watching and Learning 3: Final Report of the External Evaluation of England's National Literacy and Numeracy Strategies', London: Department for Education and Employment.

Galbraith, D. and Rijlaarsdam, G. (1999) 'Effective strategies for the teaching and learning of writing', *Learning and Instruction*, 9: 93–108.

Gilbert, P. (1989) 'Student text as pedagogical text', in S. de Castell, A. Luke and C. Luke (eds), *Language, Authority and Criticism*, London: Falmer Press.

Graves, D.H. (1994) *A Fresh Look at Writing*, Portsmouth, NH: Heinemann.

Harrison, C. (2002) *The National Strategy for English at Key Stage 3: Roots and Research*, London: Department for Education and Skills.

Her Majesty's Inspectorate (2000) *The Teaching of Writing in Primary Schools: Could Do Better*, London: Office for Standards in Education.

Hillocks, G. (1984) 'What works in teaching composition: A meta-analysis of experimental treatment studies', *American Journal of Education*, 93: 133–170.

Hillocks, G. (1986) *Research on Written Composition*, Urbana, Il.: National Conference on Research in English/ERIC Clearinghouse on Reading and Communication Skills.

Hillocks, G. (1995) *Teaching Writing as Reflective Practice*, New York: Teachers College Press.

Lensmire, T. (1994) *When Children Write: Critical Revisions of the Writing Workshop*, New York: Teachers College Press.

Maun, I. and Myhill, D. (2005) 'Texts as design, writers as designers', *English in Education*, 39(2), 5–21.

Miller, T. (1997) *The Formation of College English: Rhetoric and Belles Lettres in the British Cultural Provinces*, Pittsburgh: University of Pittsburgh Press.

Myhill, D.A. (1999) 'Writing matters', *English in Education*, 33(3): 70–81.

Myhill, D.A. (2001) *Better Writers*, Westley: Courseware Publications.

Riley, J. and Reedy, D. (2000) *Developing Writing for Different Purposes: Teaching about Genre in the Early Years*, London: Paul Chapman.

Riley, J. and Reedy, D. (2002) 'Children Should Be Taught Written Language', Paper presented at the International Reading Association Conference, San Francisco, April.

Sharples, M. (1999) *How We Write: Writing as Creative Design*, London: Routledge.

Torgerson, C. and Zhu, D. (2003) 'A Systematic Review and Meta-Analysis of the Effectiveness of ICT on Literacy Learning in English, 5–16 in Research Evidence in Education Library', London: Evidence for Policy and Practice Information and Co-ordinating (EPPI) Centre, Social Science Research Unit, Institute of Education, University of London.

1

The History of Writing

David R. Olson

The history of writing depends critically upon what we mean by writing.

INTRODUCTION

Paradigmatically, writing is the representation of speech. But what then about the visual signs and symbols that humans created and continue to create sometimes for communication purposes, other times for sheer self expression, and at still other times for linking themselves to the gods? To tell the history of writing, even in its paradigmatic sense, it seems essential to begin with a more comprehensive view of writing as the use of created visual marks or other artefacts for communication and expression. From this base, we may then see more clearly how representations in general relate to representations of language more specifically.

With this more inclusive notion of writing as visual communication we can include the celebrated 40,000-year-old cave drawings at Lascaux and Altamira, as well as the first markings incised on bone, in China, dating back some 10,000 years, the clay gods modelled by the Hittites some 8,000 years ago, as well as the petroglyphs carved by North American aboriginal peoples some 4,000 years ago. For it is out of these earliest attempts that the modern forms of communication we think of as 'true writing' evolved and it is from such attempts that even modern children work their way into writing and literacy. My concern in this chapter is to set out some of the transitions in visual communication and the social and cognitive conditions that contributed to the evolution of modern forms of writing.

Even the more inclusive notion of writing as visual communication rules out a huge realm of visual information, such as that of a face reddened by embarrassment, the gestures and gesticulations that accompany speech, the tracks we leave on sand or snow that may be 'read' and interpreted by others. We set them aside, not because they are unimportant, but because in such cases there is no attempt or intention on the part of the actor to express or communicate. On the other hand, smoke signals, a hand raised in greeting or anger, a headdress, or mansion indicating power or wealth, would fall within a scheme of visual communication and expression, as they are conventional signs that are intended to represent and convey information. As signs, they may be distinguished from the things they represent. Just how they represent, and how they are understood by those who 'read' them, will be a major part of the story.

The study of visual signs has traditionally focused on the structure and meaning of the sign systems themselves, that is, on what the signs represent, whether ideas, words, sounds and so on. In the more recent past, the concern has shifted to the uses of those signs and the ways they may be, and have been, interpreted as well as the traditions they help to create. In the first of these, the classical theories of writing such as those set out by Gelb (1963) and Diringer (1968) showed the evolutionary pattern of how signs that at one time represented objects and events in a somewhat direct and unmediated way, progressively shifted to represent more and more indirectly through the use of marks to indicate the abstract properties of the spoken form – words, syllables, and eventually phonemes. Briefly stated, these evolutionary accounts showed that the signs that at first represented objects or events in the world evolved into signs that attempted to represent *language* about the world.

But more functionalist orientations to writing have focused on the widely divergent uses of those signs, arguing that it was the uses and attempted uses of those signs that drove their evolution. A few tokens may adequately represent a business transaction but a richer set of signs would be required to represent a name, an event, a poem, or a law. Moreover, the uses are not only those intended by the maker of marks or signs but also the ways they are taken up and used by the recipients. Visual signs designed to represent poetry may turn out to be useful for writing curses. While we cannot be certain of the uses of the earliest drawings, carvings, and other inscriptions – were they aesthetic or were they magical? – they fall into two rough classes we usually think of as drawing and writing. However, the classes are not so well defined to be mutually exclusive, because the users of those signs may treat them as basically similar or basically different. Thus, although a religious icon and the printed word 'Jesus' may represent that person in quite different ways, viewers may treat them as equivalent objects of veneration.

In fact, just how these marks or symbols relate to the things, events, ideas, and meanings they are thought to express has been not only a philosophical puzzle but a political matter sometimes resolved only by wars and revolutions. The first actions by either a despot or an invader is to tear down the existing gods and other symbols of the culture. Think of the planting of the flag on Iwo Jima or the toppling of the statues of Saddam Hussain. Some symbols such as icons, relics, pictures, and other souvenirs would seem to be represented by *mimesis*, that is, by similarity to sharing essential features with, or having a natural connection to the things they represent. So much so that the god of the ancient Hebrews forbade the worship of graven images; presumably, the image would draw attention away from the thing the image was to represent, namely, God himself. Words, by contrast, would seem to represent by mere convention, an arbitrary relation to the thing represented, and hence much less likely to be seen as directly connected to or a participant in the thing represented.

Literary theorists distinguish these two ways of relating symbols to the things they represent as metonymy and metaphor; the first linked directly, a participant in, or part of, or bearing a strong similarity to the thing represented, the latter, standing for or taking the place of the thing represented. Images, icons, relics, sculptures, laying on of hands, representations by metonymy – they are mimetic symbols. Words, theories, models, and equations represent metaphorically; they are conveniences for thinking about the things they represent, little more than conventions. It is noteworthy that names, unlike words, are treated as if they were mimetic, as if they were intrinsically related to the person or object they designate. Hence, considerable effort goes into naming a child or a state or a building and few parents would be content to name their newborn with an arbitrary string of digits. On the other hand, it seems appropriate to name a robot R2D2.

This distinction between these two basic ways of representing is not only hard won, but it also remains controversial. Every culture treats some things as sacred and the symbols of the sacred are treated metonymically, that is, treated as if, in some sense, they embody the thing represented. Tambiah (1990) discussed the controversies about the burning of the American flag, an act that was seen by most as a desecration of the thing, the nation, it stands for. It is not regarded as merely a conventional sign even if, in fact, it is purely conventional. Names, as mentioned, are words but in addition are seen as a part of or a property of the person named, hence, the provisions against slander of 'my good name'.

It was only in the seventeenth century that signs came to be seen simply as signs. It was the Port Royal grammarians who sharply distinguished signs from things, *verba* from *res,* arguing that signs are not things but merely *representations* of things, the view we hold, at least when we are thinking scientifically, to this day. If signs are merely arbitrary and conventional and completely independent of the things they represent, what harm could there be in insulting a sign? None. Similarly, if signs such as words are merely conventional, how could words have power? They cannot. At a stroke, the world of signs was *disenchanted*. It, thus, came to be seen as ancient superstition to believe in word magic, in sympathetic medicine, or in Voodoo, the ancient practice of burning or destroying an effigy with the attempt to harm the person of whom it is an effigy. We still, of course, cringe when we see a pin poked into the eye of a person in a photo and young children will, occasionally, lick a picture of an ice-cream cone. Nevertheless, for most modern users of signs, we have adopted the Port Royal convention, passed on down to us through such famous linguists as Saussure

and Chomsky, that signs are arbitrary and conventional representations. Pictures too have come to be seen as not as mimetic but as expressions in a language of art, a view not shared by all societies nor by all members of the same society – recall the outrage expressed at the insultingly crude portrait of Churchill or the drawings of the Prophet.

Representations, then, are to be distinguished from the things they represent and they are ordinarily recognized by viewers as distinct, even if the boundary is sometimes masked or ignored. Consider the interesting drawing by the French artist Magritte who drew a picture of a pipe, smoke drifting from the barrel, which then he mischievously labelled *'Ceci n'est ce pas une pipe'* – 'This is not a pipe'. Surely, he is joking or contradicting himself. Not so, the major theme of Magritte's *ouvre* is that of playing with the possible conflicts between a thing and the representation of a thing. Hence, he portrays the artist's easel with a painting on it in such a way that you cannot tell whether you are viewing the artist's painting or the object being painted. Other artists had toyed with this quandary earlier as in Velazquez' renowned 'Les Meninas' and Escher's drawing of doves that seem to slow transform into turtles. However, it is Magritte who makes a habit of showing the troubled relation between the thing and the representation of a thing. This is not a pipe but rather *a picture of a pipe*. Woe unto him who fails to make the distinction as indeed, woe unto him who draws it too crisply.

The history of visual signs, including those that come to represent speech, is deeply embedded in the mimetic tradition, the tradition that sees resemblance or identity between sign and thing represented. The first visual signs tended to be symbols of deities, treated as objects of veneration, their form determined by resemblance or similarity to the thing represented. This was no less true for those symbols used for mundane commercial purposes, for keeping records or recording transactions, than it was for those created in the attempt to influence the gods. Furthermore, how to adequately represent one's communicative intentions, as in conventional writing, was no more obvious than how to adequately represent and communicate with an abstract and unknown god. One may compare for example the 6,000 BC Anatolian fertility goddess moulded from clay with the stained glass windows of St. Peter's Cathedral. To those who viewed them, the symbol seemed adequate to its purpose even if the forms they take are radically different. So too for the invention of signs for writing.

For there to be a history of writing, then, we must consider the structure of the symbols, the uses made of them, and, in addition, we must locate traceable lines of descent. Rather than celebrate the diversity of forms and uses, we must trace how one set of visual signs evolved into a second, often more complex set of visual marks and how those marks came to be seen as representing increasingly abstract properties of speech. In doing so, writing changed from quite diverse and special-purpose systems of signs into more or less all-purpose writing systems we employ to this day. A combination of borrowing good ideas and applying them to new and diverse uses motivated these advances.

To understand the history of writing we must set aside our literate prejudices, our tendency to assume as natural and obvious that language is an object available for inspection; that we have a natural consciousness of language. This tendency comes to literate people primarily from their identifying language with the written form and in some cases as identifying language as a distinctive 'tongue'. For nonliterate persons language is available to thought only in the most general sense, as answers to 'What did he say?' or for translating into a foreign tongue. Consequently, writing was never a matter of simply inventing a device for recording speech but rather a matter of discovering the properties of speech suitable for visual representation and communication. It was the latter task that required generations of borrowing and invention.

Consequently, while visual signs in general are natural means of communication as

any form of speaking, writing is not simply a natural communicative competence like speech. First, it was slow to evolve historically and second, is late to be acquired by children and normally requires explicit teaching. Moreover, unlike speech, writing has a relatively recent, traceable history. The great historians of writing mentioned earlier (Diringer, 1968; Gelb, 1963) traced this evolution from word signs or logographs, to syllable signs or syllabaries, and finally to alphabets that at first represented consonants only and later, in the hands of the Greeks, alphabets that represented both consonants and vowels. Consequently, three types of writing systems have been described by most writers in this tradition: logography, syllabaries, and alphabets, arranged according to Gelb's (1963: 252) *Principle of unidirectional development* 'from word to syllabic to alphabetic writing'. More recent theorists (Coulmas, 2003; Daniels, 2009; Sampson, 1985; Taylor and Olson, 1995) have shown that such systems of signs do not so easily fall into the earlier categories in that all writing systems use a variety of forms of representation including special signs for names, namely capitalization, signs for sentences, namely capitals and periods, and the like. Others (Gaur, 1987; Harris, 1986) have emphasized the ways that function and use have driven the preservation, in some cases, and the evolution, in others, of writing systems. All writing systems are attempts at communication and as those needs change, so do the writing systems.

As we have seen, it is a universal property of all so-called 'full' writing systems that they do not represent or depict the world directly but indirectly. In all of them writing is not about the world but about what one says about the world, writing is the representation of language. Consequently, all modern writing systems are based on the invention of signs that capture aspects of the sound patterns of speech rather than what those sound patterns mean or refer to. Daniels (2009) has pointed out, 'there are three known independent ancient origins of writing – the

Sumerian, the Chinese, and the Mayan – all of which served societies that had developed some degree of urbanism, and that the three languages involved were similar in basic structure: most of their morphemes are just a single syllable' (p. 36). What this means is that all writing systems began with the recognition of the fact that signs could be used to represent sound, specifically, the sound of the syllable, and that was most readily discovered, as Daniels points out, in languages that had an abundance of single syllable words. This basic insight was then exploited as writing came to be used for languages with more complex syllable structures such as Greek. It is the fact that writing brings different aspects of linguistic form into awareness that gives writing its distinctive impact on cognition; writing is not only a means of communication but also a distinctive form of representation, a representation of language.

While all modern or 'full' writing systems, then, represent language, and they all began by representing monosyllabic morphemes, under the pressure of adapting to new languages and to serve new functions they were elaborated in quite different ways. Signs may represent whole words or morphemes such as 'fee', they may represent separate syllables in multisyllable words such as 'fee/ble', they may divide syllables into 'onsets' and 'rimes', or they may take the further step of further dissolving the onsets and rimes into underlying phonological constituents and including vowels, the invention of the Greeks, to make the modern alphabet.

However, the impression that the history of writing is one of simple progress towards the alphabet is misleading. Earlier writing systems were not faltering steps towards or failed attempts at creating a transcription of language. There never was any attempt to invent an alphabet as an ideal means of representing language (Daniels, in press: 15). Rather, each step in the revision and transformation of a writing system was the result of applying a system that more or less

adequately represented one language, to a new language for which it was not well adapted, requiring revisions in the writing system. Hence, the evolutionary metaphor is somewhat misleading; as in modern biology, there never was an attempt to evolve the ideal or perfect structure but only the attempt to adapt existing structures to new requirements. If other writing systems are seen as deficient in comparison with the modern alphabet, it is only in terms of the new goals and purposes for which the alphabet was developed. Yet it is also true that the invention of the alphabet turned writing from a special purpose device into a system of communication that was capable of expressing anything that could be said; writing became in many ways the equivalent of speech.

The most general principle guiding the development and evolution of writing systems is that of serving as an effective means of storing and communicating information, through time and across space, as Innis (1951) and many others have noted. That they have come to represent the most abstract properties of spoken language is an unanticipated outcome of the attempt to develop systems to convey information unambiguously. Thus, principles of communicative effectiveness as well as principles of economy are relevant to the shaping of writing systems into more abstract forms. However, principles of conservatism and tradition are also at play. To change the writing system is to abandon a tradition and to make its literate past inaccessible, hence, the conservatism of, among others, the Chinese script. Issues of national identity whether affirming or abandoning a past, as when Serbia retains the Cyrillic alphabet to identify its link to Greek Orthodoxy whereas its neighbours adopt the Roman alphabet to show their identity with the West or as in modern Turkey's adopting the Roman script in an attempt to shed an abandoned past.

The fact that the evolution of writing systems were attempts at communication rather than attempts to represent the most fundamental and abstract properties of spoken language, namely, phonemes, has the important implication I briefly mentioned above. It implies that these revisions of writing systems were at the same time discoveries of the implicit properties of speech. This provides justification for the radical conclusion that I advanced earlier (Olson, 1994) namely, that attempts at communication had as an unanticipated outcome the discovery of the implicit properties of speech. It is this new consciousness of language that has allowed literacy to serve as a new mode of thought. As I wrote, echoing Whorf (1956): 'We introspect our language in terms of the categories laid down by our script' (p. xviii). Our linguistic categories reflect rather than determine the properties of our writing systems.

What has become more conspicuous since that was written was that technological inventions depend for their effects on how they are picked up, used, amplified, and adopted as a social practice by what has been called a 'textual community'. Without readers who themselves adopt the practice and use it in a way that is mutually comprehensible for purposes that they, as a group come to share, writing as a technology would have no social impact. No written document stands alone; it is read, discussed, interpreted, and commentaries are written and new documents created to form a tradition. It is through this tradition, existing through time and across many readers and writers that such social practices evolve into such distinctive literate forms as commerce, philosophy, science, literature, and so on. In addition, for an individual to become literate is to learn how to participate in these textual communities. It merely begins with an acquaintance with orthography, a writing system.

Yet, communicative needs do not simply create inventions out of the blue; inventions are, at least in the case of writing, adaptations of existing systems of visual communication and hence, the very possibility of a history of writing.

A HISTORY OF WRITING SYSTEMS

The earliest signs for visual communication that provide a traceable link to later forms of writing are the clay tokens developed for accounting purposes in Mesopotamia in the ninth millennium BC. The system, developed by ancient Sumerians in what is now Iraq, about the time that traditional hunter-gatherers were developing an agricultural way of life, consisted of sets of distinctively shaped tokens used to keep records of sheep and cattle and other commodities such as oil, beer, and grain. About the fourth millennium, about the time of the growth of cities, the variety of tokens increased, some were pierced so that they could be strung together, and others were placed in envelopes or *bullae* so that they could indicate a single transaction. Schmandt-Besserat (1992) has suggested that the shift from tokens to writing began when markings were made on these envelopes to indicate their contents. These markings, she suggests, constitute the first true writing. All of the eighteen signs denoting commodities such as grain, animals, and oil which later appear on standard clay tablets were derived from these marking for tokens.

Systems of signs of this sort do not yet compose a full writing system as they lack a *syntax*, a system for relating signs to each other. This began first by the invention of separate signs for number with the result that instead of representing three sheep by means of three tokens, one for each sheep, the new system could represent three sheep by two signs, one for the number three and one for the noun, sheep. Yet, even here, what we have is more of an accounting system than a full writing system. All of the world's modern writing systems evolved from systems which captured not things, and not thoughts, but the sound patterns of the language they were used to represent as we saw earlier (Daniels, 2009, p. 35).

Subsequent developments, which gave rise to the alphabet are attributable largely to the consequences of borrowing. When a script that adequately represents one language is borrowed to represent a quite different language, the signs are 'read' in a new way. Signs for one-syllable words come to be treated as signs for a single syllable of a multisyllable word. So, word signs in language A come to be treated as syllable signs when they are borrowed to represent language B as happened when Sumerian logographs were borrowed to represent a Semitic language Akkadian (Larsen, 1989: 131). A noteworthy feature of such syllable signs, or syllabaries, is that they lack signs for vowels. Distinctive signs for vowels are usually credited to the genius of the Greeks. Yet the story is less one of genius than of adapting the Semitic Phoenician syllabary to the special linguistic properties of spoken Greek. Pre-Greek scripts had reduced the complexity of their syllabaries by using a single sign for all the syllables sharing a common 'on-set' or initial sound. Thus, a single sign, say *p*, may be used to represent *pa, pe, pi, po, or pu* thereby losing any indication of the vowel differences, which, in any case, did not mark morphological or meaning differences. The Phoenician set of twenty-two graphic signs with a memorized order beginning *aleph, bet, and gemel,* was adequate for representing the full range of meanings and the signs can be seen as representing not only syllables but also the consonantal sounds of the language.

Vowels were added to the script by the Greeks about 750 BC, some have suggested especially for the transcription of the orally produced Homeric epic poems (Powell, 2002) – commercial transactions could be conducted in the scripts of the trading partners, the Phoenicians. Others (Thomas, 2009) however, have argued that even prior to the recording of the epics, Greek writing was used for such ordinary purposes as writing curses and identifying valuable objects as one's own – 'This cup belongs to Tataie' or 'I am Nestor's cup'.

While not minimizing the significance of the Greek invention of distinctive marks for vowels, it is now widely acknowledged that the development of the alphabet, like the development of the syllabary, was a more-or-less straightforward consequence of applying a script which adequately represented one language, to a second language, for which is was not completely adequate. Whereas in Phoenician vocalic differences were unimportant, in Greek, as in English, vocalic differences mark meaning differences – 'bad' is different from 'bed'. Moreover, words may consist simply of a vowel, they may begin with a vowel and words with pairs of vowels are not uncommon. To fill the gap, six of the signs representing sounds unknown to Greek speakers were borrowed to represent the isolated vowel sounds. In this way, syllables were dissolved into consonant-vowel pairings and the alphabet was born.

The structure and history of writing systems, what Gelb (1963) and more recently Daniels (2009) have called *Grammatology*, provide evidence for the claim that the implicit structure of language is not readily available even to those who are attempting to develop a writing system. Rather, the history of writing is one of the progressive discoveries of increasingly abstract properties of language. The original inventors of writing systems could not, or at least did not, simply sit down and ask themselves 'What are the basic properties of language that we should indicate with our visible signs?' Rather they worked as practitioners solving immediate problems of communication and record keeping and as the signs were applied to new languages and new tasks, the sign systems elaborated, first to capture the meanings, then the syllabic sounds, and eventually the phonemes of the language.

In learning to read and write children appear to go through a parallel discovery process. First come representations of things and events, as in drawing. Then they distinguish writing from drawing on the basis of iterative signs (Tolchinsky, 2009) claiming that *kydz* but not *kkkk* could be writing, and that writing should represent words not things. As Bruce Homer and I (Homer and Olson, 1999) showed, prereading/prewriting children when asked to write 'Three little pigs' make three small scribbles, for 'Two little pigs' they make two scribbles and so on. This indicates that they still assume that the written marks stand for the things represented, the pigs, rather than for the words of the utterance. When asked to write 'No little pigs', they may leave the paper unmarked 'Because there are no little pigs'. Still later, when they realize the writing represents sounds they may use only consonants as in representing 'book' as BK or 'boat' as BT. Interestingly, Spanish children are more likely to represent the word by its vowel sound than by its consonantal sound as when they represent 'boat' as OT (Ferreiro and Teberovsky, 1982). (If you listen to your own speech you may be surprised to hear that the 'o' sound outlasts the onset 'b' sound). Discovering the distinctive phonemes in one's speech is difficult for most children and presents an almost insurmountable hurdle to some children in learning to read an alphabetic script. Goswami (2009, p. 138) has provided both psychological and neuroscientific evidence to show that reading difficulties associated with dyslexia are traceable to difficulties in linking sounds to letters. She concluded that 'awareness of phonological structure of one's spoken language is clearly fundamental to the acquisition of literacy'.

The importance of learning to link letters to sounds should not be surprising in view of the fact that, as we saw earlier, all writing systems are composed of marks that represent the syllabic and phonological invariants of speech. Yet, there is some danger of over-attention to the issue of 'phonological awareness', which itself is as much a product of learning to read as a precondition for achieving it. Thus, reading *Harry Potter* may do as much for one's phonological awareness as hours of practice at long vowels. Of course, neither the code nor its uses should be neglected and pedagogy should be adjusted to those aspects of knowledge that are problematic for particular individuals.

So what is writing? To be sure, it is a set of signs invented to represent speech. But because of its unique relation to speech and its properties of preservation through space and time writing has come to play an incredibly diverse set of social functions – in commerce, government, literature, and science – as well as in a myriad of smaller scale, local contexts documented by Barton and Hamilton (1998). It is these uses, which have given literacy such significance and the history of writing is in large part how the potentials of writing have been taken up in various times and places. The study of writing, thereby, becomes the study of the uses of writing. To see this, consider the concept of literacy. On the one hand, it is simply the ability to decode or transform scripts into speech. However, on the other, literacy is the ability to use that competence for various culturally defined purposes. The Oxford English Dictionary captures both of these meanings: the ability to read, and, knowledge of literature.

A HISTORY OF READING

Eric Havelock (1982), one of the pantheon of heroes of our story, once pointed out, the history of writing is perhaps better described as the history of reading. For the same marks may at one time be taken, that is read, as one thing and later as another. He argued that the invention of marks, their differentiation and elaboration in various contexts of use, reflected the attempt to reduce misreadings, to reduce ambiguity. Punctuation, for example, was introduced into a writing system when it was recognized that it could forestall misreadings. Similarly, with additions to the inventory of signs; adding vowels to the set of signs was in part a response to misreadings rather than simply a discovery of an implicit property of speech by the writer. Consequently, the study of writing is at the same time the study of reading and their histories are, if not the same history, at least rather intertwined.

No history of reading exists and perhaps none is possible. Ways of reading depend not only on the properties of the text or document but on the purposes or stances of the readers. The same document could be read, for example, as the word of God, or the word of an ancient scribe, depending on whether one was a member of the faithful or an intellectual historian. Ways of reading are not uniquely individual practices but rather social practices, ways of reading that are shared by a textual community. It is within such textual communities or communities of practice that specialized and distinctive uses of writing, as for example in modern literature, evolve. Conventions of form, conventions of meaning and definition, accepted practices evolve to meet these socially shared goals. One reads and interprets documents not only according to their words but also in terms of the goals and practices in which those words are encountered. We distinguish these forms generally in terms of genres and registers – poetry as opposed to prose, philosophy as opposed to literature, and so on. Moreover, learning the conventions for these social practices is as complex and sometimes as obscure as the long-vowel rule in learning to read. To be literate is to learn to read according to those structures sets of conventions. Conversely, ways of reading dictate ways of writing. Written commentaries on sacred texts take a different form than the texts they comment on, presumably reflecting the forms that oral discourse on those topics tend to take. Hence, the history of writing and of literacy more generally is the history of the evolution of these more specialized forms of discourse. And it remains an open question as to whether there is one literacy which may be put to vastly divergent uses (Goody, 1987; Olson, 1994) or many literacies, each more or less unique with minor and incidental relations between them (Cole and Cole, 2007). Of course, it may profitably be viewed in either way (Gee, 2006).

The spread of writing and literacy, the so-called 'democratization' of writing appears to play an important part in general social change. One such change, going back to antiquity, was the association between writing and power. 'It is written' had a finality that many found irresistible. Another, more recent change, was dissolving the relation between the written and power. Modernity is identified with the increasing recognition of the right of everyone to have an opinion and a forum for expression. It removed writing from the prerogative of the rich and powerful. This move, visible in the tradition of letters to the editor, and now overwhelmingly clear in the era of internet chat rooms and blogs that rival in significance, and certainly in readership, the records of the actions of parliament. With it comes the gradual disenchantment of the written. One still finds a certain regard given to writers, a kind of regard, the hope for which keeps many of us at our computers. With the growth of literacy, there is an increasing acknowledgement that the written is always simply the expression of some writer who is more or less like the reader. Remarkably enough, until recent times, and still only for a minority, sacred texts have come to be seen, that is read, as if they were written by men not by gods. Modern readers, I suspect, do not really believe anything they read, or hear for that matter.

One relatively well-studied transformation in the ways of reading is that involved in the Protestant Reformation. The Church of Rome had, for centuries, maintained a monopoly not only on who should read and what should be read but also on how it should be read, that is, interpreted. Whether that monopoly eroded because of the more general availability of written materials or because of a loss of respect for the Church and its clergy in regions remote from Rome or both is not clear. Yet the fraying of control on how to read can be seen not only in Lutheran Protestantism but also in the rise of heretical movements throughout Western Europe (Stock, 1983). Most, if not all, heretics were literates who disbelieved in Roman orthodoxy. The well-known study of one such heretic by Carlo Ginzburg (1982) of the rustic, self-taught literate miller Menocchio, who insisted that the Biblical account of the origins of life was incorrect and that people had appeared on the earth not by the act of God but by a simple natural process known to every farmer, that of worms simply and nonmiraculously appearing on the cheese. When he refused to relent, to keep his opinions to himself, he was burned at the stake.

Luther, of course, did not deny the Bible; rather he contested the Church's authority to determine how it was read, what it really meant. He drew a strict line between what it literally meant, the meaning available to every reader, and the penumbra of tradition about its correct interpretation that was traditionally defended by the Church. Luther was not the first to recognize that the authors of the books of the Bible were men like himself who wrote for a particular purpose in a particular time and particular place to particular readers. What he succeeded in doing was recruiting a powerful following who, often for their own reasons, joined him in forming a textual community. Protestantism to this day, cherishes the view that the meaning of scripture is open to the ordinary reader, the meanings clear and transparent to all who approach with an open heart. This optimism survives even in the face of hundreds of competing sects each claiming to have discovered that true meaning.

Nonetheless the assumption that one could write and read in this direct and transparent manner, and relying only on the authority of the ordinary writer and reader, was responsible for a new way of writing, a language of description, and a new way of reading what Thomas Brown called 'the book of nature'. Reading the book of nature was to be a matter of seeing nature not as a symbol of something else but of addressing nature as an object in its own right. Alpers (1983: 81), in her careful study of Dutch artists of the seventeenth Century showed that their strategy was to 'separate the object seen from those beliefs or interpretations to which it had given rise'. Thus, one of the artists urged painters to see the clouds as clouds rather than symbols of the heavens. This new naturalism became the standard for Early Modern Science as well as the standard model for all modern descriptive

or expository prose, which imposes a sharp distinction between facts and opinions, observations and inferences, evidence and claims, and so on.

In summary, what began as a useful mnemonic, a device for keeping records some four or five millennium ago, turned into a means of communication, writing, that was readily adapted to serve diverse social practices in different ways in different contexts and cultures. Writing did so by capturing not only the basic structures of speech but also by the capacity, more developed in some cultural contexts than others, the full range of functions that speech serves. By specializing some of these functions to serve special purposes such as science and government, writing put its imprint on much of the modern world. Through such institutional arrangements as reading circles, churches, and schools, writing changed not only our ways of acting in the world but also our ways of thinking about our language, and ultimately our very selves.

REFERENCES

Alpers, S. (1983) *The Art of Describing: Dutch Art in the Seventeenth Century*. Chicago: Chicago University Press.

Barton, D. and Hamilton, M. (1998) *Local Literacies: Reading and Writing in One Community*, London and New York: Routledge.

Cole, M. and Cole, J. (2007) 'Rethinking the Goody myth', in D.R. Olson and M. Cole (eds), *Technology, Literacy and the Evolution of Society*, Cambridge: Cambridge University Press. pp.305–324.

Coulmas, F. (2003) *Writing Systems. Cambridge Textbooks in Linguistics*, Cambridge: Cambridge University Press.

Daniels, P. (2009). 'Grammatology', in D.R. Olson and N.G. Torrance (eds), *Cambridge Handbook of Literacy*, Cambridge: Cambridge University Press. pp.25–45.

Diringer, D. (1968) *The Alphabet: A Key to the History of Mankind* (third edn.), New York: Funk & Wagnalls.

Ferreiro, E. and Teberosky, A. (1982) *Literacy before Schooling*, Exeter, NH: Heinemann.

Gaur, A. (1987) *A History of Writing* (Paperback edn) London: The British Library. (Original, 1984.)

Gee, J. (2006) 'Oral discourse in a world of literacy', *Research in the Teaching of English*, 41(2): 153–159.

Gelb, I. (1963) *A Study of Writing* (second edn.), Chicago: University of Chicago Press.

Ginzburg, C. (1982) *The Cheese and the Worms: The Cosmos of a Sixteenth-Century Miller*, Markham, ON: Penguin Books.

Goody, J. (1987) *The Interface between the Oral and the Written*, Cambridge: Cambridge University Press.

Goswami, U. (2009) 'The basic processes in reading: Insights from neuroscience', in D.R. Olson and N.G. Torrance (eds), *Cambridge Handbook of Literacy*, Cambridge: Cambridge University Press. pp.134–151.

Harris, R. (1986) *The Origin of Writing*, London: Duckworth.

Havelock, E. (1982) *The Literate Revolution in Greece and its Cultural Consequences*, Princeton, NJ: Princeton University Press.

Homer, B. and Olson, D.R. (1999) *Literacy and Children's Conception of Language, Written Language and Literacy*, 2: 113–137.

Innis, H. (1951) *The Bias of Communication*, Toronto: University of Toronto Press.

Larsen, M.T. (1989) 'What they wrote on clay', in K. Schousboe and M.T. Larsen (eds), *Literacy and Society*, Copenhagen: Copenhagen University, Centre for Research in the Humanities. pp.121–148.

Olson, D.R. (1994) *The World on Paper: The Conceptual and Cognitive Implications of Writing and Reading*, Cambridge: Cambridge University Press.

Powell, B. (2002) *Writing and the Origins of Greek Literature*, Cambridge, UK: Cambridge University Press.

Sampson, J. (1985) *Writing Systems*, Stanford, CA: Stanford University Press.

Schmandt-Bessarat, D. (1992) *Before Writing*, Austin: University of Texas Press.

Stock, B. (1983) *The Implications of Literacy*, Princeton, NJ: Princeton University Press.

Tambiah, S.J. (1990) 'Relations of analogy and identity: Toward multiple orientations to the world', in D.R. Olson and N.G. Torrance (eds), *Modes of Thought*, Cambridge: Cambridge University Press. pp.34–52.

Taylor, I. and Olson, D.R. (eds) (1995) *Scripts and Literacy: Reading and Learning to Read Alphabets, Syllaries and Characters*, Dordrecht: Kluwer.

Tolchinsky, L. (2009) 'The configuration of literacy as a domain of knowledge', in D.R. Olson and N.G. Torrance (eds), *The Cambridge Handbook of Literacy*, Cambridge: Cambridge University Press. pp.468–486.

Thomas, R. (in press) 'The origins of western literacy: Literacy in ancient Greece and Rome', in D.R. Olson and N.G. Torrance (eds), *Cambridge Handbook of Literacy*, Cambridge: Cambridge University Press.

Whorf, B.L. (1956) 'Science and linguistics', in *Selected Writings of Benjamin Lee Whorf*, Cambridge, MA: MIT Press. pp.207–219.

INTRODUCTION

Theoretical perspectives

This section of the *Handbook* sets out to map the landscape in terms of the theoretical frameworks which underpin research in writing and writing development and to provide a touchstone upon which the thinking and insights in subsequent chapters can be tested. The field of research in writing is relatively young, unlike the well-developed parallel fields in language acquisition or reading, and its impact on instructional design and pedagogy has been limited. Indeed, Hayes and Flower's (1980) model of the writing process was arguably a turning point in the field, triggering a growth in empirical studies, which still flourishes today. However, that is only part of the story.

The field of writing research is not a unified, coherent one and it is characterized by theoretical frameworks, which adopt very different methodological, epistemological, and ontological stances. This difference in values and assumptions can often be seen in the way writing researchers refer to each other's work. The influential work of Graves (1983) on process approaches to writing and the value of the writing conference, which

had a significant influence on classroom practice in the US and the UK, is critiqued by Smagorinsky as 'reportage'. He argued that Graves represented 'classroom observation as research' (1987:340) and that using close observation of selected students, without looking for counterevidence for their claims, results in outcomes, which are little more than 'a narrative string of anecdotes' (1987: 332). Yet, whilst research, which is close to classroom practice may be challenged on the grounds of its limited methodological rigour, the more scientific, positivist approaches adopted by cognitive psychology are taken to task by Nystrand for their narrow conceptualization of writers 'as solitary individuals struggling mainly with their thoughts' (Nystrand, 2006:20).

It is a specific intention of this *Handbook* to offer a broad and balanced account of research in writing and writing development, rather than to present research predominantly from one theoretical orientation. Thus, this section is structured around what are, broadly speaking, the three theoretical frameworks within writing research is conducted: psychological, sociocultural, and linguistic. Psychological research is principally concerned with exploring and understanding the cognitive processes involved in writing and focuses very much on the writer as an individual, managing complex cognitive operations. Sociocultural research, in contrast, is much more interested in the contexts of writing, how writers shape and are shaped by the community within which they write, and the ways in which writing is a socially situated, meaning-making activity. The third theoretical framework, linguistic, draws upon understandings derived from corpus studies and textual analysis and describes how language works in texts and contexts to create meaning. One way of considering these three domains is to characterize them as, respectively, principally writer-oriented, context-oriented, and text-oriented. Each of these theoretical perspectives has its research community, its own discourse, its own methodological preferences, and often its own publication outlets and conferences.

This section, then, gives voice to key thinking about the psychology of writing, sociocultural theories of writing, and linguistic insights into writing development. All too often, the three theoretical frameworks operate in isolation and independent of each other; by offering them here cheek by jowl, it is our hope that readers will read not only with the text, but also across the text, building a more integrated, multiple-voiced framework for researching writing development. It seems axiomatic that an appropriate pedagogical understanding of writing development and appropriate instructional designs must take account of all three perspectives, acknowledging the cognitive demands made upon the novice writer, the role of linguistic experience in writing development, and the complex interplay of social and cultural influences upon the learner writer within a community of writers.

WRITING AS A COGNITIVE PROCESS

The first four chapters in this section of the Handbook present cognitive psychological insights into writing and writing development.

In Chapter 2, **Denis Alamargot and Michel Fayol** offer an overview of the development of cognitive psychological models of the writing process through the 1980s to the present time and illustrate that many of these models provide limited insight into writing development, because they draw on data derived from adults. Alamargot and Fayol show how the writing process is described as a complex task requiring the simultaneous management and control of a number of constraints, and that for novice writers, the cognitive demands of transcription and orthography are costly. They present a detailed critical analysis of the main developmental models proposed by Bereiter and Scardamalia (1987) and Berninger and Swanson (1994) and indicate the directions that future research in this area might follow.

Common to all cognitive models of the writing process is the identification of three subprocesses: *generation*, the creating of ideas, *translation*, the verbal production of text from ideas, and *revision*, the editing and reviewing of the written text. The next three chapters take each of these in turn and explore them in depth. In Chapter 3, **David Galbraith** considers the subcomponent of generation in the writing process. He outlines how cognitive models have attempted to explain how writers generate ideas for writing through probing long-term memory and critiques such explanations as reducing the generation of ideas to no more than recall or information retrieval. Such models seem unable to account for the creative component in writing, the discovery of ideas rather than the retrieval of ideas. Galbraith then offers the dual-processing model as an alternative explanation of the generation process, which accounts for text production, which includes actively creating new ideas for writing. The dual-process model conceptualizes the generation of ideas as a creative, knowledge-constituting process where thinking and writing occur simultaneously—we write to discover what we think. This chapter is followed by a detailed exploration of the process of translation by **John R. Hayes** in

Chapter 4. He outlines the pathway from idea to text and the resources which support writing, especially the role of working memory. For novice and developing writers, the demands of handwriting and spelling and writers' relative linguistic inexperience use up valuable capacity in working memory, which hinders cognitive attention to more sophisticated aspects of text creation. Hayes explores the pattern of 'bursts' in the translation process, the pattern of writing and pausing, which characterizes text production, and questions whether these represent sequential or parallel process. In other words, do we pause to think and then write to convert that thought into words on a page, or are the pausing and writing sequences more interrelated with thinking co-occurring during bursts of writing. Research does indicate, however, that developmentally, with increasing transcriptional fluency and linguistic experience, the writing bursts lengthen.

In Chapters of this section, **Lucile Chanquoy** offers an analytical review of cognitive research into the revision stage of the writing process. She outlines how revision is conceptualized in the various models of the writing process and describes specific models of revision, which include both online revision processes conducted during text production and post hoc revision once writing is complete. Research findings related to different patterns and practices in revision are outlined, particularly with reference to the concepts of surface and deep revision, and the role of cognitive and metacognitive knowledge in revision. Finally, the chapter addresses the difficulties by young or developing writers in acquiring effective revision strategies, including how children might develop appropriate evaluation, detection, and correction strategies.

WRITING AS SOCIAL PRACTICE

This section provides an overview of sociocultural theoretical perspectives on writing, and outlines how sociocultural theories view writing as a socially situated act of social practice, an act of connection and communication with others, and classrooms as socially determined communities of practice, which shape both written texts and writing processes. In Chapter 6, **Triantafillia Kostouli**, taking the notion of writing as social practice as a foundation, develops this thinking in the light of the theoretical approach of Critical Analysis of Writing Practices. She explores how writers' interactions with their writing and with the school context influence both their understanding of what it means to be a writer and their writing practices. It illuminates how social contexts shape and construct writer identities and positionings, and how written text is not a static, determinate, fixed entity but one coconstructed through collaboration, mediation, and negotiation.

Recognizing the tensions between school, home, and the workplace in what is valued as writing, and acknowledging the potential conflict between powerful and less powerful communities and their associated literacies, **Jon Smidt** explores how learners and teachers negotiate the various social discourse roles available to them in Chapter 7. Developing as a writer involves being socialized into practices, values, and ways of making meaning, which reflect the values of the school and the teacher more strongly than the values of the writer, and can be reduced to developing mastery of a set of cultural norms. Through the lens of the ecological theory of writing development, Smidt presents a multidimensional view of writing and shows how writers can choose to affirm dominant discourses or actively resist and challenge them.

The notion of resistance, and the way writing is intrinsically linked to issues of power and identity is developed further by **Hilary Janks** in Chapter 8. This chapter explores the interrelationships between writing, language, and power and how critical literacy pedagogy might support learners in developing critical social consciousness and an awareness of writing as a form of social action. It demonstrates how common discourses of critical literacy variously foreground domination, access, diversity, or design and argues these are interdependent forces, and that critical literacy can be a positive, reconstructive pedagogy. The chapter also engages with the 'access' paradox: that providing access to dominant written forms perpetuates their hegemonic dominance, whilst denying access maintains the marginalization of minority groups. The chapter argues that learning to write and developing as a writer are intimately connected with issues of social identities, language, and justice.

Finally, in Chapter 9, **Brian Street** introduces and develops the thinking of New Literacy Studies and of the New London Group regarding the notions of multi and of multiple literacies. He describes how, in contemporary society, the singular noun 'literacy' with its finite, uncontested interpretation demands reconceptualization in order to take account of students' various and diverse social, cultural, and linguistic resources. Both of these new research traditions have addressed this issue and the chapter considers where and how we might build on their insights at the same time as acknowledging the differences between them. It argues that the school curriculum frequently fails to acknowledge and develop the multiple literate practices of its students, particularly those from urban or socially disadvantaged students who are not part of the mainstream culture. For these students, there is a dissonance between their own ways of being literate and participative citizens and the dominant literacies required by the school curriculum. The chapter concludes by arguing that writing development requires schools to find connections between community and home literacies and conventional schooled literacies.

WRITING AS LINGUISTIC MASTERY

The cognitive and social demands of writing are underpinned by writers' linguistic experiences and the language resources, which they can draw on as writers. This section provides an insight into differing linguistic theories and perspectives, which have informed an understanding of children's development in writing. In Chapter 10, **Rose** presents a historical and cultural account of the development of genre-based literacy pedagogy, which draws on Hallidayan functional linguistics and the influential work of the Sydney School. Rose illustrates how functional linguistics has played a valuable role in scaffolding children's mastery of different written genres. Interpreting genres as staged goal-oriented social processes, functional linguistics has provided descriptions of typical features and constructions in different genres, which provided teachers and learners with a language resource for talking about written genres. It has also facilitated a pedagogical approach, which allows connections to be made between the language experiences of the family, community, school, and workplace.

Defining their theoretical framework as social semiotic rather than linguistic, **Gunther Kress and Jeff Bezemer** in Chapter 11 develop the notion of linguistic mastery, which goes beyond control of verbal language. The chapter addresses social semiotic theory, sociolinguistics and the multiple modes in which texts can create meaning. Firstly, the chapter outlines the changing nature of writing in the twenty-first century, the increasing emphasis on verbal-visual interplay in written texts, and the impact of technology allowing the easy creation of written texts with multimodal features, such as websites. It explains the concept of 'design', as posited by the New London group and explores how this informs new ways of looking at writing. Specifically, the chapter highlights the potential disjuncture between children's life experiences of written texts and the demands of the writing curriculum and signals the implications of multimodality for a pedagogy not simply of writing but of communication.

The final two chapters in this section spotlight thinking explicitly upon grammar and the contested place of grammar and grammar teaching within a theory of writing development. This international debate is comprehensively illustrated by **Terry Locke** in Chapter 12. He shows how debates about the appropriateness and value of grammar in support of writing development have been ongoing, often vitriolic and confusing, and certainly not restricted to any particular country. Whether grammar has anything to offer the writing classroom has been a controversial issue, in the US, England, Australia, and New Zealand. In a range of settings, the debate has been muddied, as it has been appropriated by political and policy agendas, which have sometimes bestowed on grammar a kind of redemptive power in the face of supposedly declining literacy standards. This chapter documents some of these debates and explores some of the confusions surrounding them. These confusions relate to terminology; the articulation of questions about the relationship between writing, pedagogy, and grammar; and the formulation of research questions themselves. It concludes with a critical analysis of the evidence from research concerning the impact of teaching grammar on children's writing development and suggests other ways or framing a research agenda around grammar, writing, and pedagogy.

The concluding chapter in this section complements the previous chapter, but rather than considering the controversies of grammar teaching, offers a constructive view of how linguistics can and might support children's development of confidence and competence as writers. **Craig Hancock** signals the historical tendency to concentrate on grammar solely as an error-correction tool, emphasizing what writers must to do or avoid. He posits instead that grammar informs understanding of the effectiveness of writing. Greater metalinguistic awareness of how different linguistic structures, shapes, and patterns can create different meanings enhances student writers' ability to make and justify decisions for themselves. Finally, the chapter argues for an integrative approach to the writing curriculum, one which does not see language as meaningfully neutral, correct, or inaccurate but which instead places language study at the heart of writing instruction and emphasizes the organic relationship between form and meaning.

REFERENCES

Graves, D. (1983) *Writing: Teachers and Children at Work*, New Hampshire: Heinemann.

Hayes, J.R. and Flower, L.S. (1980) 'Identifying the organization of writing processes', in L.W. Gregg and E.R. Steinberg (eds), *Cognitive Processes in Writing*, Hillsdale, NJ: Lawrence Erlbaum Associates. pp. 3–30.

Nystrand, M. (2006) 'The social and historical context for writing research', in C. MaCarthur, S. Graham, and J. Fitzgerald (eds), *Handbook of Writing Research*, New York: Guilford. pp.11–27.

Smagorinsky, P. (1987) 'Graves revisited: A look at the methods and conclusions of the New Hampshire study', *Written Communication*, 14(4): 331–342.

Modelling the Development of Written Composition

Denis Alamargot and Michel Fayol

INTRODUCTION

A developmental model of written production should predict both the course of the writing processes (i.e., the processing strategies) and the characteristics of the end product (i.e., the textual quality and quantity), in the light of the writer's general development, his or her specific writing expertise and the learning context. If, however, we accept this definition, writing a chapter, which describes just that such a model becomes an extremely challenging undertaking, in that a model with this degree of advancement does not yet exist.

The absence of such a model certainly cannot be ascribed to a dearth of developmental research. Although research on written production over the last 30 years has mainly concerned adults and expert writers, major advances have also been made regarding its educational and developmental aspects, both in experimental studies (Berninger et al., 2002; Bourdin and Fayol, 1994; Bourdin et al., 1996; Chanquoy et al., 1990; Graham, 2006; Swanson and Berninger, 1996) and theoretical models (Bereiter and Scardamalia, 1987; Berninger and Swanson, 1994; De La Paz and Graham, 2002; Graham et al., 2005; McCutchen, 1996, 2000; Scardamalia and

Bereiter, 1991). The absence of detailed models of the development of written composition stems rather from the fact that conceptions of writing research have been based on two different and, until now, relatively independent approaches to verbal production (Fayol, 2002). Put rather simplistically, there are two main lines of research on verbal production. The first one, involving research of a largely fundamental nature, is inspired mainly by generativist-type linguistic models and seeks to establish an integrative psycholinguistic theory of verbal production. It focuses almost exclusively on the production of words and sentences, the basic units of formal linguistics. The aim of the second one, which is initially more reliant on social demand, is to form one or several production models in order to improve the way in which utterances or texts are organized, and therefore the way in which they are processed by those who are called upon to perceive and understand them. These two approaches mirror the opposition between the two categories of units constituted by the sentence and the discourse. They correspond to two linguistic conceptions and essentially remain juxtaposed, each conducting its own research without paying much attention to the data and models generated by the other's research.

Lexical and syntactic processing has, therefore, been studied from a psycholinguistic perspective that is strongly inspired by models of oral verbal production. This research was initially based mainly on Levelt's model (Levelt, 1989, 1999; Levelt, Roelofs, and Meyer, 1999), derived from the research carried out by Garrett (1980) and closely associated with the analysis of production errors. Subsequently, systematic use has been made of the classic paradigms of experimental psychology, particularly reaction time measures, often associated with a priming task. These studies have paid very little attention to the question of development, even though Levelt (1998) he points out that this was a central issue for early psycholinguistics research.

Text composition, which involves processes that go beyond isolated words and sentences, has been studied from a cognitive perspective, allying information processing, rhetoric, and communication. Here, composition is regarded as a problem-solving activity, where a communicative goal has to be reached by managing a set of varied constraints, including the characteristics of the recipient, the type of text, and the availability of domain knowledge and linguistic knowledge. Hayes and Flower's initial model (1980) is a perfect illustration of this approach. Emphasis is placed on the planning, formulation, and revision components, as well as on the management of constraints in the course of the activity and the dynamics of the resulting processes (Flower and Hayes, 1980). The methods developed within this framework, notably think-aloud protocols (Hayes and Flower, 1983) and double and triple tasks – (Kellogg, 1987, 1988; Levy and Ransdell, 1996a), are therefore intended to define the time course of processes and/or attentional demands.

Although these two approaches are based on different paradigms, they share the same cognitivist conception that written production is a complex and composite activity which can only be properly studied if it is broken down into separate components and/or levels.

Both approaches are, therefore, faced with the same problem of how to choose the most plausible and functional means of doing so. Apart from this mutual concern, the two approaches are characterized by different objectives. In the case of the former, the aim is to identify the units involved in writing (semantic, orthographic, phonological and graphemic units, and motor programmes), together with the various processes and their time course in a system of modular processing, organized according to a precise architecture. In order to do so, researchers have to reduce the field of possibilities and generally focus on the production of isolated units (word, letter, and sentence production), sacrificing the ecological validity of the tasks they administer and the role of superordinate dimensions. For the latter, it is a case of identifying not so much the individual units that are processed as the larger processing components (planning, formulation, revision, and execution), the strategies for their implementation and the effect of their use on the resulting text quantity and quality. Here, researchers regard the activity as a single, complex whole, and this sometimes leads them to adopt a global viewpoint, thus neglecting the more fine-grained analysis of individual processes. Models, therefore, remain relatively imprecise insofar as the natures of the linguistic and orthographic processes involved in formulation are concerned. This is all the more paradoxical, given that these processes lie at the heart of the writing activity and impose certain constraints (Fayol, 1999).

This neglect by writing models in particular and by the cognitive approach to writing in general, does not pose a problem when studying expert writers. The latter are supposed to have acquired their language's orthographic rules and proceduralized the motor programmes that allow them to transcribe and execute a message without incurring any of the costs associated with these processes. Accordingly, formulation processes are generally regarded as relatively accessible and free of constraints for expert writers, although more precise data have revealed that even in adults, the written modality has a higher implementation cost than the oral one (Bourdin and Fayol, 2002). This is obviously not true for beginning writers, for whom graphomotor skills and spelling, which are still in the process of being acquired and structured, represent the bulk of the processes, constraints, and difficulties. In our opinion, no developmental approach to written composition can be complete without analyzing:

- The introduction (construction of processes and representations) of the formulation component in all its dimensions, including spelling which, up to now, has mainly been tackled within the framework of classic psycholinguistics.
- The functional development of this component, in terms of learning, the automation of certain processes and strategic control.
- The real-time management of the implementation of the different components, whose interactiveness depends on their respective efficiency at a given level of expertise.

The aim of this chapter is not to present a fully formed model of the development of written composition – a model which is currently beyond our reach – but more modestly to provide a description and critical analysis of the main developmental models proposed by Bereiter and Scardamalia (1987) and Berninger and Swanson (1994); and to disentangle the various dimensions and constraints which affect the development of written production, in order to propose new leads for future modelling.

In order to achieve this, we need, firstly, to combine the contributions of the two aforementioned psycholinguistic and cognitive approaches, in order to improve our understanding of (a) the development of the formulation component and its constituents and (b) the role played by this component in the way the processes are managed – notably through coordinating the implementation of the planning and revision components. Secondly, we need to determine the influence of the factors underlying the development of

the components, in particular (a) the child's degree of maturation, which modifies his or her memory and metacognitive capacities, and (b) the practice of written production, whether this concerns explicit acquisition through various interventions (supports and training) or implicit acquisition through regular contact with written forms.

FROM A GENERAL TO A DEVELOPMENTAL MODEL OF WRITTEN PRODUCTION

Several publications have described and discussed existing models of written production and their successive updates (for summaries, see Alamargot and Chanquoy, 2001; Butterfield, 1994; Fayol, 1997a, 2002; Levy and Ransdell, 1996b; MacArthur et al., 2006; Scardamalia and Bereiter, 1991; Zesiger, 1995). All these authors agree that the activity of written composition draws on two types of knowledge: knowledge relating to the content being evoked (theme of the text) and linguistic knowledge (lexical, syntactic, and rhetorical features). It also calls upon temporary memory (generally referred to as working memory) to maintain and handle information. It, therefore, takes place in a dynamic situation, where the text being produced depends on the goals that have been set, the recipient, the production conditions, and the text produced so far. There is also general agreement as to the existence of three components – planning, formulation, and revision. Planning relates to the retrieval of knowledge about the theme from memory, the organization of this knowledge and the way the goals are taken into account. In short, it is about defining the content and nature of the text according to the person to whom it is being addressed (the recipient) and the effect it is intended to have on the latter. Putting something into text involves the linguistic dimension and raises the problem of linearization. While the content that is evoked generally has a multidimensional structure, the text, like language in general, is one-dimensional. The words, clauses, sentences, and different parts of the texts follow on from each other in linear fashion. The transition from a multidimensional organization to a unidimensional one raises problems that are specific to writing. Even if they play a major role, it is not enough just to select words and produce sentences. The textual sequence also has to be chosen according to the content, the recipient and the writer's linguistic abilities. Moreover, in the case of written composition, the orthographic and graphic dimensions present an additional difficulty (compared with oral communication): the motor component of handwriting is less automated than that of speech, and in French as in English, words cannot be transcribed simply by making deductions from their oral form (Jaffré and Fayol, 2005). Writers return to their text in order to reread what has already been produced, detect gaps and errors, and revise the previous version of the text more or less extensively.

While each of these components has to function correctly in order for the composition to be achieved efficiently, they must also be coordinated and managed in order to ensure their seamless implementation and the fluency of the production. This is an aspect that has received a great deal of attention and has led researchers to conclude that written composition depends on the functional cost of each of these components and on whether or not an individual has sufficient attentional and memory capacity at a given time to both manage and coordinate the functioning of each component.

This general framework of text composition is not without its critics. The chief criticism relates to the fact that it is based on data yielded by studies of adults. It cannot, therefore, be immediately transposed to children, nor is it necessarily adapted to learning issues. A second criticism, which leads on from the first one, is that the formulation component and its constituent processes have never been properly defined and subjected to detailed investigation. A third criticism

centres on the varying degrees of importance given to the different components during real-time production. Despite the data reported by Kellogg (1987, 1988), we only have very general information about the dynamics of composition, which encompasses all the dimensions involved, from planning to graphic execution. A fourth criticism concerns the precise effects of processing overload on the various components that have been implemented (e.g., do orthographic difficulties have an impact in real time on the planning of ideas?). Despite these limitations, this framework has nonetheless been the driving force behind numerous studies of the evolution of performances over the 6- to 20-year age range and on the factors thought to influence this evolution. It has also led to the construction of two developmental models.

Bereiter and Scardamalia's (1987) model

The first study of the evolution of written composition was conducted among adolescents by Bereiter and Scardamalia (1987). These authors distinguished between two categories of strategies: the knowledge-telling strategy and the knowledge-transforming strategy. They showed that written composition initially takes the form of the straightforward transcription of knowledge (knowledge-telling strategy). The text is composed by formulating ideas as and when they are retrieved from long-term memory, without any reorganization of the text's conceptual content or linguistic form. This composition mode, which is exclusive to beginning writers, may result in a good-quality production, as in the case of narratives, for example. This is because the sequence of events generally corresponds to the order in which they are retrieved from memory and thus to the order in which they are formulated (Fayol, 2003a). It may also be adopted by expert writers, in certain situations where the compositional requirements and quality constraints are not fundamentally important (writing a shopping list, drafting a memo, drawing up a brief report, etc.).

The other, so-called knowledge-transforming strategy, is more elaborate. It is more frequently observed in adolescents (from the age of 14 years onwards) and adults. It consists in reorganizing domain knowledge in line with rhetorical and linguistic constraints (and vice versa), and the state of the text produced so far (Scardamalia and Bereiter, 1991). It requires the writer to solve a problem with major constraints, underlain by a dialectic between 'that which must be said' (content space) and 'that which can be said, to whom and in what way' (rhetorical space). This problem requires the writer to constantly monitor the gap between production (the text underway) and intention, and to reduce this gap by creating new contents (under the influence of pragmatic/rhetorical constraints) or new rhetorical/pragmatic goals (under the influence of domain constraints). In other words, this strategy assumes that the writer will continuously switch his or her focus between the text's conceptual content and its linguistic form, until he or she achieves a satisfactory match between the intention and the communicative intent. This means that information cannot be formulated as and when it is retrieved, but must instead be modified and adapted, and the writer must return to the text produced so far in order to modify its form and content. This compositional strategy is obviously costly in terms of cognitive resources and time on task. It assumes that the writer has been able to develop not only sufficiently advanced domain knowledge for modifications and adjustments to be made, but also pragmatic and rhetorical knowledge in order to vary and modulate the formulations according to the textual and contextual parameters.

Berninger and Swanson's (1994) model

The second model was devised by Berninger and Swanson (1994). The authors' twofold

objective was to create a developmental version of Hayes and Flower's model (1980) and to provide a more in-depth definition of formulation, for according to them, the latter's initial development determines subsequent development, first of revision then of planning. Formulation encompasses two processes. The first process, text generation, involves the transformation of ideas that are retrieved into linguistic representations. This subprocess is dedicated to the processing of words, sentences, paragraphs, and texts. The second process, transcription, is the translation of representations into written symbols. This allows phonological and orthographic coding (spelling and grammar), text segmentation (punctuation and cohesion) and fine motor skill (graphomotor execution) operations to take place. One of the characteristics of this model is that it sets a specific timetable for the emergence and complexification of the three components.

Formulation is the first component to appear, but there is a set order in which its processes are implemented. Text generation can only become operational once transcription has undergone gradual automation. Difficulties linked to transcription may thus compromise text generation performances for reasons of limited capacity. The working memory resources allocated to transcription are so great that they prevent text generation from taking place. This is why oral text composition by young children brings better results than written composition (Fayol, 1991; Simon, 1973). Once transcription has become sufficiently efficient, text generation can steadily graduate from single words to grammatical clauses, then to paragraphs combining several sentences. The next component to develop is revision, which is initially restricted to surface corrections of words and portions of sentences (with attention being focused on spelling and punctuation), before being extended to paragraphs and then to the text as a whole (concerning form and content in equal measure).

The planning component appears at a later stage, gradually moving from a local mode of operation (anticipating the following sentence) to a global mode (anticipating the content and organization of the text as a whole). Initially, this component is unable to manage the linkage of two sentences. As it develops, however, it allows the writer to plan a growing number of contents prior to their production, giving rise to the formulation of sentences organized in their correct sequence (*pre-planning*). In this, it is helped by recourse to pre-established textual schemas (e.g., the narrative schema). The final phase in the evolution of these processes means that the writer no longer has to rely exclusively on these schemas but can also plan the text according to the various different constraints.

Berninger and Swanson's (1994) model is useful, because it specifies the importance of memory systems during writing, in particular the storage and processing capacities of working memory. While its processing capacity is assumed to play a crucial role in high-level skills, its storage capacity is mainly called upon during transcription (see Swanson and Berninger, 1996, for experimental validations). These authors consider that the management of the components and their processes is undertaken by a general metacognitive process, which is not exclusive to the three writing processes and which regulates all cognitive activities.

Discussion of developmental models

Overall, two key points arise from the analysis of the various models described in the foregoing section. First of all, regarding models of written composition by adults, while a great deal of research has been looked at planning and revision, the problems raised by formulation have been neglected. This component, which is only vaguely defined in Hayes and Flower's model (1980), is only partially studied in Levelt's model (1989), which restricts itself to lexical and syntactic production. When it comes to

development, Bereiter and Scardamalia's model does not even mention formulation, as though it were not a problem. Berninger and Swanson's model, on the other hand, gives it pride of place and raises the problem of its development and its gradual coordination with the other components.

Secondly, the factors likely to affect modification, notably the improvement of written composition, have only been broached elusively. Bereiter and Scardamalia (1987) indicate that the adoption of the knowledge-transforming strategy depends on an increase in planning abilities (making it possible to construct increasingly complex goals) and in short-term memory span (for the active maintenance of the constraints inherent to the problem-solving activity). They do not, however, cite any empirical data to support this conception. Nor do they mention the possible impact of instruction and its relationship with increased abilities. This dimension is rather better defined by Berninger et al., who take the view that the functioning of these three components is constrained by the writer's working memory span and metacognitive knowledge. According to them, these two dimensions are responsible for writing development and inter-individual differences. This notion of the twofold control of processes via the automation of 'low-level' components, which frees up resources and allows a greater number of processes to be engaged, and metacognition, which permits the management of production according to goals and products, is particularly interesting. It accounts for the effects of the proceduralization of processes as a result of practice and conscious strategies of process implementation.

Berninger and Swanson's (1994) model is vastly superior to most of the others when it comes to accounting for the development of the components and their gradual coordination, be it automatic or strategic. However, it remains silent on the questions relating to the acquisition of linguistic, lexical, syntactic, and textual representations, as well as to the development and implementation of the enunciative dimensions in the course of composition.

It also remains elusive as to metacognitive management and its development. Lastly, it fails to tackle the question of instruction and its possible effects on composition processes and performances, as though the evolution we observe were somehow 'natural'.

For this reason, a number of questions common to the two main psycholinguistic and cognitive-enunciative approaches have started to emerge over the last ten years and the answers they have prompted indicate a coming together of these approaches. It would, therefore, appear to be necessary to include formulation (its management and development) in these models, specifying the interactions between the low- and high-level components, and to improve our definition of the developmental factors, particularly the impact of maturation (memory capacity and metacognitive capacity) and practice (supports, training, and implicit learning).

FORMULATION IN WRITTEN COMPOSITION: THE NARRATIVE

Composing a written text requires conceptual and communicative knowledge to be mobilized in a coordinated fashion, together with linguistic knowledge and know-how, and motor procedures, to ensure fluent formulation and execution. Obviously, when one of these components is lacking, composition cannot be conducted efficiently. This situation mainly arises in young children, because they either do not possess or have not yet fully mastered the necessary knowledge and know-how. Narrative is the only type of text that very young children produce, dealing with events, which they themselves have experienced or observed. Accordingly, in order to investigate and analyze the evolution of formulation, with a view to clarifying our understanding of the nature of the difficulties children encounter, together with the way in which they gradually overcome them, we will restrict the scope of our investigation to the narrative. We will look more specifically at changes in the production of narrative by children between six and ten years, with a view to specifying the development of representations and processes, notably in formulation.

In order to study this evolution, we must have recourse to two paradigms: one for the analysis of linguistic markers (e.g., connectives and punctuation marks) and the other for that of temporal parameters (e.g., pauses and flow rates). Currently, the use of verbal protocols, be they simultaneous or deferred, is not really feasible with children, due to the cost of their implementation and the risk of interference. Double and triple task paradigms, which allow us to assess the cognitive cost of carrying out a particular component are also difficult to use. Eye movements are now starting to be studied in adult populations, but we do not yet know whether it will one day be possible to extend this method to children. Accordingly, we will restrict ourselves to the results of research on markers and on the length and speed of production.

A four-dimensional model of narrative development

Studying the development of narrative text means distinguishing between four dimensions: a *conceptual dimension* involving the communicative intent, the content, and the recipient of the message (Fayol, 1997a; Levy and Ransdell, 1996b; Rijlaarsdam, van den Bergh and Couzjin, 1996); a *rhetorical dimension* dealing with the overall organization of the message, that is, the narrative structure (Bronckart, 1985); a *linguistic dimension*, that is, translation, taking into account the lexical choices that are strongly linked to the content of the narrative and some more general dimensions, for example, syntactic choices, morphological constraints and spelling (Bock and Levelt, 1994; Levelt, 1989); and a *graphomotor dimension* relating to the transcription of the message.

In addition, text production is a highly demanding activity, which requires the efficient online coordination of all the previously mentioned dimensions (Fayol, 1999; Torrance and Jeffery, 1999): constructing ideas and conceptual relations; accessing lexical items, choosing syntactic frames, and so on. Narration forces the author to manage two complementary constraints inherent to the linearity of text production. On the one hand, new information has to be introduced, without which the narrative would be of no interest. On the other hand, continuity must be ensured between those elements that have already been introduced and those, which emerge as the narrative unfolds. This assumes that the author possesses not only information about the content of the narrative but also knowledge of several marker systems—punctuation, connectives, pronouns, and articles – which must be used appropriately in the translation process. This also implies that the author must be capable of mobilizing this range of knowledge and know-how in real time so that the composition process unfolds smoothly. The time management of all these dimensions and the corresponding processes poses many problems for adults as well as children.

Regarding the conceptual dimension, the producer of a text (e.g., a narrative) already possesses an intention and a content, even if the relevant information for the narration is not all quickly and easily accessible. The narrator's task is, therefore, to focus on an event and to communicate the corresponding information by selecting the most appropriate items as a function of the objective being pursued, the recipients and the conceptual and linguistic knowledge of the interlocutors. If the author considers the chosen event to be sufficiently interesting, he or she starts the narration. This requires the mental representation of situations and events, as well as their temporal or causal relations, to be easily accessible so that it can be converted into text form for the recipient. According to Schank and Abelson (1977), actions are organized in terms of the goals pursued by the actors, who produce these actions in order to overcome the obstacles, which stand in the way of

attaining these goals. Formulation is made possible by causal networks (Trabasso et al., 1985). These networks appear as chains of events, linked together temporally, causally, or by other means. The more strongly two events are related, the easier it is for the narrator to retrieve the second one, provided that the first one is already available (i.e., expressed in written form) (Caron et al., 1988). As a consequence, pauses between causally related events are shorter than those between temporally related ones. More generally, the less closely two successive events or states are related, the longer the pause between them.

The question of textual structures (i.e., the rhetorical dimension) occupies an intermediate position between content-based and textualization-based approaches to written composition (Fayol, 1991). The rhetorical dimension relates to the fact that the linguistic formalization of narratives is not limited to the mere listing of characters, places, objects, and events but follows a narrative superstructure. Every narrative consists of a frame specifying times, places, and characters. This frame is introduced at the start of the narrative as a result of the practical constraints imposed by the need for effective communication. Then comes a trigger, introducing an obstacle, which generally hinders the main character in the attainment of his or her objectives. This obstacle induces an emotional reaction, together with the construction of a subgoal, designed to remove or bypass the obstacle. The main character makes one or more attempts, with varying degrees of success, until the final result is achieved (Mandler and Johnson, 1977; Stein and Glenn, 1979). The canonical organization of narratives plays a key role, because the narrative structure, which roughly follows the order of events (Fayol 1985, 1991), constitutes a plan for the retrieval of information from memory. It operates as a cue system for items grouped into categories (e.g., beginning, complication, and ending). The activation of a higher-level category makes it possible to retrieve all the elements contained within it and thus not only provides information about what needs to be formulated but also makes it possible to remember what has already been formulated. This results in the facilitation effects of the narrative structure on performances in recalling and summarizing stories (Kintsch et al., 1977; Stein and Nezworski, 1978). As a consequence, composing a narrative text is easier and less costly than producing a description (Chanquoy et al., 1990) (e.g., pauses are shorter at the beginning of narratives than at the beginning of descriptions).

Regarding the linguistic dimension, the main problem encountered in written composition is how to manage the linearization process. All narrative refers to an underlying referent (that which is described and related), which is represented mentally in a coherent fashion by the individual producing the message. This mental representation ('mental model', according to Johnson-Laird, 1983; 'model of situation', according to van Dijk and Kintsch, 1983) is always multidimensional (i.e., has many relationships linking its elements together). However, language production, whether oral or written, is strictly linear and time-dependent: only one piece of information can be related at any one time (Grimes, 1975; Levelt, 1981, 1982, 1989). The main problem confronting writers is how to present information in a linear format (i.e., to linearize information) when such information is rarely stored in a linear structure in the mental model, except for very simple narratives, where the linearization is largely determined by the chronological order of events. The linearization process involves at least three different kinds of operations: defining a starting point (which corresponds to the laying of a foundation in Gernsbacher's (1997) model of text comprehension), selecting a path and marking out the surface structure. First, the speaker/writer must select a starting point or origin, which corresponds to a particular point of view (i.e., the beginning of a narrative; the starting point of a description) (Bronckart, 1985); the rest of the information in the text must be set out in respect

of that origin (Costermans and Bestgen, 1991). For example, in English, new characters or objects putting in an appearance for the first time are preceded by an indefinite article (e.g., a man entered). Subsequent references use definite articles (e.g., the man), pronouns (e.g., he) or demonstrative adjectives (e.g., this man). Second, s/he has to determine a path leading from the beginning to the end of the reported events (Levelt, 1982; Linde and Labov, 1975). This path may or may not be easy to determine: it is easy to define in simple narratives, but much more difficult to map out in complex stories. This path includes a chain of events that are more or less strongly related by causal or temporal links (see above). Narratives describe a sequence of events in which connections can differ in nature and degree, ranging from the simple parallel unfolding of two activities (e.g., the man was walking/a car was passing) to a causal connection (e.g., the shot was fired/the man fell). There are markers (e.g., preterite and past continuous tenses) which make it possible to distinguish between foreground actions and background facts and situations (e.g., the man was walking/a noise caught his attention) (Bonnotte and Fayol, 1997; Fayol et al., 1993). Third, he or she must establish and mark the relationships between the statements in the text. According to the 'nextness' principle (Ochs, 1979; Segal, Duchan and Scott, 1991), unless otherwise indicated, two linguistic items which are close 'on the text/discourse surface' go together (i.e. are strongly related to each other). However, two consecutive statements in an oral or written discourse may either pertain to successive states or events which are strongly related to each other in the mental model of the situation being described, or pertain to states or events which are weakly related to each other in that mental model. Hence the need for a system of markers indicating the strength and/or nature of the link between adjacent statements. This set of markers is the punctuation/connectives paradigm (Fayol, 1997b; Heurley, 1997; Noordman and Vonk, 1997; Townsend, 1997).

The graphomotor dimension is rarely taken into account, because most studies dealing with written composition have dealt with adults' or adolescents' production processes. As the production of letters and words is highly automated, the impact of composing in the written modality is weak, and can be ignored in most cases. However, Bourdin and Fayol (2002) have provided evidence that when adults are requested to compose texts from words that are not thematically related, their productions are of poorer quality in the written modality than in the oral one. This result is not observed when adults compose texts from thematically related words (i.e., script related). It is easy to see why the impact of the graphomotor constraints might be far greater on children's composition.

The evolution of narrative composition in children

Narrative superstructure development

Scripted knowledge of ordered sequences of events, or 'scenic' knowledge of spatial arrangements, is vital for the understanding and production of stories. This is knowledge, which is shared by the interlocutors, and which permits efficient communication, emphasizing the essential items of information while taking familiar facts and situations as given. When an unexpected event intervenes or an obstacle arises, the sequence of events does not progress as usual and the situation becomes a potential narrative subject. This is something which has to be discovered by children and which will be more or less reinforced depending on their social environment and culture (Fayol, 1991). To summarize, knowledge of script-like event sequences and the regularities, which characterize them allows the authors of narrative texts to construct mental models of situations in order to produce texts.

The development of these chains of events, though emerging somewhat later, approximately replicates the development of scripts, for reasons, which are easy to identify. These all rest on chronological-causal relations between facts associated with goals. However, the unpredictability of an event can only be assessed if the usual scenario is known. Before the age of five years, children's productions contain very few focused chronological-causal sequences (Applebee, 1978; Pitcher and Prelinger, 1963). When producing narratives, the youngest ones simply juxtapose sequences of facts without establishing interrelations, which can be clearly be identified by adults: the characters' reactions and objectives are missing. Nevertheless, questions posed to four- and five-year-olds reveal that they are in fact aware of how events are linked and motivated (Trabasso and Nickels, 1992; Trabasso et al., 1992). Development, therefore, seems to have more to do with the ability to mobilize knowledge, notably with regard to the elements involved in the sequencing of events, than with new acquisitions (van den Broek, Lorch and Thurlow, 1996). Texts gathered from six- to eight-year-olds often have a level of organization equivalent to that which Applebee (1978) attributes to children of five years. Furthermore, there is a clear development between the ages of six and ten years, moving from the juxtaposition of facts without any discernible relationship between them to the integration of events into one or more chronological-causal chains, via a stage at around nine years when narratives are based on an often dominant script, as well as on the narration of an unexpected event (Fayol, 1991). In other words, the ability to compose coherent stories primarily develops at around four to eight years and is increasingly refined between eight and ten years, sometimes without any change between nine and eleven years (Fitzgerald, 1984). Nevertheless, there are major and persistent inter-individual differences (Peterson and McCabe, 1983).

In summary, research on the development of the production of chronological-causal chains has revealed that the acquisition and implementation of these chains begins at a very early age, since they are available from the age of five, if not earlier (Sperry and Sperry, 1996). However, the study of written composition reveals that the construction of mental models corresponding to these chains undergoes further development between six and ten years. This suggests that, because of the specific communication situations which distinguish it from the spoken modality (Fayol, 1997a), together with the new constraints imposed on processing, the transition to the written modality induces difficulties in the ability to mobilize knowledge relating to causal chains. Numerous studies have shown that the canonical organization of narratives (i.e., *the narrative superstructure*) has an impact on the behaviour of adults and children alike (Mandler, 1987). For instance, narratives containing all the constituents of the conventional order are remembered better than those, which do not respect these constraints (Yussen et al., 1991). This effect has been observed in children, of different cultures, from four to five years of age. Nevertheless, younger subjects tend to recall certain narrative categories less well than adults do—notably reactions and goals (Mandler et al., 1980). As research on the impact of causal chains has shown, the earliest narratives rarely respect the narrative superstructure: trigger/complication – endeavour/action(s) – resolution. Very young children tend to produce a summary of the event as they would in everyday speech and subsequently expand on this. It is not until children reach the age of seven or eight years that the narrative superstructure becomes dominant in written compositions. Notably, the positioning of the frame specifying times, places and characters at the start of the narrative only occurs at a relatively late age, at around eight or nine years (Fayol, 1991). The advent of this formally identifiable frame coincides with the standardized use of the imperfect in French (e.g., 'il arrivait': he was just coming) or the past continuous in English, together with the pluperfect, as well as expressions such as 'the day before' (i.e., 'la veille' in French) and 'the next day' (i.e., 'le lende-

main' in French). These verbal forms and expressions belong to narrative conventions, which vary from culture to culture.

In all probability, the acquisition of the narrative superstructure is linked to a process of implicit learning, through exposure to a corpus of written narratives. Varnhagen, Morrison and Everall (1994) have shown that recall and production performances depend on educational level, regardless of age. These findings suggest that the prolonged and repeated reading of and exposure to narrative texts help children acquire the characteristic regularities of the narrative superstructure. Accordingly, individuals who do not benefit from such exposure fail to develop this schema. Cain (1996) confirmed that children with a low level of comprehension are precisely those whose narrative productions diverge most from the narrative superstructure and that these subjects have also had less contact than others with written narratives (see also Dickinson and Tabors, 1991). More importantly, Fitzgerald and Spiegel (1983) developed a training programme for the discovery and use of the *narrative superstructure* in writing. Children taught in this way showed a significant improvement in production as well as in comprehension.

Overall, the acquisition and use of the *narrative superstructure* in written composition allows narrators to adhere more closely to the conventional character of written narratives during production. It does not, however, reduce the narration to chronological-causal relations. It constitutes a conventional rhetorical organization, which can only be acquired through exposure to a corpus of texts presenting the corresponding regularities. It depends strongly on direct contact with written narratives. However, explicit tuition-based learning proves effective both in production and in comprehension.

Formulation development in narrative

Looking more specifically at the translation component, the production of a narrative for a listener/reader requires certain lexical and syntactic choices to be made. The author, like the recipient, must make use of marker systems so that they are associated with facts or procedures in a more or less regular manner (i.e., the linearization problem) and produce a message that is orthographically correct and execute adequate sequences of letters at a graphomotor level (i.e., the transcription problem).

Linearization in production brings with it the need to juxtapose information which may be more or less closely related (Fayol, 1997a, 1997b). This requires the existence of a system of markers indicating the degree (punctuation) and nature (connectives) of the relations between clauses or successive paragraphs (Fayol, 1997b; Heurley, 1997). This system supplies the reader with indications as to the segmentation of information (i.e., separating facts from one another) and its integration (i.e., constructing a unified representation from the set of propositions). Both corpus-based studies and experimental research have shown that adults do indeed use these markers in a manner appropriate to their function.

Connectives are acquired at a very early stage and in an order, which can be found in all languages (Kail and Weissenborn, 1991), and are used in speech at an early age, even when children are handling unfamiliar subject matter (French and Nelson, 1985; Hudson and Shapiro, 1991). We might, therefore, expect them to emerge very early on in children's initial written productions. Corpus analyses have shown, however, that this is far from being the case and that it is often necessary to wait until the third grade (nine years) for them to appear (Fayol, 1991). This 'delay' is due to the fact that the event sequences that are recounted do not require the use of markers other than *and* or *then/after* and because the texts produced by very young subjects have no thematic unity. Once these sequences start to comprise chronological-causal relationships between events, written compositions include the relevant connectives. It, therefore, appears that, as far as the most elementary connectors are concerned, their

occurrence in written narratives between the ages of five and ten years is not a developmental problem but has to do with the degree of elaboration of the content reported in the text (Fayol and Mouchon, 1997).

Things are very different when we come to consider punctuation marks. Both their form and function are acquired in parallel when children learn the written language. Although this discovery continues from the age of six to twelve years, it respects the regularities characteristic of adult production from the very outset. The occurrence of a full stop, with or without a capital letter, delimits episodes or blocks of information, which possess a thematic unity, and this is confirmed by the associated pause lengths (Foulin et al., 1989). The comma appears later and is immediately applied to segmentations with a lower level of importance. The other punctuation marks appear later (Ferreiro and Zucchermaglio, 1996). Our understanding of the acquisition of punctuation is more advanced in the field of production than in that of comprehension. However, the observed facts are consistent with those relating to the functioning of connectives. In the same way, as for the *narrative superstructure*, these results suggest that the errors and difficulties displayed by beginning writers are due most of the time not to some sort of inability but to inadequate contact with texts and/or the impossibility of simultaneously performing writing tasks and marking the relevant relations between adjacent clauses. It is not learning but implementation that causes the problems.

In French as well as in English, spelling raises many problems. In both languages, the orthographic forms of words frequently differ from regular phoneme-grapheme mapping. As a consequence, people have to memorize orthographic forms. Graham (1999), like Juel (1988) before him, reported that spelling performances account for a large and significant proportion of the variance (40–50% for the former, approximately 30% for the latter) observed in beginning writers' written composition. Spelling is not the only factor to exercise constraints. Graphomotor execution also places a considerable burden on beginners. As early as the 1970s and 1980s, a number of authors found that oral productions were qualitatively and quantitatively better than written ones in young children (e.g., Hidi and Hildyard, 1983; King and Rentel, 1981; Simon, 1973). Correlational studies revealed that graphic performances were significantly associated with composition performances. Graham et al. (1997) demonstrated that graphomotor execution directly influences the fluency and quality of written composition and accounts for a significant proportion of the variance associated with the fluency and quality of written composition: approximately 60% in the first year of primary school and no less than 40% in the fourth year. Inter-individual differences in graphomotor execution, therefore, explain a significant proportion of variance, both at the beginning and in the course of primary education. Connelly, Dockrell, and Barnett (2005) have reported that in an examination setting (but not in free time; see Walczyk, 2000) the fluency of first-year university students' handwriting still accounts for some 30% of the variance in the quality of their essays. These data suggest that graphomotor performance could be one of the factors that are causally involved in variations in the quality of compositions. A series of experimental studies has confirmed the findings of the correlational approaches. Bourdin and Fayol (1994) found that when children and adults were required to recall series of words in their order of presentation, the former performed better in the oral modality than in the written one up to the third year of primary school. Adults achieved more or less equivalent scores in both modalities, if not slightly higher ones in the written modality. Furthermore, when the adults had to perform the recall task by writing in capital letters, which are familiar to them but rarely used, their performances dropped towards the level of the children. Here, therefore, the graphic

dimension of production clearly influenced the number of words that were recalled. These results were subsequently extended to sentence production, using the same paradigm (Bourdin and Fayol, 1996).

It is studies introducing practice that have yielded the most convincing arguments in favour of a causal relationship between graphic performance and written verbal composition performance. Berninger et al. (1997), Jones and Christensen (1999), and later Graham et al. (2000) showed that instructing and training children who were experiencing difficulty in learning to write in the first year of primary school brought both immediate and delayed improvements, not just in writing itself but also in the composition of sentences (Graham et al., 2000) and texts (Berninger et al., 1997; Jones and Christensen, 1999). The same procedure was followed for spelling. However, the data reported by these English-speaking authors only concerned the lexical dimension of spelling and could not, therefore, be easily generalized to written French, where the morphology of number and gender raises specific problems on account of its largely silent nature (see Fayol, 2003b; Pacton and Fayol, 2004). Correlational studies show that spelling performances account for a major proportion of the variance (40–50%) observed in beginning writers' written composition (Graham, 1999). Additional instruction and practice in spelling have been found to induce significant improvements in the quantity of written production in the second year of primary school (Berninger et al., 1997). Berninger et al. (2002) demonstrated the value of intervening both on spelling and written composition in order to achieve improvements in composition, including the spelling of words.

Conclusion: articulating representations and processing

From a cognitive perspective, the composition a written narrative is a complex activity, which simultaneously mobilizes different representational levels and procedures.

We have, therefore, distinguished between a conceptual, chronological-causal type of representation, a rhetorical representation—the narrative superstructure, which refers to a conventional textual organization, several linguistic subsystems, including the spelling of words and morphemes, which can be used to mark specific items of information, and the graphomotor dimension, which constrains the nature and speed of production. These distinctions are based on empirical data, which show that acquisition, difficulties, and functioning vary according to these dimensions.

The acquisition of the chronological-causal dimensions of actions and that of the organization of goals and actions constitute a prerequisite for producing narratives. This demands specific knowledge associated with concrete situations, as well as inferential abilities, which continue to develop between the ages of six and fifteen years (Barnes, Dennis and Haefele-Kalvaitis, 1996). Most of this knowledge is probably acquired via action schemas when children interact with their physical and social environment. The acquisition of conventional narrative forms goes beyond these organizations, even if it does take account of them. They contribute information, the aim of which is to provide sufficient data for the recipient to be able to understand the narrative. While this pragmatic and textual dimension is just as fundamental as the previous one, it cannot be acquired under the same conditions. As studies of difficulties and comparisons of populations and the effects of training have shown, it is both frequent and prolonged contact with written narratives and interaction with adults (and peers?) on the topics of these texts that encourage acquisition. The same reasoning applies to the more specifically linguistic aspects. Learning the markers and their processing requires a corpus of examples and a set of activities involving the interpretation and production of linguistic markers.

Each of the dimensions we have considered may be affected by specific difficulties

(Liles et al., 1995). Each may also be the subject of preventive or corrective action. For example, it is possible to induce the learning of the narrative superstructure by means of direct teaching coupled with exercises. These observations establish continuity between acquisition and learning, which deserves to be studied more extensively and in greater depth. Moreover, the comparison of performances of children of the same age who are asked to produce or understand narratives reveals the gap in performance between judging the narrative nature of a text (is it a narrative?) and producing a narrative text (Stein and Glenn, 1979; Stein and Nezworski, 1978). Children of five years of age who are presented with texts corresponding more or less to the conventional narrative organization systematically choose the one, which conforms most closely to the canonical organization, just as adults do. However, the productions of children of the same age have usually not reached this level. This type of performance gap suggests that we need to distinguish between the availability of knowledge and its implementation.

According to the capacity-based view, the management of a complex task, such as processing a narrative, requires the coordinated mobilization of different items of knowledge and procedures. This coordination itself may be costly and lead to performances, which are poorer than those that might be expected on the basis of assessments of the subject's knowledge. This lowering of performance with reference to potential may vary as a function of the level of development and inter-individual differences. This line of reasoning also leads us to evoke, on the one hand, the impact of memory capacity and metacognitive guidance on performance enhancement, and on the other, the effect of activities in which certain components are made easier. Increases in working memory capacities and metacognitive abilities occur as the individual matures, whereas knowledge enrichment and improvements in processing procedures appear to come from practice. The following section describes and discusses these two developmental factors.

FACTORS IN THE DEVELOPMENT OF WRITTEN COMPOSITION: MATURATION AND PRACTICE

The maturation effect: Increases in working memory and metacognitive capacities

As the learning of written production occurs at a relatively late stage (at around the age of five to six years for academic learning) and is spread over time (approximately ten years for the basic acquisition of composition), this learning is reliant on the child's general abilities, notably the development of working memory processing and storage, and the development of metacognitive and metalinguistic abilities (Kellogg, 2008).

The hypothesis that text composition expertise develops as a result of an increase in working memory capacities brought about by maturation is entirely plausible (see Chanquoy and Alamargot, 2002, for a discussion). For a long time now, we have known that memory span, especially for figures, regularly increases with age (Woodworth and Schlosberg, 1964; for summaries, see Dempster, 1981; Gaonac'h and Fradet, 2003; Gaonac'h and Larigauderie, 2000). The impact of maturation on working memory can be conceived of in different ways. According to Pascual-Leone (1970, 1987), maturation brings about the direct expansion of the processing space (one unit every two years), in particular the 'central processor', referred to as 'M space' for 'Mental Energy', which allows schemas be activated, transformed, and coordinated. The stance adopted by Case (1985), a fellow neo-Piagetian, is slightly different, in that he asserts that it is not general memory capacity that increases but operative efficiency (automation of operative schemas). This improvement in processing leads to a reduction in the amount of

processing space (referred to as operative space) in favour of working memory storage space. This is then followed by an indirect increase in the number of units that can be processed simultaneously (see also Case, Kurland, and Goldberg, 1982).

In written production, the effect of maturation is most marked in young children, and for the lowest levels of processing (i.e., proximodistal maturation determines access to graphomotor skills, while the constitution of the phonological register determines access to alphabet and orthographic learning—Hitch, Woodin, and Baker, 1989). That said, the effect of maturation has rarely been investigated in the more advanced ages of 14–15 years, even though it probably constitutes a decisive factor in the evolution of processing components such as planning and revision. Thus, while Bereiter and Scardamalia (1987) evoke the increase with age of short-term memory capacities and planning span as a condition governing access to the knowledge-transforming strategy, they clarify neither the mechanisms nor the timescale. Thus, while the maturation of working memory may well be a factor for the development of written composition, it will only be fully understood once there has been further research on the function and development of working memory. Only now are we beginning to glimpse the relationship between memory capacities and composition performances in adults, in the wake of Kellogg's (1996) model and the early experimental studies conducted by Levy and Ransdell (1996b). The developmental aspect of this research (i.e., in children and even more so in adolescents) has been somewhat neglected (see, however, Swanson and Berninger, 1996; Alamargot et al., 2007) and needs to be systematized.

The various models of development and of expert writers often presuppose the existence of a close relationship between metacognition (in the form of metacognitive skills or metacognitive knowledge) and the development of compositional expertise. Metacognition is mentioned in the context of reasoning and reflexive analysis (planning—Hayes, 1996; Hayes and Nash, 1996), the assessment of the gap between intention and text production (revision—Hayes et al., 1987; Scardamalia and Bereiter, 1983; Butterfield, Hacker, and Plumb, 1994), and the management and coordination of writing processes (monitoring—Butterfield et al., 1996). As Allal emphasizes (2000:148–149),

> Cognitive regulations are involved in the construction of the conceptual, linguistic and metalinguistic knowledge required for writing and they intervene implicitly throughout the process of text production. Metacognitive regulations entail the active management of cognitive resources with respect to a given goal and, in the case of writing, the use of explicit strategies for articulating different bodies of knowledge (conceptual, linguistic, and metalinguistic) needed for text production.

Scardamalia and Bereiter (1983) attempted to improve the metacognitive management of writing processes in young writers by proposing a relatively simple guidance procedure called CDO (Compare, Diagnose, and Operate). For writers, this involves firstly, assessing the potential gap between the written composition and the intention ('Compare'), secondly, identifying the origin of any discrepancy that is discovered ('Diagnose'), and finally, deciding which type of modification needs to be made in order to close this gap ('Operate'). This procedure can be applied either immediately after each sentence in the text has been written or once the whole text has been completed. Bereiter and Scardamalia (1987) described a series of experiments conducted in order to confirm the relevance and effectiveness of this 'alternating procedure' in fourth-, sixth- and eighth-graders (nine, eleven, and thirteen years old respectively). Results showed that the CDO procedure prompted considerable alterations to the initial version, whatever the age group and whatever the condition for applying the procedure (after each sentence or after the whole text). Although the majority of these alterations were positive, there were nonetheless a great many unwise modifications as well,

which is why there was no improvement in the overall quality of the texts. For the authors, the CDO procedure had a positive effect, because it encouraged revision behaviour in young writers (from nine to thirteen years old). However, due to their continuing lack of expertise, these young writers were unable to conduct a reflexive and metacognitive analysis of the consequences of their revisions. In the light of the study by Bereiter and Scardamalia (1987), De La Paz et al. (1998) took a closer look at the effect of the CDO procedure on eighth-graders (thirteen years old) with learning and writing difficulties. Their results showed that students using the CDO procedure revised more frequently, produced more meaning-preserving revisions that improved their text, and revised larger segments of text more frequently. However, like Bereiter and Scardamalia (1983, 1987), the authors also noted the presence of a considerable number of ill-advised revisions with CDO. The students tended to 'change for the sake of change', without being fully able to measure the consequences of their actions (failure in constructive assessments).

The relative failure of the CDO procedure suggests that no analysis of the relationship between metacognition and compositional processes can afford to ignore the underlying development of metacognitive abilities. Metacognitive development (Flavell et al., 1997), especially in its metalinguistic aspect (Gombert, 1990), brings about a redefinition of the representation of one's own knowledge and linguistic processes (Karmiloff-Smith, 1986, 1988). For this reason, the management of compositional processes probably requires a degree of maturity and the development of the metacognitive function. In their model, Berninger and Swanson (1994) give metacognition (conceived of as metacognitive knowledge influencing writing processes in working memory) pride of place. Using a 'Thinking about Writing' test, the authors sought to ascertain the extent to which compositional performances (i.e., text quality) are linked to metacognitive knowledge of writing components (planning, formulation, and revision) and from what age. Several conclusions can be drawn from the results: (i) These links are coherent at the developmental level, albeit not as numerous as one might expect. Metacognitive knowledge becomes increasingly strongly associated with the quality of writing processes as the writer becomes older. Thus,

> metacognition about writing tends not to be related to quality of writing in intermediate grade children but begins to be related to quality of writing in junior high students (Berninger and Swanson, 1994:76).

The writer, therefore, needs to achieve a certain degree of maturity in order to be able to analyze his or her writing processes and modify them. (ii) Where a relationship does exist between processes and metacognition (e.g., in junior high students), it does not involve the three components defined by Hayes and Flower (1980) but rather more general aspects, such as general knowledge about writing and sensitivity to audience. The actual metacognitive analysis of the planning, formulation, and revision processes emerges at a later stage and therefore could well be one of the conditions for the development of expertise in advanced writers. Here, once more, in line with the maturation hypothesis of working memory development, relations between metacognition and writing processes in writers aged 14–15 years and above has remained largely unexplored until now.

The practice effect: Supports and training

In developmental models, the question of instruction and the hopefully inevitable effects it has on production processes and performances is generally left to one side, as though the evolution that is observed had a 'natural and predetermined' character. Yet, instructed and related practice play a central role in the learning and development of written production and can be regarded as a second factor for development, interacting with – or at the very least acting alongside – maturation. Even studies which deal explicitly with interventions and seek to gauge their impact remain few and far between, although various instructional situations have been designed and tested in the literature (for a review of the efficiency of these various situations, see Graham, 2006; Harris et al., 2008).

The experiments described earlier with regard to the development of narratives are a case in point. These varied interventions may involve different processing levels (graphomotor skills, spelling, or text), different processes (planning, formulation, or revision) or even the overall management of the activity (self-regulation: Graham and Harris, 1996). To understand the impact of these interventions, and therefore more generally the effect of instruction and practice, it would seem important to distinguish between two forms of intervention at the conceptual level: supports and training programmes. Based on different principles, these two forms each have a different impact on the development of written production. Supports are intended to make writing processes easier during the actual activity, by mobilizing a body of knowledge and/or boosting a specific writing process. These supports are built into the writing activity and bring a direct benefit within the context of the task (e.g., providing vocabulary related to ingredients when writing a recipe). They either physically modify the task environment (access to information and a variety of documentary sources, such as dictionaries, vocabulary lists, etc.) or take the form of an instruction, which encourages the subject to adopt a more suitable writing strategy ('Make a plan first', 'Read through each sentence you have written', etc.). Bereiter and Scardamalia's CDO procedure (1983) described earlier falls into this category. Writing supports have a close temporal relationship with the production phase. They may be provided immediately before (activation of concepts, vocabulary, etc.), during (supports available in the task environment – instruction, guidance, vocabulary list, etc.) and/or immediately after composition (advice on rereading the text; carrying out final assessments/editing, etc.). We can expect to observe two complementary effects: the assisted process is more efficient (direct effect), and this in turn may enable the writer to allocate more cognitive resources to other costly processes (indirect effect).

Unlike writing supports, training programmes are intended to bring about the automaticity of existing processes and/or the acquisition of new skills. Spread over several sessions, training consists in isolating and practising one or several processes, which will subsequently be called upon during the writing activity. Training brings about a long-term benefit, thanks to a learning effect. This benefit is not restricted to writing tasks. For instance, training in fine motor skills (prehension, oculomotor coordination) helps young children to improve all their graphomotor processes, whatever the nature of the writing tasks they are given. The interventions studied by Berninger et al. (1997), Jones and Christensen (1999), and Graham et al. (2000) in the case of graphomotor skills or by Berninger et al. (2002) and Graham et al. (2002) in the case of spelling, all come under this heading (see previous section).

We believe that these two categories of support and training should be further defined, according to whether they are intended to improve a particular writing process (planning, translating, revision, and graphomotor execution) or the way in which all the writing processes are managed (control and monitoring). In the former, supports are generally used to make controlled processes easier (high-level processes: planning and revision), whereas training is intended to bring about the automation or proceduralization of lower-level processes (spelling and graphomotor execution). In the latter, supports generally make it easier for the writer to construct an accurate representation of the task and the recipient in order to govern all the processes – goal-setting). Training, meanwhile, seeks to bring about the acquisition and/or

improvement of metacognitive strategies for regulating the writing processes (self-regulation; see, e.g., the SRSD programme established by Graham, Harris, and colleagues; see De La Paz and Graham, 2002, for an experimental validation).

Finally, if we consider the effect of instruction and practice as a factor for development, two levels can be described. On the one hand, instruction and practice enable the writer to acquire and implement the knowledge and representations required for written verbal production. On the other hand, rather like maturation, they have the effect of increasing (albeit relatively) the cognitive resources dedicated to a particular process. As a result of practice or supports, the process either consumes less or benefits from additional resources freed up by the supported or practised process. This relative increase in resources, therefore, takes place either via the instantiation of expert and more efficient strategies of knowledge storage and retrieval (Ericsson and Kintsch, 1995—facilitated retrieval of knowledge and processing procedures) or via a relative increase in resources thanks to the automation of certain processes (Fayol, 1999; McCutchen, 1996; Anderson, 1993; Cowan, 1988, 1993). This twofold influence on working memory capacity (increased by maturation or practice) needs to be investigated in greater depth, in order to relate maturation-induced increases in specific memory capacity (i.e., dedicated to writing processes) to ones in general memory capacity. This twofold analysis would shed light on some of the difficulties encountered by writers and would allow us to fine-tune interventions focusing on either general or specific capacity.

GENERAL CONCLUSION

In order to formalize the development of written production, we need to regard formulation as a central component. For reasons of capacity, its acquisition and mode of functioning govern the introduction and evolution of the other components, that is, revision and planning. It is vital to study the development of formulation, especially transcription, in greater depth. Although the findings of psycholinguistic research are relevant here, there remain a number of unanswered questions. Some could probably be tackled using a modified version of Levelt's model, while others require a considerable shift in perspective. Several dimensions need to be taken into account.

Studying written formulation

Up to now, studies and theorizations have only really tackled oral verbal production. However, written language production raises specific questions. The data yielded by neuropsychology research and experimental studies show that writing is a relatively autonomous activity. In particular, it cannot be regarded as the straightforward transcription of the phonological form of an utterance, even if the production of written words shares several stages with oral verbal production (for a review, see Shanahan, 2006).

We still need to hone our definition of these stages, and indeed of the relationship between the oral and written modalities, especially in the case of 'opaque' orthographic systems (i.e., where there are no straightforward phoneme-grapheme correspondences) (Bonin, Peereman, and Fayol, 2001), followed by the processing of letters or sequences of letters which have no phonological correspondent (Fayol, Largy, and Lemaire, 1994; Pacton et al., 2001). A comparative, interlingual approach, comparing, say, the acquisition of the handwriting and orthographic systems of relatively transparent languages (e.g., Spanish and Swedish) and relatively opaque ones (e.g., English and the production of French) would be highly worthwhile, allowing us to identify the nature of orthographic processes, the various stages of acquisition and the constraints exerted by the language system. Morphological processes could be studied from the same perspective.

Teaching formulation

It is no exaggeration to say that the data collected over the last three decades have allowed major advances to take place in our understanding of the difficulties encountered by children and adults in written verbal production. These advances have not been solely theoretical, but have virtually always been accompanied by interventions whose effects have then been assessed, thereby highlighting the effectiveness of certain intervention modes (see, in particular, research by Berninger and Graham). It would doubtless be possible to draft a set of guidelines based on these results, designed to help primary school teachers teach written production more efficiently. Most research up to now has focused on the production of words or, at best, sentences, mainly in relation to the teaching of grammar, and sometimes with a view to inducing the construction of syntactically more complex sentences. However, assessments of these interventions have all shown that there is no improvement in terms of the quality and quantity of the texts that are produced (Elley et al., 1975; Legrand, 1966: 75–101). It is vital to identify the knowledge and know-how needed for written production and to assess different modes of intervention, as has been done for the other components. In particular, specific research is needed on the use of determiners and pronominal forms, verbal forms, especially past tenses, punctuation, and connectives (see Costermans and Fayol, 1997; Fayol, 1997a, 2002). All these markers require the conditions of the utterance to be taken account (Fayol, 2002) – a dimension that is virtually absent from English-language studies.

Understanding the impact of other types of acquisition and knowledge: the notion of pacemaker

Another dimension concerns the relationship between reading, speech, and writing

(Shanahan, 2006). The handful of studies that have been published on this subject tend to focus on the relations between word perception and orthographic production. Very little empirically valid research has probed the effect of text reading on children's and adults' appropriation of more or less extensive rhetorical forms. Similarly, the effect of feedback from the production of textual structures on reading comprehension has virtually never been explored. These are new and important fields, where researchers can go beyond fundamental research on the constitution and organization of rhetorical knowledge and know-how and develop educational research on the learning and implementation of this knowledge and know-how.

Understanding the impact of the activity itself: the epistemic effect of monitoring

Monitoring and regulating one's activity is a source of learning. Research on the management of processes has been conducted from an exclusively synchronic perspective: authors have looked solely at the nature and function of monitoring and regulating mechanisms (Oomen and Postma, 2001) and the disorders that may affect them. To our knowledge, no study has ever looked at the effect of feedback from corrections on subsequent production. Yet this is a crucial question, which concerns not only language learning, that is, a dynamic process of assimilating and adapting to the characteristics of the corpus, but also the rehabilitation of patients and pupils who display learning disorders. It may seem surprising that this issue has so rarely been tackled. Here, once more, it is probably a consequence of the design of production models, which concern skilled adults and tackle performances from a synchronic point of view, and of the often implicit reference to a formal linguistics, where the question of development or learning is seldom, if ever, raised.

REFERENCES

Alamargot, D. and Chanquoy, L. (2001) *Through the Models of Writing*, Dordrecht-Boston-London: Kluwer Academic Publishers.

Alamargot, D., Lambert, E., Thebault, C., and Dansac, C. (2007) 'Text Composition by Deaf and Hearing Middle School Students: Effects of Working Memory', *Reading and Writing*, 20(4): 330–360.

Allal, L. (2000) 'Metacognitive Regulation of Writing in the Classroom', in A. Camps and M. Milian (eds), *Metalinguistic Activity in Learning to Write*, Amsterdam: Amsterdam University Press. pp. 145–166.

Anderson, J.R. (1993) *Rules of the Mind*, Hillsdale, NJ: Lawrence Erlbaum Associates.

Applebee, A.N. (1978) *The Child's Concept of Story: Age Two to Seventeen*, Chicago: The University of Chicago Press.

Barnes, M.A, Dennis, M., and Haefele-Kalvaitis, J. (1996) 'The Effect of Knowledge Availability and Knowledge Accessibility on Coherence and Elaborative Inferencing in Children from Six to Fifteen Years of Age', *Journal of Experimental Child Psychology*, 61: 216–241.

Bereiter, C. and Scardamalia, M. (1983) 'Levels of Inquiry in Writing Research', in P. Mosenthal, S. Walmsley, and L. Tamor (eds), *Research on Writing: Principles and Method*, New York: Longman. pp. 3–25.

Bereiter, C. and Scardamalia, M. (1987) *The Psychology of Written Composition*, Hillsdale, NJ: Lawrence Erlbaum Associates.

Berninger, V.W. and Swanson, H.L. (1994) 'Modifying Hayes and Flower Model of Skilled Writing to Explain Beginning and Developing Writing', in E.C. Butterfield (ed.), *Advances in Cognition and Educational Practice (Vol. 2: Children's Writing: Toward a Process Theory of Development of Skilled Writing)*, Greenwich, CT: JAI Press. pp. 57–82.

Berninger, V.W., Vaughan, K.B., Abbott, R.D., Abbott, S.P., Rogan, L.W., and Brooks, A. (1997) 'Treatment of Handwriting Problems in Beginning Writers: Transfer from Handwriting to Composition', *Journal of Educational Psychology*, 89(4): 652–666.

Berninger, V.W., Vaughan, K., Abbott, R.D., Begay, K., Coleman, K.B., Curtin, G., Hawkins J.M., and Graham, S. (2002) 'Teaching Spelling and Composition Alone and Together: Implications for the Simple View of Writing', *Journal of Educational Psychology*, 94(2): 291–304.

Bock, K. and Levelt, W.J.M. (1994) 'Grammatical Encoding', in M.A. Gernsbacher (ed.), *Handbook of*

Psycholinguistics, New York: Academic Press. pp. 945–984

Bonin, P., Peereman, R., and Fayol, M. (2001) 'Do Phonological Codes Constrain the Selection of Orthographic Codes in Written Picture Naming?', *Journal of Memory and Language*, 45: 688–720.

Bonnotte, I. and Fayol, M. (1997) 'Cognitive Representations of Predicates and the Use of Past-tenses in French: A Developmental Approach', *First Language*, 17: 75–101.

Bourdin, B. and Fayol, M. (1994) 'Is Written Language Production Really More Difficult than Oral Language Production?', *International Journal of Psychology*, 29: 591–620.

Bourdin, B. and Fayol, M. (1996) 'Mode Effects in a Sentence Production Task', *CPC/Current Psychology of Cognition*, 15: 245–264.

Bourdin, B. and Fayol, M. (2002) 'Even in Adults, Written Production Is Still More Costly than Oral Production', *International Journal of Psychology*, 37: 219–22.

Bourdin, B., Fayol, M., and Darciaux, S. (1996) 'The Comparison of Oral and Written Modes on Adults' and Children's Narrative Recall', in G. Rijlaarsdam, H.v.d. Bergh, and M. Couzijn (eds), *Theories, Models and Methodology in Writing Research*, Amsterdam: Amsterdam University Press. pp. 121–141.

Bronckart J.P. (ed.) (1985) *Le Fonctionnement des Discours*. Neuchâtel: Delachaux and Niestlé.

Butterfield, E.C. (1994) *Advances in Cognition and Educational Practice (Vol. 2) Children's Writing: Toward a Process Theory of the Development of Skilled Writing*, Greenwich, CT: JAI Press.

Butterfield, E.C., Hacker, D.J., and Albertson, L.R. (1996) 'Environmental, Cognitive and Metacognitive Influences on Text Revision: Assessing the Evidence', *Educational Psychology Review*, 8(3): 239–297.

Butterfield, E.C., Hacker, D.J., and Plumb, C. (1994) 'Topic Knowledge, Linguistic Knowledge and Revision Processes as Determinants of Text Revision', in E.C. Butterfield (ed.), *Advances in Cognition and Educational Practice (Vol. 6: Children's writing: Toward a Process Theory of the Development of Skilled Writing)*, Greenwich, CT: JAI Press. pp. 83–141.

Cain, K. (1996) 'Story Knowledge and Comprehension Skill', in C. Cornoldi and J. Oakhill (eds), *Reading Comprehension Difficulties*, Mahwah, NJ: Erlbaum. pp. 167–192.

Caron, J., Micko, H.C., and Thuring, M. (1988) 'Conjunctions and the Recall of Composite Sentences', *Journal of Memory and Language*, 27(3): 309–323.

Case, R. (1985) 'A Developmentally-Based Approach to the Problem of Instructional Design', in S.S. Chipman, J.W. Segal, and R. Glaser (eds), *Thinking and Learning Skills: Current Research and Open Questions (Vol. 2)*, Hillsdale, NJ: Lawrence Erlbaum Associates. pp. 545–562.

Case, R., Kurland, D.M., and Goldberg, J. (1982) 'Operational Efficiency and the Growth of Short Term Memory Span', *Journal of Experimental Child Psychology*, 33: 386–404.

Chanquoy, L. and Alamargot, D. (2002) 'Mémoire de Travail et Rédaction de Textes: Evolution des Modèles et Bilan des Premiers Travaux', *L'Année Psychologique*, 102: 363–398.

Chanquoy, L., Foulin, J.-N., and Fayol, M. (1990) 'Temporal Management of Short Text Writing by Children and Adults', *Cahiers de Psychologie Cognitive*, 10(5): 513–540.

Connelly, V., Dockrell, J.E., and Barnett, J. (2005) 'The Slow Handwriting of Undergraduate Students Constrains Overall Performance in Exam Essays', *Educational Psychology*, 25: 97–105.

Costermans, J. and Bestgen, Y. (1991) 'The Role of Temporal Markers in the Segmentation of Narrative Discourse', *C.P.C./European Bulletin of Cognitive Psychology*, 11: 349–370.

Costermans, J. and Fayol, M. (eds) (1997) *Processing Interclausal Relationships: Studies in the Production and Comprehension of Text*, Mahwah, NJ: Lawrence Erlbaum Associates.

Cowan, N. (1988) 'Evolving Conceptions of Memory Storage, Selective Attention and Their Mutual Constraints within the Human Information Processing System', *Psychological Bulletin*, 104(2): 163–191.

Cowan, N. (1993) 'Activation, Attention and Short Term Memory', *Memory and Cognition,* 21(2): 162–167.

De La Paz, S., and Graham, S. (2002) 'Explicitly Teaching Strategies, Skills, and Knowledge: Writing Instruction in Middle School Classrooms', *Journal of Educational Psychology*, 4: 687–698.

De La Paz, S., Swanson, P.N., and Graham, S. (1998) 'The Contribution of Executive Control to the Revising by Students with Writing and Learning Difficulties', *Journal of Educational Psychology*, 90(3): 448–460.

Dempster, F.N. (1981) 'Memory Span: Sources of Individual and Developmental Differences', *Psychological Bulletin*, 89(1): 63–100.

Dickinson, D.K. and Tabors, P.O. (1991) 'Early Literacy: Linkages between Home, School and Literacy Achievement at Age Five', *Journal of Research in Childhood Education*, 6: 30–44.

Elley, W.B., Barham, I.H., Lamb, H., and Wylie, M. (1975) The Role of Grammar in a Secondary School Curriculum, *New Zealand Council for Educational Studies*, 10: 26–41.

Ericsson, K.A. and Kintsch, W. (1995) 'Long Term Working Memory', *Psychological Review*, 102(2): 211–245.

Fayol, M. (1985) Le Récit et sa Construction. *Neuchâtel*, Paris: Delachaux et Niestlé.

Fayol, M. (1991) 'Stories: A Psycholinguistic and Ontogenetic Approach to the Acquisition of Narrative Abilities', in G. Pieraut Le Bonniec and M. Dolitsky (eds), *From Basic Language to Discourse Basis Processing*, Amsterdam: Benjamin. pp. 229–243.

Fayol, M. (1997a) *Des Idées au Texte*. Paris: Presses Universitaires de France.

Fayol, M. (1997b) 'On Acquiring and Using Punctuation: A Study in Written French', in J. Costermans and M. Fayol (eds), *Processing Interclausal Relationships*, Mahwah, NJ: Erlbaum. pp. 157–178.

Fayol, M. (1999) 'From On-line Management Problems to Strategies in Written Composition', in M. Torrance and G. Jeffery (ed.), *The Cognitive Demands of Writing*, Amsterdam: Amsterdam University Press. pp. 13–23.

Fayol, M. (ed.) (2002) *Production du Langage: Trait des Sciences Cognitives*, Vol. 10, Paris: Herm-Science.

Fayol, M. (2003a) 'Text and Cognition', in T. Nunes and P. Bryant (eds), *Handbook of Children's Literacy*, Amsterdam: Kluwer Academic Publishers. pp. 181–198.

Fayol, M. (2003b) 'L'acquisition/apprentissage de la Morphologie du Nombre. Bilan et Perspectives', *Rééducation Orthophonique*, 213: 151–166.

Fayol, M. and Mouchon, S. (1997) 'Production and Comprehension of Connectives in the Written Modality. A Study of Written French', in C. Pontecorvo (ed.), *Writing Development: An Interdisciplinary View*, Amsterdam: John Benjamins. pp. 193–204.

Fayol, M., Hickmann, M., Bonnotte, I., and Gombert, J.E. (1993) 'The Effects of Narrative Context on French Verbal Inflections: A Developmental Perspective', *Journal of Psycholinguistic Research*, 4: 453–478.

Fayol, M., Largy, P., and Lemaire, P. (1994) 'When Cognitive Overload Enhances Subject-Verb Agreement Errors', *The Quarterly Journal of Experimental Psychology*, 47A: 437–464.

Ferreiro, E. and Zucchermaglio, C. (1996) 'PIZZA or PIZA? How Children Interpret the Doubling of Letters in Writing', in C. Pontecorvo, M. Orsolini, B. Burge, and L.B. Resnick (eds), *Children's Early Text Construction*, Mahwah, NJ: Lawrence Erlbaum Associates. pp. 177–206.

Fitzgerald, J. (1984) 'The Relationship between Reading Ability and Expectations for Story Structures', *Discourse Processes*, 7: 21–41.

Fitzgerald, J. and Spiegel, D.L. (1983) 'Enhancing Children's Reading Comprehension through Instruction in Narrative Structure', *Journal of Reading Behavior*, 15: 1–17.

Flavell, J.H., Green, F.L., Flavell, E.R., and Grossman, J.B. (1997) 'The Development of Children's Knowledge about Inner Speech', *Child Development*, 68: 399–347.

Flower, L. and Hayes, J.R. (1980) 'The Dynamic of Composing: Making Plans and Juggling Constraints', in L.W. Gregg and E.R. Steinberg (eds), *Cognitive Processes in Writing*, Hillsdale, NJ: Lawrence Erlbaum Associates. pp. 31–50.

Foulin, J.N., Chanquoy, L., and Fayol, M. (1989) 'Approche en Temps Réel de la Production des Connecteurs et de la Ponctuation', *Langue Française*, 81: 21–39.

French, L.A. and Nelson, K. (1985) *Children's Acquisition of Relational Terms: Some Ifs, Ors, and Buts*. New York: Springer Verlag.

Gaonac'h, D. and Fradet, A. (2003) 'La Mémoire de Travail: Développement et Implication dans les Activités Cognitives', in M. Kail and M. Fayol (eds), *Les Sciences Cognitives et l'école*, Paris: Presses Universitaires de France. pp. 91–150.

Gaonac'h, D. and Larigauderie, P. (2000) *Mémoire et Fonctionnement Cognitif: La Mémoire de Travail*, Paris: Armand Colin.

Garrett, M.F. (1980) 'Levels of Processing in Sentence Production', in B. Butterworth (ed.), *Language Production: Speech and Talk. (Vol. 1: Speech and Talk)*, New York: Academic Press. pp. 177–220.

Gernsbacher, M.A. (1997) 'Two Decades of Structure Building', *Discourse Processes*, 23: 265–304.

Gombert, J.E. (1990) *Le Développement Métalinguistique*, Paris: Presses Universitaires de France.

Graham, S. (1999) 'Handwriting and Spelling Instruction for Students with Learning Disabilities: A Review', *Learning Disability Quarterly*, 22: 78–98.

Graham, S. (2006) 'Strategy Instruction and the Teaching of Writing: A Meta-analysis', in C. MacArthur, N.L. Graham, and J. Fitzgerald (eds), *Handbook of Writing Research*, New York–London: Guilford Press. pp. 187–207.

Graham, S., Berninger, V.W., Abbott, R.D., Abbott, S.P., and Whitaker, D. (1997) 'The Role of Mechanics in Composing of Elementary School Students: A New Methodological Approach', *Journal of Educational Psychology*, 89: 170–182.

Graham, S. and Harris, K.R. (1996) 'Self-Regulation and Strategy Instruction or Students who Find Writing and Learning Challenging', in M. Levy and S. Ransdell (eds), *The Science of Writing: Theories, Methods, Individual Differences and Applications*, Mahwah, NJ: Erlbaum. pp. 347–360.

Graham, S., Harris, K.R., and Mason, L. (2005) Improving the Writing Performance, Knowledge, and Self-Efficacy of Struggling Young Writers: The Effects of Self-Regulated Strategy Development. *Contemporary Educational Psychology*, 30: 207–241.

Graham, S., Harris, K.R., and Chorzempa, B.F. (2002) 'Contribution of Spelling Instruction to the Spelling, Writing, and Reading of Poor Spellers', *Journal of Educational Psychology*, 94: 669–689.

Graham, S., Harris, K.R., and Kink, B. (2000) 'Is Handwriting Causally Related to Learning to Write? Treatment of Handwriting Problems in Beginning Writers', *Journal of Educational Psychology*, 92: 620–633.

Grimes, J.E. (1975) *The Thread of Discourse*, The Hague: Mouton.

Harris, K., Graham, S., Mason, L., and Friedlander, B. (2008) *Powerful Writing Strategies for all Students*, Baltimore, MD: Brookes.

Hayes, J.R. (1996) 'A New Framework for Understanding Cognition and Affect in Writing', in C.M. Levy and S. Ransdell (eds), *The Science of Writing: Theories, Methods, Individual Differences and Applications*, Mahwah, NJ: Lawrence Erlbaum Associates. pp. 1–27.

Hayes, J.R. and Flower, L.S. (1980) 'Identifying the Organization of Writing Processes', in L.W. Gregg and E.R. Steinberg (eds), *Cognitive Processes in Writing*, Hillsdale, NJ: Lawrence Erlbaum Associates. pp. 3–30.

Hayes, J.R. and Flower, L.S. (1983) 'Uncovering Cognitive Processes in Writing: An Introduction of Protocol Analysis', in P. Mosenthal, S. Walmsley and L. Tamor (eds), *Research on Writing: Principles and Methods*, New York, NY: Longman. pp. 206–219.

Hayes, J.R. and Nash, J.G. (1996) 'On the Nature of Planning in Writing', in C.M. Levy and S. Ransdell (eds), *The Science of Writing: Theories, Methods, Individual Differences and Applications*, Mahwah, NJ: Lawrence Erlbaum Associates. pp. 29–55.

Hayes, J.R., Flower, L., Schriver, K.A., Stratman, J.F., and Carey, L. (1987) 'Cognitive Processes in Revision', in S. Rosenberg (ed.), *Advances in Applied Psycholinguistics: Reading, Writing and Language Learning (Vol. 2)*, Cambridge: Cambridge University Press. pp. 176–240.

Heurley, L. (1997) 'Processing Units in Written Texts: Paragraphs or Information Blocks?' in J. Costermans and M. Fayol (eds), P*rocessing Interclausal Relationships*, Mahwah, NJ: Erlbaum. pp. 179–200.

Hidi, S. and Hildyard, A. (1983) 'The Comparison of Oral and Written Productions of Two Discourse Types', *Discourse Processes*, 6: 91–105.

Hitch, G.J., Woodin, M.E., and Baker, S. (1989) 'Visual and Phonological Components of Working Memory in Children', *Memory and Cognition*, 17(2): 175–185.

Hudson. J.A. and Shapiro, L.R. (1991) 'From Knowing to Telling: The Development of Children's Scripts, Stories, and Personal Narratives', in A. McCabe and C. Peterson (eds), *Developing Narrative Structure*, Hillsdale, NJ: Lawrence Erlbaum Associates, Inc. pp. 89–136.

Jaffré, J-P. and Fayol, M. (2005) 'Orthography and Literacy in French', in R.M. Joshi and P.G. Aaron (eds), *Handbook of Orthography and Literacy*, L.E.A. pp. 81–104.

Johnson-Laird, P.N. (1983) *Mental Models*, Cambridge, MA: Cambridge University Press.

Jones, D. and Christensen, C.A. (1999) 'Relationship between Automaticity in Handwriting and Students' Ability to Generate Written Text', *Journal of Educational Psychology*, 91: 44–49.

Juel, C. (1988) 'Learning to Read and Write: A Longitudinal Study of 54 Children from First to Fourth Grades', *Journal of Educational Psychology*, 80: 437–447.

Kail, M. and Weissenborn, J. (1991) 'Conjunctions: Developmental Issues', in G. Pieraut Le Bonniec and M. Dolitsky (eds), *From Basic Language to Discourse Basis Processing*, Amsterdam: Benjamin. pp. 125–142.

Karmiloff-Smith, A. (1986) 'From Metaprocesses to Conscious Access: Evidence from Children's Metalinguistic and Repair Data', *Cognition and Instruction*, 23: 95–147.

Karmiloff-Smith, A. (1988) 'A Model of Representational Change in Language Acquisition', Paper presented at the 2ème Congrés Mondial de la Langue Basque, Vitoria Gasteiz.

Kellogg, R. (2008) 'Training Writing Skills: A Cognitive Development Perspective', *Journal of Writing Research*, 1(1): 1–26.

Kellogg, R.T. (1987) 'Effects of Topic Knowledge on the Allocation of Processing Time and Cognitive Effort to Writing Processes', *Memory and Cognition*, 15(3): 256–266.

Kellogg, R.T. (1988) 'Attentional Overload and Writing Performance: Effects of Rough Draft and Outline

Strategies', *Journal of Experimental Psychology: Learning, Memory and Cognition*, 14(2): 355–365.

Kellogg, R.T. (1996) 'A Model of Working Memory in Writing', in C.M. Levy and S. Ransdell (eds), *The Science of Writing: Theories, Methods, Individual Differences and Applications*, Mahwah, NJ: Lawrence Erlbaum Associates. pp. 57–72.

King, M. and Rentel, V. (1981) 'Research Update: Conveying Meaning in Writing Texts' *Language Arts*, 58: 721–728.

Kintsch, W. Mandel, T.S., and Kozminsky, E. (1977) 'Summarizing Scrambled Stories', *Memory and Cognition*, 5: 547–552.

Legrand, L. (1966) `L'enseignement du Français à l'Ecole Elémentaire'. *Neuchatel*, Paris: Delachaux and Niestlé Aùitiés.

Levelt, W.J.M. (1981) 'The Speaker's Linearization Problem', *Phonological Transactions of the Royal Society of London* B, 295: 305–315.

Levelt, W.J.M. (1982) 'Linearization in Describing Spatial Networks', in S. Peters and E. Saarinen (eds), *Processes, Beliefs, and Questions*, Dordrecht: Reidel. pp. 199–220.

Levelt, W.J.M. (1989) *Speaking: From Intention to Articulation*, Cambridge, MA: MIT Press.

Levelt, W.J.M. (1998) 'The Genetic Perspective in Psycholinguistics. Or: Where do Spoken Words Come From?' *Journal of Psycholinguistic Research*, 27: 167–180.

Levelt, W.J.M. (1999) 'Models of Word Production', *Trends in Cognitive Sciences*, 3(6): 223–232.

Levelt, W.J.M., Roelofs, A., and Meyer, A.S. (1999) 'Multiple Perspectives on Lexical Access. Reply to Commentaries', *Behavioral and Brain Sciences*, 22(1): 61–72.

Levy, C.M. and Ransdell, S. (1996a) 'Writing Signatures', in C.M. Levy and S. Ransdell (eds), *The Science of Writing: Theories, Methods, and Applications*, Mahwah, NJ: Lawrence Erlbaum Associates. pp. 149–161.

Levy, C.M. and Ransdell, S. (eds) (1996b) *The Science of Writing: Theories, Methods, Individual Differences, and Applications*, Mahwah, NJ: Laurence Erlbaum Associates.

Liles, B.Z., Duffy, R.J., Merritt, D.D., and Purcell, S.L. (1995) 'Measurement of Narrative Discourse Ability in Children with Language Disorders', *Journal of Speech and Hearing Research*, 38: 415–425.

Linde, C. and Labov, W. (1975) 'Spatial Network as a Site for the Study of Language and Thought'. *Language*, 51: 924–939.

MacArthur, C., Graham, N.L., and Fitzgerald, J. (eds) (2006) *Handbook of Writing Research*, New York-London: Guilford Press.

Mandler, J. (1987) 'On the Psychological Validity of Story Structure', *Discourse Processes*, 10: 1–29.

Mandler, J. and Jonhson, N.S. (1977) 'Remembrance of Things Parsed: Story Structure and Recall', *Cognitive Psychology*, 9: 111–151.

Mandler, J., Scribner, S., Cole, M., and De Forest, M. (1980) 'Cross-Cultural Invariance in Story Recall', *Child Development*, 51: 19–26.

McCutchen, D. (1996) 'A Capacity Theory of Writing: Working Memory in Composition', *Educational Psychology Review*, 8(3): 299–325.

McCutchen, D. (2000) 'Knowledge, Processing, and Working Memory: Implications for a Theory of Writing', *Educational Psychologist*, 35(1): 13–23.

Noordman, L.G.M. and Vonk, W. (1997) 'The Different Functions of a Conjunction in Constructing a Representation of the Discourse', in J. Costermans and M. Fayol (eds), *Processing Interclausal Relationships*, Mahwah, NJ: Erlbaum. pp. 75–93.

Ochs, E. (1979) 'Planned and Unplanned Discourse', in T. Givon (ed.), *Syntax and Semantics (XII): Discourse and Syntax*, New York: Academic Press. pp. 51–80.

Oomen, C.C.E. and Postma, A. (2001) 'Effects of Time Pressure on Mechanisms of Speech Production and Self-Monitoring', *Journal of Psycholinguistic Research*, 30(2): 163–184.

Pacton, S. and Fayol, M. (2004) 'Learning to Spell in a Deep Orthography', in R.A. Berman (ed.), *Language Development Across Childhood and Adolescence*, John Benjamin: Amsterdam. pp. 163–176.

Pacton, S., Perruchet, P., Fayol, M., and Cleeremans, A. (2001) 'Implicit Learning out of the Lab: The Case of Orthographic Regularities', *Journal of Experimental Psychology: General*, 130: 401–426.

Pascual-Leone, J. (1970) 'A Mathematical Model for the Transition Rule in Piaget's Developmental Stages', *Acta Psychologica*, 32: 301–345.

Pascual-Leone, J. (1987) 'Organismic Processes for Neo-piagetian Theories: A Dialectical Causal Account of Cognitive Development', *International Journal of Psychology*, 22: 531–570.

Peterson, C. and McCabe, A. (1983) *Developmental Psycholinguistics: Three Ways of Looking at a Child's Narrative*, New York: Plenum.

Pitcher, E.G. and Prelinger, E. (1963) *Children tell Stories: An Analysis of Fantasy*, New York: International Universities Press.

Rijlaarsdam, G., van den Bergh, H., and Couzjin, M. (1996) *Theories, Models, and Methodology in Writing Research*, Amsterdam: Amsterdam University Press.

Scardamalia, M. and Bereiter, C. (1983) 'The Development of Evaluative, Diagnostic and Remedial

Capabilities in Children's Composing', in M. Martlew (ed.), *The Psychology of Written Language: Developmental and Educational Perspectives*, New York, NY: Wiley and Sons. pp. 67–95.

Scardamalia, M. and Bereiter, C. (1991) 'Literate Expertise', in K.A. Ericsson and J. Smith (eds), *Toward a General Theory of Expertise: Prospects and Limits*, Cambridge: Cambridge University Press. pp. 172–194.

Schank, R.C. and Abelson, R. (1977) *Scripts, Plans, Goals, and Understanding*, Hillsdale, NJ: Erlbaum.

Segal, E.M., Duchan, J.F., and Scott, P.T. (1991) 'The Role of Interclausal Connectives in Narrative Structuring: Evidence from Adults' Interpretations of Simple Stories', *Discourse Processes*, 14: 27–54.

Shanahan, T. (2006) 'Relations among Oral Language, Reading and Writing Development', in C. MacArthur, N.L. Graham, and J. Fitzgerald (eds). *Handbook of Writing Research*, New York-London: Guilford Press. pp. 171–183.

Simon, J. (1973) La Langue Ecrite de l'Enfant. Paris: P.U.F.

Sperry, L.L. and Sperry, D.E. (1996) 'Early Development of Narrative Skills', *Cognitive Development*, 11: 443–465.

Stein, N.L. and Glenn, C.G. (1979) 'An Analysis of Story Comprehension in Elementary School Children', in R.O. Freedle (ed.), *New Directions in Discourse Processing*, Norwood, NJ: Ablex. pp. 53–120.

Stein, N.L. and Nezworski, T. (1978) 'The Effect of Organization and Instructional Set on Story Memory', *Discourse Processes*, 1: 177–193.

Swanson, H.L. (1999) 'What Develops in Working Memory? A Lifespan Perspective', *Developmental Psychology*, 35: 986–1000.

Swanson, H.L. and Berninger, V.W. (1996) 'Individual Differences in Children's Working Memory and Writing Skills', *Journal of Experimental Child Psychology*, 63: 358–385.

Torrance, M. and Jeffery, G. (ed.) (1999) *The Cognitive Demands of Writing*, Amsterdam: Amsterdam University Press.

Townsend, D.J. (1997) 'Processing Clauses and their Relationships during Comprehension', in J. Costermans and M. Fayol (eds), *Processing Interclausal Relationships*, Mahwah, NJ: Erlbaum. pp. 265–282.

Trabasso, T., Secco, T., and van den Broek, P. (1984) 'Causal Cohesion and Story Coherence', in H. Mandl, N. Stein, and T. Trabasso (eds), *Learning and Comprehension of Text*, pp. 83–111. Hillsdale, NJ: Erlbaum.

Trabasso, T. and Nickels, M. (1992) 'The Development of Goal Plans of Actions in the Narration of a Picture Story', *Discourse Processes*, 15: 249–275.

Trabasso, T., Stein, N.L., Rodkin, P.C., Munger, M.P., and Baughn, C.R. (1992) 'Knowledge of Goals and Plans in the On-line Narration of Events', *Cognitive Development*, 7: 133–170.

van den Broek, P., Lorch, E.P., and Thurlow, R. (1996) 'Children's and Adults' Memory for Television Stories: The Role of Causal Factors, Story Grammar Categories, and Hierarchical Level', *Child Development*, 67: 3010–3028.

van Dijk, T.A. and Kintsch, W. (1983) *Strategies of Discourse Comprehension*, New York: Academic Press.

Varnhagen, C.K., Morrison, F.J., and Everall, R. (1994) 'Ageing and Schooling Effects in Story Recall and Story Production', *Developmental Psychology*, 30: 969–979.

Walczyk, J.J. (2000) 'The Interplay between Automatic and Control Processes in Reading', *Reading Research Quarterly*, 35: 554–566.

Woodworth, R.S. and Schlosberg, H. (1964) *Experimental Psychology*, New York: Holt, Rinehart and Winston.

Yussen, S.R., Stright, A.D., Glysch, R.L., Bonk, C.E., Lu, I., and Al-Sabaty, I. (1991) 'Learning and Forgetting of Narratives Following Good and Poor Text Organization', *Contemporary Educational Psychology*, 16: 346–374.

Zesiger, P. (1995) Ecrire. Approches Cognitive, *Neuropsychologique et Développementale*. Paris: Presses Universitaires de France.

Writing about What We Know: Generating Ideas in Writing

David Galbraith

An old cliché about writing is that writers should write about what they know. The intention being to exhort writers, young writers in particular, to write about things in terms of their own experience rather than, for example, to make up stories about spaceships and pop stars. There is some truth in this: writers do write more fluently and coherently about familiar topics than they do about unfamiliar topics. However, as we shall see, simply writing about what one knows has also been identified as one of the main weaknesses of novice writers.

There are two senses in which simply writing about what you know is problematic. The first is that writing does not just involve the unmediated transcription of knowledge. It also involves actively transforming knowledge in order to satisfy broader communicative goals. The second is that it implies that the writer already knows what they will be going to write about. However, as E.M. Forster famously asked, 'How can I know what I think until I see what I say?' Exhortations to write about what you know imply that the writer should stick to thoughts that they already have rather than that they

should explore the possibilities of thoughts that they do not as yet fully understand.

These two senses suggest that over and above writing about what one knows, one needs also to (i) go beyond this in order to create a coherent text that achieves the writer's goals with respect to the reader, and (ii) that 'what we know' is something that may only emerge in the course of writing rather than being something preexisting about which we can write. In this chapter, I will outline the classic cognitive models of how the writer's knowledge is realized as text and then describe how they account for the transformation and/or constitution of knowledge during writing. I will then consider an alternative account of these processes based on a different conception of how knowledge is mentally represented.

KNOWLEDGE TELLING

Hayes and Flower's original model of the writing process (Hayes and Flower, 1980; see Alamargot and Fayol, this volume, for an overview) was based on their analysis of protocols collected from writers thinking aloud as they wrote. Their aim was to identify the main components of the process and create a model of how these were combined in the course of writing. This model was deliberately constructed as a high-level model corresponding to writer's introspections about how writing was carried out. Fine-grained detail about how different components of the process were implemented by the cognitive system was left to be filled out by a combination of current research into basic features of the cognitive system and future research about how these were instantiated during writing. Their analysis of the protocols suggested that three main kinds of process were involved: *planning*, which involved the formulation of goals, and the generation and organization of ideas in order to satisfy those goals; *translation*, which, as the name implies, involved the translation of ideas into language; and *reviewing*, which involved reading over the text that the writer had already written, and editing it so that it satisfied their goals better. These processes used resources from the task environment (including the writing assignment and the text produced so far) and from the writer's long-term memory and were coordinated by a 'monitor' or central executive, which was responsible for deciding which processes should be carried out when.

For present purposes, the key feature of this model is the strong distinction between planning, where the creation of content takes place, and translation, where content is formulated as language. This means that what the writers say in their text is exclusively determined by the planning component of the writing process: translation is concerned with how best to express what the writer thinks, and reviewing is concerned with reading and editing the way this thought is expressed. To understand their claims about how writers generate the content of their text, therefore, we need to look in detail at their model of the planning process and how it interacts with the task environment and the

writer's long-term memory. Figure 3.1 shows their model of the generating subcomponent of the process.

According to this model, in order to work out what to say about the topic, the writer starts by using the specifications in the writing assignment to construct a set of cues with which to probe long-term memory. If content is successfully retrieved and then positively evaluated, it is either noted down on paper or stored mentally for later translation into text. This content then acts as a new probe for memory so that each retrieval episode consists of associative chains of content being retrieved from memory. If they cannot retrieve appropriate content, then they (or more strictly speaking the monitor) have to decide what to do next. This may be to pursue a different goal – for example, to go and read a book about the topic, or to read the assignment more closely – or it may be to carry on generating content by probing memory again with a different set of cues.

Note, also, that the monitor plays a role even if the writer successfully generates content in that the writer has to decide what to do next. This decision process is under the control of the monitor and depends in part on the writer's overall writing strategy. The writer might, for example, decide to translate the content into full text or to consider how to organize the idea in relation to other already generated content. Alternatively, they might decide to carry on generating further content in note-form. Hayes and Flower characterized differences in the overall strategy used by writers as corresponding to different configurations of the monitor. Some writers, for example, prefer to generate content freely before they turn to organizing: they would be characterized in terms of the model as prioritizing the goal of generating in the early stages of the writing process. Other writers may prefer to attempt a perfect first draft and engage in full cycles of generating, organizing, translating, and reviewing before moving on to the next episode of generating.

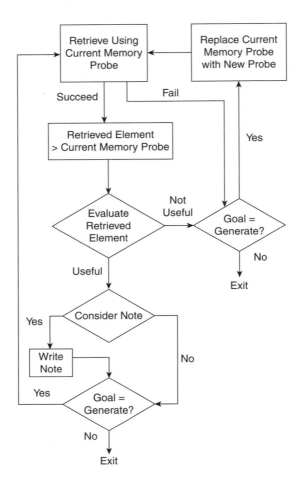

Figure 3.1   The generating component of the writing process as conceived in Hayes and Flower's model (1980:13).

This model of idea generation as a process of retrieving content from long-term memory is a general assumption in current cognitive models of writing. It is virtually identical to the knowledge-telling model described by Bereiter and Scardamalia (1987) (see Figure 3.2). Although they use this model to characterize the writing processes of younger and less expert writers, and contrast it with the knowledge-transforming model employed by older and more expert writers, it is still embedded as the idea generation component of the more advanced model.

COGNITIVE OVERLOAD

Given this model of how ideas are generated during writing, the main finding of research on the factors affecting retrieval is that idea generation can be reduced when it has to be combined with other components of writing. Subsequent research has focused on strategies for reducing the effects of this conflict between different components of writing.

Caccamise (1987), for example, asked college students to carry out what was essentially a knowledge telling task. They were

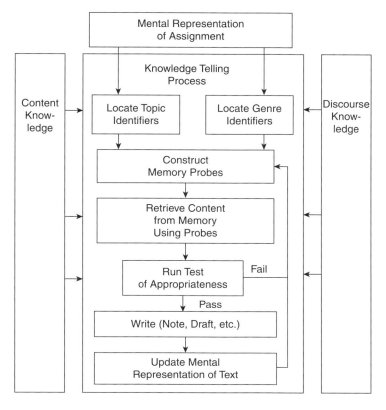

Figure 3.2   Bereiter and Scardamalia's (1987:8) model of the knowledge telling process.

asked to say everything that came to mind about a topic without worrying about repetitions or how well organized or expressed what they said was. She gave them four different topics varying in how familiar they were and asked them either to assume an audience of fifth grade school children or an audience of fellow college students. Her first, straightforward, finding was that the students produced many more ideas about familiar topics than unfamiliar ones, and that ideas produced about the familiar topic were much more organized than the ideas produced about unfamiliar ones. More interestingly, she also found that when children were given as the audience, although the students produced just as many ideas, these were much less organized and were produced much less fluently. She concluded that the audience

was not typically included as part of the memory probes used to search memory, but that the audience constraint was imposed after retrieval as part of an editing process. She also suggested that, because of the limited capacity of short-term memory this editing process could not be carried out very effectively, and recommended that under such circumstances writers should be encouraged to generate their ideas first without regard to the audience and only concern themselves with editing once ideas had been retrieved.

Caccamise's results suggest that idea generation can be impaired by conflicts with relatively high-level processes like adapting to audience constraints. A series of studies by Bourdin and Fayol (1994) comparing written and spoken recall with varying age groups suggests that low-level processes involved in spelling and handwriting can also impair retrieval. In simple word-recall tasks, Bourdin and Fayol found that both second and fourth grade children recalled substantially fewer items when their responses were written (i.e., using relatively less practised handwriting and spelling skills) than when their responses were spoken (i.e., they could rely on more automatic speech production skills). There was no corresponding difference for adults. In fact, recall was slightly better with written responses for adults. Similar results were found for a more complex sentence production task (Bourdin and Fayol, 1996). However, when the composition task was substantially more complex (Bourdin and Fayol, 2002), they found that even adults perform worse in writing compared to speaking. This suggests that even when spelling and handwriting are very well practised, they can still have a residual effect on memory retrieval if working memory resources are overloaded by other resource-demanding processes.

A study by Glynn et al. (1982) suggests that idea generation is reduced whenever it has to be combined with other components of the writing process. Following Hayes and Flower (1980), they identified four distinct operations in writing: (a) generating ideas, (b) sequencing or organizing ideas, (c) expressing ideas in sentences, and (d) complying with spelling and grammatical conventions. The extent to which these operations had to be carried out at the same time was manipulated by instructing writers to divide the writing of a brief letter into two separate ten-minute sessions and varying the number of operations that which had to be carried out during the preliminary draft. The resulting four preliminary draft formats successively removed one of the operations. In the polished sentences condition, writers had to write a complete, polished version of the letter on the first draft. In the mechanics-free sentences condition, they had to write the complete text, but without worrying about mechanics (spelling and punctuation). In the ordered notes condition, they were instructed to write their ideas

down in brief three or four word notes, and to ensure these were organized into a logical order. Finally, in the unordered notes condition, they were instructed to jot their ideas down in note-form as before, but not to worry about the order in which they were expressed. Glynn et al. found that the number of ideas generated in the preliminary drafts was progressively lower as the number of constraints present increased, with the fewest ideas being generated in the polished sentences conditions and the most ideas being generated in the unordered notes condition. They concluded that generating ideas was more productive when it was carried out in note-form prior to the production of text than when it was carried out at the same time as producing the text.

One implication of this general line of research is that it is important for other components of the writing process to be carried out as automatically as possible. Being able to write or type fluently and having well-developed language skills should reduce cognitive overload and facilitate more fluent retrieval of content from long-term memory. In addition, strategies for managing the writing process that help reduce cognitive load should also enable more fluent idea generation. The most thorough investigation of the effectiveness of different drafting strategies was carried out by Kellogg in a series of experiments (Kellogg, 1988, 1990; see Kellogg, 1994, for a review). Kellogg (1988) distinguished two different ways in which writers might reduce cognitive load during writing. An outline strategy, in which writers generate and organize their ideas prior to writing, before focusing their attention on translation and revision processes, should minimize the attention required for translating ideas during planning. A rough-drafting strategy, which involves translating text without worrying about how well-expressed it is, leaving monitoring of expression to revision of the draft after writing, should further reduce the burden on formulating content during text production. In combination, then, outlining followed by rough drafting should in theory provide for the most efficient distribution of resources during writing since it will separate both planning from translation and translation from revision. Kellogg (1988) tested this by manipulating two variables. Writers were instructed either to make a hierarchical outline before writing, or to start writing immediately. Then, when they produced the text itself, they were instructed either to write the text freely, without worrying about how well it was expressed, returning later to revise, or to attempt to produce a polished text on the first draft. The effect on the distribution of processes during writing (as indicated through directed retrospection) and the quality of the final text were measured. The results were very clear. First, the manipulations did indeed lead to a redistribution of processing during writing. In the outline conditions, writers showed much less evidence of planning during text production, presumably because this had largely been completed prior to writing. In the rough draft conditions, revision was reduced during the initial draft and postponed until later. Second, outlining was associated with higher quality final drafts but rough drafting showed no effect, despite the fact that revision had been postponed and should, therefore, have been able to draw on more attentional resources.

A later study by Kellogg (1990) suggested that the construction of a hierarchically organized outline prior to writing is associated with a higher quality final product than is the construction of an ordered list of ideas, and that this in turn is associated with higher quality final text than a simple clustering strategy. Furthermore, this is true despite the fact that more ideas tend to be generated using a clustering strategy than when an outline is constructed. Kellogg's (1994) general conclusion is that the effectiveness of the outlining strategy is a consequence of the fact that it enables writers to organize their ideas better prior to writing, as well as that it then enables them to devote more resources to formulating these ideas effectively in text. (But see Galbraith and Torrance, 2004, for

evidence that these studies may underestimate the effectiveness of certain forms of rough-drafting strategy.)

KNOWLEDGE TRANSFORMING

The research we have considered so far has concentrated on how retrieval of ideas can be improved by automating other components of the writing process – particularly the low-level skills involved in transcription and the language skills involved in formulating ideas in text – and by strategies for managing the writing process itself. Studies comparing the writing processes of experts and novices (see Hayes and Flower, 1986, for a review of research on adults, and Bereiter and Scardamalia, 1987 for a review focusing on the developmental literature) have, however, suggested that these are not the only ingredients involved. Experts not only manage the cognitive conflict involved more effectively but also appear to direct their writing towards different goals. While novice writers appear to define writing as primarily a matter of expressing what they know about a topic, expert writers define it as a matter of achieving communicative goals. In Flower's (1979) words, whereas novices produce 'writer-based' prose; experts produce 'reader-based' prose.

This difference in the goals towards which writing is directed represents a fundamental shift in focus and has wide-ranging consequences for the way that writing is carried out. Experts typically develop much more elaborate and interconnected sets of goals for their writing, building these networks gradually and modifying them in the course of writing. As a result, they spend longer planning, during, as well as before, writing: Bereiter and Scardamalia (1987) report that adult protocols typically contain ratios of thought to text of around 4:1, whereas children of 10 or so years old show ratios of thought to text more like 1:1. Flower and Hayes (1980) report that, whereas novices generate the majority (70%) of their ideas in response to the topic alone, experts generate the majority of their ideas (60%) in response to their rhetorical goals. Moreover, revision is no longer a matter of assessing how well the writer's ideas are expressed in language but becomes a matter of assessing how well the text satisfies the writer's goals. As a reflection of this, Hayes and Nash (1996) revised model of writing no longer treats the revision process as a simple matter of reading and editing text or as an independent component of the writing process. Instead, it is treated as a combination of the more basic processes of text interpretation, reflection, and text production, and involves generating and organizing ideas, both during and after writing, in order to satisfy rhetorical goals.

Bereiter and Scardamalia (1987) formalized these differences in their knowledge transforming model of writing (see Figure 3.3), stressing that this should not be seen simply as an evolution of the knowledge telling model but that it involved a radical change in the way that the writing task is defined by the writer and in the way that it is carried out. Thus, although it retains the knowledge telling model (and hence Hayes and Flower's model of idea generation) as a characterization of the process whereby content is retrieved from memory, this is embedded within a dialectic between content and rhetorical problem spaces. This is intended to capture two features of the writing process. First, it reflects the fact that ideas are represented, not just as a reflection of the writer's

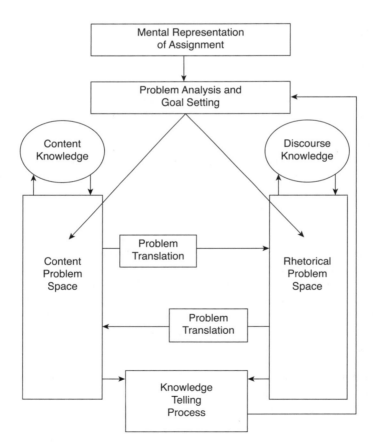

Figure 3.3   Bereiter and Scardamalia's (1987) knowledge-transforming model of writing.

knowledge (content space), but also in terms of their rhetorical function within the text (rhetorical space). Second, writing is not simply a matter of adapting content to the rhetorical context, but is an emergent process in which content is formulated as the text develops. Thus, not only is content retrieved in response to a more elaborated representation of the assignment as a rhetorical problem, but it is also formulated in the context of, and as a contribution to, the series of rhetorical acts gradually emerging in the text. The contrast between the knowledge telling model and the knowledge transforming model is a contrast between writers who ask themselves questions like, 'What do I know about this?', 'Does this sentence correspond to the idea I want to express?', 'What else do I know about this?', and writers who, having thought about the goals they want to achieve, say things like, 'If I want to achieve this, then the first step I need to take is …', 'I can do this by saying …' 'Having said that, what do I need to do next …'. Content is retrieved, as and when it is needed, in order to develop the text further towards the writer's goals. In consequence, writing well involves not just satisfying rhetorical goals, but in the course of doing so, developing one's understanding of the topic.

A training study conducted by Scardamalia et al. (1984) with a group of sixth grade students provides a good illustration of how this translates into practice. Training took place over 19 weeks and included procedural facilitation, modelling of writing by both teachers and pupils, and explicit instruction in various problem-solving strategies. The key theoretical ingredient was procedural facilitation. This involved providing students with prompt cards to be used during planning. These prompt cards were grouped according to their rhetorical function (e.g., elaborate, improve, goals, and organization) and consisted of cues like 'A better argument would be', 'An example of this would be', 'My main point is', 'But many readers won't agree that', and so on. These prompts were used extensively throughout the course of

instruction – in demonstrations by the teacher, in modelling by students for one another, and during practice writing exercises – and were designed to help the students set rhetorical goals and use these to guide the generation of content during writing. In posttests, Scardamalia et al. (1984) found that, in contrast to a control group, the training group increased the number of reflective thoughts included in think aloud protocols collected during planning, and produced what were judged to be more reflective essays. They noted, however, in a more detailed analysis, that students did less well on ratings concerned with 'developing a coherent and well-thought-out position' on a topic, and suggested that this could reflect a gap between attempt and execution.

One feature that distinguishes Bereiter and Scardamalia's approach is that they place less emphasis on strategies like outlining. This is partly because they see the knowledge transforming model as applying across the writing process as a whole, and partly because they want to emphasize that, what matters about planning is not so much *when* it takes place as *how* it is carried out. In a study investigating how writers of different ages (students from Grades four, six, and eight, as well as a group of adults) set about constructing the main point of their texts, Bereiter et al. (1988) found that, over and above the amount of time spent planning, the main difference between older and younger writers was in how the writers went about constructing their main points. As part of the study, the participants were asked to think aloud while planning and the resulting protocols were scored for evidence of six different kinds of constructive moves, which Bereiter et al. (1988) assumed to be characteristic of a knowledge transforming approach to writing. Although, they did find a strong relationship between the length of time spent planning and the quality of the main points identified in the plans, they also found that the better main points were associated with a greater number of constructive moves. Notably, this was not just a consequence of the difference in the ages of the groups: the same relationships were apparent within the different age groups. A subsequent path analysis showed that grade level influenced the number of constructive moves the writer made, which then influenced the level of the main point in the plan, which in turn influenced the level of the main point in the text. The crucial feature being that grade level did not have a direct influence on level of main point (as would be expected if the results were just a consequence of differences between the age groups in existing knowledge) but only influenced it via the number of constructive moves made during planning. (See also, a more recent study by Galbraith et al. (2005) showing that when the amount of time spent preplanning is held constant the quality of the finished text correlates strongly with the extent to which extra content is added to satisfy rhetorical goals during preplanning.)

In summary, the knowledge transforming model represents an important extension of Hayes and Flower's model of idea generation. Although it shares the same basic mechanism of generating ideas – the retrieval of content from long-term memory – it emphasizes the rhetorical nature of the goals towards which writing is directed, and claims that this involves a redefinition of writing, rather than simply an evolution of a knowledge telling approach. This means that, although Bereiter and Scardamalia might accept that using outlining to reduce cognitive load could facilitate planning, they would argue that it is not sufficient. Only once writing is redirected towards rhetorical goals does it become a means of developing the writer's understanding, rather than simply a means of making content generation more fluent.

Although this model of writing captures important features of the writing process, I want to argue in the remainder of this chapter that it is only a partial account and that it has two particularly problematic features. First, although one of its attractive features is its claim to account for the common experience of writing as a source of discovery, this is only an implication of the model, which was not

directly tested in the development of the model. Second, the knowledge-telling model, which is embedded within the knowledge-transforming model as its account of how content is generated to satisfy goals, does not on the face of it explain how novel content is formulated during writing.

DISCOVERY THROUGH WRITING

The research we have discussed so far has focused on the processes involved in writing rather than on the effects of these processes on the writer's thought. The claim that writing develops understanding is an implication of the model, rather than something that has been empirically tested. Subsequent research has investigated this more directly, and examined the conditions under which writers discover new ideas through writing (Galbraith, 1992, 1999; Galbraith et al., 2006).

These experiments used the same general procedure. Writers were asked to rate how much they felt they knew about a topic and then to list their ideas about the topic, both before and after writing. They were then asked to rate the similarity of the ideas contained in the two lists. In some experiments, they were also asked to rate the similarity of the ideas within lists, again, both before and after writing. This enabled Galbraith and his colleagues to identify whether the processes carried out during writing had led to a change in what the writer thought about the topic or in how organized their thoughts were, and whether any such changes were associated with subjective changes in knowledge.

This research has focussed on the conditions under which two different types of writer, selected using Snyder's self-monitoring scale (Snyder, 1986), generate new ideas during writing. High self-monitors are, in Snyder's words, 'particularly sensitive to the expression and self-presentation of relevant others in social situations and use these cues as guidelines for monitoring (i.e., regulating and controlling) their own verbal and non verbal self-presentation'. By contrast, low self-monitors' 'self-presentation and expressive behaviour … seems, in a functional sense, to be controlled from within by their affective states (they express it as they feel it) rather than moulded and tailored to fit the situation'. Galbraith selected these two types of writers, because they seemed to embody the contrast between knowledge-telling and knowledge-transforming approaches to writing: low self-monitors would be expected to prioritize the direct expression of their beliefs about the topic, whereas high self-monitors would be expected to generate content to satisfy their communicative goals. (A recent study by Klein et al., 2004, showing that high self-monitors vary the thoughts they list before a discussion with different audiences, whereas low self-monitors do not, supports this assumption.)

Galbraith (1992) asked low and high self-monitors either to write notes in preparation for an essay (planning) or to write an essay without preplanning (text production), and measured the extent which writers developed new ideas in these different conditions using the methods described in the preceding section. If, as Bereiter and Scardamalia suggest, discovery depends on the extent to which writers generate content in response to rhetorical goals, one would expect the high self-monitors to produce more new ideas after writing than the low self-monitors. If, furthermore, the process involves deliberate problem-solving and this is impaired when the capacity of working memory is overloaded, then one would expect a greater number of new ideas to be produced after planning in note-form than when writers had to produce full text at the same time as planning. This was, partly, what Galbraith found. The high self-monitors discovered more new ideas after writing notes than the low self-monitors did, and this was reduced when the high self-monitors had to write full text. This suggests that discovery depends on the extent to which content generation is directed towards the satisfaction of rhetorical goals and that it is reduced when the writer has to

deal with the extra cognitive load of producing well-formed text. However, if this were the case, one would also expect the low self-monitors to generate even less new ideas when writing full text. In fact, Galbraith found that the low self-monitors generated a high number of new ideas after writing full text, just as many in fact as the high self-monitors did when they made notes. In other words, discovery also appeared to occur when writing was assumed not to be directed towards rhetorical goals, and when cognitive load should be at its highest. Furthermore, in direct contrast to what the knowledge transforming model would predict, the new ideas produced by the high self-monitors after writing notes were not associated with subjective increases in writers' knowledge. By contrast, there was a clear positive correlation between the number of new ideas produced by the low self-monitors after writing full text and increased knowledge of the topic.

Overall, Galbraith (1992) concluded that, although there was evidence that adapting thought to rhetorical goals does affect the generation of content, this was not associated with the development of the writer's understanding. In addition, there was also evidence that dispositionally guided text production, far from being a matter of retrieving existing ideas from memory, involved actively creating novel content, and that this led to the development of the writer's understanding.

In a later study, using a similar method but focusing on different forms of text production, Galbraith (1999) found that the number of new ideas produced by low self-monitors was at its greatest when writing was not planned beforehand, and that outlining before writing reduced the difference between the low and high self-monitors, with low self-monitors experiencing a reduction in new ideas and high self-monitors an increase in new ideas compared to nonplanned writing.

More recently, Galbraith et al. (2006) again replicated the finding that low self-monitors discover more new ideas after nonplanned text production than high self-monitors, but also found evidence of a difference in the effect of outline-planned writing on low and high self-monitors' thought. Thus, although, as in previous experiments, the high self-monitors produced more new ideas when they were allowed to make an outline before writing, Galbraith et al. (2006) found that the high self-monitors' ideas were less coherently organized after writing. In other words, although high self-monitors did appear to produce more new ideas when they were asked to make an outline before writing than when they just wrote an unplanned draft, as one might expect if outlining helps them to develop a fuller representation of the rhetorical problem, this appeared to lead to less coherently organized thoughts about the topic. By contrast, low self-monitors produced more new ideas after writing a spontaneous draft, and in both planned and unplanned writing maintained the coherence of their thoughts before and after writing.

For present purposes, the key point about these results is that they appear to contradict important features of Bereiter and Scardamalia's knowledge transforming model. First, they consistently suggest that, although writers who are sensitive to rhetorical content, and readily adapt their thought to the communicative context, do generate new ideas during writing, these new ideas are not associated with the development of understanding, and in fact appear to reduce the coherence of the writer's thought. Second, they consistently suggest that writers whom one would expect to translate their existing ideas into text, and who typically do not adapt their thought to the demands of the communicative context (low self-monitors), also generate new ideas during writing, and that these new ideas are coherently organized and associated with the development of their understanding. In other words, precisely the wrong kinds of people, according to the knowledge-transforming model, appear to develop their understanding through writing.

KNOWLEDGE CONSTITUTING

By themselves, these empirical findings are suggestive, but not conclusive, evidence against the knowledge transforming model. Further research is needed directly examining the processes involved when low and high self-monitors develop their ideas before we can conclusively rule out a knowledge transforming account of the findings. The problem is that these empirical findings tie in with a more conceptual problem in the model. This stems from the assumption that generating ideas is a matter of retrieving pre-existing content from memory. While this can account for the fact that different content is retrieved when the rhetorical context drives memory search than when content is retrieved associatively, it does not explain how this can be new content that develops the writer's understanding. Bereiter and Scardamalia (1987: 349–351) acknowledge this problem when they discuss memory search procedures, pointing out that 'One of the most formidable challenges to theories of language use is to explain how it is that skillful speakers and writers are able to think so quickly of material fitting multiple constraints'. They consider the possibility that this could be a consequence of spreading activation within a network of fixed semantic units but conclude that it would be impossible for such a network to store explicitly all the different possibilities that might be required by different rhetorical contexts. Instead, they suggest a process of heuristic search, in which the rhetorical problem is progressively redefined until it 'provides cues that activate appropriate nodes in memory'. However, it is not clear how, given their assumption that memory nodes consist of fixed units, this resolves the issue. Surely, all that heuristic search – or more refined rhetorical planning – achieved in this context is retrieval of more specific content. In other words, although they recognize the problem, it is not clear that heuristic search provides a solution to it.

Both Hayes and Flower and Bereiter and Scardamalia appeal to information processing models current at the time they were writing. These have come to be characterized as symbolic models of representation and typically assumed that content was explicitly represented in long-term memory. At just about this time, alternative, connectionist theories of representation began to appear (McClelland, Rumelhart and the PDP group, 1986). In such models, content is not stored as fixed, explicit representations in a separate long-term memory, waiting to be retrieved for manipulation in short-term memory. Instead, it is *synthesized* as and when it is needed in a contextually appropriate form.

To give you an idea of the principles of the processing involved, consider the very simple, 'toy' network shown in Figure 3.4.

This network consists of simple units, very loosely analogous to neurons in the brain, with three basic properties: (i) each unit sums up the activation it receives via connections (shown as arrows in the diagram) from other units in the network; (ii) if the total activation it receives is higher than its threshold for activation, then (iii) the unit will fire and pass

activation on to all the other units it is connected to in the network. In themselves, the units or nodes in such networks do not represent anything at all, they simply sum up activation from incoming connections and transmit it through outgoing connections to units further up the network. In the network shown in Figure 3.5, these units are organized in three layers. For the sake of this example, you can think of the input layer as a perceptual layer, receiving input from the external environment (each unit might be a photoreceptor in the retina for example), the hidden layer as the network's conceptual representation of this input, and the output layer as the network's response to the perceptual input (e.g., the name of an object perceived in the environment).

The key feature of this network is that its knowledge is not represented by the hidden units within the network. This same set of units has different patterns of activation for different inputs and only develops these patterns of activation in the presence of a particular input. Rather it is the connections

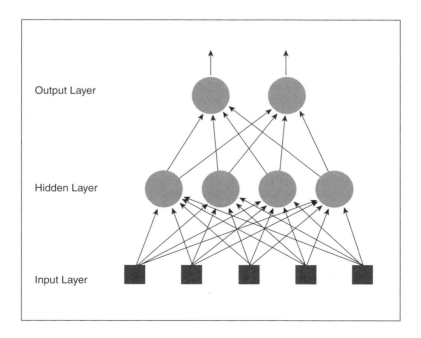

Figure 3.4   A simple feed-forward network.

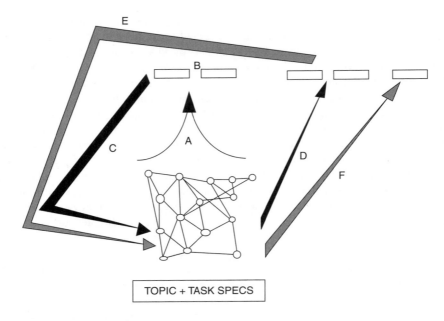

Figure 3.5   Writing as a knowledge-constituting process (Galbraith, 1999).

between the units, which are fixed and which guide processing, and which constitute the network's knowledge of the world. This knowledge is not directly accessible, but reveals itself, implicitly, in the response it causes the network to synthesize in a particular context. Thus, when the visual image of a cat for example appears on the input layer, the connections linking the input layer will pass activation on to the hidden layer, and cause a particular pattern of activation to appear across these hidden units, which will in turn pass activation on through the connections linking the hidden layer to the output layer, causing a particular pattern of activation at the output layer corresponding to the word 'cat'. Equally, if the input pattern were to be the visual image of a dog, for example, the *same* set of connections would result in a different pattern across the hidden layer, and the production of the response 'dog' at the output layer. In other words, the network's knowledge is represented by the strength of the connections between units, and these have their effects, implicitly, by guiding activation round the network, enabling it to

synthesize different responses to different inputs. In such networks then knowledge is synthesized anew in a contextually specific form each time it is used rather than being stored explicitly as a fixed piece of information in long-term memory.

Galbraith (1999) invoked these principles to provide an account of writing as a knowledge constituting process. The first important feature to note about this model is that it does not deny that content is represented sometimes as individual events which can be accessed via a process of retrieval. Writers do sometimes remember (or try to recall) what it is they want to say. Rather, it claims that such knowledge is stored in a separate – *episodic* – memory system, operating (perhaps) according to the principles assumed by Hayes and Flower and Bereiter and Scardamalia, whereas language production draws on a different – *semantic* – memory system, and operates according to connectionist principles. (See McClelland et al. (1995) for evidence of two such complementary memory systems, and Rogers and McClelland, 2004, for a connectionist model of semantic memory.) According to Galbraith, the knowledge constituting process is prompted specifically by the requirement to formulate thought in explicit propositions.

In the knowledge-constituting model, shown in Figure 3.5, the writer's semantic memory is represented by the network of units at the centre of the diagram, with the writer's knowledge, or disposition towards the topic as Galbraith (1999) calls it, represented by the fixed weights connecting the units. Given an input (TOPIC + TASK SPECS), the units within the network are activated according to the strength of the connections between the input pattern and the units in the network. The units then pass activation between themselves until they settle into stable state. This represents the 'best fit' the network can find between the various pieces of information in the network, and corresponds to the message the writer wishes to convey (labelled A in the diagram). In terms of the 'toy' example I have just described, the TOPIC + TASK SPECS are analogous to the input layer, the writer's semantic memory to the hidden layer and A to the output layer. This message is then formulated as an utterance (labelled B in the diagram). (Note that the transformation of A (the message) into B (the utterance) could be considered to be a further network, with an input layer at A passing activation through a hidden layer (not shown) to an output layer at B.)

By themselves, steps A and B could be seen as a replacement for the idea generation component of Bereiter and Scardamalia's knowledge-transforming model. The only difference being that, rather than simply involving the retrieval of existing content, this would involve synthesizing content, as if for the first time, in response to a contextually specific set of goals. A particular virtue being that this would provide a mechanism whereby novel content could be created in response to altered rhetorical goals. Furthermore, since knowledge is represented implicitly in such networks, the writer would, quite literally, be 'finding out what they think by seeing what they say'.

However, the second part of the model (as represented by the steps labelled C, D, E, and F in the diagram) makes further claims which mean that it cannot simply be added to the knowledge transforming model as a more up to date account of how content is synthesized in text. The first claim is that the initial proposition formulated by the network (at B in the diagram) is only a partial, 'best fitting', representation of the input. When the input initially occurs, it activates a wide range of units within semantic memory according to the strength of the links between the input and the nodes within the network. However, once these units have been activated, constraint satisfaction between the units will mean that some ultimately 'lose out' and hence are not incorporated in the message to be formulated in language. Furthermore, limitations in the expressive capabilities of the writer's linguistic resources mean that not all of the content will be formulated in language.

In order, then, to fully capture the writer's implicit knowledge, further cycles of text production are required. Galbraith (1999) suggests that this involves negative connections (labelled C in the diagram) from the output at B to the units in semantic memory. (Mannes and Kintsch, 1991, include a similar assumption in their model of planning by constraint satisfaction.) This has the effect of reducing the activation of units corresponding to the initial proposition, and enables previously suppressed units to influence the next output synthesized by the network. This following synthesis of content is labelled D in the diagram. The network continues with succeeding cycles of negative feedback (labelled E) and utterance synthesis (labelled F) until all the content activated by the input has been formulated.

There are alternative ways in which feedback from the initial proposition could take place. For example, feedback may involve adding the previous output utterance to the input to the network, rather than a direct influence on the network itself. For present purposes, however, the key point is that the writer's implicit disposition will only be fully realized in the text to the extent that it is allowed to continue to guide the production of successive propositions. This only occurs if the sequence of propositions is allowed to unfold without interruption by external, rhetorical constraints. The writer's response to the initial prompt is not represented by a single proposition but is instead spread, discursively, across the set of propositions. Thus, in this model, progressive refinement of thought is achieved in the text itself, and involves successive dispositional responses to emerging propositions rather than a progressive redefinition of rhetorical constraints.

This emphasis on the dispositionally driven nature of text production brings the hypothesis into direct conflict with the knowledge transforming model's claim that discovery depends on the adaptation of thought to external rhetorical goals. Taken together, the different aspects of the model explain why writers in Galbraith's experiments develop their understanding when they write full text (express thought in explicit propositions) rather than when they plan in note-form and why it is the low self-monitors (dispositionally guided writers) rather than the high self-monitors who do so. It also suggests why, in Scardamalia et al. (1984) training study, in which students were asked to consult cue cards after each succeeding sentence, the children did not produce particularly coherent text. The knowledge constituting model assumes that this was because external rhetorical goals interrupted the text production process before the writer's implicit disposition towards the topic had been fully constituted in the text.

CONCLUSION

The knowledge-constituting model suggests that, during text production, idea generation involves the synthesis rather than the retrieval of content. Nevertheless, it does not deny that retrieval of existing content or explicit planning to satisfy rhetorical goals are an important aspect of writing. Reflectively surveying memory plays a valuable role in identifying relevant content, and explicitly formulating rhetorical goals ensures that it is appropriate to the rhetorical context. However, in order for this potential content to be realized in the text, and in order for it to capture the writer's implicit understanding, it has to be dispositionally synthesized in the course of text production. This means that a dual process model is required to account for writing as a whole.

According to the dual process model, then, both rhetorical planning and dispositional text production are required for effective writing. Rhetorical planning is assumed to operate on an episodic memory of previously entertained propositions (ideas that the writer has read, heard, or formulated themselves in the past). Ideas are retrieved from this memory in the way described in Hayes and Flower's model and writers vary in the extent to which memory search is guided by their rhetorical goals. Because it involves explicit consideration of content and possible ways of organizing it, it is subject to working memory constraints, and operates best when thought is represented economically in note-form. Dispositional text production is assumed to operate through parallel constraint satisfaction within the writer's semantic memory, and is responsible for constituting content suggested by planning in a series of explicit propositions in the text. In general, the two processes interact with each other. Planning delivers potential content for realization in the text, and unpredicted formulations in the text lead to revision of the writer global plan. Writers vary in the extent to which they prioritize the two processes. Low self-monitors appear to prioritize dispositional goals, with the result that they are more likely to constitute their thought in text, but perhaps at the expense of producing less clearly structured text. High self-monitors appear to prioritize rhetorical goals, with the result that they are more likely to consider a wider range of rhetorically appropriate content, but at the expense of constituting their own understanding in the text.

The dual process model casts many of the phenomena I have reviewed here in a different light. First, it suggests that, over and above the cognitive overload engendered by having too many things to think of at once, another fundamental conflict in writing is between writers' dispositional and rhetorical goals. The writer's disposition, when conceived of as the fixed weights in a constraint satisfaction network, consists of the writer's distinctive point of view about the world. It is who they are. This means that writing arouses profoundly conflicting emotions: elation when one finds oneself discovering a new insight; fear when one feels oneself entering unexplored territory with unpredictable consequences; alienation when external constraints or our own preconceptions prevent us from constituting our thought; loneliness when what we say is misunderstood by others.

Second, the model implies a different view of the role of language in writing. The main focus in cognitive models of writing to date has been on the thinking behind the text and on the need to reduce the load on working memory to enable the writer to do it more effectively. Hence, the emphasis has been either on the need to plan separately from producing text, or on the need to automate language processes so that they do not consume the working memory resources required for thinking. If the knowledge-constituting process is as is suggested here, then language skills have a much more essential role. They are the vehicle through which thought is constituted externally, and hence enable the writer to gain access to their implicit disposition about a topic. Text production in general, rather than being something that gets in the way of thinking, is in fact where thinking takes place.

Let me conclude with a final comment on 'writing about you know'. I suggested initially that this was bad advice, partly because it could encourage a knowledge-telling model of writing, and partly because it assumes that

the writer already knows what they want to say. The knowledge-constituting model suggests that, insofar as they are taken to mean that one should let one's writing be dispositionally guided, there is also a sense in which this, and other romantic exhortations like 'be true to yourself', are good advice. According to the dual process model, however, the more analytic process of adapting thought to rhetorical goals is equally important, and the conflict between the two processes is a necessary one. The reason why there is a perennial conflict between romantic approaches to writing, which focus on personal expression, and more classical approaches which focus on rhetorical skill, is that they both capture an essential component of the writing process.

REFERENCES

Bereiter, C. and Scardamalia, M. (1987) *The Psychology of Written Composition*, Hillsdale, NJ: Lawrence Erlbaum Associates.

Bereiter, C., Burtis, P.J., and Scardamalia, M. (1988) 'Cognitive Operations in Constructing Main Points in Written Composition', *Journal of Memory and Language*, 27: 261–278.

Bourdin, B. and Fayol, M. (1994) 'Is Written Language Production more Difficult than Oral Language Production – A Working-Memory Approach', *International Journal of Psychology*, 29(5): 591–620.

Bourdin, B. and Fayol, M. (1996) 'Mode Effects in a Sentence Production Span Task', *Cahiers De Psychologie Cognitive-Current Psychology of Cognition*, 15(3): 245–264.

Bourdin, B. and Fayol, M. (2002) 'Even in Adults, Written Production Is Still more Costly than Oral Production', *International Journal of Psychology*, 37(4): 219–227.

Caccamise, D.J. (1987) 'Idea Generation in Writing', in A. Matsuhashi (ed), *Writing in Real Time: Modelling Production Processes*, New York, NY: Longman Inc. pp.224–253.

Flower, L. (1979) 'Writer-based Prose: A Cognitive Basis for Problems in Writing', *College English*, 41(1): 19–37.

Flower, L.S. and Hayes, J.R. (1980) 'The Cognition of Discovery: Defining a Rhetorical Problem', *College Composition and Communication*, 31: 21–32.

Galbraith, D. (1992) 'Conditions for Discovery through Writing', *Instructional Science*, 21: 45–72.

Galbraith, D. (1999) 'Writing as a Knowledge-Constituting Process', in M. Torrance and D. Galbraith (eds), *Knowing What to Write*, Amsterdam, NL: Amsterdam University Press. pp.139–160.

Galbraith, D. and Torrance, M. (2004) 'Revision in the Context of Different Drafting Strategies', in L. Chanquoy, L. Allal, and P. Largy (eds), *Revision in Writing*, Dordrecht, NL: Kluwer Academic Publishers. pp.63–86.

Galbraith, D., Ford, S., Walker, G., and Ford, J. (2005) 'The Contribution of Different Components of Working Memory to Planning in Writing', *L1 – Educational Studies in Language and Literature*, 15: 113–145.

Galbraith, D., Torrance, M., and Hallam, J. (2006) 'Effects of Writing on Conceptual Coherence', *Proceedings of the 28th Annual Conference of the Cognitive Science Society*. pp.1340–1345.

Glynn, S. M., Britton, B., Muth, D., and Dogan, N. (1982) 'Writing and Revising Persuasive Documents: Cognitive Demands', *Journal of Educational Psychology*, 74: 557–567.

Hayes, J.R. and Flower, L.S. (1980) 'Identifying the Organization of Writing Processes', in L.W. Gregg and E.R. Steinberg (eds), *Cognitive Processes in Writing*, Hillsdale, NJ: Lawrence Erlbaum Associates. pp.3–30.

Hayes, J.R. and Flower, L.S. (1986) 'Writing Research and the Writer', *American Psychologist*, 41(10): 1106–1113.

Hayes, J.R. and Nash, J.G. (1996) 'On the Nature of Planning in Writing', in C.M. Levy and S. Ransdell (eds), *The Science of Writing: Theories, Methods,* *Individual Differences and Applications*, Mahwah, NJ: Lawrence Erlbaum Associates. pp.29–56.

Kellogg, R.T. (1988) 'Attentional Overload and Writing Performance: Effects of Rough Draft and Outline Strategies', *Journal of Experimental Psychology: Learning, Memory and Cognition*, 14: 355–365.

Kellogg, R.T. (1990) 'Effectiveness of Prewriting Strategies as a Function of Task Demands', *American Journal of Psychology*, 103: 327–342.

Kellogg, R.T. (1994) *The Psychology of Writing*, New York: Oxford University Press.

Klein, O., Snyder, M., and Livingston, R.W. (2004) 'Prejudice on the Stage: Self-Monitoring and the Expression of Group Attitudes', *British Journal of Social Psychology*, 43: 299–314.

Mannes, S.M. and Kintsch, W. (1991) 'Routine Computing Tasks: Planning as Understanding', *Cognitive Science*, 15(3): 305–342.

McClelland, J.L., McNaughton, B.L., and O'Reilly, R.C. (1995) 'Why there are Complementary Learning Systems in the Hippocampus and Neocortex: Insights from the Successes and Failures of Connectionist Models of Learning and Memory', *Psychological Review*, 102: 419–457.

McClelland, J.L., Rumelhart, D.E., and the PDP research group (1986) *Parallel Distributed Processing: Volumes 1 and 2*, Cambridge, MA: MIT Press.

Rogers, T. and McClelland, J. (2004) *Semantic Cognition*, Cambridge, MA: MIT Press.

Scardamalia, M., Bereiter, C., and Steinbach, R. (1984) 'Teachability of Reflective Processes in Written Composition', *Cognitive Science*, 8: 173–190.

Snyder, M. (1986) *Public Appearances, Private Realities: The Psychology of Self-Monitoring*, New York: W. H. Freeman and Company.

From Idea to Text

John R. Hayes

When we write, we are aware that we propose ideas for inclusion in the text, that we formulate language in our heads to capture some of these ideas, and then try to write that language down before it fades from memory. We also know that we sometimes change what we have written or are about to write. We have some idea, then, about the processes that are involved when we move from idea to text. Identifying these processes and how they work together is important for understanding the nature of writing and for providing a solid basis for teaching writing. In what follows, I will address these questions:

- What is the path from idea to text?
- How are sentences put together?
- What resources support writing?
- What factors limit fluency?
- What constrains text production?
- Are writing processes sequential or parallel?

WHAT IS THE PATH FROM IDEA TO TEXT?

The model shown in Figure 4.1 was proposed by Chenoweth and Hayes (2001) to describe the path from idea to text for adult writers.

According to this model, the *proposer* sends an idea package, either in verbal or nonverbal form, to the *translator*. For extended texts, the *proposer* would also provide planning and goal-setting functions. The *translator* then creates a new language string based on the idea package. The language string is then vetted by the *evaluator/reviser* and, if accepted, is passed to the *transcriber* to be turned into text. The *reviser* can call for change at any point in the process from idea generation to transcribed text. The *reviser* makes changes by calling recursively on the other writing processes.

HOW ARE SENTENCES PUT TOGETHER?

In Kaufer, Hayes, and Flower (1986, Study 1), six skilled writers and six less skilled writers provided think-aloud protocols as they wrote essays on the topic 'My job' for a teenage audience. Analysis of these data revealed a number of interesting features of composition writing. First, the writers did not typically produce whole sentences. Rather they constructed sentences from proposed

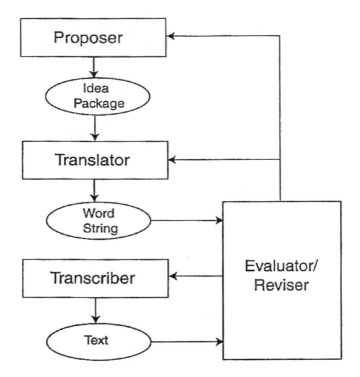

Figure 4.1   Model of the text production process from Chenoweth and Hayes (2003, p. 113).

sentence parts in a complex activity involving idea generation, evaluation, planning, and reading the text produced so far. Figure 4.2 shows a representative protocol segment of a writer constructing one of the sentences in her essay. Dashes indicate pauses of two seconds or more. Items 1, 4, 6, 7, 9, 12, and 17 are proposed sentence parts. Items 10, 13, and 15 reflect evaluations. Items 2, 3, 5, and 8 seem to reflect goal setting and in items 11 and 14, the writer reads a part of the sentence that has already been transcribed.

Sentence parts are rapidly produced bursts of language intended for inclusion in the text that are usually terminated by a pause. We have called these *pause-bursts* or *P-bursts*. Items 1, 4, 5, 6, and 7 are examples of P-bursts. In some cases, the language burst is terminated by an evaluation and at other times by a revision. For example, item 9 is terminated not by pause but by the evaluation represented by item 10. We have called such

bursts *revision-bursts* or *R-bursts*. The reason for making the distinction is this. With P-bursts, the production process appears to run out of steam. For example, when the writer represented in Figure 4.2 says 'The best thing about it is that …' she has said all language that she has planned for the text at this point. She does not know where the sentence is going and needs to plan more language before she can proceed. The length of the P-burst (in this example, seven words) seems to reflect a kind of limit to the capacity of the production process at that moment. In research described later in this chapter, the length of the P-burst has been used to identify capacity limitations in the writing processes.

The observation that texts are typically composed of short language bursts has been confirmed in several studies (Chenoweth and Hayes, 2001, 2003; Hayes, 2007; Hayes and Chenoweth, 2007;). It appears that text

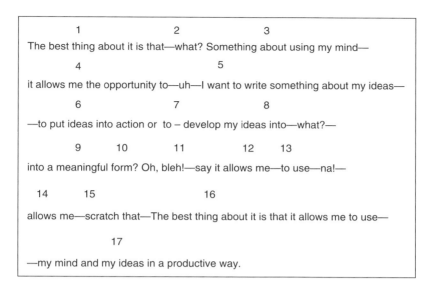

Figure 4.2   Protocol of a writer composing one sentence of an essay.

composition typically occurs by constructing sentences from language bursts.

WHAT RESOURCES SUPPORT WRITING?

The physical task environment

In their study of essay writing, Kaufer and his colleagues found that 66% of sentence composing episodes involved rereading earlier parts of the sentence being composed (1986, Study 1). Rereading may facilitate translation by refreshing the writer's memory for features of the already composed parts of the sentence such as number, tense, or content. However, only 8% of episodes involved rereading sentences that the writers had completed earlier. It may be that in composing longer essays, writers make more extensive use of previously composed sentences.

Chenoweth and Hayes (2003) studied writers typing one-sentence descriptions of multipanel cartoons. In some conditions, the writers' texts were visible to them and in

other conditions, they were not. Surprisingly, participants took less time to finish the task when their texts were not visible to them. The reduced writing time was attributable to a reduction in the number of revisions. In the invisible condition, writers made only 45% as many revisions as in the visible condition. Thus, visibility of the text in the task environment was an important trigger for the revision process. However, it is not the only trigger. In the invisible condition, writers were still able to make revisions to their text, presumably based on memory for what they had typed.

Some writers produce written outlines (plans) for their essays before they began to produce formal sentences (Kaufer et al., 1986, Study 1). These outlines, consisting of short written notes, are texts in their own right as they involved proposing, translating, transcribing, and in some cases revising. The outlines then became part of the writer's task environment for writing the essay. In some cases, the outlines were extremely sketchy, consisting of little more than a general topic, but in other cases, they were quite detailed. The outlines consisted of two sorts of notes: ordered lists of topics and directions (or goals) to the writer, for example, 'Keep it simple'. Kaufer et al. (1986) concluded that the order of topics in the outline is often closely related to the list of topics in the final essay but that the two are typically not identical. Changes are often made while transforming the outline into formal text.

Thus, it is evident that the physical task environment, and particularly, the text-written-so-far, provides important support for the writer.

Long-term memory

There is no doubt that long-term memory is essential for writing. After all, it contains the writer's knowledge of vocabulary, grammar, audience, topic knowledge, and even the writer's biography. If there were no long-term memory, there would be no writing. However, this does not mean that the relation between long-term memory and writing is simple. The following examples illustrate some of the complexities.

Kellogg (1987) explored the impact of topic knowledge on writing. In his study, participants wrote persuasive essays on a topic related to the United Nations. The participants were divided into high- and low-knowledge groups on the basis of their U. N. related knowledge. While they were writing, they were required to respond as rapidly as possible to a prompt presented at unpredictable times. Response times to the prompt were used as an index of the effort that the writing task demanded of the writers. The essays were then evaluated for overall quality.

The easy prediction would be that writers with high topic knowledge would write the better essays. What Kellogg (1987) found was that the overall quality of the essays was about the same for the high- and low-knowledge groups. However, the effort involved in writing the essays was significantly higher for the low-knowledge group.

In Study 1 by Kaufer et al. (1986), more experienced writers wrote significantly longer essays than less experienced writers. However, the more experienced writers also constructed their sentences from significantly longer sentence parts (P-bursts) than less experienced writers. This result was unexpected. Knowledge stored in long-term memory appears to influence both fluency and burst length. The association between fluency (measured here by essay length) and burst length has been confirmed in a number of subsequent studies (Chenoweth and Hayes, 2001, 2003; Hayes, 2007; Hayes and Chenoweth, 2007).

Kaufer et al. (1986, Study 3), tested the hypothesis that there was a grammatical structure to the language bursts. They examined protocols from an experienced writer and from a less experienced writer. Each wrote essays on six topics. From these protocols, the researchers selected all of the language bursts that ended with a pause (P-bursts). Then they counted how many of these bursts terminated at the end of a clause or a phrase. Of the 205 bursts examined, 36% ended at clause boundaries; 26% ended at phrase boundaries that were not also clause boundaries, and 39% ended at places that were neither clause nor phrase boundaries. Thus, as expected, knowledge of grammatical structure, stored in long-term memory, appear to be an important factor in determining where a P-burst ends but it was not the only factor.

To explore the relation between linguistic experience and written fluency, Chenoweth and Hayes (2001) recruited American college students who had studied French or German for either three or five semesters and collected think-aloud protocols from them as they composed essays in their first language (L1) and their second language (L2). They found that greater linguistic experience was associated with increased writing rate. Students wrote faster in their L1 than in their L2 and students with five semesters of experience wrote faster in L2 than students with three semesters of experience. However, the authors also found that the relations between linguistic experience and P-burst length exactly mirrored those for writing rate.

Chenoweth and Hayes (2001) also found a relation between linguistic experience and revision. They observed that the percentage of bursts that were R-bursts (bursts terminated by a revision) decreased as linguistic experience increased. For example, 26% of bursts were R-bursts when writers composed in L2, but only 13% when they composed in L1. In addition, they found that the percentage of proposed bursts that were included in the final texts increased as linguistic experience increased. For example, 78% of proposed bursts were accepted when writers composed in L2 in contrast to 87% accepted when they composed in L1. These results suggest that the revision process terminates more bursts in progress (in an R-burst, the translation process is terminated by revision) and rejects more bursts that have been produced for writers with less linguistic experience than for writers with more linguistic experience. Chenoweth and Hayes (2001) interpret this result as follows:

1. The process of translating ideas into language requires more cognitive resources for writers with less linguistic experience than for writers with more linguistic experience.
2. During *translation*, resource limitations hamper writers with less linguistic experience in applying their grammars (and other principles of felicity of expression) to the language string being generated.
3. This resource limitation results in more errors in the generated string.
4. If some of these errors are detected during *translation*, the percentage of R-bursts will increase.
5. If some of the errors are not detected until after translation is complete, when demands on cognitive resources are reduced and grammatical rules can be more fully applied, more proposed parts will be rejected and acceptance rates will decline.

These researchers hypothesized that all four of the effects they observed: increased writing rate, increased burst length, decreased percent of R-bursts, and increased acceptance rates could be attributed to the facilitating effects of increased linguistic experience on the *translation* process.

Presumably, linguistic experience allows the writer to acquire many kinds of knowledge for storage in long-term memory. This includes not only knowledge of grammar but also of vocabulary, audience, genre, and so on. Knowledge stored in long-term memory is clearly critical for skilled writers.

Working memory

There are several productive ways to explore the role of working memory in writing. I will mention three. One is to study individual differences in working memory and to relate those differences to writing performance. Another is to note how writing processes interfere with secondary task performance and to infer from this how heavily a working memory resource is being used by the writing process. The third is to interfere with some aspect of working memory and to note the effects on writing.

Individual differences

Since working memory involves both the storage and processing of information, a task to measure an individual's working memory should involve both storage and processing. Daneman and Carpenter (1980) were the first to propose such a task. In their task, participants read a sequence of sentences aloud and recalled the last word of each sentence. Thus, participants were required both to store information and simultaneously to process it. The participants' working memory was measured by the numbers of words they could remember. This measure is called a *reading span* because the processing activity participants engage in is reading. Ransdell and Levy (1999) provided a brief review of the tasks whose performance is predicted by reading span.

Ransdell and Levy (1999) have designed a task similar to reading span that they call *writing span*. In this task, participants are presented lists of words and must compose a sentence incorporating each word. As in the reading span task, the participants' writing span was measured by how many of the presented words they could remember. These authors found that their writing span measure significantly predicted measures of writing quality, writing fluency, and reading comprehension. The authors proposed that individuals with high span perform better in reading and writing tasks, because they can use their memory resources more flexibly than individuals with low spans.

Impact of writing on secondary tasks

Kellogg (2001) has made very effective use of this paradigm to assess the cognitive demands of various writing processes. In this study, participants wrote two essays; one handwritten and the other typed. They were randomly assigned to write either narrative, persuasive or descriptive texts. While writing, the participants were required to respond as rapidly as possible to a tone presented at unpredictable times and to report whether they were *planning*, *translating*, *reviewing*, or doing some unrelated activity. Reaction time results indicated that the three processes interfered about equally with the secondary task. Reaction times were shorter for narrative than for persuasive and descriptive texts and they were shorter for handwritten than for typed texts. Kellogg (2001) suggested that familiarity was responsible for the advantage of the narrative genre and the handwriting mode over the alternatives.

Kellogg (1996) has proposed that visual working memory plays a role in *planning* and *editing*. A study by Kellogg, Olive, and Piolat (2007) provides some evidence to support this position. In a dual task study, these authors asked participants to write definitions of abstract (hard to image) and concrete (easy to image) words. Participants were also asked to engage in one of two secondary tasks, each of which required the participant to respond rapidly to a change in a sequence of stimuli. One of the secondary tasks required verbal working memory and the other required visual working memory. These authors found that writing descriptions of concrete nouns increased response times to both of the secondary tasks. In contrast, writing definitions of abstract terms increases response times only to the verbal secondary task. This suggests that visual working memory was involved in writing processes when participants were writing about materials that were easy to visualize. Thus, visual working memory might well be involved in tasks that require writers to compose from visual sources such as writing instructions for assembling devices.

Interfering with working memory

I will discuss studies that use one of two procedures for interfering with verbal working memory: exposure to unattended speech and articulatory suppression. In the unattended speech procedure, the participant is exposed to irrelevant speech while writing but directed to ignore it. In the articulatory suppression procedure, the participant is asked to rapidly repeat a syllable such as *la la la* or *the the the* while writing. This method has been shown to reduce working memory capacity (Longini, Richardson, and Aiello, 1993). Salame and Baddeley (1982) found that articulatory suppression was substantially more effective than unattended speech in interfering with verbal working memory.

Unattended speech

In a series of studies, Levy and Marek (1999) used unattended speech to test Kellogg's model (1996). In Experiment 1, the participants transcribed a passage from one computer window to another. The authors found no effect of unattended speech on either the speed or accuracy in performing this task. In Experiment 2, participants edited a three-paragraph article with planted errors. The authors found no effect of unattended speech on the number of errors detected. In Experiment 3, participants were asked to construct sentences including all five of a list of five presented words. Here, the authors found that unattended speech reduced sentence quality and the percent of presented words that were included in the sentences but did not influence the time required to formulate sentences. The authors noted that the results of all three experiments were consistent with Kellogg's (1996) model which held that verbal working memory was involved in *translation* but not in *transcription* or *revision*.

Articulatory suppression

Chenoweth and Hayes (2003) studied the effect of articulatory suppression on fluency and burst length. Participants were shown a sequence of wordless cartoons on a computer screen and asked to type a single sentence summarizing the cartoon. During articulatory suppression trials, participants repeated the syllable *tap* 120 times a minute in time to a metronome. During control trials, participants tapped a foot in time to the metronome.

Chenoweth and Hayes (2003) obtained these results:

- Articulatory suppression had no significant effect on start time (the time between the appearance of the cartoon and the first keystroke) nor on the number of words written. This result was replicated in Hayes and Chenoweth (2007) and Hayes (2007). The result is of interest, because if articulatory suppression influenced the *proposing* process, we would expect to see that effect most clearly in an increase in start time.
- Articulatory suppression had no significant effect on the number of words written. This result has not been consistently observed. Kellogg (2004) has found that a memory load of six digits reduced the number of words written in a sentence production task and Hayes (2007) found that articulatory suppression reduced number of words written in the cartoon-description task.

- Articulatory suppression increased writing time (the time from first to last keystroke) and decreased writing rate (words in final text divided by writing time) each by about 20%. Increases in writing time and decreases in writing rate due to articulatory suppression were also found by Hayes and Chenoweth (2006), Hayes and Chenoweth (2007), and Hayes (2007). We can conclude that articulatory suppression does substantially reduce written fluency.
- Articulatory suppression had no effect on the number of R-bursts.
- Most dramatically, articulatory suppression caused a 34% decline in P-burst length from 12.5 words to 8.2 words. Similar reductions in burst length due to articulatory suppression were found by Hayes and Chenoweth (2007) and Hayes (2007). Clearly, articulatory suppression has a very strong effect on P-burst length.

The effect of linguistic experience and articulatory suppression on fluency (writing rate) and on P-burst length made it seem likely that the locus of both effects was in the *translation* process. The *proposing* process was viewed as a poor candidate for two reasons:

1. It seemed unlikely that linguistic experience in L2 would influence the (prelinguistic) *proposing* process.
2. The absence of an effect of articulatory suppression on start time also suggested that the *proposing* process was not affected by articulatory suppression.

The *revision* process also seemed an unlikely locus for two reasons:

1. Articulatory suppression did not influence the number of R-bursts.
2. By definition, P-bursts did not involve overt revision. Thus, the revision process is not active during P-bursts. (It is possible, of course, that a language burst might be terminated by a revision that was considered but not carried out.)

Finally, it was widely believed that typing is a highly automated skill in adults and as such requires minimal verbal working memory resources (see Levy and Marek, 1999; Kellogg, 1999, for example). Given these considerations, the most likely locus for the effect of articulatory suppression on both fluency and burst length appeared to be the *translation* process.

WHAT CONSTRAINS TEXT PRODUCTION?

Pinning down the source of language bursts

In an effort to rule out the *transcription* process as a possible source of bursts, Hayes and Chenoweth (2006) asked skilled typists to transcribe a text from one computer window to another. The researchers found that language bursts were essentially absent during the *transcription* task. Average burst length, if it could be called that, was more than 80 words (reported in Hayes and Chenoweth, 2007). The authors concluded that the *transcription* process could be ruled out as a significant source of bursts.

All of the earlier studies of language bursts in writing involved both proposing ideas and translating those ideas into newly composed language strings. To provide further evidence that the *translation* process *by itself* could be the source of language bursts, Hayes and Chenoweth (2007) studied an editing task that involved the creation of new language (translation) but not the proposing of new meaning. Participants were asked to translate doubly passive sentences into active voice. For example, sentences such as *John was robbed by the man who was hit by the Fed-Ex truck* were to be rewritten as *The Fed-Ex truck hit the man who robbed John.*

If proposing new meaning was the only source of language bursts, one would expect that this task could be completed virtually without pause, as was the case in the transcription task. However, if the *translation* process produces bursts whenever it creates new language, then we would expect that the edited sentences would be constructed out of sentence parts (bursts) with pauses in between as were the sentences in earlier studies.

The results of the study were quite clear. Participants are typically required between two and three bursts to complete the task. The *translation* process, then, is definitely a source of language bursts.

WHAT CONSTRAINS FLUENCY

The findings presented up to this point were consistent with the position that the *translation* process was the bottleneck responsible for language bursts and for the slowing of writing rate when verbal memory resources were limited. However, a surprising result of the Hayes and Chenoweth study (2006) of a transcription task cast doubt on that position.

The researchers found that writing rate in the transcription task was significantly slowed under articulatory suppression. This result was not consistent with Levy and Marek's (1999) conclusion that verbal working memory was not involved in *transcription*. Further, the result raised the possibility that the slowing of writing rates under articulatory suppression observed in other studies (Chenoweth and Hayes, 2003; Hayes and Chenoweth, 2007) resulted from articulatory suppression slowing the act of typing rather than slowing the *translation* process.

If the act of typing is slowed because articulatory suppression interferes directly with the *transcription* process, then we would expect that articulatory suppression would slow typing rate in a sentence generation task as well. However, since the transcription task used by Hayes and Chenoweth (2006) involved both reading and transcription, Kellogg's 1999 model would predict that the effect of articulatory suppression would be on the reading part of the task and not the transcription part. That is, the typing rate would slow down, because it was limited by the rate at which the participant can read the source text, not because the *transcription* process itself was slowed by articulatory suppression. Reading of the text-written-so-far did occur in Chenoweth and Hayes' (2003) cartoon-description task. However, in this study, the participants were not reading the text that they were currently typing. This makes it seem unlikely that an effect of articulatory suppression on reading would have an effect on typing rate in the cartoon-description task.

There are two questions, then, that we would like to answer:

1. To what extent can the reduction in writing rate due to articulatory suppression observed in Hayes and Chenoweth's (2006) transcription task account for the reduction in writing rate observed in Chenoweth and Hayes's cartoon-description task?
2. How does articulatory suppression slow writing rate in sentence production tasks?

There appears to be three possibilities:

A. It interferes only with translation
B. It interferes only with typing
C. It interferes with both translation and typing

Study design

To address these questions, this study (Hayes, 2007) directly compared the cartoon-description task (Chenoweth and Hayes, 2003) with the transcription task (Hayes and Chenoweth, 2006) by partially replicating both with the same participants. This allowed within-subjects comparisons of the measures in each study. I will describe this study (Hayes, 2007) in greater detail than other

studies in this chapter, because it is not yet available in print.

The study involved 21 undergraduates with an average typing rate in the transcription task of more than 40 words per minute. The study had three phases. In phase 1 and phase 3, participants transcribed texts from one computer window to another. In phase 2, participants wrote single sentences to describe the gist of a sequence of multipanel cartoons. In each phase, participants performed under two conditions: in the articulatory suppression condition, participants said the word 'tap' aloud in time to a metronome that clicked 120 times a minute while transcribing the texts. In the control condition, they tapped a foot in time to the metronome while transcribing. For both tasks, participants were given practice before the experimental trials.

The materials for Phases 1 and 3 were four of the six texts used by Hayes and Chenoweth (2006). The materials for phase 2 were 16 of the 24 multipanel cartoons used by Chenoweth and Hayes (2003).

RESULTS

Replication of earlier studies

As Table 4.1 shows, the study successfully replicated the major results (i.e., results with a p-value less than 0.01) obtained in Chenoweth and Hayes (2003) and in Hayes and Chenoweth (2006). Further, the present

Table 4.1 Replication of results of Chenoweth and Hayes (2003) and Hayes and Chenoweth (2006)

Cartoon-description Task	Chenoweth and Hayes (2003)		Current Study	
	AS/Control	Significance	AS/Control	Significance
Writing Time	1.18	p=.005	1.22	p=.009
Writing Rate	0.81	p<.001	.74	p<.001
P-burst word length	0.63	p<.001	.61	p<.001
Transcription Task	Hayes and Chenoweth (2006)		Current Study	
	AS/Control	Significance	AS/Control	Significance
Writing Rate	0.87	p<.006	0.82	p<.001

study found, as did Chenoweth and Hayes (2003), that articulatory suppression had no significant effect on start time, revision time, number of R-bursts, and the number of deletes per hundred characters.

There were two failures to replicate earlier findings. First, Hayes and Chenoweth (2006) found that there were more uncorrected errors in the articulatory suppression condition than in the control condition (p = 0.038). In the present study, no such difference was found. Second, Hayes and Chenoweth (2003) found that articulatory suppression had no significant effect on the number of words written. In the present study, articulatory suppression significantly reduced both the number of words and the number of characters written by about 10%.

The effects of articulatory suppression on writing rate

Articulatory suppression reduced writing rate in both tasks. In the cartoon-description task,

articulatory suppression decreased writing rate by reducing the length of the sentences written and by increasing writing time. Figure 4.2 shows these effects. Increased writing time accounts for about two-thirds of the reduction in writing rate and reduced sentence length, about one-third. A parallel analysis for the transcription task would not be appropriate since the experimenter limited the length of the sessions to approximately three minutes.

Where does the time go when people transcribe or compose?

While performing the two tasks, participants engaged in at least four objectively observable activities. They paused before starting to type; they typed; they edited and/or revised what they had typed; and they paused in the midst of typing. A key-trapping program captured the time that participants devoted to each of these activities. Table 4.3 shows these data for the control conditions of the two tasks.

Table 4.2 Effects of articulatory suppression in the cartoon-description and transcription tasks

Cartoon-description task	Control	Articulatory suppression	Significance
Characters	98.20	89.13	p =.025
Write Time	26.21	31.91	p =.009
Write Rate	4.00 cps	2.95 cps	p <.001
Transcription task			
Write Rate	5.29 cps	4.33 cps	P<.001

Table 4.3 Time spent by writers in various activities in the transcription and cartoon-description tasks

	Transcription (control)		Cartoon-description (control)	
	Time (seconds)	Time (percent)	Time (seconds)	Time (percent)
Start	1.17	0.72	4.60	14.93
Edit	19.21	11.87	5.17	16.78
Pause	1.65	1.02	2.61	8.47
Type	139.78	86.39	18.43	59.82
Total	161.81	100.00	30.81	100.00

In the transcription task, as one would expect, participants spent most of their time typing – about 85%. They spent about 12% of their time editing but very little getting started or pausing in the midst of typing. In contrast, in the cartoon-description task, participants spent more time on editing and much more on starting and pausing. The most surprising observation was that participants spent nearly 60% of their composing time typing.

If participants were writing an essay rather than a single sentence as they were in the cartoon-description task, we would expect substantial increases in the activity of the *proposing* and *translating* processes with a corresponding increase in start and pause time.

What changes when articulatory suppression slows writing in the cartoon-description task?

Table 4.4 shows the three components of writing time for the cartoon-description task in both the control and the articulatory suppression condition.

Articulatory suppression caused a significant increase in typing time and pausing time but had almost no effect on editing time. Extra pause time accounted for about 45% of the increase and extra typing time, for about 55%. Thus, articulatory suppression slowed writing rate in the cartoon-description task by increasing both pause time and typing time. In this task, it is difficult to attribute the increase in typing time to anything but a slowing of the *transcription* process. As noted in the foregoing section, it is difficult to attribute reduced writing rate to

reduced reading speed. Further, the increase in pause time cannot be attributed to the *transcription* process. Remember, pauses were essentially absent in the transcription task. Thus, there appear to be at least two bottlenecks that increase writing time when verbal working memory is limited. One seems fairly certain to be located in the *transcription* process and outside of it. It is plausible that the second bottleneck is located in the *translation* process.

Writing rate decreased under articulatory suppression both because writing time increased and because sentence length decreased. It is difficult to attribute the decrease in sentence length to any particular process with confidence. However, participants always wrote a complete sentence when performing this task. It is possible, then, that when the *translation* process is forced to operate with reduced resources, it may omit optional elaborations of the core ideas being expressed.

Cross task comparisons

In both tasks, typing rate in the articulatory suppression condition was slower than in the control condition, replicating results of earlier studies. Although articulatory suppression might plausibly have influenced typing rate in the transcription task by slowing reading, it is less plausible that it could have done so in the cartoon-description task. Rather, it seems more plausible to believe that articulatory suppression reduced typing rate in both tasks by interfering directly with the *transcription* process. This conclusion is not consistent with Kellogg's claim that the

Table 4.4 How articulatory suppression influences typing, editing, and pausing time

	Control	AS	Difference	Significance
Typing time	18.43	21.63	3.20	p <.004
Editing time	5.17	4.97	−0.20	NS
Pausing time	2.91	5.31	2.70	p <.001

Table 4.5 Typing rates by task and experimental condition

	Transcription task	Cartoon-description task
Control	6.04 cps	5.43 cps
AS	5.02 cps	4.16 cps

transcription process makes little use of verbal working memory.

Typing in the transcription task was significantly faster than in the cartoon-description task in both experimental conditions. These two tasks differ in that the cartoon-description task involves the *proposing* and *translating* processes, but the transcription task does not. This suggests that the *proposing* and *translating* processes slowed the typing process in the cartoon-description task.

Are writing processes sequential or parallel?

Writers engage in a variety of processes including proposing ideas, translating ideas into language, and revising and transcribing them. Clearly, these processes can interact with each other. We have just discussed evidence that typing in a sentence-composing task may be slowed by other writing processes. One way this could happen is that the processes are being carried out in parallel and each process, by its operation, reduces the resources available for the other processes. Another possibility, proposed by Chenoweth and Hayes, is that the processes do not overlap in time (2003:113–115). In this view, for example, writers translate an idea into words and then stop translating to transcribe those words into text. Only when translation is complete does the writer return to generating ideas. Two processes interact because the prior process leaves an output in a buffer that constitutes a memory load for a later process. For example, the *translation* process may leave a string of words in a buffer for the *reviser* to evaluate and the

transcriber to turn into text. Maintaining that buffer reduces the working memory capacity available for other processes.

If this model were correct, we would expect the memory load to decrease as the string is transcribed and, as a result, the typing rate would increase. Chanquoy, Foulin, and Fayol (1990) carried out a study that provides some evidence that such a model is plausible. Participants in the study composed sentences with three clauses. The authors found that writing rate increased from first clause to last clause. The authors suggested that all of the clauses were composed and stored in memory before transcription began. Typing rate increased as the number of clauses that had to be held in memory decreased.

However, Alamargot, Dansac, Chesnet, and Fayol (2007) have provided dramatic evidence that parallel processing does occur during transcription. These authors studied adult writers carrying out a writing-from-sources task. They used the Eye and Pen system (Alamargot, Chesnet, Dansac, and Ros, 2006) that allowed them to simultaneously record the participants' handwritings on a graphic tablet and their eye-movements with a head mounted camera. Results indicated that participants were definitely looking away from the text that they were handwriting at least 10% of the time.

Clearly such data force a reevaluation of the Chenoweth and Hayes (2003) position that writing processes operate sequentially. One might abandon that position entirely. However, I believe a more conservative position would be to believe that transcription, because it is generally a very demanding task, usually but not always requires the writer's full attention.

SUMMARY

Relatively noncontroversial claims with strong empirical support

- When writers compose text, they construct sentences from relatively short sentence parts – strings of rapidly produced words terminated by a pause – that are intended for inclusion in the text. We have called these P-bursts.
- Writers become more fluent and produce longer sentence parts (P-bursts) as their linguistic experience increases.
- Writers become less fluent and produce shorter sentence parts as their verbal working memory resources are reduced.
- Grammatical structure is an important factor determining where language bursts end.
- Writers use the text-produced-so-far to facilitate both text production and text revision.
- Writers with more linguistic experience compose sentence parts that have fewer errors and are more likely to be included in the final text than writers with less linguistic experience. Put differently, writers with more linguistic experience are more efficient writers.

Relatively more controversial claims with some empirical support

- The *translation* process is a primary source of language bursts.
- The *transcription* process makes use of substantial resources both of time and of verbal working memory.
- Both the *translation* and the *transcription* processes contribute to the slowing of writing rate when verbal working memory is limited.

Areas of uncertainty

Using response time to a secondary task as a measure of resource use, Kellogg (2001) found that *proposing*, *translating*, and *reviewing* are about equally demanding or cognitive resources. Hayes (2007) using an articulatory suppression method, found that *translating* and *transcribing* used substantially more verbal memory resources than did *proposing* and *revising*. These results can be consistent if we posit that *proposing* and *reviewing* use more of other cognitive resources than *translating* does and that all of these resources add up to the same total for the three writing processes. However, the methods used in these two studies are different enough that it is hard to have confidence in such a neat additive scheme. It would be helpful to know if a change in task that selectively increased the use of verbal working memory in the translator as measured by articulatory suppression methods also increased resource use during translation as measured by response time in a secondary task.

Chenoweth and Hayes have proposed that the various writing processes operate without temporal overlap (2003:113–115). At present, there is no data bearing on the temporal overlap of the *proposing*, *translating*, and *revising* processes with each other. The data that is available (Alamargot et al., 2007) indicates that the *transcription* process can overlap with other writing processes by as much as or more than 10% of the time. Data such as Alamargot and his colleagues have collected can help us understand to what extent writing processes are parallel and to what extent they are sequential.

CONCLUSIONS

Modern versions of Hayes' model such as that described in Chenoweth and Hayes (2001) are generally consistent with the available data. However, they are still quite incomplete. Here are two major gaps that need to be filled.

Firstly, it is fairly well-established that writers construct texts from language bursts and the length of the bursts is positively related to fluency. However, we do not yet have a clear model of how language bursts are formed from proposed ideas. Ideally, such a model would account for how language is selected to match ideas, how the length of bursts is related to the complexity of the ideas being expressed, why bursts tend to end on clause and phrase boundaries, why burst length increases with the writer's linguistic experience and with the availability of verbal working memory, and how the current burst is coordinated with the text-written-so-far.

Secondly, Bereiter and Scardamalia (1987) and Berninger and Swanson (1994) have made critically important contributions to the modelling of writing development, but this work needs to be carried further. A comprehensive model of writing development should include the development of executive functions promoting the ability to stay focused and to switch perspective, the development of memory skills, the mastery of transcription skills, the increase in vocabulary and spelling knowledge, the development of audience awareness and of rhetorical skills, the sharpening of metacognitive skills, and the amassing of world knowledge. Such a model could be of considerable value to curriculum designers.

In the last quarter of a century, our field has made a good deal of progress. However, we still have a long way to go.

REFERENCES

Alamargot, D., Chesnet, D., Dansac, C., and Ros, C. (2006) 'Eye and Pen: A New Device for Studying Reading During Writing', *Behavior Research Methods*, 38(2): 278–299.

Alamargot, D., Dansac, C., Chesnet, D., and Fayol, M. (2007) 'Parallel Processing before and after Pauses: A Combined Analysis of Graphomotor and Eye Movements during Procedural Text Production', in M. Torrance, L. ven Waes, and D. Galbraith (eds), *Writing and Cognition: Research and Applications (Vol. 20)*, Amsterdam: Elsevier. pp.13–29.

Bereiter, C. and Scardamalia, M. (1987) *The Psychology of Written Composition*, Hillsdale, NJ: Lawrence Erlbaum.

Berninger, V.W. and Swanson, H.L. (1994) 'Modifying Hayes and Flower's Model of Skilled Writing to Explain Beginning and Developing Writing', in E.C. Butterfield (ed.), *Children's Writing: Toward a*

Process Theory of the Development of Skilled Writing (Vol. 2), Greenwich, Connecticut: JAI Press. pp.57–82.

Chanquoy, L., Foulin, J., and Fayol, M. (1990) 'Temporal Management of Short Text Writing by Children and Adults', *Cahiers de Psychologie Cognitive/ European Bulletin of Cognitive Psychology*, 10(5): 513–540.

Chenoweth, N.A. and Hayes, J.R. (2001) 'Fluency in Writing: Generating Text in L1 and L2', *Written Communication*, 18(1): 80–98.

Chenoweth, N.A. and Hayes, J.R. (2003) 'The Inner Voice in Writing', *Written Communication*, 20(1): 99–118.

Daneman, M. and Carpenter, P.A. (1980) 'Individual Differences in Working Memory and Reading', *Journal of Verbal Learning and Verbal Behavior*, 19: 1–18.

Hayes, J.R. (2007, September 7). 'Temporal Patterns in Text Production', Talk presented at Université de Poitiers.

Hayes, J.R. and Chenoweth, N.A. (2006) 'Is Working Memory Involved in the Transcribing and Editing of Texts?' *Written Communication*, 23(2): 135–149.

Hayes, J.R. and Chenoweth, N.A. (2007) 'Working Memory in an Editing Task', *Written Communication*, 24(4): 283–294.

Kaufer, D.S., Hayes, J.R., and Flower, L.S. (1986) 'Composing Written Sentences', *Research in the Teaching of English*, 20(2): 121–140.

Kellogg, R.T. (1987) 'Effects of Topic Knowledge on the Allocation of Processing Time and Cognitive Effort to Writing Processes', *Memory and Cognition*, 15: 256–266.

Kellogg, R.T. (1996) 'A Model of Working Memory in Writing', in C.M. Levy and S. Ransdell (eds), *The Science of Writing: Theories, Methods, Individual Differences, and Applications*, Mahwah, NJ: Lawrence Erlbaum Associates. pp.57–72.

Kellogg, R.T. (1999) 'Components of Working Memory in Text Production', in M. Torrance and G. Jeffery (eds), *The Cognitive Demands of Writing: Processing Capacity and Working Memory Effects in Text Production (Vol. 3)*, Amsterdam, Amsterdam University Press. pp.25–42.

Kellogg, R.T. (2001) 'Competition for Working Memory among Writing Processes', *American Journal of Psychology*, 114(2): 175–191.

Kellogg, R.T. (2004) 'Working Memory Components in Written Sentence Generation', *American Journal of Psychology*, 117: 341–361.

Kellogg, R.T., Olive, T., and Piolat, A. (2007) 'Verbal and Visual Working Memory in Written Sentence

Production', in M. Torrance, L. van Waes and D. Galbraith (eds), *Writing and Cognition: Research and Applications (Vol. 20)*, Amsterdam: Elsevier. pp.97–108.

Levy, C.M. and Marek, P. (1999) 'Testing Components of Kellogg's Multicomponent Model of Working Memory in Writing', in M. Torrance and G. Jeffery (eds), *The Cognitive Demands of Writing: Processing Capacity and Working Memory Effects in Text Production (Vol. 3)*, Amsterdam: Amsterdam University Press. pp.25–41.

Longini, A.M., Richardson, A.T.E., and Aiello, A. (1993) 'Articulatory Rehearsal and Phonological Storage in Working Memory', *Memory and Cognition*, 21: 11–22.

Ransdell, S. and Levy, C.M. (1999) 'Writing, Reading, and Speaking Memory Spans and the Importance of Resource Flexibility', in M. Torrance and G.C. Gaynor (eds), *The Cognitive Demands of Writing: Processing Capacity and Working Memory Effects in Text Production (Vol. 3)*, Amsterdam: Amsterdam University Press. pp.99–113.

Salame, P. and Baddeley, A.D. (1982) 'Disruption of Memory by Unattended Speech: Implications for the Structure of Working Memory', *Journal of Verbal Learning and Verbal Behavior*, 21: 150–164.

Revision Processes

Lucile Chanquoy

INTRODUCTION

'Writing is rewriting' say teachers to their pupils from time to time. To paint a fuller picture, rewriting is also reading, understanding, and writing combined.

Indeed, several complex revising operations are involved, at the same time, including rereading, detection, perception, diagnosis, and correction processes. For instance, detecting an error requires a rereading of the text and perceiving an inadequacy between the written text and the author's initial representation temporarily stored in memory; diagnosing this error requires one to determine its nature; correcting the error leads to a modification to the written text, if the reviser possesses the necessary means for implementing this change (e.g., Butterfield et al., 1996). To elaborate on these operations more specifically, in this chapter, first, the revision processes are described in terms of general writing models and then through models specifically assigned to revision (see also the review of Becker, 2006). The second part of this chapter is dedicated to an overview of experimental inquiries into the revision processes aimed at helping novice and/or beginner writers to revise their texts.

WHAT IS REVISION?

A definition

The most complete definition of revision remains that provided by Fitzgerald (1987: 484) twenty years ago. She wrote:

> Revision means making any changes at any point in the writing process. It involves identifying discrepancies between intended and instantiated text, deciding what could or should be changed in the text and how to make desired changes, and operating, that is, making the desired changes. Changes may or may not affect meaning of the text, and they may be major or minor.

In this definition, revision is a cognitively complex and costly process and means both the implementation of a correction and the different procedures used to revise. Revision can thus be defined as an examination of the text already produced, which involves rereading, eventually followed by corrections or modifications, which engages editing (Temple et al., 1993). These two activities aim at improving the text quality (Torrance et al., 2007; Van den Bergh and Rijlaarsdam, 2001) and can occur at any point in time during writing (Faigley et al., 1985). This definition mainly implies external revision where visible changes are made to the text. However, it is important to consider mental revision, conceived as a process of evaluating and clarifying the writer's thoughts (McCutchen et al., 1997).

For instance, Hayes and Flower (1983) have distinguished reviewing from revising: reviewing means evaluating both the intended and the written text, and it is a mental activity; conversely revising is editing, and thus external. The same distinction is proposed by Scardamalia and Bereiter (1983) who distinguished revising and reprocessing. Of course, this second type of revision, due to its internal aspect, seems more difficult to empirically analyze, except while using verbal protocols.

The revising process in the models of writing

Hayes and Flower's model

In 1980, Hayes and Flower proposed a model which is the most well-known writing model to date. In their model, the process of revising, which they labelled reviewing, is conceived as being recurrent throughout the text production. This process is divided into two subprocesses: reading and editing, which constitutes checking and correcting the text already produced. The reading subprocess allows the writer to find errors and to evaluate the appropriateness between the text and the writer's goals; the editing subprocess is conceived as a system of production rules, used to solve problems. Theses subprocesses are recurrent, and can interrupt the other writing processes or occur after that the entire text has been written.

Later, Flower and Hayes (1981) elaborated further on the revising process, arguing that revision can be considered both as an internal (evaluation) and external phenomenon (effective corrections). More precisely, Hayes and Flower (1983) distinguished between reviewing and revising activities. Reviewing is necessary to evaluate what is written or what has been planned, and it leans more towards being a mental process. Conversely, revising leads to physical modifications, which can be spotted in the text's surface (external revisions). A deeper exploration of Hayes and Flower's proposal will be taken up in a later section.

The revising process in recent writing models

In 1996, two new models of writing were published in Levy and Ransdell's (1996) book, 'The science of writing'. The first model was formulated by Kellogg (1996). Kellogg's objective was to integrate within one model the writing processes and the different components of working memory, as conceived earlier by Baddeley and Hitch (1974). Summarizing this model, the working memory architecture is composed of a central executive for complex processing (i.e., reasoning, reflecting, etc.) and two slave registers, the visuospatial sketchpad and the phonological loop, storing visuospatial and phonological representations, respectively. Following Brown et al.'s (1988) model, Kellogg (1996) conceived of writing as comprising three systems – formulation, execution, and monitoring – wherein monitoring corresponds to revision. This in turn comprises two basic processes. It implies reading the text for the purpose of possibly initiating a correction in the text. The first process (reading) allows the writer to regularly reread/verify both the text representation and the already written text. The editing process enables the detection and the diagnosis of text problems, resulting in the creation of a new version of text, once the problems have been solved. The most important thing to note here is not the definitions proposed by Kellogg for the different writing processes, but the proposal he made about the cognitive cost of these processes on working memory. Concerning revision (or monitoring), Kellogg postulates that reading solicits both the phonological loop and the central executive while editing only involves the central executive. Even when this subprocess taps into no more than one component, it is costly, because there exist several forms of editing, which make heavy demands on working memory.

Before presenting specific models of revision, the next section outlines the revision processes depicted in some models which aim at describing or explaining the development of writing.

Revision in developmental models

In order to explain how a writer becomes an expert, Bereiter and Scardamalia (1987) and Scardamalia and Bereiter (1987) have proposed two writing strategies. The first, labelled the Knowledge Telling Strategy, is used by novices who produce a text by formulating ideas as they are retrieved from their memory, without any conceptual or linguistic reorganization. It is made of three main components: (1) the mental representation of the assignment, (2) the knowledge about content and discourse, stored in long-term memory, and (3) the knowledge-telling process, in order to produce the text. Seven processing stages are implied in this process, and it seems that none of them are dedicated to revision. This strategy has been summarized by McCutchen (1988) as a *'think it, write it'* procedure, allowing young writers to produce a text without using a processing mechanism that is too costly on their cognitive capacities. The second strategy, used by more expert writers, is the Knowledge Transforming Strategy. Very sophisticated types of processing are involved in this strategy. For example, a writer can readjust her/his text according to linguistic, conceptual, rhetorical, etc. aspects. In order to 'transform text rather than simply to tell', an important part of the writing process is engaged for planning and revising, even if the authors do not describe the strategy using these terms.

In their reformulation of Hayes and Flower's (1980) model in order to explain the development of the writing process, Berninger and Swanson (1994) have modelled three successive steps showing how young writers progressively integrate writing processes and subprocesses. They show that the three writing processes as defined by Hayes and Flower (1980) – planning, translating, and reviewing – can interact with each other as they reach a more mature stage in expert writers, while in beginner writers the processes are developing with specific speeds. Indeed, those processes are not operational at the beginning of learning how to write, but appear in a precise order during the course of this learning. Through many experiments, Berninger and her colleagues made it apparent that translating appears before planning and reviewing processes (e.g., Berninger et al., 1992, 1994). Planning would first concern very local (sentence by sentence) portions of a text before concerning larger text portions. Concerning revision, the reviewing process would first appear at an isolated word level, then at a sentence level, at a paragraph level, and finally at a text level–from a local to a global perspective. Writers initially perform revision after a text has been written, before being able to process revisions while writing. In addition, revision is only an external process, which means that it only concerns the physical text and not an eventual mental representation. These three processes would be constrained by writers' working memory capacity and metacognitive knowledge about revision (see Alamargot and Chanquoy, 2001, 2004; Chanquoy and Alamargot, 2003).

To summarize ...

According to writing models, revision can be conceived both as an internal process, which compares a mental representation of the intended text with the text already written, and as an external operation of reading and of editing the produced text. On the one hand, Bartlett (1982) summarizes revision by three subprocesses: detection, identification, and modification of the erroneous text segment. On the other hand, revision is equally a process of return to mental thoughts, before writing them (McCutchen et al., 1997). Revision can be considered as a complex activity of internal and external evaluation of both text representation and production, and if some dissonances are detected and if the writer possesses the means for this, evaluation is followed by internal and/or external corrections. In this view, revision is a process aiming at improving both the future text and the already written text. This very complex process weighs heavily on writers' limited working memory capacities (Beal, 1996; McCutchen, 1996). This is more precisely described in the next section.

Specific models of revision

Scardamalia and Bereiter (1983, 1986)

From an educational perspective, Scardamalia and Bereiter (1983, 1986) conceive of revision through a technique of procedural facilitation and describe a system explaining how the revising process works as a self-regulated procedure, composed of three recursive and cyclic operations respectively labelled Compare, Diagnose, and Operate (or the CDO procedure). They consciously intervene during specific cycles of revision, and allow the writer to revise the text sentence per sentence during writing pauses.

According to the authors, as two types of mental representation are built and stored in long-term memory during text production – a representation concerning the actual text and a representation of the intended text – the CDO procedure would execute when these two representations conflict: (1) the *Compare* operation compares the actual text and the intended text, in order to perceive an inadequacy between them; (2) the *Diagnose* operation identifies the nature of the problem and finds a correction; (3) the *Operate* operation realizes the correction *via* two components (choosing a tactic and generating a change in the text). The modification of a text segment leads to a new textual representation, and leads subsequently to a new CDO cycle. However, the implementation of a revision cycle does not predictably lead to a revision.

This first model is relatively simple as it only implicates an intended text and a 'real' text. A difference between these two texts leads the writer to implement a CDO sequence in order to reduce the distance between internal and external texts. The next model is much more complex.

Flower et al. (1986) and Hayes et al. (1987)

Flower et al. (1986) and Hayes et al. (1987) have elaborated a complex model describing revising processes (or strategies) and the necessary knowledge involved during revision. This model is still currently referred to as a central framework among revising models. The authors define revision as an intentional and strategic activity, which is consciously implemented by the writer. The model is composed of four controlled – and thus cognitively costly – operations: (1) the task definition, (2) the text evaluation, (3) the selection of a strategy, and (4) its execution.

The *task definition*, which is fundamental, strategic, and conscious, is elaborated through the writer's textual and contextual knowledge and through metacognitive knowledge about revision, depending on her/his objectives. The task definition leads to a mental representation of the task and is essential, because it orients all the revising process.

The *evaluation* requires the writer to read, comprehend, and criticize her/his own text in order to identify potential problems. It comprises two subprocesses: problem detection and diagnosis. The problem detection requires comparing the writer's initial intentions (i.e., the intended text) and the text produced so far. As alluded to earlier in this chapter, Hayes et al. (1987) distinguish between three evaluation levels: (1) comparison between intention and text; (2) comparison between text plan and writer's goals; (3) text evaluation (spelling, grammar...). The problem identification (or diagnosis) follows the detection and leads the writer to choose a strategy.

According to the problem representation, a *strategy* is selected, because the detection is not systematically followed by a modification in the text. The writer can decide either to ignore the problem, if it is judged to be too simple or too complex, or s/he can decide to rewrite the problematic segment. If the latter path is chosen, four revision strategies are available: (1) to postpone the problem solving; (2) to look for more information to better understand the problem; (3) to rewrite the text or a text segment with the goal of preserving the basic idea; (4) to revise the text with the goal of preserving and enhancing the expression of the already produced text. Depending on the chosen strategy, the *execution* leads the writer to realize the required modifications.

Each of these four steps is necessarily and strategically subordinate to the preceding step, even though the writer does not inevitably carry out each of them. The last three steps of the model correspond globally to the CDO procedure (Scardamalia and Bereiter, 1983, 1986).

In conclusion, in Flower et al.'s (1986) and Hayes et al.'s (1987) models, the knowledge stored in the writer's memory plays a fundamental role during the different stages of revision. Revision necessitates a constant interaction between several types of knowledge (referential, linguistic, pragmatic, etc.), and the different revising processes, subprocesses, and strategies. As Alamargot and Chanquoy (2001) emphasized, text revisions are the concrete or visible results of a set of very complex mental activities that involve many decision-making stages, ending in (possible) written corrections. Revision could thus be defined as a decisional activity that is controlled at a metacognitive level.

Hayes' (1996) new model and the importance of reading during revision

In 1996, Hayes not only proposed a new version of the original Hayes and Flower's (1980) model and his own (1996) model of writing, but also focused on the importance of reading and comprehension during revision. Starting at Hayes et al.'s (1987) model, Hayes has specified the function of the evaluation process by considering it as a process of reading comprehension, which allows the writer to detect and diagnose text problems. This process enables the writer to build a representation of the text meaning, through different kinds of knowledge. The writer's reading function is thus quite different from the reader's reading function in the way that the writer does not simply read to understand, but with an idea in mind for detecting a problem in the text. Thus, revision cannot be simply considered as a writing process but is 'a composite of text interpretation, reflection, and text production' (Hayes, 1996:15).

This model has three components: (1) the control structure, which Hayes considered as fundamental and defined as a 'task schema' (i.e., a set of knowledge for revision) and which involves a goal, several revising activities, attentional goals, revising criteria, and strategies; (2) three processes concerning the different activities involved in revising (reflection, critical reading, and text production), and (3) the resources in long-term memory and working memory.

Globally, this model emphasizes the importance of reading and writing during revision. Three kinds of reading are involved: reading to evaluate, reading source texts, and reading to define tasks (see Hayes, 2004). Thus, reading and writing, as complex but necessary activities in revision, both imply heavy costs on the cognitive resources. In two experiments, Roussey and Piolat (in press) have analyzed the cognitive effort associated with critical reading and comprehension reading processes and the associated revising performance. They showed that critical reading was more effortful than comprehension reading and that critical reading was more effortful for syntax errors than for spelling errors.

In the previous models, the knowledge stored in long-term memory is fundamental to the execution of the revision subprocesses. Revision indeed necessitates a constant interaction between linguistic knowledge and contextual knowledge, and between processes defining the task, evaluating the text, detecting errors, and selecting appropriate strategies. It is also important to consider available resources in working memory, and indeed revision can be defined as a demanding process for the working memory system. The fundamental role of working memory has been described in a new model of revision, presented in the next section.

Butterfield, et al.'s (1996) procedural model

Due to its procedural characteristics, the smoothness of its definitions, and the fact that it is the first autonomous cognitive architecture of revision, Flower et al.'s (1986) and Hayes et al.'s (1987) model has allowed researchers to investigate revision in greater conceptual detail. This conception has inspired Butterfield et al. (1996) who have certainly elaborated the most complete model of revision, considering all the formalized components. Their model has the advantage of showing the importance of both long-term and working memory processes during revision and the significance of metacognitive knowledge. It has two interactive components: the environment and the cognitive-metacognitive system.

The environment comprises the rhetorical problem and the actual text being revised. The rhetorical problem space allows the reviser to specify the theme, the addressee, and the importance of the text segment to be revised. The actual text is defined through its format, genre, and lexical and syntactic units. It is not the most important part of the model for the authors, because they postulate that revision mainly concerns a mental representation of the text. Indeed, even whether external and internal modifications are realized, Butterfield et al. consider that revisions are always mental processes, since they are systematically elaborated at a mental level before being visible – or not – on the paper (or on the screen).

The cognitive-metacognitive system is divided between long-term memory and working memory. Revising processes implemented within working memory correspond to the processes described in Flower et al.'s (1986) and Hayes et al.'s (1987) models. These processes allow for (1) representation of rhetorical problems and evaluation of the text, (2) reading to represent and comprehend the text, (3) detection and diagnosis of a text's problems, (4) selection, modification, or creation of strategies to solve these problems, and finally (5) translation of revisions from the (mentally) represented text to the actual text.

Comparatively, long-term memory is used to free resources in working memory. For instance, an already-revised text segment could transfer from working memory to long-term memory. This memory has two levels, cognition and metacognition, which interact *via* the monitor and the control (see also: Butterfield et al. 1995). The cognitive component of long-term memory stores different kinds of knowledge (i.e., about the topic or writing standards), three strategies (thinking, reading, and writing), and a representation of the main characteristics of the text that is being revised. Automated strategies are implemented in long-term memory, without any load on working memory, while controlled strategies are performed in working memory and necessitate cognitive resources. In addition, the different kinds of knowledge stored in long-term memory are constantly interacting with the different processes of defining the task, evaluating the text, detecting errors, and selecting strategies to solve these errors.

In long-term memory, metacognition is built of knowledge models, which are the same as those in cognition, and understanding of strategies, whose strategies are equally the same as in cognition. In addition, the same distribution would exist at the metacognitive level and at the cognitive level, between knowledge on the theme, on the language, and on the written activity. Metacognitive strategies and metacognitive knowledge respectively enable the reviser to know when, where, how, and why it is necessary to use, evaluate, and control cognitive strategies and cognitive knowledge. This kind of control and evaluation is believed to be automatically released in long-term memory. Of course, there are constant interactions between all the components of the environment and of the cognitive-metacognitive system.

One of the advantages of Butterfield et al.'s (1996) model is that it took into account the task environment and, within the cognitive-metacognitive system, that it specified the role of long-term and working memory during revision. This model is thus the most complete one available on revision. Furthermore, by distinguishing cognition and metacognition, the authors have emphasized and formalized what Flower et al. (1986) noticed about the difference between activated knowledge and available knowledge, pointing out that activated knowledge is the more important one. A failure during the revising process can thus be explained both by a lack of knowledge and by an impossibility to activate the necessary knowledge.

This model emphasizes the metacognitive components, which allow strategic analyses during revision. As with Hayes (1996), Butterfield et al. (1996) limit the border between comprehension and production. They open interesting perspectives by integrating revision knowledge and operations within a general cognitive system, composed of memory registers. This type of architecture goes farther than the simple definition or description of revision processes to inquire into their modes of operation within a limited capacity system. This last aspect has been more particularly studied by researchers during recent years.

Conclusion

The different models of revision – models, which are either specifically conceptualized or 'embedded' in more general writing architectures – have evolved in order, firstly, to describe as precisely as possible the different processes involved during revision, secondly, to consider the great difficulty of this activity, necessitating a writer's and a reviser's careful reading of the text in order to detect some errors or problems, and thirdly, to introduce

long-term memory, working memory, and a metacognitive system in order to dynamically explore the revision process. Globally, revision is unanimously considered as a very complex process, weighing heavily on writers' attention and limited capacities in working memory.

The classification of revision activities

Beyond the descriptions of revising processes and subprocesses, it is important to be able to classify the effective (external) revisions made in a text. With this objective in mind, some authors have tried to categorize revisions according to a certain number of criteria. For instance, Sommers (1980) has defined four operations involved in revising a text: deletion, substitution, shifting, and reorganization. These four operations can be realized in four linguistic levels: word, phrase, sentence, or idea. To extend this statement, Monahan (1984) has added four dimensions to classify revisions: (1) the revision moment (for example, on the draft or on the final copy); (2) the revision text level (to revise a word, a phrase, a clause, a sentence, a paragraph, or the whole text); (3) the nature of the revision (addition, deletion, rearrangement, and embedding); (4) the revision objective (to revise for a better text presentation, for checking spelling, for improving the style, in order to emphasize transitions, etc.).

In order to consolidate the proposals of these two authors, two large categories of revising activities have been described by Chanquoy (1997a; see equally: Chanquoy and Veaute, 1994; Chanquoy, Piolat, and Roussey, 1996):

(1) 'Surface' revisions are modifications concerning the text surface, such as: adding, shifting, substituting, or deleting (to use words from Sommers, 1980 and Monahan, 1984) a punctuation mark; rewriting a word or a text segment for a better readability; checking spelling errors (both lexical and grammatical).

(2) 'Deep' or 'semantic' revisions modify the text meaning and comprise additions, deletions, shifting, substitutions, rearrangements or reorganization and transformations of words, phrases, clauses, sentences, or longer text segments.

Two other indicators are added to these categories:

(a) The 'off-line' location of revision—for example, at the beginning, middle, or end of the text.
(b) The 'on-line' location of revision during the writing activity—for example, during the elaboration of a plan, during draft writing, during text final version writing, during a specific revising stage, etc.

Moreover, for both categories, corrections can be considered as correct, erroneous, or neutral (i.e., a neutral correction does not improve or decrease the text quality).

Arguably, the most complete classification is Faigley and Witte's (1981, 1984) taxonomy, which takes into account both syntactic and semantic aspects of revision (see Table 5.1). The authors have distinguished six types of operations and six linguistic levels and have taken into account the revised text level, wherein revisions can be surface changes or semantic revisions, changing the meaning of the text. Surface revisions can be formal (e.g., spelling, punctuation, etc.) or made in order to preserve the text meaning (additions, deletions, etc.). Semantic revisions may concern microstructural changes or macrostructural changes.

Of course, the foregoing classifications only concern revisions achieved in the produced text. It is currently impossible to make such a categorization for mental revisions.

Recently, in order to help researchers to classify revisions, some computer-assisted processing methods have been elaborated, not only to measure the number of revisions and to locate them in the text, but also to compute the number of added or deleted letters, with comparison to the total number of typed letters, when the writer is using a word processor (e.g., Severinson Eklundh and Kolberg, 2003; Piolat, 2007).

Having considered a range of cognitive models of revision processes and taxonomies of revision activity, the remainder of this chapter is more specifically dedicated to the presentation of some studies made in a 'psycho-educational' perspective, in order both to better understand revision and to elaborate educational means in order to help writers during the revising stage of writing.

WHAT KIND OF REVISION HELP IS AVAILABLE FOR NOVICE AND/OR BEGINNER WRITERS?

The influence of topic, theme, genre, addressee, and author on revision

The writer's knowledge of the theme associated with his/her knowledge about linguistic rules and on the activity of revision in

Table 5.1 Faigley's and Witte's taxonomy of revision – with respect to Faigley and Witte (1981: 403, Fig. 1)

Surface revisions		Semantic revisions	
Formal changes (conventional editing revisions)	Preserving meaning changes (paraphrases)	Microstructural changes (minor revisions)	Macrostructural changes (major revisions)
Spelling	Addition	Addition	Addition
Tense	Deletion	Deletion	Deletion
Number and modality	Substitution	Substitution	Substitution
Abbreviation	Permutation	Permutation	Permutation
Punctuation	Distribution	Distribution	Distribution
Format	Consolidation	Consolidation	Consolidation

general, allows for more error detection and correction. For instance, Butterfield et al. (1994) have shown that an appropriate knowledge about the theme leads to more revisions that require less cognitive effort. However, these revisions mainly concern the text surface (e.g., spelling, punctuation, etc.) and thus semantic revisions remain rare (see also: Hacker et al., 1994). Conversely, according to Butterfield et al. (1994), or McArthur et al. (1991), the text genre has no significant impact on the nature and the frequency of revisions. Concerning the addressee, Traxler and Gernsbacher (1992, 1993) made it apparent that a feedback from the addressee has a positive effect on the revision of descriptive texts.

Beal (1996) asserts that the revision process also includes the ability to evaluate the text's communicative quality. This means that the writer has to reread and evaluate the text as it will be perceived by the reader, to anticipate possible sources of ambiguity and to add information so as to clarify the text. This remains a very difficult activity, even with more expert writers.

Finally, it seems that the most prominent factor involved in increasing the number of revisions in the amelioration of a text is the authorship. Indeed, in both novice and expert writers, revisions are more frequent in others' texts than in the writer's own texts (see Bartlett, 1982; Daneman and Stainton, 1993; Cameron et al., 1997).

The role of cognitive and metacognitive knowledge

When writers do not revise, is it due to a lack of knowledge about the revising process? To reply to this question, Plumb et al. (1994) have proposed a hypothesis with two nonexclusive facets: Writers either do not revise because they lack appropriate knowledge about revision, and/or because they do not use their stored knowledge about revision.

According to Butterfield et al.'s (1996) model, the first part of the hypothesis refers to a deficit at the cognitive level (knowledge

deficit) and the second part of the hypothesis refers to a deficit at the metacognitive level (processing deficit). This last deficit would be linked to a poor task comprehension or to the difficulty to implement a particular strategy. For the authors, this second kind of deficit is much more complex to explain, because several variables are involved: writers may fail to revise as a result of a lack of efficient strategies, an absence of appropriate knowledge activation, an inadequate perception of the task, or a lack of motivation.

Plumb et al.'s (1994) results validate the processing deficit hypothesis as described by Butterfield et al. (1996). Thus, even whether the knowledge relative to the theme and discourse is necessary and important for the revision process, this kind of knowledge is not sufficient. Indeed, except for spelling revisions, having knowledge about *how* to correct other kinds of errors is not sufficient to detect them. As opposed to Flower et al. (1986), Bartlett (1982), or Fitzgerald's (1987) ideas, who assert that error detection and correction depend on separated pieces of knowledge and on different processes, Plumb et al. (1994) have shown that knowledge about how to correct a text is not sufficient to operate this correction in the text.

Now, another question must be answered: Why is it important to possess explicit knowledge about revising in order to revise? Some answers about the failure of revision have been provided by studies carried out by (Wallace and Hayes, 1991; Wallace et al., 1996). Three main reasons are invoked: a lack of revision skills; a lack of coordination in the procedures needed for revision; and an inappropriate definition of the revision task or activity. According to Wallace and Hayes (1991), if the failure to revise is either due to a lack of basic skills or a lack of executive procedures, then simply telling writers to revise would, of course, be ineffective. However, if this failure is – totally or not – the result of an inappropriate task definition, then instructions about this task should have an effect. To verify this postulate, Wallace and Hayes (1991) outlined for an experimental group of students the main differences between local and global revision. A control group's and an experimental group's revisions were analyzed both for global revision and for text quality. Results showed that the experimental group made more global revisions and higher quality revisions than the control group. Wallace and Hayes' (1991) study obviously points out that metacognitive factors play a key role in revision practices, at least for competent college writers. It is clear, in this study, that a writer's task definition largely influences one's revision activities. Finally, relevant training can lead writers to change their task definition and, thus, it is possible to consider the possibility of metacognitive training in writing, as suggested by Hayes (2001).

The importance of tutorials to guide revision

With beginner writers, revision stresses the problem of self-evaluation and self-correction. This is particularly important among young and/or inexperienced writers (Hayes and Flower, 1986; Beal, 1993; Chanquoy, 1997a). Indeed, while experts consider revision as an activity concerning the global text (whole-text task), novices consider it at a more local level (sentence-level task). Inexperienced or beginner writers define revision as consisting in changing words, suppressing errors, and deleting parts of text (Sommers, 1980), and therefore make essentially low-level revisions, while experienced or expert writers have more sophisticated revising strategies (Faigley and Witte, 1981). It is thus important, on an educational perspective, to help beginner writers to revise their texts more efficiently and at a deeper level. To meet this objective, some researchers have formulated some tools to guide the revision process:

(a) Teacher's feedback (Matsuhashi, 1987; Englert et al., 1991; Beal, 1993; Goldstein, 2004)
(b) Collaborative (or peer) revising (Beal et al., 1990; Sitko, 1992; Beal, 1993, 1996)
(c) Computer-assisted revising (Daiute and Kruidenier, 1985; Owston et al., 1992; Piolat and Roussey,

1995; Zammuner, 1995; Holdich et al., 2003; Figueredo and Varnhagen, 2006; etc. and see the meta-analysis made by Goldberg et al. in 2003 about the effect of computers on student writing)
(d) Self-questioning guides (Scardamalia and Bereiter, 1983; Chanquoy and Veaute, 1994; Chanquoy et al., 1996; Chanquoy, 1997b)
(e) Process-oriented writing instructions (McGarrell and Verbeem, 2007), etc.

For example, Piolat and Roussey (1995) have used a computer-assisted production procedure to help participants both in writing and revising. With the help of simplified word-processing software, the writer can revise his/her text by simply using an optical pencil to signal sections needing modification. Chanquoy and Veaute (1994), in a longitudinal study (from third to fifth grade), have constructed two revision guides built as self-questioning lists: a surface guide, with questions about the text's form (spelling, vocabulary, and punctuation) and a depth guide with surface questions plus questions leading to semantic modifications. Results showed that, in contrast to a certain number of studies (e.g., Bartlett, 1982; Scardamalia and Bereiter, 1983; Juel et al., 1986; Matsuhashi, 1987, etc.), children revise their texts both spontaneously and with the help of the guides even from a very young age. Surface revisions are most often spelling and punctuation corrections. Meaning revisions are more varied: changes of verb tenses, modifications of noun phrases, replacements, changes in the sentence orders, word additions or deletions, etc. Finally, the impact of revision guides is sensitive and positive. Globally, all the studies on procedural facilitations of revision show that providing beginner writers with prompts or lists can help them in their revising activities and lighten the cognitive load associated with revision (see Dix, 2006).

Reducing working memory load

Working memory and revision
Nowadays, increasingly numerous works are interested in the role of working memory limited capacity on the revising processes

(see for example: Hacker, 1994; Hacker et al., 1994; McCutchen, 1994; Swanson and Berninger, 1994; Chanquoy, 2001; Hayes, 2006, etc.).

As shown by models presented in the first part of this chapter, limited capacities of working memory deeply constrain writing and revising processes and can lead to cognitive overload in novice or beginner writers, especially if they have not yet automated some of the low-level writing processes (e.g., Berninger and Swanson, 1994). More precisely, Hacker (1994) and Hacker et al. (1994) explain the fact that writers revise text surface elements more than text meaning by the claim that surface revisions are not only easier to make but also less resource-demanding. In the same way, Fitzgerald and Markham (1987) show that working memory is more called upon for error detection in meaning or coherence than for spelling error detection. Indeed, detection and diagnosis operations— if they are not limited to the text surface— necessitate simultaneously the processes of accessing and maintaining in working memory a written text representation and a mental text representation (McCutchen, 1996). The frequency and the nature of revisions would largely depend on the general cost of the writing process, which is linked to the writer's working memory capacity and expertise (Berninger et al., 1996; Swanson and Berninger, 1996). From this perspective, it is possible to consider experimental paradigms, which would serve to lighten the cognitive load associated with the revising process. For example, deferring the revising activity until after the whole text has been written would probably lead to more corrections. Indeed, the writer would in this case carry out two separate tasks: a writing task, and, only afterwards, a revising task.

Reducing load by introducing visible helps in the text

Graham et al. (1995) observe that, in children and/or novice writers, revision is limited for several reasons: the failure to clearly define

goals and intentions; the difficulty of implementing text evaluation; the difficulty in determining what needs to be modified and how; the lack of control and appropriate knowledge, etc. Considering these reasons, it is possible to create experimental paradigms to reduce the cognitive load associated with revision. For example, as error detection and correction require different kinds of knowledge and skills, helping beginner writers to select correct knowledge and appropriate skills should lead to more efficient text revisions.

Following McCutchen et al. (1997), the objective of Chanquoy's (2002) study was to investigate firstly, if the location of an error and/or secondly, if a list of solutions to correct it could help novice writers to correctly revise their texts. In this experiment, there was manipulation of some factors that were hypothesized to influence problem detection (i.e., knowledge of error location) and problem diagnosis/correction (i.e., knowledge about possible solution to correct the error). Participants in third, fourth, and fifth grades were divided into three groups: one control group and two experimental groups. The children in the control group were asked to revise a text in which errors had been introduced and they had to underline errors and to correct them, without any help. The children in the 'cued' group had to revise the same text in which errors were boldfaced; their task was to write down the correction under the erroneous part of text. The children in the 'cued + solution' group were asked to revise the same text with boldfaced errors and they were helped by a list of solutions that was provided under the printed text. They had to choose the correct answer among a list of three possible corrections for each error. Two types of errors were introduced: spelling and grammatical errors. The percentage of correctly *versus* incorrectly revised errors was analyzed.

Results showed that approximately 50% of the errors were correctly revised and that, of course, third and fourth graders made fewer correct revisions than fifth graders. Regardless of the grade, correct revisions were less frequent for control groups than that for both experimental groups. Spelling errors were responded to with more correct revisions than grammar errors. However, the frequency of correct revisions largely depended on the group: the control group revised more grammar than spelling errors while the 'cued' group revised more spelling than grammar errors; finally, there was no difference in correctly revised errors for the 'cued plus solution' group. On the other hand, fourth and third graders (mainly) made about 25% of incorrect revisions, both for spelling and grammar errors.

The usefulness of knowledge of error location varies both with grade level and the nature of the help (bold-printed errors *versus* bold-printed errors plus solutions). Knowledge about error location facilitates its detection, but not systematically its diagnosis, at least for the younger children. To conclude, this kind of cueing intervention, as already noticed by McCutchen et al. (1997) could lead writers to define revision task as a local rather than a global process. To verify this assertion, it is necessary to replicate this experiment by introducing meaning errors, which need to consider the text as a whole.

Reducing load by differing revision

Chanquoy (1997b) suggested that revision during writing would mainly lead to surface modifications (i.e., spelling, punctuation, etc.), while revision after writing, which would be less resource-demanding, would lead to deeper modifications. Correction after writing would be more efficient than during writing, because there would be no competition between writing and revising processes for the limited working memory capacities. To validate these hypotheses, Chanquoy (1997b) asked the experimental groups of third graders and fifth graders to revise their texts either during or after writing (but refrained from doing so with the control group). The experiment began and ended with a pre- and post-test without any instruction about revision. Results showed that children revised their texts, even if they were not explicitly told to revise. In support of the hypotheses, older children made more revisions than the youngest. Also, experimental groups revised more than the control group, which means that revisions were more frequent during experimental steps, when precise instructions about revision were provided either during or after the writing process. More specifically, surface revisions were more numerous than deep revisions, but only in the third grade. Correct revisions were always more frequent than neutral or erroneous revisions, for both grades and all groups. Finally, there were few differences between 'on-line' and 'after' groups. This last result was surprising. It was expected that on-line revision, competing with the other writing processes for working-memory limited resources, would lead to fewer corrections than postponed revision.

To try to explain these results and in order to examine if the delay in revising has any effect on the frequency and nature of revisions, Chanquoy (2001) led an experiment that focused on three occasions of revising instead of two. The objective was twofold: to study how children develop revision skills and to analyze the frequency and nature of revisions, depending on different conditions, designed in order to modify the load associated with the revising process, according to the timing of revision.

Third, fourth, and fifth graders were asked to write a text, and to revise it either during writing or afterwards. Three experimental conditions were designed, and all children in all grades participated in all of them: (1) on-line revision (texts were simultaneously written and revised); (2) after writing revision (writing – revising – rewriting); (3) postponed revision (texts were written on a draft on one day, then revised and recopied the day after). The text length, the frequency of errors and the frequency and the nature of revisions were analyzed (i.e., frequency, because these data were adjusted with the text length). The main results showed the effect of children's grade level on revision, and that postponing the revising process helps children to increase the frequency and the depth of their revisions. More precisely, compared to all grades, third graders showed the clearest difference between the three revising conditions, with more revisions from the control to the delayed condition: third graders largely benefited thus from delayed revising conditions. When their cognitive resources were not divided between both writing and revising processes, they revised more intensively, even if their revisions were mainly surface corrections. With the lower percentage of revisions, fourth graders have largely benefited from the two postponed revising conditions. Similarly, fifth graders revised more during 'after-writing' and 'postponed revision' conditions than during on-line revising condition.

Globally, the delay between writing and revising allowed children to have a more detached view of their text (Perl, 1979) and perhaps to evaluate their texts for a reader, in order to anticipate possible sources of ambiguity and to add information to make the content clearer (Beal, 1996). Separating writing and revising processes seems to be efficient to support writers revising their text, specifically to read their text and to take into account text meaning, instead of just correcting formal errors.

Nevertheless, in this experiment, children were not deliberately taught (nor explicitly helped) to revise texts. It is thus possible to combine postponed revision with clear instructions about revision, such as using revision guides (Chanquoy, 1997a) or revising cards (Daiute and Kruidenier, 1985; De La Paz et al., 1998).

CONCLUSION

It seems now that the revising process is precisely defined and described in both specific and general models. However, some questions remain about the subprocesses of revision and the types of necessary knowledge, and how they are implemented.

On a more practical side, it is equally important to find means to distinguish and to analyze mental and external revisions. Currently, as assumed by Alamargot and Chanquoy (2001), it is only possible to postulate that internal revision would preferentially take place early on during the writing process, during planning activities, while external revision would concern visible corrections done on the draft or on the final copy. However, is it not possible to consider that each visible revision has previously been a mental one? In this case, the level of representation implied by the revision seems to be more important and more crucial than the simple nature of revision (mental or external). However, this last remark does not help to distinguish on the paper (or the screen) which revision is external or internal!

Similarly, it is credible to postulate that revision, regardless of its nature, can both interrupt writing processes and appear in parallel with these processes, or be considered as a final verification, depending on the cognitive demands of both writing and revising. At least for expert writers, most surface (or mechanical) revisions can be realized 'cost-free' to cognitive processes during writing, without interrupting the global writing process, whereas semantic revisions could both be realized during writing or during a stage specifically dedicated to revision. This seems relatively easy to validate but underlies a more complex question about the automated or controlled nature of revision. Currently, some researchers consider that the revising process is deliberated, while others postulate that a part of revision can be automated (e.g., the editing subprocess of Hayes and Flower, 1980) while another part remains deliberate (e.g., reviewing). But what can we say about reading for revision?

Concerning this last question, Hacker (1994) has emphasized that revision necessitates reading and Hayes (1996) has shown that revision necessitates reading comprehension. It seems evident that revision begins with a reading of the text, which allows the reviser to build a mental representation of the produced text and to revise it. According to Daiute and Kruidenier (1985), revision can be considered as an internal dialogue between the writer and the writer-reviser. The efficiency of revision would thus depend on the cognitive resources involved during reading: the less costly the reading process is, the more resources there are available for revising (Hacker, 1994). It is clear that, for revising, the writer must be able to reread his/her text, and therefore to have sufficient resources and appropriate reading skills. This double activity can be held during the course of writing, that is to say that the reviser is in a situation of completing a triple-faceted task (to read, to revise, and to write) during revision.

In conclusion, revision is – as writing was defined some years ago – a very complex activity, which weighs heavily on the limited capacities of a writer's working memory, and more particularly on verbal working memory (Hayes, 2006). As for writing, the different revising subprocesses compete for limited resources in working memory. This fact is largely used to explain why writers, regardless of their expertise, revise more on the surface of a text than for its meaning, simply because surface revisions consume fewer cognitive resources (e.g., Fitzgerald and Markham, 1987; Hacker et al., 1994; McCutchen, 1994). To test precisely how many resources are needed for a subprocess, it could be possible to borrow the method used by Levy and colleagues (e.g., Lea and Levy, 1999; Levy et al., 1999; Levy and Marek, 1999), which consists in successively loading one of the two working-memory slave systems and the central executive to measure the cost of the different writing subprocesses. The same can be done with revision subprocesses in a developmental perspective.

All these preceding points mean that there is still a lot to do in revision research, not only to explain but also to solve revision failures. These last years, revision research has tended to focus on error detection and correction, to improve the surface of the text, more than on structural or meaning-related revisions. However, semantic corrections raise the question of whether the revisions lead to an improvement in text quality (see for instance, van den Bergh and Rijlaarsdam, 2001).

REFERENCES

Alamargot, D. and Chanquoy, L. (2001) 'Through the models of writing in cognitive psychology', in *International Series on the Research of Learning and Instruction of Writing*. Dordrecht: Kluwer Academic Publisher.

Alamargot, D. and Chanquoy, L. (2004) 'Apprentissage et développement dans l'activité de rédaction de textes', in A. Piolat (ed.), *Ecriture et Sciences Cognitives*. Marseille: Presses Universitaires de Provence. pp.125–146.

Baddeley, A.D. and Hitch, G. (1974) 'Working memory', in G.A. Bower (ed.), *Recent Advances in Learning and Motivation. Vol. 8*, New York: Academic Press. pp.47–90.

Bartlett, E.J. (1982) 'Learning to revise: Some component processes', in M. Nystrand (ed.), *What Writers Know: The Language, Process, and Structure of Written Discourse*, New York: Academic Press. pp.345–363.

Beal, C.R. (1993) 'Contributions of developmental psychology to understanding revision: Implications for consultation with classroom teachers', *School Psychology Review*, 22: 643–655.

Beal, C.R. (1996) 'The role of comprehension monitoring in children's revision', *Educational Psychology Review*, 8(3): 219–238.

Beal, C.R., Garrod, A.C., and Bonitatibus, G.J. (1990) 'Fostering children's revision skills through training in comprehension monitoring', *Journal of Educational Psychology*, 82(2): 275–280.

Becker, A. (2006) 'A review of writing model research based on cognitive processes', in A. Horning and A. Becker (eds), *Revision. History, Theory and Practice*, West Lafayette: Parlor Press. pp.25–48.

Bereiter, C. and Scardamalia, M. (1987) *The Psychology of Written Composition*, Hillsdale, NJ: Erlbaum.

Berninger, V.W. and Swanson, H.L. (1994) 'Modification of the Hayes and Flower model to explain beginning and developing writing', in E. Butterfield (ed.),

Advances in Cognition and Educational Practice. Vol. 2: Children's Writing: Toward a process theory of development of skilled writing, Greenwich, CT: JAI Press. pp.57–82.

Berninger, V.W., Cartwright, A.C., Yates, C.M., Swanson, H.L., and Abbott, R.D. (1994) 'Developmental skills related to writing and reading acquisition in the intermediate grades', *Reading and Writing: An Interdisciplinary Journal*, 6: 161–196.

Berninger, V.W., Fuller, F., and Whitaker, D. (1996) 'A process model of writing development across the life span', *Educational Psychology Review*, 8(3): 193–217.

Berninger, V.W., Yates, C., Cartwright, A., Rutberg, J., Remy, E., and Abbott, R. (1992) 'Lower-level developmental skills in beginning writing', *Reading and Writing: An Interdisciplinary Journal*, 4: 257–280.

Brown, J.S., McDonald, J.L., Brown, T.L., and Carr, T.H. (1988) 'Adapting to processing demands in discourse production: The case of handwriting', *Journal of Experimental Psychology: Human Perception and Performance*, 14(1): 45–59.

Butterfield, E.C., Albertson, L.R., and Johnston, J. (1995) 'On making cognitive theory more general and developmentally pertinent', in F. Weinert and W. Schneider (eds) *Memory Performance and Competence: Issues in Growth and Development*, Hillsdale, NJ: L. Erlbaum Associates. pp.181–205.

Butterfield, E.C., Hacker, D.J., and Albertson, L.R. (1996) 'Environmental, cognitive, and metacognitive influences on text revision: Assessing the evidence', *Educational Psychology Review*, 8(3): 239–297.

Butterfield, E.C., Hacker, D.J., and Plumb, C. (1994) 'Topic knowledge, linguistic knowledge, and revision processes as determinants of text revision', in E.C. Butterfield (ed.), *Advances in Cognition and Educational Practice. Vol. 2: Children's writing: Toward a process theory of the development of skilled writing*, Greenwich, CT: JAI Press. pp.83–141.

Cameron, C.A., Edmunds, G., Wigmore, B., Hunt, A.K., and Linton, M.J. (1997) 'Children's revision of textual flaws', *International Journal of Behavioral Development*, 20(4): 667–680.

Chanquoy, L. (1997a) 'Thinking skills and composing: Examples of text revision', in J.H.M. Hamers and M. Overtoom (eds), *Inventory of European Programmes for Teaching Thinking*, Utrecht: Sardes. pp.179–185.

Chanquoy, L. (1997b) 'Revising written texts: How could we help children to revise?' Paper presented at the Seventh Annual Meeting of the Society for Text and Discourse, Utrecht (The Netherlands), July, 10–11, 1997.

Chanquoy, L. (2001) 'How to make it easier for children to revise their writing? A study of text revision from 3rd to 5th grades', *British Journal of Educational Psychology*, 71: 15–41.

Chanquoy, L. (2002) 'Text revision and cognitive demands in 3rd, 4th, and 5th graders', Proceedings of the Conference on Language, Culture and Communication for the 50th birthday of the Letter Faculty of the University of Barnaoul, Russia. Vol. 2, pp.139–150.

Chanquoy, L. and Alamargot, D. (2003) 'Approche développementale des modèles de rédaction de textes et de leurs relations avec la mémoire de travail', *Le Langage et L'Homme: Logopédie, Psychologie, Audiologie*, XXXVIII(2): 171–190.

Chanquoy, L. and Veaute, J.L. (1994) 'La révision de textes écrits: Etude longitudinale chez l'enfant de 8 à 10 ans', *Conference of the French Society of Psychology*. Montpellier, France, October 6–8.

Chanquoy, L., Piolat, A., and Roussey, J.Y. (1996) 'Effects of self-questioning on text revising. A study with 8-, 10- and 14-year-old children', *Communication for the International Conference 'The Growing Mind'*. Geneva (Switzerland), September, 14–18.

Daiute, C. and Kruidenier, J. (1985) 'A self-questioning strategy to increase young writers' revising processes', *Applied Psycholinguistics*, 6: 307–318.

Daneman, M. and Stainton, M. (1993) 'The generation effect in reading and proofreading. Is it easier or harder to detect errors in one's own writing?' *Reading and Writing: An Interdisciplinary Journal*, 5: 297–313.

De La Paz, S., Swanson, P.N., and Graham, S. (1998) 'The contribution of executive control to the revising by students with writing and learning difficulties', *Journal of Educational Psychology*, 90(3): 448–460.

Dix, S. (2006) 'What did I change and why did I do it? Young writers' revision practices', *Literacy*, 40(1): 3–10.

Englert, C., Raphael, T., Anderson, L., Anthony, H., Stevens, D., and Fear, K. (1991) 'Making writing strategies and self-task visible: Cognitive strategy instruction in writing in regular and special education classrooms', *American Educational Research Journal*, 28: 337–373.

Faigley, L. and Witte, S. (1981) 'Analysing revision', *College Composition and Communication*, 32: 400–414.

Faigley, L. and Witte, S.P. (1984) 'Measuring the effects of revisions on text structure', in R. Beach and L.S. Bridwell (eds), *New Directions in Composing Research*, New York: Guilford Press. pp.95–108.

Faigley, L., Cherry, R.D., Jollifre, D.A., and Skinner, A.M. (1985) *Assessing Writers' Knowledge and Processes of Composing*, Norwood, NJ: Ablex.

Figueredo, L. and Varnhagen, C.K. (2006) 'Spelling and grammar checkers: Are they intrusive?' *British Journal of Educational Technology*, 37(5): 721–732.

Fitzgerald, J. (1987) 'Research on revision in writing', *Review of Educational Research*, 57(4): 481–506.

Fitzgerald, J. and Markham, L.R. (1987) 'Teaching children about revision in writing', *Cognition and Instruction*, 4(1): 3–24.

Flower, L.S. and Hayes, J.R. (1981) 'A cognitive process theory of writing', *College Composition and Communication*, 32: 365–387.

Flower, L.S., Hayes, J.R., Carey, L., Schriver, K., and Stratman, J. (1986) 'Detection, diagnosis, and the strategies of revision', *College Composition and Communication*, 37: 16–55.

Goldberg, A. Russell, M., and Cook, A. (2003) 'The effect of computers on student writing: A meta-analysis of studies from 1992 to 2002', *The Journal of Technology, Learning, and Assessment*, 2(1): 3–51.

Goldstein, L.M. (2004) 'Questions and answers about teacher written commentary and student revision: teachers and students working together', *Journal of Second Language Writing*, 13(1): 63–80.

Graham, S., McArthur, C., and Schwartz, S. (1995) 'Effects of goal setting and procedural facilitation on the revising behavior and writing performance of students with writing and learning problems', *Journal of Educational Psychology*, 87(2): 230–240.

Hacker, D.J. (1994) 'Comprehension monitoring as a writing process', *Advances in Cognition and Educational Practice*, 6: 143–172.

Hacker, D.J., Plumb, C., Butterfield, E.C., Quathamer, D., and Heineken, E. (1994) 'Text revision: Detection and correction of errors', *Journal of Educational Psychology*, 86(1): 65–78.

Hayes, J.R. (1996) 'A new framework for understanding cognition and affect in writing', in C.M. Levy and S. Ransdell (eds), *The Science of Writing*. Mahwah, NJ: L. Erlbaum Associates. pp.1–28.

Hayes, J.R. (2001) 'Commentary on the book – Through the models of writing', in D. Alamargot and L. Chanquoy (eds), *Through the Models of Writing*, Dordrecht: Kluwer Academic Publishers. pp.228–236.

Hayes, J.R. (2004) 'What triggers revision?' in L. Allal, L. Chanquoy, and P. Largy (eds), *Revision. Cognitive and Instructional Processes*, Dordrecht: Kluwer Academic Publishers. pp.9–20.

Hayes, J.R. (2006) 'Is working memory involved in the transcribing and editing of texts?', *Written Communication*, 23(2): 135–149.

Hayes, J.R. and Flower, L.S. (1980) 'Identifying the organization of writing processes', in L.W. Gregg and E.R. Steinberg (eds), *Cognitive Processes in Writing*, Hillsdale, NJ: Erlbaum. pp.3–30.

Hayes, J.R. and Flower, L.S. (1983) 'Uncovering cognitive processes in writing: An introduction of protocol analysis', in P. Mosenthal, S. Walmsley, and L. Tamor (eds), *Research on Writing: Principles and Methods*, New York: Longman. pp.206–219.

Hayes, J.R. and Flower, L.S. (1986) 'Writing research and the writer', *American Psychologist*, 41: 1106–1113.

Hayes, J.R., Flower, L.S., Schriver, K.A., Stratman, J., and Carey, L. (1987) 'Cognitive processes in revision', in S. Rosenberg (ed.), *Advances in Psycholinguistics, Vol. 2: Reading, writing, and language processing*, Cambridge: Cambridge University Press. pp.176–240.

Holdich, C.E., Chung, P.W.H., and Holdich, R.G. (2003) 'Improving children's written grammar and style: revising and editing with Harry', *Computers & Education*, 42: 1–23.

Juel, C., Griffith, P.L., and Gough, P.B. (1986) 'Acquisition of literacy: A longitudinal study of children in first and second grade', *Journal of Educational Psychology*, 78(4): 243–255.

Kellogg, R.T. (1996) 'A model of working memory in writing', in C.M. Levy and S. Ransdell (eds), *The Science of Writing*, Mahwah, NJ: L. Erlbaum Associates. pp.57–72.

Lea, J. and Levy, C.M. (1999) 'Working memory as a resource in the writing process', in G. Rijlaarsdam and E. Espéret (series eds), and M. Torrance and G. Jeffery (eds), *Studies in Writing: Vol. 3. The cognitive demands of writing: Processing capacity and working memory in text production*, Amsterdam: Amsterdam University Press. pp.63–82.

Levy, C.M. and Marek, P. (1999) 'Testing components of Kellogg's multicomponent models of Working Memory in writing: The role of the phonological loop', in M. Torrance and G. Jeffery (eds) *Studies in Writing: Vol. 3. The cognitive demands of writing. Processing capacity and working memory effects in text production*. pp.25–41. Amsterdam: Amsterdam University Press.

Levy, C.M. and Ransdell, S. (eds) (1996) *The Science of Writing: Theories, Methods and Applications*, Mahwah, NJ: L. Erlbaum Associates.

Levy, C.M., White, K., Lea, J., and Ransdell, S. (1999) 'Contributions of the visuo-spatial sketchpad, phonological loop and central executive to writing and recall', in E. Espéret, and M.-F. Crété (eds), Proceedings of the 1998 Writing Conference. Poitiers: Editions de la MSHS. pp.41–47.

Levy C.M., and Marek, P. (1999) 'Testing components of Kellogg's multicomponent model of working memory in writing: The role of the phonological loop', in M. Torrance and G.C. Jeffery (eds), *The Cognitive Demands of Writing*, Amsterdam: Amsterdam University Press. pp.13–24.

Matsuhashi, A. (1987) 'Revising the plan and altering the text', in A. Matsuhashi (ed.), *Writing in Real Time*, Norwood, NJ: Ablex. pp.197–223.

McArthur, C.A., Graham, S., and Schwartz, S. (1991) 'Knowledge of revision and revising behavior among students with learning disabilities', *Learning Disability Quarterly*, 14: 61–73.

McCutchen, D. (1988) '"Functional automaticity" in children's writing: A problem of metacognitive control', *Written Communication*, 5: 306–324.

McCutchen, D. (1994) 'The magical number three, plus or minus two: Working memory in writing', in E.C. Butterfield (eds), *Advances in cognition and Educational Practice. Vol. 2: Children's writing: Toward a process theory of the development of skilled writing*, Greenwich, CT: JAI Press. pp.1–30.

McCutchen, D. (1996) 'A capacity theory of writing: Working memory in composition', *Educational Psychology Review*, 8(3): 299–325.

McCutchen, D., Francis, M., and Kerr, S. (1997) 'Revising for meaning: Effects of knowledge and strategy', *Journal of Educational Psychology*, 89(4): 667–676.

McGarrell, H. and Verbeem, J. (2007) 'Motivating revision of drafts through formative feedback', *ELT Journal*, 61(3): 228–236.

Monahan, B.D. (1984) 'Revision strategies of basic and competent writers as they write for different audience', *Research in the Teaching of English*, 18(3): 288–304.

Owston, R.D., Murphy, S., and Widerman, H.H. (1992) 'The effects of word processing on students' writing quality and revision strategies', *Research in the Teaching of English*, 26(3): 249–275.

Perl, S. (1979) 'The composing processes of unskilled College writers', *Research in the Teaching of English*, 13(4): 317–336.

Piolat, A. (2007) 'Les usages et les inconvénients d'un traitement de texte pour réviser un texte', in J. Bisaillon (ed.), *La Révision Professionnelle: Processus, stratégies et pratiques*, Québec: Editions Nota Bene. pp.189–211.

Piolat, A. and Roussey, J.Y. (1995) 'Environnements d'apprentissages informatisés et réécriture de textes', *Repères*, 10: 49–66.

Plumb, C., Butterfield, E.C., Hacker, D.J., and Dunlosky, J. (1994) 'Error correction in text. Testing the processing-deficit and knowledge-deficit hypotheses', *Reading and Writing: An Interdisciplinary Journal*, 6: 347–360.

Roussey, J.Y. and Piolat, A. (in press). 'Critical reading effort during text revision', *The European Journal of Cognitive Psychology*.

Scardamalia, M. and Bereiter, C. (1983) 'The development of evaluative, diagnostic, and remedial capabilities in children's composing', in M. Martlew (ed.), *The Psychology of Written Language. Developmental and Educational Perspectives*, New York: Wiley. pp.67–95.

Scardamalia, M. and Bereiter, C. (1986) 'Research on written composition', in M. Wittrock (ed.), *Handbook of Research on Teaching* (third edn.), New York: McMillan. pp.778–803.

Scardamalia, M. and Bereiter, C. (1987) 'Knowledge telling and knowledge transforming in written composition', in R. Rosenberg (ed.), *Advances in Applied Psycholinguistics, Vol. 2: Reading, writing, and language learning*, Cambridge: Cambridge University Press. pp.142–175.

Severinson Eklundh, K. and Kollberg, P. (2003) 'Emerging discourse structure: computer-assisted episode analysis as a window to global revision in university students' writing', *Journal of Pragmatics*, 35: 869–891.

Sitko, B.M. (1992) 'Writers meet their readers in the classroom: Revising after feedback', in M. Secor and D. Chamey (eds), *Constructing Rhetorical Education*, Carbonale, IL: Southern Illinois University Press. pp.278–294.

Sommers, N. (1980) 'Revision strategies of student writers and experienced writers', *College Composition and Communication*, 31: 378–387.

Swanson, H.L. and Berninger, V.W. (1994) 'Working memory as a source of individual differences in children's writing', in E.C. Butterfield (ed.), *Advances in Cognition and Educational Practice. Vol. 2: Children's writing: Toward a process theory of the development of skilled writing*, Greenwich, CT: JAI Press. pp.31–56.

Swanson, H.L. and Berninger, V.W. (1996) 'Individual differences in children's working memory and writing skills', *Journal of Experimental Child Psychology*, 63: 358–385.

Temple, C., Nathan, R., Temple, F., and Burris, N.A. (1993) *The Beginnings of Writing* (third edn.), Boston: Allyn and Bacon.

Torrance, M., Fidalgo, R., and García, J.-N. (2007) 'The teachability and effectiveness of cognitive self-regulation in sixth-grade writers', *Learning and Instruction*, 17(3): 265–285.

Traxler, M.J. and Gernsbacher, M.A. (1992) 'Improving written communication through minimal feedback', *Language and Cognitive Processes*, 7: 1–22.

Traxler, M.J. and Gernsbacher, M.A. (1993) 'Improving written communication through perspective-taking', *Language and Cognitive Processes*, 8(3): 311–334.

Van den Bergh, H. and Rijlaarsdam, G. (2001) 'Changes in cognitive activities during the writing process and relationships with text quality', *Educational Psychology*, 21(4): 373–385.

Wallace, D. and Hayes, J.R. (1991) 'Redefining revision for freshmen', *Research in the Teaching of English*, 25(1): 54–66.

Wallace, D.L., Hayes, J.R., Hatch, J.A., Miller, W., Moser, G., and Silk, C.M. (1996) 'Better revision in eight minutes? Prompting first-year college writers to revise globally', *Journal of Educational Psychology*, 88: 682–687.

Zammuner, V.L. (1995) 'Individual and cooperative computer-writing and revising: Who gets the best results?', *Learning and Instruction*, 5(1): 101–124.

A Sociocultural Framework: Writing as Social Practice

Triantafillia Kostouli

INTRODUCTION

This chapter, building upon the notion of writing as social practice, sets out to outline the basic premises of a new approach to school writing, referred to as Critical Analysis of Writing Practices. This draws upon and extends assumptions and terms from Critical Discourse Analysis (Blommaert, 2005; Chouliaraki and Fairclough, 1999; Fairclough, 2003, 2004, 2006; Rogers, 2003, 2004; Wodak and Ludwig, 1999), neo-Vygotskian research (Wertsch, 1985, 1991, 1998), activity theory (Bazerman, 1988; Berkenkotter and Huckin, 1995; Prior, 1998), and poststructuralist feminist research (Baxter, 2003). Integrated, these perspectives may help us account for a little-researched issue (Street, 2005b; Van Eng et al., 2005), namely for writing development and learning processes as coconstructed within school contexts through their interaction with wider social forces. Critical Analysis of Writing Practices is proposed as an approach with an explicitly political agenda; this is dedicated to uncovering how societal asymmetries, power hierarchies, and ideological models leading to the marginalization of particular social groups, are reproduced and/or are contested through the writing acts and texts produced in local classroom communities. Drawing upon data from the Greek educational system, the discussion is situated within a wider 'cross-national perspective' (Foster and Russell, 2002) to identify how social practices (consisting of different kinds of texts and writing events) validate, sustain, and/or redefine national as well as transnational meanings and ideologies – voices of authority (in Heller and Martin-Jones's [2001] terms).

Critical Discourse Analysis has been developed as an approach to language study concerned with raising awareness about the ideological underpinnings of linguistic choice (Van Dijk, 1998; Weiss and Wodak, 2003; Wodak and Meyer, 2001). Restated in school contexts (see Lewis et al., 2007), the extensions introduced capture the ways by which students are constructed as specific kinds of writers and indeed learners (Bourne, 2002; Hruska, 2004); how they are positioned and repositioned as subjects by different and even competing discourses (see Sunderland, 2004). Two key assumptions underpin the field of Critical Analysis of Writing Practices. The first is this: analysis should combine the close textual investigation of patterns of language use in written discourses with the micro-analytic account of the resources shaping the emergence of writing activities as specific kinds of learning contexts. Microanalysis (see Bloome et al., 2005; Boden and Zimmerman, 1991) reveals the situated construction of inequalities; alternatively, the contexts constructed around written texts are not taken a priori as 'learning' contexts; these are rather seen as shaping learning opportunities, which, as studies have shown (Kostouli, 2005b; O'Connor, 2003; Rex, 2006; Santa Barbara Classroom Discourse Group, 1992, 1995), are usually taken up by some (and not necessarily all) students. The second assumption builds upon and extends the premise on the contextually shaped nature of meanings: language is seen as a context-bound phenomenon, which can be properly understood by paying attention to the different kinds of local and global contexts; these contexts, rather than seen as bounded units, with the higher-order ones enveloping smaller ones, are proposed to interpenetrate one another (see Duranti and Goodwin, 1992; and for a review on writing, see Kostouli, 2005a).

Critical Analysis of Writing Practices attempts to establish links between the 'micro' and 'macro' contexts, through the construct of 'social practices' (or 'communicative practices' in Hank's [1996] terms). This is used to account for the ways by which local actors oscillate between the prefabricated meanings suggested by social structures and the meanings emerging in local occasions through the agency of language producers (Fairclough, 2003). Proceeding beyond single occasions to capture the way social practices work as mediational tools in a cultural landscape of meanings (see also Farrell, 2006; Gunnarsson et al., 1997; Sarangi and Roberts, 1999; Smart, 2006 as regards workplace communication), this chapter builds upon a redefined notion, the 'nexus of social practices' (Norris and Jones, 2005). The proposal outlined in this chapter, then, links the descriptive analysis of text patterns and the interactive strategies used in different kinds of writing contexts (such as one-to-one writing conferences and whole-class interactions around texts) to processes such as empowerment and learning as attested through shifting positionings and multiple identities. Attention is directed towards unveiling how, through an intertextual universe of texts and writing activities, certain meanings, voices (in Bakhtin's [1981, 1986] terms), and specific identity positionings are proposed, negotiated, taken up, and/or rejected by local actors within school communities.

This suggestion represents a considerable divergence from (or, rather, an enrichment of) interactionist approaches prevailing in first (Wells, 1999; Wells and Chang-Wells, 1992) and second language research (Flowerdew, 2000; Hall and Verplaetse, 2000; Lantolf, 2000; Lillis, 2001; Tardy, 2006); these tend to define learning (in line with Lave and Wenger, 1991; Rogoff, 1990) as increasing participation to communities of practice (Larson and Marsh, 2005). More recent ESL-based work on academic socialization has foregrounded a different approach to learning: this is seen as a process that involves 'struggles over access to resources, conflicts and negotiations between differing viewpoints arising from different degrees of experience and expertise' (Morita, 2004: 577). In the discussion outlined in the following section, learning, redefined as a socially displayed process, is linked to the multiple positionings and different forms of identity negotiated in writing communities vis-à-vis wider discourses (Norton, 2000; Wortham, 2006); the learning trajectories coconstructed are traced through the positionings established (temporarily or consistently) by participant members against global discourses. These positionings are realized textually (through the linguistic forms and the macro-organizational patterns in the written texts produced) and interactionally (through the strategies used and the units constructed around texts). This account of learning, then, proceeds beyond textual evidence to trace how, through the trajectories coconstructed, planning and brainstorming activities give rise to texts, which are redrafted in revision activities; it is through these trajectories (defined, after Hopper [1995: 57], as 'pathways through communicative episodes') that writing communities emerge as specific kinds of learning contexts (Gutierrez, 1994; Roth et al., 2005). The critical study of writing practices as they emerge and get reshaped within a learning community requires that we proceed beyond single instances of observable social practices to accomplish two goals: (1) unveil the political nature of the realities constructed by participants in local communities; learning trajectories are, thus, seen as an integral means participants use for confirming and/or contesting wider social forces (capturing, among others, the policies that shape classroom practices) and (2) step out of the realities analysts describe to engage in an emancipatory goal. The latter suggests that researchers collaborate with local actors (teacher and students) to redefine school communities as dialogic places (see also Freedman and Delp, 2007), that is, as places where multiple voices coexist and contesting discourses of nondominant groups are acknowledged and validated.

SOCIAL THEORY AND WRITING RESEARCH

On the structure versus agency distinction

In extending research on the way classroom strategies, and interactive units from writing, conferences, to brainstorming or planning sessions (Allal et al., 2005; Gutierrez et al., 1995, Gutirerez and Stones, 2000; Hicks, 1996; Mariage, 2000) index and redefine wider social forces, and how texts are used by children and teachers to negotiate literate identities (see also, Lewis, 2001), the discussion needs to bring into the forefront a distinction of central importance within social theory. Stated as the 'structure *versus* agency' duality, the relationship between the individual and the society (or, in this case, the local

community and the global social forces) has been regarded as the acid test of any social theory. An issue of central importance for social theory has been to capture whether it is the actions of individuals or the workings of broader social structures that influence the reproduction of social life. Indeed, given current new developments (on global cultures and glocalization created by fusions of meanings drawn from the national, global, and local levels of activity [see Lam, 2004; Pahl and Rowsell, 2006 for implications to literacy research]), modern social theorists investigate further issues; whether, for instance, the relationship between the individual and the society may have been actually altered as a result of these social changes. Bringing this problem into writing research, I suggest that writing research be revisited as part of social theory. I view writing researchers as researchers concerned with unveiling the way by which writing, as a semiotic tool working independently and/or in combination with speaking and image to form multimodal aggregates (see Royce and Bowcher, 2007), contributes to the reproduction of social life and to social change. Indeed, the perspective of Critical Analysis of Writing Practices outlined in this chapter aims to bring social theory, discourse analysis, and writing research together in an attempt to describe, interpret, and explain the ways in which a nexus of social practices '... represent and become represented by the social world' (Rogers et al., 2005: 366).

In social theory, structure is used to refer to 'regular, relatively fixed, objective and generalized features of social life' (King, 2005: 215). Structure usually refers to constraints posed by social institutions or systems. Agency, on the other hand, refers to the actions undertaken by an individual or groups of individuals. The issue social theory grapples with is this: How do actors negotiate structure? Central in this respect is the work by Giddens (1981, 1984) and Bourdieu (1977). While an extensive review cannot be possible within this chapter, it should be stated that Giddens in his 'structuration theory' attempts to explain the reproduction of institutional orders through the agency of individuals. According to Giddens, social structures are constituted by human agency, and yet at the same time they are seen as the very medium of this constitution. Indeed, as Giddens argues, social life, being highly complex and temporal, is constantly being reproduced through the relationship between the individual and society. In addressing this relationship, Bourdieu proposes the construct of 'habitus', used in reference to perceptual structures and embodied dispositions created in an individual over time; these are proposed to organize the way individuals see the world and act in it. Bourdieu has been criticized for his tendency to 'reduce dynamic and uncertain social interaction to the inevitable reproduction of institutional forces' (King, 2005: 229). Current research within social theory proceeds away from structure *versus* agency, seen as static ontologic poles, to focus on the dynamic contexts of social relations created between interacting individuals and groups. From proposals of people following rules in private isolation, current work suggests that individuals should be seen as able to 'act relatively predictably and to create social order'; people are proposed to 'routinely accept certain common understandings of what is appropriate, and these understandings become binding and constraining' (King, 2005: 231).

How do these issues shape language use and indeed writing practices? Fairclough (1989, 1995, 2003) has noted that social theorists have rarely drawn upon linguistic work to illustrate the ways by which social structures are constituted; indeed, little research has been conducted on the linguistic processes by which social change is enacted. On the other hand, sociolinguistics, while linking linguistic practice within social issues, has been accused of only 'weakly' making the link with social theory. Sociolinguistics has been accused of borrowing from social theory concepts, such as class, race, ethnicity, and gender, and treating them as if they were 'real things' (see Coupland et al., 2001;

Erickson, 2004). Fairclough's response, through the framework of Critical Discourse Analysis, has been to call for a 'transdisciplinary' inquiry that would bring linguistic resources to account for issues of power and domination, as these are constituted in various sociohistorical contexts (Fairclough, 1989, 1995, 2003). This approach has been criticized, however, from a number of angles. Erickson (2004), for instance, suggests that too much attention has been given to broader 'global' issues at the expense of 'local' issues.

In attempting to forge links between 'micro' and 'macro' contexts, the construct of social practices has been proposed as an intermediate factor. Fairclough (2003) conceptualizes the notion of social practices as a construct oscillating between social structures, on the one hand (which are seen as abstract entities), and local events, on the other. Fairclough (2003: 23) construes a social structure (used in reference to an economic structure, a kinship system, or a language) as 'defining a potential, a set of possibilities', while local events capture what actually happens. Fairclough (2003) advises us, however, that the relationship between structure and events is a very complex one. Events are not in any simple or direct way the effects of abstract social structures. Their relationship is mediated by 'social practices', consisting of the articulation of the following elements, namely: action and interaction, social relations, persons (with beliefs, attitudes, histories, etc.), the material world, and discourse (Fairclough, 2003: 25).

As an example of a social practice, Fairclough proposes the classroom lesson – a proposal reminiscent of Christie's (2002) construal of lessons as 'macro-curriculum genres'. While detailed work needs to be done to unveil the set of assumptions these two proposals build upon, in this chapter, which focuses on classroom-based activities, finer distinctions are introduced. I distinguish lower-level social practices (capturing the units, such as reading and writing events, within a classroom lesson) from compound social practices, constituting a 'nexus of social practices'. This notion, similar to Bazerman's (1994) construct of 'genre sets', is used to capture the higher order structure coproduced by local actors as they coordinate various mediational tools, including texts, within communities to attain specific social actions. In creating this structure, actors may exercise their agency in different ways, while building upon intersubjective understandings that bind them in their local action.

Extended to school-situated learning processes, Fairclough's notion of 'social practices' represents a richer perspective compared to others proposed thus far; consider, for instance, Gee's (1996, 2004) proposal developed within the field of New Literacies Studies. Gee has proposed a useful distinction between Discourses (with a capital D) and discourses; the former is used in reference to certain, systematic ways of talking, listening, acting, interacting, and using tools and objects; through these, people display and recognize a particular social identity. How are Discourses realized? As Knobel (1999) suggests, Gee is not clear on this relationship (see also Lemke [1995], on a detailed analysis of various frameworks addressing such linkages). Given that these notions will be used in this chapter, certain clarifications are necessary. Let me begin by distinguishing between the term 'discourse', used (in line with traditional discourse analysis [Brown and Yule, 1983]) in reference to 'language above the sentence level' or to 'language in use'. To distinguish written from spoken units, the terms 'written texts' and 'interactive units' will be used, respectively. These local discourses are proposed to reflect plural discourses or Discourses. The notion of Discourses is used in line with Foucault (1972) to denote forms of 'knowledge' – powerful sets of assumptions, expectations, explanations – structuring the ways we think about things, and prescribing 'natural' behaviour. Given that a discourse presents particular relationships as self-evident and 'true', Discourses are linked to power. As Foucault

suggested, in a certain Discourse, certain forms of knowledge are excluded from being considered as true.

How do these distinctions pertain to educational contexts? How do these inform the way children negotiate constraints posed by institutional Discourses? Extending Fairclough's approach, I suggest that a complete analysis of the way local actors use writing processes to negotiate agency and structure – and assert their voice or identity (Canagarajah, 2004; Prior, 2001) – should not just involve a detailed engagement with the way a specific social practice is coconstructed. Attention needs to be directed toward unveiling how through an intertextual universe of social practices (created out of a series of texts and writing activities), certain meanings, and voices and specific identity positionings (capturing what school regards as 'appropriate' ways of reading, writing, and acting) are taken up and/or contested by local actors within school communities.

IDENTITIES IN DISCOURSES AND TEXTS: FROM POSITIONS TO POSITIONINGS

In an attempt to develop ways of addressing the relationship between local discourses and global ideological Discourses, positioning theory has been developed (Davies and Harré, 1990; De Fina et al., 2006). 'Positioning' refers to 'the process through which speakers adopt, resist and offer "subject positions" that are made available in Discourses or 'master narratives'" (Benwell and Stokoe, 2006: 43). In general, there are two basic ways of conceptualizing the relationship between subject positions proposed by Discourses and the identities taken up by local actors in situated cases. The first and more traditional one construes of identities as reproductions of the positions suggested by master narratives, cultural discourses, and institutional norms. The other, which is more in line with ethnomethodological views, focuses on positions as interactively shaped and locally occasioned. Positioning is indexed through a variety of linguistic means. Current interactional work (De Fina et al., 2006; Leander, 2002a,b; Litosseliti and Sunderland, 2002; McCarthey, 2002; McCarthey and Moje, 2002) attends to how actors index their positionings against discourses, how they use language to reaffirm and take up the subject positions proposed to them, and how they use linguistic resources to resist, negotiate, or modify these positions, exercising, thus, agency in identity construction.

How do these notions relate to educational research? Writing research has recently taken up the notion of student agency as exercised through the construction of school genres. Different directions may be singled out. On the one hand, we may note research focusing on how students exercise agency when faced with a new task. Indeed, as work on academic literacies and identities has attested (Ivanič, 1998), instead of viewing texts as 'reflecting … a pre-defined subjectivity' (Canagarajah, 2004: 270), writing may be seen as the means through which meanings are negotiated and different kinds of identities may be constructed. Canagarajah (2004) has delineated a taxonomy of strategies multilingual writers employ to create images of their selves that appeal to them and display these to their readers various types of identity; these may contest or validate or transcend established discourses 'to create a new voice for themselves' (Canagarajah, 2004: 270). Working in school literacies, Dyson (1993, 1999, 2002) has illustrated how young students draw upon community funds to produce texts in school; pop culture themes were found to serve as an important textual and social scaffold, shaping children's appropriation of new genres. According to Dyson, the way children use these cultural resources reveals their power to improvise, reconfigure, and rearticulate their own meanings – a significant aspect to literate learning in contemporary postmodern world. Similarly,

Kamberelis (2001) has described how through the 'lamination' of numerous different speech genre fragments derived from popular culture, two fifth grade boys engaged with tasks in a biology unit, negotiating, at the same time, new identities for them. According to Kamberelis, the boys, by reanimating 'pop culture discourse in internally persuasive ways to express their scientific identities and task commitments' (p. 115), repositioned themselves away from their earlier identities (as relatively tough, marginal members of the community) to ones valued by the class for the depth of their popular culture knowledge and for creativity.

It is worth noting that this research deals with cases where students had received no explicit instruction on the task they set out to implement. If these students' textual response is seen as an initiating unit or as a text in an intertextually built chain of events (see Prior, 2004), it is worth attending to how classroom forces (i.e., instructional contexts) work to negotiate, contest, and/or reshape those identities and meaning making resources. The work of Pappas et al. (2004) on science literacies with second graders from a diverse ethnolinguistic population is illustrative (see also Gee and Clinton, 2000). Analyzing a series of read alouds, Pappas et al. (2004) have illustrated how classroom processes shaped student-proposed narrative meanings and everyday understandings of science toward more authoritative meanings; the rich intertextual references to everyday meanings were gradually replaced with ones favoring the school-valued view of science as decontextualized. Similarly, in her analysis of reading practices in American classroom communities, Anagnostopoulos (2003) illustrated that the reader positions taken up by teacher and students cannot be understood if research focuses on local factors; rather, the classroom should be seen as a space through which local actors negotiate and/or affirm a system of constraints posed by Chicago's Academic Standards Exam (CASE). As illustrated, this exam projects specific reader 'positions': 'good' readers of literature were those skilled at the reproduction of facts and details. Interestingly, the opposite process can also take place. More recent work on multimodality building upon the New London Group (2000) (Kress et al., 2001, 2005; Ranker, 2007; Stein, 2004) illuminated opposing forces at work: how students by 'resourcing given sources' (in Stein's, 2004 terms) succeeded at extending prevailing but limited notions of school genres. Ranker, for instance, attests that the narratives produced by an eight-year-old child were constructed out of redesigned material borrowed from several media, such as comic books, video games, web sites, and television cartoons. Indeed, as the work by Kress et al. attests, through this negotiation, the notion of school science may also be extended; 'science texts' were found to be constructed by British children through an interplay of verbal and visual resources (see also Unsworth, 1993 for the Australian context).

In light of the foregoing, it appears that to account for the specific kinds of writer identities, students take up and negotiate within local textual universes, we need to attend to both local texts and the interactive units constructed. In my proposal, I illustrate how a series of constantly evolving nexuses of social practices works to establish positionings that reinscribe into classroom communities wider ideological resources suggesting specific writer identities. It is interesting to attend to whether local classroom communities reproduce or modify these identities. It is through such positionings to wider social discourses that acts of empowerment are claimed. Power or, more aptly, empowerment, rather than seen as acquired as a direct outcome of one's appropriation of the genres of schooling (Johns, 2002; Schleppegrell, 2004; but see Freadman, 1994), is redefined as a local accomplishment; this is shaped and reshaped out of the positionings participants adopt in local communities as they renegotiate global educational discourses defining specific 'literate identities' and specific notions of 'success'.

POWER, DISCOURSES, AND INSTITUTIONS

A central concern of work in Critical Discourse Analysis is the relationship between discourse, power, and ideology within institutional settings. While initially power has been linked to institutions, in his 'theory of structuration', Giddens (1981: 51) argues that social actors should not be seen as completely overpowered by institutional dominance; institutions are presented to have a transformative capacity and a potential for both domination and emancipation; this is proposed to be embedded in the everyday practices of organizational life. According to Foucault (1980), power is a form of action or relation between people, which is negotiated in interaction and, as such, it is never fixed or stable. Indeed, power has been proposed to be located in different kinds of strategies.

Foucault has been criticized for his failure to provide an analysis of the agents, and social relations through which power, knowledge, and discourse emerge as regulative devices. However, the idea of power as enacted within relationships and, thus, as something which can be contested at every moment in every interaction has been taken up in analyses of interactions within ESL communities (Norton, 2000) as well as within various institutions (see Mayr, 2004). Critical Discourse Analysis sets out to illustrate how discourses produce and maintain relations of power, domination, and inequality, assumed to be 'natural' by speakers. Working on gender within a Feminist Post Structuralist Discourse Analysis, Baxter (2003: 8) defines power 'as a "net-line organization" which weaves itself discursively through social organizations, meanings, relations and the construction of speakers' subjectivities or identities'. In line with Blackledge (2005), I propose a view of empowerment as arising out of the way meanings shift and change as they are recontextualized (i.e., taken from one context to get constructed anew in another [see Silverstein and Urban, 1996]) in local communities.

In capturing the way this recontextualization process is constructed through writing acts and processes in educational contexts, let me outline the wider picture. Among the issues that need to be addressed, as of theoretical and methodological significance, the following may be included. Theoretical ones: How do students' writing practices index ideological positions? How do texts enact 'power' and/or contribute to constructing power relations? How can we integrate notions such as empowerment and identities (drawn from social theory) with the textual analysis of texts? How is writing used to effect social change? How do, through the genres local actors use, positionings are claimed, identities are negotiated and asserted? How can standard, stage-like accounts of 'writing development' be reinterpreted in a social practice framework to help us account for the dynamic processes of identity formation? Methodological ones: What is the power of the researcher (usually an outsider of a community) to unveil the political underpinnings of any text and/or any writing activity and identify writer identities? How can one diminish the authorial voice suggesting a specific reading on the workings of a specific community (i.e., of a specific social reality, Gergen, 1999)? How can one gain access to the hidden resources and acts of silencing that carry significant, community-inscribed ideological meanings?

WRITING AS SOCIAL PRACTICE: AGENCY, RECONTEXTUALIZATIONS, AND POWER DYNAMICS

Outlining 'mainstream' sociocultural research

Before delineating the way Critical Analysis of Writing Practices addresses some of these issues, it is important that I note this: any work that builds upon and explores the view of writing as social practice represents a paradigm shift from 'mainstream' sociocultural, Vygotskian-informed research, which basically subscribes to a view of writing as social action (for recent reviews see Englert et al., 2006; Prior, 2006). In general, this research is constituted of three distinct strands. The first one is classroom-based, focusing on the strategies teachers or certain peers (taken a priori as experts) use to scaffold new meanings within a learning community of novices (Hogan and Pressley, 1997; Mercer, 1995; Mercer and Littleton, 2007; Rojas-Drummond, 2003; Sharpe, 2006). This research basically focuses on one component taken out of the rich and highly complex – as well as deeply political – bidirectional processes involving the negotiation of different meanings (but see Gibbons, 2003 on this), divergent understandings and the projection of new identities. The second line of work is a product-based one; it attends to the appropriation of school genres as indexed in and through the register choices and macrostructural patterns used by children of different age and social groups in their written texts (Donovan and Smolkin, 2002; Kamberelis, 1999). Situated between these two is the third, more dynamic research strand; this traces the way oral interactions and various mediational tools (such as diagrams of text structures) shape students' writing processes (for a review on school processes see Englert et al., 2006 and for academic as well, Prior, 2006). Different arguments have been outlined, moving away from earlier and more static work on orality *versus* literacy, seen as binary constructs (Chafe, 1982; Tannen, 1982), to trace their interdependence (Horowitz, 2007; Poole, 2003). More interesting findings are attested by recent research conducted mainly with regard to the appropriation of science literacies (Crawford, 2004; Haneda, 2000; Kelly and Chen, 1999); this work basically suggests that the paths from oral classroom discourses to students' written texts are not linear but fragmented and circular (see also Prior, 1998 on academic literacies). While this fragmentation has been reported on school literacies, it has not been adequately accounted for.

Consider an interesting case. In their analysis of the texts written in a high school physics class, Kelly and Chen (1999) documented limited appropriation of scientific discourse; this was attributed to gaps in instructional processes. Indeed, suggestions were made for the need of explicit instruction on the norms of scientific discourse (i.e., examination of what counts as an 'empirical claim', a 'theoretical assertion', or a 'consistent argument'). However, working on summary writing in academic contexts, Macbeth (2006) attests similar difficulties, though the solution proposed is different. Macbeth suggests that notions such as 'summary' or 'empirical claim' are highly indexical and, as such, they cannot be adequately understood unless seen as part of students' active and repeated engagement with tasks. How can these findings be accounted for? A different line of more pedagogically oriented research suggests that new pedagogies – such as project work (Moje et al., 2001) or inquiry units (Haneda and Wells, 2000; Wells and Chang-Wells, 1992; Wells and Claxton, 2002) may facilitate students' appropriation of school genres. However, Moje et al. (2001) suggested, as a result of their work with a project-based pedagogy, that critical pedagogies may, in fact, exclude marginalized groups from appropriating school-valued discourses. This is due to the unique demands they place upon students by virtue of the disciplinary, interactional, and instructional classroom Discourses project pedagogies promote. They cite Delpit, who argues that many students from nonmainstream backgrounds come to school expecting and even needing interactions that centre on the authoritative role of the teacher; as a result, project-based pedagogy – with its emphasis on inquiry and collaboration – introduces a Discourse (i.e., a stance toward knowledge and meaning making) that is unfamiliar to those children (Moje et al., 2001: 472). As suggested below, to be helpful, analyses of local processes need to inquire into how

these index wider social issues or Discourses (see also Moje, 1997).

GENRES, IDENTITIES, AND EMPOWERMENT: EVIDENCE FROM A GREEK CLASSROOM

In delineating the way specific kinds of literate identities emerge and power relations are established, in my research, I combine the analysis of situated practices in Greek elementary classrooms with the political goal of radically revising the texture of daily classroom life. Working with a group of teachers, the goal has been to revise the static view of writing they operated with, created through monologic patterns of interaction. In the new curriculum designed and implemented collaboratively, writing is seen as a tool for negotiating social meanings, for constructing identities, and new ways of communicating with the world – ways that foster dialogue (see, Linell, 1998) with the multiplicity of meanings proposed by all participants (for a similar point with regard to monologism and dialogism in American classrooms, see Nystrand et al., 1997).

The data (a videotaped series of thematic units) were taken at various intervals from the classrooms. From one sixth-grade classroom (referred to as the focal classroom), data were obtained from the first day of school in September to the last day in mid-June. Some data were also taken from the previous year, when those children were attending the fifth grade and worked with the same teacher. Moving away from the notion of classrooms as bounded units (see Maybin, 2006, 2007; Street, 2005a), attention is directed to the way classrooms communicate with social life. To accomplish this goal, thematic or inquiry units were constructed so that children come in contact with various communities and critically engage with their meanings and resources (see also Comber and Simpson, 2001). Figure 6.1 presents a limited intertextual universe, two units

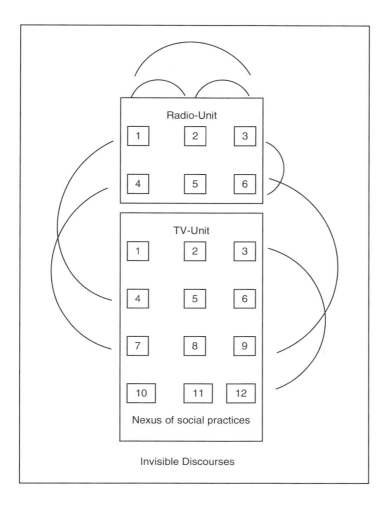

Figure 6.1   Genre sets/nexuses of social practices and Discourses in a classroom community.

constructed around two themes, radio and TV, selected by the children. During these units, children visited the local radio station to present their problems (limited yard space, sports facilities, etc.) by reading texts they had prepared in groups. The interaction with the journalists was broadcast, creating live response from the city mayor and citizens. The next day writing conferences were constructed, with children discussing the social effects of their texts. These conferences diverge significantly from the ones usually constructed in process and genre-pedagogies (see Johns, 2002). A further illustration might

be pertinent. In the reflection they engaged in, some children expressed their disappointment with the way they were treated by the journalists, who asked them 'meaningless' questions. This discussion is an important part of the trajectory toward the new literate identity of critical actors teachers and students negotiated in this classroom; children, thus, reflected upon a discursive practice (interview with the journalists) and captured the identities of 'small kids' projected to them by the journalists; for this group of children, journalists, with their questioning style, rejected the identities the children wished to project, as 'active members of their community' engaging in important projects. Given this critical perspective, how is writing to be defined? How is writing development and learning to be conceptualized? Before addressing this issue, certain preliminaries are necessary on the research methodology employed.

From describing to coconstructing a universe of writing practices. Building on the premise that the use of any research methodology is not a neutral choice but rather 'reveals the researcher's view of "knowledge"' (Gergen and Gergen, 1999: 61), in this project, the researcher and the researched are seen as collaborators in the coconstruction of local meanings. Challenging the positivist view, I begin with the premise that there does not exist an objective world that can be described by researchers through experimental methods. I acknowledge, in line with postconstructionist approaches, that social realities are constructed through language. Knowledge is seen as constructed through discourse; it is seen as contextual, localized, and perspectival, rather than as universal (see also Canagarajah, 2005). In light of this, then, I do not propose that ideological meanings exist out there in the community and can be read off texts. I attend to how a locally constructed textual universe reinscribes various kinds of ideological meanings: it is not through specific discourse acts and other semiotic practices that ideologies are formulated; these are reproduced and reinforced through textual universes. The aim, therefore, is to unveil the way textual patterns and ways of communicating (including patterns of silence or not participation) work to make certain meanings (over others) within local communities. This methodology provides space for the coexistence and juxtaposition of many different accounts; participants' voices are acknowledged, since these are seen as the versions of 'social realities' participants themselves construct. The implications of these to writing, text production, and development are summarized in the following section.

First: Within this universe, written texts and genres are not seen as arising out of static templates; these are seen as shaped out of a universe of meanings negotiated (see also Prior, 1998, 2005). Building upon Silverstein and Urban's (1996) notion of 'the natural histories of discourse', I suggest that to capture text production we need to attend to how different kinds of semiotic resources are used, how meanings are projected, how they are taken up from one unit and get negotiated in the next one(s). Each unit – once completed – functions as a context that proposes a set of resources that can be recontextualized for the construction of any new one. Meanings are, thus, not transferred; they get recontextualized (see also Kostouli, 2006). This notion (presented through the arc lines between units in Figure 6.1) captures the changes meanings undergo as they are used for different purposes within each universe of social practices.

Secondly: On Discourses, local units and empowerment, the following can be proposed. Figure 6.1 presents a series of numbered units; each captures a day's textual work. Each unit consists of lower- level activities or social practices, within which participants engaged, among others, in reading different kinds of texts on these topics (from narrative to multimodal informational to argumentative texts) and engaged in various kinds of writing activities, such as taking notes, creating questionnaires, planning the content to be included in their texts, inscription (i.e., producing texts), and revising these texts in groups and/or in whole-class writing conferences. Planning and revising, thus, rather than seen as mental processes only, are revisited as socially displayed and collaborative acts. It should be added, however, that the new curriculum participants wished to implement presented them with new requirements for assessing the 'effectiveness' or 'quality' or 'success' of their texts as well as the meaning of their reading and writing practices (for similar lines along this, see Bloome et al., 2005). Alternatively, the meaning of the activities constructed – and of the literate identities projected – had to be negotiated against a new Discourse. Analyses revealed, however, that the textual universe created was, in fact, a hybrid one, containing meanings from two Discourses, the traditional, skills-based one and the new one.

To unveil the construction of power and empowerment, the questions asked are these: If meanings move from one unit to the next and may combine different Discourses, what is the direction of this shift? Toward asserting authoritativeness or not (see on this, Kostouli, 2007)? Which Discourse and whose voice is foregrounded out of this process? Who gets silenced and by which (direct or indirect) processes? Used in classroom discourse, Bakhtin's notion of polyphony implies that at any unit, many voices, from different ideological points and Discourses, may appear in the texts and interactive units constructed. The notion of polyphony, however, does not entail that equal space is provided to all discourses.

The implications of this proposal to text construction and writing development cannot, apparently, be outlined in the limited space of this chapter. It can be noted, however, that writing is revisited as one among the means or tools local agents use – both teacher and students – within their communities to negotiate and redefine their positionings not just against one another but vis-à-vis dominant discourses; as attested (Kostouli, 2006, 2007), through the writing acts taken, and the kinds of activities they engaged in as well as through the texts constructed, local actors are repositioned; they learn a way of asserting their voice and exercising their agency. Writing is thus used for negotiating the multiple discourses competing for 'envoicing' (Prior, 2001) within the discursive space of local communities.

How can we account for writing development? Building upon a rather static view of text as a bounded notion – a construct that has prevailed in Discourse Analysis – most work on writing development in school contexts (within an experimental perspective) tends to corroborate a stage-like individual progression to 'better', 'more complex' texts; this needs to be revisited. The data analyzed thus far seem to propose a different approach to writing development; this is seen as reflecting the position – which may be temporary – constructed by a student vis-à-vis the discourses brought in and projected by the teacher and the other students; the linguistic forms and the text patterns need to be seen as the means by which this student negotiates his/her agency against these discourses with the aim to affirm or modify them.

CONCLUSIONS

This study set out to outline the basic premises constituting a new approach to writing and school writing in particular, which is seen as part of a social practice. Revisiting schools and classroom communities away from earlier notions stressing fixity, writing is proposed to arise out of the complex interplay between local and global resources. As suggested, accounts of text production and indeed of writing development need to move away from proposals stressing their nature as individual accomplishments to attend their dialogic emergence. Further research from different cultural contexts is needed to enrich our understandings of the factors shaping this process: how meanings get negotiated, how genres emerge in local communities out of different design patterns (New London Group, 2000), how, through teaching acts, certain identity positions are projected and get recontextualized in the social practices constructed. In this approach, classroom interaction is revisited as a polycontextual structure (in Leander's [2002a,b] terms; see also Stroud and Wee, 2007) created out of multiple interacting contexts (consisting of written texts, whole-classroom settings, and peer-group settings). What are the implications of this perspective to classroom-shaped processes of literacy learning? Further theoretical work needs to be undertaken, addressing in detail the way the framework outlined in this chapter relates to Vygotskian work used to inform educational practices (see Daniels, 2001; Kozulin et al., 2003; Moll, 1990) and to Cultural Historical Activity Theory (CHAT); while drawing upon some similar notions, CHAT has been used principally in academic contexts and workplaces (but see Wells and Claxton, 2002) to account for novices' ways of exercising their agency as they get socialized into the constraints of new communities.

A further issue is how this framework on writing may be used to inform teacher practice. The way sociocultural research may be used for teacher education has been addressed (see Hawkins, 2004). Critical Analysis of Writing Practices foregrounds the need for teachers to develop a critical stance toward their own processes; teaching and learning processes have been presented as deeply political processes. These have been described as the means through which a local culture of certain meanings (rather than others) is constituted. Attention should, therefore, shift away from simply presenting teachers with a list of strategies assumed to work as devices scaffolding students' appropriation of school literacies. Attention needs to be directed toward helping them unveil the political implications of their choices, from their local teaching strategies to the kinds of activities implemented. The issue is not whether this kind of questioning or the other should be used; rather, work should focus on how, through this kind of questioning, I, as a teacher, privilege certain voices over others and exclude some children from the meaning-making process. Furthermore, the work on the Greek context, though succinctly presented, gives us insights into the way educational changes should be seen; while such changes are proposed to take place once new curricula and new syllabuses are introduced, as found, change has to be interactively coconstructed over a long process. Research should, therefore, shift away from policies as top-down structures to revisit policies 'as a discourse that develops over time' (see Walford, 2003: 3).

An important line of research concerns the interplay between school and out-of-school literacies (Alvermann, 2005; Hull and Schultz, 2001, 2002 on the American context; Myhill, 2005 on British school context) and the use of new and digital literacies (Lankshear and Knobel, 2003). It is well known that out-of-school literacies may not be always validated in school contexts (see Mahiri, 2004). It is worth investigating how this interplay redefines not just school writing processes but our theoretical accounts of what learning is. It is important that we inquire more into the discourses children draw in to enact resistance to school-projected identities and meanings. If power implies resistance, as Weber and Foucault have suggested, we should also consider more carefully the discourses certain teachers operate with; these, though intended to empower students, may actually work to disempower them. An analysis of the linguistic and textual strategies of resistance is important for our understanding of the way power relations are coconstructed in society and education. Finally, in the period we live and in which 'historical boundaries are blurred by the constant borrowing and rehashing of cultural artefacts (Miles, 2001: 87), we need to inquire into the role of schooling and the changes that need to be introduced so that we help children develop creative new ways for not just reproducing given meanings but for responding to unknown 'new' demands.

REFERENCES

Allal, L., Mottier, Lopez, L., Lehraus, K., and Forget, A. (2005) 'Whole-class interaction in an activity of writing and revision', in T. Kostouli (ed.), *Writing in Context(s): Textual Practices and Learning Processes in Sociocultural Settings*, Boston: Springer. pp.69–91.

Alvermann, D.E. (ed.) (2005) *Adolescents and Literacies in a Digital World*, New York: Peter Lang.

Anagnostopoulos, D. (2003) 'Testing and student engagement with literature in urban classrooms: A multi-layered perspective', *Research in the Teaching of English*, 38(2): 136–212.

Bakhtin, M.M. (1981) *The Dialogic Imagination*, Tr. C. Emerson and M. Holquist (eds), Austin: University of Texas Press.

Bakhtin, M.M. (1986) *Speech Genres and Other Late Essays*, Tr. V.W. McGee, C. Emerson, and M. Holquist (eds), Austin: University of Austin Press.

Baxter, J. (2003) *Positioning Gender in Discourse*, Basingstoke: Palgrave Macmillan.

Bazerman, C. (1988) *Shaping Written Knowledge: The Genre and Activity of the Experimental Article in Science*, Madison, WI: Wisconsin University Press.

Bazerman, C. (1994) 'Systems of genre and the enactment of social intentions', in A. Freedman and P. Medway (eds), *Rethinking Genre*, Madison: University of Wisconsin Press. pp.79–101.

Benwell, B. and Stokoe, E. (2006) *Discourse and Identity*, Edinburgh: Edinburgh University Press.

Berkenkotter, C. and Huckin, T.N. (1995) *Genre Knowledge in Disciplinary Communication*, Hillsdale, NJ: Lawrence Erlbaum Associates.

Blackledge, A. (2005) *Discourse and Power in a Multilingual World*, Amsterdam: John Benjamins.

Blommaert, Jan (2005) *Discourse: A Critical Introduction*, Cambridge: CUP.

Bloome, D., Carter, St.P., Otto, Sh., and Shuart-Faris, N. (eds) (2005) *Discourse Analysis and the Study of Classroom Language and Literacy Events – A Microethnographic Perspective*, Mahwah, NJ: Lawrence Erlbaum Associates

Boden, D. and Zimmerman, D.H. (eds) (1991) Talk and Social Structure: Studies in Ethnomethodology and Conversation Analysis, Cambridge: Polity Press.

Bourdieu, P. (1977) *Outline of a Theory of Practice*, Cambridge: Cambridge University Press.

Bourne, J. (2002) *'Oh, what will Miss say!' Constructing texts and identities in the discursive processes of school writing', Language and Education*, 16(4): 241–259

Brown, G. and Yule, G. (1983) Discourse Analysis, Cambridge: Cambridge University Press.

Canagarajah, A.S. (2004) 'Multilingual writers and the struggle for voice in academic discourse', in A. Pavlenko and A. Blackledge (eds), *Negotiation of Identities in Multilingual Contexts*, Clevedon: Multilingual Matters. pp.266–289.

Canagarajah, A.S. (2005) *Reclaiming the Local in Language Policy and Practice*, Mahwah, NJ: Lawrence Erlbaum Associates.

Chafe, W. (1982) 'Integration, and involvement in speaking, writing and oral literature', in D. Tannen (ed.), *Spoken and Written Language: Exploring orality and literacy*, Norwood, NJ: Ablex. pp.35–54.

Chouliaraki, L. and Fairclough, N. (1999) *Discourse in Late Modernity: Rethinking critical discourse analysis*, Edinburgh: Edinburgh University Press.

Christie, F. (2002) *Classroom Discourse Analysis: A functional perspective*, London: Continuum.

Comber, B. and Simpson, A. (eds) (2001) *Negotiating Critical Literacies in Classrooms*, Mahwah, NJ: Lawrence Erlbaum Associates.

Coupland, N., Sarangi, Sr., and Candlin, Ch. N. (2001) *Sociolinguistics and Social Theory*, Harlow, England: Pearson.

Crawford, T. (2004) 'What counts as knowing: Constructing a communicative repertoire for student demonstration of knowledge in science', *Journal of Research in Science Teaching*, 42(2): 139–165.

Daniels, H. (2001) *Vygotsky and Pedagogy*, London: RoutledgeFalmer.

Davies, B, and Harré, R. (1990) 'Positioning: The discursive production of selves', *Journal for the Theory of Social Behaviour*, 20: 43–63.

De Fina, A., Schifrin, D., and Bamberg, M. (eds) (2006) *Discourse and Identity*, Cambridge: Cambridge University Press.

Donovan, C.A. and Smolkin, L.B. (2002) 'Children's genre knowledge: An examination of K-5 students' performance on multiple tasks providing differing levels of scaffolding', *Reading Research Quarterly*, 37(4): 428–465.

Duranti, A. and Goodwin, C. (eds) (1992) *Rethinking Context: Language as an Interactive Phenomenon*, Cambridge: Cambridge University Press.

Dyson, A.H. (1993) *Social Worlds of Children Learning to Write in an Urban Primary School*, New York: Teachers College, Columbia University.

Dyson, A.H. (1999) 'Coach Bombay's kids learn to write: Children's appropriation of media material for school literacy', *Research in the Teaching of English*, 33, 367–402.

Dyson, A.H. (2002) 'Writing and children's symbolic repertoires: Development unhinged', in S.B. Neuman, and D.K. Dickinson (eds), *Handbook of Early Literacy Research*, New York: The Guilford Press. pp.126–141.

Englert, C.S., Mariage, T.V., and Dunsmore, K. (2006) 'Tenets of sociocultural theory in writing instruction research', in C.A. MacArthur, S. Graham, and J. Fitzgerald (eds), *Handbook of Writing Research*, New York: Guilford. pp.208–221.

Erickson, F. (2004) *Talk and Social Theory: Ecologies of Speaking and Listening in Everyday Life*, Cambridge: Polity.

Fairclough, N. (1989) *Language and Power*, London: Longman.

Fairclough, N. (1995) *Critical Discourse Analysis: The Critical Study of Discourse*, London: Longman.

Fairclough, N. (2003) *Analyzing Discourse: Textual Analysis for Social Research*, London: Routledge.

Fairclough, N. (2004) 'Semiotic aspects of social transformation and learning' in R. Rogers (ed.) *An Introduction to Critical Discourse Analysis in Education*, Mahwah, NJ: Lawrence Erlbaum Associates. pp.225–235.

Fairclough, N. (2006) 'Semiosis, ideology and mediation: A dialectical view', in I. Lassen, J. Strunk, and T. Vestergaard (eds), *Mediating Ideology in Text and Image*, London: Routledge. pp.19–35.

Farrell, L. (2006) *Making Knowledge Common: Literacy and Knowledge at Work*, New York: Peter Lang.

Flowerdew, J. (2000) 'Discourse community, legitimate peripheral participation, and the nonnative-English-speaking scholar', *TESOL Quarterly*, 34(1): 127–150.

Foster, D., and Russell, D.R. (eds) (2002) *Writing and Learning in Cross-National Perspective: Transitions from Secondary to Higher Education*, Mahwah, NJ: NCTE and LEA.

Foucault, M. (1972) *The Archeology of Knowledge*, London: Tavistock.

Foucault, M. (1980) 'The eye of power', in C. Gordon (ed.) *Power/Knowledge: Selected interviews and other writings 1972–1977*, New York: Pantheon. pp.146–165.

Freadman, A. (1994) 'Anyone for tennis?' in A. Freedman and P. Medway (eds), *Genre and the New Rhetoric*, London: Taylor & Francis. pp.43–66.

Freedman, S.W. and Delp, V.K. (2007) 'Conceptualizing a whole-class learning space: A grand dialogic zone', *Research in the Teaching of English*, 41(3): 259–268.

Gee, J.P. (1996) *Social Linguistics and Literacies: Ideology in Discourses* (second edn.), New York: Falmer Press.

Gee, J.P. (2004) *Situated Language and Learning: A Critique of Traditional Schooling*, New York: Routledge.

Gee, J.P. and Clinton, K. (2000) 'An African American child's science talk: Co-construction of meaning from the perspectives of multiple discourses', in M.A. Gallego and S. Hollingsworth (eds), *What Counts as Literacy: Challenging the school standard*, New York: Teachers College. pp.118–135.

Gergen, K.J. (1999) *An Invitation to Social Construction*, London: Sage.

Gergen, M. and Gergen, K.J. (eds) (1999) *Social Construction: A Reader*, London: Sage.

Gibbons, P. (2003) 'Mediating language learning: Teacher interactions with ESL students in a content-based classroom', *TESOL Quarterly*, 37(2): 247–273.

Giddens, A. (1981) *A Contemporary Critique of Historical Materialism (Vol. 1)*, London: Macmillan.

Giddens, A. (1984) *The Constitution of Society: Outline of the Theory of Structuration*, Cambridge: Polity Press.

Gunnarsson, B-L., Linell, P., and Nordberg, B. (eds) (1997) *Professional Discourse*, London: Addison Wesley Longman.

Gutierrez, K.D. (1994) 'How talk, context, and script shape contexts for learning: A cross-case comparison of journal sharing', *Linguistics and Education*, 5: 335–365.

Gutierrez, K.D. and Stone, L.D. (2000) 'Synchronic and diachronic dimensions of social practice: An emerging methodology for cultural-historical perspectives on literacy learning', in C.D. Lee and P. Smagorinsky (eds), *Vygotskian Perspectives on Literacy Research: Constructing meaning through collaborative inquiry*, Cambridge: Cambridge University Press. pp.150–164.

Gutierrez, K.D., Rymes, B., and Larson, J. (1995) 'Script, counterscript, and underlife in classrooms: James Brown vs. Brown vs. Board of Education', *Harvard Educational Review*, 12: 123–131.

Hall, J.K. and Verplaetse, L.St. (eds) (2000) *Second and Foreign Language Learning through Classroom Interaction*, Mahwah, NJ: Lawrence Erlbaum Associates.

Haneda, M. (2000) 'Modes of student participation in an elementary school science classroom: From talking to writing', *Linguistics and Education*, 10(4): 459–485.

Haneda, M. and Wells, G. (2000) 'Writing in knowledge-building communities', *Research in the Teaching of English*, 43: 430–457.

Hanks, W.F. (1996) *Language and Communicative Practices*, Boulder, CO: Westview Press.

Hawkins, M.R. (ed.) (2004) *Language Learning and Teacher Education: A Sociocultural Approach*, Clevedon: Multilingual Matters Ltd.

Heller, M. and Martin-Jones, M. (eds) (2001) *Voices of Authority: Education and linguistic difference*, Westport, CN: Ablex.

Hicks, D. (1996) *Discourse, Learning, and Schooling*, Cambridge: CUP.

Hogan, K. and Pressley, M. (1997) *Scaffolding Student Learning: Instructional approaches and issues*, Cambridge, MA: Brookline Books.

Hopper, R. (1995) 'Episode trajectory in conversational play', in P. Ten Have and G. Psathas (eds), *Situated*

Order: Studies in the social organization of talk and embodied activities, Boston: University Press of America, Inc. pp.57–71.

Horowitz, R. (ed.) (2007) *Talking Texts: How Speech and Writing Interact in School Learning*, Mahwah, NJ: Lawrence Erlbaum Associates.

Hruska, B.L. (2004) 'Constructing gender in an English dominant kindergarten: Implications for second language learners', *TESOL Quarterly*, 38(3): 459–485.

Hull, G. and Schultz, K. (2001) 'Literacy and Learning Out of School: A Review of Theory and Research', *Review of Educational Research*, 71(4): 575–611.

Hull, G. and Schultz, K. (eds) (2002) 'Schools out!: Bringing Out-of-School Literacies with Classroom Practice'. New York: Teachers College Press.

Ivanič, R. (1998) *Writing and Identity: The Discoursal Representation of Identity in Academic Writing*, Amsterdam: John Benjamins.

Johns, A. (ed.) (2002) *Genre in the Classroom: Multiple Perspectives*, Mahwah, NJ: Lawrence Erlbaum Associates.

Kamberelis, G. (1999) 'Genre development and learning: Children writing stories, science reports and poems', *Research in the Teaching of English*, 33: 403–460.

Kamberelis, G. (2001) 'Producing heteroglossic classroom (micro)cultures through hybrid discourse practice', *Linguistics and Education*, 12: 85–125.

Kelly, G.J. and Chen, C. (1999) 'The sound of music: Constructing science as sociocultural practices through oral and written discourse', *Journal of Research in Science Teaching*, 36(8): 883–915.

King, A. (2005) 'Structure and Agency', in A. Harrington (ed.), *Modern Social Theory: An Introduction*, Oxford: Oxford University Press. pp.215–232.

Knobel, M. (1999) *Everyday Literacies: Students, Discourse and Social Practice*, New York: Peter Lang.

Kostouli, T. (2005a) 'Introduction: Making social meanings in contexts', in T. Kostouli (ed.), *Writing in Context(s): Textual practices and learning processes in sociocultural settings*, Boston: Springer. pp.1–26.

Kostouli, T. (2005b) 'Co-constructing writing contexts in classrooms: Scaffolding, collaboration, and asymmetries of knowledge', in T. Kostouli (ed.) *Writing in Context(s): Textual practices and learning processes in sociocultural settings*, Boston: Springer. pp.93–116.

Kostouli, T. (2006) 'The role of intercontextuality in the co-construction of genre meanings: Evidence from Greek classrooms', paper presented at the Joint AAAL and ACLA/CAAL Conference of Applied Linguistics, Montreal, Canada.

Kostouli, T. (2007) 'Principles of "effective" teaching and learning in literacy classrooms: A multi-layered approach to dialogic discourse', paper presented at the 6th IAIMTE conference, Exeter, England.

Kozulin, A., Gindis, B. Ageyev, V.S., and Miller, S.M. (eds) (2003) *Vygotsky's Educational Theory in Cultural Context*, Cambridge: CUP.

Kress, G., Jewitt, C., Bourne, J., Franks, A., Hardcastle, J., Jones, K., and Reid, E. (2005) *English in Urban Classrooms: A Multimodal Perspective on Teaching and Learning*, London: RoutledgeFalmer.

Kress, G., Jewitt, C., Ogborn, J., and Tsatsarelis, Ch. (2001) *Multimodal Teaching and Learning: The Rhetorics of the Science Classroom*, London: Continuum.

Lam, W.S.E. (2004) 'Border Discourses and Identities in Transnational Youth Culture', in J. Mahiri (ed.) *What They Don't Learn at School: Literacy in the lives of urban youth*, New York: Peter Lang. pp.79–97.

Lankshear, C. and Knobel, M. (2003) *New Literacies: Changing Knowledge and Classroom Learning*, Buckingham: Open University Press.

Lantolf, J.P. (ed.) (2000) *Sociocultural Theory and Second Language Learning*, New York: Oxford University Press.

Larson, J. and Marsh, J. (eds) (2005) *Making Literacy Real: Theories and Practices for Learning and Teaching*, London: Sage.

Lave, J. and Wenger, E. (1991) *Situated Learning. Legitimate Peripheral Participation*, New York: Cambridge University Press.

Leander, K. M. (2002a) 'Polycontextual construction zones: Mapping the expansion of school space and identity', *Mind, Culture and Activity*, 9(3): 211–237.

Leander, K.M. (2002b) 'Locating Latanya: The situated production of identity artifacts in classroom interaction', *Research in the Teaching of English*, 37(2): 198–250.

Lemke, J. L. (1995) *Textual Politics: Discourse and Social Dynamics*, London: Taylor and Francis.

Lewis, C. (2001) *Literacy Practices as Social Acts: Power, Status and Cultural Norms in the Classroom*, Mahwah, NJ: Lawrence Erlbaum Associates.

Lewis, C., Enciso, P., and Moje E.B. (eds) (2007) *Reframing Sociocultural research on Literacy: Identity, agency and power*, Mahwah, NJ: Lawrence Erlbaum Associates.

Lillis, T.M. (2001) *Student Writing: Access, Regulation, Desire*, London: Routledge.

Linell, P. (1998) *Approaching Dialogue: Talk, interaction and contexts in dialogical perspectives*, Amsterdam/Philadelphia: Benjamins.

Litosseliti, L. and Sunderland, J. (eds) (2002) *Gender Identity and Discourse Analysis*, Amsterdam: John Benjamins.

Macbeth, K.P. (2006) 'Diverse, unforeseen, and quaint difficulties: The sensible responses of novices learning to follow instructions in academic writing', *Research in the Teaching of Writing*, 41(2): 180–207.

Mahiri, J. (ed.) (2004) *What They Don't Learn at School: Literacy in the Lives of Urban Youth*, New York: Peter Lang.

Mariage, T.V. (2000) 'Constructing educational possibilities: A sociolinguistic examination of meaning-making in "sharing chair"', *Learning Disability Quarterly*, 23(2): 79–103.

Maybin, J. (2006) Children's Voices: Talk, Knowledge and Identity. Basingstoke: Palgrave Macmillan.

Maybin, J. (2007) 'Literacy under and over the desk: Oppositions and heterogeneity', *Language and Education*, 21(6): 515–530.

Mayr, A. (2004) *Prison Discourse: Language as a Means of Control and Resistance*, Basingstoke: Palgrave Macmillan.

McCarthey, S.J. (2002) *Students' Identities and Literacy Learning*, Newark: International Reading Association.

McCarthey, S.J. and Moje, E.B. (2002) 'Identity matters', *Reading Research Quarterly*, 37(2): 228–238.

Mercer, N. (1995) *The Guided Construction of Knowledge*, Multilingual Matters: Clevedon.

Mercer, N. and K. Littleton (2007) *Dialogue and the Development of Children's Thinking: A sociocultural perspective*, London: Routledge.

Miles, St. (2001) *Social Theory in the Real World*, London: Sage.

Moje, E.B. (1997) 'Exploring discourse, subjectivity, and knowledge in chemistry class', *Journal of Classroom Interaction*, 32: 35–44.

Moje, E.B., Collazzo, T., Carrillo, R., and Marx, R.W. (2001) 'Maestro, what is "Quality"? Language, literacy and discourse in project-based science', *Journal of Research in Science Teaching*, 38 (4): 469–498.

Moll, L.C. (ed.) (1990) *Vygotsky and Education: Instructional Implications and Applications of Socio-Historical Psychology*, Cambridge: Cambridge University Press.

Morita, N. (2004) 'Negotiating participation and identity in second language academic communities', *TESOL Quarterly*, 38(4): 573–603.

Myhill, D. (2005) 'Prior knowledge and the (re)production of school written genres: An analysis of British children's meaning-making resources', in T. Kostouli (ed.), *Writing in Context(s): Textual practices and*

learning processes in sociocultural settings, Boston: Springer. pp.117–136.

New London Group (2000) 'A pedagogy of multiliteracies: Designing social futures', in B. Cope and M. Kalantzis (eds), *Multiliteracies: Literacy Learning and the Design of Social Futures*, New York: Routledge. pp.9–37.

Norris, S. and R.H. Jones (eds) (2005) *Discourse in Action: Introducing Mediated Discourse Analysis*, London: Routledge.

Norton, B. (2000) *Identity and Language Learning: Gender, Ethnicity, and Educational Change*, London: Longman /Pearson Education.

Nystrand, M., Gamoran, A., Kachur, R., and Prendergast, K. (1997) Opening Dialogue: Understanding the Dynamics of Language and Learning in the English Classroom, New York/London: Teachers College Press.

O'Connor, K. (2003) 'Communicative practice, cultural production, and situated learning', in St. Wortham and B. Rymes (eds.), *Linguistic Anthropology of Education*, Westport, CT: Praeger. pp.61–91.

Pahl, K. and Rowsell, J. (eds) (2006) *Travel Notes from the New Literacy Studies: Instances of Practice*, Clevedon: Multilingual Matters.

Pappas, C.C., Varelas, M. Barray, A., and Rife, A. (2004) 'Dialogic inquiry around information text: The role of intertextuality in constructing scientific understandings in urban primary classrooms', in N. Shuart-Farris and D. Bloome (eds), *Uses of Intertextuality in Classroom and Educational Research*, Greenwich: Information Age Publishing. pp.93–145.

Poole, D. (2003) 'Linguistic connections between co-occurring speech and writing in a classroom literacy event', *Discourse Processes*, 35(2): 103–134.

Prior, P. (1998) *Writing Disciplinarity: A Sociohistoric Account of Literate Activity in the Academy*, Mahwah, NJ: Lawrence Erlbaum Associates.

Prior, P. (2001) 'Voices in text, mind, and society: Sociohistoric accounts of discourse acquisition and use', *Journal of Second Language Writing*, 10(1–2): 55–81.

Prior, P. (2004) 'Tracing process: How texts come into being', in Ch. Bazerman, and P. Prior (eds) *What Writing Does and How it Does It: An introduction to analyzing texts and textual practices*, Mahwah, NJ: Lawrence Erlbaum Associates. pp.167–200.

Prior, P. (2005) 'Toward the ethnography of communication: A response to Richard Andrews' "Models of argumentation in educational discourse"', *Text*, 25(1): 129–144.

Prior, P. (2006) 'A sociocultural theory of writing', in C.A. MacArthur, S. Graham, and J. Fitzgerald (eds),

Handbook of Writing Research, New York: Guilford. pp.54–66.

Ranker, J. (2007) 'Designing meaning with multiple media sources: A case study of an eight-year old student's writing process', *Research in the Teaching of English*, 41(4): 402–434.

Rex, L.A. (ed.) (2006) *Discourse of Opportunity: How talk in Learning Situations Creates and Constrains*, Cresskill, NJ: Hampton Press.

Rogers, R. (2003) *A Critical Discourse Analysis of Family Literacy Practices: Power in and out of Print*, Mahwah, NJ: Lawrence Erlbaum Associates.

Rogers, R. (ed.) (2004) *An Introduction to Critical Discourse Analysis in Education*, Mahwah, NJ: Lawrence Erlbaum Associates.

Rogers, R., Malancharuvil-Berkes, E., Mosley, M., Hui, D., and O'Garro Joseph, Gl. (2005) 'Critical Discourse Analysis in Education: A review of the literature', *Review of Educational Research*, 75(3): 365–416.

Rogoff, B. (1990) *Apprenticeship in Thinking: Cognitive Development in Social Context*, New York: Oxford University Press.

Rojas-Drummond, S. (2003) 'Guided participation, discourse and the construction of knowledge in Mexican classrooms', in S. Goodman, T. Lillis, J. Maybin, and N. Mercer (eds), *Language, Literacy and Education: A Reader*, Stoke on Trent: Trentham Books. pp.35–54.

Roth, W.M., Hwang, S.W., Coulart, M.I.M., and Lee, Y.J. (2005) *Participation, Learning, and Identity: Dialectical perspectives*, Berlin: Lehmanns Media.

Royce, T.D. and Bowcher, W. (eds) (2007) *New Directions in the Analysis of Multimodal Discourse*, Mahwah, NJ: Lawrence Erlbaum Associates.

Santa Barbara Classroom Discourse Group (1992) 'Constructing literacy in classrooms: Literate action as social accomplishment', in H. Marshall (ed.), *Redefining Student Learning: Roots of Educational Change*, Norwood, NJ: Ablex. pp.119–150.

Santa Barbara Classroom Discourse Group (1995) 'Constructing an integrated inquiry-oriented approach in classrooms: A cross case analysis of social, literate and academic practices', *Journal of Classroom Interaction*, 30(2): 1–15.

Sarangi, S. and Roberts, C. (eds) (1999) Talk, Work and Institutional Order: Discourse in medical, mediation and management settings, Berlin: Mouton de Gruyter.

Schleppegrell, M.J. (2004) *The Language of Schooling: A functional linguistics perspective*, Mahwah, NJ: LEA.

Sharpe, T. (2006) '"Unpacking" scaffolding: Identifying discourse and multimodal strategies that support learning', *Language and Education*, 20(3): 211–231.

Silverstein, M., and Urban, G. (1996) 'The natural history of discourse', in M. Silverstein and G. Urban (eds), *Natural Histories of Discourse*, Chicago: Chicago University Press, pp.1–17.

Smart, Gr. (2006) *Writing the Economy: Activity, Genre, and Technology in the World of Banking*, London: Equinox.

Stein, P. (2004) 'Re-sourcing resources: Pedagogy, history and loss in a Johannesburg classroom', in M.R. Hawkins (ed.), *Language Learning and Teacher Education: A Sociocultural Approach*, Clevedon: Multilingual Matters. pp.35–51.

Street, B.V. (2005b) 'Recent applications of new literacy studies in Educational Contexts', *Research in the Teaching of English*, 39(4): 417–423.

Street, B.V. (ed.) (2005a) *Literacies across Educational Contexts: Mediating learning and teaching*, Philadelphia: Caslon.

Stroud, C. and Wee, L. (2007) 'A pedagogical application of liminalities in social positioning: Identity and literacy in Singapore', *TESOL Quarterly*, 41(1): 33–79.

Sunderland, J. (2004) *Gendered Discourses*, Basingstoke: Palgrave Macmillan.

Tannen, D. (ed.) (1982) *Spoken and Written Language: Exploring Orality and Literacy*, Norwood, NJ: Ablex.

Tardy, C. (2006) 'Appropriation, ownership, and agency: negotiating teacher feedback on academic settings', in K. Hyland and F. Hyland (eds), *Feedback in Second Language Writing: Contexts and issues*, Cambridge: CUP. pp.60–78.

Unsworth, L. (ed.) (1993) *Literacy Learning and Teaching: Language as Social Practice in the Primary School*, Melbourne: MacMillan Education Australia.

Van Dijk, T.A. (1998) *Ideology: A Multidisciplinary Approach*, London: Sage.

Van Eng, A., Dagenais, D., and Toohey, K. (2005) 'A socio-cultural perspective on school-based research: Some emerging considerations', *Language and Education*, 19(6): 496–512.

Walford, G. (2003) 'Introduction: Investigating Education Policy', in G. Walford (ed.), *Investigating Educational Policy through Ethnography*, Amsterdam: Elsevier. pp.1–15.

Weiss, G. and Wodak, R. (2003) *Critical Discourse Analysis: Theory and Interdisciplinarity*, Basingstoke: Palgrave Macmillan.

Wells, G, and G. Claxton (eds) (2002) *Learning for Life in the 21st century: Sociocultural Perspectives on the Future of Education*, Oxford: Blackwell.

Wells, G. (1999) *Dialogic Inquiry: Towards a Sociocultural Practice and Theory of Education*, New York: Cambridge University Press.

Wells, G., and Chang-Wells, G. (1992) *Constructing Knowledge Together: Classrooms as Centers of Inquiry and Literacy*, Portsmouth, NH: Heinemann.

Wertsch, J. (1985) *Vygotsky and the Social Formation of Mind*, Cambridge: Cambridge University Press.

Wertsch, J. (1991) *Voices of the Mind*, Cambridge, Mass.: Harvard University Press.

Wertsch, J. (1998) *Mind as Action*, New York/Oxford: Oxford University Press.

Wodak, R. and Ludwig, Ch. (eds) (1999) *Challenges in a Changing World: Issues in Critical Discourse Analysis*, Passagen Verlag.

Wodak, R., Meyer, M. (eds) (2001) *Methods of Discourse Analysis*, London: Sage.

Wortham, St. (2006) *Learning Identity: The Joint Emergence of Social Identification and Academic Learning*, Cambridge: Cambridge University Press

7

Developing Discourse Roles and Positionings – An Ecological Theory of Writing Development

Jon Smidt

This chapter points to the need for an *ecological theory* of writing development. It takes the view that development of writing at school implies learning to negotiate the voices and roles offered by the genres of school writing. This approach, inspired by Mikhail Bakhtin's (1986) ideas about the dialogical relationship between individual utterances and what he calls 'speech genres', calls for a discussion of the relationships between individual writers, their texts, discourses in the classroom with teachers and fellow students, culture-specific norms and expectations for writing at school, values and beliefs in the societies the writers inhabit, and writers' sense of who they are or want to be in their writing.

We will explore the relevance and use of an ecological theory of writing development in classroom research by looking at three very different studies of writers at different age levels. In all of these studies, writers adopt and negotiate social discourse roles available to them in the genres of school writing, and social interaction between actual participants in particular classrooms is seen as participation also in a larger world of values and discourses. We shall ask what these studies may tell us about writing development as a personal negotiation of cultural genres and values.

DISCOURSE ROLES AND POSITIONINGS

Before turning to the three studies, the reader is invited to consider a set of terms that capture the Bakhtinian double perspective of individual utterances and speech genres in actual situational contexts. We suggest that the terms 'discourse roles' and 'positionings' may be helpful in understanding how actual writers struggle textually with the culturally given genres that they meet at school.

The tradition from George Herbert Mead stressed the importance of *social roles* in the development of identities (Goffman, 1990). 'There are all sorts of different selves',

Mead wrote, 'answering to all sorts of different social reactions. It is the social process itself that is responsible for the appearance of the self' (1967: 142). School is just one of the arenas for the trying out of social roles, but certainly an important one for young people in our societies, and any classroom invites to – often demands – the adoption of various roles. Most of these roles imply the use of language, as when a student enters the role of participant in a debate or a presenter of literary texts or simply a student answering test questions. These are all examples of school genres, and they invite – or demand – the adoption of social roles, to be expressed in language. Cherry (1988), in a study of academic writing, used the Aristotelian term *persona* about 'the roles authors create for themselves in written discourse given their representation of audience, subject matter, and other elements of context' (Cherry, 1988: 268ff., see further discussion in Ivanic, 1998: 89ff.). In the context of this handbook, it is natural to ask how the trying out of textual roles or discourse roles influences the development of writing.

The tradition from Mikhail Bakhtin has focused on the way people *position* themselves dialogically through their utterances. Bakhtin, in his essay on 'The Problem of Speech Genres', said about real-life dialogues: 'Each rejoinder, regardless of how brief and abrupt, has a specific quality of completion that expresses a particular position of the speaker, to which one may respond or may assume, with respect to it, a responsive position' (1986: 72). Ongstad (1999), elaborating on Bakhtin, speaks about self-positioning as triadic: in any utterance, speakers or writers position themselves in relation to the topic (reference), in relation to given ways of speaking about it and their own sense of how they want to present themselves (expressivity), and in relation to former and expected listeners or readers (addressivity) (cf. Bakhtin, 1986: 84 ff.).

Smidt (2002), discussing the relevance of the terms discourse roles and positionings, concluded that it may be useful to keep both

terms. *Discourse roles* (or *textual roles*) would then 'refer to the discoursal presentation of selves offered by culturally patterned ways of writing as student writers try their hands at being political commentators, entertainers, philosophers, writers of fiction, or journalists'. *Positionings*, on the other hand, would refer to:

> ... the students' unique and always changing stances *within* these roles and genres, and in relation to topic, form, expected readers, and the norms of school writing. Thus, the overlapping concepts of positionings and discourse roles emphasize the connection between the unique utterance and the cultural expectations of speech genres. (Bakhtin, 1986; Smidt, 2002: 424)

With these concepts, we can turn to our three examples. The first study follows a group of children in primary school, the second one presents the 'double histories' of two high school writers and their teacher over a period of two years, while the third examines and discusses the efforts of nonacademic adult students to develop 'discoursal selves' in higher education.

DEVELOPMENT – CHALLENGING NORMS AND VALUES

In *Writing Superheroes* (1997) Anne Haas Dyson followed a group of second grade children in a Californian inner city school through third grade, using ideas especially from Bakhtin to interpret what she observed. An important theme in Dyson's studies of young children is 'the link between composing a text and composing a place for oneself in the social world' (Dyson, 1993: 229). In this particular classroom, the teacher provided an institution called Author's Theater, giving the children the opportunity to compose texts to be acted out with classmates as actors and audience. The enacted stories often featured superheroes from the media – Ninja Turtles, X-Men, and the like – and Dyson shows how the stories became part of the complicated relationships between the children in the classroom, as the authors chose whom to invite as actors in their 'stories'. The tensions and conflicts of gender, race and social class – in this classroom and in the larger world – came to the surface. For instance, Tina, an Afro-American girl, tired of all the male heroes in the superhero stories, started composing her own stories with female heroes. To do so, Tina actively used the social roles of 'story writer' and 'director', which the Author's Theater in this classroom invited to, and in doing so she challenged the power relations in her classroom as well as the genre of Superhero stories and the ideological values they imply. Writing is here – as it often is – closely linked with other social activities and with spoken language, as the social roles of story writer and director are as much enacted physically and orally as in writing. Nevertheless, Dyson also shows the power of the written word, as Tina takes the decisions about participants in her 'story'.

Therefore, in this classroom, composing a text very definitely was a way of positioning oneself socially. Dyson shows how written texts are sites for acting out conflicts in social worlds. Some of the titles of chapters in her book illustrate various aspects of the ways texts are integrated in the social life of the classroom: 'The Ninjas, the Ladies, and the X-Men: Text as Ticket to Play', 'The "Trials and Tribulations" of Emily and Other Media Misses: Text as Dialogic Medium', 'The Coming of Venus Tina: Texts as Markers and Mediators of Tough-Talking Kids', 'Transformed and Silenced Lovers: Texts as Sites of Revelation and Circumvention'. So, on the one hand, positioning oneself textually means positioning oneself in a social world, as here in second grade classroom of friends and competitors. On the other hand, the study shows that positioning oneself in a text also means appropriating the words and signs of others, culturally mediated in texts of all sorts and loaded with values, like the good guys and bad guys of popular media:

> Thus, our texts are formed at the intersection of a social relationship between ourselves as composers and our addressees and an ideological one between our own psyches (or inner meanings) and the words, cultural signs, available to us. (Dyson, 1997: 4)

Dyson's analysis of what happened in this writing classroom shows how writers may use writing to confront and challenge, even change the 'rules of the game'. In fact, the texts written and performed in this classroom were not only results of the social setup of the environment for writing ('Author's Theater' etc.) and the cultural influences from the media, but also actively influenced and changed ideas and relationships in the class. From a Bakhtinian point of view, the genres, words, and cultural signs available – like the superhero stories in this case – may be an inevitable point of departure but never the end of the story. As Dyson says, '[c]omposers, ... are not so much meaning makers as meaning negotiators, who adopt, resist, or stretch available words' (ibid). Dyson also makes a strong case for teachers like the one she followed in this study, who see sociocultural diversity and even conflict as a resource rather than a problem in the writing development of young children.

DEVELOPMENT AND THE SOCIAL MEANING OF WRITING

In 'Double Histories in Multivocal Classrooms' Smidt (2002) reports the 'double histories' of two student writers and their teacher over a period of two years in Norwegian upper secondary school. The two students, Siri and Olav, started out with different ideas about themselves as writers and about the social meaning of writing at school. Siri positioned herself from the start as a feminist with a strong interest in social and political issues like (in her own words) 'environmental protection, racism, school, rape and incest, oppressed people, witch practices' (Smidt, 2002: 427). These were topics she wanted to write about. At the same time, she was critical to the – in her view – limited and limiting genres of expository writing at school. For Olav, writing at school was a school assignment, no more – and so he tried to find ways of doing the writing assignments as efficiently as possible, with as little personal involvement as he could.

School writing in Norwegian upper secondary school usually gives students a choice between a certain number of topics and genres, and Siri's and Olav's teacher allowed for even more freedom of choice than usual during the first two years. In the third and final year, the options were more limited, as the teacher knew what genres his students should be able to cope with in the final exams, and felt an obligation to prepare them for that. The two students position themselves differently in their choice of topic and genre. Not surprisingly, Siri regularly chose topics and genres, which allowed her to adopt discourse roles that matched her self-image, for instance the discourse roles of a political activist or a literary writer, and in her texts, she positioned herself very strongly in these roles. Olav, on the other hand, chose 'safe' tasks, where things could be done 'correctly', for instance by following models provided by his teacher. Siri stretches and challenges the norms and genres of school writing, Olav tries to find the correct and most profitable solutions given the school context.

This study demonstrates the multidimensional situatedness of students' development as writers. First, Siri's and Olav's writing development is strongly motivated by their ideas about the social meaning of writing at school, and their ideas about who they are or want to be. Secondly, their teacher and the social practices and genres of his classroom are clearly important in Siri's and Olav's development as writers. In the interaction between students and teacher, there is a reciprocal positioning. The students in their writing positioned not only themselves, but also their teacher, Siri addressing him as a literary adviser, Olav expecting him to be the schoolteacher who knows the rules. Correspondingly, in his written response to

Siri and Olav, the teacher positioned himself and the students differently (cf. Sperling, 1994, 1995). This is the *interactional* dimension in writing development. However, Siri's and Olav's teacher (and the genres and social practices of his classroom) stood in a constant dialogic relationship with the norms of school writing of Norwegian upper secondary school. In his response to his students, the teacher made interpretations of the norms and requirements of Norwegian upper secondary school writing, negotiating these norms as he tried to adjust his responses to his two very different addressees. This is the *sociocultural or ideological* dimension in writing development.

Thus, the double histories of these student writers and their teacher suggest that writing development is multidimensional, involving students' own changing and developing sense of their 'discoursal selves' (Ivanic, 1998) and the social meaning of writing, in constant dialogue with teachers' responses, the genres and topics offered in a certain school culture, and the teacher's and students' own negotiations of these norms. Moreover, the study shows that the reciprocal positionings of students and teachers are not only shaped in a sociocultural environment; but they are also part of this environmental context and actively influence and change it.

DEVELOPMENT – STRUGGLING TO CREATE A DISCOURSAL SELF

In *Writing and Identity* (1998), Roz Ivanic examined and discussed the efforts of eight adult students trying to find their way into academic writing. Ivanic shows how they struggled to find out how to present themselves in writing in the new and unfamiliar world of higher education. For these eight, as for many other students, the process of becoming members of an academic 'community of practice' (Lave and Wenger, 1991) implied imitating and borrowing, intertextually, the 'voices' of other texts, some of them immediately present, some echoes of reading or writing in other situations. In one case, Ivanic offers an analysis of how one of the students, Rachel, a Social Work student, deals with an assignment in her fourth year in university to write a case story drawn from a professional placement as a social-worker (Ivanic, 1998: 128). In her analysis, Ivanic shows how this student moves between several different 'subject-positions' (or positionings) in her essay:

... some major, some minor; some of which she identifies with, some of which she feels ambivalent about, and some of which she rejects. Of these, her positioning as an apprentice social-worker is in itself multi-faceted. I show how these identities manifest themselves in specific discoursal choices. (Ivanic, 1998: 132)

Ivanic, building on Fairclough (1992), talks about the practices and discourse types available in a certain social situation, the values, beliefs and power relations that these practices represent, and the 'possibilities of selfhood' they afford (Ivanic, 1998: 64). She shows how writing development means negotiating the 'possibilities of selfhood' that students see in this social situation, and at the same time, negotiating their own sense of who they are – their 'autobiographical selves'. Ivanic sees:

... every act of academic writing as, among other things, the writer's struggle to create a discoursal self which removes the tension between their autobiographical self and the possibilities for selfhood available in the academic community. (336)

Writing development might be understood as learning to write in the ways preferred and privileged in a certain 'discourse community', for instance a discipline in higher education, but Ivanic shows this to be only half the story. Although academic membership is guarded by (sometimes) explicit and (more often) tacit rules, Ivanic in her analysis shows that there are more than one ways of becoming a member – 'academic discourse is not monolithic' (281). There are different and sometimes contesting norms and traditions in different disciplines and often even within one discipline, and they are never static.

Moreover, with the help of Halliday, Ivanic is able to show how the eight students she worked with, position themselves individually, using the discursive resources they have in multiple ways. In other words, this study supports the idea that writing development implies negotiating sociocultural norms and rules, but is not determined by them.

What all three studies have in common is the insistence that writing is developed in complex relationships between individual writers and their sense of who they are in different social situations, their fellow students and teachers, the social practices and genres afforded, the discourse roles they adopt, and the positionings they make. This multidimensional view of writing is what is indicated by speaking of an 'ecological theory of writing development'.

THE MULTIDIMENSIONAL DIALOGUES – AN ECOLOGICAL THEORY OF WRITING DEVELOPMENT

Gregory Bateson (1972) used the metaphor of 'ecology' about human relationships, including the use of language. David Barton (1994) explains how the metaphor may also be used in the study of literacy:

Originating in biology, ecology is the study of the interrelationship of an organism and its environment. When applied to humans, it is the interrelationship of an area of human activity and its environment. It is concerned with how the activity – literacy in this case – is part of the environment and at the same time influences and is influenced by the environment. An ecological approach takes as its starting-point this interaction between individuals and their environments. (Barton, 1994: 29)

Used about writing development, the metaphor of 'ecology' turns our attention to the influence of all participants in the writing classroom, student writers, classmates, and teachers, as well as the represented cultures and norms, as we have seen in our three examples – Tina's superheroes in the second grade classroom, Siri and Olav positioning their teacher as well as themselves in upper secondary school writing, Rachel negotiating the norms of writing in university. Hardly any theory today would question the importance of contexts in the development of writing. As Nystrand, Gamoran, and Carbonaro (1998) said, a classroom consists of many different modes of discourse, and 'an ecological perspective is indispensable for understanding how these different modes of discourse can interact to promote overall literacy development'. However, there have been debates about the definition of 'context' – what contexts are we talking about, and how much is determined by the cultural contexts of the writing practices? One such debate is the one between *social interactionists* and *social constructionists*. For social interactionists like Rommetveit (1974) and Nystrand (1986, 1989, 1990), the critical context for writing is the dialogic relationship between writer and reader. On the other side, Swales (1990), Fairclough (1992), and others have stressed the importance of the cultural and ideological contexts and speak about the ways writers are constrained by the norms of their 'discourse communities'. In other words, Rommetveit and Nystrand represent a microsocial perspective on context, while Swales and Fairclough represent a meso- or macro-social view. In this chapter, we have made the point that both perspectives are needed to understand how writing is developed in a school setting.

A theory is needed that allows us to study how individual students, like second-grader Tina, high-school students Siri and Olav, or university student Rachel, in social interaction with teachers and peers, interpret and negotiate, experiment and struggle with the genres, norms, and values that are represented in their classroom. According to Bakhtin, individual utterances enter a world of multiple voices and ways of speaking ('speech genres'). Each individual utterance makes a new contribution to the chain of utterances by placing itself – as it must do – in some relation to previous utterances and voices (Bakhtin, 1981, 1986). This is, of course, also the case for student writers – and their teachers. Their texts too are utterances, responding in various ways to the topics and forms of writing that are available to them at school. Therefore, if we agree with Bakhtin, even the small contributions made by individual student writers influence the contexts of writing for those that follow.

So, it is possible to think and talk about the development of writing as something that develops in the social practices of 'literacy events' (Barton 1994), in which there are many active parts. Teachers of writing normally have ideas about what counts as good writing, as Siri's and Olav's teacher had, and so have their students. Teachers and students can challenge, negotiate, sometimes even change the 'rules of the game' to some extent, as Tina did, but this is a dialogical process, since challenging and changing presuppose given values or conventions.

As we have seen in the three reported studies, any classroom is part of a larger world, and as Bakhtin pointed out, our words are filled with the meanings and values of others (1986: 89). While Nystrand (1990) warned against a too rigid social constructionist view of writing, in which the interaction between actual writers and readers may seem to lose attention, others, such as Ivanic (1998) and Evensen (2002), have stressed the importance of combining social interactionist and social constructionist theories for discovering how individual writers in real-life interaction with others struggle to find their way into the sociocultural roles and genres of various discourse communities. Evensen (2002), in a study of teenager Kari's writing development, shows how a text about her favourite music instrument is a meeting place, a 'diatope' as Evensen calls it, for her understanding of the immediate audience she is addressing, as well as culturally given genres and conventions of writing. There is, in Evensen's view, a 'double dialogue' going on in Kari's text – between Kari and her addressees. In Evensen's study of Kari's writing, this 'double dialogue' is connected to a textual theory of foregrounding and backgrounding, as Evensen demonstrates how she tries to give her readers the necessary cultural backgrounding to understand what she is writing about. The social interactionist perspective – Kari's sense of what her readers need – therefore implicates a wider view of positions and genres available to her in her school setting.

Halliday (1994), from his social-semiotic and systemic functional perspective, also takes a double view of context, seeing the *situational context* of an utterance or text, which, in the case of writing at school, includes interaction with teacher and class, as an instance of the more abstract *cultural context*. The context of situation interacts with contexts of culture – including what is understood as the 'rules' and genres of school writing: what counts as good writing in terms of what you are allowed to write, and how, and for what purpose. In Halliday's terms, the writer needs to have a sense of *'field'* ('what is actually taking place'), 'tenor' ('who is taking part'), and 'mode' ('what role is language playing') (Halliday and Martin 1993: 32f). These are aspects of the context of situation that imply wider cultural contexts.

RELEVANCE FOR RESEARCH AND PRACTICE

A question to be raised at the end of this chapter is what implications an ecological theory of writing development may have for researchers and for teachers of writing. Of course, it is impossible to combine a sociocultural – situated – theory of writing development with the notion that there are universal answers to pedagogical problems. Moreover, obviously, the three reported studies, from a Californian inner city primary classroom, from a Norwegian upper secondary classroom, and from an English university, can never be seen as representative of writing development at different age levels. They do, however, illustrate important points

in an ecological theory of writing development and open for discussions about the aims and objectives of education in writing.

Looking at the three studies in terms of Ongstad's Bakhtinian triad of self-positioning, it seems that Dyson's focus is on the content or referential side of writing – the children position themselves in relation to topics, issues, values, and relationships in and around the text in the literacy events of the classroom. Ivanic's focus is more on the form, the voices in available linguistic resources, and the values that go along with them, the possible ways of presenting oneself in certain discourse communities (expressivity). However, all three studies emphasize the relational side of writing: positioning oneself towards other speakers and writers (addressivity).

For Halliday and his followers, development of writing requires learning to understand and use the culturally given ways of expressing oneself in different fields of life and society. Halliday speaks about different 'registers' for different social situations. Genre pedagogy in Australia and other countries have been inspired by Halliday to give explicit genre instruction to students to teach them how to communicate in the social situations they may meet, in education, and in other social situations (Cope and Kalantzis (eds), 1993). It is, however, not quite clear in Halliday's theory to what extent individual writers may challenge or change the genres and registers. This point is, on the other hand, very strongly highlighted in all of the three reported studies.

In Dyson's study the social practices of writing and performing stories in the classroom give the children an opportunity not only to learn the structures of 'stories', but also to learn to use writing to challenge values and power structures.

Siri's and Olav's histories as writers illustrate two (among a great many) roads in writing development, linked to their respective ideas of the social meaning of writing at school. For Olav, writing development means learning the rules. In his school writing, he learns how to make strategic choices, using writing instrumentally to get on in his school career. Siri, on the other hand, develops new ways of using writing to present her views to the world, challenging traditional values and established beliefs. However, while their developmental roads vary, both writers in this process position themselves as writers, developing writer's identities ('discoursal selves') and presenting themselves to social worlds through the discourse roles they choose and their positionings in them. Their positionings influence not only the responses from their teacher, but also the context of their writing in classroom.

In the academic world of Ivanic's students, the norms and expectations of writing are more often unspoken than explicit, and at the same time writers feel the pressure to qualify as members of the academic community by developing 'right' ways of saying and writing things. However, as Ivanic demonstrates, there are many ways of positioning oneself even in an academic community. In Ivanic's view, it is important to see writing as a site of struggle in which writers are negotiating an identity (Ivanic, 1998: 332). Writing development (and research in writing development) requires what she calls 'Critical language awareness': an awareness of the norms of writing and the power relations behind them, in order to point to the possibilities of challenging and changing them (339).

In this chapter, I have suggested that an ecological theory of writing development contributes to our understanding of how writers develop writer identities as they position themselves in textual roles in sociocultural worlds. To be a full participant in a democratic society today people need to understand the whats, the hows, and whys of written communication. They need to know something about the world around them, and they need to know the important genres of their society and different ways of expressing themselves in different situations. They also need to know that writing can be used actively to affirm privileged ways of speaking and writing or to resist and challenge them.

REFERENCES

Bakhtin, M. (1981) *The Dialogic Imagination. Four Essays* (Tr. and ed.) M. Holquist, Austin, TX: University of Texas Press.

Bakhtin, M. (1986) *Speech Genres and Other Late Essays*, Tr V.W. McGee (eds) C. Emerson and M. Holquist, Austin, TX: University of Texas Press.

Barton, D. (1994) *Literacy. An Introduction to the Ecology of Written Language*, Oxford: Blackwell.

Bateson, G. (1972) *Steps to an Ecology of Mind*, New York: Ballantine Books.

Cherry, R. (1988) 'Ethos versus Persona: Self-representation in written discourse', *Written Communication*, 5(3): 251–276.

Cope, B. and Kalantzis, M. (eds) (1993) *The Powers of Literacy: A Genre Approach to Teaching Writing*, Pittsburgh, PA: University of Pittsburgh Press.

Dyson, A.H. (1993) *The Social Worlds of Children Learning to Write in an Urban Primary School*, New York: Teachers College Press.

Dyson, A.H. (1997) *Writing Superheroes. Contemporary Childhood, Popular Culture, and Classroom Literacy*, New York: Teachers College, Columbia University.

Evensen, L.S. (2002) 'Convention from below: Negotiating interaction and culture in argumentative writing', *Written Communication*, 19(3): 382–413.

Fairclough, N. (1992) *Discourse and Social Change*, Cambridge UK: Polity Press.

Goffman, E. (1990) *The Presentation of Self in Everyday Life*, London: Penguin Books. (Original work published 1959.)

Halliday, M.A.K. (1994) *An Introduction to Functional Grammar* (second edn.), London and New York: Edward Arnold.

Halliday, M.A.K. and Martin, J.R. (1993) *Writing Science: Literacy and Discursive Power*, London and Pittsburgh: University. of Pittsburgh Press.

Ivanic, R. (1998) *Writing and Identity: The Discoursal Construction of Identity in Academic Writing*, Amsterdam/Philadelphia: John Benjamins.

Lave, J. and Wenger, E. (1991) *Situated Learning. Legitimate Peripheral Participation*, Cambridge: Cambridge University Press.

Mead, G.H. (1967) *Mind, Self and Society from the Standpoint of a Social Behaviorist*, Chicago and London: The University of Chicago Press, Phoenix Books. (Original work published 1934.)

Nystrand, M. (1986) *The Structure of Written Communication. Studies in Reciprocity Between Writers and Readers*, Orlando: Academic Press.

Nystrand, M. (1989) 'A social-interactive model of writing', *Written Communication*, 6(1): 66–85.

Nystrand, M. (1990) 'Sharing words: The effects of readers on developing writers', *Written Communication*, 7: 3–24.

Nystrand, M., Gamoran, A., and Carbonaro, W. (1998) *Towards an Ecology of Learning: The Case of Classroom Discourse and its Effects on Writing in High School English and Social Studies*, Albany NY/ Madison WI: National Research Center on English Learning and Achievement/Wisconsin Center for Education Research Report Series 2.34.

Ongstad, S. (1999) 'Self-positioning(s) and students' task reflexivity – a semiotic macro concept exemplified', *Journal of Structural Learning and Intelligent Systems,* 14(2): 1–28.

Rommetveit, R. (1974) *On Message Structure: A Framework for the Study of Language and Communication*, London: Wiley.

Sperling, M. (1994) 'Constructing the perspective of teacher-as-reader: A framework for studying response to student writing', *Research in the Teaching of English*, 28: 175–203.

Sperling, M. (1995) *Revealing the Teacher-as-Reader: A Framework for Discussion and Learning* (Center for the Study of Writing Occasional Paper No. 40). Berkeley: National Writing Project.

Smidt, J. (2002) 'Double histories in multivocal classrooms: Notes toward an ecological account of writing', *Written Communication*, 19(3): 414–443.

Swales, J. (1990) *Genre Analysis: English in Academic and Research Settings*, Cambridge: Cambridge University Press.

8

Writing: A Critical Literacy Perspective

Hilary Janks

INTRODUCTION

Peter was a bright young twelve-year-old in my Grade 7 class at a comprehensive school in London, where I was working as a supply teacher in the early 1980s. He was difficult, always finishing first so that he would have time to make a nuisance of himself. Sporting a glass eye, he was a real toughie. When I introduced free-writing journals one Friday afternoon, the students, egged on by Peter, tested me. They wanted to know exactly how free? Could they use swear words? I told them that as far as I was concerned they could fill a page with the worst swear word they could think of, but they would have to take responsibility for what they wrote in their journals if their parents or another teacher found their books. That seemed to satisfy them and no one ever exercised this option.

Peter took his empty exercise book home and on Monday morning returned to school and announced that he had finished. He handed me his journal filled from cover to cover with his writing. Before he could blink, I had pasted a second exercise book into the back of his journal. His determination to finish ahead of the class, as was his wont, had required him to spend much of his weekend writing. In this concentrated effort, he must have discovered that writing could be pleasurable, because this most uncooperative of students went on to fill five more books with his ideas, his hopes, his concerns, and his disappointments.

This was the first time that these students had been given complete control over their writing. Their journals became a safe space where they could write about what mattered to them. It became a space in which they could drop their bravado in front of their peers, and show an interest in school. No one but I would know. For the first time they could use writing to address an interested adult who responded to the meanings they were communicating, rather than to their grammar and form. They had to write at least three pieces of any length every week and although this work was not assessed and did not count 'for marks', most of the students wrote more than the minimum. They begged for time in class to write in their journals. Ironically, for them it was a way of avoiding work. In this space, they had freedom to be whoever they wanted to be and the power to choose what they would write. Many chose to include drawings and photographs of their interests, their families or people with whom they identified – usually pop stars or sporting heroes. Twenty-five years later, I have no difficulty understanding why students, who resist writing in school, will spend hours writing on *My Space* or *Facebook*. Now students can choose their audience from a networked community across the globe and multimodal text production has become easier and more sophisticated with greater access to the new digital technologies. The contrast with educational settings is extreme. From primary to tertiary education, students' writing is still largely controlled by the teacher and the set-topic essay is still the norm in both language and content subject classrooms, in a range of educational contexts.

CRITICAL LITERACY

Freire's approach to literacy teaching depends on people using writing to make meanings that matter to them. While this is not a sufficient condition for critical writing, it is a necessary condition. For Freire,

If learning to read and write is to constitute an act of knowing, the learners must assume from the beginning the role of creative subjects. It is not a matter of memorizing and repeating given syllables and phrases …

Insofar as language is impossible without thought, and language and thought are impossible without the world to which they refer, the human word is more than mere vocabulary – it is word-and-action. The cognitive dimensions of the literacy process must include the relationships of men [sic] with their world (Freire, 1972a: 29).

Freire was the first to challenge our assumptions about literacy as simply teaching students the skills necessary for reading and writing. He helps us to understand that reading and writing the word cannot be separated from reading and writing the world.

Freire's two seminal books, *Cultural Action for Freedom* (1972a) and *Pedagogy of the Oppressed* (1972b), show how, in the process of learning, to read both the *word* and the *world* critically, adult literacy learners regain their sense of themselves as agents who can act to transform the social situations in which they find themselves. In the late 1970s, Fowler, Hodge, Kress and Trew (1979) laid the theoretical ground for 'critical linguistics' (Fowler and Kress, 1979: 185–213). This was followed by developments in the field of critical discourse analysis (Fairclough, 1989, 2003; Gee, 1996, 1999).

Most of the early work focused on critical reading, and it was only towards the end of the 1990s that the first books on critical writing were published. Apart from the work spearheaded by Freire on adult education, most of the theoretical work on critical writing is on academic writing in higher education (Clark and Ivanič, 1997; Ivanič, 1998; Kamler and Thomson, 2006; Lillis, 2001). This work, which sees writing as a social practice, pays careful attention to the disciplinary norms that writers in the academy have to master. Academic texts are exclusive and excluding for both writers and readers. Writing is fundamentally bound up with questions of power and identity. Writers, new to the academy, often experience a sense of alienation when they try to penetrate new discourse communities and writers, new to research, struggle to find an authoritative position from which to speak.

Kress and Van Leeuwen's (2001; Kress, 2003) work on multimodality has had a profound effect on our understanding of literacy. He argues that the new digital technologies have enabled a profound semiotic shift in which our communication system now relies on a wide range of representational resources, such that 'writers' for screen rather than page have to orchestrate a range of simultaneous message streams using different modes of meaning making. Even texts that are predominantly verbal have design features such as font, font size, and *font style*, **colour**, s p a c i n g, and layout.

In addition to lexical, grammatical, content and sequencing choices, writers and publishers have to decide on the overall design of the page. These design features are an important part of the message. For example, Badenhorst's (2007) book for postgraduate students on research writing looks like a school textbook. Despite her erudition and grounded approach to research writing, many researchers will find it difficult to engage with the ideas because of the format in which they are presented.

Examples of critical writing practice for primary and secondary schools can be found in critical literacy materials for classrooms. As early as 1984, the Inner London Education Authority's English Centre, produced workbooks with a critical edge. In particular, *Changing Stories* introduced the idea of rewriting texts by asking students to consider different versions of traditional tales and by inviting them to write their own endings (Mellor, Hemming, and Leggett, 1984). Mellor went on to establish Chalkface Press in Australia which produced a series of workbooks that included the examination and rewriting of texts that were racist, sexist, or elitist (for example, Forrestal et al., 1992; Mellor and Patterson, 1996). Martino (1997) and Kenworthy and Kenworthy (1997) used postcolonial theory to challenge colonial texts and to explore texts that developed the practice of 'writing back'. In the Critical Language Awareness Series, which I edited, every workbook includes critical writing activities as does Christensen's (2000) *Reading, Writing and Rising Up*. Vasquez's (2004) work with young children includes many classroom projects in which three to five year-olds learn to use writing – petitions, letters, plays, stories – as a form of social action. As yet, however, the practice of critical writing has not been developed as the main focus of critical literacy work in schools as it was, for example, in Kamler's (2001: 55–78) work with 70 to 85-year-old women on stories of ageing.

The purpose of the project was to confront the narrow range of negative images of ageing pervasive in our culture and to produce new stories written from the perspective of the older women (Kamler, 2001: 55).

In this project, older women were given the opportunity to use writing to frame their subject positions differently. According to Lakoff (2004), this act constitutes social change.

Frames are mental structures that shape the way we see the world. As a result, they shape the goals we seek, the plans we make, the way we act and what counts as good or bad outcomes of our actions. In politics, our frames shape our social policies. To change our frames is to change all of this. Reframing is social change (Lakoff 2004: xv).

The move from critical reading to critical writing is important, because it enables us to think about where we might go after we have deconstructed a text. Because texts are constructed word by word, image by image, they can be deconstructed – unpicked, unmade, the positions produced for the reader laid bare, but what then? A critical approach to writing enables us to transform the texts that we have deconstructed, to remake the word. It helps us to think about how we are positioning ourselves and our readers by the choices we make as we write and to consider how the words we use to name the world may privilege some at the expense of others. If repositioning texts is tied to an ethic of social justice then writing and rewriting can contribute to the kind of identity and social transformation that Freire's work advocates.

The journal-approach to writing, used with Peter, is of course not necessarily critical in the Freirean sense of the word. Education has to do more than produce fluent writers who enjoy using writing to produce meanings and texts that matter to them. Writers need a critical social consciousness to produce texts that make a difference to the ways in which we 'name' and understand the world. They also need access to schooled literacies – to the standard variety of the dominant language, to dominant genres and to the social and rhetorical sophistication needed to write for a range of audiences and purposes. These are harder for students to master if they have no experience of meaningful, pleasurable, fluent writing on which to build.

THE INTERDEPENDENT[1] MODEL FOR CRITICAL LITERACY EDUCATION

From the discussion so far, I have suggested that critical writing is a form of social action that works with questions of control, identity, positioning, standard languages, dominant genres, and access. In order to develop these ideas more systematically, I turn now to the interdependent model for critical literacy education that I have been developing since 1998. In this model (Janks, 2000), I argue that the theoretical concepts in the field of critical literacy: domination or power, access, diversity, and design/redesign are *crucially interdependent*. The model is summarized in Table 8.1. In this model, the concept of

'design' has been adapted from the work of Kress (2000) and the concept of redesign from the New London Group (1996).

In brief, *power* stands for the orientation in critical literacy that tries to understand how discourse works to produce, maintain, or contest structured relations of power in the society, and the ways in which texts privilege some interests to the detriment of others. Critical literacy education provides the means for seeing how power is instantiated in texts and with the literacy skills needed to read against these texts. For Foucault (1976), discourse also has the power to produce us as particular kinds of subjects. It is necessary to recognize that differences such as language, gender, race, class, and ethnicity, result in social stratification and inequality. *Diversity* is the word I use for social difference. Because difference is structured in relation to power, it affects people's life chances and the kind of resources that they have access to. *Access* within a critical literacy orientation

Table 8.1   The interdependent model for critical literacy

Power without access	This maintains the exclusionary force of powerful discourse.
Power without diversity	Without difference and diversity, powerful forms lose the ruptures that produce challenge and creative transformations.
Power without design	The deconstruction of power, without reconstruction or design, removes human agency.
Access without power	Access without a theory of power leads to the naturalisation of powerful discourses without an understanding of how these powerful forms came to be powerful.
Access without diversity	This fails to recognise that difference fundamentally affects pathways to access and involves issues of history, identity and value.
Access without design	This maintains and reifies powerful forms without considering how they can be transformed.
Diversity without a theory of power	This leads to a celebration of diversity without any recognition that difference is structured in dominance and that not all discourses/genres/ languages/literacies are equally powerful.
Diversity without access	Diversity without access to powerful forms of language ghettoises students.
Diversity without design	Diversity provides the means, the ideas, the alternative perspectives for reconstruction and transformation. Without design, the potential that diversity offers is not realised.
Design without power	Design, without an understanding of how powerful discourses/practices perpetuate themselves, runs the risk of an unconscious reproduction of these forms.
Design without access	Runs the risk of whatever is designed remaining on the margins.
Design without diversity	This privileges powerful forms and fails to use the design resources provided by difference.

focuses on issues pertaining to linguistic and discoursal access and tries to address the question of unequal access to different literacies. *Design* is the concept used to refer to multimodal text production. It focuses on the production rather than the reception of texts.

In this model, writing should be seen as one kind of design. The word *writing* cannot be extended metaphorically to nonverbal texts in the way that *reading* can. While we can talk about reading gestures, film, clothing, photographs, bodies, space, and so on, we do not talk about writing them. The word 'design', unlike the word 'write', *does* work across multiple modalities – multiple forms of meaning making or semeiosis – you can design a dress, a page, a poster, furniture, or a classroom. I therefore use 'design' as catch-all word for imagining and producing texts. 'Imagining' sees design as a blueprint for production in which there is a 'deliberateness about choosing the modes for representation and the framing for that representation' (Kress and van Leeuwen, 2001: 45). However, in text production there is no clear separation between designing and producing in that the ongoing process of semiotic choice and change, made easy by digital technologies, enables ongoing revision and redesign. 'The boundary between design and production is … blurry' (Kress and van Leeuwen, 2001: 55) as designers, including writers, use the process of production to discover and shape their ideas.

Redesign refers to the practice of combining and recombining semiotic resources so as to create possibilities for transformation (The New London Group, 1996; Cope and Kalantzis, 1997). In my own work, I have used the word *reconstruction* for the transformative move as it takes us beyond the practice of deconstruction and suggests that power can also be productive (Janks, 2000). Because all texts are constructed, they can be reconstructed, to offer a different representation of the world.

Now when I teach critical reading, I ask students to imagine alternative designs and

then to deconstruct those (Janks, 2000, 2005). The ability to read texts critically, including our own texts, creates the conditions for transformative redesign. The ongoing cycle of text construction-deconstruction-reconstruction/redesign is captured by Paulo Freire when he says that,

> To exist, humanly, is to *name* the world, to change it. Once named, the world in its turn reappears to its namers as a problem and requires of them a new *naming* (1972a: 61).

In this way, Freire links literacy – writing, reading and rewriting the word and the world – to human agency and the power to effect social transformation. Design, which is where writing is located in my model, is therefore essential to the integrated model, because it moves us beyond critique to action. Instead of simply deconstructing texts to expose the power relations at play, there is an expectation that readers will rewrite both the words and the world they refer to. From a Freirean perspective, critique should lead to social transformation through action. In terms of this model, design needs to take power, diversity, and access seriously. The argument is that it is the inter-dependence of design (which includes writing), with the other more social orientations, that *makes* it critical. It places design in a dialectical relation to the world. The shaded rows in Table 8.1, all pertain to design. They will form the basis of the discussion on writing that follows. When each row is illustrated, it will be reinserted into the text.

WRITING AND POWER

Taking power seriously means that we have to attend to the ways in which our writing works to position our readers and to examine whose interests are served by this positioning. We need to understand the possible power effects of our choices. We need to understand how our ideational choices construct participants, processes, and circumstances from a particular perspective; we need to attend to our choices of mood and modality, which encode relations of authority and agency between writers and readers; we need to think about how textual choices work to foreground and background ideas, to construct cause and effect, to position information as old or new (Halliday, 1985). We need control over grammar and lexis so that we can produce the nuances we need to realize the meaning potential that language affords us. What is selected from the range of lexical and grammatical options determines how this potential is realized.

These ideas can be illustrated with reference to a talk that I gave at a conference entitled 'Critical literacy methods, models, and motivation'. When I first thought of the title for this talk, I wanted to call it 'Critical literacy: methods, models, and *motives*'. It sounded right. I liked the balance created by the two three-syllable words followed by the three two-syllable words, and the rhythm created by the alliteration. However, the word *motives* bothered me. Murderers have motives. The word *motives* keeps bad company. We think of people as having 'hidden' or 'ulterior' motives. We think of motives as being self-interested more often than we think of them as being pure. The word *motivation*, on the other hand has had a better press. It is associated with a beneficial psychological force that enables us to do good things. We think of people who are 'highly motivated' as achievers, as having positive attitudes. As teachers, we all want motivated learners but are likely to distrust students with motives. Therefore, harnessing all the positive connotations of the word 'motivation', I changed my title.

We also need to understand how when we use language, we draw unconsciously on our communities' resources for naming the world, on the discourses, the 'saying (writing)-doing-being-valuing-believing combinations' (Gee, 1990: 142) that we inhabit. When Foucault says that 'discourse is the power which is to be seized' (1970), it is precisely because of the power of discourse to produce us as particular kinds of human subjects.

We need to be able to rewrite the texts of spin-doctors, advertising agencies, branding machines, war-mongers, homophobes, chauvinists, and racists to create different, more equitable versions of our social world. Practice in reconstructing the words of others, enables us to reposition our own texts. As writers, we are held accountable for the way we 'name' the world. In the end, our ethical stance will determine how our writing is judged. Writing provides one of the means of 'speaking truth to power' (Foucault, 1970), of 'writing back' (Pennycook, 1998), of imagining and articulating a more just world (Freire, 1972a, b).

Power without design	The deconstruction of power, without reconstruction or design, removes human agency.

The work of feminist linguists, such as Spender (1980), Cameron (1985, 1990) and Threadgold (1997), is a case in point. Their analysis of the sexist nature of English, changed the way we use the language. For example, in writing, the use of nonsexist pronouns is now standard requirement for the publication of academic texts.

Design without power	Design without an understanding of how powerful discourses perpetuate themselves, runs the risk of unconscious reproduction of these forms.

In an analysis of an advertisement for pension plans for domestic workers (Janks, 1997), I was able to show how the advertisers, while attempting to harness new postapartheid discourses of workers' rights and employers' obligations to provide pensions, nevertheless continue to draw on old paternalistic apartheid discourses. In the advertisement, the employer infantalises her employee by making unilateral decisions for her. In this way, the discourses we inhabit continue to speak through us and are unconsciously reproduced, even when we are consciously trying to reframe the discourse pertaining to domestic workers.

WRITING AND DIVERSITY

Heath's (1983) longitudinal study in the Piedmont Carolinas, where she researched the language practices of three communities, a white working class community, a black working class community, and a middle class community of mainstream white and black families, demonstrated convincingly that different communities have different 'ways with words'. Although children from all three communities attended the same school, 'mainstream language values and skills were the norm' (1983: 4) in education. Here power intersects with diversity, privileging the language practices of the already privileged.

Her study centred on the language and literacy practices in the three different communities. The project of schooling has to recognize that literacy is not equally valued across all communities. In South Africa, for example, there is little print material in African languages and there is not a culture of writing in these languages. The teaching of literacy is further compounded in multilingual classrooms where students are expected to master the standard variety of the language of education, which is often not the language of their home or community. In South Africa, for example, where parents have the right to choose the language in which their children will be educated, there are few resources for using African languages across the curriculum. As a result of what Ndebele calls a 'predetermined pragmatism' based on 'limited choices' (1986: 220), most African

parents opt for English as the medium of teaching and learning. African parents are not alone. 'Content and language integrated learning is an increasing curriculum trend in Europe' (Graddol, 2006: 86). There is an ever-increasing demand for English, and China alone is producing 20 million new users of English every year.

Now that there are more nonnative speakers of English than native speakers, hybrid varieties are developing as nonnative speakers who speak different home languages use English as a lingua franca. The use of English as a global language has necessitated a greater tolerance for different varieties of English in spoken communication. In writing, the standard variety remains the norm. 'Hidden armies of copy editors [ensure that] only standard forms reach print' (Graddol, 2006: 115).

The genre theorists in Australia went beyond teaching children standard English and argued that children from marginalized communities also needed access to the dominant genres needed for success in school: Recount, Report, Procedure, Explanation, Exposition, and Discussion. They analyzed the linguistic and structural features of these genres so that they could be taught explicitly. In the process, the dominant genres were reified and there was little room for creativity or transgression. Western norms were privileged and indigenous forms ignored. For example, although not regarded as a dominant genre, Western norms for narrative are assumed. Corson (2001: 47) cites studies in Australia that show the spatial rather than temporal organization of aboriginal narratives. Based on the movement of characters from place to place, 'moving and stopping narratives' are created. There is little place in schools for diverse 'ways with words'.

| Design without diversity | This privileges powerful forms and fails to use the design resources provided by difference. |

Literature on the other hand provides abundant evidence for how writing is enriched by writers who are able to capture the rhythms and perspectives of different 'ways with words'. Only in the name of literary aesthetics are the linguistic gatekeepers, the discourse police, held at bay.

In *The Bonesetter's Daughter*, Amy Tan (2001) is able to capture LuLing's English, the 'choppy talk' (42) that she had taught herself in Hong Kong and China:

> Lootie[2] give me so much trouble. Maybe I send her go Taiwan, school for bad children. What you think' (43). Later she says to her daughter Ruth, 'You wish I dead? You wish no mother tell you what to do. Okay, maybe I die soon' (46).

Roberts (2003) similarly captures the cadences of Bombay English in *Shantaram*. Here Prabakar invites Karla to a celebration lunch:

> We will have it a very nice lunches! My good self, I have kept it a complete empty stomach for filling up to fat. So good is the food. You will enjoy so much, the people will think you are having a baby inside your dress (246).

Alice Walker has done the same for Ebonics, Bosman for an Afrikaans-inflected English.

Chinua Achebe, rather than using an African variety of English, has instead worked to capture the idiom of Nigeria in English. Here we see time measured by the slow rhythms of the seasons and the crops, belief in the power of potions and the voice of the Oracle, and the importance of the land.

> And so they killed the white man and tied his iron horse to their sacred tree ... This was before the planting season began. For a long time nothing happened. The rains had come and yams had been sown. The iron horse was still tied to sacred silk-cotton tree ... They have a big market in Abame on every other Afo day and, as you know the whole clan gathers there. That was the day it happened. ... They must have used a powerful medicine to make themselves invisible until the market was full. And they began to shoot. ... Everybody was killed. ... Their clan is now completely empty. Even the sacred fish in their mysterious lake have fled and the lake has turned the colour of blood. A great evil has come upon their land as the Oracle has warned (Achebe, 1958: 125–126).

These writers extend the possibilities for English with their different perspectives and sensibilities.

Diversity without design	Diversity provides the means, the ideas, the alternative perspectives for reconstruction and transformation. Without design, the potential that diversity offers is not realized.

Schools need to embrace students' multilingual resources and their community funds of knowledge so that all students' identities are validated in the classroom and have a place in their writing.

WRITING AND ACCESS

Difference is structured in relation to power, which results in social hierarchies. The different languages and varieties that we speak are not equally valued in the communities and countries in which we live, or in the global arena, nor do they provide equal access to material, educational, and economic resources. This produces a system of social distinction, providing linguistic capital to those who have access to the valued languages or varieties. Moreover, the 'chances of access' (Bourdieu, 1991: 56) are not equally distributed across the society.

> Words, utterances are not only ... signs to be understood and deciphered; they are also *signs of wealth*, intended to be evaluated and appreciated, and *signs of authority*, intended to be believed and obeyed (Bourdieu, 1991: 66, italics in the original).

For Bourdieu, the different power attributed to different varieties is a form of 'symbolic power'. It is 'symbolic' because it depends on people's belief in the social distinctions; a language's legitimacy depends on people 'recognising' its legitimacy (1991: 170). Bourdieu calls this 'misrecognition', because he sees it as an example of institutionally manufactured compliance or consent. Given that the education system is a key institutional apparatus for the privileging of a particular language (or variety) and for legitimating its dominance, it is ironic that it often fails to provide marginal students with *knowledge of* and *access to* the legitimate language. Instead it succeeds in teaching them *recognition of* (misrecognition of) its legitimacy (1991: 62, my emphasis). As a teacher of English, a globally dominant language, one is currently faced with an irresolvable contradiction (Granville et al., 1998; Janks, 1995).

> If you provide more learners with access to the dominant variety of the dominant language, you ... maintain its dominance. If, on the other hand, you deny students access, you perpetuate their marginalization in a society that continues to recognize this language as a mark of distinction. It is this contradiction that Lodge (1997) has called *the access paradox*. The access paradox recognizes that domination without access, excludes students from the language or the language variety that would afford them the most linguistic capital, thereby limiting their life chances. It restricts students to the communities in which their marginalized languages are spoken. On the other hand, access without a theory of domination, naturalizes the power of the dominant language ... and devalues students' own languages (Janks, 2004: 36).

What is needed is a language pedagogy that reverses this – that gives mastery of English, together with a critical view of its status as a global language. The Sydney School's approach to teaching genre, which focused on access, needed to counter the legitimating force of this reifying pedagogy by embracing cross-cultural instantiations of these genres and opening up possibilities for redesign.

Access without design	This maintains and reifies powerful forms without considering how they can be transformed.

Education needs to produce students who understand why linguistic diversity is a resource for creativity and cognition, who value all the languages that they speak and who are wary of linguistic hegemony and the tyranny of standard norms.

Unfortunately there is no point in encouraging writers to exploit all their linguistic resources and to bring their 'community funds of knowledge' (Moll, 1992) and 'ways with words' into the centre, unless simultaneously we work to make the centre more inclusive.

Design without access	Runs the risk of whatever is designed remaining on the margins.

Greater inclusivity requires social action to prevent gatekeeping practices, which excludes voices that are different. This is starting to happen. Editors of academic journals are beginning to ask referees to assist with editing the written language of articles whose content is worthy of dissemination but whose language the journal would reject. Where universities still demand linguistically flawless doctoral theses, some universities now allow students to have their work edited while others have taken the small step of informing examiners that the candidate is not writing in his or her main language. In addition, cultural flows are now less unidirectional: Japanese Manga comics, Hong Kong action movies, Bollywood films, and Spanish telenovelas are no longer on the margins.

CONCLUSION

Twenty million bloggers are now claiming their place as makers, rather than just consumers, of information on the internet. When we write, we want readers to enter our world. We can play with the word *design*, and suggest that as writers we have designs on our readers. We work hard to entice them into our way of seeing and understanding the world. We use language in combination with other signs to construct our version of reality and we work to position our readers. Nearly forty years ago, Bolinger (1980) described language as a loaded weapon. As writers, we need to recognize the power of words to do good or harm, to be used in the interests of all or only some. Ultimately, the choice is an ethical one which affects how we 'name' our world and, in so doing, ourselves.

NOTES

1   In Janks (2000) this model is called 'a *synthesis* model for critical literacy education'. Because the model theorises different emphases in critical literacy in relation to one another, the model is more than a synthesis. I now refer to it as the *interdependent* model of critical literacy. In addition, I now use the concept of power, rather than the concept of domination so as not to privilege a Marxist theory of power.

2   Ruthie.

REFERENCES

Achebe, C. (1958) *Things Fall Apart*, London: Heinemann.

Badenhorst, C. (2007) *Research Writing Breaking the Barriers*, Pretoria: Van Schaik.

Bolinger, D. (1980) *Language the Loaded Weapon*, Harlow: Longman.

Bourdieu, P. (1991) *Language and Symbolic Power*, Cambridge: Polity Press.

Cameron, D. (1985) *Feminism and Linguistic Theory*, London: Macmillan.

Cameron, D. (1990) *The Feminist Critique of Language*, London: Routledge.

Christensen, L. (2000) *Reading, Writing and Rising Up: Teaching about social justice and the power of the written word*, Milwaukee: Rethinking Schools.

Clark, R. and Ivanic, R. (1997) *The Politics of Writing*, London: Routledge.

Cope, B. and Kalantzis, M. (2000) *Multiliteracies: Literacy Learning and the Design of Social Futures*, London: Routledge.

Corson, D. (2001) *Language, Diversity and Education*, Mahwah: Lawrence Erlbaum and Associates.

Fairclough, N. (1989) *Language and Power*, London: Longman.

Fairclough, N. (2003) *Analysing Discourse*, London: Routledge.

Forrestal, P., Cook, C., and Dainutis, J. (1992) *Making Meanings*, Scarborough: Chalkface Press.

Foucault, M. (1970). The Order of Discourse. Inaugural Lecture at the College de France. In M. Shapiro (Ed.), *Language and Politics.* Oxford: Basil Blackwell.

Foucault, M. (1976) *History of Sexuality*, Volume 1. Harmondsworth: Penguin.

Foucault, M. (1984) 'The Order of Discourse. Inaugural lecture at the Collège De France', in M. Shapiro (ed.), *Language and Politics*, Oxford: Basil Blackwell. pp.108–138.

Fowler, R., Hodge, B., Kress, G., and Trew, T. (1979) *Language and Control*, London: Routledge and Kegan Paul.

Fowler, R. and Kress, G (1979) 'Critical Linguistics', in R. Fowler., B. Hodge., G. Kress, and T. Trew (eds), *Language and Control*, London: Routledge and Kegan Paul. pp.185–213.

Freire P. (1972a) *Cultural Action for Freedom*, Harmondsworth: Peguin.

Freire, P. (1972b) *Pedagogy of the Oppressed*, Harmondsworth: Penguin.

Gee, J. (1990) *Social Linguistics and Literacies*, London: Falmer Press.

Gee, J.P. (1996). *Social Linguistics and Literacies: Ideology in Discourses* (2nd ed.). London and New York: Taylor & Francis.

Gee, J. (1999) *An Introduction to Discourse Analysis*, London: Routlege.

Graddol, D. (2006) *English Next*, British Council. http://www.britishcouncil.org/learning-research-englishnext.htm. Downloaded 23 September 2007.

Granville, S., Janks, H., Joseph, M., Mphahlele, M., Ramani, E., Reed, Y., and Watson, P. (1998) 'English With or Without G(u)ilt: A Position Paper on Language in Education Policy for South Africa', *Language and Education*, 12: 254–272.

Halliday, M.A.K. (1985) *An Introduction to Functional Grammar*, London: Arnold.

Heath, S.B. (1983) *Ways with Words*, Cambridge: Cambridge University Press.

Ivanic, R. (1998) *Writing and Identity*, Amsterdam: John Benjamins Publishing Company.

Janks, H. (1995) *The Research and Development of Critical Language Awareness Materials for Use in South African Schools*, Unpublished Doctoral Thesis. Johannesburg: University of the Witwatersrand.

Janks, H. (1997) 'Critical discourse analysis as a research tool', *Discourse*, 18(3): 329–342.

Janks, H. (2000) 'Domination, access, diversity and design: a synthesis for critical literacy education', *Educational Review,* 52(2): 175–186

Janks, H. (2004) 'The access paradox', *English in Australia,* 12(1): 33–42.

Janks, H. (2005) 'Deconstruction and Reconstruction: Diversity as a productive resource', *Discourse,* 26(1): 31–43.

Kamler, B. (2001) *Relocating the Personal,* Albany: State University of New York.

Kamler, B. and Thomson, P. (2006) *Helping Doctoral Students Write,* London: Routledge.

Kenworthy, C. and Kenworthy, S. (1997) *Aboriginality in Texts and Contexts,* Fremantle: Fremantle Arts Centre Press.

Kress, G. (2000) 'Multimodality', in B. Cope and M. Kalantzis (eds), *Multiliteracies: Literacy learning and the design of social futures,* London: Routledge. pp.182–202

Kress, G. (2003) *Literacy in the New Media Age,* London: Routledge.

Kress, G. and Van Leeuwen, T. (2001) *Multimodal Discourse,* London: Arnold.

Lakoff, G. (2004) *Don't Think of an Elephant, Know Your Values and Frame the Debate,* White River Junction: Vermont, Chelsea Green.

Lillis, T. (2001) *Student Writing: Access, Regulation, Desire,* London: Routledge.

Lodge, H. (1997) *Providing Access to Academic Literacy in the Arts Foundation Programme at the University of the Witwatersrand in 1996 – The Theory behind the Practice,* Unpublished Master's Dissertation, Johannesburg, University of The Witwatersrand.

Martino, W. (1997) *From the Margins,* Fremantle: Fremantle Arts Centre Press.

Mellor, B. with J. Hemming and J. Leggett. (1984) *Changing Stories,* London: Inner London Education Authority English Centre.

Mellor, B., Patterson, A., and O'Neill, M. (1987) *Reading Stories,* Scarborough: Chalkface Press.

Mellor, B., and Patterson, A. (1996). *Investigating Texts.* Scarborough: Chalkface Press.

Moll, L. (1992). Literacy research in community and classroom. A sociocultural approach. In J. G. R. Beach, M. Kamil and T. Shanahan (Ed.), *Mulitdisciplinary Perspectives on Literacy Research.* Urbana, Illinois: National Council of Teachers of English.

Moll, L., Amanti, C., Neffe, D., and González, N. (1992) 'Funds of knowledge for teaching: Using a qualitative approach to connect homes and classrooms', *Theory into Practice,* 31(2): 132–141.

Ndebele, N.S. (1987) 'The English Language and Social Change in South Africa', in D. Bunn and J. Taylor (eds), *From South Africa New Writing, Photographs and Art,* Tri-Quarterly, No. 69, Chicago: Northwestern University.

New London Group. (1996) A pedagogy of multiliteracies: designing social futures. *Harvard Educational Review, Cambridge,* 66, 60–92.

New London Group (2000) 'A Pedagogy of Multiliteracies', in B. Cope and M. Kalantzis (eds), *Multiliteracies: Literacy learning and the design of social futures,* London: Routledge. pp.9–37.

Pennycook, A. (1998) *English and the Discourses of Colonialism,* London: Routledge.

Roberts, G. (2003) *Shantaram,* London: Abacus.

Spender, D. (1980) *Manmade Language,* London: Routledge and Kegan Paul.

Tan, A. (2001) *The Bonesetter's Daughter,* London: Flamingo.

Threadgold, T. (1997) *Feminist Poetics,* London: Routledge.

Vasquez, V. (2004) *Negotiating Critical Literacies with Young Children,* Mahwah: Lawrence Erlbaum and Associates.

Multiple Literacies and Multi-literacies

Brian V. Street

This chapter introduces and develops the thinking of New Literacy Studies and of the New London Group regarding the notions of multi and of multiple literacies and their implications for educational practice and in particular, the designing of programmes for literacy learning. The New Literacy Studies (NLS) adopts a 'social practice' approach to literacy, drawing upon ethnographic perspectives that study literacy practices across different cultural contexts and recognizing the plurality, therefore, of the literacy experience. Developments in Literacy Studies have been usefully summarized in articles by Gee (2000), Finnegan (1988), Besnier and Street (1994), and Street (1995). Books by Barton and Hamilton (1998), Barton, Hamilton, and Ivanic (1999), Maybin (1994), Street and Lefstein (2007), and Street (1995, 2005) provide fuller accounts of the new approaches. The New London Group (NLG) likewise argues the need to pluralize the notion of literacy but locates this in the context of developments that Gee et al. (1996) term 'the new work order' and Kress and others refer to as 'multimodality' (Kress 2003; Kress and Street, 2006; Kress and van Leeuwen, 1996). NLG first came to wider attention through an article in the *Harvard Educational Review* (NLG, 1996) and a subsequent book edited by Cope and Kalantzis (2000) entitled *Multiliteracies: literacy learning and the design of social futures.* The authors advocate a response to the new conditions in which 'literacy' is encountered, in terms of the 'multi-literacies' of visual literacy, computer literacy, graphic literacy, and so on; and of the pedagogies that might be addressed to this new situation. They argue that those working in education need to develop pedagogies that will prepare students for these new conditions, these new 'multi-literacies'.

The present chapter takes up the challenge posed by these two emerging traditions by attempting to locate the arguments about 'multi-literacies' presented by NLG in the context of the more ethnographic perspective offered by NLS. In particular, it contrasts the concept of 'multi-literacies' with that of 'multiple literacies' and discusses the implications of adopting the different terms for conceptualization of literacy practices in contemporary society in general and for the development of students' writing in educational contexts in particular. After describing the major contributions in each area, the chapter offers a critical review of the strengths and weaknesses of each. It argues that those developing the concept of a 'pedagogy of multi-literacies' need to locate the concept in a broader understanding of these positions and the critiques of them. This, then, has implications for those in education struggling with both new communicative demands in the wider world and the increasing regulatory pressures of governments and formal institutions of education, such as the National Literacy Strategy in the UK and the 'No Child Left Behind' programme in the USA. The chapter concludes with some indicative examples of work in educational contexts that builds on the insights developed here in supporting students' writing development.

'NEW LITERACY STUDIES'

An alternative to the dominant model of literacy has developed in recent years amongst researchers and amongst practitioners who take a view of reading and writing that is more 'social' in its orientation. Both teachers and researchers have been forced by their exposure to educational situations on the ground to recognize that literacy varies from one context to another, that readers and writers have different conceptions of the meanings of what they are doing, and that these meanings are not just 'individual' or 'cognitive' but derived from cultural processes (Pahl and Rowsell, 2005; Street, 1984, 2005). The academic and schooled literacy of dominant western elites represents only one form of literacy amongst many, just as the forms of language amongst such elites is only one dialect amongst many. In everyday life, in communities and neighbourhoods, in workplaces in urban and rural environments, what it means to engage in reading and writing varies considerably (Barton and Ivanic, 1991). With respect to writing development, for instance, the focus on spelling correctly or on punctuation that characterizes schooled literacy is seen by NLS scholars less important than a focus on communication and on the social relations involved. Ethnographic research on the actual uses and meanings of literacy practices in specific social contexts

has revealed a multiplicity of literacies that by the very weight of evidence throw into doubt the certainties and simplicities of the dominant model with its single (western-based) Literacy (Street, 1993).

I have characterized the dominant view of literacy as an 'autonomous' model of literacy (Street, 1984). According to this view, literacy is a neutral technique, which can be applied across all social and cultural contexts with generally uniform effects. The model is rooted in earlier psychological theories of individual cognitive development and social theories of progress and development, from simple to complex society, and from 'traditional' to 'modern'. The major tenet of this perspective is that there is a 'great divide' between oral and written forms of communication (Finnegan, 1988). In societies characterized by mainly oral modes of communication, it is assumed that certain features of 'modern' society are lacking, notably the ability to dissemble oneself from immediate meanings and contexts, use of formal logic, and a 'modernising' perspective on life (Goody, 1977, 1968, 1987; Lerner, 1958). The acquisition of literacy, then, has major implications for both individuals and for societies. As individuals acquire literacy, so their worldviews expand: they are able to juxtapose different sets of ideas critically and so develop scientific and logical thinking. Economic and political institutions are believed to change with the spread of literacy, so that rational economic planning and capitalist entrepreneurship replace barter and exchange (Anderson and Bowman, 1965). In world terms, such a change leads to a new world order in which the model offered by western 'developed' societies is imitated by 'under developed' societies. According to Anderson (1965) and to earlier UNESCO (1976) approaches to education, the spread of literacy is associated with most features of modernization, notably economic take off, rational health planning, female emancipation, and so on. In political terms, patrimonial social orders give way to bureaucratic and democratic systems, where promotion is on merit, not kinship or social position, and decision making is democratically ordered through such institutions as political parties, voting, and a division of political and judicial institutions. That all of this follows from the spread of literacy tends to be taken for granted amongst development economists and policy makers at a macro level, whilst amongst researchers it provides the basic focus for enquiry – how literacy leads to these effects and in what conditions becomes a dominant research question.

At the individual level, similar changes are believed to follow from the acquisition of literacy. As with the social level, the major feature of literacy is seen to be the ability to lay different ideas out side by side and to evaluate them critically. Logic, critical thought, and scientific perspectives then follow. Individuals who might be rooted in restricted modes of thought are able to develop elaborated and critical thinking and to make rational choices better. A great deal of psychological research is devoted to the cognitive implications of the acquisition of literacy (Olson, 1977, 1994; Olson and Torrance, forthcoming) [see also Olson, this volume]. The theoretical roots of these ideas are also to be found in technological determinism – a belief that social progress follows from specific technical developments such as the printing press, or television, or currently computing and information technology; from theories of cognitive development at individual level tested through experimental methods (though often apparently validated through more speculative methods cf. Ong, 1982); modernization theory and the concept of progress derived from eighteenth century European Enlightenment thinking (Oxenham, 1980).

Much of this appears 'natural' in the everyday discourse of many contemporary western societies. Media representations of literacy and its significance pathologize those with difficulties in reading and writing, whether adults or 'failed' school children. Schools are berated for failing the society if literacy levels are seen to fall – by various measures

rooted in the autonomous model. The issue of 'falling standards' has dominated public debate about literacy in a number of societies in recent years (Hirsch, 1987). Adult literacy campaigns have been created, in both the developed and developing world contexts, to overcome this 'disadvantage' and their publicity tends to reinforce the popular conception of literacy. In the UK, the National Literacy Strategy could be seen as grounded in these ideas (Marsh, 2004; Pahl and Rowsell, 2005; Stephens, 2000; Street, 1998).

The *strengths* of the autonomous model of literacy are claimed to be its focus on individual and technical skills and its ability to 'deliver' in pedagogic terms, mastery of reading and writing through an ability to separate out the social and cultural 'interference' of traditional beliefs and mindsets. The implications of this view for pedagogy and for programmes are examined briefly in the conclusion to this article. The *weaknesses* of the autonomous are that it is insensitive to cultural variation, narrowly economistic, and ethnocentric in its focus upon western forms of literacy at the expense of local traditions and meanings (cf. critiques by Street, 1984, 1993; Finnegan, 1988).

Because of these problems with dominant views of literacy, new models have been developed in recent years that attempt to take a more critical and a more culturally relative perspective. These have been termed the 'New Literacy Studies' (NLS) (cf. Gee, 1990; Street, 2005). Key concepts within this new orientation are those of 'literacy events' and 'literacy practices'. The former derives from the work of Shirley Brice Heath (1983) who wrote one of the earliest and definitive 'ethnographies' of literacy as social practice. She employed the term 'literacy events' to refer to any situation or event in which reading and/or writing were salient. Simple in its formulation, the concept nevertheless had great power in facilitating research, enabling researchers to focus upon actual uses of reading and writing in context rather than the speculative accounts evident in either the autonomous model or in critical literacy.

I have found it useful to extend this concept to refer not only to events and behaviours but to take account also of the conceptualizations that actors themselves bring to the events and the cultural assumptions that underpin these, which refer to as 'literacy practices' (Street, 1984, 2000). Literacy practices are located at a broader, more abstract level and so enable us to describe not only the immediate settings of literacy but also the cultural concepts and practice that are brought to bear on the event. Comparison can process using both of these concepts to compare and analyse the literacy events and literacy practices of many different communities, both in and out of school, as Heath did in her early ethnography (1983) and many have done since in applying these insights to the support that teachers might give to pupils in their development of writing (Hull and Schultz, 2002; Pahl and Rowsell, 2005; Street, 1993).

Amongst high school children in Philadelphia, for instance, writing may be used out of school to develop rap songs or poems about personal identity, so that what matters are that the vocabulary used is recognizable to peers and that the 'right' to write at all has been established (Camitta, 1993; Shuman, 1993). In a pacific atoll on the other hand, it may be sermons that represent the major use of writing and the 'voice' of the pastor evokes hierarchy and shared religious meanings in which the congregation are relatively passive (Besnier, 1995). Again amongst villagers in Iran, the uses of literacy may be associated with, on the one hand Islamic learning and reading the Quran and on the other with the practicalities of selling fruit to the city, requiring literacy for writing labels on boxes, keeping lists and invoices, writing cheques, and reading inventories (Street, 1984). In a Zafimaniry village in Madagascar, literacy is highly valued ideologically, and children are encouraged to attend the local French-based school where they learn to incant texts and learn scribing by rote, but in real everyday life it plays no real part, has little bearing on work activities or on the epistemological bases for classification or inquiry (Bloch, 1993): in that sense literacy remains a sign of something else rather than a material practice of real importance. Again, in contemporary South Africa, researchers have identified multiple forms of literacy practices that vary between urban and rural areas, amongst political activists in settlement sites and agricultural workers in traditional farms, for taxi drivers in Cape Town or election campaigners taking messages about the 'New South Africa' to nonliterate voters (Prinsloo and Breier, 1996; Stein, 2007).

In all of these cases, the close ethnographic study of literacy in social context, based upon a broader conception of literacy as a social practice, forces us to suspend our own conceptions of what 'literacy' means and to be open to variation. The theoretical roots of this approach are in the ethnography of communication, and in the disciplines of anthropology and sociolinguistics. Its *strengths* are that it is grounded in accounts of real social practice, whereas the autonomous model derives its evidence either from experiments on individual skills or from general inferences and speculations about social change, a charge also levelled against much critical literacy. Its implications for pedagogy are for the use of 'real' materials in teaching and for an emphasis on meanings rather than the formalist precisions of the autonomous model or the sometimes-narrow political agendas that have dominated critical literacy. Its *weaknesses* are that it complicates the design of programmes and curricula in ways that might actually prevent anything being done, that is it is hugely demanding on designers and organizers but most especially on teachers who have to become virtually ethnographers themselves, sensitive to the cultural variations amongst their learners and able to address the different literacy needs of both the immediate environment and those their students are likely to enter (Heath, 1983). Recent applications of NLS to educational contexts have responded vigorously to these criticisms and demonstrated the importance of taking account of learners' home and community contexts in building on these 'funds of knowledge' for educational purposes (Bloome, 1989; Hull and Schultz, 2002; Pahl and Rowsell, 2005; Street, 2005). It is the relationship between these sensitivities to the local and awareness of the larger changes in society to which learners are currently exposed that leads me to consider here the other major tradition in literacy studies that is currently impacting on education and learning – that of the New London Group and its Pedagogy of Multi-literacies.

NEW LONDON GROUP

The 'New London Group' (NLG) (Cazden et al., 1996) have put forward the notion of multi-literacy to refer multiple forms of literacy associated with channels or modes, such as computer literacy and visual literacy. The NLG are interested in channels and modes of communication that can be referred to as 'multiliteracies'. Gunther Kress in particular is interested in the notion of visual literacy, so for him multi-literacy signals a new world in which the reading and writing practices of literacy are only one part of what people are going to have to learn in order to be 'literate' (Kress and van Leeuwen, 1996). They are going to have to learn to handle the icons and the signs, the Word for Windows package with all its combinations of signs, symbols, boundaries, pictures, words, texts, images, etc.

Those who espouse this perspective argue that the nature of the world is changing radically and that the ethnographic approach simply privileges 'lost' or 'disappearing' world views and ways with words: to persist with them is simply to disadvantage their users in a world where power will lie with those who can command the genres of power (McLaren and Lankshear, 1994). These claims are rooted more broadly in recent critical revision of the Enlightenment claims for rationality, science, and objectivity. A number of researchers, often working under the label 'post modernism', have argued that these changes are as significant as those characterized in such dramatic terms as 'traditional to modern', or preliterate to literate. The major features of this change are to be found in the workplace and in the nature of labour markets, work processes, the relations of worker and 'boss', the production of goods, and their distribution across the world. These are 'New Times' in which 'Fast Capitalism' supplants the simple economic imperatives of early capitalist development (Gee et al., 1996; O'Connor, 1994).

Whilst these changes can be observed at a material level, in the 'global' nature of markets, the interrelation of economic processes in different parts of the world, the 'democratization' of workplaces with 'flat' rather than hierarchical relations and the immediate targeting of production to consumer choices, they are also evident, though not always so visibly, in intellectual and ideological shifts in the modern world order. The dominant view of the 'modern' world was of rational, linear thinking based on belief in science and objective truth: the new world order turns out to be less predictable, less logical, more vicarious and disordered, and more multifaceted in both cultural and linguistic terms. This 'post-modern' world has different communication systems and needs, is more sensitive to and dependent on variation rather than standardization and in some senses is less optimistic in that it denies a simple unilinear 'progress' from simpler to complex or from traditional to modern. The post in postmodern is not a sequential term but a shift of plane.

The meanings of literacy, then, have shifted radically in this new world order. The kinds of 'reading' and writing required of workers is quite different from that in the 'modern' era (O'Connor, 1994). The major quality required of new labour forces is flexibility, an ability to move between different orders of communication – spoken, written, visual, and computer-based. Some researchers have argued that this shift involves in some sense the 'end of language' in that analysis must focus far more on semiotic systems – on systems of signs such as icons, visual representations, and computer display – rather than on language-based writing systems (Kress, 2003). It is a world of international road signs, standardized labels on clothing, recognizable televisual images, commercial logos, bank by phone, or by computerized display in multiple languages. In this sense, literacy takes on a much broader meaning: there are 'multi-literacies' – computer literacy, visual literacy, technological literacy as well as the extended metaphors of political literacy and cultural literacy (Hirsch, 1987). Academic literacy and the narrow modernist view of 'schooled' literacy (Cook-Gumperz, 1986) are not necessarily well-suited to this new world order and certainly does not train new members of society to handle the complexity of the world they are entering. The implications for pedagogy and for education generally are immense and are scarcely realized. Indeed, it could be argued that the current emphasis in a number of western societies on 'back to basics' and the scare stories about 'illiteracy' and 'falling standards' represent a resistance to these changes and a harking back to a safer and more certain world order in which a single 'literacy' characterized a single dominant world view that was more stable and persistent. Literacy, then, remains a sign by which we know the world we live in, it refers not simply to the skills of reading and writing but to the way we think about ourselves as working and thinking beings: the literacy of the modern era is, then, a very different literacy than that of the postmodern era.

The theoretical roots of this view are in sociology and critical theory. Its *strengths* lie in its ability to locate literacy in the larger world context and to address the workplace needs of the contemporary world. Its *weaknesses* are that it is too theoretical, and often presented in inaccessible language; it is ungrounded in actual descriptions of social or even individual practice, being dependent on large and often vague generalization, and that beneath an apparently radical exterior it remains rooted in an 'autonomous' model of literacy that assumes acquiring forms of literacy will provide access to forms of power (Cope and Kalantzis, 1993).

From an NLS perspective, there is a problem regarding generalization and lack of ethnographic specificity in some of the accounts of 'New Times' offered in NLG. Are all factories going the way that chapter suggests? Are hierarchies really being flattened? Is not some of the rhetoric of fast capitalism itself a way of justifying new forms of exploitation and inequality as though they were inevitable and just the product of collective action, or the neutral market, rather than serving the interests of particular elites (cf. Gee et al., 1996). Kress (2003), a member of the NLG, has also criticized the further extensions of 'multi-literacy' into, for instance, political literacy, or emotional literacy, thereby using the term as a metaphor for competence [see also Moss, this volume].

If the 'multi-literacies' position is located within what is outlined in the foregoing section as an autonomous model of literacy, then it is subject to the critiques levelled against that model: that is, from an ethnographic perspective, critiques of its ethnocentrism, reification and technological determinism, and its location in evolutionary theories of progress and modernization. If, on the other hand, the multi-literacies position is to be located within New Literacy Studies, then it has to take account of the critiques regarding 'romanticism, relevance, and relativism' levelled against those studies, such as the problems of accumulating empirical accounts of literacy in different cultures without a general theory, as well as the problems found by practitioners and agencies with the sheer complexity and perhaps unrealistic demands laid upon those attempting to implement the model. By bringing these positions together, this chapter aims to offer an overview for those concerned to take account of the 'new literacies' whilst maintaining practical and realistic educational programmes.

IMPLICATIONS FOR POLICY AND PROGRAMMES IN WRITING AND DEVELOPMENT

I conclude, then, with a brief discussion of the implications of the different approaches detailed here for the design of programmes in the development of writing and reading, whether at school level, and for the nature of teaching and learning more generally. The autonomous model of literacy that has underpinned much educational theory and policy, with its emphasis on individual skills and cognition, has tended to support a technical pedagogy for both reading and writing – with the emphasis frequently on reading, to the chagrin of writing specialists (cf. Stannard and Huxford, 2007), focused on rote learning, skill manipulation, and lack of critical enquiry or interaction. The argument here is that the skills must be learnt – often the 'hard way' – and then it is up to the newly literate to decide what to do with them, whether to read Marx or the Bible. Both the NLS and the NLG approaches would critique this approach represented in the USA by the 'No Child Left Behind' framework (see critiques in Larson, 2007) and in the UK by aspects of the National Literacy Strategy (see critiques that follows, by Marsh, 2004). The New Literacy Studies, in contrast, has been concerned to help develop a pedagogy that builds on the knowledge of language and of writing and reading that learners bring from home, as in Hull and Schultz's (2002) attempt to bridge the home/school boundaries or Street's (2005) edited volume of examples from 20+ sites of such practical combining of theory and practice, home and school. It is ultimately to these practical applications that the NLG paper also was addressed, with its focus not simply on defining the new 'multi-literacies' but its concern for a 'pedagogy of multi-literacies'.

Marsh (2004), a researcher at Sheffield University in the UK offers a critique of UK programmes that in some ways combines both the NLS and the NLG approaches:

> … the National Literacy Strategy Framework privileges particular types of texts and producers of texts. All references to producers of texts use the words 'writer', 'author' or 'poet', and there is no mention of producers, directors or creators. It could be argued that the term 'author' is used in a generic sense to include authorship of televisual and media texts, but the word is most frequently used in conjunction with terms that relate to the written word. This privileging of the written word is clearly stated in supporting documentation. The *Teachers' Notes on Shared and Guided Reading and Writing at KS2* (DfEE, 1998) suggest that, 'Although the emphasis in the Literacy Hour is upon books, children should have plenty of opportunity to read a range of media texts' (DfEE, 1998: 7). This marginalization of media texts can also be identified in the current National Curriculum (DfEE/QCA, 1999). Media texts are not mentioned at all in the key stage 1 orders [ages 5–7]. At key stage 2 [ages 8–10], it is suggested that the reading curriculum should include: a range of modern action by significant children's authors; long-established children's action; a range of good-quality modern poetry; classic poetry and myths, legends and traditional stories (DfEE/QCA, 1999: 54). This tradition is, as I have contended, long-established within primary literacy education. In a small note on ICT tucked away within the margins of the text, it is suggested that, 'Pupils could use moving image texts (for example, television, film, multimedia) to support their study of literary texts and to study how words, images and sounds are combined to convey meaning and emotion' (DfEE/QCA, 1999: 54). This is a clear prioritisation of print-based texts, with media texts used merely to support children's understanding of the former. (Marsh, 2004: 258)

Marsh calls upon much of the literature cited here to propose an alternative approach to the literacy curriculum. She begins with a reference to Kress:

> … the primary literacy curriculum needs to reconsider the definition and scope of literacy in a new media age and adapt accordingly (Kress, 2003), recognising that the kinds of texts, which are important and relevant to contemporary children's lives are very different from those promoted … in the early years of the twentieth century. Thus, the development of a culturally-relevant pedagogy (Ladson-Billings, 1995) is not so much concerned

with simply reflecting and valuing children's cultural choices in an effort to ensure that schooling is relevant and meaningful, important as this is, but with ensuring that the kinds of texts that are created and analysed within the literacy curriculum are embedded within popular, socio-cultural literacy practices, practices which are transforming the epistemological foundations of literacy. (Lankshear and Knobel, 2003; Marsh, 2004: 259)

How, then, might we identify such popular, 'socio-cultural literacy practices' and build on them for contemporary pedagogy? In a recent summary of case studies in UK schools, Street, Lefstein, and Pahl (2007) have shown how the picture may be improving beyond the narrow focus indicated by Marsh. Using detailed ethnographic perspectives to describe actual practices in classrooms where teachers were supported to combine a range of 'new literacies', through partnerships with such organizations as Creative Partnerships, they conclude:

... the cases have demonstrated how the actual practices of the classroom do not just replicate the intentions of policy-makers, curriculum designers and testers. In the case of the Creative Partnerships project, teachers were seen to 'take hold' of the external designs in their own local ways. Likewise, in ... punctuation lessons, the class's interactional routines can be seen to be just as important as the curricular prescriptions (if not more so) in terms of the approach to literacy and punctuation that ultimately emerges from the lessons. This finding is supported by the other lessons in both Lefstein and Pahl's larger studies: National Literacy Strategy curricular prescriptions have been assimilated into existing interactional dynamics and local meanings. (Street, Lefstein, and Pahl, 2007: 151)

This seems an appropriate place, then, to conclude this chapter by pointing forward to how the new approaches to literacy – as social practice, as 'multiple' and as 'multi' – are being taken up in classrooms and are being used by teachers used to adapt and move beyond the more narrow and regulatory prescriptions of policy makers. I will provide three indicative examples of how teachers are using these new theories to support their students writing practices, one taken from the work of Millard in UK schools in a book by Pahl whose contribution was cited in the preceding section; one from

a text that I cited as part of an address to the National Reading Conference in the USA where the issues signalled in this chapter were of great concern; and a further example of work with students at the interface of school and university in the UK.

Pahl and Rowsell recently edited a volume, *Travel Notes from the New Literacy Studies* (2006) in which they attempted to bring together new work in literacy theory of the kind outlined in this chapter with actual examples of educational interventions that they hope will contribute to 'a transformative literacy pedagogy' (Pahl and Rowsell, 2006: 12). Whilst the whole book, and the authors' other volume (2005), provide manifold examples of such work, I will offer here just one indicative example that speaks well to the concerns of the present volume with writing and development. Millard's chapter in the 2006 Pahl and Rowsell volume summarizes a number of research projects on teacher/pupil interactions around writing and the ways in which teachers can draw upon their pupils' home experiences in developing national curriculum requirements (Millard, 2006: 234). The example I provide here, taken from work in a primary school in England, focuses on 'narrative framing' that takes account both of new approaches to writing derived from New Literacy Studies and also of the significance of multi modality in children's writing down of narrative texts. Millard argues that:

... children's narrative interests can be openly imported directly into their school work (i.e., not 'found' as smuggled in references to an otherwise school-formulated meanings) allowing both boys and girls to work with personal preferences. In *The Castle of Fear* (Millard, 2005) and *Writing of Heroes and Villains* project (Millard, 2004), pupils aged nine-to-ten years old were encouraged to incorporate their individual knowledge of narrative characterisation and plot structure taken from more visual modes, into the planning and creation of new print-based narratives, which had embedded within them elements of the imposed curriculum objectives set for their stage of education. The teacher's planning encouraged pupils to move between drawing and writing in a seamless flow, allowing personal preferences for different modalities to be selected in arranging individual texts, creating characters and in generally designing a new work. To support creative work, pupils were encouraged not only to draw on examples from the school texts they were sharing which were, *The Lion the Witch and the Wardrobe* and *The Hobbit*, but also from the selections of video clips they watched at home which featured villains and their schemes to undermine the protagonists. (Millard, 2006: 238)

She illustrates this argument through a commentary she recorded from a pupil who had always appeared eager to write and who was considered an exemplary pupil in this aspect by his teacher but who revealed his real preferences when allowed choice to plan in class. He says:

I'm not into writing. I like organising my ideas in pictures. Whenever Miss J (the classroom teacher) asks Chris to draw his ideas I want to do that too. When the Misty Mountain song was read to us, I got a picture of a dark moon and I swooped in over the mountains to a castle and then deep down into the dragon's lair. (Millard, 2006: 239)

Millard comments: 'His picture sequence is clearly drawing from his understanding of film action, shot in perspective with the focus moving slowly in on the dragon's lair. Designated a 'clever' boy, he has not often been encouraged to sketch out his ideas for writing in images, however, his response on this occasion shows clearly how the affordances of the visual mode enables him to articulate ideas of narrative structuring by means of the image, acquired through his preference for filmed narratives (Millard, 2006: 239).

Writing teachers today, confronted by pupils with the kind of knowledge of film, images and new technologies evident in this case, can, suggests Millard, build on the new modes involved rather than feeling threatened by them or seeing them as somehow separate or even inferior from traditional written forms. In this case, the pupil is already successful at writing, so is not using new modes simply as a substitute; rather he is able to blend the different modes and to build a more sophisticated text that well meets national curriculum standards.

I cited a similar example in a paper for the USA National Reading Conference (Street, 2006) for an older pupil of Hispanic background in California, who again combined visual and written mode to greater effect than when previously made to work only in written mode. Cowan (2005) taught in an Hispanic Academic Summer Program in California and he recalled some years later how one student responded to a call for writing and what he took his responses to mean:

Joaquin submitted just one short piece of writing but two pieces of artwork, including a full-page drawing that used distinctive iconography (see Figure in Cowan, 2005: 147): an Aztec pyramid, an Aztec warrior, a mythological god in the figure of a feathered serpent, and a Mexican flag. This kind of artwork, most often created by Latino adolescents in the United States and identifiable by its use of distinctive iconography like Mesoamerican pyramids, figures from Aztec and Mayan mythology, lowrider cars. (Cowan, 2005: 147)

Cowan asked Joaquin about how he chose what to submit. He answered:

I really didn't know how to use certain words and use certain styles of writing to express everything. But I knew how to draw it and put it out there ... It's the same sort of thing, like when they found the first drawings in the caves. It was just the bison and people hunting, they didn't have written language but right there they were saying, we were hunters, we survive, we did it. So just by looking at that you read off of it. (Cowan, 2005: 147)

Cowan commented on this response in the context of an interview he conducted with Joaquin some years later:

When he was twelve, Joaquin felt better able to express his meanings visually than through his writing. He sees drawing as an ancient, efficient means of making meaning, that a viewer has only to see an image and 'read off of it' to apprehend its meaning. I asked Joaquin what he would have said about this drawing in 1994.

Back then, 1 just would have been like, oh I like Aztecs so I put these here. And I like pyramids, they're here ... I would have said these were things that make up me ... I could have probably said something like that's actually me [Aztec warrior], that's actually my house [pyramid] and that's what I believe [feathered serpent] and that's where I come from [flag of Mexico]. It was that simple. (Cowan, 2005: 148)

Cowan was duly chastened by his own earlier interpretation of Joaquin's work and now sees, through the student's eyes but with hindsight, meanings that he originally missed.

Joaquin is now a skilled artist striving to become a film-maker, confident of his visual abilities and developing his writing abilities to translate his visions for films into screenplays. In the summer of 1994, Joaquin had created a memorable text, a drawing that 'pretty much tell[s] a story in one picture' (Cowan, 2005: 148), a semiotic narrative that used cultural icons to tell where he came from, and that was worth keeping. He 'put' his cultural heritage 'out there' so that any reader of the anthology could 'read off of it'. But his teacher at that time:

> couldn't read or comprehend it until years later, because I saw it as an elaborate doodle, not as a visual text communicating a particular meaning. Unbeknown to me when I was teaching HAP students, Joaquin and his peers were communicating messages about their cultural heritage through visual texts that they created and that we published. (Cowan, 2005: 148)

I also commented on this text, in the context of a paper for the National Reading Conference where teachers and researchers were struggling with exactly the issues raised by new approaches to writing and new understandings of multimodality:

> That Cowan saw the drawing at the time as 'an elaborate doodle' is a reminder to us all that pupils are often doing things that have elaborate meaning to them but that we as teachers or researchers may not have the time – or the lenses – to 'see' as they appear to their producers. In considering the kinds of literacies that might be appropriate for new times, we may have to take into account not only the modality, in Kress's terms, in this case the relationship between visual and written modes, but also the deeper social and cultural meanings associated with such production, in this case the historical associations of Aztec iconography and their ideological meanings to an Hispanic boy in contemporary California. (Street, 2006: 39)

Finally, I describe a programme for students in their last years of school in the UK who are applying for university places.

The Academic Language Development Programme, held at King's College London by members of the Language and Literacies Group there, builds on awareness of writing issues faced by students as they progress from school to university and in particular on the insights brought to such writing tasks by work in the field of 'academic literacies' (Lea and Street, 1998, 2006). In helping students develop the writing genres required for applying to university, we realized that different modes of communication were also involved and tried to make both explicit in our teaching sessions. We defined genres as types of text, both spoken and written, such as student discussions, written notes, letters, and academic essays. We wanted to help students be more aware of the different language and semiotic practices associated with the requirements of different genres in academic contexts. (The following account is adapted from Lea and Street, 2006.)

In one of the early sessions, I gave a presentation on genre switching (see Figure 9.1). I explicitly drew attention to the fact that prior to having a discussion or to writing down points from classroom discourse, just having thoughts and ideas about a subject already involves certain kinds of representation, with different language entailments than required in other forms or genres. Thoughts may, for instance, be free flowing, they may not always operate in sentences and they may include images and other nonlinguistic semiosis such as colours. Then, when the students were asked to move into group talk and discussion, they were required to provide explicitness, to take account of their interlocutor and to employ specific language features and defined speech patterns. The shift from free flowing thoughts/ideas to some explicitness in discussion with others we identified as a shift to a different genre, although as Gunther Kress has pointed out (personal communication), it also involves a shift of 'mode' – from internal thought to external speech). Likewise, as the students shifted from talk and discussion to taking notes, new requirements came into play, such

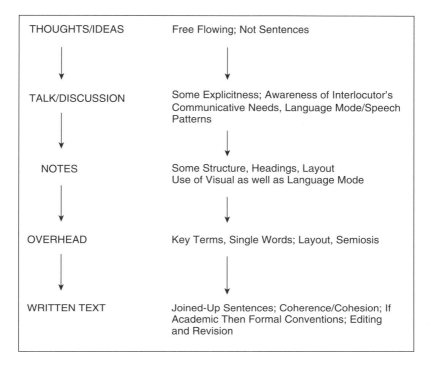

Figure 9.1   Genre/Mode Switching.

as the need for explicit attention to language structure, use of headings, and use of visual as well as language 'modes' such as lay out.

The tutors encouraged students to make presentations to the whole class using overhead projector slides and again drew attention to the particular genre and mode features of an overhead slide, such as highlighting of key terms, use of single words and lay out. Finally, students were asked to provide a page of written text based upon the discussions and overheads and these required joined up sentences; attention to coherence and cohesion, use of formal conventions of academic writing, and attention to editing and revision. Each genre and mode had different qualities or, as Kress might say, 'affordances' [see also Kress, this volume]. In their educational histories, students had not always been made explicitly aware of these qualities as they moved between different genres in their schoolwork. They had rarely been given time to dwell on and develop the distinctive

features of each genre, or to address the question of the relationship of these different genres to each other, including the fluid overlap of the boundaries of each genre. In the Programme, teachers asked, for instance, how do genres and modes vary across disciplines, subjects, and fields? Students from science disciplines appeared less familiar with extended prose but adept at structured lay out and use of visual signs, whilst social science students had had more written work to do in their school practice but had not necessarily differentiated its features from those of talk and visual layout as explicitly as we were doing in these sessions. In some cases, the students reported that the teachers in their regular school would follow a discussion by asking them to 'write it up' without necessarily making explicit the different requirements as they switched genre from speech to writing or from notes to essays. In the Academic Literacy Development Programme, explicit attention was focused on such switching, transformation, and the changing of meanings and representations from one genre and mode to another. We discussed how this often involves a different 'mix' of two or more genres and modes, such as the notion that writing always creates meaning through layout as well as through the use of words. Attention to these issues constituted a basic premise of the pedagogy in the course.

These examples, then, indicate some of the fruitful ways in which the approach to writing adopted by many researchers and practitioners in the New Literacy Studies could link with the insights about multimodality in the work of the New London Group, to provide policy and practice in education that could help us 'see' and then build upon and develop students' own literacy practices.

REFERENCES

Anderson, C.A. and Bowman, M. (ed.) (1965) *Education and Economic Development*, London: Frank Cass.

Barton, D. and Hamilton, M. (1998) *Local Literacies: Reading and Writing in One Community*, London: Routledge.

Barton, D. and Ivanic, R. (eds) (1991) *Writing in the Community*, London: Sage.

Barton, D., Hamilton, M., and Ivanic, R. (eds) (1999) *Situated Literacies: Reading and Writing in Context*, London: Routledge.

Besnier, N. (1995) *Literacy, Emotion and Authority: Reading and Writing on a Polynesian Atoll*, Cambridge: Cambridge University Press.

Besnier, N. and Street, B. (1994) 'Aspects of Literacy', in T. Ingold (ed.), *Encyclopedia of Anthropology*, London: Routledge. pp.527–562.

Bloch, M. (1993) 'The Uses of Schooling and Literacy in a Zafimaniry Village', in B. Street (ed.), *Cross-Cultural Approaches to Literacy*, Cambridge: Cambridge University Press. pp.62–86.

Bloome, D. (ed.) (1989) *Classrooms and Literacy*, Norwood, NJ: Ablex.

Camitta, M. (1993) 'Vernacular Writing: Varieties of Literacy among Philadelphia High School Students', in B. Street. (ed.) *Cross-Cultural Approaches to Literacy*, Cambridge: Cambridge University Press. pp.228–246.

Cazden, C., Cope, B., Fairclough, N., and Gee, J. (1996) 'A Pedagogy of Multiliteracies: Designing Social Futures', *Harvard Educational Review*, 66(1): 60–92.

Cook-Gumperz, J. (1986) *The Social Construction of Literacy*, New York: Cambridge University Press.

Cope, B. and Kalantzis, M. (eds) (1993) *The Powers of Literacy: A Genre Approach to Teaching Writing*, London: Falmer Press.

Cope, B. and Kalantzis, M. (2000) *Multiliteracies: Literacy Learning and the Design of Social Futures*, London: Routledge.

Cowan, P. (2005) 'Putting it out there: Revealing Latino Visual Discourse in the Hispanic Academic Summer Program for Middle School Students', in B. Street (ed.) *Literacies Across Educational Contexts: Mediating Learning and Teaching*, Philadelphia: Caslon Publishing. pp.146–148.

Department for Education and Employment (DfEE) (1998) *Teachers' Notes on Shared and Guided Reading and Writing at KS2*, London: Her Majesty's Stationery Office.

Department for Education and Employment (DfEE)/ Qualifications and Curriculum Authority (QCA) (1999) *The National Curriculum*, London: Her Majesty's Stationery Office.

Finnegan, R. (1988) *Literacy and Orality*, Oxford: Blackwell.

Gee, J.P. (1990) 'Orality and Literacy: from the Savage Mind to Ways with Words', in J.P. Gee (ed.) *Social Linguistics and Literacy: Ideology in Discourses*, Falmer Press: London. pp.27–48.

Gee, J.P. (2000) 'The New Literacy Studies: from "Socially Situated" to the Work of the Social', in D. Barton, M. Hamilton, and R. Ivanic (eds) (2000) *Situated Literacies: Reading and Writing in Context*, London: Routledge. pp.180–196.

Gee, J., Hull, G., and Lankshear, C. (1996) *The New Work Order: Behind the Language of the New Capitalism*, London: Allen and Unwin.

Goody, J. (ed.) (1968) *Literacy in Traditional Societies*, Cambridge: Cambridge University Press.

Goody, J. (1977) *The Domestication of the Savage Mind*, Cambridge: Cambridge University Press.

Goody, J. (1987) *The Interface Between the Written and the Oral*, Cambridge: Cambridge University Press.

Heath, S.B. (1983) *Ways with Words*, Cambridge: Cambridge University Press.

Hirsch, E.D. Jr. (1987) *Cultural Literacy: What Every American Needs to Know*, Boston: Houghton Mifflin.

Hull, G. and Schultz, K. (2002) 'Locating Literacy Theory in Out-of-School Contexts', in G. Hull and K. Schultz.

(eds), *School's Out: Bridging Out-of-School Literacies with Classroom Practice*, New York: Teachers College Press. pp.11–31.

Kress, G. (2003) *Literacy in the New Media Age*, London: Routledge.

Kress, G. and Street, B. (2006) 'Multi-Modality and Literacy Practices', Foreword in K. Pahl and J. Rowsell (eds), *Travel Notes from the New Literacy Studies: Case Studies of Practice*, Clevedon: Multilingual Matters. pp.vii–x.

Kress, G. and van Leeuwen, T. (1996) *Reading Images: The Grammar of Visual Design*, London: Routledge.

Ladson-Billings, G. (1995) 'Towards a Theory of Culturally Relevant Pedagogy', *American Educational Research Journal*, 32: 465–491.

Lankshear, C. and Knobel, M. (2003) *New Literacies: Changing Knowledge and Classroom Learning*, Milton Keynes: Open University Press.

Larson, J. (ed.) (2007) *Literacy as Snake Oil 2*, Portsmouth NJ: Peter Lang.

Lea, M.R. and Street, B.V. (2006) 'The "Academic Literacies" Model: Theory and Applications', *Theory into Practice, Fall*, 45(4): 368–377.

Lea, M.R. and Street, B.V. (1998) 'Student Writing in Higher Education: An Academic Literacies Approach', *Studies in Higher Education*, 23(2): 157–172.

Lerner, D. (1958) *The Passing of Traditional Society*, New York: Glencoe Free Press.

Marsh, J. (2004). 'The Primary Canon: A Critical Review', *British Journal of Educational Studies*, 52(3): 249–262.

Maybin, J. (ed.) (1994) *Language and Literacy in Social Practice*, Multilingual Matters/ Open University: Clevedon.

McLaren, P. and Lankshear, C. (1994) *Politics of Liberation: Paths from Freire*, London: Routledge.

Millard, E. (2004) 'Writing about Heroes and Villains: Fusing Children's Knowledge about Popular Fantasy with School-Based Literacy Requirements', in J. Evans (ed.) *Literacy Moves On*, London: David Fulton. pp.144–164.

Millard, E. (2005) 'To Enter the Castle of Fear: Engendering Children's Story Writing from Home to School at KS2', *Gender and Education*, 17(1): 57–73.

Millard, E. (2006) 'Transformative Pedagogy: Teachers Creating a Literacy of Fusion', in K. Pahl and J. Rowsell (eds) *Travel Notes from the New Literacy Studies: Case Studies in Practice*, Clevedon: Multilingual Matters Ltd. pp.234–253.

New London Group. (1996) 'A pedagogy of multiliteracies: designing social futures', *Harvard Educational Review*, 66(1): 60–92.

O'Connor, P. (1994) *Thinking Work: Theoretical Perspectives on Workers' Literacies*, Victoria: Deakin University Press.

Olson, D. (1977) 'From Utterance to Text: the Bias of Language in Speech and Writing', *Harvard Educational Review*, 47: 257–281.

Olson, D. (1994) *The World on Paper*, Cambridge: Cambridge University Press.

Olson D. and Torrance, N. (forthcoming) (eds) *Cambridge Handbook of Literacy*, Cambridge: Cambridge University Press.

Ong, W. (1982) *Orality and Literacy: The Technologising of the Word*, London: Methuen.

Oxenham, J. (1980) *Literacy: Writing, Reading and Social Organisation*, London: Routledge and Kegan Paul.

Pahl, K. and Rowsell, J. (2005) *Literacy and Education: The New Literacy Studies in the Classroom*, London: Sage.

Pahl, K. and Rowsell, J. (eds) (2006) *Travel Notes from the New Literacy Studies: Case Studies in Practice*, Clevedon: Multilingual Matters Ltd.

Prinsloo, M. and Breier, M. (eds) (1996) *The Social Uses of Literacy: Case Studies from S. Africa*, Amsterdam: John Benjamins.

Shuman, A. (1993) 'Collaborative Writing: Appropriating Power or Reproducing Authority?' in B. Street (ed.), *Cross-Cultural Approaches to Literacy*, Cambridge: Cambridge University Press. pp.247–271.

Stannard, J. and Huxford, L. (2007) *The Literacy Game*, London: Routledge.

Stein, P. (2007) 'Literacies In and Out of School in South Africa', in B. Street and N. Hornberger (eds), *Encyclopedia of Language and Education, Vol. 2: Literacy*, New York: Springer. pp.309–320.

Stephens, K. (2000) 'A Critical Discussion of the New Literacy Studies', *British Journal of Educational Studies*, 48(1): 10–23.

Street, B. (1984) *Literacy in Theory and Practice*, Cambridge: Cambridge University Press.

Street, B. (ed.) (1993) *Cross-Cultural Approaches to Literacy*, Cambridge: Cambridge University Press.

Street, B. (1995) *Social Literacies: Critical perspectives on Literacy in Development, Ethnography and Education*, London: Longman.

Street, B. (1998) 'New Literacies in Theory and Practice: What are the Implications for Language in Education?', *Linguistics and Education*, 10(1): 1–24.

Street, B. (2000) 'Literacy "Events" and Literacy Practices: Theory and Practice in the "New Literacy Studies"', in K. Jones and M. Martin-Jones (eds), *Multilingual Literacies: Comparative Perspectives on*

Research and Practice, Amsterdam: J. Benjamins. pp.17–30.

Street, B. (ed.) (2005) *Literacies Across Educational Contexts: Mediating Learning and Teaching*, Philadelphia: Caslon Publishing.

Street, B. (2006) 'New Literacies for New Times', in J. Hoffman and D. Schallert (eds), *55th Yearbook of the National Reading Conference NRC Inc.*, Oak Creek, Wisconsin. pp.21–42.

Street, B. and Lefstein, A. (2007) *Literacy: An Advanced Resource Book*, London: Routledge.

Street, B., Lefstein, A., and Pahl, K. (2007) 'The National Literacy Strategy in England: Contradictions of Control and Creativity', in J. Larson (ed.), *Literacy as Snake Oil 2*, Portsmouth NJ: Peter Lang. pp.123–154.

UNESCO (1976) *The Experimental World Literacy Programme: A Critical Assessment*, Paris: UNESCO.

Writing as Linguistic Mastery: The Development of Genre-Based Literacy Pedagogy

David Rose

This chapter outlines the genre-based approaches to teaching reading and writing developed over the past three decades in what has become known as the Sydney School (Martin, 2000, 2006; Martin and Rose, 2005). The pedagogy has been designed through a series of large-scale action research projects with teachers in various educational contexts, informed by functional linguistics and genre and register theory (Christie, 1999; Cope and Kalantzis, 1993; Hasan and Martin, 1989; Martin, 1998; Martin and Rose, 2003, 2008; Painter and Martin, 1986), by the educational sociology of Basil Bernstein (1990, 1996; Christie and Martin, 2007), and by Halliday's ground-breaking work on language development (1975, 1993, 2004), and its ongoing elaboration by various scholars, especially Painter's work on language learning in the home (1984, 1986, 1996, 1998, 2004). With respect to the breadth and detail of its linguistic focus, and its uniquely designed teaching strategies, Hyland (2007) describes the Sydney School as 'perhaps the most clearly articulated approach to genre both theoretically and pedagogically' (see also Hyon, 1996; Johns, 2002). The term genre-based refers hereafter to these approaches.

There have been three major phases in the pedagogy's development: the initial design of the writing pedagogy in the 1980s, with a handful of genres in the primary school; the extension of the writing pedagogy in the 1990s, to genres across the secondary school curriculum and beyond; and the development of the reading pedagogy from the late 1990s, integrating reading and writing with teaching practice across the curriculum at primary, secondary, and tertiary education levels. The strategies developed in the initial stage are now standard literacy teaching practice in primary schools across Australia and increasingly internationally, as well as in ESL and academic literacy programs. The latest reading and writing strategies have been consistently shown to accelerate literacy development at twice to over four times expected rates, at the same time as they close the gap in any class between the most and least successful students (Culican, 2006; McRae et al., 2000; Rose, Farrington, and Page, 2008). After reviewing developments in each of these three stages, the chapter concludes by positioning genre-based pedagogy in relation to other approaches in the literacy field.

THE GENRE WRITING PEDAGOGY

The two key dimensions of the genre writing pedagogy developed in the 1980s were an analysis of the kinds of texts that students are expected to write in the primary school, and a consistent method for supporting all students to write successfully. The pedagogy was developed in an ongoing partnership between teachers and discourse linguists, in the context of a school system that had largely abandoned the explicit teaching of writing in favour of a progressivist ideology of personal development. The whole language movement, which came to dominate Australian education faculties and school syllabi from the late 1970s, prescribed the teaching of grammar and composition in both the classroom and teacher training. Teachers were told not to impose direct instruction in writing on children, but to encourage them to write from personal experience, without any models (even for handwriting and spelling), followed by an 'editing' process in which the teacher would provide feedback on their efforts. In consequence, the most common kinds of writing to be found in primary schools included just two genres (examples from Martin and Rose, 2008):

[1]

On Sunday the 9ᵗʰ of November Jesse my friend and me Conal, went to the park called Jonson park me and Jesse played on the playaquitmint and it was very fun but me and Jesse both like the same peace of equipment I don't know wa …

As this kind of text makes an observation about something that has happened to the writer (going to the park to play), and comments about how they felt about it (what they liked), it was termed an **observation/comment**.

The other common kind of text records a series of events unfolding through time, which was termed **recount**:

[2]

Last Sunday me and My family went to the blue Mountains to go and see my dads friends. There were two children as well One of the childrens name was Hamish, Hamish was about 12 years old and his brother was about 19 or 18 years old. So when we arrived we all had lunch and we had chicken, bread, salad and a drink. after we had lunch I went on the tramplen after I went on the tramplen for about half an hour we went to go to a rugby leeg game for about 3 hours and I got an ice-cream and a packet of chips after the rugby leeg game I went on the tramplen agin and I got another ice-cream and after I had finished my ice-cream we went home. I had a great day.

As so-called 'process writing' replaced literacy teaching in Australia, this genre became ubiquitous. As more curriculum time was devoted to writing in progressivist classrooms, the recounts became longer, but the genre did not develop. The writer of text [2] could be any age from 6 to 14, depending on social background. Without explicit teaching, the writing of children from literate middle class families would naturally begin earlier and develop faster, while those from oral cultural backgrounds, such as Indigenous Australian children, may still be writing no more than these two genres, with very little elaboration, by the time they reached high school (Rose, 1999).

On the other hand, some students were writing stories that teachers tended to assign greater value to, which included a complicating event that was then resolved. Following Labov and Waletzky (1967), these stories were classified as **narratives**:

My ghost story

[3]

When I was 13, I was walking down the road with my best friend Mitchell.

It was my birthday and my parents weren't home, so we went to egg people houses (sic). One the way home around midnight we had to walk past the tip. The story that was going round at the time that there lived a ghost in the tip.

As we were about half way past, we heard a weird nosie.

We went to investigate, when we got there a rat was rolling a tin can. We heard the nosie again except it wasn't tin can.

We went to investigate again we saw this thing floating in the air like something invisible was taking it along with them.

We were so scare that we screamed so loud that the whole town could here us.

Everyone came and by that time the ghost left.

Everyone thought we were just causing trouble.

Every since we never walk around town after 6:00pm.

The End!!!

In addition to stories, factual texts were also being written in the primary school. Some factual texts classified and described things; these were termed **reports**:

Crocodile

[4]

Crocodiles are from the reptile family. Crocodiles are like snakes but with two legs on each side of the crocodiles body.

Crocodiles have four legs and the crocodiles have scales all over its body. Crocodiles have a long gore [jaw] and they have a long powerful tail so it can nock its enems into the water so it can eat the animal.

Crocodiles live on the ege of a swamp or a river. They make there nests out of mud and leaves.

Crocodiles eat meat lke chikens, cows and catle and other kinds of animals.

Crocdils move by there legs. Crocodiles can walk on legs. Crocodiles have four legs. Crocodiles also have scals all over there body and they have a powerfall tail to swim in the water.

Crocdils have eggs they do not have (live) babys.

Crocodiles can carry there egg(s) in there big gore.

Much rarer were texts that explain phenomena with a sequence of events, or **explanations**:

Our planet

[5]

Earth's core is as hot as the furthest outer layer of the sun. They are both 6000c°.

Earth started as a ball of fire.

Slowly it cooled.

But it was still too hot for Life.

Slowly water formed

and then the first signs of life, microscopic cells.

Then came trees.

About seven thousand million years later came the first man.

As children were generally not shown how to write these genres, their primary source for models was experience outside of school. For most children this was predominantly oral experience, while a few, such as the 8-year-old writer of text [5] were able to draw on experience from their reading. As teachers had no terms for the texts they wanted from their students other than 'stories', they were unable to provide encouragement other than 'write more', and to correct their syntax and punctuation. Indeed the teacher's written comment on the explanation [4] was 'Where is your margin? This is not a story'.

With this kind of hands-off approach to writing in the primary school, only a handful of students would independently develop the writing skills they needed for success in secondary school, an approach that seemed custom-designed to maintain unequal school outcomes, with just 10–20% of Australian students matriculating to university while 50–60% accessed no further education (Rose, 2005). If this inequitable trend was to be subverted, it was clear that teachers needed some explicit tools to recognize the kinds of writing their students needed to learn and tools to teach their students how to write them.

The first step in the research program was to identify and name the kinds of texts that were found, developing a map of genres written in the school. Martin (e.g., 1998) characterized genres as staged, goal oriented social processes: social because writers shape their texts for readers of particular kinds; goal oriented because a text unfolds towards its social purpose; staged, because it usually takes more than one step to reach the goal. Following Martin's model, genres were distinguished by recurrent global patterns. For example, story genres were distinguished on the presence or absence of a time line (observation/comment *versus* others), and the presence or absence of a complicating event (recount *versus* narrative); factual genres were distinguished on whether they explained processes or described things (explanation *versus* report); argument genres were distinguished between those that argued for a point of view, or discussed two or more points of view (exposition *versus* discussion). Secondly the organization of each genre was distinguished by recurrent local patterns, such as the narrative stages Orientat ion^Complication^Resolution identified by Labov and Waletzky (1967), or the stages of an exposition described in traditional rhetoric, Thesis^Arguments^Restatement of Thesis. So, in addition to the names for various genres, the stages that characterized each genre were also named, developing an explicit

metalanguage that teachers and students could use for talking about writing.

This map of written genres and their staging then formed the basis for designing an explicit writing pedagogy. Halliday's and Painter's work on oral language learning had shown that caregivers continually model and elaborate on children's spoken efforts, contradicting the Piagetan/Chomskyan hypothesis of individuated language acquisition that whole language pedagogy was predicated on. From Halliday and Painter, the principle of 'guidance through interaction in the context of shared experience' was adapted by Rothery (1989, 1994/2008, 1996) for classroom language learning contexts. Rothery's challenge was to make learning to write a comparable activity to learning to speak for all students, irrespective of their home background and academic strengths. To achieve this, she and her colleagues designed a teaching/learning cycle, illustrated in Figure 10.1.

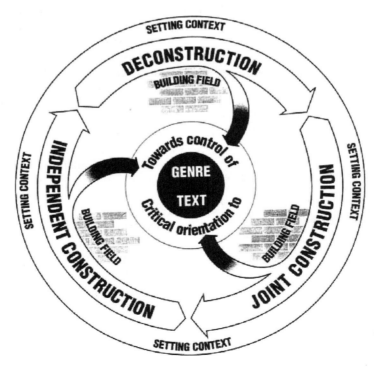

Figure 10.1   Teaching/learning cycle (Rothery, 1994/2008).

The cycle features three main stages – Deconstruction, Joint Construction, and Individual Construction. Deconstruction involves teachers guiding students to recognize the cultural context, staging, and key linguistic features in model texts, of the genre they are expected to write. Joint Construction involves guiding the whole class to construct another text in the same genre, which is jointly scribed on the blackboard. Independent Construction involves students writing a third text, in the same genre, on their own. All three stages of the pedagogy involve building field (so that students are familiar with the content of the texts they are reading and writing), and setting context (so that students understand the social purpose of the genre). The ultimate goal of the cycle is for students to take control of the genre, both in terms of being able to write it and also reflect critically on its role.

For the Sydney School, Joint Construction is the phase of the cycle that provides the link between language learning in the home and language learning at school. This phase is illustrated in the following section with a Year 6 class in an Australian primary school (from Martin and Rose, 2007). Most of the students in this class come from immigrant non-English speaking backgrounds (Arabic and Vietnamese) and have learned spoken English at school. The students are working on the exposition genre, exemplified in text [5] with one student's successful independent construction following this lesson.

Exposition for: Should an amphitheatre be built in Wiley park?

[5]

I strongly believe that the amphitheatre in Wiley Park should be built for these following reasons, such as: it attracts more people to the area, shops and public transport will earn a larger profit, people will become more interested in Wiley park, and it is suitable for all ages.

My first reason is that it will bring more people to our area because there are not many main

attractions in our community and it can be something to remember our bi-centenary by in years to come.

Another point to mention is shops will earn more money, for example, the new restaurant which will be built with in the amphitheatre. And not to forget Public transport which will create more money for the government and will be more easier for the disabled to travel by if they wish to do so.

And last but not least it is not only for the grown ups but it is also suitable for children for example, there will be entertainment such as concerts, plays and shows. In my opinion from a child's point of view I think it's going to be fun and it's about time the council did something like this.

I hope I have convinced you that we should have a amphitheatre at Wiley Park.

In Exchange 1, the class is working on previewing arguments in the Thesis, and using a topic sentence to introduce arguments in each paragraph. The issue here is why students should go to school. At this point *I strongly believe that children should go to school* has been scribed on the board, and the class is working on how to complete this introduction. In this dialogue, the teacher is asking students for a phrase, which will allow them to preview their arguments in the exposition's thesis.

Exchange 1

T	...Filippa?
Filippa	***I strongly believe that children should go to school*** *for these main reasons... um, and I'm going to list them all.*
T	Sorry, say that again.
Lisa	*For these main reasons.*
T	*For these main reasons.* Who can think of a different word other than main?
Sts	*For the following reasons.*
T	*For the following reasons.* Who can think of another word?
Loukia	*Listed.*
T	*For these listed reasons*, um. Who can think of another word?
Filippa	*For these reasons shown here.*
T	*For these reasons written here.* O.K. Who thinks *main reasons*. Hands up. Quick. A show of hands. *Main.* These *listed*. I've forgotten what the other ones were.
Sts	*Following* [in unison]
T	OK. Looks like *following.*
Sts	*For the following reasons.*

T   *For the following reasons* [scribes]. Now, trying to think, um, before we go on, before we list all of them, we want to include those things that you mentioned for that introduction, don't we? So how can we talk about that? Who can think? *I strongly believe children should go to school for the following reasons.* Filippa?

Filippa   You could, um, learn a wide range - a wide range of subjects and um religions and um ...

T   Right. Who can keep going from that? ...

Following several cycles of students selecting ideas, with the teacher guiding, encouraging, and elaborating, the class consensus is for *the following reasons*. This phrase is an important piece of superstructure for expositions, classifying the thesis' supporting arguments in order to preview them. Nominalising the logical meaning of 'because' as *following reasons* is the kind of grammatical metaphor these students will have to learn to read and write in secondary school (see following section). Scaffolding of this kind is a powerful technique for apprenticing young writers into a more mature control of genres and their linguistic features, because it so strongly reflects their experience of learning spoken language in the home, with its continual cycles of caregivers encouraging and extending on children's efforts.

GENRES ACROSS THE CURRICULUM

During the 1990s two major developments for genre-based writing pedagogy were its institutionalization in state syllabi and/or teacher professional development and teaching materials throughout Australia (e.g., Board of Studies NSW, 1994/2007), and the extension of the action research program from the primary school to the secondary school and beyond. The institutionalization of the pedagogy occurred despite vociferous opposition from whole language proponents in education faculties (Hyland, 2007; Martin et al., 1987), which continued as pedagogic fashion switched from progressivism to critical theory in the 1990s, and to currently fashionable constructivist positions (see Conclusion). At the same time, the functional linguistic basis of the pedagogy has been attacked by conservative advocates of traditional school grammar (Martin, 2000). However, as the pedagogy's demonstrable utility continues to grow, these campaigns have succeeded only in slowing its uptake.

The extension into the secondary curriculum and beyond was spurred by major economic changes that Australia underwent in the 1990s, from heavily protected manufacturing based on deskilled immigrant labour, towards internationally competitive service and information industries. In this context, the Sydney School was funded to research the literacy demands of the country's major industrial sectors, and of related secondary school curriculum subjects, in a project known as *Write it Right*. Informed by Bernstein's (1990) sociological model of relations between education and production, reading and writing demands were explored in science-based industries and the secondary science and maths curricula, and in media and public administration sectors and English, history, and geography curricula. Key publications from this project include Christie and Martin, 1997; Coffin, 1996/2008, 1997; Humphrey, 1996/2008; Iedema, 1995/2008; Iedema et al., 1994/2008; Martin and Veel, 1998; Rose et al., 1992/2007; Veel and Coffin, 1996.

The *Write it Right* research identified close parallels in the genres and their discourse patterns that students are expected to read and write in the secondary school, and those found in the workplaces that education prepares them for, at various vocational levels. The map of genres developed in the earlier stage of the research was considerably expanded, distinguishing specific types within each family of genres, including types of stories, text responses, arguments, histories, reports, explanations, and procedures. Table 10.1 summarizes the major types, their social purposes, and expected stages (described in depth in Martin and Rose, 2008).

Table 10.1: Major genres in the school curriculum

	Genre	Purpose	Stages
Stories	Recount	Recounting events	Orientation Record of events
	Narrative	Resolving a complication in a story	Orientation Complication Evaluation Resolution
	Exemplum	Judging character or behaviour in a story	Orientation Incident Interpretation
Text responses	Personal response	Reacting emotionally to a text	Evaluation Reaction
	Review	Evaluating a literary, visual or musical text	Context Description of text Judgement
	Interpretation	Interpreting the message of the text	Evaluation Synopsis of text Reaffirmation
	Critical response	Challenging the message of the text	Evaluation Deconstruction Challenge
Arguments	Exposition	Arguing for a point of view	Thesis Arguments Reiteration
	Discussion	Discussing two or more points of view	Thesis Arguments Reiteration
Histories	Autobiographical recount	Recounting life events	Orientation Record of stages
	Biographical recount	Recounting life stages	Orientation Record of stages
	Historical recount	Recounting historical events	Background Record of stages
Explanations	Sequential explanation	Explaining a sequence	Phenomenon Explanation
	Factorial explanation	Explaining multiple causes	Phenomenon Explanation
	Consequential explanation	Explaining multiple effects	Phenomenon Explanation
Reports	Descriptive report	Classifying and describing a phenomenon	Classification Description
	Classifying report	Classifying and describing types of phenomena	Classification Description
	Compositional report	Describing parts of wholes	Classification Description
Procedures	Procedure	How to do experiments and observations	Purpose Equipment Steps
	Procedural recount	Recounting experiments and observations	Purpose Method Results

In the process of working closely with secondary teachers, the writing pedagogy was also refined and expanded, and teaching materials were developed that aimed to provide teachers with a high level of critical skills in both text analysis and pedagogy. Curriculum sequences were mapped out that could lead students from writing recounts in progressivist classrooms to linguistic mastery of genres across the primary and secondary curricula. Such a learner pathway is illustrated here with key genres in the history curriculum, drawing on work by Coffin, 1997. In Bernstein's terms, this pathway builds a stairway of recontextualization, from everyday discourse to academic history.

As history recounts the past in stages or episodes, the first step students have to make, from personal stories to histories, is to manage episodic time alongside serial time, from 'sequence in time' to 'setting in time', from 'and then' to 'the next period'. And alongside managing time, students also need to shift from writing about themselves (first person) to writing about others (third person), and from stories of individuals (specific) to histories of institutions (general).

The second step is then from historical recounts to historical explanations, as this involves moving from temporal to causal connections between events. To explain causality, historical explanations draw heavily on grammatical metaphor; they tend to nominalise events as abstract things, that are related by causal verbs such as *x is caused by y, results in y, is associated with y*, and so on. For example, in the following text [6], *the impact of immigration is determined not only by the number of jobs migrants take, but also by the jobs they create,* in other words 'abstraction y is determined by abstraction x' (For descriptions of grammatical metaphor see Halliday, 1994; Halliday and Martin, 1993; Rose, 2006).

Thirdly, some explanations are organized, not by sequence in time but rhetorically, beginning with the event being explained and then unfolding through a set of relevant factors or consequences. Since these factors and consequences are not ordered in time with respect to one another, students have to learn to put them into a sequence appropriate to the explanation. In other words, they have to organize the text independently of the sequence of events, since texture is no longer determined by chronology.

Finally, students must learn to negotiate contested interpretations of history, using argument genres. As with explanations, arguments unfold rhetorically rather than chronologically; but unlike explanations, their notion of cause is also rhetorical. They are concerned with why a contestable reading of the past is motivated, not simply with what caused what. So, cause is not just deployed to relate events, but to organize the rhetorical structure of the argument, presenting evidence and then drawing conclusions and countering other positions.

From the textures outlined in the foregoing, it is possible to design a spiral curriculum that leads learners through the genres of history, and the linguistic hurdles each one presents, illustrated in Figure 10.2.

READING TO LEARN

As writing skills develop ultimately from experience with reading, which is the crucial mode of learning in formal education, the genre-based approach to writing has been extended over the past decade into teaching reading, using carefully designed strategies to support students to recognize language patterns in written texts, enabling them to read with critical understanding, and then to use these language patterns in their writing. This methodology, known as *Reading to Learn* is designed to be integrated with classroom practice across the curriculum, at all levels of education (Martin, 2006; Martin and Rose, 2005; Rose, 2004, 2005, 2007; Rose and Acevedo, 2006; Rose et al., 2004, 2008, www.readingtolearn.com.au). It approaches reading first from the perspective of genre, followed by the patterns in which a text's field unfolds through the

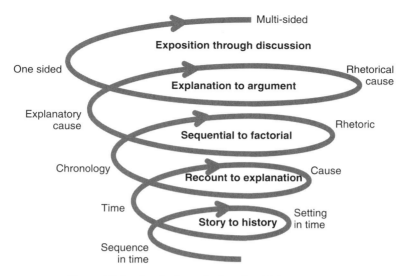

Figure 10.2   A spiral curriculum for history genres.

genre, and finally the wordings within sentences that realize these discourse patterns. The methodology is illustrated in the following section with a lesson in which adult ESL students, many of whom have weak English and/or literacy skills, learn to read and write a discussion about immigration in Australia, in an academic preparation course. An extract of the reading text is presented as text [6]. The first paragraph presents the Issue, the second paragraph presents one position on immigration's impact on employment, and the third presents the author's opposing position.

Plus to immigration equation

[6]

Both before and since the White Australia policy of the 1950s, immigration has been a political hot potato – yet the economic evidence shows immigration has been extremely good for the nation. In spite of the facts, today's economic nationalist parties – One Nation, the Australian Democrats, Advance Australia, the Greens and Australia First – espouse policies of greatly reduced or zero net migration. They do so for several reasons.

The most common argument against allowing migrants in numbers is based on a lopsided view of the impact on Australia's economy. The Advance

Australia party wants to call a "halt to all immigration until we have solved our unemployment problems" as if the only impact of migration is to take jobs which might otherwise be available to unemployed Australians.

But the impact of immigration is determined not only by the number of jobs migrants take, but also by the jobs they create. Population growth through migration creates demand for housing, goods and services which is met through higher production which in turn leads to higher employment. Depending on the size and composition of the migrant intake, most studies show the net impact of immigration on unemployment is positive. ...

Before reading this text, the lesson began with a discussion about immigration and the Australian economy and political parties, building the field of the text. This was followed by the teacher outlining the social function and stages of the discussion genre (see Table 10.1 in the foregoing section), and then a summary of the text's field, as it unfolds through each phase of the discussion, in terms accessible to all students. This stage is known as Preparing before Reading in the *Reading to Learn* methodology. The text was then read aloud and discussed paragraph by paragraph.

The next stage, known as Detailed Reading, supports students to read the text themselves, sentence by sentence. A carefully designed scaffolding interaction cycle is used to prepare all students to identify the word groups in each sentence, which they highlight as they go. In each cycle, particular students are asked to identify and say the wordings in turn, ensuring that all students participate equally. Student responses are always affirmed, and the meaning of the identified wording may be elaborated, by defining words, explaining concepts, or discussing the students' knowledge. These cycles are illustrated for one sentence in Exchange 2, each cycle beginning with a Prepare move.

Exchange 2: Detailed reading

T	Now in the next sentence the author tells us that some political parties want a separate national economy for Australia, and they want less or no immigration. So I'll read this. *In spite of the facts, today's economic nationalist parties – One Nation, the Australian Democrats, Advance Australia, the Greens and Australia First – espouse policies of greatly reduced or zero net migration.*	Prepare sentence
T	Now, it starts off by saying *'in spite of the facts'*, and I'll tell you what that means. *'In spite of the facts'* means that even though the facts are there, they are not looking at the facts. They're still going this way [demonstrates by walking across].	Elaborate
St	Ignore?	Select
T	Ignoring the facts, that's right. *In spite of the facts.*	Affirm
T	And then it tells us which parties. And I'll ask these people at this table to tell me [indicating table]. Today's...? Can you tell me what kind of parties?	Prepare
Sts	*Economic nationalist parties*	Identify
T	Exactly.	
	So that's what I want you to highlight – *economic nationalist parties* – if you can just highlight those three words?	Instruct
	[checking students' highlighting] That's perfect ... that's exactly right, *economic nationalist parties*. Beautiful ... perfect ... OK ... we're on the right track.	Affirm
T	Then it tells us the names of these parties. You guys can tell me the names of these parties. Don't highlight them, just tell me the names, have a look.	Prepare
Sts	*One Nation, the Australian Democrats, Advance Australia, the Greens, Australia First.*	Identify
T	So the author has mixed all these parties up, and they're all very different. But he's grouping them together and he's calling them *'economic nationalist parties'.*	Elaborate
T	Can you see what they espouse? Two policies. *Policies of ...?*	Prepare
Sts	*Greatly reduced or zero net migration.*	Identify
T	Exactly.	Affirm
	Let's highlight those two. *Policies of ...*	Instruct
Sts	*Policies of*	Identify
T	And then those two policies ...	Prepare
Sts	*Greatly reduced*	Identify
T	*Greatly reduced*	Affirm
Sts	*Zero net*	Identify
T	*... or zero net migration.*	Affirm
T	So, *greatly reduced*? What do you think that means? [demonstrates by pointing downwards]. Can we say that in a simple way?	Prepare
St	Much less	Select
T	Much less, that's exactly right, Tatyana, much less.	Affirm
T	*Zero net*? 'Net' means what you have in the end. So if you have one minus one [writing equation on board $1 - 1 =$], what do you get?	Prepare
Sts	Zero.	Identify
T	Zero, that's right.	Affirm
	That's *zero net.*	Elaborate

Preparation moves enable all students to identify the wordings in the text, and elaborations extend their understanding, in terms of either the field (e.g., grouping different parties as 'economic nationalist parties'), or language (e.g., defining conjunctions 'in spite of', or technical terms 'zero net'). Elaborations can also open up critical discussion by students, of both language patterns and the text's field. While neo-Vygotskyan theories often focus on the learning potential of the elaborating ('feedback') move in 'IRF' cycles (e.g., Mercer, 2000), Reading to Learn treats preparation moves as equally important, and carefully designs both to ensure equal access for all learners to written meanings. Working through texts in this fashion enables all students to read them with critical understanding, no matter what the starting levels of the students, or the difficulty of the text.

The wordings that students identified and highlighted in this lesson were the lexical items presenting the key information in each sentence. In the next stage, Preparing for Writing, these wordings are written as dot point notes on the class board, by students taking turns to scribe, as other students dictate the highlighted words to them. When one side of the board has been filled with notes, they are then used to write a new text on the other side of the board, in a stage known as Joint Rewriting, again with students taking turns to scribe while the whole class selects what to write, guided by the teacher. As students select the wordings, and scribe the sentence on the board, the teacher may elaborate with language issues at various levels, from text organization, to grammatical issues, to spelling, pronunciation, and even handwriting. Importantly, the processes of reading and writing are not interrupted to study language systems that are typical concerns of language teaching; rather the elaborations occur rapidly as the text unfolds. If need be, these systems can be studied in extension activities following Detailed Reading and Rewriting. Text 3 is an extract of the discussion that this class rewrote from their notes.

A balanced view of migration

[3]

Political parties have been arguing about immigration since the 1950s. We know from the economy that immigration is excellent for the nation.

Parties that want to protect the national economy want to lessen or eliminate migration. These parties have three main arguments. They have an unbalanced view of how migration affects the economy. Some parties think that migrants take jobs from unemployed Australians.

However, migrants take some jobs but they also produce new jobs. More people need more houses, more goods and more services so more of these are produced and this more jobs. Research shows that the effect of immigration is good, although it depends on who comes and how many people come ...

In terms of mode, this text is closer to what this group of students would be expected to write at this stage of their academic preparation course. The level of metaphorical and idiomatic language has been reduced, while holding the field of the text constant. In the process, students with varying backgrounds have learnt to read highly metaphorical, idiomatic academic English, to identify the key information in each sentence, to write this information as notes, and to use it to write their own text – fundamental skills required for academic study. At the same time, they have encountered and practised using a variety of English language features in both oral and written modes. This level of scaffolding support ensures that all students will be able to independently construct successful new discussions, at the same time as they acquire a plethora of the language resources that realize them.

CONCLUSION

Genre-based pedagogy has been designed to enable learners to make connections between the repertoires of meanings they bring from their experience in the family, community, school, workplace, and the reservoir of meanings that have evolved in modern societies for controlling the social and natural worlds. The research base of the pedagogy has been concerned on one hand to map the genres through which control is exercised, and on the other to design pedagogic strategies that will enable all learners to make these genres part of their own repertoires. Over the past 25 years, this action research project has achieved some remarkable successes. Measures of its success include the take up of genre writing pedagogy throughout Australia, and increasingly internationally, in countries such as Indonesia where it is now mandated for the entire primary and secondary school systems, as well as the extraordinary rates of literacy development reported for Reading to Learn (Culican, 2006; McRae et al., 2000; Rose et al., 2008); while other literacy pedagogies report significant improvements, few can claim consistent literacy development rates at twice to over four times what is normally expected.

However the pedagogy is still evolving, and its future development will emerge from the diversifying contexts in which it is currently being applied across the globe, from early years literacy programs in east Africa, where teachers often have to manage multilingual classes of 80 or more children with minimal resources, to national curricula in nations as large and diverse as Indonesia, to postgraduate academic programs in China, Latin America, and South Africa, and the complexifying multimodal learning environments of western schools. The particular cultural, linguistic, and pedagogic issues of each context helps to shape the design of the theory as a whole, as well as each component of the pedagogy. This chapter has focused on the design of classroom interaction cycles and learning sequences, for learners to build connections between their existing repertoires and the genres of schooling. However, this access for learners would not be possible without programs that support teachers to expand their pedagogic repertoires, to build connections between their existing practices and the linguistic knowledge and scaffolding

strategies of genre-based approaches. Where the aim of the classroom strategies is to provide learners with metalinguistic tools to recognize and use the language patterns of the texts they encounter, the aim of the teacher training programs is to provide teachers with both metalinguistic and metapedagogic tools for analyzing and carefully planning their classroom practices. Designing such training programs has been a major focus of the action research to date (see Koop and Rose, 2008; Rose 2007; Rose and Acevedo, 2006).

The third level of the action research program is metatheoretical, designed to provide teachers and researchers with tools for constructing relations between genre-based pedagogic theory and other positions in the crowded literacy education field. To this end, the metatheoretical perspective of Basil Bernstein's educational sociology (1990, 1996) provides an overview that is useful for interpreting both the principles of genre-based pedagogy and the antipathy with which it has often been received. In Bernstein's analysis, schematized in Figure 10.3, pedagogic theories may be contrasted along two axes: whether the focus of change is primarily on the psyche of the learner or on relations between social groups, and whether the focus of pedagogy is primarily on transmission of textual performances (skills and knowledge), or on acquisition of competences (personal, cultural, and critical).

Pedagogies focused on change within individuals through transmission of textual performances include, for example, traditional approaches to grammar or curriculum instruction, intended to transmit systematized knowledge using lectures, demonstration, drills, and practice tasks, as well as phonics, spelling and 'sight word' drills, and basal reader programs. The tacit theory of learning implicit in these kinds of activities is made overt in certain dimensions of behaviourist psychology. Broadly, learning is conceived as a process of individuals practising behaviours demonstrated by teachers or texts. Acquisition is then demonstrated by

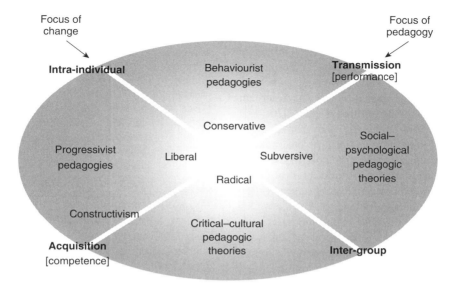

Figure 10.3   Types of pedagogy (adapted from Bernstein, 1990).

performances for which the criteria are made explicit and visible to the learner, and reinforced by positive or negative evaluation. These kinds of approaches have often been associated with conservative political positions, such as the mandating of phonics programs by the Bush administration in the US. Bernstein (1990, 1996) describes their association with 'old middle class' occupations in economic production, but comments that they have also produced generations of radical thinkers.

Throughout the twentieth century, such traditional approaches have been opposed by progressivist education movements in North America and the UK, associated particularly with liberal political positions and 'new middle class' occupations in the production and distribution of semiotic resources, 'agents of symbolic control'. As liberalism valorizes individual freedom and opportunity, these pedagogies conceive learning as a creative process emerging within individuals, which may be constrained or crippled by transmission pedagogies, that are caricatured as 'teacher-centred' or 'rote learning'. As teacher training was professionalized from the

1960s, this view was legitimated in Piaget's theory of innate cognitive development and Chomsky's hypothesis of innate language acquisition, and in the ESL field by Hymes' notion of communicative competence. The focus of these pedagogies is on competences emerging within the person of the learner; the teacher's role is primarily to facilitate this process by 'immersing' the learner in a language environment and encouraging expression of personal experience. As learners are not given overt external criteria for textual performances, Bernstein describes them as 'invisible' pedagogies.

A third position in the model is occupied by critical pedagogic theories, such as Freire's 'critical consciousness', Bourdieu's critique of 'symbolic violence', or the critical-cultural theories of Giroux and others. These pedagogic theories are associated with radical politics; they expect social change as learners acquire a critical awareness of power relations. As with progressivism, the focus of pedagogy is still on the person of the learner but the competences to be acquired are critical and/or cultural dispositions. As they are opposed to transmission of hegemonic discourses, criteria for textual performances also remain invisible to the learner. These radical positions have had less direct influence on mainstream teaching practice, but may be absorbed into liberal movements, such as Freire's appropriation by North American adult education theorists in the 1970s and 1980s. More recently, they have been absorbed to varying degrees in constructivist theories, which straddle the progressivist and critical quadrants in a smorgasbord of opposition to transmission pedagogies (see Muller, 2000, for a detailed review).

The fourth position in the model is concerned with changing power relations between social groups by transmitting textual performances. This is the position occupied by Vygotskyan social psychology and genre-based pedagogy, theories that treat learning as a social process in which teachers model activities for learners. As genre-based pedagogy advocates explicit teaching of textual performances, it has been attacked from each of the competence positions above. Nevertheless, unlike behaviourist pedagogies, the contents and practices of transmission are viewed as social semiotic resources that have evolved as means for exercising power and control in contemporary societies, and so are distributed differentially between social groups. Genre-based theory regards the endemic inequality of schooling as the fundamental problem for literacy pedagogies to address. However, it does not start from an oppositional stance to transmission pedagogies, or to the ideological positioning of learners, or the discourses of the academy. Rather the goal of genre-based pedagogy is to give all learners the opportunities in education that are currently restricted to the few who matriculate to tertiary study. Its strategy is to provide teachers with tools for analyzing texts and scaffolding learning that will enable all their students to realize their potential. This position is neither conservative, liberal nor radical, but rather subverts the inequity of educational outcomes simply by giving students and teachers the tools they need to succeed.

REFERENCES

Bernstein, B. (1990) *The Structuring of Pedagogic Discourse*, London: Routledge.

Bernstein, B. (1996) *Pedagogy, Symbolic Control and Identity: Theory, Research, Critique*, London: Taylor and Francis.

Board of Studies NSW (1994/2007) *English K-6 Syllabus*, Sydney: Board of Studies NSW http://k6.boardofstudies.nsw.edu.au/files/english/k6_english_syl.pdf.

Christie, F. (ed.) (1999) *Pedagogy and the Shaping of Consciousness: Linguistic and Social Processes*, London: Cassell.

Christie, F. and Martin, J.R. (eds) (1997) *Genres and Institutions: Social Practices in the Workplace and School*, London: Cassell.

Christie, F. and Martin, J.R. (eds) (2007) *Knowledge Structure: Functional Linguistic and Sociological Perspectives*, London: Continuum.

Coffin, C. (1996/2008) *Exploring Literacy in School History*, Sydney: Metropolitan East Disadvantaged Schools Program. Republished 2008. Sydney: Adult Migrant English Service.

Coffin, C. (1997) 'Constructing and Giving Value to the Past: An Investigation into Secondary School History', in F. Christie and J.R. Martin (eds), *Knowledge Structure: Functional Linguistic and Sociological Perspectives*, London: Continuum. pp.196–230.

Cope, B. and Kalantzis, M. (eds) (1993) *The Powers of Literacy: A Genre Approach to Teaching Writing*, London: Falmer.

Culican, S. (2006) *Learning to Read: Reading to Learn, A Middle Years Literacy Intervention Research Project*, Final Report 2003–2004, Catholic Education Office: Melbourne. http://www.cecv.melb.catholic.edu.au/Research and Seminar Papers.

Halliday, M.A.K. (1975) *Learning How to Mean: Explorations in the Development of Language*, London: Edward Arnold.

Halliday, M.A.K. (1993) 'Towards a language-based theory of learning', *Linguistics and Education* 5.2: 9–116.

Halliday, M.A.K. (2004) *An Introduction to Functional Grammar* (second edn.), London: Arnold. (first edn., 1994).

Halliday, M.A.K. and Martin, J.R. (1993) *Writing Science: Literacy and Discursive Power*, Pittsburgh: University of Pittsburgh Press.

Hasan, R. and Martin, J.R. (1989) *Language Development: Learning Language, Learning Culture*, Norwood, NJ: Ablex.

Hasan, R. and Williams, G. (eds) (1996) *Literacy in Society*, London: Longman.

Humphrey, S. (1996/2008) *Exploring Literacy in School Geography*, Sydney: Metropolitan East Disadvantaged Schools Program, Republished 2008, Sydney: Adult Migrant English Service.

Hyland, K. (2007) 'Genre pedagogy: Language, literacy and L2 writing instruction', *Journal of Second Language Writing* 16: 148–164.

Hyon, S. (1996) 'Genre in three traditions: Implications for ESL', *TESOL Quarterly*, 30(4): 693–722.

Iedema, R. (1995/2008) *Literacy of Administration*, Sydney: Metropolitan East Disadvantaged Schools Program, Republished 2008, Sydney: Adult Migrant English Service.

Iedema, R., Feez, S., and White, P. (1994/2008) *Media Literacy*, Sydney: Metropolitan East Disadvantaged Schools Program, Republished 2008, Sydney: Adult Migrant English Service.

Inghilleri, M. (2002) 'Britton and Bernstein on Vygotsky: divergent views on mind and language in the pedagogic context', *Pedagogy, Culture and Society*, 10(3): 467–482.

Johns, A.M. (ed.) (2002) *Genres in the Classroom: Applying Theory and Research to Practice*, Mahwah, NJ: Lawrence Erlbaum.

Koop, C. and Rose, D. (2008) *Reading to learn in Murdi Paaki: changing outcomes for Indigenous students*, Literacy Learning: The Middle Years, 16(1): 41–46.

Labov, W. and Waletzky, J. (1967) 'Narrative Analysis: Oral Versions of Personal Experience', in J. Helm (ed.) *Essays on the Verbal and Visual Arts*, Seattle: University of Washington Press. pp.12–44.

Leigh, A. and Ryan, C. (2008) *How Has School Productivity Changed in Australia?* Canberra: Australian National University http://econrsss.anu.edu.au/~aleigh/.

Martin, J.R. (1998) 'Mentoring Semogenesis: "Genre-based" Literacy Pedagogy', in F. Christie (ed.), *Pedagogy and the Shaping of Consciousness: Linguistic and Social Processes*, London: Cassell. pp.123–155.

Martin, J.R. (2000) 'Grammar meets genre – reflections on the "Sydney School"', *Arts: The Journal of the Sydney University Arts Association,* 22: 47–95.

Martin, J.R. (2006) 'Metadiscourse: Designing Interaction in Genre-based Literacy Programs', in R. Whittaker, M. O'Donnell, and A. McCabe (eds), *Language and Literacy: Functional Approaches*, London: Continuum. pp.95–122.

Martin, J.R. and Rose, D. (2003) *Working with Discourse: Meaning Beyond the Clause*, London: Continuum.

Martin, J.R. and Rose, D. (2005) 'Designing Literacy Pedagogy: Scaffolding Asymmetries', in R. Hasan, C.M.I.M. Matthiessen and J. Webster (eds), *Continuing Discourse on Language*, London: Equinox. pp.251–280.

Martin, J.R. and Rose, D. (2007) 'Interacting with text: the role of dialogue in learning to read and write', *Foreign Languages in China*, 4(5): 66–80.

Martin, J.R. and Rose, D. (2008) *Genre Relations: Mapping Culture*, London: Equinox.

Martin, J.R. and Veel, R. (1998) *Reading Science: Critical and Functional Perspectives on Discourses of Science*, London: Routledge.

Martin, J.R., Christie, F., and Rothery, J. (1987) 'Social Processes in Education: A reply to Sawyer and Watson (and others)', in I. Reid (ed.) *The Place of Genre in Learning: Current Debates*, Geelong: Typereader Publications 1. pp.55–58.

McRae, D., Ainsworth, G., Cumming, J., Hughes, P., Mackay, T. Price, K., Rowland, M., Warhurst, J., Woods, D., and Zbar, V. (2000) *What has Worked, and Will Again: the IESIP Strategic Results Projects*, Canberra: Australian Curriculum Studies Association, 24–26, www.acsa.edu.au.

Mercer, N. (2000) *Words and Minds: How we Use Language to Work Together*, London: Routledge.

Muller, J. (2000) *Reclaiming Knowledge: Social Theory, Curriculum and Education Policy*, London: Routledge.

Painter, C. (1984) *Into the Mother Tongue: A Case Study of Early Language Development*, London: Pinter.

Painter, C. (1986) 'The Role of Interaction in Learning to Speak and Learning to Write', in C. Painter and J.R. Martin (eds), *Writing to Mean: Teaching Genres Across the Curriculum*, Applied Linguistics Association of Australia (Occasional Papers 9). pp.62–97.

Painter, C. (1996) 'The Development of Language as a Resource for Thinking: A Linguistic View of Learning', in R. Hasan and G. Williams (eds), *Literacy in Society*, London: Longman. pp.50–85.

Painter, C. (1998) *Learning through Language in Early Childhood*, London: Cassell.

Painter, C. (2004) 'The "Interpersonal First" Principle in Child Language Development', in G. Williams and A. Lukin (eds), *Language Development: Functional Perspectives on Species and Individuals*, London: Continuum. pp.133–153.

Painter, C. and Martin, J.R. (eds) (1986) *Writing to Mean: Teaching Genres across the Curriculum*, Applied Linguistics Association of Australia (Occasional Papers 9).

Rose, D. (1999) 'Culture, Competence and Schooling: Approaches to Literacy Teaching in Indigenous School Education', in F. Christie (ed.), *Pedagogy and* the Shaping of Consciousness: Linguistic and Social Processes, London: Cassell. pp.217–245.

Rose, D. (2004) 'Sequencing and Pacing of the Hidden Curriculum: How Indigenous Children are Left Out of the Chain', in J. Muller, B. Davies, and A. Morais (eds), Reading Bernstein, Researching Bernstein, London: Routledge Falmer. pp.91–107.

Rose, D. (2005) 'Democratising the Classroom: A literacy Pedagogy for the New Generation', Journal of Education, 37: 127–164, www.ukzn.ac.za/joe/joe_issues.htm.

Rose, D. (2006) 'Grammatical Metaphor', in K. Brown (ed.), Encyclopedia of Language and Linguistics (second edn.), Oxford: Elsevier. pp.66–73 (first edn. 1993, ed. R Asher).

Rose, D. (2007) A reading-based model of schooling. Pesquisas em Discurso Pedagógico, 4: 2, 1–22, http://www.maxwell.lambda.ele.puc-rio.br.

Rose, D. and Acevedo, C. (2006) 'Closing the Gap and Accelerating Learning in the Middle Years of Schooling', Australian Journal of Language and Literacy, 14(2): 32–45, www.alea.edu.au/llmy0606.htm.

Rose, D., McInnes, D., and Korner, H. (1992) Scientific Literacy, Sydney: Metropolitan East Disadvantaged Schools Program. Republished 2007, Sydney: Adult Migrant Education Service.

Rose, D., Lui-Chivizhe, L., McKnight, A., and Smith, A. (2004) 'Scaffolding Academic Reading and Writing at the Koori Centre' Australian Journal of Indigenous Education, 30th Anniversary Edition, 41–9, www.atsis.uq.edu.au/ajie.

Rose, D., Rose, M., Farrington, S., and Page, S. (2008) 'Scaffolding Literacy for Indigenous Health Sciences Students', Journal of English for Academic Purposes, 7(3): 166–180.

Rothery, J. (1989) 'Learning about Language', in R. Hasan and J.R. Martin (eds), Language Development: Learning Language, Learning Culture, Norwood, NJ: Ablex. pp.199–256.

Rothery, J. (1994/2008) Exploring Literacy in School English (Write it Right Resources for Literacy and Learning), Sydney: Metropolitan East Disadvantaged Schools Program. Republished 2008, Sydney: Adult Migrant Education Service.

Rothery, J. (1996) 'Making Changes: Developing an Educational Linguistics', in R. Hasan and G. Williams (eds), Literacy in Society, London: Longman. pp.86–123.

Veel, R. and Coffin, C. (1996) 'Learning to Think like an Historian: The Language of Secondary School History', in R. Hasan and G. Williams (eds), Literacy in Society, London: Longman. pp.191–231.

Writing in a Multimodal World of Representation

Gunther Kress and Jeff Bezemer

INTRODUCTION

The contemporary multimodal communicational world poses sharp questions about the likely future development of writing. Increasingly, writing is one of several *modes of representation* used in modally complex texts, and in many such texts, it is not the central means for making meaning. When we compare a textbook from 1935 with a contemporary one, we note that there tends to be less writing and the writing that there is differs from the writing of seventy years ago, syntactically, and textually. Although images were present on the pages of textbooks 'then', there are more images 'now'; images 'now' look and function differently from those found before. Writing and image also interact in ways that were not conceived of in seminal comments by Roland Barthes on that subject, even in the 1960s (Barthes, 1973). Curricular content is represented differently; and the manner in which the materials are laid out on the page points to social and epistemological changes, which cannot be explained by a focus on representational practices alone. The *page* is used differently to the way it had been: it now has a different semiotic function. It has become a *site of display* with quite specific social and

semiotic potentials. If, going one step further, we compare a contemporary textbook with 'pages' on the web dealing with the 'same' issues, we see that modes of representation other than image and writing – moving image and speech for instance – have found their way into the design and shaping of texts, with significant effects on writing.

Here we aim to show what a *(social) semiotic* (Hodge and Kress, 1988) – rather than a *(socio-)linguistic* – account of such changes might look like. We explore the relation between the 'make-up', the 'shape' of *texts* – their *designs* – and the implications for what it means to be a writer, a reader, or a learner in the twenty-first century (cf. New London Group, 1996). That requires attention to social origins of texts as much as to their semiotic effects; to the potentials of modes as well as to their interactions within a multimodal text; it needs attention to the potentials and constraints of media – the printed media, such as the book or the electronic media of screens, such as the web. To mark the fundamental differences we need changes in focus, metaphors, and 'orientation' – for instance, from *writing* to *text-making*; from *composition* to *design;* and from (adherence to) *convention* to *rhetoric*. The shifts in text-making practices involve new attention to *mode* and *medium*, to *genre*, and to *sites of display*. In short, understanding these developments, let alone speculating about future directions for writing, requires a new set of theoretical tools.

Divergent, contradictory, and confusing views dominate debates on the cultural effects of contemporary practices in writing; usually they invoke practices of 'the past'. The views range from cultural pessimism (Postman, 1993; Tuman, 1992) to concerns about economic performance, as witnessed in OECD (Organization for economic Cooperation and Development) sponsored studies such as PISA, TIMMS, and PIRLS. Less prominent, if equally and firmly expressed, are beliefs in the empowering potential of such changes (Kaplan, 1995). The theoretical frame presented here should help put debates on writing on a firmer footing than nostalgia or euphoria.

REPRESENTATION AS SOCIAL AND SEMIOTIC PRACTICE: SOME CONCEPTS

Our theoretical approach is a social semiotic rather than a linguistic one. That has far-reaching consequences. Texts are seen as always multimodal; this makes text-making and texts the relevant larger frame. The term 'writing' no longer stands as a synonym for text or text-making (as in 'I'm just not getting anywhere with my writing'); instead, it refers either to the *mode* of writing *or* the *practices/processes* of writing. So, in thinking about the 'future of writing', we take that to be about the mode of writing as cultural technology. Writing-as-mode always needs to be seen in conjunction with specific media. Modes are looked at in terms of their semiotic potentials, so that quite similar questions can be asked about image and writing; not as in a linguistic framework: 'do images have words and sentences? – but in a semiotic one: 'what are resources for 'arrangements'? (e.g., syntax, or layout) or for 'emphasis'?

(e.g., type of font, or bolding), and more generally, 'what are the semiotic resources of this mode?'. Using this perspective, we believe that we can begin to provide a fuller, more insightful and plausible account of the place, the uses and the functions of writing in the twenty-first century.

Given this theoretical take, we introduce some central categories of the theory that stands behind such assumptions.

Sign-makers and signs

In a social semiotic account of representation as meaning-making, those who produce as well as those who 'use' texts – visual artists, editors, writers, teachers, and students – are *sign-makers*. *Signs* are units in which meaning and form are brought together in a relation *motivated* by the *interest* of the sign-maker. The process of sign making is always subject to the availability of semiotic resources and to the *aptness* of the resources to the meanings, which the sign-maker wishes to realize. In principle, there are always limitations of resources, even if always differently. In many classrooms around the world, there exist the severest constraints on resources both for teachers and children. Yet we treat the design of a text as the sign-maker's apt representation of her or his interest.

Interest

The *interest* of the producer of texts is two-fold: *representational* – 'how is my interest in this phenomenon best realized given the resources I have available?' and *communicational* – 'how can I best realize my social relation with this audience?' The text-maker's interests (as well as the text-*remaker's*) are shaped by the social, cultural, economic, political, and technological environments in which signs are made. At the same time, sign-makers have to be aware of the media of distribution for their signs and that awareness is factored into the making of the sign.

Design

Given the complex relation of modal affordance, rhetor's interest, and the variability and complexity of social environments, *design* moves into the centre of attention in the making of complex signs-as-texts. The shift, conceptually, from *composition* to *design* mirrors a social shift from competence in a specific practice conceived in terms of understanding of and adherence to convention governing the use of a mode – writing, say – to a focus on the *interest* and *agency* of the *rhetor* and the *designer* in the making of signs-as-texts. *Design* is the practice in which modes, media, and sites of display, are brought together with the rhetor's purposes, the designer's interests and the characteristics of the audience into potential alignment and coherence with each other. From the designer's perspective, *design* is the mediating process of giving shape to the interests, purposes, and intentions of the rhetor in relation to the assumed characteristics of a specific audience given the semiotic resources available for realizing/materializing these purposes as *apt* material, complex signs, that is, as *texts*.

Text

Text is the material form in which rhetorical purposes and the processes of design are given realization through the semiotic resources available to the designer. A text is a semiotic entity, which, internally, is semiotically cohesive and which is coherent in meaning; texts have relations of coherence with relevant semiotic entities in their environment. A text is a *complete* semiotic entity, given *completeness* by the social occasion in which it was produced. A text functions as a message in communication.

Mode

A *mode* is a socially and culturally shaped resource for making meaning; that is, it is the product of social-semiotic work on a specific *material* over significant periods. Image, writing, layout, speech, moving image, and gesture are examples of modes, all used in texts. What is to count as mode is treated as a matter for decision by communities and their social-representational needs. For the 'ordinary' user of writing, font is part of that mode. For a typesetter or graphic designer, the meaning potentials – the affordances – of font are such that it can be used as mode; that is, meaning can be made through the affordances of font.

Meanings are made in a variety of modes and always with more than one mode. Modes have differing *semiotic resources*. The mode of writing for instance, has syntactic, grammatical, lexical, and textual resources; it has graphic resources such as font type, and font size; and it has resources for framing, such as punctuation and the use of space of the site where writing appears. The modes of speech and writing share aspects of grammar, syntax, and lexis; these are cultural resources which are the product of social work over long periods. Speech and writing differ absolutely in their materiality: sound in one case and (graphic) marks on a surface in the other. Beyond the shared cultural resources, speech has the material resources of loudness/softness (intensity of energy), pitch and pitch variation – intonation – (frequency of vibration of the vocal chords), tonal/vocal quality, length, and silence. Image has resources such as position of elements in a framed space, size, shape, colour, icons of various kinds – lines, circles – as well as resources such as spatial relations of depicted elements to each other; and, in the case of moving images, the temporal succession of images, 'movement' as well as the changing relations to each other of elements of an image.

That is, modes have different *affordances* – potentials and constraints for making meaning. These differences in affordance mean that modes can be used to do different kinds of semiotic work. This enables sign makers to design texts in relation to their interests and their rhetorical intentions for designs of meaning, which, in modal ensembles, best meet the rhetor's interest and her/his sense of the characteristics of the audience.

Medium

Medium has a material and a social aspect. Materially, medium is the substance in and through which meaning is realized and through which meaning becomes available to others (cf. 'oil on canvas'). From that perspective, print (as paper-and-print), is medium; by extension, the book is medium, if differently; the screen another; and the 'speaker-as-body-and-voice' yet another. Socially, a medium of distribution involved in communication is (the result of) semiotic, sociocultural, and technological practices (cf. film, newspaper, billboard, radio, television, theatre, a classroom, and so on). From this perspective, 'textbook' is one medium and web-based learning-resources for students are (becoming) another.

Reconfigurations of the *media landscape* – notably the ubiquity of the screen – will have effects on writing. Semiotically, it will have effects in changes to the uses, forms, and valuations of the mode of writing. The logic of writing had provided the logic for the organization of the book. The screen is the medium dominated by image and its logic: when writing appears on the screen, the logics of the image will come more and more to shape the mode of writing, in all respects (Kress, 2003). Socially, book and screen provide different potentials for semiotic action by sign-makers.

Site of display

If we take a sheet of A4 paper, we can write an announcement on it and pin it on a wall; we have created a poster. We can also fold it, write an announcement on the front page and fill the other three pages with a diverse range of information; we have created a booklet. We can also fold it twice, cut it in four pieces and write an announcement on all four parts: we have created flyers. In all three instances, we have reshaped the material medium of paper to create a *site of display*, which is apt for our interests. It is the space that becomes available as medium for the display of text as complex sign.

In textbooks of the 1930s, the chapter was the site of display of a coherent, integral 'unit of knowledge' (e.g., an account of the human digestive system); now, in contemporary textbooks, the double-page spread is used as a site of display for a 'unit of work' (a 'lesson', or a 'demonstration'). As a site of display, a *chapter* is organized first and foremost as a conceptual, epistemological 'site'; the *double page spread* is organized first and foremost as a material, semiotic, and pedagogic site. Hence, the size of a chapter in a 1930s textbook was determined by the author's sense of 'completeness' and of 'justice to the subject matter'; in a contemporary textbook by contrast, it is the space of *the double page spread*, which shapes what content will appear and how. Both the older and the newer textbook were/are integrated into other units and categories: to a curriculum for instance and its syllabus, to organization of teaching, such as the number and length of lessons. Representation responds in a complex chain to social factors via diverse cultural and semiotic resources with far-reaching effects on the future of the mode of writing.

FROM WRITING AND COMPOSITION TO THE MULTIMODAL DESIGN OF TEXTS

Where before *competence* in relation to one mode, *writing*, was seen as sufficient for the task of *composition*, we now need to understand the semiotic potentials of all modes involved in the *design* and making of multimodal texts. Where texts consist of image and writing say, specific forms of textual cohesion and coherence emerge and theoretical means are needed for making sense of these. Where previously grooved routines of convention could serve as reliable guides in composition, in a multimodal world there is a need to assess on each occasion of text-making what the social relations with an audience are, what resources there are for making the text, what media are going to be used, and how these fit with what is to be communicated and with a clear understanding of the characteristics of the audience. Hence, a rhetorical approach to text-making is essential.

Text making is a *semiotic act* in which meaning is *the* issue in every aspect, because it is also a *social act* with social consequences. So *composition* seen as competent performance is replaced by *design* seen as the attempt to make constantly varying rhetorical purposes effective. In a multimodal approach, it is not possible to think about representation in general and about writing in particular without taking note of the profound changes in social forms, structures, and processes, which characterize the present and will continue to do so into the foreseeable future. These have shaping effects on semiotic forms, processes, and possibilities of meaning, representation, the making of texts and, in this, on writing. Current changes in *power* and in *principles* and *agencies of control* are – among others – about a shift from 'vertical' to 'horizontal' structures, from hierarchical to more open, participatory relations. This has effects such as the disintegration of social frames, leading to changes in *genres*, access to and notions of authorship and canonicity. This wholesale change in social relations means that *participation in semiotic production* now describes the characteristics of communication more accurately.

That has profound effects on writing in two ways. New text-production is multimodal, in which image can have a major and writing a minor role with effects on the role, functions, and forms of writing. The *social* change has already led to an emphasis on

agency as *semiotic production*. While this may well be an illusion seen in wider frames, it is the case that young people act out of such understandings of their power in relation to writing, to reading and to the making of text generally. In other words, the social changes manifest themselves in an assumption of significant agency on the part of the young in the domain of their own cultural/semiotic production.

These social-representational changes also characterize features of the contemporary media landscape: by the *participatory affordances* of current media technologies – blurring former distinctions of production and consumption, of 'writing' and 'reading'; the *global and local 'reach'* of media (obliterating the difference of global and local) – with severe effects on genres; by *contents both global and local*; by *ubiquity, convergence, and connectivity,* so that occasions of semiotic production – text-making/'writing' – are not tied to sites and times; and by *multimodality*, that is, representations in many modes, each chosen for the aptness of its communicational potentials.

Production and *participation* as the ruling metaphors in communication and the consequential individual dispositions of agency have deep effects on writing, reading, and textual processes. With former structures of power, the characterization of the relation of media 'audience' to media production had been that of 'consumption'. With new distributions of power, *production* and *participation* are the ruling dispositions of those who had previously been seen as 'audience'. *Youtube* (founded in 2006 and sold within 18 months to Google for 1.6 billion US$) witnesses a daily uploading of 60 000 videos. That can stand as a metaphor for the changed social relation to media: *producing* for an unknown and potentially vast group, *distribution* via existing, new, or yet to be created 'sites': *production* for the new media, new sites, in full 'democratic'(?) *participation*.

All aspects of text-making are drawn into that, with far-reaching effects. In many contemporary social practices, there seems little or no concern about what were, until the mid-eighties or so, central questions, for instance questions of 'authenticity' of authorship of certain kinds of texts. In *downloading, 'mixing', cutting and pasting, 'sampling', and recontextualization*, questions such as 'where did this come from?' 'who is the original/originating author' seem not an issue. Much like the use, in former times, of a ruined castle or monastic building as a quarry, a source of building materials – a large chunk here as a lintel, or another there as part of a wall – texts are taken as 'resources' to be 'mined' for the making of new texts. There is an absolute need to understand the practices, aesthetics, ethics, and epistemologies of contemporary forms of text production. At the moment, these are discussed in terms of nineteenth-century models, where terms such as 'plagiarism' or 'mere copying' are too often too readily to hand: that is, the

invocation of models from an era where conceptions of authorship were clear and legally buttressed.

NEW MODAL CONFIGURATIONS

In this section, we will explore a number of multimodal texts drawn from textbooks and web-based learning resources to show how contemporary modal configurations afford new epistemological commitments and engagements as well as new social relations between designers and readers.

Writing and image

Figures 11.1–11.3 depict examples of learning resources for secondary school Science.

Animal Nutrition : Nutrition in Mammal 161

Digestion is the first stage of nutrition. It takes place in the *alimentary canal*. We shall now consider this process in detail.

The Alimentary Canal (fig. 148).

Food taken in at the mouth passes into and along a tube called the *alimentary canal*, the other end of which opens at

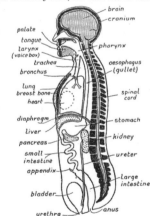

FIG. 148.—Chief internal organs of Man (simple scheme)

the hind end of the body. The opening is the *anus*. From the *mouth* onwards the parts of the alimentary canal are the "back of the mouth" (*pharynx*), the gullet (*œsophagus*), the *stomach*, and the gut (*intestine*). The whole of the canal, including the mouth cavity, is lined with a soft pink tissue
11

CHAPTER XVIII

ANIMAL NUTRITION : NUTRITION IN THE MAMMAL

Introduction—In the Biology section of Part II we studied the structure of some simple animals and plants, and their life processes, *i.e.* how they obtain and use food, how they move, respire, excrete, and reproduce. In the present section we shall consider the structure and life processes of some higher animals and plants.

How Food is Used—We have already studied the chief *food-stuffs* (p. 156). They are the useful constituents of various substances used as food.

Food is used for two purposes within the body of an organism. It supplies *energy*, including *heat*, and it supplies substances which the living organism builds up into *protoplasm*. An organism needs energy because its active tissues expend energy. Some food-stuffs supply this energy. Active tissues also "wear away" and must be replaced. Growing organisms make additional tissue. New tissue, whether to replace waste or for growth, is made from certain food-stuffs which are built up into protoplasm.

Carbohydrates (p. 156) are the main source of energy. *Fats* (p. 158) supply heat. *Proteins* (p. 157), *salts*, and *water* are used in making protoplasm. **Respiration** is the process by which food sets free energy in the body of an organism. This will be studied in the next chapter. **Nutrition** includes the intake of food, and all the changes it undergoes in being converted into protoplasm. In this chapter we shall study the nutrition of those higher animals which are classed as

Mammals—A **Mammal** is a backboned animal (**Vertebrate**). Its young are born alive: they do not "hatch" from eggs. They are suckled by the mother, who produces milk for this purpose. The Mammal has two pairs of limbs, each with (usually) five digits, and its body is more or less clothed with hair.
160

Figure 11.1   Fairbrother, Nightingale, and Wyeth (1935), pp.161–

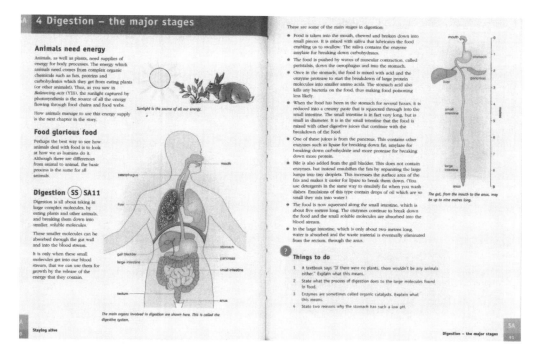

Figure 11.2   Science Education Group (2002), pp. 90–91. Reprinted by permission of Harcourt Education.

All deal with the digestive system. Figure 11.1 is from a textbook published in 1935, Figure 11.2 from a textbook published in 2002, and Figure 11.3 from an online learning resource mediated via the screen, accessed in November 2005. The 1935 textbook uses both image and writing to introduce the main organs involved in digestion ('The pharynx and upper part of the gullet are in the neck … The oesophagus is a narrow muscular tube.'). In the contemporary learning resources, the organs are introduced solely through image. The text thus suggests a shift from a former design in which image *illustrated* a detailed written account to the present, where a constellation of image and writing serves *complementary* functions.

A general communicational (here a pedagogic) question that arises from observations like these is: Do such changes in graphic design make a difference to how readers/ viewers engage with that text?, to what students attend?, and how they learn? Where writing is used, the text is ordered by the logic of sequence. It might be argued that this shapes engagement with the text. In writing, as in speech, something has to be mentioned first, something else second, and something else last, and meaning attaches to being first and last, and so on. In the 1930s textbook, the sentence 'From the mouth onwards the parts of the alimentary canal are the "back of the mouth" (*pharynx*), the gullet (*oesophagus*), the *stomach*, and the gut (*intestine*)' precedes the sentence 'The pharynx and upper part of the gullet are in the neck' and this is the 'logical', sequential order which readers are expected to follow in their attempts to make sense of the digestive system.

By contrast, where image is used, a different 'logic' seems to operate: the organs involved in the digestive system are not introduced in sequence. Rather, in the image all the organs are simultaneously present. Hence, the

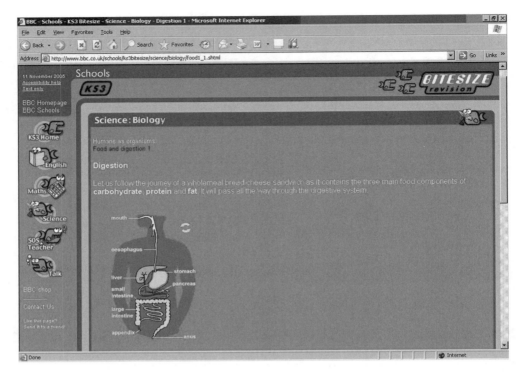

Figure 11.3   www.bbc.co.uk/bitesize, 1 November 2005. Reprinted by permission of BBC.

drawing does not specify a reading path as writing does: readers/viewers (students) can decide for themselves which organs to attend to in which order. In the screen-mediated learning resource (Figure 11.3), however, the mode of animation is used and the organs 'light up' in sequence, one after another. Thus, the learner loses some control over the reading path again to the designer. In that way, the designer uses the affordances of the mode of animation and the medium of the screen to shape pedagogy (and students' learning), without losing the epistemological affordances of the mode of image.

The affordance of image has other implications for designers and learners. In a drawing, designers have to show the relative position and size of the oesophagus, while in writing, they can but need not do so: they can refer to the oesophagus without detailing these (spatial) features at all. If (s)he does, as

in 'the oesophagus is a narrow tube', the 'picture' that is suggested is far less specific than the drawing has to be, leaving much room for interpretation on the part of the learner. The 'epistemological commitment' of writing and image differ. If the oesophagus is shown to have a certain width then the viewer is entitled to infer that that is its width; no such commitment follows from the written account. A designer's choice between writing and image, therefore, has significant implications for what does and what does not become available for students to learn with. Additionally, it has implications for the order in which these potentials become available.

Writing, speech, and moving image

On the web, *moving image* and *speech* can be used alongside or instead of writing. These

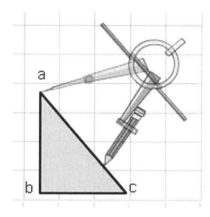

Figure 11.4   Adapted from: lgfl.skoool. co.uk/content/keystage3/maths/pc/ learningsteps/RSTLC/launch.html, 1 August 2007.

modes afford a whole new set of resources for representing the world of Science, Mathematics, and other school subjects. In other words, different 'translations' – 'transductions' (Kress, 2003) can now be made from one mode to another. The textbook may 'transduct' artefacts and actions into writing and image; on the web, artefacts and actions may be transducted into moving image and speech, as Figure 11.4 shows. It is a (partial) screenshot of an animation on rotational transformations. The 'scene' uses several modes: it *shows* – mode of image, it *tells* – mode of speech, and it *describes* – mode of writing, how to rotate an angle.

Below the image of the protractor, there is a written textual element: it is there in the mode of writing; as it is also read out aloud – performed – it is also present in the example in the mode of speech. The text reads as follows.

> Put pointer of compass on point 'a'. Open out compass to length of 'ac'. Draw a curve which passes through 'c'. This ensures that the length of the lines in the image will be the same as in the original triangle. This makes sure that the length of 'ac' (the image) is the same as 'ac' (the original) because the size of an object doesn't change during rotation.

Here there is transduction from *artefact* (a mode of three-D material entities) to *writing*, with effects similar to those discussed before. These have effects on specificity and generality, as well as on ordering. The voice-over reading of the written 'script' uses *speech* for the transduction of the modes of *artefact* and *action*. There is the use of the mode of *moving image* for the transduction of *action*. In this example, 'tone' is used to foreground particular lexical items; in the written text-element, foregrounding is done syntactically. Below is our transcript of the voice-over version; we have marked the boundaries between *intonation units* using a double slash, and we have underlined the items where the major pitch movement occurs (a 'fall' in each case). The element with the major pitch movement is, thereby, marked as providing 'new information'. This creates a contrast of 'given' and 'new' information within each 'information unit' (cf. Halliday, 1967).

Put pointer of *compass* // on point *a* //. Open *out* // compass to length of a *c* //. Draw a *curve* // which passes through *c* //. This *ensures* // that the length of the lines in the *image* // will be the same as in the original *triangle* //. This makes *sure* // that the length of *a c* // the *image* // is the same as *a c* // the *original* //. Because the size // of an *object* // doesn't change during *rotation* //.

If we compare the written and spoken text-elements, we see that the two modes provide two distinctive readings (and different potentials for learning) in each case. In the first, three sentences of the written element, the readers' attention is drawn to the element that is mentioned first – the *action* to be performed: *put, open out, draw* – and to the imperative mood, thus foregrounding *action* as *command*.

In the spoken version, the listener's attention is drawn to *the object involved* – 'compass', *location* – 'point a', *extent* of action – 'out', and so on. What ensues is a contrapuntal organization, with the mode of writing highlighting action-as-commands – *put, open out, draw* – and the mode of speech highlighting *objects and attendant circumstances – location, shape*.

In this example, there is also use of the mode of *moving image*, which combines the affordances of still image and its spatial organization with temporal organization: it unfolds in time. That brings distinct increases in semiotic resources. Elements can now appear and disappear, and through that, movement can be suggested. In the scene that we are looking at here, the first element to appear is the triangle. Then the compass appears, placed with its pointer at 'A'. Then two movements take place: the 'opening out' of the compass and the inscription of a curve. Then the compass disappears again. As such, the moving image represents the demonstration of how to use a compass rather differently from the written and spoken text-elements. For instance, it is *specific* about what 'opening out' and 'drawing a curve' entails. 'Drawing a curve' is displayed as a movement of the compass whereby one of its legs retains its position and the other leg, which leaves a trace, makes a gentle, clockwise turn.

The example shows that as we transduct to a complex of image, writing, speech, and moving image, quite different resources become available for use, resources of *lexis* or of *depiction*, with implications for generality and specificity, and syntactic resources with implications for the arrangement of constituents as well as for the social relations of maker of message and 'reader' – the relation of 'command' for instance. Therefore, for the designer of the learning resource the question becomes one of 'aptness of the level of specificity-generality and arrangement' for the specific occasion. There are also implications for pedagogy: in one mode, commands are given (writing and speech), in another, actors can be back-grounded ((moving) image); in one mode, reading paths are set by the learner (image), in another, by the designer (moving image). That in turn will lead to design decisions about use of modes. It also strongly sets the 'ground' for engagement and learning.

MULTIMODAL TEXTS: NEW FORMS OF COHESION, NEW PRACTICES OF READING?

Present ideas about coherence and cohesion have been developed in an era when 'language' was socially and semiotically dominant. Relations between, say, images and writing were not seen as part of the remit of explanation by linguistic theories. If we want to understand the makeup of multimodal texts, how they function in their wider environment, and above all, understand the manner in which we engage with and make sense of them, we need to ask questions around principles of cohesion and coherence, which apply to them. Here, we will explore some notions originally established for language within Linguistics and see whether they are needed and can prove useful as semiotic categories.

Chunking up

Staying with the example of textbooks or learning resources for now, we can say that notwithstanding the impact of social, economic and political change and educational reforms, many curricular entities, such as 'the poem', or pedagogic entities, such as the exercise, continue to feature in learning resources. In the 1930s textbook in Figure 11.5, we find an introduction which provides a historical context for a poem, which appears on the pages of the book. Questions about the poem are then put. The next section of the textbook continues with 'language study', introducing curricular entities such as *metaphor* and *simile* using examples drawn from the poem and asks questions in relation to these.

We recognize the special curricular and pedagogic status of textual entities not just lexically (via headings) but also through the use of indentation, font, and numbering. The use of quite distinctive margins tells us which part of the overall text belongs together to form a poem, or a paragraph. The numbering

> ### LESSON NINE
>
> ### LITERATURE
>
> ' L'ALLEGRO.'
>
> The Elizabethan age was succeeded by a period of religious and political strife, which culminated in the triumph of Puritanism under Oliver Cromwell. Therefore the expansive development of literature was restricted, and thought mainly concentrated on one particular book—the Bible. The dominating figure of this age is John Milton, the great Puritan poet ; but he is so supremely an artist that he blends the perfection of ancient art, as learnt from the Renaissance, with the religious turmoil of his time, which has had so profound an effect on his work. His most famous poem is the epic *Paradise Lost*, which relates the story of ' man's first disobedience and its fruit.' He also wrote many shorter poems, of which the following is an example.
>
> #### L'ALLEGRO
>
> Haste thee, Nymph, and bring with thee
> Jest, and youthful jollity,
> Quips, and cranks, and wanton wiles,
> Nods, and becks and wreathéd smiles,
> Sport that wrinkled Care derides,
> And Laughter holding both his sides.
> Come, and trip it as you go,
> On the light fantastic toe ;
> And in thy right hand lead with thee
>
> 85

Figure 11.5   Mamour (1934), pp.85. Instructional text reprinted by permission of Macmillan.

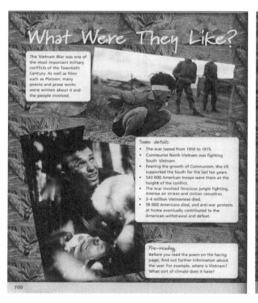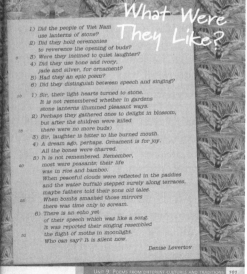

Figure 11.6   Brindle, Machin, and Thomas (2002), pp.100 101. © 2002 Folens Limited, on behalf of the authors Keith Brindle, Roger Machin, and Peter Thomas.

of the questions tells us that this part of the text belongs together to form an *exercise*, a series of things to do. In other words, the designers have used a limited set of semiotic resources to 'entextualize' certain curricular and pedagogic entities. In textbooks from the 1980s, we do not see significant differences. We find the same curricular entities: intro-duction/background to the poem, presenta-tion of the poem followed by questions; and they are entextualized using the same semi-otic resources: numbering, indentation, and font. However, comparing both these with Figure 11.6, an excerpt from a textbook from the year 2000, we see a dramatic change. The same curricular and pedagogic entities are there, but the range of semiotic resources used to turn them into distinctive textual enti-ties has become wider and different. As well as indentation, font, and numbering there is the use of font-colour, background colour, bullet-point lists, and lines. In other words, what belongs together is marked off much more sharply now than before. Text is *chunked up* into readily recognizable entities.

Layout

Simultaneously with the move towards *chunking up* text, we can see that the *place-ment* of the various text-elements has changed. In the 1930s and 1980s, placement was strictly linear: textual entities were 'pushed' onto pages without much attention to how this played out spatially. Authors would include instructions in their manu-scripts such as 'Insert Figure 4 about here'. What mattered was not where on the page a sentence appeared, but where in a sequence of entities a curricular entity appeared. 'Content' provided the principle for ordering. Textual entities, in other words, were not placed according to semiotic principles ('laid out') on the page but placed in a sequence given by requirements of content. In the con-temporary textbook by contrast, placement on the page – layout – has become a resource for making meaning. We can change the

arrangement of the textual entities on the page and find that each layout means differ-ently, as well as discovering that there are 'ungrammatical' layouts. In the 1930s and 1980s examples, the various curricular enti-ties formed a clear sequence: one was sup-posed to read from page 1 through to the last page, and to read, on each page, from the top left corner to the bottom right corner. The order in which learners engaged with these curricular entities was fixed, and it was fixed by the designer. In contemporary texts, the entities are clearly semiotic and are not nec-essarily organized in that way. They are more 'spaced out', spread across the pages, and it is often up to the reader to decide which entity to engage with first. Take the images and text blocks on the left page of Figure 11.6, for instance. These are simultaneously present, and it is up to the reader to decide whether to read the block giving 'some details' before or after 'reading' the colour photo. However, the *reading path* is still constrained. Given 'west-ern' semiotic conventions around reading direction, we are not supposed to read the right page before the left page.

Creating 'Text'

Observations on the increased *chunking up* of text and the emergence of *layout* as a semiotic resource raise the questions, 'how are these chunks tied together?' and 'how do they relate to each other?' How do they form a unified whole as opposed to being a collec-tion of unrelated entities? In addressing this question, we believe it is useful to follow Halliday and Hasan's (1976), distinction between information structure and cohesion. Information structure is about the ordering of the text into units of information on the basis of the distinction into given and new. Cohesion is about 'a potential for relating one element in the text to another, wherever they are and without any implication that everything in the text has some part in it.' (p. 27).

We take the distinction of given and new information as a basic requirement of all semiotic (inter)action: in interaction, we need to present something as a shared stating point, from where we can build into new informational terrain. In the old textbooks, *information structure* was based on linearity. In the 1930s example, background information of the poem *preceded* the poem itself. In the 2000 example, that information structure is realized not through placement in sequence (linearity) but through placement on the two-page spread (layout): the textual entities on the left of the two-page spread constitute the given, and those on the right page the new. Much of the textbook is organized like this. The next two-page spread for instance shows the poem of the left page and the 'exploring the poem' on the right: by now, we know the poem and it can be the 'point of departure' for the next informational chunk.

In a written text, cohesion is realized through reference, substitution, ellipsis, conjunction, or lexical cohesion. The question for multimodal texts in contemporary communication is: can the 'chunks' on the contemporary page be related, as they can be in a written text? Our answer would be: 'yes' in terms of general semiotic principles, and 'no' in the means specific to a particular mode.

To give just one example, that of *reference*. Linguistic items can have the property of *reference*, that is, 'instead of being interpreted semantically in their own right, they make reference to something else for their interpretation.' (Halliday and Hasan, 1976: 31). We can find examples of such items in the poem on the right side of the two-page spread in Figure 11.6. 'They', in line 3, refers to 'the people of Viet Nam' – it is a reference item. If we consider the title written on top of the left page (and reiterated on the right page), 'What were they like', we have another reference item, 'they', but now we are less clear about the item to which it refers. It may refer to 'the people involved' in the 'chunk' in the top left corner, or any other group of people named in writing. It may also refer to the people depicted on either or both images.

While this example may suggest a 'loss' of cohesion, or at least an increasing ambiguity of reference, our analysis suggests that there are also 'gains', or new potentials for cohesion, resulting from the increasing availability of graphic resources, including *shape, size, colour, sharpness, punctuation, indentation, placement, lines (boxes, vectors), and type of font.*

Selecting audiences

Coherence in textbooks is based to a large extent on a consistent rhetoric: addressing the same audience throughout. If textbook series differentiate between different audiences, and they usually do, in terms of 'key stage', 'year' or 'level', there are separate books for each of them. In other words, different media are prescribed for different audiences. When writing was the dominant mode, these media would vary in their writing to construct different audiences. In the contemporary textbook, the whole range of lexico-grammatical and graphic resources is used to do so.

On the web, such differentiation works differently. Often 'educational' websites have separate entries for students, teachers, and children. Not only do such sites allow learners to choose themselves the text that they think is apt for their learning, but also allow learners to access all other texts – not only those for other year groups, but also those for teachers or for 'experts'. 'The Poetry Archive', a website which 'exists to help make poetry accessible, relevant, and enjoyable to a wide audience' may serve as an example (see www.poetryarchive.org.uk; retrieved 1 August 2007).

The point we want to make repeats the point about the social generating semiotic forms, which we have made several times. In this case, we have a text-entity, which addresses a very different audience to that of the text-book with significant effects in all aspects of the multimodal text, writing included.

Outlook: writing in a multimodal communicational world

What are the implications of multimodality for a pedagogy of writing and for writing itself? The future uses, shapes, potentials of writing as well as conceptions of writing pedagogies need to be considered within a clear sense of social environments. Pedagogy is a specific instance of a larger-level social practice with its relations, processes, and structures, characterized by a focus on particular selections and shaping of 'knowledge' (as 'curriculum') and learning (as engagement with and transformation of that 'curriculum' in relation to the learner's interest), in or out of institutions such as schools, university, and the like. Social relations in pedagogic settings shape engagement with the cultural technologies of representation (modes), production ('tools'), and dissemination (media): they are active in selection and shaping of modes to be used in representation. In this way, they shape valuations of *writing* (compared to *image* for instance), conceptions of 'canonicity', and shape individual dispositions, and make what was socially produced and is culturally available seem natural, normal, routinized, and grooved.

At the moment, the school is caught between different conceptions of authority and agency in relation to production of knowledge, to the authoring of texts, the authority/canonicity of knowledge, and of semiotic forms. But learning has long since left the confines of institutions such as school, university, college, and the like. and forms of pedagogy have to accommodate to 'life-long', life-wide' learning, that is, learning at *all times*, by those who have every right for their interests to be taken with utmost seriousness, in *all sites*, in *all phases* of professional and personal life. In school, many young people see themselves as authors of the knowledge they want, of the kinds of texts that meet their social, personal, and affective needs and in that, they come into conflict with the sharply differing conceptions

and practices of the school. Hence, conceptions of pedagogy held by 'the school' are at loggerheads with those held – however implicitly – by those in school. In that stand-off, conceptions of pedagogy will need to be developed which accommodate the conflicting interests of generation, of power, of politics, and of an ever more globalizing market-dominated economy. Clearly, the agency of learners has to be taken as the central plank. Equally clearly, that the insights, understandings, values, and knowledge, which are the results of centuries and millennia of social and cultural work cannot and should not suddenly be ditched.

These considerations apply for pedagogies for/of *writing*. *Pedagogically*, the agency and the centrality of writers and of readers, of those who make meanings, has to be the starting point. *Semiotically*, *writing* has to be seen at all times as part of *multimodal design* arising from a specific *rhetorical interest*. In such designs, the affordances of all modes are judged and used in relation to that. Given its long history of social preponderance, *writing* has present social valuations, which are part of its social affordances. *Design* is prospective and therefore always necessarily innovative and transformative rather than competent implementation of conventionally given practices. Social agency and the interested process of design engage with the affordances – socially and semiotically – of the media and the means/resources of production.

In that context, a pedagogy of writing has to be seen as an integral part of a framing pedagogy of communication, in which *writing* has a specific place. Components of that pedagogy are multimodal representation and sensitivity to media and their affordances. In a globalizing environment, both in local manifestations, e.g., London as a microcosm of the global, and in manifestations beyond the local – with profoundly different conceptions of social positions, semiotic resources, and notions of 'the public domain' – pedagogies of communication have to be sensitive to the particularities of the specific locality.

ACKNOWLEDGEMENTS

This article draws on an ongoing research project, 'Gains and Losses: Changes in Representation, Knowledge and Pedagogy in Learning Resources' (2007–2009), funded by the Economic and Social Research Council (RES-062-23-0224).

REFERENCES

Barthes, R. (1973) *Mythologies*, St Albans: Paladin.

Brindle, K., Machin R., and Thomas P. (2002) *Folens GCSE English for AQA/A*, Dunstable: Folens.

Fairbrother, F., Nightingale E., and Wyeth F.J. (1935) *General Science, Part III*, London: G. Bell and Sons.

Halliday, M.A.K. (1967) *Intonation and Grammar in British English*. The Hague: Mouton.

Halliday, M.A.K. and Hasan R. (1976) *Cohesion in English*, London: Longman.

Hodge, R. and Kress G. (1988) *Social Semiotics*, Cambridge: Polity Press.

Kaplan, N. (1995) 'Politexts, Hypertexts, and Other Cultural Formations in the Late Age of Print', *Computer-Mediated Communication Magazine*, 2(3).

Kress, G. (2003) *Literacy in the New Media Age*, London: Routledge.

Mamour, A. (1934b) *The Complete English, Book I*, London: Macmillan.

New London Group (1996) 'A Pedagogy of Multiliteracies: Designing Social Futures', *Harvard Education Review*, 66: 60–92.

Postman, N. (1993) *Technopoly: The Surrender of Culture to Technology*, New York: Vintage Books.

Science Education Group (2002) *Salters GCSE Science Y11*, Oxford: Heinemann.

Tuman, M. (1992) *Word Perfect: Literacy in the Computer Age*, Pittsburgh: Pittsburgh University Press.

Grammar and Writing – The International Debate

Terry Locke

INTRODUCTION

As a way of framing the debate, let me start with an actual instance (Elley et al., 1979), a controlled trial that was conducted in New Zealand around 30 years ago. This study was one of the three deemed to be high, high/medium, or medium/high in quality in a systematic review undertaken in 2004 by an English Review Group (of which I was a member) based at the University of York and in association with the Evidence for Policy and Practice Information and Coordinating Centre (EPPI-Centre) of the University of London (Andrews et al., 2006).[1] The research question for this review was: 'What is the effect of grammar teaching in English on 5 to 16-year-olds' accuracy and quality in written composition?' The review focused on two aspects of 'grammar teaching': the teaching of formal sentence grammar/syntax and the teaching of 'sentence-combining'. The New Zealand study was in the former category.

The avowed purpose of the study was to 'determine the direct effects of a study of transformational-generative grammar on the language growth of secondary school pupils' with 12 variables chosen for analysis (Elley et al., 1979: 98). The investigation, a controlled trial, was conducted in a large coeducational high school in Auckland. Within the school, '250 pupils of average ability were taught, observed and regularly assessed for a period of three years, from the beginning of their third-form year, in February 1970, to the latter part of their fifth-form year, in November, 1972', i.e., from age 13/14 to 15/16. Because classes in the school were streamed by ability, the researchers were able to exclude extremes of ability, thus making it 'easier to identify systematic differences between teaching programmes' (Elley et al., 1979: 17). The experimental pupils were classified into eight classes of 31 pupils, matched on the basis of 'general ability, reading comprehension, reading vocabulary, English language usage, and with the proportions of children from each sex, ethnic group, contributing school and subject options' (Elley et al., 1979: 19).

The three courses studied by the three groups were as follows:

1. A Transformational Grammar (TG) course, which included the grammar, rhetoric, and literature strands of the Oregon English Curriculum developed in 1961 (three classes).
2. A Reading-Writing course (RW), which was the Oregon course with extra reading and creative writing substituted for the transformational grammar strand (three classes).

3. A rather typical New Zealand English programme (LLE) based around a series of textbooks (*Let's Learn English*), which offered a range of exercises in composition, comprehension, and a more traditional 'functional' grammar (two classes).

In their conclusion, the researchers reported that 'in the first two years of the study, no differences in language skills appeared between the three groups' (Elley et al., 1979: 97). The transformational grammar classes liked writing less than the other groups. In Form 4 (Year 10, 14/15-year-olds), only one comparison (from 30 possible) showed significant differences (on essay content). In Form 5 (Year 11, 15/16-year-olds), only two of the 12 variables listed showed any significant differences (sentence-combining test and English usage test). Again, in the School Certificate Examination, there were no significant differences between the three groups. In attitude tests, TG (Transformational Grammar) and LLE (Let us Learn English) pupils (those formally taught grammar) saw sentence study as 'repetitive' and 'useless' (Elley et al., 1979: 98). Elley et al. concluded that:

> Transformational grammar, as represented in the Oregon Curriculum, seems to have no more effect on writing style, or on the variety in transformation used, or on conventional usage, than traditional grammar, or than no grammar at all. Whatever it takes to produce a competent writer, it seems that the knowledge and skill outcomes of a course in transformational grammar are neither necessary nor sufficient for this purpose. (1979: 96)

In designing their project, Elley and his team studied carefully the results and research designs of all the relevant studies they could find. They believed the subject 'accessible to empirical study' and were concerned 'that the crucial experiment had not yet been conducted' (Elley et al., 1979: 15). As their own reports tell us, they developed a set of stringent guidelines for themselves aimed at eliminating the mistakes made by their predecessors. The results, then, should have been the end of the matter. However, as we know, this was not to be the case. The enduring nature of the grammar/writing controversy is the subject of the next section.

BONES OF CONTENTION

> Predictably, the corruption of writing pedagogy began in the sixties. In 1966, the Carnegie Endowment funded a conference of American and British writing teachers at Dartmouth College. The event was organized by the Modern Language Association and the National Conference [sic] of Teachers of English. The Dartmouth Conference was the Woodstock of the composition professions [sic]: It liberated teachers from the dull routine of teaching grammar and logic. (Mac Donald, 1995: 4)

Does the teaching of grammar impact positively on students' writing development? This question needs to be considered in relation to a broader one of the place of knowledge about language in the English/literacy classroom. Both have been bones of contention. However, the debates, while controversial, unsettled, and frequently confused historically, have been played out in different ways in different educational and policy environments. In this section, I will be commenting on the debates in four settings: New Zealand, England, the US, and Australia.

The piece of journalese cited in the epigraph to this section targets the 1966 Dartmouth Conference as the seminal event, which drove grammar from the Eden of effective writing pedagogy. This conference was perhaps the last time that English teachers approached a consensus on a range of issues in an international forum. As American participant, Herbert Muller, commented, the role of grammar was certainly an issue the conference dealt with. He reported general agreement with the conclusion that grammatical knowledge did little to improve speaking and writing and that 'the teaching of grammar has been chiefly a waste of time' (1967: 68). However, the conference was split on whether knowledge about language should be taught explicitly and if so at what stage. Linguists, on the back foot, found it hard to argue for the utility of linguistic knowledge but wanted to defend it as a humanistic study. As we shall see, the Dartmouth Conference threw a long shadow.

New Zealand

Elley et al.'s research was prompted by attendance by two of its English Department staff, Ian Barham and Malcolm Wyllie, at a 'series of lectures in 1968–1969 sponsored by the Auckland English Association on alternative approaches to the teaching of English'. The consequent discussions were described as 'lively' and as giving rise to 'certain basic questions about the role of grammar' (1979: vi). The influence of Dartmouth (or the 'corruption' if you like) had reached New Zealand. A New English Syllabus Committee (NESC) was set up in November, 1969 and, over a period of 14 years produced a new syllabus (Department of Education, 1983). The document embodied a personal growth model of English[2] and contained no mention of the term 'grammar'. Even in the list of understandings of language in Language Aim 1, there was no suggestion that a knowledge of language structure should be part of an English programme.

Writing in the late 1970s, Elley et al. began their research report with the statement that 'Generations of teachers of English language have been schooled against a background of faith in the undoubted benefits of instruction in formal grammar' (1979: 1). Writing of their own time, however, they noted a turning of the tide, a 'Dover Beach' sort of erosion of faith prompted by 60 years of research failing to find a positive effect on writing from the teaching of grammar. 'Nevertheless', they wrote, 'the value of grammar is a regular topic for heated debate, in newspapers, in school staffrooms and in parent-teacher meetings' and in curriculum-related decision-making (1979: 2). At the time of writing,

... it is now clear that large numbers of New Zealand teachers have deliberately abandoned the teaching of grammar altogether, and now place their faith in 'naturalistic' approaches to the teaching of communication skills, through wide reading, dramatic activities, extensive writing, and informal discussion of the students' own productions. (1979: 3)

Other teachers had taken up more recent grammars, such as the Oregon curriculum's transformational grammar, or New Zealand versions of Hallidayan grammar. English needed guidance on the place, if any, of grammar in the curriculum and their research aimed at providing it.

It is probable that while the research left certain questions unanswered (as I will be discussing later), it did contribute to a decline in the formal teaching of grammar in New Zealand classrooms in the 1980s. The absence is reflected in an NZATE (New Zealand Association for the Teaching of English) position paper on teaching writing, which has no mention at all of grammar or even knowledge about language (Anon, 1989).[3]

When a new curriculum for English was developed in the early 1990s (Ministry of Education, 1994), the grammar debate reignited. The document had a section on 'Exploring and learning about language', which suggested that 'Learning how to make their knowledge of language explicit provides a basis from which they [students] can make informed and conscious choices of language'. It was deemed desirable for students to explore and develop an understanding of grammar, viewed as 'the way words and phrases are formed and combined' (1994: 17). However, beyond this isolated mention, grammar was distinctly absent. There was no mention of it as supporting learning in the 'Principles of learning and teaching in English', and in the 'Exploring language' strand for written language, the word had no place in the wording of the curriculum's achievement objectives.

Prominent poet, novelist, and critic, C. K. Stead (1997) lambasted the new curriculum on a number of fronts including grammar, arguing that English teachers had backed away from language teaching, claiming that even though conventions of language change, these conventions should still be taught. He noted the absence of the 'dread g-word' from the national curriculum and the need to include it. The response of the New Zealand Association for the Teaching of English (NZATE) to such criticism was to initiate the Exploring Language project with the Ministry of Education, which produced a resource for all New Zealand teachers with the same name (Ministry of Education, 1996). The resource aimed at establishing a common metalanguage for all teachers, primary and secondary, and included a 'grammar toolbox' (Gordon, 2005). However, planned professional development for teachers on how grammatical (and other linguistic) knowledge might be applied pedagogically never eventuated. In the New Zealand context, questions raised by Elley et al. in the late 1970s – 'Has grammar an important place in the crowded curriculum at all? If so, which type?' and so on (1979: 2) – have remained unanswered, even as a new curriculum for schools is on its way to being mandated.

Australia

Of the 31 studies, the EPPI Review identified for in-depth review on syntax and sentence-combining, 28 originated from the US, two from Canada, and one from New Zealand (Andrews et al., 2004: 34). The absence of Australia reflects more than anything the form the grammar/writing debate took in that country. Certainly, up until the 1980s, the situation in Australia generally paralleled that of its trans-Tasman neighbour. Christie (2005), for instance, identifies the teaching of grammar in classrooms as having been a controversial issue since the 1960s. However, the decision by M.A.K. Halliday to move from England to Australia in 1976 as Foundation Professor of Linguistics at the University of Sydney was to profoundly affect the shape of the debate there.

As Christie represents the situation in Australia (and the UK), the 1970s saw the emergence of two schools of thought on language and language learning in schools. These groups, which she terms *linguists* and *non-linguists*, had a number of features in common, including disenchantment with traditional English teaching, 'with its joyless pursuit of parts of speech and correction of "faulty sentences"' (2004: 149). However, the groups 'differed sharply about what should constitute knowledge about language for teachers, and about how such knowledge should be used' (2004: 149–150). Influenced by Dartmouth and the personal growth model of English espoused by John Dixon and others, the nonlinguists saw teachers as language growth facilitators and 'eschewed linguistic knowledge, on the grounds of its alleged preoccupation with "structure" and indifference to meaning' (2004: 150). Operating out of a less individualistic discourse than the nonlinguists, the linguists constructed the child as a social being,

> ... growing in participation in complex sets of social processes, where language was an essential resource for articulating experience and knowledge, and where language itself was an interesting phenomenon to speculate about and to learn. (2004: 150)

The linguists were committed to teachers mastering an extensive metalanguage and applying this in their classroom programmes.

The major outcome of the linguists' approach was the Australian genre school, spearheaded in the early 1980s by the theoretical writings of Gunther Kress, Jim Martin, and Joan Rothery, which drew in varying ways on Hallidayan grammar to put the text/context nexus and concepts such as 'genre' and 'register' at the core of metalinguistic understanding.[4] Added to the debate about whether to teach grammar was the question: What or whose grammar?[5] The systemic functional (SF) grammar lobby was powerful one in Australia, but not without its opponents.

A flavour of the grammar/writing debate in the Australian context can be obtained readily by reading Cope and Kalantzis' (1993a) attack on progressive English with its supposed emphasis on 'whole language' and 'process writing', which they described

as inexorably tied to a middle-class discourse, as favouring students 'whose voice is
closest to the literate culture of power in
industrial society', as reproductive of educational inequity, as reducing teachers to
managers, as tied to an unworkable analogy
between orality and literacy, and as often
ending up with a 'fragmented, eclectic pho-
tocopier curriculum' (1993b: 6). Stung by
such criticism, Dixon and Stratta hit back,
suggesting the Genre School was itself confused about how many genres there were and
questioning the simple connection between
text-type and purpose. Further, they saw the
short-list of written genres as arbitrary and
untheorized, shortcomings in the way typical
school-based genres were defined, and the
notion of 'staged structure' as problematic, that is, as tending to produce 'normative' genre definitions (a bad practice)
and as creating a disjunction with the 'real'
world (1995: 84–86). Critics such as Paul
Richardson (1994) also took issue with the
way in which the genre theorists constructed
their metalinguistic frame, taking issue not
just with the way grammar was being used in
classrooms but with a tendency for genres
themselves to be seen as normative rather
than dynamic.

More than a decade on, the terms of the
debate in Australia remain very much un-
changed. Beginning as an approach to writing, genre and functional grammar have
become coupled with critical literacy to produce a powerful model of subject English.
The model has become a cornerstone of a
number of state curriculums (for example,
Queensland and New South Wales). However,
the model has no general, policy mandate.
Nor is the question of the place of grammar
in the writing curriculum a settled one. Critics
such as Sawyer continue to assert that:

> Politicians find these approaches to literacy appeal-
> ing since they promise the electoral magic of
> 'grammar'. The overwhelming amount of research
> showing no correlation between a conscious
> knowledge of grammar and the ability to write
> is simply ignored because 'grammar' is the only
> thing voters can remember 'doing' in English.
> (1995: 5)

However, advocates such as Christie (2004,
2005) and Williams (for example, 2004)
argue for the important contribution SF grammar is playing in the development of an
educational linguistics capable of constructing a metalanguage for discussing the
increased range of multimodal and digital
texts in society, arguing that 'students need a
metalanguage in order to deal in particular
with their literacy needs', including writing
(Christie, 2004: 153).

England and Wales

In England and Wales during the 1970s and
1980s, policy and practice in relation to the
grammar/writing question was in accord with
the Dartmouth 'consensus' and reflected in
the Bullock Report (Department of Education
and Science, 1975), which viewed grammar
as related to teacher's professional knowledge and as contributing to a teacher's ability
to help students with their writing, and a
child's 'language competence [as] growing
incrementally through the interaction of reading, writing, speaking and listening' (Andrews
et al., 2006: 41). The formal teaching of
grammar was not countenanced. However, as
Andrews has pointed out, it would be simplistic to suggest that a 'concern for accuracy, clear expression and a degree of
knowledge about language' was missing
from classrooms at this time (2005a: 71).

In the late 1980s, the political and policy
climate changed rapidly, as a Conservative
Government began a period of rule, which
lasted for nearly twenty years. Following their victory in 1983, a series of educational reforms were instituted, which led to
far greater state control over curriculum.
According to Urzsula Clark, 'The curriculum
envisaged by this reversal amounted to a res-
toration of a grammar school curriculum,
with the privileged text in English returning
to the teaching of standard English, its grammar, and its literature' (2005: 37).

What distinguishes the situation in England
from that in Australia and New Zealand is

the extent to which educational policy drove the reignition of the grammar in classrooms debate. With some irony, Andrews et al. note that despite the weight of research evidence to the contrary, the Kingman Report (Department of Education and Science, 1988), reflected 'a conviction amongst curriculum writers and policy makers in England that grammar teaching to young learners of English is a good thing; [and] that it will improve their written English and their ability to talk about language' (2006: 40).

As in Australia and elsewhere, the grammar/writing debate in England Wales might be thought of as having two aspects: Whether and what kind? In respect of the first of these, recent government thinking has been underpinned by two publications from the Qualifications and Curriculum Authority (QCA), *The Grammar Papers* (QCA, 1998), and *Not Whether But How* (QCA, 1999), the latter of the two appearing to close down debate on the question! The National Literacy Strategy (NLS) (operating for 7 to 11-year-olds from 1997 and for 11 to 14-year-olds from 2002) was underpinned by the belief that students would write better if their knowledge about language was increased and a programme was developed aimed at using sentence grammar to improve, through explicit teaching, students' ability to write sentences. Teaching resources such as *Grammar for Writing* (Department for Education and Employment, 2000) were produced aimed at providing 'all pupils [with] extensive grammatical knowledge' (2000: 7). Behind the policy is what might be called the 'knowledge for choice' argument. An explicit knowledge about language, it is argued, maximizes a student's ability to make qualitative decisions at critical moments during the composition process.

In her discussion of the 'grammar wars' in England, Clark (2005) has paid particular attention to the question – What kind of grammar? In her view, Conservative ministers attempted to impose an outmoded, prescriptive, Latinate grammar in their drive to impose grammar teaching in schools. As in Australia and New Zealand, however, university-based linguists had a role to play in the grammar/writing debate.[6] The work of Halliday and others had produced grammar approaches which, with their emphasis on the social, cultural, creative, and critical aspects of language and their focus on power relations in the social context, were incompatible with government purposes. Professor Ronald Carter (1994, 1996), a linguist influenced by Halliday's approach, led the multimillion pound Lanuage in the National Curriculum (LINC) project to develop support materials to foster growth in language understanding among pupils, but the resultant materials were scrapped by the Government.

Given the economic investment in the National Literacy Strategy in England and Wales, it is hardly surprising that the response of the Department for Education and Skills (DfES) to the EPPI Review's findings on the teaching of grammar should be a defensive one, taking the line of 'eclecticism', that is, arguing that a 'wide range of methods and approaches was encouraged' in schools (Andrews et al., 2006: 41). It is certainly true that revisions to terminology in use in NLS resources have reflected more modern grammars. However, while 'eclecticism' can sound positive, it may well be concealing a patchiness in approaches to introducing metalanguage into classroom discourse and a general confusion among teachers as to whether, why, and how grammar should be taught.

The United States

The abbreviation SLATE stands for 'Support for the Learning and Teaching of English' and, according to the website of the National Council of Teachers of English (NCTE) in the US, 'represents the commitment of caring English language arts teachers to use our intellectual leadership and professional knowledge to make a difference in decisions affecting our classrooms and our students.' One SLATE service is to offer a series of 'starter sheets', #3 of which is entitled 'On the

Teaching of Grammar'. This 'Fact Sheet' has an epigraph: 'Research over a period of nearly 90 years has consistently shown that the teaching of school grammar has little or no effect on students' (Hillocks and Smith, 1991). The document succinctly presents sets of bullet points on what the research shows both *not* to work and to work, as well as implications for 'teaching grammar as an aid to writing'. The foregoing quotation from Hillocks and Smith represents the tenor of the section on what does not work, i.e., the teaching of what is termed 'formal grammar' in a systematic, decontextualized way. What *is* described as working is the discussion of grammar points in the context of writing and systematic practice in sentence combining and expanding. Elley et al. (1979) figure in the references (NCTE, 1995: 7–8), yet another indication of the way in which this study became a kind of reference point for subsequent treatments of the 'grammar' question.

The SLATE starter sheet was prepared by Constance Weaver, who in 1995 had already produced one influential text on grammar and teaching and was about to release another (Weaver, 1979, 1996). The first of these was published by NCTE itself. To what extent is the starter sheet indicative of an unproblematic consensus in the US? To answer this question and to clarify the state of the grammar/writing debate in the US, it is instructive to compare two contributions, one by Weaver et al. (2006) and the other by Kolln and Hancock (2005) to a double issue of the journal *English Teaching: Practice and Critique* on the topic of 'Knowledge About Language in the English/Literacy classroom'.[7]

Weaver et al.'s contribution can be thought of as showcasing an approach to grammar, which is nicely encapsulated in the abstract:

Drawing on theory and practice, the authors argue that, rather than trying to 'cover' all grammatical skills, something traditionally done in many classrooms, and with limited results, teachers can more successfully teach less grammar with better results by focusing on key grammatical options and skills in the context of actual writing, throughout the writing process and over time. (2006: 77)

Two assumptions implicit here, which I will return to later, are that explicit grammatical knowledge is best taught at the point of need and that such knowledge opens up choices to writers in their acts of composition (the choice argument alluded to earlier). The authors conclude that: 'A conscious knowledge of certain aspects of grammar, along with the ability to use and manipulate them, does have much to offer writers' (2006: 100).

Martha Kolln has long advocated the use in classrooms of what she calls a 'rhetorical grammar', for different purposes 'from the remedial, error-avoidance or error-correction purpose of so many grammar lessons. I use rhetorical as a modifier to identify grammar in the service of rhetoric: grammar knowledge as a tool that enables the writer to make effective choices' (1996: 29). Citing Tchudi and Tchudi (1991: 164), Kolln and Hancock represent the situation in the US thus: 'Over the years, *grammar* has probably generated more discussion, debate, acrimony, and maybe even fistfights than any other component of the English/language arts curriculum' (2005: 12). In her section of the joint article, Kolln describes the historical nonrealization of a 'scientifically grounded, rhetorically focused, professionally supported, and publicly embraced grammar' in American public schools from the perspective of one who supports such a grammar. Kolln identifies a 'confluence' of forces responsible for this nonrealization:

... the ascendancy of generative grammar, NCTE policy, including the 1963 Braddock report and the 1986 Hillocks update, whole language approaches to language acquisition, the ascendancy of process approaches within composition, the primacy of literature within English curriculums at all levels, minimalist grammar and its anti-knowledge stance, political pressures against the imposition of an elitist language, a general lack of preparation for those in the teaching profession, and a general public failure to recognize grammar as anything but a loose collection of prescriptive mandates. (2005: 11)

Interestingly, in relation to previous discussion in this chapter, Kolln identifies the Dartmouth Conference and Dixon's *Growth*

Through English as contributing to the 'storm that overtook grammar' (2005: 16). Weaver herself is viewed as having played a major role in helping develop NCTE policy on the issue.

It is clear, however, that Weaver's position (and that of NCTE) is not simply antigrammar. So, what is the debate about? Let us start with a point of agreement. Both positions would agree that the decontextualized teaching of a formal, traditional, school grammar with an emphasis on error identification and correction is of no use. As I see it, Kolln's lament is to a large extent about the loss of a particular kind of conversation around the place of grammar.[8] Kolln tellingly compares the NCTE convention programme of 1963, with over 50 papers offered in its language section, with the programme thirty years later, which had no presentation on language structure or linguistics out of the 1000 given.[9] You could say that Kolln's regret relates to debates she sees as suppressed by the hegemony of the 'grammar in context' approach. One of these is the question of: Which or whose grammar best suits classroom pedagogy? With her rhetorical focus, Kolln is predisposed to favour a 'top-down', context-oriented grammar (as favoured in the LINC project). However, reference to Halliday and systemic functional grammar is notably absent from Weaver et al. (2006) and Kolln and Hancock (2005). With this question unaddressed, the question of what *teachers* should know about language is difficult to answer. As Kolln argues, the question is also hard to answer as long as the debate is couched around the role of 'grammar as an aid to writing' (Kolln and Hancock, 2005: 20). A further question relates to the question of 'systematic' instruction or the lack of it. If grammatical knowledge (either for teachers and students) is *not* systematized, then how can the chance element inherent in the grammar at the point of need argument be addressed? On what systematic foundation can teachers plan for the *if*, *when*, and *how* of grammar instruction?[10] As Andrews et al. (2006) put it in relation to the

UK context, when is 'eclecticism' just a nice-sounding word for chancy?

Another debate, which should be mentioned here, and alluded to by Carter (1996) in his discussion of the LINC project, relates to the issue of dialect and language variation. The debate is referred to by Kolln and Hancock (2005). However, its relevance to the grammar/writing debate is most fully addressed by Wheeler (2006) in the same double issue. The question might be put thus: How can explicit grammar instruction support the learning of standard varieties of English? Writing in 2005, Kolln alludes to antielitist arguments recognizing 'the legitimacy of the home-language dialects' of students as an antigrammar force (2005: 17). Ironically, however, Wheeler, arguing strongly from the *same* principle of legitimacy, mounts a research-based case for the use of particular, explicit grammar-based strategies – that is, contrastive analysis and code-switching – as powerful tools in both affirming African American English as a dialect and supporting the learning of standard English.[11]

THE EPPI REVIEW REVISITED: ITS CONTRIBUTION TO THE DEBATE AND WHERE TO FROM HERE

The 2004, EPPI Review was undertaken in order to 'shed some conclusive light' on the effects of grammar teaching on writing in respect of two aspects, the teaching of formal sentence grammar/syntax and the teaching of a technique known in the USA as 'sentence-combining'. In presenting its findings, the review group was at pains to accept limitations implicit in its particular review methodology (see Andrews, 2005b).

It was also at pains to make clear its role in the grammar/writing debate – what it was *not* doing and what it *was*. 'We were looking to gauge the effectiveness of a particular pedagogical approach and to generalize the results through synthesis, *not* to give finely grained accounts of the teaching of grammar in different contexts' (Andrews et al., 2006: 44). The choice of the word 'effect' in the guiding question actually effected a predisposition towards selecting particular kinds of research designs over others, that is, designs which isolated particular kinds of pedagogical interventions from their contexts. That itself was deemed to be problematic.

In relation to the first of these aspects, the teaching of formal grammar/syntax, the review asserted that it 'appears to have no influence on either the accuracy or quality of written language development for 5-16-year-olds' (2006: 51). Such a result was hardly surprising. The review really was traversing old ground. Elley et al. (1979), one of the three studies viewed as of reasonable quality had drawn a similar conclusion almost thirty years before and had itself reviewed a second of the EPPI Review's studies considered worthy of in-depth review, Bateman and Zidonis (1966).[12] The finding was controversial in England and Wales, because in that setting a policy decision had been made to mandate the teaching of formal grammar (of a sort) and huge amounts of money had been invested to support the policy. However, as this chapter indicates, policy making in other settings has rather assumed the first of the EPPI Review's findings as a given.

The Review begins to recast the debate, however, when it draws a comparison with its second finding – that teaching 'sentence combining appears to have a more positive effect on writing quality and accuracy' (2006: 51) – with its first.

> For instance, the teaching of syntax appears to put emphasis on 'knowledge about' the construction of sentences. Sentence-combining suggests a pedagogy of applied knowledge – at its best, applied in situations of contextualized learning; at its worst, drilling. (2006: 52)

A shift is being signalled here from a body of metalinguistic knowledge (with a focus on syntax) to practical approaches that appear to offer positive support at some point in the writing process.

A different kind of shift in the terms of the debate can be achieved by, perhaps ironically, deconstructing the syntax of the EPPI Review question, which focused on 'the effect of grammar teaching ... on ... accuracy and quality in written composition' (2006: 43). A systemic functional grammarian would call this a major example of nominalization. And like all nominalizations, it suppresses certain kinds of information and privileges other sorts. Highlighted here is causality and its connectedness to a specific intervention ('grammar teaching'). Grammar teaching is rather fuzzy, and could mean a huge range of things. Also highlighted is composition as product rather than process. Totally suppressed is the teacher who has presumably guided the process (suppressed) that has led to the product, i.e., an accurate, quality (as adjudged by some measure not stated) composition (in some genre or other). The suppressed information can be seen, I think, as offering clues as to how the debate needs to be recast. If writing is as much process as product, what are the identifiable stages in successful composition and how can these be best supported pedagogically? Are these stages the same for all types of composition? What implicit knowledge understandings contribute to the successful accomplishment of a particular stage? And would making these understandings explicit, add something positive to the learning process? If the answer to the last question is yes, how systematic do these understandings need to be made? Are some systems, for example, Hallidayan grammar, better than others?

Questions such as these, I suggest, are the ones that need to be asked. Asking them will prompt rather different research questions from those asked by the EPPI Review team. And they will be questions, which will not be answered by one, particular research design. Meanwhile, by way of conclusion, let me return to the study by Elley et al. (1979) in my own country and some other findings of that three-year study. Tellingly, the researchers found that good writers in the third form were still the best writers in the fifth form.

> The good writers stayed good; the poor improved but little. More important, they all showed only a modest growth in written composition skills over the two-year period. The actual mean gain

was only 2.92 (out of 32 points), or 60 percent of one standard deviation. The increase was statistically significant, but by no means reassuring. So, whatever the components of an effective writing programme in the secondary school may be, it seems unlikely that the three courses studied in this project have a produced a formula for dramatic improvement. (1979: 101)

Such concluding comments make sobering reading. Thirty years on, the 'formula' remains elusive. Prompted by the same debate as the EPPI Review, the New Zealand researchers trialled three different sets of conditions to see if they would work to improve students' writing. No set worked. As suggested earlier, the debate clearly needs to be recast, and the research agenda also.

NOTES

1 For ease of reference, I will be terming this the 'EPPI Review'.

2 Influenced by the theories of John Dixon (1975) and others. For a discussion see Locke, 2007.

3 In a 1991 retrospective on grammar teaching in New Zealand schools, Elizabeth Gordon described the writers of the 1945 Thomas Report on the Post-Primary Curriculum as thinking that 'grammar had become a sterile study, that it was taught mechanically, and extended a dead-hand influence on the whole of English teaching' (1991: 22). Clearly, curriculum policy antipathy to formal grammar teaching in New Zealand goes back a long way.

4 A useful overview of the genesis of the Australian Genre School and its conceptual frame can be found in Cope, B., and Kalantzis, M. (Eds.) (1993a). *The Powers of Literacy: A Genre Approach to Teaching Writing*. Pittsburgh: University of Pittsburgh Press.

5 Starting as it does with the social context, systemic functional (or Hallidayan) grammar might be described as 'top down'. More traditional descriptive grammars, which start from units such as words, phrases and clauses, can be described as 'bottom-up' grammars. In general, New Zealand and the United Kingdom have espoused bottom-up grammars, though the LINC Project (see Carter, 1994: 257) had 'complete texts at the centre of interest'. Writing in *Exploring Language*, Elizabeth Gordon wrote that its terminology 'follows the Quirk grammar closely' and references Quirk, R., Greenbaum, S., Leech, G., and Svartvik, J. (1985) *A Comprehensive Grammar of the English Language*. London: Longman.

6 For a substantial retrospective on the situation in England and elsewhere, see Hudson, R., and

Walmsley, J. (2005). 'The English Patient: English Grammar and Teaching in the Twentieth Century', *Journal of Linguistics*, 41 (3), 593–622.

7 Edited by the author. Volume 4, Number 3 can be accessed at http://education.waikato.ac.nz/research/journal/view.php?id=10&p=1 and Volume 5, Number 1 at http://education.waikato.ac.nz/research/journal/view.php?id=11&p=1.

8 As a means of re-establishing the conversation, Kolln, Hancock and others have set up an interest group, the Assembly for the Teaching of English Grammar (ATEG), which is an official assembly of NCTE (Kolln and Hancock, 2005: 20).

9 By way of trans-Atlantic comparison, one might note that in England and Wales, the LINC Project was in full swing from 1989 until 1992 (see Carter, 1994).

10 Weaver et al would see part of the solution to this problem as a resource bank of 'mini-lessons' for teachers to utilize at the point of need (2006: 82).

11 A major point of Wheeler's (2006) article is to draw attention to sensitive issues surrounding the legitimacy of African American English as a dialect. From her perspective, the mere naming of African American English as a dialect is a political act and a risky business. A comparable story is told by Gordon (2005) about the political climate in New Zealand, which rendered a suggestion that Maori (the indigenous language) be used as a linguistic comparison with English untenable.

12 Interestingly, Elley et al. rate Bateman and Zidonis (1966) less favourable methodologically than the EPPI Review.

REFERENCES

Andrews, R. (2005a) 'Knowledge about the teaching of [sentence] grammar: The state of play', *English Teaching: Practice and Critique*, 4(3): 68–75.

Andrews, R. (2005b) 'The place of systematic reviews in educational research', British *Journal of Educational Studies*, 53(4): 399–416.

Andrews, R., Torgerson, C., Beverton, S., Freeman, A., Locke, T., Low, G., Robinson, A., and Zhu, D. (2004) 'The Effect of Grammar Teaching (syntax) in English on 5 to 16 year olds' Accuracy and Quality in Written Composition', *Research Evidence in Education Library*, London: EPPI-Centre, Social Science Research Unit, Institute of Education.

Andrews, R., Torgerson, C., Beverton, S., Freeman, A., Locke, T., Low, G., Robinson, A., and Zhu, D. (2006) 'The effect of grammar teaching on writing development', *British Educational Research Journal*, 32(1): 39–55.

Anon. (1989) 'Teaching writing: A position statement', *English in Aotearoa*, 10: 9–10.

Bateman, D. and Zidonis, F. (1966) *The Effect of a Study of Transformational Grammar on the Writing of Ninth and Tenth Graders*, Urbana, IL: NCTE.

Carter, R. (1994) 'Knowledge about language in the curriculum', in S. Brindley (ed.), *Teaching English*, London and New York: Routledge. pp.246–258.

Carter, R. (1996) 'Politics and knowledge about language: The LINC Project', in R. Hasan and G. Williams (eds), *Literacy in Society*, London: Longman. pp.1–3.

Christie, F. (2004) 'Revisiting some old Themes: The role of grammar in the teaching of English', in J. Foley (ed.), *Language, Education and Discourse: Functional Approaches*, New York/London: Continuum. pp.145–173.

Christie, F. (2005) 'Developing dimensions of an educational linguistics', in R. Hasan, C. Matthiessen, and J. Webster (eds), *Continuing Discourse on Language: A Functional Perspective, Vol. 1*, London/Oakville: Equinox. pp.217–250.

Clark, U. (2005) 'Bernstein's theory of pedagogic discourse: Linguistics, educational policy and practice in the UK English/literacy classroom', *English Teaching: Practice and Critique*, 4(3): 32–47.

Cope, B. and Kalantzis, M. (eds) (1993a) *The powers of literacy: A genre approach to teaching writing*, Pittsburgh: University of Pittsburgh Press.

Cope, B. and Kalantzis, M. (1993b) 'Introduction: How a genre approach to literacy can transform the way writing is taught', in B. Cope and M. Kalantzis (eds), *The Powers of Literacy: A genre approach to teaching writing*, Pittsburgh: University of Pittsburgh Press. pp.1–21.

Department of Education (1983) *English: Forms 3–5, Statement of Aims*, Wellington: Department of Education.

Department of Education and Employment (2000) *Grammar for Writing*, London: Her Majesty's Stationery Office.

Department of Education and Science (1975) *A Language for Life (The Bullock Report)*, London: Her Majesty's Stationery Office.

Department of Education and Science (1988) *Report of the Committee of Inquiry in the Teaching of the English Language (The Kingman Report)*, London: Her Majesty's Stationery Office.

Dixon, J. (1975) *Growth Through English (Set in the Perspective of the Seventies)*, Edgerton: NATE/Oxford University Press.

Dixon, J. and Stratta, L. (1995) 'What does genre theory offer?' in W. Sawyer (ed.), *Teaching Writing: Is Genre the Answer?*, Springwood, NSW: Australian Education Network. pp.77–91.

Elley, W. B., Barham, I. H., Lam, H., and Wyllie, M. (1979) *The Role of Grammar in the Secondary School Curriculum* (Wellington, New Zealand Council for Educational Research).

Gordon, E. (1991) *Grammar teaching in NZ schools: Past, present, and future*, English in Aotearoa, 15: 19–30.

Gordon, E. (2005) 'Grammar in New Zealand schools: Two case studies', *English Teaching: Practice and Critique*, 4(3): 48–68.

Hillocks, G., Jr. and Smith, M. (1991) 'Grammar and usage', in J. Flood, J. Jensen, D. Lapp, and J. Squire (ed.), *Handbook of Research on Teaching the English Language Arts*, New York: Macmillan. pp.591–603.

Hudson, R. and Walmsley, J. (2005) 'The English Patient: English grammar and teaching in the Twentieth Century', *Journal of Linguistics*, 41(3): 593–622.

Kolln, M. (1996) 'Rhetorical grammar: A modification lesson', *English Journal*, 85(7): 25–31.

Kolln, M. and Hancock, C. (2005) 'The story of English grammar in United States Schools', *English Teaching: Practice and Critique*, 4(3): 11–31.

Locke, T. (2007) 'Constructing English in New Zealand: A report on a decade of reform', *L1 – Educational studies in language and literature*, 7(2): 5–33.

Mac Donald, H. (1995) 'Why Johnny can't write', *The Public Interest*, 3–13 (Summer).

Ministry of Education (1994) *English in the New Zealand Curriculum*, Wellington: Learning Media.

Ministry of Education (1996) *Exploring Language: A Handbook for Teachers*, Wellington: Learning Media.

Muller, H.J. (1967) *The Uses of English: Guidelines for the Teaching of English from the Anglo-American Conference at Dartmouth College*, New York: Holt, Rinehart and Winston.

National Council of Teachers of English (NCTE) (1995). #3 'On the Teaching of Grammar', *Slate Starter Sheet*, Retrieved 29 August, 2007 from http://beta.ncte.org/library/files/About_NCTE/Issues/teach-grammar.pdf.

Qualifications and Curriculum Authority (1998) *The Grammar Papers*, London: Qualifications and Curriculum Authority.

Qualifications and Curriculum Authority (1999) *Not Whether But How*, London: Qualifications and Curriculum Authority.

Quirk, R., Greenbaum, S., Leech, G., and Svartvik, J. (1985) *A Comprehensive Grammar of the English Language*, London: Longman.

Richardson, P. (1994) 'Language as personal resource and as social construct: Competing views of literacy pedagogy in Australia', in A. Freedman and P. Medway (eds), *Learning and Teaching Genre*, Portsmouth, NH: Boynton/Cook Publishers. pp.117–142.

Sawyer, W. (ed.) (1995) *Teaching Writing: Is genre the answer?*, Springwood, NSW: Australian Education Network.

Stead, C.K. (1997) 'The English Patient', *Metro*, 84–90 (April).

Tchudi, S.J. and Tchudi, S.N. (1991) *The English Language Arts Handbook: Classroom strategies for teachers*, New Jersey: Boynton Cook.

Weaver, C. (1979) *Grammar for Teachers: Perspectives and definitions*, Urbana, IL: National Council of Teachers of English.

Weaver, C. (1996) *Teaching Grammar in Context*, Portsmouth, NH: Boynton/Cook.

Weaver, C., Bush, J., with Anderson, J. and Bills, P. (2006) 'Grammar intertwined throughout the writing process: An "inch wide and a mile deep"', *English Teaching: Practice and Critique*, 5(1): 77–101.

Wheeler, R. (2006) '"What do we do about Student Grammar – all those missing *-ed's* and *-s's*?" Using Comparison and Contrast to Teach Standard English in Dialectically Diverse Classrooms', *English Teaching: Practice and Critique*, 5(1): 16–33.

Williams, G. (2004) 'Ontogenesis and Grammatics: Functions of metalanguage in pedagogical discourse', in G. Williams and A. Lukin (eds), *The Development of Language: Functional Perspectives on Species and Individuals*, London and New York: Continuum. pp.241–256.

13

How Linguistics Can Inform the Teaching of Writing

Craig Hancock

The spirit of poetry, like all other living powers, must of necessity circumscribe itself by rules, were it only to unite power with beauty. It must embody in order to reveal itself; but a living body is of necessity an organized one – and what is organization but the connection of parts to a whole, so that each part is at once end and means! This is no discovery of criticism; it is a necessity of the human mind – and all nations have felt and obeyed it. ... (Samuel Taylor Coleridge, Lectures on Shakespeare)

The form is mechanic when on any given material we impress a predetermined form, not necessarily arising out of the properties of the material, as when to a mass of wet clay we give whatever shape we wish it to retain when hardened. The organic form, on the other hand, is innate; it shapes as it develops itself from within, and the fullness of its development is one and the same with the perfection of its outward form. Such is the life, such the form. (Samuel Taylor Coleridge, Lectures on Shakespeare)

One difficulty in addressing the core concern of this chapter – how linguistics can inform the teaching of writing – is that neither linguistics nor the teachings of writing are monolithic fields. The central position I will be taking – that this is fundamentally a functional question, a question about how language itself functions within an effective text – is likely to be interpreted differently by a linguist than it would for a writing teacher, since linguistics has 'functional' schools as well as schools

that are more formal (structural or generative). Schools of linguistics that may think of themselves as 'progressive' have some views about language in common with more traditional approaches to composition. These linguistic schools have varying views about how language is acquired, about to what extent the underlying forms are innate or learned. If language is a mechanical system, essentially meaningfully neutral, essentially innate, then there may be little value to the writer or writing teacher in exploring its nature, little value in parsing sentences or learning the systems for describing its underlying formality. If, on the other hand, the forms of language are inherently, organically linked to discourse context and to meaning, and if these forms are not at all innate, but acquired over a lifetime of interactive use, then linguistics may have an enormous amount to offer the writing teacher and writing student, insights that go well beyond the minimum needed to write conventionally or correctly. It may very well be, in turn, that composition specialists have a great deal to offer the discipline of linguistics, which has as its primary field of study the very tools every writer puts to use. Recent insights in linguistics – essentially over the past twenty-five years, a small period in the evolution of a technical discipline – have the potential to radically transform the relationship between language knowledge and language use. This means overcoming an elitist tradition in linguistics, which, with a few very important exceptions, has not highly valued pedagogical applications, and an enormous predisposition within the field of English in general, composition less so, to devalue knowledge about language (Hudson and Walmsley, 2005; MacDonald, 2007). My goal will be to make the case for a robust collaboration and give at least a rough feel for how that collaboration might have immediate practical applications.

SOME BACKGROUND ON GRAMMAR

Traditional school grammar

It may be a rough truth to say that most people consider traditional school grammar and grammar to be one and the same, since school grammar has, historically at least, been the view of grammar presented to them in school or the grammar cast out of school in the liberal movements of the sixties and seventies, the grammar most soundly discredited by the empirical studies that fail to show a quick crossover between instruction in grammar and improvement in writing. Though it brings with it a terminology that carries over into other, more scientifically grounded grammars – *noun, verb, adjective, adverb, modifier, conjunction, preposition, auxiliary, transitive verb, intransitive verb, subject,* and *predicate* are core examples – it also can be said to define those terms fairly poorly and to move too quickly from word types to sentence types without enough attention to intermediate word groups, like the phrase and the clause. It tends to carry with it a number of prescriptive rules that seem arbitrary and capricious, having more of a life in the handbooks than they do in the practice of successful writers. For a good, critical look at some of these 'myth rules', see Schuster (2003) and the Language Mavens chapter in

Pinker (2000). 'Once introduced, a prescriptive rule is very hard to eradicate, no matter how ridiculous' (Pinker, 2000: 387). These include rules against splitting infinitives, starting sentences with *and, but,* or *because,* ending sentences with prepositions, and so on. I like to debrief my students on what they know about grammar when entering college, and questionable rules seem to be the bulk of it. 'Don't use *I* when you write.' 'Don't use contractions.' 'You can't write the way you speak.' Even when clearly more rhetorical than grammatical – rules about the number of sentences in a paragraph, for example – students think of them as grammar precisely because they are constraining and prescriptive. Grammar is error and error is grammar in much of the public mind.

This unreflective mix of prescriptive and descriptive also carries over into traditional attempts to reinforce or enforce Standard English, a position that puts it at war with more grounded formal grammars and the goals of more progressive pedagogy. To a traditionalist, what is standard is *proper* or *correct.* Variations from it are thought of as *improper* or *wrong.* Writing is very often *corrected* along these lines. This, of course, has been roundly criticized by those in composition who offer true revision as a contrast to mere correction and who work hard to position writing as a meaning-making activity, equal to literature in the pantheon.

Some aspects of traditional school grammar date back to attempts to move up in social class by displacing some of the stigmatized features of less prestigious dialects. Because we now value diversity, those goals make us uncomfortable. 'Language differences are perhaps what most often prompt teachers and many others to unwarranted judgments about the ability and knowledge of their students. Those who grew up in working-class neighbourhoods, as I did, will recall teachers' animosities to *how* we said things. What we said did not matter much, as long as we said it in a fashion that met that teacher's view of 'correctness'. For example, my seventh and eighth grade English teacher had clear rules about usage that she expected us to meet. When we did not, we were sure to meet some degree of public embarrassment, from simple correction to sarcastic humiliation. ... Although I would like to think that this verbal dictatorship has had little effect on me over the years, it certainly had the effect, at the time, of shutting down student talk, except for the surreptitious, illegal kind' (Hillocks, 1995: 17).

The big problem, as Pinker sees it, is that this happens because the language maven, whether columnist or zealous teacher, has two major blind spots: 'a gross underestimation of the linguistic wherewithal of the common person' and 'complete ignorance of the modern science of language' (Pinker, 2000: 412–413).

Traditional school grammar also gives us the metalanguage that undergirds much of the conventionality of language in written form. Terms like 'run-on sentence' and 'sentence fragment' come out of traditional grammar, and the 'rules' for punctuation, presented as rules and not as somewhat flexible conventions, use a terminology drawn largely from school grammar traditions. I found sixty-four technical terms in the punctuation sections of the fifth edition of Diana Hacker's *A Writer's Reference* (2003), perhaps the best selling composition handbook in the United States. To follow the rules for commas, for example, students need to read and make sense of sentences that include *coordinating conjunction*, *introductory word group*, and *nonrestrictive modifiers* (further broken down into *adjective clauses*, *adjective phrases*, and *appositives*.) The handbook is in the awkward position of trying to explain these difficult concepts at the point of explaining the rule. Unless punctuation can be mastered intuitively, someone who wants to diligently follow the system must confront a rather baffling array of new concepts and their terms.

Perhaps the best case for traditional grammar is that it is a pedagogical grammar, though its efficacy has been robustly challenged. When the public hears that we do not

need to teach grammar, they may suspect that we no longer care about whether or not students can write 'correctly' or follow routine discourse conventions. Even the most progressive educators seem to echo the need for students to master Standard English and use conventional punctuation. The most telling argument against systematic instruction in traditional grammar is the fairly accurate observation that you can't get there from here, that memorizing definitions for 'parts of speech' – *a noun is a person, place, or thing* – does not give us the basis we need for writing conventionally and correctly, and time might be better spent in actual reading and writing, with the occasional 'correcting' going on at point of need. I will take this position up later on in 'the case for minimalism'. As an alternative to traditional grammar or more formal grammars, it makes some sense. Fortunately, these are not the only alternatives.

Structural grammar

Structuralist approaches to grammar, from the start, have taken pains to put the description of language on more scientific grounds. In some ways, as in the seminal work of Leonard Bloomfield (1933), that has meant limiting attention to formal elements, those elements that can be most readily observed and measured. It is certainly a descriptive rather than prescriptive approach, more interested in language in present use than that in history. Since speech has predated writing by thousands of years and since many languages that need to be described have never been written down, speech is given primacy in the system. This, of course, puts it at odds with prescriptive approaches, in part, because it will recognize usage patterns discouraged by traditional grammar to be rule-driven, grammatical, even widely used.

A structural grammar amends classifications of words by trying to give them a more scientific ground. As much as possible, that means definition by formal characteristics rather than semantic ones. A noun is a noun if it can be made plural by adding 's', or if it can follow a determiner (itself a term not recognized in traditional grammar). A verb is a verb if it can change form to reflect tense and aspect. Structural linguistics recognizes phonetic, morphemic, and syntactic systems. They describe the way sounds come together to make syllables and words, the way meaningful units combine in the making of words, and the various patterns that occur when words come together in sentences. It makes a far clearer distinction between word class – which tells us something about the potential of a word – and its role within a particular instance of use. Therefore, 'Tuesday' is clearly a noun, because it passes the noun class tests, but that does not keep it from modifying a noun in a phrase like 'Tuesday seminar' or acting adverbially in a sentence like 'They left Tuesday'.

It is interesting that the earliest attacks on grammar in the schools came largely from the structuralist camps, and they were not antigrammar positions as much as they were antitraditional grammar (Kolln and Hancock, 2005). Susan Peck McDonald cites the rise of a structural grammar as in many ways abetting the antigrammar positions in the sixties since it was the intellectual underpinning for the 'Students' Right to Their Own Language' (CCCC, 1974), an official NCTE position statement. Since structural grammar takes the spoken language as primary, and since it takes a disinterested, nonjudgmental stance, perhaps it leaves a writing teacher caught between a felt need to enforce the forms and structures felt to be appropriate to writing and the need to affirm the value of diverse dialects and the communities they represent. In the United States, that has literally been black *versus* white, though McDonald points out that the current demographic, with so many students bringing languages other than English to school, has changed the teaching situation dramatically (2007).

If structural grammar gives us a far more accurate, scientific view of language, but a nonjudgmental view based on speech, what can it do to help in the carryover from speech to writing? One answer may be in the corpus grammars (see Biber et al., 1999); now, with the help of the huge power of computers, we can look at a great many texts from different contexts and registers and begin to build an understanding of how language changes, not just in writing, but in different genres of writing, which may put pressure on the language to work in specialized ways, or may be evolving their own formal conventions. To some extent, these are functional, not just formal questions, which might best be answered with a functional or organic notion of the relationship between meaning and form.

There is no question, though, that a grounding in structural grammar puts us in a position where we can read (and disagree with) a traditional handbook. It puts us in a position where we can critically evaluate many of the formal conventions of writing. That kind of grounding does not come easily, and it is not the kind of carryover from grammar study to writing that is likely to show up in a short term, controlled, holistically rated assessment. I will return to those questions later.

Generative grammar

Generative grammar is an extension of formal grammar into its mental roots. It has undergone major revisions since its dramatic introduction in the late fifties, but it has remained essentially an attempt to explain the underlying, innate, universal aspects of grammar, the inheritance of all humans by virtue of being human, which make language itself possible. It tries to describe the 'finite forms' that make possible an infinity of expressions. Chomsky's (1957, 1965) early point was that behaviorist views of language and language acquisition cannot account for the complexities of language 'competence.' An early division between 'competence' and 'performance' (our awkward efforts at putting innate competence into practice) freed the linguist to study largely 'competence' and formulate a highly abstract, formal, decontextualized, almost mathematical view of language. The best way to test the grammaticality of an utterance is to ask a native speaker, for whom it will or will not feel right. In the earliest versions, this involved a differentiation between the 'deep structure' of an utterance and various 'surface structure' variations, with the deep structure rules as primary and variations described in terms of 'transformational' rules. In effect, it describes how primary meanings are both generated and transformed and has thus generally been called *generative* or *transformational* grammar in its various pedagogical applications.

Kolln (Kolln and Hancock, 2005) faults a faddish interest in generative grammar for being part of a 'perfect storm' that displaced a developing interest in the far more practical structural grammar in the fifties and sixties. When generative grammar failed – and it tended to do so rather dramatically – it was often thought of as a failure of linguistics to address teaching needs, not just as a failure of one radically abstract approach. Susan Peck MacDonald extends the blame to structural grammar itself for setting up a binary opposition between prescriptive and descriptive. She points out the rather unfortunate confluence of an interest in linguistics at a time in which 'linguistics had little to offer English' (2007: 609).

Any serious school of linguistics acknowledges the intuitive or unconscious way in which grammar functions within discourse. To a generative grammarian, this unconscious system is not so much learned, as activated, and it is activated in a fairly predictable, biological way. 'Acquiring language is less something that a child does than something that happens to the child, like growing arms instead of wings, or undergoing puberty at a certain stage of maturation' (Chomsky, 1996: 563). 'People know how to talk in more or less the sense that spiders know how to spin webs' (Pinker, 2000: 5). We are biologically programmed to do this. For better or worse, this has become a position used to support a minimalist attention to grammar.

There are two theoretical positions that undergird minimalism. One is that language is not so much learned, but both innate and acquired, not from direct instruction, but from exposure. The other is that form at this level is not context sensitive; it has little or nothing to do with meaning. Though minimalism is a pedagogical position, not a linguistic one, I will explore it in some detail in the next section before moving on to more useful alternatives, which tend to see language as learned rather than acquired, as context sensitive, and as meaning-making.

One pedagogical approach coming out of generative grammar that has been able to gather some proponents and demonstrate some efficacy is sentence-combining. In sentence combining, practising writers are given very short 'kernel' sentences and asked to combine them into more complex structures. Terms often used to describe the goals are 'syntactic fluency' and 'syntactic maturity'. The theory would be that a mature writer has a wide range of syntactic options available and that complexity is a later development. It is interesting that one study reported on by Hillocks (1986) shows holistically assessed ratings going down for some students who have added complexity. This would seem to argue for including conscious attention to choices as rhetorical options.

Minimalism as a program

One of the most appealing presentations of minimalism as pedagogical approach comes by way of Rei Noguchi (1991). He begins with a rather sympathetic description of the situation a poor composition teacher finds herself in, dealing with awkward sentences from a student who knows little or nothing about language. As Noguchi points out, the grammar of the language is systematic, and it is very difficult to isolate any one part of that system without bringing into play so much of the rest. The idea of a sentence for example, cannot be a 'complete thought' if the student insists that what we clearly see as a fragment is 'complete' in his own mind. If we fall back on a more formal definition, for example that a sentence is 'a group of words having a complete subject and complete predicate,' (Noguchi, 1991: 39) we are then faced with the difficult task of explaining *complete subject* and *complete predicate*. Is subject the actor? Does it come first? Quite often that is the case, but not always.

Traditional grammar, structural grammar, and generative grammar give us a systematic description of forms. Writing, though, carries with it prescriptive constraints. There is not a quick and easy connection between the two. What Noguchi advocates, instead, is using the beginning writer's intuitive understanding of grammar as a means toward dealing with those aspects of grammar most closely tied to meeting the conventions of writing. The idea of a sentence, for example, can be addressed through appending tag questions, a tool within a native speaker's repertoire, which can then lead us back to the sentence's subject. If you believe that grammar is largely a system of forms and that native speakers have this system available intuitively, then a direct appeal to this intuitive system can help us bypass the need for a more systematic understanding. Given the short time most writing teachers have available to work with students, this has appeal.

Minimalist approaches seem predicated on the notion of innateness and tend to assume that the primary reason for learning grammar, its primary value for writing, would be in avoidance of error. We do not need to teach, in effect, what has already been acquired, what is already there. 'Prescriptive rules are useless without the more fundamental rules that create the sentences. … These rules are never mentioned in the style manuals or school grammar because the authors correctly assume that anyone capable of reading the manuals must already have the rules … When a scientist considers all the high-tech mental machinery needed to arrange words into ordinary sentences, prescriptive rules are, at best, "inconsequential little decorations"' (Pinker, 2000: 384).

If the forms of language are simply neutral conveyors of meaning, then they will not have an important role in the higher level concerns of text. 'If the study of grammar and mechanics is brought to bear on the composing process at all, it is likely to influence only the most concrete levels, the planning and editing of specific sentences. But such study would have no effect on the higher-level processes of deciding on intentions and generating and organizing ideas' (Hillocks, 1986: 226). Hillocks says further on in the same text that even the 'planning and editing of specific sentences' would not benefit from systematic knowledge. 'The study of traditional school grammar is not designed to help children generate sentences but only to parse already-generated sentences. Thus, the study of grammar is unlikely to be helpful even in the planning of specific sentences. The study of mechanics and usage (what might be called "conventional correctness") is likely to have effect only in the last-minute editing done during transcription or in the editing process following it' (1986: 226–227).

If we think of language as something to be acquired, that it can be acquired with little or no formal instruction, and that it has little or no connection to the meaning-making features of discourse, then it is an easy step to advocate minimalist intervention. For Erica Lindemann (2001), this means that knowledge about language is and can be very valuable to the writing teacher, but need not be passed on to the typical student. 'To *teach* English requires a second kind of knowledge, a 'conscious understanding' of linguistic principles', but 'what teachers must know about written English is not necessarily the same body of information that our students must be required to memorize' (Lindemann, 2001: 60). This is a position shared with Constance Weaver (1996), who also advocates enough knowledge about language to keep teachers from imposing regressive prescriptivism, but does not advocate passing knowledge on. If we think of grammar as 'the functional command of sentence structures that enable us to comprehend or produce language, then we do not need to teach grammar at all: the grammar of our native language is what we learn in acquiring that language' (Weaver, 1996: 2). Both Weaver and Lindemann argue against formal instruction in part by citing the studies that show that instruction in formal grammar does not carry over. Both admit the need for some sort of intervention in order to help students master the conventions of writing and avoid 'error,' but that does not require a comprehensive understanding of language. 'Only a few of the frequently occurring errors in the Connors-Lunsford study and only a few of the status-marking, very serious, or serious errors in Hairston's study require for their elimination an understanding of grammatical concepts commonly taught. And these few kinds of errors can be understood by comprehending only a few grammatical concepts' (Weaver, 1996: 115).

Hillocks, to his credit, is a bit less sure. 'Even the most liberal authorities ... recognize a need to attend to the mechanics of writing, although they would abjure the traditional naming of parts of speech and parsing of sentences' (1986: 138). According to Hillocks, two questions need to be addressed. The first is how much error is acceptable, which is 'not answerable by research. Teachers and institutions must decide for themselves on acceptable error types and rates' (1986: 139). The other question is how much knowledge about grammar is necessary to deal with those errors. 'Very little research on the teaching of mechanics has been conducted. The teaching of grammar and correctness has had, at best, mixed results even for teaching correctness. We do not know how much grammar or what grammatical knowledge writers must have to copyread with accuracy' (1986: 140).

Certainly, one serious objection that can be raised about minimalism is concern about the wise teacher 'guiding' the acquisition of language without mentoring the student into the knowledge base that underlies the teaching. Susan Peck MacDonald has described the results of minimalist teaching over a few

generations as a general 'erasure of language' from the discipline base of English, at least in the states. English teachers in training, with little or no formal understanding of language from their own schooling, often have no more than a course or two in linguistics to build up their competence, possibly courses that reiterate the research-driven position that grammar itself is harmful, irrelevant, or unimportant. 'We send out teachers who lack the intellectual capital about language that an older generation possessed, but who, meaning well, may then try to reinvent knowledge about language in ad hoc ways or repeat old nostrums that would horrify the scholars of the sixties who thought the old nostrums had been laid to rest' (MacDonald, 2007: 619).

Another very telling criticism is that teaching grammar 'in context' is fundamentally misleading, since the grammar understood by the context advocates is not a context sensitive grammar. Context is simply a 'point-of-need', not a place where rhetorically nuanced choices can be made through deeper understanding of a form/meaning interconnection. Any truly contextualized grammar may have to reclaim the term from its current, more narrow use. 'The truth is that teaching grammar and knowledge about language in positive, contextualized ways which make clear links with writing is not yet an established way of teaching and it is, as yet, hugely under-researched' (Myhill, 2005: 81). Myhill goes on to criticize grammar in context advocates for not holding their own teaching up to any serious reflection.

The rejection of decontextualised, and with it by implication, prescriptive, grammar teaching was rooted in insightful critique of what was happening in English classrooms. In contrast, the 'grammar in context' principle is both less sharply critiqued and considerably less clearly conceptualised. There has been little genuine discussion or consideration of what 'in context' means. Frequently, observations of classroom practice indicate that the notion of 'in context' means little more than grammar teaching which is slotted into English lessons, where the focus is not grammar, but some other feature of English learning (2005: 82).

Systemic functional grammar (SFG)

Mary Schleppegrell, in *At Last: the Meaning in Grammar* (2007), joins a number of thoughtful educators decrying the overly simplistic, reductionist views on language and grammar, 'the purportedly research-driven notions that grammar is no more than a set of rules for accuracy in language use and that grammar plays no role in writing development' (2007: 121. see also Micciche, 2004). Though teachers routinely help students change phrasing and organization and consider the effect of choices on intended audience, they will not necessarily think of that as 'grammar' if it is not in the service of fixing a fixed number of prescriptively named problems.

> Teachers are intuitively teaching grammar by focusing students' attention on language alternatives ... but few teachers feel competent in explaining or presenting in explicit ways the options and affordances of systems such as conjunction or modality that offer a range of meaning-making options (2007: 121–22).

For Schleppegrell, one important key is the insight afforded in systemic functional grammar, which helps reveal 'how different language choices construct more or less powerful texts ..., what is valued in student writing ... how language develops over time' (2007: 122).

It is interesting that the first major text in systemic functional grammar, the first edition of Halliday's introduction to functional grammar, was published in 1985, around the time The National Council of Teachers of English was reaffirming its stance against the systematic teaching of grammar and Hillocks (1986) was releasing his meta-analysis of research on the teaching of writing, which echoed the negative views of Braddock et al. (1963). For many in the United States, those publications closed the books on the issue without hint of the possibility that other, functional approaches to the problem were not only possible, but also under serious development.

Traditional and formal approaches are not well suited to judging the effectiveness of a sentence. Technically, we can tell whether a sentence is grammatical by appealing to the intuitions of a native speaker. A formal grammar, structural or generative, can give us the formal rules behind that, rules we might use to help along a nonnative speaker making adjustments from their own native language. We can tell whether a sentence is 'correct' by appealing to the rules of a prescriptive grammar, including the rules codified in a typical manual of style or a typical handbook. It is easy to understand how this might have an important, but peripheral connection to what many of us consider to be the real work of writing, making of meaning and the making of human connections. A functional grammar, in contrast, gives us a way to explore the effectiveness of a choice. It heals the split between grammar and meaning. It connects form to meaning and form to purpose. Through this lens, it is possible to look at an evolving sentence as deeply tied to an unfolding purpose. The form is not innate and it is not neutral. Forms have evolved, in fact, to carry out human purposes. They have evolved, and are evolving, to meet human needs. The forms themselves are discourse sensitive, not merely neutral in the construal and construction of meaning. 'The approach that is likely to be most effective will be one that recognizes *meaning* and *use* as central features of language and that tackles grammar from this point of view' (Bloor and Bloor, 2004: 2).

The kinds of meaning that SFG recognizes at the level of the sentence are kinds of meaning writing teachers routinely value at the level of the whole text. Language helps us represent the world, including the interior world of our thoughts and emotions. It helps us establish and carry out interpersonal relations and interactions. It helps us carry out purposes that require more than a single utterance in the form of messages or texts. These three primary metafunctions – the *ideational*, *interpersonal*, and *textual* – are carried out in and through the grammar. They are, in fact, realized through resources in the language at the level of the clause. 'The entire architecture of language is arranged along functional lines. Language is as it is because of the functions in which it has evolved in the human species' (Halliday and Matthiessen, 2004: 31).

It is hard to get a working feel for systemic functional grammar in this kind of overview, in part because it is a systematic view, not merely a loose collection of functional observations. But it is possible to look at the 'processes' within a clause, essentially governed by the verb, as a representation of the world, be it material, behavioral, mental, verbal, relational, or existential. The clause, at the same time, will isolate some aspect of the representation to be the subject of a proposition or offer or request for information or goods and services. The focus of a statement or question, in other words, will not always be the doer of the process. And the sentence, even in casual discourse, is rarely a complete thought, but a move in a series of related moves, a portioning-out of the purpose of the text, for which we have thematic options (starting point), emphasis options (often clause ending), and various ways for extending meaning across the highly variable boundaries of the sentence.

Systemic functional grammar is, in effect, a systematic study of how the higher order concerns of discourse are realized and in and through the grammar. It is more truly a grammar in context, because it does not view form itself as independent of context, but as deeply context sensitive. It gives us a rich repertoire of tools already available in the language, but largely functioning below conscious awareness, by bringing those natural resources to conscious light.

If language is not just a meaningfully neutral, biologically innate system, but a system that has evolved to meet human needs, then it is highly possible that the system is still evolving. Since writing is fairly new to most of humanity, and since the uses of language are changing radically with the evolution of technical disciplines, it should not surprise us that language itself has been changing to help make that possible. 'School-based texts are difficult for many students, precisely because they emerge from discourse contexts that require different ways of using language than students experience outside of school (Schleppegrell, 2004: 9). Schleppegrell argues that 'researchers and educators need a more complete understanding of the linguistic challenges of schooling. In the absence of an explicit focus on language, students from certain social class backgrounds continue to be privileged and others to be disadvantaged in learning, assessment, and promotion, perpetuating the obvious inequalities that exist today' (2004: 3). In *The Language of Schooling*, Schleppegrell draws on SFG as a way to make more explicit the demands of more academic texts.

Cognitive linguistics

For the most part, cognitive linguistics has grown up under the shadow of generative paradigm, and so its practitioners have tended to describe their own approach in contrast to this, though acknowledging certain points in common – that a theory of language needs also to be a theory of human cognition, that it needs to account for the human ability to generate an endless supply of novel utterances, and that a 'non-trivial theory of language learning is needed'(Goldberg, 2006: 4). It nevertheless differs from generative grammar in some startling ways. Croft and Cruse (2004) give these three core, contrasting hypotheses: 'Language is not an autonomous cognitive faculty'; 'Grammar is conceptualization'; and 'Knowledge of language emerges from language use' (2004: 1).

To the extent that 'language is not an autonomous cognitive faculty', it is not separate from our sensory motor or social experiences of the world. Since grammar itself is 'conceptualization', there is not a distinct difference or mechanical separation between the meanings of language and the forms it finds itself in. There is, in fact, much more a word-grammar cline, with a great deal of dynamic movement as words form constructions and constructions become lexicalized, free to take on new meanings, just as words do. There is not a one-to-one 'truth function' between a language construct and an outside world. 'An expression implies a particular construal, reflecting just one of countless ways of perceiving and portraying the situation in question' (Langacker, 2008:.4.). What we have come to think of as language governing 'rules' may be much more like patterns, a 'grammaticalization' that occurs over time and becomes routinized through frequency. The verb process 'giving' is not di-transitive because it follows the rules of di-transitive constructions, but because the very nature of giving involves a giver, some entity to be given, and some entity, generally a person, that it is given to. Perhaps one problem with formal, abstract grammar is that it pulls us away from this heavily localized centre of language. 'Grammar cannot be a fixed property of human brains, but is emergent, constantly undergoing revision as it is deployed and redesigned in everyday talk' (Ford, Fox, and Thompson, 2003: 119). 'Grammar is not a static, closed, or self-contained system, but is highly susceptible to change and highly affected by language use' (Bybee, 2003: 145). It is shaped and constrained by the functions it serves, including 'a multi-faceted interactive function, involving communication, manipulation, expressiveness, and social communion' (Langacker, 2008:7).

Moreover, knowledge about language, what the generativists call 'competence', is not something we are born with, but something that emerges over a lifetime of use. For Tomasello, the key cognitive processes that make language acquisition possible are 'intention reading' and 'pattern finding' processes (2003: 6). 'The process of acquiring language conventions serves to focus children's attention on aspects of experience that they might not otherwise have focused on. The relation between children's language and cognition is a two-way street' (Tomasello, 2003: 63).

The implications for education are enormous. Minimalist approaches are built on far less solid ground if grammar is not something innate and activated in early childhood, simply put to use as adults, but rather a far more detailed, concrete, contextual system that develops over a lifetime of interaction and use. In addition, study of grammar would not be a study of a 'formal' system, but a conceptual system, deeply grounded in context. Language is not a neutral system, to be attended to only when it runs counter to prescriptive rules, but deeply tied to cognition and to discourse. The form of the text and the language of the text are its meaning, in a very fundamental way.

One very important branch of cognitive linguistics, most closely tied to George Lakoff and Mark Johnson, has been exploring the essentially metaphoric nature of all language, including a great deal that generally happens below our conscious attention. The most seminal text was Lakoff and Johnson's *Metaphors We Live By*, originally published in 1983. The line of thinking has been developed in a number of follow-up texts, including *Women, Fire, and Dangerous Things* (Lakoff, 1987) and *Philosophy in the Flesh* (Lakoff and Johnson, 1999). A particularly useful summary is provided in *Afterword, 2003* to the most recent edition of *Metaphors We Live By*. Lakoff and Johnson show unequivocally in example after example that metaphor is deeply conceptual. It does not involve similarities so much as mappings across different domains. Many of our most primary metaphors – that *up* is *more*, for example, or that *warmth* is *affection* – are deeply tied to our most fundamental sensory-motor experience of the word. Moreover, if we consistently express something metaphorically – for example, that time is money, that it can be spent, saved, or wasted – it is also a key cultural conception.

From the perspective of cognitive linguistics, there is not a clear distinction between literary language and the language of everyday life. Mark Turner extends this to the nature of narrative, which is not simply a literary form, but a deeply human way of understanding our place in the world. 'Narrative imagining – story – is the fundamental instrument of thought. Rational capacities depend on it. It is our chief means of looking into the future, of predicting, of planning, and of explaining. It is a literary capacity indispensable to human cognition generally'. To Turner, 'the mind is essentially literary' (1996:4–5).

CONCLUSIONS AND IMPLICATIONS

One problem with bringing a complex knowledge about language into the teaching of writing is still the problem of time, the problem of managing resources. Language itself can more than make up the bulk of the curriculum in a semester long or yearlong course. In addition, most writing teachers are currently faced with students who know little or nothing about language to start, students who may have substantial misunderstanding to impede them. Minimalism seems almost inevitable. At the same time, though, we have students who take English classes essentially every year of their education. There is no reason at all that their education should not include a systematic understanding of how language works. There is no excuse for the continuation of blatantly harmful and inaccurate or incomplete descriptions of language in the name of expediency. We can and should lobby for the integration of a linguistically sound language study into the curriculum, and this should include approaches to language that are reading and writing friendly, that do not simply see language as meaningfully neutral, as correct or incorrect.

Certainly, any approach to language needs to acknowledge the intuitive nature of much of our understanding. Language cannot work as language without a certain degree of automaticity. That said, it does not follow that language is simply a behaviour or an instinct. The questions at this stage should be of knowledge about language, not simply a question of what behaviours will be encouraged, discouraged, or permitted. Knowledge about language brings with it the possibility of a student becoming an agent, capable of carrying out his or her own purposes. It seems to me unconscionable in a number of ways to simply think of language as an unconscious system that merely needs to be acquired. If experts disagree on the nature of language, then we can do what we do in any discipline, which is to pass on an acknowledgment of those differing understandings as part of what the discipline of linguistics is all about. We can certainly do more than we currently do to make language itself a very rich and interesting topic, not merely a few shallow definitions and a loose collection of constraints.

Knowledge about language, not just behaviour, can be directed toward four major goals: mastery of standard English without denigration of the vernacular; mastery of the routine conventions of written discourse, including punctuation; understanding of the relationship between syntactic choice and rhetorical effect in the construction of various kinds of text; and understanding the special kinds of language that come into play in the technical disciplines.

I believe that students should have far more opportunity to write in genres that call for the vernacular – first person narration, dramatic monologue, conversation within story and play, more colloquial genres such as jokes, or advertising. They should have far more opportunity to explore and record the kinds of language they find around them in their homes and in their communities. Highly valued literary texts that use these dialects can be part of that mix. It does no good to affirm the students' right to their own language if the only response to it is correction. In exploring ways in which local language differs from the standard, students can also deepen their understanding of Standard English and its functional role in tying together larger communities. Knowledge about language gives us a chance to celebrate local dialects without fear of being imprisoned in them or held back by them. It is not an either/or choice and need not be framed as such.

Perhaps a first step for helping students master the conventions of written discourse is to rewrite those conventions in a reader-friendly way without resorting to narrowly focused distortions, such as 'a sentence is a complete thought' or 'put commas where you hear the pauses'. The grammar of speech is an intonation system, and it may very well help to bring that system to conscious light as a meaning-portioning system. But if we are to decide that students will be judged at least partly on the ability to put commas before conjunctions linking independent clauses (a U.S. pattern), then we should help them understand both *independent clause* and *conjunction*. My students come to college with the notion that a 'run-on sentence' is a sentence that runs on too long, and this gives most of them no way to recognize the pattern when we see it or alter it in productive ways. We need to simply decide what a successful writer ought to be able to do and then give them the knowledge they need to do it. A theory of innateness in grammar has somehow translated over into an expectation that someone will absorb writing conventions largely from exposure, but there is no clear evidence to support this.

Systemic functional grammar is a particularly rich area for form/meaning connections. I suspect that cognitive linguistics has at least an equal potential, though I believe it has yet to develop a pedagogical program that would use a deeper understanding of language as an adjunct to reading and writing. Martha Kolln's *Rhetorical Grammar* (2007), now in its fifth edition, is a useful attempt to merge a structural grammar with insights about rhetorical application. We can use concepts like *given* and *new* as counters to the complete thought concept of a sentence. Unity and coherence can only happen if meaning extends outward toward other sentences and in harmony with the larger purposes of the text. Repetition of various kinds is an essential part of this. Intonation grammar helps us see default positions for emphasis, generally at the end of a clause, but also in marked themes and non-restrictive word groups.

For the most part, these are insights that can bring almost immediate payoff without a need for grounding in a whole system. I like to introduce the concept of effectiveness as separate from correctness and then help students tie various choices to differences in message structure or in meaning.

'Genre' is a hugely useful category. As presented first by Swales (1990), genre has a much wider application than has historically been the case in literary studies. It is 'staged' (often requiring more than a single step) and purposeful. It evolves in the context of culture, and so is inherently dynamic. One very useful way to approach an exploration of the functionality of language is to do so through genre, getting students to explore the kinds of forms and the kinds of language that show up, the functional reasons for that (which versions are the most effective and why) and then have patterns of possibility, patterns of expectation to work with, in reading or writing in those genres.

Composition has at least given lip service these last few decades to 'writing across the curriculum', but has not fully embraced the possibility that the functional nature of those disciplines may be pushing the resources of language in unique ways. At any rate, it may be the provenance of the writing teacher to know more about the demands of disciplines other than English, to know of the ways in which perspective is brought in, the ways in which statements are qualified, and so on, as part of the way a discipline has to operate as a collegial discipline. If speech tends to be grammatically complex (more clauses and less meaning per clause), the general tendency in writing, as Halliday has pointed out, it toward a lexical density (more meaning per clause.) This is an inevitable process, since the evolution of a technical discipline requires a great deal to be shared as given; it is also a process that can become self-important and dysfunctional, and even in its best uses, very difficult to adjust to. Our normal way of understanding (construing) the world is with processes, participants, and circumstances. Technical language, though, often nominalizes those processes in what Halliday calls 'grammatical metaphor'. 'Where the everyday "mother tongue" of commonsense knowledge construes reality as a balanced tension between things and processes, the elaborated register of scientific knowledge reconstrues it as an edifice of things' (Halliday and Martin, 1993: 15). Joseph Williams (1993) advises us largely to unpack the nominalizations, use active verbs, and leave actors in the core sentence roles, but that can be naïve English teacher advice to someone reading and writing in the technical disciplines. It does not help to tell a science student to avoid the passive without first asking why passives are eight times more likely to show up in academic texts, or why most passives are agentless (Biber et al., 1999). The truth is that these forms are highly functional, useful in ways that go well beyond a mere 'style'.

Perhaps goals like these will help us to mine the insights of linguistics in practical ways. I would like to suggest a reciprocal pressure; linguists themselves need to look toward experts in reading and writing for questions worth exploring in their own field. A totally disinterested inquiry is in danger of missing the point.

The best, I believe, a systematic pedagogy based on a belief in the organic relationship between form and meaning, is yet to come.

REFERENCES

Biber, D., Conrad, S., Finegan, E., Johansson, S., and Leech, G. (1999) *Longman Grammar of Spoken and Written English*, Essex, UK: Longman.

Bloomfield, L. (1933) *Language*. New York: Henry Holt.

Bloor, T. and Bloor, M. (2004) *The Functional Analysis of English* (second edn.), New York: Oxford.

Braddock, R., Lloyd-Jones, R., and Schoer, L. (1963) *Research in Written Composition*, Urbana, Il: National Council of Teachers of English.

Bybee, J. (2003) 'Cognitive Processes in Grammaticalization', in Michael Tomasello (ed.), *The*

New Psychology of Language, Mahwah, NJ: Lawrence Erlbaum. pp.145–168.

Chomsky, N. (1957) *Syntactic Structures*, The Hague: Mouton.

Chomsky, N. (1965) *Aspects of the Theory of Syntax*, Cambridge: MIT.

Chomsky, N. (1996) 'Language and Problems of Knowledge', in A.P. Martinich (ed.), *The Philosophy of Language* (third edn.), New York: Oxford. pp.558–577.

Conference on College Composition and Communication (1974) 'Students' Right to Their Own Language', *College Composition and Communication*, Vol. XXV, special issue.

Croft, W. and Cruse, D.A. (2004) *Cognitive Linguistics*, New York: Cambridge.

Ford, C.E., Fox, B.A., and Thompson, S.A. (2003) 'Social Interaction and Grammar', in M. Tomasello (ed.), *The New Psychology of Grammar*, Mahwah, NJ: Lawrence Erlbaum. pp.119–144.

Goldberg, A.E. (2006) *Constructions at Work: The Nature of Generalizations in Language*, New York: Oxford.

Hacker, D. (2003) *A Writer's Reference (5th edn.)*, Boston: Bedford/St. Martin's.

Halliday, M.A.K. and Martin, J.R. (1993) *Writing Science: Literacy and Discursive Power*, Pittsburgh: Univ. of Pittsburgh Press.

Halliday, M.A.K. and Matthiessen, C.M.I.M. (2004) *An Introduction to Functional Grammar* (third edn.), New York: Oxford.

Hancock, C. (2005) *Meaning-Centred Grammar: An Introductory Text*, London: Equinox.

Hillocks, G. Jr. (1986) *Research on Written Composition*, Urbana, Ill: NCTE.

Hillocks, G. Jr. (1995) *Teaching Writing as Reflective Practice*, NewYork: Teachers College Press.

Hudson, R. and Walmsley, J. (2005) 'The English Patient: English Grammar and Teaching in the Twentieth Century', *Journal of Linguistics*, 41(3): 593–622.

Kolln, M. (2007) *Rhetorical Grammar: Grammatical Choices, Rhetorical Effects* (fifth edn.), New York: Pearson.

Kolln, M. and Hancock, C. (2005) 'The Story of English Grammar in United States Schools', *English Teaching: Practice and Critique*, 4(3): 11–31.

Lakoff, G. (1987) *Women, Fire, and Dangerous Things: What Categories Reveal about the Mind*, Chicago: Univ. of Chicago Press.

Lakoff, G. and Johnson, M. (1999) *Philosophy in the Flesh*, New York: Basic Books.

Lakoff, G. and Johnson, M. (1980, Afterword, 2003) *Metaphors We Live By*, Chicago: Univ. of Chicago Press.

Lakoff, G. and Johnson, M. (2003) *Metaphors We Live By: With a new Afterword*, Chicago: University of Chicago Press.

Langacker, R.W. (2008) *Cognitive Grammar: A Basic Introduction*, New York: Oxford.

Lindemann, E. (2001) *A Rhetoric for Writing Teachers.* New York: Oxford.

MacDonald, S.P. (2007) 'The Erasure of Language', *College Composition and Communication*, 58(4): 585–625.

Micciche, L. (2004) 'Making a Case for Rhetorical Grammar', *College Composition and Communication*, 55(4): 716–737.

Myhill, D. (2005) 'Ways of Knowing: Writing with Grammar in Mind', *English Teaching: Practice and Critique*, 4(3): 77–96.

Noguchi, R. (1991) *Grammar and the Teaching of Writing: Limits and Possibilities*, Urbana, Ill: NCTE.

Pinker, S. (2000) *The Language Instinct: How the Mind Creates Language*, New York: Harper Collins.

Schleppegrell, M.J. (2004) *The Language of Schooling: A Functional Linguistics perspective*, Mahwah, NJ: Lawrence Erlbaum.

Schleppegrell, M.J. (2007) 'At last: The Meaning in Grammar', *Research in the Teaching of English*, 42(1): 121–128.

Schuster, E. (2003) *Breaking the Rules: Liberating Writers Through Innovative Grammar Instruction*, Portsmouth, NH: Heinemann.

Swales, J. (1990) *Genre Analysis: English in Academic and Research Settings*, New York: Cambridge.

Tomasello, M. (2003) *Constructing a Language: A Usage-Based Theory of Language Acquisition*, Cambridge, MA: Harvard.

Turner, M. (1996) *The Literary Mind: The Origins of Thought and Language*, New York: Oxford.

Weaver, C. (1996) *Teaching Grammar in Context*, Portsmouth, NH: Boynton/Cook.

Williams, J.M. (2003) *Style: The Basics of Clarity and Grace*, New York: Longman.

INTRODUCTION

In the beginning: The development of writing in early childhood

This section provides an overview of the development of writing in early childhood (and into middle childhood) from contrasting points of view. Firstly, the discussion acknowledges that mastery of the ability to transform spoken language into a written form is hugely challenging for young children, given the demands of the multidimensional nature of the task. Psychology offers explanation of the way that writing is an example of human processing in action. This highly complex task requires the simultaneous orchestration of a number of activities; and in so doing, it places great demand on the cognitive system. Across the different theories of the writing process, two ideas are central to understanding the challenge that writing presents to the novice. One is the assumption of limited capacity and the other of a control mechanism.

Limited capacity suggests that the brain is able to process only constrained amounts of information. This means that when writers have ideas to record, and if, as is the case with young children, they have difficulty converting the sounds they can hear within the words into written symbols, and problems also in manipulating the pencil, or knowing how to form the letters, there is little cognitive capacity spare to organize the ideas into a text and thus to compose effectively.

The notion of a control mechanism suggests that in the brain there is a mechanism with an executive function, which oversees the processing, storage, retrieval, and utilization of information. The amount of cognitive capacity required by the control mechanism reduces, as the writer becomes more proficient in carrying out the various interrelated tasks. Thus for educators, the central message from psychological theory is that if emergent writers are given instruction in and the opportunity to practise the transcriptional skills of handwriting and spelling, they become more able to compose written texts of length and quality.

Secondly, this section draws upon socialcultural theory and acknowledges that it took humankind several millennia to develop ways to make a permanent record of ideas and thought through an alphabetic code system. It, therefore, recognizes the remarkable achievement of many 4- and 5-year-old children when they discover how to use marks to represent oral language and so achieve access to a 'second order symbolic system'

(Vygotsky, 1978). The underlying principle is that all language learning is a meaning-making, problem-solving process with the learner as the active participant at its centre, albeit supported by more expert others. The stance that this section takes is that children negotiate a place for writing within their individual symbolic repertoire and capitalize upon a range of semiotic and social processes and ideological position. The nature of the early childhood literacy discussed is realized differently in the lives of children in varying societal and curricula circumstances.

The discussion of this achievement is informed by the disciplines of psychology, linguistic and sociocultural theory in the eight chapters, which make up this section. The individual chapters in this section are underpinned by a number of shared recognitions:

i) A prerequisite conceptual grasp is required of the nature and purpose of written language broadly, and of texts and of print more specifically in order for a child to learn to write

ii) The complementarity of reading and writing in the decoding and encoding dimensions and how the experience of texts informs both understanding of structure and develops literary awareness

iii) The influence of the social context in facilitating early writing development

iv) The extent to which the peer culture and personal experience empower literacy learning and impact on the nature and production of the child's texts

v) The cognitively challenging process of learning to write through which children's intellectual development is enhanced

In Chapter 14, **Deborah W. Rowe**, through a comprehensive, systematic literature review of studies, traces the key trends in early writing research beginning with a brief outline of work conducted during the seminal period from the 1930s through to the 1980s, and then focuses in detail on research conducted in the last two decades—the period from 1990 to early 2008. Rowe describes the ways in which children respond to their physical, social, and cultural environments as they experiment with ways of recording written language alongside their developing understanding of the world.

The consideration of the texts that children produce reflects the evolving nature of written language and how it is complexly intertwined with other symbolic systems of drawing and semiotics. Historical and comparative issues in early childhood literacy are addressed. The innate drive of human beings to make and represent meaning lies at the heart of this chapter, and sets the scene for the chapter, which follows. It affirms the stance that early writing attempts are evidence of the way that children explore ways to represent meanings for themselves as social agents rather than merely research subjects.

In Chapter 15, **Anne Haas Dyson** offers a perspective that places each childhood experience at the centre of an individual's literacy development. It sees children as transporters and transformers of their personal and cultural experiences in their early attempts to communicate. It is through the process of writing that children are able to expand, reconfigure and rearticulate their own childhoods using a process of recontextualization. Dyson defines the term 'recontextualization' as the way that children appropriate multiple sources when they write. The data collected through observation in early-years classrooms evidence the way that pupils are influenced as learners by their lives within their social communities more fundamentally than is often recognized or valued by school educators. The chapter discusses the impressive ability of young children to draw upon and respond flexibly to multiple sources of music and song, the media, sport reporting and popular culture to generate novel and powerful texts.

In Chapter 16, **Judy Parr, Rebecca Jesson,** and **Stuart McNaughton** argue that, if written language is parasitic on spoken language, extending and capitalizing upon children's oral competence to develop their writing is crucial. This chapter draws upon the theory and research findings, which offer suggestions on the way that an explicit focus on enhancing speaking and listening benefits children's written language. Activity-based work in stimulating purposeful environments, where language opportunities are rich, are described. The implementation of a pedagogy, which maximizes the potential of talking to generate ideas, structure texts, and for rehearsal of arguments are developed. Ways of working such as the teacher using scaffolded discussion, 'recruiting talk' where the spoken word is both the raw material for writing and a tool to manipulate this material, the language experience approach, talk as a textual platform, the writing conference, and deliberately making connections through intertextual talk are all investigated.

Given that the Roman and Greek alphabetic writing systems were the last and most refined to be developed in the history of literacy, it is not surprising that complete competency with the written English language system takes young learners many years to achieve. In Chapter 17, **Charles Read** describes how children's early awareness of the alphabetic system through to its mastery gradually develops through myriad purposeful encounters with print (and, most valuably, scaffolded by more advanced writers) before formal schooling takes place. In the early stage of literacy development, children consolidate the ability to decode through the encoding of the sounds of speech into graphemes as they write to communicate personal messages. This is, as Read suggests, the heart of the matter, the child grasps the alphabetic principle that letters (or more precisely, spellings) represent phonemes. It is during the writing process that the relationship between the individual sounds of language and the letters that represent those sounds becomes clear to the child and also memorable. The process of writing has the advantage over reading, in that children demonstrate through their texts a developing grasp of grapheme-phoneme correspondence. In addition, the chapter discusses various stage theories related to the spelling aspect of writing and offers fruitful avenues for further research.

Punctuation as a dimension of writing bridges both the compositional and transcriptional aspects of writing continuous text and is a relatively under investigated area in early childhood literacy. In Chapter 18, **Nigel Hall** draws on evidence from both the work of others and his own research findings, to discuss how children achieve understanding of both the semantic function and surface feature conventions of punctuation within the English writing system. The data provide evidence of how children gradually become aware of a symbolic system, which has no sound referent and then begin to punctuate their writing given appropriate experience and support. Hall considers how children acquire an early understanding of punctuation based on graphic information prior to developing linguistic reasoning. He looks at how children later develop understanding of grammatical punctuation, the apostrophe, and the punctuation of speech.

Young writers employ technology when they first begin to mark-make. The ability to grip a writing tool in order to make marks on a surface with the intentionality to convey meaning (and that is seen by them as distinct from drawing) requires conceptual understanding of a 'second order symbol system' referred to earlier, knowledge of orthography and highly developed fine motor skills. In Chapter 19, **Carol Christensen** discusses how learning the correct formation of letters at the appropriate developmental stage facilitates both composition of written texts and consolidates familiarity with grapheme—phoneme correspondence and hence aids spelling. She argues that the rapid coding of orthographic information, speed of finger movement and rapid production of alphabetic letters (orthographic-motor integration) supports the ability to transcribe ideas into text, by releasing cognitive capacity. The beneficial effect is an enduring one. The chapter also explores controversial issues such as the continued need for the hard-won skill to fluently handwrite texts in a technological age replete with personal computers, laptops, e-mail, and mobile phone texting. Christensen argues strongly that not only is handwriting an important facet of an individual's personality but a kinaesthetic capability, which greatly enhances the production of ideas and text generation in both the early and later stages of learning to write.

The General Introduction to this Handbook argues that learning to write is a multidimensional challenge for young learners. The writer has to think what to say, organize, and structure the intended communication, consider how to break each word into its constituent sounds and then transform those sounds into written symbols by physically forming each symbol in order to make a mark. In **Chapter 20,** Pietro Boscolo investigates the optimal conditions and for what reasons and in what situations both beginner and more experienced writers become engaged and sufficiently motivated to undertake the task, and in so doing, they become more proficient. It re-affirms that as pupils invent and experiment, in a supportive context, they become more appreciative and knowledgeable of the tool for communication that writing is. Therefore, as children perceive and use written language for authentic and personally chosen purposes, they generate hypotheses about, and value, the power of the system itself.

In **Chapter 21**, Jackie Marsh builds on the previous chapter by suggesting further important ways in which the immense challenge that writing presents can be met. Indisputably, it is a challenge that requires a powerhouse of motivation and level of interest. Marsh, in this chapter, suggests that a pervasive and accessible source of motivation, and one that is largely untapped by formal education, is children's abiding fascination (even obsession) with popular culture. In their out-of-school lives, DVDs, comic books, computer programmes, TV, and mobile phones contribute substantially to and shape pupils' literacy development in general, and their writing in particular. Popular culture, Marsh argues, has a profound effect on children's identities, social networks, and cultural practices. The research findings cited provide evidence of imaginative ways in which teachers can harness this engagement with popular culture in order to encourage children to make their own texts and artefacts (often multimodally), whilst not negating the enjoyment, emotional satisfaction and intrinsic educative value of classical children's literature.

REFERENCE

Vygotsky, L.S. (1978) *Mind in Society*, Cambridge, MA: Harvard University Press.

Early Written Communication

Deborah Wells Rowe

The study of young children's written communication has a long history that goes back at least as far as Hildreth's (1936) study of developmental sequences in young children's name writing. She reports that her interest in preschoolers' writing happened somewhat accidentally, as part of conducting comprehensive mental examinations of 3- to 6-year-olds. In the course of administering these tests, she noted that many children were eager to write their names on their drawings, and so, she began to include name writing as a regular part of her assessment routine. These informal observations by a sensitive social scientist led to a systematic investigation of name writing, and her findings that young children's writing progressed developmentally from unorganized scribbles to marks that were progressively more writing-like.

This early work received relatively little attention by literacy researchers for the next four decades – perhaps because the prevailing reading readiness perspectives assumed that composing should be delayed until children had learned to read independently. (See Teale and Sulzby [1986a] for an historical review of this period.) Nevertheless, Hildreth's investigation foreshadowed several key themes that would be taken up again by emergent literacy (Teale and Sulzby, 1986b) researchers in the 1970s, namely: (a) preschoolers begin to learn about writing before formal schooling; (b) scribbles and other unconventional forms of preschool writing reflect children's hypotheses about print; and (c) young children learn about writing through everyday interactions with more accomplished writers. Though these themes have been developed and reframed in important ways, they remain central to current understandings of early writing.

In this chapter, I trace key trends in early writing research beginning with a brief outline of work conducted during the seminal period from the 1930s through the 1980s, and then focus in detail on research conducted in the last two decades – the period from 1990 to early 2008. My primary purpose is to provide an analysis of the theoretical and topical landscape of current research on early writing and to identify new trends that hold promise for moving the field forward in the next decade.

SCOPE AND METHODS FOR THE REVIEW

My review of early writing research during the seminal period from the 1930s through the 1980s is primarily intended to provide background to the current period. I identified seminal studies based my experience as an early literacy researcher and by examining reference lists provided by previous reviews (Sulzby and Teale, 1991; Yaden et al. 2000). For the period from 1990 to early 2008, I conducted a systematic literature search for studies relating to early writing. I used electronic databases to search for studies of young children's writing (birth through age six) and augmented this method with hand searches of 16 prominent English language journals that publish research on literacy or early childhood learning (i.e., *Australian Journal of Early Childhood, Developmental Psychology, Early Childhood Education Journal, Early Childhood Research Quarterly, Journal of Early Childhood Literacy, Journal of Literacy Research, Journal of Research in Reading, Language Arts, International Journal of Early Childhood, Learning & Instruction, Reading and Writing Quarterly, Reading Research Quarterly, Reading Teacher, Research in the Teaching of English, Yearbook of the National Reading Conference, Young Children*). Research monographs published during this period were also included.

Using these procedures, I located 129 research reports related to young children's writing published from 1990 to early 2008. To identify current and emerging trends, I separated studies published from 1990 to 1999 from those appearing between 2000 and early 2008. All studies were categorized according to the topical focus of research questions and the underlying theoretical framework. Though each study was assigned to only one type of theoretical framework, studies with multiple research foci were categorized into more than one topical focus category.

SEMINAL RESEARCH ON EARLY WRITING: THE 1930s THROUGH THE 1980s

Though the roots of early writing research go back to the 1930s (Hildreth, 1936) it was Read's (1971) seminal investigation of developmental spelling patterns (for more detail see Read, this volume) and Clay's (1975) study of the 'principles' (i.e., hypotheses) organizing children's early writing attempts that actually heralded a ground-swell of interest in preschool writing. Their work, along with other seminal work conducted from an emergent literacy perspective (e.g., Ferreiro and Teberosky, 1982; Goodman, 1980; Harste et al., 1984; Sulzby, 1985) created a kind of Copernican Revolution in our perspectives on preschool literacy. Researchers established that children's 'scribbles' were not only visually organized like writing (i.e., linearity, units) but that young authors also used their marks to express meanings (Harste et al., 1984). This work directly challenged the notion of *convention* as the watershed criterion for identifying the beginnings of writing, replacing it, instead, with the construct of *intention*. In her work on the 'roots of literacy', Yetta Goodman (1986) defined reading and writing as 'human interaction with print when the reader and writer *believe* that they are making sense of and through written language' (p. 6) (italics added for emphasis.) Harste et al. (1984) argued that 'intentionality' – the child's intention to use marks to represent a linguistic message – was a basic characteristic of young children's unconventional writing activity.

Overall, the emergent literacy perspective challenged educators to see preschoolers as active literacy learners who constructed hypotheses about print. The majority of research on young children's writing in the 1980s and 1990s was conducted from cognitive and sociocognitive perspectives that focused attention on individual child writers, their texts, and their interactions. Topically, much

Table 14.1 Topical foci in early writing research: 1930s through the 1980s

Topic		Exemplar Studies
Text patterns	Forms: types of marks used for writing	Bissex, 1980; Clay, 1975; Hildreth, 1936
	Differences between writing and drawing	Harste et al., 1984; Sulzby, 1985
	Directionality, space, page arrangement	Clay, 1975; Harste et al., 1984
	Genre	Harste et al., 1984; Newkirk, 1989
	Concept of word	Clay, 1975
	Intentionality (meanings)	Bissex, 1980; Clay, 1975; Goodman, 1980; Harste et al., 1984
	Form/meaning relationships	Bissex, 1980; Clay, 1975; Ferreiro and Teberosky, 1982
	Spelling	Henderson and Beers, 1980; Read, 1971
Writing processes	Writing/play connections	Isenberg and Jacobs, 1983; Roskos, 1988
	Composing processes (drafting, revision)	Graves, 1979; Sowers, 1985
Writing as sociocultural practice		Dyson, 1989; Heath, 1983

of this research focused on describing patterns in the marks children used in their texts or developmental patterns in children's spelling (see Table 14.1). Researchers interested in the writing processes of elementary writers extended their studies to include younger 5- and 6-year-old school entrants and described writing processes such as drafting and revising. Finally, a few researchers began to explore preschoolers' interactions with writing during play.

Many studies published during this period were implicitly rooted in an autonomous model of literacy (Street, 1995). Researchers searched for universal principles and patterns of early writing and used research designs that either controlled or ignored the social context for writing. As a result, much of the research produced during this period, presented an idealized child writer who progressively constructed more sophisticated hypotheses about writing and who produced increasingly more conventional writing performances. There was relatively little attention to either individual or cultural difference in seminal research on young children's written communication. An exception was the research of Heath (1983) and Dyson (1989). While both of these researchers were interested in describing what children knew about literacy, both also attempted to understand children's writing in relation to the cultural patterns of their homes and communities.

CURRENT TRENDS IN EARLY WRITING RESEARCH: 1990–2008

Writing as a sociocognitive activity

In the last two decades, researchers have worked to both extend and reframe the field's understanding of early writing. Table 14.2 displays the topical foci for the 129 studies identified for this review. For ease of comparison, I have grouped current studies under the same three superordinate categories used for seminal research: text patterns, writing processes, and writing as sociocultural practice. When current research foci are compared to those seen in Table 14.1, it is clear that many seminal topics of study have continued to be important in the period from 1990 to the present, but that current researchers have also expanded the array of research questions in important ways.

Text patterns

Most research aimed at describing children's text patterns has been rooted in cognitive and sociocognitive perspectives that serve as the basis for the emergent literacy perspective (Goodman, 1990; Sulzby and Teale, 1991). This view assumes that children's texts appear unconventional to adult eyes, because

Table 14.2 Topical foci and number of studies in early writing research: 1990–2008

Topic		1990–1999[1]	2000–2008[2]	Total[3]
Text patterns	Text patterns (multiple aspects)	13	6	19
	Multimodality	6	9	15
	Genre	6	6	12
	Spelling	5	7	12
	Name writing	2	3	5
	Writing/drawing relationships	2	3	5
	Computer writing	3	1	4
	Oral language/writing link	2	1	3
Writing processes	Social interaction during writing (sociocognitive)	7	7	14
	Writing/play connection	11	0	11
	Metacognition/writing	1	1	2
	Writing/reading connection (sociocognitive)	0	1	1
Writing as social practice	Social interaction during writing (sociocultural)	9	19	28
	Identity	4	14	18
	Gender/writing	5	3	8
	Home literacy practices	3	1	4
	ELL/bilingual writing	1	5	6
	Writing/reading connection (sociocultural)	0	1	1
Theoretical framework	Cognitive/sociocognitive	55	39	94
	Sociocultural	15	20	35

[1]Number of identified studies, 1990 to 1999 = 70.
[2]Number of identified studies, 2000 to early 2008 = 59.
[3]Total number of identified studies = 129.

they reflect the current state of children's hypotheses about print (Besse, 1996; Ferriero, 1990; Ferreiero et al. 1996; Goodman, 1990; Kamii et al. 2001; Schickedanz, 1990). Therefore, a major goal of early writing research has been to describe the textual patterns children produce and then to analyze them as indices of their understandings about print. Both in the seminal period and in current research, a considerable amount of attention has been devoted to describing textual patterns such as the forms (i.e., types of marks) children use for writing, speech-print links, depiction of word units, directionality and spatial arrangement of marks, differences between marks used for writing and drawing, spelling patterns, and genre-specific text features. Table 14.2 shows that text patterns remain one of the most studied areas of childhood writing.

Writing forms

With regard to writing forms, current research (Green, 1998; Kenner, 2000; Sulzby, 1996) generally confirms patterns observed during the seminal period (e.g., Clay, 1975; Dyson, 1985; Ferreiro and Teberosky, 1982; Harste et al., 1984). Writing begins with scribbles that are largely undifferentiated and over time moves in a general trajectory toward forms that have more writing-like characteristics including linearity, appropriate directional patterns, and individual units (Yang and Noel, 2006). Recent research also confirms that children experiment with spatial arrangement of text on the page (Kenner, 2000; Sipe, 1998; Yang and Noel, 2006; Zecker, 1999). Cross-linguistic research (Pine, 2005) supports seminal observations (Harste et al., 1984) that young children produce graphic forms and exhibit visual noticing behaviours that reflect the writing systems of their cultures.

An emerging trend in the last decade has been increased study of the writing forms and processes of children between birth and age 3. Of the 129 studies included in this review, 10 include children in this age group. Lancaster's (2001, 2007) research with 1- and 2-year-olds has shown that these youngsters use symbolic principles to inform mark making. However, overall, they show less concern about writing forms than the processes of marking and interacting with others around writing. At this age, writing forms and their meanings remain fluid. Children often transform both the form and meaning of marks within the composing event.

Name writing

Because name writing is the cultural context in which many children have the most adult assistance, and because of children's intense personal connection to their names, there has been an increasing interest in studying the forms children produce when asked to write their names. Preschoolers' produce more conventional writing forms and move toward conventionality more quickly in name writing than when writing other words (Levin, Both-DeVries, Aram, and Bus, 2005). Several researchers (Bloodgood, 1999; Haney et al., 2003; Martens, 1999; Welsch et al., 2003) have also shown that the forms children produce in name writing are related to more general understandings about print such as letter identification and concept of word. Findings are mixed as to whether name writing is related to phonological awareness (Haney et al., 2003; Welsch et al., 2003).

Developmental trajectory of forms

A current interest of researchers has been the debate about whether children move sequentially through a predictable series of stages, each with a characteristic form for writing. Data from individual interviews conducted by Piagetian researchers (Besse, 1996; Ferreiro, 1990; Ferreiro and Teberosky, 1982; Grossi, 1990; Kamii et al., 2001; Pontecorvo and Zucchermaglio, 1990; Yaden and Tardibuono, 2004) have tended to support stage theory, while researchers observing children in natural contexts have found more variability in the forms that children produce at any point in time (Green, 1998; Kenner, 2000; Sulzby, 1996). The consensus among the latter group of researchers is that, while there is a rough progression toward more conventional writing forms, at each moment in time, children produce a variety of forms. When children add new forms to their repertoires, old ones are not necessarily abandoned (Sulzby, 1996).

Spelling

Young children's spelling patterns have remained an active area of interest during the last two decades comprising 9.3% of identified studies (n = 12). This research has resulted in considerable consensus that spelling development occurs in a fairly predictable way with children constructing a series of qualitatively different hypotheses about how speech is represented in print (Fresch, 2001; Henderson and Beers, 1980; Hughes and Searle, 1991; Korkeamaki and Dreher, 2000; Mayer and Moskos, 1998). In general, research shows that children progress from spellings where there is no link between letters and sounds to spellings where letters are used to represent some or all of a word's sounds.

Next, children begin to use orthographic rules and visual strategies. In a final stage, conventional spelling becomes well established. However, some debate remains about the best scheme for dividing and labelling spelling stages (Bear and Templeton, 1998; Gentry, 2000; Read, 1971).

Genre knowledge

As seen in Table 14.2, genre research has been a particularly active area of investigation in the last two decades (9.3% of identified studies; n = 12). Kress (1997) has argued that learning to write is not a generic process, but instead involves learning the demands and potentials of different genres. There is considerable evidence that preschoolers construct texts that reflect syntactic and semantic features of genres such as stories, lists, labels, signs, poems, letters, and e-mails (Chapman, 1994, 1995; Donovan, 2001; Mavers, 2007; Wolf, 2006; Wollman-Bonilla, 2003; Zecker, 1999). Overall, children's ability to produce genre-appropriate meanings outstripped their ability to record them in writing (Donovan, 2001; Zecker, 1999). Children's stories were more generally conventional than their information pieces such as science reports (Kamberelis and Bovino, 1999). Genre knowledge, like other aspects of children's authoring, appears to develop early, become more complex with age (Chapman, 1995; Donovan, 2001; Kamberelis, 1999; Kamberelis and Bovino, 1999; Smolkin and Donovan, 2004), and to be expressed differently depending on the complexity of the task (Borzone de Manrique and Signorini, 1998).

Researchers working from sociocultural perspectives have extended the scope of genre research by investigating its cultural basis for genre knowledge and the power structures inherent in it. Bloome et al. (2003) demonstrated that African-American preschoolers' written narratives often reflected community storytelling patterns, rather than school-based story structures. They argue that school pref-erences for hierarchical narrative structures have the potential to marginalize children who use other genre structures rooted in out-of-school experiences. As children gain experience in school, some appear to build genre knowledge by appropriating cultural forms of writing and reworking them to create hybrids that fit specific school tasks and audiences (Chapman, 1995; Dyson, 1999; Kamberelis and Bovino, 1999; Power, 1991; Solsken et al. 2000; Wollman-Bonilla, 2000).

Writing and drawing

A trend of growing importance in early writing research has been investigation of the connections between children's writing and other sign systems. Perhaps, because adults often assume that very young children's unconventional marks are drawing rather than writing, one line of seminal work in this area focused on establishing whether preschoolers distinguish writing from drawing (e.g., Ferreiro and Teberosky, 1982; Harste et al., 1984). Table 14.2 shows that five current studies specifically addressed writing/drawing relationships. Lancaster's (2007) recent research with 1- and 2-year-olds found that these youngest preschoolers did not distinguish between writing and drawing, but instead made use of the structural features of both systems. Rowe (2008) on the other hand, found that most 2-year-olds used different marks to distinguish drawing from writing within a composing event, though across events they did not use consistent types of mark for writing and drawing. For older preschoolers, both seminal and more recent research has supported the conclusion that, by age three, many children have different action plans for writing and drawing and are developing an understanding of differences in the two modes of representation (Brenneman et al., 1996; Landsmann, 1996). However, this conclusion has recently been called in to question. Levin and Bus' (2003) study of 2- to 4-year-olds found that even after children begin to produce writing-like forms, they may be 'drawing print' (p. 891). The question as to what understandings children have about writing and drawing, and whether drawing precedes writing remains open to further investigation.

WRITING AS SEMIOTIC ACTIVITY

Multimodal composing

Almost all researchers observing young children's authoring have commented on their tendencies to combine writing with other semiotic systems such as talk, drawing, gesture, and dramatic play. Researchers working from semiotic perspectives (Kress, 1997; Siegel, 1995, 2006) are currently expanding the line of research exploring the connections between writing and other sign systems (e.g., art, oral language, gesture, gaze, movement, and music) with an eye toward more fully understanding the multimodal nature of children's texts and authoring processes. While adults and older children are more likely to have adopted dominant views of writing as separate from other forms of communication, very young children have less cultural experience and so are less constrained by boundaries between sign systems (Kress, 1997). Authoring for young children involves language, vocalization, gesture, gaze, bodily action, and graphic production (Lancaster, 2001, 2006; Williams, 1999; Wright, 2007).

Both seminal and more recent studies document children's flexible interweaving of semiotic systems (e.g., Berghoff and Hamilton, 2000; Clyde, 1994; Gallas, 1998; Kress, 1997; Lancaster, 2001; Rowe, 1994; Upitis, 1992). Most often described have been authoring practices that combine writing, art, and oral language (Olson, 1992), but researchers have also noted children's connections between writing, music, dance, dramatic play, and drama (Gallas, 1994; Rowe, 1994; Rowe et al. 2001, 2003; Siegel, 2006; Upitis, 1992). Researchers have also begun to investigate children's interweaving of linguistic (i.e., print) and visual resources (i.e., font, colour, and layout) as they compose on computers (Mavers, 2007; Siegel, 2006). From a semiotic perspective, meaning-making can be considered a process of design (Mavers, 2007) in which multimodal authoring practices allow children to draw on meanings formed in a variety of sign systems and to gain access to authoring events using nonlinguistic forms of communication (Clyde, 1994; Harste, 2000). Several researchers have described transmediation (Genishi et al. 2001; Siegel, 1995) or transduction (Kress, 1997) – movement of meanings across sign systems – as an important part of multimodal authoring activities. Multimodal authoring appears to be particularly important for beginning writers, those whose strength is not language, or who are learning English as another language (Genishi et al., 2001; Harste, 2000; Rowe et al., 2001).

When researchers broaden the semiotic boundaries of authoring, another outcome is an increasing focus on the embodied and material nature of authoring practices. Young children perform their early writings with gesture, facial expression, and pantomime (Lancaster, 2007; Williams, 1999; Wright, 2007). Embodied practices such as gaze and body posture carry important meanings, and are closely monitored by adults who interact with young authors (Lancaster, 2001). Multimodal authoring practices are also strongly influenced by the physical materials that are available in the environment (Kress, 1997). As Kress (1997) points out, the materiality of the objects is important in that children are adopting and adapting culturally significant elements of complex signs when they combine paper, writing tools, and objects from their environment, with gesture, talk, and drama.

Overall, it is clear that, very early, children begin to wrestle with the characteristic visual arrays and meaning potentials of a variety of sign systems. Throughout the early years, children's texts and writing performances are decidedly multimodal. Though some research continues to cast children's multimodal writing as a step along the way toward more mature, print-only texts, semiotic perspectives reframe children's multimodal texts and writing performances in relation to more expansive views that celebrate and normalize composing with multiple sign systems (Dyson, 2004; Harste et al., 1984; Siegel, 1995) and that connect multimodal composing to the increasing multimodality of children's twenty-first century textual experiences (Kress and Van Leeuwen, 2006; Mavers, 2007; New London Group, 1996; Wright, 2007). This trend suggests that childhood writing will increasingly be studied as one facet of a more complex multimodal design process in which pictures, gestures, music, and movement join reading and writing as 'basic' resources for composing (Dyson, 2004; Siegel, 2006).

Writing/play connections

As seen in Table 14.2, children's writing (and reading) in play contexts was a particularly active research area in the 1990s (8.5% of identified studies, n = 11). Naturalistic studies of children's spontaneous dramatic play show that children often write as part of the literate roles they took on in play (Neuman and Roskos, 1991). This observation led to the design of a number of studies where literacy materials and props were added to dramatic play centres with the goal of providing more opportunities for literacy-related play, including writing. Results show that writing and reading activities increase in literacyenriched play centres (Christie and Enz, 1992; Morrow, 1991; Neuman and Roskos, 1991, 1992, 1993; Vukelich, 1991b) and that adult scaffolding further increases literacy-related play in these centres (Morrow and Rand, 1991; Vukelich, 1991b). When studying the impact of literacy-enriched play contexts on children's understandings of the functions of writing, mixed results were obtained (Neuman and Roskos, 1993; Vukelich, 1991a).

Social interaction and writing

Another line of current research directly explores how children's individual authoring processes are formed and shaped in social interaction (10.8% of identified studies, n = 14). Most studies exploring these questions have adopted sociopsycholinguistic (Harste et al., 1984) or sociocognitive perspectives (Vygotsky, 1978) that focus attention on the ways writing is socially mediated in interactions with others.

There is a large body of research studying how children interact with adults and peers during writing, and describing the impact of those interactions on their print hypotheses. With regard to adult interaction styles, adults were found to scaffold toddlers', preschoolers', and kindergarteners' writing by tracking the child's forms and meanings and matching their contributions to the child's current needs and independent writing level (DeBaryshe et al. 1996; Lancaster, 2001; Lysaker, 2000). Following Vygotsky (1978), researchers have described such interactions as developing shared consciousness with an adult and suggested that social interaction of this type supports children in crossing the zone of proximal development. Adult scaffolding allows children to do things collaboratively that they cannot yet accomplish on their own (DeBaryshe et al. 1996; Lancaster, 2001; Lysaker, 2000). At the same time, the level of control exerted by adults during writing has been shown to affect children's talk and writing products. Less controlling adult styles encourage children to produce more forms of emergent writing (Fang, 1999; Gutman and Sulzby, 2000) and to talk more as they write (Burns and Casbergue, 1992; Zucchermaglio and Scheuer, 1996). However, children also produce less conventional texts when adults exert less control on the course of writing.

Peer interaction also appears to support writing in important ways. When writing with others, peers observe demonstrations of culturally appropriate writing forms, processes, and meanings (Chapman, 1996; Harste et al., 1984; Rowe, 1994; Wollman-Bonilla, 2001b). Young writers often link their texts to those of other authors with whom they interact – sometimes sticking close to the form and content of another author's text and sometimes using it only as a starting point for their texts (Dyson, 1998; Rowe, 1994). Even in cases where children's authoring processes appear imitative, they are engaged in constructive work (Dyson, 1989; Kress, 1997; Newkirk, 1989; Rowe, 1994).

Social interaction also appears to play an important role in children's construction and testing of literacy hypotheses. Constructivist theories of learning suggest that literacy learning occurs through a cycle of hypothesis testing in which children attempt to use their existing hypotheses to account for their experiences (Ferreiro and Teberosky, 1982; Goodman, 1990; Harste et al., 1984; Piaget, 1976; Short et al. 1996). When children cannot assimilate the new information into their existing schemes, the anomalies motivate a re-examination of the situation, and the construction and testing of new hypotheses. Social interaction becomes an integral part of children's authoring in several ways. As they interact with others, young writers confirm their existing literacy hypotheses (Rowe, 1994) and encounter challenges to their understandings that push them to clarify, expand, and refine their ideas and texts (Condon and Clyde, 1996; Rowe, 1994). Social interaction encourages children to shift stances to consider the audience's perspective and monitor the effectiveness and appropriateness of their texts (Graves, 1984; Rowe, 1994; Wollman-Bonilla, 2001a). Gregory (2001) found that peers benefit from writing activities, even if one is a more accomplished writer.

Another line of research in this area has described the roles that hearing (Condon and Clyde, 1996; Dyson, 1989; Labbo, 1996; Rowe, 1994; Rowe et al., 2001; Wiseman, 2003) and deaf children (Troyer, 1991; Williams, 1999) take when writing with peers

including observing other authors; providing assistance to another author by scribing, providing spellings, or ideas; mirroring other authors' texts and processes; sharing different parts of a writing task to complete a single text; and working collaboratively to coauthor texts. Children use talk to negotiate and define their roles (Troyer, 1991), to request and provide help and information (Jones, 2003; Rowe, 1994; Sipe, 1998; Williams, 1999), and to challenge and question peers' authoring practices (Rowe, 1994; Schultz, 1997; Williams, 1999).

Overall, these studies represent a substantial shift in the focus and methods used to study early writing as compared to the seminal period. In the last two decades, researchers have been increasingly interested in directly studying the role of social interaction in young children's literacy learning. For preschoolers, social relationships with adults motivate participation in writing. Adults' interactive styles affect the amount and type of children's emergent writing. Social interaction offers information about writing in the form of demonstrations, opportunities to ask for and to receive help, and a social nudge to consider audience perspectives on one's writing.

WRITING AS SOCIOCULTURAL PRACTICE

The focus of the cognitive and sociocognitive research reviewed thus far has been on describing young children's hypotheses about print, and the impact of social interaction on those hypotheses. Researchers working from sociocultural perspectives reframe the constructive work of composing as local, ideological, and positional. In these studies, it matters where, when, and with whom research is conducted. The goal is not to search for universals or to present portraits of generic child writers, but instead to understand how particular writers engage in the local writing practices of specific classrooms and communities. An important question in this line of research is how children's hypotheses, texts, and writing processes are shaped by cultural practices around writing in their communities or classrooms, and also how their participation as writers helps shape community practices. This interest in local writing practices has led to careful descriptions of the writing events in which child take part, and also to an expansion of the types of child writers studied. The latter trend is especially evident in a growing line of research studying the writing of young children who are bilingual or who are learning English as another language.

The cultural basis of home and school writing practices

When writing is seen as a socially situated act, young children's hypotheses and writing strategies are assumed to be rooted in the literacy practices of particular local communities. As a result, the culture- and class-based nature of young children's writing is an expanding area of investigation for researchers working within sociocultural frames. Perhaps, because of the difficulty of conducting research in children's homes, or because of the field's focus on schooled literacy, in the last two decades, only a few researchers have directly investigated how young children experience writing at home or in their communities (e.g., Hicks, 2002; Purcell-Gates, 1996; Reyes, 2006). However, a number of researchers have conducted depth interviews of parents (e.g., Compton-Lilly, 2003; Meier, 2000) or observed children's use of community- and home-based writing practices in classroom settings (e.g., Bloome et al., 2003; Dyson, 1993, 2003). These studies demonstrate that children come to school with a wide variety of writing attitudes, definitions, purposes, and experiences that serve as resources for organizing their first writing attempts. Parents, children, and teachers may hold differing views of 'good'

writing and of appropriate writing experiences for young children. Meier (2000) found that parents and children from a Spanish/English bilingual community in the U.S. valued conventional forms of writing and alphabet practice over more open-ended emergent literacy activities planned by teachers. Social class may also affect children's experiences with writing. Working in Israel, Korat and Levin (2002) found that low-SES and high-SES mothers held different beliefs and engaged in different kinds of interactions with their children around spelling. Further, as children launch into writing, they may use it for culturally based purposes appropriated from their homes and communities. Ballenger (1999), for example, found that the Haitian-American preschoolers in her study used writing to maintain connections with their parents, build friendships, and become part of a community – all highly valued cultural activities in the children's homes. A number of researchers have shown how children use home-based popular culture texts along with oral and literate traditions as resources for writing in classroom settings (Bloome et al., 2003; Dyson, 1993, 2003). Home literacy experiences have been shown to affect children's understandings about writing (Purcell-Gates, 1995, 1996; Senechal et al 1998). For example, Purcell-Gates' (1996) found that low SES children who saw and had opportunities to participate in many uses of written language were more likely to understand that print is symbolic and can be used for a variety of purposes.

Despite findings of culturally and class-based variation in children's writing experiences, it is also clear that broad categories describing social class, ethnicity, and home language are not necessarily good predictors of individual children's home literacy experiences. Researchers have observed considerable variation in the writing practices of low income and minority homes (Purcell-Gates, 1996; Taylor and Dorsey-Gaines, 1988; Teale, 1986). Families who share similar ethnic or social class backgrounds may not share the same literacy values, beliefs, and writing practices.

English language learners and writing

As seen in Table 14.2, a recent trend in early writing research is the study of young children who are bilingual or learning English as another language (4.6% of identified studies, n = 6). This work investigates how home-based cultural and linguistic practices affect how and what young children learn about writing. A primary conclusion of this work is that children who are learning English as another language do not constitute a monolithic group. Studies of young writers show that some children have support from parents and community members in speaking and writing both their L1 and English at home (Moll et al. 2001; Reyes, 2006) while other children live in close-knit communities where English is rarely spoken or written (Qian and Pan, 2006). For young bilingual writers, learning is often bidirectional between parents and children, and between L1 and L2 (Gort, 2006; Reyes, 2006). As with monolingual children, writing in both L1 and L2 is meaning driven (Moll et al., 2001) and choices of which language to use in writing are related to children's identities in relation to different audiences (Kennedy, 2006; Reyes, 2006).

Writing and classroom culture

Researchers are also beginning to turn the cultural lens inward to examine school writing practices. Though a good deal of the existing research on early writing has been conducted with white, middle-class children, or in mainstream preschool contexts, the cultural basis for observed writing practices has been less frequently analyzed than when children belong to 'other' writing communities. As early writing is reframed as a cultural

practice, researchers are beginning to highlight the cultural basis for school literacy (Ballenger, 1999; Meier, 2000; Wilson, 2000). Rowe (2008), for example, highlighted the connections between middle-class child-rearing practices and teacher interactions around writing in an emergent literacy preschool. Overall, this line of work challenges a view of writing that normalizes middle-class and schooled practices and reveals ways that children from diverse backgrounds may be silenced, or marginalized, when their writing does not match expected mainstream patterns (Bloome et al., 2003).

Researchers have also investigated *what* children learn about writing as they participate in the temporary cultures of classroom writing communities (Larson, 1995, 1999; Larson and Maier, 2000; Manyak, 2001; Power, 1991). For example, Kantor et al. (1992) tracked the way that preschoolers and their teachers coconstructed meanings about literacy in classroom activities. They concluded that each activity's materials, purposes, and participant structures framed literacy in distinctive ways. Power (1991) studied the ways her first graders' coconstructed a uniquely situated definition of text by constructing joint understandings of 'pop ups' as a valued convention for writing in her classroom.

Following Lave and Wenger (1991), some literacy researchers (Larson, 1999; Manyak, 2001) have argued that preschool and elementary children learn these culturally situated literacies through legitimate peripheral participation in communities of practice.

This notion has spurred investigators to document *how* children participate in authoring events. The focus of this work is on understanding how social participation structures give children access to roles and knowledge needed to become members of the classroom writing community (Larson and Maier, 2000). Shifts between roles as experts and novices (Manyak, 2001), and as teacher, author, coauthor, and as one who overhears, allow the social distribution of knowledge about writing, and give children access to central roles in writing events well before they can take them up independently (Larson, 1995, 1999; Larson and Maier, 2000). Through participation, children learn valued relations to text, to other participants, and to the world.

Writing and identity

Especially in the last decade, researchers working from a sociocultural perspective have begun to explore writing as an act of self-definition (13.9% of identified studies, n = 18). Learning to write involves much more than adding new skills to children's cognitive repertoires. It requires that children take on new cultural identities and affects their sense of self in profound ways (Compton-Lilly, 2006; Dyson, 2001; Manyak, 2001; Rowe et al., 2001; Solsken, 1993). In classrooms, where young children select their own topics, writing involves assuming a 'social voice' (Dyson, 2001). For example, children's choices to write about insects or video games position them in particular ways in relation to their peers, the ongoing dialogue in their classroom, and to the texts and practices of the larger society (Compton-Lilly, 2006; Dyson, 2001, 2003; Van Sluys, 2003). Dyson's (2003) research with first graders has demonstrated that young writers use texts to construct social affiliations with their peers, as well as to accept and resist the ways they are positioned by others. However, because children are simultaneously positioned in the overlapping communities of official and peer cultures (Dyson, 1993; Rowe et al. 2001), the same writing activities often have very different meanings for their positions as students in the official world and as friends in the peer world. For example, Rowe and her colleagues (Rowe et al., 2001; Rowe and Leander, 2005) found that struggling first-grade writers sometimes resisted participating in official classroom writing activities where they only had access to lower status roles that were inconsistent with

their powerful identities in the peer world. Overall, this line of research reveals that young children's writing functions as much to establish 'who I am in relation to you' as to serve other communicative purposes (Van Sluys, 2003).

Writing as gendered practice

Researchers have also conducted ideological analyses of the gendered nature of authoring practices and the ways that writing may reify or transform the social positions occupied and available to young authors (6.2% of identified studies, n = 8). Solsken (1993) has explored the ways children's orientations toward literacy were framed by gender and class relations in their families and the larger society. She found that middle-class, 5- and 6-year-old boys' and girls' literacy biographies were impacted by societal ideologies about gender, especially the division of labour in the children's homes in which mothers took major responsibility for supporting children's literacy. For the boys in Solsken's study, writing was preferred over reading, both because it was less directly identified with their mothers and because it provided more opportunities for initiative and productivity. Girls' invested in writing in ways that were consistent with female qualities, using it to maintain bonds of affection and nurture and to entertain themselves and others.

In school writing contexts, gender and ethnicity have been shown to affect the ways young writers are positioned in composing events by their peers, with girls and ethnic outsiders sometimes having limited access to powerful roles (Gallas, 1998; Henkin, 1995, 1998). On the other hand, children sometimes also use writing as an opportunity to challenge gender boundaries by creating characters that break with traditional gender roles and stereotypes (MacGillivray and Martinez, 1998).

Overall, defining writing as social practice has helped to establish that writing is neither generic nor politically neutral. Children learn situated ways of making meaning with print that vary according to the literacy practices of their homes and classrooms. When children write, they take up, adapt, or resist positions in existing systems of power relations. Negotiating their places in these cultural systems is a key part of writing.

EMERGING TRENDS AND FUTURE DIRECTIONS IN EARLY WRITING RESEARCH

Though this review has undoubtedly failed to locate some instances of early writing research, my goal has been to look as comprehensively as possible at what has been studied in the last two decades. My conclusion is that the topical and theoretical landscape of early writing research is changing. The field is increasingly moving toward a view of child writing that is more semiotically complex, more socially and culturally situated, and more ideologically positioned. This review points to recent semiotic and sociocultural turns in early literacy research as important forces that are now shaping emerging lines of study and that will likely guide future investigations.

Semiotic perspectives have begun to take multimodal composing seriously, recognizing it not only as an early childhood phenomenon, but also an essential aspect of all writing in new literacies environments (New London Group, 1996). We have only scratched the surface in understanding how young children begin to coordinate and understand the social potentials of the multimodal tools available to them. In the next decade, researchers will undoubtedly expand our understandings of children's transmediation practices (Siegel, 2006) and multimodal 'symbol weaving' (Dyson, 1993). At the same time, recent research exposes young children's composing as an active, embodied process strongly affected by materials and spaces. This suggests that important contributions

might be made by following the spatial turn emerging in some research with older writers (Leander, 2002; Sheehy, 2004; Wilson, 2004). Exploring early writing as it is embedded in sociospatial practices of classrooms and communities (Lefebvre, 1991; Soja, 1996) opens the dialectical interplay between the material, social, and cognitive aspects of writing as an area for future investigation.

The trend toward seeing early writing as a sociocognitive process has been important in the last decades, and there is now a growing trend toward viewing social interaction from sociocultural perspectives (Gee, 2003; Lave and Wenger, 1991; Rogoff, 2003). When literacy is viewed as a social practice, the focus moves from individual children's minds and cognitive hypotheses to a study of their *participation* in local literacy events (Gee, 2001). Such a perspective continues to give a role to individual participants, but at the same time argues that their knowledge and actions are inextricably part of a web of sociocultural relations. By focusing research attention on the cultural practices of children's homes and communities, the field is beginning to move away from a search for universal principles, and toward a more complex understanding of early writing as situated in local childrearing practices and community beliefs about writing. The current trend has already launched interesting new lines of research that recognize the diversity of young bilingual children's early writing experiences that explore children's flexible, recontextualization (Dyson, 2001) of home, community, and school writing practices. Finally, researchers are also beginning to explore how even the youngest children's writing experiences are embedded in structures of power and privilege. Emerging lines of sociocultural research related to gender, social class, and language group open new possibilities for understanding what and how very young children learn to write.

I close this review with the observation that the study of early writing has the potential to be an exceptionally generative space for developing theoretical understandings of writing beyond the early years. Young children do what comes naturally when they write; they are freer to be textual scavengers under the guise of play. They make use of their current sociocultural understandings and compose with available materials and embodied tools, initially, without too much worry about adult conventions. As a result, their texts and actions often look strange to adult eyes – and, therein, lies the advantage. When sensitive social scientists take seriously the charge to see writing, and occasions for writing, through the eyes of particular children situated in particular locations, early childhood composing provides a laboratory for challenging our own restricted cultural categories, and in turn for developing more complex models of the sociocultural and sociocognitive processes involved in learning to write.

REFERENCES

Ballenger, C. (1999) *Teaching Other People's Children: Literacy and Learning in a Bilingual Classroom*, New York: Teachers College Press.

Bear, D. and Templeton, S. (1998) 'Explorations in spelling: Foundations for learning and teaching phonics, spelling, and vocabulary', *Reading Teacher*, 52: 222–242.

Berghoff, B. and Hamilton, S. (2000) 'Inquiry and multiple ways of knowing in a first grade', in B. Berghoff, K. Egawa, J.C. Harste, and B. Hoonan (eds), *Beyond Reading and Writing: Inquiry Curriculum and Multiple Ways of Knowing*, Urbana, IL: National Council of Teachers of English.

Besse, J.M. (1996) 'An approach to writing in kindergarten', in M. Orsolini, B. Burge, and L.B. Resnick (eds), *Children's Early Text Construction*, Mahwah, NJ: Lawrence Erlbaum Association. pp.127–144.

Bissex, G. (1980) *GYNS at Work: A Child Learns to Read and Write*, Cambridge, MA: Harvard University Press.

Bloodgood, J. (1999) 'What's in a name? Children's name writing and name acquisition', *Reading Research Quarterly*, 34: 342–367.

Bloome, D., Katz, L., and Champion, T. (2003) 'Young children's narratives and ideologies of language in classrooms', *Reading & Writing Quarterly*, 19: 2005–2223.

Borzone de Manrique, A.M. and Signorini, A. (1998) 'Emergent writing forms in Spanish', *Reading and Writing: An Interdisciplinary Journal*, 10: 499–517.

Brenneman, K., Massey, C., Machado, S.F., and Gelman, R. (1996) 'Young children's plans differ for writing and drawing', *Cognitive Development*, 11: 397–419.

Burns, M.S. and Casbergue, R. (1992) 'Parent-child interaction in a letter-writing context', *Journal of Reading Behavior*, 24: 289–312.

Chapman, M.L. (1994) 'The emergence of genres: Some findings from an examination of first grade writing', *Written Communication*, 11: 348–380.

Chapman, M.L. (1995) 'The sociocognitive construction of written genres in first grade', *Research in the Teaching of English*, 29(2): 164–192.

Chapman, M.L. (1996) 'More than spelling: Widening the lens on emergent writing', *Reading Horizons*, 36: 317–339.

Christie, J. and Enz, B.J. (1992) 'The effects of literacy play interventions on preschoolers' play patterns and literacy development', *Early Education and Development*, 3: 205–220.

Clay, M. (1975) *What Did I Write?*, Auckland, New Zealand: Heinemann.

Clyde, J.A. (1994) 'Lessons from Douglas: Expanding our visions of what it means to "know"', *Language Arts*, 71: 22–33.

Compton-Lilly, C. (2003) *Reading Families: The Literate Lives of Urban Children*, New York: Teachers College Press.

Compton-Lilly, C. (2006) 'Identity, childhood culture, and literacy learning: A case study', *Journal of Early Childhood Literacy*, 6(1): 57–76.

Condon, M. and Clyde, J.A. (1996) 'Co-authoring: Composing through conversation', *Language Arts*, 73: 587–596.

DeBaryshe, B.D., Buell, M.J., and Binder, J.C. (1996) 'What a parent brings to the table: Young children writing with and without parental assistance', *Journal of Literacy Research*, 28: 71–90.

Donovan, C.A. (2001) 'Children's development and control of written story and informational genres: Insights from one elementary school', *Research in the Teaching of English*, 35: 394–447.

Dyson, A. (1985) 'Individual differences in emerging writing', in M. Farr (ed.) *Advances in Writing Research: Children's Early Writing Development*. Vol. 1, Norwood, NJ: Ablex. pp.59–125.

Dyson, A. (1989) *Multiple Worlds of Child Writers: Friends Learning to Write*, New York: Teachers College Press.

Dyson, A. (1993) *Social Worlds of Children Learning to Write in an Urban Primary School*, New York: Teachers College Press.

Dyson, A. (1999) 'Transforming transfer: Unruly children, contrary texts, and the persistence of the pedagogical order', *Review of Research in Education*, 24: 141–171.

Dyson, A. (2001). 'Where are the childhoods in childhood literacy? An exploration of (outer) school space', *Journal of Early Childhood Literacy*, 1: 9–39.

Dyson, A. (2003). *The Brothers and Sisters Learn to Write: Popular Literacies and School Cultures*, New York: Teachers College Press.

Dyson, A. (2004) 'Diversity as a "handful": Toward retheorizing the basics', *Research in the Teaching of English*, 39(2): 210–214.

Fang, Z. (1999) 'Expanding the vista of emergent writing research: Implications for early childhood educators', Early Childhood Education Journal, 26: 179–182.

Ferreiro, E. (1990) 'Literacy development: Psychogenesis', in Y. Goodman (ed.), *How Children Construct Literacy: Piagetian Perspectives*, Newark, DE: International Reading Association. pp.12–25.

Ferreiro, E. and Teberosky, A. (1982) *Literacy Before Schooling*, Portsmouth, NH: Heinemann.

Ferreiro, E., Pontecorvo, C., and Zucchermaglio, C. (1996) 'PIZZA or PIZA? How children interpret the doubling of letters in writing', in C. Pontecorvo, M. Orsolini, B. Burge, and L.B. Resnick (eds), *Children's Early Text Construction*, Mahwah, NJ: Lawrence Erlbaum. pp.145–163.

Fresch, M.J. (2001) 'Journal entries as a window on spelling knowledge', *Reading Teacher*, 54(5): 500–513.

Gallas, K. (1994) *The Languages of Learning: How Children Talk, Write, Dance, Draw, and Sing their Understanding of the World*, New York: Teachers College Press.

Gallas, K. (1998) *Sometimes I Can be Anything: Power, Gender, and Identity in a Primary Classroom*, New York: Teachers College Press.

Gee, J.P. (2001) 'Foreword', in C. Lewis (ed.), *Literacy Practices as Social Acts: Power, Status, and Cultural Norms in the Classroom*, Mahwah, NJ: Lawrence Erlbaum Associates. pp.xv–xix.

Gee, J.P. (2003) 'A sociocultural perspective on early literacy development', in S.B. Neuman and D. Dickinson (eds), *Handbook of Early Literacy Research*, New York: Guilford Press. pp.30–42.

Genishi, C., Stires, S.E., and Yung-Chan, D. (2001) 'Writing in an integrated curriculum: Prekindergarten English language learners as symbol makers', *The Elementary School Journal*, 101(4): 399–416.

Gentry, J.R. (2000) 'A retrospective on invented spelling and a look forward', *Reading Teacher*, 54(3): 318–332.

Goodman, Y. (1980) 'The roots of literacy', in M.P. Douglas (ed.), *Claremont Reading Conference. 44th Yearbook*, Claremont, CA: Claremont Colleges. pp.1–32.

Goodman, Y. (ed.) (1990) *How Children Construct Literacy: Piagetian Perspectives*, Newark, DE: International Reading Association.

Gort, M. (2006) 'Strategic codeswitching, interliteracy, and other personal of emergent bilingual writing: Lessons from first grade dual language classrooms', *Journal of Early Childhood Literacy*, 6(3): 323–454.

Graves, D. (1979) 'What children show us about revision', *Language Arts*, 65: 312–318.

Graves, D. (1984) 'A case study observing the development of primary children's composing, spelling, and motor behaviours during the writing process', in D. Graves (ed.), *A Researcher Learns to Write: Selected Articles and Monographs*, Exeter, NH: Heinemann. pp.141–165.

Green, C.R. (1998) 'This is my name', *Childhood Education*, 74(4): 226–231.

Gregory, E. (2001) 'Sisters and brothers as language and literacy teachers: Synergy between siblings playing and working together', *Journal of Early Childhood Literacy*, 1: 301–322.

Grossi, E.P. (1990) 'Applying psychogenesis principles to the literacy instruction of lower-class children in Brazil', in Y. Goodman (ed.), *How Children Construct Literacy: Piagetian Perspectives*, Newark, DE: International Reading Association. pp.99–114.

Gutman, L.M. and Sulzby, E. (2000) 'The role of autonomy-support *versus* control in the emergent writing behaviours of African-American kindergarten children', *Reading Research and Instruction*, 39(2): 170–184.

Haney, M.R., Bissonnette, V., and Behnken, K.L. (2003) 'The relationship among name writing and early literacy skills in kindergarten children', *Child Study Journal*, 33(2): 99–114.

Harste, J.C. (2000) 'Six points of departure', in B. Berghoff, K. Egawa, J.C. Harste, and B. Hoonan (eds), *Beyond Reading and Writing: Inquiry Curriculum and Multiple Ways of Knowing*, Urbana, IL: National Council of Teachers of English. pp.1–16.

Harste, J.C., Woodward, V.A., and Burke, C.L. (1984) *Language Stories and Literacy Lessons*, Portsmouth, NH: Heinemann.

Heath, S.B. (1983) *Ways with Words*, Cambridge: Cambridge University Press.

Henderson, E. and Beers, J. (1980) *Developmental and Cognitive Aspects of Learning to Spell: A Reflection of Word Knowledge*, Newark, DE: International Reading Association.

Henkin, R. (1995) 'Insiders and outsiders in first grade writing workshops: Gender and equity issues', *Language Arts*, 72(6): 429–434.

Henkin, R. (1998) *Who's Invited to Share? Using Literacy to Teach for Equity and Social Justice*, Portsmouth, NH: Heinemann.

Hicks, D. (2002) *Reading Lives: Working Class Children and Literacy Learning*, New York: Teachers College Press.

Hildreth, G. (1936) 'Developmental sequences in name writing', *Child Development*, 7: 291–303.

Hughes, M. and Searle, D. (1991) 'A longitudinal study of the growth of spelling abilities within the context of the development of literacy', in J. Zutell, S. McCormick, L. Caton, and P. O'Keefe (eds), *Learner Factors/Teacher Factors: Issues in Literacy Research and Instruction, Fortieth Yearbook of the National Reading Conference*. Chicago: National Reading Conference.

Isenberg, J. and Jacobs, E. (1983) *Playful Literacy Activities and Learning: Preliminary Observations*, ERIC Document Reproduction Service.

Jones, I. (2003) 'Collaborative writing and children's use of literate language: A sequential analysis of social interaction', *Journal of Early Childhood Literacy*, 3(2): 165–178.

Kamberelis, G. (1999) 'Genre development and learning: Children writing stories, science reports, and poems', *Research in the Teaching of English*, 33(4): 403–463.

Kamberelis, G. and Bovino, T.D. (1999) 'Cultural artifacts as scaffolds for genre development', *Reading Research Quarterly*, 34(2): 138–170.

Kamii, C., Long, R., and Manning, M. (2001) 'Kindergarteners' development toward "invented" spelling and a glottographic theory', *Linguistics and Education*, 12: 195–210.

Kantor, R., Miller, S.M., and Fernie, D.E. (1992) 'Diverse paths to literacy in a preschool classroom: A sociocultural perspective', *Reading Research Quarterly*, 27: 185–201.

Kennedy, E. (2006) 'Literacy development of linguistically diverse first graders in a mainstream English classroom: Connecting speaking and writing', *Journal of Early Childhood Literacy*, 6(2): 163–189.

Kenner, C. (2000) 'Symbols make text: A social semiotic analysis of writing in a multilingual nursery', *Written Language and Literacy*, 3(2): 235–266.

Korat, O. and Levin, I. (2002) 'Spelling acquisition in two societal groups: Mother child interaction, maternal beliefs and child's spelling', *Journal of Literacy Research*, 34(2): 209–236.

Korkeamaki, R.-L. and Dreher, M.J. (2000) 'Finnish kindergarteners' literacy development in contextualized literacy episodes: A focus on spelling', *Journal of Literacy Research*, 32(3): 349–393.

Kress, G. (1997) *Before Writing: Rethinking the Paths to Literacy*, London: Routledge.

Kress, G. and Van Leeuwen, T. (2006) *Reading Images: The Grammar of Visual Design*, London: Routledge.

Labbo, L. (1996) 'A semiotic analysis of young children's symbol making in a classroom computer center', *Reading Research Quarterly*, 31(4): 356–385.

Lancaster, L. (2001) 'Staring at the page: The function of gaze in a young child's interpretation of symbolic forms', *Journal of Early Childhood Literacy*, 1(2): 131–152.

Lancaster, L. (2006) *Grammaticisation in Early Mark Making: A Multimodal Investigation*, Cheshire, UK: Manchester Metropolitan University.

Lancaster, L. (2007) 'Representing the ways of the world: How children under three start to use syntax in graphic signs', *Journal of Early Childhood Literacy*, 7(3): 123–154.

Landsmann, L.T. (1996) 'Three accounts of literacy and the role of environment', in C. Pontecorvo, M. Orsolini, B. Burge, and L. Resnick (eds), *Children's Early Text Construction*, Mahwah, NJ: Lawrence Erlbaum. pp.101–126.

Larson, J. (1995) 'Talk matters: The role of pivot in the distribution of literacy knowledge among novice writers', *Linguistics and Education*, 7: 277–302.

Larson, J. (1999) 'Analyzing participation frameworks in a kindergarten writing activity: The role of overhearer in learning to write', *Written Communication*, 16: 225–257.

Larson, J. and Maier, M. (2000) 'Co-authoring classroom texts: Shifting participant roles in writing activity', *Research in the Teaching of English*, 34(4): 468–497.

Lave, J. and Wenger, E. (1991) *Situated Learning: Legitimate Peripheral Participation*, Cambridge, England: Cambridge University Press.

Leander, K. (2002) 'Silencing in classroom interaction: Producing and relating social spaces', *Discourse Processes*, 34(2): 193–235.

Lefebvre, H. (1991) *The Production of Space* (D. Nicholson-Smith, Trans.). Oxford, England: Blackwell.

Levin, I., Both-DeVries, A., Aram, D., and Bus, A. G. (2005) 'Writing starts with own name writing: From scribbling to conventional spelling in Israeli and Dutch children', *Applied Psycholinguistics*, 26: 463–477.

Levin, I. and Bus, A.G. (2003) 'How is emergent writing based on drawing? Analyses of children's products and their sorting by children and mothers', *Developmental Psychology*, 39(5): 891–905.

Lysaker, J. (2000) 'Beyond words: The relational dimensions of learning to reading and write', *Language Arts*, 77(6): 479–484.

MacGillivray, L. and Martinez, A.M. (1998) 'Princesses who commit suicide: Primary children writing within and against gender stereotypes', *Journal of Literacy Research*, 30(1): 53–84.

Manyak, P. (2001) 'Participation, hybridity, and carnival: A situated analysis of a dynamic literacy practice in a primary-grade English immersion class', *Journal of Literacy Research*, 33: 423–465.

Martens, P.A. (1999) 'Mommy, how do you write "Sarah"?: The role of name writing in one child's literacy', *Journal of Research in Childhood Education*, 14(1): 5–15.

Mavers, D. (2007) 'Semiotic resourcefulness: A young child's email exchange as design', *Journal of Early Childhood Literacy*, 7(2): 155–176.

Mayer, C. and Moskos, E. (1998) 'Deaf children learning to spell', *Research in the Teaching of English*, 33: 158–180.

Meier, D.R. (2000) *Scribble Scrabble. Learning to Read and Write: Success with Diverse Teachers, Children, and Families*, New York: Teachers College Press.

Moll, L.C., Saez, R., and Dworin, J. (2001) 'Exploring biliteracy: Two student case examples of writing as social practice', *The Elementary School Journal*, 101(4): 435–449.

Morrow, L.M. (1991) 'Relationships among physical design of play centers, teachers' on literacy in play, and children's literacy behaviors during play', in S. McCormick and J. Zutell (eds), *Learner Factors/ Teacher Factors: Issues in Literacy Research and Instruction, Thirty-Eighth Yearbook of the National Reading Conference*, Chicago: National Reading Conference. pp.77–86.

Morrow, L.M. and Rand, M. (1991) 'Promoting literacy during play by designing early childhood classroom environments', *Reading Research and Instruction*, 35: 85–101.

Neuman, S.B. and Roskos, K. (1991) 'The influence of literacy-enriched play centers on preschoolers' conceptions of the functions of print', in J. Christie (ed.), *Play and Early Literacy Development*, Albany: State University of New York Press. pp.167–187.

Neuman, S.B. and Roskos, K. (1992) 'Literacy objects as cultural tools: Effects on children's literacy behaviours in play', *Reading Research Quarterly*, 27: 203–225.

Neuman, S.B. and Roskos, K. (1993) 'Access to print for children of poverty: Differential effects of adult mediation and literacy-enriched play settings on environmental and functional print tasks', *American Educational Research Journal*, 30: 95–122.

New London Group (1996) 'A pedagogy of multiliteracies: Designing social futures', *Harvard Educational Review*, 66(1): 60–92.

Newkirk, T. (1989) *More than Stories: The Range of Children's Writing*, Portsmouth, NH: Heinemann.

Olson, J.L. (1992) *Envisioning Writing: Toward an Integration of Drawing and Writing*, Portsmouth, NH: Heinemann.

Piaget, J. (1976) *The Grasp of Consciousness: Action and Concept in the Young Child*, Cambridge, MA: Harvard University Press.

Pine, N. (2005) 'Visual information-seeking behavior of Chinese- and English-speaking children', in A. Makkai, W.J. Sullivan, and A.R. Lommel (eds), *LACUS Forum XXXI: Interconnections*, Houston, TX: LACUS. pp.289–300.

Pontecorvo, C. and Zucchermaglio, C. (1990) 'A passage to literacy: Learning in a social context', in Y. Goodman (ed.), *How Children Construct Literacy: Piagetian Perspectives*, Newark, DE: International Reading Association. pp.59–98.

Power, B.M. (1991) 'Pop-Ups: The rise and fall of one convention in a first grade writing workshop', *Journal of Research in Childhood Education*, 6: 54–65.

Purcell-Gates, V. (1995) *Other People's Words: The Cycle of Low Literacy*, Cambridge, MA: Harvard University Press.

Purcell-Gates, V. (1996) 'Stories, coupons, and the TV Guide: Relationships between home literacy experiences and emergent literacy knowledge', *Reading Research Quarterly*, 31(4): 406–428.

Qian, G. and Pan, J. (2006) 'Susanna's way of becoming literate: A case study of literacy acquisition by a young girl from a Chinese immigrant family', *Reading Horizons*, 47(1): 75–96.

Read, C. (1971) 'Preschool children's knowledge of English phonology', *Harvard Educational Review*, 41:1–34.

Reyes, I. (2006) 'Exploring connections between emergent biliteracy and bilingualism', *Journal of Early Childhood Literacy*, 6(3): 267–292.

Rogoff, B. (2003) *The Cultural Nature of Human Development*, Oxford: Oxford University Press.

Roskos, K. (1988) 'Literacy at work in play', *Reading Teacher*, 41: 562–566.

Rowe, D.W. (1994) *Preschoolers as Authors: Literacy Learning in the Social World of the Classroom*, Cresskill, NJ: Hampton Press.

Rowe, D.W. (2008) 'Social contracts for writing: Negotiating shared understandings about text in the preschool years', *Reading Research Quarterly*, 43(1): 66–95.

Rowe, D.W., Fitch, J.D. and Bass, A.S. (2001) 'Power, identity, and instructional stance in the writers' workshop', *Language Arts*, 78: 426–434.

Rowe, D.W., Fitch, J.D., and Bass, A.S. (2003) 'Toy stories as opportunities for imagination and reflection in writers' workshop', *Language Arts*, 80(5): 363–374.

Rowe, D.W. and Leander, K. (2005) 'Analyzing the production of third space in classroom literacy events', in B. Maloch, J.V. Hoffman, D.L. Schallert, C.M. Fairbanks, and J. Worthy (eds), *54th Yearbook of the National Reading Conference*, Oak Creek, WI: National Reading Conference. pp.318–333.

Schultz, K. (1997) '"Do you want to be in my story?": Collaborative writing in an urban elementary classroom', *Journal of Literacy Research*, 29(2): 253–287.

Senechal, M., LeFevre, J.-A., Thomas, E.M., and Daley, K.E. (1998) 'Differential effects of home literacy experiences on the development of oral and written language', *Reading Research Quarterly*, 33(1): 96–116.

Schickedanz, J.A. (1990) *Adam's Righting Revolutions: One Child's Literacy Development from Infancy Through Grade One*, Portsmouth, NH: Heinemann.

Sheehy, M. (2004) 'Between a thick and a thin place: Changing literacy practices', in K. Leander and M. Sheehy (eds), *Spatializing Literacy Research and Practice*, New York: Peter Lang. pp.91–114.

Short, K.G., Harste, J.C., and Burke, C.L. (1996) *Creating Classroom for Authors and Inquirers* (second edn.), Portsmouth, NH: Heinemann.

Siegel, M. (1995) 'More than words: The generative power of transmediation for learning', *Canadian Journal of Education*, 20(4): 455–475.

Siegel, M. (2006) 'Rereading the signs: Multimodal transformations in the field of literacy education', *Language Arts*, 84(1): 65–77.

Sipe, L. (1998) 'Transitions to the conventional: An examination of a first grader's composing process', *Journal of Literacy Research*, 30: 357–388.

Smolkin, L.B. and Donovan, C.A. (2004) 'Developing conscious understanding of genre: The relationship between implicit and explicit knowledge during the five-to-seven shift', in J. Worthy, B. Maloch, J.V. Hoffman, D.L. Schallert, and C.M. Fairbanks (eds), *53rd Yearbook of the National Reading Conference*, Oak Creek, WI: National Reading Conference. pp.385–399.

Soja, E.W. (1996) *Thirdspace: Journeys to Los Angeles and Other Real-and-Imagined Places*, Malden, MA: Blackwell Publishers.

Solsken, J. (1993) *Literacy, Gender, and Work in Families and in School*, Norwood, NJ: Ablex.

Solsken, J., Willett, J., and Wilson-Keenan, J.-A. (2000) 'Cultivating hybrid texts in multicultural classrooms: Promise and challenge', *Research in the Teaching of English*, 35(2): 179–212.

Sowers, S. (1985) 'Learning to write in a workshop: A study in grades one through four', in M. Farr (ed.), *Advances in Writing Research. Children's Early Writing Development Vol. 1*, Norwood, NJ: Ablex Publishing Corp. pp.297–342

Street, B.V. (1995) *Social Literacies. Critical Approaches to Literacy Development, Ethnography and Education*, London: Longman.

Sulzby, E. (1985) 'Kindergarteners as writers and readers', in M. Farr (ed.), *Advances in Writing Research. Children's Early Writing Vol. 1*, Norwood, NJ: Ablex. pp.127–200.

Sulzby, E. (1996) 'Roles of oral and written language as children approach conventional literacy', in C. Pontecorvo, M. Orsolini, B. Burge, and L.B. Resnick (eds), *Children's Early Text Construction*, Mahwah, NJ: Lawrence Erlbaum Association. pp.25–46.

Sulzby, E. and Teale, W. (1991) 'Emergent literacy', in R. Barr, M. Kamil, P. Mosenthal, and P.D. Pearson (eds), *Handbook of Reading Research Vol. II*, New York: Longman. pp.727–758.

Taylor, D. and Dorsey-Gaines, D. (1988) *Growing Up Literate. Learning from Inner-City Families*, Portsmouth, NH: Heinemann.

Teale, W. (1986) 'Home background and young children's literacy development', in W. Teale and E. Sulzby (eds), *Emergent Literacy*, Norwood, NJ: Ablex. pp.173–206.

Teale, W. and Sulzby, E. (1986a) 'Introduction. Emergent literacy as a perspective for examining how young children become writers and readers', in W. Teale and E. Sulzby (eds), *Emergent Literacy*, Norwood, NJ: Ablex. pp.vii–xxv.

Teale, W. and Sulzby, E. (eds) (1986b) *Emergent Literacy*, Norwood, NJ: Ablex.

Troyer, C. (1991) 'From emergent literacy to emergent pedagogy: Learning from children learning together', in J. Zutell, S. McCormick, L. Caton, and P. O'Keefe (eds), *Learner Factors/Teacher factors: Issues in Literacy Research and Instruction*, Chicago: National Reading Conference, pp.119–126.

Upitis, R. (1992) 'Can I Play You My Song?', *The Compositions and Invented Notations of Children*, Portsmouth, NH: Heinemann.

Van Sluys, K. (2003) 'Writing and identity construction: A young author's life in transition', *Language Arts*, 80(3): 176–184.

Vukelich, C. (1991a) Learning about the functions of writing: The effects of three play interventions on children's development and knowledge about writing. Paper presented at the National Reading Conference. Palm Springs, CA.

Vukelich, C. (1991b) 'Materials and modeling: Promoting literacy duirng play', in J. Christie (ed.), *Play and Early Literacy Development*, Albany: State University of New York Press. pp.215–231.

Vygotsky, L.S. (1978) *Mind in Society*, Cambridge, MA: Harvard University Press.

Welsch, J.G., Sullivan, A., and Justice, L.M. (2003) 'That's my letter!: What preschoolers' name writing representations tell us about emergent literacy knowledge', *Journal of Literacy Research*, 35(2): 757–776.

Williams, C.L. (1999) 'Preschool deaf children's use of signed language during writing events', *Journal of Literacy Research*, 31: 183–212.

Wilson, A. (2004) 'Four days and a breakfast. Time, space and literacy/ies in the prison community', in K. Leander and M. Sheehy (eds), *Spatializing Literacy Research and Practice*, New York: Peter Lang. pp.67–90.

Wilson, C. (2000) *Telling a Different Story: Teaching and Literacy in an Urban Preschool*, New York: Teachers College Press.

Wiseman, A.M. (2003) 'Collaboration, initiation, and rejection: The social construction of stories in a kindergarten class', *Reading Teacher*, 56(8): 802–810.

Wolf, S.A. (2006) 'The mermaid's purse: Looking closely at young children's art and poetry', *Language Arts*, 84(1): 10–20.

Wollman-Bonilla, J.E. (2000) 'Teaching science writing to first graders: Genre learning and recontextualization', *Research in the Teaching of English*, 35: 35–65.

Wollman-Bonilla, J.E. (2001a) 'Can first-grade writers demonstrate audience awareness?' *Reading Research Quarterly*, 36: 184–201.

Wollman-Bonilla, J.E. (2001b) 'Family involvement in early writing instruction', *Journal of Early Childhood Literacy*, 1: 167–192.

Wollman-Bonilla, J.E. (2003) 'E-mail as genre: A beginning writer learns the conventions', *Language Arts*, 81(2): 126–134.

Wright, S. (2007) 'Young children's meaning-making through drawing and "telling": Analogies to filmic textual features', *Australian Journal of Early Childhood*, 32(4): 7–49.

Yaden, D., Rowe, D.W., and MacGillivray, L. (2000) 'Emergent literacy. A matter (polyphony) of perspectives', in M. Kamil, P. Mosenthal, P.D. Pearson, and R. Barr (eds), *Handbook of Reading Research Vol. III*, Mahwah, NJ: Lawrence Erlbaum. pp.425–454.

Yaden, D. and Tardibuono, J.M. (2004) 'The emergent writing development of urban Latino preschoolers: Developmental perspectives and instructional environments for second-language learners', *Reading and Writing Quarterly*, 20: 29–61.

Yang, H.-C. and Noel, A.M. (2006) 'The developmental characteristics of four- and five-year-old preschoolers' drawing: An analysis of scribbles, placement patterns, emergent writing, and name writing in archived spontaneous drawing samples', *Journal of Early Childhood Literacy*, 6(2): 145–162.

Zecker, L.B. (1999) 'Different texts, different emergent writing forms', *Language Arts*, 76(6): 483–490.

Zucchermaglio, C. and Scheuer, N. (1996) 'Children dictating a story: Is together better?' in C. Pontecorvo, M. Orsolini, B. Burge, and L. Resnick (eds), *Children's Early Text Construction*, Mahwah, NJ: Lawrence Erlbaum. pp.83–98.

15

Writing in Childhood Worlds

Anne Haas Dyson

Almost 20 years ago, Loris Malaguzzi, the founder of the Italian municipal preprimary system (Reggio Emilia), visited my then university home in Berkeley, California. I asked him if the children in his schools wrote and how that writing began. He told me, through a translator, that writing began when children put little gifts in each other's mailboxes – a small piece of candy, perhaps, or a bit of ribbon. The small gift was a shared pleasure, a mediator of a relationship. To use contemporary academic language, within this practice – this frame for action – children could move into offering each other, not small treats, but written notes, even if the note contained only their name.

This story is as good as any for a description of how written language might become a useful tool in young children's lives. Children do explore print's qualities as an interesting object – the shape of its symbols, their linear march, their arrangement on a page (Clay, 1975). Indeed, educational programs themselves may place primary emphasis on surface-level 'basics' (i.e., letters, their formation, their names, and sounds). Still, in order to take ownership of and manipulate written symbols, young children need some intention to communicate, to bend those symbols to some end. In Vygotsky's words,

if writing is to be more than a set of 'hand and finger habits' for children, it must be 'relevant' to their lives (Vygotsky, 1978: 117–118). A major source for that relevance can be found in children's shared practices as children.

Listen, for example, to six-year-old Lyron during his classroom writing time early in his first-grade year. He has asked (to put it mildly) if other children are going to write about a favourite pastime – floor hockey, a kind of hockey where you 'don't need ice skates ... just regular shoes' but still can play like those professional hockey players appreciated in his northern U.S. state:

Lyron: Janette, write about floor hockey!
Janette: I am (irritated, as in 'I already said I was')
Lyron: Jon, are you?

Lyron now adds classmates to his own text about who is going to be playing field hockey.

Lyron: I'm writing Janette first. (He has her name tag.)
Jason, your turn.... Here you go, Jason.

As Lyron adds each name, his voice is full of anticipation, seemingly assuming others' pleasure at being included. His voice could be that of a child offering others' sweets rather than a place in a text (from a project described in Dyson, 2006). Viewing televised professional hockey and playing in locally organized child teams were part of Lyron's sense of himself, tied to his family pastimes, his northern location, his peer pleasures, and his gender identity (despite Janette, a rare *girl* hockey player). Composing time offered a new venue for hockey play; that familiar practice was transformed to fit the symbolic possibilities and social arrangements of the textual 'playground', as it were. Still, as is typical of young children's composing, Lyron's narrative play happened primarily through the talk and drawing that accompanied his writing. These media allowed teams of children to be spatially located on a drawn playing field and dramatically positioned in a moment in time (when the coach was yelling, when a goal was made or missed).

In this chapter, I discuss how children may negotiate a place for writing within their symbolic repertoire and the semiotic, social, and ideological processes that negotiation entails. I consider too how those processes, and the writing development they mediate, may be tied to the very stuff of childhood relationships and play; such linking of written language to shared pleasures (i.e., to the use of popular literacies [for an expansion on this theme, see Marsh, this volume] is shaped by curricular constraints and possibilities, themselves tied to societal and political contexts for education.

To help illustrate these ideas, I use samples of children writing from selected research projects of my own. All the studied classrooms have been urban public schools in the U.S., all racially integrated ones in which African-American children have been a dominant group; many of the focal children, like Lyron, have been African-American and from low-income and working-class neighborhoods. The studies' conclusions, though, have not been about any one population of children but about the phenomenon of interest – the symbolic and social dynamics that help explain the changing nature of children's writing in their lives together as children as well as students. Given the socioeconomic, political, and cultural differences in the nature

of both childhood resources and school curricula, the conception of child literacy discussed herein will be realized differently in the lives of children in varying societal and curricular circumstances (Prinsloo and Stein, 2004).

In the section to follow, I provide a theoretical landscape for this chapter by laying out its sociocultural and dialogic stance on popular literacies, childhood agency, and development itself.

WRITING AND THE CONSTRUCTION OF CHILDHOODS: DEFINING THE THEORETICAL LANDSCAPE

Whenever Lyron composed (drew, talked, and wrote) about floor hockey, he was, in part, appropriating for his own use the discourse of – the expected ways of communicating about – sport in his society: he drew scoreboards, playing fields, and players with hockey sticks; he reported whether his team won or lost. At the same time, he appropriated the expected textual voice in his official classroom world, where personal narratives were valued: he wrote an apparently true story about his anticipated or lived experiences. Finally, the listing of peers and an expectation of reciprocity (of those he listed including him in their texts) were part of the communicative expectations of his unofficial peer world; indeed, he accompanied his writing with drawings of 'fake' narratives for amusing – or irritating – peers (e.g., of his classmate Jon flipping over when he went after a hockey puck).

As Lyron's composing illustrates, any seemingly simple child's text may mediate a hybrid space, in which children take action in diverse social spheres (Dyson, 1993, 2003, 2006). Understanding such spaces requires an understanding of composing as a dialogic act, of children's worlds as manifestations of situated child agency, and of development as shaped by sociocultural dynamics.

ENTERING CONVERSATIONS: WRITING AS DIALOGUE

In the view of the Russian language philosopher Bakhtin (1981, 1986), any utterance, be it oral or written, is a dialogic response; it takes shape in a stratified world filled with a diversity of kinds of social voices. An utterance, then, is both a communicative act in the moment and linked to the communicative past; the voices that have filled our everyday lives provide the resources – the used words – from which we construct our present response. All utterances are thus enacted speech genres or kinds of voices, be they short conversational rejoinders or lengthy novels; their formation is guided by expected ways of taking a turn in typical situations for communication.

In contemporary childhoods, young children may come in contact with a great diversity of voice types, emanating from human and technological sources of all kinds. Ways of reporting news, of advertising products and services, of celebrating, communicating, or praying through song – all are kinds of voices enacted through different technologies (e.g., video, radio, and animation), using different kinds of symbol systems (e.g., written language, drawing, and music), and implicating different ideologies about how the world works (e.g., the nature of gender roles, of power, and of family relations).

Children may draw on these voices in their own dramatic play, when they become singing stars, superheroes, mommies, babies, and all manner of appealing others (Garvey, 1990). Through such play, children negotiate their identities, including those of gender, race, and class (Dyson, 1997; Mitchell and Reid-Walsh, 2002; Paley, 1984). Who can be the 'hockey player'? the 'superhero'? the damsel needing – and deserving – saving?

In school, children learn to enter into new kinds of conversations that emphasize the written medium. In so doing, they must use their resources – the symbolic tools and cultural material – of their previous communicative experiences. Among these resources,

then, are the practices and symbolic stuff of their own childhoods.

CHILDHOOD AGENCY: PLAYING IN SCHOOL

Playful practices, and their realization in the social relations of children, may seem antithetical to the 'work' required by the official school world. A dominant view of schooling is that it serves as 'competitive skills preparation' (Fass, 2007: 254), particularly for children deemed 'at risk' of school failure (and of threatening national economic health [www.nochildleftbehind.gov.]). Given this view and, also, societies' urgent need to provide schooling for their youngest citizens, children's unofficial or child-controlled literacy practices and relations may seem unimportant, even trivial.

Yet, it is hard to keep children's communicative experiences and cultural resources outside the school door. Adults do shape children's entry into cultural practices, including those involving written language; but children themselves contribute to the maintenance and transformation of those practices (Gazkins et al., 1992). This is because practices, as contexts for participation, are actively constructed, not simply given (Bauman, 2004). In school, children use their experiential, linguistic, and textual resources to help construct meaningful frames (i.e., meaningful social practices) to organize their actions.

In so doing, children may construct unofficial or peer-governed contexts that both appropriate from and rework official practices (cf., Corsaro, 1985, 2003; Dyson, 2006, 2008; Goffman, 1961; Levinson, 1998). Children may spend a significant amount of time sitting side-by-side at their desks, as teachers circulate or work in one-to-one conferences with children. Whether they 'should' or 'should not', young children tend to be drawn to other children and to play. Indeed, even in highly structured literacy activities, children may engage in playful banter and spontaneous competitions (Glupcynski, 2007; Sahni, 1994). Children's textual productions may begin to mediate familiar peer relations and childhood practices. Composing, then, may become all wound up in the dialogic dynamics of the unofficial world, that is, in the production of texts or utterances that anticipate, and respond to, peers.

This negotiation of unofficial practices may be hastened by the very nature of children's resources for entering into official school writing. For example, given the directive to write a story, children may draw upon characters, themes, plots, and images from sports media, radio, video games, cartoons, and TV shows – all cultural material that may be drawn from their experiences enjoying and enacting narratives (Dyson, 1997; Marsh and Millard, 2000; Newkirk, 2002). Such material, though, may be more familiar to, and more valued by, other children than by their teachers. Similarly, young schoolchildren may 'write' by drawing, potentially an important medium for children's narrative play (e.g., Thompson, 2006), not to mention its importance in the visual images of popular media texts (Kress, 2003). Nevertheless, in the official school world, drawing may be viewed as irrelevant, a distraction, or, perhaps, as a 'planning' strategy for child writing, not as a major means for text production (i.e., for deliberately arranging symbols for some end), particularly since the tested 'basics' are written language skills, not drawing skills (Anning and Ring, 2004). Children's recontextualization of familiar symbolic tools and material thus situates their development within hybrid practices linked to official and unofficial worlds.

DEVELOPING WRITERS AND THE TRAJECTORIES OF PRACTICES

Like all learners, young schoolchildren must use familiar frames of reference to recontextualize salient aspects of new activities (new concepts, new symbolic tools, and new social practices (Miller and Goodnow, 1995; Nelson, 1996). This reframing of material within familiar practices allows children a sense of competence and agency – indeed, it allows them sense. In a dialectic fashion, children also recontextualize the cultural stuff of their everyday worlds (e.g., images, storylines, and typified and particular voices) within the frameworks of new activities. This remixing of cultural materials poses challenges as children translate and transform material across symbolic borders (e.g., from audiovisual sources to printed pages), social relations (e.g., from peer play in unofficial spaces to individual display in official spaces), and ideologies (e.g., about what is a worthy text).

For researchers, this movement of material across practices and social worlds implies that child writing cannot be studied only by examining child texts or by studying child participation in one kind of writing genre. Rather, children's participation in any one practice is linked to their experiences with other communicative practices. In borrowing and revoicing symbolic material from their landscape of possibilities, children juxtapose, blend, and differentiate practices. Ideally, they are not moving forward on some kind of imaginary pathway to literacy but manoeuvring with more control, more flexibility, on expanding textual landscapes of diverse voices.

For educators, recontextualization processes imply that the pedagogic goal of writing instruction is not the mastery of a particular text type but a disciplining of discourse flexibility and adaptability; that disciplining involves learning about the 'options, limits, and blends' of symbol use across practices (building on the nonliteracy work of Miller and Goodnow, 1995: 12). In the following section, I illustrate the key features of recontextualization processes and the dynamic interplay they generate between official literacy practices and the construction of unofficial childhood ones.

CHILD WRITERS AT WORK AND PLAY

Most efforts to expand visions of children's resources for school learning have focused on community or family culture, including teacher studies documenting household 'funds of knowledge' (i.e., varied forms of household activities, for example, gardening, cooking, carpentry (Gonzalez, Moll, and Amanti, 2005), as well as family languages and cultural practices like storytelling (Reyes, 2001; Wiley, 2005). Herein, I am stressing an overlapping but distinctive set of resources found in children's lived experiences, that found in children's participation in collective meaning making with other children, including that meaning making tied to the use of commercial media (Storey, 2001).

Because this media material originates outside school and yet has a clear role in childhood relations and play inside school, it allows one to trace that material as it becomes all wound up in children's school writing. The key means for this transformation are the processes of recontextualization illustrated in the sections to follow. As is also illustrated, this transformation of symbolic and cultural material has ramifications for the social organization of writing itself and, potentially, for the enactment of a literacy curriculum responsive to children's worlds and contemporary times. I begin, next, with three first graders, one a football fan, the other two aspiring singers.

REFRAMING OFFICIAL PRACTICES: HYBRID PRODUCTIONS

Through a year-long ethnographic study in an urban, multiracial first grade, I documented children's reliance on nonacademic social worlds to negotiate their entry into school literacy (Dyson, 2003). Those worlds provided these San Francisco Bay children with agency and meaningful symbols, including those from popular music, films, animated shows, and sports media. The children's media appropriations were useful, in part, because they provided them with a range of cultural material, among them, communicative genres, models of textual structures and elements, technological conventions, actual spoken utterances, and conceptual content, including a pool of potential characters, plots, and themes. The use of that material posed productive developmental challenges in differentiating symbol systems and social practices.

AN ILLUSTRATION OF THE TEXTUAL POSSIBILITIES OF SPORTS

Consider, for example, Marcel, a member of a friendship group of African-American children who called themselves 'the brothers and the sisters'. Like many children, particularly boys, Marcel was intensely interested in sports, especially football. He and his close friends Wenona and Noah constructed an unofficial 'figured' or constructed world that coexisted along with the official one (Holland, et al., 1998). In that world, the children had varied roles and appealing identities. Their (imagined) coach was based both in Minnesota (where he had a co-ed hockey team, the Mighty Ducks, based on a movie of the same name) and in Texas (Dallas, Texas, to be exact), where Wenona was a cheerleader and the boys played for the Cowboys, a professional football team.

The children's sports play involved a range of interrelated communicative practices, initially carried out primarily through talk and drawing; these included *planning their agendas*, particularly given their need to travel and, also, to do their homework, *reporting the results of*, and *narrating highlights of, actual and imagined games* (the latter featuring themselves), and *evaluating the relative merits of teams*. During the daily open-ended composing period, children's popular pleasures, like football, initially were evident in simple sentences like those modelled by their teacher (e.g., 'I like a player or a team'). As the children gained experience, writing became more embedded within their play. Guided by a clear sense of a communicative frame (a 'typified voice', in Bakhtin's, 1986, sense), child writers adapted, stretched, and appropriated new resources, all the while manipulating the elements of the written system (e.g., letters, words, and syntax).

To illustrate, consider an early text of Marcel's, one that was deceptively simple (see Figure 15.1). As in that text, Marcel first wrote sports reports by borrowing the symbolic material and graphic arrangement of a television score-reporting practice. Moreover, his choice of teams was related to his sports play, as suggested in the talk accompanying its production, excerpted next:

Marcel is sitting by Lakeisha on one side and a parent volunteer, Cindy, on the other. Lakeisha is his "fake sister" and understands that he plays for a winning team – Dallas. Cindy is not a relative; she understands Marcel as a little boy who, she

Figure 15.1   Writing in childhood worlds.

thinks, has the facts about Dallas's fate in the football playoffs wrong.

Marcel: (to Lakeisha) I know what I want to write about. 'The Dallas Cowboys (beat) Carolina'. (In the unofficial world, Dallas always wins.)

Cindy: They [Dallas] *lost*. Did you watch the game?

... [omitted data]

Marcel: They're out! Out of the playoffs?

Cindy: They're like the 49ers now.

Marcel changes his plans. He still starts with *The Dallas* but then produces the text in Figure 15.1.

Marcel: (to Cindy) This says, 'Dallas against Minnesota. In Texas. 15 to 48'.

...

(to Lakeisha) I be home tomorrow, only me and Wenona will be home late.'Cause me and Wenona got practice .... I still got to go to football practice. ... Wenona got cheerleading.

Marcel and Wenona will be late home tomorrow. The Dallas Cowboys may be out of the playoffs, but Marcel's 'still got to go to football practice', and Wenona's still got to go to cheerleading.

In this event, one can hear and see the converging of practices when Marcel translates (or remixes) the audiovisual display of sports scores to a paper and pencil display. For example, Marcel's event highlights concepts of directionality and page arrangement. However, Marcel's arrangement is not the result of a child engaging solely with print (as in Clay, 1975) but of a child recontextualizing written language across practices. Marcel does not follow the left-to-right conventions of a prose report; he arranges team names and scores vertically, as on a TV screen.

The converging of different practices is notable too in the complex interplay of what is written and what is read. In the official writing practice, his teacher emphasized that the children should monitor how their spoken and written words match. But a sports announcer's practice is to read a more elaborate text than the one displayed.

One can literally hear Marcel as he shifts voices, precariously positioned between practices. He initially writes *The* before he writes *Dallas*, a prose reporting style since he has a sentence planned, 'The Dallas Cowboys beat Carolina'. After a parent volunteer corrects his report, Marcel writes a screen-like display of team names and scores to accurately report the previous week's play in which Dallas beat Minnesota. Between his columns of team names, Marcel writes *in Texas*, which would not be written on such a display, but which an announcer might read. Marcel himself adopts an announcer voice as he rereads his text to the parent volunteer, 'Dallas against Minnesota. In Texas. 15 to 48'. In so doing, he reads the unwritten 'against', but not the written *the*.

Beyond these symbolic and discursive challenges, there are the social ones having to do with the situated reality of 'truth': What is true in his unofficial world (that Dallas always wins) is not true in the world more generally. And, finally, there are the gender ideologies embedded in all football related events, ideologies that could become salient when they entered the official world through whole class sharing, as they did when his teacher led a class discussion about the truth of a child's assertion that only boys like football.

In sum, when Marcel translated cultural material (e.g., names, informational displays, kinds of texts, and text sequencing conventions) across the boundaries of different practices, the symbolic knowledge embedded in his everyday and playful practices could be disrupted and brought into reflective awareness. At the same time, so too could the social knowledge and ideological assumptions of those practices.

RADIO SONGS, GIRL GROUPS, AND TEXTUAL RESOURCES

In a related way, the 'fake sisters' Vanessa and Denise, along with their fake siblings, were singers and chanters of varied kinds of texts (e.g., church songs, jump rope rhymes, and soul songs and raps from the radio). Out on the playground, the girls played girl-singing group. One child would be the lead and the others would be back-up singers, coming in at appropriate times with an accompanying line. Collectively, they composed coherent stanzas through semantic consistency and repetitive structures that were genre appropriate. The girls would disagree about the appropriate back-up line, eventually coming to a consensus.

Although the girls did jointly write songs, they did not do so in the official world; they did not think their teacher was 'used to' their radio songs. Nonetheless, the children's skill at collaboratively composing did have transformative power in the official world. Their collaboration involved adapting their efforts to the material constraints and official expectations that each child would produce an individual text. In the following example, Denise and Vanessa are not jointly writing a love song but, rather, a scary story inspired by a television show involving horror stories (a show with which Vanessa seemed more familiar).

Working in their separate writing workshop books, Denise and Vanessa divide their respective pages into four sections and then begin composing in different sections. In Denise's words, they are 'writing a [scary] story that goes together but in different books'. In her book, Denise begins to write about one boy and two girls playing together. In hers, Vanessa skips the top section and, in the second, writes:

> And a litte girl play with a litte boy but the boy was a vapyr and the boy beis [bites] her

As the girls are writing, Vanessa has a question

Vanessa: What's the title going to be?
...
Denise: 'One Boy and Two Girls'.
Vanessa: That's not good.
Denise: What should it be then? 'The Man and Two Women'.
Vanessa: That's not good either.

Denise becomes more tentative.

Denise: The Happy Scary Thing?
Vanessa: No. 'The Thing That Make You Shiver. Things That Makes You Shiver!'

Denise: No! (firmly)
Vanessa: 'One Boy and Two Girls' don't make sense (equally firmly)
...
Denise: Well, what should it be?... I know what it should be called. 'The Vampire'.
Vanessa: Ah, whatever you want (resigned) Wait! (excited) It should be, 'Be Careful What You Wish For'.

This appeals to Denise.

Denise: And a girl could say, 'I wish I was a vampire'. And she could turn into a vampire.
Vanessa: And the boy was already one.

Denise writes and then reads:

Denise: 'I wish I was a vampire'
...
Vanessa: 'I said, to myself on a star'. NO, 'I wish to a star'.
Denise: Write yours! We won't have time to share!

As they did on the playground, the girls negotiated vocal parts and made decisions about what lines would sound good when they performed their text during sharing time. Vanessa in particular searched for the right words, given her ear for the 'scary story' genre. At the same time, the girls reframed unofficial media materials within their official concerns as dutiful first-grade writers; they made explicit references to 'making sense' and to page arrangement (not only voice arrangement) and to text details like 'titles' and 'ends', just as their teacher modelled. This blend of practices supported their sophisticated composing decisions (example in full in Dyson, 2003).

The preceding examples illustrate children drawing from diverse cultural resources to find entry into, and a guiding practice within which to extend, official writing. Although the project from which the child data was drawn was focused on a particular child culture, there is evidence that, cross-culturally, childhoods are differentially but substantially linked to collective meaning-making and that, during composing, the playful practices of childhood can appear, given some minimum space for child agency and social interaction.

CROSS-CULTURAL POSSIBILITIES

Illustrations of the diversity of children's popular resources and the potential for official exploitation when recontextualized in school are available (including, e.g. descriptions of pedagogical interventions in Australian [Comber and Kamler, 2005] and U.K. classrooms [Marsh and Millard, 2000]).

To illustrate, Kenner (2005), located in London, discusses how television and computer technologies allowed preschoolers in multilingual, immigrant families access to a diversity of traditional and popular texts, themselves recontextualized in new media. An *imam* taking phone-in questions on religious matters, young women dancing to Arabic popular music, an Australian soap opera transformed into a Hong Kong noodle bar saga – all could be merely a click away. With the encouragement of parent volunteers, the children appropriated from these texts to create ones of their own (e.g., a poster for a movie, a newspaper composed of clippings from native-language newspapers, including clippings about movie and sports stars). (For a practice-sensitive discussion of children's multimodal and multilingual productions, see Pahl and Roswell, 2005.)

What is emphasized in this chapter, though, is the way in which children appropriate from the diversity of their communicative experiences, whether or not doing so is sanctioned or even recognized by the school and, moreover, the way in which the use of popular literacies themselves are linked to the construction of childhoods.

For example, Prinsloo (2004) documented the range of multilingual (Xhosa, English, and some Afrikaans words) and multimodal meaning making on display in a group of Cape Town girls' playing of two games, variations of tag and skipping games accompanied by verbal play and display. Within those frames were borrowings from school, local, and popular culture (including a song much loved by Marcel, Denise, and their friends ['I Believe I Can Fly' (Kelly, 1996)]). Just as with the San Francisco Bay Area girls described earlier, the discursive flexibility of the South African children was evident on multiple levels (grammatical, phonological, lexical, and discursive). Unlike in the study of the Bay Area children, Prinsloo was not able to document with any ease the girls' use of that discursive flexibility in official school contexts, as their literacy curriculum, as in other 'non-elite schools', focused on drills and 'the basics' (Prinsloo, 2004, p.302).

Sahni (1994, 2001) studied young children in a similar rote situation in a rural Indian school; the school's main material resources were the mats on which they sat and their chalk and slates. Prior to her intervention, the literacy curriculum emphasized rote learning; there was no provision for child composing (as opposed to child copying or transcribing teacher dictation). However, the children, like all others discussed in this chapter, had symbolic and social resources available in their own childhood pleasures. Thus, Sahni intervened, initially relying on what she had learned about the children, particularly their knowledge and enjoyment of song and poetry. She also began with familiar school practices – like copying and transcribing teacher dictation, but the children copied favorite and then jointly composed productions. Soon the social relations and imaginative substance of children's lives began to mediate their productions.

For instance, one of the children, Sakun, drew and wrote about her friends playing hopscotch and, as she did so, those friends participated playfully in her production:

Shakun: (in Hindi) So, Alima, you take that side [of the hopscotch chalk drawing] and Geeta, you be on this side.

Geeta: OK and then who wins?

Shaun: Uh … you lose and Salima wins.

Geeta: Why am I losing? Why not Salima? I play much better than her.

Salima watches smiling, as Geeta argues good naturedly.

Shakun: No, no, no. You lose this time (Sahni, 1994: 151).

Evident in the foregoing examples, and throughout this chapter, is the way in which the unofficial world of children may reconfigure the expected social organization of writing itself. The official world typically expects and evaluates children's productions as individual accomplishments, not as communicative mediators or dialogic turns. Within the unofficial world, though, writing is embedded in peer dialogues – in the claims and counterclaims of children like Lyron, Marcel, Denise, and Shakun. The potential ramifications of that social embeddedness for the official world are discussed in the section to follow.

FROM INDIVIDUAL PRODUCTIONS TO COMMUNAL DIALOGUES: IDEOLOGIAL TENSIONS AND CURRICULAR POSSIBILITIES

When writing becomes embedded in peer relations, it potentially generates a diversity of related practices and communicative options that spread throughout a socially-bound space, like that information among peers. These interconnected practices help constitute a local child culture. Within these practices are not only potential symbolic and linguistic resources but also ideological tensions that could be of use in the official world.

SOCIETAL THEMES IN TEXTUAL PLAY

The social practices being mediated by textual play are potentially all wound up with issues that are not typically considered part of writing time, issues like the roles of gender and race in character identities, the nature of power, the relationship between 'action' and 'violence' (Newkirk, 2002) in plot development, and even the suitability of pretend fighting as a source of fun. Part of becoming a sophisticated writer in varied

sorts of social spaces is learning that words can reverberate differently – elicit different responses – in a socially and ideologically complex society (Bakhtin, 1981).

To illustrate, consider the fate of 'fighting' as textual play in two urban classrooms serving primarily low-income children; the rooms are not directly comparable, given the differences in children's ages, in geographic regions, and in reigning educational policy. Still, similar unofficial practices figured in strikingly different ways into the official organization of writing.

In a San Francisco Bay classroom for 7- to- 9-year-olds, children (particularly boys) brought their playground superhero play into the classroom composing time. Similar to master early childhood teacher Vivian Paley (2004), the children's teacher had a classroom stage (an 'Author's Theater'); she encouraged her children to bring stories with 'action' (as opposed to 'information' pieces) to that stage. There, the stories would be acted out by chosen peers. That stage soon became an official prime site for superhero dramas, and the dramas themselves arose from a complex of unofficial practices, including intense oral negotiations about author's choices of characters and of peers to play those characters (Dyson, 1997). Since the superheroes were well known, particularly from television shows, most children were knowledgeable enough about those heroes to engage in such negotiations.

In and of itself, the transformation of superhero play to classroom composing posed issues of symbolic, social, and ideological differentiation. There were symbolic challenges, like translating the fun of swift movement in playground chase games to drawn motion lines, projectile arches, and dense scribbles of chaotic action, and to the lexical demands of written words that, at least conventionally, follow each other in staid lines. Most relevant in this section, though, are the social transformations and ideological tensions brought about by Author's Theater. For example, in 'fair play' on the playground, superhero teams of 'good guys' fought 'bad guys' in variants of chase games. These playground chase games, which involved all child players, did not transform easily into 'fair' composing time play, where 'main' characters had to be named and could indeed get more play than others. Moreover, 'fighting' was taken for granted by playground superhero fans as a 'good thing'; on the official classroom stage, some children's 'saving the world' actions were others' 'violence', and watching such 'violence' on the television was forbidden in their homes.

Because there was a public forum, so to speak – that is, a regular classroom discussion of children's responses to their composing and theatre productions – these varied issues figured into the official curriculum. 'Character motivations', 'setting', 'plot lines' were all discussed, as were any assumptions about who could play what role (e.g., boys' assumptions that girls' right [unlike boys' right] to play certain gender-specific roles depended on physical similarity to media characters, including perceptions of race). These public discussions reverberated in child composers' oral negotiations and textual decision-making (i.e., their ideological 'consciousness awaken[ed]', in Bakhtin's terms [1981: 345]). The discussions also reverberated in the official curriculum more generally. For example, social studies lessons and composing time blended as the class discussed how the definition of 'powerful' depended on the nature of the stories being told; thus, the physical power of superhero stories contrasted the nonviolent power featured in historical accounts of civil rights leaders.

A half a continent away, and a decade later, a classroom in Michigan (attended by Lyron) was concentrating on practising traditional writing conventions by writing and editing personal narratives; there was no public forum, just a quick sharing time in which children read their composed texts. Still, playground practices slipped into and transformed the children's composing; among those practices was another chase game, this one locally referred to as 'war', informed by a cartoon series (see Dyson, 2007).

Initially, the textual war games took place primarily through the drawing and talking of boys in close physical proximity to each other. As in other examples throughout this chapter, the children's 'individual' productions unfolded in interaction with other children; their products were linked. However, as had happened in the Bay Area classroom too, issues arose, including gender issues sparked by a girl's decision to play (i.e., that is, to write 'war' stories). This textual and social action had ideological reverberations in the unofficial world (i.e., boys objected since girls, to quote Lyron, 'don't even know about war'). More intense dialogic encounters among boys and girls, mediated by more elaborate written texts, followed – but their loud play with gendered war had official ramifications; specifically, they led to the teacher's understandable decision to ban the topic of war.

What matters herein, though, is that in this curricular situation, questions about child texts that focused on characters' motives, plot resolutions, or children's varied evaluative reactions to the featured 'action' were not part of official 'basics'. Teachers do have the responsibility to maintain what they judge as an emotionally safe, ethical context for child learning; but, without some kind of public forum about child texts, they cannot support children's awareness of the heteroglossia surrounding all texts and, thus, an authorial thoughtfulness about their composing decisions. The absence suggests a monologic view of language production, a view that seems out-of-synch with the socioculturally complex times in which we live.

LANGUAGE IDEOLOGIES AND PLAYFUL POSSIBILITIES

A monologic view of texts is also implicated in curricular views of 'good' – including grammatically correct – language. In contrast, children, as described herein, play with *situated* voices appropriated from family, community, school, and media; these voices reflect the languages, language variants, and registers that comprise their realized worlds. Textual play with these voices potentially promotes communicative flexibility and adaptability, not to mention language learning itself.

For example, Reyes (2001) discusses young children's use of code-switching between Spanish and English as a kind of social play mediated by writing, a play that furthered biliteracy. Similarly, in appropriating appealing voices, young speakers of marginalized language variants (like African-American English) may write new kinds of registers or variants (e.g. see Dyson, 2008). Yelling at the 'bad gies [guys]' through textual battles, for instance, calls for a different kind of voice than, say, inviting a peer to a pretend (if written about) birthday party, or appropriating the voice of an appealing poetic verse.

Still, in order to support children's discursive flexibility – their playful powers – the official curriculum would need to incorporate explicit acknowledgement of and respect for linguistic diversity. One way of doing that is through the use of literature in which characters speak in a multilingual world, or through (following Sahni [1994]) transcribing children's songs or folk games in local languages, whether or not commercial texts are available. Even allowing children to construct – or (re)produce – grocery product boxes in multilingual societies can generate children's critical awareness of the differential power of languages in varied spheres (Alexander and Bloch [n.d.], a video production for teachers and parents of young Xhosa-speaking South African children).

Play with, and a critical awareness of, situated language seems especially important given the world children are growing up in, an ever more interconnected world of diverse languages and, indeed, new variations of English. A comfort with such a world would seem to promote both sociopolitical sophistication about, and aesthetic openness to, the diverse rhythms of languages.

ON THE RELEVANCE OF CHILD WRITING

This chapter began with a well-known educator's story about how writing began in young children's use of classroom mailboxes to exchange small presents. These exchanges constituted an important cultural practice – a shared way of producing meaning in their lives. That practice was a comfortable social space within which new kinds of symbolic exchanges, mediated by writing, could grow.

Too often writing's foundational 'basics' are thought of as simply a set of skills – writing one's letters, learning one's sound/symbol connections, 'stretching out' and transforming spoken sounds into written symbols. But the *basics* of writing, as conceptualized herein, are not found in these skills, however important. Rather, they are found in mobilizing and adapting – in recontextualizing – one's experiential and semiotic possibilities for the communicative situation at hand.

Thus, throughout this chapter, I have aimed to illustrate how children, in varied cultural spaces and social situations, have used each other and enacted practices to make their ventures into school writing 'relevant to life' (Vygotsky, 1978:.118). Such illustrations were found in the busy sports-filled lives (and language) of Marcel and his friends, the collaborative productions of the radio-singing stars (and composers), and the increasingly action-packed dramas of the superheroes and the warriors.

The emphasis on children's lives together in no way discounts the responsibility of policy makers and classroom teachers to plan for and guide student learning and to assess progress toward agreed upon goals. Nor is this emphasis meant to suggest that children's unofficial worlds should merge with the official. The very existence of children's unofficial worlds is energized, at least in part, by their desire for social spaces and agendas that they can control (Chudacoff, 2007; Corsaro, 2003).

The emphasis on children's worlds, though, does underscore that educators are not in sole control of children's learning. Children's actions are based on their own interpretations of what is, or perhaps could, go on in, and around the official world. By providing space and time for children's symbolic and social actions during composing, and by paying attention to those actions and to the interconnections among children's productions, educators may themselves learn about children's interest in and emerging control of unexpected literacy practices and unbenchmarked (or assessed) conventions, as well as about the social and ideological tensions in their worlds. Children's efforts to build on their communicative experiences – to recontextualize them in new practices – pose intellectually rich challenges and, at least potentially, thought-provoking issues about what is good and fair in their often multimodal texts.

All around the world, children engage in playful practices with other children. They sing, dance, tell stories, imagine worlds, and, more and more, they include in their play the voices heard from media productions. Through these practices, children define themselves as agents in their worlds. If valued by the adult world, these practices may be seen as enacting intentions and mobilizing resources that will support children as they venture into new symbolic possibilities, meet new audiences, and join in new practices within worlds they themselves are helping to make.

AUTHOR NOTE

The project reported herein benefited from the much appreciated support of the Spencer Foundation and, also, of the University of Illinois at Urbana/Champaign. The findings and opinions expressed are, of course, my sole responsibility. I thank my hard-working research assistant, Sophie Dewayani.

REFERENCES

Alexander, N. and Bloch, C. (n.d.) Feeling at Home with Literacy [video]. Capetown, South Africa: Project for Alternative Education in South Africa.

Anning, A. and Ring, K. (2004) *Making Sense of Children's Drawings*, Berkshire: Open University Press.

Bakhtin, M. (1981) 'Discourse in the novel', in C. Emerson and M. Holquist (eds), *The Dialogic Imagination: Four Essays by M. Bakhtin*, Austin: University of Texas Press. pp.254–422.

Bakhtin, M. (1986) *Speech Genres and Other Late Essays*, Austin: University of Texas Press.

Bauman, R. (2004) *A World of Others' Words: Cross-Cultural Perspectives on Intertextuality*, Malden, MA: Blackwell.

Chudacoff, H.P. (2007) *Children at Play: An American History*, New York: New York University Press.

Clay, M. (1975) *What Did I Write?*, Auckland: Heinemann.

Corsaro, W. (1985) *Friendship and Peer Culture in the Early Years*, Norwood, NJ: Ablex.

Comber, B. and Kamler, B. (eds) (2005) *Turn-Around Pedagogies: Literacy Interventions for At-Risk Students*, Newtown, NSW, Australia: Primary English Teachers Association.

Corsaro, W.A. (2003) *'We're Friends, Right?' Inside Kids' Cultures*, Washington, DC: Joseph Henry Press.

Dyson, A.H. (1993) *Social Worlds of Children Learning to Write in an Urban Primary School*, New York: Teachers College Press.

Dyson, A.H. (1997) *Writing Superheroes: Contemporary Childhood, Popular Culture, and Classroom Literacy*, New York: Teachers College Press.

Dyson, A.H. (2003) *The Brothers and Sisters Learn to Write: Popular Literacies in Childhood and School Cultures*, New York: Teachers College Press.

Dyson, A.H. (2006) 'On saying it right (write): "Fix-its" in the foundations of learning to write', *Research in the Teaching of English*, 41: 8–44.

Dyson, A.H. (2007) 'School literacy and the development of a child culture: Written remnants of the "gusto of life"', in D. Thiessen and A. Cook-Sather (eds), *International Handbook of Student Experiences in Elementary and Secondary School*, Dordrecht, The Netherlands: Kluwer. pp.115–142.

Dyson, A.H. (2008) 'Staying in the (curricular) lines: Practice constraints and possibilities in childhood writing', *Written Communication*, 25: 119–159.

Fass, P. (2007) *Children of a New World: Society, Culture, and Globalization*, New York: New York University Press.

Garvey, C. (1990) *Play* (enl. edn.), Cambridge, MA: Harvard University Press.

Gazkins, S., Miller, P.J., and Corsaro, W. (1992) 'Theoretical and methodological perspectives in the interpretive study of children', in W. Corsaro and P.J. Miller (eds), *Interpretive Approaches to Children's Socialization*, San Francisco: Jossey-Bass. pp.5–23.

Glupzynski, T. (2007) 'Understanding young children's experiences with a scripted literacy curriculum', PhD dissertation, Teachers College, Columbia University.

Goffman, E. (1961) *Asylums*, Garden City: Anchor Books.

Gonzales, N. (2005) 'Beyond culture: The hybridity of funds of knowledge', in N. Gonzales, L. Moll, and C. Armanti (eds), *Funds of Knowledge*, Mahwah, NJ: Erlbaum. pp.19–46.

Holland, D., Lachiotte, W., Skinner, D., and Cain, C. (1998) *Identity and Agency in Cultural Worlds*, Cambridge, MA: Harvard University Press.

Kelly, R. (1996) I believe I can fly. On *Space Jam* [CD], New York: Atlanta Records.

Kenner, C. (2005) 'Bilingual children's uses of popular culture in text-making', in J. Marsh (ed.), *Popular Culture, New Media and Digital Literacy in Early Childhood*, London: Routledge. pp.73–88.

Kress, G. (2003) *Literacy in the New Media Age*, London: Routledge.

Levinson, B. (1998) 'Student culture and the contradictions of equality at a Mexican secondary school', *Anthropology and Education Quarterly*, 29: 267–296.

Marsh, J. and Millard, E. (2000) *Literacy and Popular Culture*, London: Sage.

Miller, P. and Goodnow, J.J. (1995) 'Cultural practices: Toward an integration of culture and development', in J.J. Goodnow, P.J. Miller, and F. Kessel (eds), *Cultural Practices as Contexts for Development, No. 67, New Directions in Child Development*, San Francisco: Jossey Bass. pp.5–16.

Mitchell, C. and Reid-Walsh, J. (2002) *Researching Children's Popular Culture: The Cultural Spaces of Childhood*, New York: Routledge.

Nelson, K. (1996) *Language in Cognitive Development: The Emergence of the Mediated Mind*, Cambridge: Cambridge University Press.

Newkirk, T. (2002) *Misreading Masculinity: Boys, Literacy, and Popular Culture*. Portsmouth, NH: Heinemann.

Pahl, K. (2005) 'Narrative spaces and multiple identities: Children's textual explorations of console games in home settings', in J. Marsh (ed.), *Popular Culture, New Media and Digital Literacy in Early Childhood*, London: Routledge Falmer. pp.126–145.

Pahl, K. and Rowsell, J. (2005) *Literacy and Education*, London: Paul Chapman.

Paley, V.G. (1984) *Boys and Girls: Superheroes in the Doll Corner*, Chicago: University Of Chicago Press.

Paley, V. (2004) *A Child's Work: The Importance of Fantasy Play*, Chicago: University of Chicago Press.

Prinsloo, M. (2004) 'Literacy is child's play: Making sense in Khwezi Park', *Language and Education*, 18: 291–314.

Prinsloo, M. and Stein, P. (2004) 'Children's early encounters with literacy in South African classrooms', *Perspectives in Education*, 22(2): 67–84.

Reyes, M. de la Luz (2001) 'Unleashing possibilities: Biliteracy in the primary grades', in M. de la Luz Reyes and J.J. Halcon (eds), *The Best for Our Children: Critical Perspectives on Literacy for Latino Students*, New York: Teachers College Press. pp.96–121.

Reyes, M. de la Luz and Halcon, J.J. (eds) (2001) *The Best for Our Children: Critical Perspectives on Literacy for Latino Students*, New York: Teachers College Press.

Sahni, U. (1994) 'Building circles of mutuality: A sociocultural analysis of literacy in a rural classroom in India', PhD dissertation, University of California, Berkeley.

Sahni, U. (2001) 'Children appropriating literacy: Empowerment pedagogy from young children's perspective', in B. Comber and A. Simpson (eds), *Negotiating Critical Literacies in Classrooms*, Mahwah, NJ: Erlbaum. pp.19–36.

Storey, J. (2001) *An Introductory Guide to Cultural Theory and Popular Culture* (third edn.), Essex: Pearson Education Limited.

Thompson, C. (2006) 'The "ket aesthetic": Visual culture in childhood', in J. Fineberg (ed.), *When We Were Young: New Perspectives on the Art of the Child*,

Vygotsky, L.S. (1978) *Mind in Society*, Cambridge, MA: Harvard University Press.

Wiley, T.G. (2005) *Literacy and Language Diversity in the United States* (second edn.), Washington, DC: Center for Applied Linguistics.

Agency and Platform: The Relationships between Talk and Writing

Judy Parr, Rebecca Jesson, and Stuart McNaughton

Writers on early literacy development (e.g., Clay, 1991; Dyson, 2000; Roskos, Christie, and Richgels, 2003; Teale and Sulzby, 1989) have claimed that children's early reading and writing are embedded in a larger developing system of communication. There is a general belief that, potentially, the components can work together to help the child negotiate the world and make sense of experiences within it (Lewis, 2000). However, it is only relatively recently through integrative movements such as 'comprehension as construction', 'reader response', or 'whole language' that interconnectedness has been deliberately fostered (Nelson and Calfee, 1998).

In this chapter, we focus on exploring talk and writing from a pedagogical stance, considering talk as something that can be employed deliberately and proactively. Most contemporary curricula for early writing make the assumption that talk impacts on children's writing. We explore why we would expect talk to make a difference, both to what and to how children write, and consider the

empirical evidence regarding the influence of talk on the writing of young children. Finally, drawing on examples from our own literacy context, we propose theoretical rationales for instructional practices that have been designed to make relationships more effective.

THE INFLUENCE OF TALK ON WRITING: THEORY AND PRACTICE

The presence of talk in the act of writing is impressive to those who observe classrooms. Thirty years ago, Britton (1970) employed the metaphor of writing in classrooms 'floating on a sea of talk'. This metaphor captures the idea that talk links the teacher, the young writer, and the writing, thereby supporting and sustaining writing, enabling interconnections to be made. More recently, Dyson (2000: 47) observed how young children are 'typically quite audible writers'. As they work, talk that is both official and unofficial pervades. Speech and saying, according to

Dyson (2006), 'thread' themselves throughout writing time. For Dyson (2000), the talk has added significance; reflecting and constructing the social and cultural identities of the participants in the classroom practices, connecting literacy events with social interactions and relationships see also Chapter 15, this volume.

What are the theoretical and empirical bases to these claims of the significance of talk to the act of writing and to the development of the child? The place of talk was prominent in models of the writing process and familiar oral language was posited to be the basis for one of these, the 'knowledge telling' model (Bereiter and Scardamalia, 1987). In this way of composing, the writing unfolded much like a conversation as opposed to the alternative model where material was transformed for the reader. Two lines of thought with respect to talk and writing connect to this. One was a simplistic view that the conventions of writing simply had to be grafted on to an intact oral system; the other the view that there are important differences in terms of structure and mode between spoken and written language (Vygotsky, 1962). With respect to mode, writing uses marks not sounds and is permanent. Analyses of structure are afforded by linguistic frameworks, which examine how the spoken and written modes differ, for example, at the levels of 'pronunciation', grammar and syntax, and meaning (Crystal, 1987) or with respect to a number of dimensions (e.g. lexical variety) along which particular genre, either spoken or written, will vary (Holme, 2004). Debates about the relative similarity or difference of speaking and writing are reflected in the view of talk as aiding or inhibiting writing development (Sperling, 1996).

The starting point for our analysis is the general theoretical position that language learning and use have their origins in social interaction (Vygotsky, 1978; Wittgenstein, 1953). From a sociocultural perspective on learning and development, learning to write is embedded within and develops from routine social interactions with literate others (Heath, 1983). Children are socialized to become more expert writers through active participation in meaningful literacy activity, and it is language that mediates experience (Vygotsky, 1962). To this activity children bring basic capabilities to learn and make sense and these are applied and developed within the social structures provided (McNaughton, 1995). The research literature on talk and writing is, therefore, viewed in terms of this general position, looking at how talk builds the psychological resources of the child, and at the roles of teacher, peer, and child talk within the structured literacy events of classrooms.

A range of functions are linked to the talk observed in classrooms. Amongst these are the functions of planning and self-regulation. Young writers' self-regulatory talk during writing may be patterned after the talk of others including more expert others involved in guiding the young writer. Bruner (1986: 175) describes how more expert adults 'loan' children their consciousness about language and language use. As they engage in talk with more expert writers, young writers are seen to internalize and transform what occurs on the external plane and this takes the form of inner speech (Vygotsky, 1978) that guides the child's thinking (Wertsch and Stone, 1985). Such talk, it is argued, helps to regulate and orchestrate the complex processes involved in writing – the planning, the encoding, the checking, and evaluating.

This executive function of talk, whereby children talk aloud to formulate a plan or to rehearse, can resemble playing with language and trying something out- an oral draft literally, to hear the language, to attend to the nature of sound (Clay, 1975; Ferreiro and Teberosky, 1982). Children may read aloud what they have written as a way to evaluate, to see whether it sounds right, semantically and syntactically. This latter strategy is not unproblematic. As Dyson (2006) illustrates, when children are urged by their teacher to listen to their own voices to help them in writing, what sounds right will vary with development and for sociocultural and situational reasons. What sounds right reflects the writer's sociocultural and linguistic resources, resources that can be at variance with those of the school. Some of this talk aloud is not simply for self. Spelling a word aloud or saying a portion of text aloud may be a form of problem solving or rehearsal, but it is also a performance offered to others, a way of being with and among others (Bomer and Laman, 2004). The read aloud performance may be to test out the message on an audience – to invite participation and appreciation.

Children are thus supported in writing not only by their appropriation of adult, specifically teacher, talk but also supported by what Dyson calls more unofficial events, those events that are governed by their relationship with others through the use of language experienced in settings like the home or peer group. Their appropriation draws on many voices as the words of others are 'assimilated, reworked, and re-accentuated' (Bakhtin, 1986: 89). Young writers often revoice interactions with adults in interacting with each other, guided by a sense of how a voice should sound in a particular situation; they are grappling with writing's demands within their relationships with other children (Dyson, 2006).

This revoicing is illustrated in the work of McCarthey (1994). She considered teacher talk and interaction in relation to subsequent student talk and text, and concluded that students went through cyclical phases in internalizing the social interaction. At first, they participated, appropriating from the interaction, then transformed as they took control. They then made the transformation public and, finally, the interaction was integrated back into social practices, a process termed conventionalization. However, McCarthey notes how the children both internalized and resisted as they drew on classroom discourse (not just language but social forms of participation) and as they transformed it.

The interaction among participants can contribute significantly to the process of learning to write as it occurs through both direct and peripheral participation in joint activity (Larson, 1995) as well as outside the predominantly dyadic interactions (termed 'cross-play' by Goffman, 1981). The multiple and overlapping texts that participants bring create the intertextual space for the social distribution and appropriation of literacy knowledge to occur (Larson, 1995).

Occasions for talk around print are contained within structured literacy events, which have a purpose, together with roles and expectations of what is to be discussed, and how (Heath, 1983). Within these settings, learners appropriate the patterns of interaction, not just the language but also concepts, habits, dispositions, culture, and relationships (Daiute and Dalton, 1993; Dyson, 1989, 2003). Literacy events in the classroom, like 'writing workshop', are seen to contain structures that Bakhtin (1986) would call speech genres, that is stable, socially defined types of utterances and these become ways of thinking that are helpful for writing (Bomer and Laman, 2004). Likewise, the talk of teachers in conference interactions, where teachers respond in ways that are intended to scaffold children's writing development, is organized within, and is itself constitutive of, social activity or events (Dyson, 2000).

Teachers use talk and joint activity to create a shared communicative space; an 'inter-mental development zone' (Mercer, 2004), which is constantly reconstituted with ongoing dialogue. These discussions can be jointly constructed, or conversations in which, although there is joint responsibility, the adult assumes the greater level of responsibility. In relation to writing, teacher-led talk and discussion may be used to cue prior knowledge and build content; to make intertextual links – language and process links between texts and between reading and writing; to build metalinguistic awareness; to make specific what is to be learned and what success will look like; to provide feedback to young writers and also feed-forward in the sense of how to move on in their writing development.

More explicit efforts to help children to acquire ways of thinking that are helpful for writing are exemplified in instructional conversations where children are supported to acquire 'schooled discourse' (Goldenberg, 1992). These conversations are designed to weave into instructional activities, communicative, cultural-historical dimensions, deliberately using the child's cultural-historical knowledge as an instructional resource. Instructional conversations aim to take advantage of intertextuality in bridging the worlds of child and teacher and allowing each to voice different readings of 'text'. Such conversations can directly influence writing. For example, Patthey-Chavez and Clare (1996) traced the ongoing effects of common topics and concerns developed from scaffolded discussion on increased fluency and appropriate syntax use in the writing of bilingual children. Likewise, in the widespread junior school literacy practice of morning talks, where children take an extended conversational turn, they are encouraged to give complete descriptions of an object or event and to structure talk in a way more similar to written discourse. Here children are seen to practice literate discourse in preparation for writing (Cazden, 2001).

RECRUITING TALK IN RELATION TO WRITING: THEORETICAL STANCES

Two closely related theoretical ideas can be derived from this research base. One involves seeing children as agentive, whose talk either as individuals or as part of a community enables creative expression and negotiation of meaning in oral and written forms to develop. Approaches that foster this function of talk focus typically around writers' developing notions of voice and authorship. The second approach views talk as creating textual platforms. This perspective draws on theory about intertextuality created in talk and oral preparation for literacy as well as talk that enables opportunities for 'input' at different linguistic levels such as vocabulary. Interacting with others provides a frame for using text level, sub text, and word level features in writing. The spoken word is both the raw material for writing and a tool to manipulate this material (Dyson, 2000).

How do actual instructional approaches reflect these ways of understanding relationships between talk and writing? As examples, we now examine in more detail approaches to recruiting talk in relation to writing that characterize the experience of young writers in our particular educational context. The first two owe much to two of our foremost New Zealand educators (Marie Clay and Sylvia Ashton-Warner). The third is not an established approach, rather concepts in lieu of an approach and our introduction of these concepts here is to argue for an increasing significance across the range of approaches used in effective literacy instruction. Together the three illustrate both perspectives: seeing children as agentive using talk to enable in oral and written forms of communication and viewing talk as creating textual frames or platforms for writing.

The first, the language experience approach, is a relatively fluid literacy event with numerous participants, a collective event. The second involves a more dyadic instructional event, where the expert guides the developing writer through scaffolded interaction, aiming to withdraw gradually as the interaction is internalized. Examples like this characterize deliberate tutoring in Reading Recovery (Clay, 2005) as well as effective writing conferences in ordinary classrooms with young writers. The third would be designed deliberately to foster connections between and among texts. This intended approach draws on the notion of intertextuality, and the significance of talk both mediating between and among texts and guiding the learner to make these connections.

Talk as agency: Learners negotiating meanings

A major premise of the theoretical base we draw on is that children are active participants in their own learning. As such, they are meaning makers, attempting to make sense of classroom literacy events and constructing frameworks for their understanding (Dyson, 2002). This theory of development aligns with sociocultural views of writing as a communicative act in classroom activities that encourage and promote children's own agency through meaning making and communication and prioritising children's experiences and linguistic resources.

Both writing and speaking are communicative acts. As such, many approaches to the teaching of writing value that communication for the role it has to play in the developing understanding and expression of the writer's identities. Communicating as speakers, children's audiences are present and responsive; as writers their audience is remote (Bereiter and Scardamalia, 1987). In classrooms, however, it is possible to harness the potential of the learning community as an immediate and responsive audience for writers, as well as seek out other more remote audiences for children's writing. Classroom activities that focus on this aspect of agency promote children's developing notions of their own voice as authors, as well as their sense of themselves as participants in a communicative process, as critics and respondents. This often entails the involvement of peers in the writing process as the most immediate of audiences. Such classroom literacy events focus on the related notions of authenticity and audience and aim to immerse children in authentic literacy activities for real audiences.

These major understandings underpin many components of writers' workshop approaches to writing: 'writing flourishes when children's expression is valued in all its forms' (Graves et al., 2004: 90). Notions of authenticity can be seen when children are encouraged to self-select most of their writing topics and genre, generating ideas continuously (Graves, 1983). Learners in writing workshops write at their own pace, seek response and feedback, and choose which of

their works, if any, they will publish. The writing is the learner's own expression of voice and plays an active role in shaping and reflecting learners' identities (Capello, 2006).

Within workshops and other classroom structures for authentic writing are approaches designed to foster notions of both voice and audience. Peer response can be harnessed at varying stages throughout composition. Collaborative planning (Higgins et al., 1992) builds on the support of peers as an immediate audience before writing, peer conferencing occurs during the writing process, and author's theatre is an opportunity for writers to take centre stage when work is ready to be published. Written response from peers can also be used; peer response journals promote an understanding of audience, as does the use on online chat rooms and communities (Beach et al., 2005). Publication celebrations (Atwell, 1998) where various community members are invited to respond to children's work and website publications (Flood et al., 2005) also encourage children to consider audience when writing.

Promoting children's agency in writing through authentic meaning making and the incorporation of children's linguistic and cultural resources as authors is, in the New Zealand context, addressed through the collective endeavour of language experience. Language experience activities are a familiar part of early literacy learning and teaching in many settings, but have a particular historical foundation in New Zealand classrooms. Language experience lessons include talking, writing, and reading activities, which are based around a shared classroom event or experience and which use the language of the learner as the starting point for literacy development. They are one of a variety of approaches to writing described in the New Zealand Ministry of Education support materials for teachers (*Effective Literacy Practice in Years 1 to 4*, 2003).

Language experience is most often described as growing from the 'organic method' of teaching and learning first articulated by Sylvia Ashton-Warner (1963). Ashton-Warner railed against the imposition of what she saw as an unnatural curriculum upon the creative energies of the child. She wrote passionately about the need for literacy to be meaningful to children, and advocated for learners' own voices to be the basis of literacy instruction, 'I reach into the mind of the child, bring out a handful of the stuff I find there, and use that as our first working material .... For it's here, right in this first word, that the love of reading is born ... (Ashton-Warner, 1963: 15).

The New Zealand language experience lesson, one of an array of writing contexts, has a common format. Initial stages focus around a planned, joint activity. The teacher purposefully sets up an event for the learners that will be 'vivid' or 'unusual' (Elley et al., 1996). As the learners 'do' and 'talk' the experience, they are constructing meaning. The children are engaged in the experience and also in discussion about the experience; the teacher is eliciting the children's own language, and recognizing the unique worldview and emerging linguistic understandings that each learner brings to the experience. During discussion, children's ideas are explored and their language is recorded. The shared event is, thus, the vehicle for authentic classroom talk and meaning construction about a joint experience. This may then be followed up by construction of a written text about the experience as a shared or guided writing lesson, and as a text for future reading. 'The key feature of this approach is that it uses talk about children's experiences as the basis for writing' (*Effective Literacy Practice in Years 1 to 4*, 2003: 102).

To understand fully how this approach recruits talk in the development of writing, it is necessary to elaborate its collective nature, an under-theorized aspect of earlier explanations, linked as they were to more individualistic psychological theories of the 1960s and 1970s. Wenger (1999) analysis of learning provides a means for this. He suggests that

learning is the result of learners engaging in and contributing to the practices of their communities. In classrooms, therefore, students learn through engaging in meaningful practices and having access to resources that enhance their participation. Individual learning occurs through the interaction between joint experiences and individual developing competence. Understandings are based on that negotiation of meaning, which learners help to shape. For educators and researchers, using these ideas as a frame of reference allows us to see language experience activities as potentially powerful contexts for literacy learning, recruiting talk through a joint negotiation of meaning, participation in authentic events, and the exploration of literate identities.

Wenger characterizes meaning-making as a process, which he calls 'negotiation of meaning' (1999: 53). In the language experience lesson, meaning is negotiated in an overt sense as learners express their developing understandings and these are built on or interpreted by others. The recording of these understandings in written format is also, in many ways, a negotiation between the teacher's literate experience and the meanings supplied by learners.

The activities of language experience also illustrate negotiation of meaning through Wenger's concepts of participation and reification. As learners participate in the doing and talking event, through writing they are also involved in the process of 'reifying' their experience (1999: 59). The group records the experience, developing their competence and creating an object for future reference. It is common to create a wall story, for example, which records the experience and conveys group understandings. The lesson then becomes part of the community's shared repertoire – based on shared participation and reification of these shared events. The participants are active learners by virtue of their engagement with the experience. Through its reification in terms of pictures, drawings, captions, description, and interpretation, the negotiated meaning becomes part of the class' shared history. Through this shared history of learning, the community of practice arises.

Wenger's analysis allows us to see how participation in a learning community has implications for the individual learner. Classroom learning communities are contexts for identity, because they offer a past and a future that can be experienced as a 'personal trajectory' (1999: 215). Language experience activities provide a valuable context to interweave the identities of participating learners. Drawing as it does on learners' voices, the lesson 'incorporates the members' pasts into its history' (1999: 215) by celebrating the meanings brought by the learners, and allowing learners to have central place in the constitution of practice. This allows an understanding that all members of the classroom community are also members of many other communities simultaneously. Learners' identities are formed through their participation in all of their communities. Wenger argues that the experience of multimembership means that learners are at risk of not fitting within a particular community. This can be overcome by communities that seek to include the multimembership of group members (1999: 216). In terms of classroom literacy events, the importance of recognizing children's existing literacies is imperative.

The second way that language experience activities can enhance participants' identities is by creating an environment where students want to learn, or as Wenger puts it, 'opening trajectories of participation that place engagement in its practice in the context of a valued future' (1999: 215). Language experience lessons encourage students to make generalizations and see connections – the links between thinking, talking, reading, and writing within the context of participating in an authentic experience. The objects created in this lesson are furthermore valued for future learning. Engaging in shared events and having one's understandings reified encourages alignment – seeing oneself as part of something bigger, wanting to be part of the larger literacy exercise.

Talk as textual platform: Guiding writing

In contrast to the planned immersion approach of language experience, there are more specific tutorial events. When teachers, through talk, make the most of teachable moments around writing they create the opportunity for meaningful but strategic linguistic input to support writers. Under ideal conditions, the interactions provide graduated assistance to learners. The maintenance of a 'quality zone' allows the teacher to enable a learner to operate beyond his/ her independent capacity (Mercer, 1995). The teacher constructs various scaffolds – asking questions, modelling actions, and directing the child's practice. The teacher, through talk and action, fine-tunes the problem presented to the child, together with the help given (Cazden, 2001). Several specific instructional approaches illustrate these features; talk around text is one of these.

TALK AROUND A CHILD'S TEXT

Joint interactions in which a more expert person provides guidance for a less expert person characterize both reading and writing instruction. In New Zealand classrooms, teachers are encouraged to vary instructional approaches depending on the level of support required by learners to achieve desired goals. Shared, guided, interactive, and independent contexts for reading and writing are distinguished by the level of support afforded. In addition, teachers guide writers as they engage in the writing process by entering conversations focused on the students' writing (*Effective Literacy Practice in Years 1 to 4*, 2003). Teaching in response to individual needs in writing is the basis of these one-on-one interactions around evolving work.

The scaffolding properties of such interactions, the guided participation that occurs with teaching (Rogoff, 1990), have been extensively analyzed for reading activities, however, there are fewer examples for writing. A notable exception is Clay and Cazden (1990) analysis of writing in Reading Recovery sessions for children who, after one year at school, are making lower than expected progress. They applied the well-known features of the scaffolding model to the writing portion of Reading Recovery to conclude that the teacher's help in writing serves similar functions to that she gives in reading; promoting emerging skill, allowing the child to work with the familiar, introducing the unfamiliar in a measured way, and dealing constructively with errors (Clay and Cazden, 1990).

The model can be applied also to the more general case of writing conferences in which interactions have an established routine and provide a familiar structure that support learning. However, while the pattern is familiar and constant, the conversation is adapted to individual need, focusing attention on memorable examples from which the child can learn (Kelly et al., 1996). During conferences teachers make moment-by-moment or in-flight decisions (Cazden, 1988) that have the potential to move children's writing forward in meaningful ways. Effective conferences require teachers to have developed deep understandings about their writers; to have knowledge about writing and how it develops and an awareness of the nature and purposes of instructional talk. The success of the interaction lies in the degree of match between what needs to be learned and what and how it is being taught. Effective conferences provide writers with opportunities to interact with a reader and to craft meaning for another; to develop metacognitive awareness in relation to the writing process and the self-regulatory strategies needed for reflecting on their texts (Glasswell, 1999), together with what Graves (1983) calls the personal responsibility needed to become a writer.

Successful interactions in a conference have several hallmarks (Glasswell and Parr, n.d). One is that the talk is goal directed. The teacher and child engage around a topic that focuses their talk and actions on the present and on the child's growing competence.

Teachers spend time trying to understand where the children are as writers. In Reading Recovery, this is known as 'roaming around the known' (Clay, 1993), attempting to find in tasks, texts, and talk the development of shared understandings, goals, and ways of acting. Developing writers are similarly focused, trying to figure out what they are meant to do and why; how they might learn to do it better, learning from what the teacher says and does (McNaughton, 2002). Second, both need to focus efforts in a forward-looking direction, sharing the goal that the writer will, over time, be able to undertake more of the task independently. Finally, an effective interchange involves the writer receiving just the right amount of the right kind of support at the right time for just the right period so that transfer of responsibility happens (Tharp and Gallimore, 1988).

The following conference between an expert teacher and a young writer in his first year at school (from Glasswell, 1999) illustrates these principles. What the teacher decides to talk about is guided by her knowledge of what the child can already do as a writer; by the history of her interactions with him over time and by her professional understanding of what he needs to learn next. The child, Charlie, initiates the interaction inviting Eleanor, his teacher, to respond to his piece about how he hurt his leg. In the first part, they discuss his invented spellings, following his lead about what he has been working on with respect to encoding (New Zealand children are encouraged to take risks in writing). She supports his self-evaluation, encouraging him to take responsibility, building his capability by asking him to identify what he got right and by confirming and praising his self assessment. Eleanor provides just the right amount of support in pursuing the goal she has for him of self-regulation, prompting him to take responsibility for what he is able to do independently.

1) T: Right, Charlie Barley! *(Both laugh).*
2) C: *(Charlie shares his book with Eleanor)* I tried hard but I didn't get some …

3) T: (*Eleanor smiles and laughs and turns his book around to see his writing*). OK! What does this say? (*Eleanor re-voices Charlie's written words with enthusiasm*) 'I …. HURT my leg!' I hurt my leg! Is this an 'h' here? What letters did you get right there?

4) C: (*Charlie looks at his book and points out letters he identifies as correct in the spelling of the word 'hurt'*)

5) T: The /h/ and the /t/! Pretty good, eh?

6) C: Mmmm (*smiles and nods- meaning yes*)
Then, they read the story together (turns 8-16); clarifying a word he has attempted to spell (turn 12). Eleanor responds as an interested, empathic reader (turn 16)

7) T: (reads from Charlie's book, re-voicing his written text.) I hurt my leg. Is that your title, is it?

8) C: Mmm (*nods meaning yes*)

9) T: What's after that?

10) C: (*Charlie takes over reading, revoicing his written text*) I hurt my leg. I fell over on the driveway.

11) T: (*revoicing Charlie's written text with rising intonation to clarify the upcoming word which Charlie has attempted to spell*). On the …?

12) C: (*rereads*) driveway.

13) T: driveway?

14) C: Mmm. That's all!

15) T: Oh, did you? My goodness!

The next series of turns show how Eleanor actively guides Charlie to an understanding of an audience and of an audience's understanding. She wants to enhance his monitoring of meaning in his writing. Eleanor models difficulty working out the meaning of his text, inviting him to share her confusion. Revoicing the text with deliberate expression, she makes it more salient for him to think about. She pauses, allowing him the opportunity to respond before she tells him explicitly that they need to say something else and asks him to close his eyes to better 'see' what she is driving at. She revoices the text again, pausing expectantly. When understanding does not dawn, she adjusts her support to a higher level asking a question intended to lead Charlie to think in particular ways about the problem at hand. Then she tells him that they need to write the cause and effect sequence into the piece 'so people will know' and she rehearses

for him a clarified version (which, incidentally, he appropriates in his writing next day in terms of the intent but not the syntactical construction. Charlie seems to have begun the task of experimenting independently).

16) T: OK! (*Eleanor revoices again from Charlie's text. Her voice is slow and thoughtful*) I hurt my leg (title). I hurt my leg. I fell over on the driveway. (*Eleanor pauses. She looks puzzled and seems to be thinking.*)

17) T: We need to say something else here. It sounds (*pausing*) Listen, when I read it- when I read it to you (*pausing*). Close your eyes and listen.

18) C: (*Charlie closes his eyes.*)

19) T: (*Eleanor revoices Charlie's text again slowly and deliberately*) I hurt my leg … I fell over on the driveway. (*She pauses, looking at him and then continues with a question.*)

20) T: So … did you hurt your leg and THEN (*said loudly for emphasis*) you fell over on the driveway or did you hurt your leg BY (*said loudly for emphasis*) falling over on the driveway?
(*Another writer interrupts and a few seconds is spent talking with the child*)

21) T: (*returning her attention to Charlie*) OK. So did you hurt your leg and THEN you fell over on the driveway, or did you hurt your leg BECAUSE you fell over on the driveway?

22) C: Because of

23) T: OK Well, maybe we need to say that-so people will know.

24) T: (*rehearsing a clarified version of the story*) I hurt my leg BECAUSE (*said loudly for emphasis*) I fell over on the driveway!

25) T: Would you like to write ……..

This brief conference well illustrates talk that is both responsive and sensitive in its guidance. The support system is finely tuned to provide different levels of support as appropriate. The conference talk is goal directed, forward looking with the right amount of support offered.

Deliberately creating connections: Intertextual talk

The analysis we offer of the third approach to using talk suggests the need for a more deliberate focus than might currently occur in

New Zealand classrooms. The analysis again draws on the notion of talk as textual platform building on the Bakhtian idea of speech genres, namely, stable, socially defined types of utterances that give rise to helpful ways of thinking about the written word. It also draws on notions of explicit guidance and of enabling children to develop more control and awareness in their writing. Nevertheless, in this analysis, teachers' talk about text and particularly around the relationships between texts, it is argued, has the potential to help children build metalinguistic knowledge; to understand how texts work to achieve their communicative purposes and, specifically, to understand the 'linguistically contextualized' (Gee, 1990, 2001) nature of the language of the school.

The idea of intertextuality, generally considered as a social construction involving the juxtaposing of texts or connections made between texts, has been widely discussed (e.g., Shuart-Faris and Bloome, 2004). Interconnections can be seen in two ways: 'seeing a text as a kind of pastiche of bits and pieces from other texts or seeing it as part of a vast interrelated network composed of prior texts, present texts, and even future texts' (Nelson, 1998: 269). Furthermore, making connections can be understood as a form of transfer when an unfamiliar activity incorporates some features of a more familiar one (McNaughton, 2002).

As in the language experience lesson, children's language resources, their own, culturally situated oral text, can be the basis for teaching about writing. In a similar way to writing conferences, their oral texts, containing familiar content and using familiar language, can be resituated or recontextualized in school-like forms (Dyson, 1997). But also, their prior knowledge about and previous experience with texts can be garnered in the service of writing. We have analyzed transcripts of teachers in teacher-led parts of writing lessons and in guided reading to identify how, through talk, they connect with what children already know and have experienced. We see connections as being of four

main types and present, in some instances, brief examples from lessons to illustrate, commenting on how such talk serves writing.

Content-based connections

One form of connection is through a focus on comparing or contrasting content (e.g., themes, concepts, arguments, and characters). In an example from our work, the teacher is working with a group in a Year-1 classroom. She has seized a teaching moment and taken an opportunity that presented itself when one of the children skipped ahead looking at the pictures and noticed a snake. The child asked whether 'Rags' (in the book title) was the dog or the snake. Realizing that the child is thinking about the previous book where the snake was the main character, the teacher uses this confusion as a teaching opportunity. The point she makes about telling a story from a point of view draws on the fact that the books (in this series) have some of the same characters but, in different stories, a different character is fore-grounded and tells it from his/her viewpoint.

Structurally based connections

Another form of connection made in teacher-led talk involves a specific reference to how texts work, largely linguistically, to achieve their purpose. This might include identifying features of text like the elements of structure at text or local level (main point, topic sentence, or elements of story schema like complication and resolution) or language resources like choice of particular words, the use of figurative language, or the use of grammatical structures like passive constructions or tense. In our example (with Year-5 children), the teacher is making a link between the text they are reading (the second chapter of 'No Safe Harbour' by David Hill) and a movie text that has a similar setting/context. The link, however, is to do with the schematic structure of the narrative and the notion of build-up to a climax.

1) T: Just quickly, tell the person next to you what you think is going to happen next.
2) C: [talking]
3) T: OK thank you. What do you think B ... could happen next?
4) C1: Um on the way the ferry starts leaving they might hit a sand bar or something and they might have to turn at the right place and smash into the sand bar and tip over or else it could just crash beside some rocks on the wharf.
5) T: Gee that's a lot to happen on one page isn't it [Teacher laughs] Well done.
6) C2: Or they could both drown.
7) T: Yes only chapter two but yes good thinking. J ...?
8) C3: Well they might start rescuing each other.
9) T: Yeah I know that you all know that the boats going to sink and as someone just said it's on the front. But I don't think it's going to start sinking in chapter two. Why do I think its not ... Why do you think that L ...?
10) C4: Cos um if they sink they'll probably die and there won't be anything to say at the end.
11) T: Could be ... and do you think the author's going to want to keep us in suspense a little bit longer just yet?
12) C: [A few children say ...] Yeah.
13) T: Okay if you went to the movies ... who has seen Titanic?
14) C: [Some children raise their hands]
15) T: Like from the minute Jack got on the boat, did you just want it to sink next?
16) C: [A few children say No]
17) T: Did a whole three hour movie have to keep going first?
18) C: [A few children say: Yeah]
19) T: OK it's the same, probably the same with this book.

Process-based connections

A third way in which connections are made highlights for learners the links between the processes of reasoning or problem-solving strategies used to make meaning in both reading and writing. These strategies and processes may involve predicting, questioning, or searching for evidence to confirm

or disconfirm. Examples include showing that the act of summarizing to capture the gist is used both to aid comprehension when reading and to make decisions about adding to or revising written text. In a writing lesson we observed, the Year-4 children are using a familiar and much loved text 'Greedy Cat' to generate some content for an argument that they are going to write. They are cued to pose questions in order to produce argument points to use in their writing in the same way that a reader might generate questions in order to locate material in a text to test predictions or to establish content to help comprehension.

Connections with children's cultural and linguistic resources

The final type of connection is one that is familiar to, and is the most common form of connection made by, New Zealand primary teachers (Parr and McNaughton, 2007), namely, making the connection between experiential text and either reading or writing. Activating prior knowledge may aid comprehension or aid retrieval of relevant content in writing. One example of this comes from a lesson with older children researching mangroves. The teacher aims to help understanding of a text describing how mangroves work to clean the environment through an analogy to something the children are likely to understand through their past experience.

1) T: Have you ever put something like a carnation into dye and seen what happens? Did you guys do that last year?

And the discussion continues about the process of absorption.

These examples show teachers in classrooms using talk as a textual platform, to make explicit for children the intertextual nature of language, the borrowings, revoicing, and echoes. Given the theoretical significance of making such connections, our argument is that perhaps established approaches might be adapted to better focus on such connections.

CONCLUSION

We have described theoretical rationales for the role of talk in writing and these have been applied to and elaborated with descriptions of instructional practices. There is a rich empirical base for arguing that the assumed functions of talk in terms of promoting agency and textual platforms are present in well-tried approaches that are designed to recruit talk to promoting writing. We have suggested that an underutilized focus in writing instruction is making intertextual connections explicitly.

Much of what we have presented is in the form of idealized descriptions. They are ideal in two ways. The first is that clearly some talk taking place in structured literacy events does not function effectively to build agency and to create platforms. We need extended analyses of these 'failures' to be effective (e.g., Glasswell et al., 2003). Analyses of when the instruction breaks down are necessary so that we understand better how to create the most effective conditions especially for those children whose linguistic and cultural resources are not well matched with classroom talk and classroom events (Dyson, 1997).

They are ideal in a second sense. What is surprising from an examination of this research base is that there are few examples of deliberate systematic investigation of the assumed significance of talk to writing. Rich descriptions are available and these are often associated with teachers known to be effective (e.g., Dyson, 1989, 1997, 2003; Glasswell, 1999). Transfer of ideas from collaborative discussions to writing has been demonstrated by Reznitskaya et al. (2008). But Pearson et al. (2007) note that a specific research base, which demonstrates the effects of talk on aspects of writing, in their case on the use of shared vocabulary, is missing. We conclude this chapter with a suggestion that one aspect of further research would be to investigate more deliberately the effects of various approaches, testing out the properties that enable these approaches to be maximally effective, and establishing how and in what ways they are effective for developing writers.

REFERENCES

Ashton-Warner, S. (1963) *Teacher*, London: Secker and Warburg.

Atwell, N. (1998) *In the Middle: New Understandings About Writing, Reading, and Learning* (second edn.), Portsmouth, NH: Boynton/Cook.

Bakhtin, M.M. (1986) *Speech Genres and Other Late Essays*, Tr. V.M. McGee, Austin, TX: University of Texas Press.

Beach, R., Friedrich, T., and Williams, D.J. (2005) 'Writing and response in the secondary school', in R. Indrisano and J.R. Paratore (eds), *Learning to Write, Writing to Learn: Theory and Research in Practice*, Boston: International Reading Association. pp.156–175.

Bereiter, C. and Scardamalia, M. (1987) *The Psychology of Written Composition*, Hillsdale, NJ: Lawrence Erlbaum.

Bomer, R. and Laman, T. (2004) 'Positioning in a primary writing workshop: Joint action in the discursive production of writing subjects', *Research in the Teaching of English*, 38: 420–462.

Britton, J. (1970) *Language and Learning*, Harmondsworth, UK: Penguin.

Bruner, J. (1986) *Actual Minds, Possible Worlds*, Cambridge, MA: Harvard University Press.

Cappello, M. (2006) 'Under construction: Voice and identity development in writing workshop', *Language Arts*, 83(6): 482.

Cazden, C. (1988) *Classroom Discourse: The Language of Teaching and Learning*, Portsmouth, NH: Heinemann.

Cazden, C. (2001) *Classroom Discourse: The Language of Teaching and Learning* (second edn.), Portsmouth, NH: Heinemann.

Clay, M.M. (1975) *What Did I Write?*, Auckland, New Zealand: Heinemann.

Clay, M.M. (1991) *Becoming Literate: The Construction of Inner Control*, Auckland: Heinemann Education.

Clay, M.M. (1993) *Reading Recovery: A Guidebook for Teachers in Training*, Auckland, New Zealand: Heinemann.

Clay, M.M. (2005) *Literacy Lessons Designed for Individuals*, Portsmouth, NH: Heinemann.

Clay, M.M. and Cazden, C.B. (1990) 'A Vygotskian interpretation of reading recovery', in L.C. Moll (ed.), *Vygotsky and Education: Instructional Implications and Applications of Sociohistorical Psychology*, Cambridge: Cambridge University Press.

Crystal, D. (1987) *Child Language, Learning, and Linguistics: An Overview for the Teaching and Therapeutic Professions* (second edn.), London: E. Arnold.

Daiute, C. and Dalton, B. (1993) 'Collaboration between children learning to write: Can novices be masters?' *Cognition and Instruction*, 1: 281–333.

Dyson, A.H. (1989) *Multiple Worlds of Child Writers: Friends Learning to Write*, New York: Teachers College Press.

Dyson, A.H. (1997) *Writing Superheroes: Contemporary Childhood, Popular Culture and Classroom Literacy*, New York: Teachers College Press.

Dyson, A.H. (2000) 'Writing and the sea of voices: Oral language in, around and about writing', in R. Indrisano and J.R. Squires (eds), *Perspectives on Writing: Research Theory and Practice*, Newark, DL: International Reading Association. pp.45–65.

Dyson, A.H. (2002) 'The drinking god factor: A writing development remix for "all" children', *Written Communication*, 19(4): 545–577.

Dyson, A.H. (2003) *The Brothers and Sisters Learn to Write: Popular Literacies in Childhood and School Cultures*, New York: Teachers College Press.

Dyson, A.H. (2006) 'On saying it right (write): "Fix-its" in the foundations of learning to write', *Research in the Teaching of English*, 41: 8–42.

Elley, W., Cutting, B., Mangubhai, F., and Hugo, C. (1996) 'Lifting literacy levels with story books: Evidence from the South Pacific, Singapore, Sri Lanka, and South Africa', Paper presented at the World Conference on Literacy, Philadelphia, PA.

Ferreiro, E. and Teberosky, A. (1982) *Literacy Before Schooling*, Portsmouth, NH: Heinemann.

Flood, J., Lapp, D., and Buhr, W.I.R. (2005). 'Middle school writing: 9 essential components model', in R. Indrisano and J.R. Paratore (eds), *Learning to Write, Writing to Learn: Theory and Research in Practice*, Boston: International Reading Association. pp.120–136.

Gee, J.P. (1990) *Social Linguistics and Literacies*, London: Falmer.

Gee, J.P. (2001) 'Reading as situated language: A sociocognitive perspective', *Journal of Adolescent and Adult Literacy*, 44: 714–725.

Glasswell, K. (1999) 'The patterning of difference: Teachers and children constructing development in writing'. PhD thesis, University of Auckland, Auckland, New Zealand.

Glasswell, K. and Parr, J.M. (nd) 'Making the most of teachable moments in writing'. Unpublished paper, University of Auckland.

Glasswell, K., Parr, J.M., and McNaughton, S. (2003) 'Working with William: Teaching, learning and the joint construction of a struggling writer', *The Reading Teacher*, 56(5): 494–500.

Goffman, E. (1981) *Forms of Talk*, Philadelphia: University of Pennsylvania Press.

Goldenberg, C. (1992) 'Instructional conversations: Promoting comprehension through discussion', *The Reading Teacher*, 46: 316–326.

Graves, D. (1983) *Writing: Teachers and Children at Work*, Portsmouth, NH: Heinemann.

Graves, D., Tuyay, S., and Green, J. (2004) 'What I've learned from teachers of writing', *Language Arts*, 82(2): 88.

Heath, S.B. (1983) *Ways with Words: Language, Life and Work in Communities and Classrooms*, New York: Cambridge University Press.

Higgins, L., Flower, L., and Petraglia, J. (1992) 'Planning text together: The role of critical reflection in student collaboration', *Written Communication*, 9(1): 48–84.

Holme, R. (2004) *Literacy: An Introduction*, Edinburgh: Edinburgh University Press.

Kelly, P.R., Klein, A.F., and Pinnell, G.S. (1996) 'Learning through conversation', *Running Record*, 8: 1–3.

Larson, J. (1995) 'Talk matters: The role of pivot in the distribution of literacy knowledge among novice writers', *Linguistics and Education*, 7: 277–302.

Lewis, M. (2000) 'The promise of dynamic systems approaches for an integrated account of human development', *Child Development*, 71: 36–43.

McCarthey, S.J. (1994) 'Authors, text, and talk: The internalization of dialogue from social interaction during writing', *Reading Research Quarterly*, 29: 201–231.

McNaughton, S. (1995) *Patterns of Emergent Literacy: Processes of Development and Transition*, Auckland, New Zealand: Oxford University Press.

McNaughton, S. (2002) *Meeting of Minds*, Wellington, New Zealand: Learning Media.

Mercer, N. (1995) *The Guided Construction of Knowledge: Talk Amongst Teachers and Learners*, Clevedon: Multilingual Matters.

Mercer, N. (2004) 'Development through dialogue', in T. Grainger (ed.), *The RoutledgeFalmer Reader in Language and Literacy*, London: RoutledgeFalmer. pp.121–137.

Ministry of Education (2003) *Effective Literacy Practice in Years 1 to 4*, Wellington: Learning Media.

Nelson, N. (1998) 'Reading and writing contextualized', in N. Nelson and R.C. Calfee (eds), *The Reading Writing Connection: Ninety-Seventh Yearbook of the National Society of the Study of Education*, Chicago, IL: University of Chicago Press. pp.266–285.

Nelson, N. and Calfee, R. (1998) 'The reading-writing connection viewed historically', in N. Nelson and R.C. Calfee (eds), *The Reading Writing Connection: Ninety-Seventh Yearbook of the National Society of the Study of Education*, Chicago, IL: University of Chicago Press. pp.1–52.

Parr, J.M. and McNaughton, S. (2007) 'Making connections: The nature and occurrence of links in literacy teaching and learning', Paper presented to the Annual Meeting of the American Educational Research Association, Chicago, April.

Patthey-Chavez, G.G. and Clare, L. (1996) 'Task, talk and text: The influence of instructional conversation on bilingual writers', *Written Communication*, 13: 515–563.

Pearson, P.D., Hiebert, E.H., and Kamil, M.L. (2007) 'Vocabulary assessment: What we know and what we need to learn', *Reading Research Quarterly*, 42(2): 282–296.

Reznitskaya, A., Anderson, R.C., Dong, T., Li, Y., Kim, I-L and Kim, S-Y. (2008). Learning to think well: Application of argument schema theory to literacy instruction. In C. Block and S. Parris (Eds.) *Comprehension Instruction: Research-Based Practices* (2nd ed.). New York: Guilford Publishing. pp.196–213.

Rogoff, B. (1990) *Apprenticeship in Thinking*, New York: Oxford University Press.

Roskos, K.A., Christie, J.F., and Richgels, D.J. (2003) 'The essentials of early literacy instruction', *Journal of National Association for the Education of Young Children*, www.naeyc.org/resources/journal, accessed May, 2007.

Shuart-Faris, N. and Bloome, D. (eds) (2004) *Uses of Intertextuality in Classrooms and Educational Research*, Greenwich, CT: Information Age Publishing.

Sperling, M. (1996) 'Revisiting the writing-speaking connection: Challenges for research on writing and writing instruction', *Review of Educational Research*, 66(1): 53–86.

Teale, W. and Sulzby, E. (1989) 'Emergent literacy: New perspectives', in D.S. Strickland and L.M. Morrow (eds), *Emerging Literacy: Young Children Learn to Read and Write*, Newark, Delaware: International Reading Association. pp.1–15.

Tharp, R. and Gallimore, R. (1988) *Rousing Minds to Life: Teaching, Learning and Schooling in Social Context*, Cambridge: Cambridge University Press.

Vygotsky, L. (1962) *Thought and Language*, Cambridge, MA: MIT Press.

Vygotsky, L. (1978) *Mind in Society. The Development of Higher Psychological Processes*, Cambridge, MA: Harvard University Press.

Wenger, E. (1999) *Communities of Practice: Learning, Meaning, and Identity*, Cambridge: Cambridge University Press.

Wertsch, J.V. and Stone, C.A. (1985) 'The concept of internalization in Vygotsky's account of the genesis of higher mental functions', in J. Wertsch (ed.), *Culture, Communication and Cognition: Vygotskian Perspectives*, Cambridge, England: Cambridge University Press. pp.162–179.

Wittgenstein, L. (1953) *Philosophical Investigations*, Tr. G.E.M. Anscomb, Oxford, England: Blackwell and Mott.

17

Learning to Use Alphabetic Writing

Charles Read

The initial process of learning to use alphabetic writing is worthy of a chapter in a handbook such as this one, because it is essential for writing in most languages, and it includes complexities, some of which are not immediately evident, that confound some children and even some adult learners. Truly learning to write alphabetically must achieve *productivity*; that is, one must be able, in principle at least, to write any word in one's vocabulary, whether or not one has seen it in print.[1] Young children and adults of low literacy may be able to write a few words, such as their own name, by printing a memorized string of letters, but productive alphabetic literacy for tens of thousands of words is not normally acquired by a prodigious feat of memorization. Instead, one must master a specific kind of system.

ALPHABETIC WRITING

An alphabetic writing system is one in which spellings (letters or sequences of letters) represent individual speech sounds, mainly. In linguistic terms, graphemes represent phonemes. In this respect, alphabetic writing contrasts with syllabaries, such as those used for Japanese, and with morphographic writing, such as the systems used for the various forms of Chinese. In syllabic writing, the symbols represent entire syllables, and in morphographic writing, the symbols represent *morphemes*, or individual meaningful units. In Chinese, these morphemes are usually one syllable in length, but as in other languages, but to a greater extent than most, one pronunciation may express different meanings (such as the syllable *case* in English). The various meanings are typically represented by different symbols in a morphographic writing system. Thus, the real target is the meaning unit, not the pronunciation, although many Chinese characters include references to pronunciation, secondarily.

Alphabetic writing has come to be very widely adopted. Even languages that normally employ a nonalphabetic writing system, such as Japanese or Chinese, have alphabetic alternatives for special purposes, such as electronic transmission or communications for foreigners, as on the supplementary street signs in major Chinese cities. Languages use a variety of alphabets, such as those employed for Arabic, English, Korean, Russian, and Thai, but they are all using the same basic insight: that syllables can be thought of as composed of individual speech sounds, each of which can then be represented by conventional spellings. Even when an orthography includes many anomalies, as that of English notoriously does, it may still be fundamentally alphabetic.

Each type of writing system has advantages and disadvantages. One advantage of Chinese characters is that they can be read across the vast territory in which they are used, crossing boundaries of dialects and even languages. A character may be pronounced one way in the North and a completely different way in the South, but its meaning is usually the same. One disadvantage is that mastering the system does indeed require a massive effort of memorization. Literacy in Chinese means learning tens of thousands of characters, although relationships among characters make this accomplishment more attainable than it would be if the characters were arbitrary.

To some extent, alphabetic writing has the opposite advantages and disadvantages. The set of symbols is small: in English, the twenty-six letters of the alphabet plus a number of digraphs, such as *th* and *sh*, and other multiletter spellings. Having mastered the alphabetic principle and a relatively small number of sound-spelling correspondences, one can write thousands of words. These spellings are not as portable as in Chinese; a reader of another language, even a closely related one like Dutch, cannot comprehend a text in English in the way that a speaker of Cantonese can glean the meaning of a text written in Mandarin. However, probably the most significant disadvantage of alphabetic writing is that essential first step: one must grasp the alphabetic principle and learn to analyze syllables into their component speech sounds. While that analysis may seem transparent to people who have mastered it, it is not self-evident and in fact poses difficulty to many learners. We will consider that difficulty in the following section. It may help to explain why alphabetic writing was historically the last form to be invented, long after syllabic and morphographic writing, not to mention pictographs.

Classic accounts of writing systems are those of Gelb, 1963, and Coulmas, 1989. For a deeper and more extensive discussion of writing systems in relation to learning to read, see Gleitman and Rozin, 1977.

LEARNING TO WRITE ALPHABETICALLY

Learning to write, in any system, is not a single cognitive step but rather involves components of knowledge and skill. In this section, we will consider some of these components. These are not put forward as stages in a developmental sequence but as logical components of the learning process. Some of them presuppose others, but actual development, as with any other complex skill, typically proceeds at an irregular pace and in a sequence that varies from one person to another.

A primitive but essential component of learning to write is the notion that symbols can represent language. A child may scribble an apparently random mark, or a familiar symbol or letter, and announce that it 'says' something. While there may be no discernible relationship between the mark and the message, a notable and quite specific cognitive achievement is implied: the idea that a mark can represent a particular linguistic unit, such as a word or sentence. Note that not all symbols do that; an icon such as the Christian cross carries great meaning to some people but does not stand for a particular word or sentence, as a piece of writing does.

A second component (again, not necessarily second in sequence) of learning to write is learning to recognize and to create conventional symbols – not scribbles but letters, for example. Recognizing a letter often goes with knowing its conventional name, but it might mean simply knowing that that shape *is* a letter, one of a particular set of marks. Likewise, forming or manipulating letters might involve pencil and paper or a keyboard or a set of plastic letters.

A third component is associating one or more of these recognizable symbols with something, such as connecting *M* with McDonalds restaurants. Knowing that an *M* of a particular size, shape, color, and location is associated with a certain restaurant is generic symbolic behavior, but connecting any *M* with the restaurant or, better yet, the name, is closer to writing.

Still closer to alphabetic writing is knowing that a letter is connected, not to just one object or one word, but to many – that *M* is connected not only to McDonalds but also to Max or to Michigan. 'Knowing' in this context does not mean that a child could articulate this concept, of course, but simply that the child makes multiple connections, which might be demonstrated in various ways. As the example suggests, the connection is often to the initial sound or letter of a word or syllable, but not necessarily.

The two most critical components of alphabetic literacy, however, are acquiring 'phonemic awareness' and learning the alphabetic principle, that spellings represent speech sounds. Phonemic awareness is essentially the concept that syllables are made up of individual speech sounds, or phonemes. Demonstrating the critical role of this concept in learning to read and write is arguably the most important outcome from literacy research of the 1980s and 1990s. Conceiving of a syllable as made up of speech sounds is necessarily an abstraction, not a physical reality. Within syllables and words, speech sounds blend and influence each other, so that what we think of an individual sound, say /p/, is actually a class of different pronunciations in different contexts. The actual sounds, and the ways in which they are classified, differ from one language to another. What counts as a /p/ in Hindi is not what counts as a /p/ in English. Moreover, unlike syllables, not all speech sounds are pronounceable by themselves, and even those that are, rarely occur in isolation except in instructional settings. For more on the structure of speech in relation to alphabetic writing, see Gleitman and Rozin, 1977, and Liberman et al., 1989.

Research tasks that have been used to measure phonemic awareness include recognizing or creating rhyme or alliteration, or pronouncing syllables with a phonemic manipulation, such as saying a syllable with an initial sound added or deleted. These same tasks can be used instructionally to foster phonemic awareness. For more on phonemic awareness and its development, see Bradley and Bryant, 1985, and Goswami and Bryant, 1990.

The alphabetic principle, that letters (more precisely, spellings) represent phonemes, is of course the heart of the matter. Both of these concepts, phoneme and spelling, are abstractions in the sense that they name classes of physically different entities, and the mapping between the two becomes harder to recognize within a syllable than at the beginning or end. While it may seem a simple step from knowing that *M* somehow goes with words that begin with /m/ to learning the true nature of alphabetic writing, that is actually a considerable accomplishment. For more on that principle, see Rozin and Gleitman, 1977.

Beyond mastering the alphabetic principle in this fundamental sense, there are the aspects of spelling that are generally the focus of formal instruction: learning to use the *standard* sound-spelling correspondences of an alphabetic orthography, including contextual constraints (e.g., /k/ is spelled CK in English only at the ends of syllables). In addition, there are nonalphabetic functions of orthography, which reflect relationships in meaning or historical derivation (e.g., *sign* reflects its relationship to *signal* and *signature*, not solely its pronunciation; /f/ is spelled PH in words of Greek origin). Critics of English orthography have been urging reform for at least four centuries (Venezky, 1970: 30–33), but embodying relationships in meaning may aid the fluent reader, even though it creates difficulty for the learner. There are also complications that serve no known purpose for the reader or the writer, of course.

Whatever intricacies of orthography a child must master in school, the most significant cognitive achievement comes at the outset: mastering the alphabetic principle. Historically, alphabetic writing was the last major system to develop, thousands of years after other forms. A reasonable speculation is that prior to the gradual emergence and spread of alphabetic writing, even literate people did not have access to the conception that makes it possible, the notion of identifiable speech sounds within syllables. While this conception seems transparent to those of us who write alphabetically, it may not have been to writers before the invention of the alphabet, and it may not be to nonalphabetic writers today. Although puns and other jokes, as well as the recognition of mispronunciations and misunderstandings, often have to do with individual speech sounds, it may be that such events do not ordinarily stimulate phonemic awareness at the level required to learn alphabetic writing.

DOES PHONEMIC AWARENESS DEVELOP OUTSIDE OF ALPHABETIC WRITING?

Liberman et al. (1977) raised essentially this question, referring to phonemic awareness as 'phonetic segmentation':

> On the one hand, the increase in ability to segment phonetically might result from the reading instruction that begins between [ages] five and six. Alternatively, it might be a manifestation of some kind of intellectual maturation. The latter possibility might be tested by a developmental study of segmentation skills in a language community such as the Chinese, where the orthographic unit is the word and where reading instruction therefore does not demand the kind of phonetic analysis needed in an alphabetic system (pp. 212–213).

Morais et al. (1979) tested this question by comparing literate and illiterate adults in rural Portugal. They concluded:

> Awareness of speech as a sequence of phones is thus not attained spontaneously in the course of general cognitive growth, but demands some specific training, which for most persons, is probably provided by learning to read in the alphabetic system. (p. 323, abstract)

Read et al. (1986) studied literate adults in China, as had been suggested by Liberman et al., adapting the methodology of Morais et al. They found a nearly absolute distinction: adults who had once learned alphabetic writing for Chinese or some other language could identify and manipulate speech sounds within syllables, while those who were equally literate in Chinese characters but had never written alphabetically could not. They concluded:

> We can now add [to the evidence of Morais et al.] that [the skill of locating and manipulating phonemes within syllables] does not develop even with seven years of schooling and forty years of reading and writing non-alphabetically in a language rich in implicit examples like rhymes, minimal pairs, and phonetic radicals [within Chinese characters], not to mention Spoonerisms. Once a segmental conception has developed, however, it may outlast the fluency in reading [alphabetically]. (p. 43)

Thus, a reasonable conclusion on the evidence so far is that for many, if not most, people, it is learning to read and write alphabetically that stimulates phonemic awareness, rather than the other way around. One can recognize puns, rhymes, mispronunciations, and other everyday speech events without perceiving them as turning upon individual speech sounds. For most people, only alphabetic writing actually *requires* phonemic awareness.

DIFFICULTY IN ACHIEVING PHONEMIC AWARENESS

Not only does phonemic awareness not necessarily emerge as a result of cognitive maturation, experience with spoken language, or even nonalphabetic literacy, but in fact it is difficult for some learners to achieve. Considering the long historical period required for the genesis of alphabetic writing, perhaps it is not surprising that the phonemic principle continues to be obscure to many children and adult learners today. Most of the evidence for this difficulty comes from studies of reading, in part because reading research is far more extensive and better funded than research on writing processes.

Both of the recent reports of major national panels in the United States on reading research and educational practice give extensive attention to phonemic awareness and its development. Snow et al. (eds) 1998, call it 'key to understanding the logic of the alphabetic principle and thus to the learnability of phonics and spelling' (p. 52). The technical report of the National Reading Panel (2000a) begins with half a chapter on phonemic awareness instruction, concluding from a meta-analysis of ninety-six controlled comparisons that 'teaching children to manipulate phonemes in words was highly effective across all the literacy domains and outcomes', including both reading and spelling (pp. 2–3). The widely distributed summary of that report (2000b) goes further, concluding that 'PA training was the cause of improvement in students' phonemic awareness, reading, and spelling' (p. 7). While both versions make clear that phonemic awareness is not a sufficient condition for learning to read and write, they strongly imply that it is a necessary one and that for many children, explicit instruction is essential.

In one of the most complete and reliable accounts combining evidence from basic and instructional research, Adams (1990: 328–329) sums up the situation this way:

> In contrast [to word awareness], the development of phonemic awareness is often slow and difficult. Among those children who will successfully learn to read but are not sensitive to phonemes before reading instruction is begun, phonemic awareness seems to develop alongside their word recognition skills. On the other hand, an absence or lack of phonemic awareness appears to be characteristic of children who are failing or have failed to learn to read.

Although phonemic awareness is not spontaneously acquired, it can be successfully taught. Furthermore, when reading instruction is methodically coupled with such training, the success rates are dramatic.

Considering that some degree of phonemic awareness appears to be a prerequisite for achieving productive alphabetic writing, as opposed to producing memorized sequences of letters, the evidence that while it may be difficult, it is teachable, is crucial.

Cooper et al. (2002) studied the development of phonological awareness, defined as the segmentation and blending of phonemes, in a relatively small sample of children from kindergarten to second grade. Their analysis suggests that receptive and expressive oral language development contributes significantly to phonological awareness, which in turn influences the acquisition of early reading.

CHILDREN'S INVENTED SPELLING

While these prerequisites to alphabetic writing may not emerge spontaneously, even in adulthood, some children do begin to write productively before formal instruction. Read (1971, 1975, 1986) describes this phenomenon, analyzing spellings produced by thirty-two preschool children. The analysis focuses on nonstandard spellings, because those must be to some extent created, rather than copied from dictation or print. In order to create spellings, these children must have acquired some degree of phonemic awareness and understanding of the alphabetic principle. In addition, they knew some letter names and some conventions of standard spelling. This partial knowledge gave them what they needed to begin writing messages to parents, captions on drawings, or brief narratives, such as:

YUTS A LADE YET FEHEG AND HE KOT FLEPR

Once a lady went fishing, and she caught Flipper. (C. Chomsky, 1979)

The above example illustrates the role of partial knowledge of letter names and standard spellings. The author wanted to write 'once' (a standard beginning for stories), but how to spell it? 'Once' and 'went' begin with the sound /w/, and so does the name of the letter *Y*. Letter names often begin with a sound that the letter conventionally represents, so why not use *Y* to represent /w/?

Read's emphasis, however, was on other, less evident, phonological bases for children's invented spelling. One example in the forego-ing is the use of *E* to spell the vowel of 'fishing' and 'Flipper' (/I/). In the sample reported in Read (1975), this spelling occurred in nearly 23% of the instances of that vowel by children younger than six years, second only to the standard spelling *I* and far more frequently than any other spell-ing. Why should *E* be the most frequent nonstandard spelling? Read's proposal involves the name of the letter *E*, which begins with a vowel sound very similar to that in 'Flipper'. Spellings of this same sort occur frequently for virtually all vowels that do not correspond directly to letter-names. As in spelling 'once' with a *Y*, a child who has a considerable degree of phonemic awareness along with a partial knowledge of letter names and standard spelling corre-spondences can build on that knowledge to invent spellings as needed.

A different sort of phonetic judgment is seen at the end of 'FLEPR'. What follows the /p/ is really just one sound – an /r/-coloured vowel in American pronunciation or simply a vowel in most British production. Therefore, it is not correct to say that in this spelling, which is typical of young children's writing, a vowel sound has been omitted. Rather, a single vowel sound is represented by a single letter, the most plausible one for American pronunciation.

Even more striking to most parents and teachers is the spelling *CHR* for /tr/, as in CHRIE for 'try'. At the beginning of a syl-lable in English, /tr/ is *affricated*, that is, produced in a way that creates considerable turbulence; this is not true, for example, of the /t/ in 'tie', which is released more abruptly, producing a different sound. Phonetic nuances such as these have to be built into software that produces synthetic speech; without them, the speech does not sound natural. A related affricated sound is the one we usually spell *CH* in standard spelling, as in 'chime'. A child who knows that and who wants to spell initial /tr/ as in 'try', faces a choice: is it more like the sound spelled *CH* or the one spelled *T*? Phonetically, there is no simple answer to this question; it is a choice between two different similarities. It is entirely plausi-ble that the affrication is more salient to some children, so that they choose CHR for /tr/.

In Read's sample, some of these invented spellings occurred even at age six or seven. This is not surprising, because some teachers and some curricula, such as some Montessori schools, encourage children to write more fluently, not stopping to check spellings at first and not avoiding words whose standard spelling they do not know. Treiman (1993) provides an in-depth account of the spelling of 43 first-graders in one classroom in the United States. She observes many of the spelling patterns that Read described as well as others, and she considers more closely the context in which those spellings occur, including nonphonological influences. In other publications, Treiman has examined various aspects of children's invented spell-ing in detail, including the role of letter names (Treiman and Kessler, 2003; Treiman et al., 2001) and that of syllable structure, including the distinction between the onset and the rime of syllables (Treiman and Zukowski, 1996).

Invented spelling and the development of spelling more generally have been studied in languages other than English. In such stud-ies, one can see the language-specific inter-actions among sound system, orthography, and instruction that yield differing patterns of development. For examples, see Leong and Joshi, 1997; Read, 1986, Chapter 4; Perfetti et al. (eds), 1997; and Treiman (ed.), 1997.

WHAT WE CAN LEARN FROM INVENTED SPELLINGS

These young spellers do not contradict the observation that acquiring the foundations of alphabetic writing can be difficult for many learners. What the invented spellings show is that in some home and (pre)school contexts, with a considerable degree of phonemic awareness and partial knowledge of letter names and standard spellings, some children can extend that knowledge in order to spell new words. In doing so, they seem to assume that spelling is a productive system, not just a big set of words to be memorized. In extending their knowledge to meet their needs, they seem to rely much more than adults do on phonetic relationships, such as those between letter names and the sounds they wish to represent. In several striking cases, they perceive those relationships accurately and represent them in a manner that is plausible, both linguistically and in relation to their partial knowledge of spelling.

Another lesson to be learned from children's invented spelling is that writing provides a window into cognitive development, different from and in some ways clearer than the window provided by reading. Far more research, and far more debate over instruction, has concentrated on the development of reading than of writing. Because writing yields a durable and tangible product, and because the writing process can be more directly observed than that of reading, it gives us an opportunity to study the development of literacy in detail and at various levels.

A parallel might be seen in asking readers to read aloud, a venerable and legitimate technique in instruction and research. However, reading aloud is not necessarily the same as silent reading, and the result, even when recorded or transcribed, is difficult to analyze. In the study of children's invented spelling, we see the potential for understanding developmental processes through writing.

These developmental processes are not simply the inverses of those in reading at the same age (Read, 1981), though that is what the commonplace 'encode/decode' terminology suggests. Young writers are also young readers, but they write in their own way words that they can read in standard orthography. They do not appear to assume that each word, or each phoneme, must have a unique representation or the same representation in writing as in reading. In fact, their reading often employs more varied strategies, with more attention to context, than their writing at the same age (Bissex, 1980). Studying writing in detail yields insights into development,

but not necessarily the same developments as in reading, or at the same pace. However, Ehri (1997) argues, "reading and spelling are one and the same, almost" in that they draw upon the same knowledge about the alphabetic system and the spellings of words.

Because the invented spellings illustrate so clearly what their writers do and do not know, they also help us to construct a better basis for instruction. Besides knowing that young spellers have a grasp of the alphabetic principle, we can tell which letter-names and which standard spellings they know. We can also see which phonological or other relationships shape their spellings. We may avoid giving inappropriate or even misleading corrections. For example, seeing a spelling like CHRIE for 'try', many parents and teachers might be inclined to explain that 'try begins with a /t/'. The more emphatically they pronounce 'tuh-rye', the less the initial phoneme sounds like the beginning of 'try', or the more they lengthen the release of the /t/ of 'try', the more they make it sound like what we spell *CH*. By distorting or exaggerating the sound in question, our instruction risks conveying the wrong message: that alphabetic spelling does not relate to sounds in a comprehensible way. Rather, the invented spelling represents one real and quite salient similarity, while the standard spelling represents another. Any practical alphabetic orthography categorizes sounds in some way; it is not, and should not be, a detailed phonetic transcription. Repeatedly, young spellers show that they too group sounds together in order to spell them, but they form different categories from those embodied in standard spelling in some cases, some of which reflect quite salient phonetic relationships.

FROM THE SCIENCE OF DEVELOPMENT TO THE ART OF INSTRUCTION

One widely adopted but controversial application of what we know about development has been by advocates of 'whole language' instruction, such as Sandra Wilde (1992; see especially Chapter 4). Starting from the observation that some young children write with pleasure if they do not stop to worry about the standard spelling of every word at first, Wilde urges teachers to encourage children to do so: 'Allowing children the freedom to write independently is the basic principle underlying the use of invented spelling in the classroom' (p. 57).

Wilde's approach relies in part on children learning to write from extensive experience with reading and being read to, as well as experience in writing: 'A large part of learning spelling and punctuation … occurs through large amounts of exposure to written language as a reader and practice in written language as a writer' (p. 61). Other scholars have challenged this tenet as requiring further substantiation, at least (Brown, 1990; Graham, 2000).

However, Wilde and other responsible advocates do not rely entirely on spontaneous or 'naturalistic' learning. Wilde recommends teaching standard spelling and punctuation in response to individual children's needs and levels of development. She suggests 'mini-lessons' for a whole class and individual interventions in response to what each child is ready to learn. She emphasizes teaching children to use classroom resources, including dictionaries and the teacher, to learn standard spelling for themselves, as they need it. What Wilde opposes is the traditional curriculum of periodic lists of words to be spelled and rules to be learned, on one schedule for an entire class without regard to individual differences. Although her recommendations rely on rich experience with written language, she does not suggest that it is sufficient for learning to read and spell.

It is reasonable to suppose that effective instruction builds on what children already know, even as it teaches conventional representations. This supposition has not, however, been put to a rigorous and extensive empirical test. Some other resources for teachers present solid information about English orthography and spelling development. Henderson (1990) discusses formal and informal spelling instruction in the elementary grades on the basis of the history of English spelling. Somewhat similarly, Henry (2003) distinguishes 'layers' of spelling in English – Anglo-Saxon, Latin, and Greek – as units of learning to spell. Bear et al. (2007) integrate spelling with the development of vocabulary and word knowledge more generally.

BEYOND SOUND-SPELLING CORRESPONDENCES

In languages with phonemically regular orthographies, such as Dutch, Spanish, Finnish, or Korean, mastering the standard sound-spelling correspondences is the main task in learning to write alphabetically. In almost all such cases, there are some contextual variations to be learned (e.g., sounds that have more than one spelling depending upon their position within a word) and a list of exceptional spellings for words borrowed from other languages, but the vast majority of words can be spelled properly with a small number of rules for each phoneme. Even in languages with more complex orthographies, such a set of rules constitutes the truly alphabetic part.

In English, another large piece of the orthography is not alphabetic but morphographic, akin to the writing system of Chinese, though using letters instead of characters. As noted earlier, *sign* embodies the same morpheme (meaningful unit) as in *signal* and *signature*, and the spelling makes that relationship evident, at the cost of departing from purely alphabetic representation. The same can be said of many other morphologically or historically derived forms. Perhaps the most frequent examples are the suffixes that mean {plural} for nouns or {past tense} for verbs; each is pronounced in three different ways, depending on the preceding sound, but these morphemes are spelled more consistently: -s or –es for {plural} and –ed for {past tense}. Consider, for instance, the pronunciations and spelling of *raced*, *raised*, and *rated*. Chomsky and Halle (1968), among many others, argued that this morphological consistency benefits the adult who is reading for meaning, although it may complicate the task of the child who is trying to master alphabetic writing. Treiman (1993, Chapter 10); Beers and Beers, 1992; Templeton, 1992, and Leong, 2000 all present evidence about learning such morphological and derivational relationships and their role in spelling.

ARE THERE STAGES IN MASTERING ALPHABETIC WRITING?

Given that some of the skills and knowledge needed for alphabetic writing appear to form a logical progression and that some spelling patterns are clearly more sophisticated than others, some scholars have hypothesized a sequence of stages in spelling development. In particular, the late Edmund H. Henderson and his students have done so, as in Templeton and Bear (1992). They have proposed approximately six stages that incorporate some of the features of invented spellings. Within that volume, Linnea Ehri (Chapter 12) presents a noteworthy overview and critique, along with her own proposal of four broader stages.

However, Varnhagen (1995) challenged the basic concept of stages as proposed by Henderson and his colleagues, pointing out that 'progression from stage to stage is not invariant' and suggesting that children 'appear to have the entire range of strategies available to them from a very early age' (p. 260). Varnhagen et al. (1997) analyzed the spellings in stories written by children in grades one to six. They examined the use of final silent –*e* to mark a 'long' vowel sound, as in *mate* versus *mat*, and the spellings of past tense in regular verb endings. Varnhagen et al. found not a progression of stages but rather steep development, particularly

between first and second grade. Instead of stages, they propose that spelling consists of multiple strategies that interweave. One should note, however, that they examined only two spelling patterns and that a finer-grained analysis earlier, for example, between kindergarten and second grade, might reveal more stage-like progression.

There is clearly an opportunity for research on this issue, because confirming or disconfirming that writing development proceeds in a predictable way is essential to understanding development, and that understanding in turn must underlie effective instruction and evaluation. No one doubts that spellings develop from crude first attempts to the standard forms, which in some languages incorporate multiple levels of representation, and that they pass through some recognizable variants along the way. However, the more consistency and depth we can find in this progression, the more spelling can tell us about the nature of development in literacy generally.

CONCLUSIONS

Within the last twenty-five years or so, we have come a long way in the study of how alphabetic writing develops. At one time, spelling 'errors' were classified in relation to standard spellings, as letters omitted, inserted, transposed, or substituted, for example. Although such analyses could be voluminous, not much insight came from them. We now know why: at early stages of development, what a learner writes is not merely an imperfectly remembered standard spelling. In fact, a learner may never have even seen the standard spelling of a word that she wishes to write. Rather, the spellings that learners produce are in many instances the result of an active effort, based on the sound of the word, including its syllabic structure, and a partial knowledge of the principles of standard spelling, including letter-names, sound-spelling correspondences, and spelling patterns, as well as, later in development, whatever the learner knows (or supposes) about the history and morphology of the word. We now know that spelling is like reading in that while focusing on the message, the learner attempts to integrate multiple kinds of information.

Because of that progress, we now appreciate that we are studying the development of alphabetic writing, not merely the memorization of spellings. We now know that writing at the level of spelling is comparable in complexity, though not generally parallel in processes, to reading at the level of word identification. Both are fundamental and in a sense pedestrian; they exist to serve the higher level thinking that really characterizes writing and reading. Nevertheless, spelling and word identification are both cognitive accomplishments in their own right, drawing upon multiple kinds of knowledge and following various courses of development that deserve further inquiry.

NOTE

1 This does not mean that one can spell any word correctly. It means that one can spell any word in a manner that reflects the orthography of the language, subject to the variations and errors that affect any human performance.

REFERENCES

Adams, M.J. (1990) *Learning to Read: Thinking and Learning About Print*, Cambridge, MA: MIT Press.

Bear, D., Invernizzi, M., Templeton, S., and Johnston, F. (2007) *Words Their Way: Word Study for Phonics, Vocabulary, and Spelling Instruction* (fourth edn.), Englewood Cliffs, NJ: Prentice Hall.

Beers, C.S. and Beers, J.W. (1992) 'Children's spelling of English inflectional morphology', in Templeton, Shane, and Bear, Donald R. (eds), *Development of Orthographic Knowledge and the Foundations of Literacy*, Hillsdale, NJ: Erlbaum Associates.

Bissex, G.L. (1980) *Gnys At Wrk: A Child Learns to Read and Write*, Cambridge, MA: Harvard University Press.

Bradley, L. and Bryant, P. (1985) *Rhyme and Reason in Reading and Spelling*, Ann Arbor: University of Michigan Press.

Brown, A.S. (1990) 'A review of recent research on spelling', *Educational Psychology Review*, 2(4): 365–397.

Chomsky, C. (1979) 'Approaching reading through invented spelling', in Lauren B. Resnick and Phyllis A. Weaver (eds), *The Theory and Practice of Early Reading*, Vol. 2, Hillsdale, NJ: Erlbaum Associates. pp.43–65.

Chomsky, N. and Halle, M. (1968) *The Sound Pattern of English*, New York: Harper & Row.

Cooper, D.H., Roth, F.P., Speece, D.L., and Schatschneider, C. (2002) 'The contribution of oral language skills to the development of phonological awareness', *Applied Psycholinguistics*, 23: 399–416.

Coulmas, F. (1989) *The Writing Systems of the World*, Oxford: Blackwell.

Ehri, L. (1992) 'Review and commentary: Stages of spelling development', in Templeton, Shane and Bear, Donald R. (eds), *Development of Orthographic Knowledge and the Foundations of Literacy*, Hillsdale, NJ: Erlbaum Associates.

Ehri, L. (1997) 'Learning to read and learning to spell are one and the same, almost', in Perfetti, C.A., Rieben, L., and Fayol, M. (eds), *Learning to Spell: Research, Theory, and Practice across Languages*, Mahwah, NJ: Erlbaum Associates.

Gelb, I.J. (1963) *A Study of Writing*, Chicago: University of Chicago Press.

Gleitman, L.R. and Rozin, P. (1977) 'The structure and acquisition of reading I: Relations between orthographies and the structure of language', in A.S. Reber and D.L. Scarborough (eds), *Toward a Psychology of Reading*, Hillsdale, NJ: Erlbaum Associates, Chapter 1.

Goswami, U. and Bryant, P. (1990) *Phonological Skills and Learning to Read*, Hove, East Sussex: Erlbaum Associates.

Graham, S. (2000) 'Should the natural learning approach replace spelling instruction?', *Journal of Educational Psychology*, 92(2): 235–247.

Henderson, E.H. (1990) *Teaching Spelling* (second edn.), Boston: Houghton Mifflin.

Henry, M.K. (2003) *Unlocking Literacy: Effective Decoding and Spelling Instruction*, Baltimore: Paul H. Brookes Publishing.

Leong, C.K. (2000) 'Rapid processing of base and derived forms of words and grades 4, 5, and 6 children's spelling', *Reading and Writing*, 12(3–4): 277–302.

Leong, C.K. and Joshi, R.M. (eds) (1997) *Cross-Language Studies of Learning to Spell: Phonologic and Orthographic Processing*, Dordrecht: Kluwer Academic.

Liberman, I.Y., Shankweiler, D., and Liberman, A.M. (1989) 'The alphabetic principle and learning to read', in Shankweiler, Donald and Liberman, Isabelle Y. (eds), *Phonology and Reading Disability: Solving the Reading Puzzle*, Ann Arbor: University of Michigan Press, Chapter 1.

Liberman, I.Y., Shankweiler, D., Liberman, A.M., Fowler, C., and Fischer, F.W. (1977) 'Phonetic segmentation and recoding in the beginning reader', in A.S. Reber and D. Scarborough (eds), *Toward a Psychology of Reading*, Hillsdale, NJ: Erlbaum Associates, Chapter 5.

Morais, J., Cary, L., Alegria, J., and Bertelson, P. (1979) 'Does awareness of speech as a sequence of phones arise spontaneously?', *Cognition*, 7: 323–331.

National Reading Panel (2000a) *Teaching Children to Read: An evidence-based assessment of the scientific research literature on reading and its implications for reading instruction: Reports of the subgroups* [Full Report], Washington, DC: National Institute of Child Health and Human Development. Available online at: http://www.nichd.nih.gov/publications/pubskey.cfm?from=reading.

National Reading Panel (2000b) *Teaching children to read: An evidence-based assessment of the scientific research literature on reading and its implications for reading instruction*, Washington, DC: National Institute of Child Health and Human Development.

Perfetti, C.A., Rieben, L., and Fayol, M. (eds) (1997) *Learning to Spell: Research, Theory, and Practice Across Languages*, Mahwah, NJ: Erlbaum Associates.

Read, C. (1971) 'Pre-school children's knowledge of English phonology', *Harvard Educational Review*, 41: 1–34.

Read, C. (1975) *Children's Categorization of Speech Sounds in English*, Urbana, IL: National Council of Teachers of English.

Read, C. (1981) 'Writing is not the inverse of reading for young children', in Carl H. Frederiksen and Joseph F. Dominic (eds), *Writing: The Nature, Development, and Teaching of Written Communication*, Hillsdale, NJ: Erlbaum Associates. pp.105–118.

Read, C. (1986) *Children's Creative Spelling*, London: Routledge & Kegan Paul.

Read, C., Zhang, Y., Nie, H., and Ding, B. (1986) 'The ability to manipulate speech sounds depends on knowing alphabetic writing', *Cognition*, 24: 31–44. Reprinted in Paul Bertelson (ed.) (1987) The Onset of Literacy: Cognitive Processes in Reading Acquisition, Cambridge, MA: MIT Press.

Rozin, P. and Gleitman, L.R. (1977) 'The structure and acquisition of reading II: The reading process and the acquisition of the alphabetic principle', in A.S. Reber and D.L. Scarborough (eds), *Toward a Psychology of Reading*, Hillsdale, NJ: Erlbaum Associates, Chapter 2.

Snow, C.E., Burns, M.S., and Griffin, P. (eds) (1998) *Preventing Reading Difficulties in Young Children*, Washington, DC: National Academy Press.

Templeton, S. (1992) 'Theory, nature, and pedagogy of higher-order orthographic development in older students', in S. Templeton and D.R. Bear (eds), *Development of Orthographic Knowledge and the Foundations of Literacy*, Hillsdale, NJ: Erlbaum Associates.

Templeton, S. and Bear, D.R. (eds) (1992) *Development of Orthographic Knowledge and the Foundations of Literacy*, Hillsdale, NJ: Erlbaum Associates.

Treiman, R. (1993) *Beginning to Spell*, Oxford: Oxford University Press.

Treiman, R. (ed.) (1997) *Spelling. Special issue of Reading and Writing: An Interdisciplinary Journal, 9*, [Also published as Treiman, R. (ed.) Spelling. Dordrecht, The Netherlands: Kluwer.]

Treiman, R. and Kessler, B. (2003) 'The role of letter names in the acquisition of literacy', in R. Kail (ed.), *Advances in Child Development and Behavior*, 31:105–135. San Diego: Academic Press.

Treiman, R., Sotak, L., and Bowman, M. (2001) 'The roles of letter names and letter sounds in connecting print and speech', *Memory & Cognition*, 29: 860–873.

Treiman, R. and Zukowski, A. (1996) 'Children's sensitivity to syllables, onsets, rimes, and phonemes', *Journal of Experimental Child Psychology*, 61: 193–215.

Varnhagen, C.K. (1995) 'Children's spelling strategies', in Virginia Berninger (ed.), *The Varieties of Orthographic Knowledge II: Relationships to Phonology, Reading, and Writing*, Dordrecht: Kluwer.

Varnhagen, C.K., Mccallum, M and Burstow, M. (1997) 'Is children's spelling naturally stage-like?', *Reading and Writing*, 9(5–6): 451–481.

Venezky, R.L. (1970) *The Structure of English Orthography*, The Hague: Mouton.

Wilde, S. (1992) *You Kan Red This!*, Portsmouth, NH: Heinemann.

18

Developing an Understanding of Punctuation

Nigel Hall

INTRODUCTION

One of the less-studied aspects of written language development is how children come to understand punctuation. As recently as 1999, Beard commented that, 'Punctuation has rarely been discussed at length in literacy education publications', and part of the reason for this is that there has been so little research on the topic. This is, perhaps, rather surprising, for probably the aspect of language knowledge most frequently complained about is punctuation. Only recently, for over a year, the world's best selling nonfiction book was a tirade about people's failures to punctuate correctly, what the author termed a 'zero tolerance approach to punctuation' (Truss, 2003).

Such complaints about poor punctuation are nothing new, for despite the mythologies of politicians, which suggest that everything was better in the past, these complaints have been present for centuries, and constant across the twentieth century. Why does learning to punctuate seem to present such a problem? There are a number of possible general reasons.

Firstly, like all aspects of written language, punctuation has been and always will be a site of contestation. On the one hand, punctuation is not a static concept and even if we restrict the discussion to early modern and modern English, it has changed fairly dramatically across time (Nunberg, 1990). These changes have seldom been the consequence of explicit personal invention; it has been usage and need determining what survives and what disappears. On the other hand, there has to be conventions or rules, for without these, punctuation would be utterly idiosyncratic and the chances of using it to facilitate effective communication would be either lost or severely hindered. This contestation is most dramatically marked in education, for while language and punctuation continually evolve, so governments and other agencies attempt to lock it down and keep it fixed. Unfortunately, children are caught in the middle; they are taught the rules whilst at the same time popular culture and advertising increasingly play havoc with them (for a detailed review of punctuation issues, see Hall, 1996).

Secondly, and still related to contestation, defining punctuation and its marks has become increasingly difficult. As punctuation has shifted from a more elocutionary nature to a more grammatical nature, so definitions have had to become more flexible. Nevertheless, most English grammar textbooks from the sixteenth to the nineteenth century have two or three pages with almost identical lists of punctuation marks and almost identical, brief definitions of their use. Today, life is more complex, for easy access to graphic tools within computer technology has begun to offer multiple ways to signify particular relations between parts of texts normally marked by conventional punctuation. For example, an examination of a range of contemporary children's books would reveal many different ways of representing the marking of speech without using quotation marks. Speech might be signalled by colour, by typeface, by typestyle (bold, underlining, etc.), by type size, by space, by position on a page, or by combinations of these features, and different voices might also be represented by different typographic devices. Thus, when children look for models of punctuation, they are offered considerably more than the conventional marks of traditional punctuation.

Thirdly, beginning writers are faced with a formidable challenge. They have to control the creation of the meaning, the graphic and grammatical representation of this meaning, its conversion into a set of phoneme/grapheme relationships and represent all this neatly on a piece of paper using an awkward writing instrument that needs to be held in a particular way [for further discussion of the challenge that writing presents for individuals, see this volume, Chapter 33]. However, there is some carry over of knowledge from what they know about oral language. It is relatively easy for a learner to recognize that writing uses mostly the same words as spoken language, that they are organized in generally similar ways, and that they need to make sense just as they do in spoken language. Nevertheless, one thing for which there is no carry over is punctuation. Punctuation marks are not normally present in speech; they are a very distinctive property of written language. Thus, when punctuation is introduced to children, usually by teachers, they are shown some very small physical marks (indeed, the most important are close to being invisible), but these marks cannot be easily fitted into children's existing schemas of what language is about. As a result, punctuation can seem abstract, arbitrary, imposed, and generally meaningless to young learners.

Finally, the ways in which punctuation has been taught for the last five hundred years have been highly formal (Michael, 1987). Punctuation as an object in schooling derives from a discourse that locates it as a system bounded by a set of rules controlling correct usage. The teaching of punctuation is centred on a range of belief systems and ideological positions about the nature of the object, and the nature of teaching and learning, and in school, these tend to position it as an autonomous object to be learned in a relatively decontextualized manner (Street and Street, 1991). It is a language of instruction rather than a language of use, which tends to position the children as learners of an apparently neutral and unproblematic set of skills in which writing itself is mainly a device for learning language skills rather than having a genuine communicative experience. Teachers and textbooks have tended to teach children that punctuation is a set of rules imposed upon writers rather than a set of tools for writers so that they can make their meanings as clear as possible. Thus, learning to punctuate has been mostly about getting it right rather than exploring what it offers to writers.

In what follows, we review evidence from existing studies of how children develop early understanding of punctuation prior to developing linguistic reasoning relating to punctuation. We then look in more detail at how children develop understanding of grammatical punctuation, the apostrophe, and the punctuation of speech. In each of these sections, there is a brief review of the literature and then a discussion of some issues arising from a major study carried out in the UK.[1]

BEGINNING TO PUNCTUATE: PRELINGUISTIC PUNCTUATION

Until very recently, papers by Calkins (1980), Ferreiro, and Teberosky (1983), Edelsky (1983), Cordiero, Giacobbe, and Cazden (1983), Cazden, Giacobbe, and Cordiero (1985), Cordeiro (1988), and Kress (1982) were the only published studies on this topic relating to children (for a full review see Hall, 1996). While very different in approach, and all rather limited in scope, there are some points of agreement between them. All the authors suggest that learning to punctuate is not a passive process in which children simply learn a set of rules and can then punctuate accurately. Cordiero, Giacobbe, and Cazden (1983) write about 'the hypotheses young children try to act upon', Edelsky (1983) writes that 'Children's writing seemed to develop through internal and individual process of hypothesis creating/testing and schema development tapping'; Ferreiro and Teberosky (1983) explain that 'what appears as confusion is actually the child's systematization, operating from bases very different from the adult's'; and Kress (1982), in an analysis of one child's texts, suggests that 'The child may be searching for a unit which can express some unified coherent concept which the child needs to express'. The reasoning behind these comments was almost all based upon postwriting analysis of children's written texts. Calkins had briefly interviewed children, some comments from the teacher's notebook were collected in the Cordiero studies, and Edelsky visited the classroom three times during the year. However, overall, relatively little, if any, data was collected about the behaviour of children as they were actually working in classrooms. Indeed, to a large extent, the children themselves seem missing from most of these studies. A few later studies have strongly reinforced the notion that learning to punctuate is not about passively accepting rules (Anderson, 1996; Martens and Goodman,

1996; Arthur, 1996; Ruiz, 1996); yet in total, these studies are relatively small and largely disconnected to each other.

There is a fairly fundamental division in the way children understand punctuation. The first and earliest category is what we, here, term *Pre-linguistic Punctuation*. The second is what we term *Linguistic Punctuation*. However, while understanding punctuation almost invariably begins with our first category, there is also a considerable degree of overlap between this and the second category, and elements of the first category continue to appear up to the age of eleven, and in many cases may do so into and throughout adulthood (Ivanic, 1996). In the prelinguistic phase of understanding punctuation a number of phases can be observed.

Resistance

In this first phase, despite being introduced to and taught about punctuation, children simply failed to use it (Hall, 1998). Although the term 'resistance' is used here, it is important not to imply that the children's resistance to using punctuation was an explicit policy on their part. It clearly was not, for when children were reminded by the teacher to put a full stop at the end, they would do so with enthusiasm, and often with a statement of the sort 'Oh yeah, I forget that'. Their general approach to teacher requests was one of compliance and acquiescence. The reasons for resistance are several.

As indicated in the foregoing section, young writers are coping with a substantial cognitive burden in that the multilayered demands of the writing task are considerable. The school experience of these children had positioned phonic knowledge and spelling as the most important elements of literacy. Thus, the children's primary effort at the beginning of the year was directed at putting words on paper to represent a simple message using correct spelling. It is not surprising that the tiniest marks were seen as less important.

Everyday, children queued up to ask the teacher about spellings; not once in the two years of this study was any child heard asking the teacher about the use of a punctuation mark.

In addition to appearing to have no significance, there is something of a paradox in that the most important punctuation mark—the full stop—is visually the smallest. It was noticeable that when punctuation marks began to occur in the children's independent writing, most commonly, they were the more visually salient marks of exclamation and interrogation.

As readers, children were able to cope perfectly well without the need for punctuation. The books the children were reading at this point contained relatively little text, and mostly showed only one sentence on a page. Full stops are pretty redundant when both their position on a line and position on a page suggest that a sentence has ended. This was compounded by the children at this stage tending to read with relatively staccato intonation, in which each word receives equal stress, thus sentence demarcation in oral reading was seldom present. It was the individual word, which was the focus of attention rather than the sentence or text.

For the children as writers, punctuation was equally redundant. Except where legibility was an issue, children seldom had difficulty in reading back what they had written, and often managed to read with normal intonation. They knew what they had written; they did not need to insert punctuation marks into it.

While there is not time to explore it in this chapter, it should be noted that resistance to using punctuation was not only widespread but also extremely persistent.

Moving to graphic punctuation

Children do not go on ignoring punctuation forever. It becomes impossible for children to ignore the increasing emphasis teachers put upon it; endless repetitions of requests to remember punctuation and endless admonitions ultimately have some effect. However, it seems that even as children begin to incorporate punctuation into their independent writing, the ways in which they use it owe little to convention or linguistics. The argument of Hall (1999) is that this incorporation is actually fairly consistent in that the full stop and comma are positioned on the page according to space rather than any underlying linguistic principle, what Hall terms graphic punctuation. Graphic punctuation tends to be manifested through.

End-of-line punctuation

This is relatively common in classrooms and is well recognized by teachers and reported by researchers. Typically, the child puts a full stop at the end of every line. In the group of children studied, its most frequent occurrence came while the children were writing only two or three lines. However, the notion of end-of-line punctuation was a frequent element in the children's talk about punctuation.

End-of-page and end-of-piece punctuation

Here, the child, typically, writes without including any punctuation but once s/he reaches the end of a page or the end of a piece, adds a full stop. Sometimes, there may be a full stop at the end of the first line (regardless of whether it actually marks a sentence) and another at the end of the piece. At this point, an exaggerated full stop is often written, as if to say, 'That's it, I've finished now'. This was probably the commonest usage of punctuation by the children during their second year in school. The omission is no longer simply a case of punctuation having no significance for the child; it is much more likely that the child's efforts have gone into generating the meaning of a piece. Once a story starts being written, meaning overrides attention to punctuation.

Distribution of punctuation according to length of unit

This was relatively uncommon and only one child used this as a strategy. This child had written a piece with only one full stop. When she had finished, the researcher asked her if there was anything she wanted to add or change, and the child said, 'full stops'. She went slowly through the piece, appearing to read it carefully before including a number of full stops. Her explanations for their placement invoked notions such as 'it was too long', 'from there to there', and having not put one in the line above. For her, the distribution of full stops was according to graphic balance—there needs to be so many, they must not be too close together, nor must they be too far apart.

In this phase, it was as if punctuation had separate roots from writing, was not intrinsic to meaning-making, and was a set of objects that are added to render a piece of text graphically acceptable. The function of punctuation seemed to be to fulfil a teacher's request for marks to be present. It was not intrinsic to the act of writing, and for so many of the children, for so much of their time, it was something added after the writing had been done.

MOVING TOWARDS LINGUISTIC PUNCTUATION

Children do eventually become aware that punctuation is not just about graphic placement and do begin to move towards linguistic punctuation. Clear evidence for this came from children's discussions during a punctuation problem-solving task (Hall and Holden-Sim, 1996). Working with a researcher, a group of three children had composed a text about their teacher. The beginning of the text read (as laid out in the original):

> She is my friend and.
> Sometimes she is a bit bossy.
> And she shouts a lot and
> She tells us to do our work

When invited to see if any changes needed to be made, one child, Rachel, wanted to write a full stop after the word 'lot' in line 3. There then followed an energetic debate for some minutes. David claimed, 'You're not supposed to put full stops in the middle' (referring to the middle of a line). Fatima said, 'So that's how you know that (referring to the 'and' after 'lot') goes with that (referring to line 4). This debate continued for several minutes with Rachel and Fatima defending their position. However, David was adamant and in frustration eventually grabbed the pen, crossed out the 'and' and rewrote it at the beginning of line 4 and thus everyone could be satisfied.

In this extract, David is clearly arguing using graphic reasons and his ultimate move is to physically rearrange the text to satisfy his graphic requirements. Rachel, and especially Fatima, although incorrect, were offering arguments that recognized elements of the grammatical structure of the text. They still left the full stops at the end of lines 1 and 2, but the transition towards linguistic reasoning was clearly underway. Within a few weeks Fatima had written a 25-line text in which the full stops clearly marked semantic units within the text. It seems that the move towards linguistic punctuation is not initially marked by the segmentation of conventional sentence demarcation, but by the marking of units that make sense to children as coherent meanings (see also Kress, 1982).

Grammatical punctuation

Today, punctuation is primarily recognized as being mainly organized according to grammatical principles, but this has not always been the case. The punctuation sections of early modern books on grammar were often aimed at how texts should be read aloud rather than how texts should be written. As a consequence, the major grammatical stops were marked in reading by a relative duration of pausing; in many systems a full stop or period represented a count of four, a comma a count of three, a semicolon a count of two, while a colon represented a count of one (as can be found in *Punctuation Personified*, 1824, the first ever book on punctuation for children). Across the eighteenth and nineteenth centuries the grammatical basis of punctuation became fairly well established, although Bruthiaux (1993) claims that prosodic use of punctuation was still strong in public life and Cruttenden states that even amongst grammarians who advocate a syntactic use of punctuation, elocutionary considerations are still alive (1990: 59).

Research into children's understanding of grammatical punctuation beyond the prelinguistic stage is very limited, and any such study is inevitably linked to children's understanding of grammar and its link to writing, and the metalanguage associated with it. What seems to be generally acknowledged is that in children's early writing, the syntax is close to the syntax of speech (Kress, 1982; Perera, 1984). However, there is also evidence that even in these early stages, writing is not, as Bracewell rather starkly puts it, 'simply visible speech' (1980: 407). McDonnell Harris (1977), working in an experimental setting, came to the conclusion that for the children concerned, writing was not the same as talk written down. In Perera's study (1984) the eight-year-old children's written and oral production was very similar, some constructions appeared in speech but did not appear in writing and vice versa. As children become more familiar with the structure of written language, the linear structure of oral language is gradually replaced by the hierarchical structure of more mature writing (Hunt, 1965, 1970; Kress, 1982; Perera, 1984). The language that children now begin to write includes subordinated and embedded clauses, passive constructions, cleft sentences, longer clauses and noun phrases, explicit references, and cohesion devices that ensure that the text constitutes a whole and as this happens so the need for grammatical punctuation increases (Lurcat, 1973). Ferreiro and Pontecorvo's (1999) report on a study of children in the

second grade, and who spoke/wrote either Spanish or Italian. Analysis of the seven-year-old children's punctuation use in a narrative text suggested that the children held some ideas about the structure of written language, but did not appear to possess a sufficiently strong command of punctuation to be able to mark syntactic relations, conventionally. Calkins (1980) compared grade three children in two classes and found that the children in the class in which punctuation was taught in context had a far better understanding of the nuances of punctuation, in particular the developing understanding of the comma, than the children in the class in which punctuation was taught by rote.

The most recent and substantial study into young children's understanding of grammatical punctuation is by Wassouf (2007, and her study was part of a larger study that also involves the two main studies in the two following sections). This study involved 96 children aged from seven to eleven and was concerned with uncovering children's oral reasoning about punctuation. Wassouf identified a number of issues for children but three of the most important are: the persistence of graphic reasoning, the relationship between prosody and punctuation, and a reliance on a relatively intuitive notion of making sense.

The persistence of graphic reasoning

Having developed theories of punctuation according to graphic principles, some children find it hard to leave them behind. When older children relied on graphic principles, they talked about the number of words between two punctuation marks, or between the beginning of the text and the first punctuation mark inserted. Their beliefs as to how many words should separate two marks or how many words should be written at the beginning of a text before punctuation could be used varied greatly and ranged from vague idea of an appropriate length to more precise word count. The length of a sequence of the text was also used as a criterion to decide whether that sequence was a sentence or not. Also, when examining texts, the correctness or otherwise of a full stop was often defended according to whether it was followed by a capital letter (although this is unlikely to reflect their use when writing). Such reasoning became less common with the oldest children but was still regularly seen in the reasoning of the seven-, eight-, and nine-year-olds.

Prosody and punctuation placement

Despite the general recognition by linguists that punctuation is essentially grammatical, prosodic reasoning and explanation lives on in schooling. Even very early on teachers tend to stress listening to what has been written, and teachers can often be seen reading aloud children's texts writing that have been produced without full stops and/or commas. The teachers often do not breathe while reading, sometimes pretending to go blue in the face in order demonstrate the necessity of punctuation. The words 'pausing' and 'breathing' tended to dominate teacher explanations and demonstrations (even though there is evidence of deaf children successfully learning to use punctuation without being able access prosody at all) (Ruiz, 1996). It is certainly the case that giving grammatical explanations to young children is difficult, but the focus on prosodic explanation results in such reasoning staying in children's minds. As a consequence, even the oldest children in her study still relied heavily on it, something that sometimes leads to curious consequences. There was one example in which a grammatical explanation would have clarified whether a comma was needed after 'know' in '*I know I'll buy him some CDs*, some socks, etc.' The ten-year-old children, however, did not use grammar. One child read this section aloud with a deep breath and a pause after 'know' and declared, 'There, it

does need a comma!' Another child promptly read it without a pause or deep breath and said, 'No it doesn't!' Children of all ages in Wassouf's study used prosodic reasoning without realizing that it would only work if the underlying grammatical structure supported it. As a consequence, across the age range, decisions about whether or not to use particular punctuation marks, especially the comma, were often erratic. She believes that teachers need to be more careful in not over-emphasizing the importance of punctuating according to prosodic rules.

Reliance on a relatively intuitive notion of making sense

All the children in Wassouf's study were being explicitly and regularly taught grammar as part of the stipulated National Curriculum, but hardly ever did any child draw on a grammatical explanation to justify a decision about the use of punctuation. Their reasoning was either, if appropriate, prosodic or based on 'whether it made sense'. In over 30 hours of intense discussion about the use of full stops and commas, only a couple of times was the metalanguage of grammar used to support a reason for, or for not, using a particular punctuation mark. However, the notion of a unit of text making sense is a major move forward from graphic reasoning. The expression of 'it doesn't make sense' had a meaning close to 'it is wrong' or 'it is illogical'. These arguments, although in terms of semantics, were very close to grammatical justifications, as though the children, unable to express their ideas in grammatical terms, reverted to semantic notions instead. It seems that the children used this more general kind of explanation when they had a feeling that some punctuation use was appropriate or inappropriate but did not know how to explain why. It is clear from this and the previous issue that the most useful explanations for the use of punctuation, grammatical ones, had not yet been absorbed by the children to a level that they felt comfortable using them in practice.

THE APOSTROPHE

Since its introduction to the English language in the sixteenth century, the apostrophe has been a problematic and contentious punctuation mark (Sklar, 1976). Despite sometimes being used correctly, many times, it is not, or else it is omitted from where it should be written. Even in more contemporary times when the rules governing the apostrophe's use have become relatively fixed, still many people, young and old, are experiencing problems with being able to use it accurately.

Despite the longevity and persistence of these difficulties, just eight studies have been conducted about how writers' understand the apostrophe: three with adult-age learners and five with children, four of these only in the last decade. Perhaps unsurprisingly, the focus of most of these studies was the possessive apostrophe. More fundamentally, no study has considered young children's learning and understanding of the apostrophe in a comprehensive way. From the five studies conducted with children, several main findings emerge, but the overall one is that the possessive apostrophe is confusing for children to learn and understand, at any age. At all ages many children were found to have strong tendencies to write an apostrophe before a final letter 's' in plural spellings (Pascoe, 1997; Bryant, Nunes, and Bindman, 2000). In addition, several of the studies found that intervention generally makes a positive difference to young children's performances with using the apostrophe (Cordiero, Giacobbe, and Cazden, 1983; Bryant, Devine, Ledward, and Nunes, 1997; Stuart, Dixon, and Masterson, 2004); specifically that, morpho-syntactic awareness improves their use of the possessive apostrophe (Bryant et al., 1997), and after being taught the possessive apostrophe, they use the mark more in their writing (Cordiero et al., 1983; Bryant et al., 1997; Bryant et al.,

2000). Both the Bryant et al. investigations suggest there may be advantages to forging stronger links between spelling and grammar while Pascoe's research (1997) drew attention to limitations posed by thinking about the concept of possession simply in terms of 'belonging' and 'ownership'.

Sing (2006) is the only researcher to have looked specifically at children's understanding of the apostrophe across a sustained age period (7 to 11 years of age), and did so by focusing solely on children's oral reasoning about the apostrophe rather than their use of it. In this British study, she found that children's learning and understanding of the apostrophe did not always progress in a neat linear or consistently positive way. The development of the children's knowledge was often coupled with confusions, misunderstandings, misinterpretations and missed cases of omission and possession, and these difficulties were still common among some eleven-year-old children in her study. A number of findings emerged from Sing's analysis.

Metalanguage issues—using the term 'apostrophe'

The term 'apostrophe' was particularly, though not exclusively, problematic for a number of the younger children; they experienced particular difficulties with its pronunciation and even with just being able to remember it. This however, did not halt or inhibit their discussions about the apostrophe as they resorted to using a range of alternative references instead. Some children called it by another name such as 'comma', some pointed to the mark they wanted if they could see it written in the text, while others characterized it in various ways, e.g., *'just like a straight line'* or *'one of those things at the top'*. In a number of cases, the children's remarks indicated that the apostrophe's strong graphic resemblance to several other punctuation marks was a source of some confusion. An even greater terminological confusion arose with the possessive apostrophe.

Confusion associated with the notion of 'possession' and 'belonging'

The term 'possessive apostrophe' is well established in both the research and descriptive literature relating to punctuation, but it carries with it some problems. In the classrooms observed by Sing, the most common word associated with the apostrophe was 'belong' or 'belonging', which is clearly related to the notion of possession and ownership. The children at eight or nine were doing exercises in which they had to insert apostrophes in sentences like 'Sally picked up Peter's book', and had no problem with teacher explanations that the apostrophe showed the book *belonged* to Peter. This word, or associated words, then showed up constantly in their discussions related to the texts on which they worked. However, this became slightly confusing to the children when confronted with 'Peter's house'. When asked whether the house actually belonged to Peter, many started to change their minds about the need for an apostrophe. Even more problematic for them was meeting the words, 'three days time', and trying to work out whether an apostrophe was needed. All the children, even the eleven-year-olds, rejected the apostrophe, for as days 'were not owned, they could not belong to anything. Thus, the children's notion of belonging was actually hindering their ability to identify other types of possessive noun phrases, such as those with an abstract, inanimate sense. The possessive apostrophe is a complex mark (see Quirk, Greenbaum, Leech, and Svartvik, 1985, for a comprehensive explanation) and notions like 'belonging', while designed to simply things for children, can create deep level, and possibly long lasting confusion.

Lacking knowledge of the use and meaning of morphemes

The children's difficulties with understanding the full extent of the possessive meaning also became apparent through their frequent misunderstandings of the final 's' morpheme in certain plural words. Regular plural noun spellings terminate with the letter 's' as do singular and plural possessive nouns (plus an apostrophe). Thus, the important distinction for children to realize is the grammatical and semantic role played by the apostrophe and the 's' morpheme when written in the spelling of different noun types. That they fail to recognize this difference is indicated by the large number of children prepared to put an apostrophe before the 's' in the plural noun spelling of *'mornings'*. It seems that one of the primary meanings children gain from ritualistic exercises in which they put possessive apostrophes in lists of sentences is that a final 's' designates possession. Thus, what might seem like a secure knowledge of the possessive apostrophe in singular possessive structures, is actually revealed as uncertainty when faced with regular plural noun spellings.

UNDERSTANDING THE PUNCTUATION OF SPEECH

If children's understanding of punctuation is as a whole under-researched, then research on their understanding of speech is close to nonexistent. Ferriero and Zuchermaglio (1996) found that Argentinian and Mexican seven- and eight-year-olds used more punctuation during direct speech than in the rest of their story texts, but little of this involved quotation marks. When speech boundaries were marked, it was often by other punctuation marks such as full stops or exclamation marks. Even with reading, despite the frequency with which direct speech appears in books for young children (Baker and Freebody, 1989) and despite some enthusiastic intonation in reading some direct speech ('Who's been sleeping in my bed?'), children often have difficulty in working out who is speaking, and when there is a change of speaker (Perera, 1996). This is particularly the case when there is no straightforward signalling of direct speech by reporting clauses (e.g., 'he said', 'she shouted').

Does the rarity of research into children's understanding of the punctuation of speech reflect a view that it is unproblematic? At first sight, the speech mark seems as if it ought to be the easiest of punctuation marks to use; after all, you simply put them around the text that forms the quotation. The authors of England's *National Literacy Strategy: Framework for Teaching* (DFEE. 1998) seem to agree with this, demanding that six-year-olds can 'identify speech marks in reading, understand their purpose, use the term correctly' and that seven-year-olds can 'use the term speech marks' and 'use speech marks and other dialogue punctuation appropriately in writing and to use the conventions which mark boundaries between spoken words and the rest of the sentence.' However, this punctuation mark turns out to have many kinds of problems for children, especially younger children. The following observations mostly come from, as yet, unpublished material from a research project (Hall, Sing, and Wassouf, 2002).

Young children can have difficulties in identifying boundaries between speech and nonspeech in sentences. One six-year-old child observed by the first author put short strokes at the top of the line several times in his two-line piece that did not contain any speech. He claimed they were speech marks and were needed because it was him saying it; thus, he confuses authorial voice with the voices of anyone cited. However, he could be viewed as correct; after all, almost all children's writing is read out aloud by them to the teacher.

Children have many problems distinguishing between direct and indirect speech (a distinction the British NLS *Framework for Teaching* does not demand until children are nine or ten). Even in reading, young children misread the punctuation of speech (Perera, 1996). Names for speech marks are inconsistent, and despite every English child being taught the term 'speech marks' the earliest

published use of it so far found is from 1977. They are more commonly known as quotation marks, inverted commas and 'sixty-sixes' and 'ninety-nines' (and by several other names across just the twentieth century, including by Ballard (1930) 'lip marks'). Many children in our studies, even ten- and eleven-year-old, continued to use these other terms, or, in quite a few cases, could not remember any terms, invented their own or simply pointed, e.g.:

> I'm not sure/and that's your/you know how the/it's like erm/kind of/two like little things and er/in the air kind of/ (I) /speech marks I think

The designation of speech in books (specially children's books) is immensely varied. As indicated in the introduction, the models available to children in their reading books are hugely varied. It should be also said that a number of high level literary novels, some prize winning books, have either left out conventional speech punctuation, or have modified it. The children in our study would spend quite a lot of time debating what punctuation marks should look like, especially speech marks. There was huge concern that the shape was exactly right, and this may be a consequence of the emphasis on 'correctness' in many classrooms. Thus, echoes of graphic punctuation persist even among the older age groups.

The punctuation of speech does not simply involve speech marks. Representing speech is aided by many other marks and devices. Does one follow a reporting clause with a colon, a comma, or nothing at all? Does one start a quotation with a capital letter or not? Should there be a final punctuation mark inside quotation marks or outside? What does one do about a quote within a quote? These are serious issues for children and in our study, discussion of them took up some time and as children brought different sources of information about punctuation to their discussions there was often uncertainty and disagreement. This is troubling to children working in a school system, which makes accuracy and correctness key features of assessment.

In our study, we worked with children from age seven to eleven. While there was a definite improvement across the year groups in the correct use of speech marks, their detailed discussions revealed that to some extent these correct responses were sometimes based more on intuition than on reasoned argument. Although it sometimes occurred, it was relatively rare to actually hear children using the metalanguage associated with speech, e.g.:

Jos ... you have to/you have to like say/erm/oh what d'you call it?...
Jam ...reported speech...
Jos ...past tense
Jam it would be past tense if/if it was reported speech...

It seems that many of the oldest children still overused the terms 'ninety-nines' and 'sixty-sixes', rather than the formal terms taught to them (e.g., '...you could have a '99' there then a '66' going that way') there was some confusion about sentences within speech marks, particularly whether each sentence needed speech marks, and how quotations actually ended (e.g., 'because you always put a full stop after you've got some speech').

On a simply correction test given to the oldest children towards the end of our study, they managed only 75% accuracy with the punctuation of speech, which suggests that despite it appearing straightforward there is more difficulty with it for children than educationalists have allowed for.

way, and the documentation (as in so much educational material about the teaching of punctuation) completely failed to recognize the subtleties of punctuation that so easily perplex children when seeking to understand it. What is often forgotten by the people who write such documents is that as written language use progresses so the punctuation problems children have to solve increase in difficulty. Older children may make punctuation errors, but this is often because the problems they are trying to solve by using punctuation have become much more complex. The children who were studied, despite not having full command of the punctuation of speech by the age of eleven, were very impressive in the way they discussed it. They were highly strategic in the way they approached discussion, drawing on different sources of evidence and weighing up carefully all the arguments for and against a particular usage. They sustained long discussions about the issues and approached the tasks reflectively. It is a pity that so much teaching of punctuation fails to imbue children with a real interest in it, such as that displayed by the children under discussion.

NOTE

1 *The Development of Punctuation Knowledge in Children Aged Seven to Eleven*. Economic and Social Research Council Project, R0002383348 (2000–2002).

CONCLUSION

The children in Hall, Wassouf's, and Sing's studies certainly did increase their understanding of punctuation as they moved through schooling. However, the manner of this progress certainly did not reflect the simplicity of the developmental structures outlined in the documents that guided how children should be taught about it. Progress did not proceed in a straightforward linear

REFERENCES

Anderson, H. (1996) 'Vicki's story: A seven-year-old's use and understanding of punctuation', in N. Hall and A. Robinson (eds), *Learning About Punctuation*, Clevedon: Multilingual Matters.

Anon (1824) *Punctuation Personified*, London: John Harris.

Arthur, C. (1996) 'Learning about punctuation: A look at one lesson', in N. Hall and A. Robinson (eds), *Learning About Punctuation*, Clevedon: Multilingual Matters.

Baker, C. and Freebody, P. (1989) *Children's First School Books*, Oxford: Blackwell.

Ballard, Phillip (1930) *Fundamental English: First Series, Book Three*, London: University of London Press Ltd.

Beard, R. (1999) *National Literacy Strategy: Review of Research and other Related Evidence*, London: Department for Education and Employment.

Bracewell, R. (1980) 'Writing as a cognitive activity', *Visible Language*, 14: 400–422.

Bruthiaux, P. (1993) 'Knowing when to stop: investigating the nature of punctuation', *Language and Communication*, 13(1): 27–43.

Bryant, P., Devine, M., Ledward, A., and Nunes, T. (1997) 'Spelling with apostrophes and understanding possession', *British Journal of Educational Psychology*, 67(1): 91–110.

Bryant, P., Nunes, T., and Bindman, M. (2000) 'The relations between children's linguistic awareness and spelling: The case of the apostrophe', *Reading and Writing: An Interdisciplinary Journal*, 12: 253–276.

Calkins, L. (1980) 'When children want to punctuate: basic skills belong in context', *Language Arts*, 57(5): 567–573.

Cazden, C, Cordiero, P., and Giaccobe, M. (1985) 'Spontaneous and scientific concepts: Young children's learning of punctuation', in G. Wells and J. Nichols (eds), *Language and Learning: An Interactional Perspective*, Brighton: Falmer Books. pp.107–123.

Cordiero, P. (1988) 'Children's punctuation: An analysis of errors in period placement', *Research in the Teaching of English*, 22(1): 62–74.

Cordiero, P., Giacobbe, M.E., and Cazden, C. (1983) 'Apostrophes, quotation marks, and periods: Learning punctuation in the first grade', *Language Arts*, 60(3): 323–332.

Cruttenden, A. (1990) 'Intonation and the comma', *Visible Language*, 25(1): 54–73.

Department for Education and Employment (1998) *National Literacy Strategy: Framework for Teaching*. London: Department for Education and Employment.

Edelsky, C. (1983) 'Segmentation and punctuation: Developmental data from young writers in a bilingual program', *Research in the Teaching of English*, 17(2): 135–156.

Ferreiro, E. and Pontecorvo, C. (1999) 'Managing the written text: the beginning of punctuation in children's writing', *Learning and Instruction*, 9(6), online.

Ferreiro, E. and Teberosky, A. (1983) *Literacy before Schooling*, London: Heinemann Educational.

Ferreiro, E. and Zucchermaglio, C. (1996) 'Children's use of punctuation makers: The case of "quoted speech"', in C. Pontecorvo, M. Orsolini, B. Burge,

and L.B. Resnick (eds), *Children's Early Text Construction*, Mahwah, NJ: LEA. pp.177–205.

Hall, N. (1996) 'Learning about punctuation: An introduction and overview', in N. Hall and A. Robinson (eds), *Learning About Punctuation*, Clevedon: Multilingual Matters.

Hall, N. (1998) 'Young children and resistance to punctuation', *Research in Education*, 60: 29–40.

Hall, N. (1999) 'Young children's use of graphic punctuation', *Language and Education*, 13(3): 178–193.

Hall, N. and Holden-Sim, K. (1996) 'Debating punctuation: Six-year-olds figure it out', in N. Hall and J. Martello (eds), *Listening to Children Think: Exploring Talk in the Early Years*, London: Hodder & Stoughton.

Hall, N., Sing, S., and Wassouf, C. (2002) The Development of Punctuation Knowledge in Children Aged Seven to Eleven. Working document for ESRC Project R0002383348.

Hunt, K. (1965) Grammatical Structures Written at Three Grade Levels. NCTE Research Report No. 3. Champaign, Illinois: National Council of Teachers of English.

Hunt, K. (1970) Syntactic Maturity in Schoolchildren and Adults. Monographs of the Society for Research in Child Development, Special No. 134(1).

Ivanic, R. (1996) 'Linguistics and the logic of nonstandard punctuation', in N. Hall and A. Robinson (eds), *Learning About Punctuation*, Clevedon: Multilingual Matters. pp.148–169.

Kress, G. (1982) *Learning to Write*, London: Routledge and Keegan Paul.

Lurcat, L. (1973) 'L'Acquisition de la Ponctuation', *Revue Française de Pédagogie*, 25: 14–27.

Martens, P. and Goodmans, Y. (1996) 'Invented punctuation', in N. Hall and A. Robinson (eds), *Learning About Punctuation*, Clevedon: Multilingual Matters.

McDonnell Harris, M. (1977) 'Oral and Written Syntax Attainment of Second Graders', *Research in the Teaching of English*, 11:117–132.

Michael, Ian (1987) *The Teaching of English from the Sixteenth Century to 1870*, Cambridge: Cambridge University Press.

Nunberg, G. (1990) *The Linguistics of Punctuation*, California: Centre for the Study of Language and Information.

Pascoe, M. (1997) *The Problem of the Apostrophe*, MA thesis, University of Liverpool.

Perera, K. (1984) *Children's Writing and Reading: Analysing Classroom Language*, Oxford: Blackwell.

Perera, K. (1996) 'Who says what? Learning to "read" the punctuation of direct speech', in N. Hall and A. Robinson (eds), *Learning About Punctuation*, Clevedon: Multilingual Matters.

Quirk, R., Greenbaum, G., Leech, G., and Svartvic, J. (1985) *A Comprehensive Grammar of the English Language*, London: Longman.

Ruiz, N. (1996) 'A young deaf child explores punctuation', in N. Hall and A. Robinson (eds), *Learning About Punctuation*, Clevedon: Multilingual Matters.

Sing, S. (2006) *Making Sense of the Apostrophe: Young Children's Explorations into the World of Punctuation*, PhD thesis, Manchester Metropolitan University, Manchester.

Sing, S. and Hall, N. (in press) 'Listening to children think about punctuation', in E. Carter (ed.), *Why Writing Matters: Issues of Access and Identity in Writing Research and Pedagogy*, Amsterdam: John Benjamins.

Sklar, E. (1976) 'The possessive apostrophe: The development and decline of a crooked mark', *College English*, 38(2): 175–183.

Street, B. and Street, J. (1991) 'The schooling of literacy', in Barton, D. and Ivanič, R. (eds), *Writing in the Community*, London: Sage. pp.143–166.

Stuart, M., Dixon, M., and Masterson, J. (2004) 'Use of apostrophes by six- to nine-year-old children', *Educational Psychology*, 24(3): 251–261.

Truss, L. (2003) Eats, Shoots and Leaves: The Zero Tolerance Approach to Punctuation. London: Profile Books.

Wassouf, C. (2007) The Development of Key Stage 2 Children's Understanding of Grammatical Punctuation, PhD thesis, Manchester Metropolitan University, Manchester.

Wilde, S. (1996) 'Just periods and exclamation points: the continued development of children's knowledge about punctuation', in N. Hall and A. Robinson (eds), *Learning About Punctuation*, Clevedon: Multilingual Matters.

The Critical Role Handwriting Plays in the Ability to Produce High-Quality Written Text

Carol A. Christensen

Given the diversity and complexity of cognitive processes involved in the production of high-quality written text, it seems counterintuitive to suggest that handwriting is a key element in students' ability to create original and well-structured text. However, there is a sound theoretical basis and mounting empirical evidence to suggest that the relationship between handwriting and quality of written text is strong and surprisingly robust.

The focus of handwriting in the curriculum for most of the last century was on legibility, neatness and strict motor control. Good penmanship was central to curriculum in literacy for much of the twentieth century (Schlagal, 2007). However, more recently, handwriting has been seen as unimportant and irrelevant to contemporary education (Medwell and Wray, 2007).

Schlagal argues that in recent decades two factors have pushed handwriting to the margins of curriculum. There has been a de-emphasis on basic skills with their concomitant requirement for regimes of extended practice. A focus on spelling, grammar and handwriting has been replaced by an emphasis on personal communication. Second, the contemporary focus on electronic forms of communication, particularly with regard to word processing, has led some educators to argue that there is no longer any need to teach low-level skills such as handwriting (Schlagal, 2007).

In addition, it seems that research in the 1980s on emergent writing which demonstrated that children could create meaningful texts before having access to the formal writing system led to a curriculum focus on semantics, creativity, genre and pragmatic awareness (Hall, 1987; Teale and Sulzby, 1986; Wray and Lewis, 1997) as well as a focus on processes such as planning, monitoring and revising (Hayes and Flowers, 1980), rather than emphasizing on handwriting-related skills such as letter formation and legibility (Medwell and Wray, 2007).

It seems ironic, then, that to some extent, when handwriting is addressed in contemporary curriculum documents, the traditional emphasis found in early documents on neatness, motor control and script-style remains (Medwell and Wray, 2007). Thus, current curriculum does not reflect recent research on the importance of handwriting or on the need for speed and fluency which underpins writers' ability to produce high-quality written text.

COGNITIVE PROCESSES IN WRITING

The multiplicity of cognitive processes involved in writing include: ideation related to the ability to generate original and creative ideas; syntactic awareness involved in the production of grammatically accurate text; pragmatic awareness and sensitivity-to-audience required to produce text that communicates clearly and appropriately with the reader; technical accuracy related to spelling; and awareness of aspects of text such as genre. The number and complexity of these processes mean that, when attempting to produce text, novice writers can experience significant problems with capacity limitation of working memory or cognitive load.

Cognitive load refers to the attentional demands required to perform intellectual tasks (Sweller, 1988). Essentially, the human mind has sufficient cognitive resources to attend to only one conscious intellectual activity at a time. Thus, attention is often referred to as the scarce cognitive resource (Lesgold et al., 1988). This means that in order to perform complex intellectual tasks, an individual must be able to manage the potentially competing attentional demands that tasks may pose. This can be done in one of two ways. First, individuals can sequence tasks that have high cognitive loads. Process writing enables the writer to sequentially focus attention on one element of writing at a time. This is effective in a number of situations; however, it is not possible to sequence all the attention-consuming aspects of tasks at all times.

Automaticity provides the alternative to sequencing the cognitive processes needed to write (LaBerge and Samuels, 1974). Automaticity is defined as the ability to recall information from memory quickly, accurately and effortlessly (Schneider and Shriffrin, 1977). One characteristic of expertise is automaticity, so that experts have their knowledge available in such a way that they can retrieve and use information without consuming attention. This effortless retrieval of sub-components of complex tasks means that experts consume relatively few cognitive resources in the execution of low-level aspects of tasks and, therefore, have most of their attentional resources available for sophisticated, higher-order aspects of tasks (Bransford et al., 2000). In other words, in addition to sequencing, expert writers can manage cognitive load through automaticity.

Handwriting is one aspect of written language that cannot be sequenced in order to manage cognitive load. If novice writers focus attention on the process of getting letters and words on the page, then they do not have sufficient attentional resources to focus on higher-order and centrally important processes such as ideation, pragmatic awareness or sensitivity to genre. Thus, theoretically, automaticity in handwriting is an essential prerequisite to the production of high-quality, creative and well-structured written text. Indeed, over the last 20 years, in addition to theoretical analysis, there has been a steady accumulation of empirical support for the notion that handwriting plays a central role in allowing the production of high-quality written text.

THEORETICAL ASPECTS OF HANDWRITING AND WRITTEN TEXT

Graham et al. (1997) argued that the necessity to switch attention from higher-order processes to the mechanical aspects of writing can interfere with planning, which in turn impacts on the complexity and coherence of written work. They suggested that switching attention from the composing process to handwriting may affect the coherence and complexity of written work (Graham and Weintraub, 1996). Graham et al. (2000) suggested that the need to switch attention from the composing process to the mechanical demands of handwriting, for example, having to think about how to form a particular letter, may result in a writer forgetting his or her ideas or plans for the text. Similarly, McCutchen (1996) argued that the physical act of writing text is so demanding for young writers that they develop an approach to production of written text (knowledge telling) that minimizes the use of self-regulatory processes (e.g. planning, monitoring and revising). Thus, the cognitive load of handwriting, by exerting competing attentional demands, may make it difficult for the writer to translate his or her intentions into text.

In a review of the literature, Berninger (1999) argued that there was substantial evidence to show that both transcription and working memory processes constrained the development of children's ability to compose text. This applied to children who were identified as learning-disabled as well as children without learning disabilities.

In addition to problems with allocation of attention, if writers lack fluency in handwriting, they may not be able to get their ideas on the page fast enough to keep up with their thoughts. In other words, there is interference with content generation as well as with recall of ideas for text already planned. Graham and Weintraub (1996) argued that speed is an important aspect of handwriting. If handwriting is very slow, then students may not be able record their thoughts in a way that keeps pace with their generation of ideas. Thus, they may forget their ideas before they get them on paper. Graham et al. found that speed of handwriting was significantly related to children's quality of composition.

Berninger's simple view of writing (Berninger et al., 2002) suggested a theory of writing which consisted of three components. The first related to lower-level skill related to transcription including spelling

and handwriting. The second refers to text generation processes or composing. The third related to executive functioning including planning, monitoring and revising. This model has underpinned a number of studies which have examined developmental processes contributing to children's ability to create written text.

Berninger et al. (1991) developed a model which accounted for the relationship between lower-order skills, higher-order elements of writing such as composing and executive management, and performance on written tasks. This model was based on developmental constraints. They suggested that constraints operate at multiple levels in a dynamic relationship. Thus, Berninger et al. (1992) suggested that some sensory and motor capacities need to develop before the ability to integrate sensory-motor information, which underpins handwriting. This is followed by the development of higher-order cognitive skills related to writing. Berninger et al. (1992) argue that problems with rapid coding of orthographic information, speed of finger movement and rapid production of alphabetic letters (orthographic-motor integration) may constrain the ability to transcribe ideas into text.

In addition to its impact on composition, handwriting can impact on children's attitude to writing. Berninger et al. (1991) suggested that if children find the acquisition of handwriting skills difficult, they tend to avoid writing tasks. This, in turn, impacts on their sense of self-efficacy in regard to writing and, consequently, they display arrested development in written language. Graham and Weintraub (1996) also argued that students' motivation may be impacted because of experiences of frustration with the writing process.

It should be kept in mind that handwriting is not just motor act. It requires the integration of motor behaviour with the knowledge of orthography (Berninger and Graham, 1998). Memory for orthographic information, particularly letter shapes, contributes more to handwriting skill than the motor component of writing. Orthographic–motor integration refers to the ability to recall and produce letter shapes, groups of letters and words. Thus, handwriting requires the writer to mentally code and rehearse the visual representation of patterns of letters in words, and to integrate these patterns with motor activities (Berninger, 1994).

EMPIRICAL EVIDENCE FOR THE IMPACT OF HANDWRITING ON WRITTEN TEXT

While there is growing evidence that handwriting plays a significant role in writers' ability to produce written text, there is variability in some research findings. In part, this is due to diversity in data collection methods based on a range of assessment methods for both handwriting and composition of written text. Assessment of handwriting has included asking students to create a piece of text, to write letters of the alphabet from memory, to copy single letters and to copy a piece of text.

There is also diversity in participants in research on handwriting. They have been drawn from a range of backgrounds and characteristics, including normally developing young, novice writers, older students and adults. Participants have included normally achieving students, as well as, students with reading and writing disabilities. In addition to a range of data collection methods and participants, a variety of analysis techniques have been used, including correlational studies, structural equation modelling, quasi-experimental and experimental designs.

Despite this variety in approach, there is consistency in a number of research findings. Much of the research has investigated the relationship between handwriting and two distinct aspects of written text. The first is compositional fluency, which refers to the facility with which a writer can produce text. It is often measured by the amount of text produced in a specified time. The second is the quality of written text. Measures of quality often consider issues such as: originality and creativity of thoughts and ideas contained in the text, logical sequencing and

organization of the text, use of appropriate genre-specific structures, coherence of concepts expressed, detail and comprehensiveness of the coverage of the topic, sensitivity to audience and clarity of expression which is underpinned by pragmatic awareness.

Research on handwriting and fluency of composition shows a strong and enduring relationship across a range of participant ages and methodological approaches. Research on handwriting and quality of written text is less consistent, but nevertheless points to a critically important variable.

It should be noted that the relationship between handwriting and fluency and the quality of written text is due to working memory limitations and cognitive load. There is limited evidence of a relationship between the appearance of handwriting and written text (Parker et al., 1991).

Handwriting and production of written text for young students

As long ago as 1976, Rice found that for students in grade 2, the speed of handwriting predicted academic achievement as well as ability to complete written assignments. More recently, a number of studies have found significant correlations between fluency in handwriting and students' ability to produce written text. Biemiller et al. (1993), working with children in grades 1–6, reported correlations of between .34 and .76 between fluency of handwriting and fluency in composition. Similarly, Meltza et al. (1985) found correlations of .27 between speed of writing the alphabet and fluency in composition and .30 for quality of written text for students in grades 4–9.

To more carefully control for influences involved in writing, Graham et al. (1997) used structural equation modelling to examine the relationships among handwriting, spelling and written language. They assessed 300 children in grades 1, 2 and 3 (primary) and 300 children in grades 4, 5 and 6 (intermediate) on two measures of handwriting: an alphabet task and a copying task. They also used a standardized spelling assessment and measured fluency and quality of composition. They found that mechanics related to spelling and handwriting accounted for 66% of the variance in compositional fluency in primary grades and 41% of the variance in intermediate grades. Mechanics accounted for a smaller proportion of the variance in quality of text: 25% in quality of composition for primary children and 42% of the variance for intermediate children. The impact of handwriting was also indicated in that Graham et al. reported that the relationship between spelling and composition was indirect and accounted for by its correlation with handwriting.

Jones and Christensen (1999), working with children in grade 1 in Australia, found a much stronger relationship between speed and accuracy of handwriting and quality of written text than was observed in other studies. They found that when reading was controlled, handwriting accounted for 53% of the variance in written text.

Using Berninger et al.'s (1991) constraints model, Berninger et al. (1992) examined the hypothesis that development of written text consists of two components. First, a process of text generation allows the writer to convert ideas into spoken language. Second, a transcription process converts spoken language into written text. They administered a number of measures to 300 children in grades 1, 2 and 3. The data supported their hypothesis that text generation was followed by transcription. They found that lower-level developmental variables are related to early writing skill. Specifically, rapid and automatic production of alphabet letters, rapid coding of orthographic information and speed of finger movement were the best predictors of both handwriting and composition skills.

Taken as a whole, correlational studies indicate that the ability to produce letters automatically accounts for a remarkably large proportion of the variance in compositional fluency and, depending on the age of students, a large proportion of the variance in quality of written text.

Relationship with learning disabilities

It seems that in much the same way that phonological awareness is a core area of deficit for children with reading disabilities (Stanovich, 1986), handwriting may be a core area of difficulty for students experiencing learning disabilities related to writing.

Weintraub and Graham (1998) compared a group of fifth-grade students with learning disabilities who were good and poor handwriters with a matched control group. They found that students with learning disabilities had slower handwriting and had difficulty in increasing their handwriting speed when required to do so. The inability of students to modify the speed of their handwriting to match task demands points to a difficulty in executive control which affects many students with learning disabilities.

Gregg et al. (2007) examined the writing of students with and without dyslexia. They found that fluency in handwriting along with spelling and vocabulary accounted for more of the variance in scores of quality of text for students identified with dyslexia than for other students.

Martlew (1992) compared the performance of a group of 10-year-old children identified as experiencing dyslexia with a group of same-aged peers and a group of spelling-age-matched, younger children. She found that the children with dyslexia were more similar to the younger spelling-matched group than their peers, indicating that automatized movement patterns accumulated from errors in both letter formation and spelling.

There is some evidence to suggest that handwriting difficulties may be particularly problematic for capable students experiencing problems in written language; in other words, students whose achievement in other areas indicates potential greater than their current achievement in written language. Yates et al. (1994) found that transcription skills were the best variables to differentiate good and poor writers among intellectually talented students in elementary grades.

Development of handwriting skills as students mature

In addition to the evidence of the role of handwriting on young children's written text quality, there seems to be emerging evidence to support the idea that difficulties in lower-order processes underpin writing difficulties for older students. Thus, it appears that children who demonstrate difficulties in handwriting do not 'grow out' of problems without intervention. Data from studies of adolescents and adults demonstrate that handwriting problems can be detected in older students through to university.

Smits-Engelsman and Van Galen (1997) conducted a longitudinal study of 16 children, in grades 2, 3 and 4, who were identified as dysgraphic because of poor handwriting. They found that without instructional assistance, the children appeared to be unable to improve their writing over the span of a year. Similarly, Mojet (1991) found that children aged 8–12 years generally showed an improvement in fluency as they grew older. However, poor handwriting persisted for children experiencing difficulties.

Berninger and Swanson (1994) examined the handwriting and composition of 300 primary, intermediate- and junior-grade students. They suggested that handwriting is critical in the development of all components of writing. However, transcription (the ability of students to get their ideas on the page) accounted for a decreasing proportion of variance in compositional fluency as students developed from primary to junior high school.

In contrast, Christensen and Jones (2000) reported that the relationship between handwriting and quality of written text is surprisingly robust from early elementary school to adolescence. They found that handwriting accounted for between 49% and 67% of the variance in quality of written text. For grade 1 students, it accounted for 49% of variance; this increased to 67% in grade 2. It reduced to 55% in grade 3 and 49% in grade 5. However, for grade 10 students, a remarkable 67% of variance was accounted for by handwriting.

Impact of handwriting for older students

Working with post-secondary students, Harrison and Beres (2007) examined the writing of 42 students with or without writing difficulties. They found that older students with writing difficulties over-emphasized lower-order skills (spelling and handwriting) when writing text. These students showed awareness of these difficulties and frequently commented on the nature of the problems they were experiencing.

Connelly (2006) argued that there had been increasing enrolments of students with dyslexia in universities. These students frequently rated writing as one of their greatest areas of difficulty. Connelly found that, compared with an age-matched control group, students with writing disabilities did not experience difficulties in higher-order processes such as idea generation or organization. However, they were significantly lower on measures of lower-order transcription skills; fluency in handwriting and spelling.

Connelly et al. (2005) examined the impact of low-level skills on undergraduates performing writing tasks under high- and low-pressure situations. They found that handwriting constrained performance more when students were working under exam conditions (high pressure) than when they wrote a formative class essay. They found that handwriting was significantly related to tutors' marks, number of words written (compositional fluency) and overall score of the essay. Thus, Connelly et al. suggest that low-level skills such as handwriting constrained undergraduate performance to a significant extent.

Connelly et al. (2006) looked at the fluency of transcription and higher-order writing skills (use of vocabulary, organization and coherence) with three groups of college students: students with dyslexia, an age-matched control group without dyslexia and a spelling match control. Scores for essay writing for the students with dyslexia and the spelling matched control group did not differ. However, the age-matched control was significantly better than the other two groups. Fluency in handwriting as measured by the alphabet task was significantly related to writing quality for the group of students with dyslexia and spelling-matched controls, but not for the age-matched students. This can be explained in terms of cognitive load. If mature writers have automated handwriting skills, then handwriting does not exert an influence on their ability to produce written text. However, if writers lack automaticity in handwriting, regardless of their age, then their ability to produce good-quality written text is impaired.

In addition to its impact on composition, competence in handwriting can influence how long it takes for students to complete written assignments and their competence in taking written notes during lectures. This seems to have a consequential impact on how often they write (Graham, 1992; Graham and Weintraub, 1996). Thus, handwriting can indirectly impact on older students' overall achievement as these critical areas of study are compromised.

Peverly et al. (2007) examined a little-recognized impact of handwriting for adolescents and adult learners: note-taking. They argued that the ability to record accurate and appropriate notes is critical to success in tertiary education. They also argued that if handwriting represents a high cognitive load, then attentional resources are not available for more sophisticated and complex aspects of note taking; holding lecture information in working memory; selecting, constructing and transforming important information using a range of cognitive and metacognitive strategies to transfer information to the page; and maintaining continuity of the lecture (Christensen et al., 1992; Kobayashi 2005; Piolat et al., 2005).

Peverly (2006) argued that issues of cognitive load related to transcription continue to

exert an influence into adulthood. He suggested that automaticity in transcription is essential to reduce the burden on working memory to enable writers to engage in the metacognitive processes necessary to produce competent text. Thus, the requirement for essay writing and taking lecture notes for tertiary students means that handwriting continues to be as important for adult learners as it is for children.

EVIDENCE FROM INTERVENTIONS IN HANDWRITING

Perhaps the most convincing evidence for the impact of handwriting on written language skills is provided by studies that have looked at interventions to enhance the handwriting of students with compromised skills. While there are only a limited number of these studies, they nevertheless have demonstrated that children experiencing difficulties in handwriting can experience significant benefit from a handwriting program.

Brooks et al. (1999) provided 17 grade 4 and 5 students, experiencing learning disabilities in writing, with a program that covered both transcription (handwriting and spelling) and composition skills. They found that students improved in automaticity in handwriting as well as in their ability to compose text.

Jones and Christensen (1999) identified 19 six- and seven-year-olds who had handwriting problems and 19 age- and reading-matched peers in the same classrooms. They measured proficiency in handwriting, quality of written language and reading. At the commencement of the study, the control group students scored significantly more on measures of handwriting and quality of written language. Children with handwriting problems were given approximately 10 minutes per day of handwriting intervention for 8 weeks. The control group had normal grade 1 writing instruction. Although the control group's scores were initially significantly higher, at the conclusion of the intervention the experimental group matched the control group on measures of handwriting and quality of written text.

There is also evidence that a handwriting intervention can be effective for older students. In a study with students in grades 8 and 9 who were experiencing handwriting problems, Christensen (2005) found that a handwriting intervention significantly improved both the quality and quantity of text that students could produce.

TEACHING STRATEGIES TO DEVELOP AUTOMATICITY IN HANDWRITING

Handwriting is a specific skill that requires the integration of the knowledge of orthography with a series of motor activities. Thus, programs must specifically teach orthographic–motor integration related to handwriting. There is little evidence that programs focusing on general fine motor activities in the absence of orthographic–motor integration will have a marked effect on improving handwriting. For example, Sudsawad et al. (2002) compared the effects of three conditions, kinaesthetic training, handwriting and no treatment, on the handwriting of 45 six- and seven-year-olds who had kinaesthetic and handwriting difficulties. They report that kinaesthetic training did not result in any gains in handwriting performance.

Legibility and penmanship

Traditionally, instruction in handwriting has focussed on penmanship, neatness and disciplined control of the pencil. While not having a clear direct influence on children's ability to produce high-quality written text, nevertheless, legibility can impact on their achievement. There appears to be a consistent relationship reported on legibility of handwriting and perceptions of quality of written text. Studies comparing the judgments on written text, differing only in legibility, demonstrated that papers which are written more neatly score higher than those with poorer legibility (Briggs, 1980; Chase, 1986; Hughes et al., 1983).

However, the relationship between handwriting and quality of written text depends on issues of cognitive load rather than penmanship. Thus, the focus of handwriting instruction should be on developing automaticity in orthographic-motor integration rather than penmanship.

Efficacy of practices in handwriting

Sassoon (2003) has written extensively on the need to teach handwriting. She suggests that it is critical for very young children to develop habits of correct letter formation. Preschool activities can consist of pre-writing patterns which encourage the development of correct motor behaviours to form letters (e.g. downward strokes). Sassoon argues that young children should be discouraged from engaging in 'spontaneous' writing unless they can form letters correctly. As soon as children have the prerequisite skills (e.g. the ability to sit still and focus for a short time), they should begin formal handwriting instruction. These lessons should be systematic, short and repetitive, and lead children to feel a sense of satisfaction with mastery of the skill. Teaching of letters should follow a letter-family sequence where letters of similar shape are taught together. She also suggests that cursive writing be encouraged as early as possible.

There are relatively few studies that have specifically investigated instructional efficacy of various teaching strategies in handwriting. One notable exception is a study conducted by Berninger et al. (1997). They assigned children in first grade who had difficulty in handwriting to one of five treatment conditions:

a Writing letters after seeing a teacher modelling the process

b Writing letters after looking at a written model with arrows to indicate the direction in which it should be formed
c Writing letters while looking at an unmarked copy
d Writing letters from memory after looking at a copy with direction arrows
e Writing letters from memory after looking at an unmarked copy

In addition to the experimental groups, a control group worked on phonological awareness.

Berninger et al. hypothesized that writing from memory would facilitate the development of retrieval paths and subsequently facilitate automaticity in handwriting. They also suggested that direction arrows would facilitate the creation of memory routines.

Children in all handwriting groups improved more in proficiency in handwriting than children in the control group. Moreover, the group which wrote letters from memory after looking at a copy with arrows had better scores on a measure of fluency in writing text than the other treatment groups and the control group. Thus, it appears that approaches that encourage children to retrieve letter shapes from memory, particularly where directional arrows are used to cue actions, are more effective than other approaches.

Graham et al. (2000) looked at the impact of supplementary handwriting instruction for 38 grade 1 students who wrote slowly and were experiencing difficulty in learning to write. Half of the students were assigned to handwriting intervention. The program was based on a model that suggested that writing requires: retrieval and holding letters in memory, accessing corresponding motor program, setting parameters such as size of letter and speed of writing, and executing the production of the text (Ellis, 1982; Margolin, 1984; van Galen, 1991). Thus, children in the handwriting condition learned the names of the letters of the alphabet, were taught how to form each letter, adjusted parameters of speed and fluency by rewriting text at a faster pace, and practiced writing single letters, words and sentences.

The other half of the students was assigned to a control group which was provided with instruction in phonological awareness. The children were provided with 27 lessons, each of 15 minutes in duration. Assessment which immediately followed the conclusion of the sessions indicated that the children in the handwriting condition performed better than control group students on measures of handwriting, as well as fluency in production written text. However, differences in quality of written text were not detected, nor did the program lead to enhanced motivation and attitude towards writing. The advantages that the experimental group obtained from the program were maintained at a 6-month follow-up. However, they seemed to be slightly attenuated, leading to the suggestion that a longer-term or more powerful intervention may be necessary for enduring improvement to be experienced by children with handwriting difficulties.

In a series of studies, Berninger et al. (2006) examined the relationship between intervention in handwriting and children's ability to produce written text. Working with grade 1 children, they compared an intervention that focused on orthographic-free motor activities such as tracing plastic letters, motor-free orthographic activities such as touching and naming letters on a keyboard, and direct instruction in handwriting. They found that the handwriting program was more effective in developing automaticity in handwriting than either of the orthographic motor-free activities. In a second study, they found that neither motor training nor orthographic training added to the impact of direct instruction in handwriting. It was also noted that one aspect of the intervention that seemed to be effective was the combination of a skill-based component which focused on writing letters and short composition activities.

These two studies also appeared to show that handwriting intervention enhanced reading. However, a third study indicated that handwriting added to a reading program failed to demonstrate improved reading skills.

Finally, they examined a multi-layered approach to building skills of third and fourth graders at risk of writing difficulties. The intervention included a comprehensive approach to building composition skills, including transcription, text generation and executive functions such as planning, monitoring and revising. They found that students showed significant improvement on measures of composition as well as in high-stake tests involving written language.

Jones and Christensen (1999) implemented a program with grade 1 students which included encouraging students to use conventional letter formations and facilitating speed and efficiency. Letter shapes were first modelled by the teacher. Modelling was followed by guided and independent practice. Children wrote letters with and without paper. For example, they drew letters in the air, jumped on the floor, used finger paint and traced letters on their desks. On paper, letter tracks were used to provide students with practice. Children used coloured pencils to repeatedly follow the tracks. They found that the program significantly improved children's handwriting as well as the quantity and quality of compositions they could write.

It is not clear the extent to which opportunities to write extended text will enhance handwriting. Graham (1992) suggested that improvement in handwriting could occur as a result of students having frequent opportunities to write. However, Christensen (2005) found that for grade 8 and 9 students with handwriting difficulties, opportunities to write extended text did not result in gains in handwriting, or quantity or quality of written language. It may be that if students have a significant lack in proficiency in handwriting, an explicit skills-based program is essential to develop automaticity. However, students whose handwriting is developing normally, or only lagging slightly behind age expectations, may be able to develop automaticity through everyday experiences in writing text. This points to the need to carefully screen students to ascertain their level of proficiency in relation to the development of their peers, and then to tailor a program according to individual needs.

Relatively few studies have examined teachers' capacity to change practices in relation to developing skills in handwriting. However, in one study, Jones (2004) worked with teachers working with kindergarten-aged children. She provided two groups of 15 teachers with 1 hour of professional development. One group was told of the importance of teaching handwriting and given some tips on how to develop written language skills. They were not given any concrete information on how to teach handwriting. The other group was given information on how to teach handwriting.

The key to the instructional approach adopted in the study was on developing fluency rather than neatness or disciplined control in writing. Teachers were encouraged to use large fluent strokes with their students – writing on a white board, finger-painting or writing in the air. One useful technique was to use bubble letters. Children were given large sheets of paper on which were drawn bubble shapes of letters. The bubbles contained a green star to mark the starting position and a red star where the stroke should stop. They also contained arrows to indicate the direction in which the letter should be made. Children selected three coloured pencils and drew 'rainbow' letters. The emphasis was on teaching children the shape of the letters using large, fluid strokes. Other than the 1 hour of professional development, no intervention was carried out with the teachers or students.

Jones visited each classroom mid-semester to observe how teachers taught handwriting. She found significant differences on every dimension of handwriting instruction that she observed, with the exception of one (providing parents with information on Beginner's Alphabet Script). Teachers who attended the written language professional development focused on careful pencil control. They used tightly constrained lined pages and commercially available texts as a basis for their handwriting program. In comparison, teachers in the handwriting professional development group did not utilize any of these programmatic approaches. They focused on: fluency rather than control; early intervention and early assessment; and identification and intervention with children who were at risk of experiencing difficulties. In a surprising finding, these teachers introduced the letter-shapes at a rate of approximately one per day early in the year. Later, they returned to each letter to provide extended practice in writing the letter. Control group teachers tended to teach each letter-shape for one week before moving on to the next.

Differences between the two classrooms at the end of the year were quite marked in terms of both handwriting, fluency of composition and quality of written text. Classes taught by teachers who completed the handwriting professional development had significantly higher scores on an alphabet measure of automaticity in handwriting, wrote significantly more text and had higher quality of written text scores. In a follow-up a year later, after children had been dispersed across a number of teachers who had not been involved in either of the professional development session, the differences between the two groups were sustained and dramatic. Handwriting children scored 40% higher than control group children in handwriting, wrote 65% more text and scored 30% higher on quality of written text. The handwriting children also made significantly fewer errors in spelling when composing a piece of text. Although they wrote significantly more text, they made 50% fewer spelling errors at both post and delayed post tests.

Instruction for older students

Adolescents who experience difficulties in producing written text present particular instructional challenges. These students have often failed in writing for many years. Inability to write often leads to frustration and development of a lack of a sense of self-efficacy around writing tasks. Given that

these students may have been exposed to instruction for more than 7 years, it would seem reasonable to suggest that it is not possible for them to develop the necessary automaticity in writing to become proficient in production of written text. Thus, persisting with teaching handwriting is likely to be a fruitless exercise and some form of compensatory mechanism, such as computer use, should be put in place.

While relatively few studies have examined the ability of older students to develop automaticity in handwriting, the available evidence suggests that it is possible for these students to become proficient in handwriting and that a structured, sequenced handwriting program can have a dramatic impact on students' written language.

Christensen (2005) identified two groups of grade 8 and 9 students who scored more than two standard deviations below the mean of their peers on an alphabetic task that measured fluency in orthographic–motor integration (handwriting). The instructional intervention for one group consisted of writing a journal for 20 minutes per day, 4 days per week for 8 weeks. The other group spent the same amount of time working on a handwriting program. The program provided structured practice in writing letters and words. The skills sequence commenced with single letters based on shape (e.g. letters based on an anti-clockwise circle, 'a', 'o', 'c', came first, then letters based on a stroke 'l', 'i', 'j', etc). When students had practised each letter of the alphabet, they moved onto two-letter sequences and then three-letter sequences and words. A key feature of the instruction was regular, timed mastery tests. Before students could progress from practising one letter to the next, they needed to complete a time trial where they wrote more than 58 letters in 45 seconds.

Although the two groups were equivalent at pretest, at the conclusion of the intervention the handwriting group had significantly higher scores in fluency in handwriting. In addition, handwriting students wrote significantly more text (an indicator of fluency in composition) and had higher scores in quality of text.

Frequency and durations of lessons

To a large extent, instruction to develop automaticity in handwriting requires regimes of practice that are similar to those required to develop automaticity in other skills. The key is engagement in short, frequent practice sessions. Sessions should be of limited duration – 10–20 minutes and conducted frequently – daily if possible.

Evidence from intervention studies suggests that in order for students to develop fluency in composition there should be two elements in an effective program. First, students need to develop handwriting skill by practicing writing letters and words in isolation from other tasks. Second, they should have opportunities to use their skills in writing extended text (Graham and Weintraub, 1996).

Role of teacher verbal mediation in practice

The efficacy of teacher verbal mediation in handwriting is unclear. Verbal mediation occurs when the teacher demonstrates and provides students with a series of verbal cues to guide their movements (e.g. 'the stroke starts at the top and...').

There is some evidence to suggest that the verbal description of how to form letters correctly may facilitate learning correct letter formation for very young, beginning writers (e.g. kindergarten children) (Graham and Weintraub, 1996). However, Berninger et al. (1997) found that verbal mediation was not effective for older students. These students performed better when they were provided with visual models of letters with directional arrows to indicate the path of the movement they should follow. It appears that for older students, teacher verbal mediation may actually interfere with their internal cognitive processes of retrieving the orthographic and motor information they require to produce letters and words on the page.

Impact of style and script

Relatively little research has been conducted into the impact of various forms of script on the development of automaticity in handwriting. Peters (1985) argued that, based on kinaesthetic learning, there was a strong relationship between accuracy in spelling and fluent, joined-up (cursive) handwriting. Thus, Medwell and Wray (2007) suggested that, in Britain, Peters' work led to reform of the practice of handwriting to focus on use of a script style that included entry and exit strokes and the joining of letters as early as possible. However, there has been a dearth of empirical support for claims of the impact of cursive style on proficiency in handwriting.

Graham et al. (1998) analysed the writing of 600 students in grades 4–9. They found that students who used a combination of manuscript and cursive letters were the most fluent. Students using a mixed style were also judged to have higher scores on a measure of legibility. However, there were no significant differences in speed or legibility for students who used either manuscript or cursive exclusively.

This finding contrasts with Jones (2004) who found that children who used a mixture of printing and cursive had lower scores on a measure of automaticity in handwriting, as well as lower scores in quality of written text than either students who used printing only or cursive only. Jones' data appeared to indicate that students could automate either printing or cursive, and that alternating between these two styles was an indicator of lack of automaticity – at least for the sample of students she examined. The explanation for these apparently contradictory findings could reside in a number of factors, including the age of the students (Jones' students were younger than those of Graham et al.), the script the students were using or an unidentified aspect of the instructional conditions under which the students were learning to write.

In summary, existing research seems to indicate that carefully structured regimes of practice in handwriting can lead to increases in automaticity of handwriting, with consequential improvements in fluency of composition and quality of written text. Practice in handwriting should include short, frequent lessons of practicing production of letters and words, as well as using handwriting skills to compose text. The focus for both young children and older students should be on building fluency rather than rigid pencil control or precise letter positioning between lines. The role of verbal mediation is not clear. However, it appears that teacher verbal instructions may be useful for very young children in the beginning stages of learning to write, but not for older writers.

Given the impact that automaticity in handwriting has on children's ability to produce written text and the paucity of evidence on the nature of effective practices in building that automaticity, there appears to be a critical need for studies to examine issues such as style and script, regimes of practices and teaching strategies related to efficacy in developing proficiency in handwriting.

UTILITY OF COMPUTERS IN REPLACING THE NEED FOR HANDWRITING

Many educators believe that the ready availability of computer technology has obviated the need for students to be able to master written text. Two issues arise from this proposition. First, the ability to produce written text remains an important facet of schooling. In order to complete class work and many assessment tasks, students from kindergarten to tertiary education must have automaticity in handwriting in order to complete written tasks. Given the relative ease with which interventions have been able to effect significant change in handwriting, even with older students who have experienced many years of frustration and failure,

it seems reasonable to teach handwriting to both young writers, as well as older students who are experiencing difficulties.

Second, the same relationship holds between word-processed text and keyboarding skills, as holds between handwriting and written language. If writers allocate attention to the low-level activity of typing, then they do not have sufficient cognitive resources to attend to the complex higher-order aspects of writing. Christensen (2004) examined the relationship between handwriting and handwritten text, as well as typing and typed text, for 276 students in grades 8 and 9. She found significant correlations between handwriting and written text and corresponding correlations between typing and typed text.

Connelly et al. (2007) looked at fluency in handwriting and typing for grade 5 and 6 students. There was a strong relationship between handwriting and keyboarding skills. Specifically, speed and legibility of handwriting accounted for 71% of the variance in keyboarding. This suggests that merely switching a student to a keyboard is unlikely to ameliorate difficulties in text generation that result from handwriting. These students are likely to experience the same difficulties in typing.

Finally, there appears to be some evidence to suggest that keyboarding does not confer a significant advantage in terms of students' production of written language. Interestingly, in the Connelly et al. study, children were consistently faster at handwriting than keyboarding. In keeping with cognitive load theory, children's handwritten compositions were of higher quality than typed texts. Connelly et al. found that keyboard texts were up to 2 years developmentally behind handwritten texts.

Berninger et al. (1998) assigned two groups of elementary-aged children (spelling disabled only or spelling and handwriting disabled) to one of two conditions (pencil or computer response). They found that using a computer keyboard provided no benefit over handwriting to these children.

Finally, in a study of the impact of writing on pre-schoolers' ability to recognize letters,

Longcamp et al. (2004) asked two groups of 38 children to either copy letters by hand or type letters. They found that handwriting letters was more effective in developing letter recognition than typing.

In could be argued that, as keyboard strokes require less intricate fine motor control than handwriting, there could be some students who would benefit from utilizing personal computers rather persevering with hand-produced text. However, taken as a whole, the evidence seems to suggest that there is little support for keyboarding to replace instruction in handwritten text for the majority of students.

In conclusion, handwriting is a key but frequently neglected factor facilitating young children's ability to produce written text. Researchers have consistently found significant correlations between measures of proficiency in handwriting and fluency in composition as well as quality of the compositions. It also appears that many students who are identified as having writing disabilities have a core difficulty in handwriting. In addition to regression studies, intervention studies have shown that practice in handwriting, both for young, novice writers and older students, can build proficiency in handwriting, and consequent fluency and quality of written text.

This work has significant implications for curriculum development. Handwriting should form a core part of the curriculum for young children. The aim should be to enhance children's ability to write letters and words quickly and effortlessly. The focus should be on fluency in letter production rather than the traditional approach characterized by neatness and good 'penmanship'.

REFERENCES

Berninger, V. (1994). *Reading and Writing Acquisition: A Developmental Neuropsychological Perspective*. Madison, WI: Brown & Benchmark.

Berninger, V. (1999). 'Coordinating transcription and text generation in working memory during composing: Automatic and constructive processes', *Learning Disabilities Quarterly*, 22(2): 99–112.

Berninger, V. and Graham, S. (1998). 'Language by hand: A synthesis of a decade of research on handwriting', *Handwriting Review*, 12(1): 11–25.

Berninger, V. and Swanson, H. L. (1994). 'Modifying Hayes and Flower's model of killed writing to explain beginning and developing writing'. In E. Butterfield (ed.), *Children's Writing: Towards a Process of Theory of the Development of Skilled Writing*. Greenwich, CT: JAI Press. pp. 57–81.

Berninger, V., Mizokawa, D., and Bragg, R. (1991). 'Theory-based diagnosis and remediation of writing disabilities', *Journal of Educational Psychology*, 29: 57–79.

Berninger, V., Yates, C., Cartwright, A., Rutberg, J., Remy E., and Abbott, R. (1992). 'Lower-level developmental skills in beginning writing'. *Reading and Writing: An Interdisciplinary Journal*, 4: 257–280.

Berninger, V., Rutberg, J., Abbott, R., Garcia, N., Anderson-Youngstrom, M., Brooks, A., a nd Fulton, C. (2006). 'Tier 1 and Tier 2 early intervention for handwriting and composing', *Journal of School Psychology*, 44(1): 3–30.

Berninger, V., Abbott, R., Rogan, L., Reed, E., Abbott, S., Brooks, A., Vaughan, K., and Graham, S. (1998). 'Teaching spelling to children with specific learning disabilities: The mind's eye ear and eye brat the computer or pencil', *Learning Disabilities Quarterly*, 21(2): 106–122.

Berninger, V., Vaughn, K., Abbott, R., Abbott, S., Rogan, L., Brooks, A., Reed, E., and Graham, S. (1997). 'Treatment of handwriting problems in beginning writers: Transfer from handwriting to composition'. *Journal of Educational Psychology*, 89: 652–666.

Berninger, V., Vaughn, K., Abbott, R., Begay, K., Coleman, K. B., Curtain, G., Hawkins, J. M., and Graham, S. (2002). 'Teaching spelling and composition alone and together: Implications for the simple view of writing', *Journal of Educational Psychology*, 94(2): 291–304.

Biemiller, A., Regan, E., and Gang, B. (1993). *Studies in the Development of Writing Speed: Age Task and Individual Differences*. University of Toronto: On, Canada. Unpublished manuscript.

Blass, T. and Siegman, A. (1975). 'A psycholinguistic comparison of speech, dictation, and writing'. *Language and Speech*, 18: 20–34.

Bransford, J., Brown, A., and Cocking, R. (2000). *How People Learn: Brain, Mind, Experience, and School*. Washington, DC: National Academy Press.

Briggs, D. (1980). 'A study of the influence of handwriting upon grades using exam-grade classrooms'. *Educational Review*, 32: 185–193.

Christensen, C. (2004). 'Relationship between ortho-graphic-motor integration and computer use for the production of creative and well-structured written text', *British Journal of Educational Psychology*, 74(4): 551–564.

Christensen, C. (2005). 'The role of orthographic-motor integration in the production of creative and well-structured written text for students in secondary school', *Educational Psychology*, 25(5): 441–453.

Christensen, C., Massey, D. R., and Isaacs, P. (1992). 'Cognitive strategies and study habits: An analysis of the measurement of tertiary students' learning', *British Journal of Educational Psychology*, 61: 290–299.

Christensen, C. and Jones, D. (2000). 'Handwriting: An underestimated skill in the development of written language', *Handwriting Today*, 2: 56–69.

Connelly, V. (2006). 'Contribution of lower order skills to the written composition of college students with and without dyslexia', *Developmental Neuropsychology*, 29(1): 175–196.

Connelly, V., Dockrell, J., and Barnett, J. (2005). 'The slow handwriting of undergraduate students constrains overall performance in exam essays', *Educational Psychology*, 25(1): 99–107.

Connelly, V., Gee, D., and Walsh, E. (2007). 'A comparison of keyboarded and handwritten compositions and the relationship with transcription speed', *British Journal of Educational Psychology*, 77(2): 479–492.

De la Paz, S. and Graham, S. (1997). 'Effects of dictation and advanced planning instruction on the composing of students with writing and learning problems', *Journal of Educational Psychology*, 89(2): 203–222.

Ellis, A. (1982). 'Spelling and writing (and reading and speaking)'. In A. Ellis (ed.), *Normality and Pathology in Cognitive Functions*. London: Academic Press. pp. 113–146.

Graham, S. (1990). 'The role of production factors in learning disabled students' compositions', *Journal of Educational Psychology*, 82(4): 781–791.

Graham, S. (1992). 'Issues in handwriting instruction', *Focus on Exceptional Children*, 89: 223–234.

Graham, S. and Weintraub, N. (1996). 'A review of handwriting research: Progress and prospects from 1980 to 1994', *Educational Psychology Review*, 8(1): 7–87.

Graham, S., Harris, K., and Fink, B. (2000). 'Is handwriting causally related to learning to write? Treatment of handwriting problems in beginning writers', *Journal of Educational Psychology*, 92(4): 620–633.

Graham, S., Weintraub, N., and Berninger, V. (1998). 'The relationship between handwriting style and speed and legibility', *Journal of Educational Research*, 91(5): 290–296.

Graham, S., Berninger, V., Abbott, R., Abbott, S., and Whitaker, D. (1997). 'Role of mechanics in composing of elementary school students: A new methodological approach', *Journal of Educational Psychology*, 89(1): 170–182.

Gregg, N., Coleman, C., Davis, M., and Chalk, J. C. (2007). 'Times essay writing: Implications for high-stakes tests', *Journal of Learning Disabilities*, 40(4): 306–318.

Hall, N. (1987). *The Emergence of Literacy*. Sevenoaks: Hodder and Stoughton.

Harrison, G. and Beres, D. (2007). 'The writing strategies of post-secondary students with writing difficulties', *Exceptionality Education in Canada*, 17(2): 221–242.

Hayes, J. and Flowers, L. (1980). 'Identifying the organization of writing processes'. In L. Gregg and E. Steinberg (eds.), *Cognitive Processes in Writing*. Hillsdale, NJ: Erlbaum. pp. 3–30.

Hidi, S. and Hildyard, A. (1983). 'The comparison of oral and written productions in two discourse types', *Discourse Processes*, 6(2): 91–105.

Jones, D. (2004). 'Automaticity of the transcription process in the production of written text'. Unpublished doctoral dissertation. University of Queensland, Brisbane, Australia.

Jones, D. and Christensen, C. (1999). 'Relationship between automaticity in handwriting and students' ability to generate written text', *Journal of Educational Psychology*, 91(1): 44–49.

Kobayashi, K. (2005). 'What limits the encoding effect of note taking? A meta-analytic examination', *Contemporary Educational Psychology*, 30: 242–262.

LaBerge, D. and Samuels, S. J. (1974). 'Toward a theory of automatic information processing in reading', *Cognitive Psychology*, 6(2): 293–323.

Lesgold, A., Rubison, H., Feltovich, P., Glaser, R., Klopfet, D., and Wang, Y. (1988). 'Expertise in a complex skill: Diagnosing X-ray pictures'. In M. T. Chi, R. Glaser, and M. Farr (eds.), *The Nature of Expertise*. Hillsdale, NJ: Erlbaum. pp. 311–342.

Longcamp, M., Zerbato-Poudou, M., and Velay, J. (2004). 'The influence of writing practice on letter recognition in preschool children: A comparison between handwriting and typing'. *Acta Psychologica*, 119(1): 67–79.

Margolin, D. (1984). 'The neuropsychology of writing and spelling: Semantic, phonological, motor and perceptual processes', *The Quarterly Journal of Experimental Psychology*, 36(3): 459–489.

Martlew, M. (1992). 'Handwriting and spelling: Dyslexic children's abilities compared with children of the same chronological age and younger children of the same spelling level', *British Journal of Educational Psychology*, 62(3): 375–390.

McCutchen, D. (1996). 'A capacity theory of writing: Working memory in composition', *Educational Psychology Review*, 8(2): 299–325.

Medwell, J. and Wray, D. (2007). 'Handwriting: What do we know and what do we need to know?', *Literacy*, 41(1):10–15.

Meltza, L., Fenton, T., and Persky, S. (1985). 'A developmental study of the components of written language in children with and without learning difficulties', Paper presented at the annual meeting of the American Educational Research association, Chicago, ILL.

Mojet, J. (1991). 'Characteristics of the developing handwriting skill in elementary education'. In J. Wann, A. Wing, D. Wolpert, and N. Sovik (eds.), *Development of Graphic Skills*. London: Academic Press. pp. 53–75.

Parker, R., Tindal, G., and Hasbrouck, J. (1991). 'Progress monitoring with objective measures of writing performance for students with learning disabilities', *Exceptional Children*, 58(1): 61–73.

Piolat, A., Olive, T., and Kellogg, R. (2005). 'Cognitive effort during note taking'. *Applied Cognitive Psychology*, 19(3): 291–312.

Reece, J. (1992). 'Cognitive processes in the development of written composition skills: The role of planning, dictation, and computer tools'. Unpublished doctoral dissertation, La Trobe University, Bundora, Canada.

Rice, R. (1976). 'The use of handwriting rate for predicting academic achievement and suggesting curriculum modifications', *Dissertations Abstracts International*, 37: 1887A .

Scardamalia, M., Bereiter, C., and Goleman, H. (1982). 'The role of production factors in writing ability'.

In M. Levine, W. Carey, and A. Crocker (eds.), *Developmental Behavioral Pediatrics*. Philadelphia: W. B. Saunders. pp 477–490.

Schlagal, B. (2007). 'Best practices in spelling and handwriting'. In S. Graham, C. MacArthur, and J. Fitzgerald (eds.), *Best Practices in Writing Instruction: Solving Problems in the Teaching of Literacy*. New York: Guliford Press. pp. 179–201.

Schneider, W. and Shriffrin, R. (1977). 'Controlled and automatic human information processing: Detection, search and attention'. *Psychological Review*, 84(1): 1–66.

Smits-Engelsman, B. and Van Galen, G. (1997). 'Dysgraphia in children: Lasting deficiency or transient developmental delay?', *Journal of Experimental Child Psychology*, 67(2): 164–184.

Stanovich, K. (1986). 'Matthew effects in reading: Some consequences of individual differences in the acquisition of literacy', *Reading Research Quarterly*, 21(4): 360–407.

Sudsawad, P., Trombly, C., Henderson, A., and Tickle-Degnen, L. (2002). 'Testing the effect of kinesthetic training on handwriting performance in first-grade students', *American Journal of Occupational Therapy*, 56(1): 26–33.

Sweller, J. (1988). 'Cognitive load during problem solving: Effects on learning', *Cognitive Science*, 12(3): 257–285.

Teale, W. and Sulzby, E. (eds.) (1986). *Emergent Literacy: Writing and Reading*. Norwood, NJ: Ablex.

Van Galen, C. (1991). 'Handwriting: Issues for a psychomotor theory', *Human Movement Science*, 10(2): 165–191.

Weintraub, N. and Graham, S. (1998). 'Writing legibly and quickly: A study of children's ability to adjust their handwriting to meet common classroom demands'. *Learning Disabilities: Research and Practice*, 13(2): 146–152.

Wray, J. and Lewis, D. (1997). 'Handwriting: what do we know and what do we need to know?', *Literacy*, 41(1): 10–15.

Yates, C., Berninger, V., and Abbott, R. (1994). 'Writing problems in intellectually gifted children', *Journal for the Education of the Gifted*, 18: 131–155.

Engaging and Motivating Children to Write

Pietro Boscolo

As teachers of language skills regret, pupils in the upper grades of primary and middle school often do not enjoy writing. There may be several reasons for this low level of motivation, but two seem to be particularly relevant. Firstly, whereas in preschool and the early grades of primary school, children use writing as a way of expressing their feelings and experiences, in the upper grades of primary school, writing is often based on stereotyped text genres and, consequently, is perceived by students as being a limited-purpose and routine activity. Secondly, since writing tasks become more demanding and are more rigorously assessed by teachers in the upper grades, the children feel vulnerable when asked to write. This sense of inadequacy can be even stronger in children who, due to their social background and/or limited linguistic competence, have difficulty carrying out school tasks requiring the use of written language. Thus, the perception of writing as a routine and not very interesting activity as well as the threat of harsh assessment, both contribute to some children developing a negative attitude and low perceptions of themselves as competent writers. This, in consequence, reduces the motivation to write.

Despite exploring practically all aspects of school writing over the past three decades, researchers into writing initially neglected aspects connected with motivation. Daly and Miller's (1975a, b) analysis of university students' anxiety related to academic writing (*writing apprehension*) represents a lone study, conducted before the development of writing research and overshadowed by subsequent studies on self-efficacy in writing. The two main approaches, which have dominated writing research since the 1980s—cognitive and socioconstructivist—have exerted a relevant but indirect influence on the study of motivation to write. On the one hand, cognitively-oriented scholars have emphasized the complexity of writing processes and the difficulties that young and novice writers have to deal with. In general, these researchers have been more concerned with devising instructional methods enabling young students to face the cognitive and linguistic obstacles when writing, such as procedural facilitation (Bereiter and Scardamalia, 1987) and self-regulation strategies (e.g., Harris and Graham, 1996), than with contrasting the negative effects of such obstacles on less-competent students' attitude to writing.

The socioconstructivist approach to literacy learning, on the other hand, which views writing as a situated activity and emphasizes its social and cultural dimensions, has strongly criticized traditional writing instruction as being based on a formal view of genres and unauthentic tasks, and has described the conditions which can make writing a meaningful experience for young students. Although the motivational consequences of this view of writing have not been made explicit by writing researchers, with very few exceptions (e.g., Oldfather and Dahl, 1994), this approach has contributed greatly to underlining the conditions which may foster motivation to write in the classroom. However, a decisive contribution to the conceptualization of motivation to write has come from research on motivation at the end of the 1980s, when some motivational constructs—in particular, interest and self-efficacy—were applied to the study of writing.

The present chapter comprises three parts. In the first part, motivation to write is conceptualized in terms of two motivational dimensions: the meaningfulness of writing activities and tasks proposed in the classroom, and students' sense of their own competence. In the second part, the findings and implications of studies, which have tested the effectiveness of instructional practices aimed at stimulating students' motivation to write are analysed. Lastly, a profile of a student with a high level of motivation to write is described and discussed.

CONCEPTUALIZING MOTIVATION TO WRITE

As mentioned in the foregoing, research on motivation has provided a few relevant constructs to investigate the problems of learning to write. However, a more basic contribution of this research field is to clarify the meaning of motivation itself in relation to a specific school subject. What emerges from the variety of theoretical frameworks and constructs,

which characterize current research is that motivation to learn a specific school subject should not be traced back to a single and more or less simple 'drive' or 'will'. Instead, it is a pattern of cognitive, metacognitive, and affective variables, which determine the way a student approaches—or tries to avoid—the subject (Brophy, 1999, 2004; Covington, 1999). Moreover, motivation is not a characteristic *of* the student, but is 'distributed' in the learning environment (Stipek, 2002; Volet and Järvelä, 2001; Wigfield and Eccles, 2002). In the case of writing, the way a student approaches a writing task is influenced by his or her competence level in writing, as well as by the way writing tasks are organized and proposed in his or her instructional context. In turn, the attractiveness and relevance of writing activities depends on the teacher's ideas about writing, which are more or less implicitly transmitted to students through teaching.

Two constructs are particularly helpful to conceptualize motivation to learn a specific subject (Brophy, 1999). One is the meaningfulness of the activities a student is engaged in; that is, the extent to which a learning task is perceived by the student as relevant to his or her personal objectives. While learning to compose texts, students not only acquire cognitive and linguistic skills and knowledge, but also learn a lot of things *about* writing. For instance, they come to view writing as an engaging or, alternatively, a repetitive activity, and a subject more or less relevant to their future study and lives. In sum, students develop a set of beliefs, many of which are implicit, about the function and role of school writing (Boscolo and Gelati, 2007; Bruning and Horn, 2000). The other construct is a student's sense of competence, that is, the extent to which he or she feels able to engage in a task, especially as a consequence of previous experiences of success or failure in the subject. This second aspect is particularly important when, as in the case of writing, a subject is perceived as demanding and relevant in the curriculum. Consistent with this conceptualization, we argue in this chapter that motivation to write is an attitude to, or view of, writing. It is based on a set of beliefs that students develop about writing, and themselves as writers, through the various situations in which they are asked to write and use their written productions. In turn, students' attitude towards writing influences their approach to specific writing tasks, and the degree to which they are willing to engage in them.

Motivation in its various aspects is not fixed and unchangeable. In the early grades of primary school, children experience the different functions of writing: narrating personal events, describing people and objects, inventing short poems, and so on (Chapman, 1994). These genres have different motivational potentials, since they may be perceived by children variously as enjoyable, boring, easy, or demanding. In the primary upper grades and in middle and high schools, knowledge elaboration tends to become the main function of school writing. The multi-genre nature of writing is progressively restricted to essays and compositions in which students are basically required to expose, in a correct and possibly personal form, what they have learned (Boscolo and Hidi, 2007). The different functions of writing through school grades may have different motivational consequences in terms of meaningfulness and sense of competence. If the progressive reduction of writing genres traditionally adopted in school—from free narration of personal experiences to elaboration of knowledge—is based on meaningful learning experiences through which students can progressively learn different functions of writing, the motivational consequence should be positive. Instead, the consequences would most probably be negative if students experience a genre as boring and/or a source of failure.

Our use of the expressions 'writing activity' and 'writing task' might induce one to consider them synonymous. In fact, this is not so. In the neo-Vygotskian perspective that we adopt, the meaning of writing activity refers to how a task is organized. As Wertsch (1985) pointed out, 'an activity or activity setting is grounded in a set of assumptions about appropriate roles, goals, and means used by the participants in the setting' (pp. 212). In this perspective, an activity setting determines the significance of the operations involved in the activity—such as, in the case of writing, the teacher's moves (directions, guide, feedback, etc.) on the one hand, and students' writing behaviours on the other. Therefore, the way a task is organized reflects both the role of writing in the curriculum and the teacher's view of writing and writing instruction. A view of writing as mainly focusing on reproducing text types or, alternatively, on student's personal elaboration of knowledge and experience, has implications for the ways specific writing tasks are organized in the classroom, and how writing is related to other disciplines and evaluated by the teacher. This, in turn, bears some consequences on students' view of, and attitude to, writing.

On the basis of the conceptualization of motivation to write in terms of a student's perception of the meaningfulness of school writing and sense of competence, empirical studies on motivation to write can be grouped into two categories: studies on the instructional methods, which may make writing attractive to students, and studies on self-efficacy in writing and its relation to a student's performance. Most studies on instructional methods have been conducted within the framework of research into the varying levels of interest of the pupils.

MOTIVATING STUDENTS TO WRITE: A MATTER OF TOPIC AND ACTIVITIES

Topic as a source of interest

At the end of the 1980s, the concept of interest, as elaborated by cognitive scholars in the previous decade (Hidi and Baird, 1986; Kintsch, 1980; Schank, 1979), was applied to writing research. Interest has been defined as a motivational variable, as well as a psychological state that takes place during interactions between people and objects in the environment, and is characterized by increased attention, concentration, and affect (Hidi, 1990, 2001; Renninger, Hidi, and Krapp, 1992). Experiencing interest involves positive affect, which can be assumed to be combined or integrated with cognition (Renninger, 2000). Another general characteristic of interest is its content or object-specificity. Rather than being globally interested, individuals have interest in specific activities, subjects, topics, or tasks.

Most researchers agree about the distinction between two types of interest: situational and individual (or personal). Situational interest is evoked rather suddenly by something in the environment that focuses attention and represents an action that may or may not have a long-term effect on the individual's knowledge and value systems; in other words, it may or may not develop into a long-standing, individual interest. The adjective 'situational' has been used as a generic label for various sources of interest. In and out of the school setting, the 'interesting' features, which stimulate an individual's attention and search for information often emerge from oral and written discourse. Discursive situations, which may be sources of interest include an article in a journal, a lecture, or a TV program, for example. Situational interest stimulated by oral or written texts has been called *text-based* (Hidi and Baird, 1988). The second type or category, individual interest, refers to a relatively enduring predisposition to attend to events and objects, as well as to reengage in activities (Krapp, 2000; Renninger, 2000). This predisposition develops slowly, tends to be long lasting and is associated with increased knowledge and values (Renninger, 1992, 2000).

The first application of the concept of interest in writing is with regard to the topic. Hidi and McLaren (1990, 1991) analysed the influence of topic on writing performance. Since interest stimulates intellectual activity, the authors assumed that when children can

choose to write about a topic, which they find interesting, they will write better than children who are allowed no choice. In an early study, Hidi and McLaren (1990) hypothesized that the interest of a topic would influence primary school students' production of expository texts. In a first phase of the study, teachers and fourth- and sixth-graders rated a list of topics for their levels of interest. In a subsequent phase, the same students were asked to write a composition on either a topic rated as highly interesting (space travel) or not so interesting (such as living in a city). Results showed that written expositions on the high-interest topic were not qualitatively better; the quality of compositions was more related to students' level of knowledge about the topic rather than the amount of interest in it. The authors concluded that even with highly interesting topics, writing may appear to be daunting if students do not have sufficient content knowledge.

While in Hidi and McLaren's (1990, 1991) studies the topic has been considered a source of situational interest, in subsequent studies in writing, topic interest has been viewed as a form of individual interest. In their study on interest, knowledge, and narrative writing, Benton et al. (1995) used a different measure of interest from Hidi and McLaren (1990, 1991). Ninth-graders and undergraduate college students wrote a story about baseball. After the students had finished their compositions, their knowledge of and interest in the topic were evaluated. The interest measure included a 7-point scale of students' interest in baseball and five questions regarding their experiences playing or watching baseball. On the basis of the interest measure, participants were placed in high- and low-interest groups. In a follow-up study, Albin et al. (1996) investigated how individual differences in undergraduate students' interest in two topics (baseball and soccer) were related to narrative writing. The results indicated that interest in baseball was significantly related to writing quality, controlling for gender, discourse, and topic knowledge. In addition, students wrote more topic-relevant information on the baseball story—a relatively high interest topic—than on the relatively low interesting topic of soccer. This result was confirmed by Renninger et al. (2002), who reported that if a topic identified as individual interest (i.e., topics about which individuals had increased knowledge and value) was inserted in a passage, 11-year-old students were likely to write longer reconstructive recalls and attend better to the meaning of the text.

Classroom activity as a source of interest

These early studies of interest in writing were based on the assumption of the similarity between reading and writing from a motivational point of view: since the attractiveness of the topic is a motivational source of reading, it should be equally so for writing. In fact, topic may be a good source of interest for reading, but a weak one for writing. Being interested in a topic does not necessarily imply that one is interested in writing about that topic. In the last decade of the twentieth century, under the influence of the social constructivist approach to literacy learning, a second phase of studies followed, related to a shift in perspective from an emphasis on the level of interest in a topic to a broader view of writing as a meaningful activity. According to this perspective, motivation to write may emerge in classroom activities in which writing has a relevant role and is viewed as meaningful by the students themselves. Motivation to write is not only a matter of a student's interest in a topic, although a topic may be, and usually is, a source of interest for a writing task. Instead, it is the student's orientation to writing, which is triggered, stimulated, and to some degree maintained by the attractive features of the activity, which emerge in a specific situation (Boscolo and Cisotto, 1997; Bromley, 1999; Gambrell and Morrow, 1996; Hidi et al., 2002; Hiebert, 1994; Miller and Meece, 1999; Nolen, 2001, 2007; Oldfather

and Dahl, 1994; Oldfather and Shanahan, 2007).

What are the features that make writing a meaningful activity? Two, in particular, are underlined in the studies cited in the preceding section: a close relationship between writing and classroom activities, and also its collaborative dimension. Traditionally, writing is taught and evaluated separately from other subjects, although it may also be related to some (for instance, writing the report of a scientific experiment carried out in the classroom). Moreover, writing is usually perceived by teachers and students, as basically an individual, solitary activity. Each student has to write by and for him- or herself, thus allowing the teacher to evaluate a written text 'objectively'. In primary school, there may be many occasions to link writing to classroom activities, which allow students to experience writing as a collaborative enterprise. For instance, an opportunity to write may be provided by the students' and teacher's decision to write a set of criteria to be followed in order to form classroom groups (Boscolo and Cisotto, 1997). In this case, writing is not only needed for the final report (list of criteria), but is also used in various ways during the preparation phase in which students discuss the best criteria, argue, and take notes to be provisionally organized as homework. The problem of forming groups gives rise to lively discussion, during which the teacher may suggest using writing to record the students' own and schoolmates' proposals, to prepare a plan of activities, and/ or make a first draft of what emerged. In the following discussions, notes can be used by children to compare points of view, and prepare a final text, to which every child contributes. This helps students understand that there are various types of writing—some more informal, such as notes, and others more structured, such as a report or list of rules— which may accompany an activity and take/ give meaning from/to each moment of it.

A different but similar example can be found in the teaching of history. The discovery of America—a topic children usually find intriguing, though they are not particularly eager to write about it—may provide the opportunity of experiencing a variety of uses of writing. Writing may be used by children (fifth graders) to express their initial explanation of an event to start a discussion, to hypothesize about the reasons for Columbus's enterprise, to interpret what appears to be an amazing event (a ship load of slaves taken by Columbus), to make comments on contrasting documents, and so on (Boscolo and Mason, 2001). Similarly, writing can be used in science teaching, when students are asked to change their beliefs on a scientific phenomenon by carrying out an experiment. In this case too, they can individually form impressions and personal comments as a basis for a classroom discussion, in which the various points of view and comments are expressed, compared, and discussed (Boscolo and Mason, 2001).

Students, therefore, can realize that writing is a flexible tool, through which they can learn better as well as participate more actively in classroom activities. They also realize that writing can be used to fulfil many objectives and in various subjects, such as science, social studies, and mathematics. That is, writing is portrayed as a multidisciplinary activity, which entails a multiplicity of genres. Students can also perceive writing as a collaborative activity, which is central to a social constructivist view of literacy learning. Classroom collaboration is the condition for creating a community of discourse practices through which students may discover the functions of reading, writing, and other literate practices, and through them, their identities as learners (e.g., Nolen, 2001, 2007; Oldfather and Dahl, 1994). Nolen (2001, 2007) has used the expression 'literate communities' to describe classrooms in which reading and writing have a social function and writing is experienced as a means of expression and communication. This does not only mean finding a 'true' audience, different from the teacher, or making students write (planning, transcribing, and/or revising) in pairs or small groups. Writing is a tool for

communication, because not only what one writes can be read by somebody else, or something can be written together with companions, but it can also be performed in an interactive context. When the production of a text is aimed at achieving a common objective (for instance preparing a brochure for an exhibition organized by the school, or a playbill for a school performance), the planning, writing, and revising of this text can be made in collaboration. The final text is, therefore, communicated as well as the salient phases of its production. However, communicating may also regard, although less obviously, forms of individual writing, such as those used by many students to learn. This includes the moments when students take notes during a classroom discussion or lecture to prepare a report, or just record some concepts emerging from the discussion, which they have been impressed by. These forms of writing may turn out to be useful in subsequent classroom discussions, as elements for giving students a first idea of a community of discourse. Showing also that individual writing, such as note taking, has an interactive component, may help students understand the close links between writing and classroom activities.

Hidi et al. (2002) have examined how a combination of motivational and instructional variables can be utilized in an intervention program to improve students' emotional and cognitive experiences during the writing of argument. The program was aimed at teaching students (sixth graders) writing of argument (writing arguments on stimulating topics, such as 'Should girls play on boys' teams?' and 'Should violence be taken out of cartoons on television?'). The intervention, lasting eight weeks, included classroom discussions on the topics, lectures, and notes on the characteristics of writing an argument, and classroom exercises treating a problem from another point of view. At each stage, writing was used as a tool for fixing ideas and preparing a draft as a basis for discussion. The results showed that the quality and quantity of the participants' written arguments significantly improved after the activity.

It also emerged that general interest in writing, enjoying writing in several genres, and feeling efficacious about such writing are closely related and may have reciprocal developmental influences on each other.

Teaching writing as a meaningful activity is not only important in elementary school. In the following example, taken from an intervention study conducted with ninth graders in a literature class (Boscolo and Carotti, 2003), writing is used as a tool for literary comprehension. Initially, the students are invited to express and justify their reactions to reading a literary text assigned as individual homework. The reactions are usually expressed orally during class conversations, but sometimes the students themselves prefer to write them. The students then take notes of their impressions and reflections during literary reading in the classroom, and their teacher's comments. The notes are discussed and integrated by new teacher comments. Organizing these notes is assigned as homework. The students are invited to identify significant keywords to describe characters or places or events of the literary text they are reading. It is a 'card indexing', which requires a student's personal elaboration of a text. For instance, in a novel by the Italian novelist Italo Calvino, the theme of hybrid is emphasized and discussed. The students then use this theme to interpret the text. It is a selective reading by which the students discover and practice tools, which are also useful for future text analysis. Moreover, the students write the 'minutes' of some particularly interesting lesson by organizing their notes. Finally, they write a final report of their work, which is discussed in the classroom. Some of the tools used for text analysis (e.g., the role of irony in authorial voice) are applied to a new literary text. It is a 'transfer' task, in which the students are asked to use the concepts they have learned, and is also an occasion for making them aware of the elaborative function of writing.

In these examples, the source of interest is the writing environment itself. That is, it is the activity, which requires children's writing; the supportive, but not evaluative attitude, of the teacher; and the collaborative climate, which gives meaning to writing. Interest in the activity 'transfers' to writing, a student finds writing interesting if the instructional situation allows him/her to discover and practice the attractive, unusual, and challenging aspects of the activity, which may not, and usually do not, emerge from traditional writing tasks.

On authentic writing tasks

Bruning and Horn (2000), synthesizing the results of studies on motivation and writing, argued that several conditions in the learning environment are necessary to support young writers' positive perceptions of themselves as writers and their engagement in writing; among them, fostering authentic writing goals and contexts. This includes writing for true communicative or expressive objectives, closely related to meaningful classroom activities.

The adjective 'authentic' is often used in relation to writing tasks that involve children in immediate uses of writing for enjoyment and communication (Bromley, 1999; Bruning and Horn, 2000; Hiebert, 1994). Of course, writing in a classroom may be appreciated by students when faced with a real problem that can be solved using writing. An example may be a letter to the city council in which students protest about the inefficiency of a service and/or suggest a solution. Authentic writing, however, is not only aimed at achieving a practical goal. Studies in writing, mostly conducted from a social constructivist perspective, have emphasized the social dimension of writing, and the importance of making students aware, at different school levels, that writing is a fundamental tool of communication. However, we think that stressing the social dimension of writing does not only mean emphasizing communication. Writing is a social activity not only because we use it to communicate with others, but also because we can share our writing with others and discuss and comment on it.

What children come to realize in primary school is that writing is a flexible tool by which many functions and goals can be achieved. Flexibility does not only regard the use of writing as a tool for learning various subjects. In elementary school, 'playing' with writing is an activity students are willing to engage in. Playing means, for instance, manipulating stories by changing characters, their motives, or the sequence of episodes to obtain a new, more amusing or curious end, albeit within the constraints of text coherence. It may mean rewriting a short text avoiding certain word categories, or composing a meaningful 'cento' using words taken from titles of newspaper articles and reader passages; or creating images and metaphors with colours to describe the seasons. This writing is called 'creative' because it is aimed at creating 'new' meanings, that is, making children discover novel and challenging uses of language. Children not only enjoy practising it, but it also tests and increases their linguistic competence, obviously under the teacher's guidance. Moreover, they can collaborate to produce results (e.g., a short poem), which will be appreciated by the teacher and schoolmates (Boscolo, 2002). This type of writing is also authentic, although, in our opinion, the adjective 'meaningful' is preferred. Recently, Boscolo, Gelati and Galvan (submitted) found that fourth graders who participated in an intervention study on creative writing, were not only more able to write creatively at the end of the intervention, but also reported that they liked writing more than the control group students who did not participate.

Of course, the use of challenging tasks may contribute to motivation to write if children are able to manage them, as studies on interest (e.g., Mitchell, 1993; Renninger, 1992) and particularly on self-efficacy show.

SENSE OF COMPETENCE IN WRITING

Most studies on sense of competence[1] in writing have been conducted in the theoretical framework of Bandura's (1986) social cognitive theory of human functioning, in which the concept of self-efficacy has an essential role. Self-efficacy beliefs can be defined as students' judgements of their capability to organize and execute the course of action required to achieve a certain type of performance (Pajares and Valiante, 2006). If a student believes that his or her action can produce the desired outcome, he or she has the incentive to persevere in the face of difficulties. Self-efficacy belief in writing may be different in relation to specific skills and genres. A student may feel more efficacious in writing an essay than, say, a tale. Moreover, within a specific genre various writing skills are involved. For instance, a student may feel efficacious in idea generation, and much less efficacious about writing a coherent text.

A student's self-efficacy beliefs are closely connected to competence in a domain, on the one hand, and self-regulation skills, on the other. Students form their self-efficacy beliefs taking information from various sources, but the most influential source is the outcome of previous performance: a successful outcome tends to raise self-efficacy, whereas a failure tends to lower it. A successful performance does not only depend on a student's ability in a domain or subject, but also on how he or she is able to plan writing time, organize knowledge related to an assignment, seek help in case of difficulties, overcome anxiety, and so on—in a word, to regulate him—or herself. Self-regulation refers to the self-initiated feelings, thoughts, and actions that writers use to improve their writing skills as well as the quality of the text they are writing (Zimmerman and Kitsantas, 1999, 2002, 2007). The more self-regulatory skills a student has for writing, the more self-efficacious he or she feels. Zimmerman and Bandura (1994) assessed students' self-efficacy, goal setting, and self-evaluation at the beginning of the semester, and found that self-efficacy beliefs were predictive of self-evaluative standards and their final grades in the writing course.

There is also evidence of a close relationship between self-efficacy beliefs and interest. Zimmerman and Kitsantas found that high school girls' perception of self-efficacy for writing predicted their interest in the task and their level of proficiency. A relevant result of Hidi et al.'s (2002) study cited earlier was that students' self-efficacy beliefs predicted not only their general interest in writing, but also interest in writing specific genres.

Students' sense of efficacy has been found to differ as a function of gender and development. Typically, girls report greater confidence in their writing capabilities, at least in middle school. Subsequently, boys have a stronger sense of efficacy. A study by Pajares and Valiante (1999) showed that, although girls outperformed boys in writing, girls and boys reported the same self-efficacy. However, when asked, girls said that they were better than boys. From a developmental perspective, Pajares, Valiante and Cheong (2007) analysed the data of more than one thousand students from grades 4 to 11. Writing self-efficacy was found to diminish from elementary to middle school and remained at the same level in high school.

How can teachers help students cultivate their sense of writing efficacy? Several studies have emphasized that student self-perceived competence and control are closely related to the stimulating features of an instructional environment (e.g., Brophy, 1999; Harter, 1992; Pajares and Johnson, 1994; Pajares, 1997; Renninger, 1992). An optimal learning environment for writing—and, in general, literacy—is one, which provides students with tasks and activities of an appropriate level of difficulty ('challenge') and autonomy. Being able to choose and manage challenging but solvable tasks and problems helps students perceive themselves as competent learners. This self-perception, in turn, is believed to foster their engagement and motivation in literate activities (Gambrell and Morrow, 1996; Guthrie and Wigfield, 2000; Turner, 1995). Instead, it is highly improbable that a student can view as interesting a task, which he or she does not feel able to deal with successfully. In general, teaching students how to manage the difficulties of writing, that is how to self-regulate, is the best support of their self-efficacy beliefs—in writing as in all subjects (Zimmerman and Kitsantas, 2007).

The classroom conditions in which students have the opportunity to share and compare their opinions, discuss, and work collaboratively may foster self-efficacy (Walker, 2003). Hidi et al. (2002) found that collaborative group work did not affect all students equally. In their intervention study, only boys responded positively to the effect of this variable. According to the authors, this unexpected result might be due to the traditionally 'solitary' learning of writing in school, in contrast with an unusual collaborative setting. While this finding and the suggested interpretation deserve to be analysed in further studies, it should be noted that a 'challenging' task and situation, such as writing about interesting topics in collaboration, may be not sufficient to change a view of writing in terms of sense of competence and meaningfulness, that students have formed over time. Making students feel more efficacious as well as perceiving writing as a meaningful experience is not an objective, which can be attained in a few sessions, thanks to stimulating topics and tasks. Motivating students to write means, in our view, proposing tasks. This can make them increasingly aware that writing has various dimensions—individual and collaborative, new and 'old' genres, creative and, unavoidably, boring tasks—which complement each other.

THE DEVELOPMENT OF INTEREST (AND OTHER VARIABLES) IN WRITING

Recently, Hidi and Renninger (2006) have described a developmental thread, from situational interest to the development of individual interest as a predisposition. More specifically, they argued that individual interest may develop from situational, and this development involves four phases. According to the model, in the first phase, situational interest for a particular content is *triggered*. If the triggered situational interest is sustained, the second phase, referred to as *maintained situational* interest, evolves. In the third phase, this type of interest shifts into an *emerging individual* interest, in which knowledge is accruing, fuelled by individuals' curiosity about the content of their interest and increased effort to self-regulate and identify with the content of their interest. In the fourth and final phase, referred to as a *well-developed individual* interest, the person has an increased ability to self-regulate, a broadened knowledge base, and increased value for the content.

Lipstein and Renninger (2007) have applied the four-phase model to writing through a questionnaire and interview study conducted with 12- to 15-year-old students. Students' responses to the questionnaire and interview were used to identify several variables: interest in writing, conceptual competence, goal setting and strategy use, effort, self-efficacy, and feedback preferences. On the basis of questionnaire responses, the authors identified students at four phases of interest in writing, by adopting a descriptive methodology, which draws on commonalities across a group of students. Profiles of students located in each of the four phases were developed, and the relations among the variables were examined. At the triggered situational interest phase, a student is stimulated by the topic, but has no vision of writing as a purposeful activity. Moreover, he or she reports no value for writing, and expresses little confidence in his/her ability. The feedback he or she prefers is manageable and specific, related to punctuation or spelling. At the maintained situation interest phase, students sometimes report they write on their own, outside of school. They are literal in their understanding of teacher's comments on their writings. Differently from students at the triggered interest phase, they enjoy expressing their ideas about a topic. These students seem to have mastered the writing conventions.

Students at the phase of emerging individual interest are more confident in their ability to write, and view writing as a part of their identities. They do not draw a sharp distinction between school writing and writing for themselves. They are willing to revise their work, but clearly prefer to have positive feedback from the teacher, and do not like restrictions to their writing. Lastly, students with a well-developed interest have a strong sense of audience and look for feedback about the clarity of their writing. They focus more on procedural aspects of writing and are aware of the close relation between a writer's ideas and the ways in which he or she expresses them. They also have strong self-efficacy beliefs.

TO CONCLUDE: A PROFILE OF THE MOTIVATED-TO-WRITE STUDENT

At the beginning of this chapter, we highlighted two basic dimensions for a conceptualization of motivation to write: a student's sense of competence and the meaning that writing assumes for him or her. After reviewing studies on the conditions that can influence a sense of competence and the meaning of writing, a conclusive question could be: What is the profile of a motivated-to-write student? Lipstein and Renninger (2007) provided persuasive 'portraits' of students at different levels, or phases, of interest in writing. The main focus of their study was interest, although the development of interest in writing has been integrated with analyses of other motivational variables, such as self-efficacy, goal setting, type of preferred feedback, and so on. However, we think that the profile of a motivated student should take into account other aspects besides interest. A first aspect is valuing: a motivated-to-write students is one who values writing, in that he or she views it as a tool by which various communicative objectives can be attained through various genres, although in school he or she has experienced and/or enjoyed only a few of these. 'Valuing' seems to be a more appropriate term than 'being interested', in that a sense of relevance is implicit; although we should not forget that value is an essential component of individual interest (Renninger, 1992). A motivated student is not necessarily one who 'likes' writing, but one who willingly uses this tool when needed, and gains satisfaction from writing.

Motivation is not only interest and value, as explored in this chapter. A motivated-to-write student is also realistically aware of his or her competence and efficacy in the experienced genres, which contribute to his or her satisfaction when writing. Whereas writing instruction at the various school levels seems to be based on the implicit assumption that learning to write—and learning to read—is acquiring a 'general' ability to be utilized in any domain, the sense of competence in writing is also an awareness of the multiple meanings of writing. Lastly, a motivated student is one who has learned how to manage the difficulties of writing; that is, one who knows not only what to write, but also how to use the available external and internal resources to attain a communicative objective.

All these dimensions should be considered from a developmental perspective. Development, in this case, does not regard only motivational variables or dimensions, but also the role of writing experiences and teacher instructional strategies at the different school-grade levels. The way a primary school student values writing is most probably different from a middle or high school student, and not only because interest, as well as writing and self-regulation skills, change with school grade. This remark may sound banal, however, empirical evidence is lacking on how teaching practices, on the one hand, and student writing experiences, on the other, interact to produce motivation or demotivation to write. Longitudinal studies of how students' views of writing are formed, and possibly modified, are needed.

NOTE

1 The expression 'sense of competence' is a generic label for two constructs often used as synonyms: self-perception of competence and self-efficacy. In fact, self-perception of writing competence (or self-concept in writing) refers to an individual's evaluation of his or her ability in a domain (e.g., 'I find it easy to write a coherent essay', 'I view myself as a poor writer'), whereas self-efficacy refers to an individual's belief about his or her capability to carry out a specific task (e.g., 'How able do you feel to use verb tenses correctly in a two-page composition?', '... to organize ideas in clear paragraphs?') (Pajares, 1996, 1997).

REFERENCES

Albin, M.L., Benton, S.L., and Khramtsova, I. (1996) 'Individual differences in interest and narrative writing', *Contemporary Educational Psychology*, 21: 305–324.

Bandura, A. (1986) *Social Foundations of Thought and Action: A Social-Cognitive Theory*, Englewood Cliffs, NJ: Prentice-Hall.

Benton, S.L., Corkill, A.J., Sharp, J.M., Downey, R.G., and Khramtsova, I. (1995) 'Knowledge, interest and narrative writing', *Journal of Educational Psychology*, 87: 66–79.

Bereiter, C. and Scardamalia, M. (1987) *The Psychology of Written Composition*, Hillsdale, NJ: Lawrence Erlbaum Associates.

Boscolo, P. (2002) La scrittura nella scuola dell'obbligo. Insegnare e motivare a scrivere. [Writing in compulsory school. Teaching and motivating to write]. Roma (Italy): Laterza.

Boscolo, P. and Carotti, L. (2003). 'Does writing contribute to improving high school students' approach to literature?', *L1—Educational Studies in Language and Literature*, 3: 197–224.

Boscolo, P. and Cisotto, L. (1997) Making writing interesting in elementary school. Paper presented at the 7th biannual meeting of the European Association for Research on Learning and Instruction, Athens, Greece, August 26–30.

Boscolo, P. and Gelati, C. (2007) 'Best practices in promoting motivation for writing', in S. Graham, C.A. MacArthur, and J. Fitzgerald (eds), *Best Practices in Writing Instruction*, New York-London: Guilford. pp.202–221.

Boscolo, P. and Hidi, S. (2007) 'The multiple meanings of motivation to write', in S. Hidi and P. Boscolo (eds), *Motivation and Writing: Research and School Practice*, Oxford: Elsevier. pp.1–14.

Boscolo, P. and Mason, L. (2001) 'Writing to learn, writing to transfer', in P. Tynjälä, L. Mason, and K. Lonka (eds), *Writing as a Learning Tool: Integrating Theory and Practice*, Dordrecht: Kluwer. pp.83–104.

Bromley, K. (1999) 'Key components of sound writing instruction', in L.B. Gambrell, L.M. Morrow, S.B. Neuman, and M. Pressley (eds), *Best Practices in Literacy Instruction*, New York and London: Guilford Press. pp.152–174.

Brophy, G. (1999) 'Toward a model of the value aspects of motivation in education: Developing appreciation for particular learning domains and activities', *Educational Psychologist,* 34: 75–85.

Brophy, J. (2004) *Motivating Students to Learn* (second edn.), Mahwah, NJ, and London: Lawrence Erlbaum Associates.

Bruning, R. and Horn, C. (2000) 'Developing motivation to write', *Educational Psychologist*, 35: 25–37.

Chapman, M.L. (1994) 'The emergence of genres: Some findings from an examination of first grade writing', *Written Communication*, 11: 348–380.

Covington, M.V. (1999) 'Caring about learning: The nature and nurturing of subject-matter appreciation', *Educational Psychologist*, 34: 127–156.

Daly, J.A. and Miller, M.D. (1975a) 'The development of a measure of writing apprehension', *Research in the Teaching of English*, 9: 242–249.

Daly, J.A. and Miller, M.D. (1975b) 'Further studies in writing apprehension: SAT scores, success expectations, willingness to take advanced courses and see differences', *Research in the Teaching of English*, 9: 250–256.

Gambrell, L.B. and Morrow, L.M. (1996) 'Creating motivating contexts for literacy learning', in L. Baker, P. Afflerbach, and D. Reinking (eds), *Developing Engaged Readers in School and Home Communities*, Mahwah, NJ: Lawrence Erlbaum Associates. pp.115–136.

Guthrie, J. and Wigfield, A. (2000) 'Engagement and motivation in reading', in M.L. Kamil, P.B. Mosenthal, P.D. Pearson, and R. Barr (eds), *Handbook of Reading Research, Vol. 3*, Mahwah, NJ: Lawrence Erlbaum Associates. pp.403–422.

Harris, K.R. and Graham, S. (1996) *Making the Writing Process Work: Strategies for Composition and Self-Regulation*, Cambridge, MA: Brookline.

Harter, S. (1992) 'The relationship between perceived competence, affect, and motivational orientation within the classroom: processes and patterns of change', in A.K. Boggiano and T.S. Pittman (eds),

Achievement and Motivation: A Social-Developmental Perspective, Cambridge: Cambridge University Press. pp.77–114.

Hidi, S. (1990) 'Interest and its contribution as a mental resource for learning', *Review of Educational Research*, 60: 549–571.

Hidi, S. (2001) 'Interest, reading, and learning: Theoretical and practical considerations', *Educational Psychology Review*, 13: 191–208.

Hidi, S. and Baird, W. (1986) 'Interestingness: A neglected variable in discourse processing', *Cognitive Science*, 10: 179–194.

Hidi, S. and Baird, W. (1988) 'Strategies for increasing text-based interest and students' recall of expository texts', *Reading Research Quarterly*, 23: 465–483.

Hidi, S. and Boscolo, P. (2006) 'Motivation and writing', in C.A. MacArthur, S. Graham, and J. Fitzgerald (eds), *Handbook of Writing Research*, New York-London: Guilford. pp.144–157.

Hidi, S. and McLaren, J. (1990) 'The effect of topic and theme interestingness on the production of school expositions', in H. Mandl, E. De Corte, N. Bennett, and H.F. Friedrich (eds), *Learning and Instruction: European Research in an International Context. Vol. 2.2*, Oxford: Pergamon. pp.295–308.

Hidi, S. and McLaren, J. (1991) 'Motivational factors in writing: The role of topic interestingness', *European Journal of Psychology of Education*, 6: 187–197.

Hidi, S. and Renninger, K.A. (2006) 'The four-phase model of interest development', *Educational Psychologist*, 42: 111–127.

Hidi, S., Berndorff, D., and Ainley, M. (2002) 'Children's argument writing, interest and self-efficacy: An intervention study', *Learning and Instruction*, 12: 429–446.

Hiebert, E.H. (1994) 'Becoming literate through authentic tasks: Evidence and adaptations', in R.B. Ruddell, M.R. Ruddell, and H. Singer (eds), *Theoretical Models and Processes of Reading*, Newark, DL: International Reading Association. pp.391–413.

Kintsch, W. (1980) 'Learning from text, levels of comprehension, or: Why anyone would read a story anyway', *Poetics*, 9: 87–98.

Krapp, A. (2000) 'Interest and human development during adolescence: An educational-psychological approach', in J. Heckhausen (ed.), *Motivational Psychology of Human Development*, London: Elsevier. pp.109–128.

Lipstein, R.L. and Renninger, K.A. (2007) '"Putting things into words": The development of 12–15-year-old students' interest for writing', in S. Hidi and P. Boscolo (eds), *Writing and Motivation*, Oxford: Elsevier. pp.113–140.

Miller, S. and Meece, J. (1999) 'Third graders' motivational preferences for reading and writing tasks', *The Elementary School Journal*, 100(1): 19–35.

Mitchell, M. (1993) 'Situational interest: Its multifaceted structure in the secondary school mathematics classroom', *Journal of Educational Psychology*, 85: 424–436.

Nolen, S.B. (2001) 'Constructing literacy in the kindergarten: Task structure, collaboration and motivation', *Cognition and Instruction*, 19: 95–142.

Nolen, S.B. (2007) 'The role of literate communities in the development of children's interest in writing', in S. Hidi and P. Boscolo (eds), *Motivation and Writing: Research and School Practice Oxford*, Elsevier. pp.241–255.

Oldfather, P. and Dahl, K. (1994) 'Toward a social constructivist reconceptualization of intrinsic motivation for literacy learning', *JRB: A Journal of Literacy*, 26: 139–158.

Oldfather, P. and Shanahan, C.H. (2007) 'A cross-case study of writing motivation as empowerment', in S. Hidi and P. Boscolo (eds), *Motivation and Writing: Research and School Practice*, Oxford: Elsevier. pp.257–279.

Pajares, F. (1996) 'Self-efficacy beliefs in academic settings', *Review of Educational Research*, 66: 543–578.

Pajares, F. (1997) 'Current directions in self-efficacy research', in M.L. Maehr and P.R. Pintrich (eds), *Advances in Motivation and Achievement*, Vol. 10, Greenwich, CN: JAI Press, pp.1–49.

Pajares, F. and Johnson, M.J. (1994) 'Confidence and competence in writing: The role of writing self-efficacy, outcome expectancy, and apprehension', *Research in the Teaching of English*, 28: 313–331.

Pajares, F. and Valiante, G. (1999) 'Grade level and gender differences in the writing self-beliefs of middle school students', *Contemporary Educational Psychology*, 24: 390–405.

Pajares, F. and Valiante, G. (2006) 'Self-efficacy beliefs and motivation in writing development', in C.A. MacArthur, S. Graham, and J. Fitzgerald (eds), *Handbook of Writing Research*, New York-London: Guilford. pp.158–170.

Pajares, F., Valiante, G., and Cheong, Y.F. (2007) 'Writing self-efficacy and its relation to gender, writing motivation and writing competence: A developmental perspective', in S. Hidi and P. Boscolo (eds), *Writing and Motivation*, Oxford: Elsevier. pp.113–140.

Renninger, K.A. (1992) 'Individual interest and development: Implications for theory and practice', in K.A. Renninger, S. Hidi, and A. Krapp (eds), *The Role of Interest in Learning and Development*, Hillsdale, NJ: Lawrence Erlbaum Associates. pp.361–395.

Renninger, K.A. (2000) 'Individual interest and its implications for understanding intrinsic motivation', in C. Sansone and J.M. Harackiewicz (eds), *Intrinsic and Extrinsic Motivation*, San Diego, CA: Academic Press. pp.373–404.

Renninger, K.A., Ewen, L., and Lasher, A.K. (2002) 'Individual interest as context in expository text and mathematical word problems', *Learning and Instruction*, 12: 467–491.

Renninger, K.A., Hidi, S., and Krapp, A. (eds) (1992) *The Role of Interest in Learning and Development*, Hillsdale, NJ: Lawrence Erlbaum Associates.

Schank, R.C. (1979) 'Interestingness: Controlling inferences', *Artificial Intelligence*, 12: 273–297.

Stipek, D. (2002) *Motivation to Learn* (second edn.), Boston: Allyn and Bacon.

Turner, J.C. (1995) 'The influence of classroom contexts on young children's motivation for literacy', *Reading Research Quarterly*, 30: 410–441.

Volet, S. and Järvelä, S. (eds) (2001) *Motivation in Learning Contexts*, Pergamon: Elsevier.

Walker, B.J. (2003) 'The cultivation of student self-efficacy in reading and writing', *Reading and Writing Quarterly*, 19: 173–187.

Wertsch, J.V. (1985) *Vygotsky and the Social Formation of Mind*, Cambridge, MA, and London: Harvard University Press.

Wigfield, A. and Eccles, J. (2002) *Development of Achievement Motivation*, San Diego, CA: Academic Press.

Zimmerman, B.J. and Bandura, A. (1994) 'Impact of self-regulatory influences on writing course attainment', *American Educational Research Journal*, 31: 845–862.

Zimmerman, B.J. and Kitsantas, A. (1997) 'Developmental phases in self-regulation: Shifting from process to outcome goals', *Journal of Educational Psychology*, 89: 29–36.

Zimmerman, B.J. and Kitsantas, A. (1999) 'Acquiring writing revision skill: Shifting from process to outcome self-regulatory goals', *Journal of Educational Psychology*, 91: 1–10.

Zimmerman, B.J. and Kitsantas, A. (2002) 'Acquiring writing revision proficiency through observation and emulation', *Journal of Educational Psychology*, 94: 660–668.

Zimmerman, B.J. and Kitsantas, A. (2007) 'A writer's discipline: The development of self-regulatory skill', in S. Hidi and P. Boscolo (eds), *Motivation and Writing: Research and School Practice*, Oxford: Elsevier. pp.51–69.

21

Writing and Popular Culture

Jackie Marsh

INTRODUCTION

Children and young people are immersed in a wide variety of forms of popular culture in their everyday lives and these texts, and artefacts have a profound effect on their identities, social networks, and cultural practices. 'Popular culture' in this context can be defined as the: 'daily, vernacular, common, cultural environment around us all … the television we watch, the movies we see, the fast food, or slow food, we eat, the clothes we wear' (Browne, 1987:2) and includes the texts and artefacts we consume as well as produce. It is inevitable that literacy is bound up in this heady mix and there is now much evidence that attests to the central role that popular culture plays in children and young people's out of school literacy lives (Knobel, 2005; Marsh, 2005; Pahl, 2005).

The aim of this chapter is to examine the potential role that popular culture can play in the writing curriculum in schools. Since the last decade of the twentieth century, there has been a body of work that has examined the use of popular culture in the literacy/ English curriculum, some of which was analysed in a previous review of the field by Marsh (2003). In this chapter, therefore, I will focus only on research published since 2003. In addition,

I draw only from studies conducted in school or college classrooms. Research into the potential role that popular culture can play in the literacy/ English curriculum has extended to informal educational institutions, such as after-school clubs and care centres (Alvermann, 2005; Alvermann and Eakle, 2007), but this work is beyond the scope of this chapter.

The chapter is structured into three main sections. In the first section, I review research that has revealed the way in which popular culture creeps into children and young people's written texts in classrooms despite any overt intention to enable this to happen on the part of teachers. The second section moves on to consider research in which popular cultural texts have been introduced deliberately into the writing curriculum by educators in order to motivate and engage pupils in schooled writing activities. The third section considers the adaptation of out-of-school popular cultural writing practices for educational purposes, and explores the way in which these practices are challenging the boundaries of writing as it is instantiated in the curriculum. Finally, in the conclusion, I consider the research that still needs to be undertaken if we are to gain a fuller understanding of the potential role that popular culture can play in the writing curriculum. My aim in this chapter is not to offer an exhaustive account of research in this field, for that would need a more extensive publication than is possible here, but to outline what I consider to be the key issues and questions that need to be considered in any consideration of the relationship between popular culture and writing in schools. Some of this work not only indicates the significant role that teachers' subject knowledge and pedagogical content knowledge plays in the construction of a writing curriculum that utilizes popular culture (Pahl and Rowsell, 2005; Larson and Marsh, 2005), but it also points to the way in which the curriculum needs to offer spaces in which pupils themselves can embed their out-of-school practices in classroom tasks, as the following section outlines.

SCHOOL WRITING INFORMED BY POPULAR CULTURE

There is a rich range of research, that indicates that even when teachers do not deliberately introduce popular cultural forms into the classroom, the influence of popular culture can be seen in children's writing. Pupils' popular cultural interests seep into their written texts and become an integral part of their compositions. This phenomenon has been traced most carefully by Anne Haas Dyson (1994; 1996; 1997; 1999; 2001; 2003). In a series of detailed ethnographic case studies of classroom life, Dyson has identified how media culture permeates children's texts as they use the 'textual toys' that litter their popular cultural landscape in their written compositions. The children in the elementary classrooms that she observed wrote stories and other texts that drew from their everyday lives and these texts invariably included themes and motifs from television and film, popular music, and sports. This work was undertaken in classrooms in which the teacher made room for children's out-of-school pleasures to enter into classroom life. [For further

discussion see Dyson Chapter 15.] However, other children have managed to sneak popular culture into classrooms under the noses of disapproving teachers. Vasquez (2005), for example, reports on the actions of a boy who introduced icons from Pokémon onto the cover of his journal, indiscernible to his teacher, because she was unaware of the discourses related to Pokémon.

The children in Dyson's studies were able to draw on their own cultural resources, because the teachers concerned adopted pedagogical practices that valued what children brought to the site of learning. This was also the case in a more recent case study undertaken by Ranker (2007), who examined the media influences on the writing of an eight-year-old boy. The use of a writing workshop approach (Calkins,1983; 1994) to the teaching of writing enabled the child studied to draw on resources from his everyday cultural interests and this included comic books, the Internet, television, and video games. Characters, plots, and textual forms were adapted from these sources and used in various ways in the child's written narratives. Newkirk (2002:138) also reported on the work of a teacher, Mike Anderson, who identified the following discourses, common in popular culture, that children draw upon in their writing: good versus evil, heroes and underdogs, action/excitement/adventure; magical powers, and friendship.

An overview of this body of research, therefore, suggests that pupils use popular culture in numerous ways in their writing and Table 21.1 offers a summary of the key elements on which pupils draw as they mine these cultural interests.

Ranker (2007) makes clear, as did Dyson (2001; 2003) before him, that children do not adopt themes and characters from popular culture in an uncritical manner, but they refashion and recontextualize them. Willett (2005), in a study of eight- and nine-year-olds' writing, also identifies the role that parody and pastiche play in pupils' adaptations of media texts. If the concept of design proposed by the New London Group (1996) is

Table 21.1   How popular culture informs children's school-based writing

		Examples	Sources
Element drawn from popular cultural texts in children's school-based writing	Themes	Pupils draw on themes common in popular cultural texts e.g. good versus evil; heroes and underdogs; action/excitement/adventure; magical powers and friendship.	Dyson (1999; 2001; 2003) Newkirk (2002)
	Plots	Pupils develop plots based on narratives encountered in television and films, video games.	Dyson (2001; 2003) Ranker (2007) Willett (2005)
	Settings	Pupils use settings from popular culture for their writing e.g. football field.	Dyson (2003)
	Characters	Pupils introduce characters from popular culture e.g. Donkey Kong; Grim Reaper.	Dyson (1999) Graham (2004) Ranker (2007) Willett (2005)
	Story grammar	Pupils develop narratives that draw on the story grammars of non-linear texts e.g. video games.	Graham (2004) Ranker (2006; 2007)
	Textual forms/layout	Pupils use and adapt layouts used in popular texts, such as comic strips.	Ranker (2007)

utilized in any analysis of text production in schools (Walsh, 2007), then it becomes clear that what children are engaged in as they reuse and repurpose popular cultural texts for schooled purposes is a process of redesign, not simple replication. The research considered in this section suggests that the voice of individual pupils can become stronger in their writing if they have the freedom to choose topics and themes. However, this can also be the case if it is their teachers who are the ones to introduce popular texts to the classroom, a process explored in the next section of the chapter.

INTRODUCING POPULAR CULTURAL TEXTS INTO THE WRITING CURRICULUM

A number of studies have examined the impact of projects in which popular cultural texts have been introduced into classrooms in order to promote engagement in schooled literacy practices. For example, during the last few years, there has been an increased interest in the use of film to inform the literacy/English curriculum. Film forms a significant part of children and young people's leisure practices (Livingstone and Bovill, 1999; Marsh et al., 2005), and it is, therefore, a valuable medium to use within the classroom. Previous to the period of focus in this chapter, a number of studies had indicated the potential value of the use of film in raising children's attainment in writing (Oldham, 1999; Parker, 1999). In 2004, the Primary National Strategy (PNS) and the United Kingdom Literacy Association (UKLA) published a study in which teachers in three Local Authorities (LAs) in England used films and drama to promote writing (PNS/UKLA, 2004). In 2005–2007, the British Film Institute worked with over 35 LAs in England in a project in which lead practitioners were trained in the use of film in the literacy/English curriculum. Findings from these two projects indicate that the use of film increased children's attainment in writing (including the areas of composition and effect, text structure and organization, and sentence structure and punctuation). The project also enhanced children's attitudes to writing and impacted positively on their self-esteem as writers (Marsh and Bearne, 2007;

PNS/UKLA, 2004). In addition, a project in which early-years teachers embedded the use of film and popular cultural texts into the communications, language, and literacy curriculum led to enhanced levels of motivation and engagement in writing tasks (Marsh et al., 2005).

Film is only one aspect of the moving image media, that children encounter in their everyday lives. Computer games are also key texts that pupils engage with on a regular basis (Livingstone and Bovill, 1999; Marsh et al., 2005) and these have also been used to inform the writing curriculum. Millard (2005) outlines a study in which a class of eight- and nine-year-olds created stories in which they could incorporate themes and narrative structures from computer and adventure games. Millard suggests that this activity resulted in gendered texts, in which boys drew primarily from film and television and girls from traditional fairy tales in the construction of their narratives. The teacher led the children in class discussion in which they could reflect critically on these gendered patterns, a critical approach to the use of popular culture in the curriculum, that was promoted by Alvermann, Moon, and Hagood (1999).

This focus on the use of computer games in the writing curriculum was a feature of a study conducted by Bearne and Wolstencroft (2005) with a class of eight- and nine-year-olds. The children compared and contrasted the narrative features of a traditional fairy tale, *Red Riding Hood*, with a popular video game, *Lara Croft*. They then developed the *Red Riding Hood* story as a computer game, writing both instructions for the game and the story. The findings indicate that the children were able to draw from their out-of-school knowledge of computer games to enhance aspects of their classroom narratives, such as voice, structure, pace, and viewpoint. Beavis (2004; 2007) has also embedded computer games into the writing curriculum of schools in Australia, broadening the scope of the work to move from writing reviews of games to their design, suggesting that such work can attend to the

'3D' model of literacy proposed by Green (1988), that is, such work can engage pupils in consideration of the cultural, critical, and operational aspects of texts.

Whilst the work outlined in the foregoing section has considered popular culture texts in the literacy/English curriculum in their own right, a number of studies have provided pupils with opportunities to compare and contrast popular texts with canonical ones. Alvermann, Huddleston, and Hagood (2004) describe a process in which a secondary teacher constructed a unit of work for English in which the discursive practices embedded within the World Wrestling Federation (WWF) were compared and contrasted to classical literature, namely, *Julius Caesar*, *Beowulf*, and *Sir Gawain and the Green Knight*. Similarly, Davies and Pahl (2006) depict a post-16 college classroom in which students compared and contrasted lyrics composed by the rap singer, Eminem, with the poetry of William Blake. They use the concept of 'third space' (Bhabha, 1994; Gutierrez et al., 1999; Moje et al., 2004) to outline how projects of this kind combine out-of-school literacy practices with traditional literacy activities in order to construct a hybrid curriculum in which popular/canonical/home/school can be integrated in meaningful ways.

The enjoyment of hip-hop music, such as that produced by singers like Eminem, has been an extensive popular culture practice over the last decade. Educational researchers have explored ways in which hip-hop can inform the school curriculum (Duncan-Andrade and Morrell, 2005; Meacham, 2004; Morrell and Duncan-Andrade, 2004, 2006). Meacham, for example, has reported on work in which pupils have formed a hip-hop band and undertaken curriculum work related to this process, e.g., developing business plans, writing contracts, and so on (Meacham, 2004). Morrell and Duncan-Andrade (2004) present a series of vignettes in which they outline how hip-hop was drawn upon in a number of English units that focused on exploring themes in poetry and song through expository writing. As in the Davies and Pahl (2006) example, students compared and contrasted the lyrics of hip-hop artists such as Nas and Grand Master Flash with canonical poets, including Coleridge and Eliot. The units of work not only offered students opportunities to draw on their own 'funds of knowledge' (Moll et al., 1992), but also to understand the role that poets play in societies. Morrell and Duncan-Andrade stress, however, that hip-hop should not just be seen as a bridge to canonical texts for students who may not otherwise wish to make those links, but can and should be studied as a worthy subject in its own right (2004: 266).

In this section, the focus has been on the introduction of popular cultural *texts* into the classroom. In the next section, I move on to consider the introduction of popular cultural *practices* into writing curricula.

INTRODUCING POPULAR CULTURAL PRACTICES INTO THE WRITING CURRICULUM

Children and young people have always been engaged in a wide range of writing practices outside of school, such as diary writing. However, with the advent of new technologies, it would appear that the range of practices in which they engage has proliferated, including, for example, blogging, use of email, instant messaging and chat rooms (Davies, 2009), text messaging using mobile phones (Shortis, 2007), and the use of social networking sites such as MySpace or Bebo (Demos, 2007; Dowdall, in press), or virtual worlds such as Club Penguin™ or Barbie Girls™ (Marsh, 2009). The majority of these practices embed children within a social network in which they exchange news and views with other users and it may be this factor which has increased children and young people's engagement in writing, as they have distinct purposes and diverse audiences for their writing. There are a number of popular contemporary out-of-school writing practices that have begun to become adopted into writing curricula in schools. In this section, I will review research focused on emailing, texting, virtual worlds, and blogging.

Merchant (2003) describes a cross-school project involving 7- to 10-year-olds in which children collaborated using email to write stories based on two popular narrative genres: sword and sorcery adventures and sci-fi stories. The findings suggest that this online collaboration offers potential for the development of more equal writing partnerships than might ensue offline. Further, the email narratives contained a number of features more normally found in spoken discourse, including the use of informal language and a looser grammatical structure, indicating the blurring of boundaries between spoken and written discourse and innovatory textual practices in online communication (Shortis, 2007). In a second project involving email exchanges between pupils, Merchant et al. (2006) outline how 8- to 10-year-old children constructed 'digital shoeboxes', that is, shoeboxes in which they placed texts and artefacts that represented aspects of their lives and identities, drawing from the concept developed in the 'Home-School Knowledge Exchange Project' (Greenhough et al., 2005). These shoeboxes were then photographed using a digital camera. The children sent the photographs to a partner in another school and they discussed the contents of each others' shoeboxes via email. The authors of the report argue that:

> By using such technologies, the pupils in this study were provided with a real purpose for writing and a context for exchanging information about themselves and their interests. They were able to move beyond traditional print-based writing practices using the multi-modal affordances of the screen to communicate ideas and perform identities. At times they moved seamlessly across different software platforms such as PowerPoint, Photoshop, First Class, Word, and were also able to search the Web to select relevant information. In this way they orchestrate new ways of making meaning that are becoming increasingly important in a digital world. (Merchant et al., 2006: 36)

Merchant has more recently moved on to examine the literacy practices afforded in virtual worlds. There are a number of virtual worlds currently popular with children and young people in their out-of-school literacy practices, including: Barbie Girls™, Club Penguin™, Habbo Hotel™, Neopets™, and Webkinz™. Many of the sites enable users to create and dress-up an avatar, decorate their avatar's home, buy and look after pets, and play games in order to earn money to purchase items for their avatars and homes. The virtual worlds also enable interactive chat and in many of the worlds, this is tightly controlled and monitored in order to allay parental concerns regarding Internet safety. In a project designed to ensure such online safety, Merchant (2007a) describes how one LA in England designed a literacy-rich 3D virtual world in which pupils from ten different primary schools could participate. In the virtual world, children can encounter a range of text-types and engage in text-messaging and MSN-type chat. However, Merchant (2007) warns that educators' tendencies to over-focus on replicating offline literacy practices in such online worlds can undermine the potential these spaces have for developing pupils' digital literacy skills.

In addition to virtual worlds, another prevalent out-of-school writing activity is blogging. Blogs, or weblogs, consist of online posts, which authors place on to their blog pages, with the most recent entries appearing first. Blog entries can concern a number of things, such as author's everyday lives (similar to diary entries), news, politics, and entertainment, amongst other categories. Blogs enable commentators to make comments on the entries, although this facility can be disallowed by blog authors. This commenting facility means that blogs offer rich potential for social exchanges and collaboration (Davies and Merchant, 2007; Lankshear and Knobel, 2006). Blogs can also contain images and links to other sites which enable bloggers to embed video and podcasts (audio files) into their blogs. The practice of blogging has become widespread, with estimates that the number of blogs is currently in excess of 60 million, although the number of active blogs may be much fewer than that. In Marsh (2009), a project is outlined in which a teacher allowed children aged 7–8 to create blogs in class as part of a project on dinosaurs. The children posted regular entries to their blog in which they documented their project findings and used the blog to upload comments to each other regarding the content of their posts. This activity drew on children's out-of-school interests in addition to enabling them to engage in a writing project in which collaboration and critical review was valued.

In many of the projects discussed in this section, pupils were engaged in the authoring of texts that included a number of modes, not just the written word. In 2003, Gunther Kress outlined the way in which the subject English was being transformed in a new media age due to two shifts: one in the primary mode of communication (from word to image) and the other a shift in dominant media (from page to screen). He stressed that the transformations precipitated by these moves would be profound:

> It is already clear that the effects of the two changes taken together will have the widest imaginable political, economic, social, cultural, conceptual/cognitive, and epistemological consequences. (Kress, 2003:1)

The implications of this paradigmatic shift have been widely discussed (Carrington, 2005; Lankshear and Knobel, 2006; Merchant, 2007b) and there is now widespread evidence that the popular cultural practices in which children and young people engage involve multimodal practices, that is, the design of texts that include word, image, sound, and animation (Bearne, 2003; Flewitt, 2008). In the case of the blogging project outlined in the preceding section, children drew on a variety of web sources, as well as their own productions, to mix and match in the production of new texts, reflecting the type of creative activities already well embedded in a 'DIY Internet' (Sharp, 2006) culture. Thus, the blog contains short films and animations created by the pupils in which the written word was integrated with a range of other modes. Recent research that has examined the relationship between digital cultures and writing, suggests that children and young people are developing a range of complex authoring skills across various modes (Erixon and Nixon, 2007) and that these writing practices can be embedded in curricula in exciting ways. For example, Beavis (2007) and Burn (2007) suggest that computer games can be used both to promote traditional writing practices and to engage children in game authoring.

There is a need to assess the impact of these curricula and pedagogical changes on a broader range of skills, understanding, and knowledge appropriate for the demands of the digital age and work in this area is beginning to emerge (Bearne et al., 2007; Marsh, in press; Merchant, 2007b; Walsh, 2007).

Table 21.2 outlines some of the competences/outcomes that were developed in the blogging project (Marsh, 2009), although the table is not intended to offer an exhaustive list.

This is not to suggest that schools should be moving away from a focus on the written word. Far from it, traditional texts and practices are still a central feature in the lives of many children and young people. Rather, schools need to broaden the writing curriculum to include these multimodal practices if they are to reflect the out-of-school literacy interests and practices of their pupils. Introducing popular culture into a contemporary writing curriculum will inevitably involve multimodal forms and work such as that outlined in this section is just a foreshadow of future textual productions. There is much more research needed in the years ahead in order to ascertain the value and outcomes of

Table 21.2 Skills, knowledge and understanding developed in the blogging project

Key competences	Examples
Understanding of the affordances of various modes and the ability to choose appropriate modes for specific purposes	Pupils produced a wide range of multimodal texts that required understanding of the affordances of modes and how modes could work best together to achieve goals. These included: texts that were solely written or oral or consisting of only still images or moving images; texts combining one or more of these modes; animated films; live action films; podcasts; photostories.
Understanding of various media and the ability to choose appropriately for specific purposes	Children used a wide range of media in the production of texts and made critical judgements about which media to use.
Skills in the various modes that enabled them to decode, understand and interpret, engage with and respond to and create and shape texts	Children developed a wide range of skills including: knowledge of the alphabetic principle and abilities in reading and writing print; ability to read both still and moving images; understanding of the features of various genres; understanding of the principles of transduction in the production of multimodal texts; ability to navigate texts across media, follow hyperlinks, read radially etc.
Ability to analyse critically a range of texts and make judgements about value, purpose, audience, and ideologies	In the development of multimodal texts, children were reviewing a wide range of online and offline texts in order to inform their work. They also regularly reviewed their own and peers' work.
Ability to relate texts to their social, cultural, historical contexts and literary traditions	Children were able to relate multimodal texts to their social, cultural and historical contexts and were adept at recognizing intertextuality.
Ability to select and use appropriately other texts for use in the design process	Children produced texts that remixed media content. Children made animated and live action films that incorporated music.
Ability to collaborate in text production, analysis, and response	Children were successful in collaborating with both known and unknown others in the production and analysis of texts. Social networking software, for example, enabled them to comment on others' work and develop an understanding of the value of networks.

merging school and home writing interests and, in the final section of this chapter, I will reflect on what I consider to be the main priorities in setting our future research agenda in this area.

CONCLUSION

Over the last five years, as I have indicated in this chapter, there has been a wealth of work conducted in classrooms that attests to the value of embedding children and young people's popular culture into the writing curriculum. This builds on a substantial body of work conducted previously in this area (see Marsh, 2003, for a review). One might be forgiven for thinking that there are few areas left untouched in this search for evidence of the efficacy of this approach to the teaching and learning of writing. However, there are a number of issues that demand further consideration by researchers in the years ahead. The first and most urgent of these is the need to review the nature of the writing curriculum itself in a digital age.

Part of the difficulty lies in the fact that distinctions are still being made between 'traditional' literacy, focused on print, on paper, and the alphabetical principle, and 'new literacies', which incorporate a range of modes and include a variety of media. A more fruitful way forward would be to focus instead on the notion of communication (Street, 1997) and refer to communicative texts, practices, and events as they are instantiated across modes and media. In this conceptual framework, 'literacy' would signify engagement with lettered representation (Kress, 2003) on both paper, screen, and the wider environment and the interaction between literacy and other modes such as sound, image, and gesture would be accepted as normal practice. The production and analysis of multimodal, multimedia texts would then be embedded within curricula frameworks and emphasis placed on developing learners' skills, understanding and knowledge

with regard to communication across all modes and media. In this model, there would be little need to maintain the distinction between 'traditional' and 'new' literacies, between 'writing' and 'authoring' of multimodal texts. Whether or not this work takes place in a subject titled 'English' is a moot point.

In relation to the development of the subject of English, we are in a period characterized by immense change and uncertainty (Kress, 2003; 2006) [see also Kress in Chapter 11]. There are numerous phrases used that relate to the more extensive engagement with multimodal multimedia texts such as 'media literacy' (Ofcom, 2006), 'digital literacy' (Merchant, 2007b), 'new literacies' (Lankshear and Knobel, 2006), 'multimodal literacy', 'visual literacy', and 'information literacy', to name but a few. Many of these developments share common features and foci, with an emphasis on the analysis and production of multimodal texts across a range of media. One might argue that this proliferation of literacies presents few problems as they all point to slightly different issues and have distinct histories, but in reality this multiplicity is leading to theoretical and conceptual confusions, in addition to contributing to political nervousness regarding further developments. We appear to be at a key juncture in curriculum development and need to consider the implications for the subject English (Green, 2006; Kress, 2006). A focus on the development of the subject so that it encompasses the analysis and production of multimodal, multimedia texts and involves integration of activities that currently occur in areas of the curriculum such as media studies, ICT, or 'information literacy' is timely. Whether or not this subject continues to be titled 'English' or 'Communication, language, and literacy' or even 'Communication Studies' appears at the moment to be the least of the challenges faced, given the lack of common understanding about what the subject should look like in theory and practice. In the face of this turmoil, the work of Kress (2006) has been significant to furthering understanding of how the subject should be shaped in the twenty-first century and he emphasizes the need for it to focus, above all else, on meaning:

> In a society dominated by the demands of the market, by consumption therefore, by its constant and insistent demands for choice—no matter how spurious that choice may be—there is an absolute demand that the curriculum overall should include a subject that has *meaning* as its central question, has as its central concern principles for making choices. (Kress, 2006: 3)

In relation to the role of popular culture in such a curriculum subject, it is clear that pupils, whether they bring popular culture into the curriculum themselves or respond to teachers' invitations to engage with it, find it motivating and empowering, and engage in questions of meaning in relation to these texts and artefacts. However, there is a need for more focused studies on the way in which the use of popular culture impacts on attainment in literacy. The use of a range of methodologies is essential here, including the use of experimental and quasi-experimental studies, despite (or perhaps because of) a previous lack of attention to these research designs in this field. In addition, further longitudinal, ethnographic case studies of classroom writing, such as those conducted by Dyson (1996; 1999; 2001; 2003) are needed if we are to have a detailed understanding of the processes at work as children create multimodal texts in which they draw from their out-of-school knowledge. Finally, research, which offers insights into the way in which educators can begin to assess the skills, knowledge and understanding developed in the production of multimodal texts is required if we are going to be able to take this work forward in meaningful ways. Incorporating popular culture into the writing curriculum should not be simply a utilitarian means of getting pupils to sign up to more conventional school-based writing practices, it should instead be predicated on the need to develop pupils who can be confident and competent authors in the twenty-first century. We will only be able to do this if we are

able to offer the children and young people we teach a curriculum that is underpinned by research on development, continuity, and progression, although this is not to suggest the creation of a lock-step, linear approach to the teaching and learning of writing in a digital age. Nevertheless, in this task we must not get too caught up with writing and multimodal production as a set of skills to be defined and measured for, as Dyson reminds us, popular culture is a social practice in which children are constructed as competent agents of their worlds:

> There is pleasure and power in learning to craft movement, sound and, yes, written words. But it's the breadth of the symbolic repertoire, the sense of competent agency, and the social sophistication to shift one's actions to suit local conditions, that allow children to become full participants in their presents and in their travels into their futures. (Dyson, 2003:3)

As we travel ever still further into the digital future, it is this aspect of authorship that needs to take central place in any writing curricula that celebrates and embraces popular culture.

REFERENCES

Alvermann, D.E. (2005) 'Ned and Kevin: An online discussion that challenges the "not-yet-adult" cultural model', in K. Pahl and J. Rowsell (eds), *Travelnotes from the New Literacy Studies*, Clevedon, UK: Multilingual Matters.

Alvermann, D.E. and Eakle, A.J. (2007) 'Dissolving learning boundaries: The doing, re-doing, and undoing of school', in D. Thiessen and A. Cook-Sather, *International Handbook of Student Experience in Elementary and Secondary School*, New York: Springer. pp.143–166.

Alvermann, D., Huddleston, A., and Hagood, M.C. (2004) 'What could professional wrestling and school literacy practices possibly have in common?', *Journal of Adolescent and Adult Literacy*, 47: 532–540.

Alvermann, D.E., Moon, J.S., and Hagood, M.C. (1999) *Popular Culture in the Classroom: Teaching and Researching Critical Media Literacy*, Newark, Delaware: IRA/NRC.

Bearne, E. (2003) 'Rethinking literacy: Communication, representation and text', *Reading—Literacy and Language*, 37(3): 98–103.

Bearne, E. and Wolstencroft, H. (2005) 'Playing with texts: The contribution of children's knowledge of computer narratives to their story writing', in J. Marsh and E. Millard (eds), *Popular Literacies, Childhood and Schooling*, London: RoutledgeFalmer. pp.72–92.

Bearne, E., Clark, C., Johnson, A., Manford, P., Mottram, M. and Wolstencroft, H. with Anderson, R., Gamble, N. and Overall, L. (2007). *Reading on Screen*. University of Leicester: United Kingdom Literacy Association.

Beavis, C. (2004) 'Critical perspectives on curriculum and ICTs: The 3D model, literacy and computer games', *Interactive Educational Multimedia*, 9: 77–88. Online. Available http: <http://www.ub.es/multimedia/iem/down/c9/Curriculum_and_ICTs.pdf> Accessed 15 November, 2007.

Beavis, C. (2007) 'Writing, digital culture and English curriculum', *L1—Educational Studies in Language and Literature*, 7(4): 23–44.

Bhabha, H.K. (1994) *The Location of Culture*, London: Routledge.

Browne, R. (1987) 'Popular culture: Medicine for illiteracy and associated ills', *Journal of Popular Culture*, 2(3): 1–5.

Burn, A. (2007) '"Writing" computer games: Game literacy and new-old narratives', *L1—Educational Studies in Language and Literature*, 7(4): 45–67.

Calkins, L. (1983) *Lessons from a Child: On the Teaching and Learning of Writing*, Exeter, NH: Heinemann.

Calkins, L. (1994) *The Art of Teaching Writing*, Portsmouth, NH: Heinemann. (Original work published 1986.)

Carrington, V. (2005) 'New textual landscapes, information and early literacy' in J. Marsh (ed.), *Popular Culture, New Media and Digital Literacy in Early Childhood*, London: RoutledgeFalmer.

Davies, J. (2009) 'Online connections, collaborations, chronicles and crossings', in M. Robinson, R. Willett, and J. Marsh (eds), *Play, Creativity and Digital Cultures*, London: Routledge.

Davies, J. and Merchant, G. (2007) 'Looking from the inside out: Academic blogging as new literacy', in Knobel, M. and Lankshear, C. (eds), *A New Literacies Sampler*, New York: Peter Lang. pp.167–197.

Davies, J. and Pahl, K. (2006) 'Blending voices, blending learning: Lessons in pedagogy from a post-16 classroom', in E. Bearne and J. Marsh (eds), *Literacy and Social Inclusion: Closing the Gap*, Stoke-on-Trent: Trentham. pp.89–102.

Demos (2007) *Their Space-Education for a Digital Generation*. Online. Available http: <http://www.demos.co.uk/files/Their%20space%20-%20web.pdf> (Accessed 20 August, 2007).

Dowdall, C. (2009) 'The texts of me and the texts of us: Improvisation and polished performance in social networking sites', in M. Robinson, R. Willett, and J. Marsh (eds), *Play, Creativity and Digital Cultures*, London: Routledge.

Duncan-Andrade, J. and Morrell, E. (2005) 'Turn up that radio teacher: Popular cultural pedagogy in new century urban schools', *Journal of School Leadership*, 15: 284–308.

Dyson, A.H. (1994) 'The Ninjas, the X-Men, and the ladies: Playing with power and identity in an urban primary school', *Teachers College Record*, 96: 219–239.

Dyson, A.H. (1996). 'Cultural constellations and childhood identities: On Greek gods, cartoon heroes, and the social lives of schoolchildren', *Harvard Educational Review*, 66: 471–495.

Dyson, A.H. (1997) *Writing Superheroes: Contemporary Childhood, Popular Culture, and Classroom Literacy*, New York: Teachers College Press.

Dyson, A.H. (1999) 'Coach Bombay's kids learn to write: Children's appropriation of media material for school literacy', *Research in the Teaching of English*, 33: 367–402.

Dyson, A.H. (2001) 'Where are the childhoods in childhood literacy? An exploration in outer (school) space', *Journal of Early Childhood Literacy*, 1: 9–39.

Dyson, A.H. (2003) *Brothers and Sisters Learn to Write: Popular Literacies in Childhood and School Cultures*, New York: Teachers College Press.

Flewitt, R. (2008) Multimodality, in J. Marsh and E. Hallet (eds), *Desirable Literacies* (second edn.), London: Paul Chapman. pp.122–139.

Erixon, P.O. and Nixon, H. (2007) 'Editorial: Teaching writing in a changing semiotic landscape', *L1—Educational Studies in Language and Literature*, 7(4): pp.1–6.

Graham, L. (2004) '"It's Spiderman!" Popular culture in writing journals in the early years', Paper presented at the ESRC Research Seminar Series, Children's Literacy and Popular Culture, 11 February, 2005. Online. Available http:<http://www.shef.ac.uk/literacy/esrc/seminar6.html> (Accessed 16 July, 2007).

Green, B. (1988) 'Subject-specific literacy and school learning: A focus on writing', *Australian Journal of Education*, 32(2): 156–179.

Green, B. (2006) 'English, literacy, rhetoric: Changing the project?', *English in Education*, 40(1): 7–19.

Greenough, P. Scanlan, M., Feiler, A., Johnson, D., Yee, W.C., Andrews, J., Price, A., Smithson, M., and Hughes, M. (2005) 'Boxing Clever: using shoeboxes to support home school knowledge exchange', *Literacy*, 39(2): 97–103.

Gutierrez, K.D., Baquedano-Lopez, P., Alvarez, H., and Chiu, M.M. (1999) 'Building a culture of collaboration through hybrid language practices', *Theory into Practice*, 38: 87–93.

Knobel, M. (2005) 'Technokids, Koala Trouble and *Pokémon*: Literacy, new technologies and popular culture in children's everyday lives', in J. Marsh and E. Millard (eds), *Popular Literacies, Childhood and Schooling*, London: RoutledgeFalmer. pp.11–28.

Kress, G. (2003) *Literacy in a New Media Age*, London: Routledge.

Kress, G. (2006) 'Editorial', *English in Education*, 40(1): 1–4.

Lankshear, C. and Knobel, M. (2006) *New Literacies: Everyday practices and classroom learning* (second edn.), Maidenhead, Berkshire: Open University Press. (first edn. 2003).

Larson, J. and Marsh, J. (2005) *Making Literacy Real: Theories and Practices for teaching and Learning*, London, New Dehli, Thousand Oaks, CA: Sage.

Livingstone, S. and Bovill, M. (1999) Young People, New Media: Report of the Research Project: Children, Young People and the Changing Media Environment. London: London School of Economics and Political Science.

Marsh, J. (2003) 'Early childhood literacy and popular culture' in N. Hall, J. Larson, and J. Marsh (eds), *Handbook of Early Childhood Literacy*, London: Sage. pp.112–125.

Marsh, J. (ed.) (2005) *Popular Culture, New Media and Digital Technology in Early Childhood*, London: RoutledgeFalmer.

Marsh, J. (2009) 'Productive pedagogies: Play, creativity and digital cultures in the classroom', in M. Robinson, R. Willett, and J. Marsh (eds), *Play, Creativity and Digital Cultures*, New York and London: Routledge.

Marsh, J. and Bearne, E. (2007) *Moving Literacy On: Evaluation of the BFI Training Scheme for Lead Practitioners in Moving Image Education*, Sheffield: University of Sheffield/ UKLA.

Marsh, J. and Millard, E. (eds) (2005) *Popular Literacies, Childhood and Schooling*, London: Routledge-Falmer.

Marsh, J., Brooks, G., Hughes, J., Ritchie, L., Roberts, S., and Wright, K. (2005) *Digital Beginnings: Young Children's Use of Popular Culture, Media and New Technologies*, Sheffield: University of Sheffield.

Online. Available http: <http://www.digitalbeginnings.shef.ac.uk/> (Accessed 18 November, 2007).

Meacham, S. (2004) 'Literacy and "Street Credibility": Plantations, Prisons and African American Literacy from Frederick Douglass to Fifty Cent', Paper presented at ESRC Conference, Children's Literacy and Popular Culture Seminar Series, University of Sheffield, 20 March, 2004.

Merchant, G. (2003) 'E-mail me your thoughts: Digital communication and narrative writing', *Literacy*, 37(3): 104–110.

Merchant, G. (2007a) 'Daleks and other avatars', Paper presented at the UKLA Conference, University of Swansea, July, 2007.

Merchant, G. (2007b) 'Writing the future in the digital age', *Literacy*, 41(3): 118–128.

Merchant, G., Dickinson, P., Burnett, C., and Myers, J. (2006) 'Do you like dogs or writing? Identity performance in children's digital message exchange', *English in Education*, 40(3): 21–38.

Millard, E. (2005) 'To enter the castle of fear: Engendering children's story writing from home to school at KS2', *Gender and Education*, 17(1): 57–73.

Moje, E.B., Ciechanowski, K.M., Kramer,K., Ellis,L., Carrillo, R., and Collazzo, T. (2004) 'Working towards third space in content area literacy: An examination of everyday funds of knowledge and discourse', *Reading Research Quarterly*, 39: 38–70.

Moll, L., Amanti, C., Neff, D., and Gonzalez, N. (1992) 'Funds of knowledge for teaching: Using a Qualitative Approach to Connect Homes and Classrooms', *Theory into Practice*, 31: 132–141.

Morrell, E. and Duncan-Andrade, J. (2004) 'What youth do learn in school: Using hip-hop as a bridge to canonical poetry', in J. Mahiri (ed.), *What They Don't Learn in School: Literacy in the Lives of Urban Youth*, New York: Peter Lang. pp.247–268.

Morrell, E. and Duncan-Andrade, J. (2006) 'Popular culture and critical media pedagogy in secondary literacy classrooms', *International Journal of Learning,* 12(9): 273–280.

Newkirk, T. (2002) *Misreading Masculinity: Boys, Literacy and Popular Culture*, Portsmouth, NH: Heinemann.

New London Group (1996) 'A pedagogy of multiliteracies: Designing social futures', *Harvard Educational Review*, 66(1), 60–92.

Ofcom (2006) *Media Literacy Audit: Report on Media Literacy amongst Children*, London: Ofcom. Online. Available http: <http://www.Ofcom.org.uk/advice/media_literacy/medlitpub/medlitpubrss/children/children.pdf> (Accessed 20 August, 2007).

Oldham, J (1999) 'The book of the film: Enhancing print literacy at KS3', *English in Education*, 33(1): 36–46.

Pahl, K. (2005) 'Children's popular culture in the home: tracing cultural practices in texts' in J. Marsh and E. Millard (eds), *Popular Literacies, Childhood and Schooling*, London: RoutledgeFalmer. pp.29–53.

Pahl, K. and Rowsell, J. (2005) *Literacy and Education: Understanding the New Literacy Studies in the Classroom*, London: Sage.

Parker, D. (1999) 'You've read the book, now make the film: Moving image media, print literacy and narrative', *English in Education*, 33: 24–35.

Primary National Strategy/United Kingdom Literacy Association (2004) *Raising Boys' Achievement in Writing*, Royston: UKLA.

Ranker, J. (2006) '"There's fire magic, electric magic, ice magic, or poison magic": The world of video games and Adrian's compositions about gauntlet legends', *Language Arts*, 84(1): 21–33.

Ranker, J. (2007) 'Designing meaning with multiple media sources: A case study of an eight-year-old student's writing processes', *Research in the Teaching of English*, 41(4): 402–434.

Sharp, D. (2006) 'Participatory culture production and the DIY Internet: From theory to practice and back again', *Media International Australia Incorporating Culture and Policy*, 118: 16–24.

Shortis. T. (2007) 'Revoicing txt: Spelling, Vernacular Orthography and "Unregimented Writing"', in S. Posteguillo, M.J., Esteve, and M. L. Gea-Valor (eds), *The Texture of Internet Netlinguistics in Progress*, Cambridge: Cambridge Scholars Publishing. pp.2–21.

Street, B. (1997) 'The Implications of the New Literacy Studies for Education', *English in Education*, 31(3): 45–59.

Vasquez, V.M. (2005) 'Resistance, power-tricky and colorless energy: What engagement with everyday popular cultural texts can tell us about learning and literacy', in J. Marsh (ed), *Popular Culture, New Media and Digital Literacy in Early Childhood*, London: RoutledgeFalmer. pp.201–218.

Walsh, C. (2007) 'Creativity as capital in the literacy classroom: youth as multimodal designers', *Literacy*, 41(2): 79–85.

Walsh, M. (2007) *Literacy for E-Learning and Multimodal Classroom Contexts, 2006*. Sydney, Australia: Australian Catholic University, School of Education.

Willett, R. (2005) '"Baddies" in the classroom: media education and narrative writing', *Literacy*, 39: 142–148.

SECTION III

INTRODUCTION

Conceptual and empirical issues in writing development

This section is primarily concerned with longitudinal notions of development and with some of the dimensions that this development can follow. The section builds on much of the previous one by discussing how the form, structure, and content of writing may develop at different points in our lives and in the different contexts and settings provided in school and the world beyond

Chapter 22 is concerned with morphemes and children's spelling. Morphemes are the smallest units of meaning and their study, morphology, is an underresearched area in literacy studies. Although a great deal of debate has focused on the educational implications of the phoneme-grapheme correspondences of the English writing system, English orthography may be more accurately described as a 'morpho-phonemic' system. An awareness of the rules that govern combinations of morphemes, from single letter suffixes to whole root words, may reveal patterns and consistencies that are not apparent at the phoneme-grapheme level. **Peter Bryant** and **Terezinha Nunes** provide an

account of their recent work in the field, especially the links between morphemes and spelling, and indicate important new implications for policy and practice.

The next chapter discusses what may be meant by 'maturity' in writing, a term that is often used in discussions of how writing develops. **Richard Hudson** examines the assumption that the 'linguistic maturity' of a piece of writing (or speech) can be measured in terms of the linguistic patterns that it contains. He raises key questions for writing research about which linguistic patterns are found more often in more mature writing and what external influences determine how these linguistic patterns develop, while also alerting us to a number of challenges that face anyone who engages in this research

Peter Smagorinsky's chapter moves beyond the intratextual elements of writing development that have been discussed in previous chapters to examine developmental aspects of texts as a whole. His chapter is based on a paper given at the international seminar series in which the origins of the *Handbook* lie. The experiences of visiting two famous European churches, and of trying to read them as 'texts', are used to make a case for a broadened notion of textuality. The chapter embraces a semiotic view of textuality and literacy that regards any configuration of signs as a potential text.

Smagorinsky argues that, while 'new literacies' studies have recently received much attention, multimodal literacies have in fact been around since the first drawings on cave walls and have served educational purposes for millennia. He draws on his recent studies of the design of living spaces by high school students and concludes that the quality of writing or other composition is a function of readers' and writers' relationships and expectations, rather than a static quality of the text. Understanding the cultural construction of expectations is important in understanding any judgment relative to quality.

In the chapter entitled 'The Content of Students' Writing', **Brenton Doecke** and **Douglas McClenaghan** confront the developmental issues that are evident in what is written about. One of the long-standing criticisms of 'school literacy' is that emphases on attainment can result in writing that does not go beyond writing that Hartog[1] once described as 'something, about anything, for no-one in particular'. Recent centralizing trends in state and national educational policy have drawn attention to the range of content that is available in different curriculum areas. These trends also risk overlooking key sources of content, both in the 'real world' and in the world of the imagination. The authors' arguments centre on what can be gained from focusing on what pupils and students have to communicate in their writing and from focusing on social spaces where they *want* to communicate. This involves extending an examination of what students' writing is 'about' to the social exchanges and networks in which they participate, including those beyond the school. The chapter is illustrated by cases of students' writing, which the chapter authors use to convey a sense of imaginative and critical engagement in writing development.

Children writing poetry is of particular interest, because the main focus of the communication is likely to be on the text itself, as an object capable of being appreciated in its own right because of its structure, unity, and fit. The structure exaggerates certain features of the text, helping make it conspicuous in some way and allowing its unity and fit to be better appreciated in the context of what the writer is attending to and what the poem conveys. These textual qualities bring with them distinctive educational gains from student engagement. Yet the writing of poetry may become a casualty of recent centralized initiatives in education policy. The issues of reliably assessing attainment and progression in poetry writing risk a diminution of its place in the curriculum. In Chapter 26, **Anthony Wilson** accepts that the concept of progression within the poetry writing of children is a relatively new one in the field of writing research. He also accepts that claims for poetry's importance in the curriculum, what has been described as the 'jewel in the crown of the verbal arts', are largely based on opinion formed from practice rather than empirical studies. This is borne out by the fact that poetry does not seem to feature in the established models of writing that are discussed elsewhere in this *Handbook* (see, for instance, Chapters 2–5), leaving descriptions of its worth based not on studies of young people's writing but on rhetoric.

The chapter addresses this issue by reporting on a small-scale research study of the poetry writing of children aged 10–11. It argues that progression in poetry can indeed be planned for and uses Bereiter and Scardamalia's concept of knowledge-telling and knowledge-transformation to help synthesize writing and creativity theory with insights about young writers' use of language, form, and models in poetry. In proposing a concept of poetry writing as knowledge discovery, the chapter argues that poetry writing can be an aid to language development, enabling children to engage with creative habits of mind and extending their schemas of what writing can achieve.

In Chapter 27, **Debra Myhill** reminds us that the concept of writing development in writers between ages 11 and 16 has received far less pedagogical and empirical attention than the development of writing in the early years and primary/elementary education.

Understanding of what it means to become a 'better writer' in this older age phase is often limited to broad, generalized principles of improvement. She argues that the common association of linguistic mastery with basic or functional literacy is unfortunate and risks contributing to an impoverished view of linguistic development, which reduces development to the avoidance of error or 'bad grammar' and the acquisition of functional literacy.

Noting the absence of large-scale, robust enquiries, which specifically explore linguistic development in children in the secondary phase, the chapter reports a two-year project, funded by the UK Economic and Social Research Council, which involved a detailed linguistic analysis of writing samples, classroom observation, and post hoc interviews with students.

The findings support a view of writers as designers, with development as a writer in the secondary school phase being described as a process of moving along the trajectories from speech patterns to writing patterns, from declaration to elaboration, and from translation to transformation. The conclusions are that linguistic development in the secondary phase is about acquiring the possibilities of choice, about having a design repertoire to draw upon, and about crafting sentences and texts to satisfy the rhetorical demands of the task.

Ellen Lavelle takes account of the fact that writing development is a life-long process, with distinctive demands being experienced at each stage of educational provision and through adulthood. Her chapter focuses on the college years, in which the demands on students' ability to handle complex discursive genres interface with increasingly sophisticated technological support for the content, style, and multimodal refinement of written language.

Writers' beliefs about writing play a powerful role in this process. In particular, self-efficacy, the belief that one can succeed at a particular task, is a powerful factor affecting both learning and writing performance. Given the complexity and rigor of the writing process, college students often lack a sense of self-efficacy as academic writers. This chapter reviews the self-efficacy and writing research and then extends those ideas to the teaching of writing at the college level.

In Chapter 29, **Brian Huot** and **Jeff Perry** review progress toward a new understanding for classroom writing assessment by returning to Michael Scriven's distinction between formative and summative assessment. Their chapter differentiates between assessment, grading, and testing, and reviews the major contributions to the literature on responding to student writing. Their argument is that realizing how and why assessment has been an underresearched aspect of the teaching of writing provides writing teachers with a powerful tool for improving the teaching of writing. Assessment is an important and integral part of the ways in which a writer negotiates the writing process, providing the criteria for decisions about texts and the process of producing these texts. In addition to discussing ways in which assessment can and should be a positive component of effective writing pedagogy, Huot and Perry provide some new language for use when discussing writing assessment that may promote the teaching and learning of writing in a school context.

Section III ends with a chapter by **Gert Rijlaarsdam** and **his colleagues** that discusses the role of readers in writing development. For many years, writing has been portrayed in research literature as a way of problem-solving. Chapter 30 discusses the usability in writing instruction of pretesting texts with real readers. This provides a way to embody the often-omitted final stage of the problem-solving model: the implementation and evaluation of the problem 'solution'—the written text. The chapter authors focus on pretesting texts through reader observation instead of through readers' comments. They use observation as a means to collect feedback on the qualities of the text for the purpose of revision, enhancing the writer's audience awareness as part of the writer's expertise.

They conclude from the research results and examples discussed that actual readers and actual reading processes deserve a place in effective writing instruction. Reader feedback, reader observation, and role-switching between writers and readers can be essential complements to a cognitive, process-oriented view on writing education.

They offer a number of recommendations linked to an educational environment for writing students that presents them with ample opportunities to get to know their audience, to collect real responses to their texts, and to make discoveries about 'what works' in communicative tasks.

NOTE

1 Hartog, P.J. (1908) *The Writing of English* (second edn.), Oxford: Clarendon Press.

Morphemes and Children's Spelling

Peter Bryant and Terezinha Nunes

WHAT ARE MORPHEMIC SPELLING RULES?

Morphemes are units of meaning. Some words have one such unit, but many have more than one. There is only one morpheme in the adjective 'glad', while 'gladly', an adverb, and 'gladness', a noun, contain two morphemes each. All three words share the same root morpheme, 'glad'; but the added '-ly' ending in 'gladly' and '-ness' in 'gladness' turns the first of these two words into an adverb and the second into an abstract noun. The '-ly' and -ness' endings are affix morphemes and each of them crops up in a large number of words in a rule-like way. Whenever you put '-ly' or '-ness' on the end of an adjective you generate an adverb in the first case and an abstract noun in the second.

In many languages, morphemes have a profound effect on the way that words are spelled (see Jaffré, 1997). This is because the same morphemes tend to be spelled in the same way in different words. The result is a set of morphemic spelling rules, which transcend the basic alphabetic rules and, as we shall see, play a great part in children's successes and failures in learning to read and write.

Spelling the same sound differently

The endings of the words 'socks' and 'fox' sound the same, but are spelled differently. The reason is that 'socks' is a two-morpheme, and 'fox' a one-morpheme word. The word 'socks' consists of the root morpheme 'sock' and the /s/ ending which is the plural morpheme. The plural morpheme at the end of English regular plural words is always spelled as '-s' or as '-es'. 'Fox', however, is a one-morpheme word and the /ks/ ending in one-morpheme words is invariably spelled as '-x' or as '-xe' (e.g. 'axe'). So, the decision about which way to spell these two words and any other word ending in /ks/ rests on their morphemic structure.

The same link between morphemes and spelling exists in many other languages as well. French is full of instances in which the choice between alternative spellings is settled by the word's morphemic structure. Consider the two phrases 'j'ai mangé' and 'je mangais'. Both verbs end in the identical /e/ sound, but it is spelled as '-ais' in the imperfect (first person singular) and as 'é' in the perfect verb, and the same, of course, is true of other French verbs (Brissaud and Bessonnat, 2001).

The Greek orthography offers more ways to spell vowels than there are vowels. Anyone writing modern Greek, therefore, has choices to make about how to spell some of its vowels. However, when these vowels are part of an affix morpheme, there is a clear rule for which spelling should be used. The inflectional affixes for the nominative, neuter, single nouns, and for the first person, singular present tense verbs sound exactly the same. The sound for both is /ɔ/, which is spelled either as omicron, 'o', or as omega, 'ω'. The neuter noun ending is always spelled with an 'o' (e.g., δώρο ('gift')), and the first person verb ending with an 'ω' (e.g. γελώ ('I laugh')). Again, morphemes settle the way this sound is spelled when the sound is part of an affix.

Spelling different sounds the same

Another morphemic rule, which is commoner in English than in other scripts, is that particular morphemes tend to be spelled in the same way in different words even when their sound varies in speech from word to word. Let us return to the English regular plural noun ending. In some words we pronounce it as /s/ and in others as /z/: 'cats', 'rocks', and 'coughs' are in the first of these groups; and 'trees', 'dogs', and 'cabs' in the second. English spelling disregards this phonological difference: every regular plural noun has an 's' ending in English.

Another powerful example is the past ending in English regular past verbs. Invariably the correct spelling for this ending is '-ed', but we pronounce it as /d/ ('killed'), or as /t/ ('kissed'), or as /id/ ('wanted') in different words. The same pattern of morphemic constancy affects some root morphemes in English. The root morphemes in 'heal' and 'health', and in 'muscle' and 'muscular' are the same. They are spelled in the same way, despite differences in the pronunciation of the vowel sound in the first pair of words and of the root's final consonant cluster in the second.

Spelling morphemes that have no sound

A third link between spelling and morphemes is the fact that writing sometimes provides information that is not to be found in speech. Plural endings in French nouns, adjectives, and verbs are usually silent in speech, but appear in writing (Fayol et al., 1999). The verbs, the adjectives, and the nouns in the two sentences 'Il aime la grande maison' and 'Ils aiment les grandes maisons' sound exactly the same as each other in speech but they are spelled differently, because of the written plural endings in the second sentence. The sounds of the three words, therefore, tell us nothing about their singularity or plurality, but the spelling does, because the plural inflectional morphemes are written ('-s' in nouns and adjectives, '-nt' in verbs) but not spoken.

In English, the apostrophe works in the same way. Plural and possessive nouns sound the same in speech but differ in script: plurals do not have an apostrophe and possessives do. The two phrases 'The girl's drink' and 'the girls drink' sound exactly the same in speech, but the apostrophe tells us in the first sequence that the drink in question belongs to a singular girl: the '-'s' is a possessive affix for a singular noun. The absence of an apostrophe in the second sequence is explicit enough information that 'girls' is a plural noun and thus that 'dance' in this case must be a verb.

The most important point to be made about these three links between morphemes and spelling is that they all go beyond the alphabetic code. This code is based entirely on the correspondence between single letters or sequences of letters and sounds, and it cannot do the job performed by any of these three rules. No amount of alphabetic knowledge will tell you to spell 'socks' in one way and 'fox' in another, and it actually goes against alphabetic correspondence rules to spell the /t/ ending in 'kissed' as '-ed'.

LEARNING OR NOT LEARNING THE RULES

Morphemic spelling rules exist, but does anyone learn them and does anyone use them? We cannot be sure that anyone does, because there is another way to learn how to spell the endings of 'socks' and 'fox' differently, and how to spell the endings of 'cats' and 'dogs' in the same way. The alternative is sometimes called 'word-specific knowledge' and sometimes 'lexical knowledge'. These two terms refer to the obvious and important fact that, as we learn to read, we become familiar with the spelling of specific words.

Readers do build up a sizeable store of memories for the spellings of a great number of words. This store is essential, especially for people reading and writing in an orthography as complex as English. How else are they able to learn to write 'Gloucester', not 'Gloster', and to remember that 'reign' has one meaning and 'rain' another? You have to remember the spelling of these specific words to get them right: no phonemic or morphemic rules, however sophisticated, will do that job for you.

It follows that people might also use this store of word-specific knowledge to bypass morphemic spelling rules completely. They might learn the correct spelling for 'socks' and 'fox' simply by coming across these particular words in written text and remembering how each one is spelled, without understanding that the 's' ending on 'socks' represents the plural morpheme or that 'x' is the commonest ending for one-morpheme words that end in a /ks/ sound.

The suggestion that most children might ignore morphemic spelling rules and rely on word-specific knowledge instead is a reasonable one. Many children are not taught about morphemes at school. The amount of direct teaching about morphemes and spelling given to children in schools in England is extremely small, and a recent study of teachers in schools in London (Hurry et al., 2006) revealed that many of them have hazy and

not completely correct knowledge of what morphemes are and that their ability to explain the link between morphemes and spelling is not well developed. A simple search through the National Primary Strategy website, which in the UK provides general guidance to the teaching of literacy in primary school, illustrates the way that this guidance is conceived, even if it does not tell the whole story. The word 'phoneme' appears 72 times; the word morpheme, in contrast, only 3; the words 'prefix' and 'suffix' do not appear at all. Of course, there are large variations across countries and across schools within countries, but it is fair to say that in the UK at least most children are given little instruction about morphemes and spelling. By and large, they have to discover much about the links between morphemes and spelling for themselves.

The absence of teaching is echoed by a marked lack of interest shown by many psychologists in the possibility that morphemes might play a part in children's literacy learning. Several psychological models of children's reading, including quite recent ones, leave out these rules altogether. An example is Share's influential 'self-teaching' theory (Share, 1996), which suggests that the core to the development of children's reading is their initial learning the rules of the alphabet. This gives them the tools to begin to decipher new words, which they then recognize when they encounter them subsequently. Thus, the core of the theory is that the children's alphabetic knowledge allows them to construct an increasingly well-endowed bank of word-specific knowledge, as they grow older. Morphemes play no part in this theory, though there is no reason why they should not. It would be quite possible to add morphemic rules to Share's stimulating, but possibly limited, approach. The question we must turn to is: Whether there is any need to do so? This can be reformulated as: Do morphemic spelling rules play any systematic part in children's learning to read?

We shall look at three kinds of evidence to answer this question:

- Evidence on how well and how easily children learn the conventional spellings for morphemes, such as the '-ed' ending, and the '-s' spelling for the plural
- Evidence on children's morphological awareness and its relation to their learning about morphemic spelling rules
- Evidence on the effects of explicit instruction about morphemes and their relation to spelling

How well and how easily do children learn the conventional spellings for morphemes?

When English-speaking children start to write words, they learn to use grapheme-phoneme correspondences quite rapidly (Read, 1971; Treiman, 1993). They plainly have more difficulty with spelling morphemes and particularly with morphemic spelling rules that transcend grapheme-phoneme correspondences. A good example is the '-ed' spelling for the end of regular past verbs. This spelling pattern transgresses grapheme-phoneme correspondences: we never pronounce the '-ed' at the end of regular past verbs and we use the '-ed' spelling to represent three sounds, as noted earlier on.

Young children find it hard to learn this spelling rule (Beers and Beers, 1992), and the main barrier is that it flouts grapheme-phoneme rules. Varnhagen et al. (1997) reported that over 75% of Canadian Grade-1 children (6-year-olds) wrote the past tense ending phonetically (e.g., 'helpt' for 'helped' and 'grabd' for 'grabbed') and that none of them used the correct '-ed' spelling.

This problem persists. Nunes et al. (1997a) showed this in a large-scale three-year longitudinal study of children who were 6-, 7-, or 8-year-olds when the study began. During the project, Nunes et al. took measures of the children's progress in learning the spelling for various morphemes and in particular the past verb inflection, and they also measured the children's awareness of morphemes in spoken language.

Table 22.1 gives the words that Nunes et al. asked the children to write. These ended

Table 22.1 Spelling tasks in the three-year longitudinal study (Nunes et al., 1997a)

	/d/ sound ending	/t/ sound ending
Regular verbs	called	dressed
	covered	kissed
	filled	laughed
	killed	learned
	opened	stopped
Irregular verbs	found	felt
	heard	left
	held	lost
	sold	sent
	told	slept
Non-verbs	bird	belt
	cold	except
	field	next
	gold	paint
	ground	soft

either in a /t/ or in a /d/ sound and were divided into three sets. The words in the first set were regular verbs, and so their endings were spelled as '-ed' whether the final sound was /d/ or /t/. In the second set, the words were irregular past-tense verbs which do not conform to the '-ed' spelling rule, and whose endings, therefore, are spelled phonetically. All the words in the third set were one-morpheme words: this meant that their /d/ and /t/ endings were spelled phonetically. Thus, Nunes et al. compared words that obeyed morphemic spelling rules with words that conformed to grapheme-phoneme correspondence rules.

Figure 22.1 shows us how the children managed to do so at various points in the project. The children did much better with grapheme-phoneme correspondences than with morphemic spellings: the nonverb and the irregular past verb endings were strikingly easier for the children to spell than the regular past tense '-ed' ending. This was almost certainly not due to differences in the children's familiarity with specific words, since the mean frequency with which the words appear in children's texts is much the same for the three sets (Nunes and Bryant, 2008). So, the difference is the result of children understanding the link between sounds and letters rather than the link between morphemes and letters.

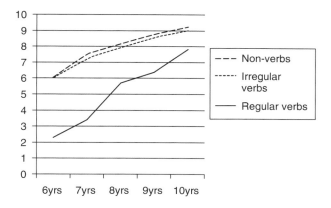

Figure 22.1   Mean number of correct spellings of the endings in regular and irregular verbs and in non-verbs by children of different ages (Nunes et al. 1997a).

The children's errors supported this conclusion. Most of the mistakes that the children made with the regular verbs were 'phonetic' errors. The children tended to spell 'kissed' as 'kist' or 'kisst', for example, and 'killed' as 'kild' or 'killd'. So, word-specific knowledge was not the explanation for the differences between the sets: the children had never seen 'words' like 'kild' and they wrote the words that way, because they were using traditional grapheme-phoneme correspondences, which they knew well by then.

The results in Figure 22.1 also show that the children got better as they grew older at spelling the word endings in all three sets. By the time that they reached the age of 9 and 10 years, the children were making few mistakes in spelling the two easier sets of words. However, at the same time, their average score for the regular verbs still fell well below 80%. The '-ed' ending continued to cause a lot of difficulty to some of the children, even though at that age, they had been taught a lot about spelling and had spent a great deal of time reading English text.

Other evidence suggests that the past tense is not a special case. Children also initially have much difficulty when the morphemic spelling rule settles the choice between two alternatives, both of which fit well with grapheme-phoneme rules. An example is the rule for spelling /z/ ending words as 's' if they are two-morpheme words like 'dogs' and 'trees' but not if they are one-morpheme words like 'jazz' or 'laze' or 'please'.

In fact, many experts have suggested that this particular distinction is quite an easy one for children to learn. Charles Read (1971, 1986), an American linguist, reported that young children hardly ever spelled /z/ ending plurals as '-z' and argued that this showed that they knew something about the connection between morphemes and spelling. Treiman (1993) confirmed Read's observation about children's reluctance to write plurals as /z/, and claimed that this could be due to the fact that the letter 'z' appears infrequently in English texts.

Recently, however, Kemp and Bryant (2003) found that children really do have a lot of difficulty with /z/ ending plural words, or at any rate with some of them. They asked children aged from 5 to 8 years to write plural words that ended in a /z/ sound. Each of the plural words that the children had to write was part of a sentence that made it clear that this word was a plural noun. Sometimes in these words, the /z/ ending in the plural word came immediately after a consonant ('*fibs*. The naughty boy told *fibs* to his mother') and sometimes it followed a vowel ('*fleas*. That poor little dog has got *fleas*').

The children made many mistakes in spelling the ending of the plural words in which the sound immediately preceding the /z/ ending was a vowel (e.g., 'fleas'). They managed to spell the /z/ ending correctly only 73% of the time. They spelled 20% of these plural endings either as '-ze' or as '-se': these are incorrect spellings for plural endings but correct spellings for one-morpheme words in which the /z/ ending is immediately preceded by a long vowel ('freeze', 'please'). So, there was a great deal of confusion about the plural ending even though all the words were familiar to the children in this study.

The children did much better with the other set of plural words — the 'fibs' type words in which the sound just before the /z/ ending is a consonant. They spelled the plural ending correctly as '-s' 91% of the time, and they hardly ever used the '-se' (1%) or '-ze' (2%) singular endings with these words. This was almost certainly due to the children detecting a specific pattern in English spelling. Nearly every English word in which the /z/ ending follows a consonant is spelled as '-s'. This is because nearly every English word of this sort is a two-morpheme word—either a plural word or a third person singular present tense verb (e.g., '(he) runs'). There are a few exceptions, which are all words that children are unlikely to know— words like 'adze' and 'bronze'. Thus, children probably do well with these 'fibs' words by learning a simple but specific rule that the /z/ ending is always spelled as '-s' when it follows a consonant. It may seem odd that they spot this pattern, especially since no teacher ever tells them about it. However, different researchers (Ferreiro and Teberosky, 1982; Karmiloff-Smith, 1992; Tolchinsky, 1988; Treiman, 1993; Lehtonen and Bryant, 2005) have shown that children are quite sensitive to what seem to be form rules in spelling: i.e., they rarely use or accept as appropriate spellings combinations of letters (or letter-like forms) that are nonexistent or very rare in the orthography, which they are

learning. So, the children seem to be using some form of rule, but the rule in itself is very different in nature from the general morphemic spelling rule that plural inflections are spelled as '-s'.

Knowledge of the pattern 'no z after consonants' is no help with /z/ ending words in which a long vowel sound comes just before this ending. In some of these words, the /z/ ending is spelled as '-s', because they are two-morpheme words ('trees', 'he sees'). In others, it is spelled as '-se' or as '-ze' ('freeze' 'praise'), and these are all one-morpheme words. Here is an example of how everyone has two possible ways to learn to spell the endings of these words. They can rely either on word-specific knowledge or on morphemic spelling rules. In the more difficult 'fleas' task, in which the /z/ ending was preceded by a vowel the children did spell the plural ending correctly more often than not, even though they made a lot of mistakes. This relative success does not establish that the children had any knowledge of the spelling rule, because it may have been due to the children's word-specific knowledge.

The best way to eliminate word-specific knowledge is to ask children to spell pseudowords (words which obey the phonological constraints of the language, but have no meaning) that are either clearly in the plural or clearly singular. This can be done by embedding the pseudowords in sentences, which make it obvious whether they refer to a plural noun or not. Kemp and Bryant (2003) did this in a further experiment with children in the same age range as the in the first study. They asked children to write a series of pseudowords with /z/ endings. Each pseudoword was embedded in a sentence, which made it clear whether the word was a plural or singular noun. There were three sets of these pseudowords:

1. Plural words: the /z/ ending followed a consonant (correct spelling '-s')—Example: '*stogs*. There are five *stogs* in my garden'.
2. Plural words: the /z/ ending followed a long vowel (correct spelling '-s')—Example: '*prees*. How many *prees* can you see up there?'

3. Singular words: the /z/ ending followed a long vowel (correct spelling '-se' or '-ze')—Example: '*preeze*. That man keeps a big *preeze* in his cupboard'.

Again the young children made a great deal of mistakes in spelling the endings of the words with vowels sounds just before the /z/ sound (the prees/preeze words in sets 2 and 3). On average in set 2, the children only spelled 37% of the plural words with the correct '-s' ending. In set 3, they spelled only 49% of the one-morpheme pseudowords with the correct '-se' or '-ze' endings. They did much better, as in the earlier study, in spelling plural words with a consonant just before the /z/ ending (the *stogs* words in set 1): here they were right 74% of the time.

It seems, therefore, that young children in the early stages of learning to read and spell are as uncertain about the rule for spelling plural inflections as they are about the rule for past tense inflections. It also seems that many children ingeniously discover for themselves a spelling pattern, which helps them with some plural words ('fibs' and 'stogs') though not with others ('trees' and 'prees'). In general, we can conclude that children tend not to follow the morphemic spelling rules that we have been discussing and probably other morphemic spelling rules as well during the first few years of learning to read and write.

Some difficulties persist. The evidence strongly suggests that at the age when children are able to spell past tense endings correctly, they are still completely at sea with the rule for the possessive apostrophe. This difficulty is probably due to the fact that plural and possessive nouns in English sound exactly the same. The morphemic distinction is represented in writing, but not in speech; 'dogs' sounds just the same as 'dog's' in speech but the two words are quite different in writing. In England, pupils are introduced to the possessive apostrophe when they are around 9 years. Bryant et al. (1997) looked at how well 9-, 10-, and 11-year-old children understand the role of the apostrophe.

They gave children a set of written sentences, each with a missing word and there was a blank space where the word should have been. The experimenters dictated each sentence, including the missing word, and asked the children to write this word into the blank space. The missing word was a plural noun in half the sentences (e.g., 'The dogs are barking') and a singular, possessive noun in the other half ('Is this the boy's football?'): the missing word is underlined in both examples. Bryant et al. wanted to find out whether the children could work out whether each word was plural or possessive and assign the apostrophe accordingly.

The children were generally reluctant to use the apostrophe, which meant that they were right most of the time with plural words and wrong most of the time with the possessives. The 9-year-olds hardly ever put in an apostrophe, and when they did use apostrophes they were as likely to do so with the wrong words as with the right ones (see also McMillan, 1999). The 10- and 11-year-olds also tended to leave the apostrophe out, but at least they assigned more apostrophes to the possessive than to the plural words.

There are now many other examples of the difficulties that children have, often for many years, in learning the conventional spellings for morphemes. We have summarized these recently (Nunes and Bryant, 2006), but we will provide one further striking example here. This concerns the endings '-ion' and '-ian', and '-ness'. Nouns ending in '–ion' are normally abstract nouns, like 'education' and 'dictation', that are derived from verbs. Nouns ending in '–ness' are also abstract nouns like 'happiness' and 'cheerfulness', and they are derived from adjectives. In contrast, a noun ending in '-ian' usually concerns a person, and tends to be about what the person does ('a magician') or about the person's nationality ('the Egyptian'). These spellings, for reasons that are not completely clear, are particularly hard for English school children. Figure 22.2 shows how often the suffixes '-ion' and '-ness' were written correctly by a sample of over 700 children in

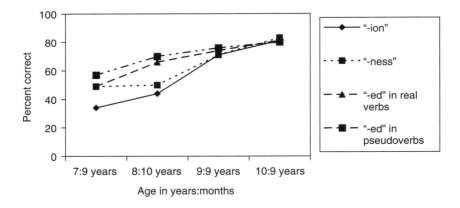

Figure 22.2   Percentage of children who spelled each suffix ('-ion', '-ness', and '-ed') correctly by age level (Nunes and Bryant, 2006).

eight different schools in Oxford and London. Nine- and ten-year-old children only managed to get a mean score of 80%. This level of success is not at all impressive, given that there is no ambiguity in the spelling if you know about the suffixes.

These examples suggest that, at least under the current conditions of instruction, young children do not easily use morpheme-grapheme correspondences, even when these seem to involve relatively simple rules. English children clearly take some time to learn morphemic spelling rules, if they learn them at all. In cases where the spelling for particular morphemes either flouts grapheme-phoneme correspondences, as with the '-ed' past tense and the '-ion' and '-ian' endings, or where morphemes determine which of the two or more spellings to use for the same sound, as in /z/ ending words, most children younger than about 10 years face some difficulty. Their difficulties demonstrate that they have not mastered, and probably do not understand, the relevant morphemic rules.

We need to know the obstacles. Are children in this age range simply unable to link morphemes and spelling or are there built-in obstacles in the orthography that they happen to be learning? We have focused on English-speaking children who have the particular problem that different sets of rules clash in

their orthography. The grapheme-phoneme correspondence rules, which they are taught explicitly, are in conflict with several of the morphemic rules. Perhaps it would be easier to learn about morphemes and spelling in an orthography in which there is no clash between these rules and the system of grapheme-phoneme correspondences.

Greek is a good example of an orthography in which morphemic spelling rules are important but do not clash directly with the grapheme-phoneme rules (Bryant et al., 1999). Greek words obey grapheme-phoneme conversion rules. Once you know these rules you can read every word in the language and you will produce the right sound irrespective of whether you have heard the word before or not. However, spelling is not quite so easy, and the reason is the fact, noted earlier, that there is more than one way of spelling three of the five Greek vowel sounds.

1. 'o' and 'ω' both signify /ɔ/ as in 'hot'
2. 'ε' and 'αι' both signify /e/ as in 'wet'
3. 'η', 'ι', 'u',' oι' 'ει' all signify /i/ as in 'seat'

Greek spellers, therefore, have to make a choice when they write a word with one of these three vowels. How they make this choice may depend on whether the vowel is in the stem or in an affix. There is no simple rule for vowels in stems. The speller has to rely on word- or stem-specific knowledge when deciding whether to use 'o' or 'ω' to represent the vowel /ɔ/ when it occurs in a word's stem. Sometimes 'o' is the right spelling (e.g., τόπι(ball)) and sometimes 'ω' (e.g., φωνή(voice)). Grapheme-phoneme correspondence will tell the speller what the possible choices are (e.g., between 'o' and 'ω'), but only specific learning will settle the choice.

However, word-specific knowledge is one way but not the only way to decide which vowel spelling to use in an affix morpheme. Morphemic knowledge is the alternative, because each affix is always spelled in the same way. The sound /ɔ/ at the end of a verb is the inflection for the first person singular present tense and its correct spelling is always 'ω' (e,g, γελώ('I laugh'), βγαίνω('I go out')). The same sound at the end of a noun is an inflection for the nominative, neuter, singular nouns, which is always spelled as 'o' (e.g. μήλο(apple), δώρο(present)).

At the time that of the research that we are about to describe, the practice in Greek schools was not to teach the children directly and explicitly about the links between morphemes and spelling. Thus, when children spelled the vowel sounds correctly in affixes in real words they could be doing so either through word- specific knowledge or through knowledge of morphemic spelling rules. In Greece, where all the children receive the same textbooks from the government, the focus of instruction was on phonology, and, like English children, they had to work out the rules for themselves.

Again, the best way to eliminate word-specific knowledge in spelling tasks is to work with pseudowords. If children spell inflections correctly, they must be using the morphemic rules. If they are better at spelling inflections in real words than in pseudowords, they must to some extent be using word-specific knowledge.

Chliounaki and Bryant (2007) used both kinds of task in a longitudinal study of Cretan children, whom they tested on three separate occasions spread over a period of just under two years. The children were 6-year-old in the first of the three sessions, 7-year-old in the second, and 8-year-old in the third and final session. In each of these sessions, we asked them to spell a large set of real words and an equal number of pseudowords.

Figure 22.3 shows that the children spelled the vowel correctly more often in real words than in pseudoword inflections. The difference demonstrates some reliance on word-specific knowledge, since this knowledge can only help them with real and familiar words and not at all with pseudowords. It also shows that when the children were 6-year-old, their scores for pseudoword inflections were rather low but better than one would expect by chance. Random choices would result in an average score of around 12 out of 32 correct choices. In the first session, the average score for correct spelling was 15.7. We looked at how many individual children produced scores in this pseudoword task that were significantly above chance level in this session, and we found that 22.2% of our sample reached this level and were, therefore, using morphemic spelling rules. In the next session, nearly a year later, that figure was 63.3% and in the final session when the children were 8-year-old, it was 77.8%. Thus, we found that a reasonable minority of Greek children already knew quite a lot about morphemic spelling rules in their first year at school, and we also found a sharp rise in the children's knowledge and use of these rules over the next two years.

This early start and rapid improvement on the part of Greek pupils contrasts with most of the results that we have reported for English children. The contrast may be due to the differences in the English and Greek orthographies. The regularity of the Greek orthography may have made it easier for the children to detect the connection between morphemes and spelling.

The study also threw some light on how the Greek children manage to infer morphemic

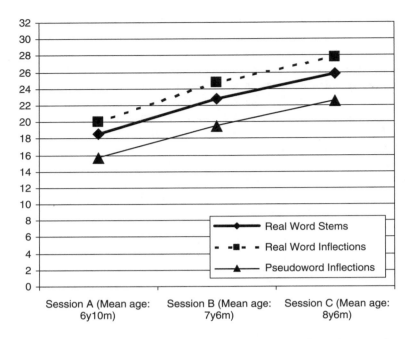

Figure 22.3   The Greek children's (N = 90) mean scores for spelling the vowel sounds correctly (out of 32) in Sessions 1, 2, and 3 (Chliounaki and Bryant, 2007).

spelling rules. It was already clear from the results that the children were able to spell inflections in real words quite some time before they could spell them in pseudowords. In all three sessions, we found many children whose scores on real word inflections were significantly above chance while their scores on pseudoword inflections were not, but we only found one child in one session whose score on pseudoword inflections was significantly above chance level, while his equivalent real word score was not. This pattern raises an interesting possibility, which is that the children first build up a bank of word-specific knowledge about the spelling of their endings, and then use this knowledge as the basis for making inferences about the rules underlying these spellings.

One way to test this hypothesis is to look at correlations across time. The hypothesis that word-specific knowledge is the basis for learning about morphemic spelling rules predicts that the children's scores with real word inflections (a measure of their word-specific knowledge) in earlier sessions should be

related to their spelling of pseudoword inflections (a measure of their knowledge of morphemic spelling rules) in later sessions, and that the vice versa relation (pseudoword in earlier sessions and real word inflections in later sessions) should be much weaker. It also predicts that the children's real word stem spelling in earlier sessions should not be related to how well they learn to write pseudoword inflections any better than earlier. Pseudoword inflection scores are related to later real word inflection scores, because according to the hypothesis knowledge of how to spell inflections is specifically based on the children's word-specific knowledge of real word inflections and not on their knowledge of real word stems.

Figure 22.4 presents two cross-lagged correlation analyses, which test these prediction. The first analysis (A) shows that the predicted pattern did occur (Prediction 1). The children's spelling of real word inflections in Session 1 predicted their spelling of pseudoword inflections in Session 2, but their pseudoword spelling in Session 1

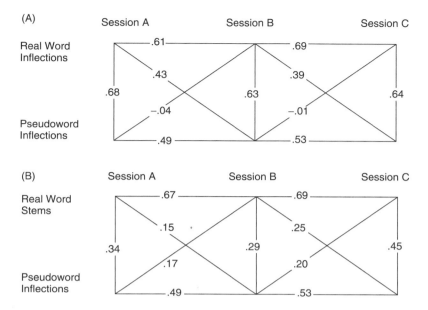

Figure 22.4   Two cross-lagged partial correlations (with age, IQ, and the outcome measure at Time 1 controlled) between Greek children's spelling scores (A) for real word inflections and pseudoword inflections, and (B) for real word stems and pseudoword inflections (Chliounaki and Bryant, 2007).

did not predict their real word inflection scores in Session 2. Exactly the same pattern holds in the relations between Session 2 and Session 3. The second analysis (B) confirmed (see Prediction 2) that the children's scores for spelling stems did not predict their pseudoword inflection spelling in the next session any more than their pseudoword inflection spelling scores predicted their success in spelling stems. Together the analyses established that Greek children's learning about the rules for spelling inflections is firmly rooted in their initial bank of word-specific knowledge of word endings.

CHILDREN'S MORPHOLOGICAL AWARENESS AND ITS RELATION TO THEIR LEARNING ABOUT MORPHEMIC SPELLING RULES

There are different possible reasons why children, and particularly English-speaking children, find it hard to learn about morphemes and spelling. One, which we have touched on, is that many morphemic spelling rules clash with alphabetic conventions. Another possibility is that children's knowledge about morphemes is too weak for them to be able to form rules about the links between morphemes and spelling for themselves. This argument is akin to the widely accepted claim for the existence of a strong relationship between children's phonological awareness and their success in reading. It is not surprising that several researchers began to ask whether there might also be a similar link between morphological awareness and children's literacy (e.g., Carlisle, 1988; 1995; 2000; Sénéchal, 2000).

In this section, we shall concentrate on the possibility that children's awareness of morphology is related to their use of morphemic spelling. A central aim of the study by Nunes et al. (1997a), which we mentioned earlier, was to measure longitudinally the relation between children's morphological awareness

Table 22.2 The sentence and word analogy tasks devised by Nunes et al. (1997a).

The Sentence Analogy Task			
The tester uses puppets to present the sentences. The first puppet 'says' the first sentence in the pair; the second puppet 'says' the second sentence. Then the first puppet says the first sentence in the second pair and the child is encouraged to help the second puppet and say his sentence. Each item presents the corresponding pairs e.g.,			
Tom helps Mary	*First pair*	*Second pair*	_____
Jane threw the ball	Jane throws the ball	Jane kicked the ball	_____
The cow woke up	The cow wakes up	The cow ran away	_____
The Word Analogy Task			
The tester uses puppets to present the words. The first puppet 'says' the first word in the pair; the second puppet 'says' the second word. Then the first puppet says the first word in the second pair and the child is encouraged to help the second puppet and say his word. Each item presents the corresponding pairs e.g.,			
First pair		*Second pair*	
anger	angry	strength	_____
teacher	taught	writer	_____
walk	walked	shake	_____

and their ability to use morphemic spelling rules, and particularly the rule about the '-ed' ending for past tense verbs. We have already described how we gave the children three types of words to spell: (1) regular past verbs, (2) irregular past verbs, and (3) non-verbs. The main measures of morphological awareness were Sentence Analogy and Word Analogy, which are described in Table 22.2.

The children's scores in these two tasks significantly predicted their performance in three spelling tasks 15 months later, even after controls for differences in IQ and in their spelling at the time when they were given the morphological awareness tasks. In this initial comparison, the outcome measure was the children's spelling of real words, which could have been influenced by word-specific knowledge. In another comparison in the same longitudinal project, Nunes et al. (1997b) asked children to spell pseudoverbs embedded in sentences, which made it clear that they were past verbs (e.g., crelled. Harry is crelling his book. Maybe he will crell mine tomorrow. He crelled another one this morning.). At the time of this test, the children were aged between 9- and to 11-years. Again, the children's morphological awareness scores predicted the number of times that they correctly ended the past tense pseudoverbs with an '-ed'.

Several other studies support the idea that morphological awareness is a predictor of children's ability to spell words using morphemic spelling rules, independently of the children's general verbal ability in English (Green et al., 2003) and in other languages (Hebrew: Levin et al., 1999; Dutch: Rispens et al., 2007; Danish: Arnback and Elbro, 2000; Greek: Bryant et al., 1999: and also Harris and Giannouli, 1999; French: Sénéchal, 2000). The contribution of morphology is not restricted to spelling, but also appears in word reading and comprehension (e.g., Carlisle and Addison Stone, 2003; Deacon and Kirby, 2004; Leong and Parkinson, 1995; Nagy et al., 2006; Totereau et al., 1997).

There is evidence that the connection also works the other way: learning to read and spell affects children's morphological awareness.

Nunes et al. (2006) carried out two studies of the consequences of learning to spell on children's awareness of morphemes. The aim of the first study aim was to see whether the children's progress in spelling could predict their growth in morphological awareness. Nunes et al. used children's ability to spell with the '-ed' ending as our longitudinal predictor and the children's scores in the sentence analogy and word analogy tasks about a year later as our outcome measures.

After controlling for the children's age and verbal ability, the children's spelling ability was still a significant predictor of their awareness of morphology. Thus, the more they learn about spelling, the more aware they become of morphology.

Levin et al. (1999) found similar reciprocal influences between morphological knowledge and reading and spelling in a study of Israeli children learning to read and write Hebrew (see also Derwing et al., 1995). There is, therefore, consistent support for the idea of a two-way street between morphological awareness and spelling.

THE EFFECTS OF EXPLICIT INSTRUCTION ABOUT MORPHEMES AND THEIR RELATION TO SPELLING

The evidence that we discussed in an earlier part of this chapter that many children find it hard to work out morphemic spelling rules for themselves, raises the question whether they would fare any better if they were taught formally about these rules. The rules themselves are a potential support. Knowing when to write '-ion' and when '-ian' at the end of a word should, in principle, be an immense help to children who otherwise make frequent spelling mistakes with these two endings. Yet, intervention studies about morphemes and spelling are still comparatively rare. The fullest account of them can be found in Nunes and Bryant's book (2006) on teaching children morphemic spelling rules.

One of the earliest intervention studies in this field was done by Solveig Lyster (2002), a Norwegian psychologist, whose intervention was with a large group of 6-year-old children and their preschool teachers in their last year before school (at the time of this project children in Norway did not go to school until after their seventh birthday). She divided the children into three groups: a Phonological group, a Morphological group, and a Control group.

The study contained a Pre-test, Intervention period, and finally a Post-test. The Pre-tests were about children's awareness of phonology (including rhyme and phoneme tasks) and a morphology task, which dealt with compound words like 'fire-engine'. The intervention lasted 17 weeks with one session per week. The children in the Phonology groups were taught about sounds in words with the help of various rhyme and phoneme tasks during these intervention sessions. The teaching given to the Morphology group was about the relationship between prefixes and suffixes to the meaning of word and the grammar of sentences. The Control group children were visited by the experimenters but not taught anything special or unusual.

In the posttest, the children were given a battery of measures of their use of phonological and orthographic rules and awareness of syntax. There was no direct measure of their morphemic spelling.

The intervention had an effect: the children in the two intervention groups did significantly better in the posttests than the children in the control group, but there was very little sign of any specific effects of intervention. The Morphology group children as well as the Phonology group children did better in the posttest phonology tasks than the children in the Control group. The Morphology training made children particularly aware of syntax. Perhaps if there had been more direct measures of children's use of morphemes in reading and spelling, the project would have shown other specific effects of teaching preschool children morphology.

Another relatively early intervention study was carried out by Nunes et al. (2003) with 7- and 8-year-old children in English schools. The study consisted of a pretest in which the children's knowledge of morphological and phonological spelling rules and their general level of ability in reading and spelling were assessed. The measures included standardized tests of reading and spelling as well as specific tasks that were devised by the experimenters to measure children's use of the phonological and morphological spelling rules, which were to be taught during the intervention period. The pretests were followed by a 12-week intervention, carried out with small groups of children. After this, the children were given a posttest with the same measures as in the pretest. The purpose of the study was to compare the effects of different kinds of intervention on the progress that the children made between the pre- and the posttest.

There were five intervention groups. The first two (Phonology Alone and Phonology with Writing) were taught about phonologically based spelling rules. The phonology group was taught these rules orally whereas the phonology with writing group was taught with written examples as well. The next two groups (Morphology Alone and Morphology with Writing) were taught about morphological spelling rules. Again, the first of these two groups was taught orally while the second had to write examples as well. One example of the games given to the children in these two groups was about agentive endings, like '-ian' at the end of 'mathematician' and '-er' at the end of 'teacher'. Nunes et al. asked these children to complete sentences like 'A person who does magic is a?' Finally, the experimenters included a large Control group as the fifth group. They gave the children the pre- and posttests, so that they could use their scores as a baseline to measure the effects of the teaching given to the children in the other four groups.

Nunes et al. found that the children in all four intervention groups made more progress in reading than the children in the control group did. There were no significant differences in the posttest reading task between the four intervention-groups. Teaching morphological rules improved children's reading as much as teaching phonological rules did. The two morphology intervention groups did better in the posttest measures of spelling according to morphemic rules than the other groups did. Thus, the study established that morphological teaching has an effect.

Having settled that, it is quite possible to teach children about morphemes and spelling in general, we can now ask whether this is true of even the most difficult of morphemic spellings. One obvious candidate is the spelling of endings with the sound /ən/, like 'education' and 'mathematician'. These words end in exactly the same sound but are spelled differently for morphemic reasons, which we have already given. The morphemic rules for spelling '-ion' and '-ian' are hardly ever taught at school.

Nunes and Bryant (2006) decided to take the 'ion'/'ian' distinction as a test case in a series of studies about teaching morphemic spelling rules. They began with 'laboratory' studies. The first was designed to find out whether it is possible to teach children explicitly about this morphemic spelling rule. All the children in the study took a pretest, which was designed to measure how well they spelled words and pseudowords with '-ion' endings. Next, the children were given two 'intervention' sessions in which we taught them something about spelling. The children were divided into four groups (three experimental groups and a control group). One group was the Explicit group: whenever the children in this group produced a spelling or made a judgment about spelling they were told whether they were right or wrong, and the experimenter discussed the '-ion/-ian' difference with them. The Implicit group children were given the same games with the same words except that there was no explicit discussion of the rule in the intervention sessions. The children in the Implicit group were told whether they were right or not and what the right spelling was if they made the wrong decision. However, they were given no time to discuss the rule. The third group was called the Mixed group, because they went through a mixture of these two procedures. In the first part of each of the games that they played, the teaching procedure was the same as that used for the Implicit group, and in the second, it was the same as that used for as the Explicit group. The fourth group was a Control group. The Control children also went to two intervention sessions, but during these sessions, we

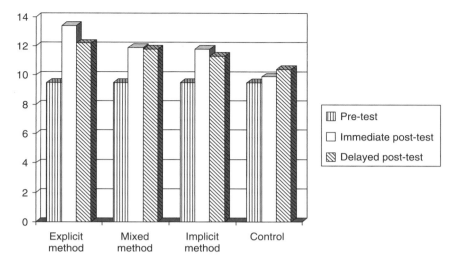

Figure 22.5 The mean number (out of 16) of correctly spelled '-ion' and '-ian' endings in real words by the three intervention groups and the control group (Bryant and Nunes, 2006).

taught them about a completely different aspect of literacy. They were encouraged to analyse texts and make inferences about them, in order to improve their reading comprehension.

Figure 22.5 shows that the children in all three experimental groups spelled the real words a great deal better in the immediate posttest than they had in the pretest, and their scores in this posttest were much higher than those of the children in the Control group. The children in the Explicit group improved a great deal more sharply than the other two experimental groups did between the pretest and the immediate posttest. Two months later in a delayed posttest there was a general levelling out of the scores of the three experimental groups, but the children in the Explicit group continued to outperform the control group children.

The experimenters also tested children's spelling of pseudowords, but did not use pseudowords during the intervention, and so these provided an especially stringent test of the effectiveness of our teaching about morphemes. As Figure 22.6 shows, all three experimental groups spelled the pseudowords

in the immediate posttest a great deal better than the control group did and this difference lasted quite well over the next two months.

Later, Nunes and Bryant carried out a classroom study. Teachers randomly assigned their 9-year-old pupils to two groups, a Taught group and a Control group. The teachers gave the children in the Taught group classroom versions of the spelling games used in the laboratory study in two lessons only. They talked to the children about the spelling rule that underlies the distinction between the two endings, as we had done with the Explicit group in our earlier study. They did not teach the Control group children about morphemes but taught them about making inferences when reading, to improve reading comprehension.

The results of this classroom study were much the same as in the preceding laboratory study. In the immediate posttest, the Taught group spelled the '-ion' and '-ian' endings in real words (Figure 22.7) and in pseudowords (Figure 22.8) much better than the Control group managed to do. The Taught group were still ahead of the Control group two months later, but the difference was a great

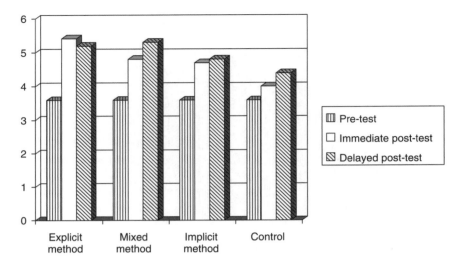

Figure 22.6 The mean number (out of 8) of correctly spelled '-ion' and '-ian' endings in pseudowords by the three intervention groups and the control group (Bryant and Nunes, 2006).

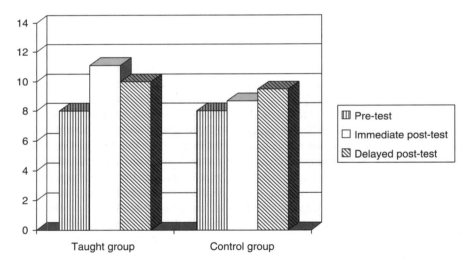

Figure 22.7 The mean number (out of 16) of correctly spelled '-ion' and '-ian' endings in real words in the classroom intervention study (Bryant and Nunes, 2006).

deal smaller with both kinds of word, and it was not statistically significant.

This classroom study showed that it is possible to teach children an entirely unfamiliar rule in the classroom as well as in the laboratory, and that this can be done in two lessons only, though sustainable effects might require a bit more teaching.

Nunes and Bryant's next question was whether their intervention would work when they had no control over how it was administered. They reasoned that if, they were to send their materials and programme to schools, different schools would deliver this programme to their children in varying ways.

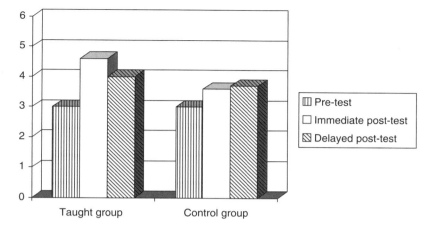

Figure 22.8   The mean number (out of 8) of correctly spelled '-ion' and '-ian' endings in pseudowords in the classroom intervention study (Bryant and Nunes, 2006).

Nunes and Bryant devised two programmes to send to schools, one called Morphology with spelling and the other Morphology only. They organized the two programmes into seven sessions and put the material on a CD, which was sent to the teachers who were going to carry out the interventions. The researchers met with the teachers for approximately one hour before the teachers started the programme, and during this hour they discussed what morphemes are, their importance for spelling, and how the games could be used in the classroom. These teachers taught classes of 9-year-old children.

In the Morphology Alone programme, the teachers emphasized the way that spoken words are constructed from morphemes while in the Morphology with Spelling programme, they concentrated both on assembling words with units of meaning and on the spelling of the morphemes. Otherwise, the two programmes were very similar. Both consisted of the same series of games, which emphasized syntax and a wide variety of derivational and inflectional affixes. In the games about parts of speech, children were given sentences with a missing word and several choices for that missing word. Thus one sentence, with appropriate pictures, said

'We saw a _____ in the town centre' and the alternatives for the missing word appeared on the screen — e.g., 'car', 'computer', 'sing', 'buses'. Two of these choices were possible, and the other two for different reasons were not.

Other games were about affixes. The children saw pictures of a 'bicycle' and a 'tricycle' and were asked to explain what in the two words described the most important difference between them. They were asked about words like 'uniform' and 'binoculars' in order for them to reflect on and discuss the significance of these two words' prefixes. Finally, the material included made-up words like 'biheaded' and 'bitailed', and the children were asked to produce drawings showing a 'biheaded monster' and a 'bitailed horse'. Another example was the affix 'en', which is a prefix, as in 'enlarge' and a suffix as in 'lengthen'; in both cases, it has the same function of forming a verb.

Some of the material in these games was designed to engage children's imagination and promote generalization of a rule by using pseudowords. For example, one game includes a picture of two strange looking men each holding a box and the caption reads 'They are montists. They look after _____ which they keep in their little black boxes.' In this case, the children would need to strip off the suffix to find the stem.

Both programmes were successful. All three groups, Morphology Alone, Morphology with Spelling, and the Control group, improved in their spelling of morphemes from pre- to posttest. However, the improvement was far greater in the two intervention groups, Morphology alone and Morphology with Spelling than in the Control group did. Again, explicit instruction about morphemes worked. It improved children's spelling by telling them about rules, which they had not been able to learn for themselves.

In the pre- and posttests, the children were also given vocabulary tests and the children in both Intervention groups made significantly more progress in their vocabulary scores from pre- to posttest than did the children in the Control group. Thus, our interventions seem to have been successful even when we had no hand in the details of the teaching itself, and the last finding that the teaching improved the children's vocabulary as well as their writing is welcome news and adds a further reason to pursue research on the effects of teaching morphemes.

SUMMARY

In this chapter, our main aim has been to persuade readers that morphemic spelling rules provide a potential resource of great value for teaching children about spelling, but that the importance of these rules has not been properly recognized either by psychologists or in education. We presented three lines of evidence to support this view. They were on:

- How children learn the conventional spellings for morphemes, such as the '-ed' ending and the '-s' spelling for the plural
- Children's morphological awareness
- The effects of explicit instruction about morphemes

With the first of these, we established that children do learn about morphemic spelling rules, even in the absence of systematic teaching about them, but that this learning takes a long time, is difficult for many children, and is often incomplete.

The second line of evidence led us to more positive conclusions. Children are aware to some extent of the structure of morphemes in the language though there are large individual differences among children in the extent of this awareness. These differences are important, because there is a strong, two-way relation between children's morphological awareness and their success in learning morphemic spelling rules.

The aim of the third line of evidence was to answer a counterfactual 'What if?' question. 'What would happen if we didn't leave it up to children to discover so much about the connection between morphemes and spelling for themselves? What if we gave children the systematic teaching about morphemic spelling rules, which they don't receive at the moment?' The consistent answer that the results of intervention experiments provide is a positive one. Teaching certainly helps children learn these rules and the signs are that children enjoy and are quite interested in this kind of teaching.

Our final conclusion is that morphemic spelling rules are a valuable but neglected resource for those learning to be literate. We can harness this resource, and we should.

REFERENCES

Arnback, E. and Elbro, C. (2000) 'The effects of morphological awareness training on the reading and spelling of young dyslexics', *Scandinavian Journal of Educational Research*, 44: 229–251.

Beers, C.S. and Beers, J.W. (1992) 'Children's spelling of English inflectional morphology', in S. Tempelton and D.R. Bear (eds), *Development of orthographic knowledge and the foundations of literacy: A memorial Festshrift for Edmund H. Henderson*, Hillsdale, NJ: Lawrence Erlbaum. pp. 230–252.

Brissaud, C. and Bessonnat, D. (2001) L'Orthographe au Collège. Pour une autre approche. Grenoble: Éditions Delagrave.

Bryant, P., Devine, M., Ledward, A., and Nunes, T. (1997) 'Spelling with apostrophes and understanding possession', *British Journal of Educational Psychology*, 67: 93–112.

Bryant, P., Nunes, T., and Aidinis, A. (1999) 'Different morphemes, same spelling problems: Cross-linguistic developmental studies', in M. Harris and G. Hatano (eds), *Learning to read and write: A cross-linguistic perspective*, Cambridge: Cambridge University Press. pp. 112–133.

Carlisle, J. (1988) 'Knowledge of derivational morphology and spelling ability in fourth, sixth, and eighth graders', *Applied Psycholinguistics*, 9: 247–266.

Carlisle, J.F. (1995) 'Morphological awareness and early reading achievement', in L.B. Feldman (ed.), *Morphological Aspects of Language Processing*, Hillsdale, NJ: Lawrence Erlbaum. pp. 189–210.

Carlisle, J.F. (2000) 'Awareness of the structure and meaning of morphologically complex words: Impact on reading', *Reading and Writing*, 12: 169–190.

Carlisle, J.F. and Addison Stone, C. (2003) 'The effects of morphological structure on children's reading of derived words in English', in E.M.H. Assink and D. Sandra (eds), *Reading Complex Words. Cross Language Studies*. New York: Kluwer Academic/Plenum Publishers. pp. 27–52.

Chliounaki, K. and Bryant, P. (2007) 'How children learn about morphological spelling rules', *Child Development*, 78(4): 1360–1373.

Deacon, S.H. and Kirby, J.R. (2004) 'Morphological awareness: just "more phonological"? The roles of morphological and phonological awareness in reading development', *Applied Psycholinguistics*, 25: 223–238.

Derwing, B.L., Smith, M.L., and Wiebe, G.E. (1995) 'On the role of spelling in morpheme recognition: Experimental studies with children and adults' in L.B. Feldman (ed.), *Morphological aspects of language processing*, Hillsdale, NJ: Lawrence Erlbaum. pp. 3–28.

Fayol, M., Thenevin, M.-G., Jarousse, J.-P., and Totereau, C. (1999) 'From learning to teaching to learn French written morphology', in T. Nunes (ed.), *Learning to read: An integrated view from research and practice*, Dordrecht, The Netherlands: Kluwer. pp. 43–64.

Ferreiro, E. and Teberosky, A. (1982) *Literacy before Schooling*, Exeter, New Hampshire: Heinemann Educational Books.

Green, L., McCutchen, D., Schwiebert, C., Quinlan, T., Eva-Wood, A., and Juelis, J. (2003) 'Morphological development in children's writing', *Journal of Educational Psychology*, 95: 752–761.

Harris, M. and Giannouli, V. (1999) 'Learning to read and spell in Greek: The importance of letter knowledge and morphological awareness', in M. Harris and G. Hatano (eds), *Learning to Read and write: A cross-linguistic perspective*, Cambridge: Cambridge University Press. pp. 51–70.

Hurry, J., Curno, T., Parker, M., and Pretzlik, U. (2006) 'Can we increase teachers' awareness of morphology and have an impact on their pupils' spelling?' In T. Nunes and P. Bryant (eds.) *Improving Literacy through Teaching Morphemes*. London: Routledge.

Jaffré, J.P. (1997) 'From writing to orthography: The functions and limits of the notion of system', in C.A. Perfetti, L. Rieben', and M. Fayol (eds), *Learning to Spell. Research, theory, and practice across languages*, Mahwah (NJ): Lawrence Erlbaum. pp. 3–20.

Karmiloff-Smith, A. (1992) *Beyond Modularity: A Developmental Perspective on Cognitive Science*, Cambridge, Mass: MIT Press.

Kemp, N. and Bryant, P. (2003) 'Do beez buzz? Rule-based and frequency-based knowledge in learning to spell plural –s', *Child Development*, 74: 63–74.

Lehtonen, A. and Bryant, P. (2005) 'Double challenge: form comes before function in children's understanding of their orthography', *Developmental Science*, 8: 211–217.

Leong, C.K. and Parkinson, M.E. (1995) 'Processing English morphological structure by poor readers', in C.K. Leong and R.M. Joshi (eds), *Developmental and acquired dyslexia*, Dordrecht: Kluwer Academic Publishers. pp. 237–259.

Levin, I., Ravid, D., and Rapaport, S. (1999) 'Developing morphological awareness and learning to write: A two-way street', in T. Nunes (ed.), *Learning to read: An integrated view from research and practice*, Dordrecht, The Netherlands: Kluwer. pp. 77–104.

Lyster, S.A.H. (2002) 'The effects of morphological versus phonological awareness training in kindergarten on reading development', *Reading and Writing: An Interdisciplinary Journal*, 15: 261–294.

McMillan, A. (1999) 'Words, letters and smurphs: Apostrophes and their uses' in T. Nunes (ed.), *Learning to read: An integrated view from research and practice*, Dordrecht: Kluwer. pp. 369–391.

Nagy, W., Berninger, V.W., and Abbott, R.D. (2006) 'Contributions of morphology beyond phonology to literacy outcomes of upper elementary and middle-school students', *Journal of Educational Psychology*, 98(1): 135–147.

National Primary Strategy website, accessed on 7 February, 2008: http://www.standards.dfes.gov.uk/primaryframeworks/literacy/

Nunes, T. and Bryant, P. (2006) *Improving Literacy through Teaching Morphemes*, London: Routledge.

Nunes, T. and Bryant, P. (2009) *Children's Reading and Spelling. Beyond the First Steps*, Oxford: Blackwell.

Nunes, T., Bryant, P., and Bindman, M. (1997a) 'Morphological spelling strategies: Developmental stages and processes', *Developmental Psychology*, 33: 637–649.

Nunes, T., Bryant, P., and Bindman, M. (1997b) 'Learning to spell regular and irregular verbs', *Reading and Writing*, 9: 427–449.

Nunes, T., Bryant, P., and Bindman, M. (2006) 'The effects of learning to spell on children's awareness of morphology', *Reading and Writing: An Interdisciplinary Journal*, 19: 767–787.

Nunes, T., Bryant, P., and Olsson, J. (2003) 'Learning morphological and phonological spelling rules: An intervention study', *Scientific Studies of Reading*, 7: 289–307.

Read, C. (1971) 'Pre-school children's knowledge of English phonology', *Harvard Educational Review*, 41: 1–34.

Read, C. (1986) *Children's Creative Spelling*, London: Routledge and Kegan Paul.

Rispens, J.E., McBride-Chang, C., and Reitsma, P. (in press) 'Morphological awareness and early and advanced word recognition and spelling in Dutch', *Reading and Writing*.

Sénéchal, M. (2000) 'Morphological effects in children's spelling of French words', *Canadian Journal of Experimental Psychology*, 54: 76–85.

Share, D. (1996) 'Phonological recoding and self-teaching: Sine qua non of reading acquisition', *Cognition*, 55: 151–218.

Tolchinsky, L. (1988) 'Form and meaning in the development of writing', *European Journal of Psychology of Education*, 3: 385–398.

Totereau, C., Thevenin, M.G., and Fayol, M. (1997) 'The development of the understanding of number morphology in written French', in C.A. Perfetti, L. Rieben, and M. Fayol (eds), *Learning to spell. Research, theory, and practice across languages*, Mahwah (NJ): Lawrence Erlbaum. pp. 97–114.

Treiman, R. (1993) *Beginning to Spell: A Study of First-Grade Children*, New York: Oxford University Press.

Varnhagen, C.K., McCallum, M., and Burstow, M. (1997) 'Is children's spelling naturally stage-like?' *Reading and Writing: An Interdisciplinary Journal*, 9: 451–481.

23

Measuring Maturity

Richard Hudson

MATURITY IN WRITING

The words *mature* and *maturity* are often used in discussions of how writing develops; for example, 'maturity of sentence structures' (Perera, 1984: 3), 'maturity as a writer' (Perera, 1986: 497), 'mature levels of language skill' (Harpin, 1976: 59), 'more mature use of syntax' (Weaver, 1996: 124, quoting Hunt, 1965). The assumption in this research is that a writer's language 'matures' as a tool for expressing ideas that presumably mature along a separate route and to at least some extent independently. Moreover, since language consists of objective patterns such as words, clauses, and so on, it is assumed that the 'linguistic maturity' of a piece of writing (or speech) can be measured in terms of the patterns that it contains. The question for writing research, therefore, is which linguistic patterns are found more often in more mature writing and what external influences determine how they develop. The purpose of this article is to review the anglophone literature, which has tried to investigate this question, starting with a number of challenges that face anyone engaging in this research.

The first challenge, of course, is deciding exactly what counts as 'mature'. An easy starting point is to define it in terms of the writer's age, which does indeed turn out to be highly relevant to the development of a wide range of linguistic patterns. For example, one common measure is the length of 'T-units' ('minimal terminable units' Hunt, 1965), a string of words that includes a main clause and all its modifiers. For the sake of concreteness, I apply this and other measures to two tiny extracts from writing[1] by pupils from year-6, Sarah, and year-9, Joanne (See Table 23.1 on next page). Sarah's five T-units are separated by *and* or by full stops, and have a mean length of 39/5 = 7.8 words; Joanne's 32 words form a single T-unit, so her mean T-unit length is 32—an extreme example of T-unit length increasing with age.

As far as age is concerned, the research evidence shows that writers tend to put more words into each 'T-unit' as they get older, as shown in Figure 23.1. This graph shows T-unit lengths reported by two separate research projects: an American study of pupils at grades 4, 8, and 12, i.e., aged 9, 13, and 17 (Hunt, 1965: 56) and a more recent British study of pupils at the ends of Key Stages (KS) 1, 2, and 3, i.e., aged 7, 11, and 14 (Malvern et al., 2004: 163). The convergence of these two sets of figures is all the

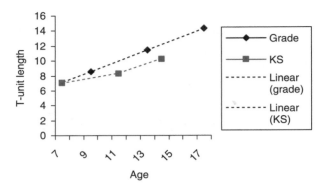

Figure 23.1   T-Unit length by age.

Table 23.1 Two short extracts of writing by children

Writer	Age	Grade	Words	Sample
Sarah	year 6	level 3	39	He had just been in a horrible battle and he had killed lots of people. When he had finished his battle he was exhausted and he was tottering and came across a beautiful lady who was singing beautiful songs ...
Joanne	year 9	level 7	32	Giles Harvey, a former Eton pupil, was one and a half times over the limit when he was involved in a head-on crash while he was racing his BMW sports car.

more remarkable for coming from two different education systems and periods.

Unfortunately, age is not the only determinant of most linguistic features. If it had been, writing could be left to develop under its own momentum in just the same way that bodies become taller and puberty sets in, and by definition, every adult would be a mature writer. The fact is that some people write better than other people of the same age write; for example, Sarah (from Table 23.1) is below average for her age group, whereas Joanne is well above average. Examiners can agree (more or less) on the grading of scripts, and it turns out that these gradings can also be related to objective measures such as T-unit length. The British study mentioned earlier also classified students' writing according to the National-Curriculum level to which it had previously been assigned by experienced examiners. The graph in Figure 23.2 (from Malvern and others, 2004:163) shows that higher-rated scripts tend to contain longer T-units (though not all level-differences are

statistically significant). (We return below to the interesting difference in this figure between the figures for KS3 (secondary) and KS1-2 (primary) writers) This finding is somewhat surprising, because an earlier literature review (Crowhurst, 1980) had concluded that T-unit length was not in fact a predictor of writing quality; the question clearly deserves more research.

Maturity, then, is a matter not only of age but also of ability. However, age and ability often (but not always) seem to pick out the same linguistic patterns—in this case, longer T-units—so more mature writing can in fact be defined as that of people who are not only older, but also more able (as defined by experienced examiners). The link to ability clearly risks circularity if we define mature writing as produced by mature writers, but the objective measures reviewed in the following section avoid this risk by isolating distinct factors whose developmental paths can be compared not only with examiners' ratings, but also with each other. For example,

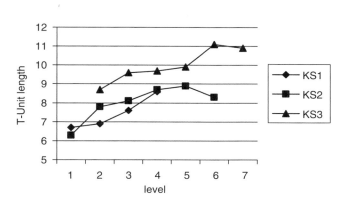

Figure 23.2   T-Unit length by quality level.

examiner-gradings correlate even more strongly with text length (the number of words in each piece of writing) and spelling (Malvern et al., 2004: 171), so these measures lend objective support to the examiners' subjective gradings. In short, there really is such a thing as 'mature writing', and there really are objective measures of maturity.

However, objective measures clearly need to be treated with a great deal of caution. For one thing:

> … more syntactically mature, in Hunt's terms, is not necessarily better … Relatively mature sentences can be awkward, convoluted, even unintelligible; they can also be inappropriate to the subject, the audience and the writer's or persona's voice. Conversely, relatively simple sentences can make their point succinctly and emphatically. Often, of course, sentence variety is best (Weaver, 1996: 130).

When applied to T-units, this means that long T-units are not inherently better or more mature than short ones; and similarly for all the other patterns reviewed below. In relation to pedagogy, it would be wrong to suggest that children should be taught to use nothing but long T-units. On the other hand, the ability to use longer T-units when needed is part of maturity, so T-units are relevant to the writer and to the overall text, if not to the individual sentence.

This caveat about objective measures is important because of the enormous variation among adult writers. The studies quoted in the following section simply report what happens without, on the whole, passing judgement on it. This is a reasonable approach when the objective measures are correlated with examiners' judgements of quality, because we can assume that the best grades for the oldest students define the ultimate target of all school writing. But what about writing beyond the school? At this level, there are no examiners, so research tends to be purely descriptive. Nevertheless, as we all know, some adults write better than others, and nobody would suggest that all adult models are equally relevant as targets for school teaching.

Another important caveat about objective measures is that they are very sensitive to register differences, so different measures are needed for defining development in different areas of language. For example, when children have to write a set of instructions they use much more mature syntax than when telling a story (Perera, 1984: 239–40; Harpin, 1976: 59); and the writing and speech of the same person typically differ even more dramatically (Halliday, 1987). If the aim is formative assessment of a student's capacity as a writer, then it is important to select writing tasks carefully.

A final reservation is that 'maturity' continues to develop throughout life, and certainly well after the end of compulsory schooling.

The evidence from comprehension in speech shows that even some apparently 'basic' areas of grammar go on developing into adulthood; for example, some 19-year-olds wrongly interpreted sentences such as *Bill asked Helen which book to read* as though the verb had been *told* (Kramer et al., 1972, quoted in Perera, 1984: 138), and even as simple a structure as 'X because Y' (as in *John laughed because Mary was surprised*) defeated one college student in ten (Irwin, 1980; Perera, 1984: 141). Given the prevalence of adult illiteracy, we may certainly expect at least as much postschool growth in writing.

WHY MEASURE MATURITY?

In spite of these reservations, objective measures are an important tool in understanding how language develops in its written mode as well as in speech. More qualitative and subjective measures are also important, so the following comments are intended to show merely why they need to be complemented by quantitative and objective measures. Indeed, the best way of validating an objective measure is to show that it correlates well with a global subjective assessment by an experienced examiner, because this defines the target of teaching in our schools. Most of the benefits listed in the following section need further research and development before we can enjoy them, but they are all the more worth listing now as a stimulus to future work.

One potential benefit is in **formative assessment**, as a tool for assessing how each student is developing and what further teaching they need. Research reveals a range of abilities which may surprise even experienced teachers. One longitudinal study of children's spoken language, for instance, found a difference at 42 months equivalent to between 30 and 36 months, between the fastest and slowest developers (Wells, 1986). I know of no similar results for writing, but there are good reasons for thinking the range of variation at

a given age may be even greater, given that some normal individuals fail to acquire even basic literacy by the end of schooling. Moreover, the growth of writing arguably consists in the learning of innumerable tiny details, so teachers need to know where students have gaps. This kind of information can be found by objective measures—but only, of course, if they measure development at the right degree of granularity.

One particular advantage of objective over subjective measures is their sensitivity to absences as well as presences. A teacher may be much more aware of the patterns that children do use in their writing than of those they do not. For example, even weak writers very rarely use specifically spoken patterns such as the words *well, sort of, these,* and *sort of thing* in the constructed example[2] (1).

(1) Well, we sort of ran out of these red bricks sort of thing.

This absence is especially significant given that the same pupils are tending to use such patterns more and more in their speech (Perera, 1990: 220).

Another important role of objective measures is in **pedagogical research**, and indeed this is probably where they have been applied most often. There is a long and well documented tradition of research on the effectiveness of grammar teaching as a method for improving writing in which the effects of the grammar teaching are assessed by means of objective measures (Andrews et al., 2004; Andrews, 2005, Elley, 1994; Hudson, 2001; Kolln and Hancock, 2005; Myhill, 2005; Perera, 1984; Tomlinson, 1994; Weaver, 1996; Wyse, 2001). One of the issues that runs through this research is the importance of choosing a relevant measure. A typical project would teach children how to recognize some rather general features of sentence structure and then test for an effect using some equally general measure such as the length of T-units discussed in the preceding section. However, why should we expect this kind of effect from this kind of teaching? In contrast, we might expect children who have practised producing complex T-units through a relevant exercise such as sentence combining to produce longer T-units—as indeed they do (Andrews, 2005; Daiker et al., 1978; Graham and Perin, 2007; Hillocks and Mavrognes, 1986; O'Hare, 1973). Similarly, teaching about a specific pattern does produce objectively measurable effects on the use of that particular pattern; for example, teaching about apostrophes improves children's use of apostrophes (Bryant et al., 2002, 2004), and similarly for teaching about morphologically-conditioned spelling (Hurry 2004; Nunes et al., 2003).

Objective measures are important in building general models of how writing develops, because there are many different possible influences whose relative importance needs to be assessed. For example, how much influence does reading have on writing? One project (Eckhoff, 1983 reported in Perera, 1986: 517) tried to answer this question by comparing the writing of children who had followed two different reading schemes, which favoured different linguistic patterns. What emerged was that the particular patterns used by the children in their writing tracked those of the books they had read in class, so the children's writing had been deeply influenced by their reading. This kind of research can only be done by careful and detailed objective analysis of both reading and writing.

Finally, we must consider a radical third application for objective measures. It is possible that they should play some role in **summative assessment**, either as a complement to the normal practice of subjective assessment by examiners or even as a replacement for it. This controversial possibility is raised starkly by a recent study of surface features of children's writing by means of computer (Malvern et al., 2004 from which Figure 23.2 was taken). This figure shows that T-unit length rises in a fairly consistent way with the 'level' of the writing as assessed by an experienced examiner. Moreover, the main inconsistency between the two measures seems if anything to call the examiners'

gradings into question, because examiners seem to be unintentionally allowing the writer's age to influence their grading. In this project, the writers spanned three very different age groups: two primary, years 2 and 6, and one secondary, year 9 (respectively, Key Stages 1, 2, and 3), but the National-Curriculum grading levels are meant to be neutral for age and the examiners were not told the writers' age. (The scripts they marked had been typed in order to hide the evidence of handwriting.) The figures show that KS3 scripts consistently had much longer T-units than KS1 or KS2 scripts of the same level, suggesting that examiners may have guessed the writer's age and expected longer T-units of older writers. Whatever the explanation may be, the findings clearly demand one. This example illustrates the possibility of using objective measures to complement and validate (or question) subjective measures.

However, it is also possible to imagine a more ambitious role for objective measures. The same project found that the six objective measures that were applied to the children's written texts correlated collectively rather well with the examiners' gradings; in fact, all the other five measures predicted these gradings even better than T-unit length. When combined, these six measures accounted for 76% of the variation in the examiners' gradings (Malvern et al., 2004: 170–1). (The best single predictor was text length, closely followed by spelling; the other measures, all of which correlated significantly with level, were word length, diversity of vocabulary, and rarity.) As the authors point out (pp. 172), it is possible that a larger collection of measures would explain even more of this variation, raising the possibility that a computer analysis might one day give very nearly the same verdict on a text, as does a human examiner. In that case, the crucial research question is whether two independent human markers come closer to agreement with each other than the computer does with either of them. If they do not, the basic marking may as well be done by computer, with possible moderation by a human.

In summary, then, objective measures contribute in three ways to the teaching of writing: in formative assessment, in summative assessment, and in testing experimental outcomes. Historically, the objective analysis was generally done by humans, but thanks to the powerful tools that are now available in computational linguistics, and no less to the fact that children increasingly use word processors, the job can quite easily be mechanized. It may not be long before teachers, or even pupils themselves, can produce an objective measure of a piece of writing as easily as they can now apply a spelling checker. This is why it is vital for us to have a proper understanding of these measures.

VOCABULARY

The vocabulary used in a piece of writing is one of the most obvious and educationally relevant things to measure objectively. A number of different and complementary measures have been applied (Read 2000: 200-5, cited in Malvern et al., 2004: 3):

- **Lexical diversity** (or 'lexical variation'), which is typically represented by the type:token ratio for the text concerned—i.e., the number of distinct words ('types') divided by the number of running words (tokens); e.g., *the man in the moon* contains five running words but only four distinct words (because *the* occurs twice), so its type:token ratio is 4/5 = 0.8. The higher the ratio, the more diversity there is. This ratio is taken as an indication of the size of the writer's total vocabulary, although the relation is clearly complex. It is important to keep the number of tokens constant, so when applied to the first 32 words in the texts in Table 23.1, this measure gives 21/32 = 0.66 for Sarah and 27/32 = 0.84 for Joanne, who therefore uses a wider range of vocabulary.
- **Lexical sophistication**, a measure of the difficulty or 'maturity' of the words used; this variable can be quantified in a number of ways, ranging from the apparently trivial matter of word length (Malvern et al., 2004: 157–8) to more sophisticated distinctions of rarity (pp.158–9).

- **Lexical density**, the balance between lexical 'content words' (such as *dog* and *attract*) and grammatical 'function words' like *the* and *is* (Ure, 1971; Halliday, 1987). This measure distinguishes writing from speech, but it also distinguishes different kinds of writing from one another. Consequently, it is less relevant to measuring maturity than to distinguishing registers. Nevertheless, it gives Joanne 0.68 (13 lexical words to 19 nonlexical) compared with 0.56 for Sarah, which locates Sarah's writing nearer to speech than Joanne's.
- **Number of errors**, the proportion of words that are 'wrong' in any respect, whether in spelling, grammar, or meaning. This measure was first developed for second-language learners (Arnaud, 1984) but the notion of 'correctness' is a little more problematic when applied to first-language learners. However, even for them, it is more or less uncontentious in areas such as spelling. On the other hand, errors are often a sign of ambition and growth; for example, Sarah makes no errors, but the more ambitious Joanne omits the comma after the (ambitious) appositive noun phrase a *former Eton pupil* and a possible hyphen in *head-on crash*.

All of these measures of vocabulary raise methodological problems, such as the need to define categories clearly and consistently and to distinguish homonyms. The problems are especially challenging in the case of lexical diversity, because the type:token ratio is very sensitive to the length of the passage being measured, because the longer the passage, the more likely it is that the next word token will involve a type that has already been used in the passage. The problem can be solved (Malvern et al., 2004), but it requires caution.

No doubt there are many other measures that could be applied to vocabulary. One variable which is particularly intriguing is the balance of word classes—what proportion of the word tokens (i.e., running words) in a text are nouns, how many are verbs, and so on. When words are analysed in this way, striking regularities emerge. For example, most kinds of adult written English show a figure very close to 37% for 'nominals', which include both common or proper nouns

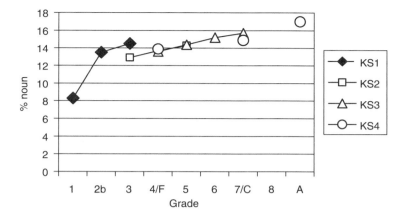

Figure 23.3 Nouniness of written work by four age groups graded at five levels.

and pronouns; but the balance between nouns and pronouns varies systematically between 'informational' and 'imaginative' writing, with about 7% pronouns in informational compared with 15% in imaginative writing (Hudson, 1994). Similarly, the balance of word classes changes systematically across children's writing and correlates with maturity. The data[3] in Figure 23.3 show that (on average) the more mature a piece of writing is, the more of its words will be nouns. We can call this measure 'nouniness'—not to be confused with either the 'noun bias', which at one time was said to be found in young children's speech (Malvern et al., 2004: 138–42) or the 'nominal style' which is discussed later in this section. The data are based on a grammatical analysis of several thousand scripts written by children of different ages (Key Stages 1–4) and graded by experienced examiners; we shall refer to this data-set below as the '**QCA data**' for reasons explained in the footnote. The grades shown are a mixture of the National Curriculum Levels 1 to 8 and the GCSE grades F, C, and A[4], with all the dangers that are inherent in trying to project two different grading schemes onto one another. However, the graph does show that the 'nouniness' of writing increases with both age and grade, so it qualifies as a valid measure of maturity;

moreover, unlike Figure 23.2, this one supports the official claim that grades are independent of age. The differences emerge in passages as short as those in Table 23.1: 15% nouns for Sarah, 31% for Joanne.

As with other measures, the nouniness of a piece of work is affected even more by the writing task than by the writer's age or the examiner's grading, and as usual, it is the non-narrative task that produces the most mature scores. Figure 23.4 shows the effect of writing task in the data reported in the foregoing section, though for some reason the effect is much less in the oldest writers than in the younger ones.

Nouniness is not the only relevant measure based on word classes. Another is 'nominality', the 'nominal style', which is sometimes contrasted with 'verbal style' (Wells, 1960). This is a more complex measure, which seems to involve two clusters of word classes:

* Nouns—i.e., common nouns and proper nouns—cluster with adjectives and prepositions.
* Verbs cluster with adverbs and pronouns—not just personal pronouns but also demonstratives, relatives, interrogatives, and compound pronouns such as *someone* and *nothing*.

This measure is certainly relevant to adult writing, where 'informational' and 'imaginative' writings have very different profiles, as

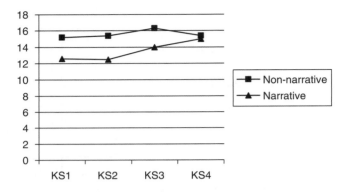

Figure 23.4   Nouniness-nouns as percent of all word tokens-at four ages and in two writing tasks.

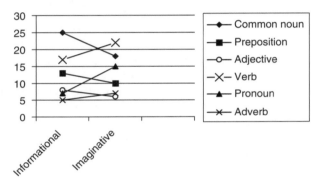

Figure 23.5   Two groups of word classes as percent of all word tokens in 'informational' and 'imaginative' adult writing.

shown in Figure 23.5. As can be seen, informational writing contains more common nouns, prepositions, and adjectives than imaginative writing, whereas the reverse is true for verbs, pronouns, and adverbs. However, even though the two sample texts are both stories, the measure distinguishes them dramatically: Sarah uses 11 'nominal' to 18 'verbal' words (0.61) contrasting with Joanne's 14 to 7 (2.0).

What do these measures mean for teachers? The answer depends, of course, on how we explain the differences being measured (see the discussion in the section 'Explaining the measures'), but two conclusions are immediately obvious. One is the banal observation that mature writing uses a wide vocabulary, however, we may choose to measure this; so

the pedagogical challenge is to find ways to help children to widen their vocabulary, with objective measures of vocabulary as a tool for assessing success. The other is that some of the measures, especially those based on word classes, are too abstract to focus on in most classes, so there can be no question of 'teaching them to use more nouns'.

SYNTAX: GENERAL TRENDS

We now turn to syntax, the grammatical patterns in which individual words are combined with one another—phrases, clauses, and (of course) sentences. These patterns may be approached in two different ways, which we can distinguish as general and specific. General patterns are defined in terms of very general categories such as 'subordinate clause' or 'finite verb', whereas specific patterns are tied to more specific categories such as 'postponed subject' or even to individual lexical items. This section considers general measures of maturity, leaving more specific measures for the next section.

There is a long tradition of educational research into general grammatical patterns dating back at least as far as Stormzand and O'Shea, 1924, which has a detailed study of the patterns found in adult writing, with a very small sample of school writing for comparison. The aim in this case was simply to decide which patterns were worth teaching at school, but later studies have generally focused much more on children's own writing. Some of the main large-scale analyses of children's writing are: Anon, 1999; Harpin, 1976; Hunt, 1965; O'Donnell et al., 1967; Yerrill, 1977. A particularly good, though ageing, survey of this literature is Perera, 1984, supported by the same author's slightly more recent chapter-length summaries (Perera, 1986, 1990).

The measures which have been applied to children's writing include the following:

- T-unit length, which I used above as an example. The advantage of separating T-units from sentence is that the latter is generally defined in

terms of punctuation, and given the unreliability of children's punctuation there would be little point in taking it too seriously.
- Coordination, especially coordination of clauses (by means of the coordinating conjunctions *and, but, or, then,* or *so*). Every research project has found that this is the favourite strategy of the immature for combining clauses into sentences (Perera, 1984: 230). The coordinating conjunction *and* occurs three times in Sarah's extract, but not at all in Joanne's. The downward trend in coordination emerges clearly from Figure 23.6 (based on the same QCA data as Figure 23.3) though the grading system again seems to interact with age more than one might hope; but, surprisingly, in this case, it is the older writers who use less mature grammar. The irregularity at Key Stage 1 (Year 2) is as expected, given that these children are still struggling to write sentences more than a few words long and coordination is an important tool for achieving this.
- Subordination, the use of subordinate clauses. As coordination falls, subordination rises (Perera, 1984: 231). This trend emerges very clearly from Figure 23.7, once again based on the QCA data, though this pattern also shows a large difference between the oldest writers (Key Stage 4) and the others, for whom grade seems to be unaffected by age. Perhaps the most interesting feature in this graph is the clear downward trend at the highest grades. This probably reflects the tendency (documented by Loban, 1963: 40) at this stage of development to replace full finite subordinate clauses (e.g. *while we were talking*) by nonfinite ones (e.g., *while talking*) or by

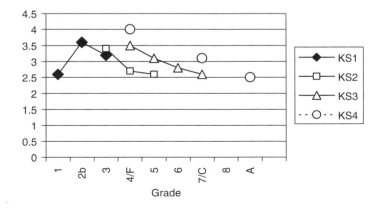

Figure 23.6   Co-ordinated clauses per 100 words by age and grade.

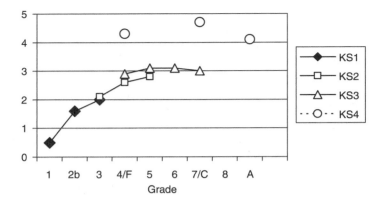

Figure 23.7   Subordinate clauses per 100 words by age and grade.

nominalizations (e.g., *during our conversation*). Both Sarah and Joanne include two subordinate clauses in the very short samples quoted, so this measure would not distinguish them.

There are other general syntactic measures that have been used, but they all illustrate the conclusion that I draw in the next section: that the more specific a measure is, the more revealing it is. For example, it is more revealing to distinguish different kinds of subordinate clauses than to lump them all together, since relative clauses show a much clearer pattern of growth than do either nominal or adverbial clauses (Perera, 1986: 496). What this means for teachers is that the very general syntactic patterns such as coordination and subordination may be best left to develop naturally, without explicit attention, because growth towards maturity will follow automatically as children learn to replace specific kinds of coordination by specific kinds of subordination or nonclausal patterns.

SYNTAX: DETAILED TRENDS

Analysing a sentence in terms of general syntactic patterns misses most of the information which is important for teachers and pupils. Every five-year-old already uses subordinate clauses freely in speech, and even

weak writers use them in writing; but it is only mature writers who use *unless* or *although* to introduce their adverbial clauses or *whose* or *with whom* in their relative clauses. This is important if, as I believe, writers mature by learning specific patterns such as these rather than by getting better at using the general patterns.

The use of specific patterns could in principle also be measured numerically by counting the mature patterns in a text using a list of these patterns which would emerge from further research. To give a flavour of this kind of research, consider the general clause pattern, which starts with a place adverbial and finishes with a delayed subject (Perera, 1986: 514). The examples quoted by Perera include the following:

(1) Here's a bus stop (spoken by a 12-year-old)
(2) About three miles down the road was a little town called Sea Palling (written by a 12-year-old)

These examples both have the same clause structure (Place adverbial + BE + Subject), which some grammarians call 'subject-verb inversion', but these two examples represent very different stages of maturity (Biber et al., 1999: 926). The first is an everyday item in the ordinary speech of any child, whereas the second is much more mature and emerges quite late in writing. The difference between them lies in the fronted place adverbial.

The everyday ones all have either *here* or *there* in this position, followed by the verb *be, come,* or *go* (Carter and McCarthy, 2006: 94). This very specific pattern is not a sign of maturity; but other examples of the same general pattern are, and especially so if they involve a verb other than *be*, such as *stands* in (3).

> (3) In the corner of the field stands an old oak tree which is said to be a thousand years old.

Examples like (3) contain what Perera calls '"mature" structures more frequent in writing than in speech' (Perera, 1986: 503) or 'constructions typical of written language' (Perera, 1990: 222). Our sample extracts contain only two clear examples of specifically written patterns, both used (as expected) by Joanne:

- Apposition (*Giles Harvey, a former Eton pupil*)—a clear case of mature syntax (Yerrill, 1977; Perera, 1984: 225).
- *While* (in: *was involved in … while he was racing …*); according to one analysis, this is found in the writing of ten-year-olds but not in the speech even of twelve-year-olds (Perera, 1990: 231).

Perera lists a great many other specifically written patterns (Perera, 1984: 247–267 1986; 1990). A full list of such patterns would be extremely valuable, especially if it was classified for relative 'maturity'. Unfortunately, no such list exists, so teachers must use their intuitions about individual cases. In doing so, however, they should be careful not to confuse maturity with difficulty or (apparent) complexity, because many of these mature patterns are easy to understand—indeed, their function is to make difficult ideas easy to understand. For example, the apparently simple (4) is actually more mature in its syntax than (5), because the long direct object has been moved out of its normal position by a process, which some grammarians call 'postponement' and which is more common in academic writing than in conversation (Biber et al., 1999:153; 930–1).

> (4) We got *ready* everything that we needed for the next day's outing to the seaside.

> (5) We got *everything that we needed for the next day's outing to the seaside* ready.

Detailed syntactic patterns are probably more important for teachers than the more general ones such as coordination and subordination, because on the one hand they are easier to spot, and on the other hand they are significant points on the route towards maturity where the teacher may be able to give specific help. Learning a new construction happens in stages, as the learner moves from partial understanding to full maturity in this particular area of the language. Mistakes are symptoms of growth, as in the following examples (Perera, 1984: 3):

> (6) In this particular rockpool that I looked in was so crammed with all kinds of marine life.
> (7) Children which had to work in the coal mines I feel bad about this.
> (8) His dog came with him to get the birds what the man killed.
> (9) Although they tried hard but they didn't win the match.

Each of these examples shows a child struggling with a mature syntactic pattern which has not yet been fully mastered.

EXPLAINING THE MEASURES

These measures of maturity are justified empirically by the research evidence, but it is time to move the discussion to a deeper level of understanding. Why do these measures work? Each of them is presumably measuring some kind of mental development in the writer, but precisely. What kind of development? The question is important for teachers, because the answer will decide what teaching strategies to adopt. At one extreme, if it is all a matter of mental growth that happens anyway with age, the best teaching strategy is simply to do nothing and leave it all to Mother Nature. At the other extreme, if it is all a matter of knowledge that can be taught, then the best strategy is direct instruction. Not surprisingly, I believe the answer is a great deal more complex (and interesting) than either of these extremes. It certainly involves at least two kinds of growth: growth of the cognitive 'infrastructure', especially working memory, and growth of the child's language.

Working memory, also known as short-term memory (Miyake and Shah, 1999), includes distinct components; one analysis (Gathercole, 1999) distinguishes phonological memory, for strings of sounds or words, from complex working memory, for manipulating words (e.g., by repeating a list of numbers in reverse order). Working memory increases sharply with age up to about age 12 for phonological memory and about 16 for complex memory, so its growth coincides with many of the developments in language; moreover, at any age there is enormous individual variation in working memory, which may account for at least some of the grading differences. As children's working memory grows, they get better both at learning new words and patterns and also at using them in longer and more demanding combinations; so some of the growth revealed by maturity measures is due directly or indirectly to growth in working memory. An obvious candidate is T-unit length. If this really does reflect nothing but the growth of working memory, then intervention is probably pointless. To the extent that longer T-units are needed in mature writing, children will get better at using them whatever the teacher does.

Knowledge of language, i.e., the linguist's 'competence', includes grammar and vocabulary, both of which continue to grow through the school years—indeed, grammar growth and vocabulary growth are strongly correlated (Bates and Goodman, 1997). There are mature constructions that many pupils even at secondary level do not understand, such as the difference between *ask* and *tell* in *John asked/told Mary what to read* (who is the reader—John or Mary?) (Perera, 1984: 137–8), or subordination by *although* (pp. 144); and the same point is even more obvious and uncontentious with vocabulary. This kind of growth can be measured directly by spotting mature patterns, but it may also be revealed indirectly through more abstract measures; for instance, the 'nouniness' discussed above may reflect the proportion of nouns in the writer's entire vocabulary. (This would be so if nouns constituted a growing proportion of new vocabulary, but at present, this hypothesis cannot be tested against research evidence.) Whatever measures we use, knowledge of language grows as the child learns the 'tools of the trade'—the words and syntax of the mature written language. This is the area where intervention by teachers may be most helpful, so we need a great deal more research on how best to intervene. 'Teachers can have a very profound effect on the rate and quality of individual development through levels of expectation, the careful provision of tasks and the quality of intervention; they cannot just rely on "skills growing with practice"' (Allison et al., 2002).

CONCLUSIONS

A great deal has already been achieved in this area. We now have a collection of tried and tested tools for measuring the maturity of writing, which have already allowed us to map out roughly the typical path that writing follows as it matures. Some of these tools are so sensitive to quality that they are at least comparable with human examiners, raising the possibility of automated marking.

These achievements reveal three areas where future research will be most productive.

- **Grammatical description**: we need a checklist of 'mature' syntactic patterns graded for relative maturity. This would allow serious research on the more precise measures described on pages 358–9.
- **Theory**: we need a theory to explain what the measures are measuring, as explained briefly in the previous section..
- **Pedagogy**: we need to know how to translate the results of the measures into teaching policies, which will at least take account of each pupil's known maturity and, if possible, enhance it.

NOTES

1 These texts are taken from the National Curriculum website at http://www.ncaction.org.uk/search/index.htm.

2 The example is based on a real one quoted by Perera.

3 The data were produced in a series of projects funded in the UK by the Qualifications and Curriculum Authority in the late 1990s and early 2000s. The studies of writing by pupils in Key Stages 1–3 (i.e., years 2, 6, and 9) were carried out by the University of Cambridge Local Examining Syndicate but have not been published; the data were kindly made available to me by the project director, Andrew Watts. For Key Stage 4 (year 11), QCA commissioned Debra Myhill of the University of Exeter; for the published results, see Anon (1999).

4 The National Curriculum for England defines 10 levels, which are meant to be independent of age and which are used in various national tests during compulsory schooling. The General Certificate of Education (GCSE), a personal qualification which is taken at the end of compulsory schooling in year 11, uses grades A (best) to F (fail); C is considered the bottom of the 'good' grades.

REFERENCES

Allison, P., Beard, R., and Willcocks, J. (2002) 'Subordination in children's writing', *Language and Education*, 16: 97–111.

Andrews, R. (2005) 'Knowledge about the teaching of [sentence] grammar: The state of play', *English Teaching: Practice and Critique*, 4: 69–76.

Andrews, R., Beverton, S., Locke, T., Low, G., Robinson, A., Torgerson, C., and Zhu, D. (2004) 'The effect of grammar teaching (syntax) in English on 5 to 16 year olds' accuracy and quality in written composition'. Unpublished. http://eppi.ioe.ac.uk/EPPIWebContent/reel/review_groups/english/eng_rv6/eng_rv6.pdf

Anon (1999) *Technical Accuracy in Writing in GCSE English: Research Findings*, London: Qualifications and Curriculum Authority.

Arnaud, P. (1984) 'The lexical richness of L2 written productions and the validity of vocabulary tests', in T. Culhane, C. Klein Bradley, and D. Stevenson (eds), *Practice and Problems in Language Testing: Papers from the International Symposium on Language Testing*, Colchester, UK: University of Essex. pp.14–28.

Bates, E. and Goodman, J. (1997) 'On the inseparability of grammar and the lexicon: Evidence from acquisition, aphasia and real-time processing', *Language and Cognitive Processes*, 12: 507–584.

Biber, D., Johansson, S., Leech, G., Conrad, S., and Finegan, E. (1999) *Longman Grammar of Spoken and Written English*, London: Longman.

Bryant, P., Devine, M., Ledward, A., and Nunes, T. (2002) 'Spelling with apostrophes and understanding possession', *British Journal of Educational Psychology*, 67. 91–110.

Bryant, P., Nunes, T., and Bindman, M. (2004) 'The relations between children's linguistic awareness and spelling: The case of the apostrophe', *Reading and Writing*, 12: 253–276.

Carter, R. and McCarthy, M. (2006) *Cambridge Grammar of English: A Comprehensive Guide. Spoken and Written English Grammar and Usage*, Cambridge: Cambridge University Press.

Crowhurst, M. (1980) *The Effect of Syntactic Complexity on Writing Quality: A Review of Research*, ERIC document number ED202024.

Daiker, D., Kerek, A., and Morenberg, M. (1978) 'Sentence-combining and syntactic maturity in freshman English', *College Composition and Communication*, 29: 36–41.

Eckhoff, B. (1983) 'How reading affects children's writing', *Language Arts*, 60: 607–616.

Elley, W. (1994) 'Grammar teaching and language skill', in R. Asher (ed.), *Encyclopedia of Language and Linguistics*, Oxford: Pergamon. pp.1468–1471.

Gathercole, S. (1999) 'Cognitive approaches to the development of short-term memory', *Trends in Cognitive Sciences*, 3: 410–419.

Graham, S. and Perin, D. (2007) Writing Next: Effective Strategies to Improve Writing of Adolescents in Middle and High Schools. A Report to Carnegie Corporation of New York. Washington DC: Alliance for Excellent Education.

Halliday, M. (1987) 'Spoken and written modes of meaning', in R. Horowitz and S.J. Samuels (eds), *Comprehending Oral and Written Language*, Orlando: Academic Press. pp.55–82.

Harpin, W. (1976) *The Second 'R''. Writing Development in the Junior School*, London: Allen and Unwin.

Hillocks, G. and Mavrognes, N. (1986) 'Sentence combining' in G. Hillocks (ed.), *Research on Written Composition: New Directions for Teaching*, Urbana, IL: National Council for the Teaching of English. pp.142–146.

Hudson, R. (1994) 'About 37% of word-tokens are nouns', *Language*, 70: 331–339.

Hudson, R. (2001) 'Grammar teaching and writing skills: The research evidence', *Syntax in the Schools*, 17: 1–6.

Hunt, K. (1965) *Grammatical Structures Written at Three Grade Levels*, Champaigne, IL: National Council of Teachers of English.

Hurry, J. (2004) 'Why morphology matters and comprehension counts', *http://www.qca.org.uk/library-Assets/media/12378_morphology_matters_comprehension_counts_janehurry.pdf*

Irwin, J. (1980) 'The effects of explicitness and clause order on the comprehension of reversible causal relationships', *Reading Research Quarterly*, 15: 477–488.

Kolln, M. and Hancock, C. (2005) 'The story of English grammar in United States schools', *English Teaching: Practice and Critique*, 4: 11–31.

Kramer, P., Koff, E., and Luria, Z. (1972) 'The development of competence in an exceptional language structure in older children and young adults', *Child Development*, 43: 121–130.

Loban, W. (1963) *The Language of Elementary School Children. A Study of the Use and Control of Language and the Relations among Speaking, Reading, Writing and Listening*, Champaign, Ill: National Council of Teachers of English.

Malvern, D., Richards, B., Chipere, N., and Duran, P. (2004) *Lexical Diversity and Language Development: Quantification and Assessment*, Palgrave Macmillan.

Miyake, A. and Shah, P. (1999) *Models of Working Memory. Mechanisms of Active Maintenance and Executive Control*, Cambridge: Cambridge University Press.

Myhill, D. (2005) 'Ways of knowing: Writing with grammar in mind', *English Teaching: Practice and Critique*, 4: 77–96.

Nunes, T., Bryant, P., and Olsson, J. (2003) 'Learning morphological and phonological spelling rules: An intervention study', *Scientific Studies of Reading*, 7: 289–307.

O'Donnell, R.C., Griffin, W.G., and Norris, R.C. (1967) *Syntax of Kindergarten and Elementary School Children: A Transformational Analysis*, Champaign, Ill: National Council of Teachers of English.

O'Hare, F. (1973) *Sentence Combining: Improving Student Writing Without Formal Grammar Instruction*, Research Report No. 15. Urbana, IL: National Council of Teachers of English.

Perera, K. (1984) *Children's Writing and Reading. Analysing Classroom Language*, Oxford: B. Blackwell in association with A. Deutsch.

Perera, K. (1986) 'Language acquisition and writing', in P. Fletcher and M. Garman (eds), *Language Acquisition. Studies in First Language Development* (second edn.), Cambridge: Cambridge University Press. pp.494–518.

Perera, K. (1990) 'Grammatical differentiation between speech and writing in children aged 8 to 12', in R. Carter (ed.), *Knowledge About Language and the Curriculum*, London: Hodder and Stoughton. pp.216–233.

Read, J. (2000) *Assessing Vocabulary*, Cambridge: Cambridge University Press.

Stormzand, M. and O'Shea, M. (1924) *How Much English Grammar? An Investigation of the Frequency of Usage of Grammatical Constructions in Various Types of Writing Together with a Discussion of the Teaching of Grammar in the Elementary and the High School*, Baltimore: Warwick and York.

Tomlinson, D. (1994) 'Errors in the research into the effectiveness of grammar teaching', *English in Education*, 28: 2–26.

Ure, J. (1971) 'Lexical density and register differentiation', G. Perren and J. Trim (eds), *Applications of Linguistics: Selected Papers of the Second International Congress of Applied Linguistics*, Cambridge 1969. Cambridge: Cambridge University Press. pp.443–452.

Weaver, C. (1996) *Teaching Grammar in Context*, Portsmouth, NH.: Heinemann.

Wells, G. (1986) 'Variation in child language', in P. Fletcher and M. Garman (eds), *Language Acquisition* (second edn.), Cambridge: Cambridge University Press. pp.109–147.

Wells, R. (1960) 'Nominal and verbal style', in T. Sebeok (ed.), *Style in Language*, Cambridge, MA: MIT Press. pp.13–20.

Wyse, D. (2001) 'Grammar for writing? A critical review of empirical evidence', *British Journal of Educational Studies*, 49: 411–427.

Yerrill, K. (1977) 'A consideration of the later development of children's syntax in speech and writing: A study of parenthetical, appositional and related items', PhD dissertation, University of Newcastle upon Tyne.

The Architecture of Textuality: A Semiotic View of Composing in and out of School

Peter Smagorinsky

This chapter was originally presented at the Economic and Social Research Council Seminar Series *Reconceptualising Writing 5-16: Cross-phase and cross-disciplinary perspectives* at Crossmead Conference Centre, University of Exeter, Devon, England, 7 May, 2004

In the last few years I've had the opportunity to take several trips from the U.S. to Europe, primarily to attend academic conferences but also, of course, to absorb as much culture as possible during my visits. As a way of introducing some ideas I'd like to develop in this chapter, I will review my experiences with two magnificent churches I visited during recent trips and my readings of them as texts; or, in some cases, my limited ability to read them, or my evolving understanding of them as I learned more about their histories. I hope that this brief account of my travels helps to set the stage for my ultimate goal with this chapter: to make a case for a broadened notion of textuality. While 'New Literacies' studies have gotten much attention of late, because of their emphasis on technology and its implications for textuality

in emerging economies (e.g., The New London Group, 1996; Street, 2003), I will argue that multimodal literacies are not so new at all, and that they have always been implicated in the emerging economy. Indeed, they have been around since the first drawings on cave walls and have served educational purposes for millennia.

First stop, Paris. Like any good tourist, I spent time in the Cathedral of Notre-Dame, among Christendom's greatest architectural achievements. As part of the reading I did in preparation for this trip, I learned that in the sixth century Pope Gregory the Great proposed that the scriptures be depicted on the walls of churches for the benefit of the largely unlettered Christian flock. In the city of Arras in northern France in 1025, religious leaders revived this idea, believing that it might enable 'illiterate people to learn what books cannot teach them' (Gies and Gies, 1994: 130). During the Middle Ages sculpture was the most esteemed artistic medium, one of the few that could be admired and understood by both aristocrats and uneducated peasants. Many European churches began to provide comprehensive theological lessons carved in stone, the Cathedral of Notre-Dame among them. Because it depicted the Biblical narrative in sculpture and other art forms so that it could be 'read' by the masses, the church was variously known as the Sermon in Stone and the Bible of the Poor.

My experience of the Cathedral of Notre-Dame was probably less informed, and certainly less inspired, than those of the illiterate worshippers for whom the chapel had been so constructed, given my own disaffiliation from formal religion and their deep faith in the church and its teachings. My interest in the church as a historical site and architectural wonder is admittedly more secular, a point I make not to demean its religious significance but to account for different readings of the church. While I can recognize depictions of the most famous Biblical narratives, many of the icons in Notre-Dame had little significance for me, either as familiar stories or as articles of faith, even as I resonated with them as deeply spiritual works of art. Like almost anyone who visits this cathedral, I found myself awed at its magnificence. Unlike many, I was incapable of engaging with it as a profoundly moving religious experience, in part because of my lack of faith and in part because of my narrow knowledge of the Biblical narrative.

I now shift to a different site on a different trip, this time to the great island city of Venice. I again confess my ignorance by saying that before visiting Italy, I did not realize that Venice was an island off the coast of the Italian mainland, or that this position enabled the city to become one of the greatest naval powers in European history—a source of power and conquest that ultimately informed my reading of the church as a text. I was also quite ignorant about its crown jewel, the Basílica de San Marco. This church provides the sanctuary for what are believed to be the bones of Christ's Apostle Mark, the possession of which gave Venice the prestige that helped it to become, over time, one of Europe's most important cities. Like the

Cathedral at Notre-Dame, the Basílica de San Marco is replete with Christian iconography, a sermon not only in stone but also in spectacular jewels, precious stones, and valuable metals. Even for someone like me with limited knowledge of the stories being told, the Basílica provides an extraordinary experience, one filled with wonder at the scope and beauty of the church's design and amazement at the riches of the church's ornamentation.

But my lack of knowledge of Biblical stories was offset by a very different knowledge, that of Venetian history, learned primarily through my reading in preparation for this much-anticipated trip. I learned that the interior decoration for the Basílica was largely the result of the fourth Crusade, perhaps the most shameful exploit in the history of Christianity (Norwich, 1989). At the beginning of the thirteenth century, the Venetians launched an assault on Constantinople under the Christian cross, ostensibly as part of their continuing campaign against the Muslims but more specifically aimed at seizing the great wealth held by their rival city. With its location at the intersection of the land route from Europe to Asia and the seaway from the Black Sea to the Mediterranean, and with its ideally contoured harbour within the Golden Horn—an asset for both trade and naval manoeuvring—Constantinople, and Byzantium before it, was a city of incomparable fortune.

Advancing the Christian faith, the motive for many Crusaders, was largely a pretense for the Venetian's venture, which was designed to enrich their church, the city-state of Venice, and individual Crusaders. The booty from this invasion is now abundantly on display in the Basílica de San Marco, contributing greatly to its glorious embellishment. I should also add that St. Mark's bones themselves were stolen by Venetians in 828 from Egypt, though for ostensibly more lofty purposes. Legend has it that when Mark went to the lagoon that ultimately became the site of the city of Venice, an angel came and said, 'Peace to you, Mark my Evangelist'.

This greeting was taken as a divine prophesy that Venice would be his final earthly resting place and justified his remains' return, however nefariously acquired.

My knowledge of the cynical design behind the fourth Crusade deeply affected my experience of the Basilica. Its incomparable beauty and splendour were, for me, compromised by the manner in which the precious materials had come at great human cost and at the price of the church's integrity. This reading of the church might not be available to those who understand Christian iconography and have spiritual engagement with the church but no knowledge of Venetian history.

My experiences in these extraordinary houses of worship have contributed to my own understanding of both the production and reading of writing. I link the composition and reading of texts together, because I think they are inseparable; a text without a reader provides only the potential for an eventual reading transaction, and a reader without a text can't do much reading. However, much writing done in school, and especially most writing done for assessment, seems to assume that texts are autonomous—that is, that they have inherent qualities without respect to particular readers, communities of readers, or textual genres that set up expectations for how texts are most fruitfully produced and understood. I am persuaded by Nystrand (1986) that textual quality is a function of readers' expectations; a good text is one that is *in tune* with whatever conventions, rhetorical qualities, vocabulary, and other qualities its community of readers anticipates. This does not necessarily mean that readers always like what authors say or how they say it; rather, an effectively written text is in dialogue with readers' expectations, even if the writer deliberately thwarts those expectations, as in a parody or text designed to be provocative. To extend Nystrand's musical metaphor, my colleagues and I have argued that texts and readers must not only be in tune with one another but also with the larger

harmonic structure of which they are all a part, with different genres (in music, for instance, freeform jazz, the minuet, the Senegalese griot form, etc.) providing different expectations for structure, presentation, grammar, and other aspects of the textual whole (Smagorinsky, 2001).

The field of education, however, does not often embrace this notion of reading and composing as what Nystrand (1986) calls *reciprocal* processes. Nystrand argues that texts do not follow the *doctrine of autonomous texts* (p. 81), i.e., the belief by Olson (1977) and others that texts must be sufficiently explicit to produce a meaning independent of what readers read into them. Many educators, for instance, might assume that the Basílica de San Marco has a fixed meaning grounded in a literal understanding of the Biblical narrative. Any constructive work on my part, they might argue, is irrelevant if it is not concerned with my comprehension of the text as it is inscribed, or how they think it is inscribed, or how the inscriber might have thought it was inscribed. The meaning of the Basílica, they might argue, is in the text, not in my transaction with it and the images that my reading evokes for me as a consequence of my experiences and knowledge of textual codes.

Curious assumptions are often at work in the formal educational arena with respect to both the reading and writing of written texts. My daughter, for instance, once took a standardized assessment of writing in which, along with countless other teenagers in countless large rooms across the U.S., she responded to a writing prompt that called for a particular type of writing. The assessment of her writing appeared to have been done by a machine, though I cannot say for sure. Among the evaluative comments was that *she appeared to have little sense of audience.* Now, how they determined that I have no idea. I do recall laughing out loud over their conclusion that kids who sit in silent rooms in uncomfortable desks while being watched like thieves writing on topics of someone else's choosing that appear to be scored by machines have little sense of audience.

This same teenager writes abundantly on her own time, often in remarkable ways: ensconced at the computer, with several Instant Messaging windows open being filled with conversations with online friends from around the world, coauthoring book manuscripts based on the Animorphs book series (see http://www.scholastic.com/animorphs/index.htm), writing sophisticated html code for her art websites, coauthoring and discussing anime art with online friends spanning the globe, dashing off her homework for different teachers, and much more (see Black and Steinkuehler, 2008, for a review of research in this area). This writing, I assume, is responsive to each other person's communicative needs, and thus shows some awareness of audience; at least, they seem to write back, which suggests to me that she knows how to get across to them. Some of her writing is in languages that are highly specialized, not just html but such dialects as *l33t* (pronounced "leet"—see http://www.bbc.co.uk/dna/h2g2/A787917), the sort of playful, original, intelligent, and fun use of language that is typically pursued with joy and passion by teenagers among themselves (Alvermann and Xu, 2003; Black, 2008; Kirkland et al., 2001), yet is viewed with opprobrium and suppressed in school, and certainly on writing assessments. Her use of these conventions—like most of the purposeful, particularly the meaningful, and enjoyable things that people do with texts—is largely discounted in schools.

One reason that my daughter and so many kids around the world find their nonacademic textual reading and writing to be meaningful and absorbing is that, unlike most of what they produce for school and assessment, it does indeed communicate with and invite response from people whom they consider to be important: their peer group, either immediate or virtual. This communicative, often affective dimension of textual exchange is not available in writing for school that has narrow evaluative criteria and is responded to primarily in terms of adherence to those

criteria; what they get back is not the informed and engaged response from a reader but critical attention to their errors in form. This error, for many kids, likely includes their limited understanding of audience, which in my view is built into requirements of the writing tasks often elicited in classrooms and on writing assessments.

As my opening illustrations suggest, I also embrace a broad view of textuality and literacy, one that takes a semiotic view that regards any configuration of signs as a potential text (Smagorinsky, 2001). And so, my daughter's anime art drawings stand as texts, as do cathedrals designed to tell a story, and musical compositions, and web pages, and other arrangements of signs that provide a meaning potential for possible readers. This perspective, while seemingly a radical idea for schools and those who assess their students, has been available for some time, having been outlined by Mead (1934), Lotman (1977), Scribner and Cole (1981), Gardner (1983), Harste et al. (1984), Wertsch (1991), Witte (1992), Smagorinsky (1995), The New London Group (1996), and Pope Gregory the Great 1,500 years ago.

I would like to illustrate what is potentially lost in typical school conceptions of composition by referring to some recent studies I've done under the sponsorship of the Spencer Foundation, each focusing on the design of living spaces by high school students. These living spaces include houses (Smagorinsky et al., 2005), the interiors of homes (Smagorinsky et al., 2006), and ranches designed to produce particular breeds of horses (Smagorinsky et al., 2004). In each case the students designed spaces that revealed their understanding of the structures and spaces and how people function in relation to them, followed conventions associated with design fields, drew abundantly on knowledge from across the school curriculum, engaged in a lengthy process of composition, drew on formal and informal knowledge from both school and personal experiences, were apprenticed into approaches to design, and inscribed their designs abundantly with personal narratives and values in relation to how they wanted to live their lives.

Significantly, they accomplished all this in classes that are outside the academic 'core' of the school, in classes not only not required for graduation but generally regarded, in the words of one teacher of these students, as 'basket weaving', a term used in the U.S. for classes that are easy and mindless. (I should point out that weaving baskets, especially those inscribed with artistry, is actually pretty hard, as one of my Native American students—himself from a community in which the weaving of baskets is an important cultural tradition—instructed me.) Yet, in such classes, I've found students working with high levels of engagement with the curriculum; further, they have exhibited sophisticated cognition and understanding of audience in their academic work. Based on my observations of classes across this school's curriculum, I believe that these levels of engagement and cognition are higher than what the students tend to reach in the core classes that they are required to take.

THE COMPOSITION AND READING OF AN ARCHITECTURAL TEXT

My own informal reading of Parisian and Venetian churches has suggested the ways in which readers may or may not be in dialogue with what its designers probably had in mind. I'll next move to a study of the development of a set of architectural plans (Smagorinsky et al., 2005) in a high school architectural design class. This study was particularly interesting, because it enabled us to examine not just student Rick's composing process, but his teacher Bill's negotiation of meaning with the student throughout the month or so during which he produced his design—a sort of interpersonal exchange not available to those of us who visit venerable churches. As a result, we were able to understand in some detail how the student's inscription of meaning in the house design was and was not aligned with his teacher's expectations,

and how their negotiation of the form of the final design represented both Rick's apprenticeship into the field of architectural design as conceived by Bill and Rick's inscription of a personal life trajectory into the drawing.

We next outline some of the major themes we found guiding Rick's design of a house under the mentorship of Bill, who worked closely with the local construction firm operated by his brothers. This firm built a particular kind of house designed for the tract housing market; i.e., houses that look roughly the same, situated on lots of the same size and shape, all required by code to sit the same distance from the suburban streets on which they were built. Bill's values were thus oriented to producing rectilinear designs that sat on rectilinear properties, typically on level plots in this generally flat part of the country. Within this setting, Rick produced his design, which he also submitted to a state-wide competition, finishing fourth.

Normative assumptions guiding text production

Bill and Rick used the term 'common sense' on a number of occasions to describe Bill's assumptions about architectural design and home construction. In many ways, Rick recognized and appreciated the reasoning behind Bill's common sense and took it up in his own work:

> He took it a step further and explained, you know, okay, like in a bathroom, it's going to be much easier on your plumber if you put everything on one side. Put your sink and your toilet on one side. Then when you put your bathtub, you put it at the end. Put the spout at that one side. Don't put a sink way over here in one corner, and then you're just going to have plumbing going everywhere. You know, just teaching us some common sense things that you really wouldn't think of.

In our reading of the data, we saw these references to common sense—or 'practical' knowledge as they referred to it on occasion—as instances of what D'Andrade (1995;

c.f. Cole, 1996) calls *cultural schemata*; that is, 'patterns of elementary schemas that make up the meaning system characteristic of any cultural group' (Cole, 1996: 126). These schemata often take on a normative value that is generalized as 'common sense' that, one presumes, ought to inform any reasonable analysis of a situation. This common sense, which we interpret to be culturally constructed, provided the common ground of agreement for the principles that guided Rick's design of his house. In terms of the sort of house that Bill envisioned his students describing—those that would sell in a competitive housing market in a period following a serious economic depression—these values were axiomatic.

Our notion that they are culturally-situated springs from the fact that in other parts of the world, housing has different requirements. Prior to their closure, for instance, I taught on military bases in Panama City, Panama. In many parts of the city, much of the housing has little or no electricity because of a combination of year-round balmy weather and extreme poverty. Bill's notion of common sense assumed that a house has electricity—hardly a surprise in a U.S. suburban-style community. On one occasion, Bill described another design principle that followed from his common sense:

> What they have to think about, and what I try to make them think about, and the process I try to make them go through is what is easy and what is convenient. And I don't mean easy as far as easy for them to draw. Easy for them to live in. When you walk in [a room], make sure the light switch is on the door handle side, so you don't have to walk into a dark room.

The housing market of the city in which Bill's brothers needed to compete for house sales, then, provided the mediating culture that contributed to his notion of a cultural schema for commonsensical design. These principles might not apply to other areas and markets in which the culture has formed around other problems and conditions that must be addressed during the design of homes.

Tensions between goals

While accepting many of Bill's common sense views about architectural design, Rick found himself often at odds with the conventions Bill invoked for his house plans. One recurring tension we found came between Rick's goals for his drawing and the expectations of the adults who read and assessed his work. Rick's house design was intended to afford a particular way of living, including his preference for odd angles and his need to have an open design to account for his feelings of claustrophobia. Bill, on the other hand, embodied the norms of the field of architecture and the subfield of southwestern, suburban, mass-market tract housing design.

Rick's projection of the house design in relation to his lifestyle needs was quite different from Bill's sense of convention and market pragmatism. Bill emphasized what could realistically be built and sold in a community such as the one they lived in. The recent economic recession and resulting housing depression had left local builders wary of building unique houses that were difficult to market. Bill's sense of housing norms and marketability was based on his knowledge of which house designs resulted in quick and thus profitable turnarounds on the market, a consequence of his close relationship with his brothers and their business, which like all local construction firms, as well as any enterprise in the region at large had struggled during the market decline.

Rick, on the other hand, had a unique vision of himself and his lifestyle that caused him to resist certain norms invoked by Bill; further, he had gone through adolescence during the economic recovery and so had no deeply rooted sense of how the market had crashed during his childhood. Rick was unconventional for his school: He had dropped out and then returned to take this course after having taken classes at the local Vocational-Technical school. He had long blond hair tied back in a ponytail and got about town on rollerblades. He was a self-described nonconformist in general, and he continually found himself at odds with the conventions governing the shapes of rooms emphasized by Bill. Rick worked against these conventions because he wanted to include unusual angles in his design.

Rick often revealed his preferences for his house's function through his narratives that illustrated how his lifestyle would be accommodated by his design decisions. He explained, for instance, one design decision as follows:

> Rick: The teacher wanted to put some coat closets in there, and I didn't. ... I couldn't think of a place to put it without taking away from the overall—he was talking about, okay, let's cut this wall down like this, and we'll make this a closet. The door will be right there. Well, at, really to me, that just wouldn't be right. To have that study, then, like that. It just doesn't look right.
>
> Q: Wouldn't be symmetrical like that?
>
> Rick: Yeah. It would, it would make it, the plan, easier. But yet not what I was shooting for. I was shooting for something just totally different. I wanted something nice and open, but at the same time I wanted some closed off areas. I used to have a—there was a door coming out here. And there was actually a patio, like a garden that you could go out in the morning and drink coffee or whatever, and it was, there was a four-foot brick wall going all the way around it. So that, you know, you had a little bit of privacy, but not too much. Which kind of fit in with the rest of the theme of—you know, your dining room, you've got a little bit of privacy, that wall there, that had no shade. But at the same time, you could still get, you could still see into the living room.

These angles created a feeling of open space for Rick. Rick said, 'I didn't want everything tight, compact ... A lot of the houses, and even the houses that won [the state high school architectural design competition], looked tight and uncomfortable to me ... I don't like feeling cramped in. I am extremely claustrophobic and I don't, I wanted something large'. Yet an open design worked against the notion of efficiency that Bill hoped to impress on his students. And in the context of the virtual neighbourhood plot that Bill had

provided for the students, Rick's preference for inefficient angles and open spaces would violate the sense of uniformity expected in such neighbourhoods.

In a sense, then, the assignment created a conundrum for Bill and Rick. The task required students to design a house that would afford their lifestyle; yet he also required that the house be situated on a plot similar to those on which his brothers built houses. This constraint produced tension between Bill and Rick in that Rick's lifestyle was not well suited for such neighbourhoods, at least from a marketing standpoint, which was paramount to Bill and irrelevant to Rick.

Tensions between writer's inscription and reader's encoding

Rick had little trouble reading his audience, given his close relationship with Bill throughout the design process. The tension resulted from the kinds of competing goals for the house's design and Bill's reluctance to recognize Rick's sense of style and notion of economy as legitimate in the context of the task. Rick's design became problematic for Bill when it departed from Bill's normative sense of what constituted practical or common sense approaches to designing a home as a commodity within the economy to which he had become enculturated, the postrecession suburban mass housing market. Rick, however, had a different purpose for his design: to embody and facilitate a specific and unique approach to living.

In one sense, Rick's composition might be read with reasonable proximity to his intentions by anyone conversant with the codes of architectural design. Readers who have inhabited American homes, even those with no experience in reading architectural plans, might have little difficulty in determining from Rick's drawing what is a hallway and what is a bedroom. In other words, he produced his design with attention to conventions typically employed by architects, and his house was not so unconventional that a lay reader would have difficulty figuring out that a square room on the second floor was a room while the narrow, rectangular figure running down the centre of the design was a hallway.

In another sense, Rick's inscription is potentially lost when the text is unmediated by his own account of his decision-making process. Our research method provided access to Rick's inscription of meaning through his accounts of narratives and other schematic tools. These narratives suggested the sorts of experiences his design might induce and how those experiences might contribute to a more meaningful life for him within the home.

Texts are in one sense static in that they are fixed upon the page. Yet Rick's narratives revealed that he inscribed his house design with abundant movement and activity that he anticipated within the house, movement of a particular kind and motivated by a particular ideology. We have described, for instance, Rick's brief story of how he hoped to negotiate the premises: 'There was actually a patio, like a garden that you could go out in the morning and drink coffee or whatever, and it was, there was a four-foot brick wall going all the way around it'. These narratives were central to the kinds of design decisions he made, and suggest the ways in which his drawings represented not simply a structure but a way of living within that structure.

Bill's encoding of meaning during his reading, however, was quite different: The octagonal rooms suggested narratives in which consumers house hunting in this neighbourhood, and thus seeking a tract home, walked through the door, saw the odd angles, and quickly walked out in search of a home more accommodating to their furniture layout, pathways for movement, and the life afforded by such a configuration. Just as importantly, Bill's narrative extended to include the contractor stuck with an unmarketable home in an economy recently troubled by low housing starts and scant new home purchases.

Identity construction through textual composition

Rick was both a product of his culture and one who resisted it. He accepted and acted within the constraints suggested by institutionalized rules such as building codes and 'common sense' rules that governed building construction in this geographical area. In doing so he accepted the trajectory of producing marketable suburban tract housing that was encouraged by his teacher and followed by his classmates. At the same time, Rick's vision of how he wanted to live, reinforced by narrative images of how a house might facilitate his particular living and spatial needs, created critical points of departure from this trajectory, particularly with regard to his angular design:

> Everybody's got this real basic shape. You see a lot of squares. And I wanted to stray away from that.

John-Steiner and Meehan (2000) have argued that creativity follows from new juxtapositions of existing ideas. Rick brought new juxtapositions (e.g., a different sense of geometry) to Bill's class and the field, yet they were discouraged, because they departed from Bill's common sense with regard to profitable architectural design and house construction. We see Rick and Bill working collaboratively, if occasionally at odds, to produce an architectural design that juxtaposed existing conventions in new ways. Rick did not invent the octagon but did, at least in this setting, introduce this shape as a new configuration. As such, it was a creative decision consistent with his belief in himself as a unique individual. We see his design of this cultural text as both an embodiment of his vision of himself and as an opportunity to develop that vision.

DISCUSSION

Undoubtedly, I've gone far afield from conventional notions of literacy in this tour of

European churches and American and Panamanian houses. I hope that these forays have shed some light on what I consider to be key issues in the teaching and learning of how to write. I would stress the following points:

1. Composition refers to the intentional, conventional design and production of a text, regardless of medium. While writing is often considered the tool of compositional tools (a metaphor variously attributed to Dewey, Vygotsky, and Luria with respect to speech), I would argue instead that it is but one among many ways in which people can communicate, construct meaning, and learn.
2. The quality of writing or other composition is a function of readers' and writers' relationships and expectations, rather than a static quality of the text. Understanding the cultural construction of expectations is important in understanding any judgment relative to quality.
3. The meaning of a piece of writing is not always apparent. I extrapolate that just as Rick's design was comprised of narratives that were not visible to the uninformed reader, what students have to say through writing is not always evident in the texts alone. Greater perspicacity may be in order on some occasions if students do not sufficiently elaborate their writing. On the other hand, certain types of expression call for economic and even cryptic textual depiction, as in an architectural drawing or a poem. When the goal is to distill meaning and suggest it through relatively parsimonious compositions, it is incumbent on the reader to read the textual codes and what they potentially represent in terms of the author's purposes in constructing the text in a particular way. In this era of standardization of student work (see Hillocks, 2002), such generous readings are greatly at risk, a problem that research into multimodality must contest if the meaning of student expression is to be taken seriously.
4. The importance of a piece of writing to the writer ought to matter in developing school opportunities for composing. Students who willingly invest time and emotional energy in their compositions are likely inscribing meaning and their emerging identities in them as well (Smagorinsky et al., 2007). Such writing is better evidence of one's ability than the uninspired writing produced during wide-scale assessments and much other school-based writing.

5. Achieving authenticity is not necessarily, and not likely, painless, but requires cognitive and emotional investment, the willingness to revise or start over, and the willingness to grow, along with whatever growing pains are required to advance the process.
6. What teachers consider to be conventional and commonsensical is not always the same as what students think is appropriate for a text. These different expectations should be made explicit and perhaps negotiated as a way to help students understand the cultural expectations into which they are composing, and to provide them with experience in articulating and defending their understanding of rules and procedures. Typically, in school, students are simply provided with rules and downgraded for violating them. As Rick's experience illustrates, students often have good reasons for breaking rules. Given the opportunity, they might be able to explain and justify their understanding of the communicative and expressive needs of their compositions and why they can produce forms more appropriate to their purposes.

I see, then, both the whole school curriculum and the whole of compositional expression as appropriate settings in which to think about writing and writing instruction. Too often, I think, writing across the curriculum is imposed on other disciplines by English teachers as a panacea for the general malaise of the educational experience. In my view, English teachers would benefit from thinking about the broader notion of text composition and the ways in which it is practiced across disciplines. In my school observations, much of the most dynamic learning has come outside English or other 'core' classes and outside the realm of writing. Often, this learning has come in parts of the school typically considered to have low academic status: home economics, agriculture, and so on.

In these classes I have observed, and often collected data, as students have composed texts of great meaning to them, such as the clothes that students in a sewing class prepared for their own wardrobes. These students almost universally took great care with their compositions, willingly revising them and meticulously producing a final product of which they were proud. At the same time, I have seen students in 'core' academic courses snoozing through lectures and dashing off assignments so that they can finish and move on to something they find worthwhile. It strikes me that rather than imposing the values and practices of English on every discipline, English teachers might benefit from thinking about how students experience school across the curriculum, observing and talking with students who are involved in the design of texts (often nonverbal) for other 'low status' classes, and rethinking how they might invigorate their own discipline by spending time with teachers and students in others.

REFERENCES

Alvermann, D.E. and Xu, S.H. (2003) 'Children's everyday literacies: Intersections of popular culture and language arts instruction across the curriculum', *Language Arts*, 81: 145–154.

Black, R.W. (2008) *Adolescents and Online Fan Fiction*, New York: Peter Lang.

Black, R.W. and Steinkuehler, C. (2008) 'Literacy in virtual worlds', in L. Christenbury, R. Bomer, and P. Smagorinsky (eds), *Handbook on Adolescent Literacy*, New York: Guilford. pp.271–286.

Cole, M. (1996) *Cultural Psychology: A Once and Future Discipline*, Cambridge, MA: Harvard University Press.

D'Andrade, R. (1995) *The Development of Cognitive Anthropology*, New York: Cambridge University Press.

Gardner, H. (1983) *Frames of Mind: The Theory of Multiple Intelligences*, New York: Basic Books.

Gies, F. and J. Gies (1994) *Cathedral, Forge, and Waterwheel: Technology and Invention in the Middle Ages*, New York: HarperCollins.

Harste, J.C., Woodward, V.A., and Burke, C.L. (1984) *Language Stories and Literacy Lessons*, Portsmouth, NH: Heinemann.

Hillocks, G. (2002) *The Testing Trap: How State Writing Assessments Control Learning*, New York: Teachers College Press.

John-Steiner, V.P. and Meehan, T.M. (2000) 'Creativity and collaboration in knowledge construction', in

C.D. Lee and P. Smagorinsky (eds), *Vygotskian Perspectives on Literacy Development: Constructing Meaning Through Collaborative Inquiry*, New York: Cambridge University Press. pp.31–48.

Kirkland, D., Jackson, A., and Smitherman, G. (March/ April 2001) 'Leroy, Big D, and Big Daddy speakin Ebonics on the internet', *American Language Review*, 22–26.

Lotman, J. (1977) *The Structure of the Artistic Text* (Tr. G. Lenhoff and R. Vroon), Ann Arbor, MI: University of Michigan, Department of Slavic Languages and Literatures.

Mead, G.H. (1934) *Mind, Self, and Society*, Chicago: University of Chicago Press.

Norwich, J.J. (1989) *A History of Venice*, New York: Vintage.

Nystrand, M. (1986) *The Structure of Written Communication: Studies in Reciprocity Between Writers and Readers*, Orlando, FL: Academic Press.

Olson, D. (1977) 'From utterance to text: The bias of language in speech and writing', *The Harvard Educational Review*, 47: 257–281.

Scribner, S. and Cole, M. (1981) *The Psychology of Literacy*, Cambridge, MA: Harvard University Press.

Smagorinsky, P. (1995) 'Constructing meaning in the disciplines: Reconceptualizing writing across the curriculum as composing across the curriculum', *American Journal of Education*, 103: 160–184.

Smagorinsky, P. (2001) 'If meaning is constructed, what is it made from? Toward a cultural theory of reading', *Review of Educational Research*, 71: 133–169.

Smagorinsky, P., Augustine, S.M., and O'Donnell-Allen, C. (2007) 'Experiences with personal, academic, and hybrid writing: A study of two high school seniors', *English in Australia*, 42(3): 55–73.

Smagorinsky, P., Cook, L., and Reed, P. (2005) 'The construction of meaning and identity in the composition and reading of an architectural text', *Reading Research Quarterly*, 40: 70–88.

Smagorinsky, P., Pettis, V., and Reed, P. (2004) 'High school students' compositions of ranch designs: Implications for academic and personal achievement', *Written Communication*, 21: 386–418.

Smagorinsky, P., Zoss, M., and Reed, P. (2006) 'Residential interior design as complex composition: A case study of a high school senior's composing process', *Written Communication*, 23: 295–330.

Street, B. (2003) 'What's "new" in New Literacy Studies? Critical approaches to literacy in theory and practice', *Current Issues in Comparative Education*, 77–91.

The New London Group (1996) 'A pedagogy of multiliteracies: Designing social futures', *Harvard Educational Review*, 66(1): 60–92.

Wertsch, J.V. (1991) *Voices of the Mind: A Sociocultural Approach to Mediated Action*, Cambridge, MA: Harvard University Press.

Witte, S. (1992) 'Context, text, intertext: Toward a constructivist semiotic of writing', *Written Communication*, 9: 237–308.

25

The Content of Students' Writing

Brenton Doecke and Douglas McClenaghan

We classify at our peril. Experiments have shown that even the lightest touch of the classifier's hand is likely to induce us to see members of a class as more alike than they actually are, and items from different classes as less alike than they actually are. And when our business is to do more than merely look, these errors may develop, in the course of our dealings, into something quite substantial.

(Britton, et al. 1975, *The Development of Writing Abilities* (11–18):1)

INTRODUCTION

School has often been a scene of conflict between the linguistic diversity that students bring with them into the schoolyard and the standard forms of language which are valued in classrooms. Students have rich linguistic resources at their disposal, in the form of community languages, dialects, slang, and the language of 'the day and hour' (Bahktin, 1981: 293), which schools have typically struggled to acknowledge. Yet the pressure to impose some sort of linguistic norm seems especially pervasive at the present moment. Standards-based reforms (Darling-Hammond, 2004) are increasingly mediating the professional practice of teachers, requiring them to judge students' literacy abilities against certain benchmarks of performance. In many educational settings, teachers have been reduced to administering a barrage of standardized tests in order to demonstrate whether their students are performing at the required level.

The paradox is that, at the very moment when many young people are engaging in an extraordinary spectrum of multimodal communications in their daily lives, schools appear to be privileging an ever more narrow range of writing practices as indicators of literacy ability (Sefton-Green, 2000). You need only think of the ubiquitous literary 'essay' that secondary school students in the Anglophone world are obliged to master (Teese, 2000; Green, 2001; Clyne, 2005; Kostogriz, 2005). Such types of school writing have little or no connection with the semiotic practices that students experience in their out-of-school lives. Rather than engaging in writing as a meaning-making activity that is infused with real purpose, students are obliged to submit written work which their teachers can classify and measure. These tendencies arguably reflect a deep uncertainty about the present, a crisis of values in 'an era of instability' (Kress, 2002; Doecke et al., 2006), which has given rise to conservative pressures to affirm the centrality of traditional forms of language and communication. They also reflect a neoliberal fetish of measurement and containment. But perhaps most startling of all, they betray a deep seated fear of the potential of young people and their capacity to exceed what is familiar and routine.

The aim of this chapter is to argue what can be gained by refocusing on what students have to communicate in their writing, and—crucially—by providing them with a social space where they *want* to communicate. Needless to say, this involves more than examining what their writing is 'about', as though the content of students' writing can ever be understood apart from the forms in which it is embodied or the contexts out of which it emerges. We believe that focusing on the content of students' writing involves recognizing how the artefacts they create emerge out of the networks in which they participate, many of which extend far beyond the school gates, showing traces of the multiple subjectivities they experience as they negotiate the situations presented to them. It means understanding their writing in a relational way, within the context of their ongoing social exchanges, including their location within the institutional structures that mediate their interactions with teachers and other students when they come to school. Above all, it means orienting instruction 'toward the future, not the past' (Vygotsky, 1962: 104), and enabling students to explore the possibilities of thought and language, meaning and communication that are open to them.

A RESEARCHER'S STANDPOINT

To focus on the content of students' writing is to set aside many of the frames of reference that teachers habitually use when reading their students' work. This is nothing new—educators gain powerful insights into school writing when the content of their students' work seems especially lively or interesting, whatever the criteria specified for assessing a particular task. Countless studies of writing pedagogy have been motivated by a desire to enable students to use their writing as a vehicle for exploring experience, in contrast to a traditional focus on the surface features of written expression and other routine tasks associated with school writing (cf. Langdon, 1961; Dixon, 1967; Murray, 1982; Graves, 1983). Reviewing this literature, you could be forgiven for thinking that these educators have been perpetually engaged in a subversive struggle to allow their students to escape the 'shades of the prison house', to challenge the dull conformity of the set task, in order to explore experiences and emotions that resist conventional classification.

Yet, as we have argued in our introductory remarks, while this approach to the teaching of writing has a long history, the conflict between responding to the content of students' writing and traditional forms of school assessment is being played out differently at the present moment. Without doubt, educators need to think again about the experiences on which young people are able to draw when they are 'doing' school writing, to reconceptualize those experiences in ways that do justice to the multiple contexts and networks in which young people operate (cf. Doecke and McClenagahan, 1997). The content of students' writing can provide a powerful counterpoint to the types of surveillance that are currently being implemented in schools, gesturing beyond the terms in which an adult world seeks to define them. Nevertheless, if the experiences of young people challenge the boundaries imposed by a conventional understanding of school writing, it is also necessary to recognize the way those boundaries have themselves been redrawn and reconstituted as a set of standards for measuring the performance of individual students. Such standards increasingly shape the professional judgements of teachers as they respond to students' writing and in doing so they impact decisively on the way students do school. Students are constantly being told where they fit into the scheme of things, whether in the form of the results of standardized tests or tertiary entrance scores. That such practices are being enacted against a background of a globalizing economy, which has substantially undermined traditional pathways into work or further education, shows how much is at stake when students engage in meaning making that challenges conventional school genres.

We shall illustrate these tensions by considering some examples of students' writing that prompt thought about the social relationships or contexts in which they might be located. Crucially, these samples of students' writing are not the product of a planned intervention by the teacher, Douglas McClenaghan, as in an action research cycle (Grundy, 1995; Carr and Kemmis, 1986). These texts emerged, instead, out of the daily routines in his classroom, forming part of the students' ongoing dialogue with him, as they negotiated their way through a prescribed course of study. The school is located in a middle class suburb of Melbourne. As a state school, it does not adopt the exclusionary practices of the wealthy private schools that have come to dominate the educational landscape in Australia, but its demographic nonetheless means that it does not face the social and economic issues of state schools in poorer suburbs.

Rather than action research, the inquiry on which this chapter is based might best be described as an attempt by this teacher to understand the institutional setting in which he works, to see further than the immediacy of the present and the day-to-day demands being made on him. This means going beyond the here and now, and coming to understand how any workplace setting is part of an extended network of social relationships that is not immediately visible to the individuals who take part in it (cf. Smith, 2005: 32, 36). Dorothy Smith calls this 'knowing the social', arguing for situated inquiry that is driven by a 'notion of the everyday world as problematic' (p. 40), as 'a territory to be discovered, not a question that is concluded in its answer' (p. 41, cf. Hamilton, 2005). The challenge, when it comes to responding to students'

writing, is for teachers to turn an ethnographer's eye on the artefacts their students create, to ask what those artefacts mean. This, indeed, is how we understand the task of refocusing on the content of students' writing.

The world in which this teacher and his students operate is constituted by a multitude of texts (cf. Smith, 2005: 101) that mediate the social relationships enacted in their institutional setting. The official, mandated curriculum defines the knowledge and skills students are expected to develop, providing what Smith calls 'a key juncture between the local settings of people's everyday worlds and the ruling relations' (p. 101). Teachers are required to map their students' literacy achievement against pre-existing continua that show expected progression points, thereby judging their performance against state-wide benchmarks. The relevant level for the samples of students' writing that we examine in this chapter is couched in the following language:

At Level 6, students write sustained and cohesive narratives that experiment with different techniques and show attention to chronology, characterization, consistent point of view and development of a resolution. They write persuasive texts dealing with complex ideas and issues and control the linguistic structures and features that support the presentation of different perspectives on complex themes and issues. They select subject matter and begin to use a range of language techniques to try to position readers to accept particular views of people, characters, events, ideas and information (Victorian Curriculum and Assessment Authority 2008; http://vels.vcaa.vic.edu.au/)

Managerial, normative, and performance based, this text discursively constructs not only how subject English should be understood, but also the trajectories that classes and students should follow (or what one such document describes as their 'typical progression' (cf. AEC, 1994: 1). To some extent, the following samples of students' writing can be read as illustrating this 'standard', which describes the level of accomplishment students are expected to meet in their final years of secondary school. However, they also challenge this construction of English literacy ability, speaking back in powerful ways to such attempts to 'transform the local particularities of people, place, and time into standardized, generalized, and, especially, translocal forms of coordinating people's activities' (Smith, 2005: 101).

The following section presents cases of students' writing, and attempts to convey a sense of their engagement in the issues they raise, as well as the rich particularity and multilayered quality of the texts they have created. In a concluding section, we shall attempt to capture their significance as illustrations of the 'content' of students' writing.

CASES

Zombie

The first text confronts any attempt to assess it as a piece of school writing, not least because the student ('Grace') has chosen to include very little written text at all, beyond the opening title—'Zombie. The Cranberries'—and a quotation from Mahatma Ghandi on the 70th slide: '… What difference does it make to the dead, the orphans and the homeless, whether the mad destruction is wrought under the name of totalitarianism or the holy name of liberty and democracy?'

This text was created as a response to an invitation by Douglas McClenaghan to his students to write a 'creative' piece of their own choice. They had previously looked at a television program which discussed a poem, 'Not Waving, But Drowning', by Stevie Smith. The program supposedly presented a film of the poem, but the class agreed that it was rather an unsatisfying re-enactment of the events in the text, and that the poem appeared to elude representation in this form. They concluded that the story, such as it is, did not comprise what was interesting about the poem, and that many important dimensions of the text were missing, although they also felt that the film of the poem did not fully exploit the potential of the medium to combine text with sound and imagery in powerful ways. What would a multimodal poem look like? Douglas McClenaghan was then able to show work done by students in previous years, which combined visual and written text in innovative ways (for an example, see McClengahan and Doecke, 2005; Doecke and McClenaghan, 2005). Grace's piece arose out of the idea that she could use slideshow software as a possible alternative to hand drawing. A number of other students also produced slideshow presentations, as though it has become a hybrid genre of its own, combining sound and visual imagery with written text.

Until the moment in Grace's slideshow where she presents the Ghandi quotation, the text consists solely of photographs, which Grace has taken from the Internet, a veritable barrage of images showing scenes of children and women suffering in wartime settings. These images are combined in a powerpoint presentation, with the Cranberries' song, 'Zombie', playing in the background, as image after image flashes up on the screen. The powerpoint lasts for the duration of the song, and the very final slide presents the lyrics:

> Another mother's breakin'
> Heart is taking over.
> When the vi'lence causes silence,
> We must be mistaken.
> It's the same old theme since nineteen-sixteen.
> In your head, in your head they're still fighting,
> With their tanks and their bombs,
> And their bombs and their guns.
> In your head, in your head, they are dying …

It is impossible not to be confronted by the text's force as a protest against war and the world that 'they' (those people who are 'still fighting,/With their tanks and their bombs,/And their bombs and their guns') have made for children. Although Grace does not interpolate with any of her own words, the way she combines images positions readers in a very complex manner, involving subtle shifts of perspective that are akin to the way a change of pronouns ('I', 'you', 'we', or 'they') can change the construction of point of view in a narrative. The dominant images are those of children and their mothers, when readers are invited to empathize ('we' are clearly meant to identify with their suffering). Men ('they') only appear as images of soldiers in uniform or as anonymous shadows towering above crouching children whose eyes are filled with fear. Yet the proliferation of faces expressing fear, bewilderment, and pain also builds up a sense of a world which is quite different from the one which 'we' know. Who, then, are 'we'? Grace answers this question by including five images (out of a total of over seventy) towards the end of the presentation without any preparation or forewarning. They are simply interleaved with the predominant images of privation and suffering, and they are all media images of affluent Western society: an image of a woman watching a wide-screen television, an image that is seemingly taken at random from a television variety show, a repeat of the woman watching the television (although there is no image on the screen; she is merely sitting back on her lounge, her back towards us, facing the screen), an image of a luxury motor car taken from an advertisement, and finally an image of a woman with her eyes closed, lathering soap on to her face, again taken from an advertisement, as shown in Figure 25.1.

Figure 25.2   SLIDE 62.

The powerpoint then switches to a black and white image of a child looking up from a gutter (Figure 25.2), and then resumes the parade of images of war and destruction: soldiers patrolling, a man with his lips sewn together, and a border patrol guard with his gun aimed towards a mother and her child. 'We' may be capable of showing sympathy for the plight of those people whose suffering has been graphically evoked by the slides, and yet the text finally raises questions about 'our' world, and the way 'our' wealth' is bound up with the misery of others. (Indeed, at this point the text combines the only other image in the text which involves written text, namely a World War One poster saying: 'Your chums are fighting. Why aren't you?', when it effectively points an accusatory finger at 'you'.)

As indicated in the foregoing section, other students also chose to construct texts in this form, covering a range of issues. One text asks: 'What is love?' ('Does it last forever? Is it a dream? A journey? A touch?

Figure 25.1   SLIDE 61.

The course of true love never did run smooth.'), amusingly juxtaposing pictures of animals copulating with more sentimental images of couples holding hands, apparently lost in each other's eyes. Another piece, provocatively titled 'Sanity', combines written text composed by the student with images of alienation and disorientation, with ghost-like sounds in the background:

It's too dark, I can't breathe
With my sunken eyes
And sallow skin
Broken nails
And limp hair
Pulling me tighter
I'm hanging here
And no one notices ...

The texts provide a small window on how these young people are experiencing the world in which they find themselves.

Charcoal Eyes

Young people's disposition to juxtapose imagery and combine texts is sometimes assumed to be a consequence of multimodal forms of communication. Although there is obviously an element of truth to this claim, the creativity shown by Grace and her peers cannot be reduced to a mere function of modern technology, as though young people are simply victims of consumer culture. Rather, it shows their capacity to appropriate contemporary media for their own purposes. Their texts combine form and content in ways that enable them to explore issues of identity and community affiliation as they are experiencing them in a period of radical uncertainty and social change. Some other students in Douglas McClenaghan's classes actually resort to very traditional media in order to address the matters that concern them, including in one instance a papier-mâché display, albeit reflecting a similar disposition or sensibility to that which we have just identified (see Doecke and McClenagahan, 2005). The sample of student writing on which we now wish to focus

was presented as a spiral bound project book, consisting entirely of black pages on which are pasted visual and written texts. The book has no title, merely a black cover. It is only when you open the book that you find the words, 'Charcoal Eyes', set against the background of an image of a young man who is staring directly at you. Moreover, the written text which follows, surrounded by white and black borders, is reminiscent of very traditional expressions of sympathy or mourning.

A few weeks before the submission of this work, Douglas McClenaghan had asked his students to do an oral presentation in which they read a poem or played a song of their choice to the class, and then presented a spoken analysis. The students were encouraged to talk not only about more than simply the text they had each chosen, but to include, where relevant, details about the poet or songwriter and the time when the text was created. 'Janine' asked if she could speak about a poem published online by a friend. When she gave her speech, she revealed to her classmates that this person had died of a drug overdose not long after writing the poem. This was a young man she knew personally, but with whom she and others shared an online community that focused substantially on their own creative writing and each other's responses to that writing.

When, a few weeks later, Douglas McClenaghan gave students the opportunity to create their own texts, Janine asked whether she could present a collection of poems, rather than write a single piece. Douglas's response was that she was in control. As mentioned in the preceding section, when setting 'creative' writing he provides examples of work produced by students from previous years, including multimedia texts that suggest the potential of combining printed text with visual imagery (see Doecke and McClenaghan, 2005). Janine is a keen photographer who studies visual arts with an emphasis on photography and digital media. She was able to recruit another young man in the class to model for photographs that she

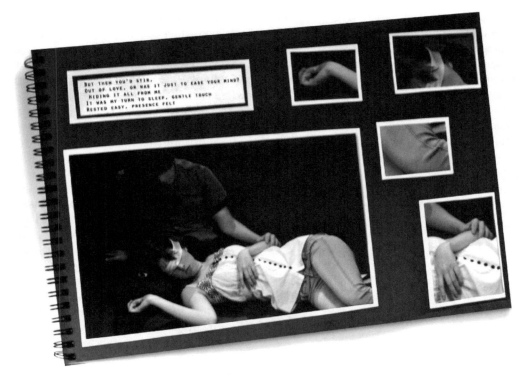

Figure 25.3   Images from *Charcoal Eyes.*

subsequently combined with her written texts.

'Charcoal Eyes' consists of a series of poems addressed to a youth who committed suicide through a heroin overdose about twelve months earlier. The occasion for writing the poems was, in fact, the anniversary of his death, which was approaching. Each poem is presented in the manner just described, within a black border on white paper, which has in turn been pasted on to a black page. The poems are arranged in chronological order in an effort to show 'the progression of emotion and grieving'. Janine explains the context and purpose of each poem in explanatory comments at the end of the book. She notes that one of the poems actually takes the form of a 'letter' written 'almost in response to the letter' she had received from the young man who had taken his own life:

It takes themes and particular lines from the original and rebuts them ... I'm unsure what you'll make of it, because although I fully understand the meaning behind each line, I'm not positive that it will make sense to anyone who hasn't read the original letter, but being of a personal nature I was uncomfortable about putting a copy in to compare with. This final poem also signifies acceptance and offers a legitimate place to leave a final goodbye.

On another page, Janine explains the selection of photographs that she includes in the text, which 'are loosely based on pictures' drawn by the young man, who was an aspiring artist. Each shot, in fact, is carefully constructed, and, taken together, the photographs employ visual imagery (a white blindfold, a black blindfold, red shoes) to convey a sense of the contradictory nature of Janine's emotions and the prospect of acceptance of what has happened. Most of the pages combine written text with photographs showing a youth and a girl in various poses. There is nothing sexualized about these poses; the overriding impression they convey is one of companionship, of two people who are content to be in each other's presence. Each photograph is juxtaposed with smaller photographs focusing on details from the main photo: a hand, a shirt collar, red shoes, a shoelace, and a belt buckle. Written and visual texts combine to confront the mystery of Jake's presence in the life of the author, and the mystery of our presence in each other's lives.

Perhaps the most memorable poem is one which, as the author explains, 'confronts the reality of his addiction and how it affected everyone around him'.

> Do you know how many heroin related deaths occurred last year?
>
> I do. 364 in total.
>
> 151 of which were suicides.
>
> And 10 by kids who were about your age.
>
> Do you know how many drug users were provided with counselling
>
> Treatment on any given day last year?
>
> I do. About 2000.
>
> 2000 people who sought help,
>
> And most were admitted for treatment.

By presenting figures relating to heroin addiction and its treatment, the poem conveys a sense of yet another voice, the official voice of a regulated society, where individuals count only as statistics. These numbers are embedded in the imaginary conversation between Janine and the young man that has run through all the poems (he is the 'you' addressed in the previous lines). The next poem is 'The Letter', in which the author 'rebuts' the letter which the young man wrote to her before he died, when she manages to reach a sense of 'acceptance'.

The Shark Net

The image shown in Figure 25.4 is taken from a text created by a student, 'Daniel', as a response to the autobiography, *The Shark Net*, by Australian writer Robert Drewe. *The Shark Net* is an account of Drewe's childhood and adolescence in Perth, Western Australia, in the 1950s and early 1960s.

An important part of the book is Drewe's imaginative recreation of the world of Eric Cooke, who, as a serial killer, terrorized Perth during much of this period, until he was caught, tried, and hanged in 1963, the second last man to be executed in Australia. The fact that Drewe's family knew Cooke is one of the most intriguing aspects of the book, troubling what might otherwise have been a nostalgic account of growing up in Perth.

Daniel took up Douglas McClenaghan's invitation to recreate *The Shark Net* by producing a short section of the novel in the form of a graphic novel. In the part of the book which Daniel chose to recreate, Cooke, as imagined by Drewe, reflects on his often brutal family history as he disposes of one of his murder weapons by throwing it into the Swan River. Many of the students in the class chose to focus on Cooke, whose extraordinary story runs parallel with Drewe's account of growing up in Perth. He is not sympathetically portrayed in the book, but Drewe does seek to understand the man, showing how Cooke was strangely bound up with his family history.

Daniel's representation of Cooke emulates and develops the manga style of graphic novel. On this page, and throughout the text, Daniel obscures the character's face. In other frames, Cooke is only shown from a distance. This emphasizes Cooke's secretiveness, the hidden life that he lived for years.

The words in each panel are taken from the book. In a section just prior to the illustration included here, Daniel combines images of Cooke walking along the banks of the Swan River, evoking a sense of his loneliness and alienation. Cooke's hair is blowing in the wind, a 'heroic' feature taken from manga. Daniel creates an image of a self-absorbed character who is almost a kind of antihero, craving for both anonymity and notoriety. The image of Cooke in Figure 25.4, where he is gazing out beyond the reader, also recalls a manga hero. Cooke is not depicted as identifiably evil or cruel. The tightly framed close-up seems to convey a sense of sadness with which

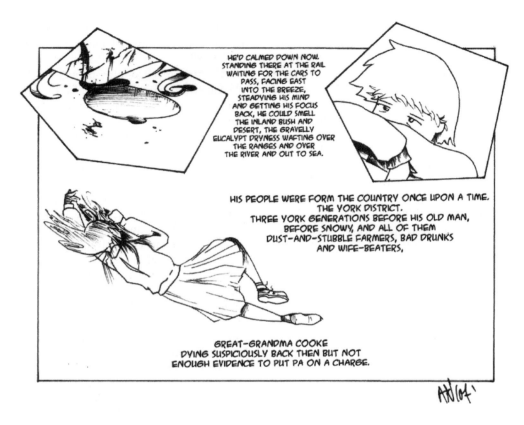

HE'D CALMED DOWN NOW. STANDING THERE AT THE RAIL WAITING FOR THE CARS TO PASS, FACING EAST INTO THE BREEZE, STEADYING HIS MIND AND GETTING HIS FOCUS BACK, HE COULD SMELL THE INLAND BUSH AND DESERT, THE GRAVELLY EUCALYPT DRYNESS WAFTING OVER THE RANGES AND OVER THE RIVER AND OUT TO SEA.

HIS PEOPLE WERE FORM THE COUNTRY ONCE UPON A TIME. THE YORK DISTRICT. THREE YORK GENERATIONS BEFORE HIS OLD MAN, BEFORE SNOWY, AND ALL OF THEM DUST-AND-STUBBLE FARMERS, BAD DRUNKS AND WIFE-BEATERS,

GREAT-GRANDMA COOKE DYING SUSPICIOUSLY BACK THEN BUT NOT ENOUGH EVIDENCE TO PUT PA ON A CHARGE.

Figure 25.4   Image from *The Shark Net* graphic novel.

readers might sympathize, but the obscured lower face also suggests that the character is hiding something. Moreover, the fact that he is looking at a point beyond the reader suggests that his needs and desires are something that we cannot easily comprehend, transcending any possibility of establishing a meaningful relationship with him.

The final image is grimly ironic. In Cooke's musings on his past, he recalls the history of violence against women in his family, including the probable murder of his great-grandmother. Daniel has chosen to focus on this particular memory. The image of a young woman lying dead reminds readers that a number of Cooke's victims were young women, and how his psyche is driven by his simultaneous attraction to and resentment of women. The power and continuing influence that an individual's past has over their lives is

a key concern in Drewe's book, and this has clearly resonated with Daniel. The picture links Cooke's horrific family past and his own horrific present, as the image could be interpreted as being both Cooke's great-grandmother and any of his female victims.

RESISTING THE CLASSIFIER'S HAND

What generalizations might be made about the content of students' writing from these samples of students' work?

Our aim in choosing such discrepant texts was precisely to capture a sense of the surprise which teachers experience when they find themselves confronted by writing which challenges their expectations in some way. Writing is often distinctive, precisely because it resists being classified easily. 'Writing', indeed, may be too limiting a word to describe the diverse forms of composition presented here (cf. Green, 2001). Yet, the professional landscape that currently prevails in most countries is one which places value on the need for things to be the same, to fall into some recognizable category.

As James Britton and his colleagues observe in *The Development of Writing Abilities (11–18)*, 'we classify at our peril' (Britton et al., 1975: 2). Having sounded this cautionary note, however, they go on to argue that 'the process of classifying seems an essential stage on the way to understanding our environment, or indeed responding to it even in more practical ways' (ibid). Their project was to refine our understanding of the categories that might be applied in assessing school writing, both the stages of development that enable us to gauge a writer's growth and those generic categories that try to capture the full range of possibilities available whenever anyone writes. Targeting 'an undifferentiated view' (p. 2) of writing which assumes that 'an English teacher has only to teach pupils 'to write' and the skill they learn will be effective in any lesson and in any kind of writing task' (p. 3). They nonetheless present their findings in a provisional way, acknowledging that the complexity of writing will always exceed any categories which might be brought to an analysis of it.

The Development of Writing Abilities (11–18) remains a fine example of research on the teaching of writing, especially at a time when so much weight is being placed on the importance of 'evidence-based' practice. Crucially, their focus on the process of writing still involves a recognition of the need for teachers 'to read what their pupils wrote for its own merits, and not with some hypothetical standard of perfection in mind' (p. 31). Their study continues to provide a framework for teachers to refine their response to students' writing in order to support their development as writers. Moreover, this support is conceived as an aspect of the social relationships that constitute any classroom,

as a place where (to borrow the words of Douglas Barnes) teachers and students come together to engage in 'meaningful communication' (Barnes, 1992). Later in their study, Britton and his coauthors argue the importance of the relationships that teachers form with their pupils, as a vital context for any exchange about their writing abilities:

> Every interaction with someone tells us something about that person; but when the interaction is between teacher and pupil, what a teacher learns from it leads not to a verdict but to further interaction. We need to distinguish writing aimed at a verdict from writing that is a link in a chain of interaction (p. 70).

This again serves to differentiate their aims from the literacy continua and assorted rubrics for assessing students' writing which have been developed since they published their study. All this seems to be directed at pronouncing a 'verdict' on the texts which students produce.

The journey, which the English teaching profession has taken in the intervening years, is reflected in the descriptor for Level 6 that has been quoted at the beginning of this chapter. The genealogy of statements, like this, obviously stretches back to texts like *The Development of Writing Abilities (11–18),* and yet far from providing a framework for interacting with any of the students whose writing we have been considering, it threatens to undermine the very possibility of such interactions. This may seem to be an extreme view—the samples of students' writing, which we have just considered, have, after all, all been produced within an educational setting that is typified by such outcomes statements, and yet they still resist being contained by those descriptors. However repressive a policy environment might be, students and their teachers are still capable of finding the creative resources within themselves to challenge its mandates, to escape 'the shades of the prison house'.

But if these examples of resistance have any significance, it is precisely because they open up possibilities which standards-based reforms deny. As long as educators remain fixated on benchmarks prescribing what students should do at each level of performance, rather than remaining alert to what their students are potentially capable of achieving, they run the risk of wasting their opportunity to engage productively with young people. That waste is reflected in the way the Level 6 statement fetishizes a disembodied concept of performance that is accomplished by no one in particular but represents the achievement of a group of undifferentiated 'students' who perform a predefined and predictable range of generic tasks. The general level at which such statements are couched conflicts with every teacher's sense that he or she is dealing with just this student, addressing just this student's needs, and attending to what just this student has to say. Despite the fact that students are constructed as the grammatical subject of the sentences that comprise this descriptor ('At Level 6, students write sustained and cohesive narratives that experiment with different techniques and show attention to chronology, characterization, consistent point of view, and development of a resolution. They write persuasive texts …', etc.), the real subject of this statement is 'Level 6', a reified concept of performance that actually displaces any appreciation of the rich specificity of the texts which students are capable of producing or the social interactions that form the context for creating and using such texts. Yet, this is not to say that such statements are ineffectual or innocuous. By mediating the relationships between teachers and their students, this descriptor forces teachers to hand down 'verdicts', rather than responding to their students' writing as a moment in their continuing exchanges with them, shutting down conversation rather than supporting it or opening it up to further possibilities. Such statements define outcomes without giving any indication of the process of reaching those outcomes, thereby eliding any recognition of the social relationships that form the indispensable condition for communicating in any classroom. Indeed, such statements construct classrooms as an undifferentiated

mass of students who all march to the same drum, and who all accomplish the same outcomes at the same time, in a steady progression towards the next level on the learning continuum, rather than as flesh and blood people who each bring different histories and values to their social interactions with one another.

We have argued that by refocusing on the content of students' writing it is possible to challenge this trend to classify their writing within a preconceived range of rubrics or stages of development. The samples of students' writing which we have been considering also show, however, that it is naïve to entertain any notion of direct communication with students in a world where social relationships are mediated in increasingly complex ways. A story is far more than a reflection of events, involving 'chronology, characterization, consistent point of view and development of a resolution' (as the Level 6 descriptor specifies), but an exchange between a storyteller and audience about their values and identities (Chambers, 1984; Reid, 1992). So it is with the content of the writing that we have been considering in this chapter. That content cannot be understood apart from the transactions between author and audience enacted by each text, which embrace both the social relationships of the classroom and the larger networks of relationships and situations in which author and audience are located. Moreover, this larger world is evident not simply in the form of identifiable 'themes' (war, drug addiction, or social alienation), but through the modes of communication that each text employs, as these students draw on the semiotic resources available to them in order to make meaning. In their different ways, each text probes issues of identity and community affiliation: Who are 'we'? Who am 'I'? What are 'my' obligations towards others around 'me'? Who are those 'others'?

To refocus on content means, in short, to refocus on the social relationships of the classroom, to regain a sense of the way classrooms provide a space for social transactions and obligations that exceed the forms of responsibility and accountability that characterize standards-based reforms. As Smith suggests, 'knowing the social' entails knowing the ways in which the social relationships that are enacted within classroom are mediated by organizational structures and controls, which stretch beyond the immediacy of any day or event, most notably in the form of benchmarking which maps students' writing against preconceived standards of performance. However, the samples of writing we have been considering also intersect with other networks of relationships that open up alternative ways of 'knowing the social', other ways in which social relationships might be enacted, even as they are mediated by official structures. Daniel's writing draws only partially on *The Shark Net*, incorporating other learning and experiences, most notably his knowledge of contemporary comic and graphic novel culture, locating his anxiety about a world which includes people like Eric Cooke within his own social space. Grace's text might easily be published on *You Tube*, as a powerful interrogation of our life styles and practices, confronting our culpability for situations beyond the horizon of the here and now. Janine's questioning of Jake (the 'you' who is addressed throughout her text) is arguably a more intensely personal dialogue—she herself wonders whether her text will be understood by an outsider—which nonetheless resonates with anyone who has lost someone dear to them.

This is to reaffirm a writing pedagogy which builds on young people's capacity to engage imaginatively and critically in the world around them, without in any way slipping back into romantic notions of individual creativity or personal expression. Referring to media education, Burn and Durran comment that 'the cultural worlds of the media leak in where they are least expected; children's developing tastes, pleasures and subversive intentions conspire to rock any neat program schools might try to set up' (Burn and Durran, 2007: 160). The writers of the texts discussed in this chapter have all drawn on their intertextual knowledge and experiences and used these in the mundane circumstances of an English classroom as a response to the invitation to write. The complexity of their textual productions demands that they be taken seriously. Rather than judging them according to predetermined levels of performance, as teachers we need to read them with genuine engagement, 'treating the student's piece as *artifice* or *craft*' (Sawyer, 2005: 143) and attempting to show 'the reading/responding mind in action as it attempts to make sense of the text' (ibid.: 140).

These texts challenge 'the classifier's hand', requiring teachers to respond to the lived experiences represented by them.

REFERENCES

Australian Education Council (1994) *A Statement on English for Australian Schools*, Carlton: Curriculum Corporation.

Bahktin, M.M. (1981) *The Dialogic Imagination: Four Essays*, Ed. M. Holquist; Tr. C. Emerson and M. Holquist, Austin, Texas: University of Texas Press.

Barnes, D. (1992) *From Communication to Curriculum* (second edn.), Portsmouth, NH: Boynton/Cook (first edn., 1975.).

Britton, J., Burgess, T., Martin, N., McLeod, A., and Rosen, H. (1975) *The Development of Writing Abilities (11–18)*, London and Basingstoke: Macmillan Education.

Buckingham, D. (2007) *Beyond Technology: Children's Learning in the Age of Digital Culture*, Cambridge: Polity.

Burn, A. and Durran, J. (2007) *Media Literacy in Schools: Practice, Production and Progression*, London: Paul Chapman Publishing.

Carr, W. and Kemmis, S. (1986) *Becoming Critical: Education, Knowledge and Action Research*, London: Falmer Press.

Chambers, R. (1984) *Story and Situation: Narrative Seduction and the Power of Fiction*, Minneapolis: University of Minnesota Press

Clyne, M (2005) 'Writing, Testing and Culture', in B. Doecke and G. Parr (eds), *Writing=Learning*, Kent Town: Wakefield Press. pp.120–128.

Darling-Hammond, L. (2004) 'Standards, Accountability, and School Reform', in *Teachers College Record*, 106(6): 1047–1085 (June).

Dixon, J. (1967) *Growth Through English: A Report Based on the Dartmouth Seminar 1966*, London: Oxford University Press.

Doecke, B. and McClenaghan D. (1997) 'Reconceptualising Experience: Growth Pedagogy and Youth Culture', in W. Sawyer and E. Gold (eds), *Reviewing English in the 21st Century*, Melbourne: Phoenix Education. pp.51–59.

Doecke, B. and McClengahan, D. (2005) 'Engaging in Valued Activities: Popular Culture in the English Classroom', in B. Doecke and G. Parr (eds), *Writing=Learning*, Kent Town: Wakefield Press. pp.247–267.

Doecke, B., Howie, M., and Sawyer, W. (2006) 'The Present Moment', in B. Doecke, M. Howie and W. Sawyer (eds), *'Only Connect': English Teaching, School and Community*, Kent Town: Wakefield Press. pp.1–3.

Graves, D.H. (1983) *Writing: Teachers and Children at Work*, London: Heinemann Educational Books.

Green, B. (2001) 'English Teaching, "Literacy" and the Post-Age: On Compos(IT)ing and Other New Times Metaphors', in C. Durrant and C. Beavis, *P(ICT)ures of English: Teachers, Learners, and Technology*, Kent Town: Wakefield Press. pp.249–271.

Grundy, S. (1995) *Action Research as Professional Development*, Murdoch, W.A.: Innovative Links Project.

Hamilton, D. (2005) 'Knowing Practice', *Pedagogy, Culture and Society*, 13(3): 285–289.

Kostogriz, A. (2005) '(Trans)cultural Spaces of Writing', in B. Doecke and G. Parr (eds), *Writing=Learning*, Kent Town: Wakefield Press, pp.104–119.

Kress, G. (2002) 'English for an Era of Instability: Aesthetics, Ethics, Creativity, and "Design"', *English in Australia*, 134: 15–24 (July).

Langdon, M. (1961) *Let the Children Write*, London: Longman.

McClenaghan, D. and Doecke, B. (2005) 'Popular Culture: A Resource for Writing in Secondary English Classrooms', in G. Rijlaarsdam, H. van den Bergh, and M. Couzijn (eds), *Effective Learning and Teaching of Writing: A Handbook for Writing in Education*, The Netherlands: Kluwer. pp.121–130.

Murray, D. (1982) *Learning by Teaching: Selected Articles on Writing and Teaching*, Montclair, NJ: Boynton/Cook.

Reid, I. (1992) *Narrative Exchanges*, London and New York: Routledge.

Sawyer, W. (2005) 'Becoming a New Critic: Assessing Students' Writing', in B. Doecke and G. Parr (eds), *Writing=Learning*, Kent Town: Wakefield Press. pp.129–148

Sefton-Green, J. (2000) 'Beyond School: Futures for English and Media', *English in Australia*, 127–128: 14-23 (May).

Smith, D. (2005) *Institutional Ethnography: A Sociology for People*. Lanham: AltaMira Press.

Victorian Curriculum and Assessment Authority (2007) Victorian Essential learning Standards. http://vels.vcaa.vic.edu.au/ (accessed September 2007)

Vygotsky, L. S. (1962) *Thought and Language*, Ed. Tr. E. Hanfmann and G. Vakar. Cambridge, Massachusetts: MIT Press.

Creativity and Constraint: Developing as a Writer of Poetry

Anthony Wilson

INTRODUCTION

The concept of progression within the poetry writing of children is a relatively new one within the field of research on writing (Dymoke, 2001, 2003; Wilson, 2005a). By far the most common literature on poetry writing by young people in the UK context is the practitioner-related 'handbook' (Wilson, 2005b: 20). Since the work of Hourd (1949), a tradition of this type of literature has arisen, which has been dominated by a mixture of poet-practitioners or inspired experts: Hughes (1967); Corbett and Moses (1986); Dunn et al. (1987); Brownjohn (1980, 1982, 1990, collected in 1994); Pirrie (1987, 1993, 1994); Rosen (1989, 1998); those collected in Barrs and Rosen (1997); Sedgwick (1997); Carter (1998a and b); and Yates (1999). As the word 'handbook' suggests, these books are practical in their approach, with an emphasis on imparting ideas for teaching poetry writing, which are then interpreted and adapted accordingly. Many of these also contain, however,

a good deal of rhetorical material, in which the author touches on elements of the theory, which underpins his or her own distinctive approach to teaching poetry writing. Of these, the best known in the UK are Hughes (1967); Brownjohn (1994); Pirrie (1994); and Rosen (1998).

This is also true of a significant literature on the merits of poetry practice, in terms of both reading and writing: Benton (1978); Wilner (1979); Stibbs (1981); Fox and Merrick (1981); Jackson (1986); Walter (1986, 1990 and 1993); Lockwood (1993); Taylor (1994); Clements (1994); Carter, 1996, 1997, and 1998a, b and c); and Rudd (1997). In describing this literature as rhetorical, one is drawing attention to the fact that research on poetry writing by children remains scant. Claims for poetry's importance within the curriculum, what Andrews (1991:128) summarizes as the 'jewel in the crown of the verbal arts', are largely based on opinion formed from practice rather than empirical studies. Some of the handbook literature, for example Pirrie (1994) and Carter (1998c), contends that poetry writing can be of benefit to young people, and does this in the context of arguments about the importance of its close study.

There is a small but nevertheless important literature based on research looking into teachers' views on teaching poetry. This suggests that for some it remains a problematic and even difficult area of the curriculum (Benton, 1986, 1999, 2000; Mathieson, 1980; Wade and Sidaway, 1990; Sedgwick, 1988 and 1990). There remains a gap, however, within the literature of writing theory as a whole, where poetry is concerned. Poetry does not feature in the models of writing established by Flower and Hayes (1980), Bereiter and Scardamalia (1987), Kellogg (1994), and Sharples (1999) leaving extant descriptions of its worth based not on studies of young people's writing but on rhetoric. This leaves poetry at something of a disadvantage.

One can only speculate upon the reasons for the comparative lack of systematic rigorous enquiry into poetry writing by young people. Perhaps the views and opinions of English teachers (Benton, 1986, 1999, 2000) are felt to be easier to research than the cognitive demands of poetry writing; it may be that critiquing problems with practice and/or curricular documentation (Walter, 1986; Benton, 1978) is perceived to be more straightforward than theorizing about such issues as progression and assessment of poetry writing, and planning for creativity within it. Furthermore, one could infer that poetry writing is not seen to be either important or interesting enough to study in depth; alternatively, one could hypothesize that poetry is felt to be too difficult a subject for close scrutiny, often allied to deeply felt personal experience and values and therefore beyond the scope of academic enquiry. One could argue, with Benton (1978), that the lack of serious enquiry into poetry writing, at least in the UK context, can be traced back to its depiction in the Bullock Report (DES, 1975: 135) as 'something odd, certainly outside the current of normal life ... numinous and therefore rarely to be invoked'.

POETRY AS 'KNOWLEDGE DISCOVERY'

The purpose of this chapter is to address this issue by reporting on a small-scale research study of the poetry writing of children aged 10–11. It has been argued before (Wilson, 2005a, 2005b, 2007) that progression in poetry can indeed be planned for and does not need to be seen by teachers as remote or impossible. Readers will be familiar with Bereiter and Scardamalia's concept of writing, moving from knowledge-telling to knowledge-transformation (1987; and Sharples, 1999). This chapter will develop those arguments further, by synthesizing writing and creativity theory with insights about young writers' use of language, form and models in poetry, to propose the concept of poetry writing as knowledge discovery. The chapter will argue that poetry writing can be an aid to language development, enabling children to engage with creative habits of mind and extending their schemas of what writing can achieve.

THE CURRENT CONTEXT

As a way of problematizing these issues, it is first necessary to report on the current context. In England, this is formed by the curricular recommendations in the National Literacy Strategy (NLS) (DfEE, 1998), the orders in the English National Curriculum (NC) (DfEE and QCA, 1999), and recommendations of the renewed Primary National Strategy (PNS) (DfEE, 2006). The status of poetry writing within the curriculum can be described as secure but mixed (Wilson, 2005a: 230).

This mixed status first became apparent with the orders of Cox (DES, 1989; Cox, 1991) who was of the view that poetry writing would never be found in formal writing attainment tasks, or Key Stage 2 National Tests, because it cannot be given accurate and consistent marks, and therefore levels, compared with other types of writing

(Wilson, 2005a: 231). Therefore, because poetry is not formally tested, it lacks the kind of rigorous assessment shown to other writing. As has been noted, this may be a contributing factor for the comparatively scant amount of research into poetry writing by young people. This would tie in with the findings of Benton (1986), who speculated that the comparatively low status of poetry writing is due to the uncertainty of teachers who find it difficult to know whether to treat their classes as artists/poets, or to respond as they would to other pieces of writing done in school. How far various curricular interventions have ameliorated these issues is discussed in the following section.

When it first appeared, the NLS (DfEE, 1998) contained the most detailed curricular material on poetry pedagogy to appear in the UK. The outline of progression within poetry writing which it implied was the first of its kind. It was far from perfect. While it offered a wide range of content, mostly in the manner of following 'conspicuous structures and forms' (Beard, 1999: 46) and 'models' (DfEE, 1998:48), the model of progression being promoted was one centred on poetic *forms* as opposed to handling of poetic *form*. Surprisingly, there were only two references to writing from first-hand experience (Wilson, 2005a: 231). Moreover, it could be argued that this privileging of forms was more about the forms themselves rather than the learning that they encouraged. To use the phrase of Jones and Mulford (1971), the NLS was not about engagement with form, but in a reversal of the Romantic ideal of faithfully reflecting on events from life (Wordsworth, in Heaney, 1988: 169), about replicating the forms themselves, apparently for their own sake.

By concentrating on a wide range of poetic forms, the NLS contained a great deal of material about how to solve problems within what Bereiter and Scardamalia (1987) and Sharples (1999) refer to as the rhetorical space thinking in the writing of texts, which seek to go beyond mere knowledge-telling towards knowledge-transformation. In theory, this would appear to be helpful for poetry writing pedagogy. The irony is that, far from giving teachers a better view of what poetry is, this concentration on forms, but not on how to use form as part of the meaning making process, came at the expense of a coherent view of content space thinking, what Sharples (1999: 23) calls the writer's beliefs about the writing topic. Thus, children were told that mastering poetic forms, from haiku and cinquain through to rap and choral poetry, was the goal, rather than exploring questions such as 'Why do we write poetry?', 'What are the challenges of writing poems?', and 'What do we learn when we write poems?' We could speculate that there was a concentration on forms as opposed to questions such as these (which are more focussed on purposes, and, perhaps, values) because they were felt to be less problematic to teach.

Evidence that responsibility for poetry's mixed status is also to be found within curricular orders (DfEE and QCA, 1999) must not be overlooked, however. It is encouraging that the NC promotes Cox's view of young writers learning, as it were, not mere technical mastery of language, but also the habits of adult or 'real' writers (1991: 24), with all that that entails about pedagogy of the writing process, from planning and drafting to revising and editing. It can also be argued, however, that the level descriptors for writing are unhelpful in describing progression for poetry, with little to guide teachers (DfEE and QCA, 1999: 58–9) as they make their assessments of poems by young writers, due to the imprecision and lack of differentiation in the language used (ibid). Furthermore, as Cox himself has accepted (1991), level descriptors are best used to assess the technical aspects of writing. Children's progress in the NC is measured via levels, and, since the introduction of league tables, these frame the debate about 'improvement' of teaching and learning in the UK context. It could, therefore, be speculated that teachers, seeing an assessment framework geared towards technical improvements within writing may well be tempted to spend little time engaged in the teaching and assessment of nontechnical writing, such as poetry, because of the tacit admission that it is harder to assess (Wilson, 2005a: 232). In crude terms, the system does not reward it. Indeed, there is some evidence (Henry, 2001; Ofsted, 2007) to suggest that this is now an established pattern, with teachers of 10 to 11- year-olds (Year 6) not including poetry writing in their curriculum until after their classes have sat the English (not Scottish and Welsh) National Tests.

THE INTERNATIONAL CONTEXT

England is not alone among English speaking countries, however, in presenting a mixed view of poetry writing within the English curriculum. Curricular recommendations in the State of New York, for example (The University of the State of New York, 2005) contain references to young children being required to write poetry only until Grade 3. The remainder of the curricular documentation for the State mentions poetry implicitly ('select a genre and use appropriate conventions, such as dialogue, rhythm, and rhyme, with assistance': 2005: 55), but only under the heading of 'Standard 2: Literary Response and Expression'.

It is also instructive to read the curricular recommendations for the State of Queensland, Australia (Curriculum Corporation, 2005) and the Province of Ontario, Canada (Ministry of Education, 2006), for they echo the approach of the NLS and PNS on more than one level. Firstly, and not surprisingly, they present poetry as one of many genres which learners are expected to engage with, including digital and other multimodal texts, in both written and reading (viewed) form. Secondly, there is a real attempt to build progression into poetry writing, but as in England, this is achieved through the use of models and forms with even less mention of writing poetry from direct experience. Of these two, the Ontario recommendations are the more consistent, moving from writing

a variation on a familiar poem, chant, or song, in Grade 1, to cinquains/shape poems modelled on the structures and styles of poems read in Grade 4, to original poems based on a model such as a haiku in Grade 6 (Ministry of Education, 2006: 44, 84, 110).

In New Zealand (Ministry of Education, 1994) poetry writing is also encouraged through the use of models, but in a context which also promotes poetry as a medium with which to explore film-making, performance, and writing from experience on similar themes (e.g., relationships and the environment). Notable among the foregoing recommendations, the New Zealand context for poetry writing also includes notes on assessment, which promote metacognition: 'students are to review their expressive writing to observe their own processes' (Ministry of Education, 1994:106). It is a rare example of what might be called a holistic approach to writing pedagogy, of which poetry is a part.

POETRY'S STATUS

This secure but nevertheless mixed status of poetry writing perpetuates what may be called a vicious cycle of indifference and, worse, ignorance, of its merits. This leaves teachers and researchers alike with little agreed language of how progression may be accounted for within it, and with no real sense of how it might aid language development. It is as though poetry's inclusion in the curriculum provides evidence that 'creativity' is thriving, despite findings (Benton, 1986, 1999, 2000) and views (Cox, 1998; Marshall, 1998; Leach, 2000; Alexander, 2003), which suggest otherwise. As Benton (2000) has said that poetry is being taught is not a guarantee that it will be taught well. The metaphor he uses to describe this is one of a 'conveyor belt'. This is useful in indicating a process of pedagogy which, ironically perhaps, places little emphasis on process itself, and concentrates upon the 'production' of poems, regardless of their worth, beyond their adherence to certain forms (Wilson, 2005b). To reassert the value of poetry writing with young people and to explore how poetry can be taught creatively, and with an awareness of development, it will be necessary to report on a small-scale piece of research.

EXAMINING DEVELOPMENT IN POETRY WRITING

Methodology

The theory proposed in this chapter is developed from a small-scale ESRC-funded doctoral study on teaching poetry writing at Key Stage 2 (KS2). This was based on an eighteen month period of teaching a class of children aged 10–11 (Year 5 and Year 6, in the UK) in a large combined school in Exeter in southwest England.

The research was a case study within the interpretative paradigm, and sought to illuminate the poetry writing processes of young children, as well as the pedagogy developed over the project. The methods one used to do this were qualitative. They included in-depth analysis of children's writing, semistructured interviews, fieldwork notes, diaries, reports and tapes of conversations, and triangulated observations (Bassey, 1995).

A central theme in the literature of poets talking about their work (Curtis, 1996; Crawford et al., 1995; Wilmer, 1994; Wilson, 1990; Koch, 1998; Brown and Paterson, 2003; Brown, 2004) is the valuing of risk-taking and experimentation within each poem as a sign of progress. Through close reading of the poems written by the children and by drawing on ideas raised in the literature, criteria were devised which were observable as signs of progress. These criteria formed two categories as a framework for analysing the writing: use of language and use of form. This became the basis for developing a coding tool, which was used to identify patterns and areas of difficulty across the group. (For further details, see Wilson, 2005a.)

Theories of learning

Underpinning the research were the constructivist theories of Bruner (1986) and Vygotstky (in Britton, 1987). In the former, we find the idea that, though a child is young and inexperienced, they may be instructed and become proficient in activities and ideas beyond their normal scope. In the latter, through the idea of the 'zone of proximal development' (Harvard, 1996: 39), we see the concept of learning being scaffolded by adults, in order that children may become self-regulatory and eventually independent (Harvard, 1996: 47, 40). Key to this, according to Harvard is the setting of goals by the adult, and their 'gradual and sensitive withdrawal from the regulatory role' (Harvard, 1996: 47). The poems by children discussed in the following section are analysed in the light of how far they can be seen represent these two key processes at work.

The cognitive load of poetry writing

Also underpinning the research was theory regarding the nature of poetry itself. The overarching aim of the teaching was to create a 'poetry-*writing*-friendly classroom' (Rosen, in Barrs and Rosen, 1997: 4, author's italics), where poems were read, discussed, performed, analysed, and brought in from home as well as written. Underpinning this goal was Auden's concept of poetry as 'memorable speech' (in Mendelson, 1996: 105), an elastic and scavenging form (Rosen, in Barrs and Rosen, 1997: 3) where risk and playfulness with language, including the appropriation of other forms of discourse, is encouraged. In terms of creativity theory, therefore, the practice sought to embody 'possibility thinking' (Craft, 2005: 19) and Andreasen and Powers' idea (1974) of 'over-inclusive' thinking, in which concepts or spaces 'coded as separate by most people [are] treated as belonging together' (Cropley, 2001: 38). Thus, the practice embodied the notion that poetry was both 'everyday' and a separate language (Koch, 1998: 19).

Koch's own example was a useful precursor in that he believed (1970, 1973), in the tradition of Bruner and Vygotsky, that children could learn the 'language' of poetry and become expert in it. This was important because, as has been stressed before (Wilson, 2007), the cognitive demands upon children of writing poetry are great. Not only do they have to unlearn the 'rules' of prose in order to apply what Strauss (1993: 3) calls its 'hedged-off area', in the current context they have to also unlearn the rules of different poetic forms each time they experience a new form or model. This may explain why children often revert to the use of rhyme in their early attempts at writing poetry, because they see it as the foremost quality which sets it apart from prose, and therefore the one they try to replicate, regardless of meaning. This may also explain, in part, why children find it hard to lay their poems out on the page as poems and not prose. Sharples (1999) and Kellogg (1994) both stress the importance of the organizational aspect of mental schemas in writing development. Children's difficulties with writing poems can perhaps be explained by their inexperience, and in cognitive terms by their limited schemas of what poetry can be, what it can include, and what it can look like.

Progress within poetry writing

Without detailed repeating what has been reported on before (Wilson, 2005a), the tools of practical criticism were used to discuss children's poems, but were rejected as a means of pronouncing on what they showed about overall development. This was partly for practical reasons. The idea of 'scoring' poems was found to be unrealistic and unpredictable and would say little about the progress being made. A more useful approach was found to be an extension of Sedgwick's notion (1997) of wanting to discover and praise individual moments within poems: or,

what Dunn (2001: 143), reporting on pedagogy with creative writing students, calls taking pleasure in 'small improvements and [...] flashes of the genuine'. Another influence was Sharples' idea (1999) of paying close attention not only to what children did better, but also to what they did differently in their poetry writing.

Long-term scaffolding of poetry writing

These signs of progress (Wilson, 2005a: 232) were organized into three strands: use of language, use of form, and use of poetic models. Wilson (2005a) discusses all three areas of progression; Wilson (2005b) reports on development in handling of poetic form; and Wilson (2007) reports on development in the use of models and literary forms. In the latter, I argue for a reconceptualization of the use of models to teach poetry writing, introducing them at points of developmental need. It is suggested that this could take two forms: early or direct scaffolding and long-term scaffolding. The former has been reported on (2007), so it is the latter of these concepts, which is explored in detail next, by looking at poems by children.

As Harvard (1996), in the preceding section, says, the hallmarks of independent learning are the increasing of the child's self-regulation and the sensitive withdrawal of the adult. These can be seen in the examples presented in the following section. They can be classified as poems written under the stimulus of modelled processes such as 'guided fantasy' (Sansom, 1994) (sometimes referred to as guided narrative), and deep or untutored modelling. It is important to point out that both of these pedagogical approaches occurred with most success towards the end of the project.

Guided fantasy is a writing exercise, which begins by being controlled by the teacher and ends with the child taking control of the material and form of the writing for themselves. The teacher asks a series of questions

('Recall a place that you know well. Describe it.', etc.), pausing to give the class time to write after each one. Through these questions the teacher takes the class on a journey, which is at once both general and completely personal to each child. At the end of a number of these questions and answers, each child will have a 'block' of writing as it were, which they are then invited to use as a starting point, by adding to it, or to quarry, by editing and refining. This exercise is compatible with Vygotskian learning theory, because it begins with goals set up by the teacher and ends with goals being explored (or discovered) after the teacher's withdrawal.

Deep or untutored modelling is the name given to poems which were written right at the end of the project, during a period of intense redrafting in which the class was encouraged to create a portfolio, which represented their best work from the project as a whole. In practice, these poems emerged as a result of children reading a range of poems for themselves, and choosing to write poems based upon them. As has been reported (Wilson, 2007), young poets have difficulty in 'going beyond' the model given to them. This can be because the model in question is not stimulating enough; or conversely because it is too strong in itself, allowing the young poet too little space to develop their own ideas, approach to the subject, or voice. Deep/untutored models have the advantage of being chosen by children themselves. This is also compatible with Vygotskian learning theory, therefore, in the sense that the goals and rationales of the writing are directed and regulated by the child from the start. The implications for a pedagogy which used this model are discussed in the following section.

Guided fantasy explored

Three poems which were generated using guided fantasy, are presented next. They are examined in terms of their own merits or signs of progress out of which a discussion emerges about creativity and schema theory in relation to progression in poetry writing.

Things are going pear-shaped

It looked like a music shop
An outline of 3 cellos in a turquoise blue
In a swimming pool
Like a pear in the fruit bowl
Don't go into a music shop with a turquoise
Background
    Tim, 10 (November)

Stimulated by guided questions about an 'art' postcard of a painting, this was Tim's second poem in the study. It is interesting because, although not very organized, the writing shows a willingness to take risks with language, through the technique of simile ('like a music shop'; 'like a pear in a fruit bowl') and the metaphor in lines 2–3. This was more than what had been asked of the class. The next example shows Tim's writing some 15 months later.

The Express

Pulling out of the London termini
The engine thumps
And the wind in my hair
Gets to 100
Passing nowhere
Brake with air
You whack off the power handle
And breaking madly
Crossing the Border of Scotland
Pulling into Waverley station
The lady saying "This train waiting"
Resting in the Scottish city
Pulling out of the London Termini
    Tim, 11 (February)

Since Hughes (1967) and Hull (1988), the idea has persisted in poetry pedagogy that what appears on the page is only a shadow of the original 'inspiration' of the writer, and thus their intentions can never be fully known. What can be observed, nevertheless, is Tim's use of rhyme, half rhyme, onomatopoeia, and repetition. Whether or not the rhyme in the poem ('hair/air/nowhere') occurs by chance is not known. Likewise, the half rhyme: 'station/waiting; city/termini'; and the assonantal 'madly/handle'. The onomatopoeic 'thump' and 'whack' seem deliberate by comparison, perhaps more closely allied to the actual speaking voice of the writer. The result of these sound effects is to emphasize and mirror the poem's subject matter, that of rapid movement, 'below the conscious levels of thought and feeling' (Eliot, in Andrews, 1991: 53).

In terms of use of language the phrase 'the wind in my hair/Gets to 100' is pleasing, a telling evocation of speed and excitement. This is formally of note also, the phrase stretched out across two lines, the line breaks slowing down the reader's experience of the moment. The description of the arrival in 'the Scottish City', with its longer lines ('And Braking madly/Crossing the Border of Scotland/Pulling into Waverley Station), and verbs in the present participle, has the effect of slowing down the reader, as the poem and the journey draw to a close. This is partly created by the way the poem uses only one 'idea' per line in the second half of the poem, a subtle and thoughtful use of form.

Creativity and constraint in guided fantasy

What gives the poem its 'finish and lift-off' (Heaney, 1980: 221), however, is the way it is bracketed by the same first and last lines. This has the effect of causing one to wonder whether this was an event that really happened, is imaginary, or is a foretelling of an event yet to happen. Together, these small signs of progress can show that there was development in Tim's poetry writing during the practice.

How far that development is due to maturation of Tim's other writing skills remains an open question. It is always a risk on the part of a teacher or observer to make claims based on the draft of another poet's work (Hughes, 1994; Paterson, 1996). It is instructive, however, to attempt to make judgements on Tim's poem in terms of recent poetry writing theory (Dunn, 2001). Writing on poetry and pedagogy Dunn uses three metaphors to describe progress. While Sharples (1999) is right to caution against using metaphors to describe writing progress, the advantage in

using them is that they can formalize that which we find hardest to express. Dunn speaks of 'surprising oneself' and 'know[ing] what might surprise others' (2001: 139); of 'saying things you didn't know you were going to say' (140); and of taking steps 'into the unknown or vaguely known' (142).

Taken together, these metaphors describe and embody risk in the poetic enterprise. They also embody great cognitive and meta-cognitive awareness, centring on the idea that it is a sign of strength and of developing maturity to discover what needs to be said, as it is being written as opposed to a plan created beforehand. Otherwise, in the words of Longley, one is in danger of 'merely versifying opinion' (1996: 119). The idea of surprising oneself, for example, demands that one has enough self-knowledge to make judgements about what would or would not be a surprise in a poem. On another level of complexity is the consideration of what would surprise others. This perhaps helps to explain why progression in poetry is difficult to demonstrate for children. Quite apart from wanting to please the teacher, it is as though there is a struggle not only to access and use stimulating material, but also to play with it and shape it so that discoveries about form and language and meaning making are made along the way. This is why guided fantasy has benefits as a strategy. It provides both the constraint required for creativity to take place (Sharples, 1999; Boden, 2004) but with enough freedom for playfulness to occur with language and form. The child is given two chances to make their writing surprising, not just one. It should be remembered that Tim's first guided fantasy poem, while showing signs of language-play, was fairly limited. This would suggest, as been reported elsewhere (Wilson, 2005a; 2007) that progress in this area is slow and nonlinear.

Flexible schema in guided fantasy

One of the central paradoxes of creativity is that in order for discoveries to make, while engaged in an activity, it is sometimes necessary to 'narrow down the possibilities at each step [of the journey]' (Sharples, 1999: 44), that is, to 'relax some of the constraints' or to begin again by returning to a previous point (ibid: 43). These creative habits of mind demand flexibility and a preparedness to take risks. They are what we might call inventive operational schema. Extending the idea of schema as cluster or map of ideas, this could be likened to a manual of instructions, which the writer develops and refines to produce a web of tactics that can help in solving problems. Tim's way of achieving this in 'The Express' is to do something at once very simple (he repeats a line; he 'back[s] up' (ibid) to a previous point) and very complex. This results in surprise or what Dunn (2001: 140) calls 'discovery'.

One cannot know whether it was a last minute decision to repeat it, or whether it was intended all along. It is an indication of significant progress, however, because of the discovery it represents in terms of the poem's content and energy; it literally takes the poem in a new direction and adds a further layer of meaning. Nevertheless, one can also speculate that it signifies discovery about the process of writing poems, that, for example, through the relatively simple technique of repetition, it is as though a whole new poem can come into being.

Knowledge telling and rigid schema in guided fantasy

In contrast to Tim's poem, it is useful now to discuss a poem, which resulted from the same stimulus, but does not display the same sense of adventure, and which is based on a limited operational schema.

The Feeling

It looks like a girl going on holiday for the first time.
It sounds like a scream or a shout.
It smells like a sunflower.
It feels like fluff or wool.
It tastes like a sweet strawberry.
It says 'I can't wait!'

It is surprised and jumpy.
Sometimes, it makes you feel sick.
Or nervous.
   Camilla, 11 (February)

This is an effective poem, which uses the techniques of simile and metaphor, some of which can be described as unusual ('like a girl going on holiday for the first time'), to describe without naming a particular feeling. In this way, it shows awareness of, while also engaging, the reader's interest by drawing them in to solve the (unasked) question, like a riddle. It is organized and purposeful, with one idea presented on each of its lines. Every one of its lines is a full sentence, except for the last, which makes an attempt at giving the poem a 'twist' both tonally and in its content. These are all signs of progress compared with Camilla's guided fantasy poem from earlier in the project. However, in spite of all of its felicities, the poem does not give off the same level of excitement, either with the material in question or with the process of writing, that Tim's demonstrates.

'The Express' is not concerned with making prose sense but with creating an experience. 'The Feeling', for all its reader-awareness, does not create an experience, but attempts to persuade the reader that one has taken place. In terms of models of writing already mentioned, the poem is stunted in its ambition by adhering, too closely, perhaps to the stimulus which prompted it, resulting in a knowledge telling approach. To refer to the theory of two major twentieth-century poets, Camilla's poem is unconscious when it needs to be conscious, and conscious when it needs to be unconscious (Eliot, 1951). It is 'forged' rather than 'hatched' (Heaney, 1980: 87, 82). Tim's poem, on the other hand seems to take pleasure connecting 'original accent' with 'discovered style' (Heaney, 1980: 43), and appears to have created purposes that break free of its original stimulus and constraints.

The problem with such discussions is that Camilla has executed the instructions of the guided fantasy to the letter in 'The Feeling'. It is a poem, which demonstrates that progress has been made, which nevertheless makes one aware of how much more could have been achieved. Unlike Tim, she has shown rigidity, not inventiveness, in her operational schema; and has produced a poem, which, while modestly effective, has not left the 'script' (Craft, 2005: 69) of the original draft. Her poem is, therefore, an example of how a creatively promoted constraint was used not as a safety net but as a straitjacket.

Freedom and flexibility in untutored modelling

Though they extended their range of the poetry language (Koch, 1998), demonstrating qualities missing from their earlier work, Tim and Camilla's poems illustrate that progress within poetry writing is nonlinear, not easy to quantify, and, above all, takes time to appear, even with careful scaffolding. Presented in the following section are two further examples of poems arising from long-term scaffolding, which also have mixed results. They are both based on poems by Allan Ahlberg. 'Slow readers going out' is based on 'Slow Reader' and can be found in Ahlberg (1983: 13); 'Bags I', which stimulated the second poem, is from Ahlberg (1989: 30–31).

> Slow readers going out
>
> I-am-go-ing-fly-ing-less-ons
> I-am-go-ing-bed
> I-am-go-ing-to-my-grand-
> ma's-house-and-never-coming-
> back.
>   Kezia, 11 (March)

This short poem, while demonstrating engagement with the original and a desire to use its techniques for new purposes, is a good instance of the difficulty children have in going beyond the model they have chosen. As in the original all of its words are hyphenated, and some broken up into separate syllables, to convey a sense of reading slowly out loud. Different from the original is that each of the poem's three sentences represents the interior speech of the speaker's head. Hinted at, but never stated, is the idea that

having flying lessons etc. would be preferable to being in the slow readers' group. Despite this sense of subtle sophistication, the poem is, finally, quite limited, with its ideas never reaching full development.

Also written at the end of the project in a phase of untutored modelling is 'Bags off'. This poem is of a different order to that of 'Slow readers going out', because it uses the chosen model as a jumping off point to create its own world, as opposed to journeying via a series of techniques or phrases, which in some way require replicating. It should be noted that the original poem is written in quatrains and has regular rhythm and rhyme. All that it shares with the following poem is the word 'Bags'.

> Bags off
>
> Bags off,
> Bags off heavens up above,
> Bags off soft white furry kittens,
> Bags off 7:00 o'clock in the midnight,
> Bags off my yellow sunflower,
> Bags off,
> Bags off,
> Bags off pigs flying higher and higher,
> Bags off babies crying,
> Bags off 2:00 o'clock in the morning,
> Bags off love flowers,
> Bags off.
>   Kezia, 11 (March)

The central technique is one of repetition, where the phrase 'Bags off' is used as a kind of battering ram to which other phrases ('heavens up above'; 'babies crying') are fused. In contrast to Tim, mentioned earlier, her poem gains impetus from explicit play with sound, via repetition, as well as meaning ('7:00 o'clock in the midnight'; 'pigs flying higher and higher'; 'love flowers') to create deliberate nonsense. Also, in contrast to Tim, there is no discernable autobiographical material in the poem, so it could be argued that it represents an adventure with pure form and meaning, requiring the reader to take it on its own terms and make of it what they will. As in 'The Express', Kezia demonstrates a flexible operational schema to achieve the effects she does. Viewed as writing from a model, one observes the confidence needed to depart almost completely from it. Viewed as an exercise in problem solving, it is as though the heavy repetition in the poem provides the constraint against which the 'free association' (Heaney, 1988: 142) of the wordplay can have full rein, where the 'tongue is suddenly ungoverned' (ibid: xxii).

Styles (1992: 74) has called children 'natural' poets. Drawing on Chukovsky's theory (1963) that a carnivalesque subversion of reality through repetition, role play, and use of metaphor are all observable attributes of young children's language, Whitehead (1995: 52) reminds us that 'language is not just a system for communicating and transmitting information'. This is arguably what Kezia discovers in the foregoing poem, namely, that confident and wholehearted wordplay can 'alert us to the poetry and incongruity which pervades our everyday use of language' (1995: 51). In terms of writing development, therefore, one could argue that it is paradoxically in their use of nonsense, where their language comes closest to the playful utterances of the very young, that developing writers are able to display greatest sophistication. This is perhaps a counterintuitive concept for teachers to reflect upon, for it challenges notions of 'linear' development. In the current pedagogical context, where the poetry curriculum is narrowed or even dispensed with in Years 6 and 9 due to the concentration on preparation for National Tests (Ofsted, 2007), it also acts as a reminder that 'attempts to by-pass [...] exploratory thinking by imposing adult information and realism too soon' (Whitehead, 1995: 46) disinherit both teachers and children from potentially rewarding experience.

Immersion and improvisation in untutored modelling

The foregoing poem, therefore, bears no semblance to the one it is based on. Yet, this poses a difficult question for teachers. Faced with writing of this kind, one could speculate that many teachers would express puzzlement and even incomprehension. The poem makes no attempt to observe the 'normal', 'poetic' niceties found in poems by children. Moreover, it can be said to represent progression in poetry writing for two reasons. Firstly, it is an example of flexible, self-regulated and independent learning, where the goals and rationales for the writing were devised not by the teacher, but in the child's own time and at their own pace. It is knowledge which is discovered and directed by the child. Secondly, while the poem was written quickly, it could be argued that it was based on a long period of immersion and 'incubation' (Wallas, in Cropley, 2001: 41; in Sansom, 1994: 60; and Nickerson, 1999: 418). To use a very old cliché, the poem is like the tip of an iceberg: what we do not see is the eighteen months of reading, sharing, discussing, performing, drafting, and redrafting of poems in which the child has been immersed and which lead up to this final period of work. One could argue that it is this which gives the child the confidence to 'improvise'. In terms of pedagogy, many poems which displayed little desire to go beyond the model were written before this poem, which was created for its own purposes.

This can also be explained in terms of creativity theory (Weisberg, 1999), which explains incubation in terms of 'immersion' (ibid: 236), in a useful analogy with jazz musicians learning to improvise:

> They learn other's solos until they can play them back effortlessly ... and this forms the basis for the development of the ability to go beyond what they have learned and to create new music. The new music may be related to the models that they have 'internalized', in the sense that often one can tell who has influenced a given player, but the new music will go beyond the music of the model, sometimes in relatively radical ways (ibid: 236–7).

Bruner (1979) describes this process as having the 'freedom to be dominated by the object' (25), where 'we get our creative second wind, at the point when the object takes over', where we 'permit[...] it to develop its own being' (ibid). It seems there are two kinds of immersion going on here.

Firstly, there is the kind suggested by the phrase 'long-term scaffolding', mentioned earlier, which relies on the patient and careful setting of goals by teachers, in the knowledge that progress may take a while to become visible. Secondly, there is the immersion of the child in the task at hand, perhaps below the levels of conscious thought, as Eliot would put it, where thinking is so rapid and intuitive as to be almost wordless. This is the state of mind, coupled with flexible operating schemas, which can allow children to make sudden progress in their poetry writing.

Writing about children's ability to use rhyme in their poems, Brownjohn (1995: 93) says that such development is possible '*if* they have received enlightened and informed teaching throughout their career' (author's italics). It would seem that much hangs on that small but important word 'if'. On one level, as Brownjohn notes, it has implications for individual schools' policies on poetry. On another, however, it requires us to consider that the deep immersion within and self-directed modelling of poetry writing actually begin much earlier in children's school careers, at the earliest stages, when language, sound, sense, and nonsense are most explicitly played with. The challenge to pedagogy in the current context, therefore, is to consider the notion that promoting poetry as 'the "wow" factor in children's language development' (Whitehead, 1995: 51) cannot be 'left' until the latter years of the primary school, when children's ability to write is more developed. Instead, it needs 'bedding [in] the ear with a kind of linguistic hard-core' (Heaney, 1980: 45) of nursery rhymes, nonsense, songs, tongue twisters, jingles, and riddles throughout the early years (Beard, 1999: 47). Without this foundation, it is probable that using more sophisticated models later on will have only limited effects.

Implications for pedagogy

Development as a writer of poetry can be described as the use of flexible operating schema in activities of long-term scaffolding which provide both freedom and constraint, and allow for improvisation and immersion. The implications for practice are serious, but need not be daunting. The main consideration, as analysis of the current context has shown, is that of time. In a climate where poetry writing is secure but not overtly valued, it is possible to imagine a situation where pedagogy remains concerned with replicating models and forms rather than the learning within them (Wilson, 2005a), and which are 'shortcuts' to poems being produced (Wilson, 2007).

For the deep and long-term scaffolding and the exploratory thinking which has been described to take place, there need to exist 'environments of possibility' (Grainger, Goouch and Lambirth, 2005: 187), where teachers' subject knowledge is considerable, as well as their 'pedagogical knowledge and awareness of the significance of creative contexts and purpose in teaching writing' (ibid). This can be described as a pedagogy of risk: as has been shown, development in poetry is slow and requires not only patience but also good knowledge of possible models and strategies. It necessitates an emphasis on choice. For children to develop flexible operating schema for writing poems, and therefore to have choices as they write, both explicit and implicit habits of mind need to be explored with them. The 'not wholly predictable' (Wormser and Cappella, 2000: 48) nature of poetry, far from being seen as a weakness, should be embraced by teachers and researchers alike. As Dunn (2001: 187) says, 'Inherent in such knowledge is that our choices narrow with every word we put down, and that these constrictions are opportunities for invention and virtuosity'. These can be present in the use of language, of form, and that of models, on a continuum from the commonplace to the effective to the ambitious. How we define invention and virtuosity, will of course, vary from person to person and teacher to teacher. What can be taught can also be observed, however, and the best place to start looking, however our views of it may change, is with those special moments when we encourage and 'identify the genuine' (ibid: 139).

REFERENCES

Ahlberg, A. (1983) *Please Mrs Butler*, London: Kestrel.

Ahlberg, A. (1989) *Heard it in the Playground*, London: Kestrel.

Alexander, R. (2003) 'Still no Pedagogy? Principle, Pragmatism and Compliance in Primary Education', *Cambridge Journal of Education*, 34(1): 7–33.

Andreasan, N.C. and Powers, P.S. (1974) 'Over-Inclusive Thinking in Mania and Schizophrenia', *British Journal of Psychiatry*, 125: 425–456.

Andrews, R. (1991) *The Problem with Poetry*, Buckingham: Open University Press.

Auden, W.H. and Garrett, J. (1935) 'Introduction to *the Poet's Tongue*', in E. Mendelson (ed.) (1996), *W.H. Auden, Prose 1926–1938: Essays and Reviews and Travel Books in Prose and Verse*. London: Faber and Faber.

Barrs, M. and Rosen, M. (eds) (1997) *A Year with Poetry: Teachers Write about Teaching Poetry*, London: Centre for Language in Primary Education.

Bassey, M. (1995) *Creating Education Through Research: A Global Perspective of Educational Research for the 21st Century*, Newark: Kirklington Moor Press/BERA.

Beard, R. (ed.) (1995) *Rhyme, Reading, and Writing*, London: Hodder and Stoughton Educational.

Beard, R. (1999) National Literacy *Strategy: Review of Research and Other Related Evidence*. London: Department for Education and Skills.

Benton, M. (1978) 'Poetry for Children: A Neglected Art', *Children's Literature in Education*, 9(3): 111–126.

Benton, P. (1986) *Pupil, Teacher, Poem*, Sevenoaks: Hodder and Stoughton Educational.

Benton, P. (1999) 'Unweaving the Rainbow: Poetry Teaching in the Secondary School I', *Oxford Review of Education*, 25(4): 521–531.

Benton, P. (2000) 'The Conveyor Belt Curriculum? Poetry Teaching in the Secondary School II', *Oxford Review of Education*, 26(1): 81–93.

Bereiter, C. and Scardamalia, M. (1987) *The Psychology of Written Composition*, Hillsdale, NJ: Lawrence Erlbaum Associates.

Boden, M.A. (2004) *The Creative Mind: Myths and Mechanisms* (second edn.), Abingdon: Routledge.

Britton, J. (1987) 'Vygotsky's Contribution to Pedagogical Theory', *English in Education*, 21(3): 22–26.

Brown, A. (ed.) (2004) *Binary Myths 1 & 2: Conversations with Poets and Poet-Editors*, Exeter: Stride.

Brown, C. and Paterson, D. (eds.) (2003) *Don't Ask Me What I Mean: Poets in their Own Words*, London: Picador.

Brownjohn, S. (1980) *Does it have to Rhyme?*, London: Hodder and Stoughton.

Brownjohn, S. (1982) *What Rhymes with 'Secret'?*, London: Hodder and Stoughton.

Brownjohn, S. (1990) *The Ability to Name Cats*, London: Hodder and Stoughton.

Brownjohn, S. (1994) *To Rhyme Or Not to Rhyme?*, London: Hodder and Stoughton.

Brownjohn, S. (1995) 'Rhyme in Children's Writing', in Beard, R. (ed.), *Rhyme, Reading and Writing*, London: Hodder and Stoughton Educational.

Bruner, J.S. (1979) *On Knowing: Essays for the Left Hand*, Cambridge, Mass: Harvard University Press.

Bruner, J.S. (1986) *Actual Minds, Possible Worlds*, Cambridge, Mass: Harvard University Press.

Carter, D. (1996) 'Peculiar Versions of the Species Song: On Individuality, Poetry and the Clwyd Poetry Project', *The Use of English*, 48(1): 1–12.

Carter, D. (1997) 'Clwyd Poetry Project: The Four Branches Project', *The Use of English*, 48(2): 108–121.

Carter, D. (1998a) 'Poetry, the National Literacy Project and Blake's "Tyger"', *The Use of English*, 49(3): 193–204.

Carter, D. (1998b) 'Metaphorical Worlds: On the Importance of Direct Experience, Metaphor, and Vision in Children's Writing', *The Use of English*, 50(1): 37–49.

Carter, D. (1998c) *Teaching Poetry in the Primary School: Perspectives for a New Generation*, London: David Fulton Publishers.

Chukovsky, K. (1963) *From Two to Five*, Berkeley: University of California Press.

Clements, N. (1994) 'Poetry on the Pulse', *Reading*, 28(2): 18–22.

Corbett, P. and Moses, B. (1986) *Catapults and Kingfishers: Teaching Poetry Writing in Primary Schools*, Oxford: Oxford University Press.

Cox, B. (1991) *Cox on Cox: An English Curriculum for the 1990s*, London: Hodder and Stoughton Educational.

Cox, B. (1998) 'Foreword', in B. Cox (ed.) *Literacy Is Not Enough: Essays on the Importance of Reading*, Manchester: Manchester University Press and Book Trust.

Craft, A. (2005) *Creativity in Schools: Tensions and Dilemmas*, Abingdon: Routledge.

Crawford, R., Hart, H., Kinloch, D., and Price, R. (eds) (1995) *Talking Verse: Interviews with Poets*, St Andrews and Williamsburg: University of St Andrews and College of William and Mary.

Cropley, A.J. (2001) *Creativity in Education and Learning: A Guide for Teachers and Educators*, London: Kogan Page.

Curriculum Corporation (2005) Statements of Learning for English. Carlton: Curriculum Corporation.

Curtis, T. (1996) (ed.) *How Poets Work*, Bridgend: Seren.

Department for Education and Employment (1998) *The National Literacy Strategy: Framework for Teaching*, Sudbury: DfEE Publications.

Department for Education and Employment and Qualifications and Curriculum Authority (1999) *English: The National Curriculum for England (Key Stages 1–4)*, London: The Stationery Office.

Department of Education and Science (1975) *A Language for Life: The Report of the Bullock Committee (The Bullock Report)*, London: Her Majety's Stationery Offfice.

Department for Education and Skills (2006) *Primary National Strategy: Primary Framework for Literacy and Mathematics*, http://www.standards.dfes.gov.uk/primaryframeworks/literacy/planning/, accessed 19/06/07.

Department of Education and Science (1989) English for Ages 5 to 16: Proposals of the Secretary of State for Education and Science and the Secretary of State for Wales (The Cox Report). York: National Curriculum Council.

Dunn, S. (2001) *Walking Light: Memoirs and Essays on Poetry* (New Expanded Edition), Rochester, NY: BOA Editions.

Dunn, J., Styles, M., and Warburton, N. (1987) *In Tune with Yourself: Children Writing Poetry: A Handbook for Teachers*, Cambridge: Cambridge University Press.

Dymoke, S. (2001) 'Taking Poetry off its Pedestal: The Place of Poetry Writing in an Assessment-Driven Curriculum', *English in Education*, 35(3): 32–41.

Dymoke, S. (2003) *Drafting and Assessing Poetry: A Guide for Teachers*, London: Paul Chapman Publishers.

Eliot, T.S. (1951) *Selected Essays*, London: Faber and Faber.

Flower, L.S. and Hayes, J.R. (1980) 'Identifying the organization of Writing Processes', in L.W Gregg and E.R. Steinberg (eds), *Cognitive Processes in Writing*, Hillsdale, NJ: Erlbaum Associates. pp.3–30.

Fox, R. (1996) (ed.) *Perspectives on Constructivism*, Exeter: University of Exeter Media and Resources Centre.

Fox, G. and Merrick, B. (1981) 'Thirty-Six Things to do with a Poem', *Children's Literature in Education*, 12(1): 50–55.

Grainger, T., Goouch, K., and Lambirth, A. (2005) *Creativity and Writing: Developing Voice and Verve in the Classroom*, Abingdon: Routledge.

Harvard, G. (1996) 'The Key Ideas of Vygotsky and their Implications for Teaching and Schooling', in R. Fox (1996) (ed.), *Perspectives on Constructivism*. Exeter: University of Exeter Media and Resources Centre.

Heaney, S. (1980) *Preoccupations: Selected Prose 1968–1978*, London: Faber and Faber.

Heaney, S. (1988) The Government of the Tongue: The 1986 T.S. Eliot Memorial Lectures and Other Critical Writings. London: Faber and Faber.

Henry, J. (2001) 'Warning to cool the test frenzy', *Times Educational Supplement*, November 2, No. 4453, 8.

Hourd, M. (1949) *The Education of the Poetic Spirit*, London: Heinemann.

Hughes, T. (1967) *Poetry in the Making*, London: Faber and Faber.

Hughes, T. (1994) *Winter Pollen: Occasional Prose* (ed) W. Scammell. London: Faber and Faber.

Hull, R. (1988) *Behind the Poem: A Teacher's View of Children Writing*, London: Routledge.

Jackson, D. (1986) 'Poetry and the Speaking Voice', *English in Education*, 20(2): 30–42.

Jones, A. and Mulford, J. (1971) *Children Using Language: An Approach to English in the Primary School*, London: Oxford University Press.

Kellogg, R.T. (1994) *The Psychology of Writing*, New York: Oxford University Press.

Koch, K. (1970) *Wishes, Lies, and Dreams: Teaching Children to Write Poetry*, New York: Harper Perennial.

Koch, K. (1973) Rose, *Where Did You Get That Red? Teaching Great Poetry to Children*, New York: Random House.

Koch, K. (1998) *Making Your Own Days: The Pleasures of Reading and Writing Poetry*, New York: Simon and Schuster.

Leach, S. (2000), 'Student Teachers and the Experience of English: How do Secondary Student Teachers View English and its Possibilities?', in J. Davison and J. Moss (eds), *Issues in English Teaching*. London: Routledge.

Lockwood, M. (1993) 'Getting into the Rhythm: Children Reading Poetry', *Reading*, 27(3): 50–53.

Longley, M. (1996) 'A Tongue at Play', in T. Curtis (ed.), *How Poets Work, Bridgend: Seren.* pp.111–121.

Marshall, B. (1998) 'English teachers and the third way', in B. Cox (ed.), *Literacy Is Not Enough: Essays on the Importance of Reading*, Manchester: Manchester University Press and Book Trust.

Mathieson, M. (1980) 'The Problem of Poetry', *The Use of English*, 31(2): 38–43.

Mendelson, E. (ed.) (1996) *W.H. Auden, Prose 1926–1938: Essays and Reviews and Travel Books in Prose and Verse*, London: Faber and Faber.

Ministry of Education (1994) *English in the New Zealand Curriculum*, Wellington: Learning Media/Ministry of Education.

Ministry of Education (2006) *The Ontario Curriculum: Grades 1–8: Language (Revised)*. Ontario: Ministry of Education.

Nickerson, R.S. (1999) 'Enhancing Creativity', in R.J. Sternberg (ed.) *Handbook of Creativity*, Cambridge: Cambridge University Press. pp.392–430.

Office for Standards in Education (2007) *Poetry in Schools: A Survey of Practice, 2006/07*, London: Ofsted.

Ofsted (2007), *Poetry in Schools: A Survey of Practice, 2006/07*. London: Ofsted. http://www.ofsted.gov. uk/Ofsted-home/Publications-and-research/Browse-all-by/Education/Curriculum/English/Poetry-in-schools/(language)/eng-GB

Paterson, D. (1996) 'The Dilemma of the Peot', in T. Curtis (ed.), *How Poets Work*, Bridgend: Seren. pp.155–172.

Pirrie, J. (1987) *On Common Ground: A Programme for Teaching Poetry*, Sevenoaks: Hodder and Stoughton Educational.

Pirrie, J. (1993) (ed.) *Apple Fire: The Halseworth Middle School Anthology*, Newcastle upon Tyne: Bloodaxe.

Pirrie, J. (1994) *On Common Ground: A Programme for Teaching Poetry* (second edn.), Godalming: World Wide Fund for Nature.

Rosen, M. (1989) *Did I Hear You Write?*, London: André Deutsch.

Rosen, M. (1998) *Did I Hear You Write?* (second edn.), Five Leaves Press: Nottingham.

Rosen, M. (1997) 'Making Poetry Matter' in M. Barrs and M. Rosen (eds), *A Year with Poetry: Teachers Write about Teaching Poetry*, London: Centre for Language in Primary Education. pp.1–5.

Rudd, A. (1997) 'Putting Poetry at the Heart of the Work', *The Use of English*, 49(1): 64–71.

Sansom, P. (1994) *Writing Poems*, Newcastle upon Tyne: Bloodaxe Books.

Sedgwick, F (1988) 'Talking About Teaching Poetry', *Curriculum*, 9(3): 126–134.

Sedgwick, F. (1990) 'The Management of Poetry in Education', *Curriculum*, 11(1): 5–15.

Sedgwick, F. (1997) *Read my Mind: Young Children, Poetry and Learning*, London: Routledge.

Sharples, M. (1999) *How we Write: Writing as Creative Design*, London: Routledge.

Sternberg, R.J. (ed.) (1999) *Handbook of Creativity*, Cambridge: Cambridge University Press.

Stibbs, A. (1981), 'Teaching Poetry', *Children's Literature in Education*, 12(1): 39–50.

Strauss, P. (1993) *Talking Poetry: A Guide for Students, Teachers and Poets*, Cape Town and Pietermaritzburg: David Philip Publishers Ltd and University of Natal Press.

Styles, M. (1992) 'Just a Kind of Music: Children as Poets', in M. Styles, E. Bearne, and V. Watson (eds.), *After Alice: Exploring Children's Literature*, London: Cassell.

Taylor, A. (1994), '"On the Pulse": Exploring Poetry Through Drama', *Children's Literature in Education*, 25(1): 17–28.

The University of the State of New York (2005) *English Language Arts Core Curriculum: Prekindergarten – Grade 12*, New York: The University of the State of New York/The State Education Department.

Wade, B. and Sidaway, S. (1990) 'Poetry in the Curriculum: A Crisis of Confidence', *Educational Studies*, 16(1): 75–83.

Walter, C. (1986) 'The Many Years of Telling: A Tradition of Failed Practice of Teaching Poetry in the Primary School', *English in Education*, 20(3): 32–38.

Walter, C. (1990) 'Sound in Content: Some Under-Regarded Possibilities for the Teaching of Poetry in School', *Education Today*, 40(2): 54–60.

Walter, C. (1993), 'A Better Way to Begin Together: The Value of a Comparative Approach to Teaching Poetry in School', *European Journal of Teacher Education*, 16(2): 179–190.

Weisberg, R.W. (1999) 'Creativity and Knowledge: A Challenge to Theories', in R.J. Sternberg (ed.), *Handbook of Creativity*, Cambridge: Cambridge University Press. pp.226–250.

Whitehead, M. (1995), 'Nonsense, Rhyme and Word Play in Young Children', in R. Beard (ed.), *Rhyme, Reading and Writing*, London: Hodder and Stoughton Educational.

Wilmer, C. (ed.) (1994) *Poets Talking: The Poet of the Month Interviews from BBC Radio 3*. Manchester: Carcanet.

Wilner, I. (1979) 'Making Poetry Happen: Birth of Poetry Troupe', *Children's Literature in Education*, 10(2): 86–91.

Wilson, R.E. (1990) *Sleeping With Monsters: Conversations with Scottish and Irish Women poets*, Dublin: Wolfhound Press.

Wilson, A. (2005a) '"Signs of Progress": Reconceptualising Response to Children's Poetry Writing', *Changing English*, 12(2); 227–242.

Wilson, A. (2005b) 'The Best Forms in the Best Order? Current Poetry Writing Pedagogy at KS2', *English in Education*, 39(3): 19–31.

Wilson, A. (2007) 'Finding a Voice? Do Literary Forms Work Creatively in Teaching Poetry Writing? *Cambridge Journal of Education*, 37(3): 441–457.

Wormser, B. and Cappella, D. (2000) *Teaching the Art of Poetry: The Moves*, New Jersey; Lawrence Erlbaum Associates.

Yates, C. (1999) *Jumpstart: Poetry in the Secondary School*, London: Poetry Society.

27

Becoming A Designer: Trajectories of Linguistic Development

Debra Myhill

INTRODUCTION

The concept of writing development in writers of age between 11 and 16 has received far less pedagogical and empirical attention than the development of writing in the early years and primary, and as a consequence understanding of what it means to become a 'better writer' in this older age phase is often limited to broad, generalized principles of improvement. In England, implicit in the national assessments of writing at age 14 and age 16 is a notion that development is characterized principally by the ability to manage a wider repertoire of genres and purposes for writing. Apart from the perennial concern for accuracy in spelling and punctuation, there is little that addresses development at a more precise linguistic level. Perhaps this is underpinned by a tacit assumption that linguistic development is a basic skill which is effectively addressed in the curriculum of the earlier age phases: the role of the secondary English teacher, therefore, is to extend the range and breadth of writing opportunities, often focusing on communicative concerns and genre issues, which operate more at text level than sentence level.

The association of linguistic mastery with basic or functional literacy is unfortunate, and parallels the association of grammar with error and correction. Thus, an impoverished view of linguistic development evolves, which reduces development to the avoidance of error or 'bad grammar' and the acquisition of functional literacy, itself a hotly contested concept. Moreover, this reductivist view of linguistic development is overlaid with professional antipathy and scepticism about the value of grammar in a writing curriculum, and opposition to policy frameworks, which appear to overvalue the importance of grammar in the writing classroom. In the words of Randy Bomer, Chair of NCTE (National Council of Teachers of English), '*English teachers do not see themselves as grammar police, on the lookout for mistakes*' (NCTE, 2006). These associations appear to be international. Elley et al. (1979) note, in New Zealand, a view that advocates '*strong doses of English grammar as a cure for some of our educational ills*' (1979: 3). In England, politician Norman Tebbit famously made a link between tolerance of grammatical inaccuracy where *'good English is no better than bad English'* and falling standards which provide *'no imperative to stay out of crime'*... (cited in Cameron, 1995: 94). Children's novelist, Phillip Pullman, satirically observes those who believe that *'teaching children about syntax and the parts of speech will result in better writing, as well as making them politer, more patriotic and less likely to become pregnant'*... (Pullman, 2005). We may have moved on somewhat since Elbow (1981: 169) argued that *'nothing helps [children's] writing so much as learning to ignore grammar'*, but the minutes of a recent meeting of the Linguistic Society of America with NCTE *'to discuss how to better integrate linguistics into the English/Language Arts curriculum'* note that NCTE was *'not eager to step in as partners in such a project (initiated by linguists)'* (LSA, 2006:1). In part, some of these responses are attributable to a tendency to use grammar as a proxy for other social values, and particularly the notion that if we teach grammar, we morally improve the nation. Cameron (1995) regards this as a view of grammar as 'verbal hygiene' and observes that the grammar debate has been less about grammar, than about *'the particular values and standards the idea of grammar has been made to symbolise'* (Cameron 1995). None of this helps a serious consideration of linguistic development in 11 to 16-year-olds.

Nevertheless, linguistic development in secondary writers is a serious issue. At age 11, young writers are on a trajectory of development, which ideally will continue not just to 16 but into adulthood. Their writing will continue to be influenced by their oral and reading experiences and their social experiences and emotional development. Few would argue that language development ceases at age 11, thus, the question of how language develops in writing beyond age 11 is important, theoretically and pedagogically. As Harpin (1976: 173) argued, *'syntactic analysis can offer insights into both the disposition*

of language resources and their employment. Such studies should be seen as a potent contribution to the knowledge base on which principled policies or programmes for writing development in school should be founded'. The purpose of this chapter is to address this issue, building on existing research on linguistic development, and reporting on a large-scale empirical study of the linguistic characteristics of writing in 13- and 15-year-olds. The chapter will illustrate that clear developmental trajectories in writing can be determined, which have implications for appropriate pedagogical or instructional designs.

EXTANT RESEARCH

The existing research on linguistic development in writing is patchy, to say the least, and much of it is also now rather old. Two large studies investigating development in middle primary were conducted by Harpin (1976) and Perera (1984). Harpin's study focused on writers aged 7–11 and analysed their writing against twelve linguistic measures, which addressed sentence length; clause length; subordination indices; the proportion of simple and complex sentences; nonfinite verb constructions in the main clause; uncommon clauses; and pronoun usages. His analysis indicated that the use of personal pronouns decreased with age, whilst clause and sentence length and the use of subordination increased. Perera's (1984) sample was similar, children aged 8–12, though the study itself was larger and more detailed and systematic. She noted that there was no clearly defined psycholinguistic theory of grammatical complexity, and her research considered grammatical complexity by considering the sequence in which children acquire constructions, on the basis that adult constructions are signs of greater linguistic maturity. Perera found that children's writing developed by moving from dependence on coordination to greater use of subordination, from using simple noun phrases to longer noun phrases with more complex structures, and from using predominantly active lexical verbs to making greater use of passives and modals. The younger writers in her sample sometimes encountered difficulties using causal and adversative connectives, and often overused the personal pronoun in subject position in the sentence. One area of linguistic mastery that seemed to be problematic across this age range was the use of reference, substitution and ellipsis, suggesting that this might be one aspect of linguistic development, which is secured in the secondary phase. More recently, Allison et al. (2002) investigated the use of subordination in writing of 5 to 9 year-old students. They found not only higher levels of subordination than had been evident in Harpin's study nearly thirty years earlier, but also coordination remained a strong characteristic of writing at this age range.

There appear to have been no large-scale, robust enquiries, which specifically explore linguistic development in children in the secondary phase, though several cross-phase studies incorporate samples from secondary (see section that follows). One study (Massey et al., 2005) does look at the writing of secondary students; though unusually compared with previous research, they look at linguistic development within an age range but across writers of differing abilities. Their research focus was exploring changes in standards in writing in public examinations over time, rather than linguistic development per se. They draw on examination scripts from different years and compare linguistic performance at different grade levels, and found that sentence length, subordination, and the use of simple sentences increased with higher grade.

Hunt (1965) and Loban (1976) both conducted linguistic analyses on writing from writers across the 5–18 age range. Hunt's study was small scale (just 54 children), and considered writing drawn from Grades 4, 8, and 12. He found no evidence that there were linguistic constructions, which acted as

markers of development, or which appear only in older writers. By contrast, Loban's larger longitudinal study of 211 children, from kindergarten through to Grade 12, found that factors that characterized language development included the use of longer sentences, greater elaboration of subject and predicate, more embedded clauses and adjectival dependent clauses, and greater variety and depth of vocabulary. An interesting cross-linguistic perspective on linguistic development is offered by an international research collaboration between Holland, USA, France, Israel, Iceland, Spain, and Sweden (Berman and Verhoeven, 2002). This project compared language production, both written and oral, across seven languages and 4 age groups (9–10; 12–13; 14–17; adults). Although this study raises some fascinating issues about the intrinsic differences between languages, it is what it reveals about linguistic development across the four age groups, which is most pertinent to this chapter. Stromqvist et al. (2002: 53) found that there was 'an important developmental leap between the 13 and 17 year olds' in lexical density and lexical diversity, which both increased between 13 and 17. Other findings, which have resonance with the findings of Harpin (1976), Loban (1976), and Perera (1984), were that clause length increased with age (Berman and Verhoeven 2002); subject noun phrases became more lexical with age, especially in expository texts (Ravid et al., 2002); the use of the passive increased with age (Ragnarsdottir et al., 2002), and syntactic complexity increased with age (Verhoeven et al., 2002).

There does seem to be some agreement across all these studies: it is evident that many linguistic constructions appear to increase in length or complexity with age: for example, sentence length, clause length, and the noun phrase. A less pronounced, but nonetheless significant trend is for there to be an increase in diversity, whether that be through greater use of the passive, lexical diversity, or an increasing ability to use an alternative to the personal pronoun in the subject position. Applebee suggested that development through the school years is characterized by an *'increasing degree of structural complexity'* (Applebee, 2000: 97).

However structural, or syntactic, complexity is not synonymous with either better writing or writing development, though it may well play a key part in that development. Writing, as a social communicative act, is more than the deployment of particular linguistic constructions—it is a meaning-making activity in which the rhetorical choices made create different shades and nuances of meaning for different audiences and contexts. Given the etymological root of text as *'textere'*, to weave, Allison et al. (2002: 109) aptly describe this as weaving *'the tapestry of vocabulary and grammar in ways which seem best to meet a particular communicative need at a particular time'*. There is no intrinsic merit in a complex sentence, or a long sentence, or a noun phrase expanded with adjectives: these are simply linguistic possibilities available to the writer as tools for shaping text. Haswell (2000: 338) argues that we should judge a sentence, not by its length or syntactical complexity, but by how effectively it is *'serving specific rhetorical motives'*, an argument which resonates with Paraskevas' belief in the importance of *'connecting grammar to rhetorical and stylistic effects'* (Paraskevas, 2006: 65).

INVESTIGATING LINGUISTIC DEVELOPMENT IN SECONDARY WRITERS

The research outlined in the preceding section indicates two things very clearly. Firstly, research, which focuses on secondary writers and their linguistic development is virtually nonexistent; and secondly, that linguistic development is about increasing both syntactical maturity and confidence in using those syntactical structures effectively in a specific writing context. Furthermore, research into writing frequently draws heavily on either a cognitive psychological perspective, or a sociocultural perspective, with less assured use of linguistic perspectives. The act of writing involves all three domains: writing is always a social communicative endeavour, embedded in a context, and mediated by social and historical practices. However, it is also a cognitive process, a problem-solving activity involving generating ideas, translating those ideas into text, and reviewing their effectiveness. Linguistic mastery overlaps both these domains, as language production is cognitive but the linguistic choices made in any text are influenced not only by linguistic capacity but also by social understandings of texts and audiences. The design of the study at the heart of this chapter was informed by this set of awarenesses and involved not just a linguistic analysis of text, but also an analysis of the social context of the classroom and writers' perceptions of their own cognitive processes.

The study was a two-year project, funded by the Economic and Social Research Council, which involved a detailed linguistic analysis of writing samples in the first year, and classroom observation and post hoc interview with writers in the second year. This chapter draws principally on the data from the first year, but full details of the project and associated publications can be found on the project website: www.people.ex. ac.uk/damyhill/patterns_and_processes.htm. The sample for the study was drawn from year 8 (aged 12–13) and year 10 (aged 14–15) students in six schools in the South-West of England. Two pieces of writing from standard classroom writing lessons were collected: the only specification regarding these pieces of writing was that it should arise from a lesson, which focused on teaching writing, rather than writing derived as a consequence of a different instructional focus. One piece of writing was a personal narrative, drawn from experience and the second an argument. Previous studies have looked predominantly at age as the key variable in development, but the Massey et al. (2005) study unusually took writing achievement or

Table 27.1 Summary of the sample stratification

		Good		Average		Weak		Total Y8	Total Y10	Total
		Y8	Y10	Y8	Y10	Y8	Y10			
Narrative	Boys	30	30	30	30	30	30	90	90	180
	Girls	30	30	30	30	30	30	90	90	180
Total Narrative		120		120		120		180	180	360
Argument	Boys	30	30	30	30	28	30	88	90	178
	Girls	30	30	30	30	30	30	90	90	180
Total Argument		120		120		118		178	180	358
Total Boys		120		120		118		180	180	358
Total Girls		120		120		120		180	180	360
Total		240		240		238		358	360	718

writing quality as the variable. We felt writing quality was a useful variable and, therefore, the writing samples were also categorized by writing quality. The writing samples were graded by the class teachers in line with national assessment standards in England, and the gradings double-checked by the Project Director. These grades permitted the stratification of the sample into Good, Average, and Weak writing by quality, and the sample was also stratified by gender. Table 27.1 gives a full outline of the sampling.

As with the studies reviewed earlier, the textual analysis at sentence level considered aspects of syntactical maturity, including sentence length, the use of subordination, and the use of passive. However, building on the methodological insights gained from an earlier study (Myhill, 1999), the analysis also looked in some detail at thematic variety and sought data not just on mean sentence length, but also on the length of the shortest and longest sentence. An outline of the variables analysed is presented in Table 27.2

In parallel to this quantitative data on linguistic constructions, the analysis collated qualitative data in order to attempt to make meaningful connections between statistical patterns discovered and their effectiveness in the context of the writing. Actual examples of all linguistic features counted were collated in a purpose-built database, permitting subsequent analysis, and a qualitative coding frame was used to capture observations about the way the various linguistic constructions were used.

CONSTRUCTING A TAXONOMY FOR LINGUISTIC DEVELOPMENT

A detailed description of the linguistic analysis of the students' writing can be found on the project website, cited earlier, and in Myhill (2008). In this chapter, however, I would like to move beyond data presentation to a more conceptual consideration of what the data means in terms of linguistic development in this age phase. Firstly, it is worth noting that the trajectories of development were more evident in the differences between weak, average, and good writing than in age-related differences, although the patterns of development between 13 and 15 broadly mirror the development pattern from weak to good. For example, the number of finite verbs used decreased between 13 and 15, and they also decreased from good to weak writing: but the strength of the difference was greater in terms of the writing quality than age. The range of achievement present in a secondary year group is wider than in the younger primary phase and it may be that age is a less helpful lens through which to view linguistic development in older writers than writing ability. In other words, what is it that good writers in this age phase do that weaker

Table 27.2 Outline of variables analysed in the study

Sentence length
 Number of sentences
 Number of words in shortest sentence
 Number of words in longest sentence
 Number of confused longest sentences
 Number of minor sentences
 Number of confused minor sentences

Thematic variety
 Number of subject openings
 Number of adverbial openings
 Number of non-finite clause openings
 Number of finite subordinate clause openings
 Number of fronted openings
 Number of *and, but, so* openings
 Number of cleft sentences

Text output counts
 Number of words
 Number of sentences
 Number of paragraphs
 Number of sentences per paragraph
 Number of words per sentence
 Number of characters per word
 Number of passive sentences

Clauses
 Number of finite verbs
 Number of finite subordinate clause
 Number of coordinate clauses
 Number of infinitive clauses
 Number of present participle clauses
 Number of past participle clauses

Other syntactical structures
 Number of subject-verb inversions (discounting questions)
 Number of subject clauses
 Number of nound phrases
 Length of longest noun phrase
 Number of coherence lapses

writers do not do? Significantly, in light of the international concern about boys' underachievement in writing, there were few gender differences evident (for a more detailed exploration of this, see Jones and Myhill, 2007).

In terms of conceptualizing linguistic development, the combination of the analysis of the quantitative and qualitative data suggests that it is possible to think of linguistic development in terms of three developmental trajectories: from speech patterns to writing patterns; from declaration to elaboration; and from translation to transformation. The three trajectories are not discrete, but overlapping, and represent a growing awareness of how words, phrases, and sentences can be shaped and manipulated to satisfy the demands of the task and the needs of the reader.

FROM SPEECH PATTERNS TO WRITING PATTERNS

The differences between speech and writing have been well understood for some time in linguistics research (see, for example, O'Donnell, 1974; Tannen, 1982; Halliday, 1985; Biber, 1988) although these are best *'thought of as trends rather than absolute distinctions'* (Crystal, 1995: 293). Syntactically, speech is more coordinated than writing, with long chained utterances and linear ordering. Writing is more lexically dense than speech and hierarchically ordered, with more integration, embeddedness, and subordination. An utterance is often incomplete or fragmented, with pauses, repetitions and ellipsis, whereas a sentence is complete: indeed, describing how young children learn to write, Kress (1994) argues that *'the sentence belongs to writing'* and that this is an important understanding to be acquired. Perera's research (1986) found that by the age of 8, children could discriminate quite confidently between speech and writing, using *'specifically oral constructions'* in speech and in writing *'grammatical constructions that are more advanced than those they use in speech'* (1986: 91). Writers in the upper end of the primary phase, therefore, know that writing is not speech written down. Nevertheless, the process of discriminating between speech and writing, and making appropriate choices for the text purpose and reader is more complex than this. Writing is a more abstract process than talking and is essentially monologic, though the writer has to imagine how the text might appear to a reader. This involves being able *'to elaborate semantic content voluntarily and consciously, and to select syntactic structures carefully: the writer has to take into account the knowledge that he or she shares with the audience'* (Lacasa et al., 2001:135). Moreover, as writers, children draw on their oral experiences and these influences do not always help them in developing mastery of written forms. Kress (1994), for example, points out that children from the professional classes have an advantage in learning to write because *'the structure of the spoken form of their dialects is very strongly influenced by the structures of writing'* (1994:3). Within our sample of secondary writing, it was evident that learning how to express ideas and thoughts in writing in ways, which do not simply mirror spoken patterns was reflected in the differing linguistic characteristics of good, average, and weak writing.

At word level, there were statistically significant differences in word length, with good writing presenting longer words. Whilst it would be unwise to suggest that the longer the words the better the writing, in English, longer words are often of Latinate or Greek origin, in contrast to the tendency for Anglo-Saxon words to be shorter. In formal writing, such as argument, it is frequently Latinate words, which establish the more formal written register, and one strategy for creating formality is to use Latinate synonyms for Anglo-Saxon words. Moreover, the shorter Anglo-Saxon words tend to be more typical of speech than writing. Where students were writing on the same topic, there were sometimes examples where the stronger writing used a longer Latinate word and the weaker writing used a shorter word, for example, *substances* and *stuff*, *environment* and *place*, *negative* and *bad*. In the personal narratives, longer words were often associated with a greater facility to describe personal feelings or to provide other descriptive detail for the reader, as in the following extract:

My progression along the narrow ledge was indeed noticeable, and it got a lot easier to walk

on and keep my balance the further I went. In fact, I was beginning to speed up now that I had walked some distance, and all of my fear almost vanished, as though it had just evaporated into thin air, vaporised by this new surge of confidence, which I had just received. That was, of course, until I reached my final destination on the route that I had just come along.

At times, signs of developmental growth are evident in attempts to use ambitious vocabulary, even though the choice may not quite succeed, as with *enhanced* in the extract that follows:

These made the path even more slippery and enhanced my thoughts of what would happen to me if I too, just like the water, went over the edge of the path and hit those deadly rocks.

Put simply, one element of linguistic development in writing is learning to make vocabulary choices in writing of words that you would be less likely to use in speech.

Another linguistic marker, which appears to be related to oral patterns influencing writing was the use of *like* as a subordinator, where another writer would use *as though* or *just as*. In Standard English, it would generally be accepted that *like* was not appropriate when used as a subordinator (though it may well become acceptable in due course) and there were no occurrences of *like* used in this way in the good writing, and few in average writing. The following two sentences exemplify the way *like* was used, and again reflect an oral usage which is very common:

I could smell the sweet smell of lavender, like I was standing in a herb garden.
    It seemed like he had stopped trying to get him and gone away.

A final linguistic pattern, which appeared to have a connection with oral patterns, was the tendency of weaker writing to be more dependent upon coordination as the joining principle of their sentences. This reflects both the linearity and chaining of spoken utterances, and the patterns of oral reportage: it is characteristic of telling, rather than writing. In the two extracts that follow, it is possible to see development even though both overuse coordination. The first example, typical of the weakest writing, is a 64-word multiple sentence with five coordinating conjunctions, which has the effect of chaining together several ideas, which would have benefited from separation. The second example, more typical of average writing, is a 60-word extract with four coordinating conjunctions. This is, however, divided into five sentences and makes use of the asyndetic coordinating comma, which was rare in the weakest writing. Nevertheless, the coordination makes the writing very linear and chronological, and the tendency to sentence boundaries after two clauses creates repeated two-part sentences, which are rhythmically flat.

It took me Quite a while to get used to the people *but* i soon got used to everyone there *and* i fitted in Quite nicely *but* sometimes it does get a bit worrying for me because I wreckon that everybody will be horrible to me *but* if im not horrible to them they won't be horrible to me *or* that's what i thought!!!

When we came out we stayed up *and* watched the stars, then fell asleep. The next morning we got up *and* walked around. We went for a walk *and* a spin in the speed boat. We packed our stuff in our boat *and* went into Salcombe. As we got there mum arrived to take our stuff *and* we went home.

There were, of course, examples of good writing where coordination was used very effectively, as in the next example, where the repetition enhances the meaning

I cried and cried and cried.

FROM DECLARATION TO ELABORATION

One aspect of writing development is becoming increasingly able to provide the reader with the appropriate detail required, and this usually involves a movement from a simple declaration or statement to a more elaborated statement. Another aspect is managing information and ideas appropriately on behalf of the reader to ensure clarity of communication. On one level, this might be thought to be reflected in sentence length. Several of the

earlier studies in linguistic development had found that sentence length increased with age (Loban, 1976; Harpin, 1976) and indeed this was confirmed in our study where sentence length increased at a statistically significant level between age 13–14 and age 15–16. However, two other findings run counter to the principle that sentence length per se is of any developmental significance. Firstly, when the analysis considered differences by writing quality, there were no significant differences in sentence length between texts of differing quality. Secondly, the qualitative analysis evaluated whether any of the long sentences present in the writing were confused or showing coherence lapses: writing of weaker quality showed a greater tendency towards this. In other words, many weaker texts contained long sentences, which were unable to communicate meaningfully and effectively. This supports the notion, expressed earlier, that whilst syntactical maturity may indeed develop with age, this is not necessarily concomitant with linguistic development in terms of writing effectiveness. Indeed, as will be outlined further in the next section, the use of short and minor sentences for rhetorical impact was a characteristic of the higher quality writing. What does appear to be developmentally significant is the ability to manage complex ideas expressed in long sentences. In the following two sentences, the first, from a good piece of writing, uses punctuation, coordination and subordination to present the proposition clearly; in contrast, the second sentence, from a weaker piece of writing struggles to express ideas and control coherence and has a particular difficulty managing the relative subordinate 'that' clauses.

However, some people might argue that these cases do not outweigh the benefits of euthanasia and that, compared to the number of satisfied people who have taken advantage of the system, these unfortunate cases are very much in the minority.

The fear about euthanasia is that some people may be persuaded into euthanasia through bad advice or by feeling that they are a burden to the family or society, with that many doctors, nurses and other people believe that every life has hope and that any life is better than no life at all.

More significant, in terms of linguistic development was what was happening within the sentence at clause or phrase level. One linguistic measure, the use of finite verbs, showed statistically significant differences, with weak writing presenting a markedly higher frequency of finite verbs per 100 words. The qualitative analysis indicated that this was principally due to the absence of explanatory or reflective detail, and in narrative, it often meant the writing was very plot-driven, with limited descriptive or emotional contextualization. This is exemplified in the two extracts given next. The first is 165 words long with 20 finite verbs and the second is 146 words with 11 finite verbs: the underlining of the finite verbs makes the greater frequency in the first extract visually apparent. The first example reveals some of the tendencies already outlined as characteristic of more limited linguistic development: overdependence on coordination, difficulty managing ideas over long sentences, and coherence lapses. However, the higher use of finite verbs is indicative of an attempt by the writer to drive the argument forward without giving justificatory or explanatory expansion. The very long single-sentence second paragraph, for example, introduces at least three arguments but does not pause to expand each argument. The use of '*or possibly*' and '*or even with*' as coordinating connectives exacerbates the feeling of an accumulation of arguments, rather than clear exposition of arguments. There is one nonfinite clause (*trying to ban brand new perfumes*) and, in general, the noun phrases are short. The second example, however, presents fewer finite verbs, because the argument is elaborated and counter-pointing arguments clearly presented (as signalled by '*This said* ...'). Longer noun phrases provide explanatory detail (*the main object. ...; the uproar, confusion and disruption* ...) and the reader is positioned to see alternative viewpoints (*a far greater detrimental impact*; *uncomfortable and restricting school uniform*). The use of

nonfinite clauses offers the reader justificatory arguments (*to achieve their maximum potential*) and further detail (*becoming obsessed with their outward appearance*).

Extract 1

I think animal testing *is* wrong. Because animals feel pain. etc, Just like we *do* so the *want* to risk a problem with a animal such as some kind of desise on them or even poison them to die. it *may* be unintentional but they *are* unfaire on animals Just because they are different to us because the *arnt* as smart and some of them *are* dependent on us for survival.

It is necessary to test these thing's on animals because if we, *test* them on humans they *may* get desies, or possibly die and that *will* cause problem's with familys or even with Goverment trying to band brand new perfumes that *wasnt* been tested so it *would* be less trouble if we on animal *gets* a reaction from this.

Thank you for your concern or the animal's but we *have* taken all of the problems to mind so that's why we *do* this to animals so we *may* find a cure for different disieses.

Extract 2

Clearly, the main object of pupils attending schools and other educational institutions *is* to gain qualifications which *will* lead to well paid and powerful jobs in the "society of tomorrow", of which they *will* be a part. To achieve their maximum potential, it *is* almost certainly crucial for them to effectively process and store all the information that *is* being passed on to them each day. Many people *would* argue that it is impossible for students to do this whilst wearing an uncomfortable and restricting school uniform. This said, there are those who *maintain* that the uproar, confusion and disruption that *would* be caused by pupils becoming obsessed with their outward appearance, and turning school into a bizarre type of fashion parade, *would* have a far greater detrimental impact on the education of the pupils in question than the slight discomfort *caused* by any school uniform.

In addition, the second piece of writing uses expansion skilfully to counterpoint with brevity in order to give weight to the argument proposed: consider the '*uproar, confusion and disruption*', the pupils '*obsessed with their outward appearance*', and the '*bizarre type of fashion parade*' set against the '*slight discomfort*' of school uniform.

FROM TRANSLATION TO TRANSFORMATION

Bereiter and Scardamalia's (1987) distinction between knowledge-telling and knowledge-transforming will be familiar to most readers. Their work with young novice writers suggested that the developmental trajectory was from writing sentence by sentence, focusing principally on what information is to be conveyed, to shaping sentences and text with the reader in mind. Kroll (1978) argued that the knowledge-telling phase was one of cognitive egocentrism, whereas Pea and Kurland (1987: 293) describe knowledge-telling as a *memory dump*. It was evident in our study that the weakest writing, even at the secondary phase, exhibited many of the characteristics of the knowledge-telling phase, with little evidence of rhetorical choices or shaping. It is possible to consider knowledge-transformation as, in part at least, about linguistic development specifically in terms of how sentences are shaped and patterned. Or, put another way, how writers develop from translating verbal ideas into a linear sentence to transforming verbal ideas into sentences, which have both content and rhetorical impact.

One area that emerged as a marker of linguistic development was thematic variety: the theme is the left-most constituent of the sentence, the starting point, and the rheme is everything, which follows in the sentence. Brown and Yule (1983) note the principle of linearization in writing, namely that '*what the writer puts first will influence the interpretation of everything else that follows*' (1983: 133). The statistical analysis of our data revealed that weak writing was more likely to have a subject theme, whereas better writing varied the theme, transforming the communicative content for the reader. The repetition of sentences beginning with a subject, as in the following example, establishes a rather flat textual rhythm and makes no real attempt to influence how the reader will read that text: in narrative, it was frequently associated with a heavy use of chronology as a narrative organizing principle.

> We were off to the beach called Sunny Cove. The wind was blowing in our faces. We are finally there. I set up the tent and looked around. I was a bit scared but it was quite fun.

Developmentally, it appears that the adverbial is the first linguistic construction to be used as a variant on the subject theme, as the best writing of 12–13 year olds and the average writing of 14–15 year olds presented more adverbials than the other writing samples. This may, of course, be because adverbials, certainly in England, are taught more than other possible ways of beginning sentences. The good writing of 14 to 15-year-olds not only used adverbials but also had a wider repertoire of thematic constructions, including nonfinite clauses, subordinate clauses and inversions. In the next example, two of the sentences open with a subordinate clause and one uses ellipsis with an adverbial start (*not just ...*). The final sentence is an inversion, and by shifting the subject to the end of the sentence, it is given prominence or end-weight (Leech and Svartvik, 1975: 174)

> When I was young, I was like a mouse. Not just because I was small, but because I didn't stop moving. My head was like a fairground. The big wheel was spinning in my brain. Something always told me that I had go get up and run somewhere, and that is exactly what I always did. When you're young (and we're talking about three here), there is a lot to discover. One of those things is stairs.

Closely linked with thematic variety was the rhetorical use of sentences of varied length. It is worth noting in the two examples cited in the foregoing section that in the first, all the sentences not only have related subject starts but they are also very similar in length: in contrast, the second has more varied length allowing the writer to create a better textual rhythm. In the most confident writing, sequences of short sentences were used to generate pace, and long and short sentences were juxtaposed for emphasis or effect. This often included the use of minor sentences, as exemplified next.

> The cellar is illuminated for a few seconds as the bulb flashes and goes out. An after-image is all that is left as the dim light is extinguished. An abandoned duvet is in the middle of the floor. A few dusty carpet squares in the corner. More dust.
>   I remember it like it was yesterday. The boredom. Fear. Grown men stumbling and slipping in the mud like a child taking its first steps. Every time I think about it a cold shiver runs down my spine. All the sadness, remorse and loneliness comes rolling back to me like a ball rolling down a hill.

Another linguistic feature evident in the foregoing examples is the effective use of the simple sentence. Repeated earlier studies (e.g., Harpin, 1976; Perera, 1984; Allison et al., 2002) have suggested that the use of subordination increases with age, though the data is strongest in studies focused on the primary age range. Our data disclosed no significant difference between the two age groups in use of subordination but a significant statistical difference did emerge between writing at the different quality levels. However, this reverses the expected pattern with good writing making less use of subordination than either average or weak. The qualitative analysis suggests that this is because the most able writers are transforming their text, not only through the expansion to provide detail, as evidenced earlier, but also through the use of both brevity and syntactical simplicity in simple sentences. The propensity towards over-long sentences often with poorly managed subordination was a marker of weaker writing, as we have seen. Thus, linguistic development is arguably not about an ever-increasing use of subordination but about mastery and control of subordination, where appropriate, set alongside judicious use of simple sentences.

WRITERS AS DESIGNERS

Developing as a writer in the secondary phase can, therefore, be described as a process of moving along the trajectories from speech patterns to writing patterns, from declaration to elaboration, and from translation to transformation. These are complementary and overlapping trajectories: thematic variety is an example of transforming sentences but the lack of thematic variety may well owe its origins to the dominance of the subject start to utterances in speech. It is possible, however, to integrate all three trajectories within an overarching principle of linguistic development—the principle of becoming a designer of writing. Sharples (1999) conceptualized writing as an act of creative design, in which writing is viewed as a problem-solving activity with a design solution. This notion of writing as design and writers as designers is implicit in Kellogg's (2006) development of Bereiter and Scardamalia's concepts of knowledge-telling and knowledge-transforming. To these, Kellogg adds a third developmental concept, knowledge-crafting, which is the final stage of writing development. He distinguishes between the three stages by drawing attention to the widening focus of the writer's attention as s/he writes—a knowledge-teller is author-focused, a knowledge-transformer is author and text-focused, and a knowledge-crafter is author, text, and reader-focused. At this stage, a writer can '*represent and manipulate the author's ideas, the text's meaning, and the imagined reader's interpretation of the text*' (Kellogg, 2006). Paraskevas (2006) expresses the same idea through the analogy of being an apprentice to a craft, where writers learn how to craft sentence and texts to satisfy their rhetorical purposes.

The connection between design and the visual presentation of written texts is the most common association (Kress and van Leeuwen, 1996; Tonfoni, 1994) but the exclusion of the verbal and the linguistic weakens the conceptualization of writing as design: '*it is important that the notion of designing embraces not only visual and presentational choices, but linguistic choices too*' (Maun and Myhill, 2005: 9). Linguistic development in the secondary phase is, thus, about acquiring the possibilities of choice, about having a design repertoire to draw upon, and about crafting sentences and texts to satisfy the rhetorical demands of the task. The pedagogical implications of this are that teaching writing with linguistic development in mind should not be about grammatical rules, error correction, or formulaic approaches to effectiveness: rather, enabling teaching will focus on extending writers' understanding of the range of options and possibilities available to them and encouraging discussion about the links between linguistic choices, rhetorical impact, and the communication of meaning. If we help maturing writers gain access to a repertoire of design choices, we may also help them to realize, as did Hemingway (1961), that *'we are all apprentices in a craft where no-one ever becomes master'*.

REFERENCES

Allison, P., Beard, R., and Willcocks, J. (2002) 'Subordination in Children's Writing,' *Language in Education*, 16(2): 97–111.

Applebee, A. (2000) 'Alternative Models of Writing Development', in R. Indrisano and J Squire (eds), *Perspectives on Writing: Research, Theory and Practice*, Newark, Delaware: IRA. pp.90–111.

Bereiter, C. and Scardamalia, M. (1987) *The Psychology of Written Composition*, Hillsdale, NJ: Lawrence Erlbaum Associates.

Berman, R.A. and Verhoeven, L. (2002) 'Cross-Linguistic Perspectives on the Development of Text Production Abilities: Speech and Writing', *Written Language and Literacy*, 5(1): 1–43.

Biber, D. (1988) *Variation across Speech and Writing*, Cambridge: Cambridge University Press.

Brown, G. and Yule, G. (1983) *Discourse Analysis*, Cambridge: Cambridge University Press.

Cameron, D. (1995) *Verbal Hygiene*, London: Routledge.

Crystal, D. (1995) *The Cambridge Encyclopedia of the English Language*, Cambridge: Cambridge University Press.

Elbow, P. (1981) *Writing with Power: Techniques for Mastering the Writing Process*, New York: Oxford.

Elley, W.B., Barham, I.H., Lamb, H., and Wylie, M. (1979) 'The Role of Grammar in a Secondary School', *Curriculum Educational Research Series No 60*, Wellington: New Zealand Council for Educational Research.

Halliday, M.A.K. (1985) *Spoken and Written Language*, Oxford: Oxford University Press.

Harpin, W. (1976) *The Second R: Writing Development in the Junior School*, London: Unwin.

Harpin, W. (1986) 'Writing Counts', in A. Wilkinson (ed.), *The Writing of Writing*, Milton Keynes: Open University Press. pp.158–176.

Haswell, R.H. (2000) 'Documenting Improvement in College Writing', *Written Communication*, 17(3): 307–352.

Hemingway, E (1961) *New York Journal-American* (11 July 1961).

Hunt, K.W. (1965) *Grammatical Structures Written at Three Grade Levels*, Champaign, Illinois: NCTE.

Jones, S.M and Myhill. D.A. (2007) 'Discourses of Difference? Examining Gender Difference in Linguistic Characteristics of Writing', *Canadian Journal of Education*, 30(2): 456–482

Kellogg, R. (2006) 'Training Writing Skills: A Cognitive Developmental Perspective', Keynote paper presented at the EARLI Writing SIG Conference, September 2006.

Kress, G. (1994) *Learning to Write*, London: Routledge.

Kress, G. and van Leeuwen, T. (1996) *Reading Images—The Grammar of Visual Design*, London: Routledge.

Kroll, B.M. (1978) 'Cognitive Egocentrism and the Problem of Audience Awareness in Written Discourse', *Research in the Teaching of English*, 12(2):269–281.

Lacasa, P., del Campo, B.M., and Reina, A. (2001) 'Talking and Writing: How do Children Develop Shared Meanings in the School Setting?', in L. Tolchinsky (ed.), *Developmental Aspects in Learning to Write*, Kluwer: Dordrecht. pp.133–162.

Leech, G.N. and Svartvik, J. (1975) *A Communicative Grammar of English*, London: Longman.

Loban, W. (1976) *Language Development: Kindergarten through Grade Twelve (Research Report 18)*, Urbana, IL: National Council of Teachers of English.

LSA (2006) Minutes of the Meeting of the Committee on Language in the School Curriculum LSA: Albuquerque http://www.lsadc.org/info/pdf_files/2006LiSCminutes.pdf [Accessed July 2006]

Massey, A.J., Elliott, G.L., and Johnson, N.K. (2005) 'Variations in Aspects of Writing in 16+ English Examinations between 1980 and 2004: Vocabulary, Spelling, Punctuation, Sentence Structure, Non-Standard English', *Research Matters: Special Issue 1,*

Cambridge: University of Cambridge Local Examinations Syndicate.

Maun, I. and Myhill, D. (2005) 'Text as Design, Writers as Designers', *English in Education*, 39(2): 5–21.

Myhill, D.A. (1999) 'Writing Matters', *English in Education*, 33(3): 70–81.

Myhill, D.A. (2008) 'Towards a Linguistic Model', *Language and Education*, 22(5): 271–288.

NCTE. (2006). Beyond Grammar Drills: How Language Works in Learning to Write The Council Chronicle Online. http://www.ncte.org/pubs/chron/highlights/125935.htm Retrieved 21 March, 2007.

O'Donnell, R.C. (1974) 'Syntactic Differences between Speech and Writing', *American Speech,* 49(1/2): 102–110.

Paraskevas, C. (2006) 'Grammar Apprenticeship', *English Journal*, 95(5): 65–69.

Pea, R. and Kurland, D. (1987) 'Cognitive Technologies for Writing', *Review of Research in Education*, 14: 277–326.

Perera, K. (1984) *Children's Writing and Reading: Analysing Classroom Language*, Oxford: Blackwell.

Perera, K. (1986) 'Grammatical Differentiation between Speech and Writing in Children Aged 8-12' in A. Wilkinson (ed.), *The Writing of Writing*, Oxford: Oxford University Press. pp.90–108.

Pullman, P. (2005, 22 January). Common Sense has Much to Learn from Moonshine. The Guardian.

www.guardian.co.uk/comment/story/0,,1396040,00.html. Accessed 6 March, 2005.

Ragnarsdóttir, H., Aparici, M., Cahana-Amitay, D., van Hell, J., and Viguié, A. (2002) 'Verbal Structure and Content in Written Discourse: Expository and Narrative Texts', *Written Language and Literacy*, 5(1): 95–126.

Ravid, D., van Hell, J., Rosado, E., and Zamora, A. (2002) 'Subject NP Patterning in the Development of Text Production: Speech and Writing', *Written Language and Literacy*, 5(1): 69–93.

Sharples, M. (1999) *How We Write: Writing as Creative Design*, London: Routledge.

Stromqvist, S., Johansson, V., Kriz, S., Ragnarsdottir, H., Aisenman, R., and Ravid, D. (2002) 'Toward a Cross-Linguistic Comparison of Lexical Quanta in Speech and Writing', *Written Language and Literacy*, 5(1): 45–68.

Tannen, D. (ed.) (1982) *Spoken and Written Language: Exploring Orality and Literacy*, Ablex: New Jersey.

Tonfoni, Graziella (1994) *Writing as a Visual Art*, Oxford: Intellect.

Verhoeven, L., Aparici, M., Cahana-Amitay, M., van Hell, J.V., Kriz, S., and Viguie-Simon, A. (2002) 'Clause Packaging in Writing and Speech: A Cross-Linguistic Developmental Analysis', *Written Language and Literacy*, 5(2): 135–161.

28

Writing through College: Self-efficacy and Instruction

Ellen Lavelle

Writing is an ideal academic assignment for college students. In addition to helping students remember facts and concepts and develop critical thinking (Sternglass, 1997), writing provides a cognitive map, one that is subject to reconstruction in the process of revision (Lavelle, 1993). However, writing is difficult. Perhaps no other academic task is so demanding. For one thing, writing imposes tremendous constraints on working memory involving a full range of demands: intentionality, theme, genre, paragraph, sentence, and lexical and grammar dimensions. Additionally, writers are faced with having to constantly alternate between global concerns such as intentionality and voice and local foci such as grammar and punctuation (Biggs, 1988). Beginning writers need to manage the physical movements of forming the letters, and even accomplished writers are constantly refining at multiple thought levels.

Writers' beliefs about writing play a powerful role as writers engage in an often difficult and elusive process (Biggs, 1988; Hounsell, 1997; Lavelle, 1993; Ryan, 1984; Silva and Nichols, 1993). In particular, self-efficacy, the belief that one can succeed at a particular task, is a powerful factor affecting both learning and writing performance. Students' beliefs in their efficacy to regulate their own learning and to master activities determine their aspirations, level of motivation, and academic accomplishments (Wood and Bandura, 1989). Self-efficacy has been shown to influence both goal level and goal commitment (Locke et al., 1984), one's choice of activities and tasks (Lent et al., 1987), and one's interpretation of feedback (Silver et al., as cited in Gist and Mitchell, 1992). In summarizing the effects of self-efficacy, Gist and Mitchell (1992) include choices, goals, emotional reactions, effort, coping, and persistence as linked to efficacy beliefs. Self-efficacy also changes as a result of learning, experience, and feedback. Most importantly, from an instructional perspective, self-efficacy is likely to be influenced by perceptions of the task and task complexity, messages of support, perceptions of accomplishments, and by modelling (Gist and Mitchell, 1992).

Given the complexity and rigour of the writing process at the college level combined with frequent shortcomings of instruction in higher education, it is not surprising that students often lack a sense of self-efficacy as academic writers. While a good deal of attention has been devoted to the examination of self-efficacy as related to college writing (cf. Pajares, 2003), implications for practice are not often clear. The purpose of this chapter is to review the self-efficacy and writing research, and also extend those ideas to the situation of teaching writing at the college level.

SELF-EFFICACY AND COLLEGE WRITING

As early as 1984, Meier et al. applied the self-efficacy model to determine how well efficacy expectations predicted writing performance, and whether cognitive and affective variables were related to efficacy expectations for college freshmen in an introductory writing course. Major findings included efficacy expectations as predictive of writing outcomes at the beginning of the course but not at the end. Depth of processing, locus of control, and anxiety were related to the amount of self-efficacy, and to the accuracy of efficacy predictions. Subjects tended to significantly overestimated their writing performance particularly in the latter portion of the course. Similarly, Shell et al. (1989) looked at the relationship between self-efficacy and outcome expectancy beliefs and achievement in writing and reading among college students. Regression analysis supported that while self-efficacy and outcome expectancy predicted reading achievement, self-efficacy alone predicted writing achievement. Finally, Pajares and Johnson (1994) investigated the writing self-efficacy, writing apprehension, and writing performance for undergraduate students in teacher education. Results indicated that self-efficacy was linked to writing performance and writing skills. Interestingly, writing apprehension was negatively correlated with writing self-efficacy, but was not predictive of writing performance.

More recently, Pajares (2003) reviewed literature on self-efficacy and writing, and supported that research findings has consistently shown that writing self-efficacy beliefs are related to writing performance for college students across a range of studies. Additionally, other variables have been linked to self-efficacy: writing apprehension (Daly and Miller as cited in Pajares, 2003), students' perceived value of writing, students' self-efficacy for self-regulation, and academic self-concept beliefs (Skaalvik, as cited in Pajares, 2003).

These studies support the link between self-efficacy and some modes of writing performance for college students. However, using a timed writing task (Shell et al., 1989; Pajares and Johnson, 1994) as an outcome measure may not be generalizeable to writing under more leisurely conditions. Indeed, task type as well as students' perception of the task influence self-efficacy for writing. Writing tasks, like other academic assignments, vary considerably not only in terms of expectations for content, organization, and fluency, but also in intention, duration, rigour, and audience. The task and students' perception of the task are major determinants of self-efficacy (cf. Gist and Mitchell, 1992).

Lavelle (1993) took mixed method approaches in a series of studies designed to define students' beliefs and strategies as related to college writing in developing the *Inventory of Processes in College Composition*. Factor analysis of writing related items yielded five scales: Elaborationist, Low Self-Efficacy, Reflective-Revision, Spontaneous Impulsive, and Procedural. Low Self-Efficacy described a fearful writing approach devoid of strategies and based on doubting skills and seeing writing as a slow and painful process. Writers scoring high on this factor, indicated that studying grammar and punctuation might improve skills, and that having their writing evaluated was a scary experience. Low Self-Efficacy scale scores were negative predictors of grade in a freshman composition course in a subsequent study, and related to writing apprehension (Lavelle, 1997).

In a follow-up, Lavelle and Zuercher (2001) validated the Low Self-Efficacy factor using interviews with students scoring high on that scale (high scores reflect low self-efficacy). The authors concluded that understanding student perceptions of writing and of themselves as writers is important in helping them gain a positive writing identity, and as a precursor to acquisition of skills. More recently, Lavelle and Guarino (2003) executed a confirmatory analysis of the Inventory of Processes in College Composition, which supported the original five factors and, in a second order analysis, found Low Self-Efficacy linked to a surface writing factor.

TEACHING WRITING

The relationship between self-efficacy and competence is a reciprocal one. Just as a sense of accomplishment promotes self-efficacy, a sense of self-efficacy promotes accomplishment. Specifically, self-efficacy fosters persistence, often in the face of peril, which drives success. This is particularly important in writing given the rigour of the process. Even great writers claim that they often sat for hours, wrote when it seemed impossible, and stayed the course. As Stafford (1978) so eloquently says in *Writing the Australian Crawl.*,

> But swimmers know that if they relax on the water it will prove to be miraculously buoyant: and writers know that a succession of little strokes on the material nearest them—without any prejudgements about the specific gravity of the topic or reasonableness of their expectations—will result in creative progress (Stafford, 1978: 23).

Self-efficacy is the buoy that supports writers as they navigate a potentially treacherous sea. It enables writers to engage in that 'succession of little strokes'. This engagement and production is particularly critical to writing, not only because writing is an ill-defined problem, but also because it is emergent process and dependent on suspended judgment and tolerance for ambiguity. Efficacious writers are also more likely to vary or alternate strategies and to use the right strategy or cluster of tactics for the particular task, rather than being locked into a particular mode such as overreliance on note cards, 'listing' of information, or grammatical rules (cf. Lavelle and Guarino, 2003). It is as though self-efficacy frees up short-term memory to explore the possibilities. If one believes that one will be successful, one is more willing to take a risk. Self-efficacy also impacts interpretation of feedback; to students low in writing self-efficacy, negative comments are more likely to be painful and personal.

Self-efficacy is a particular problem for college level writers. Writing in secondary instruction focuses largely on narrative assignments and does not prepare students for expository demands in the university. Lavelle et al. (2002) found no Low Self-efficacy factor in adapting the *Inventory of Processes in College Composition* for use with a secondary population. This may be because of the assumption that somehow, narrative writing will lead to expository skill, but if it is expository writing that is expected, it should be taught. Another problem involves the assumption that mastery of microskills necessary for writing. While mastery of grammar and punctuation is desirable, it does not guarantee quality composition and over-emphasis on microskills alone may result in some students falling through the cracks. Finally, public school teachers often do not have well-developed understandings of expository writing and are plagued by their own lack of expository writing self-efficacy (Lavelle and Bushrow, 2007), and the same may be true of many college faculty.

Self-efficacy is influenced by intentions and beliefs (Lavelle, 2003), perceptions of the task and task complexity, messages of support, perceptions of accomplishments, and by modelling (Gist and Mitchell, 1992). In the college writing course or in the college course that uses writing as an instructional or evaluative tool, it is desirable to consider these influences as they interface with objectives, tasks, and assessments. At the most general level are college students' intentions or beliefs about writing and about themselves as writers.

INTENTIONS AND BELIEFS

Intentions and beliefs directly affect the strategies that college students use in writing, which, subsequently, impact writing outcomes: Intentions->Strategies->Outcomes (Lavelle, 2003). Students' beliefs include a full range of motivations: to make a meaning, to learn, to self-express, to please the teacher, or just to get done (Lavelle, 1993). For example, when students write to learn, they are apt to engage in deep, meaningful revision as opposed to editing. On the other hand, if students write to please the teacher, they rely on the rules at the expense of meaning (Lavelle and Guarino, 2003). For example, when assigned a five-page essay, a student focused on pleasing the teacher or getting a good grade might write exactly five pages regardless of content.

Students should be encouraged to see the value of writing as a tool of learning, self-expression or communication (cf. Britton, 1978 as cited in Maimon, 2002). Miamon (2002) directly supported the relationship between writing self-efficacy and beliefs regarding the functions of writing for college students. In her research with college students, she found that students high in writing self-efficacy held more rich and varied interpretations of the functions of writing. Along the same line, instruction should focus on dispelling misconceptions about ability and writing. Lackey (1997) found that students entered the writing classroom with limited knowledge regarding writing processes or their abilities!

Tingle (2004) calls for teacher empathy as key to helping students negotiate a developmental stage linked to reorganizing writing and their own identities or selfhoods.

Here, in the psychoanalytic tradition, writing becomes a self-object, an artefact that serves to define identity. Tingle argues that all writing is autobiographical in a sense as writers destabilize and construe a new identity through the act or writing. Thus, the goal of teaching is to validate writers by connecting to their experiences and to foster developmental change in the writing classroom as 'transitional space'. He urges teachers of writing to develop an empathic perspective where they seek to truly understand the situation of writers. Indeed writing is autobiographical as writers are faced with reshaping their own products as they engage in revision. Moreover, change in one's own product is personal and can be very painful if one is not efficacious as to achieving a positive outcome.

Objectives should emphasize the role of beliefs and intentions in writing. Assignments might include reflective writings, collaborative assignments, discussions, and readings regarding the functions of writing. One tool that might be used to raise awareness of both beliefs about writing and writing strategies is the *Inventory of Processes in College Composition* (Lavelle, 1993) This 7-item scale is easy to administer and score, and is used as an instructional and diagnostic tool at several universities. Emphasizing the role of intentions in the writing process empowers students. It allows them to frame their motivations in new ways, ways that boost autonomy and writer-efficacy.

TASK PERCEPTIONS

Writing tasks, or assignments, vary greatly in terms of their attributes. They may be timed or ongoing, difficult or easy, familiar or novel, collaborative or independent, scaffolded or unsupported, personal or objective, or constrained or free form. Tasks may demand significant topical and/or genre knowledge or very little of either. In terms of assessment, tasks may be evaluated quantitatively and qualitatively and weighted heavily, lightly, or not at all in terms of contribution to the final grade. What is important is that a full range of types of tasks and assessments be advanced to foster at least some level of accomplishment for all students. Along the same line, writing tasks that are scaffolded, or backed with instructional support such as guidelines, assessment rubrics, and models, are ideal to promote accomplishment. How often have students been assigned a major paper only to hand it on the last night never having received guidelines or feedback? 'What does this teacher expect? What is required?' remain unknown, and increase the possibility of failure. To borrow Stafford's metaphor, if writers are struggling in a turbulent sea it is the guidelines that may keep them 'afloat'.

Another task dimension that affects writing efficacy is choice. Providing choices greatly empowers students by providing an opportunity for input into the writing process. Instructors should build a series of choices into the course. For example, allowing students to do the critical essay or the term paper, the journal or the report, providing several due dates for feedback (e.g., the fifth or tenth week), writing collaboratively or independently, or even having students contract for grades or providing a choice of 'tracks.' Of course, providing choices means losing power for the teacher and this is uncomfortable for instructors.

Finally, it is important to check students' perceptions of the task and of the process involved to accomplish the writing assignment. What does this assignment mean? What skills and strategies does it warrant? What might the outcome look like? How will it be evaluated?

MESSAGES OF SUPPORT/ ASSESSMENT

Feedback should be timely, succinct, and ongoing. Late feedback sends the message that the students' work is not important, other things are taking precedent, and this is erosive to writing efficacy. Comments that encourage analysis, creativity, and perspective taking move students towards more meaningful and involved writing. They validate student work and promote exploration. All writings have strengths and findings, and supporting those dimensions is critical to writing achievement. Generally, comments should be explicit in nature and focused on the structural or conceptual levels rather than implicit and at the lexical or sentential levels (Ziv, 1980; Lackey, 1997).

The quality of writing rests on a willingness to fully engage the writing task and oneself as author. When self-efficacy is low, it is as though writers leave something of themselves behind and adopt a more superficial approach—'just get it done' or 'just follow the rules', 'get the grade' (Lavelle, 1993). By teaching revision as the primary component of the writing process, instructors encourage a process perspective—one which allows students a series of opportunities not only to find success, but also to develop writing selfhood and skills. Revision is not editing. It is a comprehensive process of restructuring thinking. When students buy into revision, they develop an 'I can' mindset. A series of practice opportunities, each manageable in terms of familiarity and length, promotes success.

MODELLING

Modelling is critical in raising self-efficacy. When observing a model, students not only see an example of the requisite skills, but also identify with the model's process and share the model's success. This process of identification serves to elevate efficacy beliefs. 'Oh, I see how she does it, I think that I can do that too'. Writing and revision processes become overt and imitable. Instructors might use the computer and think out loud, as they compose. They might demonstrate various dimensions of the writing process such as alternating the level of focus, revising for voice or audience, revision at multiple levels, and the nature of rereading, making, and correcting mistakes. Students might model for each other although it is important that students serving as models have the requisite skills. It is important that modelling be followed by practice opportunities with manageable assignments and feedback.

Modelling also includes providing students with exemplary papers to raise awareness of genre, form, structure, and voice. Students should be allowed to write in a similar fashion and to adapt their own ideas to the framework or example. Of course, some students may rely too heavily on the source, but this can be remedied with feedback, clear definitions of plagiarism, and the understanding that imitation is part of the learning to write process.

CONCLUSION

Teaching writing or using writing as an instructional tool in college is an often difficult but rewarding undertaking. So often, I have heard colleagues lament the status of undergraduate writing, and I am not sure what advice to give them. However, as I talk about writing and instruction with them, it becomes obvious that they rarely consider students' beliefs about writing or about themselves as writers, the difficulty of the writing process, or the role of self-efficacy in writing instruction. Of course, they may not have had formal training in teaching writing, and they tend to go about using writing as their instructors did when they were in college. Usually, this involves few guidelines, no opportunities for discussion or revision, and having students plop the paper on the professor's desk on the last night of class.

It is beyond the scope of this chapter to advise faculty as to the many options for instruction in writing at the college level, indeed that is more the topic for

compositionists and other authors of this volume. Rather, I have tried to apply a very basic model of the development of self-efficacy to the situation of college writing. In particular, I have suggested that intentions, tasks and task perceptions, feedback and support, and assessments and modelling serve as key factors for in promoting writing self-efficacy, and I derived some suggestions for teaching from these. Since writing efficacy is a fuzzy notion, development is not obvious or readily measured. What is important is realizing that writing is difficult, that students may not bring the ideal writing background, and that self-efficacy serves as a major moderating variable in the writing process and it is malleable.

REFERENCES

Bandura, A. (1993) 'Perceived self-efficacy in cognitive development and functioning', *Educational Psychologist*, 28(2): 117–148.

Biggs, J.B. (1988) *Approaches to Learning and Essay Writing. Learning Strategies and Learning Styles.* New York: Plenum.

Gist, M. and Mitchell, T. (1992) 'Self-efficacy: A theoretical analysis of its determinants and malleability', *Academy of Management Review*, 17(2): 183–211.

Hounsell, D. (1997) 'Learning and Essay Writing, in F. Marton, D. Hounsell, and N. Entwistle (eds), *The Experience of Learning*, Edinburough: Scottish Academic Press.

Lackey, J.R. (1997) 'The effects of written feedback on motivation and changes in written performance' (ERIC Document Reproduction Service No. ED 406 690) Retrieved 2 August, 2007 from ERIC (Educational Resources Information Center Database.)

Lavelle, E. (1993) 'Development and validation of an inventory to assess processes in college composition', *British Journal of Educational Psychology*, 63(3): 489–499.

Lavelle, E. (1997) 'Writing styles and the narrative essay', *British Journal of Educational Psychology*, 67(4): 475–482.

Lavelle, E. (2003) 'The quality of university writing: A preliminary analysis of undergraduate portfolios', *Quality in Higher Education*, 9(1): 313–332.

Lavelle, E. and Bushrow, K. (2007) 'Writing approaches of graduate students', *Educational Psychology*, 27(6): 1–16.

Lavelle, E. and Guarino, A.J. (2003) 'A multidimensional approach to understanding college writing processes', *Educational Psychology*, 23(3): 295–305.

Lavelle, E., Smith, J., and O'Ryan, L. (2002) 'The writing approaches of secondary students', *British Journal of Educational Psychology*, 72(3): 399–418.

Lavelle, E. and Zuercher, N. (2001) 'Writing approaches of university students', *Higher Education*, 40(3): 373–391.

Lent, R.W., Brown, S.D., and Larkin, K.C. (1987) 'Comparison of three theoretically derived variables in predicting career and academic behavior: Self-efficacy, interest congruence and consequent thinking', *Journal of Counseling Psychology*, 34(3): 293–298.

Locke, E.A., Frederick, E., Lee, C., and Bobko, P. (1984) 'Effect of self-efficacy, goals and task strategies on task performance', *Journal of Applied Psychology*, 69(2): 241–251.

Maimon, L. (2002) 'Self-efficacy and functions of writing', *Journal of College Reading and Learning*, 33(1): 32–45.

Meier, S., McCarthy, P., and Schmeck, R. (1984) 'Validity of self-efficacy as a predictor of writing performance', *Cognitive Therapy and Research*, 8(2): 107–120.

Pajares, F. (2003) 'Self-efficacy beliefs, motivation, and achievement in writing: A review of the literature', *Reading and Writing Quarterly*, 19(2): 139–158.

Pajares, F. and Johnson, M.J. (1994) 'Confidence and competence in writing: The role of self-efficacy, outcome expectancy and apprehension', *Research in the Teaching of English*, 28(3): 313–331.

Ryan, M. (1984) 'Conceptions of prose coherence: Individual differences in epistemological standards', *Journal of Educational Psychology*, 76(6): 1226–1238.

Shell, D.F., Murphy, C.C., and Bruning, R. (1989) 'Self-efficacy and outcome expectancy mechanisms in reading and writing achievement', *Journal of Educational Psychology*, 81(1): 91–100.

Silva, T. and Nicholls, J. (1993) 'College students as writing theorists: Goals and beliefs about the causes of success', *Contemporary Educational Psychology*, 18 (2): 281–293.

Stafford, W. (1978) *Writing the Australian Crawl*, Ann Arbor, MI: The University of Michigan Press.

Sternglass, M.S. (1997) *Time to Know Them: A Longitudinal Study of Writing and Learning at the College Level*, Mahwah, NJ: Lawrence Erlbaum Associates.

Tingle, N. (2004) Self-*Development and College Writing*, Carbondale, IL: Southern Illinois University Press.

Wood, R.R. and Bandura, A. (1989) 'Impact of conceptions of ability on self-regulatory mechanisms, and complex decision making', *Journal of Personality and Social Psychology*, 56(3): 407–415.

Ziv, N.D. (1980) 'The effect of teacher comments on the writing of four college freshmen' (ERIC Document Reproduction Service No. ED 203 317) Retrieved 2 August, 2007 from ERIC (Educational Resources Information Center Database.)

APPENDIX 28A

Deep Writing	*Surface Writing*
Metacognitive, Reflective	Redundant, Reproductive
High or alternating level of focus	Focus at the local level
Hierarchical organization	Linear, sequential structure
Engagement, self-referencing	Detachment
Actively making meaning (agentic)	Passive ordering of data
Audience concern	Less audience concern
Thinks about essay as an integrated whole	Sees essay as an organized display
Thesis-driven	Data-driven
Revision	Editing
Transforming, going beyond assignment	Telling within the given context
Autonomous	Rule-bound
Teacher independent	Teacher dependent
Feelings of satisfaction, coherence and connectedness	

APPENDIX 28B

Approaches to Writing

Approach	Motive	Strategy
Elaborative voice	To self-express	Visualization, audience
Low Self-Efficacy	To acquire skills/avoid pain	Study grammar, collaborate, find encouragement
Reflective-Revision	To make meaning	Revision, reshaping, drafting
Spontaneous-Impulsive	To get done	Last minute, no planning or Revision, just like talking.
Procedural	Please the teacher	Observe rules, organize and manage writing

APPENDIX 28C

Inventory of Processes in College Composition: Sample Questions

FACTOR I Elaborative

1. Writing makes me feel good.
2. I tend to give a lot of description and detail.
3. I put a lot of myself in writing.
4. I use written assignments as learning experiences.

FACTOR II Low Self-efficacy

1. I cannot write a term paper.
2. Writing an essay or paper is always a slow process.
3. Having my writing evaluated scares me.
4. I need special encouragement to do my best writing.
5. My writing rarely expresses what I really think.

FACTOR III Reflective-Revision

1. I re-examine and restate my thoughts in revision.
2. There are many ways to write a written assignment.
3. The reason for writing an essay really matters to me.

4. My first draft is never my finished product.
5. Revision is the process of finding the shape of my writing.

FACTOR IV Spontaneous-Impulsive

1. My writing 'just happens' with little planning or preparation.
2. I often do written assignments at the last minute and still get a good grade.
3. I never think about how I go about writing.
4. Often my first draft is my finished product.
5. I plan, write and revise all the same time.

FACTOR V Procedural

1. When writing an essay, I stick to the rules.
2. I keep my theme or topic clearly in mind as I write.
3. I can usually find one main sentence that tells the theme of my essay.
4. The teacher is the most important audience.
5. My intention in writing papers or essays is just to answer the question.

Toward a New Understanding for Classroom Writing Assessment

Brian Huot and Jeff Perry

For over a hundred years, assessment has been a contested issue in the teaching of writing (Elliot, 2005; Lynne, 2004). James Berlin (1987), James Britton et al. (1975) and other early scholars in writing pedagogy characterized traditional approaches to teaching writing as employing strict attention to stylistic, mechanical, and grammatical conventions. Three to four decades ago, the new rhetoric, as it was known at the college level or whole language, as it is called for K-12[1] emphasized writing as a process and deemphasized responding to student writing primarily in terms of its approximation of stylistic and grammatical conventions. Regardless of the attention given to writing and its teaching over the last few decades, classroom-writing assessment remains underresearched, undertheorized, and underutilized as a legitimate and important part of teaching students how to write.

There are many reasons why classroom assessment has not received the same kinds of attention in the literature as other aspects of teaching writing. Grading in particular (Belanoff, 1994) and assessment in general (English Journal, 1994) are often seen as onerous, dreadful tasks, providing little opportunity for teaching and learning. Reay and William (2001) note how grading can help students create negative and counterproductive identities as learners. Overall, grading has been largely characterized as a bureaucratic record-keeping process (Boyd, 1998). As Huot (2002) has already noted, one of the reasons why assessment has not been examined as a viable means for teaching student writers is because it has been linked with grading and testing. Like Huot (2002), we contend that grading and testing are only one possible kind of assessment. In differentiating between different kinds of assessment, it is common to point to formative and summative means for evaluating students, with formative referring to assessment students can use while completing an academic performance, project, or unit and summative assessment coming at the end of an academic performance, project, or unit. Because the teaching of writing has had an historical focus on grading single drafts for correctness and adherence to stylistic conventions, summative rather than formative assessment has been the norm. Consequently, formative assessment has come to be seen as progressive, advisable, and good; whereas, summative assessment is seen as traditional, regressive, and bad.

In addition to turning to more ways to include formative assessment into the teaching of writing, the use of portfolios for classroom writing assessment has been a regular option. The primary conceptual assessment move in portfolios is that students do not receive grades until they have completed a range of work, received feedback, have chosen what writing to be revised, and produced more than one draft, while providing metawriting or reflective pieces about the process of drafting, selecting, and reflecting. However, many portfolio systems include giving midterm grades or tentative grades on individual assignments rather than delaying assessment until the end of the grading period or semester. While portfolios are still a common practice in many writing classrooms, the heyday of research and literature about them was probably at least ten years ago (Baker, 1993; Belanoff, 1994; Black et al, 1994; Camp and Levine, 1991; Huot and Williamson, 1997; Yancey, 1992; Yancey and Weiser, 1997; and several others).

In addition to portfolios, there has been a fairly constant stream of literature on responding to student writing (Anson, 1989; Bizarro et al, 1997; Horvath, 1984; Kynard, 2006; Lawson et al., 1989; Mathison-Fife and O'Neill, 2001; Phelps, 2000; Sommers, 1982; Straub, 1996; 1997; 2000), though, as some have noted, responding to student writing is an important but neglected aspect of the teaching of writing (Miller, 1994; Phelps, 2000). The literature on responding to student writing has mostly focused on different ways in which teachers can respond to students or on principles that characterize effective response (Anson, 1989; Straub, 2000; Sommers, 1982; many others). A lesser-known approach, becoming more prevalent

in the literature is to focus on the ways in which teachers read student writing (Huot, 2002; Kynard, 2006; Phelps, 2000; Zebroski, 1989).

Our chapter provides an overview and introduction to classroom writing assessment that addresses Michael Scriven's (1966) germinal distinction between formative and summative assessment, differentiates between assessment, grading, and testing, and reviews the major contributions to the literature on responding to student writing. Our argument is that realizing how and why assessment has been undertheorized, underresearched, and underutilized component for the teaching of writing provides writing teachers with a powerful tool for the teaching of writing. Assessment is an important and integral part of the ways in which a writer negotiates the writing process, providing the criteria for decisions about texts and the process of producing these texts. In addition to discussing ways in which assessment can and should be a positive component of effective writing pedagogy, we also hope to provide some new language with which we can talk about writing assessment that promotes the teaching and learning of writing in a school context.

FORMATIVE AND SUMMATIVE

The distinction between formative and summative assessment refers to whether or not an assessment comes at a time when the artefact that is being assessed can be improved, based upon the assessment. In classroom writing assessment, we can think of formative and summative in terms of whether or not the context of an assessment permits a student to improve her writing or not, with the understanding that an assessment that encourages students to improve their writing helps them improve as writers. Michael Scriven introduces the terms formative and summative assessment in his paper *The Methodology of Evaluation* published in 1966. It is important to note that Scriven's paper is about

curriculum evaluation and the most efficacious ways to evaluate instructional programs, learning and teaching styles and
innovations. This focus on curriculum provides a new context within which to understand the importance of the distinction
Scriven is making between formative and
summative evaluation. Although curricular
assessment is crucial in making decisions
about the structure and organization of educational programs, providing for an assessment that could provide feedback during an
instructional period is an important and
necessary evaluative innovation for program,
and curricular evaluation to have the best
possible effect on the various instructional
environments under evaluation. Just knowing
that a curriculum or instructional approach
was a failure does not improve the education
of the students within such a program. This
context for understanding the terms formative and summative reminds us that initially
these distinctions were not made for classroom assessment. We would assume, incorrectly it appears, that within the classroom a
student would be able to use an assessment to
improve his/her work.

While we wholeheartedly agree with the
value of formative assessment in the writing
classroom, we are not convinced that this
distinction in and of itself is of great value for
classroom writing assessment. The term
formative assessment says nothing about the
value or efficacy of the assessment's ability
to help a student learn to write better.
Formative merely alludes to the idea that the
assessment can be used for improvement. As
we noted earlier, this is a very important distinction when talking about program assessment, but it is really much less important
when thinking of classroom writing assessment, since all activities (some might say
'even' we might say 'especially' assessment)
should have strong instructional value. For
example, a teacher could give a student an
F on a paper marking all grammar, usage,
and mechanical and stylistic errors. If the
teacher allows the student to correct these
errors and improve the grade of the paper,

then we could call this formative assessment.
However, it would be hard to endorse this
practice as a valuable way to use assessment
and feedback to provide the best instruction
for students. The category of formative does
not guarantee the instructional value of an
assessment, which is one of the reasons why
we later advocate for teaching students to
assess.

Although we are not terribly enthusiastic
about the distinction between formative and
summative assessment for teaching writing,
we do believe that Scriven's distinction
between the goals of assessment and the
roles of assessment, which are related to his
notion of formative and summative are
important for an understanding of writing
classroom assessment. It's interesting to note
that while those of us interested in classroom
writing assessment have pretty much assumed
the superiority of formative over summative
assessment, Scriven makes no such assumption: 'Thus, there seems to be a number of
qualifications that would have to be made
before one could accept a statement asserting the greater importance of formative
evaluation by comparison with summative'
(1966: 7). Of course, Scriven might have
held a different opinion had he been talking
about classroom evaluation.

Interestingly, Scriven's use of formative
and summative is not even close to one of the
main points he makes in his paper. Moreover,
one of the forgotten, though more central,
ideas he advances is the notion that evaluation has both goals and roles, an idea that
has great relevance and importance for our
discussion of classroom writing assessment:

> The function of evaluation may be thought of in
> two ways. At the methodological level, we may
> talk of the *goals* of evaluation; in the particular
> sociological or pedagogical context we may further
> distinguish several possible *roles* of evaluation.
> (Scriven, 1966: 2)

In other words, although the ultimate goal
of classroom writing assessment is to accurately evaluate student performance in a
course or during a particular instructional
period, assessment can take on different roles

in our classrooms: 'But the role which evaluation has in a particular context may be enormously various' (Scriven, 1966: 3). Scriven's use of the terms formative and summative attempts to demonstrate the different roles assessment can assume: 'As a matter of terminology, I think that novel terms are worthwhile here, to avoid inappropriate connotations, and I propose to use the terms "formative" and "summative"' to qualify evaluation in these roles (Scriven, 1966: 7).

Our vision of assessment and its separation from grades or testing would certainly qualify as formative rather than summative. However, in keeping with Scriven's original ideas, we would identify our goal for assessment as instructive. Specifically, we think assessment should be used to help students learn to write better and to produce better texts. We also see a central role, as we discuss next, for assessment as part of the process of writing in which students learn to assess writing as they become better writers. We do not really see any conflict between using assessment to teach and having to assign a specific grade or score to students based upon their classroom performance, nor do we believe that students should be excluded from the summative assessment of their work, since we believe that it can have educational value. Thinking about assessment roles and goals rather than the formative or summative uses of assessment focuses needed attention in the writing classroom on the ability to judge a piece of writing and to understand what if any future revisions that writing might need to succeed, rather than when the assessment is given to the student.

ASSESSING, GRADING, AND TESTING STUDENT WRITING

When we talk about classroom assessment, we often lump together grading, testing, and assessing student writing. The strong association between these terms fosters an overall attitude among teachers that our need to

assess student writing somehow prevents us from teaching students how to write. Even self-assessment, which we of course heartily endorse, is often seen as a student's ability to know, predict, or otherwise assume the kind of grade or evaluation they will receive from someone else. Our separation of assessment from grading and testing implies that they not only differ, but that we need to begin to talk about classroom assessment in different ways that acknowledge these differences and allow us a way to see classroom assessment as a positive force for teaching writing. Ultimately, our treatment of assessment as a pedagogical tool also recognizes the importance and value of a student or writer's[2] ability to assess the value and efficacy of the text he/she is creating while he/she is creating it. We believe that being able to assess writing is part of being able to write well. While most scholarship on writing pedagogy would dismiss the idea of having students write single drafts that teachers grade rigorously for surface conventions, we believe that the separation of writing assessment from its teaching is an equal distortion and misrepresentation of the act of writing and learning to write.

Unfortunately, grading and/or testing, which is often seen as assessing writing in the classroom is more about the teacher's judgment than it is about helping to develop the student's sense of judgment about her writing. The type of decision-making, known as grading, hardly resembles the type of evaluation writers make constantly while writing and rewriting. In courses where students write papers that receive grades, even when revision is allowed or encouraged, the instructor is completely responsible for assessment. Returning graded and marked papers to students eliminates any responsibility for students to assess their own writing. Instead of focusing on improving the writing, students cannot but help focusing on improving their grades. While improving grades and improving writing are not unrelated, they are not the same thing. To compound the difference(s) between improving grades and writing, it is important to note that in at least one research study (Connors and Lunsford, 1993) almost sixty percent of all teacher commentary focused on justifying the grade of the paper. Students cannot help but be pressured into responding in ways that improve their grades regardless of what they might think about the writing itself. This grade-centred approach to teaching writing not only limits the kinds of revisions students might make, but it also misrepresents the act of writing. Instead of focusing on creating a text, students focus on what will bring them the best grade based upon their teachers' evaluation of their text. Unless students learn to assess, they will fail to assume the authority that comes with assessment for those who write. Unless students learn to assess writing as part of the process, then they remain students rather than becoming writers. This distinction between being a writer and being a student is illustrated in a couple of research studies. Sara Freedman (1984) reported that professional writers received lower holistic scores than did first-year college students, because the professional writing violated teachers' expectations for student work. In a later study (1987), Freedman and her colleague Melanie Sperling report upon an ethnographic study in which a gifted student completes revisions of her writing just to please the teacher. Both of these studies illustrate the tension between being a writer, a person who creates and discovers from a student who does assignments and follows the teacher as she is graded for her work.

Newer models for teaching student writers do attempt to decentre the classroom and the authority away from the teacher to the students, so that students have the authority to work as writers. Typical pedagogical practices in current classrooms include peer review and portfolios in which students are encouraged to make decisions and assume some authority. While these practices give students more autonomy and responsibility, they also assume that students are able to assess texts, their own and their peers in order to make decisions to improve their writing and the writing of their colleagues. Many students, however, are not equipped to make the kinds of decisions these practices assume. It is common, for example, for teachers to have to prohibit commentary on grammar, usage and mechanics for first-draft peer review or for students to rely on teachers' judgments about which papers to choose to revise from a portfolio. It just may be that an overall misunderstanding of the value of assessment for the teaching of writing has helped us create current teaching practices that require evaluative skills that our students do not posses.

Teaching students how to be better evaluators of writing and to use this skill in assessment to become better writers is not an impossible task. It may, however, take some rethinking about the teaching of writing in the same way that teaching writing as process required many writing teachers to rethink the ways in which they structured their classrooms, organized writing assignments, and ultimately evaluated student performance. As well, teaching student writers to assess and be better writers may require that we start to think about assessment as a process in which we involve students in all evaluative phases of their writing. This would involve students in setting rhetorical and linguistic targets for specific writing assignments and then helping students meet these targets through the process of writing and assessment. These targets should come from an assessment and understanding of the context(s) and purposes for writing as well as the process itself. Students not only learn that audience and purpose are important, but they also come to realize that only by assigning and then assessing the value of such rhetorical components can they reach their overall goals as writers.

For example, each writing assignment introduced in class should also contain a discussion of what makes a good assignment of this type. If students are writing narratives, then the introduction of characters and the maintenance of a comprehensible and recognizable order of events are important.

If the assignment is to review a book, movie, or other text, then students would talk about the importance of giving the reader an idea of text they have not seen as well as providing an assessment of how well the text being reviewed does its job. A separate rubric or scoring guideline can be created by the students and teachers for each writing task as it is assigned. This guideline or rubric can be revisited once students are in the actual process of writing the assignment. It is important in using assessment to teach writing, as it is important in using any other instrument to teach writing, that instruction is thoroughly integrated throughout the process of writing and throughout the instructional process that accompanies that writing. The rubric or scoring guideline that the teacher and students have created (and even revised) becomes an important part of the peer review process[3] when students are given a peer-review sheet based upon the rubric they helped create to facilitate the peer-review process. In this way, the assessment criteria that helped introduce and set the targets for the writing assignment is used by students to help them respond to each other for further revision of their papers. These same assessment criteria used to introduce the assignment and used in peer review can also be used by students to make other evaluative decisions like choosing which assignment to revise from a portfolio. Integrating assessment throughout the writing process provides students with practice and eventual expertise in using assessment to make important writing process decisions. This use of assessment also creates the necessary scaffolding to successfully guide students through the writing process.

Of all the existing forms of classroom writing assessment, none has generated more excitement or has more promise than the use of portfolios. Unlike other formal means for assessing writing, portfolios were first used inside the classroom and while their potential for use in program, curriculum, and statewide assessments is widely documented (Callahan, 1997, 1999; Murphy and Underwood, 2000; and many others), they remain a potentially powerful source for the productive use of assessment in the writing classroom. Like all popular and ubiquitous forms of practice in and outside of education, portfolios can and have been used in many ways. Murphy (1994) makes a case that it is the use of portfolios and not just the existence of some kind of portfolio that determines the value of portfolio assessment. Otherwise, portfolios can become just another name for papers in a folder, a sort of fancy checklist used to document student texts produced throughout a semester or specific grading period. While we make suggestions about the most appropriate ways to use portfolios to highlight the differences between assessment, testing and grading, our most crucial point is that for portfolios to really deliver on their promise, we must recognize and exploit the shift in assessment theory that drives portfolios in the first place.

It is probably important to remember that portfolios as a form of assessment came to use from a longstanding tradition in the visual and performing arts in which the progress of actors, artists, and students of the arts are documented through time. Theoretically, the use of portfolios challenges the idea that student progress can best be measured by the results of a single paper or performance or the aggregate of those papers or performances. On the other hand, assessing progress and quality is the hallmark of portfolio use. For example, it is safe to say that collecting, selecting, and reflecting, the three most important aspects of a writing portfolio (Yancey, 1992), are really forms of assessment in which students in concert with their teachers and peers make evaluative decisions about their writing decisions independent of grades or tests. Portfolios can disrupt the power of grades and the relegation of writers to the status of students only when they are used to delay grading and to help students create a body of work that can eventually be evaluated. We are fond of telling our students that we do not care what they can do in week four or five of a semester that we are only interested in what they have done at the end of a semester or other grading or instructional period. All writers eventually face some evaluation of their work, but to improve the writing and the skill of the writer, this evaluation needs to occur only at a meaningful juncture for which the writer has some control and assistance.

The assumptions behind most schemes for grading and testing student writing in the classroom are that writing skill and the progress of the writer can and should be measured by the sum of grades or scores received on individual assignments or writing tasks. A judgment based upon several pieces of writing constructed over an extended period cannot help but be different both for the writer/student and the teacher/evaluator. Not only is the context of the writing enriched, but the multiple drafts and various forms of writing also help to document the progressive, developmental, and fluid nature of literacy acquisition. In addition, the reflective and metawriting typically included in a writing portfolio provide insight not only into the written products but also into the process and experience of the writer. A portfolio, then, can emphasize not only the process and product of written texts but also the student's understanding of him/herself as a writer. Moving the focus of evaluation in a writing classroom from grades and tests not only changes the way we can evaluate, but it also provides us with a new sense of what we are assessing and how our assessments can best be connected to the teaching and learning of writing.

RESPONDING TO STUDENT WRITING

An important element of most writing classes is the teacher's written response to student writing. The traditional approach to this form of writing assessment, as we have mentioned, is woven into composition's historical role within American education. A brief look at the history of composition (Berlin, 1984; 1987) serves to situate the teaching of writing

within the working class of the professoriate. The compositionist was relegated to the drudgery of reading and 'correcting' stacks of papers, semester after semester. The most apparent marker of these days of cellar dwelling can be recognized in the collective view that teachers have of assessment. Among teachers of writing, assessment is enmeshed in grading, testing, and evaluation, and the negativity that accompanies writing assessment is directly tied to its history of drudgery, repetition, and tedium. To realize 'why assessment has been an under-theorized, under-researched and under-utilized component for the teaching of writing' it is important to review one of the most time-honoured traditions of writing instruction, the written response. The field of response theory illustrates the necessity for writing instructors to reflect on their own assessment practices as part of their pedagogical practice as well as the necessity of writing scholars to further their research into response theory.

The traditional focus of response theory scholarship has been the written responses of teachers as they appear on student papers. In many ways, the research on response was part and parcel of the process movement. In terms of the tradition of summative response, early scholarship on response showed that 'although commenting on student writing is the most widely used method for responding to student writing, it is the least understood' (Sommers, 1982: 148). Sommers' article, 'Responding to Student Writing,' was an early addition to response theory and challenged both composition scholars and composition teachers to question their own motives and practices. Sommer brought to light the fact that 'teachers' comments can take students' attention away from their own purposes in writing a particular text and focus that attention on the teachers' purpose in commenting' (p. 149). This understanding, that teachers can do as much harm as good through response and critique, challenged many of the traditional notions in the teaching of writing. Sommers and her colleagues researched teachers' responses to first and second drafts. The study revealed both a paradox in purpose as well as a major theme, namely, that 'there seems to be among teachers an accepted, albeit unwritten canon for commenting on student texts' (p. 153). Both the paradox and the canon will be recognizable to the majority of writing instructors. The canon consists of one-word comments and short phrases that make sense to English teachers but make little sense to their students. Some common elements of the canon are 'elaborate,' 'be specific,' 'be precise,' and 'avoid' (p. 152). The paradox that Sommers identifies is that teachers tend to write interlinear comments that deal with usage, style, and grammar, while also writing marginal notes that concern revision. These interlinear comments 'encourage the student to see the text as a fixed piece, frozen in time, that just needs editing,' while the marginal comments, 'suggest that the meaning of the text is not fixed, but rather that the student stills needs to develop the meaning by doing some more research' (p. 151). This early identification of a well-known and traditional pedagogical practice makes obvious the fact that very little thought and very little reflection was being given to teachers' responses to students' writing. Sommers' work was part of an early conversation that asked teachers to reflect on their pedagogy and the theories that informed those pedagogical practices.

Horvath's (1984) synthesis of views on written comments added to the work of scholars like Sommers. Horvath argued that 'formative' evaluation must precede 'summative' evaluation, that teachers need to approach papers 'as in process,' that 'a tolerance for error must be cultivated in both students and instructor,' that 'the simple avoidance of error should not be applauded,' and that 'errors themselves must be treated as occasions for learning' (p. 139). Horvath's work is evidence of a shifting mood in composition studies—a mood that began to look at the process of writing rather than the product of writing. He writes:

Also inappropriate are comments inhibiting or foreclosing effective revision … Such comments

may cause students to confuse ends with means, seeing adherence to conventions not as a way of enhancing communication but as an end in itself, with substance, purpose, originality going out of focus as students concentrate on expressing vapid, trite ideas, correctly (p. 142).

Horvath and Sommers argue convincingly for a thoughtful approach to commenting on student papers, and Horvath reminds us that 'written teacher responses need not be students' only source of response … conferences, class discussion, small group work, and written peer evaluation' (p. 144) can also aid students in revising and self-editing. This final reminder from Horvath, however, is left as a parting shot. As a whole, response theory continues, to this day, to focus primarily on teachers' written responses.

This trend of researching written responses is evident in the work of Connors and Lunsford (1993) in their investigation of 3,000 student papers. The study looks at the kinds of comments, initial comments versus terminal comments; the purpose of these comments, formal error corrections versus global comments written to motivate revision; and, the role of these comments: of 2000 comments, just 11% of these comments were written to give feedback on drafts in process, while 59% of these comments served to justify the grade given on the paper. The Connors and Lunsford investigation is most important, in our view, for capturing the disparity between comments meant to aid revision and comments written to justify a grade. As we discuss elsewhere, the ability of grades to interfere with the teaching of writing is an important difference between formative and summative assessment and the roles and goals of an evaluative technique.

The scholarship on response has remained primarily concerned with written responses, but we argue that scholarship that identifies written response as only an element (Mathison-Fife and O'Neill, 2001; Kynard, 2006; Huot, 2002; Phelps, 1989, 2000; Eddgington, 2005), a spoke in the wheel of response theory in general, is the more promising field of inquiry. Mathison-Fife and O'Neill (2001) illustrate that research on response needs to catch up to contemporary social constructivists theories that inform many classroom practices. They argue that 'if empirical research is to accurately interpret and evaluate teachers' response, it needs to consider the particular context in which response occurs as well as the students' and teachers' perspectives' (p. 303). Mathison-Fife and O'Neill's call to contextualize teachers' comments within the 'web of classroom practices' (p. 303) visits investigations that ask questions about context (Sperling, 1994) as well as investigations that approach teachers' response from the student perspective. Ultimately, however, Mathison-Fife and O'Neill (2001) express their disappointment that, except for one ethnographic study (Sperling and Freedman, 1987), 'all of these attempts to take student perspective into account limit their focus to teachers' written comments, not attempting to describe the response situation of the classroom' (Mathison-Fife and O'Neill, 2001: 304). For Mathison-Fife and O'Neill, the real question for response theory is how to more fully engage the student in self-assessment and a sense of self-awareness as writers.

READING STUDENT WRITING

In shifting our focus from responding to reading student writing, we are acknowledging that no matter how we respond, in writing, in a student conference, or over email, teachers must first read student writing. It follows then that everything we know about reading is important to an understanding of the way teachers read and respond to student writing. Over the last four decades or so, from Goodman's germinal article: 'Reading: A psycholinguistic guessing game to more recent scholarship,' it has been established that reading is an interpretive and creative act that extends beyond any mere decoding of words on a page. For our purposes in discussing the reading of student writing, we also contend that reading is an evaluative act.

How many times do we find ourselves complimenting or chiding an author (student or not) as we read. The question then for reading student writing is not whether we will evaluate, but how we will use that evaluation. Our point about how we can read and use our evaluation in very different ways is beautifully illustrated by Joseph Williams' article 'The Phenomenology of Error' (1981). Briefly, Williams sets up his 'puzzled' response to the anger and frustration created by so called errors in usage and style, and then, over the course of twenty odd pages, discusses the phenomenon of error. He shows, via Orwell, Barzun, E.B. White and other notable authorities on the English language, that even these language mavens commit errors of usage within the very tomes of style and usage that house their rules and principles for writing. In the end, Williams, after cleverly laying his trap, explains to his audience that 'I deliberately inserted … about 100 errors' (p. 165), most of which have gone unnoticed by the reader. The lesson of Williams' piece is in many ways the argument we wish to make in our review and discussion of writing assessment. If we sit down to read George Orwell, we situate ourselves differently than we do when we sent down to read a student's paper. Indeed, you might argue, but I do not sit down to grade Orwell's *1984*, but to enjoy or learn. Simply, we contend, what would happen if you sat down to enjoy or learn something from your students' writing? How differently would you then respond? What kinds of questions would you ask if you were no longer writing interlinear and marginal notes asking her to be 'more precise' or 'more specific'? What might you learn about the student's ethos if you were not circling his use of slang? As Zebroski noted almost twenty years ago, 'It is less important what we make of student writing than that we make something, something principled, of it. The writing teacher must believe that students texts are intrinsically worthy of being valued' (1989: 46).

Zebroski's book chapter, 'A hero in the classroom' revolves around the 'voices' (1989: 35) he hears when he reads a specific student text and the responses each of these voices compel him to write. The first of these voices he labels Simon Newman pop grammarian, and his response centres on the writer's errors in grammar usage and mechanics. Zebroski's second voice and response is from John Crowe Redemption in which he focuses on the structure of the student essay, encouraging him to use different sentence and paragraphing patterns. His third voice is Mina Flaherty whose response revolves around seeing the logic in the writer's choices and asking him what he intended to do in specific parts of the essay. Zebroski's final voice and response is from Mikail Zebroski Bahktin in which he focuses on the ideological tensions in the essay, clearly Zebroski's favoured reading and response. Zebroski's essay illustrates that as readers, teachers can have various interpretations. His voices or response impulses are a nice example of ways in which teachers can use various interpretations and evaluations available from their reading to make a pedagogical decision about what response best suits a student at this juncture in the writing process and his/her development as a writer.

Huot (2002) in his book chapter 'Reading like a teacher' outlines a series of activities he uses in preparing teachers to read and respond to student writing. These activities revolve around having student teachers read the same paper in groups for very different purposes, like a rough draft in a classroom setting versus reading a paper to decide whether or not a student should exit a specific course or be placed into another course. Student teachers also read student writing in different ways, to describe, summarize, or for other purposes. These reading-student-writing activities culminate in a final exam in which student teachers are given an essay they may or not have read before and are asked to create a student and respond to the essay within the context of the writer and situation they invent.

Eddgington reports on a study in which he used protocol analysis and tape recorded

eight teachers reading and responding to their students writing. He found,

> ... that reading and responding to student writing is not just a textual act; it is a contextual act. As these data show, personal beliefs, and values, classroom experiences, relationships with students and other contextual influence instructors. Reading student texts was a highly valued, emotional activity, and the instructors often called on different reading strategies (such as re-reading, skimming, and questioning) to assist them in understanding the student's text, ideas and arguments". (2005: p. 141)

Eddgington's study confirms Phelps' argument that responding to student writing is essentially about the ways in which we read student writing: 'The defining aspect of pedagogical response is not the teacher's rhetoric but the teacher's receptivity to the student text (and to what lies beyond it): Response is most fundamentally reading, not writing' (Phelps, 2000: 93).

CONCLUSION

We hope we have been able to convey how important we believe classroom assessment is to the effective teaching of writing. The nearly four-year old developments that lead to a new pedagogy or the teaching of writing were based in some substantive ways upon a dissatisfaction with the ways writing was being assessed in the classroom. As our review of the literature on responding to student reveals, just recognizing that writing was a process and that instruction needed to be process-based did not automatically address problems in the ways in which writing was evaluated and responded. It seems to us as we have been writing and evaluating our own progress in this essay that writing teachers have been adding various components toward a better pedagogy of assessment. The understanding of assessment as being both formative and summative was an important if not a complete step in the right direction. We hope that our distinctions between assessment, grading, and testing will be another important step. Nonetheless, we cannot overemphasize the importance of seeing classroom evaluation and response as an essentially component of reading.

Instead of a continuing research and scholarship into the ways in which instructors can and write responses to student writing, we call for a new research agenda focused upon the ways teachers read student writing in various contexts and across instructional and programmatic purposes. Concentrating on the ways in which we read student writing can only advance the ways in which we respond to student writing, making us more aware of the source(s) of our responses and the purposes for which we read and respond to student writing in an instructional context. The potential for our argument that the literature on responding to student writing needs to focus more closely on the reading of student texts is profoundly illustrated in Carmen Kynard's essay about reading and responding to her mostly urban, first-generation, and ethnically diverse, community college students. Kynard not only demonstrates the importance of reading student writing in consistently sound pedagogical ways, but she also implores teachers to:

> ... situate themselves as double readers, so to speak: one, as readers of the classroom text that was assigned with all of the political identities that the teachers bring to bear in their own interpretive frameworks; and, two, as readers of a socially constructed student's text bearing its own ideological framework. (2006: p. 372)

Kynard expands the notion of response as reading to include the various ideological and sociological factors involved in interpreting any linguistic, rhetorical, or literate activity in the classroom. This emphasis on interpretation for responding to student and teaching writing more generally brings us full circle to the beginning of our chapter in which we separated assessment from testing and grading and suggested that teachers articulate whatever interpretive/evaluative response they had in the best possible way to teach a particular student.

NOTES

1   While these two approaches are not identical, each was formulated during the same period in response to the prevailing way of teaching writing that James Berlin (1987) called current traditional rhetoric in which initial drafts of student texts were evaluated rigorously for grammar, usage, and mechanics. Nystrand et al. refer to whole language and new rhetoric collectively in their essay about the intellectual history of composition.
2   We discuss the importance, difference and tension between the identities of student and writer for the teaching of writing in a school context later in the essay.
3   See appendix 29A for a sample rubric and peer review sheet.

REFERENCES

Anson, C.M. (1989) (ed.) *Writing and response: Theory, practice and research*, Urbana, IL: NCTE.

Baker, Nancy W. (1993) 'The Effects of Portfolio-Based Instruction on Composition Students' Final Examination Scores, Course Grades, and Attitudes Toward Writing,' *Research in the Teaching of English*, 27: 155–174.

Belanoff, Pat (1994) 'Portfolios and Literacy: Why?' in Laurel Black et al. (eds), New *Directions in Portfolio Assessment*, Portsmouth, NH: Boynton/Cook. pp.13–24.

Berlin, James (1984) *Writing Instruction in Nineteenth-Century American Colleges*, Carbondale: Southern Illinois UP.

Berlin, James. (1987) *Rhetoric and reality: Writing instruction in American colleges, 1910–1985*, Carbondale, IL: Southern Illinois UP.

Bizarro, Patrick, Joan Chandler, Jane Mathison-Fife, Peggy O'Neil, and Richard Straub (1997) 'Interchanges: Reimagining Response', *College Composition and Communication*, 48: 269–283.

Boyd, R. (1998) 'The origins and evolution of grading student writing: Pedagogical imperatives and cultural anxieties', in F. Zak and C.C. Weaver (eds), *The Theory and Practice of Grading Student Writing: Problems and possibilities*, Albany, NY: State University of New York Press. pp.3–16.

Black, L., Daiker, D., Sommers J., and Stygall, G. (1994) (eds) *New Directions in Portfolio Assessment: Reflective practice, critical theory and large-scale scoring*, Portsmouth, NH: Boynton/Cook.

Britton, James N., Burgess, T., Martin, N., McLeod, A., and Rosen, H. (1975). *The Development of Writing Abilities* (11–18). London: Macmillan Educational Ltd.

Callahan, Susan (1997) 'Tests Worth Taking?: Using Portfolios for Accountability in Kentucky', *Research in the Teaching of English*, 31: 295–336.

Callahan, Susan (1999) 'All Done With the Best of Intentions: One Kentucky High School after Six Years of Portfolio Tests', *Assessing Writing*, 6: 5–40.

Camp, Roberta and Denise S. Levine (1991) 'Background and Variations in Sixth- through Twelfth Grade Classrooms', in Pat Belanoff and Marcia Dickson (eds), *Portfolios: Process and Product*, Portsmouth, NH: Boynton/Cook. pp.194–205.

Connors, R.J. and Lunsford, A.A. (1993) 'Teachers' rhetorical comments on student Papers', *College Composition and Communication*, 44: 200–223.

Eddington, Anthony (2005) '"What are you thinking?": understanding teacher reader and response through a protocol analysis study', *Journal of Writing Assessment*, 2(2): 125–148.

Elliot, Norbert (2005) *On a Scale: A social history of writing assessment in America*, New York: NY: Peter Lang.

English Journal (1994) 'English Journal Focus: Assessing Assessment', *English Journal*, 83: 37.

Freedman, Sarah W. (1984) 'The Registers of Student and Professional Expository Writing: Influences on teachers' responses', in R. Beach and L. Bridwell (eds), *New Directions in Composition Research*, New York: Guilford. pp.334–347.

Goodman, K.S. (1967) 'Reading: A psycholinguistic guessing game', *Journal of the Reading Specialist*, 6: 126–135.

Horvath, B.K. (1984) 'The Components of written response: A practical synthesis of current views', *Rhetoric Review*, 2: 136–156.

Huot, B. (2002) *(Re) articulating writing assessment for teaching and learning*, Logan, UT: Utah State UP.

Huot, B. and Williamson, M.M. (1997) 'Rethinking Portfolios for Evaluating Writing: Issues of Assessment and Power', in K.B.Yancey and I.Weiser (eds), *Situating Portfolios: Four Perspectives*, Logan, UT: Utah State University Press, pp.43–56.

Kynard, C. (2006). '"Y'all are killin me up in here": Response theory from a newjack composition instructor/sistahgurl meeting her students on the page', *Teaching English in the Two-Year College*, 34: 361–387.

Lawson, B., Sterr-Ryan, S., and Winterowd, W.R. (1989) (eds) *Encountering Student Texts: Interpretive issues in reading student writing*, Urbana, IL: NCTE.

Lynne, P. (2004) *Coming to Terms: A theory of writing assessment*, Logan, UT: Utah State UP.

Mathison-Fife, J. and O'Neill, P. (2001) 'Moving beyond the written comment: narrowing the gap between response, practice and research', *College Composition and Communication*, 53: 300–321.

Miller, R. (1994) 'Composing English studies: Toward a social history of the discipline', *College Composition and Communication*, 45: 164–179.

Murphy, S. (1994). 'Portfolios and Curriculum Reform: Patterns in Practice', *Assessing Writing* 1: 175–206.

Murphy, S. and Underwood, T. (2000) *Portfolio Practices: Lessons from schools, districts and states*, Norwood, MA: Christopher Gordon.

Nystrand, M., Greene, S., and Wiemelt, J. (1993) 'Where did composition studies come from?', *Written Communication*, 10: 267–333.

Phelps, Louise Weatherbee (1989) 'Images of student writing: The deep structure of teacher response', in Chris Anson (ed.), *Writing and response: Theory, practice and research*, Anson, Urbana, IL: National Council of Teachers of English. 37–67.

Phelps, Louise Weatherbee (2000) 'Cyrano's nose: variations on the theme of response', *Assessing Writing*, 7: 91–110.

Reay, Diane and Wiliam, Dylan (2001) '"I'll be a nothin" : structure, agency and the construction of identity through assessment', in Janet Collins and Deirdre Cook (eds), *Understanding Learning: Influences and outcomes*, London: Paul Chapman Publishing. pp.149–161.

Rose, D. (2007) 'A reading-based model of schooling'. *Pesquisas em Discurso Pedagógico*, 4: 2, 1–22 http://www.maxwell.lambda.ele.puc-rio.br.

Scriven, M. (1966) 'The methodology of evaluation', Publication #110 of the social science consortium. Lafayette, IN: Purdue University.

Sommers, N. (1982) 'Responding to student writing', *College Composition and Communication*, 33: 148–156.

Sperling, Melanie (1994) 'Constructing the Perspective of Teacher as Reader: A Framework for Studying Response to Student Writing', *Research in the Teaching of English*, 28: 175–207.

Sperling, M. and Freedman, S.W. (1987) 'A good girl writes like a good girl: Written response and clues to the teaching/learning process', *Written Communication*, 4: 343–369.

Straub, Richard (1996) 'The Concept of Control in Teacher Response: Defining the Varieties of Directive and Facilitative Commentary', *College Composition and Communication*, 47: 223–251.

Straub, Richard (1997) 'Students' Reactions to Teacher Comments: An Exploratory Study', *Research in Teaching English*, 31: 91–120.

Straub, Richard (2000) 'The Student, the Text and the Classroom Context: A Case Study of Teacher Response', *Assessing Writing*, 7: 23–56.

Tierney, R. and Pearson, P.D. (1983) 'Toward a composing model of reading', *Language Arts*, 60: 568–580.

Williams, Joseph (1981) 'The Phenomenology of Error', *College Composition and Communication*, 32: 152–68.

Yancey, K.B. (1992) (ed.) *Portfolios in the Writing Classroom: An introduction*, Urbana, IL: National Council of Teachers of English.

Yancey K.B. and Weiser, I. (1997) *Situating Portfolios: Four perspectives*, Logan, UT: Utah State UP.

Zebroski, J.T. (1989) 'A hero in the classroom.' in B. Lawson, S. Sterr-Ryan, and W.R. Winterowd (eds.), *Encountering Student Texts: Interpretive Issues in Reading Student Writing*, Urbana, IL: NCTE. pp.35–47.

APPENDIX 29A

Rubric for the First Two Drafts of the Statistics Paper

1. Are the point and argument of the paper clear?
2. Is the argument persuasive?
3. Are there relevant, current, statistical data to support the argument?
4. Are the data cited from a reputable source?
5. Are the data represented in clear and appropriate graphic form?
6. Is the paper organized in a coherent, logical fashion?
7. Does the paper consistently follow an appropriate documentation style?

Peer Review Sheet for Statistics Paper

Author _____   Reviewer_____

1. Appoint a time keeper 1(allot 5 minutes for each paper)
2. Read Student paper silently. Write down what you think the main argument of the paper is.

Main Argument

3. Compare what different readers saw as the main argument.
4. Is the argument clear and persuasive? Why? Not?
5. Are there relevant, current, statistical data to support the argument? Why? Not?
6. Where are the data cited from? Is it from a reputable source?
7. Are the data represented in clear and appropriate graphic form? Why? Not?
8. What is the organization of the paper? Is the paper easy or not to follow? Can you tell what the writer is going to say next? How can the organization be improved?
9. What one thing can the writer do to make the paper better?

The Role of Readers in Writing Development: Writing Students Bringing Their Texts to the Test

Gert Rijlaarsdam, Martine Braaksma, Michel Couzijn,
Tanja Janssen, Marleen Kieft, Mariet Raedts,
Elke van Steendam, Anne Toorenaar, and
Huub van den Bergh

INTRODUCTION

Readers helping writers to 'test' their text

For over thirty years, writing has been portrayed in research literature as a way of *problem solving* (Moss 1975; Flower and Hayes 1977; Hayes and Flower 1979; Hayes 1989; Bryson et al., 1991). The translation of this idea to the educational field followed soon after (e.g., Berkenkotter 1982; Coe et al., 1983). In this chapter, we will discuss the usability in writing instruction of *pretesting texts with real readers*, a way to embody the often-omitted final stage of the problem-solving model: the implementation and evaluation of the problem 'solution' that is the written text. We focus on pretesting texts by

writing students through *reader observation* instead of readers' comments. We use observation as a means to collect feedback on the qualities of the text for the purpose of revision, enhancing the writer's *audience awareness* as part of his/her writing expertise.

In the problem-solving view of writing, the writer is supposed to solve a communicative problem by producing a text that fulfils the communicative needs of the writer and the reader (the *task goal*), thus making the communication *effective*. The writing task is a 'problem' insofar as it is not directly obvious for the writer what the qualities of the text should be or how he should arrive at such a text. The contribution of this line of research to writing education lies in the cognitive approach to instruction: an orientation on the writer's mind, on writing processes and on the constituting strategic activities.

Modern textbooks on writing (e.g., Newsweek Education Programme, 2006; Srebanek, 2006) or online academic writing tools (e.g., Writing@CSU, 2008) almost invariably show a step-by-step guide on how to move through the stages of text composition: define the writing task, collect and process information, conduct prewriting activities, start writing or 'translating ideas into text', and revise the text. Strategic advice may be given, such as 'you probably want to sketch an outline first', 'try to delay revision on the word or sentence level', and 'do a last check on spelling errors before you hand in the text'. Peer feedback is often advised: students exchange papers and produce feedback. Peers are put in the role of the instructor, and provide advice on text improvement. Yet the 'solution' that the writer invented for the 'writing problem' is hardly ever put to the test. In this respect, writing education seems to fall short of the problem-solving metaphor. Theories on problem-solving processes (Newell and Simon 1972; Frederiksen 1984; Wilson 1993) all stipulate a final stage in which the chosen solution is *implemented*, and its success is monitored and evaluated. In writing education, this is hardly realized. Rarely does the writer get the opportunity to witness *real readers'* interaction with their text, responding to its particular qualities. The communication remains *virtual*.

Nevertheless, writing researchers who took a problem-solving view have always regarded it essential that writers develop a sense of *audience awareness* (Flower and Hayes 1980; Berkenkotter 1981), enabling them to make decisions in their writing to accommodate their readers' communicative needs. Audience awareness as part of writing expertise is subject of ongoing educational research that varies from quasi-experimental (e.g., Carvalho 2002) and experimental studies (e.g., Sato and Matsushima 2006; Midgette et al., 2008) to descriptive case studies (e.g., Zainuddin and Moore 2003), educational evaluations and recommendations (e.g., Paretti 2006). With the exception of Sato and Matsushima (2006), these studies have in

common that there is *no actual audience* for the student writer to get acquainted with. Students are postulating or are being presented with a number of presumed *audience characteristics* that they are to take into account. Descriptive and experimental studies demonstrate whether writing students actually follow these guidelines, which is taken as a symptom of developing audience awareness.

In professional strands of writing, however, such as technical and business writing, real test audiences are employed to assess text quality (e.g., Schriver 1996; De Jong 1998; Janssen and Jaspers 2002; see for an application in educational course materials McGovern (2007)). The main goal of this *pretesting* or *usability testing* is to gather factual information by which the text can be effectively improved, better suiting the readers' communicative needs and habits. De Jong and Schellens (1997) present a review of research on reader-focused text evaluation.

Beside this obvious stimulus for text revision, the question arises whether usability testing by means of real readers can also be advantageous to writing education. Already in the early 1990s, Schriver (1991; 1992) conducted research into potential learning effects of this *pretesting* for writers. Does feedback from real readers contribute to the writer's audience awareness, in a way that is transferable to future writing or revision tasks? Schriver presented writing students (college level) with a number of *readers' think-aloud protocols* in written format and had them practice to revise their texts in accordance with this feedback. She found that both junior and senior writers improved significantly in taking the reader's point of view when planning to revise, diagnose readers' problems caused by textual omissions, characterize problems from the reader's perspective, and attend to global text problems. In sum: by getting to know their *real readers' responses*, the writing students acquired concrete knowledge about their readers' communicative needs and behaviours. This knowledge helped them to anticipate potential problems in text that had not yet been commented on by any reader.

In line with the practice of *pretesting texts* in professional writing, we will discuss possibilities for enhancing audience awareness in young writers by means of factual and meaningful observations by writers and their readers.

In the next section, we discuss studies in the field of referential communication that yielded evidence for the effectiveness of observation activities, followed by studies of writer–reader role changing, and studies on writers observing readers as a way to collect feedback. In the third section, we will present two examples from educational practice, which illustrate how reader observation can be incorporated in educational practice. We conclude with an outlook on future writing classrooms, where more technical means will be available to writing students to observe actual communication processes and some recommendations for future research.

LEARNING TO WRITE BY EMPLOYING READERS: A BASIS FOR REVISION AND THEORIES OF A GOOD TEXT

Acquisition of audience awareness in referential communication

Yule (1997) defines referential communication as those 'communicative acts, generally spoken, in which some kind of information is exchanged between two speakers. This information exchange is typically dependent on successful acts of reference' (1). This kind of communication emerges in infanthood, and includes pointing at or verbally referencing to objects in the environment ('doll'), giving directions ('there'), describing qualities of or differences between objects ('big'), and telling stories about familiar people or animals in known settings ('pussy kitchen').

Within the domain of referential communication, writing is seen as a cognitive and social process. The cognitive task is to decide about the information to communicate and how to communicate it. Writers must coordinate two representations of the text; the communicative intent (What do I want to say?) and the actual text produced-so-far (What have I written?). These representations interact, that is, the intended text guides the composition of the actual text, and the actual text and its composing process may take the writer on unexpected tracks of thoughts, reasons, and arguments, and renewed intentions. Additionally, writers must consider audience and context of the writing. This social task requires that writers construe a third representation of the text: the reader's perspective (How are my readers likely to interpret my writing, apart from my own intentions and my own interpretation of what I have written?). This is well in line with the notion of 'audience awareness' as discussed in the previous section.

Basic research on *oral* referential communication was done by Sonnenschein and Whitehurst (Sonnenschein and Whitehurst 1983, 1984; Sonnenschein 1988) in the developmental perspective of younger children. They studied the effect of participating in communication vs. observing communication on the acquisition of referential skills. Their idea was that the absence of transfer they found between speaking and listening skills might stem from a lack of metacommunication, which is a more abstract, higher order skill than speaking or listening itself. Then they tested the hypothesis that *observation and evaluation* of speakers and/or listeners in communication tasks would result in metacommunicative knowledge, and that this knowledge contributes to the speaking and listening skills.

Sonnenschein and Whitehurst (1984) used a referential communication task; speakers (6 yrs) were asked to describe one object from a pair (similar or different in colour, size and shape) so clearly that a listener could identify it correctly (e.g., 'the blue triangle' or 'the big pink one'). In the listening role, students listened to a doll referring to one of the objects, and had to decide whether they could identify the object, or that the message was not clear enough (e.g., 'the triangle' or 'the big one'). In two conditions, the participants were trained in either the listener or the speaker role, thus participating in the communication. In a third condition, participants observed two dolls playing the game, and evaluated the performances of both speaker and listener: they had to decide whether the object was described adequately, and whether the listener identified it correctly. Furthermore, observation conditions varied according to activity (observation with or without evaluation), feedback on trials (yes/no) and the object of observation (listener, speaker, or both). As learning and transfer tasks, speaking skill, listening skill, and commenting skill on others' performance were measured.

Observation and evaluation of both speakers and listeners—i.e., of the complete communication—resulted in very high scores on all posttests; the transfer to speaking, writing, and evaluation tasks. This is a stunning result, indicating that it is possible to acquire such speaking and listening skills without practising them. Moreover, critical awareness was significantly higher than in the practising conditions. Observation of both roles without giving evaluative comments, however, yielded much smaller effects. Observation of only one role, either speaker or listener, yielded large learning effects, but no transfer effects, neither to the complementary mode, nor to the commenting tasks.

The researchers conclude that speaking and listening tasks are 'subordinated' to the commenting or evaluation task, in the sense that a student who masters the commenting task appears to master the speaking and listening tasks as well, but not vice versa. In addition, they conclude that an effective acquisition of speaking or listening skill can be accomplished by observation and evaluation of others performing such tasks.

This study provides some important suggestions for effective learning activities: (a) intermodal transfer can only be obtained by observation of both complementary roles in the communication, not by training in or observation of one role only; (b) learning and transfer effects increase strongly if the student adds evaluative comments to the observations. The act of commenting probably focuses the observer's perceptions on the criteria for successful communication.

Traxler and Gernsbacher (1992; 1993) applied the referential communication paradigm to writing instruction. Their goal was to make writers understand how readers envision or experience their text. This can be seen as the acquisition of audience awareness, developing the reader's perspective on the text they had written ('What have I written? What will my audience make of it?') as opposed to the text they intended to write. This would help to overcome one of the major problems for writers; their 'egocentric position' as Moffett (1968: 195) called it. Traxler and Gernsbacher (1992) showed that writers who received feedback from their readers successfully revised referential descriptions of geometric figures, whereas writers who did not receive feedback were unable to revise. The first group also succeeded in transferring their learning result to descriptions of new sets of geometric figures. Even a minimal form of feedback may help writers learn to envision how readers will interpret their texts.

In their subsequent study (1993), Traxler and Gernsbacher placed writers 'in their readers' shoes'. In three experiments, half the writers performed a reading task that their readers would subsequently perform, and the other half of the writers performed a control task. In the first and second experiments, the writers who gained their readers' perspective successfully revised their written descriptions of geometric figures, whereas writers who performed the control task could not. In the third experiment, the authors found that these effects could not be attributed to the fact that the writers were exposed to examples of other writers' descriptions, but that the reader enactment itself produced the learning effect. It was concluded that gaining their readers' perspective helps writers communicate more clearly, because perspective-taking helps writers form a mental representation of how readers interpret their texts.

Recently, Sato and Matsushima (2006) reported on the effects of an audience awareness enhancing intervention in referential writing, with students in various age groups (from seventh-grade to undergraduate). Some of the participants acted as writers and the others as readers. Writers wrote a text describing a more or less complex geometrical figure. Readers read the text and tried to draw the figure according to the description.

The researchers designed a learning arrangement in which the writing instruction focused on audience awareness: writers determining which information readers would require in order to produce the figure correctly, and how such information should be conveyed in text. It turned out that writers in this 'high audience-awareness' condition spent considerably more time planning and writing their texts than writers in a low audience-awareness condition, and that the texts written in the high audience-awareness condition were longer, containing more complex descriptions. In a second experiment, students were given 'prototype texts' containing adequate descriptions of complex figures. Students in the high audience-awareness condition, who developed prior knowledge on information needs for readers, were found to draw the figure more accurately. In a third experiment, these authors focused on the effect of reader feedback for writers, and employed secondary students (ninth-grade). Merely being told to attend to an audience did not improve the quality of texts. However, visual and verbal feedback from the readers (seventh-grade) was effective: writers could improve the texts by revising them to the received feedback. In addition, the experience of revising the text according to feedback transferred to later writing tasks.

In sum, the referential communication paradigm yielded some interesting results for writing education. Because of relatively clear 'success criteria' for written references, even young students succeed in developing an audience awareness that is productive in their subsequent writing. In the Sonnenschein and Whitehurst studies, the position of observer of 'what works' in communication was the most effective, more so than training in the speaker or listener roles that made up the posttests. The studies by Traxler and Gernsbacher demonstrated that even minimal reader feedback and reader enactment helps writers to develop a useful image of actual readers' needs. The Sato and Matsushima experiments show that an instructional focus on audience awareness primed writers and readers to communicate more effectively, and that even young writers develop a productive audience awareness due to reader feedback, which transfers to novel tasks.

Writers experiencing the reader's role: Perspective taking

Experiencing problems as a reader may motivate people to write better. When Vernon et al., 2005) introduced punctuation in writing lessons for young children, they realized that learning to punctuate accurately assumes knowledge of the writing system, of sentences and clauses, knowledge that is lacking at that early age. They decided to stimulate this awareness by having children read badly punctuated texts, which raised a number of comprehension and interpretation problems. Thus, the need to punctuate arose, due to having been in the role of the reader and experiencing typical readers' problems.

This principle was explored by Holliway and McCutchen (Holliway 2000; Holliway and McCutchen 2004). Would young writers (grades five and seven) benefit from learning to read and experience comprehension problems as their readers do? In the first of three sessions, all writers produced descriptions of three Tangram figures. In the second session, the writers received a typed version of their own description, and all writers were randomly assigned to one of three perspective-taking conditions; feedback-only, feedback and rating, and feedback and read-as-the-reader. In all three conditions, writers received some written feedback (one sentence) on their description, stating whether they had been successful in unambiguously describing the Tangram figure. In the condition feedback-only, students were asked to revise their original descriptions. In the condition feedback and rating, writers also received three descriptions written by other students in the group, rated the descriptions on informational adequacy, and wrote one sentence to the writer about what could be improved. They then revised their own descriptions. In the third condition, feedback and read-as-the-reader, writers were given three descriptions written by other students in the group, and were asked to match these descriptions with Tangram figures. Then writers revised their own original descriptions.

In the posttest writing session, writers composed descriptions for Tangrams they had not previously seen. Each set contained three separate groups of four similar looking Tangrams. Each group contained one 'Targetgram' and three distracters. For both grades, the read-as-the-reader condition scored significantly higher in revising their Tangram descriptions (second session) and writing descriptions for a new set of Tangrams. This led to the conclusion that perspective taking supports the development of referential writing ability.

The rating condition is more or less similar to regular peer feedback conditions. It did not yield an improvement of writing skill, except for new tasks (session 3) in grade five. Possibly, students in the rating condition lacked a frame of reference to evaluate adequacy, while in the condition read-as-the-reader students underwent typical reader problems, comparing a written description with the object and the distracters. They had to construct a frame of reference themselves: which quality in the text enables me to match a particular figure?

Holliway's study shows that minimal instruction can be sufficient to improve referential writing skill: if students experience a reader's role as a postwriting activity, an idea of reader's needs and a theory of 'good text'

may emerge. Essential is that the writer experiences how the text really 'works' when a reader uses the information. In this study, a realistic writer–reader experience was created, as Moffett (1968) argued for, in which the reader had to *use* the text rather than read, rate, or comment on it from a distant, nonparticipant role. Reader enactment gives way to the development of ideas about 'what works' in this type of communication; ideas that students successfully transferred to their own writing.

Learning to write by reader observation: Creating a feedback loop

A number of studies by Lumbelli et al. demonstrate the use of adult reader observations as a means to collect feedback for writers, and as a means to enhance their audience awareness. Witnessing the factual problems of readers may help to understand how reading works, what it takes, and how texts can either help or hinder reading (Crasnich and Lumbelli (2004). Lumbelli and Paoletti (2004) provided learners with audio-tapes, containing experts' spontaneous comprehension processes that *'contained all the flaws and redundancies of oral language; the expert reader's uncertainty had been fully verbalised, so that uncertainty about the possible different interpretations of the same passage could be traced back to uncertainty about which processes would most adequately integrate the explicit information, as read and decoded'* (Lumbelli and Paoletti 2004: 206). Gárate and Melero (2004) implemented a similar procedure. Eleven-year-olds learned to use counter argumentation in argumentative writing by using the modelling technique carried out by an expert reader, thereby fostering the transition from text comprehension to production. In these studies, students observed the reading behaviour of adults, while in this section, we will focus on studies receiving reader feedback from peer students.

In this vein, Couzijn (1995); Couzijn and Rijlaarsdam (1996); Couzijn and Rijlaarsdam (2004); and Rijlaarsdam et al. (2006) studied the effects of writers being confronted with real readers. His question was: do children develop knowledge about effective communication by witnessing how (peer) readers actually deal with texts? He focused on a particular text type with a strong and overt communicative effect: a manual for a simple physics experiment. First, Couzijn taught the children individually how to perform this physics experiment by manipulating a number of objects (glass bottle, cork, funnel, straw, water, etc.). He showed students the experiment by means of three illustrations, step-by-step, and added the physical explanations. He coached the student to do the experiment, until the student was able to carry out the experiment flawlessly and understood what it was about. Then, the student was asked to write a manual for a classroom peer. The manual should be so clear that the reader could perform the experiment perfectly and understand what it was about.

In the second stage, the written manuals were used by other students (not involved in the first stage) who were asked to perform the experiment while thinking aloud. These performances were videotaped. Three weeks after the initial writing session, the writer was shown two of the readers on video. Some writers observed readers of their own text, while others were confronted with readers of texts written by other writers. Some students had access to written comments by readers; others did not receive this support. Then, the student received his or her original text, with the request to improve its quality.

In this experiment, all three reader-observation conditions scored significantly better than a control group who had to revise their text without reader observation. The revised manuals showed many improvements over the first version (for the conditions 'observing one's own reader', 'observing one's own reader plus written comments', and 'observing someone else's reader', the effect sizes were 1.74, 2.56, and 0.47 respectively). For teaching practice, this would mean that after a class has written a certain communicative text, simply showing one or two readers on video actually 'using' such a text for its communicative purpose would stimulate the revision phase strongly. In a similar study, with another physics experiment, now in primary education (Grade 8), De Jong (2006) found effect sizes of respectively 1.49 and 2.0 for revisions after explicit prompting and after observing readers, with an effect size of the experimental condition of .96.

In education, however, we want to accomplish more; we aim at generalization of experiences and transfer to other tasks. Therefore, Couzijn asked participants three weeks later to write a 'letter of advice' to a new classroom mate, about how one should write a manual. In this way, the students' knowledge about the manual as communicative text type was assessed, a prerequisite for transfer to similar manual-writing tasks. Students from the 'observing one's own reader plus written comments' condition produced many more pieces of advice than students from the other conditions (effect size = 2.33).

Couzijn and Rijlaarsdam (1996) concluded that simply adding a revision task does not work, that observing readers before revising your own text improves the revision significantly, and that observing your own readers after having written your first draft helps even more. Furthermore, processing external feedback (written comments) enhances the generalization of transferrable knowledge (see also Rijlaarsdam et al., 2004).

These results indicate that in some instances, young writers are capable of constructing knowledge about what a good text entails. Without further help or instruction, they can build a set of criteria for a good text from observing what readers are doing and thinking while trying to comprehend the text. They can apply the criteria in their revisions. For the constructed knowledge to become durable and transferable, some reflective activity seems to be necessary.

Students making observations in the writing classroom: Two examples

The two classroom practices presented here have in common that student writers somehow get in touch with a communicative role that is complementary to their own writing role. 'Complementary' refers to two things: either a *communicative* complement, changing from writer to reader or vice versa; or a *learning* complement, changing from enactive learning-by-doing to vicarious learning-by-observation, or vice versa. This pedagogy relies on the notion that in an effective language curriculum, students learn to participate in various functional roles (see Figure 30.1).

First, they must be in a position to participate in communication in order to experience the effects of written and spoken text. As *writers*, they experience how their communicative intentions must be transformed into text. As writers moving into the *observer* role, they can witness, investigate, and learn how (their) texts affect readers and how readers actually read and respond (Couzijn and Rijlaarsdam 2004; Crasnich and Lumbelli 2005; Lumbelli and Paoletti 2005). Having moved from the writer role into an observer role, students may act as pure readers, feeding back their authentic responses; but they can also show signs of acting like 'instructors', adding advice for the readers to

their responses. Writers may also step into the reader's role themselves, to experience how similar texts work and then apply the newly acquired knowledge in a second round of writing (Holliway and McCutchen 2004).

Writing students can learn from observing how texts work in readers by comparing and evaluating their own writing strategies, as well as by abstracting and generalizing from their observations of readers and their experiences as an imagined reader. From all of these perspectives, they learn about effective factors in communicative texts. It is the teacher's role to organize communicative opportunities to learn from, to help students discover 'what works' in their various roles, and to help them make generalizations that can be applied in future communication.

The Yummy Yummy Case

As an example of changing writing, reading, and observing roles in writing classes, we present the *Yummy Yummy Case* (Figure 30.2). This lesson series (4 lessons, 45 minutes each) was designed to test the practical relevance of our student participation model (Figure 30.1). It stresses the acquisition of pragma-linguistic knowledge: what makes a particular text effective? Students (12–13 yrs) not just choose and apply, but experience and investigate text qualities. In this way, they develop a kind of 'tested' knowledge and

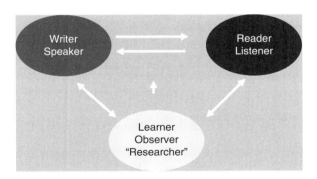

Figure 30.1   Designing interrelated communicative roles or functions in the L1 classroom (Adapted from Rijlaarsdam and Van den Bergh, 2004).

Lesson 1: Goal: writing a convincing letter of complaint, using argumentation.
Place: computer room.
Activity: Teacher presents the case to all students and students write their letters.

Imagine: you are a real fan of the *Yummy Yummy Candy Bars*. One day you read the following advertisement:

Save up for two free movie tickets!

How to get them:
On the wrapper of each Yummy Yummy Candy Bar you will find 1 saving point. Save 10 points. Send the points in an envelope to Yummy Yummy Saving Action,
PO Box 3333, 1273 KB Etten-Leur, The Netherlands.
Include a stamp of 39 cents for the mailing costs. Mention clearly your name, address, residential town, and zip code. The two free (FREE!) movie tickets will be sent as soon as possible to your address.

This offer ends on April 15th 2003.

Communicative situation: It is April 7th. Suppose you have already saved 8 points. Nearly all 10 points that are required! But alas! you cannot find any more Yummy Yummy Bars with points on the wrapper, although it is not yet April 15th. You tried a large number of shops. Strange! It seems you will not be able to collect 10 points! But you still want to get the two free movie tickets. Therefore you decide to send your 8 points and two Yummy Yummy wrappers without points.

Goal: write a letter that you send with the 8 points and the wrappers. Explain why you cannot send 10 points. Convince the Yummy Yummy Company that it isn't your fault that you didn't collect 10 points and that you still want to receive the two movie tickets. Be sure they will send you the tickets! Then address the envelope.

Note: This first version of your letter will be put in your portfolio.
•   Save your letter on a disk.
•   Print your letter and hand it in to me.
•   Give me the envelope too.
•   Send your letter to [teacher's emailaddress] (or give me your disk.)

Lesson 2: Board Meeting Yummy Yummy Candy Bars
Place: classroom.

Activity: the teacher makes six groups of 4-5 students. Each two groups are paired (A and B)
Group A: 'Management board'. The task of the board is to read and select two out of nine letters that win the movie tickets. A harsh selection must be made, because just two pairs of tickets are left in stock…).
Group B: Parallel group of 'Researchers'. The task of the researchers is to study the arguments and the criteria used by the management board during the board meeting, when they discuss and select the letters.

Goal: half of the writers have changed to 'readers', who interpret and assess the convincing qualities of each letter. As a group, they must choose the two most convincing letters and be able to explain their choice. The other half of the writers change to the 'observation of readers' position, listening and establishing 'what works' in a convincing letter of complaint. They murst be able to present a list of criteria at play.

Lesson 3: Poster composition and presentation.
Place: classroom

Activities:
A. Inquiry: The students from the research team work on listing and ordering the criteria of the *Yummy Yummy Candy Bars board* and write them on a poster. At the same time, the *Yummy Yummy* board group composes a letter to the children who did *not* win the cinema tickets.
B. Presentation: The research team presents a poster with criteria applied by the management board.
C. Presentation: The management team presents the two selected letters, referring to the poster on which the special qualities of the letters are reported.

Lesson 4: Rewriting/revision original letter & Evaluation
Place: computer room.

Activity: students all move back to their 'writing role' and use the criteria for 'convincing letters of complaint' that they, as board members or researchers, have collected and externalized. The evaluation of the lessons focuses on 'what was learned', 'what was new' and 'how did the two versions of your letter differ'.

Figure 30.2   Overview of Yummy Yummy lessons.

learn how such knowledge can be acquired. The lessons draw on implicit knowledge in students, which they groupwise collect and externalize. The developer tried to cover all roles from our student-participation model, both as participants in the communication (writers and readers) and as researchers (observers).

Prior to these lessons, the teacher made a plan and designed the worksheets. During the lessons, she stuck to her role as organizer and stimulator, and did not 'teach' about criteria. In fact, the students did all the work themselves collecting, investigating, and discussing the criteria for effective communication. Lesson 4 was a lively revising activity, indicating that students were very motivated to improve the letters. They evaluated the lessons very high (8 out of 10). Revised letters showed many improvements, especially in the domain of rhetoric. Students in the research teams made more improvements than children in the board teams (Effect size 1.30 versus 0.30; Rijlaarsdam and Braaksma, 2004). See, for similar effects of observing versus participating in writing synthesis texts, Raedts et al., 2006); argumentative texts Braaksma et al., 2002); Braaksma et al., 2004); Braaksma et al., 2001) and Couzijn (1999); for business letters in L2 Van Steendam (Van Steendam et al., 2008a and 2008b).

This Yummy Yummy lesson model shows that students (12–13 yrs) can create their own frame of reference on qualities of this particular genre: the posters presented by the 'research teams' each contained about ten items, representing at least 80% of the criteria used in the board discussion. Awareness about what works in communication was expressed (board discussion) and fed back to the whole group (research presentations). Groupwise sharing and constructing communicative awareness led to ownership of the criteria for a good text, which stimulated children to revise their own texts: it was an important experience to find that texts are actually 'improvable' and that this is within their own reach.

The Yummy Yummy Case also demonstrates that it is possible in language classes to effectively distribute writer, reader, and observer roles, when students are 'simulating' authentic readers (board teams), as has been advocated for a long time (Moffett, 1968). The key feature of the Yummy, Yummy lessons is that students are motivated to think about what

works in a text, to raise awareness about the quality of communication and, implicitly, about rhetorical strategies. The board and research teams both experience their task as a meaningful learning task that inspires and stimulates genuine dialogue about relevant content. The whole case relies on the meaningfulness of the letter of complaint, in a setting that suits students of this age quite well.

The 'Activity Morning' and storybook case

A second example from classroom practice shows how subject teachers and writing teachers from prevocational education cooperatively create motivating writing lessons, in which roles of writers, readers, and learners/observers (Figure 30.1) are distributed.

In a four-year study, Anne Toorenaar (Toorenaar and Rijlaarsdam (2005a, 2005b) investigated the learning community format, inspired by Brown and Campione (1994), Cobb and Yackel (1996), and Wells (2000). She focused on prevocational education with students preparing for 'Care and Well-being' professions (15–16 yrs). In cooperation with content-area and writing teachers, Toorenaar iteratively designed instructional units, which were then tested in classroom settings. Students learnt to work and communicate with various target groups, such as elderly people, young children, or mentally handicapped persons. Normally the students would learn from textbooks about how to communicate with such clients or audiences. In the 'community of learners' format, however, the students actually met them, and prepared and evaluated the meetings and communication tasks in the classroom.

One of the instructional units focused on the target group of young children (6–7 yrs). Teachers made arrangements for an 'activity-morning' in primary school during which ninth-grade vocational students had to guide the young children like 'professional coaches' in challenging and entertaining activities. In three preceding weeks, various activities were designed during the vocational and writing classes by students collaborating in 'design groups' of three or four peers. During the writing classes, students in 'author groups' collaboratively wrote, illustrated, and published a story book for the primary school children. Each author group took responsibility for one of the stories in the book. This lesson format was tested in two consecutive years, Y1 and Y2.

The writing teachers focused primarily on the social aspects of writing: the relationship between writers and their real audience, and the authentic purpose and context of writing (real storytelling, real entertainment). In the Y1 design, students generated ideas and content for their stories through interactive classroom discussions guided by the teacher. A teacher read aloud various kinds of stories, followed by a discussion of possible reactions from the primary school children ('Would they like this story?', 'Why or why not?'). Elaborating their ideas in stories written by themselves, author-groups would continue this discussion on a smaller scale (e.g., sharing their own history as a listener of bedtime stories). In this way, students built up 'audience awareness': they tried to understand and externalize the perspectives, needs, and wishes of their soon-to-be audience, thereby developing dialogical skills that support text production and revision (Englert et al., 2007).

In the first year, the collaborative writing processes and written stories varied strongly in quality across author groups. Therefore, two pedagogical changes were made for Y2, with a view to enhancing learning-by-observation. First, author groups watched video fragments of Y1 students reading aloud their stories in primary school. In this way, students would acquire a clearer picture of their real audience, and the authentic purpose and context of writing. They could also develop criteria for 'what works' in successful stories, based on either their own preference as listeners, or responses from the videotaped children. In addition, each author group interviewed a peer about their writing

and storytelling experience of last year. Thirdly, each author-group invented a main character, story events, and a fitting surrounding for their story, and presented their ideas for all other author groups to comment on. By means of a whole classroom discussion, guided by the teacher, students collaboratively chose the best character, most interesting events and most inspiring surrounding for their joint picture-and-story book. Each author group elaborated this idea into their own written story. Author-groups pretested their story by reading it aloud for peers, who commented on the quality of the story (appropriateness for target group) and on the read-aloud session (audibility, and voice variation).

The stories were read aloud during the activity morning with the young pupils (6–7 yrs). An independent jury consisting of primary teachers assessed all read-aloud stories. All teachers valued the Y2 stories as better, as more suitable stories to be read aloud for their young pupils. The Y2 students had clearly gotten a better grasp of criteria for successful storytelling to young pupils, by the extra activities they undertook: observation of actual storytelling and of actual listeners' responses, interview with an 'experienced' peer writer, classroom discussion about criteria for successful storytelling to the specific audience, and classroom observation of writers reading aloud their text as a pretest.

This example shows how students can be involved in various ways and roles in learning-to-write experiences: they write, they simulate readers, they observe the targeted communication (observing other students on video reading a story to small children), and apply the invented criteria during a final pretest of the written stories. It should be noted that a genuine writing task, designed for real-life communication, will lead students to genuine discussions about audience traits (young pupils), communicative goals (entertainment, understanding), and the qualities of 'good texts' that serve goals and audience.

OBSERVATION OF WRITERS AND READERS IN WRITING EDUCATION: WHAT THE FUTURE MAY BRING?

From the research results and examples discussed in the former sections, we conclude that actual readers and actual reading processes deserve a place in effective writing instruction. Reader feedback, reader observation, and role switching between writers and readers can be essential complements to a cognitive, process-oriented view on writing education. They may be considered embodiments of the 'implementation and evaluation' stage of the problem-solving process that is often taken as a metaphor for writing. Observations of real readers who actually 'use' the text for the intended communicative purpose (instruct, explain, argue, entertain, etc.) yield opportunities for writing students to collect feedback for the purpose of text revision; but students also develop transferable knowledge about readers' needs and behaviour, as well as criteria for 'effective texts' of a particular genre. Experiences with real readers probably contribute more to the development of audience awareness than the traditional practice of learning to write with an imaginary audience with postulated properties in mind.

Therefore, we advocate an educational environment for writing students that presents them with ample opportunities to get to know their audience, to collect real responses to their texts, and to make discoveries about 'what works' in communicative tasks. To this end, the concept of the 'classroom community of learners' is suitable, such as described by Brown and Campione (1994), because it allows for writing students to act as *learners* first, and *writers* second. Or better: to derive writing activities, reading or observation activities, and more reflective activities from the main goal that is *learning* (cf. Figure 30.1). The social world of the community classroom is a suitable environment in which students help each other to learn by taking up various interacting roles, thus, helping themselves in the process (Englert et al., 2007). The research

results presented in Section II form a good reference to explain why the examples of 'community of learners' presented in Section III turned out to be effective.

We expect that for practice and research, new technology can be very helpful. As a writer is his own worst critic (Moffett 1968; Traxler and Gernsbacher 1992; 1993), we must support writers to pinpoint weaker and stronger elements in their texts. Information technology can help to separate the act of writing and other acts that are supportive of observation and reflection. Schriver (1991; 1992) used audiotape recordings to present readers' responses to the writers. Couzijn (1995; Couzijn and Rijlaarsdam 1996) used videotape recordings to present real readers' responses and behaviours to written text. Lindgren (2005) used keystroke logging as input for writer reflection (see Van Waes and Leijten (2006); or the handbook for advanced users, detailing technical aspects, research backgrounds and applications: Sullivan and Lindgren (2006)). Van Steendam et al. (2008a, 2008b) and Raedts et al. (2007), both in combination with thinking-aloud and keystroke logging (see Degenhart, 2006) used Camtasia (screen recording, free trials at http://www. techsmith.com/camtasia.asp): this tool is easy to implement; recorded are actions on screen when working with word processors, PowerPoint, web-browsers, etc.; it also records audio input (thinking-aloud, and discussion in pairs). Easy to replay, and can be used as input for research, reflection, discussion, or as instruction content (two approaches for the same task: Which is better?).

RECOMMENDATIONS

For future research into reader observation as part of writing instruction, we formulate two recommendations. First is to study the relation between learner characteristics and learning activities. Most interventions studies in writing education focus on main effects, irrespective of students' individual differences, which can be significant. Meta-analyses do not report interaction effects, while their well-founded conclusions might be valid for only a part of the participating students. At least two types of individual differences are of interest when applying learning-by-observation in the writing classroom. First, the difference between high and low self-monitoring students, i.e., students with a tendency to let their task behaviour be guided by external or internal stimuli. Galbraith (1996) reported a strong interaction effect on idea generation between self-monitoring and mode of writing. High self-monitors (who are strongly directed towards rhetorical goals) tended to discover new ideas by making notes, but not by writing full text. Low self-monitors (directed towards dispositional goals, i.e., spelling out spontaneous thought) tended to discover new ideas by writing full text, but not by making notes. Thus, it is likely that low and high monitoring students may benefit differently from observational learning tasks. High self-monitors, by nature more focused on rhetorical aspects of writing, may benefit from feedback on the content of their text (their 'blind spot'), thus from observations of readers coping with content problems. Low self-monitors, by nature more focused on the intrinsic value, suitability or originality of text content, may benefit more from observation of readers dealing with rhetorical problems in their texts. A second type of individual differences to take into account is writing preference. Some students prefer to write in a planned and controlled way, relying on prewriting activities ('Mozartians'), while others like to move ahead intuitively, start writing, and rely on their capacity to shape and revise the text when the urge is felt ('Beethovians'). Kieft, Rijlaarsdam, and Van den Bergh (2008) found that students with a strong writing preference (either 'planning' or 'revising') learnt more from a writing course that was adapted to this preference. Consequently, adaptation of learning-by-observation to students' writing preference may be a useful idea. Students with a planning preference might benefit from observation as a prewriting activity, or as feedback on planning problems. On the other hand, students with a revising preference may be better off receiving feedback on their first full draft, by observations of real readers coping with particular revision problems. In general, studying interactions between learner characteristics and learning activities helps to frame a theory of effective writing instruction. See Rijlaarsdam et al. (2004) for aptitude-treatment-interactions in observing reader responses.

A second recommendation is to include process measures as dependent variables in the research design (see Braaksma et al., 2002), using think-aloud techniques; Torrance et al., 2007), using a handy self-report technique). Adding these measures into the research design is advantageous in two respects: it helps to see which cognitive subprocesses are affected by the intervention, and it makes it possible to relate resulting text quality to subprocesses, which contributes to insight in effective writing processes (Rijlaarsdam and Van den Bergh, 2004).

For writing education practice, we recommend creating learning environments in which all roles or functions of the student participation model (Figure 30.1) are implemented; a community of learners where writing students can explore interactions between texts and readers. Nowadays information technology makes it easier to observe writing processes (screen recording and keystroke logging) and reading processes (think-aloud recordings and screen recordings), thus, we would recommend that teachers and their students collect such processes and use them for instructional purposes.

The learning activity of 'pre-testing your text by observing readers' responses' can be inspired by all kinds of methods used in the design of business and technical communication. Reader demonstrations as a prewriting activity that stimulates audience awareness; readers' responses as a postwriting activity that yields feedback for revision; protocol-aided revision; groupwise comparisons and assessment of functional text qualities; demo's of complete writer-reader interactions by means of ample texts and recordings; recordings of observers who report on their findings—there is a large variety of roles and functions, and of instructional settings in which reader observations can help to improve text and/or to enhance audience awareness.

Even if students do not start out by writing, composing, or designing particular texts by themselves, they may find it useful to start as a 'researcher', studying the quality of a sample texts, documents, or hypertexts by observing their 'users' (usability testing). In this way, students can simulate descriptive research activities and accumulate knowledge that helps to understand 'what works' in written communication. This motivates students to start writing or improve their texts and to build up both genre and audience awareness.

To sum up, observation and inquiry are important learning activities in the writing classroom, stimulating the students' reflection both as writers and as readers. Most importantly, the methods presented here may assist teachers in promoting their students' self-assessment skills, in view of their lifelong learning as communicators.

ACKNOWLEDGEMENTS

This paper is a revised selection of the keynote presented at the international Writing Conference *Writing Research Across Borders*, at the University of California, Santa Barbara (22–24 February, 2008). There is some overlap with Rijlaarsdam, Braaksma, Couzijn, Janssen, Kieft, Broekkamp and Van den Bergh (2005) and Rijlaarsdam, G., Braaksma, M., Couzijn, M., Janssen, T., Raedts, M., Van Steendam, E., Toorenaar, A. And Van den Bergh, H. (2008).

Research reported from Braaksma, Couzijn and Kieft was funded by grants of the Graduate School of Teaching and Learning Amsterdam; research from Raedts and Van Steendam was funded by respectively Hasselt University Belgium and Antwerp University Belgium; research from Toorenaar is funded by the Netherlands Organization for Scientific Research.

REFERENCES

Berkenkotter, C. (1981) 'Understanding a writer's awareness of audience', *College Composition and Communication*, 32(4): 388–399.

Berkenkotter, C. (1982) 'Writing and problem solving', in T. Fulwiler and A. Young (eds), *Language Connections: Writing and Reading across the Curriculum*, Urbana, IL: National Council of Teachers of English.

Braaksma, M.A.H., Rijlaarsdam, G., and Van den Bergh, H. (2002) 'Observational learning and the effects of model-observer similarity', *Journal of Educational Psychology*, 94(2): 405–415.

Braaksma, M.A.H., Rijlaarsdam, G., Van den Bergh, H., and Van Hout-Wolters, B.H.A.M. (2004) 'Observational learning and its effects on the orchestration of writing processes', *Cognition and Instruction*, 22(1): 1–36.

Braaksma, M.A.H., Van den Bergh, H., Rijlaarsdam, G., and Couzijn, M. (2001). 'Effective learning activities in observation tasks when learning to write and read argumentative texts', *European Journal of Psychology of Education*, 16(1): 33–48.

Brown, A.L. and Campione, J.C. (1994) 'Guided discovery in a community of learners', in K. McGilly (ed.), *Integrating Cognitive Theory and Classroom Practice: Classroom Lessons*, Cambridge, MA: MIT Press/ Bradford Books. pp.229–270.

Bryson, M., Bereiter, C., Scardamalia, M., and Joram, E. (1991) 'Going beyond the problem as given: Problem solving in expert and novice writers', in R.J. Sternberg and P.A. Frensch (eds), *Complex Problem Solving: Principles and Mechanisms*, Hillsdale, NJ: Lawrence Erlbaum Associates. pp.61–84.

Carvalho, J.B. (2002) 'Developing audience awareness in writing', *Journal of Research in Reading*, 25(3): 271–282.

Cobb, P. and Yackel E. (1996) 'Constructivist, emergent, and sociocultural perspectives in the context of developmental research', *Educational psychologist*, 31: 175–190.

Coe, N., Rycroft, R., and Ernest, P. (1983) *Writing Skills: A Problem-Solving Approach*, Cambridge: Cambridge University Press.

Couzijn, M. (1995) Observation of writing and reading activities: Effects on learning and transfer. PhD Dissertation, University of Amsterdam. Dordrecht: Dorfix.

Couzijn, M. (1999) 'Learning to write by observation of writing and reading processes: Effects on learning and transfer', *Learning and Instruction*, 9: 109–142.

Couzijn, M. and Rijlaarsdam, G. (1996) 'Learning to write by reader observation and written feedback', in G. Rijlaarsdam, H. van den Bergh, and M. Couzijn (eds), *Effective Teaching and Learning of Writing. Current Trends In Research*, Amsterdam: Amsterdam University Press. pp.224–252

Couzijn, M. and Rijlaarsdam, G. (2004) 'Learning to read and write argumentative text by observation', in G. Rijlaarsdam (Series ed.), and G. Rijlaarsdam, H. Van den Bergh, and M. Couzijn (Vol. eds.), Studies in Writing. Vol. 14: Effective Learning and Teaching of Writing, Part 1, Studies in Learning to Write (second edn.), Dordrecht: Kluwer Academic Publishers. pp.241–258.

Crasnich, S. and Lumbelli, L. (2004) 'Improving argumentative writing by fostering argumentative speech', in G. Rijlaarsdam (Series ed.), and G. Rijlaarsdam, H. Van den Bergh, and M. Couzijn (Vol. eds.), Studies in Writing. Vol. 14: Effective Learning and Teaching of Writing, Part 1, Studies in Learning to Write (second edn.), Dordrecht: Kluwer Academic Publishers. pp.181–196.

De Jong, M. (1998) Reader Feedback in Text Design. Validity of the plus-minus method for the pretesting of public information brochures. Amsterdam: Rodopi. (Utrecht Studies in Language and Communication series).

De Jong., J. (2006) Leren-door-Observeren. Een experiment in het basisonderwijs [Learning through observing. An experiment in primary education]. Masters thesis. Utrecht University, The Netherlands.

De Jong, M. and Schellens, P.J. (1997) 'Reader-focused text evaluation: An overview of goals and methods', *Journal of Business and Technical Communication*, 11: 402–432.

Degenhart, M. (2006) 'Camtasia and Catmovie', in L. Van Waes, M. Leijten, and C.M. Neuwirth (Vol. eds.) and G. Rijlaarsdam (Series ed.), *Studies in Writing. Vol. 17: Writing and Digital Media*, Oxford: Elsevier. pp.180–186.

Englert, S., Mariage, T.V., and Dunsmore, K. (2006) 'Tenets of sociocultural theory in writing instruction research', in C.A. MacArthur, S. Graham, and J. Fitzgerald (eds), *Handbook of Writing Research*, New York: Guilford Press. pp.208–221.

Flower, L.S. and J.R. Hayes (1977) 'Problem-solving strategies and the writing process', *College English*, 39(4): 449–461

Flower, L. and Hayes, J. (1980) 'The cognition of discovery: Defining a rhetorical problem', *College Composition and Communication*, 31(1): 21–32.

Frederiksen, N. (1984) 'Implications of cognitive theory for instruction in problem solving', *Review of Educational Research*, 54(3): 363–407.

Galbraith, D. (1996) 'Self-monitoring, discovery through writing and individual differences in drafting strategy', in G. Rijlaarsdam, H. Van den Bergh, and M. Couzijn (eds), Studies in Writing: Vol. 1. *Theories, Models and Methodology in Writing Research*, Amsterdam: Amsterdam University Press. pp.121–144.

Gárate, M., and Melero, A. (2004) 'Teaching how to write argumentative texts at primary school', in G. Rijlaarsdam (Series ed.) and Rijlaarsdam, G., Van den Bergh, H. and Couzijn, M. (Vol. eds.), Studies in Writing. Vol. 14, Effective Learning and Teaching of Writing (second edn.), *Part 2, Studies in How to Teach Writing*. pp.323–337.

Graham, S. and Perin, D. (2007) 'A meta-analysis of writing instruction for adolescent students', *Journal of Educational Psychology*, 99(3): 445–476.

Hayes, J.R. (1989) *The Complete Problem Solver*, Hillsdale, NJ: Lawrence Erlbaum.

Hayes, J.R. and Flower, L.S. (1979) Writing as Problem Solving. ERIC Document Reproduction Service No. ED 172 202.

Holliway, D.R. (2000) It looks like a goose: Composing for the informational needs of readers. Annual Meeting of the American Educational Research Association: 1–29.

Holliway, D.R. and McCutchen, D. (2004) 'Audience perspective in young writers composing and revising. Reading as the reader', in G. Rijlaarsdam (Series ed.) and L. Allal, L. Chanquoy, and P. Largy (Vol. eds.), *Studies in Writing. Vol. 13. Revision: Cognitive and Instructional Processes*, Dordrecht: Kluwer Academic Publishers. pp.87–101.

Janssen, D.M.L. and Jaspers, J.P.C. (2002) 'Learning from readers', *Document Design*, 3(1): 13–17.

Kieft, M., Rijlaarsdam, G., and Van den Bergh, H. (2008) 'An aptitude–treatment interaction approach to writing-to-learn', *Learning and Instruction*, 18: 379–390.

Lumbelli, L. and Paoletti, G. (2004) 'Monitoring local coherence through bridging integration: From text comprehension to writing revision and planning', in

G. Rijlaarsdam (Series ed.), and G. Rijlaarsdam, H. Van den Bergh, and M. Couzijn (Vol. eds.), *Studies in Writing. Vol. 14. Effective Learning and Teaching of Writing, Part 1, Studies in Learning to Write* (second edn.), Dordrecht: Kluwer Academic Publishers. pp.197–208.

McGovern, H. (2007) 'Training teachers and serving students: Applying usability testing in writing programs', *Journal of Technical Writing and Communication*, 37(3): 323–346.

Midgette, E.P., Haria, and MacArthur, C. (2008) 'The effects of content and audience awareness goals for revision on the persuasive essays of fifth- and eighth-grade students', *Reading and Writing*, 21(1): 131–151.

Moffett, J. (1968) *Teaching the Universe of Discourse*, Boston: Houghton Mifflin Company.

Moss, A. (1975) 'Writing as problem solving: An integrative model for the teaching of composition', *Education and Urban Society*, 7(2): 187–192.

Newell, A. and H. Simon (1972) *Human Problem Solving*, Englewood Cliffs, NJ: Prentice-Hall.

Newsweek Education Program (2006) *Essay Writing for High School Students: A Step-by-Step Guide*. New York: Kaplan Publishing.

Paretti, M.C. (2006) 'Audience awareness: Leveraging problem-based learning to teach workplace communication practices', *IEEE Transactions on Professional Communication*, 49(2): 189–198.

Raedts, M., Rijlaarsdam, G., Van Waes, L., and Daems, F. (2007) 'Observational learning through video-based models: Impact on students' accuracy of self-efficacy beliefs, task knowledge and writing performances', in G. Rijlaarsdam (Series ed.), and P. Boscolo and S. Hidi (Vol. eds.), *Studies in Writing. Vol. 19. Writing and Motivation*, Oxford: Elsevier. pp.219–238.

Rijlaarsdam, G. and Braaksma, M. (2004) 'Students as researchers: Defining text quality criteria', Abstracts. Writing 2004. 9th International Conference of the EARLI Special Interest Group of Writing, Geneva. p.129.

Rijlaarsdam, G. and Van den Bergh, H. (2004) 'Effective learning and teaching of writing: Student involvement in the teaching of writing', in G. Rijlaarsdam (Series ed.), and G. Rijlaarsdam, H. Van den Bergh, and M. Couzijn (Vol. eds.), *Studies in Writing. Vol. 14. Effective Learning and Teaching of Writing, Part 1, Studies in Learning to Write* (second edn.), Dordrecht: Kluwer Academic Publishers. pp.1–16.

Rijlaarsdam, G., Couzijn, M., Janssen, T., Braaksma, M., and Kieft, M. (2006) 'Writing experiment manuals in science education: The impact of writing, genre, and audience', *International Journal of Science Education*, 28 (2-3): 203–233.

Rijlaarsdam, G. Braaksma, M., Couzijn, M., Janssen, T., Kieft, M., Broekkamp, H., and van den Bergh, H. (2005) 'Psychology and the teaching of writing in 8000 and some words', in *Pedagogy—Learning for Teaching*, BJEP Monograph series II(3): 127–153.

Rijlaarsdam, G., Braaksma, M., Couzijn, M., Janssen, T., Raedts, M., Van Steendam, E., Toorenaar, A., and Van den Bergh, H. (2008) 'Observation of peers in learning to write', *Practice and Research, Journal of Writing Research*, 1(1): 53–83.

Sato, K. and Matsushima K. (2006) 'Effects of audience awareness on procedural text writing', *Psychological Reports*, 99(1): 51–73.

Schriver, K.A. (1991) 'Plain language through protocol-aided revision', in E.R. Sternberg (ed.) *Plain Language: Principles and Practice*, Detroit (MI): Wayne State University Press. pp.148–172.

Schriver, K.A. (1992) 'Teaching writers to anticipate readers' needs: What can document designers learn from usability testing?', *Utrecht Studies in Language and Communication*, 1: 141–157.

Schriver, K.A. (1996) *Dynamics in Document Design: Creating Text for Readers*, Hoboken: John Wiley and Sons.

Sonnenschein, S. (1988) 'The development of referential communication: Speaking to different listeners', *Child Development*, 59: 694–702.

Sonnenschein, S. and Whitehurst, G.J. (1983) 'Training referential communication skills: The limits of success', *Journal of Experimental Child Psychology*, 35(3): 426–36.

Sonnenschein, S. and Whitehurst, G.J. (1984) 'Developing referential communication: A hierarchy of skills', *Child Development*, 55: 1936–1945.

Srebanek, P., Kemper, A., and Meyer, V. (2006) *Writers Inc.: A Student Handbook for Writing and Learning*, Wilmington: Great Source Education Group.

Sullivan, K.P.H. and Lindgren, E. (2006) *Computer Keystroke Logging and Writing: Methods and Applications*, Oxford: Elsevier.

Torrance, M., Fidalgo, R., and García, J.N. (2007) 'The teachability and effectiveness of cognitive self-regulation in sixth-grade writers', *Learning and Instruction*, 17(3): 265–285.

Traxler, M.J. and M.A. Gernsbacher (1992) 'Improving written communication through minimal feedback', *Language and Cognitive Processes*, 7(1): 1–22.

Traxler, M.J. and M.A. Gernsbacher (1993) 'Improving written communication through perspective-taking', *Language and Cognitive Processes*, 8(3): 311–334.

Van Steendam, E., Rijlaarsdam, G., and Sercu, L. (2008a) 'Learning to write through learning-to-revise: The effect of teaching evaluative criteria on text quality in EFL'. Manuscript submitted for publication.

Van Steendam, E., Sercu, L. and Rijlaarsdam, G. (2008b) 'The effect of strategy instruction on the quality of peer feedback in ESL/EFL'. Manuscript submitted for publication.

Van Waes, L. and Leijten, M. (2006) 'Logging writing processes with Inputlog', in L. Van Waes, M. Leijten, and C. M. Neuwirth (Vol. eds.), and G. Rijlaarsdam (Series ed.), *Studies in Writing. Vol. 17. Writing and Digital Media*. Oxford: Elsevier. pp.158–165.

Vernon, S., Alvarado, M., and Zermeño, P. (2005) 'Rewriting to introduce punctuation in the second grade: A didactic approach', in G. Rijlaarsdam (Series ed.), and G. Rijlaarsdam, H. Van den Bergh, and M. Couzijn (Vol. eds.), *Studies in Writing. Vol. 14. Effective Learning and Teaching of Writing, Part 1, Studies In Learning To Write*

(second edn.), Dordrecht: Kluwer Academic Publishers. pp.47–58.

Wells, G. (2000) 'Dialogic inquiry in education', in C. Lee and P. Smagorinsky (eds), *Vygotskian Perspectives on Literacy Research. Constructing Meaning through Collaborative Inquiry*, Cambridge: Cambridge University Press. pp.51–85.

Wilson, G. (1993) *Problem Solving and Decision Making*, London: Kogan Page.

Writing@CSU (2008) Writing Studio at Coloradu State University. See: Writing Resources / Writing Guides. URL=http://writing.colostate.edu. Last visited on July 4th, 2008.

Yule, G. (1997) *Referential Communication Tasks*, Mahwah, NJ: Erlbaum.

Zainuddin, H. and R.A. Moore (2003) 'Audience Awareness in L1 and L2 Composing of Bilingual Writers', *Teaching English as a Second or Foreign Language (TESL-EJ)*, 7(1). Electronic Journal, URL=http://tesl-ej.org/ej25/a2.html. Last visited on July 3rd, 2008.

INTRODUCTION

Challenges in writing development

Section IV of the *Handbook* examines some of the most salient challenges in research and scholarship in writing development. It begins with the key transformation in the field brought about by multilingualism. In Chapter 31, **Paul Kei Matsuda, Christina Ortmeier-Hooper,** and **Aya Matsuda** review work on the expansion of second language writing. The chapter uses the term 'second language' (or L2 for short) to include 'second language-learning', where a nonnative language is learned in a context where the target language is dominant. The chapter also uses the term to include 'foreign language-learning', where a nonnative language being learned in a context where the target language is *not* dominant. The field of second language-writing research has grown as a result of the international expansion of English as the *lingua franca* of academic and professional communication, the globalization of economy, and the migration of people across national borders.

The chapter begins with a brief historical overview of the development of second language writing research over the last century and the changing needs of second language writing instruction during this time. It then discusses various aspects of second language writing and language writers and some of key pedagogical issues. It concludes by discussing some of the new directions for second language writing research.

In Chapter 32, **Suresh Canagarajah** and **Maria Jerskey** highlight key challenges faced by advanced multilingual writers for whom English is not a first language. The term 'advanced' refers here to age and pedagogical status, not literacy proficiency, including students and academics in tertiary education. The chapter is limited to discussions of academic literacy, while recognizing that there are many other personal and professional genres of writing that are important for multilinguals.

Canagarajah and Jerskey use globalism and postmodernism as lenses through which to view multilingual writers and to describe the critical debates that relate to how teachers and researchers have addressed the development of literacy competence in tertiary educational contexts. They outline a socially-situated pedagogy for the integration of the diverse components that meet the needs of successful multilingual writers and end their chapter by suggesting some key challenges for the future.

In Chapter 33, **Julie Dockrell** addresses the enduring challenges raised by delays and difficulties in writing development. The chapter recognizes that these delays and difficulties are associated with a range of different developmental disabilities and pedagogical practices. The chapter begins by exploring the prevalence of writing difficulties and the associations between writing difficulties and other specific learning difficulties/disabilities. It argues that a descriptive analysis of the children's writing problems is insufficient to develop interventions and fails to provide adequate explanations of the cognitive processes that underpin writing. A theoretical model of the development of writing skills is needed, which provides a framework for examining the component skills, which may constrain the acquisition of text production for children. The chapter also discusses the importance of the children's motivation and instructional practices in the light of this discussion.

Nowhere are the contemporary cultural boundaries of literacy shifting more quickly than in digital online communities. Writing now crosses temporal, cultural, and linguistic borders in multicultural, multilingual, and multitasked synchronous and asynchronous networks and online communities. Students and young adults are well represented in these domains and dominate many. In Chapter 34, **Doreen Starke-Meyerring** discusses the implications for writing development of digital environments and particularly the 'contested materialities' of the new digital age. Her chapter first draws on critical theories of technologies to conceptualize digital network technologies as emerging materialities of writing. A critical understanding of technologies is seen as vital to the study and teaching of writing in digital environments, because these environments exist in and through digital technologies. Such an understanding also allows researchers, teachers, and students to analyse the contestation surrounding digital writing environments and to participate in the decision-making processes around the technologies.

The chapter goes on to outline vital ways in which these materialities of writing undergo change and contestation, focusing on the interrelated struggles that permeate all digital writing spaces. The chapter concludes with implications of these struggles over the materialities of writing in digital environments for writing development, specifically for what might be called pedagogies for critical engagement.

Writing online broadens definitions of literacy by making it possible for writers to link text, audio, video, and websites hypertextually. In contrast to printed text, in which writers largely control the sequencing of information, hypertext is nonlinear, allowing readers to click on linked items and giving them more control in the sequencing of information. By so clicking, readers control the elaboration of information they take from the author's text. Writing development in this virtual world is significantly shaped by the unique fluidity of these texts.

In Chapter 35, **Christina Haas** and **Chad Wickman** take Theodor Nelson's early definition of hypertext as 'nonsequential' writing. The branching nature of the written material allows choices to the readers in the possible use of a series of text chunks. These are connected by links that offer the reader different pathways. The chapter reviews work that examines writing itself, either in an attempt to characterize the resultant artefacts of hypertext writing or to describe the process of creating hypertext documents. It then reviews studies of the effects of writing hypertext, primarily on learning outcomes. The chapter ends by presenting and discussing a graphic synthesis of the studies reviewed and suggests some further avenues for research.

Increasingly, states and education authorities are mandating assessments of student achievement, including writing, and using the results of this high-stakes testing as a measure of accountability and performance in teaching and learning. Chapter 36, by **Marian Sainsbury**, adopts a sharp focus on writing through the lens of assessment, to investigate what is assessed, how it is assessed, and the inferences, decisions, actions, and consequences that result from the assessment. It briefly describes the political and social context in which high-stakes assessment has become prominent and sets out current views of test validity, before looking in more detail at specific examples of high-stakes writing assessment.

Recent research and publications on writing and literacy has challenged modernist conceptions of literacy that reify the oral-literate divide and elaborate ideas about writing development as the acquisition of skills for encoding abstract ideas in autonomous texts. Recent work has conceptualized multiliteracies as sociocultural practices, with 'strata' of written discourse rooted in local and historically-situated contexts. Local, 'vernacular' practices continually evolve, being influenced by institutional and political dynamics. In Chapter 37, on 'Writing in the Wider Community', **Beverly J. Moss** subjects the notion of multiliteracies to detailed discussion and critically examines the 'ideal norm' in much literacy studies research of multiple discourse communities, in which the literacy practices and languages of peoples and communities from diverse backgrounds are valued as much as those from the dominant institutions.

However, she raises the possibility that all is not as it should or could be and discusses a range of problematic issues. There may be an apparent contradiction between the ideal and the real, and local definitions of literacy may remain inadequate to help teachers understand and analyse what they hope to accomplish. Tensions also remain about what kind of writing will prepare our young people to be able to succeed in a technologically sophisticated, global society.

The chapter asks a series of timely questions about writing in the wider community and the transition that is taking place in writing studies. The questions focus on the forces that contributed to the growth of research on nonschool communities, the factors that shaped this research and the challenges facing the kind of research that may be undertaken in the future.

In the final chapter, **Robert Gundlach** provides some reflections on the future of writing development. He notes that, in discussions of nearly every domain of written communication, there is a sense of dramatic change on the horizon, often concerned with the ways in which writing is competing with, or being recontextualized by, other forms of communication.

A five-letter chalk inscription on an unoccupied sidewalk is used to illustrate the understanding of how to use written language effectively, of managing writing tools and processes to produce gestures that leave a trace. Learning to write often involves more than being taught, as it is an outcome of the interplay of interacting histories. Individuals develop along various trajectories.

The chapter argues that the increasingly pervasive use of digital technology for written communication will very likely change the character of writing development in ways that we can scarcely predict today. For instance, it is likely that writing development will become partly facilitated and possibly shaped by software to convert text to speech and speech to text. New digital tools and forms are likely to reposition written language use in a broader setting of pictures, sounds, and words both written and spoken.

Nevertheless, there is no reason to suppose that written language itself will disappear. The chapter argues that writing development will remain, at its core, a matter of composing an utterance that a reader can reconstruct from its enduring traces and can comprehend, possibly in another place and in another time.

The Expansion of Second Language Writing

Paul Kei Matsuda, Christina Ortmeier-Hooper,
and Aya Matsuda

INTRODUCTION

Second language writing is an interdisciplinary field of inquiry that draws on and contributes to various related disciplines, including applied linguistics and composition studies, which are themselves highly interdisciplinary. Second language writing research first became a major emphasis among English as a second language (ESL) teachers in U.S. higher education in the 1960s. The field continued to grow as the need for writing instruction became increasingly apparent as a result of the international expansion of English as the lingua franca of academic and professional communication. The globalization of economy and the migration of people across national borders have also expanded opportunities for advanced communication in various languages, and for that reason, the teaching of writing in second or foreign languages other than English has also began to gain attention in many countries. The recognition of the writing needs of multilingual children in schools have also fueled the growth of interest in early second language writing. The growing presence of second language writers has also been noted in composition classrooms and courses in various other disciplines, which have traditionally been designed only with native English speakers in mind. Once a concern for a relatively small number of dedicated teachers and researchers who became specialists by happenstances (Blanton and Kroll, 2002), second language writing today is relevant to all teachers who are involved in the teaching of writing—regardless of the instructional level or the disciplinary background.

A few notes about the terminology: Following the common practice in the field, the term 'second language' (or L2 for short) is used here in a broad and inclusive sense, including not only *second language* in the narrow sense (commonly referring to a nonnative language being learned in a context where the target language is dominant) but also *foreign language* (commonly referring to a nonnative language being learned in a context the target language is not dominant). As the student population diversifies, the traditional distinction between first and second languages as well as second and foreign languages has become problematic, and for that reason, it is also becoming increasingly common to refer to second language writers as *multilingual writers*. In U.S. elementary and secondary school contexts, the term *English language learners* (ELLs) is also used to distinguish a population of students from those who are already highly proficient in the target language. In U.S. higher education, a subset of students who have received a few years of high school education in English medium schools have also come to be called *generation 1.5* students, although the imprecise and inconsistent use of the term among teachers and researchers can be problematic (Matsuda and Matsuda, 2009).

This chapter begins with a brief historical overview of the development of second language writing research over the last century as well as the changing needs of second language writing instruction during this period. We will then discuss various aspects of second language writing, including the overall characteristics as well as textual features that are often associated with second language writers. Some of the key pedagogical issues will also be considered. We will conclude by discussing some of the new directions in second language writing research.

A BRIEF HISTORICAL SKETCH

Pre-history

Until well into the latter half of the twentieth century, writing was not a significant concern among second language specialists for a number of reasons. First, the literacy needs before the nineteenth century was relatively limited—people did not need a high level of literacy in a second language (or even in the first language). Second, the need to learn how to *speak* modern languages became more apparent during the nineteenth century, because the international exchange of people increased as a result of the Industrial

Revolution and other technological advancements, which made international travel safer and more affordable to a wide variety of people. Another important change that took place during this period was the rise of modern linguistics in Europe, with phonetics (the science of speech sounds) as the core of the scientific study of language. Modern scientific linguists in the latter half of the nineteenth century sought to establish their own discipline by dissociating themselves from philology, the humanistic study of language, culture, and literature, and from ancient or 'dead' languages that existed only in written forms. The move away from writing was reinforced by the popular concern about the ever widening gap between speech and writing (i.e., orthography), which prompted phoneticians to argue that language is speech and writing is its inaccurate representation.

In second language instruction, the terms 'composition' and 'writing' often meant 'written language' or 'translation' and not 'composing.' Although the term *free composition* (as opposed to translation; not to be confused with *free writing* in Elbow's [1985] sense) already existed in the late nineteenth century, it was reserved for the most advanced second language learners. The need for second language instruction in general grew rapidly after the World War I, when second language instruction became an important concern in international politics. Yet, because of the strong influence of American structural linguistics, which inherited the assumptions about writing from European structural linguistics, writing instruction was systematically excluded from the early years of second language studies. (For a detailed discussion of the emergence of second language studies, see Berns and Matsuda, 2006; Matsuda, 2001.)

The growth of second language writing research

Sustained efforts to study second language writing began in the mid-twentieth century as a result of the influx of international students in North American higher education.

During the 1950s and the early 1960s, the discussion at the Conference on College Composition and Communication (CCCC) centred on the development of placement procedures and options for second language writers, which continues to be one of the key issues in the field. Realizing that the language instruction in precollegiate intensive language programs did not sufficiently prepare students for required first-year composition courses, many institutions began to develop separate composition courses for international students (Matsuda, 1999). Second language writing during these early years was motivated primarily by pedagogical concerns, and studies emphasized direct pedagogical or administrative applications.

Some of the early research on second language writing instruction focused on the question of whether to emphasize fluency or accuracy (Brière, 1966; Erazmus, 1960; Pincas, 1962)—debate that has continued to resurface periodically throughout the history of second language writing research and instruction. The debate quickly ended as some researchers argued against free composition (the production of students' own texts) by appealing to then-popular behaviourism. Allowing students to make errors in producing their own text was considered to lead to the acquisition of incorrect forms. Instead, it was argued, writing instruction, if it were to happen at all, should be through controlled composition—carefully constructed pattern practice exercises based on descriptive grammar, followed by grammar correction by the teacher—just the way speech was being taught during this period.

Although the pattern practice pedagogy was able to help students produce a prescribed set of grammatical sentences, it quickly became clear that it did not adequately prepare students to produce a longer stretch of meaningful text, and for that reason, researchers suggested that the teaching of writing should move gradually from controlled to guided composition (Slager, 1966), which was somewhat less rigidly structured than controlled composition. Although guided composition provided prompts to have students produce a series of sentences, writing still tended to be conceptualized narrowly as the production of grammatical sentences.

Robert B. Kaplan (1966) observed that students who came from different linguistic and cultural backgrounds seemed to write texts that were incoherent in the eyes of the native-English-speaking readers, and speculated that it might be because there are paragraph patterns specific to writers' native languages and cultures. Although Kaplan's visual representations of language-specific patterns have been problematized, his idea that the seeming lack of organization is related to factors other than the writer's cognitive development helped to move second language writing research from the realm of the sentence to larger, discourse-level issues. The pedagogical approach based on Kaplan notion of *contrastive rhetoric*, at least initially, focused on pattern drills at the above sentence level. Although the study of written discourse structure became popular in the 1980s and 1990s, the tendency to overgeneralize the findings of cross-linguistic and cross-cultural research continues to be hotly debated (Casanave, 2003a).

Since the late 1960s and the 1970s, the issue of fluency versus accuracy began to resurface, as researchers influenced by Jerome Bruner's work on cognitive development (1960, 1962, 1966) began to focus more on the production and organization of meaningful text (Arapoff, 1967; Lawrence, 1972). At around the same time, an increasing number of researchers began to draw on the growing body of writing research in rhetoric and composition studies, emphasizing the similarities between first and second language writing and writers (Buckingham and Pech, 1976; Kroll, 1978; Zamel, 1976), which paved the way for the development of what might be characterized as the second language writing process movement (Krapels, 1990; Matsuda, 2003; Susser, 1994).

In the late 1970s and throughout the 1980s, second language writing researchers developed their own communities of practice, and began to generate research questions not only from classroom contexts but also from insights provided by other studies. The growth of second language writing as a research topic was facilitated by the maturing of its parent disciplines—especially applied linguistics and composition studies—which provided new theoretical and methodological tools. In applied linguistics, the development of discourse analysis in North America and text linguistics in Europe facilitated the study of second language writers' texts. In composition studies, the process movement was already in full swing, and research on the composing processes of second language writing became a major concern. A growing number of studies on writing in foreign languages other than English also began to appear in the mid 1980s (Reichelt, 1999).

In the 1980s, the growing recognition of the need for advanced literacy in academic and professional contexts in various parts of the world precipitated the growth of English for Specific Purposes and particularly English for Academic Purposes. Researchers sought to identify the writing needs across the disciplines (Braine, 1995; Horowitz, 1986; Kroll, 1979) and describe particular characteristics of written discourse in various academic and professional contexts (Bhatia, 1993; Flowerdew and Peacock, 2001; Hyland, 2004; Swales, 1990, 2004). More recently, researchers have begun to focus on the development of genre knowledge among second language writers (Tardy, 2005). Second language writing researchers have also began to integrate the sociocultural perspectives (Casanave, 2002, 2003b; Johns, 1997) in order to account for the complexity of second language writing development in its larger contexts.

The emergence of an interdisciplinary field

Toward the end of the 1980s, second language writing research began to reach a critical mass, and researchers from various disciplinary traditions began to develop a sense of identity as a coherent research field. The introduction of the term *second language writing* as an overarching term for the field (Kroll, 1990) and the creation of the *Journal of Second Language Writing* helped to solidify the status of second language writing as a field. It was also during this period that *metadisciplinary inquiry* or self-conscious inquiry into the status and history of the field as well as its theoretical and methodological orientations (Matsuda, 1998, 2005) began to increase noticeably, signalling that the field was coming of age. The end of the 1990s also saw the creation of the Symposium on Second Language Writing, the first regularly held conference dedicated to the development of knowledge in the field. Publications that provide comprehensive overviews of the field have also appeared in the first few years of the twenty-first century (e.g., Kroll, 2003; Silva and Matsuda, 2001).

Although the issue of teaching writing to nonnative language users has long attracted the attention of writing teachers from various disciplinary backgrounds, it tended to be considered as an area of specialization rather than a topic of interest to writing teachers and second language teachers at large. For this reason, much of the insights generated in the field of second language writing did not always find their way into the classroom contexts, where second language writers were often being taught by writing teachers or language teachers without much background knowledge or experience in working with second language writing (Matsuda, 1998; Valdes, 1992). In the 1990s, however, concerted efforts have been made to raise the awareness of the relevance of second language writing issues in various related disciplines and to extend the scope of the field to include younger writers, languages other than English, and countries where English is not the dominant language of society.

ASPECTS OF SECOND LANGUAGE WRITING

Second language writers: Characteristics and backgrounds

Second language writers represent a wide range of characteristics and backgrounds, which are influenced by a variety of factors, including their native language proficiency and literacy development, how they have encountered the target language, and under what circumstances they have developed their second language and writing proficiency. Research on second language writers' characteristics has distinguished between those second language writers living, working, and studying internationally in what might be deemed a more temporary situation, and those second language writers who for any number of reasons are permanent nonnative speaking residents of a country, as in the case of linguistic minorities, immigrants, the children of immigrants, or refugees.

For example, in North America, second language writing scholars note that there are differences in the ways in which resident and international second language students have acquired English and there are direct implications of these different learning contexts on their writing (Reid, 1998). Resident second language writers often learn English through immersion and as participants in the various, language interactions of their daily lives (Harklau et al., 1999; Reid, 1998). These students are often familiar with popular trends in the dominant culture. In addition, they may have strong oral fluency when it comes to day-to-day conversation, and they may be comfortable with local cultural norms and expectations (Ibrahim, 1999). Resident second language writers may have complex, ambivalent feelings about the second language and the dominant second language culture (Chiang and Schmida, 1999; Leki, 1999). They may have had many opportunities to write in the second language, but they may also have found themselves hindered by

socioeconomic circumstances and discriminatory educational practices (Fu, 1995; Ortmeier-Hooper, 2007, in press).

In contrast, international second language students often learn their second language primarily through formal foreign language instruction in their native countries or through instruction in international academic settings. Much of their prior work with a second language may have concentrated on studying language rules and forms. They may have had limited contact with proficient users of the target language and limited experience with the cultural norms and expectations of the target culture.

Across these categories, research has found that many second language writers have had limited experience with writing and writing instruction. While some second language writers may have had rigorous school experiences with writing, other second language writers will have had few school experiences with writing in both their L1 and their L2. Many second language writers may have found themselves limited to sentence-level and paragraph-level instruction on writing, particularly in those schooling situations where instruction did not include extensive writing practice with longer compositions. In the case of resident second language writers, issues of access and equity may have prevented these writers from participating in upper-level courses and a wider range of writing experiences (Fu, 1995; Villalva, 2006a, b).

Research on second language writers and their texts

It is important to note that the texts of second language writers can vary greatly from one writer to the next. Language proficiency levels, writing expertise in first language, and the kinds of writing tasks (contexts, genres, etc.) all greatly influence the texts that second language writers produce. As the CCCC Statement of Second Language Writers and

Writing states, 'most second-language writers are still in the process of acquiring syntactic and lexical competence—a process that will take a lifetime. These differences are often a matter of degree, and not all second-language writers face the same set of difficulties' (CCCC, 2001).

Studies of second language writers across various contexts have revealed some fundamental understandings of how second language writers approach the writing of their texts. In general, research comparing first and second language writers has tended to suggest that there are salient differences between the ways that second language writers develop and approach their writing tasks and the ways first language writers do (Silva, 1993). Studies have shown that second language writers often have more difficulty composing than their native speaking peers. They may plan less in their writing, have difficulty setting appropriate goals, and spend more time trying to generate material and locating suitable vocabulary for a given writing task. In addition, second language writers pause more often and have more starts-and-stops, making the process overall more time-consuming and arduous than for their native language peers.

Research on the traits of second language writers' text suggests that these texts often are seen as less effective by native-speaking readers. Second language texts are often viewed as 'simple and less complex' by native readers (Silva, 1993). Often these texts are less precise than the texts written by native-English users and present more errors both at global and local levels. At the global level, some L2 writers' text may have organization structures that seem awkward or unfamiliar to native-English readers. Some L2 writers will have had extensive experience with English grammar and sentence-level writing, but their limited experiences in writing longer compositions may result in texts that are shorter or that are lacking an overarching sense of purpose or audience. At the local level, some L2 writers' texts may exhibit difficulties with sentence structures, verb tenses, idiomatic phrases, and articles. It is often difficult for L2 writers to recognize these errors in their own writing, and studies have shown that teachers must often explicitly provide L2 writers with strategies to aid them in becoming self-editors of their own work (Ferris, 2003).

Even for those second language writers, who are highly proficient, they may have challenges and struggles as they strive to understand culturally-constructed genres and to meet the expectations of readers from the second language culture. Research on contrastive rhetoric has suggested that the norms and genres of writing are often culturally determined, and second language writers may encounter some challenges in trying to meet the expectations of new genres and new reader expectations (Kubota, 1998; Leki, 1997; Matsuda, 1997; Severino, 1993). Often the dominant traits of second language writers' texts give evidence to this mixture of challenges to master both the second language and the cultural expectations of native-language readers. Research on second language writers and their characteristics as writers has revealed a number of important traits to take into account when conducting research or teaching these writers. As the field of second language writing grows and new research emerges on different populations of L2 users, there will continue to be new theoretical and pedagogical developments in our understanding of second language writers and their texts.

Curricular design and placement issues

Second language writers can be found in educational programs at all levels and contexts, including, but not limited to: elementary schools, secondary schools, vocational schools, adult education programs, colleges, and universities. There continues to be much debate over what kinds of educational contexts best serve the needs of second language writers. Traditionally, L2 writing instruction was confined within courses designed specifically for L2 writers and taught by teachers who specialized in L2 instruction. Studies have compared the experiences of first-year college second language writers in native-speaking composition classroom and ESL composition classrooms (Braine, 1996; Harklau, 1994). They suggest that some second language writers are more comfortable in an ESL-section of a course, and they fare better academically when they have a trained second language specialist as a teacher. These courses can also be designed to provide opportunities for international second language writers to learn about the target culture.

The findings of these studies have been increasingly complicated, as more resident second language writers enter higher education and question their positioning as nonnative, 'ESL', or even 'foreign' students. In addition, there have been questions about the role of writing instruction in some second language acquisition programs. Research has shown that the kinds of writing instruction and the amount of writing instruction varied greatly across settings (Harklau, 2002). Furthermore, in ESL contexts, where the number and the diversity of the student population are growing rapidly, it is no longer possible to contain L2 writers in separate classrooms. At the college and university-level, there have been ongoing debates among second language writing specialists and administrators about the difficulty in placing second language students into appropriate composition classes (Friedrich, 2006; Preto-Bay and Hansen, 2006). Reports on cross-cultural composition classrooms, which combine first-language and second-language writers, have suggested that such blended classrooms have benefits for both sets of students (Matsuda and Silva, 1999; Reichelt and Silva, 1995/1996).

Given the growing complexity of these placement issues, as well the wide range of language experiences that L2 writers bring with them, the need for language support programs throughout an L2 writer's educational career is being recognized by L2 writing teachers and scholars (Matsuda et al., 2006; Preto-Bay and Hansen, 2006; Silva, 1994). There have been efforts to expand the conversation on L2 writers and their writing beyond writing classrooms. Scholars have considered the experiences of L2 writers across disciplinary fields, in order to examine how the writing expectations shift for those students across the curriculum (Johns, 2001; Zamel, 1995; Zhu, 2006). Researchers have also explored the importance of writing centres as a support source for L2 writers (Severino, 1993; Williams, 2004, 2006; Williams and Severino, 2004). The continued exploration of L2 writers in these sites has facilitated a growing conversation on the nature of L2 writing development across the continuum of a student's educational career.

In considering the writing development of L2 students, teachers need to be supported as well as students. In an effort to broaden the kinds of language support systems that are available to L2 writers, there have been calls for teachers to become better prepared to work with L2 writers in their classrooms and for administrators to provide sustainable professional development, encouragement, and support for all teachers working with an increasingly culturally and linguistically diverse student population. Providing teachers with resources on L2 writers and professional development in forms of workshops and support networks has become a cornerstone of the L2 writing field (Johns, 1999; Land and Whitley, 1989). These kinds of opportunities have focused on building awareness among writing teachers about the presence of L2 writers in their classrooms, as well as the needs and characteristics of those writers. In recent years, those networks of support have become more accessible and visible to composition teachers at the postsecondary level, and there is progress in making those kinds of resources more available to teachers in elementary and secondary schools.

Key pedagogical issues

In the field of second language writing, pedagogical research and publications have focused on improving the practices and strategies of teachers working with L2 writers. Specifically, research has emphasized four key pedagogical issues: the development of effective writing assignments and curriculum, teacher and peer response, the treatment of error, and assessment.

The development of effective writing assignments has been a key pedagogical issue for teachers and scholars working with second language writers. Research has found that effective writing assignments provide L2 writers with opportunities to learn about writing, to build upon their individual writing skills, and to demonstrate their areas of strength. Reid and Kroll noted that writing assignment design must be 'contextualized and authentic', include 'accessible content', 'be engaging', and 'be developed in tandem with appropriate evaluation criteria' (1995: 19). Leki (1991) suggested that writing assignments be designed to aid L2 writers in developing expertise and genre awareness. She proposed the development of writing assignments that help students to write about a given topic across a sequential genre spectrum. Second language writing researchers have also considered the social aspects of designing writing assignments. For example, Johns (1991) argued that writing courses should take 'socio-literate approach', in which teachers build assignments that encourage language minority students to consider and analyse the rhetorical and social construction of texts, exploring the purpose of a given writing task in light of a particular social environment.

Research on responding to the writing of second language students has included strategies for peers and teachers. Theoretical support for the use of peer response groups in L1 composition classrooms (Bruffee, 1984, 1993) has led to a number of empirical studies on the use of peer response groups with L2 writers (Hyland and Hyland, 2006). Some of the research has considered the influence of peer response on student writing, looking closely at how peer response improves or does not improve student writing. Second language writing researchers have also conducted discourse analysis on the interactions between reader and writer in peer response settings. The increasing diversity of second language writers and their growing presence in mainstream writing classrooms has led to research that explores the dynamics of L2 writers working in peer groups with L1 writing peers (Zhu, 2001). Recent publications have also considered the importance of training students for peer response in second language contexts (Liu and Hansen, 2002).

The treatment of error has remained an ongoing area of challenge and dispute in discussion of the writing development of L2 users. In the 1990s, John Truscott (1996) strongly argued for the abolition of grammar correction in second language writing, stating that error correction had little value—or even harmful—in helping second language students develop their writing skills. Truscott's article led to heated discussion within the field, including the 1999 debate between Dana Ferris (1999) and Truscott (1999) published in the *Journal of Second Language Writing*. Ferris (1999) argued against Truscott's premise, noting that error feedback was essential to second language writers and their writing. The debate prompted new research efforts in the role of error treatment in second language writing development. Studies over the past decade have focused upon the definition of error, the categories of errors that second language writers make, and the kinds of error feedback that are most effective. In recent years, there have been strong efforts to develop specific pedagogical strategies and response in order to improve the accuracy of L2 writers in their writing tasks (Ferris, 2002, 2003).

Studies on assessment in second language writing have examined a variety of concerns at both the classroom and the institution level. Weigle (2002) emphasized the role of 'washback'—extraneous effects of assessment—suggesting that every assessment strategy has the potential to influence a teacher's classroom practices. At the institutional level, L2 writing research on assessment has focused on the required writing examinations that many second language writers must pass in order to move forward in their educational pursuits (Johns, 1991). These high-stakes writing assessments can function as gatekeepers for second language users in educational settings, and they include writing placement exams, proficiency tests, national education benchmark testing, and exit/entrance exams. Assessment specialists in the field of second language writing have long advocated that testing and assessment are a part of the reality of second language writing and writers' lives. They argue that assessment instruments must be appropriate, equitable, and fair, particularly in terms of prompt development, scoring procedures, and the selection of readers (Hamp-Lyons and Kroll, 1996). Research in the area of L2 writing assessment is ongoing, and it has become an important area of consideration in elementary and secondary schools as high-stakes testing becomes more pervasive in these settings.

NEW AREAS OF RESEARCH

Early L2 writing

'Early L2 writing' has been defined as 'the development of L2 literacy from the writer's first encounter with a second language to the completion of high school' (Matsuda and De Pew, 2002: 262). Although research on the reading development and academic achievement of school-age second language learners has been prominent in the fields of teacher education, literacy, and second language acquisition, scholarship on the writing development of school-age second language learners has been limited. In 2002, the *Journal of Second Language Writing* (Matsuda and De Pew, 2002) dedicated a special issue to this topic, noting that published research that focused on the research and pedagogy in

relation to early ESL writers was underrepresented in the field of L2 writing.

Landmark research by Edelsky (1986) and Hudelson (1989) were early projects that highlighted the distinct nature of children and adolescents writing in a second language. Hudelson, for example, explored the pedagogical implications of second language writing for young learners, while Edelsky researched the writing approaches of elementary second language students in a bilingual setting. More recently, studies on the emergent literacy of elementary and middle-level second language students (Fu, 2003; Fu and Matoush, 2006; McCarthy et al., 2005) have considered the writing development of Asian immigrant students studying in mainstream English Language Arts classrooms and examined the importance of biliteracy in the development of L2 academic writing skills.

Research on the L2 writing among adolescents at the secondary level has examined a range of issues, including appropriate pedagogy, transitions from high school to college, out-of-school literacies, academic writing development, and identity negotiation. During the 1990s, Harklau (1994) and Fu (1995) both undertook qualitative studies examining the writing experiences of adolescent second language writers in U.S. schools. Their respective contributions found that adolescent L2 writers often had limited meaningful writing experiences in schools. Harklau (1994) compared the writing experiences of U.S. resident second language students in their ESL classrooms and in their mainstream English classrooms. Fu (1995) found that the Laotian second language students in her study were often placed in low-level classes where writing was limited to worksheets and rote activities that often stifled the students' development of meaningful English literacy.

In addition to these studies, there has also been work on the writing practices of adolescents studying English as a foreign language (EFL) in international school settings. Among these, Pennington, Brock, and Yue (1996) studied the interactions between Cantonese secondary students and their English teachers, noting the complexity of student-teacher relationships, the cultural construction of writing pedagogy, and the effects of these issues on student participation and achievement. Kobayashi and Rinnert (2002) examined the writing instruction for Japanese secondary students, and found that there was a contrast between the intensity of writing instruction offered in L2 and the minimal amount of writing instruction offered in the student's first language.

In recent years, educational policies in many Western countries have had a profound impact on the schooling of second language students. These policies and the impact of those policies on students, teachers, and schools have helped to spur a renewed interest in the school-age second language writers and their writing practices. In the United States, for example, the No Child Left Behind Act of 2001 pointedly placed the responsibility for the achievement and literacy development of English language learners in schools with administrators and teachers across the curriculum. In practice, this educational policy meant that English language learners could not be exempted from assessment tests and overall school achievement benchmarks. The effect of these kinds of national education policies can be problematic on many fronts.

At the same time, these policies have spurred interest and research in the academic writing needs of school-age second language writers. Researchers like Villalva (2006a, b) and Reynolds (2002, 2005) have looked at the kind of writing practice and rhetorical genres that adolescent second language writers have experienced in their respective school settings. Yi (2005, 2007) examined the out-of-school writing practices of Korean-American students. In addition, Harklau (2000) and Ortmeier-Hooper (2008) have considered the question of how institutional identities and representations influence adolescent second language writers and their academic writing development from high school to college.

Early L2 writing is a research area that remains unexplored on many fronts. Work on new approaches to pedagogical strategies and curriculum for young and adolescent L2 writers remains limited. Large-scale research projects are also needed to develop a broader understanding of young L2 writers across multiple and demographically diverse school settings. In particular, future research might include corpus studies on the traits of early L2 writers and their writing, or the effects of high-stakes writing assessment on middle-level and adolescent L2 writers, building on similar work done in the field of composition (Dunn et al., 2004). New research areas also include conducting comparative research projects that examines how the writing abilities of school-age immigrants and other second language learners are considered and taught within educational settings in other parts of the world.

Globalization and second language writing

The globalization of economy and politics as well as the international spread of the English language as a lingua franca of business, scientific, and academic interactions have resulted in the expansion of English language users into a broad spectrum of contexts and countries. Second language writing is an important concern for politicians, business people, engineers, and lawyers who work with their counterparts from other parts of the world. It is also important for practicing academics in many countries who are under increasing institutional pressure to publish in international research publications, which often means writing in English. But as English takes on an important role in these transaction, there have been ongoing discussions and challenges among English users about who owns English and which English is should be the target variety to be learned and used (A. Matsuda, 2006). The study of World Englishes has been at the forefront of those discussions. In light of these changes, the teaching of second language writing is no longer limited to the preparation of second language writers for advanced literacy in academic contexts.

Research on the writing development and pedagogy of students studying English in foreign language contexts has grown considerably in the last decade. Some of the regions that have been most visible include Mainland China, Finland, Hong Kong, Japan, Spain, and Taiwan, among others. In many cases, teachers and scholars from these regions have taken an interest in considering the writing pedagogies of North American composition and adapting those strategies and theories for their own students. At the same time, new questions have been raised about the nature of English writing instruction in these settings. For example, Li (1995) contrasted teacher responses to student writing in North American and Chinese settings, noting the cultural and pedagogical stances that led to these differences. You (2006) examined how globalization has led to shifting definitions of English literacy and curriculum reform at Chinese universities. The challenges presented by the institutional and national political contexts in these kinds of settings remain vastly unexplored, and new research areas include conducting empirical studies on teacher preparation, curriculum design, placement, and assessment.

Beyond foreign language settings, scholarship is also needed in the teaching of writing in other foreign language classrooms. Scholars in the field of second language writing have long advocated for a view of second language development that is inclusive of all second language writing contexts and classrooms. Historically, however, much of the research has remained focused on the use of English as the second language. More recently, there have been calls to build upon the theory and pedagogy of second language writing by considering more thoroughly the experiences of L2 writers who are learning to write in languages other than English (Reichelt, 1999). Research on writing in foreign language (FL) contexts remains limited, despite the fact that writing is often an integral part of FL classrooms and instruction. Without a more comprehensive understanding of writing in FL contexts, a theory of

second language writing remains incomplete. The uncritical acceptance of the dominance of the English language as the only target language could also have detrimental consequences to student writers who come from various linguistic backgrounds (Canagarajah, 1999, 2002; Horner and Trimbur, 2002; P. Matsuda, 2006).

The globalization of second language writing has also meant that the long cherished notions such as conventions and standards must now be revisited and reconsidered. The spread of English does not mean that more traditional, inner-circle varieties of English (Kachru, 1984)—i.e., dominant varieties in Australia, Canada, New Zealand, the United Kingdom, and the United States—are being adopted uncritically. Instead, many second language writing teachers and researchers are trying to account for the complexity of the spread as well as the diversity of the English language and explore how second language writers—and their readers—can negotiate the differences in the linguistic contact zone (Pratt, 1991), where writers and readers from various linguistic and cultural backgrounds meet one another and negotiate the differences in the context of asymmetrical power relations (Canagarajah, 2002; Kubota, 2003; Kubota and Lehner, 2004; Matsuda, 1997, 2006).

ACKNOWLEDGMENTS

We are grateful to the Graduate School of International Development, Nagoya University for its generous support in the form of a visiting researcher that enabled us to develop this chapter.

REFERENCES

Arapoff, Nancy (1967) 'Writing: A Thinking Process', *TESOL Quarterly*, 1(2): 33–39.

Berns, Margie and Matsuda, Paul Kei (2006) 'Applied Linguistics: Overview and History', in Keith Brown (ed.), *The Encyclopedia of Language and Linguistics* (second edn.), Oxford, UK: Elsevier. pp.394–405.

Bhatia, Vijay K. (1993) *Analysing Genre: Language Use in Professional Settings*, London: Longman.

Blanton, Linda L. and Kroll, Barbara (2002) *ESL Composition Tales: Reflections on Teaching*, Ann Arbor: University of Michigan Press.

Braine, George (1995) 'Writing in the Natural Sciences and Engineering', in Diane Belcher and George Braine (eds), *Academic Writing in a Second Language: Essays on Research and Pedagogy*, Norwood, NJ: Ablex. pp.113–134.

Braine, George (1996) 'ESL Students in First-Year Writing Courses: ESL versus Mainstream Classes', *Journal of Second Language Writing*, 5(2): 91–107.

Brière, Eugene. J. (1966) 'Quantity before Quality in Second Language Composition', *Language Learning*, 16: 141–51.

Bruffee, Kenneth A. (1984) 'Collaborative Learning and the Conversation of Mankind', *College English*, 46: 635–652.

Bruffee, Kenneth A. (1993) *Collaborative Learning: Higher Education, Interdependence and the Authority of Knowledge*, Baltimore, MD: John Hopkins University Press.

Bruner, Jerome. S. (1960) *The Process of Education*, Cambridge, MA: Harvard University Press.

Bruner, Jerome S. (1962) *On Knowing: Essays for the Left Hand*, Cambridge: Belknap Press of Harvard University Press.

Bruner, Jerome S. (1966) *Toward a Theory of Instruction*, Cambridge: Harvard University Press.

Buckingham, Thomas and Pech, William (1976) 'An Experience Approach to Teaching Composition', *TESOL Quarterly*, 10(1): 55–66.

CCCC Committee on Second Language Writing (2001) 'CCCC Statement on Second Language writing and writers', *College Composition and Communication*, 52(4): 669–674.

Canagarajah, A. Suresh (1999) *Resisting Imperialism in English Language Teaching*, Oxford: Oxford University Press.

Canagarajah, A. Suresh (2002) *Critical Academic Writing and Multilingual Students*, Ann Arbor: University of Michigan Press.

Casanave, Christine P. (2002) *Writing Games: Multicultural Case Studies of Academic Literacy Practices in Higher Education*, Mahwah, NJ: Lawrence Erlbaum Associates.

Casanave, Christine P. (2003a) *Controversies in Second Language Writing: Dilemmas and Decisions in Research and Instruction*, Ann Arbor: University of Michigan Press.

Casanave, Christine P. (2003b) 'Looking Ahead to More Sociopolitically-Oriented Case Study Research in L2 Writing Scholarship (But should it be called 'post-process'?)', *Journal of Second Language Writing*, 12(1): 85–102.

Chiang, Yuet-Sim D. and Schmida, Mary (1999) 'Language Identity and Language Ownership: Linguistic Conflicts of First-Year University Writing Students', in Linda Harklau, Kay M. Losey, and Meryl Siegel (eds), *Generation 1.5 Meets College Composition*, Mahwah, NJ: Lawrence Erlbaum. pp.81–96.

Dunn Jr., John, O'Neil, Peggy, Murphy, Sandra, and Huot, Brian (2004) 'High-Stakes Writing Assessment in Secondary Schools: Implications for College Composition', Colloquium presented at the Conference on College Composition and Communication, Texas.

Edelsky, Carole (1986) *Writing in a Bilingual Program: Había una Vez*, Norwood, NJ: Ablex.

Elbow, Peter (1985) *Writing with Power*, Oxford, UK: Oxford University Press.

Erazmus, Edward (1960) 'Second Language Composition Teaching at the Intermediate Level', *Language Learning*, 10: 25–31.

Ferris, Dana (1999) 'The Case for Grammar Correction in L2 Writing Classes: A Response to Truscott (1996)', *Journal of Second Language Writing*, 8(1): 1–11.

Ferris, Dana (2002) *Treatment of Error in Second Language Student Writing*. Ann Arbor: University of Michigan Press.

Ferris, Dana (2003) *Response to Student Writing: Implications for Second Language Students*, Mahwah, NJ: Erlbaum.

Flowerdew, John and Peacock, Matthew (2001) *Research Perspectives on English for Academic Purposes*, Cambridge, UK: Cambridge University Press.

Friedrich, Patricia (2006) 'Assessing the Needs of Linguistically Diverse First-Year Students: Bringing Together and Telling apart International ESL, Resident ESL and Monolingual Basic Writers', *Writing Program Administrators*, 30(1–2): 15–35.

Fu, Danling (1995) *My Trouble is my English: Asian Students and the American Dream*, Portsmouth, NH: Boynton/Cook.

Fu, Danling (2003) *An Island of English: Teaching ESL in Chinatown*, Portsmouth, NH: Heinemann.

Fu, Danling and Matoush, Mary (2006) 'Writing Development and Biliteracy', in Paul Kei Matsuda, Christina Ortmeier-Hooper, and Xiaoye You (eds), *The Politics of Second Language Writing: In Search of the Promised Land*, West Lafayette, IN: Parlor Press. pp.5–29.

Hamp-Lyons, Liz and Kroll, Barbara (1996) 'Issues in ESL Writing Assessment: An Overview', *College ESL*, 6(1): 52–72.

Harklau, Linda (1994) 'ESL versus Mainstream Classes: Contrasting L2 Learning Environments', *TESOL Quarterly*, 28(2): 241–272.

Harklau, Linda (2000) 'From the "Good kids" to the "Worst": Representations of English Language Learners across Educational Settings', *TESOL Quarterly*, 34(1): 35–67.

Harklau, Linda (2002) 'The Role of Writing in Classroom Second Language Acquisition', *Journal of Second Language*, 11(4): 329–350.

Harklau, Linda, Losey, Kay M., and Siegal, Meryl (1999) *Generation 1.5 Meets College Composition: Issues in the Teaching of Writing to U.S.-Educated Learners of English*, Mahwah, NJ: Erlbaum.

Horner, Bruce and Trimbur, John (2002) 'English only and U.S. College Composition', *College Composition and Communication*, 53(4): 594–630.

Horowitz, Daniel (1986) 'What Professors actually Require: Academic Tasks for the ESL Classroom', *TESOL Quarterly*, 20(3): 445–462.

Hudelson, Sarah (1989) *Write On: Children Writing in ESL*, Englewood Cliffs, NJ: Prentice Hall Regents.

Hyland, Ken (2004) *Disciplinary Discourses: Social Interactions in Academic Writing*, Ann Arbor: University of Michigan Press.

Hyland, Ken and Hyland, Fiona (2006) *Feedback in Second Language Writing: Contexts and Issues*, Cambridge, UK: Cambridge University Press.

Ibrahim, Awad El Karim (1999) 'Becoming Black: Rap and Hip-Hip, Race, Gender, Identity, and the Politics of ESL Learning', *TESOL Quarterly*, 33(3): 349–369.

Johns, Ann M. (1991) 'Interpreting an English Competency Examination: The Frustrations of an ESL Science Student', *Written Communication*, 5(3): 379–401.

Johns, Ann M. (1997) *Text, Role, Contexts: Developing Academic Literacies*, New York: Cambridge University Press.

Johns, Ann M. (1999) 'Opening Our Doors: Applying Socioliterate Approaches (SA) to Language Minority Classrooms', in Linda Harklau, Kay M. Losey, and Meryl Siegel (eds), *Generation 1.5 Meets College Composition: Issues in the Teaching of Writing to U.S.-Educated Learners of English*, Mahwah, NJ: Erlbaum. pp.119–142.

Johns, Ann M. (2001) 'ESL Students and WAC Programs: Varied Populations and Diverse Needs', in Susan H. McLeod, Eric Miraglia, Margot Soven, and Christopher Thaiss (eds), *WAC for the New Millennium: Strategies for Continuing Writing-across-the-Curriculum Programs*, Urbana, IL: National Council of Teachers of English. pp.141–64.

Kachru, Braj B. (1984) 'World Englishes and the Teaching of English to Non-Native Speakers: Contexts, Attitudes, and Concerns', *TESOL Newsletter*, 18(5): 25–26.

Kaplan, Robert B. (1966) 'Cultural Thought Patterns in Inter-Cultural Education', *Language Learning*, 16: 1–20.

Kobayashi, Hiroe and Rinnert, Carol (2002) 'High School Student Perceptions of First Language Literacy Instruction: Implications for Second Language Writing', *Journal of Second Language Writing*, 11(2): 91–116.

Krapels, Alexandra Rowe (1990) 'An Overview of Second Language Writing Process Research', in Barbara Kroll (ed.), *Second Language Writing: Research Insights for the Classroom*, New York: Cambridge University Press. pp.37–56.

Kroll, Barbara (1978) 'Sorting out Writing Problems', in Charles H. Blatchfold and Jacquelyn E. Schachter (eds.), *On TESOL '78: EFL Policies, Programs, Practices*, Washington, DC: TESOL. pp.176–182.

Kroll, Barbara (1979) 'A Survey of the Writing Needs of Foreign and American College Freshmen', *English Language Teaching Journal*, 33(3): 219–227.

Kroll, Barbara (ed.) (1990) *Second Language Writing: Research Insights for the Classroom*, New York: Cambridge University Press.

Kroll, Barbara (eds) (2003) *Exploring the Dynamics of Second Language Writing*, New York: Cambridge University Press.

Kubota, Ryuko (1998) 'An Investigation of L1-L2 Transfer in Writing among Japanese University Students: Implications for Contrastive Rhetoric', *Journal of Second Language Writing*, 7(1): 69–100.

Kubota, Ryuko (2003) 'New Approaches to Race, Class, and Gender in Second Language Writing', *Journal of Second Language Writing*, 12(1): 31–47.

Kubota, Ryuko and Lehner, Al (2004) 'Toward Critical Contrastive Rhetoric', *Journal of Second Language Writing*, 13(1): 7–27.

Land, Robert and Whitley, Catherine (1989) 'Evaluating Second Language Essays in Regular Composition Classes: Toward a Pluralistic U.S Rhetoric', in Donna M. Johnson and Duane H. Roen (eds.), *Richness in Writing: Empowering ESL Students*, New York: Longman. pp.284–94.

Lawrence, Mary S. (1972). *Writing as a Thinking Process*, Ann Arbor: University of Michigan Press.

Leki, Ilona (1991) 'Building Expertise through Sequenced Writing Assignments', *TESOL Journal*, 1(2): 19–23.

Leki, Ilona (1997) 'Completely Different Worlds': EAP and the Writing Experiences of ESL Students in University Courses', *TESOL Quarterly*, 31(1): 39–69.

Leki, Ilona (1999) 'Pretty much I Screwed up': Ill-Served Needs of a Permanent Resident', in Linda Harklau, Kay M. Losey, and Meryl Siegel (eds.), *Generation 1.5 Meets College Composition*, Mahwah, NJ: Lawrence Erlbaum. pp.17–43.

Li, Xiao-ming (1995) *'Good Writing' in Cross-Cultural Contexts*. Albany, NY: SUNY Press.

Liu, Jun and Hansen, Jette G. (2002) *Peer Response in Second Language Writing Classrooms*, Ann Arbor: University of Michigan Press.

Matsuda, Aya (2006) 'Negotiating ELT Assumptions in EIL Classrooms', in Julian Edge (ed.) *(Re)Locating TESOL in an Age of Empire*, Hampshire, UK: Palgrave MacMillan. pp.158–170.

Matsuda, Paul Kei (1997) 'Contrastive Rhetoric in Context: A Dynamic Model of L2 Writing', *Journal of Second Language Writing*, 6(1): 45–60.

Matsuda, Paul Kei (1998) 'Situating ESL Writing in a Cross-Disciplinary Context', *Written Communication*, 15(1): 99–121.

Matsuda, Paul Kei (1999) 'Composition Studies and ESL Writing: A Disciplinary Division of Labor', *College Composition and Communication*, 50(4): 699–721.

Matsuda, Paul Kei (2001) 'Reexamining Audiolingualism: On the Genesis of Reading and Writing in L2 Studies', in Diane Belcher and Alan Hirvela (eds.), *Linking Literacies: Perspectives on L2 Reading-Writing Connections*, Ann Arbor: University of Michigan Press. pp.84–105.

Matsuda, Paul Kei (2003) 'Process and Post-Process: A Discursive History', *Journal of Second Language Writing*, 12(1): 65–83.

Matsuda, Paul Kei (2005) 'Historical Enquiry in Second Language Writing', in Paul Kei Matsuda and Tony Silva (eds.), *Second Language Writing Research: Perspectives on the Process of Knowledge Construction*, Mahwah, NJ: Lawrence Erlbaum Associates. pp.33–46.

Matsuda, Paul Kei (2006) 'The Myth of Linguistic Homogeneity in U.S. College Composition', *College English*, 68(6): 637–651.

Matsuda, Paul Kei and De Pew, Kevin Eric (2002) 'Early Second Language Writing: An Introduction', *Journal of Second Language Writing*, 11: 261–268.

Matsuda, Paul Kei and Matsuda, Aya (2009) 'The Erasure of Resident ESL Writers', in Mark Roberge, Meryl Siegal, and Linda Harklau (eds.), *Generation 1.5 in College Composition: Teaching Academic Writing to U.S.-Educated Learners of ESL*, Mahwah, NJ: Lawrence Erlbaum Associates. pp.50–64.

Matsuda, Paul Kei, Fruit, Maria, Burton Lamm, and Tamara Lee (2006) 'Second Language Writers and Writing Program Administrators', *WPA: Writing Program Administration*, 30(1-2):11–14.

Matsuda, Paul Kei and Silva, Tony (1999) 'Cross-Cultural Composition: Mediated Integration of US and International Students', *Composition Studies*, 27(1): 15–30.

McCarthey, Sarah. J., Guo, Yi-Huey, and Cummins, Sunday (2005) 'Understanding Changes in Elementary Mandarin Students' L1 and L2 Writing', *Journal of Second Language Writing*, 14: 71–104.

Ortmeier-Hooper, Christina (2007) 'Beyond "English Language Learner": Second Language Writers, Academic Literacy, and Issues of Identity in the U.S. High School', PhD dissertation, University of New Hampshire.

Ortmeier-Hooper, Christina (2008) 'English may be my Second Language, but I'm not "ESL"', *College Composition and Communication*, 59(3): 389–419.

Ortmeier-Hooper, Christina (forthcoming) 'The Shifting Nature of Identity: Social Identity, L2 writers, and High School,' in Michelle Cox, Jay Jordan, Christina Ortmeier-Hooper, and Gwen Gray Schwartz (eds.) *Reinventing Identities in Second Language Writing*, Urbana, IL: National Council of Teachers of English.

Pennington, Martha, Brock, Mark N., and Yue, Francis (1996) 'Explaining Hong Kong Students' Response to Process Writing: An Exploration of Causes and Outcomes', *Journal of Second Language Writing*, 5(3): 227–52.

Pincas, Anita (1962) 'Structural Linguistics and Systematic Composition Teaching to Students of English as a Foreign Language', *Language Learning*, 7: 185–195.

Pratt, Mary Louise (1991) 'Arts of the Contact Zone', *Profession*, 91: 33–40.

Preto-Bay, Anna Maria, and Hansen, Kristine. (2006) 'Preparing for the Tipping Point: Designing Writing Programs to Meet the Needs of the Changing Population', *WPA: Writing Program Administration*, 30(1-2): 37–58.

Reichelt, Melinda (1999) 'Toward a More Comprehensive View of L2 Writing: Foreign Language Writing in the U.S', *Journal of Second Language Writing*, 8(2): 181–204.

Reichelt, Melinda and Silva, Tony (1995/1996) 'Cross-Cultural Composition', *TESOL Journal*, 5(2): 16–19.

Reid, Joy (1998) '"Eye" Learners and "ear" Learners: Identifying the Language Needs of International and U.S. Resident Writers', in Patricia Byrd and Joy M. Reid (eds.), *Grammar in the Composition Classroom: Essays on Teaching ESL for College-Bound Students*, New York: Heinle. pp.3–17.

Reid, Joy and Kroll, Barbara (1995) 'Designing and Assessing Effective Writing Assignments for NEW and ESL Students', *Journal of Second Language Writing*, 4:17–41.

Reynolds, Dudley (2002) 'Learning to Make Things Happen in Different Ways: Causality in the Writing of Middle-Grade English Language Learners', *Journal of Second Language Writing*, 11(3): 311–328.

Reynolds, Dudley (2005) 'Linguistic Correlates of Second Language Literacy Development: Evidence from Middle-Grade Learner Essays', *Journal of Second Language Writing*, 14(1): 19–45.

Severino, Carol (1993) 'The Sociopolitical Implications of Response to Second Language and Second Dialect Writing', *Journal of Second Language Writing*, 2(3): 181–201.

Silva, Tony (1993) 'Toward an Understanding of the Distinct Nature of L2 Writing: The ESL Research and its Implications', *TESOL Quarterly*, 27(4): 657–677.

Silva, Tony (1994) 'An Examination of Writing Program Administrators' Options for the Placement of ESL Students in First Year Writing Classes', *WPA: Writing Program Administration*, 18(1-2): 37–43.

Silva, Tony and Matsuda, Paul Kei (eds.) (2001) *On Second Language Writing*, Mahwah, NJ: Lawrence Erlbaum Associates.

Slager, William R. (1966) 'Controlling Composition: Some Practical Classroom Techniques', in Robert B. Kaplan (ed.), *Selected Conference Papers of the Association of Teachers of English as a Second Language*, Los Angeles: National Association for Foreign Student Affairs. pp.77–85.

Susser, Bernard (1994) 'Process Approaches in ESL/EFL Writing Instruction', *Journal of Second Language Writing*, 3: 31–47.

Swales, John (1990) *Genre Analysis*, Cambridge, UK: Cambridge University Press.

Swales, John (2004) *Research Genres: Explorations and Applications*, Cambridge, UK: Cambridge University Press.

Tardy, Christine (2005) 'It's like a Story': Rhetorical Knowledge Development in Advanced Academic Literacy', *Journal of English for Academic Purposes*, 4(4): 325–38.

Truscott, John (1996) 'The Case against Grammar Correction in L2 Writing Classes', *Language Learning*, 46(2): 327–369.

Truscott, John (1999) 'The Case for "The Case against Grammar Correction in L2 Writing Classes": A Response to Ferris', *Journal of Second Language Writing*, 8(2): 111–122.

Valdes, Guadalupe (1992) 'Bilingual Minorities and Language Issues in Writing: Toward Profession Wide Responses to a New Challenge', *Written Communication*, 9(1): 85–136.

Villalva, Kerry Enright (2006a) 'Hidden Literacies and Inquiry Approaches of Bilingual High School Writers', *Written Communication*, 23(1): 91–129.

Villalva, Kerry Enright (2006b) 'Reforming High School Writing: Opportunities and Constraints for Generation 1.5 writers', in Paul Kei Matsuda, Christina Ortmeier-Hooper, and Xiaoye You (eds.), *The Politics of Second Language Writing: In Search of the Promised Land*, West Lafayette, IN: Parlor Press. pp.57–68.

Weigle, Sara C. (2002) *Assessing Writing*, New York: Cambridge University Press.

Williams, Jessica (2004) 'Tutoring and Revision: Second Language Writers in the Writing Center', *Journal of Second Language Writing*, 13(3): 173–201.

Williams, Jessica (2006) 'The Role(s) of Writing Centers in Second Language Instruction', in Paul Kei Matsuda, Christina Ortmeier-Hooper, and Xiaoye You (eds.) *The Politics of Second Language Writing: In Search of the Promised Land*, West Lafayette, IN: Parlor Press. pp.109–126.

Williams, Jessica and Severino, Carol (2004) 'The Writing Center and Second Language Writers', *Journal of Second Language Writing*, 13(3): 165–172.

Yi, Youngjoo (2005) 'Asian Adolescents' Out-of-School Encounters with English and Korean Literacy', *Journal of Asian Pacific Communication*, 15(1): 57–77.

Yi, Youngjoo (2007) 'Engaging Literacy: A Biliterate Student's Composing Practices Beyond School', *Journal of Second Language Writing*, 16(1): 23–39.

You, Xiaoye (2006) 'Globalization and the Politics of Teaching EFL Writing', in Paul Kei Matsuda, Christina Ortmeier-Hooper, and Xiaoye You (eds.), *The Politics of Second Language Writing: In Search of the Promised Land*, West Lafayette, IN: Parlor Press. pp.188–202.

Zamel, Vivian (1976) 'Teaching Composition in the ESL Classroom: What Can we Learn from the Research in the Teaching of English', *TESOL Quarterly*, 10(1): 67–76.

Zamel, Vivian (1995) 'Strangers in Academia: The Experiences of Faculty and ESL Students across the Curriculum', *College Composition and Communication*, 46(4): 506–21.

Zhu, Wei (2001) 'Interaction and Feedback in Mixed Peer Response Groups', *Journal of Second Language Writing*, 10(4): 251–276.

Zhu, Wei (2006) 'Understanding Context for Writing in the University Content Classrooms', in Paul Kei Matsuda, Christina Ortmeier-Hooper, and Xiaoye You (eds.), *The Politics of Second Language Writing: In Search of the Promised Land*, West Lafayette, IN: Parlor Press. pp.129–146.

Meeting the Needs of Advanced Multilingual Writers

Suresh Canagarajah and Maria Jerskey

This chapter highlights key challenges faced by diverse adult writers for whom English is not a first language (L1). We limit ourselves to academic literacy, bearing in mind that there are many other personal and professional genres of writing that are important for multilinguals. We establish globalism and postmodernism as important sociocultural and philosophical lenses through which to view multilingual writers and describe the critical debates that relate to how teachers and researchers have addressed the development of literacy competence in tertiary educational contexts. Finally, we outline a socially situated pedagogy to integrate the diverse components that meet the needs of successful multilingual writers and address the challenges ahead.

DEFINING ADVANCED MULTILINGUAL WRITERS

We take 'advanced' in our title to refer to the age and pedagogical status, not literacy proficiency. As such, advanced multilingual writers in this chapter include students and academics in tertiary education: college-level, undergraduate students; graduate-level students and researchers; and professionals who need to write in English to conduct and/or further their academic work. Because of their advanced educational or academic professional status, the literacy demands on these writers are more complex than the demands on younger writers in primary and secondary education. Writers in higher education contexts must write extended expository essays and research papers, as undergraduates; dissertations and theses, as graduate students; and articles, chapters, and books for publication as academic professionals. The rhetorical modes employed by advanced writers are complex and serious, and stand in stark contrast to the personal and descriptive writing (often of shorter stretches of discourses) that writers in primary and secondary schools engage in. Perhaps most significantly, the writing that advanced writers need to produce is of high-stakes implications: Their writing determines whether they will graduate, receive their doctorate, become tenured in their profession, receive funding for further research, or participate in and have an influence upon academic knowledge production. What becomes fascinating but challenging for multilingual writers, is that they have to engage in this writing as they negotiate multiple languages. Their monolingual peers work within the context of a single language. Therefore, whatever their proficiency level in English, advanced multilingual writers are faced with the complex linguistic act of shuttling between multiple languages and discourses as they write in English, the lingua franca of an ever expanding transnational communicative domain.

GLOBALISM AND POSTMODERNISM IN CONTEXT

Written competence in English has taken on added significance for students and scholars in the context of globalization. The world economy and its transnational production networks demand knowledge workers from all over the world. The outsourcing and offshoring of production in this global economy has created a demand for English-speaking professionals from outside traditionally Anglophone countries. Since English remains the main language for communication in these emerging economic and production relationships, more and more people seek competence in the formal genres of writing required for this work. We see an influx of multilingual and multicultural students to Canada, the UK, Australia, and the US, despite the short decline after 9/11 (see Bollag, 2006; Mooney and MacNeil, 2006). They want to gain competence in the knowledge, codes, and discourses that will allow them to compete in emerging global economies. Their education abroad is also made possible by the new flow of capital and availability of resources in their communities thanks to globalization.

Furthermore, many developing countries give more importance to the teaching of English and English literacy in their national curriculum. We hear of policy changes in countries as diverse as China (Tsui, 2007) and Brazil (Rajagopalan, 2005) as local teachers struggle to develop English literacy competence among their students from very early stages of their schooling. The new importance given to English literacy is a reflection of the desire by many of these countries to tap into the advantages afforded by globalization. Lin and Martin (2005) bring together articles from diverse countries to show that the previous resistance to English use during decolonization is muted in the face of global opportunities that English brings to local communities.

Globalization affects academic scholars in non-Anglophone countries directly in their institutions. There is a trend to Americanize the higher education system in countries like China, India, and even UK and Australia. This shift is marked by the change of designations (from lecturer to Assistant Professor), the introduction of the tenure system, the pressure to obtain external grants, and the general corporatization of universities. To fulfill all these new obligations, local scholars are pressured to publish more in journals with a high impact factor (see Braine, 2005, for a perspective on these developments in Hong Kong). This means publishing in predominantly English language journals printed in UK or USA. If Swales' (1990) statistics on the domination of English in the academic publishing world was true in the 1980s, it is even truer now. We see a meteoric rise in submissions of English-medium articles from nonwestern and non-Anglophone communities to mainstream, Anglophone journals in the West. Graddol (1997) reports on the anglicization of scientific journals from non-Anglophone countries.

Whether English is the language of globalization, as Crystal (2003) asserts, is debatable. There are scholars who argue that other languages are also gaining importance in the context of globalization (Dor, 2004). Nevertheless, we can observe a major philosophical change that has implications for pluralizing English writing. Postmodern thinking has challenged some of the unitary and essentialized ways in which applied linguists, compositionists, and ESL (English as second language) specialists have conceived language and writing. Researchers, scholars, and teachers are thus challenged to question monolingual assumptions and consider instead: how academic styles of writing are heterogeneously defined; how English use implies multiple forms of discourse; how English comes with multiple cultures and discourses; how texts, far from objective and transparent expressions of undistorted ideas, are replete with the values, culture, and identity of the author; and how there are multiple forms of engagement with scholarship, contrary to the positivist assumptions of modernism. (For an exploration of these questions, see Horner and Trimbur, 2002; Canagarajah, 2006a, 2006b.)

All these questions allow points of entry for the values and discourses of multilingual writers even as they write in English in the high-stakes contexts of academia. Writing does not mean a one-sided and passive accommodation to what is perceived as the dominant conventions and norms of English writing. Rather, at the most personal level, the expectation of voice in writing provides some scope for difference in multilinguals' English writing. For example, the multilingualism of writers helps them to bring stylistic resources and expressive devices from their languages of proficiency to English writing. Furthermore, their own cultures of scholarship and local knowledge of their communities may critically and creatively inform their English writing.

One of the most complicated issues currently under discussion inspired by the social changes of globalization and philosophical changes of postmodernism is the status of world Englishes. English has become localized in the diverse countries to which it has traveled. As multilingual users of English outnumber native English users (Graddol, 1999) and as the lingua franca in contact situations (McArthur, 2001), the new norms and grammars of world Englishes have gained significance (Kachru, 1986). Scholars are now open to the possibility that to use a language is to

'people' it with one's own intentions and interests (to paraphrase Bakhtin). We have examples of multimodal texts on the Internet where 'English writing' involves diverse registers, codes, and genres on the same page. The reality of these hybrid texts provides spaces for other languages and localized dialects of English to coexist with standard British or American English. In business communication and professional contexts, we see multilinguals using their own grammars for successful negotiation of their objectives (Connor, 1999; Louhiala-Salminen et al., 2005). Academic writing, however, is still somewhat 'pure'. Policed by copyeditors, editors, publishers, and teachers, academic writing shows less hybridity in language or discourse conventions. However, diverse varieties of English have made their presence felt in literature for some time now (as we see in the novels of Achebe or poems of Walcott). African American scholars have used their dialect in a qualified way for voice in their academic writing (see Smitherman, 2003, for instance). Scholars consider how this thinking in literacy, globalization, and voice may open the way for diverse varieties of English for academic writing (see Horner and Trimbur, 2002; Canagarajah, 2006a). Just as Latin was displaced as the lingua franca for academic communication in the seventeenth century by European vernaculars, the time may come when 'standard written English' (currently constituted by American or British English) may give way to other and even multiple Englishes in writing.

CHALLENGES IN DEVELOPING PROFICIENCY

We now turn to the challenges in developing English literacy for multilingual writers in diverse contexts. While the challenges inherent in the social and geographical diversity of multilingual writers are already astounding, the shifts in perspective that derive from both globalism and postmodernism complexify how researchers, scholars, and educators frame their needs. These perspectives challenge traditional notions that proficiency in writing can be equated with the mastery of standard British or American grammar to produce error-free texts. They challenge the notion that writing is the mastery of a uniform set of registers and conventions that might pass for academic discourse. In addition, they challenge the notion that the acquisition of writing competence in a second language or dialect requires the writer to separate from his/her native language and native culture and focus on fitting himself/herself into expected and recognizable identities, thought patterns, and values of the target languages. Instead, effective writing requires the active negotiation of the multiple languages and identities a writer brings to construct a creative and challenging text that adds something extra to knowledge and style even as it demonstrates an awareness of the dominant conventions in the community of practice one wishes to address (Lave and Wenger, 1991; and see Li, 2007). Canagarajah (2006a) labels this bringing together of multiple discourses and identities *codemeshing*.

As writers travel toward competently creating such negotiated, code meshed, agentive texts, they face a range of challenges in diverse and complex contexts. For example, first year composition students in the US who are still in the process of learning English and/or are unprepared in academic writing skills often find themselves placed into composition courses whose goals and objectives attempt but often fail to accommodate or adapt for their lack of language proficiency and/or writing skills (Jerskey, 2006; see also Bartholomae, 1993; Harklau, 2000; Horner and Lu, 1999; Kells and Balester, 1999; Lu, 1992; McNenny and Fitzgerald, 2001; Soliday, 1996, 2002; Sternglass, 1997). Thus, a significant challenge for higher education teachers in the US becomes addressing the variety of strengths and weaknesses their multilingual students bring to their English writing (see Leki, 1992; Friedrich, 2006).

Resembling actual students from East Asian communities (see Li, 1999; Lu, 1992) and from South Asia (see Ramanathan, 2004), Yamada from Japan and Raktim from India are two fictionalized international students in US colleges who grapple with distinct challenges as writers.[1] As Japan is an *expanding circle* country where English is not used actively as a second language but, rather, as a language of 'wider communication across national and cultural boundaries' (McKay, 2002: 37), Yamada is unprepared for her struggles to be understood by US monolinguals who are unaccustomed to hearing English used as an international language. Furthermore, responses from her professors display an inconsistent range of tolerance for errors. Raktim, on the other hand, comes from an *outer circle* country where he is used to speaking in Indian English for everyday communication. His sense of fluency and comfort in English, however, is put to the test when he arrives in the US.

Although Yamada has experience writing in Japanese and has studied English as a foreign language, she finds herself unprepared to write essays for her literature course. US academic discourse requires a strongly proffered, individual point of view that is virtually nonexistent in Yamada's educational experience in Japan. The careful and deliberate sentences that Yamada can produce have no currency in her course. Yamada struggles to situate her thinking particularly in developing her own thoughts but it is exactly this disconnect that ultimately allows Yamada to negotiate and develop an authentic point of view while developing a text that can bridge the values she brings from her own culture.

Other multilingual students who have come to the US for higher education have argued that transitioning from formulaic and impersonal writing to the expected voice and process in the US was the biggest challenge for them, confirming Yamada's experience (see Li, 1999). Raktim's challenges are slightly different from Yamada's since he has already had considerable exposure to standard British English in his English classes in India. Though he might have done some writing of essays in his school, the pedagogy there remains largely product oriented (see Ramanathan, 2004).

While Raktim needs to become acculturated into more personal cognitive and affective processes of engaging with writing to represent his emerging academic voice, Yamada will need to continue not only to master competence in the syntax and acquire a larger stock of vocabulary, she will also need to become sensitized to how she can develop as a writer—using the strengths she has developed as a writer in Japanese—as she grapples with the multiple genre conventions she comes across in her US education.

The challenges for the 'Generation 1.5' are different (Harklau, et al., 1999; Schwartz, 2004; Friedrich, 2006; Ortmeier-Hooper, 2008). Ming, a 19-year-old Chinese American, has been schooled in the US, speaks Cantonese at home, and code-switches with her friends from high school who attend the same local college. While she is socialized into the local English idioms and does not sound like a 'foreigner' the way that Yamada and Raktim do when they speak, her academic writing is often written in an informal register and is peppered with grammatical errors that belie her spoken fluency. Ming needs time to master the conventions of academic writing and learn to edit her texts carefully for colloquial language. Given that, Ming is an ear learner (Reid, 2006), she is able to catch many errors in ways that Yamada still struggles with. A more complex problem for Ming and many 'Generation 1.5' students, is reconciling the assumptions that may or may not apply to her own background and experiences as she 'crosses over' into mainstream classes (Schwartz, 2004) yet shuttles back and forth between US and Chinese identities.

The rich, complex stories of multilingual students such as Yamada, Raktim, and Ming underscore the challenges they face as writers of English in Anglophone settings. Accomplished multilingual graduate students in non-Anglophone countries face a different set of challenges as they move toward professional academic careers that require writing in English. Take the case of Yuan, a Chinese graduate student in chemistry finishing his degree in Mainland China. Li (2007) studies the process of Yuan writing the first draft of an article for an English-medium journal, as part of his doctoral degree requirement. Like many nonnative graduate researchers who need to publish in English-medium journals, Yuan's greatest challenge was transitioning from the test-oriented English he struggled with as an undergraduate 'to processing and producing longer research articles in English for international publication' (76). Moreover, like many nonnative graduate researchers in non-Anglophone locations like China, Yuan's primary means of learning to write articles in English came from imitating the articles in journals he hoped to be published in. By participating in Li's case study of his efforts, Yuan developed a meta-awareness of his writing process, an awareness that proved instrumental in his engagement with and completion of his draft.

Even established advanced scholars in outer and expanding circle communities face enormous challenges as writers in English. Unlike Yuan, it is not the academic or linguistic knowledge that hinders them. They have familiarity with the academic genres, they know the language well, and they are trained well in using their research methods and instruments effectively. Rather, it is the very basic need to gain access to the research journals, books, and web access that limits them. Without these resources, they are unable to develop a convincing introductory move as described in Swales' (1990: 141) Create a Research Space model to frame their own study and findings. Other material resources such as the ability to stay connected with their colleagues for mentoring and information and the ability to find free time from their teaching responsibilities in the local institutions to compose with care and revise and edit multiple drafts limits their ability to compose effective texts. Canagarajah (1996) calls them nondiscursive requirements.

Nondiscursive requirements are not the problem for many multilingual scholars who are undergoing training in English dominant countries such as the US, UK, and Canada or are part of the faculty there. They benefit enormously from the resources already available. However, they do face cultural problems. Since many immigrate after considerable socialization in their own academic communities, they often find that the academic culture in their new environment comes with a sharp learning curve. The discourses, attitudes, and voice of scholarship are often strange and prove challenging to scholars who have been trained to be deferential to authority in their own respective communities. Kubota 2003, Sasaki 2003, and Shen 1989 write of their own challenges in transitioning to an Anglo-American academic ethos.

The challenge and need to publish for nonnative speakers of English from outside the centre has been extensively documented (Belcher, 2007; Braine, 2005; Flowerdew and Li, forthcoming). For many, like Yuan, receiving their degree and advancing in their academic careers is hinged to publishing in English-medium specialist journals. Curry and Lillis (2004) tease out factors that advanced multilingual scholars working outside English-speaking countries grapple with as they negotiate if not the demand to publish in English, then the value of publishing their research for a range of communities. Consider their profile of M.O., an associate professor of social psychology in Spain who has published extensively in Spanish research periodicals. While she does not feel external pressures to publish in English, she does feel the value of English-medium journal publications for the promotion and prestige that, she hopes, will bring funding to expand her research.

The story is slightly different and more poignant for I.G. (Curry and Lillis, 2004), an associate professor of psychology in Hungary. Unlike M.O. who feels fluent in spoken and written English, I.G. struggles with his English competency. Yet, he teaches in English to international groups of interdisciplinary professionals and has published extensively in both Hungarian and English. Like M.O., his imperative to publish in English is strategic: While his Hungarian publications lead to local funding of his research, publishing in English-medium journals provide a better forum to reach I.G.'s intended audience and they bolster I.G.'s opportunities for promotion and collaboration on an international scale. I.G.'s connection with US researchers and his collaboration with them has served to fund a laboratory, which in turn supports the work of his doctoral students and postdoctoral researchers.

For I.G., writing in English is a tremendous struggle and comes at a high emotional and time cost. It takes him twice as long to write an article in English as it does in Hungarian and, ironically, reviewers of the more prestigious journals are less willing to offer help. I.G. feels their strong preference for only highly 'accomplished English academic writing' (Curry and Lillis, 2004: 678). While I.G. is very successful, his success is evidently built on 'a large amount of work and persistence' (678).

These profiles, culled directly from available narratives and constructed fictionally from past studies and our own students, illustrate complex challenges for multilingual writers. Clearly, it is counterproductive to treat all multilingual writers as unskilled in the language and subject them to grammar-level interventions when their linguistic and literacy experiences often provide considerable strengths to build on or where the mediated support of 'literacy brokers' (Lillis and Curry, 2006) can and should be resourced. Not only are the challenges and needs important to address for the benefit of multilingual writers, it becomes increasingly clear that access to multilinguals' research and knowledge allows for a truly global perspective.

DEBATES

Researchers and teachers of writing are divided about the strategies that should be adopted to develop English literacy competence among multilingual writers. Casanave (2007) observes that while many of the debates that generate controversy in the field of L2 (second language) writing have created false dichotomies, they warrant consideration. Indeed, because of the broad range of challenges for multilingual writers as they construct English-medium texts, these conceptual and theoretical debates and their pedagogical implications are worth exploring here.

Authorship and mediation: Among the changes in our understanding of writing is the notion that writing is a mediated product (Swales, 1990). Writing has always been a social, collaborative, and situated activity. Nevertheless, the myth of individual authorship (bolstered perhaps by capitalist ideologies of personal ownership) masked the collective nature of writing (Howard, 1995). Now, we acknowledge that many other people are involved in bringing forth the finished product. Lillis and Curry (2006) outline the significant activity of the many shapers and mentors who serve as 'literacy brokers' to advanced multilingual writers in academic settings. Belcher (2007) studies the role of editors and reviewers in helping multilingual authors negotiate their revisions. She considers mentoring practices that facilitate positive revision. Many multilingual writers, however, fight shy of acknowledging the help they receive (Flowerdew, 2007). Some may not get the help they need and consider it unethical. From this perspective, we have to ask a basic question about what authorship means when many parties engage in the production of texts. A pedagogical dilemma that emerges concerns the wisdom of inculcating (and thus perpetuating) practices of self-reliance in the solitary author on one hand and, on the other, teaching negotiation strategies, i.e., ways of collaborating with others and with other texts to construct an effective piece of writing.

The underlying questions concern the values inherent in such choices: Should the production of writing in academic settings separate the scholars who are able to produce English-medium texts within the constructs and confines of an individual author? Alternatively, should the dissemination of knowledge be given a higher priority? Would the creation (or acknowledgement) of multi-authored texts threaten the reproduction of academic culture (Bourdieu, 1977) in which the single authored article, chapter, and book is valued over such collaborative efforts? If and when these issues can be untangled and resolved, so will the issues that follow.

Borrowing versus plagiarism: Just as writers collaborate with others, they also engage with multiple texts to bring forth their finished product. However, the nature of this borrowing is misunderstood. Western notions of plagiarism are applied so punitively and arbitrarily, they create confusion among writers, particularly those from cultures that value 'a close allegiance to a few acknowledged authorities' (Deckert, 1993:132) as in China or Korea (see Bouman, 2004; Cai, 1999). It is even more damaging for multilingual writers who come from oral/traditional communities where words are not owned by individuals but borrowed freely (Pennycook, 1996). In addition, memorization and quoting authorities are considered a mark of one's knowledge (Deckert, 1993; Hayward, 2004). Postmodern notions of intertextuality make us comfortable with the notion that texts do not spring forth whole from individuals, but rather from other texts. The Internet has also made 'cut and paste' easy to accomplish, not to mention other communicative practices such as remix and parody from popular culture (Faigley, 1997). If we redefine borrowing in broader terms, we can make multilingual writers adopt healthy practices of borrowing, as it derives from their culture while also shaping the borrowed words creatively to serve their own interests and voice (see Chandrasoma et al., 2004).

Description versus practice: While it is important to try to characterize what constitutes diverse academic genres for student writers, it is troubling how much we have to generalize in order to come up with monolithic descriptions and definitions. Schools such as genre analysis and corpus linguistics (Hyland and Tse, 2007) help scholars describe the registers, textual structures, and discourse conventions that make up genres as distinct as research articles (RA), book reviews, and grant proposals (see Swales, 1990). However, others wonder if texts can (or should) be generalized like this (for a critique of all forms of essentialization in writing instruction, see Zamel, 1997). Are all texts stereotypical? Do they look similar? Where does the voice and creativity of the authors come in? Moreover, though we might identify differences between an RA in literature and physics, Are we going too far when we try to distinguish an RA in literature from an RA in philosophy? In addition, especially in an age of interdisciplinarity, shouldn't disciplines (and hence their writing conventions) flow into each other and draw from each other? And what do we do with the diversity of RAs within the same discipline? Do all articles in *College, College and Communication*, or *TESOL Quarterly* adopt a similar structure? Even the register might vary in each discipline in a context when so many theoretical paradigms coexist in each field. While such description provides a convenient starting point for multilingual writers, they are better served when taught to negotiate the variability of academic discourse in context specific terms.

Accommodation versus resistance: Once the genre conventions are understood, to what extent can the multilingual writer reshape the text to suit his/her own voice, values, and interests? Scholars are now comfortable with the notion that to speak is to resist—i.e., it is by 'talking back' (hooks, 1999) that one manages to use the genre with creativity and authority, bringing one's own knowledge and values into the dominant discourse to challenge received wisdom. However, if one departs too radically from the established conventions, one's writing will be considered so idiosyncratic that it won't belong to that disciplinary community at all. Therefore, creatively merging one's discourses into the dominant discourses is treated as a pragmatic strategy of reconciliation (Canagarajah, 2006a). However, adopting the genre conventions of a context or community always involves an element of imposition and suppression (Wei et al., 2006). What is the proper attitude for multilingual authors to adopt—what is the proper balance between accommodation and resistance that will enable them to be genre-aware but critical writers?

Moving from these broader conceptual and theoretical debates, we now frame the pedagogical debates that researchers, scholars, and teachers have yet to reconcile as they address the needs of advanced multilingual writers. Because writing instruction in tertiary education has been a uniquely American pedagogical activity, a significant percentage of the scholarship emerges from US-based researchers and theorists.

Process versus product: This is an old debate that gains new ramifications in the context of multilingualism and globalization (see the special edition of *Journal of Second Language Writing*, 2003, 12(1): 'L2 Writing in the Post-Process Era'). Focusing on the 'product' went out of fashion in the 1980s with the rise of process-based instruction (Raimes, 1985, 1991; Spack, 1984; Zamel, 1982, 1987). Yet, many second language teachers feel that instruction in grammar, genre conventions, register, and style is indispensable to multilingual writers who are new to the language and culture (Johns, 2002). On the other hand, more cognitively based practitioners (Flower and Hayes, 1981) believe that teaching writers the process of planning, recursive composing, generative revising, editing, and audience awareness will help them develop the other proficiencies they require over time. Perhaps the proper balance is both proficiency and purpose dependent. While college students have the time to start with invention strategies and composing processes, professionals can directly enter their discipline-specific genres with help on registers and conventions.

Grammar versus genre: A similar debate is the extent to which students should be proficient in language before they can master genre and style conventions. Some teachers expect students who are new to English to master the basics of grammar and syntax before they are introduced to extended prose. Research has yet to prove that such mastery improves writing (see Truscott, 1996; but also Ferris, 2002). Others argue that grammar and discourse cannot be separated (Silva, 1993). The discourse of a particular genre or disciplinary writing comes with its own grammar and vocabulary and its own community of readers/writers (see Lave and Wenger, 1991). Therefore, it is possible for multilingual writers to be socialized into both together (Knapp and Watkins, 1994). Similarly, someone who has a mature understanding of his/her discipline and its knowledge paradigms and methods in his or her own L1 might not be too far in his/her ability to use the vocabulary or grammatical structures that come with that discourse in a multilingual context.

In the increasingly heterogeneous classrooms of today, a more integrated approach to grammar and genre might offer a resolution to the debate in the form of *systemic functional linguistics*. Recent research uses the paradigm of systemic functional linguistics (Halliday, 1994; Eggins, 2004) as a theory of language that can provide teachers with strategies to identify and teach the relevant linguistic features of particular genres of texts and how grammar choices function within those genres. In this way, multilingual writers can focus on the meaning-making role of language, go beyond traditional grammatical categories, and participate in the construction of effectively written texts. Schleppergrell's (2004, 2006) research with US primary and secondary school writers expands to applications for multilinguals in tertiary educational contexts by focusing on 'the language systems writers draw on and the alternatives available within those systems' Schleppergrell, 2007:123).

ENGLISH FOR GENERAL PURPOSES (EGP) VERSUS ENGLISH SPECIFIC PURPOSES (ESP)

Both sides in this debate are committed to teaching genre conventions but for different reasons. The EGP camp feels that a pedagogy of writing made up of composing generic texts helps student writers move to more specific contexts of writing (Kuriloff, 1996; Spack, 1988; Widdowson, 1983). They argue that EGP provides enough practice in primary writing concerns (i.e., paragraph structure, topic and thesis sentences, audience awareness, rhetorical modes, etc.) to develop effective writing skills. Typical first year composition classes in the US are made up of such a pedagogy: The ubiquitous five-paragraph essay falls into this curriculum. Others feel that writing is always situated and contextualized and that there is no generic writing: All meaningful and purposive writing assumes a particular community, genre conventions, and objectives that can be pragmatically taught (see Swales, 1990; but also Severino,1993 and Benesch, 1993 for a critical perspective of such pragmatism). They favour courses that are supported by Writing across the Curriculum (WAC) initiatives or by an ESP curriculum.

Based on the premises that (a) writing is an invaluable learning tool to discover and construct knowledge and (b) that specific disciplines have specific written genres and discourses that can be taught, WAC was introduced to US tertiary education curricula in the 1980s in response to a perceived lack in discipline literacy among college students regardless of their linguistic background. Similarly, ESP courses can be designed to address the linguistic and literacy needs of multilingual writers in their specific disciplines. The challenge is determining what multilingual writers (often from diverse L1 backgrounds and diverse literacy practices) will need to know in order to write effectively in their specific discipline and then creating cohesive pedagogical approaches. (See Basturkmen, 2006.)

Instruction versus socialization: Can writing be taught in the classroom through the mere interaction between the teacher and the writer? More and more, scholars feel that writing is best taught as social practice. Writing is a way for an author to engage with his/her peers in the disciplinary activities that they are mutually engaged in. Therefore, writing is best taught in the apprentice model (Lave and Wenger, 1991; Belcher, 1994). Students are asked to participate in workshops and seminars that involve engagement with their professors or colleagues to construct texts that serve a function in their research and scholarship. Though this might work well for graduate students and academic professionals, it might not be effective for undergraduates. However, some instructors feel that they can simulate the collaborative practice in the classroom through other activities. Processes such as a collaborative learning (Bruffee, 1983), authentic reading and writing, project based pedagogy (Warschauer, 2000), and other such practices help students develop writing as social practice.

CONVENTION VERSUS VOICE

At what point should writers develop their own voice in writing? Should they master the basic genre conventions first before they can consider reshaping them to suit their values and interests? Scholars in the English for Academic Purposes school have taken the orientation that it is important for multilingual writers to be introduced to genre conventions in a prescriptive or product-oriented manner before they can adopt it creatively for their purposes (Reid, 1989; Swales, 1990). Others treat this 'pragmatism' as itself ideological, colonizing students into preconstructed thought and style patterns (Benesch, 1993), and denying them practicing the critical thinking of writers. Canagarajah

(1999) finds in his ethnography of multilingual college students the desire to appropriate the conventions of academic writing to suit their purposes. They resist postponing creative and critical uses of writing for a later time.

Acquisition as unilateral versus multilateral: Traditionally, the teaching of writing to second language learners has been conceived as a unilateral progression from a lower level of language proficiency to a higher level (Johns, 1990). This progression was theorized as occurring within a single language or literacy tradition. Though this might be true for monolingual students acquiring literacy proficiency, this model does not apply for multilingual writers. The latter are moving between two languages and literacy traditions (or more), and are constantly negotiating the norms and conventions of each as they develop literate competence in English. In her concept of multicompetence, Cook (1991, 1992, 1996) captures the complex cognitive ability of multilinguals. Analogous to multitasking, multilinguals shuttle between multiple languages and literacies as they construct texts in English. Rather than comparing multilingual writers' skills with those of monolinguals, researchers and teachers can consider the kinds of negotiation that take place as multilingual writers draw from their rich linguistic and cultural backgrounds to develop literacy in English (Kobayashi and Rinnert, 2007).

L1 AS PROBLEM OR RESOURCE

In the developing multicompetence of multilingual writers, the first language doesn't have to be a problem but a resource. However, writing research has so far treated the first language as a hindrance to the acquisition of English literacy. Orientations such as contrastive rhetoric and contrastive linguistics (Kaplan, 1966, 1967; Connor, 1996) have attempted to predict the kinds of problems the first language creates for a multilingual in acquiring competence in English. Awareness of language and literacy differences from L1 to L2 can serve as positive pedagogical tools when the L1 is not conceived as deficits when they emerge in the multilingual's writing. In fact, the influence of the first language can be positive. It can help students develop a healthy distance from the norms of the second language, develop a complex language awareness between the two languages, and adopt a creative and critical stance toward writing.

WRITING AS HOMOGENOUS VERSUS HYBRID

We are now able to theorize the possibility of the other languages and cultures a multilingual writer brings to English writing when we treat texts as hybrid: There is much more happening within the bounds of a text than a single register, homogeneous genre conventions, or unitary cultural values. The changing shape of texts in the age of the Internet provides spaces for multiple influences. As texts become multivocal, we are challenged to read multiple codes and conventions in texts that merge conventions and mesh codes (see further Cope and Kalantzis, 2000).

EMERGING DIRECTIONS

What kind of pedagogy would accommodate the emerging realizations of literacy, identity, and competence in the context of globalization and postmodern thinking? Though there is no clear candidate for a dominant pedagogical model, we can illustrate shifts in the teaching of multilingual writers as follows:

Shifts in teaching multilingual writers

From:	*To:*
Deficiency/errors	Choices/opti ons
Focus on rules/conventions	Focus on strategies
Texts as transparent/objective	Texts as representational
Focus on text construction	Focus on rhetorical negotiation
Written discourse as normative	Written discourse as changing
Writing as constitutive	Writing as performative
Texts as static/discrete	Texts as fluid
Texts as context dependent	Texts as context transforming
Compartmentalize literacy traditions	Accommodate literacy traditions
L1 or C1 as a problem	L1 or C1 as a resource
Orality as a hindrance	Orality as an advantage

Teachers must keep in mind that not all textual or linguistic differences are errors. Many of the presumed errors can be choices consciously made by writers from a range of options (including choices from localized varieties of English) to achieve their communicative purposes. Even when teachers are not prepared to let students code mesh in formal writing, they have the option to help students negotiate the different grammars of world Englishes. Rather than strictly adhering to standard rules and conventions, multilingual writers can be orientated to strategies of communication that allow them to modify, resist, or reorient to the rules in a manner favourable to them. As such, there can be a scope for appropriating the dominant conventions and codes; passive acquiescence to norms results in mechanical and ineffective writing. While there is a general pedagogy for learner strategy training in English for Speakers of Other Languages (ESOL) (see Wenden, 1991), there are also descriptive studies of favourable strategies that multilingual writers may use to negotiate competing discourses effectively (see Leki, 1995; Canagarajah, 2002b). Multilingual writers benefit from a pedagogy that allows writing to go beyond narrowly defined processes of text construction. Writing becomes instead a rhetorical negotiation for achieving social meanings and functions. In other words, writing is not just constitutive, it is also performative. We do not write only to construct a rule-governed text. Although it is important for texts to be constructed sensibly in order to be meaningful, we write in order to perform important social acts (Gee, 1990; Street, 1984). We write to achieve specific interests, represent our preferred values and identities, and fulfill diverse needs. When multilingual writers understand that texts are not objective and transparent, written only to reveal certain viewpoints or information, they become engaged in constructing texts that are representational. Since writers cannot avoid displaying their identities, values, and interests in the texts they compose, a pedagogy that encourages engaging with the text to accomplish writers' preferred interests (rather than letting the dominant conventions represent their values) allows students to reflectively understand their interests in writing, the values motivating their rhetoric, and how their identities are constructed by their texts.

In order to fulfil these expectations in writing, multilingual writers can be encouraged to look at the text/context connection in a different way. Texts are not simply context-bound or context-sensitive. They are context transforming. It is for this reason that student writers should not treat rules and conventions as given or predefined for specific texts and contexts. They should think of texts and discourses as changing and changeable. Student writers can engage critically in the act of changing the rules and conventions to suit their interests, values, and identities. In other words, we are interested in not only developing competent writers, but also critical writers. Therefore, although students should be sensitive to the dominant conventions in each rhetorical context, we must also teach them to critically engage with them. We should help students demystify the dominant conventions behind a specific genre of writing, relate their writing activity to the social context in which it takes place, and shape writing to achieve a favourable voice and representation for themselves.

In such a multilingual pedagogy of writing, teachers should treat the first language and culture as a resource, not a problem. Teachers would try to accommodate diverse literacy traditions—not keep them divided and separate. If we invoke differences in communities, this is not to discount their value, but to engage with them in order to find a strategic entry point into English. Similarly, we should reconsider the role of orality in writing. Oral discourse and oral traditions of communication may find a place in writing as they prove to be valuable resources for narrative and voice for students from multilingual backgrounds. They can also help deconstruct the values behind literate traditions and expand the communicative potential of writing. Interestingly, many multilingual students come from communities that boast of precolonial literate traditions that provided a space for multimodal texts and multiliteracies (see De Souza, 2002; Viswanathan, 1993).

CHALLENGES AHEAD

It is these multilingual and non-western traditions of literacy that many Anglo-American scholars feel they should study in order to address the evolving needs of writing for an increasingly global audience (Horner and Trimbur, 2002). Even advanced Anglo-American writers now have to shuttle between discourse communities and engage with multiliteracies in the context of globalization.

Thinking primarily of the needs of Anglo-American college level writers, Horner and Trimbur (2002) argue:

[W]e should consider how writing programs can encourage writing in languages other than English. We might, for example, begin a dialogue with teachers of the other modern languages to identify shared concerns as well as differences in language pedagogy. And, where it makes sense, we should draw on students' interests and existing linguistic resources to design bilingual programs of study that seek to develop students' fluency in more than one written language and the possibilities of moving between the modern languages. (622–23)

It is perhaps useful to end this chapter by giving some pointers to researchers on some of the powerful literacy traditions multilingual students come from. An awareness of such traditions will not only help us connect better with multilingual students, but also address the needs of Anglophone writers negotiating multiliteracies and hybrid texts. Take for example the *manipravala* (mixed code) writing tradition practised in the Tamil community from precolonial times. At a time when Sanskrit was the language of religion and philosophy, Tamils mixed it with their vernacular when they started using the Tamil language for such purposes (see Viswanathan, 1993). Through such mixing, they challenged the elite and sacred status of Sanskrit while upgrading Tamil as a language suitable for discoursing on such subjects. After the encounter with British colonialism, Tamils adopted the same strategy of code mixing in their academic and literary writing. Though this tradition is only multilingual (actually exemplifying the practice of codemeshing), there are other literacy traditions in non-western communities, which are multimodal as well. De Souza (2002) describes the literacy practices of the Kashinawa in Brazil as incorporating space, colour, icons, and symbols with language to create meaning in their texts. Complex encoding and decoding skills are involved in constructing such multimodal texts in these precolonial communities. The mode of writing valued in the western communities, on the other hand, is grapho-centric (see Mignolo, 2000; De Souza, 2002).

According to the western tradition, what are valued are texts that are monolingual and unimodal (i.e., texts using written words from one language, at the exclusion of other symbol systems and languages). It is this grapho-centric tradition that still appears to influence the pedagogies dominant in writing found in tertiary educational contexts. If we want to truly reinvigorate English composition, and address the emerging challenges of multilingual writers in the context of globalization, it is important to learn from other literacy traditions from non-western backgrounds.

NOTES

1 We construct some profiles of multilingual writers to illustrate the challenges they face. Some of these students appear directly from published studies. Others are fictional composites modelled after the experiences described in publications and in our teaching experiences. In either case, we present citations that will enable readers to find out more about such students.

REFERENCES

Bartholomae, David (1993) 'The tidy house: Basic writing in the American curriculum', *Journal of Basic Writing*, 12(1): 4–21.

Basturkmen, Helen (2006) *Ideas and Options for English for Specific Purposes*, Mahwah, NJ: Lawrence Erlbaum Associates.

Belcher, Diane (1994) 'The apprenticeship approach to advanced academic literacy: Graduate students and their mentors', *English for Specific Purposes*, 13:23–34.

Belcher, Diane (2006) 'English for specific purposes: Teaching to perceived needs and imagined futures in worlds of work, study, and everyday life', *TESOL Quarterly*, 40(1): 133–156.

Belcher, Diane (2007) 'Seeking acceptance in an english-only research world', *Journal of Second Language Writing*, 16(1): 1–22.

Benesch, Sarah (1993) 'ESL, ideology, and the politics of pragmatism', *TESOL Quarterly* 27(4): 705–717.

Bollag, Burton (2006) 'Foreign enrollment at graduate schools increases, reversing a 3-year decline', *Chronicle of Higher Education*, 53(12): A45.

Bouman, Kurt (2003) 'Raising questions about Plagiarism', in Shanti Bruce and Bruce Raforth (eds), *ESL Writers: A Guide for Writing Center Tutors*, Heinemann: New Hampshire. pp.105–116

Bouman, K. (2004) 'Raising Questions about Plagiarism' in Shanti Bruce and Bruce Raforth (eds.), *ESL Writers: A Guide for Writing Center Tutors*, Heinemann: New Hampshire. pp.105–116.

Bourdieu, Pierre (1977) *Reproduction in Education, Society and Culture*, London: Sage Publications.

Braine, George (2005) 'The challenge of academic publishing: A Hong Kong perspective', *TESOL Quarterly*, 39(4): 707–716.

Brown, J.S., Collins, A., and Duguid, P. (1989) 'Situated cognition and the culture of learning', *Educational Researcher*, 18: 32–42.

Bruffee, Kenneth (1983) 'Writing and reading as collaborative or social acts', in Hays, Janice N. (ed), *The Writer's Mind*, Urbana, IL: NCTE.

Cai, Guanjun (1999) 'Texts in contexts: Understanding Chinese students' English compositions', in Cooper, Charles, and Odell, Lee (eds), *Evaluating Writing: The Role of Teachers' Knowledge about Text, Learning, and Culture*, Urbana, IL: NCTE. pp.279–97.

Canagarajah, A. Suresh (1996) 'Non-discursive requirements in academic publishing, material resources of periphery scholars, and the politics of knowledge production', *Written Communication* (13)4: 435–72.

Canagarajah, A. Suresh (1999) *Resisting Linguistic Imperialism in English Teaching*, Oxford: Oxford University Press.

Canagarajah, A. Suresh (2002a) 'Multilingual writers and the academic community: Toward a critical relationship', *Journal of English for Academic Purposes*, 1: 29–44.

Canagarajah, A. Suresh (2002b) *Critical Academic Writing and Multilingual Students*, Ann Arbor: University of Michigan Press.

Canagarajah, A. Suresh (2002c) *A Geopolitics of Academic Writing*, Pittsburgh: University of Pittsburgh Press.

Canagarajah, A. Suresh (2006a) 'The place of world englishes in composition: Pluralization continued', *College Composition and Communication* (57)4: 586–619.

Canagarajah, A. Suresh (2006b) 'Toward a writing pedagogy of shuttling between languages: Learning from multilingual writers', *College English*, 68(6): 589–604.

Canagarajah, A. Suresh (2006c) 'TESOL at forty: What are the issues?', *TESOL Quarterly* 40(1): 9–34.

Casanave, Christine P. (2007) *Controversies in Second Language Writing*, Ann Arbor: University of Michigan Press.

Casanave, Christine P. and Vandrick, Stephanie (eds) (2003) *Writing for Scholarly Publication: Behind the Scenes in Language Education*, New Jersey: Lawrence Erlbaum Associates.

Chandrasoma, R., Thompson, C., and Pennycook, A. (2004) 'Beyond plagiarism: Transgressive and non-transgressive intertextuality', *Journal of Language, Identity & Education*, 3: 171–193.

Connor, Ulla (1996) *Contrastive Rhetoric: Cross-Cultural Aspects of Second Language Writing*, Cambridge: CUP.

Connor, Ulla (1999a) 'How like you our fish? Accommodation in international business communication', in Hewings, M. and Nickerson, L. (eds.), *Business English: Research into Practice*, London: Longman. pp.115–128.

Connor, Ulla (1999b) 'Learning to write academic prose in a second language: A literacy autobiography', in Braine, George (ed), *Non-Native Educators in English Language Teaching*, Mahwah, NJ: Erlbaum. pp.29–42.

Cook, Vivian (1991) 'The poverty of the stimulus argument and multicompetence', *Second Language Research* (7): 103–117.

Cook, Vivian (1992) 'Evidence for multicompetence', *Language Learning* (42): 557–591.

Cook, Vivian (1996) 'Competence and multicompetence', in G. Brown, K. Malmkjaer, and J. Williams (eds), *Performance and competence in second language acquisition*, Cambridge: Cambridge University Press. pp.57–69.

Cope, Bill and Kalantzis, Mary (eds) (2000) *Multiliteracies: Literacy Learning and the Design of Social Futures*, London and New York: Routledge.

Crystal, D. (2003) *English as a Global Language* (2nd Ed), Cambridge: Cambridge University Press.

Curry, Mary Jane and Lillis, Theresa (2004) 'Multilingual scholars and the imperative to publish in English: Negotiating Interests, Demands, and Rewards', *TESOL Quarterly*, 38(4): 663–688.

Deckert, Glenn D. (1993) 'Perspectives on plagiarism from ESL students in Hong Kong', *Journal of Second Language Writing*, 2(2): 131–48.

De Souza, Lynn M.T.M. (2002) 'A case among cases, a world among worlds: The ecology of writing among the Kashinawa in Brazil', *Journal of Language, Identity, and Education* 1(4): 261–278.

Dor, Danny (2004) 'From Englishization to imposed multilingualism: Globalization, the Internet, and the political economy of the linguistic code', *Public Culture* (16)1: 97–118.

Eggins, Suzanne (2004) *An Introduction to Systemic Functional Linguistics* (second edn.), London: Pinter.

Faigley, Lester (1997) 'Literacy after the revolution', *College Composition and Communication* 48(1): 30–43.

Ferris, Dana R. (2002) *Treatment of Error in Second Language Student Writing*, Ann Arbor: University of Michigan Press.

Flower, Linda S. and Hayes, John R. (1981) 'A cognitive process theory of writing', *College Composition and Communication*, 32: 365–387.

Flowerdew, John (2007) 'Writing for publication in English: Plagiarism, some notes from the underground, and some reflections on stigma', Paper presented at Publishing and Presenting Research Internationally, La Laguna, Spain.

Flowerdew, John and Li, Yongyan (forthcoming) 'The globalization of scholarship: Studying Chinese scholars writing for international publication', in Rosa M. Manchon (ed), *Learning, Teaching, and Researching Writing in Foreign Language Contexts* [tentative title]. Multilingual Matters Book Series: Second Language Acquisition.

Friedrich, Patricia (2006) 'Assessing the needs of linguistically diverse first-year students: Bringing together and telling apart international ESL, resident ESL, and monolingual basic writers', *WPA (Writing Program Administration)* 29(3): 15–36.

Gee, James (1990) *Social Linguistics and Literacies: Ideology in Discourses*, London: Falmer Press.

Graddol, David (1997) *The Future of English? A Guide to Forecasting the Popularity of the English Language in the 21st Century*, London: British Council.

Graddol, David (1999) 'The decline of the native speaker', in Graddol, David and Meinhof, Ulrike (eds), *English in a Changing World. AILA Review* 13: 57–68.

Halliday, M.A.K. (1994) *An Introduction to Functional Grammar* (second edn.), London: Edward Arnold.

Harklau, Linda (2000) 'From the "good kids" to the "worst": Representations of English language learners across educational settings', *TESOL Quarterly* 34(1): 35–67.

Harklau, L., Losey, K., and Siegal, M. (eds) (1999) *Generation 1.5 Meets College Composition: Issues in the Teaching of Writing to U.S.-Educated Learners of English as a Second Language*, Mahwah, New Jersey: Lawrence Erlbaum.

Hayward, Nancy. (2004) 'Insights into cultural divides', in Shanti Bruce and Bruce Raforth (eds.), *ESL Writers: A Guide for Writing Center Tutors*, Heinemann: New Hampshire. pp.1–15.

Hooks, bell (1989) *Talking Back: Thinking Feminist, Thinking Black*, Boston: South End Press.

Horner, Bruce and Lu, Ming-Zhan (1999) *Representing the 'Other': Basic Writers and the Teaching of Basic Writing*, Urbana, IL: NCTE.

Horner, Bruce and Trimbur, John (2002) 'English only and U.S. college composition', *College Composition and Communication*, 53(4): 594–630.

Howard, Rebecca Moore (1995) 'Plagiarisms, authorships, and the academic death penalty', *College English* (57): 788–806.

Hyland, Ken and Hamp-Lyons, Liz (2002) 'EAP: Issues and directions.' *Journal of English for Academic Purposes* 1: 1–12.

Hyland, Ken and Tse, Lucy (2007) 'Is there an " academic vocabulary"?' *TESOL Quarterly*, 41(2): 235–254.

Jenkins, Jennifer (2006) 'Current perspectives on teaching world Englishes and English as a lingua franca', *TESOL Quarterly*, 40(1): 157–182.

Jerskey, Maria (2006) 'Writing Handbooks, Second Language Learners, and the Selective Tradition', PhD dissertation, New York University, New York.

Johns, Ann M. (1990) 'L1 composition theories: Implications for developing theories of L2 composition', in Barbara Kroll (ed), *Second Language Writing: Research Insights for the Classroom*, Cambridge: Cambridge University Press. pp.24–36.

Johns, Ann M. (2002) 'Introduction: Genre in the classroom', in Ann M. Johns (ed.), *Genre in the Classroom: Multiple Perspectives*, Mahwah, NJ: Lawrence Erlbaum. pp.3–13.

Kachru, Braj B. (1986) *The Alchemy of English: The Spread, Functions and Models of Non-Native Englishes*, Oxford: Pergamon.

Kaplan, Robert B. (1966) 'Cultural thought patterns in inter-cultural education', *Language Learning*, 16: 1–20.

Kaplan, Robert B. (1967) 'Contrastive rhetoric and the teaching of composition', *TESOL Quarterly*, 1(4): 10–16.

Kells, Michelle and Balester, Valerie (eds). (1999) *Attending to the Margins: Writing, Researching, and Teaching on the Front Lines*, Portsmouth, NH: Heinemann-Boynton/Cook.

Kinneavy, James L. (1993) 'Writing across the Curriculum', *ADE Bulletin*, 76(Winter): 14–21.

Knapp, Peter and Watkins, Megan (1994) *Context—Text—Grammar: Teaching the Genres and Grammar of School Writing in Infants and Primary Classrooms*, Sydney: Text Productions.

Kobayashi, Hire and Rinnert, Carol (2007) 'L1/L2 Text Construction of Multi-competent Writers in EFL Contexts: Insights and Challenges', Paper presented at the Symposium on Second Language Writing, Nagasaki, Japan.

Kroll, Barbara (ed.) (2003) *Exploring the Dynamics of Second Language Writing*, Cambridge: Cambridge University Press.

Kubota, Ryuko (2003) 'Striving for original voice in publication?: A critical reflection', in Casanave, Christine Pearson and Vandrick, Stephanie (eds), *Writing for Scholarly Publication: Behind the Scenes in Language Education*, Mahwah, NJ: Lawrence Erlbaum Associates.

Kuriloff, Peshe (1996) 'What discourses have in common: Teaching the transaction between writer and reader', *College Composition and Communication*, 47, 485–501.

Lave, Jean and Wegner, Etienne (1991) *Situated Learning: Legitimate Peripheral Participation*, Cambridge: Cambridge University Press.

Leki, Ilona (1992) *Understanding ESL Writers*, Portsmouth, NH: Boynton/Cook.

Leki, Ilona (1995) 'Coping strategies of ESL students in writing tasks across the curriculum', *TESOL Quarterly*, 29(2): 235–260.

Leki, Ilona (2003) in Kroll, Barbara (ed.) *Exploring the Dynamics of Second Language Writing*, Cambridge: Cambridge University Press.

Li, Xiao Ming (1999) 'Writing from the vantage point of an outsider/insider', in Braine, George (ed), *Non-Native Educators in English Language Teaching*, Mahwah, NJ: Lawrence Erlbaum Associates. pp.43–56.

Li, Yongyan (2007) 'Apprentice scholarly writing in a community of practice: An intraview of an NNES graduate student writing a research article', *TESOL Quarterly*, 41(1): 55–79.

Lillis, Teresa and Curry, Mary Jane (2006) 'Professional academic writing by multilingual scholars', *Written Communication*, 23(1): 3–35.

Lin, Angel and Peter Martin (eds) (2005) *Decolonisation, Globalisation: Language-in-Education Policy and Practice*, Clevedon: Multilingual Matters.

Louhiala-Salminen, L., Charles, M., and Kankaanranta, A. (2005) 'English as a lingua franca in Nordic corporate mergers: Two case companies', *English for Specific Purposes*, 24: 401–421.

Lu, Ming-Zhan (1992) 'Conflict and struggle: The enemies or preconditions of basic writing?', *College English*, 54 (December): 887–913.

Matsuda, Paul Kei (2006) 'The myth of linguistic homogeneity in U.S. college composition', *College English*, 68(6): 636–651.

Matsuda, P.K., Canagarajah, A.S., Harklau, L., Hyland, K., and Warschauer, M. (2003) 'Changing currents in second language writing research: A colloquium', *Journal of Second Language Writing*,12(2): 151–179.

McArthur, T. (2001) 'World English and world Englishes: Trends, tensions, varieties, and standards', *Language Teaching*, 34: 1–20.

McKay, Sandra Lee (2002) *Teaching English as an International Language*, Oxford: Oxford University Press.

McNenny, G. and Fitzgerald, S. H. (eds) (2001) *Mainstreaming Basic Writers: Politics and Pedagogies of Access*, Mahwah, NJ: Lawrence Erlbaum.

Mignolo, Walter D. (2000) *Local Histories/Global Designs: Coloniality, Subaltern Knowledges, and Border Thinking*, Princeton: Princeton University Press.

Mooney, Paul and McNeill, David. (2006) 'Touring Asia, U.S. Delegation promotes American Higher education', *Chronicle of Higher Education*, 53(15): A30.

Ortmeier-Hooper, C. (2008) 'English may be my second language, but I'm not "ESL" ', *College Composition and Communication*, 59, 389–419.

Pennycook, Alistair (1994) *The Cultural Politics of English as an International Language*, London: Longman.

Pennycook, Alistair (1996) 'Borrowing other's words: Text, ownership, memory, and plagiarism', *TESOL Quarterly*, 30: 210–230.

Raimes, Ann (1985) 'What unskilled ESL students do as they write: A classroom study of composing', *TESOL Quarterly*, 19: 529–534.

Raimes, Ann (1991) 'Out of the woods: Emerging traditions in the teaching of writing', *TESOL Quarterly*, 25: 407–430.

Rajagopalan, Kanivillil (2005) 'The language issue in Brazil: When local knowledge clashes with expert knowledge', in Canagarajah, A. Suresh (ed), *Reclaiming the Local in Language Policy and Practice*, Mahwah, NJ: Lawrence Erlbaum Publishers. pp.99–122.

Ramanathan, Vai (2004) *The English-Vernacular Divide: Postcolonial Language Politics and Practice*, Clevedon, UK: Multilingual Matters.

Reid, Joyce (1989) 'English as a second language composition in higher education: The expectations of the academic audience', in D.M. Johnson, and D.H. Roen (eds), *Richness in Writing: Empowering ESL Students*, New York: Longman. pp.220–234.

Reid, Joyce (2006) '"Eye" learners and "Ear" learners: identifying the language needs of International Student and U.S. Resident Writers', in P.K. Matsuda, M. Cox, J. Jordan, and C. Ortmeier-Hooper (eds), *Second-Language Writing in the Composition Classroom: A Critical Sourcebook*, New York: Bedford St. Martin's.

Robinson, V. and Kuin, L. (1999) 'The explanation of practice: Why Chinese students copy assignments', *Qualitative Studies in Education* ,12(2): 193–210.

Sasaki, Miyuki (2003) 'A scholar on the periphery', in Christine Pearson Casanave and Stephanie Vandrick (eds), *Writing for Scholarly Publication: Behind the Scenes in Language Education*, Mahwah, NJ: Lawrence Erlbaum Associates.

Schleppergrell, Mary J. (2004) *The Language of Schooling: A Functional Linguistics Perspective*, Mahwah, NJ: Erlbaum.

Schleppergrell, Mary J. (2006) 'The linguistic features of advanced language use: The grammar of exposition', in H. Byrnes (ed), *Advanced Language Learning: The Contribution of Halliday and Vygotsky*, London: Continuum. pp.134–146.

Schleppergrell, Mary J. (2007) 'The meaning in grammar', *Research in the Teaching of English*, 42(1): 121–128.

Schwartz, Gwen Gray (2004) 'Coming to terms: Generation 1.5 students in mainstream composition', *The Reading Matrix*, 4(3): 40–57.

Severino, Carol (1993) 'The Sociopolitical implications of response to second language and second dialect writing', *Journal of Second Language Writing*, 2(3): 187–201.

Shen, F. (1989) 'The classroom and the wider culture: Identity as a key to learning English composition', *College Composition and Communication*, 40(4): 459–466.

Silva, Tony (1993) 'Toward an understanding of the distinct nature of L2 writing: The ESL research and its implications', *TESOL Quarterly*, 27(4): 657–677.

Smitherman, Geneva (2003) 'The historical struggle for language rights in CCCC', in Geneva Smitherman and Victor Villaneuava (eds), *Intention to Practice: Considerations of Language Diversity in the Classroom*, Carbondale: Southern Illinois University Press. pp.7–39.

Soliday, Mary (1996) 'From the margins to the mainstream: Reconceiving remediation', *College Composition and Communication*, 47(1): 85–100.

Soliday, Mary (2002) *The Politics of Remediation: Institutional and Student Needs in Higher Education*, Pittsburgh: University of Pittsburgh Press.

Spack, Ruth (1984) 'Invention strategies and the ESL composition student', *TESOL Quarterly*, 18: 649–670.

Spack, Ruth (1988) 'Initiating ESL students into the academic discourse community: How far should we go?', *TESOL Quarterly*, 22(1): 29–51.

Sternglass, Marilyn S. (1997) *Time to Know Them: A Longitudinal Study of Writing and Learning at the College Level*, Mahwah, NJ: Lawrence Erlbaum Associates.

Street, Brian (1984) *Literacy in Theory and Practice*, Cambridge: Cambridge University Press.

Swales, John (1990) *Genre Analysis: English in Academic and Research Settings*, Cambridge: Cambridge University Press.

Truscott, J. (1996) 'The case against grammar correction in L2 writing classes', *Language Learning*, 46: 327–369.

Tsui, Amy B.M. (2007) 'Complexities of identity formation: A narrative inquiry of an EFL Teacher', *TESOL Quarterly*, 41(1): 657–680.

Viswanathan, Gauri (1993) 'English in a literate society', in R.S. Rajan (ed), *The Lie of the Land: English Literary Studies in India*, Oxford: Oxford University Press. pp.29–41.

Warschauer, Mark (2000) 'The changing global economy and the future of English teaching', *TESOL Quarterly*, 34(3): 511–536.

Wei, Z., Li, X. M., Canagarajah, A.S., and Leung, C. (2006) 'Periphery scholars publishing in professional journals', Presented at TESOL Convention, Tempe, Florida.

Wenden, Anita (1991) *Learner Strategies for Learner Autonomy*, New York: Prentice Hall.

Widdowson, H.G. (1983) *Learning Purpose and Language Use*, New York: Oxford University Press.

Zamel, Vivian (1982) 'Writing: The process of discovering meaning', *TESOL Quarterly*, 10: 67–76.

Zamel, Vivian (1987) 'Recent research on writing pedagogy', *TESOL Quarterly*, 21: 697-715.

Zamel, Vivian (1997) 'Toward a model of transculturation', *TESOL Quarterly*, 31(2): 341–351.

Causes of Delays and Difficulties in the Production of Written Text

Julie Dockrell

BACKGROUND

The ability to communicate through writing is one of the most important skills that schooling provides for children. Writing provides children with the ability to convey knowledge and ideas. New ideas may be prompted by the act of text generation itself (Galbraith, 1996). Yet, many children face challenges when learning to write; the ability to produce fluent and accurate text is an extended process stretching from the early school years to adolescence and adulthood. Part of the challenge in learning to produce written text is the complexity of the process. Writing develops over time through a complex interplay between the child's skills, the instructional context, and the demands of the writing task. It is, however, a key skill to master. By the age of eight the school curriculum incorporates aspects of writing into almost every activity; with children in primary school spending up to 50 percent of their day engaged in writing activities (McHale and Cermak, 1992). For children who experience learning difficulties the ability to accurately and efficiently convey their understandings and develop their ideas through writing is constrained.

An inability to produce sustained, accurate, and competent writing has been identified as a pervasive weakness for many children. Data collected as part of the US National Assessment of Educational Progress (Grunwald et al., 1998) noted that a significant proportion of fourth graders (16 percent) were below basic achievement levels while 60 percent had only partial mastery of the writing process. The most recent published figures illustrated a similar pattern in England. At the end of primary school, English national standards in writing were lower than in reading and 37 percent of the writing produced at this point was below national targets in 2005 [www.dfes.gov.uk/statistics]. As we shall see, difficulties are more pervasive when children have additional learning challenges. Problems in the production of written text are arguably the most prevalent developmental disability of communication skills (Lerner, 1976 cited in Hooper et al., 2002).

Delays and difficulties in text production are associated with a range of different developmental disabilities and pedagogical practices. The chapter begins by exploring the prevalence of writing difficulties and the associations between writing difficulties and other specific learning difficulties/disabilities.[1] It is argued that a descriptive analysis of the children's writing problems is insufficient to develop interventions and fails to provide adequate explanations of the cognitive processes that underpin writing. To offer appropriate interventions and to understand the nature of the difficulties that children experience it is necessary to start with a theoretical model of the development of writing skills. A robust model provides a framework for examining the component skills, which may, alone or in combination, constrain the acquisition of text production for children. The importance of the children's motivation and the instructional practices provided is considered in the light of these problems.

CHILDREN WITH WRITING PROBLEMS: PREVALENCE AND ASSOCIATED LEARNING DIFFICULTIES

Many children experience difficulties in learning. These difficulties refer to problems with acquiring, organizing, retaining, or understanding information. The problems that children experience range in terms of both the severity of difficulties and the profiles of difficulties experienced. Difficulties in written text production can occur on their own but are typically associated with other concurrent problems, which were experienced earlier in development (Grigorenko, 2007). Problems in written text production have been identified in children who experience both specific learning difficulties, as occurs when a child experiences problems with some particular task such as reading, or those with more general difficulties, as occurs when learning is slower than normal across a range of tasks.

Concern about children's writing difficulties is not new. Disorders of written expression have been discussed for more than 100 years (Ogle, 1867, cited in Hooper et al., 2002). Writing is the most common problem of 9 to 14 year old students with learning disabilities (Cobb-Morocco et al., 1992; Mayes and Calhoun, 2006). Unlike some developmental difficulties, problems in writing may not be evident until children are well into formal education, about the age of eight. The focus for identification in the early years is often on oral language (Rice and Wilcox, 1995) and in the early school years on reading decoding (Berninger et al., 2002). As we shall see both sets of skills are fundamental in underpinning written text production. Early years settings often provide opportunities for developing graphic notations—viewed by some as a precursor to writing. There are a number of notable differences between children's early graphic notations and formal writing. The production of notations in the early years is less constrained by conventional demands and typically, there is less focus on the speed and accuracy of text production. The relationship between these early graphical notations and the production of later written text is complex (see Teubal et al., 2007 for a discussion of early notations). In sum, text production difficulties may be identified relatively late but are associated with a broad range of learning difficulties.

An important early indication of writing difficulties is the amount of written text produced under timed conditions, and this correlates with the quality of written expression in the primary years (Berninger and Fuller, 1992). In general, children with learning difficulties produce shorter, less interesting and poorly organized text at both the sentence and paragraph level (Hooper et al, 2002). Texts produced are restricted to knowledge-telling (see section *Constraints on Writing*), which is underpinned by an associative linear progression. The children's texts are also marred by inordinate numbers of mechanical and grammatical errors (Anderson, 1982; MacArthur and Graham, 1987). Handwriting is less legible and the texts poorly punctuated (Graham and Weintraub, 1996). Planning for writing is also affected; students with learning difficulties are reported do very little planning and revising (Troia and Maddox, 2004). Even when specific strategies are taught, the maintenance and transfer of strategies can be a problem (Troia and Maddox, 2004). Of course, not all children with learning difficulties have all of these difficulties, nor do children experience the same sets of problems at the same time or exhibit the same severity of difficulty. This makes it challenging for researchers and practitioners to identify developmental trajectories and appropriate interventions. One potential approach to understanding the children's difficulties is to examine the extent to which particular patterns of difficulty can be linked to specific diagnostic categories of learning difficulty. Criteria for the diagnosis of learning difficulties is outlined in the International Classification of Diseases and Related Health Problems (ICD-10) (World Health Organization, 1990) and the Diagnostic and Statistical Manual of Mental Disorders (DSM-IV-TR) (American Psychiatric Association, 1994). ICD-10 has four categories of specific developmental disorder: specific developmental disorders of speech and language, specific developmental disorders of scholastic skills, specific developmental disorder of motor function, and mixed specific developmental disorder. DSM-IV-TR identifies a range of disorders usually first diagnosed in infancy, childhood, or adolescence. These include communication disorders, learning disorders, and motor skills disorders. Approaches to writing difficulties, which follow a diagnostic approach will identify groups of children, which meet diagnostic criteria and then profile and explore the writing difficulties experienced by these children.

THE LINKS BETWEEN WRITING DIFFICULTIES AND SPECIFIC LEARNING DIFFICULTIES

Poor performance in writing tasks is the behavioural manifestation of a wide range of developmental difficulties. The links between some developmental difficulties and writing problems are to be predicted. Thus, we would expect that children who are experiencing general delays in their learning will be slower in their ability to acquire basic competence in written text production and the research evidence is consistent with this hypothesis (Katims, 2001, Rousseau et al., 1993). There are also a number of specific learning difficulties, which we would expect to be associated with or cause writing problems. Handwriting requires a high level of motor coordination and high precision force regulation and, not surprisingly, children with motor coordination problems (Developmental Coordination Disorders (DCD)/dysgraphia) experience particular problems with transcription. Dysgraphic handwriting lacks consistency (Keogh and Sugden, 1985), is slow, and, typically, the children fail to progress and require specific remedial support (Smits-Engelsman et al., 1993; 1994). Overall, these difficulties restrict the production of accurate and legible texts although different diagnostic groups within DCD (overall poor control versus fine motor problems only) tend to apply different, age dependent strategies to overcome their problems (Smits-Engelsman et al., 1997). Children with oral language difficulties experience writing problems for different reasons. These children would be expected to have difficulties generating ideas to support their writing while children who have problems with word reading or text comprehension would be expected to find difficulties in producing written text. For some pupils, however, specific delays in writing may reflect the lack of appropriate instruction to match educational needs (Whittington et al., 2004). We need to be careful in evaluating the extent to which a writing problem is the result of a particular learning difficulty per se, as opposed to the result of limited or inappropriate instruction to meet the child's educational needs.

Research on the writing problems of children with specific oral language difficulties is limited. These children are typically referred to as having specific language impairment (SLI) or specific speech and language difficulties (SSLD) (Dockrell et al., 2006). Difficulties in the production of written text have been reported both for children with continuing language difficulties and those with resolved language problems, leading to the hypothesis that written language can be conceptualized as a window into residual language problems (Bishop and Clarkson, 2003; Fey et al., 2004). Specific relationships between oral language competence and the production of written text have also been identified. Phonological processes impact directly on children's spelling development, the mastery of which is a prerequisite to extended text generation (Berninger et al., 1995). In addition, wider oral language competencies such as vocabulary (Bishop and Clarkson, 2003; Dockrell et al., 2007) and oral narrative performance (Cragg and Nation, 2006) are related to written text production. A recent comparative study of dyslexic, language-impaired and, typically, developing-matched children demonstrated the ways in which different profiles of skills can impact on writing performance (Puranik et al., 2007). Language-impaired participants, but not dyslexic participants, produced fewer words and numbers of ideas than typically developing matched peers. In contrast, both dyslexic pupils and language-impaired pupils produced more spelling and grammar errors than typically developing matched peers. These authors argued that the differences between the language-impaired group and dyslexic group rested in the nonphonological dimensions of text production that were impaired in the children with oral language difficulties. However, when task complexity increased, dyslexic performance dropped to that of the language-impaired

participants. These results indicate that the children's difficulties when writing were not solely limited to the dimension of processing that was reportedly compromised. Rather, task demands had a differential negative impact on the performance of poor writers across a range of processing dimensions.

In contrast to research on the impact of oral language on writing, the relationships between reading and writing have been the subject of a significant number of research studies. Children with specific reading difficulties are indeed slow at transcription and typically compromised in their spelling (Scott, 1999). Children with specific reading difficulties include both those traditionally described as dyslexic and other poor readers. Graham and Harris (1993) categorized the wide array of writing difficulties of students with reading difficulties into three basic types: (1) lack of proficiency in text production (spelling and punctuation), (2) lack of knowledge central to the process of writing (text structure schemas and recognizing strategies that are needed), and (3) difficulty planning and revising. The below average phonological skills of poor readers is well documented and these difficulties are predicted to affect writing through poor spelling. In addition, lack of familiarity with reading texts due to inaccurate and slow reading would limit knowledge of text structures and poor reading could limit revision of the written texts produced by the children. Moreover, there is evidence from adults with dyslexia that these difficulties continue in adulthood where writing is both slower and scripts shorter than matched peers (Connelly et al., 2006; Sterling et al., 1998).

WRITING DIFFICULTIES AND CLINICAL DISORDERS

Writing difficulties have also been identified in a wide range of children with clinical disorders who nevertheless have average intelligence (Mayes and Calhoun, 2006). It is not always clear why these children should experience difficulties in text production. Children with Attention Deficit/Hyperactivity Disorder (ADHD) are rated as less proficient writers, producing more errors and writing shorter texts than typically developing children (Re, Pedson and Cornoldi, 2007). High-reported incidences of written expression problems have also been noted in children with bipolar disorders (74 percent) and children with autism (60 percent) (Mayes and Calhoun, 2006). To some extent, these problems may be linked to problems with reading and spelling. However, in the sample studied by Mayes and Calhoun (2006), both spelling and reading problems occurred in significantly fewer pupils than did writing problems. Text production draws on resources from long-term memory and working memory and therefore children who experience difficulties with attention or concentration may be particularly vulnerable to text production problems (see section on *Working Memory*). It is also possible that children who are vulnerable do not receive appropriate instruction in writing due to absences from school or an inability to benefit from the instruction when it is offered so that potential problems are exacerbated. However, the causal mechanisms in these cases are not clearly established. Thus, the extent to which particular patterns of difficulty with writing can be linked to specific diagnostic categories of learning difficulty is both complex and problematic. To provide a more detailed profile of writing difficulties, which can lead to intervention, we need to consider the writing process in greater detail.

MOVING FROM DIAGNOSTIC CATEGORIES TO AN ANALYSIS OF THE WRITING TASK AND ITS COGNITIVE COMPONENTS

Writing performance involves the integration of a range of cognitive and linguistic skills. A problem with any of these skills is likely to impact on the production of written text. As we have seen, some groups of children appear especially vulnerable to difficulties in producing written text. However, the range of children experiencing difficulties precludes a simple mapping between categories of learning difficulty and patterns of writing difficulty. Moreover, even when a specific difficulty may be seen as causally related to writing problems, for example, specific reading difficulties, the range of problems experienced with the production of written texts precludes interventions linked to the learning difficulty per se. This is because diagnostic groups reflect a heterogeneous group of difficulties (Hooper and Willis, 1989) and the writing task involves the coordination of a range of cognitive components. Moreover, there is considerable intra- and inter-subject variability in the writing task itself (Berninger, Abbott et al., 2006; Berninger, Rutberg et al., 2006). An important prerequisite in understanding delays and difficulties is an analysis of the task demands.

UNDERSTANDING THE WRITING PROCESS

To understand writing difficulties and to provide evidence-based instruction, we must be able to identify where difficulties are likely to occur. Theoretical models of the factors that underpin writing have been the focus of much discussion and development over the last 40 years (see MacArthur et al., 2006). No single model provides a comprehensive analysis of the barriers that may be experienced by children with writing difficulties. Process models, which emphasize the importance of isolating the separate components involved in text production, provide a means of identifying where pupils experience problems.

The most influential models of the processes involved in writing have been those of Hayes and Flower (1986) and Hayes (1996). In these models, three processes—planning, translating, and revising—operate recursively in the context of long-term memory and the task environment to generate writing. More recently, Berninger and colleagues have proposed the 'simple view of writing' (Berninger et al., 2002; Berninger and Amtmann, 2003). This model, shown in Figure 33.1, synthesizes diverse traditions in compositional research whereby developing writing can be represented as a triangle in a working memory environment in which transcription skills and executive functions are the vertices at the base that enables the goal of text generation at the top of the triangle to proceed efficiently. Text generation is also subject to developmental changes; as writers develop, it is argued that they move from knowledge telling to knowledge transforming (Bereiter and Scardamalia, 1987). Knowledge-telling is typical of younger or inexperienced writers. Planning is limited to idea retrieval and there is limited interaction of planning and translating with little or no reviewing of the text. In contrast, knowledge-transforming involves the interaction of planning, translating, and reviewing. Text is revised, so that it corresponds to the author's representation. The focus is on both the author's ideas and the meaning of the text.

According to Berninger (1999), transcription processes are the first in the model to develop and provide the foundation for writing, as they directly allow the writer to convert ideas and spoken language into a written form on the page. Transcription development involves both the growth of a fluent and accurate form of handwriting and a thorough knowledge of spelling. Children who are slow and labourious in forming letters and words will be restricted in their ability to generate ideas (Graham and Weintraub, 1996). A lack of automaticity in spelling increases errors and influences raters' perceptions of quality of the text (Chase, 1986). Transcription skills (handwriting and spelling) uniquely predict compositional fluency and compositional quality throughout the elementary grades (Graham et al., 1997), with handwriting accounting for 66 percent of the variance in measures of compositional fluency in the primary grades and 41 percent in intermediate grades and spelling accounting for 25 percent of the compositional quality in primary grades and 42 percent in intermediate grades (Graham et al., 1997). Berninger, Whitaker et al. (1996) claim that for younger children up to 10 years of age the

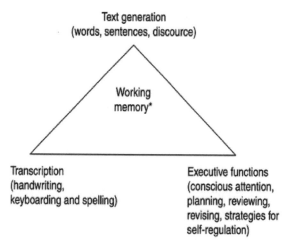

Figure 33.1 Causes of delays and difficulties in the production of written text: Simple view of writing extracted from (Berninger and Amtmann, 2003: 350).
Note: *Activates long-term memory during composing and short-term memory during reviewing.

focus of concern is the establishment of fluent translation processes. For pupils with disabilities in secondary school (Dockrell et al., in press) and pupils with dyslexia in school and higher education (Connelly et al., 2006; Hatcher et al., 2002), transcription problems continue to limit text production. Thus, transcription processes are a basic component of writing with the impact on compositional quality being more evident as children get older and when writers with difficulties face cumulative challenges when required to write expository essays in timed situations (Gregg et al., 2007).

Attention and planning are control processes that support written output. These problem-solving processes develop alongside transcription and move from being externally regulated to self-regulated. Towards the end of primary school, as transcription becomes automatized, text generation skills increase to include the selection of appropriate discourse structures for different genres and posttranslation reviewing/revising as well as advanced preplanning. The ability to coordinate these activities places additional demands on the cognitive system. Turning ideas into appropriate written text requires both executive processes and transcription skills. Early in secondary school, all the processes continue to develop but are increasingly constrained by cognitive factors such as working memory and explicit understanding of processes involved in text construction.

During text production, cognitive processes compete for limited resources and all three components in the 'simple view' draw on the same limited memory resources (see Torrance and Galbraith, 2006 for a review of the different ways to model limitations on the cognitive resources of memory in the writing process). Both Hayes (1996) and Kellogg (1996; 1999) emphasize the important role that working memory (WM) places in the writing process. Working memory is the capacity to store and manipulate information for brief periods. Hayes argues that WM is a resource available to all of the writing processes while Kellogg suggests that particular writing processes draw on different components of WM. His data support the view that translating and reading draw on verbal WM while editing and planning make use of spatial WM. Any increase in the amount demanded by one component of the writing process, such as transcription, will mean fewer cognitive resources are available for the other components. Therefore, if children are slow or inaccurate at transcription (slow handwriting and poor spelling), then we would expect their overall compositional quality will suffer as they will have to devote more resources to this area than the others do. Importantly, as we saw in the discussion of the Puranik et al. (2007) study, these processing inefficiencies can result from an interaction between the child's difficulties and the demands of the writing task. If a writing task needs to be completed quickly, children with writing difficulties are likely to be differentially impaired.

The final process to be considered is text generation. Text generation requires the child to generate ideas and to translate that language into print while maintaining the main ideas to be recorded. Children need to generate the appropriate lexicon to represent their ideas and structure these ideas into sentences. Many cognitive components of oral language generation are shared with text generation including the selection of the relevant content, lexical retrieval, and syntactic formulation (McCutchen et al., 1994). Even in secondary school, the ability to generate language efficiently is a key predictor or writing quality (Dellerman et al., 1996). For children and young people who do not possess the necessary background knowledge (McCutchen, 1986), vocabulary (Dockrell et al, 2006), or grammatical skills (Gillam and Johnston, 1992) the production of written text becomes a challenging and laborious task.

The impact of the combined demands of text generation and transcription are evident when these elements of writing are assessed separately. When the constraints posed by text generation are removed, transcription can be improved such that younger children are better at writing to dictation than free writing. By corollary, but unlike adults, they are also better able to retrieve material when they do so orally than when they have to write (Bourdin et al., 1996). The superiority of younger children's dictated stories as compared to their written stories reflects the elimination of online transcription requirements. However, text generation does not always develop before efficient transcription is established. Berninger et al. (1992) found that some beginning writers could generate the oral language to express ideas about what they were writing but could not translate the language into print. These children's stories were very difficult to read and were not very legible. Spelling was very poor but when asked about the story the children were able to produce lucid and fluent oral text indicating text generation skill. A second group of children was identified who produced legible, coherent writing with good spelling but they generated very little text. When asked to continue they claimed they could not think of anything more to say (see also Juel, 1988).

CONSTRAINTS ON WRITING

The simple view of writing provides a framework for examining children's text production. The model allows the specification of the constraints that influence the writing process (Berninger, 1996). Constraints are barriers that make writing difficult but may not be the single cause of the breakdown in writing. Constraints cover a range of child and environmental factors. In this section, the evidence base that explores some of these constraints for children with writing difficulties is explored. Factors, which are not specifically related to the writing process are initially considered followed by a brief discussion of factors, which are specified in the model.

Oral language

The simple view of writing does not specifically identify oral language as central to the writing process but as we have seen oral language is important for the generation of ideas, and it is argued that the four language systems (speaking, listening, writing, and reading) typically develop in synchrony (Shanahan, 2006). While writing is a later acquired skill it is influenced both by oral language and reading abilities. Oral language competencies and verbal reasoning contribute to composition fluency (Abbott and Berninger, 1993). In the early school years, there are parallels between oral and written modalities in writing (Hidi and Hildyard, 1983). At this point in development, oral language can be viewed as leading (Shanahan, 2006). Over time, the focus of oral language is on elaboration, whereas, the focus in writing is the development of cohesion (Gillam and Johnston, 1992; McCutchen, 1987) and knowledge transformation (section on *Understanding the Writing Process*). Although the two systems become differentiated, as children become more skilled in writing and speaking, there are continual links between them. Over time, as writing develops, it influences the other language systems.

Poor oral language skills are associated with difficulties in the fluency of producing words and clauses in text and reduced compositional quality (Berninger and Fuller, 1992; Berninger, Yates, et al., 1992). Writers who are fluent in the subskills such as retrieving words and utilizing appropriate syntactical structures are better able to produce quality writing. Both the phonological and nonphonological dimensions of oral language can have direct and indirect effects on writing (Dockrell et al., in press). To date no thresholds of oral language competence to support writing have been identified (Shanahan, 2006), but increased oral language facility is associated with increased written language proficiency (McCutchen, 1986). Even when early language problems are overcome written language continues to suffer for the children (Naucler and Magnusson, 2002). Difficulties appear to be particularly marked in the production of expository texts (Scott and Windsor, 2000) where production may be constrained by the additional cognitive demands in developing these texts.

Children with language difficulties often experience additional problems that can impact on spelling and sentence grammar. When children are slow in processing language, they may experience difficulties in processing sounds with rapid acoustic transitions and/or perceiving phonemes with low phonetic salience (e.g., t/d and s/z). These difficulties can affect both the regular past tense (ed) and tense agreement (plurals, for example, 'plays') (Montgomery and Leonard, 1998). Further research is needed but one would predict that such problems could lead to specific difficulties in spelling, which in turn could impact on sentence grammar.

Reading

Reading delays and difficulties are experienced by a significant proportion of children; some of these children will also experience difficulties with oral language (Bishop and Snowling, 2004). The impact of reading difficulties on writing needs to be considered in relation to both decoding and comprehension. Difficulties with reading decoding have been linked to the phonological dimensions of oral language. Children who have impaired phonological skills are likely to have difficulties with both word decoding and spelling. Phonological knowledge and orthographic knowledge are closely linked in developing readers and writers. Word recognition and word decoding are associated more with transcription skills than text generation skills (Abbott and Berninger, 1993). Word recognition skills provide a consistent prediction of the abilities to spell and write at all elementary/primary grade levels (Abbott and Berninger, 1993).

Recently, a study by Cragg and Nation (2006) has demonstrated the ways in which poor reading comprehenders, but age appropriate spelling, can impact on writing. The ten-year-old children in their study produced stories that were more limited and had less sophisticated story structure than matched typically developing peers. Although, their texts did not differ in length or syntactic complexity.

Thus, the impact of reading on writing may either result from poor decoding, reflecting difficulties with phonological processing, or comprehension skills, the latter reflecting nonphonological dimensions of language system. Although reading and writing rely on similar mental processes and knowledge bases the total variance shared in research studies is never more than 0.50 (see Fitzgerald and Shanahan, 2000 for a review). Thus, it is important to acknowledge the separability of the two processes and the fact that the relationship between reading and writing is likely to change over time (Fitzgerald and Shanahan, 2000). These findings point to the importance of examining other factors, which may constrain writing.

Working memory

Processing limitations in the production of text are inescapable (Torrance and Galbraith, 2006). Our ability to process information is affected both by individual constraints on processing and the task on which we are engaged. The cognitive system is constrained by the information processing resources at its disposal (Just and Carpenter, 1992; Kail and Salthouse, 1994), and processing resources are often restricted in children with learning difficulties. Specifically many children with learning difficulties experience problems with WM (Pickering and Gathercole, 2004).

Working memory plays a central role in the ability to store and process information and we have seen the critical role that WM plays in the 'simple view of writing'.

Working memory has emerged as a factor explaining a significant amount of the individual differences in writing ability in both good and poor writers. Working memory also plays an important role in writing development. Poor writers are reported to have reduced WM capacity compared to skilled writers (McCutchen, 1996). However, the ways in which working memory may limit text production differs across development. Limitations may arise as a result of a failure to acquire and practise skills or because of particular individual difficulties. As children develop, they process information more rapidly (Kail and Miller, 2006), but this increase in speed and capacity is also task and age dependent. The more automatic the low-level transcription skills are the greater the availability of the capacity-limited, WM resources for higher level composing (Berninger, 1999; McCutchen, 1996). Working memory is more predictive of text generation than transcription in 10 to 12-year-olds (Berninger and Swanson, 1994). By corollary, children with smaller working memory spans are poorer at revising than those with larger spans (Francis and McCutchen, 1994). In sum, children who are less-skilled writers but who are fluent in encoding and possess an extensive knowledge base are able to take advantage of their long-term memory resources thereby freeing up short-term memory.

Working memory is also important in the appropriate use of punctuation, planning, and revising. The use of punctuation can be central in the construction of meaning-by supporting the combination of linguistic segments. Children with writing difficulties often demonstrate problems recalling and applying the rules that govern punctuation and usage. The correct use of punctuation involves both knowledge and the ability to coordinate that knowledge and the text being constructed. This is likely to place significant demands on WM although the relevant studies to test this hypothesis are yet to be undertaken.

Planning allows us to identify goals for the writing process and generate text.

As children master basic transcription skills, written expression problems may stem from difficulties with planning and the increase in cognitive demands of these activities. As noted earlier, students with learning difficulties do very little planning even when prompted (McArthur and Graham, 1987). Explicit writing instruction designed to help improve planning behaviour is beneficial (Troia and Graham, 2002). Revision also depends on well-developed reading strategies that can be generated and coordinated efficiently and will be influenced by children's abilities to store and process information. Less-skilled writers focus on local or sentence-to-sentence revision, a strategy that interferes with the overall meaning of the text (McCutchen et al., 1997). Indeed children with writing difficulties spend a disproportionate amount of time revising lower level cognitive components of the writing process, such as spelling and word choice, rather than higher-level organization structures (Graham et al., 1993). This results in compositions that are poorly organized and which lack cohesion.

Transcription skills

A key constraint in text production for children are the transcription skills of handwriting and spelling. They limit children's ability to record, and potentially generate ideas. Pupils with motor problems are likely to have handwriting problems (Volman et al., 2006), but pupils can also have problems that are related to orthographic coding (Berninger and Amtmann, 2003). There is considerable variation in children's handwriting speeds at each grade level (Graham et al., 1998). Girls' handwriting is generally more legible than that of boys, and girls generally tend to write faster than boys, indicating a greater automaticity of letter production (Graham et al., 1998). Contextual factors such as preceding letters, connecting strokes between letters, word length, and complexity of syllables also influence the handwriting capability of the writer. The relationships between orthographic coding and handwriting is significant throughout grades one to six; at each time point, fine motor skill contributes independently through orthography to text production (Abbott and Berninger, 1993).

Although reading and spelling, as already discussed, share similar linguistic and cognitive processes spelling is more complex. In reading, several clues are available to help the reader decipher the word, whereas with spelling the writer must retrieve all the cues from memory including individual letters and graphemes in the proper order. Spelling is based on the application and integration of phonological, orthographic, and morphological principles. Typically, developing 10-year-olds are still learning to coordinate orthographic, phonological, and morphological cues in written words (Nagy et al., 2003). The process is more extended for children with learning difficulties, such that spellings produced by older children with dyslexia are similar to those of younger normal children in a number of ways including their morphological characteristics (Bourassa et al., 2006). For many children with hearing problems, spelling remains a continual challenge (Kyle and Harris, 2006).

A lack of automaticity in the retrieval of accurate spellings can inhibit the quality and fluency of written expression. Problems may interfere with both the amount and quality of writing. If a child needs to search for the letters to create a word, ideas and plans can be lost, as they overload the capacity of working memory (Graham et al., 1997). Difficulties in spelling can affect text production in a number of ways. They blur the child's message, interfere with the execution of composing processes during the act of writing, and generate negative perceptions of the writer (Graham et al., 2002). In addition, assessed written papers with fewer spelling errors obtain higher marks independently of the content (Marshall and Powers, 1969).

English-speaking children with writing difficulties typically produce recognizable spellings even when the errors are nonphonetic (Kamhi and Hinton, 2000), although exceptions are typical for both children with hearing difficulties (Kyle and Harris, 2006) and children with specific language impairments (Mackie and Dockrell, 2004). Individual differences in the early phases of the development of spelling ability are primarily caused by differences in the knowledge and use of sound-spelling information but as skills in reading and spelling progress, morphological factors become important (Nunes et al., 1997). Poor spellers may rely more on visual strategies, but it is argued that this is only because of their limited phonological knowledge (Kamhi and Hinton, 2000). Overall spelling difficulties are a major constraint in writing, and often lead students to avoid writing (Berninger et al., 2002; Graham et al., 2002).

MEETING THE NEEDS OF CHILDREN EXPERIENCING DIFFICULTIES IN LEARNING TO WRITE

In the previous sections, we have seen how children may experience difficulties with writing as a result of a number of different constraints. These constraints cause significant challenges for pupils through all phases of their school career. Motivation can be a critical catalyst in writing (Graham, 2006) and difficulties with writing lead to the avoidance of writing, which further reduces opportunities to develop writing skills (Berninger et al., 1991). Children develop a negative image of both the writing process and their own abilities to communicate ideas through writing (Gregg and Mather, 2002). Attitudes towards writing influences composition in the early years (Graham et al., 2007), and it appears that for children who have writing difficulties their dislike of the task can result in devaluing its importance (De Caso and Garcia, 2006).

A systematic and sensitive approach to intervention is required if both writing difficulties and motivational factors are to be addressed. There is evidence that teachers' adaptations for children struggling to learn to write are limited (Graham et al., 2003). Graham et al. (2003) surveyed 220 teachers and while some were making adaptations, typically, they were only making one or two adaptations. Unfortunately, even in teachers who are well prepared to meet the needs of children with writing difficulties, transfer of their knowledge and attitudes into classroom practice can be limited (Moni et al., 2007).

Overall, there is a paucity of studies investigating writing in the classroom (Hooper et al., 1994). Where data have been collected, the indication is that a limited amount of time is dedicated to the tasks 'with the time that was spent on writing largely devoted to copying tasks' (Hooper et al, 1994: 376). In a notable exception, Boscolo and Cisotto (1999) asked Year-2 teachers to identify activities used to support writing. They were able to categorize the results into two distinct approaches—rule giving and creating meaningful text. These data suggest that teachers focus either on aspects of transcription or aspects of idea generation. Clearly, the challenge for children is to coordinate both these activities. However, since there were no observational data to corroborate these results, it is not clear the extent to which the results reflect mutually exclusive practices or differences of emphasis. Nor is it known what the contribution of teaching is to the long-term writing strategies of developing writers, although there is some evidence that the differences in strategy use found in older writers may have arisen from how they were initially taught writing (Torrance et al., 1999; Whitaker et al., 1994). The importance of the curricular/instructional explanation for the differences in the writing skills of children with learning difficulties, both within and across genres, has gathered a vocal and growing number of proponents (Scott, 1999).

For children with writing difficulties even the best classroom support may not be enough; more intensive and explicit instruction will be required (Troia, 2006). The simple model of writing identifies the key instructional components in the writing process that should be evaluated and can subsequently be supported through targeted intervention. As long as translating continues to place heavy demands on writing, the management of planning will be impaired. Approaches to supporting translation skills are, therefore, a basic prerequisite to any intervention program. Providing extra instruction for transcription skills can boost the writing performance of struggling writers in the primary grades (Berninger et al., 1997). An analysis of spelling errors can provide reliable cues for spelling instruction (see Berninger and Amtmann, 2003). Handwriting (or word processing) and spelling need to be, at least, partly automated to open the way up for pupils to develop text production. Once some automaticity is established, pupils can move from word and sentence level to the development of text structures and planning and revision. A recent meta-analysis has examined the strength and consistency of the effects of different instructional practices on the quality of student writing in upper primary and secondary school (Graham and Perin, 2007). A number of effective strategies were identified, but it was argued that these strategies identified should be used in an 'optimal mix' to have the greatest effects. This mix needs to be established on the basis of pupils' response to interventions.

CONCLUSION AND FUTURE DEVELOPMENTS

Writing with technical accuracy and organizing text into planned and coherent sequences is a complex process. It is affected by the writer's expertise, the instructional support they receive and the demands of the specific writing task. Struggling writers have difficulties with basic writing skills and writing processes. Many children with learning difficulties have associated problems with text production. Written expression problems may stem from the inability to spell words, difficulties in generating ideas, the lack of automaticity of writing, and difficulties with the planning, text generation, or review and revising processes of writing. Often, these difficulties are underpinned by problems with literacy, language, or working memory. Addressing these problems requires more than simply establishing children's level of performance in comparison to peers. Careful analysis of the writing process and product and an assessment of transcription skills are required to provide appropriate intervention. In sum, children with writing difficulties require ongoing evaluation as well as direct and systematic instruction from informed practitioners if they are to develop their writing skills.

To further understand these processes, for children who are challenged by the writing process, it will be necessary to test complex developmental models both longitudinally and cross-sectionally. It is essential to fill the gap in our understanding between the behavioural manifestation, that is difficulties in writing, and the cognitive and contextual factors that underpin writing difficulties if we wish to intervene effectively.

NOTES

1   In the UK, children who experience a learning difficulty are generically referred to as having special educational needs. The category of special educational need can be further subdivided into groups of children with specific problems such as dyslexia, dysgraphia, and specific language impairment and contrasted with children who experience learning problems across the board and who are characterized by low scores on tests of general cognitive ability.

REFERENCES

Abbott R.D. and Berninger, V.W. (1993) 'Structural equation modeling of relationships among develop- mental skills and writing skills in primary and intermediate grade writers', *Journal of Educational Psychology*, 85: 478–508.

American Psychiatric Association (1994) *Diagnostic and Statistical Manual of Mental Disorders* (third revised edn.) (DSM-IV). Washington DC: American Psychiatric Association.

Anderson, P.L. (1982) 'A preliminary study of syntax in the written expression of learning disabled children', *Journal Of Learning Disabilities*, 15: 359–362.

Bereiter, C. and Scardamalia, M. (1987) The Psychology of Written Composition. Hillsdale, NJ: Erlbaum.

Berninger, V.W. (1996) *Reading and Writing Acquisition: A Developmental Neuropsychological Perspective*, New York: Westview Press.

Berninger, V.W. (1999) 'Coordinating transcription and text generation in working memory during compos- ing: Automatic and constructive process', *Learning Disability Quarterly*, 22: 99–112.

Berninger V.W. and Amtmann, D. (2003) 'Preventing written expression disabilities through early and continuing assessment and intervention for hand- writing and/or spelling problems: Research into practice', in H.L. Swanson, K. Harris, and S. Graham (eds), *Handbook of Learning Difficulties*, New York and London: Guildford Press.

Berninger, V. and Fuller, F. (1992) 'Gender differences in orthographic, verbal, and compositional fluency: Implications for diagnosis of writing disabilities in primary grade children', *Journal of School Psychology*, 30: 363–382.

Berninger, V. and Swanson, H.L. (1994) 'Modifying Hayes and Flowers' model of skilled writing to explain beginning and developing writing', in E. Butterfield (ed.), *Children's Writing: Toward a Process Theory of Development of Skilled Writing*, Greenwich, CT: JAI Press. pp.57–81.

Berninger, V., Mizokawa. D., and Bragg, R. (1991) 'Theory-based diagnosis and remediation of writing disabilities', *Journal of School Psychology*, 29: 57–79.

Berninger, V., Abbott, R., Whitaker, D., Sylvester, L., and Nolen, S. (1995) 'Integrating low-level skills and high-level skills in treatment protocol for writing disabilities', *Learning Disability Quarterly*, 18: 293–309.

Berninger, V. Abbott, R., Jones, J., Wolf, B., Gould, L., Anderson-Youngstrom, M., Shimada, S., and Apel, K. (2006) 'Early development of language by hand: Composing-, reading-, listening-, and speaking- connections, three letter writing modes, and fast mapping in spelling', *Developmental Neuro- psychology*, 29: 61–92.

Berninger, V., Hart, T., Abbott, R., and Karovsky, P. (1992) 'Defining reading and writing disabilities with and without IQ: A flexible developmental perspective', *Learning Disabilities Quarterly*, 15: 103–118.

Berninger, V., Rutberg, J., Abbott, R., Garcia, N., Anderson-Youngstrom, M., Brooks, A., and Fulton, C. (2006) 'Tier 1 and Tier 2 early intervention for handwriting and composing', *Journal of School Psychology*, 44: 3–30.

Berninger, V., Vaughn, K., Abbott, R., Abbott, S., Rogan, L., Brooks, A., Reed, E., and Graham, S. (1997) 'Treatment of handwriting problems in beginning writers: Transfer from handwriting to composition', *Journal of Educational Psychology*, 89: 652–666.

Berninger, V., Vaughan, K., Abbott, R., Begay, K., Byrd, K., Curtin, G., Minnich, J., and Graham, S. (2002) 'Teaching spelling and composition alone and together: Implications for the simple view of writing', *Journal of Educational Psychology*, 94: 291–304.

Berninger, V., Whitaker, D., Feng, Y., Swanson, H.L., and Abbott, R. (1996) 'Assessment of planning, translating, and revising in junior high writers' *Journal of School Psychology*, 34: 23–52.

Berninger, V., Yates, C., Cartwright, A., Rutberg, J., Remy, E., and Abbott, R. (1992) Lower-level developmental skills in beginning writing', *Reading and Writing: An Interdisciplinary Journal*, 4: 257–280.

Bishop, D.V.M. and Clarkson, B. (2003) 'Written language as a window into residual language deficits: A study of children with persistent and residual speech and language impairments', *Cortex*, 39(2): 215–237.

Bishop, D.V.M. and Snowling, M.J. (2004) 'Developmental dyslexia and specific language impairment: Same or different?', *Psychological Bulletin*, 130: 858-88.

Boscolo, P. and Cisotto, L. (1999) 'Instructional strategies for teaching to write: A Q-sort analysis', *Learning and Instruction*, 9(2): 209–221.

Bourassa, D., Treiman, R., and Kessler, B. (2006) 'Use of morphology in spelling by children with dyslexia and typically developing children', *Memory and Cognition*, 34: 703–714.

Bourdin, B., Fayol, M., and Darciaux, S. (1996) 'The comparison of oral and written modes on adult's and children's narrative recall', in G. Rijlaarsdam, H. van den Bergh, and M. Couzijn (eds), *Theories, Models and Methodology in Writing Research*, Amsterdam: Amsterdam University Press. pp.159–169.

Brooks, A. and Fulton C. (2006) 'Tier 1 and Tier 2 early intervention for handwriting and composing', *Journal of School Psychology*, 44: 3–30.

Chase, C. (1986) 'Essay test scoring: Interaction of relevant variables', *Journal of Educational Measurement*, 23: 1–14.

Cobb-Morocco, C., Dalton, G. and Tiverman, T. (1992) 'The impact of computer-supported writing instruction on fourth grade students with and without learning disabilities', *Reading and Writing Quarterly: Overcoming Learning Difficulties*, 8: 87–113.

Connelly, V., Campbell, S., MacLean, M., and Barnes, J. (2006) 'Contribution of lower-order letter and word fluency skills to written composition of college students with and without dyslexia', *Developmental Neuropsychology*, 29(1): 175–196.

Cragg, L. and Nation, K. (2006) 'Exploring written narrative in children with poor reading comprehension', *Educational Psychology*, 26: 55–72.

De Caso, A-M. and Garcia, J-N. (2006) 'What is missing from current writing intervention programmes? The need for writing motivation programmes', *Estudio de psicologia*, 27: 211–242.

Dellerman, P., Coirier, P., and Marchand, E. (1996) 'Planning and expertise in argumentative composition', in G. Rijlaarsdam, H. van den Bergh, and M. Couzijn (eds), *Theories, Models and Methodologies in Writing Research*, Amsterdam: Amsterdam University Press. pp.182–195.

Dockrell, J.E., Lindsay, G., and Connelly, V. (in press) 'The impact of a history of SLI on the production of written text during adolescence', *Exceptional Children*.

Dockrell, J.E., Lindsay, G., Letchford, B., and Mackie, C. (2006) 'Educational provision for children with specific speech and language difficulties: Perspectives of speech and language therapist managers', *International Journal of Language and Communication Disorders*, 41: 423–440.

Dockrell, J.E., Lindsay, G.A., Connelly, V., and Mackie, C. (2007) 'Profiling the written language difficulties of children with language and communication problems', *Exceptional Children*, 73: 147–164.

Fey, M.E., Catts, H.W., Proctor-Williams, K., Tomblin, J., and Zhang, X.Y. (2004) 'Oral and written story composition skills of children with language impairment', *Journal of Speech Language and Hearing Research*, 47(6): 1301–1318.

Fitzgerald, J. and Shanahan, T. (2000) 'Reading and writing relations and their development', *Educational Psychologist*, 35: 39–51.

Francis, M. and McCutchen, D. (April, 1994) 'Strategy differences in revising between skilled and less skilled writers', Paper presented at the annual meeting of the American Educational Research Association. New Orleans, Louisiana.

Galbraith, D. (1996) 'Self-monitoring, discovery through writing and individual differences in drafting strategy', in G. Rijlaarsdam, H. van den Bergh, and M. Couzijn (eds), *Theories, Models and Methodology in Writing Research*, Amsterdam: Amsterdam University Press. pp.21–141.

Gillam, R. and Johnston, J. (1992) 'Spoken and written language relationships in language learning impaired and normally achieving school-age children', *Journal of Speech and Hearing Research*, 35: 1303–1315.

Graham, S. (2006) 'Writing', in P. Alexander and P. Winne (eds), *Handbook of Educational Psychology*, Mahwah, NJ: Erlbaum. pp.457–478.

Graham, S. and Harris, K.R. (1993) 'Self-regulated strategy development: Helping students with learning problems develop as writers', *Elementary School Journal*, 94: 169–181.

Graham, S. and Weintraub, N. (1996) 'A review of handwriting research: Progress and prospects from 1980 to 1994', *Educational Psychology Review,* 8: 7–87.

Graham, S., Harris, K.R., and Chorzempa, B.F. (2002) 'Contribution of spelling instruction to the spelling, writing, and reading of poor spellers', *Journal of Educational Psychology*, 94: 669–686.

Graham, S., Berninger, V., Abbott, R., Abbott, S., and Whitaker, D. (1997) 'The role of mechanics in composing of elementary school students: A new methodological approach', *Journal of Educational Psychology*, 89(1): 170–182.

Graham, S., Berninger, V., and Fau, F. (2007) 'The structural relationship between writing and attitude and writing and achievement in first and third grade students', *Contemporary Educational Psychology*, 32: 516–536.

Graham, S., Perin, D. (2007) Writing next: Effective strategies to improve writing of adolescents in middle and high schools (Carnegie Corporation Report). Washington, DC: Alliance for Excellent Education. Retrieved September 7, 2007, from http://www.all4ed.org/publications/WritingNext/WritingNext.pdf.

Graham, S., Berninger, V., Weintraub, N., and Schafer, W. (1998) 'The development of handwriting fluency and legibility grades 1 through 9', *Journal of Educational Research*, 92: 42–52.

Graham, S., Harris, K.R., Fink-Chorzempa, B., and MacArthur, C. (2003) 'Primary grade teachers' instructional adaptations for struggling writers: A national survey', *Journal of Educational Psychology,* 95(2): 279–292.

Graham, S., Schwartz, S. and MacArthur, C. (1993) 'Knowledge of writing and the composing process, attitude towards writing, and self efficacy for students with and without learning disabilities', *Journal of Learning Disabilities*, 26: 237–249.

Gregg N. and Mather N. (2002) 'School is fun at recess: Informal analyses of written language for students with learning disabilities', *Journal of Learning Disabilities*, 35: 7–22.

Gregg, N., Coleman, C.D.M., and Chalk, J.C. (2007) 'Timed essay writing: Implications for high-stakes Tests', *Journal of Learning Disabilities*, 40: 306–318.

Grigorenko, E.L. (2007) 'Rethinking disorders of spoken and written language: Generating workable hypotheses', *Journal of Developmental and Behavioral Pediatrics*, 28(6): 478–486.

Grunwald, E.A., Persky, H.R., Campbell, J.R., and Mazzeo, J. (1998) *Writing report card for the nation and states*, Washington, DC: Government Printing House.

Hatcher, J., Snowling, M.J., and Griffiths, Y.M. (2002) 'Cognitive Assessment of dyslexic students in higher education', *British Journal of Educational Psychology*, 72(1): 119–33.

Hayes, J.R. (1996) 'A new framework for understanding cognition and affect in writing', in C.M. Levy and S. Ransdell (eds), *The Science Of Writing: Theories, Methods, Individual Differences And Applications*, Hillsdale, NJ; England: Lawrence Erlbaum Associates. pp.1–27.

Hayes, J.R. and Flower, L.S. (1986) 'Writing research and the writer', *American Psychologist*, 41: 1106–13.

Hidi, A. and Hildyard, A. (1983) 'The comparison of the oral and written productions in two discourse types', *Discourse Processes*, 6: 91–105.

Hooper, S.R. and Willis, W.G. (1989) *Learning Disability Subtyping: Neuropsychological Foundations, Conceptual Models, and issues in Clinical Differentiation*, New York: Springer-Verlag.

Hooper, S.R., Montgomery, J.W., Swartz, C., Reed, M.S., Sandler, A.D., Levine, M.D., Watson, T.E., and Wasileski, T. (1994) 'Measurement of written language expression', in G.R. Lyon (ed.), *Frames of Reference for the Assessment of Learning Disabilities*, New Views on Measurement Issues Baltimore: Brookes. pp.375–417.

Hooper, S., Swartz, C., Wakely W., de Kruif R., and Montgomery, J. (2002) 'Executive functions in elementary school children with and without problems in written expression', *Journal of Learning Disabilities*, 35: 57–68.

Juel, C. (1988) 'Learning to read and write: A longitudinal study of 54 children from first through fourth grades', *Journal of Educational Psychology*, 80: 437–447.

Just, M. and Carpenter, P. (1992) 'A capacity theory of comprehension: Individual differences in working memory', *Psychological Review*, 99: 122–149.

Kail, R and Miller, C. (2006) 'Developmental change in processing speed: Domain specificity and stabitlity during childhood and adolescence', *Journal of Cognition and Development*, 7: 119–137.

Kail, R. and Salthouse, T. (1994) 'Processing speed as a mental capacity', *Acta Psychologica*, 86, 199–225.

Kamhi, A.G. and Hinton, L.N. (2000) 'Explaining individual differences in spelling ability', *Topics in Language Disorders*, 20(3): 37–49.

Katims, D.S. (2001) 'Literacy assessment of students with mental retardation: An exploratory investigation', *Education and Training in Mental Retardation and Developmental Disabilities*, 36(4): 363–372.

Kellogg, R.T. (1996) 'A model of working memory in writing', in C.M. Levy and S. Ransdell (eds), *The Science of writing: Theories, Methods, Individual Differences, and applications*, Mahwah, NJ: Erlbaum. pp. 57–71.

Kellogg, R.T. (1999) 'Components of working memory in text production', in M. Torrance and G. Jeffery (eds), *The Cognitive Demands of Writing*, Amsterdam: Amsterdam University Press. pp.143–161.

Keogh, J.F. and Sugden, D.A (1985) *Movement Skill Development*, New York: Macmillan.

Kyle, F.E. and Harris, M. (2006) 'Concurrent correlates and predictors of reading and spelling in deaf and hearing school children', *Journal of Deaf Studies and Deaf Education*, 11: 273–288.

Lerner, J.W. (1976) *Children with Learning Disabilities: Theories, Diagnosis, Teaching Strategies*, Boston: Houghton Mifflin, cited in Hooper et al. (2002).

MacArthur, C.A. and Graham, S. (1987) 'Learning disabled students' composing with three methods: Handwriting, dictation and word processing', *Journal of Special Education*, 21: 22-42.

MacArthur, C., Graham, S., and Fitzgerald, J. (2006) *Handbook of Research on Writing*, New York: Guilford.

Mackie, C. and Dockrell, J. E. (2004) 'The nature of written language deficits in children with SLI', *Journal of Speech Language and Hearing Research*, 47(6): 1469–1483.

Marshall, J. C. and Powers, J. C. (1969) 'Writing neatness, composition errors, and essay grades', *Journal of Educational Measurement*, 6: 97–101.

Mayes, S. and Calhoun, S. (2006) 'Frequency of reading, math and writing disabilities in children with clinical disorders', *Learning and Individual Differences*, 16: 145–157.

McCutchen, D. (1986) 'Domain knowledge and linguistic knowledge in the development of writing ability', *Journal of Memory and Language*, 25: 431–444.

McCutchen, D. (1987) 'Children's discourse skill—form and modality requirements of schooled writing', *Discourse Processes*, 10: 267–86.

McCutchen D. (1996) 'A capacity theory of writing: Working memory in composition', *Educational Psychology Review*, 8(3): 299–325.

McCutchen, D., Covill, A., Hoyne, S.H., and Mildes, K. (1994) 'Individual differences in writing: Implications of translating fluency', *Journal of Educational Psychology*, 86: 256–266.

McCutchen, D., Francis, M., and Kerr, S. (1997) 'Revising for meaning: Effects of knowledge and strategy', *Journal of Educational Psychology*, 89: 667–676.

McHale, K. and Cermak, S. (1992) 'Fine motor activities in elementary school: Preliminary findings and provisional implications for children with fine motor problems', *American Journal of Occupational Therapy*, 46: 898–903.

Moni, K., Jobling, A., van Kraayenoord, C., Elkins, J., Miller, R., and Koppenhaver, D. (2007) 'Teachers' knowledge, attitudes and the implementation of practices around the teaching of writing in inclusive middle years' classrooms: No quick fix', *Educational and Child Psychology*, 24: 18–36.

Montgomery, J.W. and Leonard, L.B. (1998) 'Real-Time Inflectional Processing by Children With Specific Language Impairment: Effects of Phonetic Substance', *Journal of Speech, Language and Hearing Research*, 41: 1432–43.

Nagy, W., Berninger, V., Abbott, R., Vaughn, K., and Vermeulen, K. (2003) 'Relationship of morphology and other language skills to literacy skills in at-risk second grade readers and at risk fourth grade writers', *Journal of Educational Psychology*, 95: 730–742.

Naucler, K. and Magnusson, E. (2002) 'How do pre-school language problems affect language abilities in adolescence', in F. Windsor and M.L. Kelly (eds), *Investigations in Clinical Phonetics and Linguistics*, Mahwah, NJ: Erlbaum. pp.243–269.

Nunes, T., Bryant, P., and Bindman, M. (1997) 'Learning to spell regular and irregular verbs', *Reading and Writing*, 9(5-6): 427–49

Ogle, J.W. (1867). 'Aphasia and agraphia', *Report of the medical research counsel of St. George's Hospital*, 2: 83–122, cited in Hooper et al. (2002).

Pickering, S.J. and Gathercole, S.E. (2004) 'Distinctive working memory profiles in children with varying special needs', *Educational Psychology*, 24: 393–408.

Puranik, C.S., Lombardino, L.J., and Altmann, L.J. (2007) 'Writing through retellings: An exploratory study of language-impaired and dyslexic populations', *Reading and Writing*, 20(3): 251–272.

Re, A., Pedron, M., and Cornoldi, C. (2007) 'Expressive writing in children with ADHD symptoms', *Special Focus on Education*, 15: 10–16.

Rice, M.L. and Wilcox, K.A. (eds) (1995) *Building a Language-Focused Curriculum for The Preschool Classroom: A Foundation for Lifelong Communication Baltimore*, MD: Brookes Publishing Co. pp.155–169.

Rousseau, M.K., Bottge, B.A., and Dy, E.B. (1993) 'Syntactic complexity in the writing of students with and without mental retardation', *American Journal of Mental Retardation*, 98(1): 113–20.

Scott, C.M. (1999) 'Learning to write', in H.W. Catts and A.G. Kahmi (eds), *Language and Reading Disabilities*, Boston: Allyn and Bacon. pp.224–59.

Scott, C.M. and Windsor, J. (2000) 'General language performance measures in spoken and written narrative and expository discourse of school-age children with language learning disabilities', *Journal of Speech, Language, and Hearing Research*, 43: 324–339.

Shanahan, T. (2006) 'Relations among oral language, reading and writing development', in C. MacArthur, S. Graham, and J. Fitzgerald (eds), *Handbook of Writing Research*, New York: Guilford Press. pp.171–183.

Smits-Engelsman, B., Van Galen, G., and Portier, S. (1993) 'Cross-sectional and longitudinal study on developmental features of psychomotor aspects of handwriting', in Proceedings of the Sixth Handwriting Conference of the International Graphonomics Society. Motor Control of Handwriting. Telecom, Paris.

Smits-Engelsman, B., Van Galen, G., and Portier, S. (1994) 'Psychomotor Development of handwriting proficiency: A cross sectional and longitudinal study on developmental features of handwriting', in C. Faure, P. Keuss, G. Lorette, and A. Vinter (eds), *Advances in Handwriting and Drawing: A Multidisciplinary Approach*, Europia, Paris.

Smits-Engelsman, B., Van Galen, G., and Schoemaker, M. (1997) 'Theory-based diagnosis and subclassification in developmental coordination disorder', in J. Rispens, T. Van Yperen, and W. Yule (eds), *Perspectives on the Classification of Specific Developmental Disorders*, Dordretch: Kluwer Academic Publishers. (pp.229–247)

Sterling, C., Farmer, M., Riddick, B., Morgan, S., and Matthews, C. (1998) 'Adult dyslexic writing', *Dyslexia*, 4: 1–15.

Teubal, E., Dockrell, J.E., and Tolchinsky, L. (eds) (2007) *Notational Knowledge: Historical and developmental Perspectives*, Rotterdam: Sense Publishers.

Torrance, M. and Galbraith, D. (2006) 'The processing demand of writing', in C. MacArthur, S. Graham, and J. Fitzgerald (eds), *Handbook of Writing Research*, New York: Guilford Press. pp. 67-80.

Torrance, M., Thomas, G.V., and Robinson, E.J. (1999) 'Individual differences in the writing behaviour of undergraduate students', *British Journal of Educational Psychology*, 69: 189–99.

Troia, G. (2006) 'Writing instruction for students with learning disabilities', in C. MacArthur, S. Graham, and J. Fitzgerald (eds), *Handbook of Writing Research*, New York: Guilford Press. pp.324–336.

Troia, G.A. and Graham, S. (2002) 'The effectiveness of a highly explicit, teacher-directed strategy instruction routine: Changing the writing performance of students with learning disabilities', *Journal of Learning Disabilities*, 35: 290–305.

Troia, G.A. and Maddox, M.E. (2004) 'Writing instruction in middle schools: Special and general education teachers share their views and voice their concerns', *Exceptionality, 12:* 19–37.

Volman, M.J.M., van Schendel, B.M., and Jongmans, M.J. (2006) 'Handwriting difficulties in primary school children: A search for underlying mechanisms', *American Journal of Occupational Therapy*, 60(4): 451–460.

Whitaker, D, Berninger, V. Johnston, J., and Swanson, H.L. (1994) 'Intraindividual differences in levels of language in intermediate group writers: Implications for the translation process', *Learning and Individual Differences,* 6:107–130.

Whittington, J., Holland, A., Webb, T., Butler, J., Clarke, D., and Boer H. (2004) 'Academic underachievement by people with Prader-Willi syndrome', *Journal of Intellectual Disability Research*, 48: 188–200.

World Health Organization (1990) *International Classification of Diseases and Disorders* (10th edn.), Geneva: World Health Organization.

The Contested Materialities of Writing in Digital Environments: Implications for Writing Development

Doreen Starke-Meyerring

Technologies have always been central to questions of writing and writing development. As Haas (1996) observed, 'whether it is the stylus of the ancients, the pen and ink of the medieval scribe, a toddler's fat crayons, or a new Powerbook, technology makes writing possible' (p. xi). In this way, as Haas notes, 'writing *is* technology' (p. xi) and as such, it is material. This material existence of writing through and as material artefacts is also deeply intertwined with, enables, and constrains the ways in which writing works to assemble, orchestrate, and organize human activity in communities, institutions, organizations, and societies (e.g., Bazerman and Prior, 2004; 2005; Paré, 2002; 2005; Devitt, 2004; Artemeva and Freedman, 2006; Coe et al., 2002; Schryer, 1993; Smart, 2007)—what writing development researchers have also referred to as the socioeconomic materialities[1] of writing (e.g., Devitt et al., 2003; Devitt, 2004; DeVoss and Porter, 2006; Horner, 2001; Wysocki et al., 2004); the established, regularized, and normalized social practices; institutional arrangements, power structures, hierarchies, ways of material and cultural production, and their regulation in human collectives. Deeply intertwined, particular technologies and infrastructure constellations, for example, enable or constrain writing and the human activities it organizes, which in turn shape the design, use, and regulation of these technologies. As a result, a rupture or shift in one material aspect of writing is deeply implicated in the other. As Haas (1996) puts it, such shifts involve 'questions of truth, knowledge, and power' (p. 5).

For the past few hundred years, the socioeconomic materialities of writing have been shaped largely around print technologies. As such, these materialities have become settled into a somewhat stabilized equilibrium of regularized and normalized practices with laws and rules regulating diverse interests in the materialities of print technologies, for example, interests in who owns and controls access to publishing and print technologies, who owns written work, when such work can be shared with whom and under what conditions (e.g., freely or for a fee), to what extent writers are able to draw and build on existing work in creating new work, and under what conditions people write, such as the extent to which their communication is subject to surveillance and accordingly to various forms of censorship, including self-censorship.

With the emergence of digital network technologies, most notably the internet with its myriad technologies, writing increasingly takes place in digital environments. These environments take on a dizzying array of shapes, ranging from websites to blogs, wikis, so-called social-networking sites such as Facebook or MySpace, immersive virtual environments such as Second Life, peer-to-peer file sharing sites such as BitTorrent, photo or video sharing sites such as Flickr and Youtube, peer-produced news sites such as Digg.com, bookmark sharing sites such as Del.icio.us, and many more. What unites and distinguishes these digital writing environments from those in print is their materiality—their existence through the hardware and software that shape their design or what Lessig (2006) calls 'architecture'. While digital writing spaces are coded in diverse ways, they all exist in and through digital technologies, and as such they enable, constrain, challenge, reproduce, or question established practices, social orders, and hierarchies rooted in print materialities while also offering alternative practices and social orders to those established around print.

As a result, digital writing environments are highly contested in all sectors of society—in public, work place, and educational settings, as any, even cursory, glance at the major headlines in any news venue will reveal. Almost on a daily basis, we read about citizens and activists being monitored or even arrested, employees being fired, or students being sued by content industries over their use of digital files, or being disciplined over their use of blogs, social networking sites, wikis, and other digital writing spaces. For example, news stories report

about Wikipedia being banned from writing assignments in entire university departments (Cohen, 2007), about students protesting privacy invading features of corporate-sponsored digital writing spaces (Story and Stone, 2007; Calore, 2006), or about students protesting the ways in which digital technologies, such as plagiarism detection software, have been used by institutions to police their writing (CBC News, 2004; Glod, 2006). Such stories of contestation and conflict surrounding emerging digital materialities of writing abound, indicating that the ways in which we understand these changed materialities of writing has deep implications both for writing development and for organizations, institutions, and societies at large.

For students, teachers, and researchers of writing, this contestation also begs some principal and highly consequential questions: How do materialities of writing change in digital environments, how are divergent interests in these changes negotiated, and what consequences do these changes have for the socioeconomic materialities of writing—for how writing organizes human activity and how writing as a social practice is regulated? And most importantly, what are the implications of these changes for writing development?

To address these questions, this chapter first draws on critical theories of technologies to conceptualize digital network technologies as emerging materialities of writing. As the chapter shows, a critical understanding of technologies is vital to the study and teaching of writing in digital environments not only because these environments exist in and through digital technologies, but also because such an understanding allows researchers, teachers, and students of writing to analyse the contestation surrounding digital writing environments and to participate in the decision making processes around the technologies that will impact writing development as well as our organizations, institutions, and societies in important ways. The chapter then outlines vital ways in which these materialities of writing undergo change and contestation, focusing on three interrelated struggles that permeate all digital writing spaces and that have particularly significant implications for writing development: the extent to which digital writing spaces will allow for equal access; the extent to which writers will be able to share and draw on each other's work; and the extent to which digital writing spaces will be characterized by surveillance, monitoring, and policing or by designs that facilitate the voicing of dissent and participation in democratic decision making. The chapter concludes with implications of these struggles over the materialities of writing in digital environments for writing development, specifically for what we might call pedagogies for critical engagement (e.g., Bazerman, 2007; Devoss, Cushman, and Grabill, 2005; DeVoss and Porter, 2006; Hawisher and Selfe, 1999; Hicks and Grabill, 2005; Selber, 2004; Wysocki et al., 2004) that allow students to question, analyse, and engage in robust deliberation about the digital writing spaces they inhabit to participate in shaping their design, use, and regulation.

CONCEPTUALIZING DIGITAL TECHNOLOGIES AS EMERGING MATERIALITIES OF WRITING

Central to examining emerging materialities of writing in digital environments is a critical understanding of technologies—that is an understanding of technologies not as neutral tools, but rather as highly political and therefore contested dynamic material artefacts or systems of artefacts, whose design, use, and regulation are deeply implicated in reproducing, challenging, or reshaping existing social practices and orders (e.g., Benkler, 2006; Feenberg, 2002; Longford, 2005; Winner, 1986). As Winner (1986) noted, 'the things we call "technologies" are ways of building order in our world' (p. 28), which function 'similar to legislative acts' (p. 29). Longford (2005) similarly calls attention to the regulatory or (re-)ordering force of technologies, calling them silent or 'unacknowledged legislators'

(p. 72). As such, technologies always enable or constrain, privilege or marginalize certain social practices and interests at the cost of others, thus offering 'a framework of activity, a field of play' (Feenberg, 2002: 82) that is highly contested, because it presents alternative ways of ordering the activities and rights of different groups.

As Feng and Feenberg (2008) emphasize, a critical perspective examines technologies in the context of larger socioeconomic and political values, practices, and power relations that surround the emergence, design, use, and regulation of technologies. From this perspective, technologies are best thought of not as 'a thing in the ordinary sense of the term, but an "ambivalent" process of development suspended between different possibilities' (Feenberg, 2002: 15). Most importantly, as Feenberg (2002) stresses, 'technology is not a destiny but a scene of struggle. It is a social battlefield, ... in which civilizational alternatives contend' (p. 15). This critical conceptualization of technologies as highly political scenes of struggle among diverse interests in their shape, use, and regulation is particular pertinent to digital technologies, given their high malleability as they are constantly being coded and recoded, designed, and redesigned and thus constantly (re-) order social practices and arrangements. Constantly in flux, the materialities of writing in digital environments—more so than these of print—are subject to incessant contestation.

Grounded in a critical understanding of technologies, digital writing spaces, then, are scenes of struggle over the shape of these environments—of their digital materialities—as well as over the ways in which these digital materialities will enable, support, undermine, or question established socioeconomic materialities of writing, that is the existing regularized and normalized practices, social orders, and the laws or rules regulating diverse interests in these practices and orders. They are scenes of struggle over the ways in which digital technologies encode social practices and orders and whose interests these practices and orders reproduce or challenge. These struggles, therefore, evolve around a central question: To what extent will digital writing environments enable alternative practices and social orders, or to what extent will they be contested, redesigned, or regulated to reproduce established practices, norms, and orders that sustain dominant established interests (Bazerman, 2007; Feenberg, 2002; Zuboff, 1988)? In other words, in whose interests will emerging materialities of writing in digital environments be shaped and regulated?

To be sure, the responses to this question depend on the unique situatedness of each writing space—be that an online course management system, a wiki, or a so-called social networking site—the work it accomplishes, the purposes for which it has been sponsored, the discursive practices and expectations participants bring to the space, and the ways in which the digital code that inscribes the space enables, supports, constrains, or undermines those purposes and practices (Starke-Meyerring, 2008). Nevertheless, there are numerous struggles over the shape of the materialities of writing in digital environments that cut across and permeate all digital writing spaces and therefore have particularly significant implications for writing development. Of these, three are particularly foundational for the ways in which the materialities of writing in digital environment will take shape. They will serve here to illustrate the ways in which the materialities of writing in digital environments are contested: the struggle over equal access as a precondition to writing in digital environments, the struggle over ownership and the sharing of digital files, and the struggle over privacy and surveillance in digital writing spaces.

THE STRUGGLE OVER EQUAL ACCESS AS A PRECONDITION TO WRITING IN DIGITAL ENVIRONMENTS

Access to digital network technologies has long been considered central to writing and writing development. Early on, researchers noted, for example, the reduced access to computers, bandwidth, and digital infrastructure by marginalized groups and by people in marginalized regions of the world (e.g., Grabill, 2003; Knobel, 2006; Moran, 1999; Porter, 1998; Powell, 2007; Selfe, 1999; Selfe and Hawisher, 2004). Accordingly, these researchers have called on writing development researchers and teachers to study and engage in policy development around issues of access and the bridging of digital divides. Moran (1999), for example, called attention to the need for a research and teaching agenda to address issues socioeconomic inequalities in access to technologies. Selfe (1999) urged teachers and researchers of writing to pay attention to national technology literacy agendas, warning that these agendas reproduce and exacerbate existing inequalities based on race and poverty. Grabill (2003) focused specifically on issues of class as a critical factor in access to technologies for writing. Selfe and Hawisher (2004) provided rich descriptions of the various cultural, economic, social, and other factors that influence the development of 'literate lives' in the digital age.

Moreover, researchers have paid particular attention to the ways in which interfaces and larger infrastructures enable and constrain what students are able to write and learn in educational institutions (e.g., DeVoss, Cushman, Grabill, 2005; Porter, 1998; Powell, 2007), as well as in communities such as in community literacy centres (e.g., Grabill, 2007). This work has conceptualized access as a range of issues, with Porter (1998), for example, connecting issues of infrastructures, literacy practices, and community practices and Powell (2007) arguing for a conceptualization of access as practice, deeply rooted in what literacy practices are valued in local communities. Access then has been richly theorized as involving social practices around local technological interfaces and infrastructures that enable and constrain who gets to develop what kinds of literacies and for what purpose, and hence can participate in what ways in collective community endeavours.

Yet, beyond local infrastructures and literacy practices, there is also a fundamental way in which access is coded into digital network technologies—a way that perhaps most profoundly distinguishes the materialities of writing in digital environments from all other materialities of writing and communication, including those of mass media and broadcasting, a way that also has significant implications for writing and writing development. While traditional technologies of writing and communication were highly centralized and regulated by governments or a few large corporate media conglomerates, with access to publishing or broadcasting opportunities tightly controlled, digital network technologies, specifically the internet, have provided a decentralized communication infrastructure for millions of writers and have thus had what Benkler (2006) calls a vital 'corrective effect' on the failures of mass communication to provide a robust interactive public sphere. Accordingly, established communication technologies, with their tight control over access to publication or broadcasting technologies, privileged, for example, the discourse of an energy company or of the government's environmental protection agency, while that of citizens, environmental activists, or civil society organizations was more difficult to access, especially without being framed in the interests of those who controlled and sponsored established communication technologies. In short, what was published and accessible for democratic deliberation and large-scale opportunities for participation in such deliberation was highly selected and controlled.

In contrast, digital network technologies in their current design allow writers to access the corporate website, the government's environmental protection agency website, the mainstream media environmental news report, the environmentalist's blog, and the mass e-mail from the environmental civil society organization with the same ease—at roughly the same speed. Moreover, all writers participating in digital network communication,

given the same connection speed or bandwidth, can reach diverse and large audiences at the same speed as businesses or organizations can. The implications are far reaching both for individual writers and for society as a whole. For the first time in human history, culture becomes, in Benkler's (2006) words, 'writable' by the masses, with digital network technologies providing instant publishing opportunities beyond corporate or government-controlled cultural production. Accordingly, writers now also have access to, can draw on, and engage multiple audiences or even coauthors representing more diverse perspectives, and they can produce writing and participate in collaborative initiatives—from knowledge making in such collaborative enterprises as Wikipedia to online activism, without access to a publishing house or broadcasting opportunities controlled by a media conglomerate. Most importantly, as Benkler (2006) points out, digital network technologies have enabled individuals to 'monitor and disrupt the use of mass-media power, as well as organize for political action', and they have allowed individuals to create 'political salience for matters of public interest' (p. 220).

This aspect of the materialities of digital writing spaces has been enabled by a particular design of network technologies—that of packet switching guided by a principle called 'net neutrality' (Bailey, 2006; Benkler, 2006; Geist, 2008; Trans-Atlantic Consumer Dialog, 2008). Packets are the small pieces of digital information into which e-mails and other information travelling through digital networks are broken down to be reassembled at their point of destination. According to the principle of net neutrality, the flow of these packets in the network was designed in such a way that they would all be treated equally in the sense that they would be sent via the most efficient routes to their destination computer. This was true regardless of what the information in these packets was and independent of how much money someone paid, a principle according to which nobody's packets were to be blocked, slowed, accelerated, or otherwise shaped (Bailey, 2006; Benkler, 2006; Geist, 2008; Trans-Atlantic Consumer Dialog, 2008).

As a critical perspective of technologies as scenes of social struggle would suggest, this fundamental principle of emerging digital materialities of writing is being contested. Internet Service Providers (ISPs) in numerous countries have begun to change the principle of net neutrality in favour of what they call 'traffic shaping' (Bailey, 2006; Benkler, 2006; Geist, 2008; Trans-Atlantic Consumer Dialog, 2008). Traffic shaping software makes it possible for ISPs to slow packets such as those of file sharing or internet telephony services that might compete with their own fee-based services (Geist, 2006), or to block access to the website of union workers during a labour dispute (Geist, 2006). In addition to advancing the interests and services of ISPs, traffic shaping also has considerable commercial profit potential for network providers if, for example, large companies would need to outbid each other for whose site would be more easily accessible on a given network. At the same time, access to blogs or e-mails by citizens and activists, and others with limited financial resources, may be slowed down considerably, ultimately reshaping digital networking technologies and thus the materialities of digital writing spaces back into established largely centralized and controlled social orders—here in the form of a two-tiered internet.

Traffic shaping software illustrates the legislative or reordering nature of technology very visibly. If network providers are allowed the power to determine what will be accessible and in what ways, the implications for writing as well as for the kinds of societies that will be possible are more than dramatic. Traffic shaping would seriously stifle citizen participation in democratic deliberation and social activism on the web. It would also control and reduce the access writers have to existing knowledge and cultural production to critique, to continue building and innovating, and to advance knowledge. Functioning

as a silent legislator, traffic shaping software, along with legislative inaction in many countries (Trans-Atlantic Consumer Dialog, 2008), is the equivalent of legislated censorship such as that frequently reported in countries such as China or Iran. The difference is, however, that such traditional legislation is subject to much debate in the media, while the legislative function of digital technologies in the interests of certain groups remains silent, with the shift toward traffic shaping having been rated as the most underreported, but significant 2007 news item by Project Censored (2007).

Although these forms of access encoded into the design of digital network technologies have received less attention by writing development researchers, for students, teachers, and researchers of writing, much depends on how the struggle over this aspect of emerging digital materialities of writing—net neutrality—is going to play out: It will determine what kinds of voices and resources writers will be able to access, draw on, and engage with in their writing, and the extent to which writers can build on existing knowledge and culture for learning, knowledge-making, and innovation. As such, this struggle is also a primary indication of how contested emerging digital materialities of writing are and how deeply implicated these materialities are in how participatory and democratic societies will be. Most importantly, perhaps, the example of traffic shaping software as a silent legislator regulating digital materialities of writing, shows that technologies—and therefore the materialities of the writing spaces students, teachers, citizens, and others inhabit—are not neutral or somehow necessarily predetermined, but rather reflect competing interests and values in a larger social struggle over control of these materialities. While issues of access encoded in materialities of digital networks are perhaps the most central large-scale struggle over the digital materialities of writing, these questions are closely linked to another important struggle—that over questions of intellectual property and sharing.

THE STRUGGLE OVER INTELLECTUAL PROPERTY AND SHARING IN DIGITAL ENVIRONMENTS

Whether writing collaboratively or individually, writers depend on the ability to draw on, critique, and build on each other's work to create new knowledge, cultural products, and innovation (e.g., Benkler, 2006; Howard, 1999; 2007; Lessig, 2004, 2006; Litman, 2001; Porter and DeVoss, 2006). As they generate ideas through inherently social processes of invention (e.g., Bruffee, 1984; Brandt, 1990; DeVoss and Porter, 2006; Howard, 1999, 2007; Lauer, 2004; LeFevre, 1987; Lunsford, 1999; Lunsford and West, 1996; Porter, 1998; Porter and DeVoss, 2006) or shape their work through other inherently social writing processes, for instance in producing a multimedia presentation, writers must be able to draw on and share text, music, image, or video files. The processes, practices, and regulations governing the ownership of files, the ease with which they can be shared, and the ease with which they can be accessed are questioned and changed dramatically by emerging materialities of writing in digital environments, compared to those in print environments.

Most importantly, print materialities made it difficult for writers to publish and distribute their work widely and thus gave rise to industries whose business models evolved around the packaging, distribution, sale, and marketing of knowledge and cultural products, for example, in the form of journals, books, CDs, or DVDs. These industries depended on the materialities of print, specifically on the ways in which these materialities constrained the copying and distribution of files, along with regulation in the form of copyright legislation, to secure exclusive rights to the distribution of these products, with minimal exceptions for so-called fair use or fair dealing (Courant-Rife, 2007) in such products for the purpose of learning, cultural critique, and innovation. The materialities of writing in digital environments,

however, undermine such print-based business models by allowing for easy copying, sharing, publishing, and distribution of files (e.g., Bazerman, 2007; Benkler, 2006; DeVoss and Porter, 2006; Lessig, 2004; 2006; Litman, 2001). In Benkler's (2006) words, digital network technologies 'make some behaviours [here the business models of publishing rooted in print materialities] obsolete by increasing the efficacy of directly competitive strategies [here the ease of sharing and distributing files enabled by digital technologies]' (p. 18).

On the one hand, these changed materialities of writing offer new opportunities for writers to research existing work, access files, compare and engage diverse perspectives, consider and build on more work than ever possible before, and therefore ultimately to have at their disposal previously unimagined resources for knowledge-making, cultural production, innovation, and engagement in public discourse and deliberation. In particular, so-called peer-to-peer file sharing software and services, such as Napster, Grokster, BitTorrent, Gnutella, KaZaA, and many others have provided writers with easy ways to share, access, and trade each other's files on a massive, unlimited scale (Benkler, 2006; DeVoss and Porter, 2006; Geist, 2005; Lessig, 2004, 2006; Logie, 2003, 2007; Selber, 2006).

By facilitating access to such a multitude of work as well by facilitating networked interaction, this aspect of the emerging materialities of writing in digital environments has also given rise to new ways of writing— and new relationships between writers and readers, with authorship as more 'distributed and shared' (Porter and DeVoss, 2006) and boundaries between writers and readers blurring. DeVoss and Porter (2006), for example, see the rise and struggle over Napster as a sign of what they call a 'new "digital ethic" of text use and file distribution that runs counter to the usual expectations that have governed the sharing and use of print texts' (p. 179). This new digital ethic, they argue, shapes how students interact with texts—digital, print, or otherwise—and how they understand the contexts in which they write and the practices that constitute these contexts. The new digital ethic, as DeVoss and Porter emphasize, therefore, also requires attention to pedagogies and policies, such as plagiarism policies, which largely emerged around print materialities with their specific socioeconomic practices, regulations, and orders designed to privilege intellectual property for profitable distribution over sharing and practices of fair use and fair dealing.

As Howard (1999, 2007) has shown, writing policies, especially plagiarism policies, are rooted in the development of intellectual property practices and regulations in the eighteenth century that favoured the economic interests of emerging publishers and booksellers in intellectual property opportunities enabled by the printing press. As such, plagiarism policies tend to reflect Romantic notions of originality and authorship, imagining writers as lone original creative geniuses devoid of any intertextual embeddness and somehow immune to the deeply social nature of invention (e.g., DeVoss and Porter, 2006; Howard, 1999, 2007; Lunsford, 1999; Porter, 1998). Rarely does institutional understanding and regulation of writing consider the increasingly shared textual practices that characterize digital materialities of writing, which allow 'both readers and writers ... ready access to the same texts' (Howard, 2007: 5), let alone the new digital ethic of file sharing that DeVoss and Porter (2006) describe.

The ease and new ethic of sharing in digital environments has also given rise to different forms of writing such as remixes or assemblages (e.g., DeVoss and Porter, 2006; Porter and DeVoss, 2006; Johnson-Eilola, 2005; Johnson-Eilola and Selber, 2007) similar to practices of remixing in music, architecture, and popular culture (Johnson-Eilola, 2005). Remixing, according to Porter and DeVoss (2006), for example, 'is how individual writers and communities build common values; it is how composers achieve persuasive, creative, and parodic effects'.

Similarly, Selber and Johnson-Eilola (2007) emphasize an understanding of digital texts as assemblages, which they define as 'texts built primarily and explicitly from existing texts in order to solve a writing or communication problem in a new context' (p. 381). These assemblages, the authors emphasize, are not merely unoriginal derivatives of previous work; hence, they should not be valued less than traditional print-based texts with particular print-based forms of citation and quotation usage. However, remixes and assemblages often run into policies such as plagiarism policies rooted in print materialities and designed to reinforce related socioeconomic practices of text usage and intellectual property practices (e.g., Howard, 1999; 2007, Porter and DeVoss, 2006; Selber and Johnson-Eilola, 2007).

Again, as a critical understanding of technologies suggests, this aspect of emerging digital materialities of writing is highly contested, not only by attribution practices and policies rooted in print-based intellectual property practices of academic institutions, but also especially by industries whose business models have traditionally evolved around the materialities of print and their regulation in support of such business models (Benkler, 2006; DeVoss and Porter, 2006; Willinsky, 2006; Lessig, 2004, 2006; Litman, 2001; Logie, 2006). To protect their established business models, these industries have worked to reshape emerging materialities of writing in digital environments in numerous ways. For example, they have successfully lobbied for international treaties, such as the World Trade Organization agreement on Trade-Related Aspects of Intellectual Property Rights (TRIPS) and treaties by the United Nation's World Intellectual Property Organization (WIPO), as well as national legislation to pursue their interests in reshaping the use, design, and regulation of digital environments in the interests of their established print-based business models (Benkler, 2006; Courant-Rife, 2007; Lessig, 2004, 2006; Litman, 2001; Logie, 2006; Murray, 2005; Reyman, 2006); filed thousands of lawsuits against providers and users of file sharing software and services as well as against individuals and universities to outlaw, close down, or co-opt file-sharing services and to claim multibillion dollar damages from individuals and institutions (e.g., Benkler, 2006; DeVoss and Porter, 2006; Lessig, 2004, 2006); launched massive so-called education campaigns to criminalize the file-sharing practices of tens of millions of citizens, including legitimate file sharing practices, such as sampling of files, the sharing of files that are out of print, or the sharing of files that are in the public domain and are no longer restricted by copyright (Geist, 2005; Lessig, 2006); contracted with private file-sharing investigation companies; technically attacked file sharing sites with so-called decoy or fake files, spoofing software to misdirect file sharers, interdiction to prevent access to files, or swarming to spoil or slow downloads (e.g., MediaSentry and MediaDefender); and reshaped digital technologies by means of so-called digital rights management software (DRM) designed to control or lock down files—software these industries have also successfully lobbied to have legally protected against circumvention by users (Bailey, 2006; Benkler, 2006; Lessig, 2004, 2006; Litman, 2001).

These struggles over this aspect of the materialities of writing in digital environments—the ease of copying and sharing—have been financially and discursively very intense, with billions of dollars invested in protecting and expanding established business models rooted in print-based materialities of knowledge and cultural production. This aspect of emerging digital materialities of writing has also been the most widely studied by writing development researchers for their implications for writing development. For example, researchers have examined the need for emphasizing and teaching an ethic of fair use (Porter and DeVoss; 2006; DeVoss and Porter, 2006; Courant-Rife, 2007); the need for reconsidering policies governing writing, specifically institutional plagiarism policies (e.g., Selber and Johnson-Eilola, 2007; De-Voss and Porter,

2006; Howard, 1999, 2007; Marsh, 2004; Valentine, 2006), or the need for paying attention to technology legislation and its implications for the ways in which teachers and students can access and share materials for learning in online classes (e.g., Logie, 2006; Reyman, 2006). Hence, only one example, that of DRM software, may suffice here to illustrate the ways in which established print-based socioeconomic practices of regulating ownership and sharing, including print-based business models of publication and content distribution, are not only reinforced through legislation, but also directly reinscribed into the digital code as 'silent legislator' and thus into the materialities of writing in digital environments.

Digital Rights Management (DRM) software refers to digital mechanisms for monitoring and restricting access to digital files and controlling the rights individuals have in using their legally purchased content, such as an e-book, a movie, CD, MP3 file, or software program after the point of purchase (Bailey, 2006; Benkler, 2006; Lessig, 2006; Litman, 2001). DRM technologies are essentially attempts to reshape emerging digital materialities of writing to constrain their potential for the copying and sharing of files—in other words, to bend digital technologies back into the functionalities of print-based technologies and thus to protect print-based business models. To provide only one example, Adobe e-books software controls how readers can interact with a book, for example, how many pages can be copied or printed within what time frame, whether pages can be copied or printed at all, or whether a book can be read aloud, which is, for example, a vital function for visually impaired readers who need screen reading software to access a book. Often, these digital locks restrict access to works for writers well beyond restrictions imposed by print materalities or print-based legislation, which for example, easily allows a print book to be read aloud. Sometimes, these digital locks even restrict access to works that are in the public domain (Bailey, 2006; Benkler, 2006; Lessig, 2006; Litman, 2001). Similar to traffic shaping software, DRM software functions as a silent legislator regulating what writers and readers can or cannot do, what they can or cannot use. Furthermore, to prevent users from circumventing such digital locks, content industries have successfully lobbied legislators to impose fines and imprisonment (e.g., through the Digital Millennium Copyright Act (1998) in the United States) on those who try to circumvent DRM software.

Ensuring exclusive rights to the distribution of knowledge and cultural products was, of course, the hallmark of publishing business models rooted in print-based materialities not only in the cultural industry, but also in academic publishing, although the production of academic knowledge is often publicly funded. As Willinsky (2005) puts it, print-based business models of academic publishing have been characterized 'by a rather perverse property relation, in which the last investor in the research production chain—consisting of university, researcher, funding agency, and publisher—owns the resulting work outright through a very small investment in relation to the work's overall cost and value' (n. p.). Here again, the materiality of writing in digital environments undermines print-based publishing models, allowing researchers to pursue what Willinsky (2006) calls the principle of open access, the responsibility inherent in research 'to extend the circulation of such work as far as possible and ideally to all who are interested in it and all who might profit by it' (p. 5).

The potential of open-access research to inform the work of policy makers and professionals in education, medicine, and other sectors of the economy worldwide, especially in marginalized and underresourced regions, is unprecedented (Willinsky, 2006; Porter and DeVoss, 2006). Accordingly, some governments, for example, the government of the United States, recently signed into law a bill requiring publications resulting from government funded health care research to be submitted for open access in the PubMed Central online repository (Ratliff, 2008). Like other ways in which digital network technologies question the socioeconomic materialities of writing, the potential for open-access publishing is highly contested in particular by the multibillion dollar academic publishing industry (Dotinga, 2007), which has already hired an aggressive Public Relations company to undermine the open-access movement (Giles, 2007).

For academic writing, then, the way in which the struggle over the materialities of writing in digital environments plays out has particular significance for the extent to which knowledge is accessible not only to students in classrooms, but also for innovation and economic development worldwide. Like the struggle over equal access to digital writing environments, the struggle over ownership, sharing, and open access to knowledge is another important indication of the extent to which the contestation over the shape of digital environments and the kinds of writing practices they will enable or constrain is implicated in the kinds of societies and institutions we will inhabit and what individuals, organizations, and societies will be able to accomplish. Both of these major struggles—over access and ownership—are also intricately related to a third major struggle over emerging materialities of writing in digital environments—that over privacy and surveillance, a struggle whose outcomes are no less consequential for individual writers, teachers, and researchers as well as for societies at large.

THE STRUGGLE OVER PRIVACY AND SURVEILLANCE IN DIGITAL WRITING SPACES

A third and closely related vital battle over the materialities of writing in digital environments rages over the extent to which digital writing spaces are monitored and surveilled—be that to monitor and curtail political dissent, to monitor the use of intellectual property, or for other political or economic purposes (e.g., Agre and Rotenberg, 1998; Etzioni, 2000; George, 2004; Gurak, 1997; Lessig, 2005, 2006; Markel, 2005; Solove, 2004; Solove and Rotenberg, 2003; Starke-Meyerring and Gurak, 2007; Starke-Meyerring, Burk, and Gurak, 2004). Although questions of privacy and surveillance in digital writing spaces have received considerably less attention from writing development researchers than have questions of intellectual property, the struggles over privacy and surveillance are intimately related to those over access, intellectual property, and sharing. On the one hand, the reshaping of digital network technologies into large distributed surveillance spaces accompanies the fundamental shifts toward a decentralized nature of communication outside previous government and corporate media control. Given the increased space for dissenting voices to emerge and organize, the surge in digital surveillance can be likened to the surge in censorship, control, and other disciplinary mechanisms described by Eisenstein (1979) in conjunction with the printing press. Moreover, much surveillance is linked to the battle over ownership and sharing of what used to be tightly controlled intellectual property, with surveillance of intellectual property usage playing a central role in DRM and other property control strategies.

Attention to issues of privacy and surveillance is much needed in writing development research, however, because emerging materialities of writing in digital environments fundamentally change the extent to which writing and social interactions become subject to surveillance. More than ever before, the interactions of writers as well as their written products become personal data, while at the same time, writers are losing their rights to control their personal data—to control who can access, manipulate, mix, and match it under what conditions, for what purpose, and for whose benefit. In contrast to writing in print-based environments or even to interaction through other communication technologies such as telephones, emerging materialities of writing in digital environments have been shaped dramatically to facilitate massive surveillance with significant consequences for individuals, organizations, and society as a whole (e.g., Starke-Meyerring and Gurak, 2007; Starke-Meyerring, Burk, and Gurak, 2004).

First, data can now be shared, copied, searched, mined, mixed, matched, aggregated, or manipulated in previously unknown ways at unprecedented speeds for use and sale worldwide (Agre and Rotenberg, 1998; Etzioni, 2000; George, 2004; Gurak, 1997; Lessig, 2005, 2006; Markel, 2005; Starke-Meyerring and Gurak, 2007; Starke-Meyerring, Burk, and Gurak, 2004), resulting in multiple digital compilations of a writer's persona (Solove, 2004; Solove and Rotenberg, 2003) or 'digital persona' for different purposes, given the many institutional and business needs for such data. Personal data are of interest, for example, to businesses seeking information about customers—for example, to develop targeted offerings and pricing strategies that discriminate based on the socioeconomic status of customers online—or about employees—for example, to make hiring and promotion decisions. Aside from the usual e-commerce and marketing industries, the insurance industry, for example, also has a great need for personal data to determine risks and insurance rates as has the banking and credit industry to determine mortgage and lending rates. In addition, law enforcement, national security, and other government agencies have similarly strong needs for such data. With Microsoft and Google entering the business of collecting and storing personal medical and DNA data (Kawamoto, 2007), the extent of such data collection promises to be unlimited. In fact, an entire industry has emerged devoted to the lucrative business of collecting, aggregating, matching, mining, and selling personal data to businesses, banks, law enforcement, and government agencies. In short, written interactions and products in digital environments become data with audiences and purposes writers may find difficult to imagine.

Second, digital materialities of writing have been shaped such that written interactions and texts tend to be often difficult to remove by their writers as their access to the servers on which the records of these interactions and texts reside is limited, and digital writing spaces are often designed to make the removal of accounts or texts difficult, which allows for maximum data collection and mining. Lessig (2006) provides the example of Google's Gmail and its e-mail delete button, which allows only for incremental deletion of e-mails, maximizing opportunities for data collection and mining. Likewise, users of social networking sites, such as Facebook, have reported difficulties removing their accounts (Aspan, 2008). Even if users are able to close their accounts and remove their content, 'the Company may retain archived copies' (Facebook, Terms of Use, 15 Nov, 2007). As a result, data can be compiled over time and texts produced by teenage writers can remain accessible to unanticipated readers for many years to come.

Third, digital materialities of writing tend to be designed in such a way that data collection practices remain concealed to writers. Often, digital writing spaces and the policies regulating their use tend make it difficult for writers to realize when and for what purposes their interactions and texts are collected, manipulated, or transferred as data (Agre and Rotenberg, 1998; Etzioni, 2000; George, 2004; Gurak, 1997; Lessig, 2005, 2006; Markel, 2005; Starke-Meyerring and Gurak, 2007; Starke-Meyerring, Burk, and Gurak 2004). The concealed nature of data collection is inscribed in the digital code in the form of cookies, web bugs, spyware, and obscure internet browser options; enticed by ostensibly free offerings in the form of screensavers, cell phone ring tones, e-mail or social networking services; and secured by obscure and tedious privacy policies or terms of use policies, which are designed to serve the interests of maximum data collection (Markel, 2005).

These changed materialities of writing with their increased potential for massive inconspicuous data collection have wide ranging consequences not only for individuals, but also for society as a whole. Mark Poster (1990), for example, labelled digital network technologies a 'superpanopticon', invoking Foucault's (1977) key insight that societies have been moving from predominantly disciplinary control mechanisms to surveillance mechanisms, where the mechanisms of who is collecting data on whom, for

what purpose, under what conditions, and with what legitimation becomes a critical element in power relations. In addition, as Foucault demonstrated persuasively, omnipresent surveillance has important consequences for society as a whole when self-discipline and self-censorship in the face of omnipresent surveillance threaten to stifle public dissent and robust deliberation, which, of course, are vital to democratic decision making. Digital technologies, however, go far beyond Foucault's panopticon. In contrast to the panopticon, they provide decentralized opportunities for inconspicuous, but distributed, networked, and therefore ubiquitous surveillance (Lessig, 2005; Poster, 1990). As a critical perspective of technologies as scenes of social struggle would suggest, though, digital technologies do not simply accidentally support this kind of materiality of writing. Digital technologies do not by necessity enable inconspicuous omnipresent data collection. Instead, many of the data collection technologies that now characterize the internet, such as cookies, for example, were not part of the original design of the internet, but were developed to serve commercial and government interests in data collection (Lessig, 2005). As Bazerman (2007) observes, it is 'large economic stakes along with the complexity, stability and power of ...[existing] social systems' around which technologies tend to be designed or to be 'bent'.

IMPLICATIONS FOR WRITING DEVELOPMENT

Viewed through the lens of critical theories of technology, digital network technologies do not simply provide a new neutral medium into which writing practices simply travel. Rather, these technologies encode, enable, and constrain digital materialities of writing, which in various ways reproduce, compete with, challenge, question, or reshape those of print, along with its regularized and normalized socioeconomic materialities—that is the social practices, modes of production, rules, laws, orders, and expectations that evolved around print materialities. In Benkler's (2006) words, these technologies—digital or print—through their design, use, and regulation, enable and constrain 'who gets to say what to whom, and who decides' (p. 392) as well as under what conditions, and with what consequences to themselves, others, and society as a whole. As such, digital writing spaces are 'scenes of struggle' (Feenberg, 2002), with competing interests vying over their shape and the kinds of socioeconomic materialities that will be enabled or constrained. Each struggle outlined in this chapter illustrates the ways in which the economic interests of incumbent industries invested in print materialities so far have attempted to reshape or regulate digital technologies in ways that maintain and expand established print-based business models, or in the case of net neutrality and privacy, to reshape digital technologies to allow for new ways of ensuring profits, control, and surveillance. The changes in the materialities of writing in digital environments, the contestation surrounding these changes, and their consequences for writers and societies at large suggest at least two important implications for the study and teaching of writing: (1) the need for the active engagement of writing teachers and researchers in the design, use, and regulation of digital writing environments as well as for research attention to the socioeconomic materialities of writing in digital environments, and (2) the need for reconsidering writing pedagogies and policies in educational institutions.

IMPLICATIONS FOR POLICY ENGAGEMENT AND RESEARCH ATTENTION TO THE MATERIALITIES OF WRITING IN DIGITAL ENVIRONMENTS

Researchers and teachers of writing have direct stakes in the outcomes of these struggles over the materialities of writing in digital environments, because these outcomes have significant implications for writing development, e.g., what student writers, citizens, and others will be able to access, build on, what kind of knowledge they will be able to make, to what extent they will be able to participate in cultural production, in social activism, under what conditions, and with what consequences to themselves and society. Most importantly, as the examples of the contested nature of the materialities of writing in digital environments discussed in this chapter illustrate, the struggle over these materialities is deeply implicated in larger social struggles over digital technologies as ways of reordering socioeconomic practices with deep implications for societies—for how democratic, participatory, open, and collaborative they will be.

Not surprisingly, with the materialities of our core practice—writing—suspended between 'civilizational alternatives' (Feenberg, 2002), writing studies researchers have increasingly urged teachers of writing to attend to this political nature of the socioeconomic materialities of writing and to become actively engaged in the deliberation of digital technology design, use, and policy at all levels (e.g., Courant-Rife, 2007; DeVoss, Cushman, and Grabill, 2005; DeVoss and Porter, 2006; Howard, 1999, 2007; Logie, 2006; Moran, 1999; Reyman, 2006; Selber, 2004; Selfe, 1999). The difficulty here is, of course, the ways in which technologies, including writing, as mundane, everyday material systems of getting work done—as seemingly neutral tools or means to an end, remain silent and invisible—we might say, 'hidden in plain view', as do the struggles that unfold over their design, use, and regulation. As Haas (1996) notes, for example, 'it is precisely because technology is such an integral part of writing that it is often overlooked. As is often the case, what is ubiquitous becomes transparent' (p. xi). Moreover, as Feenberg (2002, 2006) has emphasized, the dominant discursive regime of technological instrumentalism—of a simplified view of technologies as mere means to an end—keeps the political nature of technologies hidden. Accordingly, as writing development researchers (e.g., Grabill, 2003; DeVoss, Cushman, and Grabill, 2005; Wysocki, 2004) have stressed, an important task researchers and teachers face is to make their highly contested nature as enabling or constraining social orders visible.

At the same time, to support this critical engagement, writing development researchers must increasingly pay attention to the socioeconomic materialities of writing (e.g., DeVoss, Cushman, and Grabill, 2005; DeVoss and Porter, 2006; Haas, 1996; Horner, 2001; Selber, 2006). As print materialities of writing had settled into a somewhat stabilized equilibrium, with fewer opportunities for the constant recoding that characterizes digital technologies, writing development research has tended to focus less on those materialities and the ways in which they enable or constrain socioeconomic materialities, but has instead focused more on students, teachers, and classrooms. As Selber (2006) notes, for example, much research on writing and technologies has 'tended to focus more on students, teachers, classrooms, and writing programs and less on the larger contexts within which people and programs are situated' (p. 2). While issues of intellectual property, fair use, and file sharing have already received considerable attention, issues of how access and privacy or surveillance are inscribed in the code and the implications these materialities have for writing and writing development have received less attention. Yet, in all of these areas, writing teachers need more research analysing the competing interests at work in shaping such spaces and examining the consequences particular designs, pedagogies, and policies for writing in digital environments, for example, such as mechanisms of access or surveillance encoded in digital technologies, plagiarism policies, or the use of plagiarism policing software, have for writers, the work they do, their ability to learn and develop as writers, and their

participation in democratic deliberation and decision making.

IMPLICATIONS FOR RECONSIDERING WRITING PEDAGOGIES AND POLICIES

As the analysis of key struggles over digital network technologies as emerging materialities of writing has shown, these technologies are never neutral, but rather contested scenes of struggle over how established socioeconomic materialities of writing—social orders, practices, and hierarchies are to be reproduced, challenged, or questioned. Writing development in digital environments, therefore, calls for what we might term pedagogies for critical engagement— pedagogies that allow students to critically analyse and engage in the design, use, and regulation of the digital writing spaces they inhabit (e.g., Bazerman, 2007; Devoss, Cushman, and Grabill, 2005; DeVoss and Porter, 2006; Hawisher and Selfe, 1999; Hicks and Grabill, 2005; Selber, 2004; Wysocki et al., 2004). Most importantly, pedagogies for critical engagement in digital writing spaces call for critical analysis and participation as well as for the reconsideration of established writing pedagogies, policies, and infrastructures from a critical perspective.

Fostering critical analysis and engagement in digital writing spaces

First, perhaps most importantly, pedagogies for critical engagement create opportunities in writing classes for critical analysis of the writing spaces in which the students participate. As Bazerman (2007) urges, 'Beyond providing students with facility in design tools and multimedia rhetoric, teachers of rhetoric need to provide students with analytic tools to understand the changing locations and informational richness of encounters they will be creating, the larger knowledge, social, and activity environments that surround the particular encounter and activity spaces they are working in, and the ways in which communications will mediate transformed work, citizenship, and personal relations' (n. p). Critical analysis here does not mean 'saying negative things' or uncovering 'hidden truths'. Rather, drawing on critical theories of technologies (e.g., Benkler, 2006; Feenberg, 2002; Winner, 1986; Longford, 2005) as well as discourse (e.g., Fairclough, 2003; Coe et al., 2002; Lemke, 1995; Paré, 2002; 2005), critical analysis involves asking critical questions about the design, use, and regulation of digital writing spaces similar to the kinds of questions students learn to ask about discourse. For example, what rhetorical work is to be accomplished in a given writing space, for whom, how, and why? Who sponsors a digital writing space (Brandt and Clinton, 2002) and why? Whose interests are being enabled or constrained and how by the design, use, and regulation of the space? How are these interests advanced or marginalized discursively? What social practices and orders are being reproduced, challenged, or contested? For instance, how are practices of access, intellectual property, and surveillance encoded, regulated, and advanced discursively in digital writing spaces as well as in the technologies through which students interact with them (e.g., browser software, institutional network services, and ISP networks)? What opportunities for participation in shaping the design, use, or regulation of digital writing spaces are available to writers or can be mobilized?

To be sure, students are deeply and, in many cases, critically engaged in the immediate digital writing spaces in which they participate. For example, students in Facebook quickly mobilized free online petition software and set up a protest blog called 'savefacebook.org' when the company introduced blatantly privacy-invading features, such as minifeeds or beacons that advertised

their activities in the site (through minifeeds) as well as all their purchases in partnering e-commerce sites (through so-called beacons) to all their 'friends' (Calore, 2006; Story and Stone, 2007). Nevertheless, examining and engaging in the politics over the socioeconomic materialities of a digital writing space, especially from a critical perspective—that is, a perspective that examines these spaces in the context of larger socioeconomic power struggles—is a more challenging task. For example, discussions around the personal and societal implications of business models that require site participants to grant a company such as Facebook 'an irrevocable, perpetual, nonexclusive, transferable, fully paid, worldwide license (with the right to sublicense) to use, copy, publicly perform, publicly display, reformat, translate, excerpt (in whole or in part), and distribute such User Content for any purpose, commercial, advertising, or otherwise' (Facebook, Terms of Use, 15 Nov, 2007) remain rare as does engagement in larger (national or international) debates and struggles for access, fair use and sharing, or privacy. No doubt, critical awareness of and engagement in these struggles is a challenging task, especially as writers transition from more stabilized print materialities to the constantly contested materialities of digital writing environments, which are, after all, 'hidden in plain view'. As Longford (2005) notes, 'the politics of [technology] has seldom hit the radar screens of average internet users and citizens' (p. 82).

Furthermore, as writing development researchers have stressed, pedagogies for writing in digital environments must not stop with analysis, but must also support students in developing the literacy practices needed to engage productively in robust deliberation in digital environments in order to participate in shaping the design, use, and regulation of digital writing spaces and the emerging social practices, orders, and interests these enable, constrain, question, challenge, or reproduce. Selber (2004), for example, advocates a heuristic for thinking about digital literacies as functional, critical, and rhetorical (productive). Similarly, Wysocki (2004), emphasizes that like analysis, 'the production—crafting— of new media texts is equally important, too, for it is how we produce and can see our own possible positions within the broad and materially different communication channels where we all now move and work with others' (p. 22).

Rooted in a critical understanding of digital writing spaces as scenes of struggle over alternative social orders, pedagogies for critical engagement, then, can also help teachers and program directors reconsider the kinds of graduates they envision from their courses and programs. Will these be passive, docile users, 'skilled in the use of technologies', participating in embattled terrain, unknowingly facilitating interests they may not even be aware of, or will they be able to critically assess the ways in which digital network technologies reproduce, challenge, or question established orders and contribute to the democratic deliberation, shaping, and regulation of these technologies and the socio-economic materialities they enable or constrain?

Reconsidering writing pedagogies, policies, and infrastructures from critical perspectives of digital technologies as emerging materialities of writing

A critical understanding of digital technologies as emerging contested materialities of writing that compete with established materialities of print calls for writing pedagogies and policies that help students critically assess, negotiate, and engage in these competing socioeconomic materialities of writing. Working from a critical perspective, teachers and researchers of writing ask to what extent established pedagogies and institutional policies regulating writing reproduce the values, practices, assumptions, or notions of authorship rooted in print materialities, possibly ignoring the ways in which

digital materialities enable, constrain, or challenge pedagogies rooted in assumptions about writing and authorship shaped by print materialities. In other words, what kinds of materialities of writing are being privileged or marginalized in writing pedagogies and policies? In whose interests? To what extent do established pedagogies and policies simply reinforce and discipline students into established practices, with students caught between alternative materialities? Perhaps most importantly, what kinds of resources are available to support teachers and students of writing in examining and negotiating the complex ways in which writing, along with the social orders it assembles, is enabled or constrained in different materialities?

To draw on one of the news examples mentioned at the beginning of the chapter, that of banning Wikipedia from assignments, pedagogies for critical engagement here would, for example, ask what reading and writing practices rooted in what materialities are assumed and valued? Why would, for example, the history of a contested region or figure be valued more if created by a single author (or a small group of authors) with particular epistemological and ideological commitments and verified by a few peer reviewers with perhaps similar commitments? Why would that history be valued less if it reflected the negotiated diverse epistemological commitments and knowledge practices of Wikipedia participants with diverse lived experiences? What might students learn by comparing the histories, and their underlying epistemologies, produced in socioeconomic materialities of writing invested in print (e.g., here in the form of peer review) and those of a wiki space? What are the consequences for writing development of simply reinforcing the practices of established materialities and banning those of emerging materialities?

Similarly, plagiarism policies require critical scrutiny for the extent to which they reproduce and reinforce established practices and assumptions rooted in print materialities, such as Romantic notions of authorship as solitary genius and restrictions on sharing and knowledge production established in print materialities (Howard, 1999, 2007). Unfortunately, as writing development researchers and specifically the CCCC Caucus on Intellectual Property (2008) have noted, at a time when resources for writing development become a high-stakes necessity to support writing teachers, students, and institutions in negotiating competing materialities of writing and to ensure the active participation of students as citizens and professionals in the shaping of these materialities, large amounts of such resources have been spent on commercial solutions, such as plagiarism policing services, to monitor and discipline students back into established practices and orders of print materialities, with considerable damage to writing development. As Howard (2008) notes, for example, such services do not work to do what they purport to do as they do not attend to the complexity of what is referred to as plagiarism, such as the local, disciplinary, or institutional situatedness of citation and other intertextual practices; practices of paraphrasing without citation; or the construction of citations. More importantly, Howard notes that these services needlessly criminalize students as inherently guilty of academic dishonesty and commercialize their work as ongoing resources for the profits of such services, contributing to a learning atmosphere that puts trust between students and teachers, and thus writing development, at risk.

In contrast, pedagogies for critical engagement would see institutions, teachers, and students working together to reconsider writing policies in light of competing materialities of writing. Rather than simply reinforcing one set of materialities over the other and disciplining students into adhering and valuing the practices associated with one over the other, pedagogies for critical engagement would examine the ways in which different materialities enable or constrain writing as a knowledge making practice, with consequences for who is included and who can say what to whom.

Simply reinforcing one over the other deprives students of vital opportunities for critical engagement. Instead, considering writing in digital environments from a critical perspective, institutions would put writing pedagogies first and provide students and teachers with appropriate development resources for negotiating and participating in this revolutionary shift in the materialities of writing.

Accordingly, pedagogies for critical engagement also entail what DeVoss, Cushman, and Grabill (2005) call a 'productive and activist understanding of infrastructure' (p. 22). As the authors argue, teachers of writing in digital environments are uniquely positioned to make vital contributions to the deliberation and shaping of infrastructures for writing in digital environments at their institutions. Writing teachers, the authors note, have a vital role to play in shaping 'rhetorically, technically, and institutionally— what is possible for our students to write and learn' (p. 37).

CONCLUSION

To return to the guiding question posed at the beginning of this chapter—how materalities of writing change in digital environments, what consequences these changes have for how writing works to organize human activity, and what implications we might draw for writing development, this chapter has emphasized the important role of a critical perspective in studying and teaching writing in digital environments. Viewed through the lens of critical theories of technology, digital writing spaces are 'scenes of struggle' (Feenberg, 2002), with competing interests vying over their shape and the kinds of socioeconomic materialities that will be reproduced, challenged, or questioned. The outcomes of these struggles have far-reaching consequences not only for individual students, teachers, and researchers of writing, but also for institutions, organizations, and societies at large. Accordingly, as the chapter has shown, as they write and teach writing in digital environments, what students, teachers, and researchers of writing participate in—knowingly or unknowingly—is nothing less than a historic struggle over the shape of the societies, institutions, and communities we will inhabit. Teachers and researchers of writing find themselves at the forefront of these struggles as they help writers develop the critical acumen to analyse what is at stake and the technological-rhetorical sophistication to participate in the shaping and regulation of the digital writing spaces, communities, and societies we will inhabit.

NOTES

1   I use the term 'materialities' in the plural sense to reflect the many ways in which writing is material, for as Horner (2001) alerts us, 'no representation of teaching or writing can exhaust the full range of their materiality' (xix). At the same time, the pluralized term reflects the diverse and locally situated nature of these materialities in particular writing spaces, societies, institutions, classrooms, and more, as well as their situatedness within complex networks of local and global policy interactions. The pluralized term is, therefore, meant to reflect the complex ways in which the particular shape and constellations of these materialities are locally situated, assembled, and negotiated—shaping and being shaped by diverse locally situated and globally networked policies.

REFERENCES

Agre, P. and Rotenberg, M. (eds) (1998) *Technology and Privacy: The New Landscape*, Cambridge, MA: MIT Press.

Artemeva, N and Freedman, A. (eds) (2006) *Rhetorical Genre Studies and Beyond*, Winnipeg: Inkshed Publications.

Aspan, M. (2008, February 11) 'How sticky is membership on Facebook? Just try breaking free', *New York Times*, Retrieved 11 February, 2008, from http://www.nytimes.com/2008/02/11/technology/11facebook.html.

Bailey, C. (2006) 'Strong copyright + DRM + weak net neutrality = digital dystopia?', *Information Technology and Libraries*, 25 (3): 116–127. Retrieved 20 March, 2007, from http://www.digital-scholarship.org/cwb/ital25n3.pdf.

Bazerman, C. (2007) 'Electrons are cheap, society is dear', Keynote address delivered at the Conference of the Canadian Association of Teachers of Technical Writing. Saskatoon, SK, May 27–29.

Bazerman, C. and Prior, P. (eds) (2004) *What Writing Does and How it Does it: An Introduction to Analyzing Texts and Textual Practices*, Mahwah, NJ: Erlbaum.

Bazerman, C. and Prior, P. (2005) 'Genre, disciplinarity, interdisciplinarity', in J. Green, R. Beach , M. Kamil, and T. Shanahan (eds), *Multidisciplinary Perspectives on Literacy Research* (second edn.), Cresskill, NJ: Hampton Press. pp.133–178. Retrieved 20 August, 2007, from http://www.education. ucsb. edu/%7Ebazerman/chapters/34.genrewith prior.html.

Benkler, Y. (2006) *The Wealth of Networks: How Social Production Transforms Markets and Freedom*, New Haven: Yale University Press.

Brandt, D. (1990) *Literacy as Involvement: The Acts of Writers, Readers and Texts,* Carbondale, IL: Southern Illinois University Press.

Brandt, D. and Clinton, K. (2002) 'Limits of the local: Expanding perspectives on literacy as a social practice', *Journal of Literacy Research*, 34: 337–356.

Bruffee, K. (1984) 'Collaborative learning and the conversation of mankind', *College English*, 46: 635–652.

Calore, M. (2006, September 6) 'Privacy fears shock Facebook', *Wired News*, Retrieved 6 September, 2006, from http://www.wired.com/news/culture/0,71739-0.html.

CBC News (2004) 'McGill student wins fight over anti-cheating website', *CBC News*. Retrieved 16 January, 2004 http://www.cbc.ca/news/story/2004/01/16/mcgill_turnitin030116.html.

CCCC-IP Caucus (2008) CCCC-IP Caucus recommendations regarding academic integrity and the use of plagiarism detection services. Retrieved 3 April, 2008, from http://ccccip.org/cccc-ip-caucus-plagiarism-detection-serv.

Coe, R., Lingard, L., and Teslenko, T. (eds) (2002) *The Rhetoric and Ideology of Genre*, Cresskill, NJ: Hampton.

Cohen, N. (2007, February 21) 'A History department bans citing Wikipedia as a research source', *New York Times*, Retrieved 21 February, 2007, from http://www.nytimes.com/2007/02/21/education/21wikipedia.html.

Courant-Rife, M. (2007) 'The fair use doctrine: History, application, and implications for (new media) writing teachers', *Computers and Composition*, 24: 154–178.

Devitt, A.J. (2004) *Writing Genres*, Carbondale, IL: Southern Illinois University Press.

Devitt, A., Bawarshi, A., and Reiff, M.J. (2003) 'Materiality and genre in the study of discourse communities', *College English*, 65: 541–558.

DeVoss, D. and Porter, J. (2006) 'Why Napster matters to writing: Filesharing as a new ethic of digital delivery', *Computers and Composition*, 23: 178–210.

DeVoss, D., Cushman, E., and Grabill, J. (2005) 'Infrastructure and composing: The *when* of newmedia writing', *College Composition and Communication*, 57(1): 14–44.

Dotinga, R. (2007, March 14) 'Open access launches journal wars', *Wired News*, Retrieved 14 March, 2007 from http://www.wired.com/news/technology/medtech/0,72704-0.html.

Eisenstein, E.L. (1979) *The Printing Press as an Agent of Social Change: Communications and Cultural Transformations in Early-Modern Europe*, Cambridge: Cambridge University Press.

Etzioni, A. (2000) *The Limits of Privacy*, New York: Basic Books.

Facebook (2007) *Privacy policy*, Version of 6 December, 2007, Retrieved 12 December 2007, from http://www.facebook.com/policy.php.

Facebook (2007) *Terms of use*. Version of Nov 15, 2007. Retrieved 2 December, 2007, from http://www.facebook.com/terms.php.

Fairclough, N. (2003) *Analysing Discourse. Textual Analysis for Social Research*, London: Routledge.

Feenberg, A. (2002) *Transforming Technology: A Critical Theory Revised*, Oxford, UK: Oxford UP.

Feenberg, A. (2006) 'What is a philosophy of technology?' in Jahn R. Dakers (ed.), *Defining Technological Literacy. Towards an Epistemological Framework*, New York: Palgrave. pp.5–16.

Feng, P. and Feenberg, A. (2008) 'Thinking about design: Critical theory of technology and the design process', in P. Kroes, P. Vermaas, A. Light, and S. A. Moore (eds), *Philosophy and Design: From Engineering to Architecture*, Dordrecht, The Netherlands: Springer. pp.105–118.

Foucault. M. (1977) *Discipline and Punish: The Birth of the Prison*, New York: Pantheon.

Geist, M. (2005) Piercing the peer-to-peer myths: An examination of the Canadian experience. First Monday, 10 (4). Retrieved November 30, 2006, from http://www.firstmonday.org/issues/issue10_4/geist/index.html.

Geist, M. (2006) Videotron rekindles fear of a two-tier internet. Retrieved 20 March, 2007, from http://www.michaelgeist.ca/content/view/1515/159.

Geist, M. (2008) 'Network neutrality in Canada', in M. Moll and L.R. Shade (eds), *For Sale to the Highest Bidder: Telecom Policy in Canada*, Ottawa, ON: Canadian Centre for Policy Alternatives. pp.73–82.

George, J. (ed) (2004) *Computers in Society: Privacy, Ethics and the Internet*, New York: Pearson Prentice Hall.

Giles, J. (2007, January 24) 'PR's "pit bull" takes on open access', *Nature*. Retrieved 24 January, 2007, from http://www.nature.com/nature/journal/v445/n7126/full/445347a.html.

Glod, M. (2006, September 22) 'Students rebel against database designed to thwart plagiarists', *Washington Post*, p. A01. Retrieved 22 September, 2006, from http://www.washingtonpost.com/wp-dyn/content/article/2006/09/21/AR2006092101800.html.

Grabill, J. (2003) 'On divides and interfaces: Access, class, and computers', *Computers and Composition*, 20: 455–472.

Grabill, J. (2007) *Writing Community Change: Designing Technologies for Citizen Action*, Cresskill, NJ: Hampton Press.

Gurak, L. (1997) *Persuasion and Privacy in Cyberspace: The Online Protests Over Lotus Marketplace and the Clipper Chip*, New Haven, CT: Yale UP.

Gurak, L. (2001) *Cyberliteracy: Navigating the Internet with Awareness*, New Haven, CT: Yale UP.

Haas, C. (1996) *Writing Technology: Studies on the Materiality of Literacy*, Mahwah, NJ: Erlbaum.

Hawisher, G. and Selfe, C. (eds) (1999) *Passions, Pedagogies, and 21st Century Technologies*, Logan, UT: Utah State University Press.

Hicks, T. and Grabill, J. (2005) 'Multiliteracies meet methods: The case for digital writing in English education', *English Education*, 34(4): 301–311.

Horner, B. (2001) *Terms of Work for Composition: A Materialist Critique*, Albany, NY: SUNY Press.

Howard, R. (1999) *Standing in the Shadow of Giants: Plagiarists, Authors, Collaborators*, Stamford, CT: Ablex.

Howard, R. (2007) 'Understanding "internet plagiarism"', *Computers and Composition*, 24, 3–15.

Howard, R. (2008) 'Expert witness report', *Blog posting*, 28 March, 2008. Retrieved 2 April, 2008, from http://rmoorehoward.blogspot.com/2008/03/expert-witness-report.html.

Johnson-Eilola, J. (2005) *Datacloud: Toward a New Theory of Online Work*, Creskill, NJ: Hampton Press.

Johnson-Eilola, J. and Selber, S. (2007) 'Plagiarism, originality, assemblage', *Computers and Composition*, 24: 375–403.

Kawamoto, D. (2007) Google invests $3.9 million in biotech start-up. *CNET News.com*, May 22, 2007.

Retrieved 2 December, 2007 from http://www.news. com/Google-invests-3.9-million-in-biotech-start-up/ 2100-1014_3-6185860.html.

Knobel, M. (2006) Memes and affinity spaces: Some implications for policy and digital divides in education. *E-Learning*, 3(3), 411-427. Retrieved 20 March, 2007. from http://www.wwwords.co.uk/elea/.

Lauer, J. (2004) *Invention in Rhetoric and Composition*, West Lafayette, IN: Parlor.

LeFevre, K. B. (1987) *Invention as a Social Act*, Carbondale, IL: Southern Illinois UP.

Lemke, J. (1995) *Textual Politics: Discourses and Social Dynamics*, London, UK: Falmer Press.

Lessig, L. (2004) *Free Culture: The Nature and Future of Creativity*, London, UK: Penguin.

Lessig, L. (2005) 'On the internet and the benign invasions of Nineteen Eighty-Four', in A. Gleason, J. Goldsmith, and M. Nussbaum (eds), *On Nineteen Eighty-Four: Orwell and our Future*, Princeton: Princeton UP. pp.183–212.

Lessig, L. (2006) *Code Version 2.0*, New York: Basic Books.

Litman, J. (2001) *Digital Copyright*, Amherst, NY: Prometheus Books.

Logie, J. (2003) 'A copyright cold war? The polarized rhetoric of the peer-to-peer debates', *First Monday*, 8(7). Retrieved 20 March, 2007, from http://www.firstmonday.org/Issues/issue8_7/logie.

Logie, J. (2006) 'Coypright in increasingly digital academic contexts: What it takes', WIDE Research Center 2006 Conference. Retrieved 20 March, 2007, from http://wide.msu.edu/widepapers/Logie-WIDEresponse.pdf/file_view.

Logie, J. (2007) *Peers, Pirates, and Persuasion: Rhetoric in the Peer-to-Peer Debates*, West Lafayette, IN: Parlor Press.

Longford, G. (2005) 'Pedagogies of digital citizenship and the politics of code', *Techné* 9(1): 68–96. Retrieved 30 November, 2006 from http://scholar.lib.vt.edu/ejournals/SPT/v9n1/pdf/longford.pdf.

Lunsford, A. (1999) 'Rhetoric, feminism, and the politics of textual ownership', *College English*, 61(5): 529–544.

Lunsford, A. and West, S. (1996) 'Intellectual property and composition studies', *College Composition and Communication*, 47: 383–411.

Markel, M. (2005) 'The rhetoric of misdirection in corporate privacy-policy statements', *Technical Communication Quarterly*, 14(2): 197–214.

Marsh, B. (2004) 'Turnitin.com and the scriptural enterprise of plagiarism detection', *Computers and Composition*, 21: 427–438.

Moran, Charles (1999) 'Access: The a-word in technology studies?', in G. Hawisher and C. Selfe (1999)

Passions, Pedagogies, and 21st Century Technologies (paragraph 205–220), Logan, UT: Utah State University Press.

Murray, L. (2005) 'Copyright talk: Patterns and pitfalls in Canadian policy discourses,' in M. Geist (ed), *The Public Interest: The Future of Canadian Copyright Law*, Toronto: Irwin. pp.15–40. Retrieved 20 March, 2007, from http://209.171.61.222/PublicInterest/one_1_murray.htm.

Paré, A. (2002) 'Genre and identity: Individuals, institutions, and ideology', in R. Coe, L. Lingard, and T. Teslenko (eds), *The Rhetoric and Ideology of Genre*, Cresskill, NJ: Hampton. pp.57–71.

Paré, A. (2005) 'Texts and power: Toward a critical theory of language' in L. Davies and P. Leonard (eds), *Social Work in a Corporate Era: Practices of Power and Resistance*, Hants, UK: Ashgate. pp.76–90

Porter, J. (1998) *Rhetorical Ethics and Internetworked Writing*, Greenwich: Ablex.

Porter, J., and DeVoss, D. (2006) 'Rethinking plagiarism in the digital age: Remixing as a means for economic development?', WIDE Research Center 2006 Conference. Retrieved 20 March, 2007, from http://www.wide.msu.edu/widepapers/devoss_porter_plagiarism.

Poster, M. (1990) *The Mode of Information: Poststructuralism and Social Context*, Cambridge, UK: Polity Press.

Powell, A. (2007) 'Access(ing), habits, attitudes, and engagements: Re-thinking access as practice', *Computers and Composition*, 24: 16–35.

Project Censored (2007) 'Top 25 Censored Stories for 2007', Retrieved 20 March, 2008, from http://www.projectcensored.org/top-stories/category/y-2007.

Ratliff, C. (2008) 'The National Institutes of Health open access mandate: Public access for public funding in IP Caucus of the CCCC', The CCCC-IP Annual: Top Intellectual Property Developments of 2007. Retrieved 10 April, 2008, from http://ccccip.org/files/TopIP2007Collection_0.pdf.

Reyman, J. (2006) 'Copyright, distance education, and the Teach Act: Implications for teaching writing', *College Composition and Communication*, 58: 30–45.

Schryer, C.F. (1993) 'Records as genre', *Written Communication*, 10: 200–234.

Selber, S. (2004) *Multiliteracies for a Digital Age*, Carbondale, IL: Southern Illinois University Press.

Selber, S. (2006) 'Beyond Napster: Institutional policies and digital economics', WIDE Research Center 2006 Conference. Retrieved 20 March, 2007, from http://www.wide.msu.edu/widepapers/Selber_responsetempl2.pdf/file_view.

Selfe, C. (1999) *Technology and Literacy in the Twenty-First Century: The Perils of not Paying Attention*, Carbondale, IL: Southern Illinois University Press.

Selfe, C. and Hawisher, G. (2004) *Literate Lives in the Information Age: Stories from the United States*, Mahwah, NJ: Lawrence Erlbaum.

Smart, G. (2007) *Writing the Economy: Activity, Genre and Technology in the World of Banking*, London, UK: Equinox.

Solove, D. (2004) *The Digital Person: Technology and Privacy in the Information Age*, New York, UP.

Solove, D. and Rotenberg, M. (2003) *Information Privacy Law*, Aspen Publishers.

Starke-Meyerring, D. (forthcoming) 'Genre, knowledge, and digital code in web-based communities: An integrated theoretical framework for shaping digital discursive spaces', *International Journal of Web-Based Communities*.

Starke-Meyerring, D. and Gurak, L. (2007) 'The internet' in W.G. Staples (ed), *Encyclopedia of Privacy*, Westport, CT: Greenwood. pp.297–310.

Starke-Meyerring, D., Burk, D., and Gurak, L. (2004) 'Americans and internet privacy: A safe Harbor of their own?', in P.E.N. Howard and S. Jones (eds), *Society Online: The Internet in Context,* Thousand Oaks, CA: Sage Publications. pp.275–293

Story, L. and Stone, B. (2007, November 30) 'Facebook users protest online tracking', *New York Times*, Retrieved 30 November, 2007, from http://www.nytimes.com/2007/11/30/technology/30face.html.

Trans-Atlantic Consumer Dialog (2008, March) Resolution on net neutrality. DOC No. INFOSOC 36-08. Retrieved 20 April, 2008, from http://www.publicknowledge.org/pdf/tacd-nn-resolution-200803.pdf.

Valentine, K. (2006) 'Plagiarism as literacy practice: Recognizing and rethinking ethical binaries', *College Composition and Communication*, 58: 89–109.

Willinsky, J. (2005) 'The unacknowledged convergence of open source, open access, and open science', *First Monday*, 10(8). Retrieved 20 August, 2007, from http://www.firstmonday.org/issues/issue10_8/willinsky/index.html.

Willinsky, J. (2006) *The Access Principle: The Case for Open Access to Research and Scholarship*, Cambridge, MA: MIT Press.

Winner, L. (1986) *The Whale and the Reactor: A Search for Limits in an Age of High Technology*, Chicago: University of Chicago Press.

Wysocki, A. F. (2004) 'Opening new media to writing: Opening and justifications', in Wysocki, A. F. Johnson-Eilola, J. Selfe, C. L. and. Sirc G (eds), *Writing New Media: Theory and Applications for Expanding the Teaching of Composition*, Logan, UT: Utah State University Press. pp.1–41.

Wysocki, A.F., Johnson-Eilola, J., Selfe, C., and Sirc, G. (eds) (2004) *Writing New Media: Theory and Applications for Expanding the Teaching of Composition*. Logan, UT: Utah State University Press.

Zuboff, S. (1988) *In the Age of the Smart Machine*, New York: Basic Books.

Hypertext and Writing

Christina Haas and Chad Wickman

This chapter treats recent empirical research on hypertext and writing. Hypertext was defined by whom many take to be its earliest theorizer, Theodor Nelson, thus:

> By 'hypertext', I mean *nonsequential writing*—text that branches and allows choices to the readers, best read at an interactive screen. As popularly conceived, this is a series of text chunks connected by links which offer the reader different pathways. (Nelson, 1981; quoted in Landow, 1992: 4)

More recently, in the glossary to their influential volume, *Remediation: Understanding new media,* Jay David Bolter and Richard Grusin define hypertext as:

> A method of organizing and presenting text in the computer. Textual units of various sizes are presented to the reader in an order that is determined, at least in part, by electronic links that the reader chooses to follow. (1999: 272)

What we find interesting about these definitions is the absence of a *writer*. In Nelson's definition, there is certainly a writer implied in the term 'writing,' but the agency in the sentence is given over to 'text' (which branches and allows) and 'links' (which offer). Equally prominent here is the reader, who takes up choices, carves pathways. The Bolter and Grusin definition is similar in this

way: there is no active agent behind the acts of 'organizing and presenting', and the reader determines the shape of the hypertext (at least in part). Landow draws upon Barthes, Derrida, and Foucault—as well as Nelson and Vannevar Bush—to argue that hypertext is both an enactment of and evidence for a paradigm shift, a blurring of the roles of reader and writer, and a decentring of authority—implicitly, the authority of the author (at least in part).

We are suggesting that the relationship between writer and hypertext is a vexed one, and that reviewing a body of work on 'hypertext and writing' turns out to be more complex—and indeed more interesting—than first imagined. Nevertheless, lest you think we are picking at nits in this interrogation of definitions of hypertext, let us offer two more nits of evidence: A Google Scholar search, conducted in late winter of 2008, using the terms 'writing hypertext' or 'authoring hypertext,' turns up 93 entries. A similar search using the terms 'reading hypertext' or 'using hypertext' results in four times as many (391).

Further, that behemoth of information, the World Wide Web, has—as Sharples (2004) notes—largely 'overtaken' hypertext as an object of study. Indeed, Kirschenbaum calls the Web 'the largest, the most popular, and socially, culturally, and economically speaking, the most *complex* hypertext system in existence' (2000: 121; emphasis in original). In a very real way, the Web and hypertext are one and the same in daily personal and academic life, that is, a worldwide system of linked information that can be used, controlled, managed—putting the world at our fingertips. Yet, those fingertips tend to belong to readers, to retrievers, to surfers—not to active, constructing writers. Of course, wikis, blogs, and personal webpages allow us to create content for the Web, and there are some who make a living creating Web content. However, in the lives of ordinary citizens—a group with whom we identify— the primary way that the Web is used is, well, in the way of a user. (See Dillon [reviewed next] for a discussion of the personal webpage as Internet genre) We do not mean to be putting forward a (mis)conception of reading as a passive, nonconstructive act; indeed, some of Haas' early work studied readers and reading as the construction of meaning (Haas, 1994; Haas and Flower, 1988). However, we do find it worrisome that the Web constructs us as consumers of information, not as writers.

It is for these reasons that we are pleased to be able to review and discuss important work that takes the *creation of hypertext* as its object of analysis. In this chapter, we focus on empirical studies of writing or authoring hypertext; that is, studies of people (primarily students) producing hypertext. The works we detail in the following section are selected; this is by no means an exhaustive review. Our selection criteria were:

- *A focus on writing itself*—pieces in which the object of study was written texts or writing processes; or that the authoring of hypertext was investigated as means of enhancing learning outcomes.
- *Timeliness*—pieces published in the 12-year period, 1996–2008, with one exception: Richard Lehrer's 1993 piece on patterns of hypertext design is also included, based on its ubiquitous presence in many of the studies we reviewed, as well as its methodological richness.

- *Empirically based*—pieces with enough detail to allow us to understand subject selection, context of the study, data sources, method of analysis, and significance of findings. We use the term 'empirical' broadly, meaning research based in systematic observation; the actual studies represent a range of methodologies and can be characterized as descriptive, text-analytic, quasi-experimental, or correlational.
- *Of high import or influence*—pieces that (1) are widely cited in the literature, (2) are conducted with particular care in terms of design and analysis, and (3) stake out new and important territory in writing studies.

Although we did not explicitly select articles to represent an international sample, 10 of the 16 works we treat were conducted by researchers in institutions outside North America, specifically, Austria, Germany, The Netherlands, the Republic of China, and the United Kingdom.

Our chapter is organized in the following way: in the first section, we treat work that examines writing itself, either in an attempt to characterize the resultant artefacts of hypertext writing or to describe the process of creating hypertext documents. We then treat a separate, but equally important, body of work, studies in which the effects of writing hypertext, primarily on learning outcomes, are examined. These research projects explore the educational outcomes that might accrue from having students produce hypertext. In a final section, we present and discuss a graphic synthesis of the studies reviewed and suggest some further avenues for research.

THE NATURE AND SHAPE OF HYPERTEXT WRITING: ARTEFACTS AND PROCESSES

In this section, we review two kinds of studies—studies of the artefacts produced through hypertext writing and studies of the cognitive and social processes utilized in the construction of hypertext writing. The studies in this section use different methods and focus on different objects of analysis, but they all attempt to account for just what this thing called hypertext writing *is*.

Analyses of the artefacts of hypertext writing

Margit Pohl's 1998 study, 'Hypermedia as a Cognitive Tool', was motivated by her observation that students developing hypertext documents do not take full advantage of innovative features for structuring information and by her desire to create grounded guidelines for educational practice. The explicit aim of this primarily descriptive study is to investigate how student writers develop hypertexts, with 'develop' understood as the structuring of information, through the use of links or document design options (distinctive fonts, headings, and white space). Students in Pohl's program (in the Department of Design and Assessment of Technology at Vienna University of Technology) were required to write hypertext documents for all assignments using a hypertext authoring system developed at the same university, an integral feature of which is an overview editor (a branching concept mapping tool).

Pohl collected a sample of 143 hypertexts, comprising a 'representative cross section of all documents created by students'. These hypertexts were analyzed via two sets of categories: one set dealt with document structure as represented in the overview editor, while the other concerned use of screen design and layout. Results indicated that most of the links (85%) in the students' hypertexts were hierarchical and that the types of links included: (1) links between the same term used on two or more nodes (the most frequent), (2) links to explanations of terms (the next most frequent), and (3) links to examples (the least frequent, but still representing about one quarter of the links). In addition, student hypertexts used bold or italic font and indentation or empty lines to signal text structure; they also used chunking (dividing content into small pieces), queuing (arranging content topically) and employing multiple modes (graphics, pictures, and formulas) in the hypertext.

In 'Hypermedia authoring with writing process guidance', Kuo-En Chang, Yao-Ting Sun, and Jie-wan Zheng (2007) also evaluate hypertext artefacts, but theirs is a quasi-experimental comparative study, using a two-way (group and gender) analysis of covariance. The researchers developed a set of writing process guidelines, consisting of questions for each of five subprocesses of writing (e.g., setting the topic, organizing, and reviewing). An experimental group (two intact classrooms of junior high school students) used these guidelines in the construction of hypertext, while a control group (two similar classrooms) composed with a webpage editor and data collection tools, but without process guidance. The researchers found that the experimental group produced better webpages (as determined by three 'experts', two computer teachers and one teacher of Chinese) in content, layout, and structure. Gender differences were also noted, with boys producing hypertexts judged better than those of girls;[1] there were no significant interaction effects.[2]

Gill Deadman (1997) also conducted a comparative study to analyse hypertext artefacts. This is primarily a descriptive study—with copious textual examples—of students' writing produced with or without a hypertext reflective writing framework ('Pupils' reflective writing within a hypermedia framework'). Twenty-four students, aged 14 and 15, engaged in two writing activities; in the first, students wrote with support of a teacher and in the second, with support from a teacher as well as the hypertext framework. The framework here—like the guidelines used in the Chang, et al., study—consisted primarily of teacher-generated questions. A sentence-by-sentence analysis of the reasoning embedded in the documents, conducted by two teachers, showed that 69% of the pupils improved their reasoning, as evidenced in the texts and as judged by two readers.³ Overall, Deadman claims, when students used the hypertext framework, their writing exhibited a move away from pure description toward more analysis.

In 'Genres and the Web', Andrew Dillon and Barbara A. Gushrowski (2000) take a different approach to hypertext artefact analysis. Set within the context of genre studies, these researchers sought not to examine features of hypertexts produced in school contexts, but to explore whether hypertextual webpages might constitute a new genre. Their study is based on a corpus of 100+ personal webpages, defined as noncommercial home pages of individuals, distinct from their personal pages on organization websites. The project had two parts: in the descriptive first part, webpages were located via two home page resources (*The People Place* and *Personal Pages Worldwide*). The researchers identified and tabulated a set of elements common to personal webpages, including email addresses, external links, photos, and brief bios. Many of these elements were hypertextual, meaning that they were linked either within the page or to sources outside the page (e.g., tables of contents, links to external or supporting content.)

In the second part of the study, the researchers created four 'common element' and four 'uncommon element' sample pages, based on elements uncovered in the first part of the study, and distributed them to 57 graduate students in Information Science. Spearman's rank-order correlation revealed a significant correlation ($p = .01$) between users' preferences for webpages and the common elements. The researchers also asked participants to examine the list of common elements (from the first part of the study) and to indicate which they believed *should* be part of a personal home page. A statistically significant positive correlation was found ($p = .01$ by Pearson's product moment correlation) between the elements selected by participants and the elements actually present in the 100 webpages analysed. The authors conclude by noting that the personal home page

may be the first unique digitized written genre, a genre that is characterized by rapid standardization.

Process Analyses of Hypertext Writing

Margit Pohl's interest in the use of concept maps for writing of hypertext documents (reviewed in the preceding section) is carried forward in her 2004 article, with Peter Purgahofer, 'Hypertext writing profiles and visualization.' In this study, a novel method—'moving window analysis' (94)—was used to extract or infer writing processes. Here, visualization refers to concept maps and other features, which allow writers to 'visualize' (and manipulate) the structure of their emerging hypertexts. University students created hypertexts using Darkstar, a hypertext authoring system (created by Purgathofer), which includes both a node editor (to develop and embed content) and an overview editor (to create and manipulate nodes and links). Also built into Darkstar is a monitoring tool, a feature that collects data about author actions in both of the editors. The monitoring tool feature provided input for the moving window analysis, which is essentially the accumulation of vectors of observation based on actions undertaken by the writer (e.g., producing text, moving or deleting nodes, and creating links). These kinds of data, according to the authors, do not reproduce the richness and fullness of the actual writing session, but they do allow for the mapping of author actions, via cluster analysis, into an easy to understand format.

Ninety-five documents (completed by university students as part of their coursework) were analysed in this way, with the activities of *writing* text, *making* nodes and links, *moving* nodes and links, *deleting* nodes and links, and *other* activities (i.e., renaming) as categories of analysis. A cluster analysis of the five categories was conducted to distinguish different 'writing profiles' for hypertext authors, and this analysis revealed five clusters, whose members differed in the amount of time they spent creating content, creating nodes and links, and editing the structure of the hypertext via the overview map. The authors conclude that the overview maps are 'very attractive tools' for users (102), that many students experimented with many of the new and potentially useful aspects of hypertext writing, and that no overall temporal patterns of activity characterize these hypertext documents.

A more conventional methodology for assessing process—think aloud protocols—is used by Shu Ching Yang in 'A dynamic reading-linking-to-writing model for problem-solving within a constructive hypermedia learning environment' (1996). While Yang notes some practical applications of the research for system design and instruction, the primary focus here is theory building, as the author attempts to build a cognitive process account of hypertext writing. Undergraduates created discourse syntheses using the Greek culture database, *Perseus*. Think aloud protocols were collected from five students (with one student completing two for a total of six protocols) as they completed what the author calls 'authentic tasks in an authentic setting' (284)—completing writing assignments in the context of an introductory course on Greek culture—in order to address the question, 'What cognitive process underlies the novice learners' problem solving when using constructive hypermedia applications?' (285). The result, a 'Reading-linking-to-writing' model (RLW) is, the researchers claim, dynamic, recursive, and idiosyncratic and attempts to account for cognitive and metacognitive processes, affective responses, physical operations, and social context, with data for the latter three drawn from observations and posttask interviews. The RLW model contains two sets of interrelated processes, procedural (refining the task, information seeking, and structuring) and systemic (executive control, reasoning, intertextuality, reflexivity, and affective response). A detailed diagram illustrates the interrelationship of these processes and a

table summarizes main activities involved in each set of processes.

In 'Learning to compose hypertext and linear text: Transfer or interference?' (2002), Martine Braaksma and her colleagues also use a think aloud protocol method, but the writing tasks here are constructed by the researchers to answer specific questions about linear and hierarchical construction, specifically what are the similar and disparate processes involved in linear conventional (i.e., linear) and hypertextual (i.e., hierarchical) writing.[4] Participants were 123 Dutch secondary school students, with an average age of 15, characterized as 'good novices' by the researchers. Think aloud protocols were collected as each participant completed four tasks: a simple and a more complex linearization task and a simple and a more complex hierarchical task. For the linearization task, students were given a hierarchical diagram and asked to render it in linear prose; for the hierarchical task, students were given a linear text and asked to construct a hierarchical diagram; order was counterbalanced.[5] The protocol statements were coded using a process-focused set of categories: goal orientation, planning, analysis, pausing, formulating, writing, evaluating, rereading, revising, and meta-analysis. It is noteworthy that the article includes a figure of the quite complex coding scheme, as well as two detailed illustrations of the coding scheme in use.

The findings suggest that hypertext writing and linear writing draw upon the same set of cognitive processes, but that 'metacognitive activities which are known to influence the quality of the written product are stimulated in hypertext writing' (28).

Next, the researchers compared good and weak novices (defined within the study as identifying the standpoint correctly) and found that more planning and more analysis were done by what were termed the stronger novices. The quality of the resultant diagrams or texts (which was, interestingly, defined in the same way as expertise, i.e., as getting the standpoint 'correct') was correlated with the cognitive activities evidenced in the protocols in order to identify relations between 'quality' and specific processes. In addition, the researchers postulate that certain cognitive processes have transfer value, specifically planning, and analysis.

Jason Ranker, in 'Composing across multiple media: A case study of digital video production in a fifth grade classroom' (2008) uses a more descriptive methodology based on field notes, screen shots of hypervideo, and transcribed audio- and video-taped classroom sessions. The focal students, two fifth-grade males, who were cocreating a hypervideo about music and baseball in the Dominican Republic. Ranker observed the boys hypervideo construction over a seven-week period; he also collected and analysed interviews with the students and their teacher over this same period. The article includes examples of coded data to illustrate the analytic method, detailed examples from the boys' work sessions, and copious examples of the hypervideo in process (via screen captures). The composing process for hypervideo in this context was shown to be both interactive (between writers and between writers and media) and nonlinear (as research like that of Braaksma and her colleagues would suggest). The researcher notes that the video editing software created both an external, visual representation of the program and an integrative centre for their work across media—books, their own writing and drawing, and the Web. He concludes that hypermedia composing environments provide writers with a broadened repertoire of resources, as well as a space in which to integrate their individual and joint thinking and meaning making.

HYPERTEXT WRITING AND ITS POTENTIAL TO ENHANCE LEARNING

The studies reviewed in this section take hypertext writing to be a means, not an end. In other words, the researchers examine the potential of hypertext writing to increase learning outcomes, with enhanced learning operationalized in a variety of ways—for example, as increased motivation, more creative thinking, more complex knowledge structures, or greater recall of content knowledge. While they look to different outcomes, the researchers in these studies all treat the act of hypertext writing as a complex practice, one that has potentially important instructional and pedagogical payoffs.

The research of Rainer Bromme and Elmar Stahl (1999, 2001, 2002, 2005; Stahl, et al., 2007) is undergirded by the assumption that hypertext must be understood conceptually as well as empirically. Accordingly, they examine the concept of hypertext through studies of metaphor and extend and refine this conceptual understanding in a series of experiments that examine how instructors can use hypertext to promote student learning. Four specific studies are of relevance and will be discussed here.

Bromme and Stahl's early work (1999) explores how teachers introduce students to the concept of hypertext and how hypertext itself might best be used as a 'cognitive tool,' that is, as an instrument to help learners become aware of and potentially restructure their own cognitive structures (268). This exploratory study, taking place across two half-year terms, lays the groundwork for the authors' later experimental research. Their objective here, however, is to identify which specific metaphors teachers use to introduce hypertext to their students, how those metaphors shape the way students' structure and discuss their hypertext documents, and whether learning effects are influenced by the organization of classroom lessons. Bromme and Stahl attempt to answer these questions, and thus 'obtain indicators pointing to the effect of hypertext production on knowledge about subject matter structures' (271), through classroom observations, analysis of hypertext documents, and learning transfer tests. Findings suggest that teachers in this study used book, computer register, and spatial metaphors to talk about hypertext with their students; the authors also found that the metaphor(s) used by individual instructors shaped the way students structured and discussed their hypertext documents. The spatial metaphor in particular showed promise both for helping students understand hypertext conceptually and for acquiring content knowledge. Bromme and Stahl thus conclude that hypertext writing, if introduced through a spatial metaphor, may help students link their own knowledge structures with those embedded in subject matter, and, in doing so, acquire deeper understandings of hypertext design and content knowledge (278).

Bromme and Stahl (2005; see 2001) build on their classroom-based research through experimental work that examines how metaphors shape students' production of hypertext documents. Their aim in this case is to test whether the process of hypertext writing, what they refer to as 'hypertext construction,' can be used as a 'method for knowledge acquisition' (p. 116). As in previous work (e.g., 2002), Bromme and Stahl suggest that knowledge acquisition and transformation may be facilitated by three features of hypertext as a textual form: nodes (e.g., individually understandable 'text units'), links (e.g., semantic relations between nodes), and multilinear structure (e.g., subject matter structured in a way that anticipates multiple [reader] perspectives). Bromme and Stahl specifically examine two groups of students that receive different introductions to the concept of hypertext: one through a book metaphor and the other through a spatial metaphor. The authors hypothesize about the number of links each group will set, structure of hypertexts produced, pauses during the construction process, verbal statements on the rationale for link setting, statements for hypertext structure, and overall knowledge acquisition. Results suggest that metaphors do shape the way students compose hypertext documents in terms of structure and complexity. Students who were introduced to hypertext through a spatial metaphor, for instance, set more links and adopted a network-like way of structuring information;

in contrast, but expectedly, students introduced to hypertext through the book metaphor set fewer links and adopted a more linear way of structuring information. Bromme and Stahl conclude that the spatial metaphor is more suitable for helping students transform knowledge, because it 'facilitates the congruence between the potential complexity of hypertext structures and content structures' (129).

Bromme and Stahl (2002) continue their experimental work in a study that examines whether adopting multiple audience perspectives affects students' learning. This study integrates findings from previous work—e.g., the spatial metaphor is used to introduce participants to the concept of hypertext—but extends that work by examining whether students can develop flexible knowledge through a combination of multiple perspectives and hypertext writing. Cognitive flexibility, for Bromme and Stahl, relates to knowledge transfer and 'the ability to structure one's own knowledge in a variety of ways in adaptation to changing situational demands' (41). As a way to examine whether hypertext writing helps students achieve such flexibility, two groups of participants were asked to link pre-existing nodes related to the topic of the Internet. The first group was required to adopt two different audience perspectives while the second group was not given a specific audience perspective at all. Bromme and Stahl use students' link setting, the structure of hypertext documents produced, students' operations and decision made in the process of producing their documents, and overall knowledge acquisition as dependent variables for measuring differences between writing tasks. Findings indicate that adopting multiple perspectives shapes both the process of producing a hypertext document and subsequent knowledge acquisition (58). Bromme and Stahl conclude, based on this experiment, that the process of hypertext writing, combined with adopting multiple reader perspectives, fosters the transfer of knowledge and ultimately cognitive flexibility.

Stahl et al. (2007) replicate Bromme and Stahl's 2002 experiment in order to examine further the relationship between multiple audience perspectives, hypertext writing, and knowledge acquisition. The authors also continue to articulate Cognitive Flexibility Theory as a framework for exploring how hypertext writing can help students combine complex subject matter with complex rhetorical structures. The setup of this study is similar to Bromme and Stahl (2002); however, three significant changes are worth mentioning. First, Stahl et al. change the content domain from the Internet to medicine. Second, they introduce a new instrument for assessing students' hypertext writing processes. Finally, the experimental group adopted two audience perspectives, as in the earlier study, but the control group adopted one audience perspective rather than an ill-defined general audience. These changes help show whether content, adopting multiple audience perspectives or adopting a single perspective as such, helps students develop more flexible knowledge. The authors determine this by examining the structure of completed hypertext documents, data on cognitive processes involved in hypertext writing, and overall knowledge acquisition. Stahl et al. conclude that, based upon replication of their first study, hypertext writing, especially when combined with multiple audience perspectives, support students' learning and knowledge acquisition.

While Bromme and Stahl (and their colleagues) have perhaps the most well-developed program of research on hypertext and learning, probably the most influential scholar in this area is Richard Lehrer; here we treat his seminal 1993 piece, 'Authors of knowledge: Patterns of hypermedia design', as well as a 1998 article from *Journal of the Learning Sciences*, coauthored with Julie Erickson, 'The evolution of critical standards as students design hypermedia documents'.

Lehrer (1993) draws on theoretical work on design as a human activity to implement and evaluate a hypermedia application, HyperAuthor, used in the context of grade-8

American history classrooms. The overarching goal is to analyse 'the fusion of a new form of literacy, hypercomposition, with a new instructional metaphor, knowledge-as-design' (221). Think aloud protocols of student writers were used to build a framework of cognitive activities for design (based loosely on Hayes and Flower, 1980), including processes of planning, transforming and translating, evaluating, and revising. Hyper-Author incorporates this framework into a set of construction tools, including those that allow students to choose the kinds of semantic relationships set up between content nodes, and reflection tools, including different forms of maps and tables. The primary research reported here is a study of ten grade-8 students in history classes, who worked in two groups (one of students judged 'more successful' in school, and one of students judged 'less successful') over six weeks to create hypermedia presentations on the American Civil War. In addition to the final hypermedia presentations, the researcher also collected: videotapes of student interactions; field notes of activities and conversations; transcripts of design interviews, in which students were queried in a direct way about their design process; and two measure of knowledge, a comparison task and an ordering task.

These multiple measures—as well as copious examples of student writing—provide a quite coherent, multifaceted, and detailed picture of student learning in a hypermedia environment. Both groups exhibited evidence of increased involvement in learning (drawn from observations of work patterns and the design interviews); patterns of collaboration (based on field notes and videotaped work sessions); rich hierarchical structures (based on the hypermedia presentations; the presentation of the more able students was more complex in structure than that of the previously less successful students); depth of knowledge (as exhibited in student 'showcase' presentations); and even long-term retention of content: the hypermedia design students retained significantly more content knowledge (as measured by Mann-Whitney U tests, with a p of <.01) than did classroom counterparts who had not participated in the hypertext design project. In conclusion, Lehrer calls for more research on and implementation of hypermedia design in schools, as well as development of appropriate assessment procedures.

Using the same design framework and the same collaborative design task, Erickson and Lehrer (1998) conducted a two-year-long classroom study of middle-school-aged social studies students. The focus here is on 'the evolution of critical standards' (351), by which the authors mean the development, among students, of consensual patterns of belief, in particular, beliefs about design and inquiry. Although the researchers acknowledge the import of content knowledge, they do not focus on knowledge outcomes in this study. Rather, in collaboration with classroom and specialty teachers (art, computer science, and library science), they designed a collaborative, long-term set of multimedia projects for the students, and analysed data from multiple sources: classroom observations; videotaped collaborative work; teacher interviews; student interviews; artefacts, including planning documents as well as finished products; and periodic assessments of design skills. The researchers acknowledge that, given their focus on the development of criteria and shared beliefs, the focus was on data that revealed such development, in particular development of students' understanding of 'good questions' and of 'good design'. Questions evolved from simple ones with straightforward answers, to provocative and generative ones. Students' understandings of and standards for design also showed development, from a focus on including lots of content arranged in a linear way to multiple, hierarchical understandings of learning as meaning making.

Like Lehrer and Erickson, Min Liu and Keith Rutledge studied collaborative student groups engaged in hypermedia authoring. Using a writing-as-design approach, in some ways similar to that of Erickson and Lehrer

(1998) and Lehrer (1993), Liu and Rutledge's 1997 article, 'The effect of a "learner as multimedia designer" environment on at-risk high school students' motivation and learning of design knowledge', reports a semester-long study of two classrooms of at-risk high school students (one the experimental group, which designed multimedia, and one a control classroom, where other kinds of computer applications were taught). A noteworthy feature of this study is that students worked with community collaborators (from a local children's museum) in the multimedia designs. Both quantitative and qualitative data were collected: quantitative data included motivation questionnaires (for both groups) and design questionnaires (for the experimental group); qualitative data, collected only from the experimental group, consisted of a listing and ranking task, observations, interviews, and analysis of multimedia designs.[6] ANOVA (Analysis of variation) was used to analyse the questionnaire responses; the listing and ranking tasks were analysed via descriptive statistics; and the data from interviews and observations were chunked and coded in an inductive manner, with agreement between coded reported at 0.95.

There were significant interaction effects between groups and pre-/posttests for intrinsic motivation, task value, and self-efficacy measures; the researchers interpret this as increased motivation in the multimedia design group. The researchers also note significant differences between control and experimental groups' pre- and posttest design questionnaires, with the experimental group reporting more planning, more collaboration, more effort and involvement, and more interest in their class, results that suggest increased knowledge of design. The researchers also describe ways in which the qualitative data support the quantitative findings; specifically, there was evidence that students spent more time on the design projects, had heightened interest in the project, gained confidence in their abilities as learners, and learned to collaborate in the assigning and completion of tasks. The article concludes with a brief discussion of the challenges of balancing audience needs with students' need to be 'creative'.

In 'The effect of hypermedia authoring on elementary students' creative thinking', Liu (1998) explores this notion of creativity and students' self-efficacy in a six-month-long study in which students spent considerable time creating hypertext projects. Students in this study were from two intact fourth-grade classes; students in both classes used a hypermedia authoring system to create hypermedia documents on topics in science. Differences between classes were that one class worked individually, while the other worked in small groups; the small group class made collaborative decisions about content and design. Data for both classes consisted of: results of the Torrance Tests of Creative Thinking for each student; final hypermedia products assessed by two independent raters, on dimensions such as 'content is creative', 'layout is innovative', and 'amount of information is appropriate' (32); and several types of qualitative data (interviews, response logs, and teacher journals). Measures of creative thinking increased in several areas, including fluency and elaboration; additionally, low and intermediate level learners seemed to benefit even more than did high ability students, and students working collaboratively demonstrated larger gains in creativity than did students working alone.

SYNTHESIS: THE CASE OF HYPERTEXT IN THE DEVELOPMENT OF THE FIELD OF WRITING RESEARCH

This chapter has reviewed recent research on hypertext and hypertext writing. The first four columns of Table 35.1 summarize the goals, methods, objects of study, and subjects of this research as a way to suggest overlap between existing research programs. The next four columns, labelled 'Theories Employed',

note the theories of writing, learning, and discourse within which the researchers set their studies. The disciplinary, international, and journal venue context is shown in the last three columns. In this concluding section, we focus on theories and contexts of research as a way to explore future directions and possible *rapprochements* between the diverse disciplines, international contexts, and general approaches to the study of hypertext and hypertext writing.

Theories that inform the studies reviewed in this chapter reflect, in part, different goals and objects of study that occupy authors' research programs. For example, Braaksma et al. (2002) and Pohl (2004), who focus on cognitive and social processes involved in hypertext writing, employ theories that extend from research on cognitive processes involved in so-called 'traditional' text production (e.g., Hayes and Flower, 1980). Bromme and Stahl's research also draw upon the cognitive process models (Hayes and Flower, 1980; Hayes, 1996), although their work most explicitly uses Bereiter and Scardamlia's (1987) view of writing as knowledge processing. The most influential writing theory remains the cognitive process model of Hayes and Flower (1980; Hayes, 1996): Lehr er (1993), Erickson and Lehrer (1998), Braaksma, et al. (2002), Pohl and Pergahofer (2004), and Chang et al. (2007) all draw upon this theoretical tradition.

In terms of learning theory, theories of learning as design (Lehrer [1993], Norman [1988], and Perkins [1986]) were most prevalent for works published in the 1990s; the cognitive tools approach of Jonassen (1992) and the cognitive flexibility theories of Jacobson and Spiro (1995) are more influential in the 2000s. This is not to suggest a break, however, as the work of Jonassen and of Jacobson and Spiro is in some ways a further development of the learning-as-design theorists.

We note an increased theoretical richness to the research, beginning in about 1999: research published after this date tends to draw upon multiple theoretical precursors.

Table 35.1 Synthesis of research along dimensions of study details, theory employed, and context

	Study Details				Theory Employed			Context of Research		
Author, Year	Goal	Object of Study	Method of Analysis	Subjects	Writing	Learning	Discourse	Disciplinary Background	National Affiliation	Journal Type
Lehrer (1993)	Examine learning outcomes: content knowledge, involvement, retention.	Think aloud protocols, qualitative data	Descriptive	8th Graders	Cognitive process (Hayes & Flower, 1980)	Knowledge as design (Perkins, 1986)	—	Educational Psychology	USA	NA
Yang et al. (1996)	Model hypertext writing processes	Think aloud protocols, observation	Descriptive	University students	Discourse synthesis (Spivey, 1983)	—	—	Finance	ROC	Educational technology
Liu & Rutledge (1997)	Examine learning outcomes: motivation, design knowledge	Questionnaire, design tasks, qualitative data	ANOVA	Secondary school students	—	Knowledge as design (Perkins, 1986; Lehrer, 1993)	—	Curriculum & Instruction	USA	Educational technology
Deadman (1997)	Analyze hypertext artifacts	Student-produced hypertexts	Descriptive, text analysis	14–15 year-olds	—	Inner speech (Vygotsky, 1986)	—	Curriculum & Instruction, Information Technology	UK	Educational technology
Liu (1998)	Examine learning outcomes: creativity scores	Creativity and skills tests, student-produced hypermedia, qualitative data	T-Tests, ANOVA	4th Graders	—	—	—	Curriculum & Instruction; Information Technology	USA	Educational technology
Erickson & Lehrer (1998)	Examine learning outcomes: shared design knowledge	Classroom discourse	Descriptive	6th & 7th Graders	Cognitive process (Hayes & Flower, 1980)	—	—	Educational Psychology	USA	Learning theory and research

Continued

Table 35.1—*(Continued)*

Author, Year	Goal	Object of Study	Method of Analysis	Subjects	Writing	Learning	Discourse	Disciplinary Background	National Affiliation	Journal Type
		Study Details			Theory Employed			Context of Research		
Pohl (1998)	Examine structure of hypertext artifacts	Student-produced hypertexts	Descriptive	University students	—	Cognitive tools (Jonassen, 1992), Knowledge as design (Norman, 1988)	—	Information Technology	Austria	Educational technology (conf. proceedings)
Bromme & Stahl (1999)	Examine learning outcomes: semantic relations	Three tests of semantic relations and structure knowledge	T-tests	Secondary school students	Writing as knowledge processing (Bereiter & Scardamalia, 1987)	Cognitive tools (Jonassen, 1992)	—	Educational Psychology	Germany	—
Bromme & Stahl (2001)	Examine effect of metaphors on hypertext writing	Student-produced hyperlinks	T-test, chi square, ANOVA	University students	Writing as knowledge processing (Bereiter & Scardamalia, 1987)	—	—	Educational Psychology	Germany	Educational technology (conf. proceedings)
Dillon & Gushrowski (2000)	Examine generic features of hypertext artifacts	Extant personal Web pages	Textual analysis, correlations	Graduate students	Social genre theory (Bazerman, 1988)	—	Structuralist (van Dijk & Kinsch, 1983)	Information Technology	USA	Information technology
Bromme & Stahl (2002)	Examine effects of audience awareness on hypertext writing and learning	Student-produced hyperlinks	ANOVA, MANOVA	University students	Writing as knowledge processing (Bereiter & Scardamalia, 1987)	Cognitive flexibility (Jacobson & Spiro, 1995)	—	Educational Psychology	Germany	NA

Braaksma et al. (2002)	Examine processes of linearizing and hierarchicalizing	Think aloud protocols	Descriptive	Secondary school students	Cognitive process (Hayes & Flower, 1980)	—	Structuralist (van Dijk & Kinsch, 1983)	Curriculum & Instruction	The N'therlands	NA
Pohl & Purgahofer (2004)	Examine processes of, and create profiles for, hypertext writing	Student-produced hypertexts	Descriptive, cluster analysis	University students	Cognitive process (Hayes & Flower, 1980) Writing as design (Sharples, 1996)	—	Social semiotic (Kress & van Leeuwen, 1996)	Information Technology	Austria	Educational technology
Bromme & Stahl (2005)	Examine effect of metaphors on hypertext writing and learning	Student-produced hyperlinks	T-test, chi square, Mann-Whitney U test	University students	Writing as knowledge processing (Bereiter & Scardamalia, 1987)	—	—	Educational Psychology	Germany	Educational technology
Stahl et al. (2007)	Examine learning outcomes: knowledge acquisition	Student-produced hyperlinks	MANOVA	University students	Writing as knowledge processing (Bereiter & Scardamalia, 1987; writing as problem solving (Hayes, 1996).	Cognitive flexibility (Jacobson & Spiro, 1995)	—	Educational Psychology	Germany	NA
Chang et al. (2007)	Examine quality of hypertext artifacts	Student-produced web pages	ANCOVA	7th Graders	Cognitive process (Flower & Hayes, 1981; via Lehrer, 1993)	—	Structuralist (authors)	Information Technology	ROC	Educational technology

Continued

Table 35.1—(Continued)

Author, Year	Study Details				Theory Employed			Disciplinary Background	Context of Research	
	Goal	Object of Study	Method of Analysis	Subjects	Writing	Learning	Discourse		National Affiliation	Journal Type
Ranker (2008)	Examine collaborative writing processes with hypermedia	Audio and video transcripts, field notes	Descriptive, case study	5th Graders	—	—	Social Semiotic (Kress & van Leeuwen, 1996); dialogic (Bahktin, 1981)	Literacy and Education	USA	Writing research
Lehrer (1993)	Examine learning outcomes: content knowledge, involvement, retention.	Think aloud protocols, qualitative data	Descriptive	8th Graders	Cognitive process (Hayes & Flower, 1980)	Knowledge as design (Perkins, 1986)	—	Educational Psychology	USA	NA
Yang et al. (1996)	Model hypertext writing processes	Think aloud protocols, observation	Descriptive	University students	Discourse synthesis (Spivey, 1983)	—	—	Finance	ROC	Educational technology
Liu & Rutledge (1997)	Examine learning outcomes: motivation, design knowledge	Questionnaire, design tasks, qualitative data	ANOVA	Secondary school students	—	Knowledge as design (Perkins, 1986; Lehrer, 1993)	—	Curriculum & Instruction	USA	Educational technology

	Purpose	Data	Analysis	Participants				Department	Country	Field
Deadman (1997)	Analyze hypertext artifacts	Student-produced hypertexts	Descriptive, text analysis	14–15 year-olds	—	Inner speech (Vygotsky, 1986)	—	Curriculum & Instruction, Information Technology	UK	Educational technology
Liu (1998)	Examine learning outcomes: creativity scores	Creativity and skills tests, student-produced hypermedia, qualitative data	T-Tests, ANOVA	4th Graders	—	—	—	Curriculum & Instruction; Information Technology	USA	Educational technology
Erickson & Lehrer (1998)	Examine learning outcomes: shared design knowledge	Classroom discourse	Descriptive	6th & 7th Graders	Cognitive process (Hayes & Flower, 1980)	—	—	Educational Psychology	USA	Learning theory and research

Likewise, it is only in 2000 and beyond that, the researchers draw explicitly on *theories of discourse*, as well as theories of writing and learning, in presenting their research. Here, the structural discourse theory of van Dijk and Kintsch (1983), the social semiotic discourse theory of Kress and van Leeuwen (1996), and the dialogic discourse theory of Bahktin (1981) are foregrounded. This move toward theoretical complexity and richness reflects a similar trend within the larger field of writing research.

The contexts for research on hypertext and hypertext writing are as diverse as the authors' research programs. Many authors come from educational psychology—a fact that may help explain common approaches to hypertext design and to hypertext as a cognitive tool. The research within educational psychology takes up in a central way the cognitive processes involved in student learning. Authors who come from an information technology background, such as Deadman (1997), Dillon and Gushrowski (2000) and Pohl and Purgahofer (2004), draw on a wider range of theories (including Vygotsky, Bazerman, Sharples, and Kress and van Leeuwen) than do those researchers centred primarily in education. We have already noted the breadth of countries represented in the research reviewed here (seven countries on three continents), but the research reviewed here (with the exception of *Journal of the American Society for Information Science*, the venue for Dillon and Gushrowski's publication) was all presented in journals with a strong educational slant.

This observation—a common venue for publication—suggests that the research projects reviewed here share a common enterprise. This common enterprise, along with the increasing theoretical richness of research on hypertext and writing, bodes well, we believe, for continuing development in how the field of writing studies understands this important technology. However, despite the commonalities in approaches, theories, and publication venue, we find strikingly little cross-citation in the work we review. A close reading of these research studies suggests groups of researchers independently pursuing common goals. If the goal of writing studies as a field is the accumulation of knowledge about writers and writing, the building of communities of researchers interested in core issues about writing, and increased visibility of writing research, then we believe there should be more direct linking between separate programs of research. We hope that this chapter has made some headway in this direction.

NOTES

1   The gender differences may be due to boys' greater interest and skill in using computers, the authors speculate, or to girls' tendency to spend their time collecting interesting pictures. No grounding, either in the data from this study or in previous research, is offered for this speculation.

2   The authors report interaction effects as not significant, with a p of $<.05$—although they reported group differences with the same p as significant.

3   Of the 24 students who participated, 8 (one third) were excluded from the analysis, because they 'couldn't engage', lost their work, were absent, or were off-task.

4   Braaksma et al., also examined quality of products, but we categorized the study as one about process, because the article emphasizes process results and because the measure of quality here is quite narrowly defined.

5   Note that the students were not actually constructing their linear texts or hierarchical structures in an hypertext environment.

6   Note that only students who completed all tasks and measures were included; boys outnumbered girls, 23 to 8. The gender imbalance in the treatment class was particularly large: 14 males and 2 females.

REFERENCES

Bakhtin, M.M. (1981) 'Discourse in the novel' (C. Emerson and M. Holquist, Trans.), in M. Holquist (ed.), *The Dialogic Imagination*, Austin, TX: University of Texas Press. (Original work published in 1935.)

Bazerman, C. (1988) *Shaping Written Knowledge: The Genre and Activity of the Experimental Article in Science*, Madison, WI: University of Wisconsin Press.

Bereiter, C. and Scardamalia, M. (1987) *The Psychology of Written Composition*, Hillsdale, NJ: Lawrence Erlbaum.

Bolter, J.D. and Grusin, R. (1999) *Remediation: Understanding New Media*, Cambridge, MA: MIT Press.

Braaksma, M.A.H., Rijlaarsdam, G., Couzijn, M., and van den Bergh, H. (2002) 'Learning to compose hypertext and linear text: Transfer or interference?', in R. Bromme and E. Stahl (eds), *Writing Hypertext and Learning: Conceptual and empirical approaches*, Amsterdam: Pergamon. pp.15–37.

Bromme, R. and Stahl, E. (1999) 'Spatial metaphors and writing hypertexts: Studies with schools', *European Journal of Psychology of Education*, 14(2): 267–281.

Bromme and Stahl (2001) 'The idea of "hypertext" and its implications on the process of hypertext writing', in W. Frindte, T. Kohler, P. Marquet, and E. Nissen (eds), *IN-TELE 99—Internet-Based Teaching and Learning 99(3) Internet Communication*, Frankfurt am Main, Germany: Peter Lang. pp.302–308.

Bromme, R. and Stahl, E. (2002) 'Learning by producing hypertext from reader perspectives: Cognitive flexibility theory reconsidered', in R. Bromme and E. Stahl (eds), *Writing Hypertext and Learning: Conceptual and Empirical Approaches*, Amsterdam: Pergamon. pp.39–61.

Bromme, R. and Stahl, E. (2005) 'Is a hypertext a book or a space? The impact of different introductory metaphors on hypertext construction', *Computers and Education*, 44(2): 115–133.

Chang, K., Sun, Y., and Zheng, J. (2007) 'Hypermedia authoring with writing process guidance', *British Journal of Educational Technology*, 38(5): 851–860.

Deadman, G. (1997) 'Analysis of pupils' reflective writing within a hypermedia framework', *Journal of Computer Assisted Learning*, 13(1): 16–25.

Dillon, A. and Gushrowski, B. (2000) 'Genres and the web: Is the personal home page the first uniquely digital genre?', *Journal of American Society for Information Science*, 51(2): 202–205.

Erickson, J. and Lehrer, R. (1998) 'The evolution of critical standards as students design hypermedia documents', *The Journal of the Learning Sciences*, 7(3/4): 351–386.

Flower, L. and Hayes, J.R. (1981) 'A cognitive process theory of writing', *College Composition and Communication*, 32(4): 365–387.

Haas, C. (1994) 'Learning to read biology: One students' rhetorical development in college', *Written Communication*, 11(1): 43–84.

Hayes, J.R. (1996) 'A new framework for understanding cognition and affect in writing', in C.M. Levy and S. Randall (eds), *The Science Of Writing: Theories, Methods, Individual Differences, and Applications*, Mahwah, NJ: Lawrence Erlbaum. pp.1–27.

Hayes, J.R. and Flower, L. (1980) 'Identifying the organization of writing processes', in L.W. Gregg and E.R. Steinberg (eds), *Cognitive Processes in Writing*, Hillsdale, NJ: Lawrence Erlbaum. pp.3–30.

Haas, C. and Flower, L. (1988) 'Rhetorical reading strategies and the construction of meaning', *College Composition and Communication*, 39(2): 167–183.

Jacobson, M.J. and Spiro, R.J. (1995) 'Hypertext learning environments, cognitive flexibility, and the transfer of complex knowledge: An empirical investigation', *Journal of Educational Computing Research*, 12(4): 301–333.

Jonassen, D.H. (1992) 'What are cognitive tools?', in P.A.M. Kommers, D.H. Jonassen, and J.T. Mayes (eds), *Cognitive Tools For Learning*, New York: Springer. pp.1–6.

Kirschenbaum, M.G. (2000) 'Hypertext', in T. Swiss (ed.), *Unspun: Key concepts for understanding the World Wide Web*, New York: New York University Press. pp.120–137.

Kress, Gunther and van Leeuwen, T. (1996) *Reading Images: The Grammar of Visual Design*, London: Routledge.

Landow, G.P. (1992) *Hypertext: The Convergence of Contemporary Critical Theory and Technology*, Baltimore: The John Hopkins University Press.

Lehrer, R. (1993) 'Authors of knowledge: Patterns of hypermedia design', in Lajoie, S.P. and Derry, S.J. (ed.), *Computers as Cognitive Tools*, Hilldale, NJ: Lawrence Erlbaum. pp.197–227.

Liu, M. (1998) 'The effect of hypermedia authoring on elementary school student's creative thinking', *Journal of Educational Computing Research*, 19(1): 27–51.

Liu, M. and Rutledge, K. (1997) 'The effect of a "learner as multimedia designer" environment on at-risk high school students' motivation and learning of design knowledge', *Journal of Educational Computing Research*, 16(2): 145–177.

Nelson, T.H. (1981) *Literary Machines*. Swarthmore, PA: Self Published.

Norman, D.A. (1988) *The Psychology of Everyday Things*, New York: Basic Books.

Perkins, D.N. (1986) *Knowledge as Design*, Hillsdale, NJ: Lawrence Erlbaum Associates.

Pohl, M. (1998) 'Hypermedia as a cognitive tool', in T. Ottmann and I. Tomek (eds), ED-MEDIA/ED-TELECOM 98 World Conference on Educational Multimedia *and* Hypermedia and World Conference on Educational Telecommunications (Proceedings). Freiburg, Germany.

Pohl, M. and Purgathofer, P. (2004) 'Hypertext writing profiles and visualization', *Computers and the Humanities,* 38(1): 83–105.

Ranker, J. (2008) 'Composing across multiple media: A case study of digital video production in a fifth-grade classroom', *Written Communication,* 25(2): 196–234.

Sharples, M. (1992) *Computers and Writing: Issues and Implementations,* Boston: Kluwer, Dordrecht.

Sharples, M. (2004) Review of R. Bromme and E. Stahl (eds), 'Writing hypertext and learning: Conceptual and empirical approaches', *Computers and Education,* 42(3): 315–317.

Spivey, N.N. (1983) 'Discourse Synthesis: Constructing Texts in Reading and Writing', PhD Dissertation, University of Texas, Austin.

Stahl, E., Bromme, R., Stadtler, M, and Jaron, R. (2007) 'Learning by hypertext writing: Effects of considering a single audience versus multiple audiences on knowledge acquisition', in M. Torrance, L. Van Waes, and D. Galbraith (eds), *Writing and Cognition: Research and Applications,* Amsterdam: Elsevier. pp. 307–322.

van Dijk, T.A, and Kintsch, W. (1983) *Strategies of Discourse Comprehension,* New York: Academic Press.

Vygotsky, L.S. (1986) Thought and Language, Cambridge, MA: MIT Press.

Yang, S.C. (1996) 'A dynamic reading-linking-to-writing model for problem solving with a constructive hypermedia learning environment', *Journal of Educational Multimedia and Hypermedia,* 5(3/4): 283–302.

36

Developing Writing in a High-Stakes Environment

Marian Sainsbury

INTRODUCTION

Writing plays a central part in communication within society, and developing the ability to write is correspondingly fundamental as an educational aim. Because of its importance, governments, on behalf of societies, wish to reassure themselves that the educational system is meeting its obligation to produce a literate population. It is this simple reasoning that underpins the pervasive and complex systems that, in some countries, have become known as high-stakes assessment of writing.

This chapter adopts a sharp focus on writing through the lens of assessment. It will investigate not only what is assessed and how it is assessed but also the inferences, decisions, actions, and consequences that result from the assessment. Test validation theory provides a structure for such an investigation: to explore these perspectives on high-stakes assessment *is* to conduct a validation study. At the same time, the nature of the writing development process itself both shapes and is shaped by assessment systems.

This chapter will briefly describe the political and social context in which high-stakes assessment has become prominent and set out current views of test validity, before looking in more detail at specific examples of high-stakes writing assessment and relating them to these principles.

THE HIGH-STAKES ENVIRONMENT

The final decades of the twentieth century and the first decade of the twenty-first have been characterized in many countries by strongly expressed public concern about the adequacy of education systems. Underlying this trend is a range of political and economic factors. Earl et al. (2003) identify the following collection of causes:

> ... roller-coaster economic conditions, dramatic swings in political ideology and leadership and an eroding consensus about societal values. Rising levels of education have led to declining public confidence in institutions, an escalation of mistrust in public figures and an irresistible demand for greater accountability in public institutions. (Earl et al., 2003: 23)

In this climate, there are several reasons why concern has focused upon education.

Public education is a system funded and structured by governments, and in which therefore governments have an expectation to be able to exert influence. Further, economic success is viewed as reliant upon the skills of the workforce, and a more efficient education system might be expected to lead to increasing prosperity. Alongside these considerations, there are ubiquitous reports that standards of achievement are too low and that students' skills are inadequate for the workplace. Public opinion cannot understand how expensive educational provision can result in so many individuals failing. Governments respond to this pressure by adopting policies of educational reform. Since these policies aim to raise levels of attainment, there must be pressure upon schools to improve and there must be a way of measuring and comparing these levels.

Thus, the high-stakes assessment context is driven by the notion of accountability. Schools must improve the achievements of their students, and they are accountable to governments and to society at large for doing so. The assessment system is often the mechanism by which this accountability is enforced. Typically, there are targets to meet in terms of test outcomes, accompanied by incentives for success and sanctions for failure. It becomes very important for teachers and school managers to succeed, and the testing, therefore, has high stakes for professionals. It may also have high stakes for the students, in the form of certification, which controls their access to opportunity.

In the United States, the high-stakes assessment system takes the form of the *No Child Left Behind* (NCLB) program (2001). This is mandated centrally by the Federal Government, but implemented by individual states, which control their own education systems. The ambitious aim of the program is to improve attainment, not just overall, but also specifically for minority groups such as students with disabilities and ethnic minorities. Each state must establish a testing programme in at least grades 3–8, covering at least mathematics and reading/language arts.

The states define their own standards of proficiency, and it is the proportion of students meeting those standards that is the accountability measure. The aim is to increase this to 100 percent of students at the end of a 12-year period. In the meantime, there is a measure known as 'adequate yearly progress', which includes separate measures for minority groups, alongside the overall measure. Koretz and Hamilton (2006) report that in many states there are systems of rewards and sanctions for schools, based on test results, and that states are increasingly introducing higher stakes for students by means of exit examinations. Hillocks (2002) found that 37 states out of 50 included assessments of writing, though not all of these were high-stakes.

In England,[1] there has been a national curriculum with associated assessment arrangements since the early 1990s. These assessment arrangements are intended as part of an accountability system, with results published for schools, local authorities, and the entire nation. In 1997, the new Labour Government added a further accountability mechanism, in the form of national improvement targets, from which were derived targets for local authorities and individual schools. These targets are expressed in terms of the proportion of pupils attaining the expected level in the tests of English and mathematics at ages 7, 11, and 14[3]. England also has a long-standing tradition of examinations at 16 and 18, the results of which carry high stakes both for individual students and for schools.

Australia has a set of national goals arising from The Adelaide Declaration (1999), supported by a National Assessment Program combining state, national, and international assessments. Nationally comparable results for pupils in years three, five, and seven form part of the program from 2008 onwards. Each year there is a national report on schooling, detailing progress towards the national goals. This system does not, however, include policies of rewards and sanctions, so is currently less high-stakes than England or the USA.

Earl and Torrance (2000) give a description of the introduction of a system of assessment for accountability in the Canadian province of Ontario. Here, the notion of accountability was intended to be more consensual, with attainment data the starting-point for local conversations about education that would build 'trust, confidence and community responsibility' (Earl and Torrance, 2000: 137). However, at the time of writing they report that progress towards this goal was disappointing, with little evidence of community conversations and the media presenting the results in a stark and competitive way. The Ontario system tests students at grades 3, 6, 9, and 10, and continues to present its results as a stimulus for reflection and discussion, rather than for sanctions or rewards.

A feature of these accountability systems is national reporting of levels of attainment, and it is here that writing emerges as a distinct element. In England, the proportion of 11-year-olds reaching the expected level in writing is currently 67 percent (DfES, 2007). There has been some increase over the previous five years, from 60 percent in 2002 (DfES, 2004). However, writing attainment remains far behind reading, in which 83 percent of pupils reach the expected level. In the USA, a measure is provided by the National Assessment of Educational Progress (NAEP), a national sampling study. The most recent results for writing, in the 2002 survey, ranged from 24 to 31 percent reaching the Proficient standard across the three grades included (Persky et al., 2003). In both countries, public concern has been expressed about this situation, with commentators dismayed at the poor levels achieved and policy-makers determined to use the means at their disposal to improve matters (DfES, 2006; AEE, 2007).

VALIDATION OF ASSESSMENTS

Against this background, assessment of writing takes place amidst high public interest and high pressure for teachers and students. Such a context increases the importance of valid assessment outcomes, at the same time as presenting distinct threats to validity.

Recent scholarship has elucidated the complex and powerful nature of test validation theory (Kane, 2006). As currently conceived, validity is not a property that inheres in an assessment. Instead, a careful process of validation is necessary. This essentially takes the form of an argument, in two stages. First, the claims made for test outcomes must be painstakingly elucidated (Kane refers to this as the 'interpretive argument'). In considering the outcome of any assessment, the exact features of the test performance are not in themselves of great interest; rather, it is the inferences that can be drawn from the performance that are important. For example, a test may require a pupil to write a 45-minute short story. However, this single performance is intended to stand for that pupil's overall mastery of story structure, sentence variation, grammar, punctuation, spelling, and so forth. Further, it may claim to represent the pupil's ability to produce any piece of writing appropriate to audience and purpose. In a high-stakes system, there are further claims: the test performance may be taken to represent teachers' ability to teach writing effectively and the school's ability to provide a good education in literacy. Still further, this can be seen as part of a whole system of assessment that claims to bring about improvements in attainment and in teaching.

Once these claims have been set out fully, the second stage of the validation process is to investigate how far each such inference is justified (Kane terms this the 'validity argument'). Although a full investigation of the validation of high-stakes writing assessment would be far beyond the scope of this chapter, the conceptual structure of validation theory provides a useful framework for presenting an overview of the current state of high-stakes writing assessment with some examples from research.

THE CONSTRUCT OF WRITING ABILITY

The simplest and best-known definition of 'validity' is that 'a test should assess what it sets out to assess'. This crude formulation does scant justice to current thinking, but nevertheless highlights an important area of claims to be investigated. The assessment, of whatever type, is intended to stand for or represent the student's overall ability and attainment in writing. This is a substantial and significant claim, which requires justification before any of the other claims of high-stakes assessment systems can be considered. Writing *ability*, in this sense, is a theoretical construct, of which individual writing *performances* give evidence.

To begin with, it is necessary to find a way of explicating what is generally meant by writing ability. This entire volume contributes to this task, but the present chapter must at least rest upon a working definition of the construct. Broadly, writing involves the complex orchestration of many elements. On the one hand, the writer makes stylistic and structural choices to produce a text suited to purpose and reader; on the other, control of the conventions of grammar, punctuation, spelling, and handwriting is necessary. The mention of purpose and audience highlights that different types of text can be distinguished, each with typical organizational and stylistic features. Genre theory (for example, Kress, 1982; Wyatt-Smith, 1997) develops these ideas more systematically. Myhill (2001) helpfully identifies two dimensions to writing ability, which she calls *creating* and *crafting*. In contrast to some previous writers, she argues that these two aspects of the writing activity are both essential and complementary:

> The effective teaching of writing sets writing in a context, values the voice of the child *and* teaches explicitly how he or she can craft language creatively for effect, through looking closely at the linguistic features of texts. (Myhill, 2001: 16; author's italics)

Although Myhill's article focuses upon the teaching of writing, these ideas are also relevant to assessment, outlining a central construct of writing to which performance on assessments should relate. In developing this complex skill, some unevenness is to be expected, as learners have greater or lesser mastery of the elements involved. This variety makes the task of assessment yet more challenging.

The writing tests used in high-stakes contexts are usually based on an explicit definition of the nature of the writing skills to be assessed. In the United States, Canada, and Australia, these definitions are universally referred to as 'standards' (Sadler, 1987), and the assessments as 'standards-based assessments'. Koretz and Hamilton (2006) trace the history of this approach to testing. In earlier times in the USA, multiple-choice tests were prevalent. However, questions were increasingly raised about the capacity of such tests to address the higher-order skills and understandings required by the curriculum. During the 1990s, a movement known as 'performance assessment' attempted to replace multiple-choice tests with more authentic tasks, requiring students to construct rather than select answers and to produce extended pieces of work, sometimes developed over days or weeks. However, performance assessments are much less manageable on a large scale than the simple tests that preceded them, and there was soon a reaction against them for this reason. The notion that education requires the development of higher-order skills, however, remained, and standards-based assessments are intended to recognize this. Thus, standards aim to encapsulate the real educational achievements that are agreed to be of importance. Assessments may range over multiple-choice and extended-answer formats, but must be aligned to the standards. For writing, the nature of the standards and the form of the assessment are of particular importance, a topic that will be returned to in a later section.

In England, the assessment system could still be described as standards-based, though this term is generally not used, but its structure is slightly different, reflecting its genesis.

There is a scale of eight levels of attainment, which applies across the first nine years of schooling, up to age 14, with pupils progressing from level to level. These eight-level 'attainment targets' were developed alongside the curriculum and matched to it, minimizing any problems of alignment. The descriptions of attainment at each level bear a strong resemblance in their content and structure to the standards developed in other countries. The assessment tradition here has always included elements of 'performance assessment', with essay examinations rather than multiple-choice tests representing the most prevalent form in the past.

CONSTRUCT REPRESENTATION IN WRITING ASSESSMENT

A central claim of high-stakes writing assessment is, therefore, that the test or task adequately represents the construct of writing, so that inferences about a pupil's actual writing ability can be drawn from the scores on the test. Since writing is a very complex construct, combining compositional and secretarial skills, creativity, and crafting, this poses considerable challenges for assessment systems. Generally, an intermediate layer of enquiry exists, in the form of standards, the explicit statements that are intended to underpin writing assessments.

In the writing attainment target of the English national curriculum, for example (DfEE, 1999) can be discerned something of the complex construct described in the foregoing section. At each level, there is a suggestion of the creative power of writing, in wording such as 'imaginative', 'lively', 'thoughtful', 'engages and sustains the reader's interest', etc.. There is mention of writing for different purposes and readers, without any attempt to delineate exhaustively the forms and purposes covered. Each level description also includes requirements for sentence structure and vocabulary, together with accuracy in spelling, grammar, punctuation, and handwriting. The ascending levels intensify the requirements for range, appropriateness, and control.

The standard underpinning the English national writing tests can, therefore, be seen as a reasonable attempt to capture the important features of writing. The next step is to evaluate the tests themselves against this standard. The mandatory national tests for ages 7,[2] 11, and 14[3] consist of two pieces of writing, of contrasting types, one shorter (about 20 minutes) and one longer (about 40 minutes), presented as unseen, on-demand prompts and written, by hand, in controlled and timed conditions (QCA, 2007). The inclusion of two tasks is an attempt to represent some variety in terms of purposes and readers. There are new tests annually, and there is further variety in the text types, purposes and audiences required from year to year, which are unpredictable. In evaluating a writing assessment, the mark scheme (scoring rubric) is as important as the test itself. In these tests, marks (score points) are awarded separately for composition and effect; text structure and organization; sentence structure and punctuation; spelling; and handwriting. This gives explicit recognition to the notion that different aspects of writing may be better developed than others. Figure 36.1 presents an annotated example of writing marked in some of these categories.

This approach has some clear characteristics that support a claim of construct representation. Firstly, it assesses writing by writing: the assessment requires composition of complete pieces. Other indications are the recognition of purpose and audience; the variety of text types; and the inclusion of composition and effect alongside other aspects of the mark scheme. On the other hand, only a small number of purposes are included each time, the set topics are not for real readers and they may or may not genuinely engage the interest of writers. The time limits pay little respect to the processes of composition; although there are authentic purposes, which require writing to a deadline, this is not generally the case.

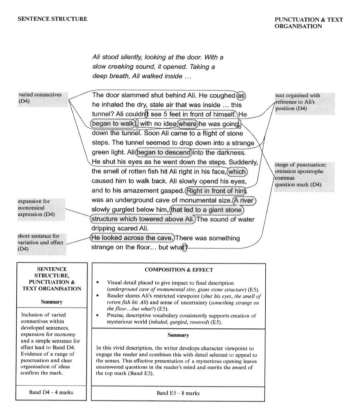

Figure 36.1: Annotated example from the mark scheme, England national curriculum tests (age 11).

In the United States, the proliferation of different states, each with its own standards, makes it more difficult to gain an overview. Writing is not, in fact, an essential requirement of NCLB, which specifies 'reading/ language arts', so high-stakes writing assessments are found in states where it is included in the 'language arts' standards. Hillocks (2002) considers only five states and identifies major differences between them in the theories of writing, wording of standards, and nature of tests.

The NAEP assessment (Persky et al., 2003) is not high-stakes for schools or individuals, but nevertheless offers the best representation of a national consensus on the construct of writing and national approaches to assessment in the USA. Its structure, or 'framework', refers to a variety of purposes and audiences but in fact identifies just three

purposes for inclusion in the assessment: narrative, informative and persuasive writing. Because of its sampling design, with individual students taking only a part of the total assessment, NAEP collects all three types of writing for all of grades 4, 8, and 12, though with different emphases: more narrative writing for the younger students, more persuasive for the older. The tasks consist of a stimulus situation, concern, or topic about which students are asked to write to a time constraint of 25 minutes. Within the overall defined purposes, there is variety of audience and form. The writing is scored on a holistic scale from one ('unsatisfactory') to six ('excellent'). Within each of these categories, there are descriptors covering content and development, structure, sentence structure, and mechanics. Figure 36.2 presents an annotated example from the NAEP assessment.

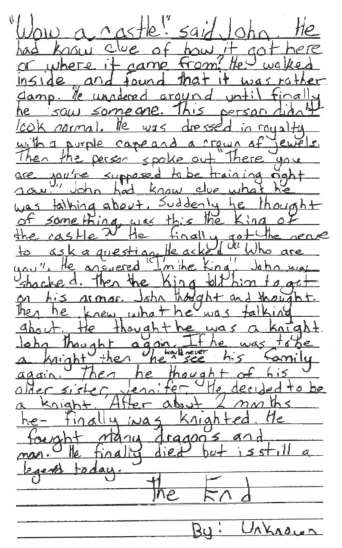

"Wow a castle!" said John. He had know clue of how it got here or where it came from? He walked inside and found that it was rather damp. He wandered around until finally he saw someone. This person didn't look normal. He was dressed in royalty with a purple cape and a crown of jewels. Then the person spoke out "There you are, you're supposed to be training right now." John had know clue what he was talking about. Suddenly he thought of something, was this the King of the castle? He finally got the nerve to ask a question. He asked "Who are you". He answered "I'm the King". John was shocked. Then the King told him to get on his armor. John thought and thought. Then he knew what he was talking about. He thought he was a knight. John thought again. If he was to be a knight then he would never see his family again. Then he thought of his older sister, Jennifer. He decided to be a knight. After about 2 months he finally was knighted. He fought many dragons and man. He finally died but is still a legend today.

                        The End

                                By: Unknown

Figure 36.2:   Annotated example from 2002 NAEP (grade 4).
This is a response to a prompt inviting the student to write a story about a castle that appears overnight. This example gains the highest score, 'excellent'. Scorer's commentary: In this paper, rated 'Excellent,' the writer uses dialogue effectively, develops characters, and provides a coherent plot. The student shows good control of language for a fourth grader and includes vivid details to illustrate the appearance of the characters — 'He was dressed in royalty with a purple cape and a crown of jewels.'

This has many characteristics in common with the England national assessment described in the preceding section: variety of form, purpose and audience, and scoring rubrics that give credit to skills in both composition and mechanics; but on-demand, time-limited tasks.

A browse of state standards sites indicates that an approach similar to NAEP is not uncommon in state standards (for example, CDE, 2006; CSDE, 2006). Often, they mention writing for different purposes and audiences (sometimes with specified text types), structuring ideas appropriately and using conventions accurately. The processes of writing: collecting ideas, drafting, reviewing, revising, publishing, also frequently appear. An example of a state that includes a writing assessment at all of grades 3–8 is Connecticut (CSDE, 2006). There are just two relevant standards: 'communicating with others', which covers both speaking and writing and mentions descriptive, narrative, expository, persuasive, and poetic modes; and 'applying English language conventions'. The latter of these is assessed by means of a multiple-choice test of editing and revising, contributing 40 percent of the outcome. There is also a 45-minute direct assessment of writing. As with NAEP, the writing purposes are narrative, expository, and persuasive, varying by grade, with the youngest students having a narrative task, the middle years an expository task and the older ones a persuasive task. Scoring of this element is, like NAEP, on a six-point holistic scale, but the criteria cover elaboration, organization, and fluency only, as the mechanical elements of writing are tested separately.

In all the examples described so far, there is an apparent intention of representing the construct of writing as well as possible within the constraints of a timed, on-demand assessment. Multiple-choice editing tests take their place in assessing mechanics, but are not claimed to represent writing as a whole. However, even in an extended writing test there are many threats to validity, particularly when the task is so predictable that it narrows the construct representation to one type of text.

Hillocks's (2002) analysis of writing assessment in a number of contrasting states identifies examples of significant narrowing in two states. In Texas, he describes how the original matrix of 16 possible text types was reduced to only four possibilities in the final assessment. Moving on to the Texas scoring criteria, he highlights a difficulty in the requirement for 'support' for reasoning within an essay. Hillocks argues that, because students cannot be assumed to have the knowledge necessary to build a logical case

in support of their position, relevant knowledge and logical links are in fact not required by the rubrics. This leads to high-scoring pieces that may be 'irrelevant, facetious, inaccurate, or sometimes false' in their arguments (Hillocks, 2002: 77).

In Illinois, Hillocks's focus is mainly on the scoring rubrics and accompanying sample papers. He demonstrates that the specific requirements set out in the rubrics make it possible to gain high scores by writing in a very formulaic way. This introduces the idea of the 'five-paragraph essay', which is pervasive in US commentaries on writing education, though not well known in the UK. The five-paragraph essay starts by stating its main theme or position and prefiguring the evidence by which it will be supported. There follow three paragraphs, each of them starting with a topic sentence related to the main theme, followed by description, detail, or examples to elaborate the point. Finally, the fifth paragraph is a conclusion restating the position and summarizing the case. Emig (1971) was the first to point out the narrowing of the notion of writing that results from such an approach, but other contributors to the current literature, as well as Hillocks, suggest that the form is still prevalent (for example, Lewis, 2001; Zigo, 2001; Dean, 2001). The narrowing of the construct of writing in tests has the potential to bring about important consequences for the teaching and learning of writing. This is a separate strand in the validation argument and will be discussed in a later section.

Some commentators take a different approach to arguing that high-stakes writing tests fail to represent adequately the writing attainment of students, using qualitative observations rather than an analysis of the tests. Albertson and Marwitz (2001) followed two eleventh-grade students in a learning support class as they produced a timed essay for the Georgia state assessment, consisting of a one-hour planning session and a later two-hour session for writing and presenting. The final essays produced by these two students did not, in the view of the researchers, do justice to the quality of the writing processes that they observed. In one case, the student collected sophisticated notes about one of the topics, but later abandoned this to write superficially on the alternative, less risky topic. The other student was willing to take risks, producing an interesting but unpolished essay, which also failed. These researchers argue that the assessment of a single short product tells very little about the rich understanding that students may have of the writing process.

SCORING AND RELIABILITY

Many of the examples of high-stakes writing assessment described in the previous section feature holistic, judgemental criteria to be applied by expert markers (readers). This is essential to construct representation, as students must be allowed to express their ideas in their own ways. However, it means that an element of subjectivity is inevitable and this whole area represents another potential threat to validity: if the scoring is inaccurate, then inferences about students' writing ability, made on the basis of the score, are unjustified. Investigations of scoring reliability are, therefore, integral to validation.

Assigning scores for writing tasks is a complex and difficult enterprise. High-stakes writing assessments typically rely on training sessions with example essays, standardization procedures, and at least an element of double marking. Congdon and McQueen (2000) carried out a systematic study involving 8285 students' writing performances and 16 raters. Each performance was rated twice, and each rater double-rated one batch of performances. The researchers revealed a high degree of variation, averaging around half a standard deviation overall, which affected reliability between raters, from day-to-day, and even between the two occasions when a rater scored the same performance.

Lumley (2002) took a different approach to his research. This involved only 24 texts and 4 raters, but yielded rich qualitative evidence in the form of think-aloud protocols. These revealed in detail the ways in which the raters were interpreting and applying the criteria. The process took place in three stages: an initial impression; rereading for specific features of the text in relation to the rating scale; and reconsidering the scores given whilst reconciling any ambiguities. Lumley highlights one example of inconsistency, where the writing is clear and coherent but not fully relevant to the task set. Here, there is evidence that raters give different weight to the contradictory judgements they have to deal with, and scoring as a result is inconsistent. Lumley's conclusion is that the design of tasks ranks alongside rater training and the specification of rating scales in the conditions necessary for valid scoring. He also identifies a need for additional guidelines for the raters addressing known areas of ambiguity.

Allingham (2000) gives an angry reaction to perceived unfairness of marking in a high-stakes environment in the context of the Ontario secondary school graduation test. He identifies a pattern similar to that described by Lumley (2002), where students are given only the lowest mark, because the composition was deemed to be 'non-compliant' to the task set. His examples include failing to set out work as three separate paragraphs and introducing opinion into an information piece. Allingham describes the resulting system as an 'utter waste of education funding on a test producing spurious data' (Allingham, 2000: 68). His article illustrates the extreme negative reaction of some educationalists when writing about students within a high-stakes testing context, something, which will recur later in the chapter.

The conclusion of this overview of the contribution of scoring to validation must be that extreme care is essential in all aspects of task design, development of rubrics, training of markers, and discussion of ambiguities before any claim to valid outcomes can be supported, and that double marking is highly desirable as a reliability check.

PORTFOLIO ASSESSMENT

In Kentucky, a very different approach to large-scale writing assessment became established during the 1990s. This assessment involves a collection of pieces of writing produced during normal classroom conditions, rather than as a test. The student selects the contents of the portfolio, but the number of pieces and types of writing is prescribed. Three grades undertake portfolio assessment. At the fourth and seventh grades, three pieces of writing are required: reflective; personal expressive or literary; and transactive. For the twelfth grade, there is an additional piece of writing, which must be transactive, but with an analytical or technical focus. For both of the older age groups, one of the pieces must be from a subject area other than English (KDE, 2007). The portfolio assessment of writing contributes towards the accountability score as part of a complex formula.

The naturalistic contexts, within which students produce their portfolios, address many of the problems of on-demand writing prompts. The self-chosen topics and the breadth of content make for a much fuller representation of the construct of writing. Hillocks describes this approach as:

> ... an opportunity for students to show their best work developed over a series of drafts, replete with feedback, revision, editing, and time to think carefully. It is writing as real writers do it. (Hillocks, 2002: 163)

A further advantage, in Hillocks's view, is a holistic scoring rubric based on an overall view of the portfolio's content. From 2006–7, however, this has been replaced by an analytic scoring rubric, where each piece of writing is scored separately for content, structure, and conventions (KDE, 2007).

The Kentucky portfolio assessment has given rise to a range of research literature. Hill (2000) describes the experience as a 'success story', recounting how, in the early years of the system, the scoring process became more accurate because of improved understanding of state standards amongst teachers. However, Lewis (2001), also writing from experience of scoring Kentucky portfolios, questions how far students' writing actually reflects authentic purposes and audiences. She believes that:

> ... although students are receiving more and different writing assignments, teachers are largely directing what students are to write in terms of form, purpose and audience. And the prompts that teachers design often limit students to contrived purposes and audiences. (Lewis, 2001:193)

She goes on to report that, even in this freer environment, the five-paragraph essay is still more prevalent than is desirable. However, Lewis also highlights the success of the Kentucky assessment in encouraging different forms of writing, whilst recognizing that the system is not yet perfect.

In the UK, the portfolio approach exists in the form of course work elements in the public examinations taken by 16- and 18-year-olds, GCSE and A-level, respectively. In these examinations, which are high-stakes for both schools and pupils, the coursework generally consists of an extended essay on a literature-related topic. At both levels, written coursework marks make up around one-third of the final result, alongside formal examinations (QCA, 2005). Thompson (2006) describes the 100 percent coursework GCSE, which was an option for schools between 1986 and 1993: a folder of work including a wide range of writing, alongside reading, speaking, and listening:

> What 100 percent coursework approaches aimed to do was move beyond the artificiality and mundanity of traditional approaches to reading and writing by asking teachers themselves to design assessment tasks which embodied genuine purposes and audiences. (Thompson, 2006: 125-126)

However, as Thompson points out, an approach which involves such freedom from central constraints was subject to political criticism from the outset and was abandoned in 1993. Public opinion is suspicious of high-stakes results not obtained under controlled conditions. A review of coursework by the Qualifications and Curriculum Authority (2005) acknowledges that the benefits of coursework outweigh its drawbacks. However, it goes on to set out a long list of ways in which procedures need to be tightened, in order to ensure reliability of marking and avoid plagiarism and inappropriate help. Clearly, a score obtained by anything other than the student's own efforts can support no valid inferences about the student's writing ability.

As with tests, the impact of portfolio assessments on teaching is another factor affecting validity, and it is to this that the next section will turn.

IMPACT AND CONSEQUENCES

The discussion up to this point has concerned the basic claim of writing assessments—that the scores can provide valid inferences about students' actual writing abilities. Within the high-stakes context, there are further claims of equal importance: that the testing regime contributes positively to practices in schools and to the raising of levels of attainment (Kane, 2006). These claims are, of course, interlinked, as the nature of testing and scoring partly determines the nature of the impact upon schools. There has been much debate about the extent to which the *consequences* of using an assessment are directly relevant to its validity. However, theorists have accepted for some years that consequential arguments are part of validation where the consequences result from inadequacies in construct representation (Messick, 1989; AERA/APA/NCEM, 1999), and this is the case in the present discussion.

Schools are under pressure to perform well on the writing assessments and to continue to improve their performance. If the assessment represents a significant narrowing of the construct of writing, then the consequences of this may be a narrowing of teaching to cover only those aspects of writing perceived to help with test performance—'teaching to the test'.

Arguments about the negative impact of testing on teaching dominate much of the research literature on high-stakes assessment. Hillocks (2002) subtitles his investigation 'How state writing assessments control learning', and identifies in particular the impact on teachers of the state testing systems in Texas and Illinois, described in the preceding section. He finds in Texas teachers an overwhelming tendency to have internalized the state standards and rubrics. They report finding them useful and adopt them as a structure for teaching. In a case study, the principal of a low-attaining school describes the writing curriculum as consisting only of tested text-types. The school has one day each week of test preparation, and nontested subjects such as science and social studies are relegated to the second half of the year, after testing has finished. In Illinois, a substantial majority of teachers report teaching the five-paragraph essay. A case study there finds teachers advised to use a writing model in which each part of the five-paragraph structure is represented by numbered and labelled boxes. Most teachers in these states, therefore, seem broadly compliant to the narrow definition of writing implied by the state assessments, teaching a reduced writing curriculum that fails to reflect the full construct of writing.

In England, Earl et al. (2003) also found evidence that teachers' practices could be affected by the pressure to achieve target levels. Their concerns include the narrowing of the whole curriculum in favour of the tested subjects as well as the narrowing of these subjects to focus upon test skills and test preparation.

Some commentators see these consequences as a serious impoverishment of the teaching of writing, directly brought about by testing. Writing specialists express horror at the way these systems can deprive students of the personal creativity and empowerment that comes with authentic writing. McCracken and McCracken (2001) list five profound losses experienced by teachers: voice and ownership, as they are forced to tell students things they do not believe themselves; time for reflection, response, renewal, relationships, reward, and relaxation; faith in their ability to succeed in the educational system; opportunity for interdisciplinary and team teaching; and ultimately, the desire even to be a teacher. Nelson (2001), in an impassioned tone typical of many writers holding such views, describes how writing should be taught:

> ... we can create classrooms and curricula that celebrate our students' writing and give them a place to tell their stories and turn their fear and anger and confusion into art, a place to give them hope in the form of their inborn gift of language as an instrument of creation. (Nelson, 2001:58)

In England, a similar view has been expressed by the acclaimed author Philip Pullman. Condemning the 'mechanistic approach' encouraged by the tests, he says:

> Proper writing just doesn't happen like that. ... There are no rules. Anything that's any good has to be discovered in the process of writing it. ... some things require to be private and tentative. Teaching at its best can give pupils the confidence to discover this mysterious state, and to begin to explore the things that can be discovered there. (Powling et al., 2003:8)

These writers see the process of writing as an essentially personal and creative act, and can, therefore, see no value at all in the artificiality of the test situation. Returning, however, to Myhill's (2001) analysis of the writing process as a combination of creating and crafting, it is possible to discern a less extreme position in some of the literature, one where crafting is valued alongside creativity and a more constructive position is advanced in relation to tests.

McClaskey (2001) provides a structure for this discussion. She distinguishes three possible approaches teachers may take within a narrow testing system. One, she calls 'embracing' the test: accepting the system and teaching narrowly with the aim of increasing scores. She recognizes that this happens, but takes a controversial position towards it:

> I ask you—*whose fault is that*? Just who do you think is implementing that test prep? It certainly isn't the textbook companies or even the principals. It's the teachers. (McClaskey, 2001: 93; author's italics)

Against this, McClaskey argues two alternative positions. One of these is to ignore the tests and continue to teach well, although she recognizes that it is necessary to have some support from school management before this is possible. The second is to 'embed' the test, including necessary test preparation but within a well-thought-out and coherent programme of work.

Several other articles detail a range of approaches that could be described as 'embedding'. Such articles are found entirely within the literature from North America, as there is a poverty of constructive engagement with issues related to formal assessment in the academic literature of the UK. Apthorp et al. (2001), Langer (2001), Wolf and Wolf (2002) and Fisher et al. (2004) all set out a range of strategies to help teachers approach the teaching of writing in an engaging and authentic way whilst still achieving improving test scores. These include the integration of reading and writing in a school-wide programme; fostering student choice and engagement; giving time to reflection; seeing the teaching of writing as cyclical and generative; explaining the procedures of the tests and examining the scoring rubrics, within this overall context. Zigo (2001) particularly stresses the value of professional development of teachers as a 'firebreak' to hold off the worst effects of state testing. Wollman-Bonilla (2004) deals specifically with persuasive writing, a frequent victim of the five-paragraph essay. She explains how meaningful issues can engage students so that they want to write persuasively, with teaching of persuasive devices and techniques integrated at the time the students need them. Earl and Torrance (2000), Hill (2000), and Parke et al. (2006) all describe improved teaching in terms of improved understanding of the standards, regarding these as embodying a rich view of the nature of writing.

These writers argue for a realistic approach within the high-stakes context, rather than rejecting the entire standards agenda. Whilst recognizing the potential shortcomings of such a system, they seek to counteract any negative impact by ensuring that students nevertheless receive a rich and rounded education in writing. The literature on the consequences of high-stakes writing assessment can thus be seen to be rather more nuanced than might at first appear.

CONCLUSION: THE VALIDATION OF HIGH-STAKES WRITING ASSESSMENT

At each stage in the validation argument outlined in the preceding sections, significant threats to validity have emerged. Given the underlying assumptions of high-stakes systems, threats to test validity are also threats to the teaching and learning of writing. In this final section, the shape of the argument will be reviewed so that necessary conditions can emerge for the defensible development of writing within a high-stakes context.

Construct representation

A writing assessment must lead to valid inferences about students' actual writing ability, not just their ability to produce a specified performance under test conditions. This has implications both for the shape of the assessment and for the approach to marking. The assessment itself should not rely upon a narrow interpretation of the standards upon which it is based, but should strive to reflect breadth and depth. One-off short tests should be supplemented wherever possible by a wider range of writing produced under nontest conditions. The scoring rubrics should be carefully designed to credit what is valued in writing, covering both creativity and crafting and avoiding criteria that could lead to formulaic writing. The marking process should include adequate training and monitoring, always mindful of the need for markers to apply the spirit of the standards and not just the wording of the rubrics.

Consequences and impact

All of the measures in the preceding paragraph will have their effects upon the consequences and impact of testing. The better the construct is represented in the assessment, the less likely it is that good teaching will be impeded by the testing regime. Alongside this, it is essential to strengthen teachers' capacity to teach writing well and their confidence in their own ability to understand what this means when confronted with high-stakes assessment. Professional development is key in this, and should include influential school managers and local officials as well as teachers. These groups need also to develop an enhanced understanding of assessment, which will help them to place high-stakes testing in its professional context, rather than allow themselves to be intimidated by it.

The professed aim of high-stakes accountability systems is, after all, to provide a better education for children, an aim shared by all professional educators. The way in which this has been implemented as high-stakes testing has been shown to have a great many flaws, which must be recognized and addressed by governments if their programmes are to have the desired effects. At the same time, however, teachers can contribute to genuine improvements, even within an accountability system, by taking a critical but constructive stance towards the requirements placed upon them. One of the most experienced commentators on educational change in recent years, Michael Fullan (1991), distinguishes between *compliance* and *capacity*. Although compliance with policies can be legally enforced, it is only by building capacity that real improvements can occur. Governments share with education professionals at all levels an obligation to ensure that the accountability systems they introduce foster capacity rather than mere compliance, for the benefit of students as well as teachers.

ACKNOWLEDGEMENTS

I am very grateful to the NFER Research Development Fund for part-funding the writing of this chapter, to Frances Brill and Chris Whetton for their valuable comments on a draft, and to Pauline Benefield and colleagues in the NFER Library for help with the literature searches.

NOTES

1 The education systems of Wales, Scotland, and Northern Ireland are devolved, so the comments on national testing refer only to England. Wales and Northern Ireland shared some of the elements described at one time or another, but do not currently share England's high-stakes culture.

2 The key stage-1 assessment for seven-year-olds now takes the form of a teacher judgement rather than a test result. Nevertheless, schools are required to administer a test of the kind described to every child, as a contribution towards that judgement.

3 The testing requirement for 14-year-olds was suddenly withdrawn in October 2008'.

REFERENCES

Albertson, K. and Marwitz, M. (2001) 'The Silent Scream: Students Negotiating Timed Writing Assessments', *Teaching English in the Two Year College*, 29(2): 144–153.

Alliance for Excellent Education (2007) *Making Writing Instruction a Priority in America's Middle and High Schools*, Washington, DC: Alliance for Excellent Education.

Allingham, P.V. (2000) 'The Ontario Secondary School Literacy Test: Mr. Harris's High-Stakes Version of B.C.'s Foundations Skills Assessment', *English Quarterly*, 32(3–4): 68–69.

American Educational Research Association, American Psychological Association and National Council for Educational Measurement (1999) *Standards for Educational and Psychological Testing*, Washington, DC: AERA.

Apthorp, H.S., Dean, C.B., Florian, J.E., Lauer, P.A., Reichardt, R., and Snow-Renner, R. (2001) *Standards in Classroom Practice: Research Synthesis*, Aurora, CO: Mid-Continent Research for Education and Learning. [online]. Available: http://www.eric.ed.gov/contentdelivery/servlet/ERICServlet?accno=ED460110_[30 July, 2007].

Australian Government Department of Education, Employment and Workplace Relations (1999) The Adelaide Declaration on National Goals for Schooling in the Twenty-first Century. [online]. Available: http://www.dest.gov.au/sectors/school_education/policy_initiatives_reviews/national_goals_for_schooling_in_the_twenty_first_century.htm [20 March 2009]

California Department of Education (2006) 'Teacher Guide for the 2006 California Writing Standards Test in Grade 4', [online]. Available: http://www.cde.ca.gov/ta/tg/sr/documents/g4wrtng06.pdf [12 October, 2007].

Congdon, P.J. and McQueen, J. (2000) 'The Stability of Rater Severity in Large-Scale Assessment Programs', *Journal of Educational Measurement*, 37(2): 163–178.

Connecticut State Department of Education (2006) '2006 Connecticut English Language Arts Curriculum Framework: A Guide for the Development of Prekindergarten—Grade 12 Literacy', [online]. Available: http://www.sde.ct.gov/sde/lib/sde/word_docs/curriculum/language_arts/february1csdeela-framework.doc [9 October, 2007].

Dean, D.M. (2001) 'The Day the Writing Died: A Play in One Act', *English Journal*, 91(1): 68–72.

Department for Education and Employment (1999) *The National Curriculum for England: English: Key Stages 1–4*, London: DfEE.

Department for Education and Skills (2004) 'National Curriculum Assessments of 7 and 11 Year Olds in England, 2003' (National Statistics First Release SFR 21/2004). [online]. Available: http://www.dcsf.gov.uk/rsgateway/DB/SFR/s000472/21-2004v3.pdf [5 September, 2007].

Department for Education and Skills (2006) 'Primary National Strategy: Literacy. Improving Writing, with a Particular Focus on Supporting Boys' Writing Development', [online]. Available: http://www.eriding.net/resources/general/prim_frmwrks/literacy/lit_index.html

Department for Education and Skills (2007) 'National Curriculum Assessments of 7 and 11 Year Olds in England, 2007' (Provisional) (National Statistics First Release SFR 24/2007). [online]. Available: http://www.dfes.gov.uk/rsgateway/DB/SFR/s000737/SFR24-2007.pdf [5 September, 2007].

Earl, L. and Torrance, N. (2000) 'Embedding Accountability and Improvement into Large-Scale Assessment: What Difference does it Make?', *Peabody Journal of Education*, 75(4): 114–141.

Earl, L., Watson, N., Levin, B., Leithwood, K., Fullan, M., and Torrance, N. with Jantzi, D., Mascall, B., and Volante, L. (2003) Watching and Learning 3: Final Report of the External Evaluation of England's National Literacy and Numeracy Strategies. London: DfES. [online]. Available: http://www.dfes.gov.uk/research/data/uploadfiles/DfES-WatchLearn%20Main.pdf [9 October, 2007].

Emig, J. (1971) *The Composing Process of Twelfth-Graders*, Urbana, IL: National Council of Teachers of English.

Fisher, D., Frey, N., Fearn, L., Farnan, N., and Petersen, F. (2004) 'Increasing Writing Achievement in an Urban Middle School', *Middle School Journal* J3, 36(2): 21–26.

Fullan, M. (1991) *The New Meaning of Educational Change*, London: Cassell.

Hill, R. (2000) 'A Success Story from Kentucky', Paper presented at the 30th Annual National Conference of the Council of Chief State School Officers on Large-Scale Assessment, Snowbird, IT, 25–28 June.

Hillocks, G. (2002) *The Testing Trap: How State Writing Assessments Control Learning* (Language and Literacy Series). New York, NY: Teachers College Press.

Kane, M.T. (2006) 'Validation', in R.L. Brennan (ed.), *Educational Measurement* (fourth edn.), Westport, CT: American Council on Education.

Kentucky Department of Education (2007) 'Writing Portfolio', Frankfort, KY: Kentucky Department of Education. [online]. Available: http://education.ky.gov/KDE/Administrative+Resources/Testing+and+Reporting+/District+Support/Writing+Portfolio.htm [9 October, 2007].

Koretz, D.M. and Hamilton, L.S. (2006) 'Testing for Accountability in K-12', in Brennan, R.L. (ed), *Educational Measurement* (fourth edn.), Westport, CT: American Council on Education.

Kress, G.R. (1982) *Learning to Write*, London: Routledge and Kegan Paul.

Langer, J. (2001) 'Succeeding Against the Odds in English', *English Journal*, 91(1): 37–42.

Lewis, S. (2001) 'Ten Years of Puzzling about Audience Awareness', Clearing House, 74(4): 191–196.

Lumley, T. (2002) 'Assessment Criteria in a Large-scale Writing Test: What do They Really Mean to the Raters?', *Language Testing*, 19(3): 246–276.

McClaskey, J. (2001) 'Who's Afraid of the Big, Bad TAAS? Rethinking our Response to Standardized Testing', *English Journal*, 91(1): 88–95.

McCracken, N.M. and McCracken, H.T. (2001) 'Teaching in the Time of Testing: What have you Lost?', *English Journal*, 91(1): 30–35.

Messick, S. (1989) 'Validity', in R.L. Linn. (ed.), *Educational Measurement* (third edn.), London: Collier Macmillan. pp.13–103.

Ministerial Council on Education, E.T.A.Y.A. (1999) The Adelaide Declaration. [online]. Available: http://www.mceetya.edu.au/mceetya/nationalgoals/index.htm [9 October, 2007].

Myhill, D. (2001) 'Writing: Crafting and Creating', *English in Education*, 35(3): 13–20.

Nelson, G.L. (2001) 'Writing Beyond Testing: "The Word as an Instrument of Creation"', *English Journal*, 91(1): 57–62.

Parke, C.S., Lane, S., and Stone, C.A. (2006) 'Impact of a State Performance Assessment Program in Reading and Writing', *Educational Research and Evaluation*, 12(3): 239–269.

Persky, H.R., Daane, M.C., and Jin, Y. (2003) *The Nation's Report Card: Writing 2002*, Washington, DC: National Center for Education Statistics. [online]. Available: http://www.eric.ed.gov/ERICDocs/data/ericdocs2sql/content_storage_01/0000019b/80/1b/06/8c.pdf

Powling, C., Ashley, B., Pullman, P., Fine, A., and Gavin, J. (2003) 'Meetings with the Minister: Five Children's Authors on the National Literacy Strategy', Reading: University of Reading, National Centre for Language and Literacy.

Qualifications and Curriculum Authority (2005) *A Review of GCE and GCSE Coursework Arrangements*, London: QCA. [online]. Available: http://www.qca.org.uk/libraryAssets/media/qca-05-1845-coursework-report.pdf [9 October, 2007].

Qualifications and Curriculum Authority (2007) *Key Stage 2 Levels 3–6 2007 Mark Schemes Pack*, London: QCA.

Sadler, D.R. (1987) 'Specifying and Promulgating Achievement Standards', *Oxford Review of Education*, 13(2): 191–209.

Thompson, P. (2006) 'Lessons of the GCSE English "100 Percent Coursework" Option, 1986–1993', in M. Sainsbury, C. Harrison' and A. Watts (eds), *Assessing Reading: From Theories to Classrooms*, Slough: NFER. pp.122–139.

US Department of Education (2001) No Child Left Behind Act 2001. Washington, DC: US Department of Education. [online]. Available: http://www.ed. gov/policy/elsec/leg/esea02/107-110.pdf [9 October, 2007].

Wolf, S. and Wolf, K. (2002) 'Teaching True and to the Test in Writing', *Language Arts*, 79(3): 229–240.

Wollman-Bonilla, J.E. (2004) 'Principled Teaching to(wards) the Test? Persuasive Writing in Two Classrooms', *Language Arts*, 81(6): 502.

Wyatt-Smith, C. (1997) 'Teaching and Assessing Writing: An Australian Perspective', *English in Education*, 31(3): 8–22.

Zigo, D. (2001) 'Constructing Firebreaks against High-stakes Testing', *English Education*, 33(3): 214–232.

Writing in the Wider Community

Beverly J. Moss

LITERACY IN THE IDEAL AND REAL WORLDS

One decade into the twenty-first century, certain concepts, though still contested, have become mainstays in writing and/or literacy studies and in related scholarly fields: multiple literacies, multiliterate, multilingualism, plurality of literacies, social practices of literacies, global networking, digital literacies, New Literacy Studies (NLS), academic or school literacy, local literacies, community literacies, literacy event, and literacy practices. Of course, this list is not exhaustive, but the items in the list signal where the field is in terms of foundational theoretical stances. On the surface, at least, we have come to generally accept that we exist in a world where there is not just one universal literacy but multiple literacies, where we belong to multiple discourse communities, and where many are multilingual. Digital literacies and multimodality seemingly dominate our present and future communicative practices. 'School literacies' have been complicated by notions of home and community literacies situated in cultural contexts where definitions of literacy are context-dependent—tied

to the social practices in which they are embedded. From this perspective, the New Literacy Studies (Street, 1993; Gee, 1991) has had a far-reaching influence in ushering in a paradigm shift in literacy studies research (see section that follows). Bruce Horner (2006), in his introduction to a special issue on 'Cross-Language Relations in Composition' in the American journal *College English,* states that 'Multilingualism … is taken as both the historical and the *ideal norm'* (italics mine) (570). And just as multilingualism, for Horner, is thought to be the ideal norm, so are multiliteracies assumed to be the ideal norm in much literacy studies research. In 1996, the New London Group, a group of ten scholars from Australia, Great Britain, and the United States, concluded that 'multiliteracies' should be the 'new approach to literacy pedagogy' (60). While the New London Group was speaking of pedagogy, their statement about multiliteracies speaks to the changing world. For the New London Group, multiliteracies as a theoretical and pedagogical approach will:

> Account for the context of our culturally and linguistically diverse and increasingly globalized societies, for the multifarious cultures that

interrelate and the plurality of texts that circulate.... Second, [multiliteracies will] account for the burgeoning variety of text forms associated with information and multimedia technologies. (1996: 60)

Gail Hawisher, Cynthia Selfe, Yi-Huey Guo, and Lu Liu (2006) in their essay in Horner's special issue observe that 'ideologies, technologies, languages, and literacies form a complex, interdependent, cultural ecology of literacy both shaping and shaped by writers' literacy practices at the macro, medial, and micro levels' (570). In this view, writers have agency in their interactions with and uses of literacy practices, but so, too, do the ideologies, technologies, and languages. Much of the writing scholarship produced over the last twenty-five years of the twentieth century and the first decade of the twenty-first century illustrate the complex interdependency of which Hawisher et al. speak. The literacy world described in the foregoing section appears to be a world that has not only made room for peoples and communities from diverse literacy and language backgrounds but has valued those literacy practices and languages as much as those practices from the dominant institutions.

The qualifiers I use to describe the literacy world that 'we have come to generally accept' are purposeful. In fact, Horner's use of *ideal norm* indicates that all is not as it should or could be. In fact, while multiliteracy and multilingualism are assumed to be the norm, in response to immigration patterns and an influx of multiple languages that comes with that immigration, several countries have waged or are waging campaigns to have one 'official' language named. Ironically, being able to communicate in the global world is seen as a common good, but the use of multiple languages in 'official' settings (government documents, for example) is seen as threatening to the common good. School systems in the name of mass literacy programs, with the encouragement and backing of local, state, and national governments, and often with the financing of 'for profit' education consulting firms, are requiring standardized curricula for teaching literacy—a one size fits all model—and a standardized literacy. This standardization in the US is often linked to high-stakes standardized tests that determine whether high school students receive a high school diploma. Graff and Duffy (2008) remind us that 'while mass public schooling today presents the most common route for individuals learning to read and write, the diversity of learners, including adult learners, in Europe and North America demands flexible understandings and pedagogies for literacy development. There is no single road to developing literacy' (51). That this warning is still necessary speaks of the apparent contradiction between the ideal and the real. Kirk Branch (2007) points to this contradiction for classroom teachers when he argues that 'a focus on local definitions of literacy—the focus of New Literacy Studies—remains inadequate to help teachers understand and analyse what they hope to accomplish by teaching, and what they hope their students will accomplish by learning, particular literacy practices' (8). So, while the current trend in literacy studies, particularly in New Literacy Studies, is to continue to encourage scholarship on local literacies as a way to achieve school literacy, Branch suggests that the trend is an ideal that is problematic.

Even in our discussions about computer technologies and digital literacies, the ideal norm and what is real can be far apart. In the ideal, the internet, specifically the World Wide Web, has provided a means for cultures to participate in cross-cultural communications. Digital technologies bring the global world to the most remote villages, making the world smaller. Presumably, this global world has an impact on community or vernacular literacies, as this contact with the wider world increases. Yet, unequal access resulting in a digital divide is still a reality. Material resources, or lack thereof, continue to contribute to who has power and who does not. Also, while digital technologies expand our definitions of writing, there is still a tension about what kind of writing will prepare our young people to be able to succeed in a technologically sophisticated, global society. What kinds of writing and other literacies should be valued is still a question.

It is within these real and ideal literacy worlds, a mythical binary at best, that the rest of this discussion will take place. For me, writing in the wider community is about the transition that is taking place in writing studies. Are we closer to the ideal norm? What are the forces that contributed to the growth of research on writing in nonschool communities? What are the current factors that shape this research? In particular, what are the challenges that are forcing scholars to rethink the role of writing in nonschool communities and the kind of research in these communities that we do? In the remainder of this chapter, I will consider those questions. I will begin with a brief discussion of the rise of research on literacies in nonschool communities or community literacies.

VALUING WHAT THEY DO AT HOME: STUDYING WRITING IN THE COMMUNITIES

Even though this chapter is concerned primarily with writing in the wider community, school or academic literacy is never far from the discussion. Like many other literacy scholars, my own interest in literacy in nonschool contexts was spurred by my motivation to validate the literacies that students from marginalized communities bring to mainstream schools from their home communities and community institutions. Often, these community literacies are considered nontraditional and lacking cultural capital particularly in relation to dominant institutions' language and literacy practices. Thus, these nontraditional literacies have been invisible, denounced as inferior, or seen as impeding children's progress in acquiring school literacy. However, with the failure of schools to adequately teach large numbers of children from diverse backgrounds,

especially children who seemed to function quite well in nonschool communities, scholars began to look to how those children were using language and literacy in their home communities. It was this turn away from school literacy—as a way to bridge a gap between nonschool and school literacy—that attracted me. The abundance of research on literacies in nonschool settings challenged and continues to question many assumptions about the intellectual and literacy experiences of children and adults from marginalized, especially minority, communities. Specifically, this research challenged the 'deficit and deprivation theories' that suggested that those from marginalized communities who spoke in nonstandard dialects were culturally deprived and/or illiterate (Farrell, 1983) and challenged the 'Great Divide Theory' that set up orality and literacy in a dichotomous relationship. These theories labelled as the autonomous model of literacy by Brian Street (1984), most often associated with Goody and Watt (1963), Ong (1982, 1986), and, most notably David Olson (1977), sought to establish literacy as a neutral technology, as a decontextualized set of skills, which contribute to higher order cognitive skills for literate individuals and societies [see also Chapter 1 in this Handbook].

As other chapters in this volume detail, a paradigm shift in literacy studies in the latter part of the twentieth century, moved literacy studies research from primarily an autonomous model to an ideological model (Street, 1994). Szwed, in his timely essay, 'The Ethnography of Literacy,' proposed:

> We [literacy scholars and educators] step back from the question of instruction, back to an even more basic 'basic,' the *social meaning of literacy*: that is, the roles these abilities play in social life; the varieties of reading and writing available for choice; the contexts for their performance; and the manner in which they are interpreted and tested, not by experts, but by ordinary people in ordinary activities. (1981: 422)

Building on Dell Hymes's (1974) theory of ethnography of communication, Szwed (1981) provides a framework for research into literacy practices in the everyday lives of 'ordinary people'.

Even more influential than Szwed's essay in 1981 was the publication that same year of psychologists' Scribner and Cole's landmark study of the literacy practices of the Vai in West Africa in the *Psychology of Literacy*. This study, using experimental design focused on the reading and writing practices of the Vai in and out of school, led Scribner and Cole (1981) to conclude that 'the metaphor of a "great divide" may not be appropriate for specifying differences among literates and nonliterates under contemporary conditions' (137). Soon after Scribner and Cole's study came two seminal works in the ethnography of literacy, Shirley Brice Heath's influential study of a working class black community, a working class white community, and a middle class integrated community in a Piedmont Carolina (US) town in *Ways with Words* (1983), and Brian Street's ethnography of literacy of a small village in Iran reported in *Literacy and Theory in Practice* (1984). Both of these studies, like Scribner and Cole, called into question the conclusions of the autonomous model of literacy and complicated how literacy is defined; in particular, these studies strongly suggested that literacy must be defined within the context of its use and that rather than looking at how literacy shapes individuals and society, we need to look at how people, especially use and shape literacy. These hugely influential studies called for more research on literacy in specific contexts, especially for the need for more ethnographies of literacy in the wider community. Heath's study, in particular, provided a model for scholars to study writing in communities with which they had some connection—communities closer to home. It also introduced to a broad audience the concept of literacy events which Heath (1982), borrowing from Teale and Sulzby, defines as 'any action sequence, involving one or more persons, in which the production and/or comprehension of print plays a role' (92). Street's (1993) study provides the field with a description of the ideological model which, in opposition to the autonomous model sees 'literacy practices as inextricably linked to culture and power structures' and as situated within social practices (12). In addition, Street also suggests a rethinking of how the field uses 'literacy practices'. For Street, 'literacy events' is subsumed under 'literacy practices'. He sees literacy practices 'as both behaviour and conceptualizations related to the use of reading and/or writing' (Street, 1993: 12). Also, important to this discussion of writing in the wider community is that these accounts of literacy and the ones that followed have come to be known as the New Literacy Studies (Gee, 1991; Street, 1993).

It is safe to say that after the publication of *The Psychology of Literacy, Ways with Words,* and *Literacy in Theory and Practice* along with the work of other scholars like Ruth Finnegan (1988) and Scollon and Scollon (1981), the shift to researching local literacies was established as valuable and viable. Around the world, scholars were studying uses of writing in the everyday lives of ordinary people. We can see the influence of these studies on later work like Niko Besnier's (1993) ethnography of a South Pacific Island community, Barton and Hamilton's (1998) ethnography of writing in a Lancaster, England community, and John Duffy's (2007) ethnography of Hmong Americans in a small Wisconsin town in the US. Studies of the 'local' and/or the 'vernacular', particularly within the framework of the new literacy studies continue to figure prominently in our discussions.

Barton and Hamilton (1998), who continue in the tradition of Scollon and Scollon, Heath, and Street, state that, 'these studies contribute to ways of talking about literacy, which properly acknowledge its situated nature and therefore offer the possibility of representing the multiplicities of literacies, which exist in any culture. Potentially, these studies can contribute to public and educational debate by providing an alternative discourse of literacy' (20). More specifically, in connecting their ethnography of literacy to educational contexts, Barton and Hamilton argue:

> Detailed ethnographic accounts can identify the many ways in which reading and writing are used and valued outside of educational contexts—or ignored for more highly valued alternatives; at the same time such accounts demonstrate the need to understand more fully the ways in which adults make use of literacy, providing the models and support that initiate children into literacy practices. (1998: 21)

Thus, ethnographies of literacies that focus on uses of writing outside the classroom provide more information about local literacy practices that may be useful to educators (see Taylor and Dorsey-Gaines' *Growing Up Literate: Learning from Inner-City Families*, 1988; Hull and Schultz's *School's Out: Bridging Out-of-School Literacies with Classroom Practices,* 2002; Weinstein-Shr's 'From Mountaintop to City Streets: Literacy in Philadelphia's Hmong Community,' 1994). As important as being useful to educators, these studies provide insight into the rich and complex vernacular literacy traditions in local communities that are often viewed as devaluing literacy or as primarily oral communities.

This paradigm shift turns our gaze, then, to local, community, or vernacular literacies. While, at times, these terms are used interchangeably, some scholars in the field offer specific definitions. For example, Gallego and Hollingsworth (2000) define *community literacies* as 'the appreciation, understanding, and/or use of interpretive and communicative traditions of culture and community, which sometimes stand as critiques of school literacies' (5). Gilmore's (1986) African-American middle school girls 'sub-rosa' literacy practices (156) and Shuman's (1986) urban adolescent girls' collaborative writing and establishing of 'storytelling rights' demonstrate vernacular or community literacies that stand as critiques of school literacies. '*Local literacies* refer to a wide range of literacy practices that are intimately connected with local or regional identities, but which are often overlooked by international

or national literacy campaigns' (Barton and Hamilton, 1998; Street, 1994 as quoted in Liddicoat, 2004: 6).

For Miriam Camitta (1993), vernacular writing 'is traditional and indigenous to the diverse cultural processes of communities as distinguished from the uniform, inflexible standards of institutions' (223). Farr's (1994) Chicago Mexicano men learning literacy *lirico* and Kalman's (1999) scribes and clients 'writing on the plaza' in Mexico are two examples. Barton and Hamilton (1998) offer one of the best definitions of vernacular literacies: 'Vernacular literacy practices are essentially ones which are not regulated by the formal rules and procedures of dominant social institutions and which have their origins in everyday life … Vernacular literacies are in fact hybrid practices which draw on a range of practices from different domains' (247). Thus, vernacular writing is often influenced by other writing traditions, particularly work of missionaries. Yet, even these 'outside' influences are not unaffected by the local traditions. Kulick and Stroud (1993), for example, conclude that in the Papua New Guinean village that they studied, the 'villagers of Gapun have their own ideas about reading and writing, generated from their own cultural concerns' (55). The cultural concerns of these local communities often lead to these hybrid practices. This hybridity is evident in numerous studies (Kulick and Stroud, 1993; Besnier, 1993; Besnier, 1995; Bloch, 1993; Reder and Reed-Wikelund, 1993; Probst, 1993). While several studies highlight the vernacular literacies outside of school, other studies highlight vernacular literacies that cross school and community boundaries (Heath, 1983; Shuman, 1986; Camitta, 1993; Finders, 1997; Barton and Hamilton, 1998).

Given the definitions of community and vernacular literacies, offered in the previous section, it is not surprising that community studies of writing are, by and large, concerned with the writing practices of marginalized or minority communities, such as Cushman's (1998) study of inner-city, low-income African-American women trying to negotiate institutional bureaucracy, Rockhill's (1993) ethnography of low-income Hispanic women in Los Angeles, or Wilson's (2000) study of 'in-between literacies of prisons' in England. Many ethnographies focus on the relationship between literacy practices and social institutions within a local community such as religious institutions (for example, Probst's 1993 study of the Aladura in Nigeria or Moss's 2003 study of literacy in African-American Churches). Several edited collections highlight the 'writing in the community' work being done around the world that has come to be known as new literacy studies. For a snapshot of this work, see the following collections: Barton and Ivanič (eds) *Writing in the Community* (1991); Street (ed) *Cross-Cultural Approaches to Literacy* (1993); Moss (ed) *Literacy across Communities* (1994); Prinsloo and Breier (eds) *The Social Uses of Literacy: Theory and Practice in Contemporary South Africa* (1996); Barton, Hamilton, and Ivanič (eds) *Situated Literacies: Reading and Writing in Context* (2000); Hawisher and Selfe (eds) *Global Literacies and the World Wide Web* (2000).

WHEN STUDYING THE LOCAL IS NOT ENOUGH: CHALLENGES TO NLS

While the paradigm shift that led to the work of Heath, Street, and the body of scholarship that has come to be known as the New Literacy Studies have proven to be invaluable in changing the way that we look at local literacies, particularly in valuing literacies in context, the end of the twentieth and beginning of the twenty-first century has seen NLS face many challenges. For an early, provocative critique of NLS, see reading psychologist Philip Gough's (1995) challenges to NLS. Gough, who embraces the autonomous model that Street and most supporters of NLS reject, believes that literacy is not social

and should not be political. For him, reading and writing are the private, independent acts that constitute literacy. Gough, like other critics of NLS, also vigorously objects to what he sees as the relativism of NLS (Gough, 1995). More current critiques of NLS highlight a tension between the local and the global or as Kirk Branch (2007) explains, between the local and the 'constructed world' (34). Brandt and Collins (2002), while taking pains to point out the strengths of NLS, question its limits. Brandt and Collins in 'Limits of the Local: Expanding Perspectives on Literacy as a Social Practice' suggest:

> As indispensable as the social-practice perspective has been to our own research and teaching, however, we wonder if the new paradigm sometimes veers too far in a reactive direction, exaggerating the power of local contexts to set or reveal the forms and meaning that literacy takes. Literate practices are not typically invented by their practitioners. (2002: 338)

Brandt and Collins (2002) seek to 'rehabilitate certain "autonomous" aspects of literacy without appealing to repudiated "autonomous models" of literacy' (339). Specifically, they acknowledge that we should look at the 'transcontextual aspects of literacy'—the travelling aspects of literacy—in other words, that we acknowledge the global. Brandt and Collins (2002) ask 'can we not see the ways that literacy arises out of local, particular, situated human interactions while also seeing how it also regularly arrives from other places—infiltrating, disjointing, and displacing local life' (343)? Calling on Bruno Latour to help them theorize this relationship between the local and the global, Brandt and Collins explain:

> With Latour's insight we are no longer confined to thinking about "the local" as that which is present in a particular context and "global" as that which is somewhere else or as something that bears down on local contexts from the outside. Latour replaces this dichotomy first by emphasizing that everything is local … However, local events can have globalizing tendencies and globalizing effects, accomplished often through the mediation of globalizing technologies. (2002: 347)

Brandt and Collins further suggest:

> Although we must always study local literacies, we can ask what is localizing and what is globalizing in what is going on. We can better acknowledge how extensively literacy is involved in globalizing enterprises. What appears to be a local event also can be understood as a far-flung tendril in a much more elaborate vine. The perspective we are advocating would allow us to acknowledge the heavy hand literacy has had in building networks across time and space—in de-localizing and re-framing social life—and in providing the centralizing powers by which larger and larger chunks of the social world are organized and connected. (2002: 347)

So for Brandt and Collins, recognizing how literacy acts on humans as well as how humans use literacy will help us see how the local penetrates the global and how the global penetrates the local.

Collins and Blot (2003), in *Literacy and Literacies: Texts, Power, and Identity*, question New Literacy Studies by suggesting that '… it still has also to account for general tendencies that hold across diverse case studies—for example, the frequent historical correlation of female gender and restricted access to literacy and schooling' (5). Collins and Blot, like Brandt and Collins (2002), acknowledge the value of situated approaches to literacy, but they point also to their shortcomings and offer a solution:

> Although we have gained insights from the richness of particular cases concerning domains of literacy and literate practices, it remains difficult to find within the work of Goody's most tenacious challengers a carefully worked out account of why literacy matters in the way that it does in the modern West. We suggest that key to such an account will be the question of power in literacy and that the ethnographic tradition falls short on just this question. (2003: 65)

Brian Street (2003) agrees with Brandt and Collins (2002) and Collins and Blot (2003) that NLS must account for the global and avoid romanticizing the local, and he sees Collins and Blot's interrogation of text, power, and identity as steps toward the impasse that NLS faces.

Kirk Branch (2007), building on Brandt and Collins' argument, takes it even further by suggesting about NLS 'that the emphasis on local meanings of literacy does not reflect in helpful ways that necessarily occurs in a literacy classroom. In such settings, almost by definition, literacy takes its meaning not from the actual classroom but from something, or some place, outside that classroom, not only from sponsors but also from a whole host of cultural expectations surrounding literacy' (34). Branch's critique is similar to Lisa Delpit's (1995) critique of progressive literacy pedagogies that do not take into account the power of dominant institutions and ideologies or the role of racism within those institutions. Branch (2007) calls for a 'rhetorical turn in addition to whatever empirical turn currently favoured in ethnographies of literacy' (34). For Branch, this rhetorical turn 'can help us understand how literacy practices become wrapped up in educational understandings, whatever they are, of the worlds in which we need to live, the worlds we teach about when we teach about literacy' (35).

John Duffy (2007) in a qualitative study of the literacy history of Hmong refugees in a small Wisconsin town uses the literacy narratives of his research participants to 'offer a critical vocabulary for talking about the ways in which people learn to read and write in diverse settings and across the boundaries of cultures, states, languages, economies, and writing systems' (6–7). Duffy's literacy study of the Hmong would be considered by Brandt and Clinton, a study that shows how a local literacy is involved in a 'globalizing enterprise'. For Duffy one cannot tell the 'story of Hmong literacy' without considering globalization, which Duffy defines as the 'welter of political, economic, religious, military, and migratory upheavals' (4). Like Kirk Branch, Duffy considers his theoretical framework 'a rhetorical conception of literacy development'. This rhetorical perspective 'views literacy development as a response to the symbolic activities of institutions, cultures, groups, or individuals' (Duffy, 2007: 200). He concludes that 'rhetorics offer the languages through which human beings come to understand a sense of the world and their place within it. Literacy is a constituent of rhetoric' (Duffy, 2007: 200). For Duffy, this framework contributes to New Literacy Studies by moving it past Brandt and Clinton's 'limits of the local' or Street's 'impasse'. Specifically, in Duffy's *Writing from These Roots*, he describes how his ethnography contributes to moving New Literacy Studies beyond the current impasse:

> That is the undertaking of this book, which attempts to contribute to the interdisciplinary project of New Literacy Studies by examining the literacy development of one people, the Hmong of Laos, in a way that connects ethnographic, historical, and theoretical perspectives. The book is *ethnographic* in that it is located in a single community and attempts to represent literacy development from the perspective of community members, communicating their diverging values, beliefs, and attitudes about reading and writing. It is *historical* in that it considers how literacy in the "ethnographic present" may be seen as a product of a culture's encounters with other cultures, states, institutions, and other powers in the past. Finally, the book offers a *theoretical* framework, and interpretive lens and language through which to understand the "general tendencies" that hold across diverse case studies. (2007: 10)

In Duffy's work, we have a model of research on writing in the wider community that answers the challenges to New Literacy Studies.

GLOBAL FORCES THAT AFFECT WRITING DEVELOPMENT

Digital Technologies

While most of the studies cited in the preceding section demonstrate that political, religious, and economic forces combined with race, gender, and class are factors that affect literacy development, specifically writing development, one of the major global forces in the twenty-first century that affects writing development is digital technology. The computer, the internet, the Web are generally touted as technologies that provide a means for people to communicate globally and, in many instances, provide opportunities for people to become multiliterate. While other chapters in this volume will provide a more detailed discussion of the role of digital technologies and writing, it is appropriate to briefly mention a few of the ways that digital literacies inform writing and local-global connections.

Even though computer technologies for those from impoverished countries and/or marginalized communities is still very much a concern, digital technologies are having an impact on global communication practices, and, therefore, global literacy practices. However, Hawisher and Selfe (2000) in their important edited collection *Global Literacies and the World-Wide Web* question what they suggest is an American and Western cultural narrative, what they call the 'global village myth' (9). Hawisher and Selfe state:

> According to this utopian and ethnocentric narrative, sophisticated computer networks—manufactured by far-sighted scientists and engineers educated within democratic and highly technological cultures—will serve to connect the world's peoples in a vast global community that transcends current geopolitical borders. Linked through this electronic community, the peoples of the world will discover and communicate about their common concerns, needs, and interests using the culturally neutral medium of computer-based communication. When individuals within the global community discover—through increased communication—their shared interests and commonweal, they will resolve their differences and identify ways of solving global problems that extend beyond the confining boundaries of nation states. (2000: 2)

Hawisher and Selfe rightly question this narrative and call for more culturally-specific studies that test the claims of the global village narrative. *Global Literacies and the World-Wide Web* (2000) is their initial response to the call. Their contributors consist of ten pairs of scholars who Hawisher and Selfe describe as follows:

> Each team is composed of at least one person who lives in, or was born in, a country other than the United States. Drawing on the talents of these teams, the volume provides a series of culturally

specific snapshots and examinations of literacy practices on the Web—in Hungary, Greece, Australia, Palau, Norway, Japan, Scotland, Mexico, Cuba, South Africa, and the United States. ... They [the snapshots] provide, most simply, a series of beginnings: incomplete, momentary, fragmentary assemblages of culturally specific information on Web literacy practices. (2000: 4)

Thus, Hawisher and Selfe and their contributors in this collection, while looking at culturally-specific literacy practices on the Web, situate those practices within national and global discourses of politics, economics, and education.

Hawisher and Selfe, with Guo and Liu (2006), in their essay 'Globalization and Agency: Designing and Redesigning the Literacies of Cyberspace', also remind us of the value of literacy narratives to 'demonstrate the multiple dimensions on which technology helps to shape the lived experiences of people within a cultural ecology' (628). This essay along with Hawisher and Selfe's collection of digital literacy narratives, *Literate Lives in the Information Age: Narratives of Literacy from the United States* (2004), illustrate that, in addition to providing valuable information about how global technologies penetrate the local and vice versa, literacy narratives are also viable paths to learning about how writing develops in the wider community (see Akinnaso, 1991).

LOCAL AND GLOBAL: PRESENT CONCERNS AND FUTURE NEEDS

I conclude this essay with a brief glance at specific kinds of communities, technologies, and cultural movements that are important 'players' in new and future writing communities: video games, hip hop culture, and disability studies. I focus on these three, not as an exhaustive list (clearly), but because they matter locally and globally and should figure prominently in discussions of writing and literacy. They matter to youth and adults, though not necessarily in the same ways or to

the same degree. Finally, they are issues that, though affected by race, gender, class, sexual orientation, age, nationality, and other identity markers, speak to groups across these markers.

'Popular literacies': Video games and literacy

Digital technologies will continue to be prominent in both local and global settings, even in communities where the absence of digital technologies speak loudly. However, many of the studies cited in the foregoing sections have already taught us that we should be wary of pronouncements about what such absence means. Graff's (1991) and Graff and Duffy's (2008) discussions of the literacy myth along with Hawisher and Selfe's (2000) warning about the 'global village myth' should signal a need for deeper, more complex interrogations of major claims about the impact of digital technologies on literacy. They should, as Hawisher and Selfe with Guo and Liu (2006) call for, point to a need for more socially situated research that helps us understand the 'complex social and cultural ecology, both local and global, within which literacy practices and values are situated' (628).

One area in particular that is garnering much attention globally is the relationship between literacy and video games. From Mackereth and Anderson's (2000) essay on 'Computers, Video Games, and Literacy: What Do Girls Think? (Statistics Included)' published in the *Australian Journal of Language and Literacy,* and Gee's provocative book, *What Video Games Have to Teach Us about Learning and Literacy* (2003) to the fall 2008 special issue of *Computers & Composition: An International Journal* devoted to gaming and literacy, scholars concerned with literacy have recognized that video gaming is a technology in which large segments of the population are engaging. In addition, Selfe and Hawisher (2007) in the introduction to their edited collection,

Gaming Lives in the Twenty-first Century: Literate Connections, situate their collection as a follow–up to Gee's *What Video Games Have to Teach Us,* and see it as 'examining Gee's claim that good computer games can provide better literacy and learning environments than US schools' (1). The strength and uniqueness of *Gaming Lives* is that the contributors provide in-depth case studies of gamers and their literacy practices. Several of the chapters, in fact, are coauthored by the gamers who are the subjects of the case studies. Selfe and Hawisher (2007), in their introduction describe *Gaming Lives* as 'focusing more precisely on the literacies acquired, practiced, and valued within digital environments of computer games ...' (1). The research reported in *Gaming Lives* is part of a large-scale international study of digital literacies that Selfe, Hawisher, and colleagues in the US and abroad are conducting to find out more about the role digital literacies play in the lived experiences of people from a range of cultural and geographic backgrounds. Because educators know little about the literacy practices used in gaming communities, case studies such as the ones that result from this large scale study become even more valuable. We need to know what kinds of writing, for example, gamers are engaging in? What is the role of race, gender, class, and/or sexual orientation in access to and reception of literacies associated with video games? What is the relationship between gaming literacies and school literacies?

Popular Literacies and Hip-Hop

Just as video games seem to have a worldwide reach, so, too, has hip-hop culture reached across oceans. In Elaine Richardson and Sean Lewis's (2000) essay, '"Flippin the Script"/ "Blowin Up the Spot": "Puttin Hip-Hop Online" in (African) America and South Africa', the authors do not focus only on South African youth's adoption of hip-hop culture; they also speak to the global spread of hip hop: 'in Japan, you might see youth dressing with Malcolm X caps worn backwards; in Hawaii, you can hear youth rapping in Hawaiian Pidgin English; in South Africa, you can experience hip-hop of the Afrikaans, English, Zulu, and other flavas and it has appeal cross-culturally' (271). Richardson and Lewis suggest that the internet provides a means for hip-hop discourses to travel and become a part of the literacy practices of youth across the globe. The popularity of hip hop music and rap videos in Europe, the UK, and Asia attest to the global market for this cultural product. This billion dollar industry reaches across the borders of the entertainment industry—music, literature, commercial television, film, sports—to fashion, advertising, and politics. Cultural movements like hip-hop with discourse practices that act as cultural critiques of dominant, hegemonic discourses, particularly associated with white patriarchal literacy practices, act simultaneously as alternatives to school literacies and as bridges to school literacy (Campbell, 2005). While African-American scholars like Richardson (2007) and Kermit Campbell (2005) examine the discourse practices and critical literacies of hip-hop primarily in African-American communities, the widespread reach of hip-hop indicates a need to study how hip-hop discourses and literacies interact with the discourses and literacies of youth cultures in communities around the world. Again, like video gaming, much of the writing that may be associated with hip-hop occurs outside of schools in nonsanctioned events, is sometimes tied to digital technology, and rightly or wrongly, associated with marginalized communities, and, is therefore, often not counted as writing.

DISABILITY STUDIES AND LITERACY

With the growth of Disability Studies as an interdisciplinary and international field, there is also a need for scholars to study writing and disability beyond the classroom. There is no shortage of scholars writing about disability, particularly using autobiography, autoethnography, and biography as method and genre (in the US, for example, see the work of Georgina Kleege, Stephen Kuusisto, and Rosemary Garland-Thompson); and there are scholars who have turned their attention to disability and the teaching of writing (Dunn, 2001; Lewicki-Wilson and Brueggemann, 2008). There are also disability studies scholars, like Brenda Jo Brueggemann (1999) who bring to the field her training as a rhetorician and compositionist and whose early scholarly path included literacy studies. And as the 2008 special issues on disability studies in Canada and disability studies in Japan in *Disability Studies Quarterly* signal, disability as a site of inquiry is worldwide. However, Disability Studies has few scholars who actually conduct scholarly inquiries into the 'writing' communities beyond school contexts. Given the deaf blogging communities, the 'Vlogs' (video logs as a counterpart to web logs), and other electronic communities that have emerged because of available computer technologies, there is a need to study what constitutes writing and text in these vlogging and blogging communities. Like the role of video games, there are literacy practices—visual, audio, and print—that are central to 'writing' in disabled communities that warrant our attention. As with literacy practices in other nonschool contexts, we have much to learn about and from the rich, complex literacy practices in these communities.

A WORD ABOUT METHODOLOGY

Even though the methodologies and theoretical framework of New Literacy Studies have been challenged, they are still prominent and viable methodologies for studying writing in socially situated settings. None of the critiques addressed in this essay—Brandt and Collins, Collins and Blot, Branch, Duffy—call for a turn away from studies of vernacular or local literacies. They do call for situating such studies within the 'global'. What we see currently and will, I think, continue to see, are ethnographies and case studies with heavy doses of critical discourse analysis and rhetorical analysis. We are also seeing the growing importance of literacy narratives, both self-written and collected. Researching writing in the wider community provides scholars, educators, and policy makers with an opportunity to understand the complexity and richness of past, current, and future writing traditions in the lives of everyday people in their varied and complex communities, to see how communities' belief systems, traditions, and power structures interact with the multiple literacies that characterize our lives. However, scholars who study writing in nontraditional contexts—the wider community—are under pressure (from critics of NLS among others) to make their research more relevant and helpful to literacy educators. In an era where 'outcomes assessment' and 'accountability' are part of the regular vocabulary of funding agencies and governments, qualitative research, particularly ethnographies of literacy, must speak to the concerns of stakeholders across the education landscape.

REFERENCES

Akinnaso, F. (1991) 'Literacy and individual consciousness,' in E. Jennings and A. Purves (eds), *Literate Systems and Individual Lives: Perspectives on Literacy and Schooling*, Albany, NY: SUNY Press. pp.73–94.

Barton, D. and Hamilton, M. (1998) *Local Literacies: Reading and Writing in One Community*, New York: Routledge.

Barton, D. and Ivanič, R. (eds) (1991) *Writing in the Community*, Newbury Park, CA: Sage.

Barton, D., Hamilton, M., and Ivanič, R. (eds) (2000) *Situated Literacies: Reading and Writing in Context*, New York: Routledge.

Besnier, N. (1993) 'Literacy and feelings: The encoding of Affect in Nukulaelae letters', in B. Street (ed.), *Cross-Cultural Approaches to Literacy*, New York: Cambridge University Press. pp.62–86.

Besnier, N. (1995) *Literacy, Emotion, and Authority: Reading and Writing on a Polynesian Atoll*, New York: Cambridge University Press.

Bloch, M. (1993) 'The uses of schooling and literacy in a Zafimaniry village,' in B. Street (ed.), *Cross-Cultural Approaches to Literacy*, New York: Cambridge University Press. pp.87–109.

Branch, K. (2007) *Eyes on the Ought to Be*, Cresskill, NJ: Hampton Press.

Brandt, D. and Collins, K. (2002) 'Limits of the local: expanding perspectives on literacy as a social practice', *Journal of Literacy Research*, 34(3): 337–56.

Brueggemann, B. (1999) *Lend Me Your Ear: Rhetorical Constructions of Deafness*, Washington, DC: Gallaudet University Press.

Camitta, M. (1993) 'Vernacular writing: Varieties of literacy among Philadelphia high school students,' in B. Street (ed.), *Cross-Cultural Approaches to Literacy*, New York: Cambridge University Press. pp.228–246.

Campbell, K. (2005) Getting *Our Groove On: Rhetoric, Language, and Literacy for the Hip Hop Generation*, Detroit, MI: Wayne State University Press.

Collins, J. and Blot, R. (2003) *Literacy and Literacies: Texts, Power and Identity*, New York: Cambridge University Press.

Cushman, E. (1998) *The Struggle and The Tools: Oral and Literate Strategies in an Inner City Community*, Albany, NY: SUNY Press.

Delpit, L. (1995) *Other People's Children: Cultural Conflict in the Classroom*, New York: The New Press.

Duffy, J. (2007) *Writing from these Roots: The Historical Development of Literacy in a Hmong-American Community*, Honolulu: University of Hawaii Press.

Dunn, P. (2001) *Talking, Sketching, Moving: Multiple Literacies in the Teaching of Writing*, Portsmouth, NH: Boynton-Cook/Heinemann.

Farr, M. (1994) 'En los idiomas: Literacy practices among Chicago Mexicanos,' in B. Moss (ed.), *Literacy Across Communities*, Creskill, NJ: Hampton Press. pp.9–47.

Farrell, T. (1983) 'I.Q. and standard English', *College Composition and Communication*, 34(4): 470–484.

Finders, M. (1997) Just Girls: *Hidden Literacies and Life in Junior High*, New York: Teachers College Press.

Finnegan, R. (1988) *Literacy and Orality*, London: Basil Blackwell.

Gallego, M. and Hollingsworth, S. (2000) 'The idea of multiple literacies,' in M. Gallego and S. Hollingsworth (eds), *What Counts as Literacy: Challenging the School Standard*, New York: Teachers College Press. pp.1–23.

Gee, J. (1991) *Social Linguistics: Ideology in Discourse*, London: Falmer Press.

Gee, J. (2003) *What Video Games Have to Teach Us about Learning and Literacy*, New York: Palgrave Macmillan.

Gilmore, P. (1986) 'Sub-rosa literacy: Peers, play, and ownership in literacy acquisition,' in B. Schieffelin and P. Gilmore (eds), *The Acquisition of Literacy: Ethnographic perspectives*, Norwood, NJ: Ablex. pp.155–168.

Goody, J. and Watt, I. (1963) 'The consequences of literacy', *Comparative Studies in Society and History*, 5(3): 305–345.

Gough, P. (1995) 'The new literacy: Caveat emptor', *Journal of Research in Reading*. 18(2): 79–86.

Graff, H. (1991) *The Literacy Myth: Literacy and Social structure in the Nineteenth Century City*, New Brunswick, NJ: Transaction Press.

Graff, H. and Duffy, J. (2008) 'Literacy myths,' in B.V. Street and N.H. Hornberger, *Encyclopedia of Language and Education* (second edn.), London: Springer US. pp.43–52.

Hawisher, G. and Selfe, C. (eds) (2000) *Global Literacies and the World Web*, New York: Routledge.

Hawisher, G. and Selfe, C. (eds) (2003) *Literate Lives in the Information Age: Narratives of Literacy from the United States*, Mahwah, NJ: Lawrence Erlbaum Associates.

Hawisher, G., Selfe, C., with Guo, Yi-Huey, and Liu, Lu (2006) 'Globalization and agency: Designing and redesigning the literacies of cyberspace', *College English*, 68(6): 619–636.

Heath, S.B. (1982) 'Protean shapes in literacy events: Ever-shifting oral and literate traditions', in D. Tannen (ed.), *Spoken and Written Language: Exploring Literacy and Orality*, Norwood, NJ: Ablex. pp.91–118.

Heath, S. B. (1983) *Ways with Words: Language, Life, and Work in Communities and Classrooms*, New York: Cambridge University Press.

Horner, B. (2006) 'Introduction: Cross-language relations in composition', *College English*, 68(6): 569–574.

Hull, G. and Schultz, K. (eds) (2002) *School's Out: Bridging Out-of-School Literacies with Classroom Practices*, New York: Teacher's College Press.

Hymes, D. (1974) *Foundations in Sociolinguistics: An Ethnographic Approach*, Philadelphia, PA: University of Pennsylvania Press.

Johnson, M. and Lacasa, P. (eds) (2008) *Computers and composition: An International Journal* (special issue), 25(3).

Kalman, J. (1999) *Writing on the Plaza: Mediated Literacy Practices among Scribes and Clients in Mexico City*, Creskill, NJ: Hampton Press.

Kulick, D. and Stroud, C. (1993) 'Conceptions and uses of literacy in a Papa New Guinean village', in B. Street (ed.), *Cross-Cultural Approaches to Literacy*, New York: Cambridge University Press. pp.30–61.

Lewicki-Wilson, C. and Brueggemann, B. (eds) (2008) *Disability and the Teaching of Writing*, New York: Bedford/St. Martin's.

Liddicoat, A. (2004) 'Language planning for literacy: Issues and implications', *Current Issues in Language Planning*, 5(1): 1–17.

Mackereth, M. and Anderson, J. (2000) 'Computers, video games, and literacy: What do girls think? (statistical data included)', *Australian Journal of Language and Literacy*, 23(3).

Moss, B. (ed) (1994) *Literacy across Communities*, Cresskill, NJ: Hampton Press.

Moss, B. (2003) *A Community Text Arises: A Literate Text and A Literacy Tradition in African-American Churches*, Cresskill, NJ: Hampton Press.

New London Group (1996) 'A pedagogy of multiliteracies: Designing social futures,' *Harvard Educational Review*, 66(1): 60–92.

Olson. D. (1977) 'From utterance to text: The bias of language in speech and writing', *Harvard Educational Review*, 47(3): 257–281.

Ong, W. (1982) *Orality and Literacy: The Technologizing of the Word*, New York: Methuen.

Ong, W. (1986) 'Writing is a technology that restructures thought', in G. Baumann (ed.), *The Written Word: Literacy in Transition*, Oxford, UK: Clarendon Press. pp.23–50.

Prinsloo, M. and Breier, M. (eds) (1996) *The Social Uses of Literacy: Theory and Practice in Contemporary South Africa*, Philadelphia, PA: John Benjamins.

Probst, P. (1993) 'The letter and the spirit: Literacy and religious authority in the history of the Aladura movement in Western Nigeria', in B. Street (ed.), *Cross-Cultural Approaches to Literacy*, New York: Cambridge University Press. pp.198–220.

Reder, S. and Reed-Wikelund, K. (1993) 'Literacy development and ethnicity: An Alaskan example', in B. Street (ed.), *Cross-Cultural Approaches to Literacy*, New York: Cambridge University Press. pp.176–197.

Richardson, E. (2007). '"She was workin' like foreal": Critical literacy and discourse practices of African American females in the age of hip hop', *Discourse and Society*, 18(6): 789–809.

Richardson, E. and Lewis, S. (2000) '"Flippin the script/blowin' up the spot": Puttin' hip-hop online in (African) America and South Africa', in G. Hawisher and C. Selfe (eds), *Global Literacies and the World Wide Web*, New York: Routledge. pp.251–276.

Rockhill, K. (1993) 'Gender, language and the politics of literacy', in B. Street (ed.), *Cross-Cultural Approaches to Literacy*, New York: Cambridge University Press. pp.156–175.

Scollon, R. and Scollon, S. (1981) *Narrative, Literacy, and Face in Interethnic Communication*, Norwood, NJ: Ablex.

Scribner, S. and Cole, M. (1981) *The Psychology of Literacy*, Cambridge, MA: Harvard University Press.

Selfe, C. and Hawisher, G. (eds) (2007) *Gaming Lives in the Twenty-First Century: Literate Connections*, New York: Palgrave Macmillan.

Shuman, A. (1986) *Storytelling Rights: The Uses of Oral and Written Texts Among Urban Adolescents*, New York: Cambridge University Press.

Street, B. (1984) *Literacy in Theory and Practice*, New York: Cambridge University Press.

Street, B. (ed) (1993) *Cross-Cultural Approaches to Literacy*, New York: Cambridge University Press.

Street, B. (1994) 'What is meant by local literacies?' *Language and Education,* 1(2): 9–17.

Street, B. (2003) 'What's "new" in new literacy studies? Critical approaches to literacy in theory and practice', *Issues in Comparative Education*, 5(2): 77–91.

Szwed, J. (1981) 'The ethnography of literacy', in M. Farr Whiteman (ed.), *Writing: The Nature, Development, and Teaching of Written Communication*, Mahwah, NJ: Lawrence Erlbaum Associates. pp.13–23.

Taylor, D. and Dorsey-Gaines, C. (1988) *Growing Up Literate: Learning from Inner-City Families*, Portsmouth, NH: Heinemann.

Weinstein-Shr, G. (1994) 'From mountaintops to city streets: Literacy in Philadelphia's Hmong community', in B. Moss (ed.), *Literacy across Communities*, Cresskill, NJ: Hampton Press. pp.49–83.

Wilson, A. (2000) 'There is no escape from the third-space theory: Borderland discourse and the 'in-between' litracies of prisons', in D. Barton, M. Hamilton, and R Ivanič (eds.), *Situated Literacies: Reading and Writing in Context*, New York: Routledge. pp.54–69.

Reflections on the Future of Writing Development

Robert Gundlach

If there is a single rallying claim in the many recent discussions of the future of reading and writing, it is, as Naomi Baron phrases it in her essay, 'The Future of Written Culture: Envisioning Language in the New Millennium', that 'the computer (and computer-based technologies)' are 'reshaping our relationship with both the written and the printed word' (2005: 7). Even in a notably balanced and thoughtful essay, 'Future Reading: Digitization and Its Discontents', in which historian Anthony Grafton seeks to look past the 'hype and rhetoric' accompanying ambitious new projects aimed at developing a digitized universal library that would provide a computer-accessible 'encyclopedic record of human experience' in text and image, Grafton asserts without qualification that '[w]e have clearly reached a new point in the history of text production'. The current 'rush to digitize the written record', Grafton adds, is properly understood as 'one of a number of critical moments in the long saga of our drive to accumulate, store, and retrieve information efficiently'. It is not likely to 'result in the infotopia that the prophets conjure up', he suggests, 'but in one of a long series of new information ecologies, each of

them challenging, in which readers, writers, and producers of text have learned to survive'. Furthermore, at present, the scene for readers and writers—the emerging new information ecology—is far from settled: '[I]t is hard to exaggerate what is already becoming possible month by month and what will become possible in the next few years' (2007: 2).

In discussions of nearly every domain of written communication, there is a sense of dramatic change on the horizon. Often the emphasis is on the ways in which writing is competing with—or being recontextualized by—other forms of communication. Studying changes in the learning environment in schools, for example, Gunter Kress and his colleagues observe that 'writing is now no longer the central mode of representation of learning materials—textbooks, Web-based resources, teacher-produced materials'. Written representation of knowledge is 'being displaced by image as the central mode', and this shift raises 'sharp questions about present and future roles and forms of writing' (Bezemer and Kress 2008: 166). Jeff Chester, examining the much-discussed phenomenon of the convergence of visual, audio, and text-centred public media, writes, 'We are on the eve of the emergence of the most powerful media and communications system ever developed'. He notes that a 'flood of compelling images', sounds, and texts are delivered 'through digital TVs, PCs, cell phones, digital video recorders, iPods, and countless mobile devices. These technologies will surround us', Chester adds, 'immerse us, always be on, wherever we are—at home, work, or play' (2007: xv).

Some commentators and scholars focus on how to harness these developments and tap their potential for engaging children and adolescents in productive uses of newly integrated and increasingly accessible digital media. Henry Jenkins, in a paper titled 'Confronting the Challenges of Participatory Culture: Media Education for the 21st Century', observes that in the United States, many 'teens are actively engaged in what we are calling *participatory cultures*', by which he means computer-mediated social networks 'with relatively low barriers to artistic expression and civic engagement, strong support for creating and sharing one's creations, and some type of informal mentorship whereby what is known by the most experienced is passed along to novices' (2006: 3). In a particularly thoughtful discussion of 'Revisioning Language, Literacy, and the Immigrant Subject in New Mediascapes', literacy scholar Wan Shun Eva Lam suggests that 'Networked electronic communication has redefined the scope of time and space in the socialization of new generations of youth', noting that 'as immigrant students (in the United States) traverse different timescapes in their daily lives, it is important to note how their identity formation and socialization in the use of language(s) are defined not only by the imagined community of the nation state but also by various imagined communities on a global scale' (2006: 175). Drawing on her analysis of recent research and her own case studies of three immigrant adolescents' communicative activities on the Internet, Lam argues that 'the new mediascapes—the changing scope of

space and time, modes of representation, symbolic materials and ways of using language associated with networked electronic media—compel us to re-think our nation-centred views of immigrant students' adaptation and their language and literacy development' (2006: 171).

Other commentators focus on what seems to be lost, if not with the emergence of new technology, then with changes the new technology seems to facilitate, toward more rapid, associative, and less traditionally sustained kinds of reading and writing. Steve Wasserman, writing in the *Columbia Journalism Review*, laments that in 'today's McWorld, the forces seeking to enroll the populace in the junk cults of celebrity, sensationalism, and gossip are increasingly powerful and wield tremendous economic clout. The cultural conversation devolves and is held hostage to these trends'. Wasserman adds: 'The terrible irony is that at the dawn of an era of almost magical technology with a potential of deepening the implicit democratic promise of mass literacy, we also totter on the edge of an abyss of profound cultural neglect' (2007: 14–15).

In the cacophony of dramatic predictions for the future of written communication, it can be difficult to reflect productively on the prospects for writing development in the future—for young children initially learning to write, for older children and adolescents developing as writers through their years in school, and for adults learning (and often relearning, possibly many times) to adapt to new writing contexts, new tools, new expectations, and new opportunities. One solution is to look at a relatively narrow aspect of the changing realm of written communication and multimedia networks and to concentrate on it. In the recent scholarly collection, *Writing and Digital Media*, for example, one team of contributors explores 'Lucidity and Negotiated Meaning in Internet Chat', while another team considers 'Knowledge Acquisition in Designing Hypervideos: Different Roles of Writing during Courses in "New" Media Production' (Van Waes,

Leijten, and Neuwirth, 2006: v). There is merit in this approach, particularly in conducting formal research, where it is crucial to formulate testable hypotheses for experimental studies or frame sharply focused questions for observational and ethnographic studies. But there is also some value, in my view, in stepping back briefly, perhaps especially here at the conclusion of a handbook that explores many aspects of writing development, to reflect in a broader way on how people will develop writing ability in the new circumstances in which many readers and writers are likely to find themselves in the years ahead.

Out walking on an autumn afternoon, not long ago, I came upon a five-letter inscription written in chalk on an otherwise unoccupied sidewalk near my home. Written entirely in upper case letters, it was apparently the work of a child who lives in the neighbourhood. The letters were these: STRTE. A box-like rectangle of chalk lines was drawn around the set of five letters, creating the impression that the text may have been designed to resemble a sign or banner. Combining my knowledge of the neighbourhood, in which children sometimes organize sidewalk races on bicycles or big-wheel riding toys, and my experience deciphering young children's early experiments with written language (see, for examples, Gundlach 1982, 1992, 2003), I arrived at the guess that STRTE was written by a six- or seven-year-old child, was meant to represent the word 'START', and that the surrounding rectangle signalled an aim to produce a sign or banner indicating the starting position of a riding course for young riders of bicycles or big-wheel toys.

If we grant the plausibility (if not the firm accuracy) of this conjecture, we can see that this small bit of discarded writing was very likely the work of a child who now, as we approach the end of the first decade of a new century, is just beginning to develop the ability to write—is very nearly at the start, so to speak, of understanding how to use written language effectively, of knowing how to create conventional written forms and novel written texts, and of managing various writing tools and processes. Assuming that this child will advance beyond the current 'STRTE' level of understanding and skill, What can we say about what lies ahead as he or she continues to develop as a writer? What will be involved as this beginner continues to develop as a writer in the years and decades to come, with the processes of learning, relearning, adjusting, and adapting possibly spanning nearly the entire twenty-first century?

Perhaps the first observation is that the tools for writing—writing's technology—available to writers and appropriated by beginning writers may vary more than is accounted for in many of the discussions of new media and written communication. This young writer wrote with chalk on a sidewalk. For this child, there was, as Roger Chartier (2004) puts it, a certain 'abstraction of text' from materiality, inasmuch as a starting-line banner, if my guess about this text is right, was simulated rather than produced directly. Nevertheless, there was a palpable materiality to this written composition: a mark made with chalk on concrete, a gesture that left a trace. Learning to write for this young writer may be like learning to write for many other young writers, involving a physical, social, and cognitive act that extends the functions not only of speaking but also of drawing and certain kinds of play (McLane and McNamee 1990).

Even this glimpse of one young child's experimentation with writing alerts us to the complexity and variability of writing development. Writing development can be shaped in crucial ways by formal writing instruction, but as recent scholarship has suggested, a premise of understanding writing development is that learning to write often involves more than being taught (Gundlach 1992, Tolchinsky 2006). Viewed more comprehensively as a dimension of language development, learning to write can be understood as an outcome of the interplay of interacting histories, which, for each individual person, are both broadly cultural and specifically biographical. Individuals begin learning to write, and continue developing as writers—when indeed particular individuals do continue to develop—along various trajectories. These trajectories are shaped by the interplay of individuals' own inclinations to experiment with writing and their experiences with writing and written language in their families, their communities, their schools, and, especially notable in our time, in the extended virtual geography, sometimes multilingual, of both public broadcast media and personal computer-based, online reading and writing activity (Danet and Herring 2007, Gundlach 2004). Generalizations about writing development must be tempered by the steady recognition—and hence the firm qualification—that people differ in the ways they learn to write and in the resources they are able and inclined to recruit to support the process. These differences are not determined exclusively, and perhaps not chiefly, by the extent to which a writer has access to advanced technology. Access to chalk, a neighbourhood sidewalk, and friends who ride bicycles may form at least a small part of the story for some beginning writers, both now and in the years ahead.

Nonetheless, the increasingly pervasive use of digital technology for written communication in cultures across the world will very likely change the character of writing development in the decades to come in ways that we can scarcely predict today. Liliana Tolchinsky makes an important contribution in her recent book, *The Cradle of Culture and What Children Know About Writing and Numbers Before Being Taught*, by emphasizing the value of focusing on the cognitive and linguistic processes involved in the individual 'child's personal work' in 'imposing certain principles on the information provided by the environment'. However, as Tolchinsky notes, 'Children's ideas [about writing and written language] are not idiosyncratic inventions—although they may appear as such—but rather reflect the selection and elaboration' of what they have

encountered in their experience of interacting with readers and writers and their encounters with written language (2003: 93). In the encounters of the future, children will come upon readers and writers who are increasingly likely to use computers to read and write. They will also find themselves engaged with computers themselves, and very possibly with machines that offer a mechanized voice reading aloud a text from the screen, whether the text has been created by another writer or by the child himself or herself. Furthermore, as speech synthesis software programs become more common for reading aloud to beginners, it is likely that speech recognition programs will also become more common and more adept in transforming a speaker's utterance into a text on a screen (see, for example, Sperber 2006). Some children's apprenticeships in the course of writing development may well become partly facilitated by—and possibly shaped by—software with features designed to convert text to speech and speech to text.

As speech recognition and speech synthesis software programs become more sophisticated, the machine itself will seem to become increasingly 'intelligent' in directing the writer's choices, in making corrections or other adjustments, and in predicting on behalf of the young writer what the unfolding text could or should include next. The processes of writing and rereading one's own writing-in-progress could thus become increasingly a matter of managing digital tools that offer meaning-inferring and choice-posing software. Writing with such digital tools may become analogous to mathematical problem solving with the use of advanced calculators and other digital problem-solving tools. Writing development may increasingly involve learning to use 'intelligent' composing and editing software effectively.

For at least some children, then, marking sidewalks with chalk may give way in future decades to experimenting with the use of digital writing tools that may resemble hand-held calculators for mathematical operations—writing tools that can create written sentences from a developing writer's speech and that can speak back, in mechanized voice, the software's best inference of the words and sentences the child has intended to enter as text. Even in such intensely mediated and highly mechanized future environments for learning to write, however, a young writer's development will likely continue to be influenced not only by access to the digital tools themselves but also by engagement with people who provide help with learning the use of the tools and, as important, for whom the writing and reading activities made possible with such tools have evident meaning and importance. Such engagement will continue to provide what Emilia Ferreiro calls a child's highly consequential 'first immersion in a "culture of literacy"'. This immersion, Ferreiro suggests in her recent comments on 'Reading and Writing in a Changing World', provides the experience of 'having listened to someone read aloud, having seen someone write, having had the opportunity to produce intentional marks, having taken part in social acts where reading and writing make sense, and having been able to ask questions and get some kind of answer' (2000: 4). It is in this kind of sociocultural context, a context that provides opportunities for a child to interact (and, importantly, to identify) with more experienced members of a cultural community and to learn from observing them, that the individual child undertakes the social and cognitive work of transforming his or her experience in a linguistic environment into individual linguistic ability.

Once children and adolescents participate in school, their academic experience is usually structured more deliberately, and they receive direct instruction aimed at helping them develop along particular trajectories as both readers and writers. But, as many scholars and educators have noted, a developing writer's experience with communication beyond the school curriculum often offers its own more or less accidental—but nonetheless powerful and thus in some ways

competing—orientation to what it means to read and write. The pervasive use of cell phones creates opportunities for speaking and writing to become nearly interchangeable for quick, everyday communication. Increasingly, older children and adolescents have access not only to cell phones that allow spoken conversation, voice mail messages, text-messages, and instant messaging dialogue, but also to computer e-mail programs that combine the use of text, sound files, photos, and video clips; to television and digital video games; and to blogs, 'facebook' and 'myspace' style personal websites.

These digital tools and forms reposition written language use in a broader setting of pictures, sounds, and words both written and spoken—a rich, mosaic-like, and sometimes kaleidoscopic mixed-medium, which children and adolescents may sometimes use to communicate quickly and efficiently and other times use to compose and then post elaborate messages that may include varying combinations of text, speech, music, visual images, photos, and videos. Tara McPherson, in 'A Rule Set for the Future', her introductory essay for the edited volume, *Digital Youth, Innovation, and the Unexpected,* notes that scholars have recently begun identifying 'the particular pleasures and possibilities of experimenting with digital media technologies. These include', she adds, 'a privileging of process over product, a sensation of mobility and control, a feeling of networked sociality, a heightened awareness of audience, learning by doing or tinkering, and an impression of mutability and transformation' (2008: 10). Furthermore, dramatic changes in writing practices brought about, or at least facilitated, by the emergence of new digital tools and attendant changes in the character of ongoing writing development are being observed not only in the extracurricular lives of children and adolescents, but also in the working lives of many adults. For example, in her recent essay, 'Writing for a Living: Literacy and the Knowledge Economy', Deborah Brandt observes that many adults report that, at work, they must adapt to

(a) changing conditions and tools for writing, (b) changing forms or genres in which they are expected to read and write, and (c) changing 'means for the treatment of others through writing (as new media presume or enact different interactive relationships)' (2005: 188).

Here, too, there is great diversity in the kinds of writing people do at work, and Brandt is careful not to suggest that changes in the technology of writing are likely to make this diversity somehow narrower. But the larger point Brandt offers is an important one: changes in the tools and conditions of writing are often associated not only with changes in form and genre but also with changes in the ongoing relationships created, sustained, and altered among people who interact through written communication, whether new writing tools and forms are used for performing tasks on the job or for communicating for other purposes in other contexts.

In recognizing this basic link between writing activity and social interaction, we are also in a position to recognize a fundamental continuity in our understanding of what it means to write, whether we are reflecting on writing in the past, the present, or the future. It is that writing can be usefully regarded as a way of speaking, a way of saying something to someone—and particularly a way of speaking across space and time. As Peter T. Daniels notes in his essay, 'The Study of Writing Systems', writing in any of the world's writing systems can be defined now, and can be understood historically, as using 'more or less permanent marks' to 'represent an utterance in such a way that it can be recovered more or less exactly without the intervention of the utterer' (Daniels, 1996: 3).

It has always been possible to compose texts that include nonlinguistic forms of representation. In fact, Daniels observes:

> It is often supposed that writing was devised for the purpose of communicating at a distance—in order to send messages that did not rely on the memory of the messenger. But this seems

to be a case of overlooking the obvious: the sending of messages, and the writing of books for posterity, are happily accidental byproducts. The earliest use of writing seems to be to communicate things that really don't have oral equivalents. (5)

But the writing systems that emerged in ancient cultures did eventually come to serve the core function of representing a writer's utterance (or a scribe's transcription of a speaker's utterance) in a way that could be decoded and comprehended by a reader familiar with the writing system, the orthography associated with the system's use in representing a particular spoken language, and the conventions of discourse appropriate to the text at hand. The written utterance to be reconstructed may have been accompanied by other kinds of information or other forms of representation—tally marks, charts, and drawings—but the composed bits of written language could nonetheless be understood as language.

This remains true of writing produced with digital tools today, and it seems likely to remain true in the future. Texts produced with new technology may well become increasingly 'epistemic, performative, multivocal, multimodal, and multimediated', as Andrea Lunsford observes (2007: 8). In the future, processes of written composition may bear little resemblance to the composing processes we know today. The forms that texts take and the recurring discourse patterns or genres that emerge may also differ dramatically from those we rely on today. The aims and practices of readers may be very different as well. Indeed, as Roger Chartier suggests, one of the 'great questions of the future' is whether 'digital textuality will be able to overcome the tendency toward fragmentation that characterizes both the structure of texts and the modes of reading that it proposes' (2004: 152). However, there is no reason to suppose that written language itself will disappear. Writing development will thus remain, at its core, a matter of learning to use written language effectively as a way of speaking, a way of composing an utterance that a reader can reconstruct from its enduring traces and can comprehend, possibly in another place and in another time.

REFERENCES

Baron, Naomi (2005) *The future of written communication: Envisioning language in the new millennium*, IBERICA, 9: 7–31.

Bezemer, Jeff and Kress, Gunther (2008) 'Writing in multimodal texts: A social semiotic account of designs for learning', *Written Communication*, 25: 166–195.

Brandt, Deborah (2005) 'Writing for a living: Literacy and the knowledge economy', *Written Communication*, 22: 166–197.

Chartier, Roger (2004) 'Language, books, and reading from the printed word to the digital text', Tr. Teresa Lavendar Fagan, *Critical Inquiry*, 31: 133–152.

Chester, Jeff (2007) *Digital Destiny: New Media and the Future of Democracy*, New York: The New Press.

Danet, Brenda and Herring, Susan C. (eds) (2007) *The Multilingual Internet: Language, Culture, and Communication Online*, Oxford: Oxford University Press.

Daniels, Peter T. (1996) 'The study of writing systems', in P.T. Daniels and W. Bright (eds), *The World's Writing Systems*, Oxford: Oxford University Press. pp.3–17.

Ferreiro, Emilia (2000) 'Reading and writing in a changing world', *Publishing Research Quarterly*, 16: 53.

Grafton, Anthony (2007) 'Future reading: Digitization and its discontents', *The New Yorker*, November 5.

Gundlach, Robert (1982) 'Children as writers: The beginning of learning to write', in M. Nystrand (ed), *What Writers Know*, New York: Academic Press. pp.129–148.

Gundlach, Robert (1992) 'What it means to be literate', in R. Beach, J. Green, M. Kamil, and T. Shanahan (eds), *Multidisciplinary Perspectives on Literacy Research*, Urbana: NCRE/NCTE. pp.365–372.

Gundlach, Robert (2003) 'The future of writing ability', in M. Nystrand and J. Duffy (eds), *Towards a Rhetoric of Everyday Life: New Directors in Research on Writing, Text, and Discourse*, Madison: University of Wisconsin Press. pp.247–263.

Gundlach, Robert (2004) 'Afterword: Words and lives: Language, literacy, and culture in multilingual Chicago', in M. Farr (ed.), *Ethnolinguistic Chicago*, Mahwah, NJ: Erlbaum. pp.381–387.

Jenkins, Henry (2006) *Confronting the Challenges of Participatory Culture: Media Education in the 21st Century*, Chicago: The MacArthur Foundation.http://www.digitallearning.macfound.org/atf/cf/%7B7E45C7E0-A3E0-4B89-AC9C-E807E1B0AE4E%7D/JENKINS_WHITE_PAPER.PDF

Lam, Wan Shun Eva (2006) 'Revisioning language, literacy, and the immigrant subject in new mediascapes', *Pedagogies: An International Journal*, 1: 171–195.

Lunsford, Andrea (2007) *Writing Matter: Rhetoric in Public and Private Lives*, Athens and London: University of Georgia Press.

McLane, Joan B. and McNamee, Gilliam D. (1990) *Early Literacy*, Cambridge, MA: Harvard University Press.

McPherson, Tara (2008) 'A rule set for the future', in T. McPherson (ed.), *Digital Youth, Innovation, and the Unexpected*, Cambridge, MA: The MIT Press. pp.1–26.

Sperber, Dan (2006) 'Reading without writing', in G. Origgi (ed.), *Text-e: Text in the Age of the Internet*, Hampshire: Palgrave Macmillan. pp.144–154.

Tolchinsky, Liliana (2003) *The Cradle of Culture*, Mahwah, NJ: Erlbaum.

Tolchinsky, Liliana (2006) 'The emergence of writing', in C.A. MacArthur, S. Graham, and J. Fitzgerald, (eds), *Handbook of Writing Research*, New York: The Guilford Press. pp.83–95.

Van Waes, Luuk, Leijten, Marielle, and Neuwirth, Christine M. (eds) (2006) *Writing and Digital Media*, Amsterdam: Elsevier.

Wasserman, Steve (2007) 'Goodbye to all that', *Columbia Journalism Review*, September/October. http://www.cjr.org/cover_story/goodbye_to_all_that_1.php?page=all

Index

Tables in italics; figures in bold